KU-302-901

P · O · C · K · E · T · S

# GERMAN DICTIONARY

## GERMAN · ENGLISH
## ENGLISH · GERMAN

COVENT
GARDEN
BOOKS

A DORLING KINDERSLEY BOOK

Produced for Dorling Kindersley by
PAGE*One*, Cairn House, Elgiva Lane, Chesham,
Buckinghamshire HP5 2JD

**PAGE*One* team**   Chris Clark, Matthew Cook,
Bob Gordon, Helen Parker

**DK Managing editor**   Jane Yorke

**German editors**   Anke Kornmüller
Christa Wiseman

Published in Great Britain by
Dorling Kindersley Limited, 9 Henrietta Street,
London WC2E 8PS

2 4 6 8 10 9 7 5 3

This edition published in 2001
for Covent Garden Books

A CIP catalogue record for this book is available from
the British Library

ISBN 1-85605-505-1

Printed and bound in Italy by LegoPrint

# GUIDE TO THE IMITATED PRONUNCIATION

The imitated pronunciation in the German–English section is designed to help English speakers pronounce the German words accurately. Read each syllable as though it were an English word, bearing in mind the following conventions:

1  The stressed syllable is printed in **bold type**.

2  **ah** is generally pronounced like the a in Southern English ask:

   **Abend, ah**-bent (evening)

   It is, however, shorter when followed by two consonants:

   **alle, ahll**-*e* (all)

3  **ay** represents a sound similar to the ay in day, as pronounced in Scotland:

   **gehen, gay**-*en* (to go)

4  The italic *e* is a neutral vowel like the e in open or the a in local

   **kommen, kom**-*en* (to come)

5  **ow** represents the vowel sound in cow:

   **aus, owss** (from)

6  EE in small capitals is pronounced like the French u in lune (or like an English ee said with pursed lips):

   **drücken, dr**EE**ck**-*en* (to press)

7  The italic **r** in the combination **er** must not be pronounced at all; it indicates that the preceding vowel is pronounced like the ur in fur:

   **hören, her**-ren (to hear)

8  The italic *k* represents a guttural sound. After a, au, o or u it is pronounced like the ch in Scottish loch:

   **Bach, bah***k* (brook)

   Elsewhere it is like a forcefully pronounced h:

   **mich, mi***k* (me)

9  g must be pronounced like the g in go:

   **Gesicht, ge-zikt** (face)

   The soft g in barrage is represented by **zh**:

   **Genie, zhain-ee** (genius)

10  s always represents sound of the s in stand, not in does:

   **Soße, zoh**-se (sauce).

# ABBREVIATIONS

| | | | |
|---|---|---|---|
| *adj* | adjective | *mil* | military |
| *abbr* | abbreviation | *mus* | music |
| *adv* | adverb | *n* | noun |
| *art* | article | *naut* | nautical |
| *Brit* | Britain | *nt* | neuter |
| *chem* | chemistry | *num* | numeral |
| *comm* | commerce | *o.s.* | oneself |
| *comp* | computing | *parl* | parliament |
| *conj* | conjunction | *pej* | pejorative |
| *elec* | electrics | *photog* | photography |
| *etw* | something | *pl* | plural |
| *f* | feminine | *pref* | prefix |
| *fam* | familiar | *prep* | preposition |
| *fig* | figuratively | *pron* | pronoun |
| *fin* | finance | *rail* | railways |
| *geog* | geography | *refl* | reflexive |
| *gram* | grammar | *relig* | religion |
| *interj* | interjection | *sb* | somebody |
| jd/jdn/jdm | somebody | *sport* | sport |
| jds | somebody's | sth | something |
| *law* | law | *theatre* | theatre |
| *m* | masculine | US | United States |
| *mech* | mechanics | *v* | verb |
| *med* | medicine | *vulg* | vulgar |

# ERKLÄRUNG DER NACHGEAHMTEN AUSSPRACHE

Die nachgeahmte Aussprache im Englisch–Deutsch Teil soll dem deutschsprachigen Benutzer des Wörterbuches helfen, die englischen Wörter korrekt auszusprechen. Jede Silbe ist so auszusprechen, als sei sie Teil eines deutschen Wortes. Dabei sind folgende Hinweise zu beachten:

1  Die Betonung liegt auf der **fettgedruckten** Silbe.

2  Das schräg gedruckte *a* wird so wie das a in der deutschen Silbe ank- ausgesprochen:

   **uncle**, *ang*-k'l (Onkel)
   **come**, *kamm* (kommen)

3  o'a wird in einem Laut ausgesprochen; die Hauptbetonung liegt auf dem o und das a klingt nur leicht nach:

   **ought**, o'at (sollte)

4  In vielen englischen Wörtern ist der Vokal der unbetonten Silbe kaum hörbar, ähnlich wie das e in Morgen oder Löffel. Dieser tonlose Vokal ist meistens durch ein *schräg gedrucktes e* bezeichnet:

   **obey**, *e*-beh (gehorchen)

   Vor l oder n fällt dieser Vokal manchmal ganz weg und wird durch ein ' gekennzeichnet:

   **table**, teh-b'l (Tisch)
   **reckon**, reck-'n (rechnen)

5  s am Ende eines Wortes wird gewöhnlich stimmhaft ausgesprochen, ähnlich dem deutschen s zwischen zwei Vokalen, z.B. in Vase. In unserer nachgeahmten Aussprache wird dieses s durch **s** bezeichnet, das stimmlose s durch **ss**:

   **scissors**, ssis-ers (Schere)

   Vor oder nach **p**, **t** oder **k** wird das s immer stimmlos ausgesprochen:

   **ask**, ahsk (fragen)
   **must**, mast (müssen)
   **clasp**, klahsp (umarmen)

6  Es gibt im Deutschen keinen Laut, der dem englischen "th" entspricht. Das stimmlose "th" ist mit der Zungenspitze zwischen den Zähnen auszusprechen, wie wenn jemand lispelt.
   Es gibt auch ein stimmhaftes "th", das fast wie ein d klingt.
   In der nachgeahmten Aussprache wird das stimmlose th mit **th** bezeichnet, das stimmhafte mit **dh**:

   **thirty**, thör-ti (dreißig)
   **this**, dhiss (dieser)

# ABKÜRZUNGEN

| | | | | |
|---|---|---|---|---|
| *adj* | Adjektiv | | *mil* | militärisch |
| *abbr* | Abkürzung | | *mus* | Musik |
| *adv* | Adverb | | *n* | Substantiv |
| *art* | Artikel | | *naut* | Seefahrt |
| *Brit* | Großbritannien | | *nt* | Neutrum |
| *chem* | Chemie | | *num* | Zahlwort |
| *comm* | Handel | | *o.s.* | sich |
| *comp* | Computer | | *parl* | Parlament |
| *conj* | Konjunktion | | *pej* | abschätzig |
| *elec* | Elektrizität | | *photog* | Fotografie |
| *etw* | etwas | | *pl* | Plural |
| *f* | Femininum | | *pref* | Präfix |
| *fam* | umgangssprachlich | | *prep* | Präposition |
| *fig* | übertragen | | *pron* | Pronomen |
| *fin* | Finanzwesen | | *rail* | Eisenbahn |
| *geog* | Geographie | | *refl* | reflexiv |
| *gram* | Grammatik | | *relig* | Religion |
| *interj* | Interjektion | | *sb* | jemand(-en/-em) |
| *jd/jdn/jdm* | jemand(-en/-em) | | *sport* | Sport |
| *jds* | jemands | | *sth* | etwas |
| *law* | Rechtswesen | | *theatre* | Theater |
| *m* | Maskulinum | | *US* | Vereinigte Staaten |
| *mech* | Technik | | *v* | Verb |
| *med* | Medizin | | *vulg* | vulgär |

# GERMAN · ENGLISH
# DEUTSCH · ENGLISCH

**Aal,** ahl, *m* eel

**Aas,** ahss, *nt* carrion

**ab,** ahp, *adv* off, from, away, down

**abändern,** ahp-enn-dern, *v* to alter

**Abänderung,** ahp-enn-der-oong, *f* alteration

**abarbeiten (sich),** ahp-ahr-by-ten (zik), *v* to overwork oneself

**abbeißen,** ahp-by-sen, *v* to bite off

**abberufen,** ahp-be-roof-en, *v* to recall, to summon away

**abbestellen,** ahp-be-shtell-en, *v* to cancel (orders), to countermand

**abbilden,** ahp-bild-en, *v* to portray, to delineate

**abbitten,** ahp-bit-en, *v* to apologize

**abbrechen,** ahp-brek-en, *v* to break off

**abbrennen,** ahp-brenn-en, *v* to burn down

**abbürsten,** ahp-bEErs-ten, *v* to brush off

**abdanken,** ahp-dahn-ken, *v* to resign, to abdicate

**abdecken,** ahp-deck-en, *v* to clear (table)

**abdrucken,** ahp-drook-en, *v* to print

**Abend,** ah-bent, *m* evening

**Abendblatt,** ah-bent-blahtt, *nt* evening paper

**Abendessen,** ah-bent-ess-en, *nt* supper

**Abenteuer,** ah-ben-toy-er, *nt* adventure

**aber,** ah-ber, *conj* but

**Aberglaube,** ah-ber-glow-be, *m* superstition

**abergläubisch,** ah-ber-gloy-bish, *adj* superstitious

**abermal(s),** ah-ber-mahl(s), *adv* again, once more

**abfahren,** ahp-fahr-en, *v* to depart, to start a journey

**Abfahrt,** ahp-fahrt, *f* departure

**Abfall,** ahp-fahll, *m* refuse, waste, offal

**abfangen,** ahp-fahng-en, *v* to catch; to intercept

**abfärben,** ahp-fair-ben, *v* to run (colours)

**abfassen,** ahp-fahss-en, *v* to draft; to seize

**abfertigen,** ahp-fair-tee-gen, *v* to dispatch, to expedite; to snub

**abfinden,** ahp-finn-den, *v* to satisfy; **sich – mit,** to come to terms with

**abfliessen,** ahp-fleess-en, *v* to flow off

**Abfluß,** ahp-flooss, *m* waste pipe; gutter

**abführen,** ahp-fEEr-en, *v* to march off; to purge

**Abführmittel,** ahp-fEEr-mitt-el, *nt* purgative

**Abgabe,** ahp-gah-be, *f* tax; duty

**Abgang,** ahp-gahng, *m* dispatch; departure; exit; discharge; abortion; waste

**abgeben,** ahp-gay-ben, *v* to deliver

**abgebrannt,** ahp-ge-brahnt, *adj* burnt down

**abgehen,** ahp-gay-en, *v* to go off, to depart

**abgelebt,** ahp-ge-laypt, *adj* decrepit; antiquated

**abgelegen,** ahp-ge-lay-gen, *adj* distant, remote

**abgemessen**, ahp-ge-mess-en, *adj* measured

**abgeneigt**, ahp-ge-ny'gt, *adj* disinclined

**Abgeordnete(r)**, ahp-ge-ord-ne-te(r), *m & f* delegate, deputy, member of parliament

**abgerundet**, ahp-ge-roonn-det, *adj* rounded off

**Abgesandte(r)**, ahp-ge-zahnn-te(r), *m & f* envoy, emissary

**abgeschmackt**, ahp-ge-shmahckt, *adj* insipid; in bad taste

**abgesehen (von)**, ahp-ge-zay-en (fon), *adv* irrespective of, apart from

**abgespannt**, ahp-ge-shpahnt, *adj* tired out

**abgestanden**, ahp-ge-shtahnn-den, *adj* stale

**abgewiesen**, ahp-ge-vee-zen, *adj* rejected

**abgewinnen**, ahp-ge-vinn-en, *v* to win from

**abgewöhnen**, ahp-ge-vern-nen, *v* to break a habit, to wean from

**abgiessen**, ahp-geess-en, *v* to pour off

**Abgott**, ahp-got, *m* idol

**abgöttisch**, ahp-gert-ish, *adj* idolatrous

**abgrenzen**, ahp-grenn-tsen, *v* to delimit

**Abgrund**, ahp-groont, *m* abyss, precipice

**abhacken**, ahp-hahck-en, *v* to chop off

**abhaken**, ahp-hah-ken, *v* to unhook; to tick off

**abhalten**, ahp-hahll-ten, *v* to detain, to restrain

**abhandeln**, ahp-hahn-deln, *v* to bargain; to discuss

**abhanden kommen**, ahp-hahn-den **komm**-en, *v* to get lost

**Abhang**, ahp-hahng, *m* slope

**abhängen (von)**, ahp-heng-en (fon), *v* to depend on

**abhängig**, ahp-heng-ik, *adj* dependent

**abhärten**, ahp-hair-ten, *v* to harden

**abhauen**, ahp-how-en, *v* to chop off, to fell

**abheben**, ahp-hay-ben, *v* to lift off; to cut (cards); to withdraw (money)

**abhelfen**, ahp-hel-fen, *v* to remedy; to redress

**abholen**, ahp-hoh-len, *v* to call for; to fetch from

**abhören**, ahp-her-ren, *v* to examine (students)

**abkaufen**, ahp-kow-fen, *v* to buy from

**abkochen**, ahp-kok-en, *v* to boil

**Abkomme**, ahp-kom-e, *m* descendant

**abkommen**, ahp-kom-en, *v* to get off/away

**abkühlen**, ahp-kEEl-en, *v* to cool

**Abkunft**, ahp-koonft, *f* origin, descent

**abkürzen**, ahp-kEErt-sen, *v*

to shorten, to abridge

**abladen**, ahp-lahd-en, *v* to unload

**ablassen**, ahp-lahss-en, *v* to reduce (price); to desist

**Ablaß**, ahp-lahss, *m* discharge; outlet

**Ablauf**, ahp-lowf, *m* drain; course; expiry; start

**ablaufen**, ahp-lowf-en, *v* to expire; to run down (clock); to flow off

**ablecken**, ahp-leck-en, *v* to lick off; to file

**ablegen**, ahp-lay-gen, *v* to lay aside, to take off

**ablehnen**, ahp-lay-nen, *v* to decline, to refuse

**Ablehnung**, ahp-lay-noong, *f* refusal

**ableiten**, ahp-ly-ten, *v* to divert, to derive (grammar)

**ablenken**, ahp-lenk-en, *v* to divert

**ablernen**, ahp-lairn-en, *v* to learn by watching

**ableugnen**, ahp-loyg-nen, *v* to deny

**Ableugnung**, ahp-loyg-noong, *f* denial

**abliefern**, ahp-leef-ern, *v* to deliver

**Ablieferung**, ahp-leef-er-oong, *f* delivery

**ablösen**, ahp-ler-zen, *v* to detach; to relieve

**Ablösung**, ahp-ler-zoong, *f* detachment, separation; relief

**abmachen**, ahp-mahk-en, *v*

to settle; to undo

**Abmachung, ahp**-mahk-oong, *f* arrangement

**abmagern, ahp**-mahg-ern, *v* to become thin

**abmalen, ahp**-mahl-en, *v* to portray

**Abmarsch, ahp**-marsh, *m* departure (troops)

**abmessen, ahp**-mess-en, *v* to measure, to survey

**abmühen (sich), ahp**-mEE-en (zik), *v* to exert oneself

**Abnahme, ahp**-nahm-e, *f* decrease, diminution; sale

**abnehmen, ahp**-nay-men, *v* to take off, to decrease; to buy

**Abnehmer, ahp**-nay-mer, *m* buyer, customer

**abneigen, ahp**-ny-gen, *v* to turn away

**Abneigung, ahp**-ny-goong, *f* aversion, disinclination

**abnutzen, ahp**-noots-en, *v* to wear out

**Abnutzung, ahp**-noots-oong, *f* wear and tear

**Abonnement, ah-bon-ne-mahng,** *nt* subscription; season ticket

**Abonnent, ah-bon-nent,** *m* subscriber

**abonnieren, ah-bon-neer-en,** *v* to subscribe

**Abort, ahp**-ort, *m* lavatory; toilet

**abputzen, ahp**-poots-en, *v* to clean, to cleanse

**abquälen, ahp**-kvail-en, *v* to torment, to torture

**abrahmen, ahp**-rahm-en, *v* to skim (milk)

**abraten, ahp**-raht-en, *v* to dissuade

**abräumen, ahp**-roy-men, *v* to clear

**abrechnen, ahp**-rek-nen, *v* to settle; to deduct

**Abrechnung, ahp**-rek-noong, *f* settlement

**Abrechnungshaus, ahp**-rek-noongs-hows, *nt* clearing-house

**Abrede, ahp**-ray-de, *f* denial; agreement

**abreden, ahp**-ray-den, *v* to dissuade

**abreiben, ahp**-ry-ben, *v* to rub off; to wear out by friction

**Abreise, ahp**-ry-ze, *f* departure

**abreisen, ahp**-ry-zen, *v* to depart

**abreißen, ahp**-ry-sen, *v* to tear off; to demolish

**abrichten, ahp**-rik-ten, *v* to train (animals); to adjust

**abrufen, ahp**-roof-en, *v* to recall

**abrunden, ahp**-roonn-den, *v* to round off

**abrupfen, ahp**-roopp-fen, *v* to pluck off

**abrutschen, ahp**-roott-shen, *v* to slip from

**absagen, ahp**-zahg-en, *v* to refuse, to put off

**Absatz, ahp**-zahts, *m* heel (of shoe); sales; paragraph

**Absatzgebiet, ahp**-zahts-ge-

beet, *nt* market, outlet (goods)

**abschaffen, ahp**-shahff-en, *v* to abolish

**Abschaffung, ahp**-shahff-oong, *f* abolition

**abschälen, ahp**-shay-len, *v* to peel, to shell

**abschätzen, ahp**-shet-sen, *v* to estimate

**Abschätzung, ahp**-shet-soong, *f* estimate

**abscheiden, ahp**-shy-den, *v* to separate

**Abscheu, ahp**-shoy, *m* loathing, abomination

**abscheulich, ahp**-**shoy**-lik, *adj* abominable

**abschicken, ahp**-shik-en, *v* to send off

**Abschied, ahp**-sheet, *m* farewell; dismissal

**abschiessen, ahp**-shee-sen, *v* to shoot off

**Abschlag, ahp**-shlahk, *m* refusal; decline (price)

**abschlagen, ahp**-shlah-gen, *v* to refuse, to knock off

**Abschlagszahlung, ahp**-shlahks-tsahl-oong, *f* instalment, part-payment

**abschleifen, ahp**-shly-fen, *v* to grind off

**abschließen, ahp**-shlees-en, *v* to lock; to settle (agreement)

**Abschluss, ahp**-shlooss, *m* conclusion, settlement

**abschmelzen, ahp**-shmelt-sen, *v* to melt off

**abschneiden, ahp**-shny-den,

*v* to cut off

**Abschnitt, ahp**-shnitt, *m* section

**abschrauben, ahp**-shrow-ben, *v* to unscrew

**abschrecken, ahp**-shreck-en, *v* to scare away

**abschreiben, ahp**-shry-ben, *v* to copy (writing)

**Abschrift, ahp**-shrift, *f* (written) copy

**abschütteln, ahp**-shEEtt-eln, *v* to shake off

**abschweifen, ahp**-shvy-fen, *v* to digress

**Abschweifung, ahp**-shvy-foong, *f* digression

**abschwören, ahp**-shver-ren, *v* to retract

**absegeln, ahp**-zay-geln, *v* to set sail

**absehen (von), ahp**-zay-en (fon), *v* to refrain from

**abseifen, ahp**-zy-fen, *v* to clean with soap

**abseits, ahp**-zites, *adv* aside; apart

**absenden, ahp**-zen-den, *v* to send off, to dispatch

**Absender, ahp**-zen-der, *m* sender

**absetzen, ahp**-zet-sen, *v* to remove (hat); to drop (off); to cancel; to dismiss; to wean

**Absetzung, ahp**-zet-soong, *f* dismissal; deduction; cancellation; weaning

**Absicht, ahp**-sikt, *f* intention, design

**absichtlich, ahp**-sikt-lik, *adj* intentional

**absolvieren, ahp**-zol-**veer**-en, *v* to absolve; to complete studies

**absonderlich, ahp**-zon-der-lik, *adj* particular, peculiar

**absondern, ahp**-zon-dern, *v* to separate; **sich –,** to seclude oneself

**abspannen, ahp**-shpahnn-en, *v* to unharness; to relax

**absparen (sich), ahp**-shpahr-en (zik), *v* to save up for

**abspenstig machen, ahp**-shpen-shtik **mahk**-en, *v* to lure away

**absperren, ahp**-shperr-en, *v* to shut off, to stop

**absplittern, ahp**-shplitt-ern, *v* to splinter off

**abspringen, ahp**-shpring-en, *v* to jump off; to break off

**abspülen, ahp**-shpEEl-en, *v* to rinse

**abstammen (von), ahp**-shtahmm-en (fon), *v* to be descended/derived (from)

**Abstand, ahp**-shtahnt, *m* distance; (fig) difference

**abstauben, ahp**-shtow-ben, *v* to dust

**Abstecher, ahp**-shtek-er, *m* excursion, short trip

**absteigen, ahp**-shty-gen, *v* to descend; to put up (hotel)

**abstellen, ahp**-shtel-en, *v* to turn off

**abstempeln, ahp**-shtem-peln, *v* to stamp

**absterben, ahp**-shtair-ben, *v* to die off

**abstimmen, ahp**-shtim-en, *v* to put to the vote

**Abstimmung, ahp**-shtim-oong, *f* vote; division

**abstoßend, ahp**-shtohs-ent, *adj* repulsive

**abstreiten, ahp**-shtry-ten, *v* to contest; to dispute

**Absturz, ahp**-shtoorts, *m* headlong fall; steep slope

**abstürzen, ahp**-shtEErt-sen, *v* to fall; to descend steeply

**Abt, ahpt,** *m* abbot

**Abtei, ahp-ty,** *f* abbey

**Abteil, ahp**-tile, *nt* compartment

**abteilen, ahp**-ty-len, *v* to divide, to partition; to classify

**Abteilung, ahp**-ty-loong, *f* department, division

**abtragen, ahp**-trahg-en, *v* to pull down (buildings); to wear out (clothes)

**abtreiben, ahp**-try-ben, *v* to abort

**abtrennen, ahp**-trenn-en, *v* to unstitch; to separate

**abtreten, ahp**-tray-ten, *v* to cede

**Abtritt, ahp**-tritt, *m* exit *theatre*; resignation; abdication

**abtrocknen, ahp**-trock-nen, *v* to dry; to wipe

**abtrünnig, ahp**-trEEnn-ik, *adj* disloyal

**Abtrünnigkeit, ahp**-trEEnn-ik-kite, *f* disloyalty

**abwarten, ahp**-vahrt-en, *v* to wait for

**abwärts, ahp**-vairts, *adv* downwards

**abwaschen, ahp**-vahsh-en, *v* to wash off

**abwechseln, ahp**-vek-seln, *v* to alternate; to change over

**abwechselnd, ahp**-vek-selnt, *adj & adv* alternate(ly)

**Abwechslung, ahp**-vek-sel-oong, *f* change

**Abweg, ahp**-vaig, *m* mistake, error

**Abwehr, ahp**-vair, *f* defence; safeguard

**abwehren, ahp**-vair-en, *v* to protect; to fend/ward off

**abweichen, ahp**-vy-ken, *v* to deviate, to differ

**Abweichung, ahp**-vy-koong, *f* deviation

**abweisen, ahp**-vy-zen, *v* to refuse; to repulse

**Abweisung, ahp**-vy-zoong, *f* refusal; rebuff

**abwendbar, ahp**-vent-bar, *adj* preventable

**abwenden, ahp**-ven-den, *v* to avert, to turn away

**abwerfen, ahp**-vair-fen, *v* to throw off; to yield

**abwesend, ahp**-vay-zent, *adj* absent; missing

**Abwesenheit, ahp**-vay-zen-hite, *f* absence

**abwickeln, ahp**-vik-eln, *v* to unroll; to settle (business)

**Abwicklung, ahp**-vik-loong, *f* settlement; completion

**abwiegen, ahp**-veeg-en, *v* to weigh

**abwischen, ahp**-vish-en, *v* to wipe off

**abzahlen, ahp**-tsahl-en, *v* to pay off; to pay in instalments

**abzählen, ahp**-tsay-len, *v* to count (out), to enumerate

**Abzahlung, ahp**-tsahl-oong, *f* part payment

**Abzählung, ahp**-tsay-loong, *f* counting; telling

**abzapfen, ahp**-tsahpp-fen, *v* to draw off

**abzehren, ahp**-tsay-ren, *v* to waste; to pine away

**Abzehrung, ahp**-tsay-roong, *f* emaciation

**Abzeichen, ahp**-tsyk-en, *nt* badge

**abzeichnen, ahp**-tsyk-nen, *v* to sketch

**abziehen, ahp**-tsee-en, *v* to pull down/off; to deduct

**Abzug, ahp**-tsook, *m* removal; retreat; proof, copy; deduction

**abzweigen, ahp**-tsvy-gen, *v* to branch off

**abzwingen, ahp**-tsving-en, *v* to extort; to obtain by force

**ach, ahk**, *interj* ah, oh, alas

**Achse, ahck**-se, *f* axis, axle

**Achsel, ahck**-sel, *f* shoulder

**acht, ahkt**, *num* eight

**Acht, ahkt**, *f* care,

attention; **sich in Acht nehmen, zik in ahkt nay-men**, to take care

**achtbar, ahkt**-bar, *adj* estimable

**Achtbarkeit, ahkt**-bar-kite, *f* respectability

**Achtel, ahk**-tel, *nt* eighth (part)

**achten, ahk**-ten, *v* to esteem, to heed

**achtenswert, ahk**-tens-vairt, *adj* worthy of esteem

**achtfach, ahkt**-fahk, *adj* eightfold

**achtlos, ahkt**-lohs, *adj* careless

**Achtlosigkeit, ahkt**-loh-zik-kite, *f* carelessness

**achtmal, ahkt**-mahl, *adv* eight times

**achtsam, ahkt**-zahm, *adj* careful; attentive (to)

**achtseitig, ahkt**-zy-tik, *adj* octagonal

**Achtung, ahk**-toong, *f* attention!, beware!; respect, esteem

**achtungsvoll, ahk**-toongs-fol, *adj* respectful

**achtungswert, ahk**-toongs-vairt, *adj* estimable

**achtzehn, ahkt**-tsain, *num* eighteen

**achtzig, ahkt**-tsik, *num* eighty

**ächzen, ehk**-tsen, *v* to groan loudly

**Acker, ahck**-er, *m* acre; field

**Ackerbau, ahck**-er-bow, *m* agriculture

**ackern, ahck**-ern, *v* to plough

**Adel, ah**-del, *m* nobility, nobleness

**adelig, ah**-del-ik, *adj* noble, titled

**adeln, ah**-deln, *v* to ennoble; to raise to the peerage

**Adelstand, ah**-del-shtahnt, *m* nobility

**Ader, ah**-der, *f* blood-vessel, vein

**Adler, ahd**-ler, *m* eagle

**adoptieren, ah**-dop-**teer**-en, *v* to adopt

**Adoption, ah**-dopts-**yohn**, *f* adoption

**Adreßbuch, ah**-dress-book, *nt* directory; address book

**Adresse, ah**-dress-*e*, *f* address

**Affäre, ah**-**fair**-*e*, *f* affair

**Affe, ahff**-*e*, *m* monkey, ape

**affig, ahff**-ik, *adj* foolish, silly

**Afrika, ahff**-ree-kah, *nt* Afrika

**AG,** *abbr* Aktiengesellschaft

**Agent, ah**-gent, *m* agent

**Agentur, ah**-gen-**toor**, *f* agency, representation

**agieren, ah**-geer-en, *v* to act (business)

**Ägypten, ay**-gEEp-ten, *nt* Egypt

**Ahn, ahn**, *m* ancestor

**ähneln, ayn**-eln, *v* to resemble

**ahnen, ahnn**-en, *v* to foresee, to suspect

**ähnlich, ayn**-lik, *adj* similar, like, resembling

**Ähnlichkeit, ayn**-lik-kite, *f* likeness, similarity

**Ahnung, ahn**-oong, *f* presentiment

**ahnungslos, ahn**-oongs-lohs, *adj* unsuspecting

**Ähre, air**-*e*, *f* ear of corn

**Aids, aydz**, *nt* Aids

**Akademiker, ah**-kah-**daym**-ik-*er*, *m* university graduate

**akademisch, ah**-kah-**daym**-ish, *adj* academic

**Akkord, ah**-kord, *m* chord

**Akkordarbeit, ah**-kord-ahr-byt, *f* piece-work

**Akku, ah**-koo, *m* rechargeable battery

**akkurat, ah**-koo-**raht**, *adj* tidy; exact; accurate

**Akrobat, ah**-kroh-**baht**, *m* acrobat

**Akt, ahkt**, *m* act; nude

**Akte, ahkk**-te, *f* file; **–nkoffer,** *m* attaché case; **–ntasche,** *f* briefcase

**Aktenzeichen, ahkk**-ten-tsy-ken, *nt* reference

**Aktie, ahkk**-tsee-*e*, *f* share (in a company)

**Aktiengesellschaft, ahkk**-tse-en-ge-**zel**-shahft, *f* public limited company

**Aktienkurs, ahkk**-tse-en-koors, *m* share price

**Aktion, ahkts**-yohn, *f* action; campaign

**Aktionär, ahkts**-yohn-**air**, *m* shareholder

**aktiv, ahkk**-teev, *adj* active

**aktuell, ahkk-too-ell**, *adj* up-to-date; topical

**Akzent, ahkk-tsent**, *m* accent; stress

**Alarm, ah**-larm, *m* alarm

**albern, ahll**-bern, *adj* silly

**Albernheit, ahll**-bern-hite, *f* foolishness, silliness

**Alge, ahll**-ge, *f* seaweed

**Alkohol, ahll**-koh-hohl, *m* alcohol

**alkoholfrei, ahll**-koh-hohl-fry, *adj* non-alcoholic

**All, ahll**, *nt* universe

**allabendlich, ahll-ah-bent**-lik, *adj* every evening

**allbekannt, ahll**-be-kahnt, *adj* universally known; notorious

**alle(r/s), ahll**-*e*(r/s), *pron* all; every; everything; *adv* finished; **–s Gute,** all the best

**Allee, ah**-lay, *f* avenue

**allein, ah**-line, *adj & adv* alone; only; *conj* but

**allemal, ahll**-*e*-mahl, *adv* always; every time; **ein für –,** once and for all

**allenfalls, ahll**-en-fahls, *adv* if need be; perhaps

**allerbeste(r/s), ahll**-er-beste(r/s), *adj* very best

**allerdings, ahll**-er-dings, *adv* to be sure, surely

**Allergie, ahll**-er-gee, *f* allergy

**allergisch, ahll**-erg-ish, *adj* allergic

**allerhand, ahll**-er-hahnt, *adj* all kinds of

**Allerheiligen, ahll**-er-**hyl**-eeg-en, *nt* All Saints' Day

**allerlei, ahll**-er-**ly**, *adj* all kinds of

**allerletzte(r/s), ahll**-er-**lets**-te(r/s), *adj* very last

**Allerseelen, ahll**-er-**zayl**-en, *nt* All Souls' (Day)

**allerseits, ahll**-er-**zites**, *adv* on every side

**alles, ahll**-es, *pron* everything

**allesamt, ahll**-*e*-**zahmt**, *adv* all (of them etc.)

**allgemein, ahll**-ge-**mine**, *adj* general; **im –en,** in general

**Allgewalt, ahll**-ge-vahlt, *f* omnipotence

**allgewaltig, ahll**-ge-**vahl**-tik, *adj* all-powerful

**alljährlich, ahll**-**yair**-lik, *adj* annual

**Allmacht, ahll**-mahkt, *f* omnipotence

**allmächtig, ahll**-**mek**-tik, *adj* omnipotent, almighty

**allmählich, ahll**-**may**-lik, *adj & adv* gradual(ly)

**Alltag, ahll**-tahk, *m* everyday life

**alltäglich, ahll**-**tayg**-lik, *adj* daily

**allwissend, ahll**-**vis**-ent, *adj* omniscient

**allzu, ahll**-tsoo, *adv* much too

**Almosen, ahll**-moh-zen, *nt* alms

**Alpen, ahll**-pen, *pl* alps; **die –,** the Alps

**Alphabet, ahll**-fah-**bayt**, *nt* alphabet

**Alptraum, ahlp**-trowm, *m* nightmare

**als, ahls,** *conj* when; than; as; such as

**also, ahll**-zo, *conj* thus; therefore; well!

**alt, ahlt,** *adj* old, antique

**Alter, ahlt**-er, *nt* age, old age; antiquity

**altern, ahlt**-ern, *v* to age, to grow old

**Altersheim, ahlt**-ers-hime, *nt* old people's home

**Altersrente, ahlt**-ers-ren-te, *f* old age pension

**altersschwach, ahlt**-ers-shvahk, *adj* decrepit

**Altertum, ahlt**-er-toom, *nt* antiquity

**altertümlich, ahlt**-er-**tEEm**-lik, *adj* ancient, antique

**altmodisch, ahlt**-moh-dish, *adj* old-fashioned

**Altpapier, ahlt**-pah-peer, *nt* waste paper

**Altstadt, ahlt**-shtaht, *f* old town

**Alufolie, ah**-loo-foh-lee-*e, f* aluminium foil

**Aluminium, ah**-loo-**min**-ee-oom, *nt* aluminium

**am (= an dem), ahmm,** *prep* at the; by the; in the; near the; to the

**Amboß, ahmm**-bos, *m* anvil

**Ambulanz, ahmm**-boo-**lahnts,** *f* ambulance; outpatients

**Ameise, ah**-my-ze, *f* ant

**Amerika, ah**-meh-ree-kah, *nt* America

**Amerikaner, ah**-meh-ree-**kah**-ner, *m* American (person)

**amerikanisch, ah**-meh-ree-**kah**-nish, *adj* American

**Amme, ah**-me, *f* (wet-) nurse

**amortisieren, ahmm**-ort-ee-**zeer**-en, *v* to pay for itself

**Ampel, ahmp**-el, *f* traffic lights

**Amsel, ahmm**-zel, *f* blackbird

**Amt, ahmt,** *nt* office; official position; job

**amtlich, ahmt**-lik, *adj* official

**Amtssiegel, ahmts**-zeeg-el, *nt* seal of office

**Amtszeichen, ahmts**-tsyk-en, *nt* dialling tone

**amüsieren, ahmm**-**EE**-**zeer**-en *v* to amuse; **sich –,** to enjoy oneself

**an, ahnn,** *prep* at; on; near; by; about; in

**Ananas, ahnn**-ah-nahs, *f* pineapple

**anbahnen, ahnn**-bahn-en, *v* to initiate; to loom

**Anbau, ahnn**-bow, *m* cultivation (soil); annex

**anbauen, ahnn**-bow-en, *v* to cultivate (soil); to extend (building)

**anbehalten, ahnn**-be-hahlt-en, *v* to keep on (clothes)

**anbei, ahnn-by,** *adv* enclosed; herewith; annexed

**anbeißen, ahnn-by-sen,** *v* to swallow (bait); to bite (off)

**anbeten, ahnn-bay-ten,** *v* to pray to; to worship

**Anbeter, ahnn-bay-ter,** *m* worshipper; admirer

**anbetteln, ahnn-bet-eln,** *v* to beg from

**anbieten, ahnn-beet-en,** *v* to offer

**anbinden, ahnn-bin-den,** *v* to tie up; to attach

**Anblick, ahnn-blik,** *m* sight; view

**anblicken, ahnn-blik-en,** *v* to glance at

**anbrechen, ahnn-brek-en,** *v* to break; to begin

**anbrennen, ahnn-bren-en,** *v* to burn (food etc.)

**anbringen, ahnn-bring-en,** *v* to bring in/on/to; to fix

**Anbruch, ahnn-brook,** *m* beginning; break

**Andacht, ahnn-dahkt,** *f* devotion; (religious) service

**andächtig, ahnn-dek-tik,** *adj* devout; attentive

**andauern, ahnn-dow-ern,** *v* to continue; to last

**Anden, ahnn-den,** *pl* Andes

**Andenken, ahnn-denn-ken,** *nt* souvenir; memory

**andere(r/s), ahnn-der-e(r/s),** *adj* other; different

**andererseits, ahnn-der-er-**zites, *adv* on the other hand

**ändern, en-dern,** *v* to change; to alter

**andernfalls, ahnn-dern-**fahls, *adv* otherwise

**anders, ahnn-ders,** *adv* otherwise; differently

**anderswo, ahnn-ders-voh,** *adv* elsewhere

**anderthalb, ahnn-dert-**hahlp, *num* one and a half

**Änderung, en-der-oong,** *f* alteration; change

**anderweitig, ahnn-der-vy-**tik, *adv* otherwise; elsewhere

**andeuten, ahnn-doyt-en,** *v* to hint; to notify

**Andeutung, ahnn-doyt-**oong, *f* hint; intimation

**Andrang, ahnn-drahng,** *m* crowd; congestion

**andrehen, ahnn-dray-en,** *v* to turn on

**androhen, ahnn-droh-en,** *v* to threaten; to menace

**aneignen, ahnn-y-gnen,** *v* **sich etw –,** to appropriate sth; to acquire sth

**aneinander, ahnn-ine-ahnn-**der, *adv* one against another; together

**anekeln, ahnn-ayk-eln,** *v* to disgust; to sicken

**anerkennen, ahnn-air-ken-**en, *v* to acknowledge

**Anerkennung, ahnn-**air-ken-oong, *f* acknowledgement; recognition

**anfachen, ahnn-fahk-en,** *v* to fan (flame)

**anfahren, ahnn-fahr-en,** *v* to arrrive; to deliver; to stop at; to run into, to hit

**Anfall, ahnn-fahl,** *m* attack; spasm

**anfallen, ahnn-fahl-en,** *v* to attack

**Anfang, ahnn-fahng,** *m* beginning

**anfangen, ahnn-fahng-en,** *v* to begin, to commence

**Anfänger, ahnn-feng-er,** *m* beginner, novice

**anfänglich, ahnn-feng-lik,** *adj & adv* original(ly); at first

**anfangs, ahnn-fahngs,** *adv* in the beginning

**anfassen ahnn-fahss-en,** *v* to take hold of

**anfertigen, ahnn-fairt-ig-en,** *v* to manufacture; to make

**Anfertigung, ahnn-fairt-ig-**oong, *f* manufacturing; making

**anfeuchten, ahnn-foyk-ten,** *v* to moisten

**anflehen, ahnn-flay-en,** *v* to implore

**anfordern, ahnn-for-dern,** *v* to demand; to claim

**Anforderung, ahnn-for-der-**oong, *f* demand; claim

**Anfrage, ahnn-frah-ge,** *f* enquiry; question

**anfragen, ahnn-frah-gen,** *v* to enquire

**anfreunden (sich), ahnn-**froyn-den (zik), *v* to

make friends

**anfügen, ahnn-**fEE-gen, *v* to join on; to add

**anführen, ahnn-**fEEr-en, *v* to lead; to quote; to dupe

**Anführer, ahnn-**fEEr-er, *m* leader; guide

**Angabe, ahnn-**gah-be, *f* declaration; statement; boasting

**angeben, ahnn-**gay-ben, *v* to declare; to denounce; to boast

**Angeberei, ahnn-**gey-ber-y, *f* showing off

**angeblich, ahnn-**gayp-lik, *adj* alleged; pretended

**angeboren, ahnn-**ge-bohr-en, *adj* inborn, innate

**Angebot, ahnn-**ge-boht, *nt* offer; bid

**angebracht, ahnn-**ge-brahkt, *adj* appropriate, fitting

**angeheitert, ahnn-**ge-hy-tert, *adj* tipsy

**angehen, ahnn-**gay-en, *v* to concern; to be tolerable

**angehend, ahnn-**gay-ent, *adj* incipient; (fig) budding

**angehören, ahnn-**ge-her-ren, *v* to belong to

**angehörig, ahnn-**ge-her-ik, *adj* belonging to

**Angehörige(r), ahnn-**ge-her-ig-e(r), *m & f* relative

**Angeklagte(r), ahnn-**ge-klahk-te(r), *m & f* accused

**Angel, ahng-**el, *f* fish-hook; door-hinge

**Angelegenheit, ahnn-**ge-lay-gen-hite, *f*

business; affair

**angeln, ahng-**eln, *v* to fish

**angemessen, ahnn-**ge-mess-en, *adj* appropriate

**angenehm, ahnn-**ge-naym, *adj* agreeable, pleasant

**angesehen, ahnn-**ge-say-en, *adj* respected

**Angesicht, ahnn-**ge-zikt, *nt* countenance; face

**angesichts, ahnn-**ge-zikts, *prep* in view of

**Angestellte(r), ahnn-**ge-shell-te(r), *m & f* employee

**angetrunken, ahnn-**ge-troonk-en, *adj* drunk

**angewöhnen, ahnn-**ge-vern-en, *v* to accustom

**Angewohnheit, ahnn-**ge-vohn-hite, *f* habit

**angezogen, ahnn-**ge-tsoh-gen, *adj* dressed; stretched

**angreifen, ahnn-**gry-fen, *v* to attack; to touch

**Angreifer, ahnn-**gry-fer, *m* aggressor; assailant

**angrenzend, ahnn-**grent-sent, *adj* adjacent, bordering

**Angriff, ahnn-**griff, *m* attack, assault

**Angst, ahnkst,** *f* anxiety, fear; **– haben (vor),** to be afraid of

**ängstigen (sich), eng-**stee-gen (zik), *v* to worry, to be worried

**ängstlich, engst-**lik, *adj* anxious; timid

**Ängstlichkeit, engst-**lik-

kite, *f* anxiousness, uneasiness

**anhaben, ahnn-**hahb-en, *v* to have on; to wear

**anhalten, ahnn-**hahlt-en, *v* to stop

**Anhalter, ahnn-**hahlt-er, *m* hitch-hiker

**Anhaltspunkt, ahnn-**hahlts-poonkt, *m* clue

**Anhang, ahnn-**hahng, *m* appendix; following, supporters

**anhängen, ahnn-**heng-en, *v,* to append, to add to

**Anhänger, ahnn-**heng-er, *m* follower, adherent; trailer; pendant

**anhänglich, ahnn-**heng-lik, *adj* attached, faithful

**Anhängsel, ahnn-**heng-sel, *nt* appendage; hanger-on; tag

**anhäufen, ahnn-**hoyf-en, *v* to accumulate

**Anhäufung, ahnn-**hoyf-oong, *f* accumulation; congestion

**anheften, ahnn-**heft-en, *v* to fasten, to tack on

**Anhöhe, ahnn-**her-e, *f* hill, rising ground; height

**anhören, ahnn-**her-ren, *v* to listen to; to hear

**Ankauf, ahnn-**kowf, *m* purchase

**ankaufen, ahnn-**kowf-en, *v* to purchase

**Ankäufer, ahnn-**koyf-er, *m* purchaser

**Anker, ahng-**ker, *m* anchor

**Ankerplatz, ahng**-ker-plahts, *m* anchorage

**anketten, ahnn**-ket-en, *v* to chain up

**Anklage, ahnn**-klahg-*e*, *f* accusation, charge

**anklagen, ahnn**-klahg-en, *v* to accuse

**Ankläger, ahnn**-klay-ger, *m* accuser; complainant

**anklammern (sich), ahnn**-klahmm-ern (zik), *v* to cling to

**Anklang, ahnn**-klahng, *m* accord; approval

**ankleben, ahnn**-klay-ben, *v* to stick on; to affix

**ankleiden, ahnn**-kly-den, *v* to dress; to attire

**anklopfen, ahnn**-klopp-fen, *v* to knock at the door

**anknüpfen, ahnn**-k'nEEp-fen, *v* to fasten/tie on; to enter into (conversation etc.)

**ankommen, ahnn**-komm-en, *v* to arrive; – **auf, owf** to depend (on)

**ankreuzen, ahnn**-kroyts-en, *v* to mark with a cross

**ankündigen, ahnn**-kEEn-de-gen, *v* to announce

**Ankunft, ahnn**-koonft, *f* arrival

**anlächeln, ahnn**-lek-eln, *v* to smile at

**Anlage, ahnn**-lah-g*e*, *f* (industrial) plant; investment; aptitude; enclosure; park

**Anlaß, ahnn**-lahss, *m* reason, cause, motive

**anlassen, ahnn**-lahss-en, *v* to leave on; to start up

**Anlasser, ahnn**-lahss-er, *m* starter (car)

**anläßlich, ahnn**-les-lik, *prep* on the occasion of

**Anlauf, ahnn**-lowf, *m* run-up; attempt; onset

**anlaufen, ahnn**-low-fen, *v* to begin, to start; (windows) to steam up

**anlegen, ahnn**-lay-gen, *v* to lay on/against; to invest; to aim at

**anlehnen, ahnn**-lay-nen, *v* to lean against; to leave ajar

**Anleihe, ahnn**-ly-*e*, *f* loan

**anleiten, ahnn**-ly-ten, *v* to guide; to instruct

**Anleitung, ahnn**-ly-toong, *f* instructions

**Anliegen, ahnn**-leeg-en, *nt* request; desire

**Anlieger, ahnn**-leeg-er, *m* resident

**anlocken, ahnn**-lock-en, *v* to attract; to lure

**anlöten, ahnn**-lert-en, *v* to solder on

**anlügen, ahnn**-lEEg-en, *v* to lie to

**anmachen, ahnn**-mahk-en, *v* to turn on; to fasten

**anmaßend, ahnn**-mahs-ent, *adj* arrogant

**Anmaßung, ahnn**-mahs-oong, *f* arrogance

**anmelden, ahnn**-mel-den, *v* to announce; to register;

**sich –,** to make an appointment, to register

**Anmeldung, ahnn**-mel-doong, *f* announcement; appointment; registration

**anmerken, ahnn**-mairk-en, *v* to note; to annotate

**Anmerkung, ahnn**-mairk-oong, *f* annotation

**Anmut, ahnn**-mooht, *f* grace, gracefulness

**anmutig, ahnn**-mooht-ik, *adj* graceful

**annageln, ahnn**-nahg-*e*ln, *v* to nail on

**annähen, ahnn**-nay-en, *v* to sew on

**annähern, ahnn**-nay-ern, *v* to approach

**annähernd, ahnn**-nay-ernt, *adj* approximate

**Annahme, ahnn**-nahm-*e*, *f* acceptance; assumption

**annehmbar, ahnn**-naym-bahr, *adj* acceptable

**annehmen, ahnn**-naym-en, *v* to accept; to assume

**Annehmlichkeit, ahnn**-naym-lik-kite, *f* agreeableness

**Annonce, ahnn**-nohnn-s*e*, *f* advertisement

**annoncieren, ahnn**-nonn-see-ren, *v* to advertise

**Anorak, ahnn**-or-ahkk, *m* anorak

**anordnen, ahnn**-ord-nen, *v* to order; to arrange

**Anordnung, ahnn**-ord-noong, *f* arrangement; direction

**anormal, ah**-nohr-mahl, *adj* abnormal

**anpacken, ahn**-pahck-en, *v* to seize

**anpassen, ahn**-pahss-en, *v* to adapt; to fit

**anpflanzen, ahn**-pflahnt-sen, *v* to plant; to cultivate

**Anpflanzung, ahn**-pflahnt-soong, *f* cultivation; plantation

**anpreisen, ahn**-pry-sen, *v* to commend; to extol

**Anprobe, ahn**-proh-be, *f* trying on

**anprobieren, ahn**-proh-beer-en, *v* to try on

**anraten, ahn**-raht-en, *v* to advise; to recommend

**anrechnen, ahn**-rek-nen, *v* to charge; take into account

**Anrecht, ahn**-rekt, *nt* right, entitlement; subscription

**Anrede, ahn**-ray-de, *f* address; speech

**anreden, ahn**-ray-den, *v* to address

**anregen, ahn**-ray-gen, *v* to stimulate; to prompt; to activate

**anregend, ahn**-ray-gent, *adj* stimulating

**Anregung, ahn**-ray-goong, *f* stimulation; stimulus

**Anreiz, ahn**-rites, *m* incentive

**anrempeln, ahn**-rem-peln, *v* to jostle; to bump into

**anrichten, ahn**-rik-ten, *v* to prepare (food); to cause

**anrücken, ahn**-rEEck-en, *v* to move near; to approach

**Anruf, ahn**-roof, *m* phone call; –beantworter, *m* answerbox

**anrufen, ahn**-roof-en, *v* to call; to ring up

**anrühren, ahn**-rEEr-en, *v* to touch; to blend

**ansagen, ahn**-zahg-en, *v* to announce

**Ansager, ahn**-zahg-er, *m* (radio/tv) announcer

**ansammeln, ahn**-zahmm-eln, *v* to collect; to amass

**ansässig, ahn**-zess-ik, *adj* domiciled; settled

**Ansatz, ahn**-zahts, *m* base; starting point; approach

**anschaffen, ahn**-shahff-en, *v* to procure; to furnish; to remit

**Anschaffung, ahn**-shahff-oong, *f* acquisition

**anschauen, ahn**-show-en, *v* to look at

**Anschauung, ahn**-show-oong, *f* point of view

**Anschein, ahn**-shine, *m* appearance; semblance

**anscheinend, ahn**-shine-ent, *adj* seeming

**anschicken (sich), ahn**-shik-en (zik), *v* to get ready for

**Anschlag, ahn**-shlahg, *m* placard; plot; touch; estimate

**anschlagen, ahn**-shlahg-en, *v* to strike (key); to tap; to fix to; to put up; to estimate

**anschließen, ahn**-shlees-en, *v* to lock; to attach; **sich etw –,** to follow sth

**Anschluß, ahn**-shlooss, *m* connection

**anschmiegen (sich), ahn**-shmeeg-en (zik), *v* to nestle against; to cling to

**anschmieren, ahn**-shmeer-en, *v* to smear on; to cheat (sb)

**anschnallen (sich), ahn**-shnahll-en (zik), *v* to fasten one's seat belt

**anschnauzen, ahn**-shnowt-sen, *v* to reprimand

**anschneiden, ahn**-shny-den, *v* to cut into; to broach

**anschrauben, ahn**-shrow-ben, *v* to screw on

**anschreiben, ahn**-shry-ben, *v* to write up; to write to

**anschreien, ahn**-shry-en, *v* to shout at

**Anschrift, ahn**-shrift, *f* address

**Anschuldigung, ahn**-shooll-dig-oong, *f* accusation, indictment

**anschwärzen, ahn**-shvairt-sen, *v* to blacken

**ansehen, ahn**-zay-en, *v* to look at; to consider

**Ansehen, ahn**-zay-en, *nt* appearance; reputation

**ansehnlich, ahn**-zayn-lik,

*adj* considerable; good-looking

**Ansicht, ahnn**-zikt, *f* view; prospect; opinion; **–skarte,** *f* (picture) postcard; **–sache,** *f* matter of opinion

**Ansiedlung, ahnn**-zeed-loong, *f* colony; settlement

**anspannen, ahnn**-shpahnn-en, *v* to stretch; to strain; to harness

**anspielen (auf), ahnn**-shpeel-en (owf), *v* to hint

**Anspielung, ahnn**-shpeel-oong, *f* allusion

**anspornen, ahnn**-shporn-en, *v* to spur on

**Ansprache, ahnn**-shprahk-e, *f* address; speech

**ansprechen, ahnn**-shprek-en, *v* to speak to; to address

**Anspruch, ahnn**-shprook, *m* claim, pretension

**anspruchslos, ahnn**-shprooks-lohs, *adj* modest

**anspruchsvoll, ahnn**-shprooks-fol, *adj* demanding

**anspucken, ahnn**-shpoock-en, *v* to spit at

**Anstalt, ahnn**-shtahlt, *f* institution

**Anstand, ahnn**-shtant, *m* decorum; decency

**anständig, ahnn**-shten-dik, *adj* decent; becoming

**Anständigkeit, ahnn**-shten-dik-kite, *f* decency

**anstatt, ahnn**-**shtahtt**, *prep* instead of

**anstaunen, ahnn**-shtow-nen, *v* to look at in amazement

**anstecken, ahnn**-shteck-en, *v* to pin to; to set alight; to infect

**ansteckend, ahnn**-shteck-ent, *adj* infectious, contagious

**Ansteckung, ahnn**-shteck-oong, *f* infection

**ansteigen, ahnn**-shty-gen, *v* to ascend, to climb

**anstellen, ahnn**-shtell-en, *v* to appoint, to employ

**Anstellung, ahnn**-shtell-oong, *f* appointment, employment, position

**anstiften, ahnn**-shtift-en, *v* to instigate

**Anstiftung, ahnn**-shtift-oong, *f* instigation; provocation

**anstimmen, ahnn**-shtimm-en, *v* to intonate; to tune

**Anstoß, ahnn**-shtohs, *m* impetus; offence

**anstoßen, ahnn**-shtohs-en, *v* to knock against; to clink (glasses)

**anstößig, ahnn**-shters-ik, *adj* offensive; obnoxious

**anstreichen, ahnn**-shtry-ken, *v* to paint

**anstrengen, ahnn**-shtreng-en, *v* to exert; to strain; **sich –,** to make an effort

**anstrengend, ahnn**-shtreng-ent, *adj* tiring

**Anstrengung, ahnn**-shtreng-oong, *f* exertion; effort

**Anstrich, ahnn**-shtrik, *m* coat of paint

**Ansturm, ahnn**-shtoorm, *m* rush; attack

**anstürmen, ahnn**-shtEErm-en, *v* to charge against

**Antarktis, ahnt**-ahrk-tis, *f* Antarctica

**antarktisch, ahnt**-ahrk-tish, *adj* Antarctic

**Anteil, ahnn**-tile, *m* share, portion; sympathy

**Antenne, ahnn**-ten-e, *f* antenna; aerial

**Antibiotikum, ahnn**-te-be-oh-te-koom, *nt* anti-biotic

**antik, ahnn**-teek, *adj* antique

**Antiquar, ahnn**-tee-kvahr, *m* antiquarian

**Antiquariat, ahnn**-tee-kvahr-e-aht, *nt* secondhand bookshop

**Antiquitäten, ahnn**-tee-kvee-tay-ten, *pl* antiques

**Antlitz, ahnt**-lits, *nt* countenance

**Antrag, ahnn**-trahg, *m* proposal

**antreffen, ahnn**-treff-en, *v* to meet; to come across

**antreiben, ahnn**-try-ben, *v* to drive (on/against); to urge (on)

**antreten, ahnn**-tray-ten, *v* to begin; to line up; to assemble; to compete

**Antrieb, ahnn**-treep, *m*

impulse; incentive; drive

**Antritt**, ahnn-tritt, m beginning

**antun**, ahnn-toon, v to inflict

**Antwort**, ahnt-vort, f answer, reply

**antworten**, ahnt-vort-en, v to answer, to reply

**anvertrauen**, ahnn-fair-trow-en, v to entrust

**anwachsen**, ahnn-vahks-en, v to grow (on); to increase

**Anwalt**, ahnn-vahlt, m lawyer; solicitor; barrister

**anwärmen**, ahnn-vairm-en, v to warm up

**anweisen**, ahnn-vy-zen, v to instruct; to transfer (money)

**Anweisung**, ahnn-vy-zoong, f direction; instruction; payment; postal order

**anwendbar**, ahnn-vent-bar, adj applicable (to)

**anwenden**, ahnn-ven-den, v to use; to apply to

**Anwendung**, ahnn-ven-doong, f use; application

**anwesend**, ahnn-vay-zent, adj present

**Anwesenheit**, ahnn-vay-zen-hite, f presence

**anwidern**, ahnn-veed-ern, v to disgust

**Anzahl**, ahnn-tsahl, f number; quantity

**anzahlen**, ahnn-tsahl-en, v to pay a deposit

**Anzahlung**, ahnn-tsahl-oong, f deposit;

part-payment

**anzapfen**, ahnn-tsahpp-fen, v to breach; to tap (trees/telephones)

**Anzeichen**, ahnn-tsy-ken, nt mark, sign, indication

**Anzeige**, ahnn-tsy-ge, f advertisement; notice; advice; denunciation; – **gegen jdn erstatten**, to report sb to the police

**anzeigen**, ahnn-tsy-gen, v to report sb to the police; to denounce

**Anzeiger**, ahnn-tsy-ger, m indicator; advertiser

**anziehen**, ahnn-tsee-en, v to draw towards; to attract; to put on (clothes)

**Anziehung**, ahnn-tsee-oong, f attraction

**Anzug**, ahnn-tsook, m suit (of clothes); approach

**anzüglich**, ahnn-tsEEk-lik, adj suggestive; pointed

**Anzüglichkeit**, ahnn-tsEEk-lik-kite, f suggestiveness

**anzünden**, ahnn-tsEEn-den, v to light

**apart**, ah-part, adj distinctive

**Apfel**, ahpp-fel, m apple

**Apfelbaum**, ahpp-fel-bowm, m apple-tree

**Apfelkuchen**, ahpp-fel-kook-en, m apple tart

**Apfelsine**, ahpp-fel-seen-e, f orange

**Apfelwein**, ahpp-fel-vine, m cider

**Apotheke**, ah-poh-tay-ke, f

chemist's (shop)

**Apotheker**, ah-poh-tay-ker, m chemist

**Apparat**, ah-pah-raht, m appliance; camera; telephone

**Appartement**, ah-pahrt-e-mong, nt flat

**Appell**, ah-pell, m appeal; roll call

**appellieren**, ah-pell-eer-en, v to appeal (court)

**Appetit**, ahp-pay-teet, m appetite; **guten –**, bon appétit

**applaudieren**, ahp-plow-deer-en, v to applaud

**Applaus**, ahp-lows, m applause

**Aprikose**, ah-pre-koh-ze, f apricot

**April**, ah-pril, m April

**Aquarell**, ahkk-vah-rel, nt water-colour; **–farbe**, f water-colour paint

**Araber**, ah-rahb-er, m Arab

**arabisch**, ah-rahb-ish, adj Arabian, Arabic

**Arbeit**, ahr-bite, f work, labour

**arbeiten**, ahr-bite-en, v to work

**Arbeiter**, ahr-bite-er, m workman, worker, labourer

**Arbeitgeber**, ahr-bite-gay-ber, m employer

**Arbeitnehmer**, ahr-bite-nay-mer, m employee

**Arbeitsamt**, ahr-bites-ahmt, nt employment exchange

**Arbeitserlaubnis,** ahr-bites-er-lowb-nis, *f* work permit

**arbeitsfähig,** ahr-bites-fay-ik, *adj* able-bodied

**Arbeitslohn,** ahr-bites-lohn, *m* wages; pay

**arbeitslos,** ahr-bites-lohs, *adj* unemployed

**Arbeitslosigkeit,** ahr-bites-loh-zik-kite, *f* unemployment

**Arbeitsplatz,** ahr-bites-plahts, *m* place of work

**Arbeitstag,** ahr-bites-tahk, *m* working day

**Arbeitszeit,** ahr-bites-tsite, *f* working hours

**Arbeitszimmer,** ahr-bites-tsim-er, *nt* study

**Architektur,** ahr-kee-teck-toor, *f* architecture

**arg,** ahrk, *adj* bad; severe; tremendous; wicked

**Argentinien,** ahrg-enn-tee-nee-en, *nt* Argentina

**Argentinier,** ahrg-enn-tee-nee-er, *m* Argentinian (person)

**argentinisch,** ahrg-enn-tee-nish, *adj* Argentinian

**Ärger,** airg-er, *m* annoyance; anger

**ärgerlich,** airg-er-lik, *adj* annoyed; annoying

**ärgern,** airg-ern, *v* to annoy; to provoke

**Ärgernis,** airg-er-nis, *nt* annoyance; scandal

**arglos,** ahrk-lohs, *adj* innocent; ingenuous

**Argwohn,** ahrk-vohn, *m* suspicion, mistrust

**argwöhnisch,** ahrk-vern-ish, *adj* suspicious

**Aristokratie,** ah-ree-stoh-krah-tee, *f* aristocracy

**Arktis,** ahrk-tis, *f* the Arctic

**arktisch,** ahrk-tish, *adj* Arctic

**Arm,** ahrm, *m* arm

**arm,** ahrm, *adj* poor

**Armband,** ahrm-bahnt, *nt* bracelet

**Armbanduhr,** ahrm-bahnt-oor, *f* wristwatch

**Arme(r),** ahrm-e(r), *m & f* poor man/woman

**Armee,** ahrm-ay, *f* army

**Ärmel,** air-mel, *m* sleeve; –kanal, *m* English Channel

**Armenhaus,** ahrm-en-hows, *nt* almshouse

**ärmlich,** airm-lik, *adj* miserable, poor

**armselig,** ahrm-zay-lik, *adj* wretched; poor

**Armseligkeit,** ahrm-zay-lik-kite, *f* wretchedness

**Armsessel,** ahrm-zess-el, *m* armchair

**Armut,** ahr-moot, *f* poverty

**arrangieren,** ahr-rahng-zheer-en, *v* to arrange

**Arsen,** ahr-zayn, *nt* arsenic

**Art,** ahrt, *f* sort, kind; species; manner

**Arterie,** ahr-tair-ee-e, *f* artery

**artig,** ahr-tik, *adj* well-behaved; polite

**Artikel,** ahr-tik-el, *m* article

**Artist,** ahr-tist, *m* artiste

**Arzneimittel,** ahrts-ny-mit-tel, *nt* medicine; drug

**Arzt,** ahrtst, *m* (male) doctor

**Ärztin,** airtst-in, *f* (female) doctor

**ärztlich,** airtst-lik, *adj* medical, medicinal

**As,** ahss, *nt* ace

**Asche,** ahsh-e, *f* ash(es)

**Aschenbecher,** ahsh-en-bek-er, *m* ashtray

**Aschenbrödel,** ahsh-en-brer-del, *nt* Cinderella

**Aschermittwoch,** ahsh-er-mit-vok, *m* Ash Wednesday

**Asiat,** ah-zee-aht, *m* Asian (person)

**asiatisch,** ah-zee-ah-tish, *adj* Asian

**Asien,** ah-zee-en, *nt* Asia

**Ast,** ahst, *m* branch (tree)

**Asthma,** ahst-mah, *nt* asthma

**Astrologie,** ahst-roh-loh-gee, *f* astrology

**Asyl,** ah-zEEl, *nt* sanctuary; (political) asylum

**Atelier,** ah-tel-ee-eh, *nt* studio

**Atem,** ah-tem, *m* breath; respiration

**Atembeklemmung,** ah-tem-be-klemm-oong, *f* difficulty in breathing; asthma

**Atemholen,** ah-tem-hoh-len, *nt* breathing

**atemlos**, ah-tem-lohs, *adj* breathless

**Atemlosigkeit**, ah-tem-loh-zik-kite, *f* breathlessness

**Atemnot**, ah-tem-noht, *f* difficult breathing

**Atemzug**, ah-tem-tsook, *m* breath

**Athen**, ah-tain, *nt* Athens

**Äther**, ay-ter, *m* ether

**Athlet**, ahtt-lait, *m* athlete

**Atlantik**, ahtt-lahnn-tik, *m* Atlantic (ocean)

**atlantisch**, ahtt-lahnn-tish, *adj* Atlantic

**Atlas**, aht-lass, *m* atlas; satin

**atmen**, aht-men, *v* to breathe

**Atmosphäre**, ahtt-mohs-fair-e, *f* atmosphere

**Atmung**, aht-moong, *f* breath; respiration

**Atombombe**, ah-tohm-bom-be, *f* atom bomb

**Atomwaffen**, ah-tohm-vahff-en, *pl* atomic weapons

**Attentat**, ahtt-en-taht, *nt* assassination attempt

**Attest**, ahtt-est, *nt* certificate, attestation

**attestieren**, ahtt-est-eer-en, *v* to attest, to certify

**Attraktion**, ahtt-rahkts-yohn, *f* attraction

**attraktiv**, ahtt-rahk-teef, *adj* attractive

**ätzen**, ett-sen, *v* to corrode; to cauterize; to etch

**au**, ow, *interj* ouch!

**auch**, owk, *conj* also,

likewise, as well

**auf**, owf, *prep* (up)on; *adv* up(wards); open

**aufatmen**, owf-aht-men, *v* to give a sigh of relief

**aufbauen**, owf-bow-en, *v* to build up; to erect

**aufbäumen (sich)**, owf-boy-men (zik), *v* to rear; to prance (horse)

**aufbauschen**, owl-bow-shen, *v* to puff (up)

**aufbehalten**, owf-be-hahl-ten, *v* to keep on (hat)

**aufbessern**, owf-bess-ern, *v* to raise (wages); to improve

**aufbewahren**, owf-be-vahr-en, *v* to keep; to take of

**Aufbewahrung**, owf-be-vahr-oong, *f* (safe-)keeping

**aufbieten**, owf-beet-en, *v* to summon; to muster

**aufblasen**, owf-blah-zen, *v* to inflate

**aufbleiben**, owf-bly-ben, *v* to stay open; to stay up late

**aufblühen**, owf-blEE-en, *v* to flourish

**aufbrauchen**, owf-browk-en, *v* to use up, to consume

**aufbrausen**, owf-brow-zen, *v* to fizz; to fly into a rage

**aufbrechen**, owf-brek-en, *v* to break open; to start (journey)

**aufbringen**, owf-bring-en, *v*

to rear; to introduce; to raise (money)

**aufdecken**, owf-deck-en, *v* to uncover; to expose

**Aufdeckung**, owf-deck-oong, *f* exposure

**aufdrehen**, owf-dray-en, *v* to turn on

**aufdringlich**, owf-dring-lik, *adj* obtrusive, insistent

**aufdrucken**, owf-drook-en, *v* to print (on); to imprint; to stamp

**aufeinander**, owf-ine-ahnn-der, *adv* one upon another, one after another

**Aufenthalt**, owf-ent-hahlt, *m* stay; delay; **–serlaubnis**, *f* residence permit

**auferlegen**, owf-air-lay-gen, *v* to impose

**auferstehen**, owf-air-shtay-en, *v* to rise from the dead

**Auferstehung**, owf-air-shtay-oong, *f* resurrection

**aufessen**, owf-ess-en, *v* to eat up, to consume

**auffahren**, owf-fahr-en, *v* to fly into a rage

**Auffahrt**, owf-fahrt, *f* drive

**auffallend**, owf-fahll-ent, *adj* striking; conspicuous

**auffällig**, owf-fel-lik, *adj* striking; conspicuous

**auffangen**, owf-fahng-en, *v* to catch; to intercept

**auffassen**, owf-fahss-en, *v* to comprehend, to conceive (ideas); to perceive

**Auffassung**, owf-fahss-oong, *f* conception,

comprehension

**auffordern, owf**-for-dern, *v* to ask; to invite

**Aufforderung, owf**-for-der-oong, *f* invitation

**auffressen, owf**-fress-en, *v* to eat up; to devour

**aufführen, owf**-fEEr-en, *v* to stage, to perform; to list

**Aufführung, owf**-fEEr-oong, *f* performance

**Aufgabe, owf**-gah-be, *f* task; exercise; registration; retirement; surrender; giving up

**Aufgang, owf**-gahng, *m* ascent; staircase; appearance, emergence

**aufgeben, owf**-gay-ben, *v* to give (up); to register; to check in

**aufgeblasen, owf**-ge-blah-zen, *adj* puffed up

**Aufgebot, owf**-ge-boht, *nt* public notice; banns

**aufgebracht, owf**-ge-brahkt, *adj* outraged

**aufgehen, owf**-gay-en, *v* to open; to rise (sun, curtain)

**aufgeklärt, owf**-ge-klairt, *adj* enlightened

**aufgeregt, owf**-ge-raykt, *adj* excited, agitated

**aufgeweckt, owf**-ge-veckt, *adj* lively; bright

**aufgreifen, owf**-gry-fen, *v* to seize, to take up

**aufhalten, owf**-hahlt-en, *v* to hold open; to detain

**aufhängen, owf**-heng-en, *v* to hang

**aufhäufen, owf**-hoyf-en, *v* to pile up

**aufheben, owf**-hay-ben, *v* to lift up; to keep up

**aufheitern, owf**-hy-tern, *v* to brighten up

**Aufheiterung, owf**-hy-ter-oong, *f* brightening

**aufhetzen, owf**-het-sen, *v* to rouse, to incite

**aufhorchen, owf**-hor-ken, *v* to prick up one's ears

**aufhören, owf**-her-ren, *v* to stop, to finish

**aufkaufen, owf**-kowf-en, *v* to buy up

**aufklappen, owf**-klahpp-en, *v* to open up/out

**aufklären, owf**-klair-en, *v* to clear up; to enlighten

**Aufklärung, owf**-klair-oong, *f* enlightenment

**aufknacken, owf**-k'nahck-en, *v* to crack open

**aufknöpfen, owf**-k'nerp-fen, *v* to unbutton

**aufkommen, owf**-komm-en, *v* to (a)rise; to come up/out; to pay (for)

**aufladen, owf**-lahd-en, *v* to load; to charge with

**Auflage, owf**-lahg-e, *f* edition (books); imposition

**auflassen, owf**-lahss-en, *v* to leave open; to shut down

**Auflauf, owf**-lowf, *m* crowd; mob; baked pudding

**auflegen, owf**-lay-gen, *v* to apply; to lay on

**auflesen, owf**-lay-zen, *v* to pick up; to glean

**auflösen, owf**-ler-zen, *v* to (dis)solve; to loosen

**Auflösung, owf**-ler-zoong, *f* dissolution; solution

**aufmachen, owf**-mahk-en, *v* to open, to undo

**Aufmachung, owf**-mahk-oong, *f* outfit; format

**aufmerken, owf**-mairk-en, *v* to mark, to take note

**aufmerksam, owf**-mairk-zahm, *adj* attentive

**Aufmerksamkeit, owf**-merk-sahm-kite, *f* attention, attentiveness

**aufmuntern, owf**-moon-tern, *v* to cheer up, to rouse

**Aufnahme, owf**-nahm-e, *f* taking up; reception

**aufnehmen, owf**-nay-men, *v* to take up/in

**aufopfern (sich), owf**-op-fern (zik), *v* to sacrifice (oneself)

**aufpassen, owf**-pahss-en, *v* to be careful; to pay attention

**aufpolstern, owf**-pol-stern, *v* to upholster

**aufpumpen, owf**-poom-pen, *v* to pump up

**aufräumen, owf**-roy-men, *v* to clear (up); to tidy (up)

**aufrecht, owf**-rekt, *adj* upright, erect

**aufregen, owf**-ray-gen, *v* to excite, to stir up

**Aufregung, owf**-ray-goong,

*f* excitement

**aufreißen, owf**-ry-sen, *v* to tear open (or up)

**aufreizen, owf**-ry-tsen, *v* to incite, to provoke

**aufrichten, owf**-rik-ten, *v* to erect

**aufrichtig, owf**-rik-tik, *adj* sincere, honest

**Aufrichtigkeit, owf**-rik-tik-kite, *f* sincerity, honesty

**Aufruf, owf**-roof, *m* calling up; appeal

**Aufruhr, owf**-roor, *m* uproar, riot, rebellion

**aufrührerisch, owf**-rEEr-er-ish, *adj* mutinous

**aufsagen, owf**-zahg-en, *v* to recite

**aufsammeln, owf**-zahmm-eln, *v* to collect

**Aufsatz, owf**-sahts, *m* essay; upper part

**aufschauen, owf**-show-en, *v* to look up

**aufschieben, owf**-shee-ben, *v* to postpone, to put off

**Aufschlag, owf**-shlahk, *m* impact; service (tennis)

**aufschlagen, owf**-shlahg-en, *v* to crash; to serve (tennis)

**aufschließen, owf**-shlees-en, *v* to unlock

**Aufschluß, owf**-shlooss, *m* disclosure, explanation

**aufschneiden, owf**-shny-den, *v* to cut open; to boast

**Aufschneider, owf**-shny-der, *m* boaster

**Aufschnitt, owf**-shnitt, *m* cut; cold meat

**aufschrauben, owf**-shrow-ben, *v* to screw on

**aufschrecken, owf**-shreck-en, *v* to startle

**Aufschrei, owf**-shry, *m* outcry; shriek

**aufschreiben, owf**-shry-ben, *v* to write down

**Aufschrift, owf**-shrift, *f* inscription; address

**Aufschub, owf**-shoop, *m* delay; adjournment

**aufschütten, owf**-shEEtt-en, *v* to pour on

**Aufschwung, owf**-shvoong, *m* swinging up; *comm* revival, upturn

**Aufsehen, owf**-zay-en, *nt* sensation, scandal

**Aufseher, owf**-zay-er, *m* overseer, inspector

**aufsetzen, owf**-zet-sen, *v* to put on; to set up

**Aufsicht, owf**-zikt, *f* supervision; care; inspection; **–srat,** *m* board of inspection

**aufsitzen, owf**-zit-sen, *v* to sit up; to mount (horse)

**aufsparen, owf**-shpahr-en, *v* to save up

**aufsperren, owf**-shpair-ren, *v* to open wide

**aufsprengen, owf**-shpreng-en, *v* to burst open; to blast open

**aufspringen, owf**-shpring-en, *v* to jump up; to bounce; to burst open

**aufstacheln, owf**-shtahk-eln, *v* to goad; to spur on

**Aufstand, owf**-shtahnt, *m* rising, rebellion

**aufständisch, owf**-shten-dish, *adj* rebellious

**aufstapeln, owf**-shtah-peln, *v* to pile/stack up

**aufstehen, owf**-shtay-en, *v* to rise, to get up

**aufsteigen, owf**-shty-gen, *v* to climb; to rise; to mount

**aufstellen, owf**-shtell-en, *v* to set up, to erect

**Aufstellung, owf**-shtell-oong, *f* erection; drawing up; list, inventory

**Aufstieg, owf**-shteek, *m* ascent

**aufsuchen, owf**-sook-en, *v* to look up; to visit

**auftauchen, owf**-towk-en, *v* to rise; to emerge

**auftauen, owf**-tow-en, *v* to thaw

**aufteilen, owf**-ty-len, *v* to divide

**Aufteilung, owf**-ty-loong, *f* division

**auftischen, owf**-tish-en, *v* to serve up, to dish up

**Auftrag, owf**-trahk, *m* order; commission; task; **–geber,** *m* client; customer; **–nehmer,** *m* person/firm accepting an order; contractor

**auftreiben, owf**-try-ben, *v* to raise; to find

**auftreten, owf**-tray-ten, *v* to appear; to step on

**Auftritt, owf**-tritt, *m*
appearance; entrance

**aufwachen, owf**-vahk-en, *v*
to wake up, to awake

**aufwachsen, owf**-vahk-sen,
*v* to grow up

**aufwärmen, owf**-vair-men, *v*
to warm up

**aufwarten, owf**-vahrt-en, *v*
to wait on

**aufwärts, owf**-vairts, *adv*
upwards

**aufwaschen, owf**-vahsh-en,
*v* to wash (up/down)

**aufwecken, owf**-veck-en, *v*
to awaken; to rouse

**aufweisen, owf**-vy-zen, *v* to
show (results)

**aufwenden, owf**-ven-den, *v*
to spend; to devote

**aufwendig, owf**-vend-ik, *adj*
costly; lavish

**aufwerfen, owf**-vairf-en, *v*
to throw up/open; to raise
(question, problem)

**aufwerten, owf**-vairt-en, *v*
to revalue; to increase in
value

**aufwickeln, owf**-vik-eln, *v*
to coil; to wind up

**aufwiegeln, owf**-veeg-eln, *v*
to stir up, to provoke

**aufwirbeln, owf**-veer-beln, *v*
to swirl up

**aufwischen, owf**-vish-en, *v*
to wipe up, to mop up

**aufwühlen, owf**-vEEl-en, *v*
to toss/rip up

**aufzählen, owf**-tsay-len, *v* to
list

**aufzehren, owf**-tsay-ren, *v*
to consume

**aufzeichnen, owf**-tsy'k-nen,
*v* to sketch; to record; to
note

**Aufzeichnung, owf**-tsy'k-
noong, *f* sketch; record;
recording; note

**aufziehen, owf**-tsee-en, *v* to
wind up; to pull up; to
rear

**Aufzug, owf**-tsook, *m* lift;
act; procession

**Augapfel, owk**-ahpp-fel, *m*
eyeball

**Auge, ow-ge,** *nt* eye; bud;
spot

**Augenarzt, ow**-gen-ahrts-t,
*m* ophthalmologist

**Augenblick, owf**-gen-blik, *m*
moment, instant

**augenblicklich, ow**-gen-
blik-lik, *adv* at present

**Augenbraue, ow**-gen-brow-
e, *f* eyebrow

**Augenlicht, ow**-gen-likt, *nt*
(eye)sight

**Augenlid, ow**-gen-leet, *nt*
eyelid

**Augenschein, ow**-gen-
shine, *m* appearance

**augenscheinlich, ow**-gen-
shine-lik, *adj* apparent

**Augenwimper, ow**-gen-vim-
per, *f* eyelash

**Augenzeuge, ow**-gen-tsoy-
ge, *m* eye-witness

**August, ow-goost,** *m*
August

**Auktion, owkts-yohn,** *f*
auction

**Auktionator, owkts-yohn-**
ah-tohr, *m* auctioneer

**aus, owss,** *prep* out of; of;
from; made of; *adv*
finished; over; off

**ausarbeiten, ows**-ahr-by-
ten, *v* to work out

**ausarten, ows**-ahrt-en, *v* to
degenerate

**ausatmen, ows**-aht-men, *v*
to breathe out, to exhale

**ausbedingen, ows**-be-ding-
en, *v* to stipulate

**ausbessern, ows**-bes-ern, *v*
to repair, to restore

**ausbeuten, ows**-boy-ten, *v*
to exploit

**ausbezahlen, ows**-be-tsahl-
en, *v* to pay out

**ausbilden, ows**-bil-den, *v* to
train

**Ausbildung, ows**-bil-doong,
*f* training; development

**ausblasen, ows**-blah-zen, *v*
to blow out

**ausbleiben, ows**-bly-ben, *v*
to stay out; to fail to
appear

**Ausblick, ows**-blik, *m*
prospect; view

**ausbrechen, ows**-brek-en, *v*
to break out

**ausbreiten, ows**-bry-ten, *v*
to spread out

**ausbrennen, ows**-bren-en, *v*
to burn out

**Ausbruch, ows**-brook, *m*
outbreak; eruption

**ausbrüten, ows**-brEEt-en, *v*
to hatch; to incubate

**ausbürsten, ows**-bEErst-en, *v*
to brush thoroughly

**Ausdauer,** ows-dow-er, *f*
endurance; perseverance

**ausdehnen,** ows-day-nen, *v*
to stretch; to expand

**Ausdehnung,** ows-day-
noong, *f* extension;
enlargement; dimension

**ausdenken,** ows-deng-ken, *v*
to think out; to imagine

**ausdienen,** ows-deen-en, *v*
to serve one's time

**ausdrehen,** ows-dray-en, *v*
to turn out

**Ausdruck,** ows-droock, *m*
expression

**ausdrücken,** ows-drEEck-en,
*v* to express; to squeeze
out

**ausdrücklich,** ows-drEEck-
lik, *adj* positive; explicit

**ausdruckslos,** ows-droocks-
lohss, *adj* without
expression

**ausdrucksvoll,** ows-
droocks-foll, *adj*
expressive; significant

**Ausdünstung,** ows-dEEnn-
stoong, *f* evaporation;
perspiration

**auseinander,** ows-ine-ahnn-
der, *adj* asunder; apart;
separate

**Auseinandersetzung,** ows-
ine-ahnn-der-zets-oong, *f*
discussion; argument;
examination; analysis

**auserlesen,** ows-air-lay-zen,
*adj* choice; select

**auserwählen,** ows-air-vay-
len, *v* to choose

**auserwählt,** ows-air-vailt,

*adj* elect; predestined

**ausfahren,** ows-fahr-en, *v* to
drive out

**Ausfahrt,** ows-fahrt, *f* drive;
excursion; exit, way out

**Ausfall,** ows-fahll, *m* loss;
cancellation; retirement;
result, outcome

**ausfallen,** ows-fahll-en, *v* to
turn out; to fall out; to
fail, to break down; to be
cancelled

**ausfechten,** ows-fek-ten, *v*
to fight out

**ausfegen,** ows-fay-gen, *v* to
sweep out

**ausfertigen,** ows-fairt-ig-en,
*v* to expedite; to draw up
(documents)

**ausfindig machen,** ows-fin-
dig mahk-en, *v* to find
(out)

**Ausflucht,** ows-flookt, *f*
excuse

**Ausflug,** ows-floock, *m*
excursion; trip

**Ausflügler,** ows-flEEg-ler, *m*
tripper

**Ausfluß,** ows-flooss, *m*
outflow; discharge

**ausfragen,** ows-frahg-en, *v*
to question

**Ausfuhr,** ows-foor, *f* export

**ausführen,** ows-fEEr-en, *v* to
carry out; to export

**ausführlich,** ows-fEEr-lik, *adj*
detailed; ample

**Ausführung,** ows-fEEr-oong,
*f* execution; completion;
model

**ausfüllen,** ows-fEEll-en, *v* to

fill out (form)

**Ausgabe,** ows-gah-be, *f*
edition; issue; expense

**Ausgang,** ows-gahng, *m*
exit, way out; upshot

**ausgeben,** ows-gay-ben, *v* to
spend; to yield

**ausgebreitet,** ows-ge-bry-tet,
*adj* spread out

**ausgebucht,** ows-ge-bookt,
*adj* fully booked

**ausgefallen,** ows-ge-fahll-
en, *adj* exceptional

**ausgehen,** ows-gay-en, *v* to
go out; to proceed from

**ausgelassen,** ows-ge-lahss-
en, *adj* boisterous;
unrestrained; left out

**ausgemacht,** ows-ge-mahkt,
*adj* made out; agreed
(upon)

**ausgenommen,** ows-ge-
nomm-en, *conj* except

**ausgesucht,** ows-ge-sookt,
*adj* choice; exceptional

**ausgezeichnet,** ows-ge-tsy'k-
net, *adj* distinguished;
excellent

**ausgießen,** ows-geess-en, *v*
to pour out

**Ausgleich,** ows-gly'k, *m*
balance; settling

**ausgleiten,** ows-gly-ten, *v* to
slip, to slide

**ausgraben,** ows-grahb-en, *v*
to dig out

**Ausguck,** ows-goock, *m*
look-out

**Ausguß,** ows-gooss, *m* sink;
drain

**aushalten,** ows-hahll-ten, *v*

to hold out; to sustain; to bear

**aushandeln, ows**-hahnn-deln, *v* to negotiate

**aushändigen, ows**-hen-dig-en, *v* to hand over

**aushängen, ows**-heng-en, *v* to hang out

**ausharren, ows**-hahrr-en, *v* to persevere

**ausheben, ows**-hay-ben, *v* to levy; to lift out; to raid

**aushelfen, ows**-hel-fen, *v* to help out

**Aushilfe, ows**-hil-fe, *f* aid; temporary help

**ausholen, ows**-hohl-en, *v* to raise one's arm to strike

**aushorchen, ows**-hor-ken, *v* to sound

**aushungern, ows**-hoong-ern, *v* to famish; to starve out

**auskämmen, ows**-kem-en, *v* to comb out

**auskennen (sich), ows**-ken-en (zik), *v* to know one's way; to be knowledgable

**auskleiden (sich), ows**-kly-den (zik), *v* to undress; to take off (clothes)

**ausklopfen, ows**-klop-fen, *v* to beat out

**auskneifen, ows**-k'ny-fen, *v* to run away

**auskochen, ows**-kok-en, *v* to boil thoroughly

**auskommen, ows**-kom-en, *v* to manage (to live); to get on with (sb)

**auskundschaften, ows**-

koont-shahft-en, *v* to reconnoitre

**Auskunft, ows**-koonft, *f* information

**auslachen, ows**-lahk-en, *v* to laugh at; to deride

**ausladen, ows**-lahd-en, *v* to unload

**Auslage, ows**-lahg-e, *f* outlay; (shop) display

**Ausland, ows**-lahnt, *nt* foreign countries; **im –**, abroad; **ins – gehen**, to go abroad

**Ausländer, ows**-len-der, *m* foreigner

**ausländisch, ows**-len-dish, *adj* foreign; alien

**Auslandsgespräch, ows**-lahnts-ge-shpraik, *nt* international call

**Auslandsreise, ows**-lahnts-ry-ze, *f* trip abroad

**auslassen, ows**-lahss-en, *v* to omit; to let out

**auslaufen, ows**-lowf-en, *v* to run out; to stop running

**ausleeren, ows**-lay-ren, *v* to empty

**auslegen, ows**-lay-gen, *v* to spread out; to display; to lay out; to interpret

**Auslegung, ows**-lay-goong, *f* interpretation; explanation

**ausleihen, ows**-ly-en, *v* to lend; **sich etw –**, to borrow sth

**ausliefern, ows**-leef-ern, *v* to deliver; to hand over; to extradite

**Auslieferung, ows**-leef-er-oong, *f* delivery; extradition

**auslöschen, ows**-lersh-en, *v* to extinguish; to obliterate

**auslösen, ows**-ler-zen, *v* to cause; to start

**ausmachen, ows**-mahk-en, *v* to put out; to switch off; **Macht es Ihnen etw aus?** Do you mind?

**Ausmarsch, ows**-marsh, *m* marching out; departure (troops)

**Ausmaß, ows**-mahss, *nt* scale; extent

**ausmessen, ows**-mess-en, *v* to measure; to take the dimensions

**Ausnahme, ows**-nahm-e, *f* exception; **–zustand**, *m* state of emergency

**ausnahmslos, ows**-nahms-lohs, *adv* without exception

**ausnahmsweise, ows**-nahms-vy-ze, *adv* as an exception

**ausnehmen, ows**-nay-men, *v* to except; to make out

**ausnutzen, ows**-noots-en, **ausnützen, ows**-nEEts-en, *v* to exploit; to utilize

**auspacken, ows**-pahck-en, *v* to unpack

**auspfeifen, ows**-pfy-fen, *v* to hiss at

**ausplaudern, ows**-plow-dern, *v* to have a good chat

**ausplündern,** ows-plEEnn-dern, *v* to loot

**auspressen,** ows-press-en, *v* to squeeze out

**ausprobieren,** ows-proh-beer-en, *v* to try out

**Auspuff,** ows-pooff, *m* exhaust (pipe, valve)

**ausrauben,** ows-row-ben, *v* to rob; to pillage

**ausräumen,** ows-roy-men, *v* to clear away

**ausrechnen,** ows-rek-nen, *v* to work out; to calculate

**Ausrede,** ows-ray-de, *f* excuse; plea

**ausreden,** ows-ray-den, *v* to finish speaking; **jdm etw –,** to talk sb out of sth

**ausreichen,** ows-ry-ken, *v* to suffice

**ausreichend,** ows-ry-kent, *adj* adequate

**Ausreise,** ows-ry-ze, *f* departure; **–erlaubnis,** *f* exit permit

**ausreisen,** ows-ry-zen, *v* to leave the country

**ausreißen,** ows-ry-sen, *v* to tear out; to run away

**ausreiten,** ows-ry-ten, *v* to go (out) riding

**ausrenken,** ows-renk-en, *v* to put out of joint

**ausrichten,** ows-rik-ten, *v* to align; to tell; to pass on

**ausrotten,** ows-rot-en, *v* to root out; to eradicate

**Ausruf,** ows-roof, *m* exclamation

**ausrufen,** ows-roof-en, *v* to exclaim; to call out

**Ausrufezeichen,** ows-roof-e-tsy-ken, *nt* exclamation mark

**ausruhen,** ows-roo-en, *v* to rest

**ausrupfen,** ows-roop-fen, *v* to pluck out

**ausrüsten,** ows-rEEst-en, *v* to furnish; to provide with; to equip

**Ausrüstung,** ows-rEEst-oong, *f* equipment; outfit

**ausrutschen,** ows-root-shen, *v* to slip

**Aussage,** ows-zahg-e, *f* assertion; statement

**aussagen,** ows-zahg-en, *v* to say; to testify

**aussätzig,** ows-zets-ik, *adj* leprous

**aussaugen,** ows-zow-gen, *v* to suck dry; to exhaust

**ausschalten,** ows-shahlt-en, *v* to eliminate; to switch off

**Ausschank,** ows-shahnk, *m* bar, pub

**ausschauen,** ows-show-en, *v* to have the appearance; **nach etw –,** to look out for sth

**ausscheiden,** ows-shy-den, *v* to separate from; to secrete

**Ausscheidung,** ows-shy-doong, *f* separation; secretion

**ausschenken,** ows-shenk-en, *v* to pour out

**ausscheuern,** ows-shoy-ern,

*v* to scour

**ausschiffen,** ows-shif-en, *v* to disembark; to put to sea

**ausschimpfen,** ows-shimp-fen, *v* to tell off

**ausschildern,** ows-shild-ern, *v* to signpost

**ausschlafen,** ows-shlahf-en, *v* to sleep enough

**Ausschlag,** ows-shlahk, *m* rash; swing; **den – geben,** to tip the balance

**ausschlagen,** ows-shlahg-en, *v* to refuse (offers)

**ausschließen,** ows-shleess-en, *v* to shut out

**ausschließlich,** ows-shleess-lik, *adj* exclusive; *adv* exclusively

**Ausschluß,** ows-shlooss, *m* exclusion

**ausschmücken,** ows-shmEEck-en, *v* to adorn

**ausschneiden,** ows-shny-den, *v* to cut out

**Ausschnitt,** ows-shnitt, *m* cutting; cut out

**ausschöpfen,** ows-sherp-fen, *v* to scoop out

**ausschreiben,** ows-shry-ben, *v* to write in full; to announce

**Ausschreibung,** ows-shry-boong, *f* invitation for tenders

**Ausschreitungen,** ows-shry-toong-en, *fpl* riot

**Ausschuß,** ows-shooss, *m* rubbish; committee

**ausschütten,** ows-shEEtt-en, *v* to pour out

**ausschwatzen**, ows-shvaht-sen, *v* to blab

**ausschweifend**, ows-shvy-fend, *adj* debauched; extravagant

**Ausschweifung**, ows-shvy-foong, *f* excess; dissipation

**aussehen**, ows-zay-en, *v* to look (have the appearance)

**Aussehen**, ows-zay-en, *nt* appearance

**aussein**, ows-sine, *v* to be out; to be over; to be switched off

**außen**, ows-en, *adv* outside; without

**Außenhandel**, ows-sen-hahn-del, *m* foreign trade

**Außenminister**, ows-sen-mee-nis-ter, *m* foreign minister

**Außenpolitik**, ows-sen-poh-lee-teek, *f* foreign policy

**außenpolitisch**, ows-sen-poh-lee-tish, *adj* as regards foreign affairs

**Außenseite**, ows-sen-zy-te, *f* outside; surface; **–r**, *m* outsider

**außer**, ows-ser, *prep* out of, beside(s), except; *conj* except; **– Betrieb**, out of order

**außerdem**, ows-ser-daim, *adv* besides; moreover

**äußere(r/s)**, oys-ser-e(r/s), *adj* outer; external

**Äußere**, oys-ser-e, *nt* appearance; outer part

**außerehelich**, ows-ser-ay-e-lik, *adj* illegitimate

**außergewöhnlich**, ows-ser-ge-vern-lik, *adj* extraordinary

**außerhalb**, ows-ser-hahlp, *prep & adv* outside; externally

**äußerlich**, oys-ser-lik, *adj* outward; apparent; external

**äußern**, oys-sern, *v* to manifest; to show

**außerordentlich**, ows-ser-ord-ent-lik, *adj* extraordinary

**äußerst**, oys-serst, *adv* extremely, exceedingly, most

**Äußerung**, oys-ser-oong, *f* utterance

**aussetzen**, ows-zet-sen, *v* to object; to disembark

**Aussicht**, ows-sikt, *f* view; prospect; outlook

**aussichtslos**, ows-sikts-lohs, *adj* hopeless

**aussöhnen**, ows-zern-en, *v* to make up (quarrel)

**Aussöhnung**, ows-zern-oong, *f* reconciliation

**aussondern**, ows-zon-dern, *v* to single out; to reject

**aussortieren**, ows-zort-eer-en, *v* to sort

**ausspannen**, ows-shpahnn-en, *v* to stretch out; to relax; to unharness

**aussperren**, ows-shpairr-en, *v* to lock out

**Aussprache**, ows-shprahk-e, *f* pronunciation; discussion

**aussprechen**, ows-shprek-en, *v* to pronounce; to say; to finish speaking

**Ausspruch**, ows-shproock, *m* saying

**ausspucken**, ows-shpoock-en, *v* to spit out

**ausspülen**, ows-shpEEl-en, *v* to rinse; to wash out

**ausstaffieren**, ows-shtahff-eer-en, *v* to equip

**Ausstand**, ows-shtahnt, *m* strike

**Ausstattung**, ows-shtahtt-oong, *f* equipment

**aussteigen**, ows-shty-gen, *v* to get out; to alight

**ausstellen**, ows-shtell-en, *v* to exhibit

**Ausstellung**, ows-shtell-oong, *f* exhibition; show

**aussterben**, ows-shtairb-en, *v* to die out

**Aussteuer**, ows-shtoy-er, *f* dowry

**Ausstieg**, ows-shteeg, *m* exit

**ausstopfen**, ows-shtopp-fen, *v* to stuff; to pad

**ausstoßen**, ows-shtols-en, *v* to eject

**ausstrahlen**, ows-shtrahlen, *v* to radiate

**Ausstrahlung**, ows-shtrahl-oong, *f* emission (rays)

**ausstrecken**, ows-shtreek-en, *v* to stretch out; to put out (hand)

**ausstreichen**, ows-shtry-ken, *v* to cross out

**ausstreuen,** ows-shtroy-en, *v* to strew (out)

**ausströmen,** ows-shtrer-men, *v* to stream out

**aussuchen,** ows-zook-en, *v* to choose, to pick

**Austausch,** ows-towsh, *m* exchange; barter

**austauschen,** ows-towsh-en, *v* to exchange

**austeilen,** ows-ty-len, *v* to distribute; to hand out; to dispense; to deal (cards)

**Auster,** ows-ter, *f* oyster

**austragen,** ows-trahg-en, *v* to carry out; to deliver (mail)

**Australien,** ows-trah-lee-en, *nt* Australia

**australisch,** ows-trah-lish, *adj* Australian

**austreiben,** ows-try-ben, *v* to drive out; to expel

**austreten,** ows-tray-ten, *v* to step out; **aus etw –,** to leave

**austrinken,** ows-trink-en, *v* to drink up

**Austritt,** ows-tritt, *m* outflow; discharge; leaving; resignation

**austrocknen,** ows-trock-nen, *v* to dry up/out; to drain; to parch

**ausüben,** ows-EEb-en, *v* to exercise; to practise; to execute

**Ausübung,** ows-EEb-oong, *f* practice; exercise; execution

**Ausverkauf,** ows-fair-kowf, *m* (clearance) sale

**ausverkauft,** ows-fair-kowft, *adj* sold out

**Auswahl,** ows-vahl, *f* selection, choice

**auswählen,** ows-vail-en, *v* to select, to choose

**Auswanderer,** ows-vahnn-der-er, *m* emigrant

**auswandern,** ows-vahnn-dern, *v* to emigrate

**Auswanderung,** ows-vahnn-der-oong, *f* emigration; exodus

**auswärtig,** ows-vairt-ik, *adj* foreign

**auswärts,** ows-vairts, *adv* abroad; outward

**auswaschen,** ows-vahsh-en, *v* to wash out

**Ausweg,** ows-vaig, *m* way out; loophole; expedient

**ausweichen,** ows-vy-ken, *v* to make way

**Ausweis,** ows-vice, *m* identity card

**ausweisen,** ows-vy-zen, *v* to expel; to deport; **sich –,** to give proof of one's identity

**Ausweisung,** ows-vy-zoong, *f* eviction; expulsion

**auswendig,** ows-ven-dig, *adv* from memory, by heart

**auswickeln,** ows-vik-eln, *v* to unwrap

**auswischen,** ows-vish-en, *v* to wipe out

**Auswuchs,** ows-vooks, *m* (out)growth

**auszahlen,** ows-tsahl-en, *v* to pay out

**Auszahlung,** ows-tsahl-oong, *f* paying out

**auszeichnen,** ows-tsy'k-nen, *v* to distinguish

**Auszeichnung,** ows-tsy'k-noong, *f* distinction; honours (exam)

**ausziehen,** ows-tsee-en, *v* to move out; to take off; to undress

**Auszubildende(r),** ows-tsoo-bil-den-de(r), *m & f* trainee

**Auszug,** ows-tsook, *m* exodus; removal; statement (accounts)

**Auto,** ow-toh, *nt* car; **–bahn,** *f* motorway; **–bahngebühr,** *f* motorway toll; **–bus,** *m* bus; **–fähre,** *f* car ferry; **–fahrer,** *m* driver

**Automat,** ow-toh-maht, *m* (vending/slot) machine

**automatisch,** ow-toh-mah-tish, *adj* automatic

**Autor,** ow-tohr, *m* author

**Autorität,** ow-tohr-ee-tait, *f* authority

**Autounfall,** ow-toh-oonn-fahll, *m* car accident

**Autovermietung,** ow-toh-fair-meet-oong, *f* car hire

**Axt,** ahkst, *f* axe

**Baby, bay-bee,** *nt* baby;
**–nahrung,** *f* baby food;
**–sitter,** *m* baby-sitter
**Bach, bahk,** *m* brook; stream
**Backe, bahck-e,** *f* cheek
**backen, bahck-en,** *v* to bake
**Backenbart, bahck-en-bart,**
*m* sideboards
**Backenzahn, bahck-en-
tsahn** *m* molar
**Bäcker, beck-er,** *m* baker
**Bäckerei, beck-e-ry,** *f*
bakery; baker's shop
**Backform, bahck-form,** *f*
baking tin
**Backofen, bahck-oh-fen,** *m*
oven
**Backpulver, bahck-pool-fer,**
*nt* baking-powder
**Backstein, bahck-shtine,** *m*
brick
**Bad, baht,** *nt* bath; spa;
**–eanstalt,** *f* swimming
baths; **–eanzug,** *m*

swimming costume;
**–ehose,** *f* swimming
trunks; **–ekappe,** *f*
swimming cap; **–emantel,**
*m* bath robe; **–emeister,** *m*
pool attendant
**baden, bahd-en,** *v* to bath(e)
**Badeort, bahd-e-ort,** *m* spa;
resort
**Badewanne, bahd-e-
vahnne,** *f* bath tub
**Badezimmer, bahd-e-
tsimmer,** *nt* bathroom
**Bagger, bahg-ger,** *m*
excavator
**baggern, bahg-gern,** *v* to
excavate, to dredge
**Bahn, bahn,** *f* railway; track;
lane; orbit; **–Card,** *f*
railcard
**bahnen, bahn-en,** *v* to make
the way
**Bahnhof, bahn-hohf,** *m*
railway station

**Bahnsteig, bahn-shtyk,** *m*
(station) platform
**Bahnübergang, bahn-EE-ber-
gahng,** *m* level crossing
**Bahre, bahr-e,** *f* stretcher;
bier
**Baisse, bay-se,** *f* fall (prices);
slump
**Bakterien, bahck-tair-i-en,**
*pl* bacteria
**bald, bahlt,** *adv* soon; almost
**baldig, bahl-dik,** *adj* early;
speedy
**balgen, bahlg-en,** *v* to
scuffle; to romp
**Balken, bahlk-en,** *m* beam;
joist
**Balkon, bahl-kohn,** *m*
balcony; circle
**Ball, bahll,** *m* ball; dance
**ballen, bahll-en,** *v* to form
into a ball
**Ballen, bahll-en,** *m* bale;
pack
**Ballett, bahl-let,** *nt* ballet
**Ballsaal, bahll-zahl,** *m*
ballroom
**Banane, ba-nah-ne,** *f*
banana
**Band, bahnt,** *m* volume,
tome; *nt* ribbon; band;
tape
**Bande, bahnd-e,** *f* band,
horde, gang
**bändigen, bend-ig-en,** *v* to
tame
**Bandmaß, bahnt-mahs,** *nt*
tape-measure
**bange, bahng-e,** *adj & adv*
afraid, anxious(ly)
**Bank, bahnk,** *f* bench;

*comm* bank; **–anweisung,** *f*
banker's order

**Bankier, bahnk**-e-eh, *m*
banker

**Bankkonto, bahnk**-kon-to,
*nt* bank account

**Bankleitzahl, bahnk**-lytt-
tsahl, *f* bank sort-code
number

**bankrott, bahnk-rott,** *adj*
bankrupt

**Bankrott, bahnk-rott,** *m*
bankruptcy; failure; crash

**Bankverbindung, bahnk**-
fair-bin-doong, *f* banking
arrangements

**Bankwesen, bahnk**-vay-zen,
*nt* banking

**bannen, bahnn**-en, *v* to
captivate; to enchant

**bar, bahr,** *adj* bare; in cash

**Bär, bair,** *m* bear

**barfuß, bahr-foos,** *adj*
barefoot(ed)

**Bargeld, bahr**-gelt, *nt* cash

**bargeldlos, bahr**-gelt-lohs,
*adj* cashless; *adv* without
using cash

**barmherzig, bahrm-hairt**-
sik, *adj* merciful;
charitable

**Barmherzigkeit, bahrm**-
**hairt**-sik-kite, *f* mercy;
compassion

**Barren, bahr**-ren, *m* (metal)
bar; ingot

**Barrikade, bahr**-re-kah-de, *f*
barricade

**barsch, bahr-sh,** *adj* rude;
rough; harsh

**Bart, bahrt,** *m* beard

**bärtig, bairt-**ik, *adj* bearded

**Barzahlung, bahr**-tsahl-
oong, *f* cash payment

**Base, bah-ze,** *f chem* base

**Basilikum, bahs-se-le-**
koom, *nt* basil

**Baß, bahss,** *m* bass (voice);
**–geige,** *f* double bass

**basteln, bahss-teln,** *v* to do
handicrafts, to make

**Batterie, bah-te-ree,** *f*
battery

**Bau, bow,** *m* building;
construction; erection

**Bauch, bowk,** *m* belly;
abdomen; **–redner,** *m*
ventriloquist;
**–schmerzen,** *pl* stomach
ache

**bauen, bow-en,** *v* to build

**Bauer, bow-**er, *m* peasant;
farmer; pawn (chess)

**Bäuerin, boy-**er-in, *f* farmer,
farmer's wife

**Bauernfänger, bow**-ern-
feng-er, *m* confidence
trickster

**Bauernhaus, bow**-ern-hous,
*nt* farmhouse

**Bauernhof, bow**-ern-hof, *m*
farmyard

**baufällig, bow**-fell-ik, *adj*
dilapidated

**Baugelände, bow**-ge-len-de,
*nt* building site; building
land

**Baum, bowm,** *m* tree;
**–schule,** *f* (tree) nursery;
**–stamm,** *m* trunk (of
tree); **–wolle,** *f* cotton

**baumeln, bowm-**eln, *v*

to dangle

**Bauplan, bow**-plahn, *m*
architect's plan

**bauschen, bow-**shen, *v* to
puff out

**Bausparkasse, bow**-shpahr-
kahs-se, *f* building society

**Baustein, bow**-shtine, *m*
building stone

**Baustelle, bow**-shtel-le, *f*
building site

**Bayer, by**-er, *m* Bavarian
(person)

**bay(e)risch, by(-e)**-rish, *adj*
Bavarian

**Bayern, by**-ern, *nt* Bavaria

**Bazillus, bah**-tsil-loos, *m*
bacillus

**beabsichtigen, be-ahp**-sik-
tig-en, *v* to intend

**beachten, be-ahk**-ten, *v* to
heed; to take notice

**beachtenswert, be-ahk**-tens-
vairt, *adj* noteworthy

**Beachtung, be-ahk**-toong, *f*
attention, notice

**Beamte(r), be-ahm**-te(r), *m*
official; civil servant

**Beamtin, be-ahm**-tin, *f*
official; civil servant

**beängstigend, be-engst**-ig-
end, *adj* alarming

**beanspruchen, be-ahnn**-
shprook-en, *v* to claim; to
take up; to demand

**beantragen, be-ahnn**-trahg-
en, *v* to apply for; to
propose

**beantworten, be-ahnt**-vort-
en, *v* to answer (to)

**Beantwortung, be-ahnt**-

vort-oong, *f* answer

**bearbeiten**, be-**ar**-by-ten, *v* to work (on sth), to deal with

**beaufsichtigen**, be-**owf**-zik-tig-en, *v* to supervize

**beauftragen**, be-**owf**-trahg-en, *v* to hire; to commission; to instruct

**bebauen**, be-**bow**-en, *v* to build upon; to cultivate (land)

**beben**, **bay**-ben, *v* to quiver

**Becher**, **bek**-er, *m* beaker; cup

**Becken**, **beck**-en, *nt* basin; pelvis; cymbals (*pl*)

**bedächtig**, be-**dek**-tik, *adj* deliberate; measured

**Bedächtigkeit**, be-**dek**-tik-kite, *f* deliberateness

**bedanken (sich)**, be-**dahnk**-en (zik), *v* to thank

**Bedarf**, be-**dahrf**, *m* need; requirement; demand

**bedauerlich**, be-**dow**-er-lik, *adj* regrettable

**bedauern**, be-**dow**-ern, *v* to regret; to sympathize; to pity

**bedecken**, be-**deck**-en, *v* to cover (with)

**bedenken**, be-**denk**-en, *v* to reflect; to think over

**bedenklich**, be-**denk**-lik, *adj* serious; critical

**Bedenkzeit**, be-**denk**-tsyt, *f* time for reflection

**bedeuten**, be-**doyt**-en, *v* to mean; to signify

**bedeutend**, be-**doyt**-ent, *adj* important, significant

**Bedeutung**, be-**doyt**-oong, *f* meaning; significance; importance

**bedeutungsvoll**, be-**doyt**-oongs-foll, *adj* significant

**bedienen**, be-**deen**-en, *v* to serve; to operate

**Bedienung**, be-**deen**-oong, *f* service; waiter/waitress; service charge;

**–sanleitung**, *f* operating instructions

**bedingt**, be-**dingt**, *adj* qualified; conditional

**Bedingung**, be-**ding**-oong, *f* condition; terms

**bedrängen**, be-**dreng**-en, *v* to pester; to put under pressure

**bedrohen**, be-**droh**-en, *v* to threaten

**Bedrohung**, be-**droh**-oong, *f* threat

**bedürfen**, be-**dEErf**-en, *v* to need, to require

**Bedürfnis**, be-**dEErf**-niss, *nt* want, need

**bedürftig**, be-**dEErf**-tik, *adj* needy, poor

**beehren**, be-**air**-en, *v* to honour with; to favour

**beeilen (sich)**, be-**ile**-en, (zik), *v* to hurry

**beeinflussen**, be-ine-**flooss**-en, *v* to influence

**beeinträchtigen**, be-ine-**trek**-tig-en, *v* to restrict; to impair; to spoil

**beenden**, be-**end**-en, *v* to end, to finish

**Beendung**, be-**end**-oong, *f* termination; completion

**beerben (jdn)**, be-**airb**-en, *v* to inherit (from sb)

**beerdigen**, be-**aird**-ig-en, *v* to bury

**Beerdigung**, be-**aird**-ig-oong, *f* funeral

**Beere**, **bair**-e, *f* berry

**Beet**, bait, *nt* (flower/vegetable) bed

**befähigen**, be-**fay**-ig-en, *v* to qualify; to enable

**Befähigung**, be-**fay**-ig-oong, *f* capacity; qualification; talent

**befallen**, be-**fahll**-en, *v* to overcome; to attack

**Befangenheit**, be-**fahng**-en-hite, *f* self-consciousness; *law* bias

**befassen (sich mit)**, be-**fahss**-en (zik mitt), *v* to occupy o.s. with

**Befehl**, be-**fail**, *m* command, order

**befehlen**, be-**fail**-en, *v* to command, to order

**befestigen**, be-**fest**-ig-en, *v* to fasten; to fortify

**Befestigung**, be-**fest**-ig-oong, *f* fastening; fortification

**Befinden**, be-**finn**-den, *nt* state of health

**befinden (sich)**, be-**finn**-den (zik), *v* to be; to feel

**beflissen**, be-**fliss**-en, *adj* zealous, studious

**befolgen**, be-**foll**-gen, *v* to follow; to observe (order)

**befördern**, be-**ferd**-ern, v to transport; to send; to promote

**Beförderung**, be-**ferd**-er-oong, f promotion; transport

**befragen**, be-**frahg**-en, v to question; to consult

**befreien**, be-**fry**-en, v to free, to liberate; to exempt

**Befreiung**, be-**fry**-oong, f release; liberation; exemption

**befremden**, be-**fremm**-den, v to seem odd

**befreunden (sich mit jdm)**, be-**froynd**-en, v to make friends with

**befreundet**, be-**froynd**-et, adj friends with

**Befruchtung**, be-**frookt**-oong, f pollination; **künstliche –**, artificial insemination

**begabt**, be-**gahpt**, adj talented, gifted

**Begabung**, be-**gahb**-oong, f talent

**begeben (sich)**, be-**gay**-ben (zik), v to proceed; to occur

**Begebenheit**, be-**gay**-ben-hite, f event

**begegnen**, be-**gaig**-nen, v to meet (by chance)

**Begegnung**, be-**gaig**-noong, f (chance) meeting

**begehen**, be-**gay**-en, v to commit; to celebrate

**begehren**, be-**gair**-en, v to desire; to wish for

**begehrt**, be-**gairt**, adj in demand

**begeistern**, be-**gy**-stern, v to inspire; **sich für etw–**, to be keen on sth

**Begeisterung**, be-**gy**-ster-oong, f enthusiasm

**Begier**, be-**geer**, f eagerness; desire; passion

**begierig**, be-**geer**-ik, adj eager for; keen; desirous

**begießen**, be-**geess**-en, v to water; fam to drink to

**Beginn**, be-**ginn**, m beginning

**beginnen**, be-**ginn**-en, v to begin, to start

**beglaubigen**, be-**glow**-big-en, v to certify

**Beglaubigung**, be-**glow**-bi-goong, f certification

**begleichen**, be-**gly**-ken, v to settle (accounts); to pay

**begleiten**, be-**gly**-ten, v to accompany; to escort

**Begleiter**, be-**gly**-ter, m companion; escort; mus accompanist

**beglücken**, be-**glEEck**-en, v to make a person happy

**beglückwünschen**, be-**glEEck**-vEEnn-shen, v to congratulate

**begnadigen**, beg-**nahd**-ig-en, v to pardon; to amnesty

**Begnadigung**, beg-**nahd**-ig-oong, f pardon; amnesty

**begnügen (sich mit)**, beg-**nEEg**-en (zik mitt), v to be satisfied with

**begraben**, be-**grahb**-en,

v to bury

**Begräbnis**, be-**grape**-niss, nt burial; funeral

**begreifen**, be-**gry**-fen, v to understand; to comprehend

**begreiflich**, be-**grife**-lik, adj comprehensible

**begrenzen**, be-**grent**-sen, v to limit

**Begriff**, be-**griff**, m idea; concept; notion

**begründen**, be-**grEEn**-den, v to justify

**Begründung**, be-**grEEnn**-doong, f justification; reason; argument

**begrüßen**, be-**grEEs**-en, v to greet, to welcome

**Begrüßung**, be-**grEEs**-oong, f greeting; welcome

**begünstigen**, be-**gEEnn**-stig-en, v to favour

**begutachten**, be-**goot**-ahk-ten, v to assess

**behaart**, be-**hahrt**, adj hairy

**behäbig**, be-**hay**-bik, adj portly; solid

**behaglich**, be-**hahk**-lik, adj comfortable; cosy

**behalten**, be-**hahllt**-en, v to keep; to retain

**Behälter**, be-**hell**-ter, m container; reservoir

**behandeln**, be-**hahnn**-deln, v to treat

**Behandlung**, be-**hahnnd**-loong, f treatment

**beharren (auf etw)**, be-**hahrr**-en, v to persevere; to insist

**behaupten**, be-**howp**-ten, *v* to claim; to assert; to maintain

**Behauptung**, be-**howp**-toong, *f* claim; assertion

**behend**, be-**hent**, *adj* agile, nimble

**beherrschen**, be-**hairsh**-en, *v* to rule; to govern; to dominate; to control; to master

**behilflich**, be-**hilf**-lik, *adj* helpful

**behindert**, be-**hin**-dert, *adj* disabled

**Behinderte(r)**, be-**hin**-derte(r), *m & f* disabled person

**Behörde**, be-**herd**-en, *f* authority

**behördlich**, be-**herd**-lik, *adj* official; authoritative

**behüten**, be-**hEEt**-en, *v* to look after; to guard

**behutsam**, be-**hoot**-zahm, *adj* cautious; careful

**bei**, by, *prep* near (to); at (the house of); on; in

**beibehalten**, by-be-hahllt-en, *v* to keep; to retain

**beibringen**, by-**bring**-en, *v* to teach; to bring forward

**Beichte**, byk-te, *f* confession

**beichten**, byk-ten, *v* to confess

**beide**, by-de, *adj* both

**beiderlei**, by-der-ly, *adj* both kinds; of both sorts

**beiderseits**, by-der-zites, *adv* on both sides

**beieinander**, by-ine-**ahnn**-der, *adv* together

**Beifall**, by-fahll, *m* applause; assent; approval

**beifügen**, by-**fEEg**-en, *v* to enclose; to append

**Beifügung**, by-**fEEg**-oong, *f* enclosure; addition; appendage

**Beigeschmack**, by-ge-shmahck, *m* aftertaste

**Beil**, bile, *nt* hatchet; chopper; axe

**Beilage**, by-lahg-e, *f* supplement (of a journal); side dish; vegetables

**beilegen**, by-lay-gen, *v* to add; to enclose; to impute; to settle (disputes)

**Beileid**, by-lite, *nt* condolence; sympathy

**beiliegend**, by-leeg-end, *adj* enclosed

**beim**, bime (= bei dem, by daim), *prep* with the; at the; near the

**beimessen**, by-mess-en, *v* to attribute; to ascribe

**Bein**, bine, *nt* leg; bone

**beinahe**, by-nah-e, *adv* almost; nearly

**Beiname**, by-nahm-e, *m* nickname; epithet

**Beinbruch**, bine-brook, *m* fracture of the leg

**beipacken**, by-pahck-en, *v* to pack up with

**Beipackzettel**, by-pahck-tse-tel, *m* instruction leaflet

**beisammen**, by-zahmm-en, *adv* together

**Beisammensein**, by-zahmm-en-zine, *nt* get-together

**Beischlaf**, by-shlahf, *m* sexual intercourse

**beiseite**, by-zyte, *adv* aside, on one side

**beisetzen**, by-zet-sen, *v* to bury

**Beisetzung**, by-zet-soong, *f* funeral

**Beispiel**, by-shpeel, *nt* example

**beispiellos**, by-shpeel-lohs, *adj* unprecedented

**beispielsweise**, by-shpeels-vy-ze, *adv* for instance; for example

**beispringen**, by-shpring-en, *v* to rush to help

**beißen**, by-sen, *v* to bite

**Beißzange**, bice-tsahng-e, *f* pliers, pincers

**Beistand**, by-stahnt, *m* assistance, support

**beistehen**, by-shtay-en, *v* to help; to stand by (sb)

**Beitrag**, by-trahk, *m* contribution

**beitragen**, by-trahg-en, *v* to contribute

**beitreten**, by-trait-en, *v* to join (club etc.)

**Beitritt**, by-tritt, *m* enrolment; joining

**Beiwagen**, by-vahg-en, *m* side-car (of motorbike)

**beiwohnen**, by-wohn-en, *v* to be present

**beizeiten**, by-tsy-ten, *adv* in time

**beizen**, by-tsen, *v* to

stain (wood)

**bejahen**, be-**yah**-en, v to answer in the affirmative; to agree with

**bejahrt**, be-**yahrt**, adj aged, advanced in years

**bekämpfen**, be-**kemp**-fen, v to fight against

**bekannt**, be-**kahnnt**, adj well-known; renowned; familiar

**Bekannte(r)**, be-**kahnnt**-e(r), m & f acquaintance

**bekanntlich**, be-**kahnnt**-lik, adv as is well known

**bekanntmachen**, be-**kahnnt**-mahk-en, v to introduce; to advertise; to announce

**Bekanntmachung**, be-**kahnnt**-mahk-oong, f (public) notice; proclamation; announcement

**Bekanntschaft**, be-**kahnnt**-shahft, f acquaintance

**bekehren**, be-**kair**-en, v to convert

**Bekehrung**, be-**kair**-oong, f conversion

**bekennen**, be-**ken**-en, v to admit; to profess

**Bekenntnis**, be-**kent**-nis, nt confession; denomination

**beklagen (sich)**, be-**klahg**-en (zik), v to complain

**beklagenswert**, be-**klahg**-ens-vairt, adj pitiable; pathetic

**Beklagte(r)**, be-**klahk**-te(r), m & f defendant; accused

**bekleiden**, be-**kly**-den, v to clothe; to fill a post; to occupy

**Bekleidung**, be-**kly**-doong, f clothing

**beklommen**, be-**klomm**-en, adj uneasy; oppressed

**bekommen**, be-**komm**-en, v to receive, to get

**bekömmlich**, be-**kermm**-lik, adj (easily) digestible

**bekräftigen**, be-**kreff**-tig-en, v to confirm

**Bekräftigung**, be-**kreff**-tig-oong, f confirmation

**bekränzen**, be-**krent**-sen, v to deck with wreaths

**bekreuzigen (sich)**, be-**kroyt**-sig-en (zik), v to cross o.s.

**bekümmern (sich)**, be-**kEmm**-ern (zik), v to be concerned about; to trouble o.s. about

**beladen**, be-**lahd**-en, v to load with

**Belag**, be-**lahg**, m coating; layer

**belagern**, be-**lahg**-ern, v to besiege; to beleaguer

**Belagerung**, be-**lahg**-er-oong, f siege

**Belang**, be-**lahng**, m importance; consequence

**belangen**, be-**lahng**-en, v to sue, to prosecute; to concern

**belanglos**, be-**lahng**-lohs, adj insignificant

**belasten**, be-**lahst**-en, v to burden; to worry; to

incriminate; to debit

**belästigen**, be-**lesst**-ig-en, v to pester; to molest

**Belastung**, be-**lahsst**-oong, f load; debit

**belaufen (sich auf)**, be-**lowf**-en (zik owf), v to amount to

**beleben**, be-**lay**-ben, v to animate, to liven up; to come alive

**belebt**, be-**laipt**, adj animated, lively; busy (street)

**Belebung**, be-**laib**-oong, f revival; animation

**Beleg**, be-**laik**, m receipt; proof; voucher

**belegen**, be-**laig**-en, v to cover; to spread; to prove; to reserve

**belehren**, be-**lair**-en, v to instruct; to inform

**Belehrung**, be-**lair**-oong, f instruction; information

**beleidigen**, be-**ly**-dig-en, v to insult; to offend

**Beleidigung**, be-**ly**-dig-oong, f insult; offence

**belesen**, be-**lay**-zen, adj well-read; scholarly

**beleuchten**, be-**loyk**-ten, v to illuminate; to light (up); to elucidate

**Beleuchtung**, be-**loyk**-toong, f illumination; lighting; elucidation

**Belgien**, bel-gi-en, nt Belgium

**Belgier**, bel-gi-er, m Belgian (person)

**belgisch**, bel-gish, *adj* Belgian

**belichten**, be-lik-ten, *v photog* to expose

**beliebig**, be-leeb-ik, *adj* any; according to one's liking

**beliebt**, be-leept, *adj* (well) liked; popular

**bellen**, bel-en, *v* to bark; to bay

**belohnen**, be-loh-nen, *v* to reward

**Belohnung**, be-loh-noong, *f* reward

**Belüftung**, be-lEEft-oong, *f* ventilation

**belügen**, be-lEEg-en, *v* to lie (to sb); to deceive (sb)

**belustigen (sich)**, be-looss-tig-en (zik), *v* to amuse (o.s.)

**Belustigung**, be-looss-tig-oong, *f* amusement; diversion

**bemächtigen (sich)**, be-mek-tig-en (zik), *v* to seize, to take possession of

**bemalen**, be-mahl-en, *v* to paint

**bemannen**, be-mahnn-en, *v* to man; to equip

**Bemannung**, be-mahnn-oong, *f* crew

**bemerken**, be-mairk-en, *v* to notice; to remark; **-swert**, *adj* remarkable; noticeable

**Bemerkung**, be-mairk-oong, *f* remark; observation; note

**bemitleiden**, be-mit-ly-den, *v* to pity

**bemittelt**, be-mit-elt, *adj* well-off, well-to-do

**bemühen (sich)**, be-mEE-en (zik), *v* to endeavour

**Bemühung**, be-mEE-oong, *f* trouble; endeavour

**benachbart**, be-nahk-bart, *adj* neighbouring, adjoining

**benachrichtigen**, be-nahk-rik-tig-en, *v* to inform

**Benachrichtigung**, be-nahk-rik-tig-oong, *f* notification

**benachteiligen**, be-nahk-ty-lig-en, *v* to prejudice, to wrong

**benannt**, be-nahnt, *adj* called, named

**benehmen (sich)**, be-nay-men (zik), *v* to behave

**Benehmen**, be-nay-men, *nt* behaviour

**beneiden**, be-ny-den, *v* to envy; to begrudge

**beneidenswert**, be-ny-dens-vairt, *adj* enviable

**benennen**, be-nen-en, *v* to name, to call

**Benennung**, be-nen-oong, *f* name, naming

**Bengel**, beng-el, *m* rascal, urchin, lout

**benötigen**, be-nert-ig-en, *v* to require; to need

**benutzen (or benützen)**, be-noott-sen (or benEEtt-sen), *v* to use

**Benutzer**, be-nootts-er, *m* user

**Benutzung**, be-noots-oong, *f* use

**Benzin**, ben-tseen, *nt* petrol

**beobachten**, be-oh-bahk-ten, *v* to observe, to watch; to examine

**Beobachter**, be-oh-bahk-ter, *m* observer

**Beobachtung**, be-oh-bahk-toong, *f* observation

**bepacken**, be-pahck-en, *v* to load, to pack

**bepflanzen**, be-pflahnt-sen, *v* to plant with

**bequem**, bek-vaim, *adj* comfortable, cosy, snug

**bequemen (sich)**, bek-vaim-en (zik), *v* to bring o.s. to

**bequemlich**, bek-vaim-lik, *adj* convenient

**Bequemlichkeit**, bek-vaim-lik-kite, *f* comfort; laziness; snugness

**beraten**, be-raht-en, *v* to advise, to counsel

**Berater**, be-raht-er, *m* adviser

**beratschlagen (sich)**, be-raht-shlahg-en (zik), *v* to discuss

**Beratung**, be-raht-oong, *f* advice; consultation; **-sstelle**, *f* advice centre

**berauben**, be-row-ben, *v* to rob, to deprive

**berauschen**, be-row-shen, *v* to intoxicate

**berechnen**, be-rek-nen, *v* to calculate

**berechnend**, be-rek-nent, *adj* calculating

**Berechnung**, be-rek-noong, *f* calculation

**berechtigen**, be-rek-tig-en, *v* to entitle; to justify

**berechtigt**, be-rek-tigt, *adj* entitled; qualified; justified

**Berechtigung**, be-rek-tig-oong, *f* authorisation; justification

**beredsam**, be-rait-zahm, *adj* eloquent

**Beredsamkeit**, be-rait-zahm-kite, *f* eloquence

**Bereich**, be-ryk, *m* area, scope; sphere

**bereichern (sich)**, be-ry-kern (zik), *v* to enrich (o.s.)

**bereifen**, be-ry-fen, *v* to fit tyres to

**Bereifung**, be-ry-foong, *f* set of tyres

**bereit**, be-rite, *adj* ready, prepared

**bereiten**, be-ry-ten, *v* to prepare, to get ready

**bereits**, be-rites, *adv* already

**Bereitschaft**, be-rite-shahft, *f* readiness; alertness; **–dienst**, *m* emergency service

**bereitwillig**, be-rite-vil-ik, *adj* willing, obliging

**Bereitwilligkeit**, be-rite-vil-ig-kite, *f* willingness, obligingness

**bereuen**, be-roy-en, *v* to regret, to repent

**Berg**, bairk, *m* mountain; hill

**bergab**, bairk-**ahpp**, *adv* downhill

**Bergarbeiter**, bairk-ar-by-ter, *m* miner

**bergauf**, bairk-**owf**, *adv* uphill

**Bergbau**, bairk-bow, *m* mining

**bergen**, bairg-en, *v* to save, to shelter; to protect

**Berggipfel**, bairk-gip-fel, *m* mountain peak

**bergig**, bairg-ik, *adj* mountainous, hilly

**Bergmann**, bairk-mahnn, *m* miner

**Bergsteigen**, bairk-shty-gen, *nt* mountaineering

**Bergsteiger**, bairk-shty-ger, *m* mountaineer

**Bergwerk**, bairk-vairk, *nt* mine; (coal-)pit

**Bericht**, be-rikt, *m* report; account; particulars

**berichten**, be-rikt-en, *v* to report

**Berichterstatter**, be-rikt-er-shtahtt-er, *m* reporter; correspondent

**berichtigen**, be-rikt-ig-en, *v* to correct; to rectify

**Berichtigung**, be-rikt-ig-oong, *f* correction

**berieseln**, be-reez-eln, *v* to irrigate

**Bernstein**, bairn-shtine, *m* amber

**bersten**, bairst-en, *v* to burst, to explode

**berüchtigt**, be-rEEk-tigt, *adj* notorious, ill-famed

**berücksichtigen**, be-rEEck-sikt-ig-en, *v* to take into consideration

**Berücksichtigung**, be-rEEck-sikt-ig-oong, *f* consideration

**Beruf**, be-roof, *m* profession; occupation

**berufen**, be-roof-en, *v* to appoint

**berufen (sich auf)**, be-roof-en (zik owf), *v* to refer to

**beruflich**, be-roof-lik, *adj* professional

**Berufsausbildung**, be-roofs-ows-bild-oong, *f* professional training

**Berufsberater**, be-roofs-be-raht-er, *m* careers adviser

**Berufsberatung**, be-roofs-be-raht-oong, *f* vocational guidance

**Berufsgeheimnis**, be-roofs-ge-hym-nis, *nt* professional secret

**Berufskrankheit**, be-roofs-krahnnk-hite, *f* occupational disease

**Berufsschule**, be-roofs-shoo-le, *f* vocational school; technical college

**Berufssportler**, be-roofs-shport-ler, *m* professional sportsman

**berufstätig**, be-roofs-tait-ik, *adj* employed

**Berufsverkehr**, be-roofs-fer-kair, *m* rush hour traffic

**Berufung**, be-roof-oong, *f* *law* appeal

**beruhen (auf)**, be-roo-en (owf), *v* to be attributable (to)

**beruhigen,** be-**roo**-ig-en, *v* to calm, to soothe, to quieten; to reassure

**Beruhigung,** be-**roo**-ig-oong, *f* calming, soothing

**berühmt,** be-**rEEmt**, *adj* celebrated, famous

**Berühmtheit,** be-**rEEmt**-hite, *f* fame, celebrity

**berühren,** be-**rEEr**-en, *v* to touch

**Berührung,** be-**rEEr**-oong, *f* touch; contact

**besagt,** be-**zahkt**, *adj* aforesaid, mentioned, said

**besänftigen,** be-**zenft**-ig-en, *v* to calm; to appease

**Besatz,** be-**zahtts,** *m* trimming

**Besatzung,** be-**sahtts**-oong, *f* garrison; crew

**besaufen (sich),** be-**zowf**-en (zik), *v fam* to get drunk

**beschädigen,** be-**shay**-dig-en, *v* to damage, to injure

**Beschädigung,** be-**shay**-dig-oong, *f* damage

**beschaffen,** be-**shahff**-en, *v* to procure, to get

**beschaffen,** be-**shahff**-en, *adj* constituted

**Beschaffenheit,** be-**shahff**-en-hite, *f* composition; constitution

**Beschaffung,** be-**shahff**-oong, *f* acquisition

**beschäftigen,** be-**sheff**-tig-en, *v* to occupy; to employ

**beschäftigt,** be-**sheff**-tigt, *adj* busy

**Beschäftigung,** be-**sheff**-tig-oong, *f* occupation, employment

**beschämen,** be-**shay**-men, *v* to (put to) shame

**Bescheid,** be-**shy't,** *m* information; reply; instruction(s)

**bescheiden,** be-**shy**-den, *adj* moderate; modest

**Bescheidenheit,** be-**shy**-den-hite, *f* modesty

**bescheinen,** be-**shy**-nen, *v* to shine on

**bescheinigen,** be-**shy**-nig-en, *v* to certify, to attest

**Bescheinigung,** be-**shy**-nig-oong, *f* attestation, certificate

**beschenken,** be-**shenk**-en, *v* to give (sb) a present

**bescheren,** be-**shair**-en, *v* to give (sb) Christmas presents

**Bescherung,** be-**shair**-oong, *f* the giving of Christmas presents

**beschießen,** be-**shees**-en, *v* to bombard, to fire on

**Beschießung,** be-**shees**-oong, *f* bombardment

**beschimpfen,** be-**shim**-fen, *v* to abuse; to affront

**beschirmen,** be-**sheerm**-en, *v* to protect; to shield

**Beschlag,** be-**shlahk**, *m* (metal) fitting; condensation; tarnish

**beschlagen,** be-**shlahg**-en, *v* to put metal fittings on; to mist over; to shoe (horse)

**Beschlagnahmung,** be-**shlahk**-nahm-oong, *f* confiscation, seizure

**beschleunigen,** be-**shloin**-ig-en, *v* to accelerate, to speed up

**Beschleunigung,** be-**shloin**-ig-oong, *f* acceleration, increase of speed

**beschließen,** be-**shlees**-en, *v* to decide, to resolve

**Beschluß,** be-**shlooss,** *m* decision; resolution

**beschlußfähig,** be-**shlooss**-fay-ig, *adj* forming a quorum

**beschmieren,** be-**shmeer**-en, *v* to spread, to smear (with)

**beschmutzen,** be-**shmoott**-sen, *v* to soil

**beschneiden,** be-**shny**-den, *v* to clip; to circumcise

**Beschneidung,** be-**shny**-doong, *f* clipping; circumcision

**beschönigen,** be-**shern**-ig-en, *v* to gloss over; to palliate

**Beschönigung,** be-**shern**-ig-oong, *f* glossing over; extenuation

**beschränken,** be-**shrenk**-en, *v* to limit

**beschränkt,** be-**shrenkt,** *adj* limited; dull

**Beschränkung,** be-**shrenk**-oong, *f* limitation

**beschreiben,** be-**shry**-ben, *v* to write on; to describe

**Beschreibung,** be-**shry**-boong, *f* description

**beschuldigen**, be-shooll-dig-en, v to accuse; to charge with a crime

**Beschuldigung**, be-shooll-dig-oong, f accusation; charge

**beschützen**, be-shEEtt-sen, v to protect

**Beschützer**, be-shEEtt-ser, m defender, protector

**Beschützung**, be-shEEtt-soong, f protection

**Beschwerde**, be-shvaird-e, f complaint

**beschweren (sich)**, be-shvair-en (zik), v to complain

**beschwerlich**, be-shvair-lik, adj exhausting; troublesome

**beschwichtigen**, be-shvik-ti-gen, v to pacify; to appease; to calm

**Beschwichtigung**, be-shvik-tig-oong, f conciliation; appeasement

**beschwindeln**, be-shvin-deln, v to cheat; to swindle; to tell lies

**beschwören**, be-shver-en, v to confirm by oath; to swear to; to implore; to conjure (spirits)

**Beschwörung**, be-shver-oong, f confirmation by oaths; entreaty; raising of spirits

**besehen**, be-zay-en, v to inspect; to view

**beseitigen**, be-zyt-ig-en, v to do away with, to eliminate

**Besen**, bay-zen, m broom

**besessen**, be-zes-en, adj possessed, frantic

**Besessene(r)**, be-zes-en-e(r), m & f possessed/frantic person

**besetzen**, be-zett-sen, v to fill (a space/seat; a vacancy); to occupy

**Besetzung**, be-zetts-oong, f cast theatre; occupation

**besichtigen**, be-zik-tig-en, v to visit; to view; to inspect

**Besichtigung**, be-zik-tig-oong, f visit; inspection

**besiegen**, be-zeeg-en, v to conquer; to vanquish

**besinnen (sich)**, be-zin-en (zik), v to think; to reflect

**Besinnung**, be-zin-oong, f consciousness

**Besitz**, be-zits, m possession; property; estate

**besitzen**, be-zit-sen, v to possess; to have

**Besitzer**, be-zit-ser, m owner, proprietor

**Besitzung**, be-zits-oong, f possession; estate

**besohlen**, be-zohl-en, v to sole (shoes)

**besonders**, be-zon-ders, adv especially; particularly

**besonnen**, be-zon-en, adj cautious; thoughtful

**besorgen**, be-zorg-en, v to acquire; to deal with; to take care of

**Besorgnis**, be-zork-niss, f concern; fear

**besorgt**, be-zorkt, adj apprehensive; anxious

**Besorgung**, be-zorg-oong, f errand; acquisition; purchase

**besprechen**, be-shprek-en, v to discuss; to review; to record

**Besprechung**, be-shprek-oong, f discussion; meeting; review

**bespritzen**, be-shprit-sen, v to squirt with water

**besser**, bess-er, adj better

**bessern**, bess-ern, v to better, to improve

**Besserung**, bess-er-oong, f improvement; reform(ation); recovery

**Bestand**, be-shtahnt, m existence; duration; stock

**beständig**, be-shten-dik, adj constant; permanent

**Beständigkeit**, be-shten-dig-kite, f stability

**Bestandteil**, be-shtahnt-tile, m ingredient

**bestärken (in etw)**, be-shtairk-en, v to confirm in sth

**bestätigen**, be-shtayt-ig-en, v to confirm; to corroborate; to acknowledge

**Bestätigung**, be-shtayt-ig-oong, f confirmation

**bestatten**, be-shtaht-en, v to bury

**Bestattung**, be-shtaht-oong, f burial; funeral

**beste(r/s)**, best-e(r/s), adj best

**bestechen**, be-*shtek*-en, v to bribe; to corrupt

**bestechlich**, be-*shtek*-lik, adj open to bribery; corruptible

**Bestechung**, be-*shtek*-oong, f corruption; bribery

**Besteck**, be-*shteck*, nt cutlery

**bestehen**, be-*shtay*-en, v to consist (**aus** of); to exist; to insist (**auf** on); to pass (exam)

**bestehlen**, be-*shtay*-len, v to rob, to steal from

**besteigen**, be-*shty*-gen, v to climb; to mount; to board (ship, bus, aeroplane); to ascend (throne)

**Besteigung**, be-*shty*-goong, f climb; ascent; accession

**bestellen**, be-*shtel*-en, v to order (goods); to give messages; to cultivate (soil)

**Bestellung**, be-*shtel*-oong, f order; commission; cultivation (soil)

**bestens**, *best*-ens, adv very well

**besteuern**, be-*shtoy*-ern, v to tax

**Besteuerung**, be-*shtoy*-er-oong, f taxation

**Bestie**, *best*-e-e, f beast, brute

**bestimmen**, be-*shtim*-en, v to decide; to appoint

**bestimmt**, be-*shtimt*, adj firm; certain; definite

**Bestimmung**, be-*shtim*-oong, f regulation; purpose

**Bestimmungsort**, be-*shtim*-oongs-ort, m destination

**bestrafen**, be-*shtrahf*-en, v to punish, to chastise; to fine

**Bestrafung**, be-*shtrahf*-oong, f punishment; reprimand; fine

**Bestrahlung**, be-*shtrahl*-oong, f radiation; radiotherapy

**bestreben**, be-*shtray*-ben, v to endeavour

**Bestrebung**, be-*shtray*-boong, f endeavour

**bestreichen**, be-*shtry*-ken, v to spread; to coat

**bestreiten**, be-*shtry*-ten, v to contest; to dispute; challenge; to deny

**bestreuen**, be-*shtroy*-en, v to sprinkle (with)

**bestürmen**, be-*shtEErm*-en, v to overwhelm; to molest

**bestürzt**, be-*shtEErtst*, adj disconcerted; alarmed

**Bestürzung**, be-*shtEErts*-oong, f consternation

**Besuch**, be-*sook*, m visit, call; attendance

**besuchen**, be-*sook*-en, v to (pay a) visit (to); to attend

**Besucher**, be-*sook*-er, m visitor

**betätigen (sich)**, be-*tay*-tig-en (zik), v to be engaged (in)

**betäuben**, be-*toyb*-en, v to stun; to anaesthetize

**Betäubung**, be-*toyb*-oong f anaesthetic

**beteiligen**, be-*ty*-lig-en, v to participate, to take part (in)

**Beteiligung**, be-*ty*-lig-oong, f participation

**beten**, *bay*-ten, v to pray; to say one's prayers

**betiteln**, be-*teet*-eln, v to name; to give a title to

**Beton**, *bay*-tong, m concrete

**betonen**, be-*tohn*-en, v to emphasize, to stress

**Betonung**, be-*tohn*-oong, f emphasis; stress

**betören**, be-*ter*-en, v to beguile

**Betracht**, be-*trahkt*, m consideration; respect

**betrachten**, be-*trahkt*-en, v to look at; to regard

**beträchtlich**, be-*trekt*-lik, adj considerable

**Betrachtung**, be-*trahkt*-oong, f consideration

**Betrag**, be-*trahk*, m amount; sum

**Betragen**, be-*trahg*-en, nt behaviour

**betragen**, be-*trahg*-en, v to amount to

**betragen (sich)**, be-*trahg*-en (zik), v to behave o.s.

**Betreff**, be-*tref*, m regard; respect

**betreffen**, be-*tref*-en, v to concern, to relate to

**betreffs**, be-*trefs*, prep concerning, with regard to

**betreiben**, be-*try*-ben, v to

pursue; to carry on (trade)

**betreten**, be-**trayt**-en, v to enter

**Betrieb**, be-**treep**, m firm; plant; operation; bustle; **–sferien**, f company holidays; **–sklima**, nt working atmosphere; **–skosten**, pl running costs; **–sleiter**, m (works) manager; **–sleitung**, f management; **–srat**, m works committee; **–sstörung**, f malfunction; **–ssystem**, nt comp operating system; **–swirtschaft**, business management

**betrinken (sich)**, be-**tring**-ken (zik), v to get drunk

**betroffen**, be-**trof**-en, adj perplexed; surprised

**betrüben**, be-**trEEb**-en, v to grieve; to afflict

**Betrug**, be-**trook**, m deception; fraud

**betrügen**, be-**trEEg**-en, v to deceive; to defraud; to cheat; to be unfaithful to

**Betrüger**, be-**trEEg**-er, m deceiver; cheat

**Betrügerei**, be-**trEEg**-e-ry, f deception, cheating

**betrunken**, be-**troonk**-en, adj drunk

**Betrunkenheit**, be-**troonk**-en-hite, f drunkenness

**Bett**, bet, nt bed

**Bettdecke**, bet-**deck**-e, f blanket; quilt

**Bettelei**, bet-e-ly, f begging

**betteln**, bet-**eln**, v to beg

**Bettlaken**, bet-**lahk**-en, nt sheet

**Bettler**, bet-ler, m beggar

**Bettuch**, bet-**took**, nt sheet

**Bettwäsche**, bet-**vesh**-e, f bed-linen

**beugen**, boyg-en, v to bend; gram to inflect, to decline, to conjugate

**Beugung**, boyg-oong, f bend(ing); inflexion

**Beule**, boyl-e, f hump; bump; swelling; bruise

**beunruhigen**, be-**oonn**-roo-ig-en, v to disturb; to alarm; to worry

**Beunruhigung**, be-**oonn**-roo-ig-oong, f alarm; uneasiness; worry

**beurkunden**, be-**oor**-koonn-den, v to certify; to document; to verify

**beurlauben**, be-**oor**-low-ben, v to give time off

**beurteilen**, be-**oor**-tyl-en, v to judge; to estimate

**Beurteilung**, be-**oor**-tyl-oong, f judgment; criticism

**Beute**, boyt-e, f booty; prey; victim

**Beutel**, boyt-el, m purse; small bag; pouch

**bevölkern**, be-**ferl**-kern, v to people; to populate

**Bevölkerung**, be-**ferl**-ker-oong, f population; inhabitants

**bevollmächtigen**, be-**foll**-mek-tig-en, v to authorize;

to give power of attorney

**bevollmächtigt**, be-**foll**-mek-tigt, adj authorized

**bevor**, be-**fohr**, conj before; **–munden**, v to impose one's will on sb; **–stehend**, adj imminent

**bevorzugen**, v to prefer

**bewachen**, be-**vahk**-en, v to guard, to watch

**bewachsen**, be-**vahk**-sen, v to grow over

**Bewachung**, be-**vahk**-oong, f watching; guarding; guard

**bewaffnen**, be-**vahff**-nen, v to arm

**Bewaffnung**, be-**vahff**-noong, f armament

**bewahren**, be-**vahr**-en, v to keep

**bewähren (sich)**, be-**vair**-en (zik), v to stand the test; to prove o.s.

**Bewährung**, be-**vair**-oong, f probation

**bewaldet**, be-**vahl**-det, adj wooded

**bewältigen**, be-**velt**-ig-en, v to accomplish; to overcome

**bewandert**, be-**vahnn**-dert, adj knowledgeable; skilled

**bewässern**, be-**ves**-ern, v to irrigate, to water

**Bewässerung**, be-**ves**-er-oong, f irrigation

**bewegen**, be-**vayg**-en, v to move; to stir; to budge

**Beweggrund**, be-**vayk**-groont, m motive

**beweglich**, be-*vayk*-lik, *adj* movable, mobile; agile

**Beweglichkeit**, be-*vayk*-lik-kite, *f* mobility

**Bewegung**, be-*vayg*-oong, *f* movement; exercise

**beweinen**, be-*vy*-nen, *v* to mourn, to weep for

**Beweis**, be-*vice*, *m* proof, evidence

**beweisen**, be-*vy*-zen, *v* to prove; to substantiate

**bewerben (sich)**, be-*vairb*-en (zik), *v* to apply for

**Bewerber**, be-*vairb*-er, *m* applicant; candidate

**Bewerbung**, be-*vairb*-oong, *f* application; candidature

**bewerkstelligen**, be-*vairk*-shtel-ig-en, *v* to achieve, to accomplish

**bewilligen**, be-*vil*-ig-en, *v* to grant, to allow

**Bewilligung**, be-*vil*-ig-oong, *f* granting; allowance

**bewirken**, be-*veerk*-en, *v* to effect; to cause

**bewirten**, be-*veert*-en, *v* to entertain (guests)

**bewirtschaften**, be-*veert*-shahft-en, *v* to cultivate (soil); to manage

**Bewirtung**, be-*veert*-oong, *f* hospitality

**bewohnen**, be-*vohn*-en, *v* to inhabit

**Bewohner**, be-*vohn*-er, *m* inhabitant; resident

**bewundern**, be-*voonn*-dern, *v* to admire

**Bewunderung**, be-*voonn*-der-oong, *f* admiration

**bewußt**, be-*voosst*, *adj* conscious, aware

**bewußtlos**, be-*voosst*-lohs, *adj* unconscious, senseless

**Bewußtlosigkeit**, be-*voosst*-loh-zig-kite, *f* unconsciousness

**Bewußtsein**, be-*voosst*-zine, *nt* consciousness

**bezahlen**, bet-*sahl*-en, *v* to pay

**Bezahlung**, bet-*sahl*-oong, *f* payment; pay; salary

**bezaubern**, bet-*sow*-bern, *v* to enchant, to charm

**bezeichnen**, bet-*sy'k*-nen, *v* to mark; to call; to designate

**Bezeichnung**, bet-*sy'k*-noong, *f* mark; name; designation

**bezeigen**, bet-*sy*-gen, *v* to show; to give signs of

**Bezeigung**, bet-*sy*-goong, *f* manifestation; show

**bezeugen**, bet-*soyg*-en, *v* to (bear) witness, to testify

**Bezeugung**, bet-*soyg*-oong, *f* testimony

**beziehen**, bet-*see*-en, *v* to move into; to cover; to obtain; **sich auf etw/jdn –**, *v* to refer to sb

**Beziehung**, bet-*see*-oong, *f* reference; connection; relationship

**beziehungsweise**, bet-*see*-oongs-vy-ze, *adv* respectively; that is

**Bezirk**, bet-*seerk*, *m* district; borough

**Bezug**, bet-*sook*, *m* cover(ing); regard; reference

**bezüglich**, bet-*sEEk*-lik, *adj & prep* concerning, with regard to

**bezwecken**, bet-*sveck*-en, *v* to aim at

**bezweifeln**, bet-*svy*-feln, *v* to doubt; to question

**bezwingen**, bet-*sving*-en, *v* to master; to overcome

**BH**, baih-hah, *m* bra

**Bibel**, beeb-el, *f* Bible

**Biber**, beeb-er, *m* beaver

**Bibliothek**, beeb-le-oh-take, *f* library; study

**Bibliothekar**, beeb-le-oh-take-ar, *m* librarian

**bieder**, beed-er, *adj* honest; straightforward; plain

**Biederkeit**, beed-er-kite, *f* straightforwardness

**biegen**, beeg-en, *v* to bend; to inflect; to curve

**biegsam**, beek-zahm, *adj* pliable; bendy

**Biegung**, beeg-oong, *f* bend; curve; inflexion

**Biene**, been-e, *f* bee

**Bienenkorb**, been-en-korp, *m* bee-hive

**Bienenzucht**, been-en-tsookt, *f* bee keeping

**Bier**, beer, *nt* beer

**Biergarten**, beer-gart-en, *m* beer garden

**bieten**, beet-en, *v* to offer; to show; to bid

**Bikini,** be-**kee**-nee, *m* bikini

**Bilanz,** be-**lahnts,** *f*
balance(-sheet)

**Bild,** bilt, *nt* picture, image,
illustration

**bilden,** bild-en, *v* to form; to
educate

**Bilderrahmen,** bild-er-**rahm**-
en, *m* picture frame

**Bildfläche,** bilt-**flaik**-e,
screen; *fig* scene

**Bildhauer,** bilt-**how**-er, *m*
sculptor

**Bildhauerei,** bilt-**how**-e-**ry,** *f*
sculpture

**bildlich,** bilt-lik, *adj*
figurative, metaphorical

**Bildnis,** bilt-niss, *nt* image,
likeness

**Bildschirm,** bilt-shirm, *m*
(television) screen;
monitor; **–text,** *m* teletext

**bildschön,** bilt-shern, *adj*
lovely; dazzlingly beautiful

**Bildung,** bild-oong, *f*
education; formation

**Billard,** bil-yart, *nt* billiards;
billiard-table

**billig,** bil-ik, *adj* cheap;
equitable; just

**billigen,** bil-ig-en, *v* to
approve of, to consent to

**Billigkeit,** bil-ik-kite, *f*
cheapness; fairness

**Billigung,** bil-ig-oong, *f*
assent, approval

**Billion,** bil-yohn, *f* Brit
billion, (US) trillion

**bimmeln,** bim-eln, *v* to ring;
to tinkle

**Bimsstein,** bims-shtine, *m*
pumice-stone

**Binde,** bin-de, *f* band;
bandage; sanitary towel

**binden,** bin-den, *v* to bind;
to tie, to fasten

**Bindestrich,** bin-de-shtrik,
*m* hyphen

**Bindfaden,** bint-fahd-en, *m*
string; twine

**binnen,** bin-en, *prep* within
(time)

**Bio-,** bee-oh, *pref* bio-;
**–graphie,** *f* biography;
**–laden,** *m* health food
shop; **–loge** (**-login),** *m* &
*f* biologist; **–logie,** *f*
biology

**Birnbaum,** beern-bowm, *m*
pear-tree

**Birne,** beern-e, *f* pear

**bis,** bis, *prep* till, until; as far
as

**bisher,** bis-hair, *adv* until
now; so far

**bisherig,** bis-**hair**-ik, *adj*
present

**Biskuit,** bis-kvit, *m* sponge
cake

**Biß,** bis, *m* bite; biting; sting

**bißchen (ein),** bis-ken
(ine), *adv* (a) little (bit);
somewhat

**Bissen,** bis-en, *m* morsel;
mouthful

**bissig,** bis-ik, *adj* snappish;
vicious; biting; caustic

**bisweilen,** bis-vy-len, *adv*
sometimes, at times

**Bit,** bit, *nt comp* bit

**Bitte,** bit-e, *f* request;
petition

**bitte,** bit-e, *interj* please; **wie
b–?,** pardon?

**bitten,** bit-en, *v* to ask, to
implore; to demand

**bitter,** bit-er, *adj* bitter

**Bitterkeit,** bit-er-kite, *f*
bitterness; sharpness

**bitterlich,** bit-er-lik, *adj* &
*adv* bitter(ly)

**Bittschrift,** bit-shrift, *f*
petition

**blähen,** blay-en, *v* to blow
out; (sich) to swell

**Blähungen,** blay-oong-en, *pl
med* wind, flatulence

**blamieren,** blahmm-**eer**-en,
*v* to show up; to expose to
ridicule

**blank,** blahnnk, *adj* shining;
bright; glittering

**Blase,** blahz-e, *f* bubble;
blister; *med* bladder

**Blasebalg,** blah-ze-bahlk, *m*
bellows

**blasen,** blahz-en, *v* to blow

**Blasenentzündung,** blahz-
en-en-ts**EEnd**-oong, *f*
cystitis

**blasiert,** blahz-**eert,** *adj*
jaded; blasé

**Blasinstrument,** blahs-in-
stroo-**ment,** *nt* wind
instrument

**blaß,** blahss, *adj* pale

**Blässe,** bless-e, *f* paleness;
pallor

**Blatt,** blahtt, *nt* leaf; blade;
petal; sheet

**blättern,** blet-ern, *v* to turn
over the pages of a book

**Blätterteig,** blet-er-tyg, *m*

puff pastry

**blau,** blow, *adj* blue

**Blech,** blek, *nt* sheet-metal; tin; *fam* nonsense

**Blechinstrument,** blek-in-stroo-**ment,** *nt* brass instrument

**Blei,** bly, *nt* lead (metal)

**bleiben,** bly-ben, *v* to stay, to remain

**bleich,** bly'k, *adj* pale, faded

**bleichen,** bly-ken, *v* to bleach; to turn pale

**bleiern,** bly-ern, *adj* leaden

**Bleistift,** bly-shtift, *m* pencil

**Blende,** blend-e, *f* aperture

**blenden,** blend-en, *v* to blind; to dazzle

**Blick,** blik, *m* glance; look; glimpse; peep

**blicken,** blik-en, *v* to look; to glance

**blind,** blinnt, *adj* blind

**Blinddarm,** blint-dahrm, *m med* appendix; **–entzündung,** *f* appendicitis

**Blindenschrift,** blin-den-shrift, *f* braille

**Blindgänger,** blint-geng-er, *m* unexploded shell; dud; dead loss

**Blindheit,** blint-hite, *f* blindness

**blindlings,** blint-links, *adv* at random

**blinken,** blink-en, *v* to shine; to gleam

**blinzeln,** blint-seln, *v* to blink; to wink

**Blitz,** blits, *m* lightning; flash; **–ableiter,** *m* lightning-conductor; **–licht,** *nt* flash

**blitzblank,** blits-**blahnk,** *adj* spick and span

**blitzen,** blits-en, *v* to be like lightning; to sparkle; *photog* to use flash

**blitzschnell,** blits-**shnel,** *adj* quick as a flash

**Block,** block, *m* block; (writing) pad

**Blockade,** block-ah-de, *f* blockade

**blockieren,** block-eer-en, *v* to blockade

**blöd,** blerd, *adj fam* stupid

**Blödsinn,** blerd-zin, *m* nonsense; imbecility; idiocy

**blödsinnig,** blerd-zin-ik, *adj* idiotic; imbecilic

**blond,** blont, *adj* fair-haired

**Blondine,** blond-een-e, *f* blonde

**bloß,** blohs, *adj* plain; naked, bare; mere; *adv* simply, only, merely

**Blöße,** blers-e, *f* nudity; clearing; opening

**blühen,** blEE-en, *v* to bloom; to blossom; to flower

**Blume,** bloom-e, *f* flower; bloom; bouquet (of wine)

**Blumenkohl,** bloom-en-kohl, *m* cauliflower

**Blumenstrauß,** bloom-en-shrows, *m* bouquet (of flowers)

**Blumentopf,** bloom-en-top'f, *m* flower-pot

**Bluse,** blooz-e, *f* blouse; smock

**Blut,** bloot, *nt* blood

**Blutader,** bloot-ahd-er, *f* vein

**Blutarmut,** bloot-arm-oot, *f* anæmia

**Blutdruck,** bloot-droock, *m* blood pressure

**Blüte,** blEEt-e, *f* blossom; flower

**bluten,** bloot-en, *v* to bleed

**Blütenblatt,** blEEt-en-blahtt, *nt* petal

**Blütenstaub,** blEEt-en-shtowp, *m* pollen

**Blütezeit,** blEEt-e-tsite, *f* prosperous time; heyday

**Blutgefäß,** bloot-ge-faiss, *nt* blood-vessel

**blutgierig,** bloot-geer-ik, *adj* bloodthirsty

**Blutgruppe,** bloot-groop-e, *f* blood group

**blutig,** bloot-ik, *adj* bloody; gory

**Blutkörperchen,** bloot-kerp-er-ken, *nt* blood-corpuscle

**Blutprobe,** bloot-prohb-e, *f* blood test

**blutsverwandt,** bloots-fair-vahnnt, *adj* closely related

**Blutverlust,** bloot-fair-loost, *m* loss of blood

**Blutvergießen,** bloot-fair-gees-en, *nt* bloodshed

**Bock,** bock, *m* buck; ram; billy-goat

**Boden,** bohd-en, *m* floor; ground; bottom; loft, attic

**bodenlos, bohd**-en-lohs, *adj*
bottomless; abysmal

**Bodensatz, bohd**-en-zahtts,
*m* sediment; grounds;
dregs

**Bodenschätze, bohd**-en-
shets-*e, pl* mineral
resources

**Bogen, bohg**-en, *m* arch;
bow; bend; sheet
(of paper)

**Bogenlicht, bohg**-en-likt, *nt*
arc-light

**Bohle, bohl**-*e, f* (thick)
plank, board; sleeper

**Bohne, bohn**-*e, f* bean

**bohren, bohr**-en, *v* to bore;
to drill

**Bohrer, bohr**-er, *m* gimlet;
drill

**Bohrinsel, bohr**-in-zel, *f* oil
rig

**Bolzen, bolt**-sen, *m* bolt;
rivet; pin

**Bombe, bom**-be, *f* bomb

**Bonbon, bom**-bong, *m & nt*
sweet

**Boot, boht**, *nt* boat

**Bord, bort**, *m* border; edge;
**an –,** *naut* aboard, on
board

**Bordell, bord**-ell, *nt* brothel

**borgen, borg**-en, *v* to
borrow; to lend

**borniert, born**-eert, *adj*
narrow-minded

**Börse, ber**-ze, *f* stock
exchange; purse

**Borste, borst**-*e, f* bristle

**bösartig, bers**-art-ik, *adj* ill-
natured; malicious

**Böschung, bersh**-oong, *f*
slope; embankment

**böse, berz**-*e, adj* bad; evil;
wicked

**Bösewicht, berz**-*e*-vikt, *m*
scoundrel

**boshaft, bohs**-hahft, *adj*
malicious; wicked

**Boshaftigkeit, bohs**-hahft-
ig-kite, *f* malice

**böswillig, bers**-vil-ik, *adj*
malevolent

**Botanik, boht**-ahn-ik, *f*
botany

**Bote, boht**-*e, m* messenger;
courier

**Botschaft, boht**-shahft, *f*
message; errand; news;
embassy; **–er,** *m*
ambassador

**boxen, box**-en, *v* to box

**boykottieren, boy**-kott-eer-
en, *v* to boycott

**Branche, brahng**-she, *f* line
of business; branch;
**–nverzeichnis,** *nt* yellow
pages

**Brand, brahnnt**, *m* fire

**branden, brahnn**-den, *v* to
surge, to roll

**Brandstiftung, brahnnt**-
shtif-toong, *f* arson

**Brandung, brahnn**-doong, *f*
surf

**Branntwein, brahnnt**-vine,
*m* brandy

**Brasilianer, brah**-zee-lee-ah-
ner, *m* Brazilian (person)

**brasilianisch, brah**-zee-lee-
ah-nish, *adj* Brazilian

**Brasilien, brah**-zee-lee-en,

*nt* Brazil

**braten, braht**-en, *v* to fry; to
roast; to bake

**Braten, braht**-en, *m* roast,
joint (of meat)

**Brathuhn, braht**-hoon, *nt*
roast chicken

**Bratkartoffeln, braht**-kart-
off-eln, *pl* fried potatoes

**Bratpfanne, braht**-fahnn-*e,*
*f* frying-pan

**Bratsche, braht**-she, *f* viola;
(bass-)viol

**Bratwurst, braht**-voorst, *f*
fried sausage

**Brauch, browk**, *m* usage;
custom

**brauchbar, browk**-bar, *adj*
useful; useable

**brauchen, browk**-en, *v* to
use; to employ; to need

**brauen, brow**-en, *v* to brew;
to mix

**Brauerei, brow**-*e*-ry, *f*
brewery

**braun, brown,** *adj* brown

**Braunkohle, brown**-kohl-*e,*
*f* brown-coal; lignite

**Brause, brow**-ze, *f* shower;
lemonade

**brausen, brow**-zen, *v* to
rush; to roar; to sprinkle

**Braut, browt**, *f* fiancée;
bride

**Bräutigam, broy**-tee-gahm,
*m* fiancé; bridegroom

**Brautjungfer, browt**-yoongf-
fer, *f* bridesmaid

**Brautpaar, browt**-pahr, *nt*
bride and bridegroom

**brav, brahf,** *adj* honest;

upright; good

**brechen, brek**-en, *v* to break; to crack; to vomit

**Brei,** bry, *m* mush, pulp, paste

**breit,** brite, *adj* broad; wide

**Breite, bry**-te, *f* breadth; width

**Breitengrad, bry**-ten-graht, *m* degree of latitude

**Bremse, brem**-ze, *f* brake

**bremsen, brem**-zen, *v* to brake

**brennen, brenn**-en, *v* to burn; to cauterize; to brand

**Brennglas, brenn**-glahs, *nt* burning-glass

**Brennessel, bren**-nes-el, *f* stinging nettle

**Brennpunkt, brenn**-poonkt, *m* focus

**Brennspiritus, brenn**-shpeer-it-ooss, *m* (methylated) spirits

**Brennstoff, brenn**-shtof, *m* fuel

**Brett,** bret, *nt* board; plank

**Brettspiel, bret**-shpeel, *nt* board game

**Brief,** breef, *m* letter; epistle

**Briefbogen, breef**-bohg-en, *m* sheet of writing paper

**Briefkasten, breef**-kahsst-en, *m* letter-box

**Briefmarke, breef**-mark-e, *f* (postage-)stamp

**Briefpapier, breef**-pah-peer, *nt* writing paper

**Briefpost, breef**-posst, *f* letter-post

**Brieftasche, breef**-tahsh-e, *f* wallet

**Briefträger, breef**-trayg-er, *m* postman

**Briefumschlag, breef**-oomm-shlahk, *m* envelope

**Briefwechsel, breef**-veck-sel, *m* correspondence

**Brillant, brill-yahnt,** *m* (cut) diamond

**Brille, bril**-e, *f* (pair of) spectacles

**bringen, bring**-en, *v* to bring; to convey; to take

**Brise, breez**-e, *f* breeze

**Brite, breet**-e, *m* Briton

**britisch, brit**-ish, *adj* British

**bröckeln, brerk**-eln, *v* to crumble; to break in small pieces

**Brocken, brock**-en, *m* fragment; scrap; crumb

**brodeln, brohd**-eln, *v* to bubble (up); to simmer

**Brokkoli, brock**-oh-lee, *pl* broccoli

**Brombeere, brom**-bair-e, *f* bramble; blackberry

**Brosche, brosh**-e, *f* brooch

**Broschüre, brosh-EEr**-e, *f* pamphlet; leaflet

**Brot,** broht, *nt* bread

**Brötchen, brert**-ken, *nt* (bread) roll

**brotlos, broht**-lohs, *adj* without means of support

**Bruch,** brook, *m* break(ing); fracture; rupture

**Bruchstück, brook-stEEk,** *nt* fragment; piece

**Bruchzahl, brook**-tsahl, *f* fraction

**Brücke, brEEck**-e, *f* bridge; viaduct

**Bruder, brood**-er, *m* brother

**brüderlich, brEEd**-er-lik, *adj* brotherly; fraternal

**Brühe, brEE**-e, *f* broth

**brüllen, brEEll**-en, *v* to bellow; to bawl; to roar

**brummen, broomm**-en, *v* to growl; to hum

**brünett, brEEn**-ett, *adj* brunette

**Brunnen, broonn**-en, *m* well; spring; fountain

**Brunnenkresse, broonn**-en-kress-e, *f* water-cress

**Brüssel, brEEs**-el, *nt* Brussels

**Brust, broosst,** *f* breast; chest; bosom

**brüsten (sich), brEEsst**-en (zik), *v* to pride o.s.; to boast about sth

**Brustkasten, broosst**-kahst-en, *m* chest; thorax

**Brustkrebs, broosst**-kreps, *m* breast cancer

**Brüstung, brEEsst**-oong, *f* parapet

**Brut,** broot, *f* brood; brooding; offspring

**brutal, broot-ahl,** *adj* brutal

**Brutalität, broot-ahl-ee-tait,** *f* brutality

**brüten, brEEt**-en, *v* to hatch; to sit on (eggs)

**Brutkasten, broot**-kahst-en, *m* incubator

**brutto, broott**-oh, *adv* gross

**Bruttolohn, broott**-oh-lohn, *m* gross wages

**Bruttosozialprodukt, broott**-oh-soh-tsee-**ahl**-proh-doockt, nt gross national product

**Buch,** book, nt book; volume; **–binder,** m bookbinder

**Buche,** book-e, f beech

**buchen,** book-en, v to book; to enter in the books

**Bücherei,** bEEk-e-ry, f library

**Bücherregal,** bEEk-er-reg-ahl, nt bookshelves

**Buchführung,** book-fEEr-oong f bookkeeping

**Buchhalter,** book-hahlt-er, m bookkeeper

**Buchhaltung,** book-hahlt-oong, f bookkeeping

**Buchhandel,** book-hahnd-el, m bookselling, book trade

**Buchhandlung,** book-hahnd-loong, f bookshop

**Buchmacher,** book-mak-er, m bookmaker

**Buchsbaum,** boocks-bowm, m box (tree)

**Büchse,** bEEck-se, f box; tin; rifle

**Büchsenfleisch,** bEEck-sen-fly'sh, nt tinned meat

**Büchsenöffner,** bEEck-sen-erff-ner, m tin opener

**Buchstabe,** book-shtahb-e, m (alphabet) letter; type

**buchstabieren,** book-shtahb-eer-en, v to spell

**buchstäblich,** book-shtayp-lik, adj literal

**Bucht,** bookt, f bay, cove;

**Buchung,** book-oong, f booking; entry

**Buckel,** boock-el, m hump, hunch; hunchback

**bucklig,** boock-lik, adj hunchbacked

**bücken (sich),** bEEck-en (zik), v to stoop; to bow

**Bückling,** bEEck-ling, m a kind of smoked herring

**Bude,** bood-e, f booth; stall; fam digs

**Büfett,** bEE-fett, nt sideboard

**Büffel,** bEEff-el, m buffalo, bison

**Bug,** boohk, m naut bow; hock, shoulder blade

**Bügel,** bEEg-el, m coathanger; stirrup; bow

**Bügeleisen,** bEEg-el-i-zen, nt iron

**bügelfrei,** bEEg-el-fry, adj non-iron

**bügeln,** bEEg-eln, v to iron, to press

**Bühne,** bEEn-e, f theatre stage; platform; **–nbild,** nt (stage) set

**Bühnenstück,** bEEn-en-shtEEck, nt (stage-)play

**Bulle,** bool-e, m bull; fam copper

**Bummel,** boomm-el, m stroll; jaunt

**bummeln,** boomm-eln, v to stroll; to dawdle

**Bummelzug,** boomm-el-tsook, m slow train

**Bund,** boont, m union,

alliance; league

**Bund,** boont, nt bundle, bunch; packet

**Bündel,** bEEnd-el, nt bundle; packet, parcel

**Bundes-,** boond-es, pref federal; **–bürger,** m German citizen; **–kanzler,** m Federal Chancellor; **–land,** nt state; Federal Republic; **–präsident,** m Federal President; **–rat,** m upper house of German parliament; **–tag,** m German parliament; **–wehr,** f German armed forces

**Bündnis,** bEEnt-niss, nt alliance, union

**bunt,** boont, adj multicoloured

**Buntstift,** boont-shtift, m crayon

**Bürde,** bEErd-e, f burden, load

**Burg,** boork, f castle; stronghold

**Bürge,** bEErg-e, m security; bail; guarantor

**bürgen,** bEErg-en, v to guarantee; to stand bail; to vouch for

**Bürger,** bEErg-er, m citizen; **–krieg,** m civil war

**bürgerlich,** bEErg-er-lik, adj middle class; civilian

**Bürgermeister,** bEErg-er-myst-er, m mayor

**Bürgersteig,** bEErg-er-shtyg, m footpath, pavement

**Bürgschaft,** bEErk-shahft, *f* pledge, guarantee

**Büro,** bEEr-**oh,** *nt* office

**Bürokratie,** bEEr-oh-kraht-**ee,** *f* bureaucracy

**bürokratisch,** bEEr-oh-**kraht**-ish, *adj* bureaucratic

**Bursche,** boorsh-*e,* *m* youth, young man

**Bürste,** bEErs-te, *f* brush

**bürsten,** bEErs-ten, *v* to brush

**Bus,** boos, *m* bus; coach

**Busch,** boosh, *m* bush, shrub; plume; tuft

**Büschel,** bEEsh-el, *nt* whisp; cluster; tuft

**buschig,** boosh-ik, *adj* bunchy; tufted; bushy

**Busen,** booz-en, *m* bosom, breast, bust

**Bushaltestelle,** boos-hahlt-e-stel-le, *f* bus stop

**Buße,** boos-*e,* *f* penitence; repentance, atonement; fine

**büßen,** bEEs-en, *v* to atone; to expiate (crime); to do penance

**Büste,** bEEst-*e,* *f* bust

**Büstenhalter,** bEEst-en-hahlt-*er,* *m* bra

**Butter,** boott-*er,* *f* butter

**Butterblume,** boott-*er*-bloom-*e,* *f* buttercup

**Butterbrot,** boott-*er*-broht, *nt* bread and butter

**bzgl.,** *abbr* bezüglich

**bzw.,** *abbr* beziehungsweise

**ca.** (= **circa**), **tseer**-kah, *adv* about, approximately

**Camcorder, kem**-korder, *m* camcorder

**campen, kemp**-en, *v* to camp

**Campingbus, kemp**-ing-boos, *m* dormobile

**Campingplatz, kemp**-ing-plahts, *m* camp site

**CD-Spieler,** see-dee-**shpeel**-er, *m* CD-player

**Cello, tchel**-loh, *nt* cello

**Celsius, tsel**-ze-ooss, *nt* centigrade

**Champagner,** shahmm-**pahnn**-yer, *m* champagne

**Champignon, shahmm**-pin-yong, *m* mushroom

**Chance, shahn**-se, *f* chance, opportunity

**Charakter,** kah-**rahck**-ter, *m* character, nature

**charakterfest,** kah-**rahck**-ter-fest, *adj* firm of character

**charakterisieren,** kah-rahck-ter-eez-**eer**-en, *v* to depict; to characterize

**Charakterzug,** kah-**rahck**-ter-tsook, *m* trait of character

**Charme, shahrm,** *m* charm

**Charterflug, tchahrt**-er-floog, *m* charter flight

**Chef, shef,** *m* principal, manager, chief, boss

**Chemie,** keh-**mee,** *f* chemistry

**Chemikalien,** keh-me-**kahl**-yen, *pl* chemicals, drugs

**Chemiker, keh**-mik-er, *m* (scientific) chemist

**chemisch, keh**-mish, *adj* chemical; **–e Reinigung,** *f* dry-cleaning

**Chiffre, shif**-re, *f* cipher; box number

**China, kee**-nah, *nt* China

**Chinese,** kee-**nay**-ze, *m*, **Chinesin,** kee-**nay**-zin, *f* Chinese (person)

**chinesisch,** kee-**nay**-zish, *adj* Chinese

**Chinin,** kee-**neen,** *nt* quinine

**Chip, tchip,** *m* crisp; *comp* chip; **–karte,** smart card

**Chirurg,** kee-**roork,** *m* surgeon

**Chor, kohr,** *m* chorus, choir

**Choral, kohr**-ahl, *m* hymn, anthem

**Christ, krist,** *m* Christian; **–baum,** *m* Christmas-tree; **–entum,** *nt* Christianity; **–fest,** *nt* Christmas; **–kind,** *nt* Infant Jesus, Christ Child

**christlich, krist**-lik, *adj* Christian

**Cola, koh**-lah, *fam* Coke ®

**Computer,** kohm-**pyoot**-er, *m* computer; **–spiel,** *nt* computer game

**Cousin,** koo-**zeng,** *m* (male) cousin

**Cousine,** koo-**zeen**-e, *f* (female) cousin

**Creme, kraim,** *f* cream; (shoe) polish

**da**, dah, *adv* there; here; then; *conj* as, since, because

**dabei**, dah-by, *adv* thereby, by it; **–sein**, *v* to be present; to be involved; **–stehen**, *v* to stand around

**Dach**, dah*k*, *nt* roof; **–boden**, *m* loft; **–decker**, *m* tiler; roofer; slater; **–gepäckträger**, *m* roof rack; **–rinne**, *f* gutter

**Dachs**, dah*k*s, *m* badger

**Dachstube**, dah*k*-shtoob-e, *f* garret, attic

**Dackel**, dah*kk*-el, *m* dachshund

**dadurch**, dah-doohr*k*, *adv* by that means; thereby

**dafür**, dah-fEEr, *adv* in return for, for that; in place of

**dagegen**, dah-**gay**-gen, *adv* & *conj* against it, in return; on the contrary

**daheim**, dah-hime, *adv* at home; indoors

**daher**, dah-hair, *adv* from that; hence

**dahin**, dah-hin, *adv* there (thither)

**dahingegen**, dah-hin-gay-gen, *adv* on the other hand; on the contrary

**dahinter**, dah-hint-er, *adv* behind it

**damals**, dah-mahls, *adv* at that time

**Damast**, dahmm-ast, *m* damask

**Dame**, dahm-e, *f* lady; (chess) queen

**damit**, dah-mit, *adv* & *conj* with it; so that

**Damm**, dahmm, *m* dam, dike; embankment, sea-wall

**dämmen**, dem-en, *v* to dam; to (hold in) check

**dämmerig**, dem-er-ik, *adj* dim, dusky

**dämmern**, dem-ern, *v* to dawn

**Dämmerung**, dem-er-oong, *f* twilight; dawn

**Dampf**, dahmf, *m* steam; vapour

**dampfen**, dahm-fen, *v* to steam; to emit steam

**dämpfen**, dem-fen, *v* to suppress, to check; to muffle, to deaden

**Dampfer**, dahm-fer, *m* steamer

**Dampfkessel**, dahmf-kess-el, *m* steam-boiler

**Dampfmaschine**, dahmf-mah-sheen-e, *f* steam-engine

**Dampfschiff**, dahmf-shif, *nt* steamship

**Dampfwalze**, dahmf-vahlt-se, *f* steam-roller

**danach**, dah-nahk, *adv* after that; later on

**Däne**, day-ne, *m* Dane, Danishman

**Dänemark**, day-ne-mahrk, *nt* Denmark

**daneben**, dah-nay-ben, *adv* beside it; next to it

**Dänin**, day-nin, *f* Dane, Danishwoman

**dänisch**, day-nish, *adj* Danish

**Dank**, dahngk, *m* gratitude, thanks; reward; **vielen –**, many thanks

**dankbar, dahngk**-bar, *adj*
grateful, thankful

**Dankbarkeit, dahngk**-bar-kite, *f* gratitude

**danke, dahngk**-*e*, *interj*
thank you

**danken, dahngk**-en, *v* to
thank

**dann,** dahnn, *adv* then; after
that, afterwards

**daran,** dah-**rahnn**, *adv* on it;
against it; near it

**darauf,** dah-**rowf**, *adv* on it

**daraus,** dah-**rows**, *adv* from
there; from it

**Darbietung, dahr**-beet-oong, *f* performance,
presentation

**darin,** dah-**rin**, *adv* in it

**darlegen, dahr**-lay-gen, *v* to
show; to exhibit; to
explain

**Darleh(e)n, dahr**-lay(-*e*-)n,
*nt* loan

**Darm,** darm, *m* intestine,
gut

**darstellen, dahr**-shtel-en, *v*
to present, to show; to
produce

**Darsteller, dahr**-shtel-er, *m*
actor

**Darstellung, dahr**-shtel-oong, *f* presentation

**darüber,** dah-**rEEb**-er, *adv*
over it; about it

**darum,** dah-**roomm**, *adv*
about it; therefore

**darunter,** dah-**roont**-er, *adv*
underneath; among

**das,** see **der**

**Dasein, dah**-zine, *nt*

existence, being

**daß,** dahss, *conj* that

**Datei,** daht-**y**, (data) file

**Daten, daht**-en, *pl* data

**Datenbank, daht**-en-bahnk,
*f* database

**Datenschutz, daht**-en-shoots, *m* data protection

**Datenverarbeitung, daht**-en-fer-ahr-bite-oong, *f*
data processing

**datieren,** daht-**eer**-en, *v* to
date

**Dattel, daht**-el, *f* date (fruit)

**Datum, daht**-oomm, *nt* date
(calendar)

**Dauer, dow**-er, *f* duration;
length of time

**dauerhaft, dow**-er-hahfft,
*adj* durable, lasting

**Dauerkarte, dow**-er-kahr-te,
*f* season ticket

**dauern, dow**-ern, *v* to last,
to continue

**Dauerwelle, dow**-er-vel-le, *f*
perm

**Daumen, dowm**-en, *m*
thumb

**Daunendecke, down**-en-deck-e, *f* duvet

**davon,** dah-**fon**, *adv* from it;
of it

**davor,** dah-**fohr**, *adv* in front
of it

**dazu,** dah-**tsoo**, *adv* with it

**dazwischen,** dah-**tsvish**-en,
*adv* between them; among
them

**Deck,** deck, *nt* deck

**Decke, deck**-e, *f* cover(ing);
ceiling; layer

**Deckel, deck**-el, *m* lid;
cover (of book)

**decken, deck**-en, *v* to cover;
to reimburse

**Deckung, deck**-oong, *f*
cover, shelter, protection

**Defekt,** de-**feckt**, *m* fault,
defect

**Degen, day**-gen, *m* sword

**dehnen, dayn**-en, *v* to
stretch; to extend

**Deich,** dy'k, *m* dike; dam;
embankment

**dein, deine(r/s),** dine, dine-e(r/s), *adj* your; *pron* yours

**Dekoration,** day-koh-rah-tse-**ohn**, *f* decoration;
window display

**delikat,** day-le-**kaht**, *adj*
delicious

**Delikatessen,** day-le-kaht-ess-en, *pl* delicatessen
(food), delicacies;
**–geschäft** *nt*, **–laden** *m*,
**–handlung** *f* delicatessen
(shop)

**Delikt,** de-**likt**, *nt* offence

**dem,** daym, *art* (dative *m* &
*nt*) (to) the; *pron* (to)
whom

**dementsprechend,** daym-ent-**shprek**-ent, *adv*
accordingly

**demgemäß,** daym-ge-mace, *adv* correspondingly;
accordingly

**demnach,** daym-**nahk**, *adv*
therefore; accordingly

**demnächst,** daym-**naikst**,
*adv* shortly, soon

**Demokratie,** day-moh-krah-

**tee,** *f* democracy

**demokratisch,** day-moh-**kraht**-ish, *adj* democratic

**Demonstration,** day-mohn-strahts-**yohn**, *f* demonstration

**demonstrieren,** day-mohn-**streer**-*en*, *v* to demonstrate

**Demut,** day-moot, *f* humility

**demütig,** day-mEEt-ik, *adj* humble; **–en,** *v* to humble; to humiliate

**Demütigung,** day-mEEt-ig-oong, *f* humiliation; abasement

**den,** dayn, *definite art* (accusative m & dative pl) (to) the

**denen,** dayn-en, *pron* (dative pl) to them, to those

**denkbar,** denk-bar, *adj* imaginable

**denken,** deng-ken, *v* to think

**Denkmal,** dengk-mahl, *nt* monument, memorial; **–schutz,** *m* protection of historical monuments

**denkwürdig,** dengk-vEErd-ik, *adj* notable; memorable

**denn,** den, *conj* for, because, since

**dennoch,** den-ok, *adv & conj* nevertheless; however; still

**Deodorant,** day-oh-dor-ahnt, *nt* deodorant

**deponieren,** day-pon-**eer**-en, *v* to deposit

**Deponie,** day-pohn-ee, *f* dump

**deprimieren,** day-preem-**eer**-en, *v* to depress

**der, die, das,** der, dee, dahs, *definite art* the; *pron* who, which

**derb,** dairp, *adj* firm, robust; rude, rough, coarse

**deren,** dair-en, *pron* (genitive f & pl) whose, of whom, of which

**dergleichen,** dair-**gly**-ken, *pron* such

**derjenige,** dair-yayn-ig-e, *pron* the one who

**derselbe,** dair-zel-be, *pron* the same

**des,** dess, *definite art* (genitive m & nt) of the

**desgleichen,** dess-**gly**-ken, *adv* likewise

**deshalb,** dess-hahlp, *adv & conj* because of that, therefore

**dessen,** dess-en, *pron* (genitive m & n) whose

**Dessert,** dess-**er**, *nt* dessert

**desto,** dess-toh, *adv* so much; **– besser,** bess-er, so much the better

**deswegen,** dess-vaig-en, *adv & conj* because of that; therefore

**Dezember,** day-**tsemm**-ber, *m* December

**Detail,** day-tie, *nt* detail

**Detektiv,** day-tek-teef, *m* detective

**deuten,** doyt-en, *v* to point out; to explain

**deutlich, doyt**-lik, *adj* distinct, clear, intelligible

**deutsch,** doytsh, *adj* German

**Deutsche(r),** doyt-she(r), *m & f* German (person)

**Deutschland,** doytsh-lahnt, *nt* Germany

**Deutung,** doyt-oong, *f* interpretation, explanation

**Devise,** day-veez-e, *f* device, motto; **–n,** *pl* foreign currency; foreign exchange

**Dia,** dee-ah, *nt photog* slide; transparency

**Dialekt,** dee-ah-lekt, *m* dialect

**Dialog,** dee-ah-lohk, *m* dialogue

**Diät,** dee-ait, *f* diet

**Diamant,** dee-ah-**mahnt**, *m* diamond

**dich,** dik, *pron* (accusative) you

**dicht,** dikt, *adj* dense; tight; solid

**dichten, dik**-ten, *v* to seal; to write poetry

**Dichter, dik**-ter, *m* poet, writer

**Dichtkunst,** dikt-koonst, *f* (art of) poetry

**Dichtung,** dikt-oong, *f* poetry

**dick,** dik, *adj* thick; fat, stout

**Dicke,** dik-e, *f* thickness; stoutness

**Dickkopf,** dik-kop'f, *m* stubborn person

**die,** see **der**

**Dieb,** deep, *m* thief, robber

**Diebstahl,** deep-shtahl, *m* theft, robbery

**Diele,** deel-*e*, *f* floorboard; plank; hall(way)

**dienen,** deen-en, *v* to serve

**Diener,** deen-*er*, *m* servant, footman, valet

**dienlich,** deen-lik, *adj* useful; expedient

**Dienst,** deenst, *m* service; duty; favour; **–bote,** *m* domestic servant

**Dienstag,** deens-tahk, *m* Tuesday

**diensthabend,** deenst-hahb-ent, *adj* on duty

**Dienstleistung,** deenst-lyst-oong, *f* service

**Dienstreise,** deenst-ryz-*e*, *f* business trip

**diesbezüglich,** dees-bet-sEEk-lik, *adj* referring to this

**dies, diese(r/s),** dees, deez-*e*(r/s), *pron* this, that

**diesmal,** dees-mahl, *adv* this time; for (this) once

**diesseits,** dees-zites, *adv* & *prep* on this side

**digital,** dee-gee-tahl, *adj* digital

**Diktat,** dik-taht, *nt* dictation

**Diktatur,** dik-tah-toor, *f* dictatorship

**diktieren,** dik-teer-en, *v* to dictate

**Ding,** ding, *nt* thing; subject; matter

**Diplom,** deep-lohm, *nt* diploma; (university) degree

**Diplomat,** deep-lohm-**aht**, *m* diplomat

**Diplomatie,** deep-lohm-aht-ee, *f* diplomacy

**direkt,** dee-reckt, *adj* direct

**Direktor,** dee-reckt-ohr, *m* director; (school) headmaster

**Direktübertragung,** dee-reckt-EEber-trahg-oong, *f* live broadcast

**Dirigent,** dee-ree-gent, *mus* conductor

**dirigieren,** dee-ree-geer-en, *v mus* to conduct

**Diskont,** dis-kont, *m* discount, rebate

**Diskussion,** dis-kooss-yohn, *f* discussion; debate

**diskutieren,** dis-koot-eer-en, *v* to discuss; to debate

**disponieren (über jdn),** dees-pohn-eer-en, *v* to tell (sb) what to do; to make arrangements

**Distel,** dist-*el*, *f* thistle

**distinguiert,** dist-ing-geert, *adj* distinguished

**doch,** dok, *conj* & *adv* still, yet, however; yes, indeed

**Docht,** dokt, *m* wick

**Dogge,** dog-*e*, *f* mastiff

**Dohle,** dohl-*e*, *f* jackdaw

**Dokument,** doh-koo-ment, *nt* document; **–arbericht,** *m* documentary

**Dolch,** dolk, *m* dagger

**dolmetschen,** dol-metsh-en, *v* to interpret

**Dolmetscher,** dol-metsh-er, *m* interpreter

**Dom,** dohm, *m* cathedral

**Donau,** doh-now, *f* Danube

**Donner,** don-er, *m* thunder

**donnern,** don-ern, *v* to thunder

**Donnerstag,** don-ers-tahk, *m* Thursday

**doof,** dohf, *adj* stupid

**Doppel,** dop-el, *nt* double, duplicate; **–bett,** *nt* double bed; **–stecker,** *m* two-way adaptor

**doppelt,** dop-elt, *adj* double, twin

**Doppelzimmer,** dop-el-tsim-er, *nt* double room

**Dorf,** dorf, *nt* village

**Dorn,** dorn, *m* thorn, prickle

**dornig,** dorn-ik, *adj* thorny

**Dörrobst,** der-ohpst; *nt* dried fruit

**dort,** dort, *adv* there

**dorther,** dort-hair, *adv* from there

**dorthin,** dort-hin, *adv* there (thither)

**dortig,** dort-ik, *adv* there (of that place)

**Dose,** doh-ze, *f* tin; can; box; **–nöffner,** *m* tin-opener

**Dotter,** dot-er, *m* yolk of an egg

**Dozent,** doht-sent *m* university lecturer

**Drache,** drahk-*e*, *m* dragon

**Drachen,** drahk-en, *m* kite; **–fliegen,** *nt* hang-gliding

**Draht**, draht, m wire

**Drama**, drah-mah, nt drama

**dramatisch**, drah-mah-tish, adj dramatic

**Drang**, drahng, m throng; pressure; urge

**drängen**, dreng-en, v to press, to push

**draußen**, drows-en, adv outside; outdoors

**Dreck**, dreck, m dirt, filth

**dreckig**, dreck-ik, adj dirty, filthy

**drehen**, dray-en, v to turn, to twist; to wind

**drei**, dry, num three

**Dreieck**, dry-eck, nt triangle

**dreieckig**, dry-eck-ik, adj triangular; three-cornered

**dreierlei**, dry-er-ly, adj of three kinds

**dreifach**, dry-fahk, adj threefold; treble; triple

**dreimal**, dry-mahl, adv three times; thrice

**dreiseitig**, dry-zy-tik, adj trilateral

**dreißig**, dry-sik, num thirty

**dreist**, dry'st, adj bold, audacious; impudent

**dreizehn**, dry-tsain, num thirteen

**dreschen**, dresh-en, v to thresh; fam to thrash

**dressieren**, dres-eer-en, v to train (animals)

**dringen**, dring-en, v to force; to urge; to penetrate; **auf etwas –,** to insist on sth

**dringend**, dring-ent, adj urgent, pressing

**drinnen**, drinn-en, adv inside

**dritte(r/s)**, dritt-e(r/s), adj third

**Drittel**, dritt-el, nt third (part)

**drittens**, dritt-ens, adv thirdly

**droben**, drohb-en, adv above, up there; on high

**Droge**, drohg-e, f drug

**drogenabhängig**, drohg-en-ahp-heng-ik, adj addicted to drugs

**Drogenmißbrauch**, drohg-en-miss-browk, m drug abuse

**Drogerie**, drohg-er-ee, f chemist's shop; drugstore

**drohen**, droh-en, v to threaten, to menace

**dröhnen**, drern-en, v to rumble, to roar, to boom

**Drohung**, droh-oong, f threat, menace

**drollig**, drol-lik, adj droll, funny, quaint

**Droschke**, drosh-ke, f (horse-drawn) carriage

**Drossel**, dross-el, f thrush

**drüben**, drEEb-en, adv over there

**Druck**, droock, m pressure; depression; print(ing)

**drucken**, droock-en, v to print; to typeset

**drücken**, drEEck-en, v to press, to squeeze; to oppress

**Drucker**, droock-er, m printer

**Druckerei**, droock-e-ry, f printing-works

**Drucksache**, droock-sahk-e, f printed matter

**Druckschrift**, droock-shrift, f block letters

**drunten**, droonnt-en, adv below, down there

**Drüse**, drEEz-e, f gland

**Dschungel**, tshoong-el, m jungle

**du**, doo, pron you

**Dudelsack**, dood-el-zahck, m bagpipes

**Duft**, dooft, m odour, fragrance

**duften**, dooft-en, v to smell (be fragrant)

**dulden**, doold-en, v to tolerate, to suffer

**duldsam**, doolt-zahm, adj (long-)suffering; tolerant

**dumm**, doomm, adj stupid, thick

**Dummheit**, doomm-hite, f stupidity

**Dummkopf**, doomm-kop'f, m blockhead; idiot

**dumpf**, doomf, adj dull, muffled; stuffy, close

**düngen**, dEEng-en, v to manure, to fertilize

**Dünger**, dEEng-er, m, manure, dung, fertilizer

**dunkel**, doong-kel, adj dark; gloomy, murky

**Dunkelheit**, doong-kel-hite, f darkness

**dunkeln**, doong-keln, v to

grow dark

**dünn**, dEEnn, *adj* thin; lean

**Dunst**, doonst, *m* vapour, steam; mist

**dünsten**, dEEns-ten, *v* to steam; to stew

**dunstig**, doons-tik, *adj* vaporous; hazy, misty

**Dur**, door, *nt mus* major

**durch**, doohrk, *prep* through; by (means of)

**durchaus**, doohrk-**ows**, *adv* throughout; quite; thoroughly

**durchblicken**, doohrk-blik-en, *v* to peep/glance through

**durchbohren**, doohrk-**bohr**-en, *v* to pierce through

**durchbrechen**, doohrk-**brek**-en, *v* to break through

**durchbringen**, doohrk-**bring**-en, *v* to get through; to support

**durchdringen**, doohrk-**dring**-en, *v* to permeate

**durcheinander**, doohrk-yn-**ahnd**-er, *adj* confused; in a mess; muddled

**Durchfahrt**, doohrk-fahrt, *f* thoroughfare, passage

**Durchfall**, doohrk-fahll, *m* diarrhoea

**durchfallen**, doohrk-fahll-en, *v* to fall through; to fail

**durchfinden (sich)**, doohrk-finn-den (zik), *v* to find one's way through

**durchführen**, doohrk-fEEr-en, *v* to carry through; to achieve

**Durchführung**, doohrk-fEEr-oong, *f* implementation; carrying out

**Durchgang**, doohrk-gahng, *m* passing through; passage; way through

**durchgehend**, doohrk-gai-ent, *adj* continuous; through (train)

**durchkommen**, doohrk-kom-en, *v* to get through; to pass (exam)

**durchkreuzen**, doohrk-kroyts-en, *v* to traverse

**durchlassen**, doohrk-lahss-en, *v* to let through

**durchlaufen**, doohrk-lowf-en, *v* to run through

**durchlesen**, doohrk-lai-zen, *v* to read through

**durchmachen**, doohrk-mahk-en, *v* to experience (hardship etc.)

**Durchmesser**, doohrk-mess-er, *m* diameter

**durchnässen**, doohrk-**ness**-en, *v* to seep through; to make wet; to soak

**durchnehmen**, doohrk-naym-en, *v* to go through

**Durchreise**, doohrk-ry-ze, *f* journey through

**durchreisen**, doohrk-ry-zen, *v* to travel through

**Durchsage**, doohrk-sag-e, *f* announcement

**durchschauen**, doohrk-**show**-en, *v* to see through

**Durchschlag**, doohrk-shlahk, *m* carbon copy

**durchschlagen**, doohrk-shlahg-en, *v* to break through; to knock through; **sich –**, to rough it

**durchschneiden**, doohrk-shny-den, *v* to cut through

**Durchschnitt**, doohrk-shnit, *m* average

**durchschnittlich**, doohrk-shnit-lik, *adj* average

**durchsehen**, doohrk-zay-en, *v* to look through

**durchsetzen**, doohrk-sets-en, *v* to enforce; **sich –**, to get one's way; to succeed

**durchsichtig**, doohrk-zik-tik, *adj* transparent

**durchstellen**, doohrk-shtel-en, *v* (telephone) to put through

**durchstöbern**, doohrk-shterb-ern, *v* to ransack

**durchstreichen**, doohrk-shtryk-en, *v* to cross out

**durchsuchen**, doohrk-sook-en, *v* to search

**Durchsuchung**, doohrk-sook-oong, *f* search

**durchtrieben**, doohrk-treeb-en, *adj* cunning

**durchweg**, doohrk-vek, *adv* through out

**durchziehen**, doohrk-tsee-en, *v* to pull through

**Durchzug**, doohrk-tsoog, *m* passage; draught

**dürfen**, dEErf-en, *v* to be allowed; may

**dürftig,** dEErft-ik, *adj* needy;
inadequate

**dürr,** dEErr, *adj* dry; barren;
arid; scrawny

**Dürre,** dEErr-*e*, *f* aridity;
drought

**Durst,** doohrst, *m* thirst; –
**haben,** *v* to be thirsty

**durstig, doorst-**ik, *adj* thirsty

**Dusche, doosh-***e*, *f* shower

**duschen, doosh-***en*, *v* to
(have) a shower

**düster,** dEEst-er, *adj* dark;
gloomy; dim

**Düsenflugzeug,** dEE-zen-
floog-tsoyg, *nt* jet (plane)

**Düsternis,** dEEst-er-niss, *f*
darkness, gloom

**Dutzend, doot-**sent, *nt*
dozen

**duzen, doot-**sen, *v* to address
a person as **du**

**D-Zug, day-**tsook, *m* fast
train

**Ebbe,** eb-*e*, *f* ebb-tide

**eben,** ay-ben, *adj & adv* even, level, flat; exact; just so

**Ebene,** ay-ben-*e*, *f* plain, level ground

**ebenfalls,** ay-ben-fahls, *adv* likewise; also

**Ebenholz,** ay-ben-holts, *nt* ebony

**ebenso,** ay-ben-zo, *adv* just so, just as

**ebnen,** ayb-nen, *v* to level, to flatten

**echt,** ekt, *adj* genuine; true; real

**Echtheit,** ekt-hite, *f* genuineness

**Ecke,** eck-*e*, *f* corner, angle, nook, edge

**eckig,** eck-ik, *adj* cornered; angular

**edel,** ay-del, *adj* noble; high-born; precious

**Edelmetall,** ayd-*e*l-mett-ahll, *nt* rare metal

**Edelstein,** ay-*e*l-shtine, *m* precious stone; jewel

**Efeu,** ay-foy, *m* ivy

**Effekten,** ef-fek-ten, *pl* effects; stock(s), securities

**egal,** ay-gahl, *adj* all the same; indifferent

**ehe,** ay-*e*, *adv* before; formerly

**Ehe,** ay-*e*, *f* matrimony; marriage; **–beratung,** *f* marriage counselling; **–bruch,** *m* adultery; **–frau,** *f* wife

**ehelich,** ay-*e*-lik, *adj* conjugal, matrimonial

**ehemalig,** ay-*e*-mahl-ik, *adj* former, previous

**ehemals,** ay-*e*-mahls, *adv* formerly

**Ehemann,** ay-*e*-mahnn, *m* husband

**Ehepaar,** ay-*e*-par, *nt* married couple

**eher,** ay-*e*r, *adv* earlier; sooner

**ehrbar,** air-bar, *adj* honourable, respectable, decent

**Ehre,** air-*e*, *f* honour; repute, credit

**ehren,** air-en, *v* to honour

**Ehrenamt,** air-en-ahmt, *nt* honorary post

**ehrenamtlich,** air-en-ahmt-lik, *adj* honorary

**Ehrengast,** air-en-gahst, *m* guest of honour

**ehrenhaft,** air-en-hahft, *adj* honourable

**Ehrenwort,** air-en-vort, *nt* word of honour

**Ehrfurcht,** air-foorkt, *f* veneration; awe

**Ehrgeiz,** air-gites, *m* ambition

**ehrgeizig,** air-gite-sik, *adj* ambitious

**ehrlich,** air-lik, *adj* honest, fair; true

**Ehrlichkeit,** air-lik-kite, *f* honesty; reliability

**ehrwürdig,** air-vEErd-ik, *adj* venerable, reverend

**Ei,** i, *nt* egg

**Eiche,** i-k*e*, *f* oak(-tree)

**Eichel,** i-k*e*l, *f* acorn

**Eichhörnchen,** i'k-hern-ken, *nt* squirrel

**Eid,** ite, *m* oath

**Eidechse,** i-deck-s*e*, *f* lizard

**Eierbecher,** i-er-bek-*e*r, *m* egg cup

**Eierkuchen, i**-er-kook-en, *m* omelet

**Eierlikör, i**-er-leek-er, *m* advocaat

**Eierstock, i**-er-shtock, *m med* ovary

**Eierschale, i**-er-shahl-e, *f* egg-shell

**Eifer, i**-fer, *m* zeal, eagerness; ardour

**Eifersucht, i**-fer-sookt, *f* jealousy

**eifersüchtig, i**-fer-sEEkt-ik, *adj* jealous

**eifrig, i**-frik, *adj* zealous, eager, keen

**Eigelb, i**-gelp, *nt* egg yolk

**eigen, i**-gen, *adj* own; particular; singular

**Eigenart, i**-gen-ahrt, *f* peculiarity; singularity

**Eigenheim, i**-gen-hym, *nt* owner-occupied house

**eigenmächtig, i**-gen-mekt-ik, *adj* arbitrary

**Eigenname, i**-gen-nahm-e, *m* proper name

**eigennützig, i**-gen-nEEtt-sik, *adj* selfish, self-seeking

**eigens, i**-gens, *adv* purposely; expressly

**Eigenschaft, i**-gen-shahft, *f* attribute; property

**Eigensinn, i**-gen-zinn, *m* obstinacy, caprice

**eigensinnig, i**-gen-zinn-ik, *adj* wilful; capricious; obstinate

**eigentlich, i**-gent-lik, *adj* real, true; essential; *adv* actually

**Eigentum, i**-gen-toom, *nt* property, estate

**Eigentümer, i**-gen-tEEm-er, *m* proprietor, owner

**eigentümlich, i**-gen-tEEm-lik, *adj* odd; peculiar; typical

**Eigentumswohnung, i**-gen-tooms-vohn-oong, *f* owner-occupied flat

**eigenwillig, i**-gen-vil-ik, *adj* wilful, self-willed

**eignen (sich), i**-gnen (zik), *v* to be suitable

**Eilbote, ile**-boht-e, *m* courier

**Eilbrief, ile**-breef, *m* express letter

**Eile, i**-le, *f* hurry, haste; promptness, speed

**eilen, i**-len, *v* to hurry

**Eilgut, ile**-goot, *nt* express freight

**eilig, i**-lik, *adj* pressing, urgent; speedy, quick

**Eilzug, ile**-tsoog, *m* semi-fast train

**Eimer, i**-mer, *m* bucket

**ein(e/s), ine**(-e/s), *indefinite art* a, an; one

**einander, ine**-ahnn-der, *adv* one another; each other

**einatmen, ine**-aht-men, *v* to inhale

**Einbahnstraße, ine**-bahn-shtrahss-e, *f* one-way street

**Einband, ine**-bahnt, *m* binding, cover (of book)

**einbilden (sich), ine**-bil-den (zik), *v* to imagine

**Einbildung, ine**-bil-doong, *f* imagination, fancy

**Einbildungskraft, ine**-bil-doongs-krahft, *f* (power of) imagination

**Einblick, ine**-blik, *m* insight

**einbrechen, ine**-brek-en, *v* to break in/through

**Einbrecher, ine**-brek-er, *m* burglar

**einbringen, ine**-bring-en, *v* to bring in

**Einbruch, ine**-brook, *m* burglary

**einchecken, ine**-tsheck-en, *v* to check in

**eincremen, ine**-kraim-en, *v* to put cream on

**eindämmen, ine**-dem-en, *v* to dam

**eindeutig, ine**-doyt-ik, *adj* unequivocal

**eindringen, ine**-dring-en, *v* to penetrate

**eindringlich, ine**-dring-lik, *adj* intrusive; forcible

**Eindruck, ine**-droock, *m* impression; imprint

**einerlei, ine**-er-ly, *adj* of the same kind, all the same

**einerseits, ine**-er-zites, *adv* on the one hand

**einfach, ine**-fahk, *adj* simple, single, plain

**Einfahrt, ine**-fahrt, *f* gateway, doorway, drive

**Einfall, ine**-fahll, *m* idea

**einfallen, ine**-fahll-en, *v* to fall in; to occur

**einfältig, ine**-felt-ik, *adj* simple-minded, foolish

**einfangen**, ine-fahng-en, *v* to capture; to arrest

**einfarbig**, ine-fahrb-ik, *adj* one colour

**Einfassung**, ine-fahss-oong, *f* border, edge

**Einfluß**, ine-flooss, *m* influence; influx

**einflußreich**, ine-flooss-ry'k, *adj* influential

**einförmig**, ine-ferm-ik, *adj* uniform; monotonous

**einfrieren**, ine-freer-en, *v* to freeze

**Einfuhr**, ine-foor, *f* import(ation)

**einführen**, ine-fEEr-en, *v* to import; to introduce

**Einführung**, ine-fEEr-oong, *f* introduction; import

**Eingabe**, ine-gahb-e, *f* petition; address

**Eingang**, ine-gahng, *m* entry; arrival; opening

**eingeben**, ine-gay-ben, *v* to give; *comp* to enter

**eingebildet**, ine-ge-bil-det, *adj* conceited

**Eingeborene(r)**, ine-ge-bohr-e-ne(r), *m & f* native

**Eingebung**, ine-gay-boong, *f* inspiration

**eingehen**, ine-gay-en, *v* to arrive; to shrink; to perish; **auf etwas –**, to go into sth

**eingehend**, ine-gay-ent, *adj* in detail; thorough

**Eingemachte(s)**, ine-ge-mahk-te(s), *nt* bottled fruit/vegetables

**eingenommen**, ine-ge-nom-en, *adj* prejudiced

**eingeschlossen**, ine-ge-shlos-en, *adj* enclosed; locked up

**eingeschrieben**, ine-ge-shreeb-en, *adj* registered (letter)

**Eingeständnis**, ine-ge-shtent-niss, *nt* confession

**eingestehen**, ine-ge-shtay-en, *v* to confess

**Eingeweide**, ine-ge-vy-de, *nt* intestines, bowels

**eingießen**, ine-gees-en, *v* to pour into

**eingreifen**, ine-gry-fen, *v* to intervene; to meddle

**Eingriff**, ine-griff, *m* intervention

**einhalten**, ine-hahlt-en, *v* to stop; to fulfil

**einhängen**, ine-henng-en, *v* to hang; to hang up (telephone)

**einheimisch**, ine-hy-mish, *adj* native, indigenous

**Einheimische(r)**, ine-hy-mish-e(r), *m & f* local (person)

**Einheit**, ine-hite, *f* unit(y); union; uniformity

**einheitlich**, ine-hite-lik, *adj* uniform; homogeneous

**einher**, ine-her, *adv* along

**einholen**, ine-hohl-en, *v* to overtake; to bring in

**einhüllen**, ine-hEEll-en, *v* to envelop, to wrap

**einig**, ine-ik, *adj* in agreement, unanimous

**einige**, ine-ig-e, *pron* a few, several

**einigen**, ine-ig-en, *v* to unite; **sich auf etw –**, to agree on sth

**einigermaßen**, ine-ig-er-mahss-en, *adv* somewhat

**Einigkeit**, ine-ig-kite, *f* unity, agreement

**Einigung**, ine-ig-oong, *f* agreement; unification

**einimpfen**, ine-im-fen, *v* to inoculate; to vaccinate

**Einkauf**, ine-kowf, *m* purchase, buying

**einkaufen**, ine-kowf-en, *v* to purchase, to buy; **– gehen**, to go shopping

**Einkäufer**, ine-koyf-er, *m* buyer

**Einkaufswagen**, ine-kowfs-vah-gen, *m* shopping trolley

**einkehren**, ine-kayr-en, *v* to stop off

**Einklang**, ine-klahng, *m* unison, accord, harmony

**Einkommen**, ine-kom-en, *nt* income; revenue

**Einkünfte**, ine-kEEnnft-e, *pl* revenue

**einladen**, ine-lahd-en, *v* to invite; to load into

**Einladung**, ine-lahd-oong, *f* invitation

**Einlage**, ine-lahg-e, *f* enclosure; investment

**Einlaß**, ine-lahss, *m* admission; letting-in

**einlassen**, ine-lahss-en, *v* to admit; to enter

**einlaufen**, ine-lowf-en, v to shrink

**einleben (sich)**, ine-lay-ben (zik), v to settle down

**einleiten**, ine-ly-ten, v to introduce; to initiate

**Einleitung**, ine-ly-toong, f introduction, preface

**einlösen**, ine-lerz-en, v to redeem, to honour (bills)

**einmachen**, ine-mahk-en, v to preserve; to bottle

**einmal**, ine-mahl, adv once, once upon a time; just; **noch –**, once more

**Einmaleins**, ine-mahl-ines, nt multiplication-table

**einmalig**, ine-mahl-ik, adj unique, single

**Einmarsch**, ine-marsh, m marching-in, entry

**einmischen(sich)**, ine-mish-en (zik), v to interfere; to meddle

**Einnahme**, ine-nahm-e, f occupation; takings

**einnehmen**, ine-naym-en, v to take medicine; to take in; to collect (taxes); to conquer

**Einöde**, ine-erd-e, f wilderness, desert

**einpacken**, ine-pahck-en, v to pack (up)

**einpflanzen**, ine-flahnt-sen, v to plant; med to implant

**einprägen**, ine-prayg-en, v to impress; to imprint; **sich etw –**, to memorize sth

**einquartieren**, ine-kvahrt-eer-en, v to quarter, to billet

**einrahmen**, ine-rahm-en, v to frame

**einräumen**, ine-roym-en, v to put in order; to accord, to grant (credit etc.)

**einreden**, ine-rayd-en, v to talk (sb) into

**einreichen**, ine-ry-ken, v to hand over; to deliver

**Einreise**, ine-ry-ze, f entry; **–bestimmungen**, fpl entry regulations

**einrichten**, ine-rik-ten, v to arrange; to put in order; to furnish

**Einrichtung**, ine-rik-toong, f arrangement; furniture, furnishing

**einrücken**, ine-rEEck-en, v to insert (advertisement); to indent

**eins**, ines, num one

**einsam**, ine-zahm, adj solitary, lonely, secluded

**Einsamkeit**, ine-zahm-kite, f solitude, isolation

**einsammeln**, ine-zahmm-eln, v to gather

**Einsatz**, ine-zahts, m insertion; stake (at games)

**einschalten**, ine-shahlt-en, v to put in; to interpolate; to switch on

**einschätzen**, ine-shett-sen, v to assess, to value

**einschenken**, ine-shenk-en, v to pour in/out

**einschiffen (sich)**, ine-shif-en (zik), v to embark

**einschl.** abbr **einschließlich**

**einschlafen**, ine-shlahf-en, v to go to sleep

**einschlagen**, ine-shlahg-en, v to knock in; to wrap up; to smash; to strike (lightning)

**einschließen**, ine-shlees-en, v to lock (up); to enclose; to include

**einschließlich**, ine-shlees-lik, adj inclusive of

**Einschnitt**, ine-shnit, m incision, cut, slit

**einschränken**, ine-shrenk-en, v to restrict; **sich –**, to cut down

**Einschränkung**, ine-shrenk-oong, f restriction

**Einschreiben**, ine-shry-ben, nt registered letter

**einschreiben**, ine-shry-ben, v to write in (a book); **sich –**, to register; to enrol

**einschreiten**, ine-shry-ten, v to interpose

**einschüchtern**, ine-shEEk-tern, v to intimidate

**einsehen**, ine-zay-en, v to look into; to understand

**einseitig**, ine-zy-tik, adj one-sided

**einsenden**, ine-zen-den, v to send in; to forward

**einsetzen**, ine-zet-sen, v to insert; to stake; **sich für etw –**, to support sth

**Einsicht**, ine-zikt, f insight; inspection

**einsichtsvoll**, ine-zikts-fol, adj intelligent; judicious

**Einsiedler,** ine-zeed-ler, *m*
hermit, recluse

**einsilbig,** ine-zil-bik, *adj* of
one syllable

**einspannen,** ine-shpahnn-
en, *v* to put (in); to
harness; to stretch over a
frame

**einsperren,** ine-shpair-en, *v*
to lock up

**Einspruch,** ine-shprook, *m*
objection, protest

**einspurig,** ine-shpoor-ik, *adj*
single-lane

**einst,** ine'st, *adv* once upon
a time

**einstecken,** ine-shteck-en, *v*
to pocket

**einstehen (für),** ine-shtay-
en, *v* to stand up (for)

**einsteigen,** ine-shty-gen, *v*
to get into

**einstellen,** ine-shtel-en, *v* to
stop; to adjust; to focus; to
employ

**einstig,** ine'st-ik, *adj* former

**einstimmig,** ine-shtim-ik,
*adj* unanimous

**einstmals,** ine'st-mahls, *adv*
at one time

**einstöckig,** ine-shterck-ik,
*adj* two-storeyed

**einstudieren,** ine-shtood-
eer-en, *v* to rehearse

**Einsturz,** ine-shtoorts, *m*
collapse, downfall, crash

**einstürzen,** ine-shtEErt-sen,
*v* to collapse

**einstweilen,** ine'st-vile-en,
*adv* meanwhile, for the
present

**einstweilig,** ine'st-vile-ik, *adj*
temporary

**eintauchen,** ine-towk-en, *v*
to immerse; to dip in

**einteilen,** ine-ty-len, *v* to
divide; to classify

**einteilig,** ine-ty-lik, *adj* one-
piece

**eintönig,** ine-tern-ik, *adj*
monotonous; tedious

**Eintopf,** ine-topf, *m* stew

**Eintracht,** ine-trahkt, *f*
harmony; union

**eintragen,** ine-trahg-en, *v* to
enter; **sich –,** to put one's
name down

**einträglich,** ine-traik-lik, *adj*
profitable, productive

**Eintragung,** ine-trahg-oong,
*f* entry (in books)

**eintreffen,** ine-tref-en, *v* to
arrive; to come

**eintreiben,** ine-try-ben, *v* to
drive in; to collect

**eintreten,** ine-tray-ten, *v* to
step in; to occur

**Eintritt,** ine-tritt, *m* entry,
entrance, admission

**Eintrittskarte,** ine-tritts-
kart-e, *f* admission ticket

**Einvernehmen,** ine-fair-
naym-en, *nt* agreement

**einverstanden,** ine-fair-
shtann-den, *adj* agreed

**Einwand,** ine-vahnt, *m*
objection

**Einwanderer,** ine-vahnn-
der-er, *m* immigrant

**einwandern,** ine-vahnn-
dern, *v* to immigrate

**Einwanderung,** ine-vahnn-
der-oong, *f* immigration

**einwandfrei,** ine-vahnt-fry,
*adj* perfect, faultless

**einweihen,** ine-vy-en, *v* to
dedicate; to consecrate; to
inaugurate

**Einweihung,** ine-vy-oong, *f*
inauguration

**einwenden,** ine-ven-den, *v*
to object, to protest

**Einwendung,** ine-ven-
doong, *f* objection, protest

**einwerfen,** ine-verf-en, *v* to
post; to smash; to throw in

**einwickeln,** ine-vik-eln, *v* to
wrap; to envelop

**einwilligen,** ine-vil-ig-en, *v*
to consent, to agree

**Einwilligung,** ine-vil-ig-
oong, *f* consent, assent

**einwirken,** ine-veerk-en, *v* to
have an effect; to
influence

**Einwohner,** ine-vohn-er, *m*
inhabitant, resident

**Einwurf,** ine-voorf, *m*
objection, rejoinder; slot

**Einzahl,** ine-tsahl, *f*
singular

**einzahlen,** ine-tsahl-en, *v* to
pay in

**Einzel-,** ine-tsel, *pref* single;
**–fahrschein,** *m* one-way
ticket; **–fall,** *m* individual
case; **–handel,** *m* retail
trade; **–heit,** *f* detail;
**–kind,** *nt* single child

**einzeln,** ine-tseln, *adj* single,
individual, particular

**Einzelzimmer,** ine-tsel-tsimm-
er, *nt* single room

**einziehen,** ine-tsee-en, v to draw/pull in(to); to collect (money); to withdraw from circulation; to move in

**einzig,** ine-tsik, adj only, sole, single, unique

**Einzug,** ine-tsook, m entry, entrance; moving in

**Eis,** ice, nt ice

**Eisbahn,** ice-bahn, f ice-rink

**Eisbär,** ice-bear, m polar bear

**Eisbein,** ice-bine, nt boiled knuckle of pork

**Eisberg,** ice-bairk, m iceberg

**Eisen,** ize-en, nt iron

**Eisenbahn,** ize-en-bahn, f railway

**eisern,** ize-ern, adj made of iron

**eisig,** ize-ik, adj icy, chilly

**Eisschrank,** ice-shrahngk, m refrigerator

**Eiszapfen,** ice-tsahpp-fen, m icicle

**eitel,** ite-el, adj vain; futile; coquetish

**Eitelkeit,** ite-el-kite, f vanity; futility

**Eiter,** ite-er, m pus

**eitern,** ite-ern, v to fester, to ulcerate; to suppurate

**Eiweiß,** i-vice, nt white of egg; protein

**Ekel,** ayk-el, m disgust; loathsome person

**ekelhaft,** ayk-el-hahfft, adj disgusting, loathsome

**ekeln,** ayk-eln, v to feel

disgust; **sich vor etw –,** to be disgusted at sth

**elektrisch,** ay-leck-trish, adj electric, electrical

**Elektrizität,** ay-leck-tree-tsee-teht, f electricity

**Elend,** ayl-ent, nt misery, wretchedness; calamity

**elend,** ayl-ent, adj miserable, wretched; needy

**elf,** elf, num eleven

**Elfe,** el-fe, f elf, fairy

**Elfenbein,** elf-en-bine, nt ivory

**Elfte,** elf-tel, nt eleventh (part)

**Ellbogen,** el-bohg-en, m elbow

**Elster,** el-ster, f magpie

**Eltern,** el-tern, pl parents

**Emaille,** ay-mahll-ye, nt enamel

**Empfang,** emp-**fahng,** m receipt, reception

**empfangen,** emp-**fahng**-en, v to receive

**Empfänger,** emp-**feng**-er, m recipient; addressee

**Empfängnis,** emp-**feng**-niss, f conception; **–verhütung,** f contraception

**Empfangsschein,** emp-**fahngs**-shine, m receipt

**empfehlen,** emp-**fayl**-en, v to recommend

**empfinden,** emp-**fin**-den, v to feel; to perceive

**empfindlich,** emp-**fint**-lik, adj sensitive; delicate

**Empfindlichkeit,** emp-**fint**-lik-kite, f sensitivity

**Empfindung,** emp-**fin**-doong, f perception, sensation, feeling

**empor,** em-**pohr,** adv up(wards)

**empören,** em-**per**-en, v to (drive to) revolt

**Empörung,** em-**per**-oong, f rising, revolt, rebellion

**emsig,** em-zik, adj industrious; busy; assiduous

**Ende,** en-de, nt end; result; conclusion; **zu – sein,** to be finished

**enden,** en-den, v to end, to finish

**endgültig,** ent-gEEl-tik, adj final; conclusive

**endlich,** ent-lik, adj final; finite; adv at last

**endlos,** ent-lohs, adj endless

**Endstation,** ent-shtats-yohn, f terminus

**Endung,** end-oong, f ending; termination

**Energie,** en-er-gee, f energy; **–verbrauch,** m energy consumption

**energisch,** en-ehrg-ish, adj energetic

**eng,** eng, adj narrow; tight; cramped

**Enge,** eng-e, f narrowness; tightness; geog straits

**Engel,** eng-el, m angel

**engherzig,** eng-hairt-sik, adj narrow-minded

**England,** eng-lahnt, nt England

**Engländer,** eng-len-der, m

**Englishman; –in,** *f*
Englishwoman

**englisch, eng-**lish, *adj*
English

**en gros,** ahng **groh,** *adv*
wholesale

**Enkel, eng-**kel, *m*
grandchild; grandson

**Enkelin, eng-**kel-in, *f*
granddaughter

**entarten,** ent-**art-**en, *v* to
degenerate

**entbehren,** ent-**bair-**en, *v* to
spare; to miss

**Entbehrung,** ent-**bair-**oong,
*f* privation, want

**entbinden,** ent-**bin-**den, *v* to
release; to absolve; to
deliver of a child

**Entbindung,** ent-**bin-**doong,
*f* delivery; release

**entblößen,** ent-**blers-**en, *v*
to bare; to deprive of

**entdecken,** ent-**deck-**en, *v*
to discover

**Entdecker,** ent-**deck-**er, *m*
discoverer

**Entdeckung,** ent-**deck-**
oong, *f* discovery

**Ente, ent-***e,* *f* duck

**entehren,** ent-**air-**en, *v* to
dishonour; to disgrace

**Entenbraten,** ent-en-**braht-**
en, *m* roast duck

**entfallen,** ent-**fahll-**en, *v* to
fall from a person's hands

**entfalten,** ent-**fahllt-**en, *v* to
unfold; to develop

**entfernen,** ent-**fairn-**en, *v* to
remove; to retire

**entfernt,** ent-**fairnt,** *adj*

distant, remote, far

**Entfernung,** ent-**fairn-**oong,
*f* distance; removal;
withdrawal

**entflammen,** ent-**flahmm-**
en, *v* to inflame; to set
ablaze

**entfliehen,** ent-**flee-**en, *v* to
flee from, to escape

**entführen,** ent-**fEEr-**en, *v* to
carry off; to abduct; to
kidnap

**Entführer,** ent-**fEEr-**er, *m*
kidnapper

**Entführung,** ent-**fEEr-**oong,
*f* kidnapping; abduction

**entgegen,** ent-**gayg-**en, *adv*
against; towards

**entgegensehen,** ent-**gayg-**
en-zay-en, *v* to look
forward to

**entgegnen,** ent-**gayg-**nen, *v*
to retort; to reply

**Entgegnung,** ent-**gayg-**
noong, *f* reply; retort

**entgehen,** ent-**gay-**en, *v* to
escape; to elude

**Entgelt,** ent-**gelt,** *nt*
remuneration;
recompense

**entgleisen,** ent-**gly-**zen, *v* to
derail

**enthalten,** ent-**hahlt-**en, *v* to
contain; **sich –,** to refrain

**enthaltsam,** ent-**hahlt-**
sahm, *adj* abstinent

**enthüllen,** ent-**hEEll-**en, *v* to
unveil; to uncover

**entkommen (aus),** ent-
**kom-**en, *v* to escape
(from)

**entladen,** ent-**lahd-**en, *v* to
unload; to discharge; **sich
–,** to discharge

**Entladung,** ent-**lahd-**oong, *f*
discharge; explosion

**entlang,** ent-**lahng,** *adv &*
*prep* along, by the side of

**entlassen,** ent-**lahss-**en, *v* to
dismiss; to discharge

**Entlassung,** ent-**lahss-**oong,
*f* dismissal

**entlaufen,** ent-**lowf-**en, *v* to
run away

**entmutigen,** ent-**moot-**ig-en,
*v* to discourage

**entnehmen,** ent-**naym-**en, *v*
to take from

**enträtseln,** ent-**rayt-**seln, *v*
to decipher

**entreißen,** ent-**rice-**en, *v* to
snatch from

**entrinnen,** ent-**rin-**en, *v* to
run from

**entrüsten,** ent-**rEEst-**en, *v* to
incense; outrage; **sich –,**
to become indignant

**Entrüstung,** ent-**rEEst-**oong,
*f* indignation

**entsagen,** ent-**zahg-**en, *v* to
renounce, to resign

**entschädigen,** ent-**shayd-**ig-
en, *v* to indemnify

**Entschädigung,** ent-**shayd-**
ig-oong, *f*
indemnification;
compensation

**entscheiden,** ent-**shy-**den, *v*
to decide

**Entscheidung,** ent-**shy-**
doong, *f* decision

**entschieden,** ent-**sheed-**en,

*adj* decided

**Entschiedenheit**, ent-**sheed**-en-hite, *f* determination; firmness

**entschließen (sich)**, ent-**shlees**-en (zik), *v* to decide, to determine

**entschlossen**, ent-**shloss**-en, *adj* determined

**Entschluß**, ent-**shlooss**, *m* decision; resolve

**entschuldigen**, ent-**shoold**-ig-en, *v* to excuse; **sich –**, to apologize

**Entschuldigung**, ent-**shoolld**-ig-oong, *f* excuse; apology

**entschwinden**, ent-**shvin**-den, *v* to vanish; to die away

**entsetzen**, ent-**zet**-sen, *v* to horrify

**Entsetzen**, ent-**set**-sen, *nt* horror; dismissal

**entsetzlich**, ent-**zets**-lik, *adj* awful, horrible

**entsinnen (sich)**, ent-**zin**-en (zik), *v* to remember

**Entsorgung**, ent-**sorg**-oong, *f* waste disposal

**entsprechen**, ent-**shprek**-en, *v* to correspond to

**entspannen (sich)**, ent-**shpahnn**-en (zik), *v* to relax

**Entspannung**, ent-**spahnn**-oong, *f* relaxation

**entspringen**, ent-**shpring**-en, *v* to escape; to originate, to spring from

**entstehen**, ent-**shtay**-en, *v* to arise; to come into existence

**Entstehung**, ent-**shtay**-oong, *f* origin, formation

**entstellen**, ent-**shtel**-en, *v* to disfigure, to deface

**enttäuschen**, ent-**toysh**-en, *v* to disappoint

**Enttäuschung**, ent-**toysh**-oong, *f* disappointment

**entwaffnen**, ent-**vahff**-nen, *v* to disarm

**entwässern**, ent-**vess**-ern, *v* to drain (land)

**entweder**, ent-**vaid**-er, *conj* either

**entweichen**, ent-**vy**-ken, *v* to escape; to disappear

**entwenden**, ent-**vend**-en, *v* to misappropriate

**entwerfen**, ent-**vairf**-en, *v* to design, to draft

**entwerten**, ent-**vairt**-en, *v* to devalue

**Entwerter**, ent-**vairt**-er, *m* ticket validating machine

**entwickeln**, ent-**vik**-eln, *v* to develop; to unroll

**Entwicklung**, ent-**vik**-loong, *f* development; **–sland**, *nt* developing country

**Entwurf**, ent-**voorf**, *m* design, sketch, outline

**entziehen**, ent-**tsee**-en, *v* to withdraw from

**Entziehung**, ent-**tseeh**-oong, *f* withdrawal; **–skur**, *f* treatment for addiction

**entziffern**, ent-**tsiff**-ern, *v* to decipher; to solve

**entzücken**, ent-**tsEEck**-en, *v* to charm, to enchant

**Entzücken**, ent-**tsEEck**-en, *nt* delight, rapture

**Entzug**, ent-**tsoog**, *m* withdrawal; **–serscheinungen**, *pl* withdrawal symptoms

**entzünden**, ent-**tsEEnd**-en, *v* to inflame

**Entzündung**, ent-**tsEEnd**-oong, *f* inflammation

**entzwei**, ent-**tsvy**, *adv* in two; asunder

**Epidemie**, epee-de-mee, *f* epidemic

**Epoche**, e-**pok**-e, *f* epoch

**er**, air, *pron* he; it

**erbarmen (sich)**, air-**barm**-en (zik), *v* to have mercy on

**erbärmlich**, air-**bairm**-lik, *adj* pitiable, miserable, wretched

**Erbe**, airb-e, *m* heir, successor

**Erbe**, airb-e, *nt* inheritance, bequest

**erben**, air-ben, *v* to inherit

**erbeuten**, air-**boyt**-en, *v* to capture; to take as booty

**erbieten (sich)**, air-**beet**-en (zik), *v* to volunteer

**erbitten**, air-**bit**-en, *v* to ask; to petition for

**erblassen**, air-**blahss**-en, *v* to turn pale

**erblich**, airp-lik, *adj* hereditary

**erblicken**, air-**blik**-en, *v* to behold, to view

**erblinden,** air-**blin**-den, *v* to go blind

**erbrechen,** air-**brek**-*en*, *v* to vomit

**Erbschaft,** airp-shahft, *f* inheritance; legacy

**Erbse,** airp-*se*, *f* pea

**Erbsensuppe,** airp-sen-zoop-e, *f* pea-soup

**Erdbeben,** airt-bayb-en, *nt* earthquake

**Erdbeere,** airt-bair-e, *f* strawberry

**Erdboden,** airt-bohd-en, *m* soil; surface of the earth

**Erde,** aird-*e*, *f* earth; world, globe

**erdenklich,** air-denk-lik, *adj* imaginable

**Erdgas,** airt-gahs, *nt* natural gas

**Erdgeschoß,** airt-ge-shohss, *nt* ground floor

**erdichten,** air-dik-ten, *v* to invent; to feign

**Erdnuß,** airt-nooss, *f* peanut

**erdrosseln,** air-dross-*eln*, *v* to throttle, to strangle

**erdrücken,** air-drEEck-en, *v* to smother

**Erdteil,** airt-tyl, *m* continent

**ereignen (sich)** air-i-gnen (zik), *v* to happen

**Ereignis,** air-i-gniss, *nt* occurrence; event; accident

**erfahren,** air-fahr-en, *v* to hear, to learn

**Erfahrung,** air-fahr-oong, *f* experience

**erfassen,** air-fahss-en, *v* to seize, to grasp

**erfinden,** air-fin-den, *v* to invent, to devise

**Erfinder,** air-fin-der, *m* inventor

**Erfindung,** air-fin-doong, *f* invention; contrivance, device

**Erfolg,** air-folk, *m* success; result, issue, outcome

**erfolgen,** air-folg-en, *v* to result; to take place

**erfolglos,** air-folg-lohs, *adj* unsuccessful

**erfolgreich,** air-folg-ryk, *adj* successful

**erforderlich,** air-ford-er-lik, *adj* necessary

**erfordern,** air-ford-ern, *v* to require, to necessitate

**erforschen,** air-forsh-en, *v* to explore

**erfreuen,** air-froy-en, *v* to gladden, to delight

**erfreulich,** air-froy-lik, *adj* pleasing; gratifying

**erfrieren,** air-free-ren, *v* to die of cold

**erfrischen,** air-frish-en, *v* to refresh

**Erfrischung,** air-frish-oong, *f* refreshment

**erfüllen,** air-fEEll-en, *v* to fulfil; to fill with

**Erfüllung,** air-fEEll-oong, *f* fulfilment; compliance

**ergänzen,** air-gent-sen, *v* to complete

**ergeben (sich),** air-gayb-en (zik), *v* to surrender; to result

**Ergebenheit,** air-gayb-en-hite, *f* devotion; attachment

**Ergebnis,** air-gayp-niss, *nt* result; issue, conclusion

**ergiebig,** air-geeb-ik, *adj* productive; prolific

**ergießen,** air-gees-en, *v* to pour/flow from

**ergreifen,** air-gry-fen, *v* to seize, to catch hold of; to move

**ergreifend,** air-gryf-ent, *adj* moving

**erhaben,** air-hahb-en, *adj* sublime; illustrious

**erhalten,** air-hahlt-en, *v* to receive; to preserve

**Erhaltung,** air-hahlt-oong, *f* preservation

**erheben,** air-hayb-en, *v* to raise, to lift

**erheblich,** air-hayp-lik, *adj* considerable

**erhellen,** air-hell-en, *v* to light up; to clear up

**erhöhen,** air-her-en, *v* to raise; to enhance; to increase

**Erhöhung,** air-her-oong, *f* elevation; increase

**erholen (sich),** air-hohl-en (zik), *v* to recover

**Erholung,** air-hohl-oong, *f* rest; recovery

**erinnern (an),** air-in-ern (ahnn), *v* to remind; **sich–,** to remember

**Erinnerung,** air-in-er-oong, *f* remembrance

**erkälten (sich)**, air-kelt-en (zik), *v* to catch cold

**erkältet sein**, air-kelt-et sine, *v* to have a cold

**Erkältung**, air-kelt-oong, *f* cold, chill, catarrh

**erkennen**, air-ken-en, *v* to recognize

**erkenntlich**, air-kent-lik, *adj* cognizant; grateful

**Erkenntnis**, air-kent-niss, *f* perception; knowledge; understanding

**Erkennung**, air-ken-oong, *f* recognition

**Erker**, airk-er, *m* alcove, balcony

**erklären**, air-klair-en, *v* to explain; to elucidate; to declare

**erklärlich**, air-klair-lik, *adj* comprehensible

**Erklärung**, air-klair-oong, *f* explanation; declaration

**erkranken**, air-krank-en, *v* to fall ill

**erkundigen (sich)**, air-koond-ig-en (zik), *v* to inquire; to make inquiries

**Erkundigung**, air-koond-ig-oong, *f* inquiry

**erlangen**, air-lahng-en, *v* to reach, to attain

**Erlaß**, air-lahss, *m* remission; relief; enactment

**erlassen**, air-lahss-en, *v* to publish (laws); to waive (debts etc.)

**erlauben**, air-lowb-en, *v* to permit, to allow

**Erlaubnis**, air-lowp-niss, *f* permission

**erläutern**, air-loyt-ern, *v* to make clear; to elucidate

**Erle**, airl-e, *f* alder(-tree)

**erleben**, air-layb-en, *v* to experience

**Erlebnis**, air-layp-niss, *nt* experience

**erledigen**, air-layd-ig-en *v* to settle; to adjust

**Erledigung**, air-layd-ig-oong, *f* settlement

**erleichtern**, air-ly'k-tern, *v* to make easy

**Erleichterung**, air-ly'k-ter-oong, *f* relief; facility

**erleiden**, air-ly-den, *v* to suffer; to sustain; to bear

**erlernen**, air-lairn-en, *v* to learn, to acquire

**erliegen**, air-leeg-en, *v* to succumb

**Erlös**, air-lers, *m* proceeds

**erlöschen**, air-lersh-en, *v* to be extinguished

**erlösen**, air-lerz-en, *v* to save, to redeem

**Erlösung**, air-lerz-oong, *f* release; salvation

**ermächtigen**, air-mek-tig-en, *v* to empower

**Ermächtigung**, air-mek-tig-oong, *f* authority

**ermahnen**, air-mahn-en, *v* to admonish, to warn

**ermäßigen**, air-maiss-ig-en, *v* to moderate; to reduce

**Ermäßigung**, air-maiss-ig-oong, *f* reduction

**ermitteln**, air-mit-eln, *v* to

ascertain, to find out; **gegen jdn –**, to investigate sb

**Ermittlung**, air-mit-loong, *f* ascertainment; investigation

**ermöglichen**, air-merg-lik-en, *v* to make possible

**ermorden**, air-mord-en, *v* to murder; to assassinate

**Ermordung**, air-mord-oong, *f* murder

**ermüden**, air-mEEd-en, *v* to tire

**ermuntern**, air-moont-ern, *v* to rouse; to liven up

**ermutigen**, air-moot-ig-en, *v* to encourage

**ernähren**, air-nair-en, *v* to nourish; **sich – von**, to live on

**Ernährung**, air-nair-oong, *f* nourishment

**ernennen**, air-nen-en, *v* to appoint; to nominate

**erneuern**, air-noy-ern, *v* to renew; to renovate

**erniedrigen**, air-need-rig-en, *v* to lower

**Ernst**, airnst, *m* seriousness; severity

**ernst**, airnst, *adj* serious, earnest; solemn, grave

**ernsthaft**, airnst-hahft, *adj* serious, earnest

**ernstlich**, airnst-lik, *adj* earnest, fervent

**Ernte**, airnt-e, *f* harvest (-time); crop

**ernten**, airnt-en, *v* to harvest, to reap

**erobern**, air-**ohb**-ern, *v* to conquer, to capture

**Eroberung**, air-**ohb**-er-oong, *f* capture, conquest

**eröffnen**, air-**erff**-nen, *v* to open; to inaugurate

**Eröffnung**, air-**erff**-noong, *f* opening; inauguration

**erörtern**, air-**ert**-ern, *v* to discuss, to argue

**Erörterung**, air-**ert**-er-oong, *f* discussion, debate

**Erotik**, air-**oht**-ik, *f* eroticism

**erotisch**, air-**oht**-ish, *adj* erotic

**erpressen**, air-**press**-en, *v* to extort; to blackmail

**Erpresser**, air-**press**-er, *m* blackmailer

**Erpressung**, air-**press**-oong, *f* extortion, blackmail

**erproben**, air-**prohb**-en, *v* to try; to experience

**erraten**, air-**raht**-en, *v* to guess

**erregen**, air-**rayg**-en, *v* to excite; to agitate

**Erregung**, air-**rayg**-oong, *f* irritation; agitation; excitement

**erreichen**, air-**ry**-ken, *v* to reach; to attain

**errichten**, air-**rik**-ten, *v* to erect; to set up

**erröten**, air-**rert**-en, *v* to blush, to redden

**Errungenschaft**, air-**roong**-en-shahft, *f* achievement

**Ersatz**, air-**zahts**, *m* substitute; compensation;

–**dienst**, *m* community service (as alternative to military service); –**reifen**, *m* spare tyre; –**teil**, spare part

**erscheinen**, air-**shy**-nen, *v* to appear

**Erscheinung**, air-**shy**-noong, *f* appearing; phenomenon

**erschießen**, air-**sheess**-en, *v* to shoot dead

**erschlagen**, air-**shlahg**-en, *v* to kill

**erschöpfen**, air-**sherp**-fen, *v* to exhaust

**Erschöpfung**, air-**sherp**-foong, *f* exhaustion

**erschrecken**, air-**shreck**-en, *v* to frighten

**erschüttern**, air-**shEEtt**-ern, *v* to shake up

**ersetzen**, air-**zet**-sen, *v* to replace; to substitute

**ersichtlich**, air-**zikt**-lik, *adj* visible, manifest

**ersparen**, air-**shpahr**-en, *v* to save, to economize

**Ersparnis**, air-**shpahr**-niss, *f* economy

**erst**, airst, *adv* at first; previously; only (just)

**erstarren**, air-**shtahrr**-en, *v* to stiffen; to grow numb/rigid

**erstatten**, air-**shtahtt**-en, *v* to restore; to render; to reimburse

**Erstattung**, air-**shtatt**-oong, *f* refund

**erstaunen**, air-**shtown**-en, *v*

to be astonished

**erstaunlich**, air-**shtown**-lik, *adj* astonishing, amazing

**erste(r/s)**, airst-e(r/s) *adj* first

**erstechen**, air-**shtek**-en, *v* to stab to death

**erstehen**, air-**shtay**-en, *v* to buy, to purchase

**ersteigen**, air-**shty**-gen, *v* to mount, to climb

**erstens**, airst-ens, *adv* first; in the first place

**ersticken**, air-**shtik**-en, *v* to stifle; to suffocate

**erstklassig**, airst-klahss-ik, *adj* first class

**erstmals**, airst-mahls, *adv* for the first time

**erstrecken**, air-**shtreck**-en, *v* to reach up to

**ersuchen**, air-**sook**-en, *v* to request

**ertappen**, air-**tahpp**-en, *v* to catch (in the act)

**erteilen**, air-**ty**-len, *v* to bestow upon, to confer upon

**ertönen**, air-**tern**-en, *v* to sound

**Ertrag**, air-**trahk**, *m* yield, produce, return

**ertragen**, air-**trahg**-en, *v* to bear; to tolerate

**erträglich**, air-**traik**-lik, *adj* bearable, tolerable

**ertrinken**, air-**trink**-en, *v* to drown

**erwachen**, air-**vahk**-en, *v* to awake

**erwachsen**, air-**vahck**-sen,

*adj* grown-up, adult

**Erwachsene(r)**, air-**vahck**-sen-e(r), *m & f* adult

**erwähnen**, air-**vain**-en, *v* to mention, to refer to

**erwärmen**, air-**vairm**-en, to warm

**erwarten**, air-**vart**-en, *v* to expect, to await

**Erwartung**, air-**vart**-oong, *f* expectation

**erwecken**, air-**veck**-en, *v* to awake; to rouse

**erweitern**, air-**vy**-tern, *v* to enlarge, to widen

**Erwerb** air-**vairp**, *m* gain, profit; acquisition

**erwerben**, air-**vairb**-en, *v* to acquire; to earn

**erwerbslos**, air-**vairbs**-lohs, *adj* unemployed

**erwidern**, air-**veed**-ern, *v* to reply, to reciprocate

**erwünscht**, air-**vEEnsht**, *adj* desired, desirable

**erwürgen**, air-**vEErg**-en, *v* to strangle

**Erz**, airts, *nt* ore, metal

**erzählen**, air-**tsail**-en, *v* to relate, to narrate, to tell

**Erzählung**, air-**tsail**-oong, *f* tale, story, narrative

**Erzbischof**, airts-**bish**-ohf, *m* archbishop

**erzeugen**, air-**tsoyg**-en, *v* to produce; to engender

**Erzeugnis**, air-**tsoyk**-niss, *nt* product, produce

**Erzeugung**, air-**tsoyg**-oong, *f* production

**erziehen**, air-**tsee**-en, *v* to rear; to educate

**Erziehung**, air-**tsee**-oong, *f* rearing; education

**erzielen**, air-**tseel**-en, *v* to achieve

**erzwingen**, air-**tsving**-en, *v* to enforce; to obtain by force

**es**, ess, *pron* it

**Esche**, esh-e, *f* ash (tree)

**Esel**, ay-zel, *m* donkey, ass

**Espe**, esp-e, *f* aspen

**eßbar**, ess-bar, *adj* eatable, edible

**essen**, ess-en, *v* to eat

**Essig**, ess-ik, *m* vinegar

**Eßlöffel**, ess-lerff-el, *m* tablespoon

**Eßzimmer**, ess-tsimm-er, *nt* dining room

**etablieren**, ay-tahb-**leer**-en, *v* to establish, to set up; **sich –**, to become established

**Etage**, ay-tah-zhe, *f* storey; floor (of building)

**Etat**, ay-**tah**, *m* balance-sheet; budget

**Etikett**, ay-tee-**ket**, *nt* label, ticket

**etliche**, et-lik-e, *pron* some; a few

**Etui**, ay-twee, *nt* case

**etwa**, et-vah, *adv* about, approximately; perhaps

**etwaig**, et-vah-ik, *adj* possible; incidental

**etwas**, et-vahss, *pron* something, some; somewhat

**euch**, oyk, *pron* (accusative

*& dative*) you, to you

**euer, eure(r/s)**, oy-er, oyr-e(r/s), *adj* your; *pron* yours

**Eule**, oyl-e, *f* owl

**Euro**, oy-roh, *m* Euro

**Europa**, oy-**roh**-pah, *nt* Europe

**Europäer**, oy-roh-**pay**-er, *m* European (person)

**europäisch**, oy-roh-**pay**-ish, *adj* European; **E–e Union**, *f* European Union

**evangelisch**, ay-fahng-**ayl**-ish, *adj* evangelical; Protestant

**Evangelium**, ay-fahng-**ayl**-e-oomm, *nt* gospel

**eventuell**, ay-vent-oo-**el**, *adj & adv* possible; possibly

**ewig**, ayv-ik, *adj* eternal, everlasting, endless

**Ewigkeit**, ayv-ik-kite, *f* eternity

**Examen**, ecks-**ahm**-en, *nt* examination

**Exemplar**, ecks-emp-**lahr**, *nt* sample; copy

**Exil**, ecks-eel, *nt* exile

**exotisch**, ecks-**oht**-ish, *adj* exotic

**Expedition**, eck-pay-dits-**yohn**, *f* expedition

**Experte**, ecks-per-te, *m* expert

**Export**, ecks-**port**, *m* export

**exportieren**, ecks-port-**eer**-en, *v* to export

**extra**, eck-strah, *adj* separate; extra

**Extrablatt**, ecks-**trah**-blahtt, *nt* special edition

**Fa.,** *abbr* **Firma**

**fabelhaft,** fahb-el-hahft, *adj* fabulous; *fam* fantastic

**Fabrik,** fah-**breeck,** *f* factory, works

**Fabrikant,** fah-brik-**ahnt,** *m* manufacturer

**Fabrikat,** fah-brik-**aht,** *nt* manufactured article; make

**Fach,** fah*k*, *nt* division; branch, line of business; **–arbeiter,** *m* skilled worker; **–ausdruck,** *m* technical term

**Fächer,** fek-er, *m* fan

**Fachmann, fahk**-mahnn, *m* expert, specialist

**fachmännisch, fahk**-men-ish, *adj* expert

**Fackel,** fah*k*k-el, *f* (lighted) torch

**fad,** faht, *adj* tasteless,

insipid, dull

**Faden,** fahd-en, *m* thread; fathom

**fadenscheinig,** fahd-en-shine-ik, *adj* threadbare; shabby

**fähig,** fay-ik, *adj* capable, able, competent

**Fähigkeit,** fay-ik-kite, *f* capability, fitness, aptitude

**fahnden,** fahn-den, *v* to search for (police)

**Fahndung,** fahnd-oong, *f* police search

**Fahne,** fahn-e, *f* flag, colours, banner

**Fahrausweis, fahr-**ows-vise, *m* ticket

**Fahrbahn,** fahr-bahn, *f* carriageway

**Fähre,** fay-re, *f* ferry

**fahren,** fahr-en, *v* to ride, to drive; to travel; to convey

**Fahrer,** fahr-er, *m* driver

**Fahrgeld,** fahr-gelt, *nt* fare

**Fahrkarte,** fahr-kart-e, *f* (travel) ticket; **–nautomat,** *m* ticket machine; **–nschalter,** *m* ticket-office

**fahrlässig,** fahr-less-ik, *adj* careless, negligent

**Fahrplan,** fahr-plahn, *m* timetable

**Fahrprüfung,** fahr-prEEf-oong, *f* driving test

**Fahrrad,** fahr-raht, *nt* cycle, bicycle; **–weg,** *m* cycle lane

**Fahrschein,** fahr-shine, *m* (bus/tram) ticket; **–entwerter,** *m* ticket machine

**Fahrschule,** fahr-shool-e, *f* driving school

**Fahrstuhl,** fahr-shtool, *m* lift

**Fahrt,** fahrt, *f* journey, drive, ride, voyage, trip; **–kosten,** *pl* travelling expenses; **–richtung,** *f* direction (of travel)

**Fährte,** fairt-e, *f* track, trail

**Fahrzeit,** fahr-tsite, *f* journey time

**Fahrzeug,** fahr-tsoyk, *nt* vessel, craft; vehicle, conveyance

**Falke,** fahlk-e, *m* falcon; hawk

**Fall,** fahll, *m* case; fall

**Falle,** fahll-e, *f* trap, snare

**fallen,** fahll-en, *v* to fall; to decrease

**fällen,** fel-en, *v* to fell, to

cut down (trees)

**fällig, fel**-ik, *adj* due, payable

**falls, fahls,** *conj* in case; provided that

**Fallschirm, fahll**-sheerm, *m* parachute

**falsch, fahlsh,** *adj* wrong, false, forged; mistaken

**fälschen, fel**-shen, *v* to forge, to adulterate

**Fälschung, felsh**-oong, *f* falsification; forgery

**Falte, fahlt**-e, *f* fold; wrinkle; pleat, crease

**falten, fahlt**-en, *v* to fold; to crease, to crumple

**faltig, fahlt**-ik, *adj* wrinkled, creased, crumpled

**Familie, fahm**-eel-ye, *f* family; tribe, stock; **–nname,** *m* surname; **–nstand,** *m* marital status

**Fang, fahng,** *m* catch, capture; prey, booty

**fangen, fahng**-en, *v* to catch, to capture, to trap

**Farbe, fahrb**-e, *f* colour, colouring, tint; paint

**farbecht, fahrb**-ekt, *adj* colour-fast

**farbenblind, fahrb**-en-blint, *adj* colour-blind

**Farbfernsehen, fahrb**-fairn-zay-en, *nt* colour television

**Farbfilm, farb**-film, *m* colour film

**färben, fairb**-en, *v* to dye; to colour; to tint

**farbig, farb**-ik, *adj* coloured

**Farbige(r), farb**-ig-e(r), *m*

*& f* coloured person

**Farbstoff, farp**-shtof, *m* dye, pigment

**Farn, farn,** *m* bracken, fern

**Fasan, fah**-zahn, *m* pheasant

**Fasching, fahsh**-ing, *m* carnival

**Faschismus, fash**-is-moos, *m* fascism

**Faschist, fash**-ist, *m* fascist

**Faser, fah**-zer, *f* fibre; filament; string

**faserig, fah**-zer-ik, *adj* fibrous; stringy

**Faß, fahss,** *nt* vat, cask, barrel, keg

**fassen, fahss**-en, *v* to seize, to take hold of; **sich –,** to compose oneself

**fast, fahsst,** *adv* almost, nearly

**fasten, fahsst**-en, *v* to fast

**Fastnacht, fahsst**-nahkt, *f* carnival-time

**fatal, fahtt**-ahl, *adj* disagreeable, vexatious, awkward

**fauchen, fowk**-en, *v* to hiss

**faul, fowl,** *adj* rotten, putrid; lazy, indolent

**faulen, fowl**-en, *v* to rot, to putrify

**faulenzen, fowl**-ent-sen, *v* to laze around, to lead an idle life

**Faulheit, fowl**-hite, *f* laziness, idleness

**Fäulnis, foyl**-niss, *f* rottenness; putrefaction

**Faulpelz, fowl**-pelts, *m* lazybones, idle person

**Faust, fowst,** *f* fist

**Fax, fax,** *nt* fax

**faxen, fax**-en, *v* to fax

**Februar, fay**-broo-ahr, *m* February

**fechten, fekt**-en, *v* to fence, to fight with swords

**Feder, fayd**-er, *f* feather; pen(-nib), quill; *mech* spring

**Federhalter, fayd**-er-hahlt-er, *m* pen-holder

**federn, fayd**-ern, *v* to be springy/elastic

**Fee, fay,** *f* fairy, elf

**Fegefeuer, fay**-ge-foy-er, *nt* purgatory

**fegen, fayg**-en, *v* to sweep; to wipe; to scour

**Fehde, fayd**-e, *f* feud, dispute, quarrel

**fehlen, fayl**-en, *v* to miss; to mistake; to be wrong

**Fehler, fayl**-er, *m* mistake; defect, blemish, flaw

**fehlerhaft, fayl**-er-hahfft, *adj* faulty, defective

**fehlerlos, fayl**-er-lohs, *adj* flawless

**Fehlgeburt, fayl**-ge-boort, *f* miscarriage

**Fehlgriff, fayl**-grif, *m* bad choice; mistake

**Fehlschlag, fayl**-shlahk, *m* failure

**fehlschlagen, fayl**-shlahg-en, *v* to miss; to fail

**Feier, fy**-er, *f* celebration

**Feierabend, fy**-er-ahb-ent, *m* closing time

**feierlich, fy**-er-lik, *adj*

ceremonious; dignified, grave

**feiern, fy**-ern, v to celebrate; to honour

**Feiertag, fy**-er-tahk, m feast-day, festival, holiday

**feig(e), fy**'k (**fy**'g-e), adj cowardly, timid; faint-hearted

**Feige, fy**-ge, f fig

**Feigheit, fike**-hite, f cowardice; timidity

**Feigling, fike**-ling, m coward

**Feile, file**-e, f file, rasp

**feilen, file**-en, v to file; to polish

**fein,** fine, adj fine, slender; elegant, graceful; refined

**Feind,** fine't, m enemy, foe, adversary

**feindlich, fine't**-lik, adj hostile, opposed, unfriendly

**Feindschaft, fine't**-shahft, f enmity, hostility

**feindselig, fine't**-zail-ik, adj hostile, inimical

**feinfühlig, fine-**fEEl-ik, adj sensitive, delicate

**Feinheit, fine**-hite, f fineness, subtlety; refinement

**Feinschmecker, fine-**shmeck-er, m gourmet

**Feld,** felt, nt field

**Feldherr, felt**-hairr, m commander-in-chief

**Feldstecher, felt**-shtek-er, m binoculars; field glasses

**Feldzug, felt**-tsook, m campaign

**Fell,** fel, nt skin, hide

**Fels,** fels, m rock; cliff; crag

**Felsen, fel**-zen, m rock; cliff; crag

**Fenster, fenst**-er, nt window; **–bank,** f window-sill; **–laden,** m shutter; **–scheibe,** f window-pane

**Ferien, fair**-yen, pl holidays; **– haben,** v to be on holiday; **–haus,** nt holiday home; **–wohnung,** f holiday apartment

**fern,** fairn, adj & adv far, distant, remote

**Fernbedienung, fairn**-be-deen-oong, f remote control

**Ferne, fair**-ne, f distance

**ferner, fair**-ner, adv further(more); farther; moreover

**Ferne(r) Osten, fair**-ne(r) ost-en, m Far East

**Ferngespräch, fairn**-ge-shpraik, nt long-distance call

**Fernglas, fairn**-glahss, nt binoculars

**Fernrohr, fairn**-rohr, nt telescope

**Fernsehapparat, fairn-**zay-ahp-ah-raht, m television set

**fernsehen, fairn**-zay-en, v to watch television

**Fernsehen, fairn**-zay-en, nt television

**Fernsprecher, fairn**-shprek-er, m telephone

**Fernsteuerung, fairn**-shtoy-er-oong, f remote control

**Fernverkehr, fairn**-fer-kair, m through traffic

**Ferse,** fair-ze, f heel

**fertig, fairt**-ik, adj ready, prepared; skilled; finished

**Fertiggericht, fairt**-ik-ge-rikt, nt pre-cooked meal

**Fertigkeit, fairt**-ik-kite, f skill, dexterity

**fertigmachen, fairt**-ik-mak-en, v to finish, to get done

**fertigstellen, fairt**-ik-shtel-en, v to complete; to finish

**fesch,** fesh, adj smart, fashionable

**Fessel, fes-**el, f fetters, shackle; ankle

**fesseln, fes-**eln, v to fetter, to chain, to shackle

**fest,** fest, adj firm, fast; constant

**Fest,** fest, nt festival; party; fête

**Festessen, fest**-ess-en, nt banquet

**festhalten, fest**-hahlt-en, v to hold fast; to detain

**Festigkeit, fest**-ik-kite, f firmness

**festklammern (sich), fest-**klahmm-ern (zik), v to cling

**Festland, fest**-lahnt, nt mainland, continent

**festlich, fest**-lik, adj festive; solemn; splendid

**Festlichkeit, fest**-lik-kite, f festivity

**festmachen, fest**-mahk-en, *v*
to fix, to attach

**festnageln, fest**-nahg-eln, *v*
to nail fast; to clinch

**Festnahme, fest**-nahm-e, *f*
arrest

**festnehmen, fest**-naym-en,
*v* to arrest

**Festplatte, fest**-plahtt-e, *f*
(hard) disk

**festsetzen, fest**-zet-sen, *v* to
arrange; to stipulate

**Festspiele, fest**-shpeel-e, *pl*
festival

**feststellen, fest**-shtel-en, *v*
to ascertain; to fix

**Feststellung, fest**-shtel-
oong, *f* evidence

**Festtag, fest**-tahk, *m*
holiday, feast-day

**Festung, fest**-oong, *f*
fortress, stronghold

**fett, fet**, *adj* fat, greasy

**Fett, fet**, *nt* fat, grease

**fettarm, fet**-ahrm, *adj* low
fat

**fettig, fet**-ik, *adj* fatty, greasy,
oily

**Fetzen, fet**-sen, *m* shred,
scrap, rag

**feucht, foykt**, *adj* damp,
moist, humid

**Feuchtigkeit, foykt**-ik-kite,
*f* moisture, humidity

**Feuer, foy**-er, *nt* fire;
**–löscher,** *m* fire
extinguisher

**feuern, foy**-ern, *v* to fire; to
light

**Feuerstein, foy**-er-shtine, *m*
flint

**Feuerwehr, foy**-er-vair, *f*
fire-brigade

**Feuerwerk, foy**-er-vairk, *nt*
firework(s)

**Feuerzeug, foy**-er-tsoyk, *nt*
(cigarette) lighter

**feurig, foyr**-ik, *adj* fiery;
ardent, passionate

**Fichte, fik**-te, *f* pine(-tree);
spruce

**Fieber, feeb**-er, *nt* fever,
(high) temperature

**fieberhaft, feeb**-er-hahft, *adj*
feverish, febrile

**Figur, feeg**-oor, *f* figure

**Filet, fee-lay,** *nt* fillet

**Filiale, fil-yahl**-e, *f comm*
branch

**Film, film,** *m* film

**filmen, film**-en, *v* to film

**Filmkamera, film-kahm-er-**
ah, *f* cine camera

**Filter, filt**-er, *m* filter;
**–zigarette,** *f* filter cigarette

**Filz, filts,** *m* felt; **–stift,** *m*
felt tip pen

**Finanz, fin**-ahnts, *f* finance;
**–amt,** *nt* Inland Revenue

**finanziell, fin-ahnts-e-ell,**
*adj* financial

**finden, fin**-den, *v* to find

**Findigkeit, fin-**dik-kite, *f*
cleverness, shrewdness

**Findling, fint**-ling, *m*
foundling

**Finger, fing**-er, *m* finger

**Fingerhut, fing**-er-hoot, *m*
thimble; foxglove

**Fingerzeig, fing**-er-tsike, *m*
indication, hint

**Fink, fink,** *m* finch

**Finne, fin**-e, *m,* **Finnin, fin**-
in, *f* Finn

**finnisch, fin**-ish, *adj* Finnish

**Finnland, fin**-lahnt, *nt*
Finland

**finster, fin**-ster, *adj* dark,
gloomy

**Finsternis, fin**-ster-nis, *f*
darkness, gloom

**Firma, feer**-mah, *f* firm,
company

**Firmenwagen, feer**-men-
vahg-en, *m* company car

**Fisch, fish,** *m* fish

**fischen, fish**-en, *v* to fish

**Fischer, fish**-er, *m* fisherman

**Fischfang, fish**-fahng, *m*
fishing

**Fischotter, fish**-ot-er, *m*
otter

**Fitneß, fit**-ness, *f* fitness

**fix, fix,** *adj* fast, fixed;
prompt, quick, nimble

**flach, flahk,** *adj* flat, plain,
even

**Fläche, flek**-e, *f* surface,
plain, plane, level

**Flachs, flahx,** *m* flax

**flackern, flahck**-ern, *v* to
flicker; to flare, to blaze

**Flagge, flahgg**-e, *f* flag

**Flamme, flahmm**-e, *f* flame

**Flannell, flahnn**-el, *m*
flannel

**Flasche, flahsh**-e, *f* bottle;
flask; **–nöffner,** *m* bottle
opener

**flattern, flahtt**-ern, *v* to
flutter; to be fickle

**flau, flow,** *adj* feeble; faint

**Flaum, flowm,** *m* down, fluff

**flechten,** flek-ten, *v* to braid; to intertwine

**Fleck,** fleck, *m* spot; place; piece of land; **blauer –,** *m* bruise

**fleckig,** fleck-ik, *adj* stained, spotted, marked

**Fledermaus,** flaid-er-mows, *f* bat

**Flegel,** flaig-el, *m* flail; boor; churl

**flehen,** flay-en, *v* to implore, to beseech

**flehentlich,** flay-ent-lik, *adj* urgent, fervent

**Fleisch,** fly'sh, *nt* flesh; meat

**Fleischbrühe,** fly'sh-brEE-e, *f* meat broth

**Fleischer,** fly-sher, *m* butcher

**Fleiß,** flice, *m* application, industry, diligence

**fleißig,** flice-ik, *adj* assiduous, industrious, diligent

**Flicken,** flick-en, *m* patch

**flicken,** flik-en, *v* to patch, to mend, to repair

**Flieder,** fleed-er, *m* lilac

**Fliege,** fleeg-e, *f* fly; bow-tie

**fliegen,** fleeg-en, *v* to fly; to race (along)

**Flieger,** fleeg-er, *m* flier; airman

**fliehen,** flee-en, *v* to flee; to fly

**Fließband,** flees-bahnt, *nt* assembly line

**fließen,** flees-en, *v* to flow, to run, to gush

**fließend,** flees-ent, *adj &* *adv* flowing(ly); fluent(ly)

**flimmern,** flim-ern, *v* to glitter, to glisten, to shimmer

**flink,** flink, *adj* agile, quick, nimble

**Flinte,** flint-e, *f* gun, musket, rifle

**Flitterwochen,** flit-er-vok-en, *pl* honeymoon

**Flocke,** flock-e, *f* flake; piece of wool

**flockig,** flock-ik, *adj* flaky, fluffy

**Floh,** floh, *m* flea; **–markt,** *m* flea market

**Floß,** flohs, *nt* raft, float

**Flosse,** flos-e, *f* fin

**Flöte,** flert-e, *f* flute

**flott,** flot, *adj* quick; lively; fun-loving

**Flotte,** flot-e, *f* fleet, navy

**Fluch,** flook, *m* curse; malediction, imprecation

**fluchen,** flook-en, *v* to curse, to swear

**Flucht,** flookt, *f* flight, escape; suite (of rooms)

**flüchten,** flEEkt-en, *v* to take flight, to flee

**flüchtig,** flEEkt-ik, *adj* fugitive, flying; hasty

**Flüchtigkeit,** flEEkt-ik-kite *f* carelessness

**Flüchtling,** flEEkt-ling, *m* fugitive; exile; refugee

**Flug,** flook, *m* flight, flying; **–blatt,** *nt* pamphlet; **–gesellschaft,** *f* airline; **–hafen,** *m* airport; **–schein,** *m* flight ticket;

pilot's licence; **–steig,** *m* boarding gate; **–verbindung,** *f* connecting flight; **–zeug,** *nt* aeroplane

**Flügel,** flEEg-el, *m* wing; grand piano

**Flunder,** floonn-der, *f* flounder

**Flur,** floohr, *f* field; *m* entrance(-hall)

**Fluß,** floohs, *m* river; running water; stream

**flüssig,** flEEss-ik, *adj* liquid, fluid

**Flüssigkeit,** flEEss-ig-kite, *f* liquid, fluid; liquidity

**flüstern,** ffEEsst-ern, *v* to whisper

**Flut,** floot, *f* flood, waves; high tide

**fluten,** floot-en, *v* to swell, to flow, to rise

**Flutlicht,** floot-likt, *nt* floodlight

**Fohlen,** fohl-en, *nt* foal; colt

**Folge,** fol-ge, *f* succession; sequence; conclusion; obedience

**folgen,** fol-gen, *v* to follow

**folgendermaßen,** fol-gend-er-mahss-en, *adv* as follows

**folgern,** fol-gern *v* to draw a conclusion

**folglich,** folk-lik, *adv & conj* consequently; hence

**folgsam,** folk-zahm, *adj* obedient, submissive

**Folgsamkeit,** folk-zahm-kite, *f* obedience

**Folie, fohl**-ee-*e*, *f* foil

**Folter, folt**-*er*, *f* torture

**foltern, folt**-*ern*, *v* to torture

**Fön, fern**-*en*, *v* to blow dry

**förderlich, ferd**-*er*-lik, *adj* conducive, useful

**fordern, ford**-*ern*, *v* to demand, to challenge

**fördern, ferd**-*ern*, *v* to further, to promote

**Forderung, ford**-*er*-oong, *f* demand; claim, debt, challenge

**Forelle, foh-rel**-*e*, *f* trout

**Form,** form, *f* shape, form; ceremony, usage

**Format, form-aht,** *nt* size

**formatieren, form-aht-eer**-*en*, *v* to format

**Formel, form**-el, *f* formula; schedule; form

**formen, form**-*en*, *v* to form, to fashion, to mould

**förmlich, ferm**-lik, *adj* formal, in due form; downright

**Formular, form**-oo-**lahr**, *nt* (blank) form

**forschen, forsh**-*en*, *v* to inquire, to investigate

**Forscher, forsh**-*er*, *m* investigator, inquirer, scholar

**Forschung, forsh**-oong, *f* research

**Forst,** forst, *m* forest

**Förster, ferst**-*er*, *m* forester

**fort,** fort, *adv* away

**fortan,** fort-**ahn**, *adv* henceforth; in future

**Fortbildung, fort**-bild-oong, *f* further education

**fortfahren, fort**-fahr-*en*, *v* to continue, to go on

**fortlaufend, fort**-lowf-ent, *adj* uninterrupted

**fortpflanzen, fort**-pflahnt-sen, *v* to reproduce

**Fortpflanzung, fort**-pflahnt-soong, *f* reproduction

**Fortschritt, fort**-shrit, *m* progress; improvement

**fortschrittlich, fort**-shrit-lik, *adj* progressive

**fortsetzen, fort**-zet-sen, *v* to continue

**Fortsetzung, fort**-zet-soong, *f* continuation

**fortwährend, fort**-vair-ent, *adj* continual; lasting

**fortziehen, fort**-tsee-*en*, *v* to move away

**Foto, foh**-toh, *nt* photograph; **–apparat,** *m* camera; **–graf,** *m* photographer; **–grafie,** *f* photography

**fotografieren, foh**-toh-grahf-eer-*en*, *v* to take photographs

**Fotokopie, foh**-toh-koh-pee, *f* photocopy

**fotokopieren, foh**-toh-koh-peer-*en*, *v* to photocopy

**Foyer, fwah-yeh,** *nt* foyer, entrance-hall

**Fracht, frahkt,** *f* freight; charge for carriage

**Frachtbrief, frahkt**-breef, *m* bill of lading

**Frack, frahck,** *m* tails

**Frage, frahg**-*e*, *f* question, inquiry; **–bogen,** *m* questionnaire

**fragen, frahg**-*en*, *v* to ask, to question, to inquire

**Fragezeichen, frahg**-*e*-tsy-ken, *nt* question mark

**fraglich, frahk**-lik, *adj* questionable

**frankieren, frahnk**-eer-*en*, *v* to pay postage

**franko, frahnk**-oh, *adv* post-paid; (carriage) free

**Frankreich, frahnk**-ry'k, *nt* France

**Franzose, frahnn-tsoh**-*ze*, *m* Frenchman

**Französin, frahnn-tser**-zin, *f* Frenchwoman

**französisch, frahnn-tser**-zish, *adj* French

**frappant, frahpp-ahnt,** *adj* striking

**Fraß, frahss,** *m* food, *fam* grub

**Fratze, frahtt**-se, *f* grimace, ugly face; tomfoolery

**Frau, frow,** *f* woman; wife; Mrs; **–enarzt,** *m* gynaecologist; **–enbewegung,** *f* feminist movement

**Fräulein, froy**-line, *nt* young lady; Miss

**frech, frek,** *adj* impudent; bold, daring

**Frechheit, frek**-hite, *f* impudence; offensiveness

**frei, fry,** *adj* free, at liberty; independent

**Freibad, fry**-baht, *nt* open-
air swimming pool

**freiberuflich, fry**-be-roof-
lik, *adj* self-employed,
freelance

**freigebig, fry**-gay-bik, *adj*
generous; liberal

**freihalten, fry**-hahlt-en, *v*
to pay for (sb)

**Freiheit, fry**-hite, *f* freedom,
liberty

**Freiherr, fry**-herr, *m* baron

**freilich, fry**-lik, *adv*
certainly, to be sure,
admittedly

**Freimaurer, fry**-mowr-er, *m*
freemason

**Freimut, fry**-moot, *m*
frankness, candour

**freisprechen, fry**-shprek-en,
*v* to acquit; to absolve

**Freispruch, fry**-shprook, *m*
acquittal

**Freitag, fry**-tahk, *m* Friday

**freiwillig, fry**-vil-ik, *adj*
voluntary; spontaneous

**Freizeit, fry**-tsite, *f* leisure,
free time; **–kleidung,** *f*
casual wear; **–park,** *m*
theme park

**fremd, fremt,** *adj* strange;
foreign; curious, odd

**fremdartig, fremt**-art-ik, *adj*
strange, singular, odd

**Fremde, frem**-de, *f*
foreign/strange country

**Fremde(r), frem**-de(r), *m &*
*f* stranger, foreigner;
**–nführer,** *m* (tourist)
guide;
**-nverkehrsamt,** *nt* tourist

office

**Fremdsprache, fremt**-
shprahk-e, *f* foreign
language

**fressen, fress**-en, *v* to eat
(of animals)

**Frettchen, fret**-ken, *nt* ferret

**Freude, froyd**-e, *f*
joy(fulness), gladness,
delight

**freudestrahlend, froyd**-e-
shtrahl-ent, *adj* radiant
with joy

**freuen, froy**-en, *v* to please;
to rejoice; **sich –,** to be
happy; **sich auf etw –,** to
look forward to sth

**Freund, froynt,** *m* friend

**freundlich, froynt**-lik, *adj*
friendly, amiable, kind

**Freundlichkeit, froynt**-lik-
kite, *f* kindness

**Freundschaft, froynt**-
shahft, *f* friendship

**freundschaftlich, froynt**-
shahft-lik, *adj* friendly

**Friede, freed**-e, *m* peace,
concord

**Friedensschluß, freed**-ens-
shlooss, *m* peace
agreement

**friedfertig, freet**-fairt-ik, *adj*
peaceable

**Friedhof, freet**-hohf, *m*
churchyard, cemetery

**friedlich, freed**-lik, *adj*
peaceable

**frieren, freer**-en, *v* to freeze;
to feel cold

**frisch, frish,** *adj* fresh; cool

**Frische, frish**-e, *f* freshness;

coolness

**Friseur, free**-zer, *m*
hairdresser

**frisieren, free**-zeer-en, *v* to
do sb's hair

**Frist, frist,** *f* space of time;
interval; date; delay

**fristen, frist**-en, *v* to delay,
to put off; to reprieve

**Frisur, free**-zoor, *f* hairstyle

**froh, froh,** *adj* glad, joyful,
delighted

**fröhlich, frer**-lik, *adj*
cheerful, glad

**Fröhlichkeit, frer**-lik-kite, *f*
cheerfulness; joyfulness

**frohlocken, froh**-lock-en, *v*
to exult, to rejoice

**Frohsinn, froh**-zin, *m*
cheerfulness

**fromm, from,** *adj* pious,
religious, devout

**Frömmigkeit, fremm**-ik-
kite, *f* piety, godliness

**Frosch, frosh,** *m* frog

**Frost, frost,** *m* frost; frosty
weather; severe cold

**Frostbeule, frost**-boy-le, *f*
chilblain

**frösteln, frerst**-eln, *v* to
shiver, to feel chilly

**frostig, frost**-ik, *adj* frosty;
frozen

**Frostschutzmittel, frost**-
shoots-mitt-el, *nt*
antifreeze

**Frucht, frookt,** *f* fruit

**fruchtbar, frookt**-bahr, *adj*
fruitful, fertile, fruit-
bearing

**Fruchtbarkeit, frookt**-bahr-kite, f fruitfulness

**Fruchtsaft, frookt**-sahft, *m* fruit juice

**früh, frEE,** *adj* early; **heute –,** this morning

**Frühe, frEE**-*e,* *f* (early) morning

**früher, frEE**-*er,* *adj* earlier, sooner; *adv* formerly

**Frühjahr, frEE**-yahr, *nt* spring

**Frühling, frEE**-ling, *m* spring

**Frühstück, frEE**-shtEEck, *nt* breakfast

**frühzeitig, frEE**-tsite-ik, *adj & adv* early; premature(ly)

**Fuchs, fooks,** *m* fox; chestnut horse; freshman

**fuchteln, fookt**-eln, *v* to gesticulate; to brandish

**Fuge, foog**-*e,* *f* joint; seam; fugue

**fügen, fEEg**-en, *v* to join, to put together; **sich –,** to submit, to accommodate oneself

**fügsam, fEEg**-zahm, *adj* tractable, accommodating

**fühlbar, fEEl**-bar, *adj* sensible, palpable; perceptible

**fühlen, fEEl**-en, *v* to feel, to touch; to sense

**Fuhre, foor**-*e,* *f* cart-load

**führen, fEEr**-en, *v* to lead, to conduct, to guide; to manage; to stock

**Führer, fEEr**-er, *m* leader; driver; manager; guide; guide-book

**Führerschein, fEEr**-er-shine,

*m* driving licence

**Führung, fEEr**-oong, *f* conduct; guidance, management

**Fülle, fEEll**-*e,* *f* plenty, abundance, profusion

**Füllen, fEEll**-en, *nt* foal, colt, filly

**füllen, fEEll**-en, *v* to fill

**Füller, fEEll**-er, *m* fountain-pen

**Füllung, fEEll**-oong, *f* filling

**Fund, foont,** *m* find

**Fundbüro, foont**-bEEr-oh, *nt* lost-property office

**fünf, fEEnf,** *num* five

**fünfzehn, fEEnf**-tsayn, *num* fifteen

**fünfzig, fEEnf**-tsik, *num* fifty

**Funk, foonk,** *m* radio

**Funke, foonk**-*e,* *m* spark, flash, flashing light

**funkeln, foonk**-eln, *v* to sparkle, to flash

**Funkspruch, foonk**-shprook, *m* radio signal

**Funktelefon, foonk**-te-le-fohn, *nt* cell-phone

**Funktion, foonk**-tse-ohn, *f* function

**funktionieren, foonk**-tsyohn-**eer**-en, *v* to function

**für, fEEr,** *prep* for

**Furcht, foorkt,** *f* fear, apprehension, anxiety

**furchtbar, foorkt**-bar, *adj* fearful, frightful, horrible

**fürchten, fEErk**-ten, *v* to fear, to be afraid of

**fürchterlich, fEErk**-ter-lik,

*adj* dreadful, terrible

**furchtsam, foorkt**-zahm, *adj* timid, apprehensive

**Fürsorge, fEEr**-zorg-*e,* *f* care, solicitude; **–unterstützung,** *f* social security

**Fürsprache, fEEr**-shprah-*ke,* *f* intercession, plea

**Fürst, fEErst,** *m* prince

**Fürstentum, fEErst**-en-toom, *nt* principality

**fürstlich, fEErst**-lik, *adj* princely

**Fuß, foos,** *m* foot, paw; **–ball,** *m* football; **–boden,** *m* floor(ing)

**Fußgänger, foos**-geng-er, *m* pedestrian; **–zone,** *f* pedestrian precinct

**Fußtritt, foos**-tritt, *m* kick

**Futter, foott**-er, *nt* food; fodder; lining (cloth)

**Futteral, foott**-er-ahl, *nt* case, covering, sheath

**füttern, fEEtt**-ern, *v* to feed; to line

g, *abbr* **Gramm**

**Gabe, gahb**-*e*, *f* gift, present; talent

**Gabel, gahb**-*el*, *f* fork

**gaffen, gahff**-en, *v* to gape; to yawn

**gähnen, gain**-en, *v* to yawn

**Galeere, gah-lair**-*e*, *f* galley

**Galerie, gah-lair-ee**, *f* gallery

**Galgen, gahll**-*gen*, *m* gallows, gibbet

**Galle, gahll**-*e*, *f* gallbladder; gall, bile; venom

**Gang, gahng**, *m* walk; path; corridor; course; **–schaltung,** *f* gears

**Gans, gahns**, *f* goose

**Gänseblume, gen**-*ze*-bloom-*e*, *f* daisy

**Gänsebraten, gen**-*ze*-braht-en, *m* roast goose

**Gänsehaut, gen**-*ze*-howt, *f* goose-flesh; goose-pimples

**Gänserich, gen**-*ze*-rik, *m* gander

**ganz, gahnts**, *adj* whole, complete, all; *adv* quite

**gänzlich, gents**-lik, *adj* entire, total, quite

**gar, gahr**, *adj* done, (well) cooked, *adv* fully, quite; **– nicht,** not at all

**Garage, gahr-ahzh**-*e*, *f* garage

**Garantie, gahr-ahnn-tee**, *f* guarantee

**Garbe, gahrb**-*e*, *f* sheaf; beam (of light)

**Garderobe, gahr-de-rohb**-*e*, *f* wardrobe; cloakroom; dressing-room

**Gardine, gahrd-een**-*e*, *f* curtain

**gären, gay**-ren, *v* to ferment; to effervesce

**Garn, gahrn**, *nt* thread, yarn, twine

**garnieren, gahrn-eer**-en, *v* to trim; to garnish

**Garnison, gahrn-ee-zohn**, *f* garrison

**Garnitur, gahrn-ee-toor**, *f* trimming, uniform; (matching) set

**garstig, gahrst**-ik, *adj* nasty, objectionable; loathsome

**Garten, gahrt**-en, *m* garden

**Gärtner, gairt**-ner, *m* gardener

**Gärtnerei, gairt**-ne-ry, *f* gardening, horticulture; garden centre, nursery

**Gas, gahs**, *nt* gas; **–herd,** *m* gas cooker; **–pedal,** *nt* accelerator pedal

**Gasse, gahss**-*e*, *f* (narrow) street, alley, lane

**Gast, gahst**, *m* guest, visitor; **–arbeiter,** *m* immigrant worker; **–freundschaft,** *f* hospitality; **–geber,** *m* host; **–haus,** *nt* inn; restaurant; **–hof,** inn, hotel; **–spiel,** *nt* guest performance; **–stätte,** *f* restaurant; **–wirt,** *m* landlord, innkeeper

**Gatte, gahtt**-*e*, *m* husband

**Gattin, gahtt**-in, *f* wife

**Gattung, gahtt**-oong, *f* kind, sort; species, genus; breed

**Gaukler, gowk**-ler, *m* juggler, conjurer, magician

**Gaul, gowl**, *m* (inferior) horse, nag, old crock

**Gaumen, gowm**-en, *m* gum(s); palate

**Gauner, gown**-er, *m* swindler, sharper, rogue

**geb.**, *abbr* **geboren**

**Gebäck**, ge-beck, *nt* biscuits, pastries

**Gebärde**, ge-baird-e, *f* gesture; gesticulation

**gebärden (sich)**, ge-baird-en (zik); *v* to behave

**gebären**, ge-bair-en, *v* to give birth

**Gebäude**, ge-boyd-e, *nt* structure, building

**geben**, gay-ben, *v* to give, to bestow, to present

**Gebet**, ge-bait, *nt* prayer, praying

**Gebiet**, ge-beet, *nt* territory; area; sphere

**gebieten**, ge-beet-en, *v* to command, to order

**gebieterisch**, ge-beet-er-ish, *adj* imperious

**gebildet**, ge-bild-et, *adj* educated

**Gebirge**, ge-beer-ge, *nt* mountain-range

**Gebiß**, ge-biss, *nt* set of teeth, denture; (bridle) bit

**geboren**, ge-bohr-en, *adj* born; née

**Gebot**, ge-boht, *nt* command(ment), order

**gebraten**, ge-braht-en, *adj* fried

**Gebrauch**, ge-browk, *m* use; application; usage

**gebrauchen**, ge-browk-en, *v* to use; to apply

**gebräuchlich**, ge-broyk-lik, *adj* in use, current

**gebraucht**, ge-browkt, *adj* second-hand

**gebrechlich**, ge-brek-lik, *adj* weak, feeble, fragile, frail

**Gebrüder**, ge-brEEd-er, *pl comm* Brothers

**Gebühr**, ge-bEEr, *f* due, duty, obligation, fee;
**–eneinheit**, *f* (telephone) unit

**Geburt**, ge-boort, *f* birth; confinement;
**–enkontrolle**, *f* birth control

**gebürtig**, ge-bEErt-ik, *adj* native

**Geburtsdatum**, ge-boorts-daht-oomm, *nt* date of birth

**Geburtsort**, ge-boorts-ohrt, *m* place of birth

**Geburtstag**, ge-boorts-tahk, *m* birthday

**Gebüsch**, ge-bEEsh, *nt* bushes, thicket, copse

**Gedächtnis**, ge-dekt-nis, *nt* memory

**Gedanke**, ge-dahng-ke, *m* thought, idea

**Gedankenstrich**, ge-dahng-ken-shtrik, *m* dash

**Gedärme**, ge-dairm-e, *pl* entrails, bowels, intestines

**gedeihen**, ge-dy-en, *v* to prosper, to thrive

**gedenken**, ge-deng-ken, *v* to remember

**Gedicht**, ge-dikt, *nt* poem, verse(s)

**gediegen**, ge-deeg-en, *adj* solid; genuine; pure

**Gedränge**, ge-dreng-e, *nt* crowd; trouble; straits

**Geduld**, ge-doolt, *f* patience

**gedulden (sich)**, ge-doold-en (zik), *v* to have patience

**geduldig**, ge-doold-ik, *adj* patient; indulgent

**geeignet**, ge-yg-net, *adj* suitable, right

**Gefahr**, ge-far, *f* danger, risk

**gefährden**, ge-faird-en, *v* to endanger

**gefährlich**, ge-fair-lik, *adj* dangerous, risky

**Gefährte**, ge-fairt-e, *m* companion, associate

**Gefallen**, ge-fahll-en, *m* favour, service

**gefallen**, ge-fahll-en, *v* to please

**gefällig**, ge-fel-ik, *adj* kind; obliging

**gefälligst**, ge-fel-igst, *adv* kindly, if you please

**gefangen**, ge-fahng-en, *adj* captured

**Gefangene(r)**, ge-fahng-en-e(r), *m & f* prisoner

**Gefangenschaft**, ge-fahng-en-shahft, *f* captivity

**Gefängnis**, ge-feng-niss, *nt* prison, jail

**Gefäß**, ge-fes, *nt* vessel, receptacle

**Gefecht**, ge-fekt, *nt* combat, action, engagement

**Gefieder**, ge-feed-er, *nt* plumage, feathers

**Geflügel**, ge-flEEg-el, *nt* poultry

**Gefolge**, ge-folg-e, *nt* retinue, entourage;

cortege

**gefräßig**, ge-**fres**-ik, *adj* gluttonous; ravenous

**Gefreite(r)**, ge-**fry**-te(r), *m & f* lance-corporal

**gefrieren**, ge-**freer**-en, *v* to freeze, to congeal

**Gefrierfach**, ge-**freer**-fahk, *nt* freezer compartment

**Gefriertruhe**, ge-**freer**-troo-e, *f* freezer

**Gefühl**, ge-**fEEl**, *nt* feeling, emotion, sense; touch

**gegen**, **gayg**-en, *prep* towards; against; about

**Gegend**, **gayg**-ent, *f* country, region; scenery

**Gegensatz**, **gayg**-en-zahts, *m* contrast

**gegenseitig**, **gayg**-en-zite-ik, *adj* opposite; mutual

**Gegenstand**, **gayg**-en-shtahnt, *m* object; theme, topic

**Gegenteil**, **gayg**-en-tile, *nt* opposite, contrary, reverse

**gegenüber**, **gayg**-en-EEb-er, *adv* opposite, facing

**Gegenverkehr**, **gayg**-en-fer-ker, *m* oncoming traffic

**Gegenwart**, **gayg**-en-vahrt, *f* presence; present

**gegenwärtig**, **gayg**-en-vairt-ik, *adj* nowadays

**Gegner**, **gayg**-ner, *m* opponent, adversary

**Gehalt**, ge-**hahlt**, *nt* salary

**gehässig**, ge-**hess**-ik, *adj* spiteful; hateful

**Gehäuse**, ge-**hoy**-ze, *nt* box, case, casing, shell

**Gehege**, ge-**hay**-ge, *nt* enclosure; park, preserve

**geheim**, ge-**hime**, *adj* secret; hidden; mysterious

**Geheimdienst**, ge-**hime**-deenst, *m* secret service

**Geheimnis**, ge-**hime**-niss, *nt* secret, mystery

**gehen**, **gay**-en, *v* to go; to walk; to work; **wie geht's?**, how are things?; **es geht**, it's all right

**Gehilfe**, ge-**hilf**-e, *m* assistant, colleague; clerk

**Gehirn**, ge-**heern**, *nt* brain(s); intellect; **–erschütterung**, *f* concussion

**Gehölz**, ge-**herlts**, *nt* copse, thicket, wood

**Gehör**, ge-**her**, *nt* hearing

**gehorchen**, ge-**hork**-en, *v* to obey

**gehören**, ge-**her**-en, *v* to belong; to be due

**gehorsam**, ge-**hohr**-zahm, *adj* obedient, docile

**Gehweg**, **gay**-wayk, *m* pavement

**Geier**, **gy**-er, *m* vulture

**Geige**, **gy**-ge, *f* violin, fiddle

**geigen**, **gy**-gen, *v* to play the violin

**geil**, **gy**'l, *adj* lewd

**Geisel**, **gy**-zel, *f* hostage

**Geißel**, **gy**-sel, *f* whip

**geißeln**, **gy**-seln, *v* to whip

**Geist**, **gy**'st, *m* ghost, spirit, spectre; intellect, mind

**geisterhaft**, **gy**-ster-hahft, *adj* ghostly

**geisteskrank**, **gy**-stes-krahnk, *adj* mentally ill

**geistig**, **gy**-stik, *adj* spiritual; intellectual, mental; *chem* alcoholic

**geistlich**, **gy**-stlik, *adj* spiritual, sacred; clerical

**Geistliche(r)**, **gy**-stlik-e(r), *m* clergyman

**geistreich**, **gy**-stry'k, *adj* witty, clever, smart

**Geiz**, **gy**'ts, *m* avarice, greed, meanness

**geizen**, **gy**-tsen, *v* to be avaricious/mean

**Geizhals**, **gy**'ts-hahls, *m* miser, skinflint

**geizig**, **gy**-tsik, *adj* avaricious, greedy, mean

**Gelächter**, ge-**lek**-ter, *nt* laughter, laughing

**Gelage**, ge-**lahg**-e, *nt* feast, carousal

**gelähmt**, ge-**laymt**, *adj* paralysed

**Gelände**, ge-**lend**-e, *nt* ground; grounds; terrain

**Geländer**, ge-**lend**-er, *nt* rail(ing), balustrade

**gelangen**, ge-**lahng**-en, *v* to arrive at, to reach

**gelangweilt**, ge-**lahng**-wylt, *adj* bored

**gelassen**, ge-**lahss**-en, *adj* calm, unruffled

**geläufig**, ge-**loyf**-ik, *adj* fluent; ready; with ease

**gelaunt**, ge-**lownt**, *adj* **gut/schlecht –**, in a good/bad mood

**gelb**, gelp, *adj* yellow

**Gelbsucht**, gelp-sookt, *f* jaundice

**Geld**, gelt, *nt* money; **–automat**, *m* cash dispenser; **–beutel**, *m* wallet; **–schein**, *m* bank note; **–strafe**, *f* fine; **–wechsel**, *m* exchange

**gelegen**, ge-lay-gen, *adj* situated, lying; appropriate

**Gelegenheit**, ge-laig-en-hite, *f* opportunity

**Gelegenheitskauf**, ge-laig-en-hites-kowf, *m* chance purchase, bargain, job-lot

**gelegentlich**, ge-laig-ent-lik, *adj* occasional, incidental

**gelehrig**, ge-lair-ik, *adj* teachable; tractable; docile

**gelehrt**, ge-lairt, *adj* learned, well-read, scholarly

**Gelehrte(r)**, ge-lairt-e(r), *m & f* scholar, scientist

**Geleise**, ge-ly-ze, *nt* track, rails

**Geleit**, ge-lite, *nt* escort, accompaniment

**geleiten**, ge-ly-ten, *v* to escort, to accompany

**Gelenk**, ge-lenk, *nt* joint, articulation; link

**gelenkig**, ge-lenk-ik, *adj* jointed; flexible

**Geliebte(r)**, ge-leep-te(r), *m & f* loved one, lover

**gelingen**, ge-ling-en, *v* to succeed, to be successful

**geloben**, ge-lohb-en, *v* to vow

**gelten**, gelt-en, *v* to have value, to be valid; to apply

**Geltung**, gelt-oong, *f* worth; validity; prominence

**Gelüste**, ge-lEEst-e, *pl* desire, longing

**gemächlich**, ge-maik-lik, *adj* leisurely, unhurried

**Gemälde**, ge-meld-e, *nt* painting

**gemäß**, ge-mes, *adj & adv* in accordance with; appropriate

**gemein**, ge-mine, *adj* common; ordinary; general; low, mean

**Gemeinde**, ge-mine-de, *f* community; parish

**Gemeinheit**, ge-mine-hite, *f* meanness; vulgarity

**gemeinsam**, ge-mine-zahm, *adj* common, mutual

**Gemeinschaft**, ge-mine-shahft, *f* community; fellowship

**Gemenge**, ge-meng-e, *nt* mixing, mingling; crowd

**gemessen**, ge-mes-en, *adj* measured; strict; slow

**Gemetzel**, ge-mets-el, *nt* slaughter, massacre

**Gemisch**, ge-mish, *nt* mixture

**Gemse**, gem-ze, *f* chamois

**Gemurmel**, ge-moorm-el, *nt* murmur(ing), muttering

**Gemüse**, ge-mEEz-e, *nt* vegetable(s); **–händler**, **–laden**, *m* greengrocer('s)

**gemustert**, ge-moost-ert, *adj* patterned

**Gemüt**, ge-mEEt, *nt* feeling, soul; mind; nature

**gemütlich**, ge-mEEt-lik, *adj* comfortable, cosy, snug; agreeable

**Gemütlichkeit**, ge-mEEt-lik-kite, *f* comfort, cosiness, snugness

**Gen**, gayn, *nt* gene

**genau**, ge-now, *adj* exact, precise; strict

**genehmigen**, ge-naym-ig-en, *v* to permit; to approve

**Genehmigung**, ge-naym-ig-oong, *f* permission; approval

**geneigt**, ge-ny'kt, *adj* sloping; inclined; disposed

**General**, gen-e-rahl, *m* general; **–probe**, *f* dress rehearsal; **–streik**, *m* general strike

**genesen**, ge-nayz-en, *v* to recover, to get well

**Genf**, genf, *nt* Geneva

**Genick**, ge-nik, *nt* neck; nape

**Genie**, zhain-ee, *nt* genius

**genieren (sich)**, shain-eer-en (zik), *v* to be embarrassed

**genießen**, ge-nees-en, *v* to enjoy

**Genosse**, ge-nos-e, *m* companion, comrade, associate

**Genre**, zhahn-re, *nt* kind; sort; species

**genug**, ge-nook, *adv* enough

**Genüge**, ge-nEEg-e, *f* sufficiency; **zur –**, enough

**genügen**, ge-nEEg-en, v to suffice

**genügsam**, ge-nEEk-zahm, adj undemanding; modest

**Genugtuung**, ge-nook-too-oong, f satisfaction

**Genuß**, ge-nooss, m enjoyment; consumption (of food)

**geöffnet**, ge-erf-net, adj open

**Geographie**, gay-oh-grahf-ee, f geography

**Gepäck**, ge-peck, nt luggage, baggage; **–aufbewahrung**, f left-luggage; **–schein**, m luggage ticket; **–träger**, m porter

**gerade**, ge-rahd-e, adj & adv straight; direct; just

**geradeaus**, ge-rahd-e-ows, adv straight ahead

**Gerät**, ge-rayt, nt tools, utensils, implements

**geraten**, ge-raht-en, v to hit upon, to get (in)to; to turn out

**geräuchert**, ge-royk-ert, adj smoked

**geräumig**, ge-roym-ik, adj spacious, roomy, extensive

**Geräusch**, ge-roysh, nt noise, sound

**gerben**, gairb-en, v to tan (hides)

**gerecht**, ge-rekt, adj just, fair, righteous

**Gerechtigkeit**, ge-rekt-tik-kite, f justice, fairness

**Gerede**, ge-raid-e, nt talk; gossip

**Gericht**, ge-rikt, nt court (of law), tribunal; dish, course

**gerichtlich**, ge-rikt-lik, adj judicial, legal, lawful

**gering**, ge-ring, adj slight, unimportant; humble; low; **–fügig**, adj trifling, petty

**geringschätzig**, ge-ring-shet-sik, adj disdainful

**gerinnen**, ge-rin-en, v to curdle; to clot

**Gerippe**, ge-rip-e, nt skeleton; framework

**gern(e)**, gairn(-e), adv gladly, with pleasure, willingly; **– haben**, v to like; **etw – tun**, to like doing sth

**Gerste**, gairst-e, f barley

**Geruch**, ge-rook, m (sense of) smell; odour

**Gerücht**, ge-rEEkt, nt rumour, hearsay

**Gerümpel**, ge-rEEmp-el, nt junk

**Gerüst**, ge-rEEst, nt scaffold(ing); stage; platform

**gesamt**, ge-zahmt, adj whole, entire, total

**Gesamtschule**, ge-zahmt-shool-e, f comprehensive school

**Gesandte(r)**, ge-zahnt-e(r), m & f ambassador

**Gesandtschaft**, ge-zahnt-shahft, f embassy

**Gesang**, ge-zahng, m singing; song

**Gesäß**, ge-zes, nt seat; bottom, backside

**Geschäft**, ge-sheft, nt business; affair; trade

**geschäftig**, ge-sheft-ik, adj busy, active

**geschäftlich**, ge-sheft-lik, adj relating to business

**Geschäfts-**, ge-shefts, pref business; **–frau**, businesswoman; **–führer**, m manager; **–mann**, m businessman; **–reise**, f business trip; **–schluß**, closing time; **–zeit**, f business hours

**geschehen**, ge-shay-en, v to happen, to occur

**Geschehnis**, ge-shay-niss, nt occurrence

**gescheit**, ge-shite, adj intelligent, shrewd, sensible

**Geschenk**, ge-shenk, nt present; gift

**Geschichte**, ge-shikt-e, f story, tale; history

**Geschick**, ge-shik, nt fate, destiny; aptitude

**geschickt**, ge-shikt, adj skilled, skilful; agile

**geschieden**, ge-sheed-en, adj divorced

**Geschirr**, ge-sheer, nt crockery, pots and pans; **–spülmaschine**, f dishwasher; **–spülmittel**, nt washing-up liquid; **–tuch**, nt dish cloth

**Geschlecht**, ge-shlekt, nt sex; gender; species, kind; generation

**geschlechtlich**, ge-shlekt-lik, *adj* sexual; generic

**Geschlechtskrankheit**, ge-shlekts-krahnk-hite, *f* venereal disease

**Geschlechtsteil**, ge-shlekts-tile, *nt* genitals

**Geschlechtsverkehr**, ge-shlekts-fer-kair, *m* sexual intercourse

**geschlossen**, ge-shlos-en, *adj* closed

**Geschmack**, ge-shmahck, *m* taste, flavour

**geschmeidig**, ge-shmy-dik, *adj* supple, flexible

**Geschöpf**, ge-sherpf, *nt* creature

**Geschoß**, ge-shoss, *nt* projectile, missile

**Geschrei**, ge-shry, *nt* shouts, shouting, shrieking, screaming

**Geschütz**, ge-shEEts, *nt* cannon, (big) gun

**Geschwätz**, ge-shvets, *nt* talk, gossip

**geschwätzig**, ge-shvets-ik, *adj* talkative, garrulous

**geschwind**, ge-shvint, *adj* quick, swift, prompt

**Geschwindigkeit**, ge-shvind-ig-kite, *f* speed, velocity; –sbeschränkung, *f* speed limit

**Geschwister**, ge-shvist-er, *pl* brother(s) and sister(s)

**Geschworene(r)**, ge-shvohr-en-e(r), *m & f* juror

**Geschwulst**, ge-shvoolst, *f* swelling, inflation

**Geschwür**, ge-shvEEr, *nt* boil, ulcer, abscess

**gesellig**, ge-zel-ik, *adj* companionable, sociable

**Geselligkeit**, ge-zel-ig-kite, *f* sociability

**Gesellschaft**, ge-zel-shahft, *f* society; company; party

**gesellschaftlich**, ge-zel-shahft-lik, *adj* social, sociable

**Gesetz**, ge-zets, *nt* law, statute

**gesetzlich**, ge-zets-lik, *adj* lawful, legal

**Gesicht**, ge-zikt, *nt* face, countenance; –ausdruck, *m* facial expression; –spunkt, *m* point of view

**Gesindel**, ge-zin-del, *nt* mob, rabble

**Gesinnung**, ge-zinn-oong, *f* disposition, mind, feeling

**gespannt**, ge-shpahnt, *adj* tense; taut; curious

**Gespenst**, ge-shpenst, *nt* ghost

**Gespräch**, ge-shprayk, *nt* conversation; dialogue

**gesprächig**, ge-shprayk-ik, *adj* talkative

**Gestalt**, ge-shtahlt, *f* form(ation), figure, shape

**gestalten**, ge-shtahlt-en, *v* to shape, to form

**Geständnis**, ge-shtent-nis, *nt* confession

**Gestank**, ge-shtahnk, *m* stench, stink

**gestatten**, ge-shtahtt-en, *v* to permit, to allow

**gestehen**, ge-shtay-en, *v* to confess, to admit

**Gestell**, ge-shtell, *nt* stand; trestle; jack

**gestern**, gest-ern, *adv* yesterday

**gestört**, ge-shtert, *adj* disturbed

**Gesträuch**, ge-shtroyk, *nt* bushes, shrubs, shrubbery

**gestreift**, ge-shtry'ft, *adj* striped, streaky

**gestrig**, ges-trik, *adj* yesterday's

**Gestüt**, ge-shtEEt, *nt* stud (farm)

**Gesuch**, ge-sook, *nt* petition; request, demand

**gesund**, ge-soont, *adj* healthy, well; wholesome; – werden, *v* to get better

**Gesundheit**, ge-zoont-hite, *f* health

**Getöse**, ge-terz-e, *nt* din, racket, row

**Getränk**, ge-trenk, *nt* drink, beverage; –ekarte, *f* wine list

**getrauen (sich)**, ge-trow-en (zik), *v* to venture, to dare

**Getreide**, ge-try-de, *nt* cereals, corn, grain

**getrennt**, ge-trennt, *adj* separate(d)

**getreu**, ge-troy, *adj* faithful, true

**Getriebe**, ge-treeb-e, *nt* gear box

**getrost**, ge-trohst, *adj* confident, hopeful

**Getümmel**, ge-tEEmm-el, *nt* turmoil, tumult; crowd

**Gewächs**, ge-veks, *nt* growth, plant; **–haus**, *nt* greenhouse

**Gewähr**, ge-vair, *f* guarantee, security

**gewähren**, ge-vair-en, *v* to grant, to give

**gewährleisten**, ge-vair-ly-sten, *v* to guarantee

**Gewalt**, ge-vahlt, *f* force, power, might

**gewaltig**, ge-vahlt-ik, *adj* mighty, strong; immense

**gewaltsam**, ge-vahlt-zahm, *adj* forcible; violent

**gewalttätig**, ge-vahlt-tait-ik, *adj* violent

**Gewand**, ge-vahnnt, *nt* garment, gown, attire

**gewandt**, ge-vahnt, *adj* agile, active, supple

**Gewebe**, ge-vayb-e, *nt* web, fabric; tissue

**Gewehr**, ge-vair, *nt* rifle, gun; weapon

**Geweih**, ge-vy, *nt* horns, antlers

**Gewerbe**, ge-vairb-e, *nt* trade, profession, line of business

**Gewerkschaft**, ge-vairk-shahft, *f* trade-union

**Gewicht**, ge-vikt, *nt* weight; stress

**gewillt**, ge-vilt, *adj* willing, disposed, inclined

**Gewinn**, ge-vin, *m* profit(s); winning(s); gain

**gewinnen**, ge-vin-en, *v* to win; to gain; to extract

**gewiß**, ge-vis, *adj* certain, sure

**Gewissen**, ge-vis-en, *nt* conscience

**gewissenhaft**, ge-vis-en-hahft, *adj* conscientious

**Gewissensbisse**, ge-vis-ens-bis-e, *pl* pang (of conscience)

**gewissermaßen**, ge-vis-er-mahss-en, *adv* to a certain extent, in a way

**Gewißheit**, ge-vis-hite, *f* certainty

**Gewitter**, ge-vit-er, *nt* thunder(storm)

**gewogen**, ge-vohg-en, *adj* kindly disposed

**gewöhnen**, ge-vern-en, *v* to accustom; **sich an etw –**, *v* to get used to sth

**Gewohnheit**, ge-vohn-hite, *f* custom, usage, habit

**gewöhnlich**, ge-vern-lik, *adj* usual; ordinary; vulgar

**gewohnt**, ge-vohnt, *adj* accustomed

**Gewölbe**, ge-verl-be, *nt* vault; arch

**Gewühl**, ge-vEEl, *nt* rummaging, wriggling; crowd, throng

**Gewürz**, ge-vEErts, *nt* spice, seasoning, condiment

**Gezeiten**, ge-tsy-ten, *pl* tide(s)

**geziert**, ge-tseert, *adj* affected

**Gezwitscher**, ge-tsvit-sher, *nt* twittering, chirping

**Gicht**, gikt, *f* gout

**Giebel**, geeb-el, *m* gable end

**Gier**, geer, *f* greed(iness); lust

**gierig**, geer-ik, *adj* greedy; lustful

**gießen**, gees-en, *v* to pour; to spill; to cast metal

**Gießkanne**, gees-kahnn-e, *f* watering-can

**Gift**, gift, *nt* poison; venom

**giftig**, gift-ik, *adj* poisonous; venomous

**Ginster**, gins-ter, *m* gorse, broom

**Gipfel**, gip-fel, *m* summit, top, peak

**Gips**, gips, *m* plaster

**Giraffe**, gee-rahff-e, *f* giraffe

**Girlande**, geer-lahnd-e, *f* garland, festoon

**Girokonto**, dsheer-oh-kohn-toh, *nt* current account

**Gitarre**, gee-tahrr-e, *f* guitar

**Gitter**, git-er, *nt* railing, fence, grille

**Glanz**, glahnts, *m* brilliance, radiance, brightness

**glänzen**, glent-sen, *v* to shine, to sparkle

**Glas**, glahs, *nt* glass

**gläsern**, glay-zern, *adj* of glass, vitreous

**glatt**, glahtt, *adj* smooth, even, polished

**Glatteis**, glahtt-ice, *nt* (black) ice

**glätten**, glet-en, *v* to smooth, to press; **sich –**, to become smooth

**Glatze, glahtt**-se, *f* bald head, bald patch

**Glaube, glow**-be, *m* belief; faith; trust

**glauben (an), glowb**-en, *v* to believe (in)

**gläubig, gloy**-bik, *adj* believing; faithful; orthodox

**Gläubiger, gloy**-big-er, *m* creditor

**gleich, gly'k**, *adj* like; equal; at once; presently

**Gleichberechtigung, gly'k**-be-rekt-ig-oong, *f* equal rights

**gleichen, gly'k**-en, *v* to be similar to, to resemble

**gleichfalls, gly'k**-fahlls, *adv* also; the same to you

**Gleichgewicht, gly'k**-ge-vikt, *nt* equilibrium

**gleichgültig, gly'k**-gEElt-ik, *adj* indifferent

**gleichmäßig, gly'k**-mes-ik, *adj* even, uniform

**Gleichmut, gly'k**-moot, *m* equanimity

**Gleichnis, gly'k**-nis, *nt* simile; parable; image, likeness

**gleichsam, gly'k**-zahm, *adv* so to speak, as it were

**Gleichstrom gly'k**-shtrohm, *m* direct current

**gleichzeitig, gly'k**-tsy-tik, *adj* at the same time

**Gleis, gly's**, *nt* rails, track; platform

**gleiten, gly**-ten, *v* to glide, to slide

**Gleitzeit, gly't**-tsite, *f* flexitime

**Gletscher, glet**-sher, *m* glacier

**Glied, gleet**, *nt* limb; joint; link

**gliedern, gleed**-ern, *v* to order, to structure

**glimmen, glim**-en, *v* to glimmer, to glow

**glimpflich, glimp**-flik, *adj* moderate, indulgent

**glitzern, glit**-sern, *v* to glitter, to sparkle

**global, gloh**-bahl, *adj* global

**Glocke, glock**-e, *f* bell

**Glockenblume, glock**-en-bloom-e, *f* bluebell

**Glockenspiel, glock**-en-shpeel, *nt* chimes; *mus* glockenspiel

**glotzen, glot**-sen, to stare

**Glück, glEEck**, *nt* (good) fortune, (good) luck; chance; happiness; – **haben**, *v* to be lucky

**glücken, glEEck**-en *v* to succeed

**glücklich, glEEck**-lik, *adj* fortunate; happy; –**erweise**, *adv* fortunately

**Glücksspiel, glEEcks**-shpeel, *nt* game of chance

**Glückwunsch, glEEck**-voonsh, *m* congratulation

**glühen, glEE**-en, *v* to glow; to make red-hot

**Glühbirne, glEE**-beern-e, *f* light bulb

**Glut, gloot**, *f* glow; heat; ardour

**GmbH,** gay em bay hah, *abbr* limited company

**Gnade, g'nah**-de, *f* grace; mercy, leniency, favour

**gnädig, g'nayd**-ik, *adj* gracious, merciful, lenient

**Gold, golt**, *nt* gold

**golden, gol**-den, *adj* golden, made of gold

**Goldfisch, golt**-fish, *m* goldfish

**Golf, golf**, *m* gulf; *nt* golf; –**platz,** *m* golf course

**gönnen, gern**-en, *v* not to grudge

**Gönner, gern**-er, *m* well-wisher, patron, protector

**Gosse, goss**-e, *f* gutter

**Gott, got**, *m* God, god, idol

**Gottesdienst, got**-es-deenst, *m* service, mass

**Gottheit, got**-hite, *f* deity

**Göttin, gert**-in, *f* goddess

**göttlich, gert**-lik, *adj* divine, godlike; funny, amusing

**gottlob, got**-lohp, *interj* thank God, thank goodness

**Götze, gert**-se, *m* idol

**Grab, grahp**, *nt* grave, tomb

**Graben, grah**-ben, *m* ditch, trench

**graben, grah**-ben, *v* to dig

**Grabstein, grahp**-shtine, *m* gravestone, tombstone

**Grad, graht**, *m* degree; grade

**Graf, grahf**, *m* count, earl

**Grafschaft, grahf**-shahft, *f* county, shire; earldom

**Gram, grahm**, *m* grief, sorrow, sadness

**grämen (sich),** gray-men (zik), *v* to grieve

**Gramm,** grahmm, *nt* gram(me)

**Grammatik,** grahmm-ahtt-ik, *f* grammar

**Granate,** grahnn-aht-e, *f* shell, grenade

**Gras,** grahs, *nt* grass

**grasen,** grah-zen, *v* to graze

**Grashalm,** grahs-hahlm, *m* blade of grass

**grassieren,** grahss-eer-en, *v* to be rife/rampant

**gräßlich,** gress-lik, *adj* horrible, awful, terrible

**Grat,** graht, *m* sharp edge

**Gräte,** grayt-e, *f* fish-bone

**gratis,** grah-tis, *adj* free (of charge)

**gratulieren (zu),** graht-oo-leer-en (tsoo), *v* to congratulate (on)

**grau,** grow, *adj* grey

**Grauen,** grow-en, *nt* fear, dread, horror

**grauenhaft,** grow-en-hahft, *adj* sinister, horrible

**grauhaarig,** grow-hahr-ik, *adj* grey-haired

**grausam,** grow-zahm, *adj* cruel, barbarous, inhuman

**gravieren,** grahv-eer-en, *v* to engrave

**graziös,** grah-tsee-erss, *adj* graceful

**greifen,** gry-fen, *v* to seize

**Greis,** grice, *m* very old man

**grell,** grel, *adj* shrill, harsh, piercing; glaring, gaudy

**Grenze,** grent-se, *f* border,

frontier; limit, edge

**grenzen,** grent-sen, *v* to border, to verge

**Grenzkontrolle,** grents-kon-troll-e, *f* border control

**Greuel,** groy-el, *m* horror, abomination; atrocity

**Grieche,** gree-ke, *m* Greek (man)

**Griechenland,** gree-ken-lahnt, *nt* Greece

**Griechin,** gree-kin, *f* Greek (woman)

**griechisch,** gree-kish, *adj* Greek

**Grieß,** greess, *m* grit, gravel; semolina

**Griff,** grif, *m* grip, seizure, capture; handle

**Grill,** grill, *m* barbecue

**Grille,** grill-e, *f* cricket

**grillen,** grill-en, *v* to grill

**Grimm,** grim, *m* anger, fury

**grimmig,** grim-ik, *adj* furious; fierce

**grinsen,** grin-zen, *v* to grin

**Grippe,** grip-e, *f* flu

**grob,** grohp, *adj* rude, coarse, uncouth

**Grobheit,** grope-hite, *f* rudeness, coarseness

**Groll,** groll, *m* resentment, grudge, malice

**grollen,** groll-en, *v* to rumble; to have a grudge

**groß,** grohs, *adj* great, big, large, spacious; tall

**großartig,** grohs-art-ik, *adj* grand, sublime

**Großbritannien,** grohs-brit-

ahnn-ee-en, *nt* Great Britain

**Größe,** grers-e, *f* greatness; size

**Großeltern,** grohs-elt-ern, *pl* grandparents

**großenteils,** grohs-en-tiles, *adv* to a large extent

**Großhandel,** grohs-hahnd-el, *m* wholesale (trade)

**großjährig,** grohs-yair-ik, *adj* of age; major

**Großmacht,** grohs-mahkt, *f* power(ful nation)

**Großmut,** grohs-moot, *f* generosity

**Großmutter,** grohs-moott-er, *f* grandmother

**Großstadt,** grohs-shtahtt, *f* large town/city

**größtenteils,** grerst-en-tiles, *adv* chiefly, mostly

**Großvater,** grohs-faht-er, *m* grandfather

**großziehen,** grohs-tsee-en, *v* to rear, to bring up

**großzügig,** grohs-tsEEg-ik, *adj* on a grand scale

**Grübchen,** grEEp-ken, *nt* dimple

**Grube,** groob-e, *f* pit, mine; hollow, cavity

**grübeln,** grEEb-eln, *v* to brood, to ponder

**Gruft,** grooft, *f* tomb, vault

**grün,** grEEn, *adj* green

**Grund,** groont, *m* ground; soil; bottom (of sea); cause, reason; **–besitz,** *m* property

**gründen,** grEEnn-den, *v* to

found, to establish

**Gründer,** grEEnn-der, *m* founder

**Grundgesetz,** groont-ge-zets, *nt* (German) Constitution

**Grundlage,** groont-lahg-e, *f* elements, rudiments

**gründlich,** grEEnt-lik, *adj* solid, profound; thorough

**Grundriß,** groont-riss, *m* ground plan; sketch

**Grundsatz,** groont-zahts, *m* principle; axiom

**Grundschule,** groont-shool-e, *f* primary school

**Grundstein,** groont-shtine, *m* foundation stone

**Grundstück,** groont-shtEEk, *nt* plot (of land)

**Gründung,** grEEnn-doong, *f* foundation

**grunzen,** groont-sen, *v* to grunt

**Gruppe,** groopp-e, *f* group, clump, cluster; **–nermäßigung,** *f* group discount

**gruselig,** grooz-el-ik, *adj* ghastly, shuddering

**Gruß,** groos, *m* greeting, regard(s); **viele Grüße,** best wishes; **Grüße an,** regards to

**grüßen,** grEEs-en, *v* to greet, to salute

**gucken,** goock-en, *v* to look, to peep

**Gulasch,** gool-ahsh, *nt* goulash

**Gulden,** goold-en, *m* florin;

Dutch guilder

**gültig,** gEElt-ik, *adj* valid, current; legal, legitimate

**Gültigkeit,** gEElt-ik-kite, *f* validity

**Gummi,** goomm-ee, *m & nt* rubber; gum; **–band,** *nt* elastic band; **–reifen,** *m* tyre; **–stiefel,** *m* rubber boot; wellington

**Gunst,** goonst, *f* favour, kindness, goodwill

**günstig,** gEEnst-ik, *adj* favourable, advantageous

**Gurgel,** goorg-el, *f* throat, gullet

**gurgeln,** goorg-eln, *v* to gargle, to gurgle

**Gurke,** goork-e, *f* cucumber; **saure –,** gherkin

**Gurt,** goort, *m* girth, girdle; belt, strap

**Gürtel,** gEErt-el, *m* girdle, belt

**Guß,** gooss, *m* pouring; shower, downpour; icing; founding; casting

**Gußeisen,** gooss-ize-en, *nt* cast-iron

**gußeisern,** gooss-ize-ern, *adj* made of cast-iron

**gut,** goot, *adj* good; *adv* well

**Gut,** goot, *nt* commodity, goods; farm; possession

**Gutachten,** goot-ahk-ten, *nt* expert opinion

**Gutdünken,** goot-dEEng-ken, *nt* judgment, opinion

**Güte,** gEEt-e, *f* goodness, kindness, virtue; quality

**Güterbahnhof,** gEEt-er-

bahn-hohf, *m* goods-station

**Güterzug,** gEEt-er-tsoog, *m* goods train

**Guthaben,** goot-hahb-en, *nt* credit

**gutheißen,** goot-hice-en, *v* to approve, to sanction

**gütig,** gEEt-ik, *adj* gracious, good-hearted

**gutmütig,** goot-mEEt-ik, *adj* good-natured

**Gutschein,** goot-shine, *m* voucher; credit note

**gutschreiben,** goot-shry-ben, *v* to credit (to)

**gutwillig,** goot-vill-ik, *adj* obliging, willing

**Gymnasium,** gim-**nahz**-yoom, *nt* grammar school

**Haag,** hahg, Den –, *nt* The Hague

**Haar,** hahr, *nt* hair; **–festiger,** *m* setting lotion; **–nadel,** *f* hairpin; **–schnitt,** *m* haircut, hairstyle; **–spange,** *f* hairslide

**haarsträubend,** hahr-shtroyb-ent, *adj* shocking, hair-raising

**Habe,** hah-be, *f* property, possession(s), fortune, belongings

**haben,** hah-ben, *v* to have

**Habgier,** hahp-geer, *f* avarice, greed

**Habicht,** hahb-ikt, *m* hawk

**Habseligkeiten,** hahp-zail-ik-kite-en, *pl* possessions, belongings; effects

**Habsucht,** hahp-sookt, *f* avarice, greed

**Hacke,** hahck-e, *f* hoe, pick-axe; heel

**hacken,** hahck-en, *v* to pick, to peck; to hack

**Hafen,** hahf-en, *m* port, harbour; **–stadt,** *f* port

**Hafer,** hahf-er, *m* oats

**Haferbrei,** hahf-er-bry, *m* porridge

**Haft,** hahft, *f* detention, confinement, imprisonment

**Haftbefehl,** hahft-be-fail, *m* warrant for arrest

**haften,** hahft-en, *v* to adhere, to be fixed to

**Haftpflicht,** hahft-pflikt, *f* liability, responsibility

**Haftung,** haft-oong, *f* liability; adhesion

**Hagel,** hahg-el, *m* hail; shower (e.g. of stones)

**hageln,** hahg-eln, *v* to hail

**hager,** hahg-er, *adj* haggard; lean, thin; slender

**Hahn,** hahn, *m* cock(-erel), rooster; tap

**Hähnchen,** hain-ken, *nt* chicken

**Hai,** hy, *m* shark

**häkeln,** hay-keln, *v* to crochet

**Haken,** hahk-en, *m* hook; peg; crook; **–kreuz,** *nt* swastika

**halb,** hahlp, *adj* half

**halber,** hahlb-er, *prep* owing to, on account of

**halbieren,** hahll-beer-en, *v* to halve, to divide into halves

**Halbinsel,** hahlb-in-zel, *f* peninsula

**halbjährlich,** hahlp-yair-lik, *adj* half-yearly; bi-annual

**Halbkreis,** hahlp-krice, *m* semi-circle

**Halbkugel,** hahlp-koog-el, *f* hemisphere

**Halbpension,** hahlp-pents-yohn, *f* half-board

**halbstündlich,** hahlp-shtEEnt-lik, *adj* half-hourly

**halbwegs,** hahlp-vaiks, *adv* tolerably, half-way

**Halbzeit,** hahlp-tsite, *f* half time

**Hälfte,** helf-te, *f* half

**Halle,** hahll-e, *f* hall; covered area; gallery

**hallen,** hahll-en, *v* to (re)sound

**Hallenbad,** hahll-en-baht, *nt* indoor swimming pool

**Halm,** hahlm, *m* blade, stalk

91

**Hals**, hahls, *m* neck, throat

**Halsband**, hahlls-bahnt, *nt* necklace, collar

**Halsschmerzen**, hahls-shmairt-sen, *pl* sore throat

**halsstarrig**, hahls-shtar-rik, *adj* stubborn

**Halstuch**, hahls-took, *nt* scarf

**Halsweh**, hahls-vay, *nt* sore throat

**Halt**, hahlt, *m* halt, stop; stability; firmness

**haltbar**, hahlt-bar, *adj* durable, solid, firm

**Haltbarkeit**, hahlt-bahr-kite, *f* durability

**halten**, hahlt-en, *v* to hold; to stop; to keep

**Haltestelle**, hahlt-e-shtell-e, *f* (bus/tram) stop

**Halteverbot**, hahlt-te-fer-boht, *nt* no stopping

**Haltung**, hahlt-oong, *f* bearing, carriage; conduct

**Halunke**, hahll-oonk-e, *m* scoundrel, rogue, ruffian

**hämisch**, hay-mish, *adj* spiteful, malicious

**Hammel**, hahmm-el, *m* mutton

**Hammelbraten**, hahmm-el-braht-en, *m* roast mutton

**Hammelfleisch**, hahmm-el-fly'sh, *nt* mutton

**Hammer**, hahmm-er, *m* hammer

**hämmern**, hemm-ern, *v* to hammer, to forge

**Hamster**, hahmm-ster, *m* hamster; hoarder

**Hand**, hahnt, *f* hand

**Handarbeit**, hahnt-ahr-bite, *f* needlework; manual work

**Handbremse**, hahnt-bremm-ze, *f* hand brake

**Handel**, hahnn-del, *m* trade; transaction

**handeln**, hahnn-deln, *v* to trade; to act, to proceed; to bargain, to deal; **sich um etw —**, to be about sth

**Handelsbilanz**, hahnd-els-bee-lants, *f* balance of trade

**Handelskammer**, hahnd-els-kahmm-er, *f* chamber of commerce

**Handelsschule**, hahnd-els-shool-e, *f* business school

**handfest**, hahnnt-fest, *adj* sturdy, stalwart, strong

**Handfläche**, hahnt-flek-e, *f* palm (of hand)

**Handgelenk**, hahnt-ge-lenk, *nt* wrist

**Handgepäck**, hahnt-ge-peck, *nt* hand luggage

**handgeschrieben**, hahnt-ge-shreeb-en, *adj* handwritten

**handgreiflich**, hahnt-grife-lik, *adj* violent

**Handgriff**, hahnt-grif, *m* grip; manipulation

**handhaben**, hahnt-hahb-en, *v* to handle

**Handkoffer**, hahnt-kof-er, *m* suitcase

**Händler**, hend-ler-, *m* trader, dealer

**Handlung**, hahnd-loong, *f* action; deed; shop

**Handschelle**, hahnt-shell-e, *f* handcuff

**Handschrift**, hahnt-shrift, *f* handwriting

**Handschuh**, hahnt-shoo, *m* glove

**Handtasche**, hahnt-tahsh-e, *f* handbag

**Handtuch**, hahnt-took, *nt* towel

**Handwerk**, hahnt-vairk, *nt* (handi)craft; trade

**Handwerker**, hahnt-vairk-er, *m* craftsman

**Handy**, hand-i, *nt* mobile phone

**Hanf**, hahnf, *m* hemp

**Hang**, hahng, *m* incline, slope; inclination

**Hängebrücke**, heng-e-brEEck-e, *f* suspension-bridge

**Hängematte**, heng-e-mahtt-e, *f* hammock

**hängen**, heng-en, *v* to hang, to suspend

**Hanswurst**, hahns-voorst, *m* buffoon, clown

**Hantel**, hahnt-el, *f* dumbbell

**hantieren**, hahnt-eer-en, *v* to handle, to manipulate

**Happen**, hahpp-en, *m* mouthful, morsel, bit

**Harfe**, harf-e, *f* harp

**Harke**, hark-e, *f* rake

**harken**, hark-en, *v* to rake

**harmlos**, harm-lohs, *adj*

harmless; innocuous

**harmonisch,** hahr-**mo**-nish, *adj* harmonious

**Harn,** harn, *m* urine

**harren (auf),** har-ren (owf), *v* to wait (for)

**hart,** hart, *adj* hard, firm, solid, severe

**Härte, hairt**-*e, f* hardness; hardiness; roughness

**härten, hairt**-en, *v* to harden; to temper (iron)

**hartgekocht,** hart-*ge*-kokt, *adj* hard-boiled

**hartherzig,** hart-hairt-sik, *adj* hard-hearted

**hartnäckig,** hart-neck-ik, *adj* stubborn, stiff-necked; chronic

**Harz,** harts, *nt* resin, rosin, gum

**Haschisch,** hahsh-ish, *nt* hashish

**Hase, hah**-ze, *m* hare

**Haselnuß, hah**-zel-nooss, *f* hazel-nut

**Haß,** hahss, *m* hate, hatred

**hassen, hahss**-en, *v* to hate

**häßlich,** hess-lik, *adj* ugly; hideous

**Häßlichkeit,** hess-lik-kite, *f* ugliness

**Hast,** hahst, *f* haste, hurry

**hasten, hahst**-en, *v* to hasten, to hurry

**hastig, hahst**-ik, *adj* hasty, hurried

**Haube, howb**-*e, f* woman's bonnet; crest

**Hauch,** howk, *m* breath, exhalation

**hauchen, howk**-en, *v* to breathe, to exhale

**Haue, how**-*e, f fam* beating, spanking

**hauen, how**-en, *v* to beat; to hew, to cut

**Haufen, howf**-en, *m* heap, group, mass; crowd

**häufen, hoyf**-en, *v* to heap (up), to accumulate; **sich —,** to mount up

**haufenweise,** howf-en-vy-ze, *adv fam* in heaps

**häufig, hoyf**-ik, *adj* frequent; numerous; usual

**Haupt,** howpt, *nt* head; chief(tain); **Haupt–** *pref* principal, main

**Hauptbahnhof, howpt**-bahn-hohf, *m* main station

**Hauptdarsteller, howpt**-dahr-shtell-er, *m* leading actor

**Hauptgericht, howpt**-ge-rikt, *nt* main course

**Häuptling, hoypt**-ling, *m* chieftain, captain

**Hauptmann, howpt**-mahnn, *m* captain

**Hauptquartier, howpt**-kvart-eer, *nt* headquarters

**Hauptrolle, howpt**-roll-*e, f* leading part

**Hauptsache, howpt**-sahk-*e, f* main thing

**hauptsächlich, howpt**-sek-lik, *adj* principal

**Hauptsaison, howpt**-say-zong, *f* high season

**Hauptspeise, howpt**-shpy-ze, *f* main course

**Hauptstadt, howpt**-shtahtt, *f* capital, metropolis

**Hauptstraße, howpt**-shtrahss-*e, f* main street

**Hauptverkehrszeit, howpt**-fer-kairs-tsite, *f* rush hour

**Hauptwort, howpt**-vort, *nt* noun, substantive

**Haus,** howss, *nt* house

**Hausarbeit, hows**-ahr-byt, *f* housework; homework

**Hausarzt, hows**-artst, *m* family doctor

**Häuserblock, hoy**-zer-block, *m* block (of houses)

**Hausflur, hows**-floohr, *m* (entrance-)hall

**Hausfrau, hows**-frow, *f* housewife

**Haushalt, hows**-hahlt, *m* household

**haushalten, hows**-hahlt-en, *v* to keep house

**Haushälterin, hows**-helt-er-in, *f* housekeeper

**Hausherr, hows**-hairr, *m* master of the house

**hausieren, howz-eer**-en, *v* to hawk, to peddle

**Hausierer, howz-eer**-er, *m* pedlar, hawker

**häuslich, hoys**-lik, *adj* domestic(ated)

**Hausmeister, hows**-myst-er, *m* caretaker

**Hausnummer, hows**-noomm-er, *f* house number

**Hausschuh, hows**-shoo, *m* slipper

**Hausschlüssel, hows**-shlEEss-el, *m* front-door key

**Haustier, hows**-teer, *nt* pet

**Haustür, hows**-tEEr, *f* front door

**Hauswirt, hows**-veert, *m* landlord

**Haut, howt,** *f* skin, hide, coat; peel

**häuten, hoyt**-en, *v* to skin, to flay

**Hautfarbe, howt**-fahr-be, *f* skin colour; complexion

**Hebamme, haip**-ahmm-e, *f* midwife

**Hebel, hay**-bel, *m* lever

**heben, hay**-ben, *v* to lift, to raise

**hebräisch, heb**-ray-ish, *adj* Hebrew

**Hebriden, heb**-ree-den, *pl* Hebrides

**Hecht, hekt,** *m* pike, jack

**Hecke, heck**-e, *f* hedge(-row); thorny bushes

**Heer, hair,** *nt* army; legion; **–führer,** *m* commander (-in-chief)

**Hefe, hayf**-e, *f* yeast

**Heft, heft,** *nt* exercise-book; knife-handle

**heften, heft**-en, *v* to fasten, to stick; to stitch

**heftig, heft**-ik, *adj* violent, vehement

**Heftpflaster, heft**-pflahst-er, *nt* (sticking) plaster

**hegen, hayg**-en, *v* to preserve; to cherish

**Heide, hy**-de, *f* heath, common; *m* heathen

**Heidekraut, hy**-de-krowt, *nt* heather

**Heidelbeere, hy**-del-bair-e, *f* bilberry

**Heidentum, hy**-den-toom, *nt* paganism

**heidnisch, hide**-nish, *adj* pagan

**heikel, hy**-kel, *adj* delicate, tricky; awkward

**heil, hile,** *adj* sound, whole, intact; cured

**Heiland, hy**-lahnt, *m* Saviour, Redeemer

**heilbar, hile**-bahr, *adj* curable

**Heilbutt, hile**-boott, *m* halibut

**heilen, hile**-en, *v* to heal, to cure

**heilig, hile**-ik, *adj* holy, sacred, hallowed, saintly

**Heiligabend, hile**-ig-ahb-ent, *m* Christmas Eve

**Heilige(r), hile**-ig-e(r), *m & f* saint

**Heiligenbild, hile**-ig-en-bilt, *nt* image of a saint

**Heiligenschein, hile**-ig-en-shine, *m* halo

**Heiligtum, hile**-ik-toom, *nt* sanctuary, sanctum

**heilkräftig, hile**-kreft-ik, *adj* curative, healing

**heillos, hile**-lohs, *adj* hopeless; frightful

**Heilmittel, hile**-mitt-el, *nt* remedy; cure

**Heilpraktiker, hile**-prahck-tik-er, *m* non-medical practitioner

**heilsam, hile**-zahm, *adj* wholesome, beneficial

**Heilsarmee, hiles**-arm-ay, *f* Salvation Army

**Heilung, hile**-oong, *f* cure

**Heim, hime,** *nt* home

**Heimat, hime**-aht, *f* home; native place

**heimatlos, hime**-aht-lohs, *adj* homeless

**Heimcomputer, hime**-kom-pyu-ter, *m* home computer

**Heimfahrt, hime**-fahrt, *f* homeward journey

**Heimkehr, hime**-kair, *f* return home

**heimlich, hime**-lik, *adj* secret, clandestine

**Heimreise, hime**-ry-ze, *f* journey home

**heimsuchen, hime**-sook-en, *v* to afflict

**heimtückisch, hime**-tEEck-ish, *adj* treacherous, spiteful

**Heimweg, hime**-vaik, *m* way home

**Heimweh, hime**-vay, *nt* home-sickness, nostalgia

**Heirat, hy**-raht, *f* marriage

**heiraten, hy**-raht-en, *v* to marry, to get married

**Heiratsantrag, hy**-rahts-ahn-trahk, *m* (marriage) proposal

**heiser, hy**-zer, *adj* hoarse, husky, raucous

**heiß, hice,** *adj* hot

**heißen, hy**-sen, *v* to call; to be called; to name; to bid;

to signify

**Heißhunger,** hice-hoong-er, *m* ravenous appetite

**heiter,** hite-er, *adj* bright, serene, clear; cheerful, gay

**Heiterkeit,** hite-er-kite, *f* cheerfulness

**heizen,** hite-sen, *v* to heat, to light a fire

**Heizkörper,** hites-ker-per, *m* radiator

**Heizung,** hites-oong, *f* heating

**hektisch,** heck-tish, *adj* hectic

**Held,** helt, *m* hero; champion

**helfen,** help-en, *v* to help, to aid; to promote; to support

**Helfer,** help-er, *m* helper

**Helfershelfer,** hel-fers-hel-fer, *m* accomplice

**hell,** hel, *adj* clear; shrill; bright; brilliant; light

**Helle,** hel-e, *f* clearness, brightness, brilliance

**Hellseher,** hel-zay-er, *m* clairvoyant

**Helm,** helm, *m* helmet; *m & nt* helm, rudder

**Hemd,** hemt, *nt* shirt

**hemmen,** hem-en, *v* to stop, to check, to impede

**Hemmung,** hem-oong, *f* inhibition

**Hengst,** hengst, *m* stallion

**Henkel,** heng-kel, *m* handle

**Henker,** heng-ker, *m* hangman, executioner

**Henne,** hen-e, *f* hen, fowl

**her,** hair, *adv* here

**herab,** hair-ahpp, *adv* down(wards)

**herablassen (sich),** hair-ahp-lahss-en (zik), *v* to condescend

**heran,** hair-ahnn, *adv* this way, near this place

**heranwachsen,** hair-ahnn-vahks-en, *v* to grow up

**herauf,** hair-owf, *adv* up(ward), up here; uphill

**heraus,** hair-owss, *adv* out of

**herausfordern,** hair-ows-ford-ern, *v* to challenge

**herausgeben,** hair-ows-gaib-en, *v* to hand over; to give in change; to publish

**herausstellen (sich),** hair-ows-shtel-en (zik), *v* to prove to be, to turn out to be

**herb,** hairp, *adj* harsh, acrid; sharp, bitter

**herbei,** hair-by, *adv* hither, here, this way

**herbeiführen,** hair-by-fEEr-en, *v* to bring about

**Herberge,** hair-bairg-e, *f* shelter; lodging; hostel

**Herbst,** hairpst, *m* autumn

**herbstlich,** hairpst-lik, *adj* autumnal

**Herd,** hairt, *m* hearth; oven

**Herde,** haird-e, *f* herd, flock

**herein,** hair-ine, *adv* in(to) this place; come in!

**hereinfallen,** hair-ine-fahll-en, *v* to be cheated

**hereinkommen,** hair-ine-kohmm-en, *v* to come in

**hereinlegen,** hair-ine-laig-en, *v* to put in(to); to swindle

**Herfahrt,** hair-fahrt, *f* journey here

**hergeben,** hair-gaib-en, *v* to give up, to hand over

**Hering,** hair-ing, *m* herring

**herkommen,** hair-kom-en, *v* to come here

**Herkunft,** hair-koonft, *f* arrival; descent, origin

**Herr,** hairr, *m* master, lord; Mr, sir; Lord; **–entoilette,** *f* men's toilet

**herrichten,** hair-rik-ten, *v* to prepare, to set in order

**herrisch,** hair-rish, *adj* domineering

**herrlich,** hair-lik, *adj* magnificent, delightful

**Herrschaft,** hair-shahft, *f* dominion, rule

**herrschen,** hair-shen, *v* to rule

**Herrscher,** hair-sher, *m* ruler, sovereign

**herrühren,** hair-rEEr-en, *v* to originate from

**herstellen,** hair-shtel-en, *v* to produce

**Hersteller,** hair-shtel-er, *m* producer; manufacturer

**Herstellung,** hair-shtel-oong, *f* production; manufacture

**herüber,** hair-EEb-er, *adv* over here; across

**herum,** hair-oomm, *adv* (a)round, round about

**herumkommen,** hair-**oomm**-kom-en, *v* to get round (places)

**herunter,** hair-**oonnt**-er, *adv* down(wards)

**hervor,** hair-**for,** *adv* forward, forth

**hervorbringen,** hair-**for**-bring-en, *v* to bring out/forth

**hervorgehen,** hair-**for**-gay-en, *v* to result from

**hervorheben,** hair-**for**-haib-en, *v* to accentuate, to emphasize

**hervorragend,** hair-**for**-rahg-ent, *adj* prominent; eminent; distinguished

**hervorrufen,** hair-**for**-roof-en, *v* to cause

**hervortreten,** hair-**for**-trait-en, *v* to step forward; to stand out (in relief)

**Herz,** hairts, *nt* heart

**herzhaft,** hairts-hahft, *adj* bold; hearty

**Herzinfarkt,** hairts-in-fahrkt, *m* heart attack

**Herzklopfen,** hairts-klohpf-en, *nt* palpitations

**herzlich,** hairts-lik, *adj* cordial, heartfelt, sincere; **–en Dank,** many thanks; **–en Glückwunsch,** congratulations; **–e Grüße,** best wishes

**Herzog,** hairt-sohk, *m* duke

**Herzschlag,** hairts-shlahk, *m* heart-beat; apoplexy

**Hetze,** het-se, *f* hunt; rush; hurry

**hetzen,** het-sen, *v* to hound; to rush; to hurry

**Hetzerei,** het-se-ry, *f* rushing

**Heu,** hoy, *nt* hay

**Heuchelei,** hoy-kel-ly, *f* hypocrisy; sham; cant

**heucheln,** hoy-keln, *v* to feign; to simulate

**heuchlerisch,** hoyk-ler-ish, *adj* hypocritical

**heuer,** hoy-er, *adv* this year

**heulen,** hoyl-en, *v* to howl, to roar, to shriek

**heurig,** hoy-rik, *adj* this year's

**Heuschnupfen,** hoy-shnoopf-en, *m* hay fever

**Heuschrecke,** hoy-shreck-e, *f* grasshopper

**heute,** hoyt-e, *adv* today; **– früh/abend,** this morning/evening

**heutig,** hoyt-ik, *adj* today's; of this day; present

**heutzutage,** hoyt-tsoo-tahg-e, *adv* nowadays

**Hexe,** hex-e, *f* witch, sorceress, enchantress

**hexen,** hex-en, *v* to practise magic/witchcraft

**Hieb,** heep, *m* stroke, blow, cuff, smack

**hier,** heer, *adv* here

**hierauf,** heer-**owf,** *adv* hereon, hereupon

**hierbei,** heer-**by,** *adv* herewith, hereby; enclosed

**hierbleiben,** heer-bly-ben, *v* to stay here

**hierher,** heer-**hair,** *adv* here (hither)

**hierhin,** heer-hin, *adv* here (hither)

**hierlassen,** heer-lahss-en, *v* to leave here

**hierzulande,** heer-tsoo-lahnn-de, *adv* in this country

**hiesig,** hee-zik, *adj* in this place/town

**Hilfe,** hilf-e, *f* help, aid, assistance, relief, support

**hilflos,** hilf-lohs, *adj* helpless

**hilfreich,** hilf-ry'k, *adj* helpful; charitable

**Hilfskraft,** hilfs-krahft, *f* assistant

**Hilfsmittel,** hilfs-mit-el, *nt* remedy, help; expedient

**Himbeere,** him-bair-e, *f* raspberry

**Himmel,** him-el, *m* heaven; sky; **–bett,** nt bed with canopy; **–fahrt,** *f* Ascension; **–reich,** *nt* kingdom of heaven; **–srichtung,** *f* direction; point of compass

**himmlisch,** him-lish, *adj* heavenly, divine

**hin,** hin, *adv* there; along; down; **– und zurück,** there and back

**hinab,** hin-**ahpp,** *adv* down (there), downwards

**hinauf,** hin-**owf,** *adv* up (there)

**hinaus,** hin-**owss,** *adv* out (there); **–gehen,** *v* to go out; to leave; **–werfen,** v to throw out

**hinderlich,** hin-der-lik, adj obstructive

**hindern,** hin-dern, v to hinder, to prevent

**Hindernis,** hin-der-niss, nt hindrance

**hindeuten,** hin-doyt-en, v to point to

**hindurch,** hin-**doohrk**, adv through(out)

**hinein,** hin-**ein**, adv into, in(side); **–gehen,** v to go in(to); **–passen,** v to fit in

**hinfahren,** hin-fahr-en, v to drive to a place

**Hinfahrt,** hin-fahrt, f outward journey

**hinfallen,** hin-fahll-en, v to fall down

**hinfällig,** hin-fel-ik, adj invalid; untenable

**Hingabe,** hin-gahb-e, f devotion

**hingeben (sich),** hin-gayb-en (zik), v to devote (o.s.)

**hingegen,** hin-**gayg**-en, adv on the other hand; on the contrary

**hingerissen,** hin-ge-ris-en, adj carried away

**hinhalten,** hin-hallt-en, v to hold out; to put off

**hinken,** hing-ken, v to limp

**hinkommen,** hin-kom-en, v to reach/get to a place

**hinlegen,** hin-layg-en, v to lay down, to put down; **sich —,** v to lie down

**hinreichend,** hin-ry'k-ent, adj adequate, sufficient

**Hinreise,** hin-ry-ze, f outward journey

**hinreißen,** hin-ry-sen, v to tear along; to carry away

**hinrichten,** hin-rik-ten, v to execute

**Hinrichtung,** hin-rik-toong, f execution

**hinschaffen,** hin-shahff-en, v to convey there

**hinsetzen,** hin-zets-en, v to put down; **sich –,** v to sit down

**hinsichtlich,** hin-zikt-lik, prep with regard to

**hinten,** hint-en, adv behind; at the back

**hinter,** hint-er, prep behind

**Hinterbliebene(r),** hint-er-**bleeb**-en-e(r), m & f bereaved person

**hintereinander,** hint-er-ine-ahnd-er, adv one after the other

**hintergehen,** hint-er-gay-en, v to deceive, to dupe

**Hintergrund,** hint-er-groont, m background

**Hinterhalt,** hint-er-halt, m ambush

**hinterher,** hint-er-hair, adv behind; afterwards

**hinterlassen,** hint-er-lahss-en, v to bequeath; to leave behind

**hinterlegen,** hint-er-laig-en, v to deposit

**Hinterlist,** hint-er-list, f cunning, deception, fraud

**Hinterrad,** hint-er-raht, nt rear wheel

**hinterrücks,** hint-er-rEEcks, adv from behind

**hinüber,** hin-EEb-er, adv over (there), across

**hin und her,** hin oont hair, adv to and fro

**hinunter,** hin-**oonnt**-er, adv down(wards); downstairs

**Hinweg,** hin-veeck, m the way there

**hinweg,** hin-**veck**, adv away

**Hinweis,** hin-vice, m reference; indication

**hinweisen (auf),** hin-vy-zen (owf), v to point (to); to indicate

**hinziehen (sich),** hin-tsee-en (zik), v to drag on

**hinzu,** hin-tsoo, adv to (a place); in addition

**hinzufügen,** hin-tsoo-fEEg-en, v to add to

**hinzuziehen,** hin-tsoo-tsee-en, v to consult

**Hirn,** heern, nt brain

**hirnverbrannt,** heern-fair-brahnt, adj crazy

**Hirsch,** heersh, m stag

**Hirt,** heert, m shepherd, herdsman

**hissen,** his-en, v to hoist

**Historiker,** his-tohr-ik-er, m historian

**historisch,** his-**tohr**-ish, adj historical

**Hitze,** hit-se, f heat, warmth

**hitzig,** hit-sik, adj hot (-headed), hasty, impetuous

**Hitzkopf,** hits-kopp'f, m

hot-headed person

**Hitzschlag, hits**-shlahk, *m* heat-stroke, sunstroke

**H-Milch, hah**-milk, *f* long-life milk

**Hobby, hobb**-ee, *nt* hobby

**Hobel, hobb**-el, *m* (wood) plane

**hobeln, hobb**-eln, *v* to plane

**Hobelspäne, hobb**-el-shpayne, *pl* (wood) shavings

**hoch, hohk**, *adj* high, elevated, lofty

**Hochachtung, hohk**-ahk-toong, *f* respect, (high) esteem

**hochachtungsvoll, hohk**-ahk-toongs-foll, *adv* faithfully

**Hochamt, hohk**-ahmt, *nt* High Mass

**Hochbetrieb, hohk**-be-treep, *m* peak period

**hochdeutsch, hohk**-doytsh, *adj* high German

**hochgradig, hohk**-grahd-ik, *adj* absolute; utter

**hochhalten, hohk**-hahlt-en, *v* to hold up

**Hochhaus, hohk**-hows, *nt* high-rise block

**Hochkonjunktur, hohk**-kon-yoonkt-oor, *f* economic boom

**Hochmut, hohk**-moot, *m* haughtiness, pride

**hochmütig, hohk**-mEEt-ik, *adj* haughty, proud

**hochnäsig, hohk**-nay-zik, *adj* arrogant

**Hochsaison, hohk**-zay-

zohn, *f* high season

**Hochschule, hohk**-shool-e, *f* university; college

**Hochsommer, hohk**-zom-er, *m* midsummer

**Hochsprung, hohk**-hproong, *m* high jump

**höchst, herkst**, *adv* highest; extremely

**Hochstapler, hohk**-shtahp-ler, *m* con man

**höchstens, herk**-stens, *adv* at the most

**Höchstgeschwindigkeit, herkst**-ge-shvind-ik-kite, *f* maximum speed

**Hochverrat, hohk**-fair-raht, *m* high treason

**Hochwasser, hohk**-vahss-er, *nt* high tide; flood

**Hochzeit, hohk**-tsite, *f* wedding, marriage

**Hochzeitsreise, hohk**-tsites-ry-ze, *f* honeymoon

**hocken, hock**-en, *v* to squat

**Hocker, hock**-er, *m* stool

**Höcker, herck**-er, *m* knob; bump; hump; hunch

**Hoden, hohd**-en, *m* testicle

**Hof, hohf**, *m* court(yard); farm

**hoffen, hof**-en, *v* to hope; to expect, to await

**hoffentlich, hof**-ent-lik, *adv* hopefully

**Hoffnung, hof**-noong, *f* hope, expectation

**höflich, herf**-lik, *adj* polite, courteous; courtly

**Höflichkeit, herf**-lik-kite, *f* politeness, courtesy

**Höhe, her**-e, *f* height, altitude; level; *mus* pitch

**Höhepunkt, her**-e-poonkt, *m* high point; peak

**höher, her**-er, *adj & adv* higher

**hohl, hohl**, *adj* hollow(ed out); concave

**Höhle, herl**-e, *f* cave(rn), hole, burrow; hovel

**Hohlmaß, hohl**-mahs, *nt* measure of capacity; dry measure

**Hohn, hohn**, *m* scorn, derision; sneer

**höhnisch, hern**-ish, *adj* scornful; sneering, mocking

**holen, hohl**-en, *v* to fetch, to come for

**Holland, hol**-ahnt, *nt* Holland

**Holländer, hol**-end-er, *m* Dutchman; **–in,** *f* Dutchwoman

**holländisch, hol**-end-ish, *adj* Dutch

**Hölle, herll**-e, *f* hell, inferno; limbo

**höllisch, herll**-ish, *adj* hellish, diabolical, infernal

**holperig, holp**-er-ik, *adj* uneven, rough, rugged

**Holunder, hohl**-oond-er, *m* elder

**Holz, holts**, *nt* wood; timber; grove

**hölzern, herlt**-sern, *adj* wooden; clumsy, stiff

**Holzkohle, holts**-kohl-e, *f*

charcoal

**Holzschnitt, holts**-shnit, *m*
wood-carving

**Homöopathie,** hohm-er-oh-paht-**ee**, *f* homeopathy

**homosexuell, hoh**-moh-sex-oo-**el**, *adj* homosexual

**Honig, hohn**-ik, *m* honey

**Honorar,** on-ohr-**ar**, *nt*
(professional) fee

**honorieren,** hon-oh-**reer**-en, *v* to remunerate

**Hopfen, hop**-fen, *m* hop
(-plant), hops

**hopsen, hop**-sen, *v* to hop,
to skip

**horchen, hork**-en, *v* to
listen

**Horde, hord**-e, *f* horde,
wandering tribe; band

**hören, her**-en, *v* to hear; to
listen to

**Hörer, her**-er, *m* listener;
(telephone) receiver

**Horizont,** hoh-ree-**tsont**, *m*
horizon

**Hormon,** hor-**mohn**, *nt*
hormone

**Horn,** horn, *nt* horn; *mus*
(French) horn

**Hornhaut, horn**-howt, *f*
horny skin; cornea

**Hornisse,** horn-**iss**-e, *f*
hornet

**Horoskop,** hor-oss-**kohp**, *nt*
horoscope

**Hörsaal, her**-zahl, *m*
lecture-hall

**Hose, hoh**-ze, *f* trousers,
breeches

**Hosenträger, hohz**-en-trayg-

er, *m* (pair of) braces

**Hospiz,** hos-**peets**, *nt*
hospice

**Hostie, host**-ye, *f* host;
consecrated wafer

**Hotel,** hoh-**tell**, *nt* hotel;
**–verzeichnis,** *nt* hotel
register

**hübsch, hEEpsh,** *adj* pretty;
polite; nice

**Hubschrauber, hoop**-
shrowb-er, *m* helicopter

**Huf,** hoof, *m* hoof

**Hufeisen, hoof**-ay-zen, *m*
horseshoe

**Hüfte, hEEft**-e, *f* hip,
haunch

**Hügel, hEEg**-el, *m* hill,
hillock

**hügelig, hEEg**-el-ik, *adj* hilly

**Huhn,** hoon, *nt* hen,
chicken; fowl

**Hühnerauge, hEEn**-er-owg-
e, *nt* med corn

**Hühnerbraten, hEEn**-er-
braht-en, *m* roast chicken

**Hühnerhof, hEEn**-er-hohf,
*m* poultry farm

**huldigen, hoold**-ig-en, *v* to
render homage

**Hülle, hEEl**-e, *f* wrapping;
wrapper, covering;
garment

**Hülle und Fülle, hEEl**-e
oont **fEEl**-e, *f* abundance

**hüllen, hEEll**-en, *v* to wrap,
to envelop

**Hülse, hEEl**-ze, *f* husk, shell,
pod; **–nfrucht,** *f* pulse
(vegetable)

**human,** hoo-**mahn**, *adj*

humane

**Hummel, hoomm**-el, *f*
(bumble-)bee

**Hummer, hoomm**-er, *m*
lobster

**Humor,** hoo-**mohr**, *m*
humour; **– haben,** *v* to
have a sense of humour

**humpeln, hoomp**-eln, *v* to
limp, to hobble

**Hund,** hoont, *m* dog, hound

**Hundehütte, hoond**-e-
hEEtt-e, *f* dog-kennel

**hundert, hoond**-ert, *num*
hundred

**hundertprozentig, hoond**-
ert-pro-**tsent**-ik, *adj* one
hundred percent

**Hündin, hEEnd**-in, *f* bitch

**Hüne, hEEn**-e, *m* giant

**Hunger, hoong**-er, *m*
hunger; starvation;
famine; **– haben,** *v* to be
hungry

**hungern, hoong**-ern, *v* to
feel hungry; to be starving

**Hungersnot, hoong**-ers-
noht, *f* famine

**hungrig, hoong**-rik, *adj*
hungry; starving

**Hupe, hoop**-e, *f* car horn

**hüpfen, hEEp**-fen, *v* to hop,
to skip, to jump

**Hürde, hEErd**-e, *f* hurdle;
fold, pen

**Hure, hoor**-e, *f* whore

**huschen, hoosh**-en, *v* to
scurry, to whisk

**husten, hoost**-en, *v* to
cough

**Husten, hoost**-en, *m* cough;

–**saft,** *m* cough mixture

**Hut,** hoot, *m* hat

**hüten,** h**EE**t-en, *v* to guard, to watch over; **sich –,** *v* to be on one's guard

**Hütte,** h**EE**tt-*e*, *f* hut, cabin, cottage; foundry

**Hyäne,** he-**ayn**-*e*, *f* hyena

**Hygiene,** hee-gee-**ayn**-*e*, *f* hygiene

**Hypothek,** hip-oh-**take,** *f* mortgage

**hysterisch,** hist-**air**-ish, *adj* hysterical

**IC,** ee-**tsay,** *abbr* **Intercity-Zug**

**ICE,** ee-tsay-ay, *abbr* **Intercity-Expreßzug**

**ich,** ik, *pron* I, (emphatic) me

**Ideal,** ee-day-**ahl,** *nt* ideal

**ideal,** ee-day-**ahl,** *adj* ideal

**idealistisch,** ee-day-ahl-**is**-tish, *adj* idealistic

**Idee,** ee-**day,** *f* idea

**identisch,** ee-**dent**-ish, *adj* identical

**Identität,** ee-dent-ee-**tayt,** *f* identity

**Idiot,** ee-dee-**oht,** *m* idiot

**idyllisch,** ee-**dEEll**-ish, *adj* idyllic

**Igel,** **eeg**-el, *m* hedgehog

**ihm,** eem, *pron* (dative m & nt) (to) him; (to) it

**ihn,** een, *pron* (accusative m) him; it

**ihnen,** **een**-en, *pron* (dative pl) (to) them

**Ihnen,** **een**-en, *pron* (dative) (to) you

**ihr,** eer, *pron* (pl & dative f) (to) her; you

**ihr, ihre(r/s),** eer, eer-*e*(r/s), *adj* her; their; *pron* hers; theirs

**Ihr, Ihre(r/s),** eer, eer-*e*(r/s), *adj* your; *pron* yours

**illegal,** ill-e-**gahl,** *adj* illegal

**illustrieren,** ill-oos-**treer**-en, *v* to illustrate

**Illustrierte,** ill-oos-**treert**-*e*, *f* magazine

**im** ( = **in dem**), im, in the

**Imbiß,** **im**-bis, *m* snack; **–stube,** *f* snack bar

**immer,** **im**-mer, *adv* always; continually; **– mehr,** more and more; **– wieder,** again and again; **für –,** for ever; **–noch,** still; **– schlimmer,** worse and worse

**Immobilien,** im-moh-**bee**-lee-en, *pl* property; **–makler,** *m* estate agent

**impfen,** **imp**-fen, *v* to vaccinate, to inoculate

**Impfung,** **imp**-foong, *f* vaccination

**imponieren,** im-pohn-**eer**-en, *v* to impress

**Import,** im-**port,** *m* import

**importieren,** im-port-**eer**-en, *v* to import

**imposant,** im-poh-**zahnt,** *adj* imposing

**impotent,** **im**-poh-tent, *adj* impotent

**imstande,** im-**shtahnd**-*e*, *adj* **– sein,** to be able (to)

**in,** in, *prep* in; at; to

**Inbegriff,** **in**-be-grif, *m* essence; inclusion

**indem,** in-**daym,** *conj* while, whilst; by, in

**Inder,** **in**-der, *m* Indian (person)

**Indianer,** in-dee-**ahn**-er, *m* American Indian

**Indien,** **in**-dee-en, *nt* India

**indisch,** **in**-dish, *adj* Indian

**industrialisieren,** in-doos-tree-ahl-ee-**seer**-en, *v* to industrialize

**Industrie,** in-doos-**tree,** *f* industry

**ineinander,** in-ine-**ahnn**-der, *adv* into one another

**Infektion,** in-fekts-**yohn,** *f* infection; **–skrankheit,** *f* infectious disease

**infizieren,** in-fee-**tseer**-en, *v* to infect

**Inflation,** in-flahts-**yohn,** *f*

inflation

**infolge**, in-**folg**-e, *prep* in consequence of

**Informatik**, in-for-**mah**-tik, *f* computer science

**Information**, in-for-mahts-**yohn**, *f* information

**informieren**, in-form-**eer**-en, *v* to inform

**Ingenieur**, in-zhayn-**yer**, *m* engineer

**Ingwer**, **ing**-ver, *m* ginger

**Inhaber**, in-**hahb**-er, *m* possessor; bearer; holder

**Inhalt**, in-**hahlt**, *m* content; **–sverzeichnis**, *nt* table of contents

**Initiative**, in-ee-tsee-ah-**teev**-e, *f* initiative

**inklusive**, in-kloo-**seev**-e, *adj* inclusive

**Inland**, in-**lahnt**, *nt* interior (of country); **–flug**, *m* domestic flight

**inländisch**, in-**lend**-dish, *adj* native, home, inland

**inmitten**, in-**mit**-en, *prep* in the middle/centre of

**innehalten**, in-e-**hahlt**-en, *v* to stop

**innen**, in-en, *adv* inside

**Innenminister**, in-en-min-ist-er, *m* Home Secretary

**Innenpolitik**, in-en-poh-lee-teek, *f* domestic policy

**Innenstadt**, in-en-**shtahtt**, *f* town centre

**innerhalb**, in-er-**hahlp**, *adv* inside; *prep* within

**innerlich**, in-er-**lik**, *adj* inner, within, internal

**innig**, in-ik, *adj* intimate, heartfelt, fond

**Innung**, in-**oong**, *f* corporation, guild; craft

**ins** ( = **in das**), ins, into the

**Insasse**, in-**zahss**-e, *m* inmate; occupant

**insbesondere**, ins-be-**zon**-der-e, *adv* in particular

**Inschrift**, in-**shrift**, *f* inscription

**Insekt**, in-**zekt**, *nt* insect

**Insel**, in-zel, *f* island, isle

**Inserat**, in-zair-**aht**, *nt* advertisement

**inserieren**, in-zer-**eer**-en, *v* to advertise

**insgesamt**, ins-ge-**zahmt**, *adv* altogether

**Installateur**, in-shtahll-ah-ter, *m* plumber

**inständig**, in-**shtend**-ik, *adj* earnest, pressing, urgent

**Instinkt**, in-**stinkt**, *m* instinct

**instinktiv**, in-stink-**teef**, *adj* instinctive

**Institut**, in-stee-**toot**, *nt* institute

**Instrument**, in-stroo-**ment**, *nt* instrument

**intelligent**, in-tel-ee-**gent**, *adj* intelligent

**Intendant**, in-ten-**dahnt**, *m* director; theatre manager

**intensiv**, in-ten-**seef**, *adj* intensiv

**Intensivstation**, in-ten-**seef**-shtahts-yohn, *f* intensive care unit

**Intercity Expreßzug**, in-ter-sit-ee ex-**press**-tsook, *m* high speed train

**Intercity-Zug**, in-ter-**sit**-ee-tsook, *m* intercity train

**interessant**, in-ter-ess-**ahnt**, *adj* interesting

**Interesse**, in-ter-**ess**-e, *nt* interest

**interessieren**, in-te-ress-**eer**-en, *v* to interest; **sich für etw –**, to be interested in sth

**Internat**, in-tair-**naht**, *nt* boarding school

**international**, in-ter-nahts-yohn-**ahl**, *adj* international

**intim**, in-**teem**, *adj* intimate

**intolerant**, in-tohl-er-ahnt, *adj* intolerant

**Invasion**, in-vahz-**yohn**, *f* invasion

**Inventur**, in-ven-**toor**, *f* stocktaking

**investieren**, in-ves-**teer**-en, *v* to invest

**inzwischen**, int-**svish**-en, *adv* meanwhile

**irdisch**, eerd-ish, *adj* earthly, worldly

**Ire**, **eer**-e, *m* Irishman

**irgend**, eerg-ent, *adv* any; **–jemand**, *pron* anybody; **–wie**, *adv* somehow; **–wann**, *adv* some time; **–wo**, *adv* somewhere

**Irin**, eer-in, *f* Irishwoman

**irisch**, eer-ish, *adj* Irish

**Irland**, eer-lahnt, *nt* Ireland, Eire

**Irländer**, eer-len-der, *m*

Irishman; **–in,** *f*
Irishwoman

**Ironie,** eer-oh-**nee,** *f* irony

**ironisch,** eer-**oh**-nish, *adj*
ironic

**irre, eer-***e*, *adj & adv* mad,
insane; muddled, confused

**Irre(r),** eer-*e*(r), *m & f*
madwoman (madman)

**irreführen, eer-***e*-fEEr-en, *v*
to lead astray

**irremachen, eer-***e*-mah*k*-en,
*v* to bewilder

**irren, eer-**en, *v* to err, to go
astray; to stray; **sich –,** *v*
to be mistaken

**Irrenanstalt, eer-**en-ahnn-
shtahlt, *f* lunatic asylum

**Irrgarten, eer-**gart-en, *m*
maze

**irrig, eer-**ik, *adj* erroneous,
wrong, false

**Irrsinn, eer-**zin, *m* insanity,
lunacy

**irrsinnig, eer-**zin-ik, *adj*
insane, mentally deranged

**Irrtum, eer-**toom, *m* error,
mistake; oversight

**irrtümlich, eer-**tEEm-li*k*, *adj*
erroneous

**Islam, ees-**lahm, *m* Islam

**isolieren, ees-**oh-**leer-**en, *v*
to isolate; to insulate

**Isolierung,** ee-zoh-**leer-**
oong, *f* isolation;
insulation

**Israel, ees-**rah-ayl, *nt* Israel

**Israeli, ees-**rah-**ay**-lee, *m &*
*f* Israeli (person)

**israelisch, ees-**rah-**ay**-lish,
*adj* Israeli

**Italien,** ee-**tah**-lee-en, *nt*
Italy

**Italiener,** ee-tah-lee-**ay**-ner,
*m* Italian (person)

**italienisch,** ee-tah-lee-**ay**-
nish, *adj* Italian

**ja,** yah, *adv* yes

**Jacht,** yahkt, *f* yacht

**Jacke,** yahk-e, *f* jacket, coat

**Jagd,** yahkt, *f* hunt(ing); chase; shooting; **–hund,** *m* hunting dog

**jagen,** yahg-en, *v* to hunt, to chase

**Jäger,** yayg-er, *m* hunter; rifleman

**jäh,** yay, *adj* sudden, impetuous; steep

**Jahr,** yahr, *nt* year

**jahrelang,** yahr-e-lahng, *adv* lasting for years

**Jahresbeitrag,** yahr-es-by-trahk, *m* annual subscription

**Jahreskarte,** yahr-es-kahr-te, *f* annual season ticket

**Jahrestag,** yahr-es-tahk, *m* anniversary

**Jahreswechsel,** yahr-es-veck-sel, *m* new year

**Jahreszahl,** yahr-es-tsahl, *f* date, year

**Jahreszeit,** yahr-es-tsite, *f* season, time of year

**Jahrgang,** yahr-gahng, *m* year; vintage; volume (of publication)

**Jahrhundert,** yahr-hoonn-dert, *nt* century

**jährlich,** yair-lik, *adj* annual, yearly

**Jahrmarkt,** yahr-markt, *m* fair

**Jahrtausend,** yahr-tow-zent, *nt* millennium

**Jahrzehnt,** yahr-tsaynt, *nt* decade

**Jähzorn,** yay-tsorn, *m* sudden anger; irritability

**Jalousie,** zhahll-oo-zee, *f* Venetian blind

**Jammer,** yahmm-er, *m* great misery, calamity

**jämmerlich,** yem-er-lik, *adj* wretched, pitiable

**jammern,** yahmm-ern, *v* to lament; to wail

**Januar,** yahnn-oo-ahr, *m* January

**Japan,** yah-pahnn, *nt* Japan

**Japaner,** yah-pahn-er, *m* Japanese (person)

**japanisch,** yah-pahn-ish, *adj* Japanese

**jäten,** yay-ten, *v* to weed

**jauchzen,** yowk-tsen, *v* to rejoice; to exult

**je,** yay, *adv* ever; each, every; *conj* **– nach,** according to

**jede(r/s),** yayd-e(r/s) *pron* each, every

**jedenfalls,** yayd-en-fahls, *adv* in any case

**jedermann,** yayd-er-mahnn, *pron* everybody; anybody

**jederzeit,** yayd-er-tsy't, *adv* at any time, always

**jedesmal,** yayd-es-mahl, *adv* each/every time

**jedoch,** yay-doch, *adv* however, still, nevertheless

**jeher,** yay-hair, *adv* von/seit **–,** always

**jemals,** yay-mahls, *adv* ever

**jemand,** yay-mahnt, *pron* someone, anyone,

anybody

**jene(r/s)**, yayn-e(r/s) *pron* that one

**jenseits**, yayn-zites, *prep* on the other side

**jetzig**, yet-sik, *adj* actual, of the present time

**jetzt**, yetst, *adv* now

**jeweils**, yay-viles, *adv* at a time

**Jh.**, *abbr* Jahrhundert

**joggen**, dshogg-en, *v* to jog

**Joghurt**, yoh-koort, *nt* yogurt

**Johannisbeere**, yoh-hahnn-is-bair-e, *f* redcurrant, blackcurrant

**Journalismus**, zhoor-nahl-ees-moos, *m* journalism

**Jubel**, yoob-el, *m* jubilation, exultation

**jubeln**, yoob-eln, *v* to jubilate, to rejoice

**jucken**, yoock-en, *v* to itch

**jüdisch**, yEEd-ish, *adj* Jewish

**Jugend**, yoog-ent, *f* youth; –herberge, *f* youth hostel

**jugendlich**, yoog-ent-lik, *adj* youthful

**Jugendliche(r)**, yoog-ent-lik-e(r), *m & f* adolescent

**Juli**, yoo-li, *m* July

**jung**, yoong, *adj* young, youthful

**Junge**, yoong-e, *m* boy, lad; *nt* young (animals)

**Jünger**, yEEng-er, *m* disciple, follower

**Jungfrau**, yoong-frow, *f* virgin

**Junggeselle**, yoong-ge-zel-e, *m* bachelor

**Jüngling**, yEEng-ling; *m* youth, young man

**jüngst**, yEEngst, *adv* recently, a short time ago

**Juni**, yoo-ni, *m* June

**Jurist**, yoor-ist, *m* lawyer, jurist

**Justiz**, yoos-teets, *f* judiciary

**Juwel**, yoo-vail, *nt* jewel, gem

**Juwelier**, yoo-vail-eer, *m* jeweller

**Kabel**, kahb-el, *nt* cable; **–fernsehen**, *nt* cable television

**Kabeljau**, kahb-el-**yow**, *m* cod

**Kabine**, kahb-**een**-e, *f* cabin

**Kachel**, kahk-*el*, *f* (glazed) tile

**Käfer**, kay-fer, *m* beetle

**Kaffee**, kahff-ay, *m* coffee

**Käfig**, kay-fik, *m* cage

**kahl**, kahl, *adj* bare, bleak; bald

**Kahn**, kahn, *m* skiff, small boat; barge

**Kai**, kay, *m* quay, jetty

**Kaiser**, ky-zer, *m* emperor

**kaiserlich**, ky-zer-lik, *adj* imperial

**Kaiserreich**, ky-zer-ry'k, *nt* empire

**Kaiserschnitt**, ky-zer-shnit, *m* Caesarean (section)

**Kakadu**, kah-kah-doo, *m* cockatoo

**Kakao**, kah-kow, *m* cocoa

**Kaktus**, kahk-toos, *m* cactus

**Kalb**, kahlp, *nt* calf

**Kalbfleisch**, kahlp-fly'sh, *nt* veal

**Kalender**, kahl-**end**-er, *m* calendar, almanac

**Kalk**, kahlk, *m* lime, chalk

**Kalorie**, kahl-oh-**ree**, *f* calorie

**kalt**, kahlt, *adj* cold; frigid; **–blütig,** *adj* cold-blooded; cool-headed

**Kälte**, kelt-e, *f* cold; frigidity

**Kamel**, kahmm-ail, *nt* camel

**Kamera**, kahmm-er-ah, *f* camera

**Kamerad**, kahmm-er-**aht**, *m* comrade, companion; **–schaft,** *f* comradeship

**Kamille**, kahmm-il-e, *f* camomile

**Kamin**, kahmm-**een**, *m* chimney (pot); fireplace

**Kamm**, kahmm, *m* comb; crest, ridge (of mountain)

**kämmen**, kem-*en*, *v* to comb

**Kammer**, kahmm-er, *f* chamber, small room

**Kampf**, kahmpf, *m* combat, fight

**kämpfen**, kemp-fen, *v* to fight, to struggle

**Kämpfer**, kemp-fer, *m* fighter, combatant, warrior

**kampflustig**, kahmpf-loost-ik, *adj* belligerent

**Kanada**, kah-nah-dah, *nt* Canada

**Kanadier**, kah-**nah**-dee-er, *m* Canadian (person)

**kanadisch**, kah-**nah**-dish, *adj* Canadian

**Kanal**, kahnn-**ahl**, *m* channel; canal; **–inseln,** *pl* Channel Islands

**Kanalisation**, kahnn-ahl-e-zahts-**yohn**, *f* drainage

**Kanaltunnel**, kahnn-**ahl**-toon-el, *m* Channel Tunnel

**Kanarienvogel**, kahnn-**ahr**-ee-en-fohg-el, *m* canary

**Kandidat**, kahnn-dee-**daht**, *m* candidate

**Kaninchen**, kahnn-**een**-ken, *nt* rabbit

**Kännchen**, ken-ken, *nt* pot

**Kanne**, kahnn-e, *f* can, pot, jug; tankard

**Kanone**, kahnn-**ohn**-e, *f*

cannon

**Kante, kahnt**-e, f edge, border, corner

**kantig, kahnt**-ik, adj edged, angular

**Kantine, kahnn-teen**-e, f canteen

**Kanzel, kahnt**-sel, f pulpit

**Kanzlei, kahnt**-se-ly, f government office; office, chambers

**Kanzler, kahnt**-sler, m chancellor

**Kap, kahpp,** nt cape, promontory, headland

**Kapelle, kahpp-el**-e, f chapel; mus band

**kapern, kahpp**-ern, v to capture; to commandeer

**kapieren, kahpp-eer**-en, v to grasp, to understand

**Kapital, kahpp-ee-tahl,** nt capital; **–anlage,** f investment

**Kapitalismus, kahpp-ee-tahl-is-moos,** m capitalism

**Kapitän, kahpp-e-tain,** m captain

**Kapitel, kahpp-it**-el, nt chapter

**Kappe, kahpp**-e, f cap; hood

**Kapsel, kahpp**-sel, f capsule, casing

**kaputt, kahpp-oott,** adj ruined; smashed, broken

**Kapuze, kahpp-oots**-e, f hood

**Karaffe, kar-ahff**-e, f carafe; decanter

**Karfreitag, kar-fry-tahk,** m Good Friday

**karg, kark,** adj mean; economical; parsimonious; scanty

**Karibik, kah-ree-beek,** f Caribbean (Sea)

**karibisch, kah-ree-bish,** adj Caribbean

**kariert, kar-eert,** adj chequered

**Karneval, kar-ne-vahl,** m carnival

**Karo, kar-oh,** nt check; diamond (shape/card)

**Karosserie, kar-oss-er-ee,** f bodywork

**Karotte, kar-ott**-e, f carrot

**Karpfen, karp-fen,** m carp

**Karren, kar-en,** m cart, dray, barrow

**Karriere, kar-ee-ayr**-e, f career; **– machen,** to make a career for o.s.

**Karte, kart**-e, f card; map, chart; ticket; **–nspiel,** nt card game; **–ntelefon,** nt card phone

**Kartoffel, kart-off**-el, f potato

**Kartoffelbrei, kart-off-el-bry,** m mashed potatoes

**Karton, kart-ong,** m cardboard(-box)

**Karussell, kar-ooss-el,** nt roundabout, merry-go-round

**Käse, kay-ze,** m cheese

**Käseglocke, kay-ze-glock**-e, f cheese-cover

**Kaserne, kah-zern**-e, f barracks

**Kasse, kahss**-e, f cash(-box); till; box-office

**Kassette, kahss-et**-e, f cassette; box

**kassieren, kahss-eer**-en, v to cash, to collect; to confiscate

**Kassierer, kahss-eer**-er, m cashier

**Kastanie, kahss-tahn-ye,** f chestnut

**Kasten, kahsst**-en, m box, trunk, case

**kastrieren, kahss-treer**-en, v to castrate

**Katalog, kah-tah-lohk,** m catalogue

**Katastrophe, kah-tah-strohf**-e, f disaster

**Kater, kaht**-er, m tom cat; hangover

**Katholik, kaht-ohl-eeck,** m Catholic

**katholisch, kaht-ohl-ish,** adj Catholic

**Katze, kahtt**-se, f cat

**Katzensprung, kahtt-sen-shproong,** m stone's throw

**Kauderwelsch, kowd-er-velsh,** nt gibberish

**kauen, kow-en,** v to chew, to masticate

**kauern, kow-ern,** v to cower, to crouch (down)

**Kauf, kowf,** m buying, purchase

**kaufen, kowf-en,** v to buy, to purchase

**Käufer, koyf-er,** m purchaser, buyer; customer

**Kaufhaus, kowf-hows,** nt department store

**kaufkräftig,** kowf-kreft-ik, *adj* having purchasing power/disposable income

**käuflich,** koyf-lik, *adj* for sale, purchasable

**kauflustig,** kouf-loost-ik, *adj* inclined to buy

**Kaufmann,** kowf-mahnn, *m* dealer, merchant

**Kaugummi,** kow-goom-ee, *m* chewing gum

**kaum,** kowm, *adv* hardly, scarcely, barely

**Kaution,** kowts-yohn, *f* security, bail

**keck,** keck, *adj* bold, daring; impudent, cheeky

**Kegel,** kay-gel, *m* skittle; cone

**Kegelbahn,** kay-gel-bahn, *f* skittle-alley

**kegeln,** kay-geln, *v* to play skittles; to bowl

**Kehle,** kayl-e, *f* throat, gullet

**Kehlkopf,** kayl-kop'f, *m* larynx

**kehren,** kayr-en, *v* to sweep; to turn (over)

**Kehrseite,** kayr-zy-te, *f* reverse; wrong side

**keifen,** ky-fen, *v* to chide, to scold, to squabble

**Keil,** kile, *m* wedge; key; **–riemen,** *m* fan belt

**Keim,** kime, *m* germ; seed-bud; ovum

**keimen,** ky-men, *v* to germinate, to sprout

**keine(r/s),** kyn-e(r/s), *pron* no, not a, not any

**keinerlei,** ky-ner-ly, *adj* not of any kind

**keinesfalls,** ky-nes-fahls, *adv* on no account

**keineswegs,** ky-nes-vaygs, *adv* by no means

**Keks,** kayks, *m* biscuit

**Kelch,** kelk, *m* goblet, cup; chalice

**Kelle,** kel-e, *f* scoop, ladle

**Keller,** kel-er, *m* cellar, basement; vault

**Kellner,** kel-ner, *m* waiter

**keltern,** kelt-ern, *v* to press (grapes)

**kennen,** ken-en, *v* to know, to be acquainted with; **–lernen,** *v* to get to know; **sich –lernen,** *v* to get to know each other; to meet

**Kenner,** ken-er, *m* expert, connoisseur

**Kenntnis,** kent-niss, *f* knowledge, information

**Kennzeichen,** ken-tsy-ken, *nt* sign, mark

**kennzeichnen,** ken-tsy-k'nen, *v* to characterize

**kentern,** kent-ern, *v* to capsize

**Keramik,** kay-rahm-ik, *f* ceramics; pottery

**Kerbe,** kair-be, *f* notch

**Kerker,** kairk-er, *m* jail, prison, dungeon

**Kerl,** kairl, *m* fellow, chap; individual

**Kern,** kairn, *m* kernel, pip, nucleus, pith; **–energie,** *f* nuclear energy

**kerngesund,** kairn-ge-zoont, *adj* thoroughly healthy

**kernig,** kairn-ik, *adj* full of pips; pithy; solid, robust

**kernlos,** kairn-lohs, *adj* seedless

**Kerze,** kairt-se, *f* candle, taper

**kerzengerade,** kairt-sen-ge-rad-e, *adj* straight as an arrow

**Kerzenständer,** kairt-sen-shtend-er, *m* candleholder

**Kessel,** kes-el, *m* kettle; cauldron; boiler

**Kette,** ket-e, *f* chain; range (of mountains)

**ketten,** ket-en, *v* to chain

**Ketzer,** ket-ser, *m* heretic

**Ketzerei,** ket-se-ry, *f* heresy

**keuchen,** koy-ken, *v* to gasp, to pant, to wheeze

**Keuchhusten,** koyk-hoost-en, *m* whooping-cough

**Keule,** koyl-e, *f* club, cudgel; leg (of meat)

**keusch,** koysh, *adj* chaste, pure, immaculate

**Kfz.,** kah eff tset, *abbr* **Kraftfahrzeug**

**kg,** *abbr* **Kilogramm**

**kichern,** kik-ern, *v* to giggle, to titter, to chuckle

**Kiefer,** keef-er, *m* jaw (-bone); *f* pine, fir

**Kiel,** keel, *m* quill(-pen); float (angling); keel

**Kieme,** keem-e, *f* gills

**Kies,** kees, *m* gravel

**Kieselstein,** keez-el-shtine, *m* pebble

**kikeriki,** keek-e-reek-ee,

*interj* cock-a-doodle-doo

**Kilo(gramm), keel**-oh (-grahmm), *nt* kilo(gram)

**Kilometer, keel**-oh-mayt-er, *m* kilometre; **–zähler,** *m* mileometer, odometer

**Kind,** kint, *nt* child

**Kinderei,** kin-de-ry, *f* childishness, nonsense

**Kindergarten, kin**-der-gahr-ten, *m* nursery school

**Kindergeld, kin**-der-gelt, *nt* child benefit

**Kinderheim, kin**-der-hime, *nt* children's home

**Kindermädchen, kin**-der-maid-*ken*, *nt* nanny

**Kinderwagen, kin**-der-vahg-en, *m* pram

**kinderleicht, kin**-der-ly'kt, *adj* very easy

**Kinderzimmer, kin**-der-tsim-er, *nt* nursery

**Kindheit, kint**-hite, *f* childhood, infancy

**kindisch, kin**-dish, *adj* childish; foolish

**kindlich, kint**-lik, *adj* childlike; simple

**Kinn,** kin, *nt* chin, lower jaw

**Kino, keen**-oh, *nt* cinema

**Kiosk, kee**-osk, *m* kiosk

**kippen, kip**-en, *v* to tilt, to tip (over), to lose one's balance

**Kirche, keerk**-e, *f* church

**Kirchenchor, keerk**-en-kor, *m* church choir

**Kirchengemeinde, keerk**-en-ge-mine-de, *f* parish

**Kirchhof, keerk**-hohf, *m* churchyard, cemetery

**Kirchturm, keerk**-toorm, *m* steeple, spire

**Kirmes, keerm**-es, *f* country fair

**Kirsche, keersh**-e, *f* cherry

**Kissen, kis**-en, *nt* cushion, pillow; **–bezug,** *m* pillowcase

**Kiste, kist**-e, *f* box, case, chest

**Kitsch,** kitsh, *m* kitsch

**kitschig, kitsh**-ik, *adj* kitschy, trashy

**Kitt,** kit, *m* putty; cement

**Kittel, kit**-el, *m* smock, overall, frock

**kitten, kit**-en, *v* to cement; to putty

**kitzelig, kit**-sel-ik, *adj* ticklish; sensitive; delicate

**kitzeln, kit**-seln, *v* to tickle, to itch

**klaffen, klahff**-en, *v* to gape, to yawn

**kläffen, klef**-en, *v* to bark, to yap, to yelp

**Klage, klahg**-e, *f* complaint, wailing, lamentation; legal action

**klagen, klahg**-en, *v* to complain, to wail; to take legal action

**Kläger, klayg**-er, *m* complainant, plaintiff

**kläglich, klayk**-lik, *adj* plaintive; lamentable

**Klammer, klahmm**-er, *f* clasp; peg; bracket

**klammern, klahmm**-ern, *v*

to clasp; to cramp; **sich – (an),** *v* to cling (to)

**Klang,** klahng, *m* sound, ring, tone

**Klappe, klahpp**-e, *f* flap, tray; valve

**klappen, klahpp**-en *v* to click; to tally; to work well

**klapperig, klahpp**-er-ik, *adj* rattling, shaky

**klappern, klahpp**-ern, *v* to rattle, to clatter

**Klapperschlange, klahpp**-er-shlahng-e, *f* rattle-snake

**Klapperstorch, klahpp**-er-shtork, *m* stork

**Klappstuhl, klahpp**-shtool, *m* folding chair

**Klaps,** klahps, *m* tap, slap; bang

**klar,** klar, *adj* clear, lucid; transparent

**klären, klair**-en, *v* to clarify; to purify; to become clear

**Klarheit, klar**-hite, *f* clarity, brightness

**Klarinette, klah**-ree-net-e, *f* clarinet

**klarlegen, klar**-layg-en, *v* to clarify, to explain

**klarmachen, klar**-mah-ken, *v* **jdm. etw –,** to make sth clear to sb

**Klarsichtfolie, klar**-zikt-foh-lee-e, *f* cling film; transparent film

**Klärung, klair**-oong, *f* clarification

**Klasse, klahss**-e, *f* class; division

**Klassik, klahss**-ik, *f* classic period

**klassisch, klahss**-ish, *adj* classical

**Klatsch, klahtsh**, *m* gossip

**klatschen, klahtsh**-en, *v* to clap; to smack; to gossip

**klatschnaß, klahtsh**-nahss, *adj* soaked to the skin

**Klaue, klow**-e, *f* claw, talon, fang

**klauen, klow**-en, *v* to pinch

**Klausel, klow**-zel, *f* clause, proviso

**Klavier, klah**-veer, *nt* piano(forte)

**kleben, klayb**-en, *v* to adhere, to stick, to affix

**klebrig, klayb**-rik, *adj* adhesive, sticky, gluey

**Klebstoff, klayp**-shtof, *m* glue, adhesive

**kleckern, kleck**-ern, *v* to slobber, to make a mess

**Klecks, klecks**, *m* ink-blot, blotch

**klecksen, kleck**-sen, *v* to make blots

**Klee, klay**, *m* clover, shamrock; **–blatt**, *nt* cloverleaf

**Kleid, klite**, *nt* dress, garment, gown; **–er**, *pl* clothes, dresses

**kleiden, kly'd**-en, *v* to dress, to clothe

**Kleiderbügel, kly'd**-er-bEEg-el, *m* coat hanger

**Kleiderschrank, kly'd**-er-shrahnk, *m* wardrobe

**kleidsam, kly'd**-sahm, *adj* becoming, fitting

**Kleidung, kly'd**-oong, *f* clothing; **–stück**, *nt* garment

**klein, kline**, *adj* small, little; short, insignificant

**Kleingeld, kline**-gelt, *nt* (small) change

**Kleinigkeit, kline**-ik-kite, *f* trifle, trivial matter

**kleinlaut, kline**-lowt, *adj* dejected, downcast

**kleinlich, kline**-lik, *adj* petty; narrow-minded

**Kleinod, kline**-oht, *nt* jewel, gem, treasure

**Kleinstadt, kline**-shtaht, *f* small town

**Kleister, kly**-ster, *m* paste

**Klemme, klem**-e, *f* clamp, vice; tight corner

**klemmen, klem**-en, *v* to squeeze, to pinch, to jam

**Klempner, klemp**-ner, *m* plumber

**Klette, klet**-e, *f* bur(dock)

**klettern, klet**-ern, *v* to climb, to clamber

**Klima, kleem**-ah, *nt* climate

**Klimaanlage, kleem**-ah-ahnn-lah-ge, *f* air-conditioning

**klimpern, klim**-pern, *v* to jingle, to tinkle; to strum

**Klinge, kling**-e, *f* blade

**Klingel, kling**-el, *f* bell

**klingeln, kling**-eln, *v* to ring a bell

**klingen, kling**-en, *v* to sound, to resound

**Klinik, klee**-nik, *f* clinic, hospital

**Klinke, klink**-e, *f* door-handle; latch; catch

**Klippe, klip**-e, *f* cliff, crag; reef, rock

**klirren, kleerr**-en, *v* to clatter, to clash, to rattle

**Klo, kloh**, *nt fam* loo

**klobig, klohb**-ik, *adj* rude, rough, clumsy

**klopfen, klop**-fen, *v* to knock, to tap, to rap, to beat

**Klops, klops**, *m* meatball

**Kloß, klohs**, *m* dumpling; lump, clod

**Kloster, klohs**-ter, *nt* cloister, monastery, convent

**Klotz, klots**, *m* log, block; trunk/stump (of tree)

**klotzig, klot**-sik, *adj* clumsy, heavy; enormous

**Klub, kloop**, *m* club

**Kluft, klooft**, *f* gap, cleft, chasm; *fam* clothes

**klug, klook**, *adj* clever; sensible; prudent; wise

**Klugheit, klook**-hite, *f* prudence, wisdom

**Klumpen, kloomp**-en, *m* lump, mass; clot

**km., abbr** Kilometer

**knabbern, k'nahbb**-ern, *v* to gnaw, to nibble

**Knabe, k'nahb**-e, *m* boy, lad

**knabenhaft, k'nahb**-en-hahft, *adj* boyish

**knacken, k'nahck**-en, *v* to crack, to snap

**Knacks, k'nahcks**, *m* crack

**Knackwurst, k'nahck-**
voorst, *f* smoked sausage

**Knall, k'nahll,** *m* crack,
crash, bang

**Knallbonbon, k'nahll-**bon-
bong, *nt* (Christmas)
cracker

**knallen, k'nahll-en,** *v* to
crack

**knallrot, k'nahll-roht,** *adj*
bright red

**knapp, k'nahpp,** *adj* tight
(-fitting); scanty; narrow

**Knappheit, k'nahpp-**hite, *f*
tightness; scantiness

**knarren, k'narr-en,** *v* to
creak, to grate, to squeak

**knattern, k'nahtt-ern,** *v* to
rattle, to crackle

**Knäuel, k'noy-**el, *nt* ball (of
thread); tangle; throng

**knauserig, k'nowz-**er-ik, *adj*
mean, stingy

**knausern, k'nowz-**ern, *v* to
be mean/stingy

**Knebel, k'nayb-**el, *m* gag;
toggle; catch

**knebeln, k'nayb-**eln, *v* to
gag

**Knecht, k'nekt,** *m* servant;
labourer

**Kneipe, k'ny-**pe, *f* pub, inn

**kneten, k'nayt-en,** *v* to
knead, to mix, to mould

**Knick, k'nik,** *m* break, bend;
flaw

**knicken, k'nik-en,** *v* to
crack, to break, to split

**Knicks, k'niks,** *m* curtsy

**knicksen, k'nik-sen,** *v* to
curtsy

**Knie, k'nee,** *nt* knee

**knien, k'nee-**en/k'neen, *v* to
kneel

**Kniff, k'nif,** *m* pinch(ing);
fold; knack, trick

**knipsen, k'nip-sen,** *v* to
punch (tickets); to snap

**Knirps, k'neerps,** *m* little
boy, nipper

**knirschen, k'neersh-**en, *v*
to creak; to gnash

**knistern, k'nist-ern,** *v* to
crackle, to rustle

**knitterfrei, k'nit-**ter-fry, *adj*
non-crease

**knittern, k'nit-**tern, *v* to
crease

**Knoblauch, k'nohp-**lowk, *m*
garlic; **–zehe,** *f* clove of
garlic

**Knöchel, k'nerk-**el, *m*
knuckle; ankle

**Knochen, k'nok-**en, *m* bone

**knochig, k'nok-**ik, *adj* bony

**Knödel, k'nerd-**el, *m*
dumpling

**Knolle, k'nohll-**e, *f* bulb,
tuber

**Knopf, k'nopf,** *m* button,
knob

**knöpfen, k'nerp-**fen, *v* to
button

**Knopfloch, k'noppf-**lok, *nt*
button-hole

**Knorpel, k'norp-**el, *m*
cartilage, gristle

**knorpelig, k'norp-**el-ik, *adj*
gristly

**knorrig, k'norr-**ik, *adj*

gnarled, knotted

**Knospe, k'nosp-**e, *f* bud

**knospen, k'nosp-**en, *v* to
bud, to shoot, to sprout

**Knoten, k'noht-**en, *m* lump;
knot; node; plot

**knoten, k'noht-**en, *v* to
knot

**knüpfen, k'nEEpp-**fen, *v* to
tie, to knot

**Knüppel, k'nEEpp-**el, *m*
cudgel, club

**knurren, k'noorr-**en, *v* to
growl, to snarl

**knurrig, k'noorr-**ik, *adj*
snarling, growling;
grumbling

**knusperig, k'noosp-**er-ik, *adj*
crisp

**k.o.,** kah oh, *adj* knocked-
out; exhausted

**Kobold, koh-**bolt, *m* goblin,
imp

**Koch, kok,** *m* cook; **–buch,**
*nt* cookery book

**kochen, kok-**en, *v* to cook;
to boil

**Kochgelegenheit, kok-**ge-
laig-en-hite, *f* cooking
facilities

**Kochgeschirr, kok-**ge-
sheerr, *nt* cooking utensils

**Kochplatte, kok-**plahtt-e, *f*
hot-plate

**Kochtopf, kok-**topf, *m*
saucepan

**Köder, ker-**der, *m* bait, lure

**Koffein, koh-fay-een,** *nt*
caffeine

**koffeinfrei, koh-fay-een-**fry,
*adj* decaffeinated

**Koffer**, kof-*er*, *m* suitcase; **–kuli**, *m* trolley; **–radio**, *nt* portable radio; **–raum**, *m* boot

**Kohl**, kohl, *m* cabbage

**Kohle**, kohl-*e*, *f* coal, carbon; charcoal

**Kohlengrube**, kohl-*en*-groob-*e*, *f* coal-pit

**kohlensäurehaltig**, kohl-*en*-zoyr-*e*-hahll-tik, *adj* carbonated

**Kohlkopf**, kohl-kopf, *m* cabbage

**kohlrabenschwarz**, kohl-**rabh**-en-shvahrts, *adj* pitch black

**Kohlrübe**, kohl-**rEEb**-*e*, *f* turnip

**Koje**, koh-*ye*, *f* berth, small cabin

**Kokain**, koh-kah-**een**, *nt* cocain

**Kokosnuß**, koh-kos-nooss, *f* coconut

**Koks**, kohks, *m* coke

**Kolben**, kolb-*en*, *m* butt (of gun); piston

**Kolik**, kohl-eek, *f* colic

**Kollege**, kol-**ayg**-*e*, *m* colleague

**Kollegium**, kol-**layg**-*e*-oomm, *nt* staff; working party

**Koller**, kol-*er*, *m* rage, frenzy

**Kolonie**, kol-on-ee, *f* colony

**Kolonne**, ko-**lon**-*e*, *f* convoy

**kolossal**, kol-os-**ahl**, *adj* colossal, enormous, huge

**Kombination**, kom-bee-nahts-**yohn**, *f* combination

**kombinieren**, kom-bee-neer-*en*, *v* to combine

**Komfort**, kom-**for**, *m* luxury

**Komiker**, koh-mik-*er*, *m* comedian; comic actor/author

**komisch**, kohm-ish, *adj* funny, comical

**Komitee**, koh-mit-**tay**, *nt* committee

**Komma**, kom-mah, *nt* comma

**Kommando**, kom-**mahnn**-doh, *nt* (word of) command, order; detachment

**kommen**, kom-*en*, *v* to come; **zu sich –**, *v* to come round; **– lassen**, *v* to send for

**Kommission**, kom-miss-**yohn**, *f* commission; committee

**Kommode**, kom-**mohd**-*e*, *f* chest of drawers

**Kommunikation**, kom-moo-nee-kahts-**yohn**, *f* communication

**Kommunismus**, kom-moo-nis-mooss, *m* communism

**kommunistisch**, kom-moo-nis-tish, *adj* communist

**Komödie**, kom-**erd**-ee-*e*, *f* comedy, play

**Kompagnon**, kom-pahnn-yong, *m* partner (in business)

**Kompaß**, kom-pahss, *m* compass

**komplex**, kom-**plex**, *adj* complicated

**Kompliment**, kom-plee-**ment**, *nt* compliment

**kompliziert**, kom-plee-**tseert**, *adj* complicated

**Komplott**, kom-**plot**, *nt* plot, conspiracy

**komponieren**, kom-pohn-eer-*en*, *v* to compose

**Komponist**, kom-pohn-**ist**, *m* composer

**Kompott**, kom-**pot**, *nt* stewed fruit

**Kompromiß**, kom-pro-**miss**, *m* compromise

**kompromittieren (sich)**, kom-proh-mit-eer-*en* (zik), *v* to expose oneself

**Kondition**, kon-deets-**yohn**, *f* condition; stamina; state of health

**Konditor**, kon-**deet**-ohr, *m* pastry-cook

**Konditorei**, kon-deet-oh-**ry**, *f* patisserie, cake shop; café

**Kondom**, kon-**dohm**, *nt* condom

**Konfektion**, kon-fekts-**yohn**, *f* ready-to-wear clothing

**Konferenz**, kon-fair-**ents**, *f* conference; **–zentrum**, *nt* congress centre

**Konfession**, kon-fes-**yohn**, *f* denomination

**Konfitüre**, kon-fee-**tEEr**-*e*, *f* jam

**Konflikt**, kon-**flikt**, *m* conflict

**Kongreß**, kong-**gres**, *m*

congress

**König,** kern-*ik,* m king

**Königin,** kern-ig-*in,* f queen

**Königreich,** kern-ig-ry'*k,* nt kingdom, realm

**Konkurrent,** kong-koor-**rent,** m competitor

**Konkurrenz,** kong-koor-**rents,** f competition

**konkurrieren,** kong-koor-**reer**-en, v to compete

**Konkurs,** kong-**koors,** m bankruptcy, insolvency

**können,** kern-en, v to be able to, to be capable of; to know how to; to be allowed to

**konsequent,** kon-ze-**kvent,** adj consistent

**Konsequenz,** kon-ze-**kvents,** f consistency; consequence

**konservativ,** kon-zair-vah-**teef,** adj conservative

**Konserve,** kon-**zairv**-e, f tinned/bottled food

**konservieren,** kon-zairv-**eer**-en, v to preserve

**Konsortium,** kon-**zorts**-ee-oomm, nt syndicate; ring

**Konsulat,** kon-zoo-**laht,** nt consulate

**Konsum,** kon-**zoom,** m consumption (of goods)

**Konsument,** kon-zoom-**ent,** m consumer

**Kontinent,** kon-tee-**nent,** m continent

**Konto,** kon-*toh,* nt account

**Kontrolle,** kon-**trol**-e, f control

**Konzept,** kon-**tsept,** nt rough draft; copy; concept

**Konzert,** kon-**tsairt,** nt concert

**Kopf,** kop'*f,* m head; skull; sense

**köpfen,** kerp-*fen,* v to behead; to lop (trees)

**Kopfhaut,** kop'*f*-howt, f scalp

**Kopfkissen,** kop'*f*-kis-en, nt pillow

**Kopfsalat,** kop'*f*-zahll-aht, m (round-headed) lettuce

**Kopfschmerzen,** kop'*f*-shmairts-en, pl headache

**Kopftuch,** kop'*f*-took, nt headscarf

**kopfüber,** kop'*f*-EEb-er, adv head over heels

**Kopfweh,** kop'*f*-vay, nt headache

**Kopie,** koh-**pee,** f copy

**kopieren,** koh-**peer**-en, v to copy

**Kopiergerät,** koh-**peer**-ge-rait, nt photocopier

**Korb,** korp, m basket, hamper, crate

**Kork,** kork, m cork; **−enzieher,** m corkscrew

**Korn,** korn, nt grain; corn

**körnig,** kern-*ik,* adj granular, grainy

**Körper,** kerp-*er,* m body; substance

**körperbehindert,** kerp-er-be-hin-dert, adj disabled

**Körpergeruch,** kerp-er-ge-rook, m body odour

**körperlich,** kerp-er-*lik,* adj

bodily, physical; substantial

**Körperteil,** kerp-er-tile, m part of the body

**korrekt,** kor-**rekt,** adj correct

**Korrektur,** kor-rek-**toor,** f correction

**korrigieren,** kor-ree-**geer**-en, v to correct; to revise

**Korruption,** kor-roopts-**yohn,** f corruption

**Kosename,** koh-*ze*-nahm-e, m pet name

**Kosmetik,** kos-**may**-tik, f cosmetics

**Kost,** kost, f food; diet

**kostbar,** kost-*bar,* adj precious, valuable; splendid

**Kosten,** kost-en, pl cost(s), charges; expenses

**kosten,** kost-en, v to cost; to taste, to try (food)

**Kostenanschlag,** kost-en-ahn-shlahk, m estimate

**kostenlos,** kost-en-lohs, adj free (of charge)

**köstlich,** kerst-*lik,* adj delicious, dainty; precious

**kostspielig,** kost-shpeel-*ik,* adj costly, dear

**Kostüm,** kost-**EEm,** nt costume; suit

**Kot,** koht, m mud, filth; excrement; dung

**Kotelett,** kot-**let,** nt cutlet, chop

**Kontaktlinsen,** kon-**tahkt**-lin-zen, pl contact lenses

**Kotflügel,** koht-**flEEg**-el, m

mud-guard

**kotzen, kot**-sen, *v fam* to
vomit

**Krabbe, krahbb**-*e*, *f* crab,
shrimp

**krabbeln, krahbb**-eln, *v* to
wriggle; to crawl

**krach, krah**k, *interj* bang,
crash, crack

**Krach, krah**k, *m* crash;
smash; *fam* row, quarrel

**krachen, krahk**-en, *v* to
crash; to burst

**krächzen, krek**-tsen, *v* to
croak, to caw

**Kraft, krah**ft, *f* strength,
power; force, validity

**kraft, krah**ft, *prep* by virtue
of

**Kraftfahrzeug, krahft**-fahr-
tsoyk, *nt* motor vehicle

**kräftig, kreft**-ik, *adj* strong,
vigorous, powerful

**kräftigen, kreft**-ig-en, *v* to
strengthen

**Kraftwerk, krahft**-vairk, *nt*
power-station

**Kragen, krahg**-en, *m* collar

**Krähe, kray**-*e*, *f* crow

**krähen, kray**-en, *v* to crow

**Kralle, krahll**-*e*, *f* claw,
talon

**krallen, krahll**-en, *v* to
scratch, to claw

**Kram, krah**m, *m* junk; stuff;
business

**kramen, krahm**-en, *v* to
rummage

**Krampf, krahmp**'f, *m* cramp,
spasm, convulsion

**krampfhaft, krahmp**'f-
haft, *adj* convulsive,
spasmodic

**Kran, krah**n, *m* crane; tap

**krank, krahn**k, *adj* ill, sick,
diseased

**Kranke(r), krahnk**-*e*(r), *m
& f* sick person, patient

**Krankenschein, krahnk**-en-
shine, *m* health insurance
card

**Krankenschwester,
krahnk**-en-shvest-er, *f*
nurse

**kränkeln, krenk**-eln, *v* to be
ill

**kränken, krenk**-en, *v* to
offend, to hurt

**Krankenhaus, krahnk**-en-
hows, *nt* hospital

**Krankenkasse, krahnk**-en-
kahss-*e*, *f* health insurance

**Krankenpfleger, krahnk**-
en-p'flayg-er, *m* nurse,
orderly

**Krankenwagen, krahnk**-en-
wahg-en, *m* ambulance

**krankhaft, krahnk**-hahft,
*adj* morbid, diseased;
pathological

**Krankheit, krahnk**-hite, *f*
illness, disease

**kränklich, krenk**-lik, *adj*
sickly, delicate

**Kranz, krahn**ts, *m* wreath,
garland

**kratzen, krahts**-en, *v* to
scratch, to scrape; to
scrawl

**kraus, krows**, *adj* curly,
frizzled; crisp

**kräuseln, kroyz**-eln, *v* to

curl, to frizzle, to crimp

**Kraut, krow**t, *nt* plant, herb;
cabbage

**Krawall, krah**-vahll, *m* riot;
brawl

**Krawatte, krah-vahtt**-*e*, *f* tie

**Krebs, krapes**, *m* crayfish;
*med* cancer

**Kreide, kry**-de, *f* chalk

**Kreis, kry**ce, *m* circle;
district, parish

**kreischen, kry**-shen, *v* to
scream, to yell, to shriek

**Kreisel, kry**-zel, *m* spinning-
top

**kreisen, kry**-zen, *v* to circle,
to revolve, to orbit

**kreisförmig, krice**-ferm-ik,
*adj* circular

**Kreislauf, krice**-lowf, *m*
circulation

**Kreissäge, krice**-zayg-*e*, *f*
circular-saw

**Kreisstadt, krice**-shtahtt, *f*
county-town

**krepieren, kray-peer**-en, *v*
to die, to perish

**Krepp, krep**, *m* crepe

**Kresse, kres**-*e*, *f* cress

**Kreta, kray**-tah, *nt* Crete

**Kreuz, kroyts**, *nt* cross;
(small of the) back

**kreuzen, kroyts**-en, *v* to
cross

**Kreuzfahrt, kroyts**-fahrt, *f*
crusade

**Kreuzgang, kroyts**-gahng, *m*
cloister; cutting

**kreuzigen, kroyts**-ig-en, *v*
to crucify

**Kreuzverhör, kroyts**-fair-her, nt, cross-examination

**Kreuzzug,** kroyts-tsook, m crusade, Holy War

**kribbeln,** krib-eln, v to prickle, to tingle; to swarm

**kriechen,** kreek-en, v to creep, to crawl

**Krieg,** kreek, m war(fare)

**kriegen,** kreeg-en, v fam to receive, to get

**kriegerisch,** kreeg-er-ish, adj warlike, martial

**Kriegserklärung,** kreeks-er-klair-oong, f declaration of war

**Kriegsgefangene(r),** kreeks-ge-fahng-en-e(r), m & f prisoner of war

**Kriegsgefangenschaft,** kreeks-ge-fahng-en-shaft, f captivity

**Kriegsgericht,** kreeks-ge-rikt, nt courtmartial

**Kriegsgesetz,** kreeks-ge-sets, nt martial law

**Kriegszustand,** kreeks-tsoo-shtahnt, m state of war

**Kriminalbeamte(r),** krim-in-ahl-be-ahmt-e(r), m detective

**kriminell,** krim-in-ell, adj criminal

**Krimi,** kree-mee, m thriller

**Krippe,** krip-e, f manger, crib; creche

**Krise,** kree-ze, f crisis

**Kritik,** krit-eek, f criticism, critique, review

**Kritiker,** krit-ik-er, m critic, reviewer

**kritisieren,** krit-eez-eer-en, v to criticise

**kritzeln,** krit-seln, v to scratch; to scribble

**Krokodil,** kroh-koh-deel, nt crocodile

**Krone,** krohn-e, f crown

**krönen,** krern-en, v to crown

**Kronprinz,** krohn-prints, m Crown Prince

**Kröte,** krert-e, f toad

**Krücke,** krEEck-e, f crutch; crook

**Krug,** krook, m jug, pitcher

**krümelig,** krEEm-el-ik, adj crumbly, crumbling

**krumm,** kroomm, adj crooked, bent, curved

**krümmen,** krEEmm-en, v to wind, to twist, to bend

**Krümmung,** krEEmm-oong, f curve, bend

**Krüppel,** krEEpp-el, m cripple, deformed person

**Kruste,** kroost-e, f crust; crackling

**Kuba,** koo-bah, nt Cuba

**Kübel,** kEEb-el, m vat, bucket

**Küche,** kEEk-e, f kitchen; cooking

**Kuchen,** kook-en, m cake

**Kuckuck,** kook-kook, m cuckoo

**Kugel,** koog-el, f ball, globe, sphere; bullet

**kugelrund,** koog-el-roont, adj round, spherical

**Kugelschreiber,** koog-el-shry-ber, m biro

**Kuh,** koo, f cow

**kühl,** kEEl, adj cool, fresh; cold, unfeeling

**Kühle,** kEEl-e, f coolness, freshness

**kühlen,** kEEl-en, v to cool

**Kühler,** kEEl-er, m radiator (of car); ice-bucket; **–haube,** f bonnet (of car)

**Kühlschrank,** kEEl-shrahnk, m refrigerator

**kühn,** kEEn, adj bold, brave, intrepid, rash

**Küken,** kEEk-en, nt chick

**kulant,** kool-ahnt, adj fair; obliging

**Kulanz,** kool-ahnts, f fairness, promptness

**Kulisse,** kool-iss-e, f (theatre) scene, wings

**Kult,** koolt, m cult

**Kultur,** koolt-oor, f culture; civilization; cultivation (soil); **–beutel,** m toilet bag

**kulturell,** koolt-oor-ell, adj cultural

**Kultusminister,** koolt-oos-min-ist-er, m minister of education

**Kümmel,** kEEmm-el, m caraway; kümmel (liqueur)

**Kummer,** koomm-er, m grief, sorrow

**kümmerlich,** kEEmm-er-lik, adj wretched, miseable, grievous

**kümmern,** kEEmm-ern, v to concern; sich um etw/jdn **–,** v to look after sth/sb

**kündbar**, KEEnt-bar, *adj* subject to notice; redeemable

**Kunde**, koond-e, *m* customer, client; **–ndienst**, *m* after-sales service

**kundgeben**, koont-gayb-en, *v* to publish, to notify

**Kundgebung**, koont-gayb-oong, *f* manifestation

**kündigen**, KEEnd-ig-en, *v* to give notice; to cancel

**Kundschaft**, koont-shahft, *f* customers, clientele; reconnaissance

**Kundschafter**, koont-shahft-er, *m* scout, spy

**künftig**, KEEnft-ik, *adj* future

**Kunst**, koonst, *f* art; skill, cleverness; **–faser**, *f* synthetic fibre; **–gegenstand**, *m* art object

**Kunstgeschichte**, koonst-ge-shik-te, *f* history of art

**Kunstgewerbe**, koonst-ge-vair-be, *nt* arts and crafts

**Kunstkenner**, koonst-ken-er, *m* art expert, connoisseur

**Künstler**, KEEnst-ler, *m* artist; artiste

**künstlerisch**, KEEnst-ler-ish, *adj* artistic

**künstlich**, KEEnst-lik, *adj* artificial; ingenious

**Kunstsammler**, koonst-sahm-ler, *m* art collector

**Kunstseide**, koonst-zy-de, *f* artificial silk

**Kunststoff**, koonst-shtoff,

*m* synthetic material

**Kunststück**, koonst-shtEEck, *nt* clever trick, feat

**Kunstwerk**, koonst-vairk, *nt* work of art

**kunterbunt**, koont-er-boont, *adj* gaudy, variegated; jumbled

**Kupfer**, koopp-fer, *nt* copper

**Kupferstich**, koopp-fer-shtik, *m* engraving

**Kuppe**, koopp-e, *f* mountain-peak

**Kuppel**, koopp-el, *f* cupola, dome

**kuppeln**, koopp-eln, *v* to pair; to matchmake; *mech* to engage the clutch

**Kupplung**, koopp-loong, *f* clutch

**Kurbel**, koorb-el, *f* crank-handle, winch-handle

**kurbeln**, koorb-eln, *v* to turn a handle, to crank

**Kürbis**, kEErb-iss, *m* pumpkin

**Kur**, koor, *f* cure; stay at a health spa; **–gast**, *m* visitor to a spa

**kurieren**, koor-eer-en, *v* to cure

**Kurort**, koor-ort, *m* health-resort; spa

**Kurpfuscher**, koor-p'foosh-er, *m* quack, charlatan

**Kurs**, koors, *m* rate of exchange; course

**Kursbuch**, koors-book, *nt* (train) timetable

**kurz**, koorts, *adj* short

**Kürze**, kEErt-se, *f* shortness; brevity

**kürzen**, kEErt-sen, *v* to shorten; to cut down

**kurzerhand**, koort-ser-hahnt, *adv* abruptly

**kurzfristig**, koorts-frist-ik, *adj* short-term

**Kurzgeschichte**, koorts-ge-shik-te, *f* short story

**kürzlich**, kEErts-lik, *adv* lately, recently

**Kurzschluß**, koorts-shlooss, *m* short-circuit

**kurzsichtig**, koorts-zikt-ik, *adj* short-sighted

**Kürzung**, kEErts-oong, *f* abridgement

**Kurzwelle**, koorts-vel-le, *f* short wave

**Kusine**, koo-zeen-e, *f* cousin

**Kuß**, kooss, *m* kiss

**küssen**, kEEss-en, *v* to kiss

**Küste**, kEEst-e, *f* coast, beach, shore

**Küster**, kEEst-er, *m* verger, sexton

**Kutsche**, koott-she, *f* coach, carriage

**Kutscher**, koott-sher, *m* coachman

**Kutte**, koott-e, *f* (monk's) habit

**Kuvert**, koo-vair, *nt* envelope, wrapper, cover

**l,** *abbr* **Liter**

**Lache, lah**k-*e,* *f* puddle, pool; laughter

**lächeln, lek-**eln, *v* to smile

**lachen, lah**k-en, *v* to laugh

**lächerlich, lek-**er-lik, *adj* laughable, ludicrous, ridiculous

**Lachs, lah**x, *m* salmon

**Lack, lah**ck, *m* lacquer, varnish

**lackieren, lah**ck-**eer-**en, *v* to lacquer

**Lackleder, lah**ck-laid-er, *nt* patent-leather

**Lade, lah-**de, *f* drawer

**Laden, lah-**den, *m* shop; shutter

**laden, lah-**den, *v* to load, to charge; to invite

**Ladendiebstahl, lah-**den-deep-shtahl, *m* shoplifting

**Ladentisch, lah-**den-tish, *m* counter (in shop)

**Laderaum, lah-**de-rowm, *m* hold (of a ship)

**Ladung, lah-**doong, *f* load, cargo; summons

**Lage, lah-**ge, *f* position, situation

**Lager, lah-**ger, *nt* camp; storehouse; stock

**Lagerhaus, lah-**ger-hows, *nt* warehouse

**lagern, lah-**gern, *v* to be stored/warehoused; to store

**lahm, lah**m, *adj* paralysed, limping, lame

**lähmen, laym-**en, *v* to paralyse, to make lame

**Lähmung, laym-**oong, *f* paralysis

**Laie, ly-**e, *m* layman, novice; outsider

**Laken, lah**k-en, *nt* (linen) sheet; shroud

**Lakritze, lah**ck-**rit-**se, *f* liquorice

**lallen, lah**ll-en, *v* to mumble, to babble

**Lamm, lah**mm, *nt* lamb

**Lampe, lah**mp-*e,* *f* lamp, light

**Lampenfieber, lah**mp-en-feeb-er, *nt* stage-fright

**Lampenschirm, lah**mp-en-sheerm, *m* lampshade

**Land, lah**nt, *nt* land, country, territory; state

**Landebahn, lah**nn-de-bahn, *f* runway

**landeinwärts, lah**nt-ine-vairts, *adv* inland

**landen, lah**nd-en, *v* to land, to disembark

**Landessprache, lah**nn-des-shprahk-*e,* *f* national language

**landesüblich, lah**nn-des-EEp-lik, *adj* customary in a country

**Landesverrat, lah**nn-des-fair-**raht,** *m* treason

**Landeswährung, lah**nn-des-vair-oong, *f* national currency

**Landgericht, lah**nt-ge-rikt, *nt* provincial court

**Landhaus, lah**nt-hows, *nt* country house

**Landkarte, lah**nt-kart-*e,* *f* map

**landläufig, lah**nt-loyf-ik, *adj* customary in a country

**ländlich, lent-**lik, *adj* rural

**Landschaft, lah**nt-shaft, *f* landscape, scenery

**Landsitz, lah**nt-zits, *m*

country-seat, villa

**Landsmann, lahnts**-mahnn, *m* fellow country-man

**Landstraße, lahnt**-shtrahs-e, *f* country road

**Landstreicher, lahnt**-shtry-ker, *m* vagrant

**Landung, lahnd**-oong, *f* landing; **–brücke,** *f* landing-stage

**Landwirt, lahnt**-veert, *m* farmer; **–schaft,** *f* agriculture

**lang, lahng,** *adj* long; tall

**lange, lahng**-e, *adv* (for) a long time

**Länge, leng**-e, *f* length

**langen, lahng**-en, *v* to suffice; to reach, to touch

**Längengrad, leng**-en-graht, *m* degree of longitude

**Langeweile, lahng**-e-vy-le, *f* boredom, tediousness

**langfristig, lahng**-frist-ik, *adj* long-term

**langjährig, lahng**-yair-ik, *adj* (of) long standing

**länglich, leng**-lik, *adj* long, elongated

**längs, lengs,** *adv & prep* along

**langsam, lahng**-zahm, *adj* slow

**längst, lengst,** *adj* longest, *adv* long ago

**langweilen, lahng**-vy-len, *v* to tire, to bore; **sich –,** *v* to be bored

**langweilig, lahng**-vy-lik, *adj* boring, tedious

**Langwelle, lahng**-vel-e, *f* long-wave

**langwierig, lahng**-veer-ik, *adj* lengthy, long lasting

**längstens, leng**-stens, *adv* at the latest

**Lappalie, lahpp**-**ahl**-ye, *f* trifle, petty matter

**Lappen, lahpp**-en, *m* rag, shred; duster

**läppisch, lep**-ish, *adj* foolish, nonsensical

**Lärche, lair**-ke, *f* larch (tree)

**Lärm, lairm,** *m* noise, din

**lärmen, lairm**-en, *v* to make a noise, to clamour

**Larve, lahrf**-e, *f* mask; pretty face; larva, grub

**lassen, lahss**-en, *v* to let, to allow (to); to leave; **etw machen –,** *v* to have sth done

**lässig, less**-ik, *adj* lazy, idle, indolent; neglectful

**Last, lahst,** *f* burden; charge; trouble

**Laster, lahst**-er, *nt* vice

**lasterhaft, lahst**-er-hahft, *adj* vicious, depraved

**Lästermaul, lest**-er-mowl, *nt* scandal-monger

**lästern, lest**-ern, *v* to blaspheme, to slander

**Lästerung, lest**-er-oong, *f* blasphemy; slander

**lästig, lest**-ik, *adj* burdensome, troublesome

**Lastkraftwagen, last**-krahft-vahg-en, *m* heavy-goods vehicle

**Lasttier, lahst**-teer, *nt* beast of burden; drudge

**Lastwagen, lahst**-vah-gen, *m* lorry

**Latein, lah**-tine, *nt* Latin; **–amerika,** *nt* Latin America

**Laterne, lahtt**-airn-e, *f* lantern

**Laternenpfahl, laht**-airn-en-p'fahl, *m* lamp-post

**latschen, laht**-shen, *v* to shuffle along; to slouch

**Latte, lahtt**-e *f* slat; bar

**Latz, lahts,** *m* bib

**lau, low,** *adj* lukewarm, tepid; half-hearted

**Laub, lowp,** *nt* foliage, leaves; **–baum,** *m* deciduous tree

**Laube, lowb**-e, *f* arbour, porch

**Laubfrosch, lowp**-frosh, *m* green frog

**Laubsäge, lowp**-zaig-e, *f* fret-saw

**Lauch, lowk,** *m* leek

**lauern, low**-ern, *v* to lie in wait

**Lauf, lowf,** *m* run(ning); path, track; (gun) barrel

**Laufbahn, lowf**-bahn, *f* career; running track

**Laufbursche, lowf**-boorsh-e, *m* errand-boy

**laufen, lowf**-en, *v* to run; to flow

**Läufer, loyf**-er, *m* runner; narrow carpet; (chess) bishop

**Laufmasche, lowf**-mahsh-er, *f* ladder (in tights)

**Laufwerk,** lowf-*vairk,* *nt* disk drive

**Lauge,** lowg-*e* *f* lye; salt solution

**Laune,** lown-*e,* *f* mood, humour

**launenhaft,** lown-en-haft, *adj* capricious, moody

**launisch,** lown-ish, *adj* moody

**Laus,** lows, *f* louse

**lauschen,** lowsh-en, *v* eavesdrop, to listen

**laut,** lowt, *adj* loud; noisy; *prep* according to

**Laut,** lowt, *m* sound, tone, note

**Laute,** lowt-*e,* *f* lute

**lauten,** lowt-en, *v* to sound; to express, to phrase

**läuten,** loyt-en, *v* to ring, to peal, to tinkle

**lauter,** lowt-er, *adj* pure; *adv* nothing but

**läutern,** loyt-ern, *v* to purify, to chasten, to ennoble

**Lautschrift,** lowt-shrift, *f* phonetic alphabet

**Lautsprecher,** lowt-shprek-er, *m* loudspeaker

**lauwarm,** low-varm, *adj* lukewarm

**Lavendel,** lah-vend-el, *m* lavender

**Lawine,** lah-veen-*e,* *f* avalanche

**Leben,** lay-ben, *nt* life, existence

**leben,** lay-ben, *v* to live, to exist

**lebend,** lay-bent, *adj* living

**lebendig,** lay-bend-ik, *adj* alive, lively; live

**Lebenserwartung,** lay-bens-er-vahrt-oong, *f* life expectancy

**Lebensfreude,** lay-bens-froyd-e, *f* joy of life

**Lebensgefahr,** lay-bens-ge-fahr, *f* mortal danger

**lebensgefährlich,** lay-bens-ge-fair-lik, *adj* extremely dangerous; critical

**Lebensgefährte,** lay-bens-ge-fair-te, *m* partner

**lebensgroß,** lay-bens-grohs, *adj* life-size

**lebenslänglich,** lay-bens-leng-lik, *adj* lifelong

**Lebenslauf,** lay-bens-lowf, *m* curriculum vitae

**Lebenslust,** lay-bens-loost, *f* joy of living; gaiety

**Lebensmittel,** lay-bens-mit-el, *pl* provisions, food; **–vergiftung,** *f* food poisoning

**Lebensunterhalt,** lay-bens-oont-er-hahlt, *m* livelihood

**Lebensversicherung,** lay-bens-fair-zik-er-oong, *f* life insurance

**Lebensweise,** lay-bens-vy-ze, *f* way of life

**lebenswichtig,** lay-bens-vik-tik, *adj* vital

**Lebenszweck,** lay-bens-tsveck, *m* purpose in life

**Leber,** lay-ber, *f* liver

**Leberfleck,** lay-ber-fleck, *m* mole, birth-mark

**Lebertran,** lay-ber-trahn, *m* cod-liver oil

**Leberwurst,** lay-ber-voorst, *f* liver-sausage

**Lebewesen,** lay-be-vaiz-en, *nt* living creature

**Lebewohl,** lay-be-vohl, *nt* farewell

**lebhaft,** laip-hahft, *adj* lively, vivacious

**Lebkuchen,** laip-kook-en, *m* gingerbread

**lechzen,** lek-tsen, *v* to be parched; to yearn for

**leck,** leck, *adj* leaky, leaking

**Leck,** leck, *nt* leak; outlet

**lecken,** leck-en, *v* to lick; to leak

**lecker,** leck-er, *adj* dainty, delicious

**Leckerbissen,** leck-er-bis-en, *m* delicacy; titbit

**Leckerei,** leck-e-ry, *f* delicacy; titbit

**Leckermaul,** leck-er-mowl, *nt* sweet-toothed person

**Leder,** lay-der, *nt* leather; hide

**ledern,** lay-dern, *adj* (made of) leather; leathery, tough

**ledig,** lay-dik, *adj* single, unmarried

**lediglich,** lay-dik-lik, *adv* purely, simply, solely

**leer,** lair, *adj* empty, unoccupied, vacant

**Leere,** lair-*e,* *f* void, vacuum, space

**leeren,** lair-en, *v* to empty, to vacate

**legen,** lay-gen, v to lay, to put; **sich –,** v to lie down; to abate, to die down

**legieren,** lay-geer-en, v to alloy (metals)

**Legierung,** lay-geer-oong, f alloy(ing)

**Legitimation,** lay-geet-eem-ahts-yohn, f proof of identity

**legitimieren (sich),** lay-geet-eem-eer-en (zik), v to prove one's identity

**Lehm,** laim, m loam; clay

**lehmig,** laim-ik, adj loamy, clayey

**Lehne,** lain-e, f (of chair) back ; arm-rest

**lehnen,** lain-en, v to lean, to recline; to prop

**Lehnstuhl,** lain-shtool, m arm-chair, easy-chair

**Lehrbuch,** lair-book, nt text-book

**Lehre,** lair-e, f advice, tuition; apprenticeship; science

**lehren,** lair-en, v to teach, to instruct

**Lehrer,** lair-er, m teacher

**Lehrfach,** lair-fahk, nt subject

**Lehrgang,** lair-gahng, m course (of lessons)

**Lehrling,** lair-ling, m apprentice, beginner

**Lehrmeister,** lair-my-ster, m master

**Lehrplan,** lair-plahn, m curriculum, teaching plan

**lehrreich,** lair-ry'k, adj instructive

**Lehrsatz,** lair-zahts, m proposition; doctrine

**Lehrstuhl,** lair-shtool, m professor's chair

**Lehrzeit,** lair-tsite, f apprenticeship

**Leib,** lipe, m body; belly, abdomen

**Leibgericht,** lipe-ge-rikt, nt favourite dish

**leibhaftig,** lipe-hahft-ik, adj real, personified

**leiblich,** lipe-lik, adj physical; bodily; natural, by birth

**Leibrente,** lipe-rent-e, f life annuity

**Leibwache,** lipe-vak-e, f bodyguard

**Leiche,** ly-ke, f corpse, dead body

**leichenblaß,** ly-ken-blahss, adj deathly pale

**Leichenwagen,** ly-ken-vahg-en, m hearse

**Leichnam,** ly'k-nahm, m corpse

**leicht,** ly'kt, adj light (in weight); easy, light; slight

**Leichtathletik,** ly'kt-aht-lay-tik, f athletics

**leichtfertig,** ly'kt-fairt-ik, adj light-hearted, frivolous

**leichtfüßig,** ly'kt-fEEss-ik, adj light-footed, nimble

**leichtgläubig,** ly'kt-gloyb-ik, adj credulous

**leichtherzig,** ly'kt-hairt-sik, adj light-hearted

**leichthin,** ly'kt-hin, adv lightly

**Leichtigkeit,** ly'kt-ik-kite, f lightness; ease

**leichtlebig,** ly'kt-laib-ik, adj easy-going, happy-go-lucky

**Leichtsinn,** ly'kt-zin, m carelessness, recklessness

**leichtsinnig,** ly'kt-zin-ik, adj careless, reckless

**leid,** lite, adj es tut mir –, I am sorry

**Leid,** lite, nt injury; wrong; harm; grief; pain

**leiden,** ly-den, v to suffer; etw/jdn nicht – können, to dislike sth/sb

**Leiden,** ly-den, nt suffering; illness; –schaft, f passion

**leidenschaftlich,** ly-den-shahft-lik, adj passionate

**leider,** ly-der, interj unfortunately

**leidlich,** lite-lik, adj bearable; passable

**Leier,** ly-er, f lyre; hurdy-gurdy; (same old) story

**Leierkasten,** ly-er-kahst-en, m barrel-organ

**leiern,** ly-ern, v to grind out a tune; to turn a handle

**leihen,** ly-en, v to lend; sich etw –, v to borrow sth

**Leihgebühr,** ly-ge-bEEr, f hire charge

**Leihhaus,** ly-hows, nt pawnshop

**leihweise,** ly-vy-ze, adv on loan

**Leim,** lime, m glue

**leimen,** lime-en, v to glue

**Leine,** line-*e,* f cord, line, thin rope; leash

**Leinen,** line-*en,* nt linen (goods)

**Leintuch,** line-*took,* nt sheet

**Leinwand,** line-*vahnt,* f canvas; screen

**leise,** ly-*ze,* adj soft, gentle, low

**Leiste,** ly-*ste,* f strip; border, skirting; groin

**leisten,** ly-*sten,* v to render, to perform; **sich etw –,** to afford

**Leistung,** ly-*stoong,* f accomplishment; capacity

**leistungsfähig,** ly-*stoongs-fay-ik,* adj efficient

**leiten,** lite-*en,* v to lead, to conduct; to manage

**Leiter,** lite-*er,* m leader, conductor; manager; f ladder, steps

**Leitfaden,** lite-*fahd-en,* m clue

**Leitsatz,** lite-*zahts,* m guiding rule

**Leitung,** lite-*oong,* f lead(ing), conduct(ing); management; **–swasser,** nt tap water

**Lektion,** lekts-**yohn,** f lesson, lecture

**Lektor,** leck-*tohr,* m editor

**Lektüre,** leck-*tEEr-e,* f reading (matter)

**Lende,** lend-*e,* f loin; hip

**lenken,** lenk-*en,* v to turn; to bend; to drive; to direct

**Lenkrad,** lenk-*raht,* nt steering wheel

**Lenkstange,** lenk-shtahng-*e,* f handlebars

**Lepra,** lay-*prah,* f leprosy

**Lerche,** lairk-*e,* f skylark

**lernbegierig, lairn**-be-geer-ik, adj eager to learn

**lernen,** lairn-*en,* v to learn, to study; to serve apprenticeship

**Lesbierin,** les-bee-er-in, f lesbian

**lesbisch,** les-bish, adj lesbian

**Lese,** lay-*ze,* f picking; harvest; vintage

**Lesebrille,** lay-ze-bril-le, f reading glasses

**lesen,** lay-*zen,* v to read

**Leser,** lay-*zer,* m reader

**leserlich,** lay-*zer-lik,* adj legible; easy to read

**Lesezeichen,** lay-ze-tsy-ken, nt bookmark

**letzte(r/s),** lets-te(r/s), adj last; latest, ultimate, final

**letztens,** lets-tens, adv lastly, finally

**letzthin,** letst-hin, adv lately

**leuchten,** loyk-ten, v to shine, to give light

**Leuchter,** loyk-ter, m candlestick; chandelier

**Leuchtfeuer,** loykt-foy-er, nt beacon

**Leuchtturm,** loykt-toorm, m lighthouse

**leugnen,** loyg-nen, v to deny; to retract

**Leumund,** loy-moont, m repute, reputation; fame

**Leumundszeugnis,** loy-moonts-tsoyk-niss, nt character reference

**Leute,** loyt-*e,* pl people

**leutselig,** loyt-zayl-ik, adj affable, condescending

**Lexikon,** lek-see-kohn, nt encyclopedia

**Libelle,** lee-bel-*e,* f dragon-fly

**liberal,** lee-be-**rahl,** adj liberal

**Licht,** likt, nt light; brightness; illumination; **–bild,** nt photograph; transparency

**lichtempfindlich,** likt-emp-find-lik, adj light sensitive

**Lichtschalter,** likt-shahlt-er, m light switch

**Lichtschutzfaktor,** likt-shoots-fahk-tor, m (sun) protection factor

**Lichtstrahl,** likt-strahl, m ray of light

**Lichtung,** likt-oong, f clearing; glade

**Lid,** leet, nt (eye-)lid

**lieb,** leep, adj dear, beloved

**liebäugeln,** leep-oyg-eln, v to ogle

**Liebe,** leeb-*e,* f love, affection, fondness

**Liebelei,** leeb-e-ly, f flirtation

**lieben,** leeb-en, v to love, to be fond of

**liebenswürdig,** leeb-ens-vEErd-ik, adj amiable, lovable

**lieber,** leeb-er, adj dearer;

*adv* rather

**Liebesbrief, leeb**-*es*-breef, *m* love letter

**Liebeserklärung, leeb**-*es*-air-klair-oong, *f* declaration of love

**Liebeskummer, leeb**-*es*-koom-*er*, *m* – **haben**, to be lovesick

**Liebespaar, leeb**-*es*-pahr, *nt* courting couple

**liebevoll, leeb**-*e*-fol, *adj* loving, affectionate; kind-hearted

**liebgewinnen, leep**-ge-vin-en, *v* to become fond of

**liebhaben, leep**-hahb-en, *v* to love, to be fond of

**Liebhaber, leep**-hahb-*er*, *m* lover; connoisseur, enthusiast

**Liebhaberei, leep**-hahb-*e*-ry, *f* hobby

**liebkosen, leep**-koz-en, *v* to caress, to fondle

**lieblich, leep**-lik, *adj* lovely; agreeable, pleasing

**Liebling, leep**-ling, *m* darling, pet; **Lieblings-,** *pref* favourite

**Liebschaft, leep**-shahft, *f* love-affair

**Lied, leet, *nt* song

**liederlich, leed**-*er*-lik, *adj* slovenly; dissolute

**Lieferant, leef**-*er*-ahnt, *m* supplier, contractor

**liefern, leef**-ern, *v* to deliver, to supply

**Lieferung, leef**-*er*-oong, *f* delivery; consignment; supply

**Lieferwagen, leef**-*er*-vah-gen, *m* (delivery) van

**Lieferzeit, leef**-*er*-tsite, *f* delivery time

**liegen, leeg**-en, *v* to lie, to be (situated)

**liegenlassen, leeg**-en-lahs-sen, *v* to leave behind

**Liegesitz, leeg**-*e*-sits, *m* reclining seat

**Liegestuhl, leeg**-*e*-shtool, *m* deck chair

**Liegewagen, leeg**-*e*-vah-gen, *m* couchette

**Liga, leeg**-ah, *f* league

**Likör, le**-ker, *m* liqueur, cordial

**lila, lee**-lah, *adj* lilac (-coloured)

**Lilie, leel**-ee-*e*, *f* lily

**Limonade, lee**-moh-nah-de, *f* lemonade

**Linde, lin**-de, *f* lime tree, linden

**lindern, lin**-dern, *v* to soften; to alleviate, to ease

**Lineal, lin**-e-ahl, *nt* ruler; rule

**Linie, leen**-ee-*e*, *f* line; rule; lineage; **–nflug,** *m* scheduled flight

**Linke, link**-*e*, *f* (political) left

**linkisch, link**-ish, *adj* clumsy, awkward

**links, links, *adv* on/to the left; on the reverse/wrong side

**Linkshänder, links**-hend-*er*, *m* left-handed person

**Linksverkehr, links**-fer-kair, *m* driving on the left

**Linse, lin**-ze, *f* lentil; lens

**Lippe, lip**-*e*, *f* lip; **–nstift,** *m* lipstick

**lispeln, lisp**-eln, *v* to lisp; to murmur; to ripple

**List, list, *f* craftiness, cunning, artifice

**Liste, list**-*e*, *f* list, register, schedule

**listig, list**-ik, *adj* cunning, crafty, wily

**Listigkeit, list**-ik-kite, *f* craftiness

**Liter, lee**-ter, *m & nt* litre

**Literatur, lit**-er-ah-toor, *f* literature

**Litfaßsäule, lit**-fahss-zoyl-*e*, *f* advertising column

**Litze, lit**-ze, *f* braid; flex

**Lizenz, lee**-tsents, *f* license

**Lkw, el kah vay, *abbr* **Lastkraftwagen,** *m* HGV

**Lob, lohp, *nt* praise, applause; good mark

**loben, lohb**-en, *v* to praise

**lobenswert, lohb**-ens-vairt, *adj* praiseworthy

**löblich, lerp**-lik, *adj* laudable, praiseworthy

**Loch, lok, *nt* hole; opening; aperture

**lochen, lok**-en, *v* to perforate

**löcherig, lerk**-*er*-ik, *adj* full of holes, perforated

**Locke, lock**-*e*, *f* curl, lock, ringlet

**locken, lock**-en, *v* to curl; to allure

**Lockenwickler, lock**-en-vik-ler, *m* curler

**locker, lock**-er, *adj* loose; spongy

**lockern, lock**-ern, *v* to loosen; to slacken

**lockig, lock**-ik, *adj* curly

**Lockmittel, lock**-mit-el, *nt* bait; temptation

**lodern, lohd**-ern, *v* to blaze

**Löffel, lerff**-el, *m* spoon; ladle

**löffeln, lerff**-eln, *v* to ladle; to eat with a spoon

**löffelweise, lerff**-el-vy-ze, *adv* by spoonfuls

**Loge, lohzh**-e, *f* (theatre) box; lodge

**Logik, lohg**-ik, *f* logic

**logisch, lohg**-ish, *adj* logical

**Lohn, lohn**, *m* reward; recompense; wage(s)

**lohnen (sich), lohn**-en (zik), *v* to be profitable

**Lohnerhöhung, lohn**-er-her-oong, *f* pay rise

**Lohnsteuer, lohn**-shtoy-er, *f* income tax

**Lokal, loh**-kahl, *nt* premises; restaurant

**Lokomotive, loh-koh-moh-tee**-ve, *f* locomotive

**Lorbeer, lor**-bair, *m* laurel, bay(-tree)

**Lorbeerkranz, lor**-bair-krahnts, *m* laurel-wreath

**Los, lohs**, *nt* lot, lottery-ticket; fate, destiny

**los, lohs**, *adj* loose, slack; **etw – sein**, *v* to be rid of sth; **Was ist –?** What is the matter?

**losbekommen, lohs**-be-kom-en, *v* to loosen

**losbinden, lohs**-bin-den, *v* to untie

**löschen, lersh**-en, *v* to extinguish; to quench; to blot (out); to unload (ship)

**lose, loh**-ze, *adj* loose; movable; dissipated

**Lösegeld, lerz**-e-gelt, *nt* ransom

**losen, loh**-zen, *v* to draw lots, to toss

**lösen, lerz**-en, *v* to loosen; to sever; to (dis)solve; to take (tickets) **sich –**, *v* to come loose; to dissolve; to solve itself

**losfahren, lohs**-fahr-en, *v* to ride/drive off

**losgehen, lohs**-gay-en, *v* to go off; to start

**loskaufen, lohs**-kowf-en, *v* to ransom, to redeem

**loskommen, lohs**-kom-en, *v* to get off; to be set free

**loslassen, lohs**-lahss-en, *v* to let go; to release

**löslich, lers**-lik, *adj* soluble

**losmachen, lohs**-mahk-en, *v* to untie, to undo, to free

**losschießen, lohs**-shees-en, *v* to fire (away); to start firing

**losschrauben, lohs**-shrowb-en, *v* to unscrew

**losspringen, lohs**-shpring-en, *v* to snap off; to jump at

**losstürmen, lohs**-shtEErm-en, *v* to (take by) storm

**lostrennen, lohs**-tren-en, *v* to sever; to unstitch

**Losung, lohz**-oong, *f* casting lots; password

**Lösung, lerz**-oong, *f* solution

**loswerden, lohs**-vaird-en, *v* to get rid of

**losziehen, lohs**-tsee-en, *v* to set out/off

**Lot, loht**, *nt* plumbline

**löten, lert**-en, *v* to solder

**Lotleine, loht**-line-e, *f* plumbline

**Lotse, loht**-se, *m* pilot (ship)

**lotsen, loht**-sen, *v* to pilot; *fam* to drag (sb) along

**Lotterie, lot**-e-ree, *f* lottery

**Lotto, lot**-oh, *nt* national lottery

**Löwe, ler**-ve, *m* lion; **–nmaul**, *nt* snapdragon; **–nzahn**, *m* dandelion

**Luchs, looks**, *m* lynx; artful person

**Lücke, lEEck**-e, *f* gap, hiatus, breach, break

**Luder, lood**-er, *nt* abomination; beast

**Luft, looft**, *f* air; gas; breath; **–ballon**, *m* balloon

**Luftdruck, looft**-droock, *m* air-pressure

**lüften, lEEft**-en, *v* to ventilate; to raise (hat)

**Luftfahrt, looft**-fahrt, *f* aviation

**Luftfracht, looft**-frakt, *f* air freight

**luftig,** looft-*ik, adj* airy;
lofty; light as air

**Luftkissenfahrzeug,** looft-
kis-en-fahr-tsoyk, *nt*
hovercraft

**luftleer,** looft-lair, *adj* void
of air

**Luftlinie,** looft-leen-ye, *f*
bee-line, as the crow flies

**Luftmatratze,** looft-mah-
trah-tse, *f* lilo, air mattress

**Luftpirat,** looft-peer-aht, *m*
hijacker

**Luftpost,** looft-post, *f* air
mail

**Luftpumpe,** looft-poom-pe,
*f* (air) pump

**Luftschloß,** looft-shloss, *nt*
castle in the air

**Luftstoß,** looft-shtos, *m* gust
of wind

**Luftverschmutzung,** looft-
fer-shmoots-oong, *f* air
pollution

**Luftwaffe,** looft-vahff-e, *f*
air force

**Luftzug,** looft-tsook, *m*
draught (of air), air-
current

**Lüge,** lEEg-e, *f* lie, falsehood

**lügen,** lEEg-en, *v* to lie, to
tell lies

**Lügner,** lEEg-ner, *m* liar

**lügnerisch,** lEEg-ner-ish, *adj*
lying, untruthful

**Luke,** look-e, *f* hatchway;
dormer-window

**Lümmel,** lEEmm-el, *m* lout

**Lump,** loomp, *m* rogue

**Lumpen,** loomp-en, *pl* rags

**lumpig,** loomp-ik, *adj*
tattered, shabby; measly

**Lunge,** loong-e, *f* lung

**Lungenentzündung,** loong-
en-ent-tsEEnd-oong, *f*
pneumonia

**lungern,** loong-ern, *v* to
loiter, to hang about

**Lunte,** loont-e, *f* fuse; brush
(fox)

**Lupe,** loop-e, *f* magnifying
glass

**Lust,** loost, *f* desire;
inclination; joy; – **auf/zu
etw haben,** *v* to feel like
doing sth

**Lustbarkeit,** loost-bar-kite, *f*
festivity, revelry

**Lüster,** lEEst-er, *m* lustre,
chandelier

**lüstern,** lEEst-ern, *adj*
longing for; lustful

**lustig,** loost-ik, *adj* happy,
jolly; amusing

**lustlos,** loost-lohs, *adj*
unenthusiastic

**Lustspiel,** loost-shpeel, *nt*
comedy

**lutschen,** loott-shen, *v* to
suck

**Luxus,** loox-ooss, *m* luxury

**Lyrik,** lEEr -ik, *f* lyric poetry,
verse

**machbar, mahk-bar,** *adj*
possible, feasible

**machen, mahk-en,** *v* to
make, to do, to matter

**Machenschaften, mahk-en-**
shahfft-en, *pl*
machination, intrigue

**Macht, mahkt,** *f* might,
power; **–befugnis,** *f*
authority; **–haber,** *m*
person in power

**mächtig, mekt-ik,** *adj*
mighty, powerful,
considerable

**Machtkampf, mahkt-**
kahmpf, *m* power struggle

**Machtstellung, mahkt-**
shtell-oong, *f* position of
power

**Machtwechsel, mahkt-veks-**
el, *m* change of power

**Mädchen, mait-ken,** *nt* girl,
maid, maiden

**Made, mahd-e,** *f* maggot,
grub, mite

**Mädel, maid-el,** *nt fam* girl

**madig, mahd-ik,** *adj*
maggoty, worm-eaten;
**jdm etw – machen,** *v* to
put sb off sth

**mag, mahg, (from mögen)**
likes, may

**Magen, mahg-en,** *m*
stomach; **–geschwür,** *nt*
stomach ulcer;
**–schmerzen,** *pl* stomach
pains

**mager, mahg-er,** *adj* lean,
thin

**Magermilch, mahg-er-milk,** *f*
skimmed milk

**Magistrat, mahgg-ist-raht,**
*m* town-council,
corporation; **–ur,** *f*
municipal council

**Mahagoni, mah-hah-gohn-**
ee, *nt* mahogany

**mähen, may-en,** *v* to mow,
to cut (grass), to reap

**Mahl, mahl,** *nt* meal, feast

**mahlen, mahl-en,** *v* to grind,
to mill

**Mahlzeit, mahl-tsite,** *f* meal,
repast

**Mähne, mayn-e,** *f* mane;
*fam* head of hair

**mahnen, mahn-en,** *v* to
remind, to admonish

**Mahnung, mahn-oong,** *f*
warning

**Mai, my,** *m* May;
**–glöckchen,** *nt* lily-of-the-
valley; **–käfer,** *m*
cockchafer, May bug

**Mailand, my-lahnt,** *nt*
Milan

**Mais, mice,** *m* maize, Indian
corn; **–kolben,** *m* corn (on
cob)

**makaber, ma-kahb-er,** *adj*
macabre

**Makel, mahk-el,** *m* stain,
blot; blemish

**makellos, mahk-el-lohs,** *adj*
immaculate

**Mäkelei, mayk-e-ly,** *f* fault
finding

**mäkeln, mayk-eln,** *v* to find
fault, to carp

**Makler, mahk-ler,** *m* broker,
commission-agent

**Makrele, mahk-rayl-e,** *f*
mackerel

**Makrone, mahk-rohn-e,** *f*
macaroon

**Makulatur, mahk-oo-laht-**
oor, *f* waste-paper; *fig*
rubbish

**Mal, mahl,** *nt* mole,

(birth)mark; time(s)

**malen, mahl**-en, *v* to paint, to depict

**Maler, mahl**-er, *m* painter, artist

**Malerei,** mahl-e-**ry**, *f* (*art of*) painting

**malerisch, mahl**-er-ish, *adj* picturesque, artistic

**Malheur,** mahl-er, *nt* misfortune, accident

**Mallorca,** mahl-**or**-kah, *nt* Majorca

**Malz,** mahlts, *nt* malt; **–bier,** *nt* malt beer; **–kaffee,** *m* malt coffee; coffee substitute

**Mama, mah**-mah, *f* mum

**man,** mahnn, *pron* one, people, they

**Manager, man**-edsh-er, *m* manager

**manch(e/er/es), mahnnk**(-e/er/es), *pron* many (a)

**mancherlei,** mahnnk-er-**ly**, *adj* different (kinds of), many, various, diverse

**manchmal, mahnnk**-mahl, *adv* sometimes

**Mandarine,** mahnn-dah-**reen**-e, *f* tangerine

**Mandat,** mahnn-**daht**, *nt* mandate, authorization; decree

**Mandel, mahnn**-del, *f* almond; tonsil

**Mangel, mahng**-el, *m* want, lack, scarcity, absence, shortcoming; **–erscheinung,** *f* shortage; *med* deficiency symptom

**mangelhaft, mahng**-el-hahft, *adj* defective, imperfect, insufficient

**mangeln, mahng**-eln, *v* to be wanting (in)

**mangels, mahng**-els, *prep* for lack of

**Mango, mahng**-goh, *f* mango

**Manie,** mahnn-ee, *f* mania

**Manier,** mahnn-**eer**, *f* manner, mode, fashion; **–en,** *pl* manners

**manierlich,** mahnn-**eer**-lik, *adj* well-mannered, well-bred; polite

**Manifest,** mahnn-ee-**fest**, *nt* manifesto

**Manko, mahng**-koh, *nt* deficiency, shortage; shortness

**Mann,** mahnn, *m* man; husband; **–esalter,** *nt* manhood; **–schaft,** *f* crew, (ship's) company; team; gang of men

**Männchen, men**-ken, *nt* little man, manikin; male animal

**Mannequin, mahnn**-e-kang, *nt* (fashion) model

**mannhaft, mahnn**-hahfft, *adj* manly, virile, brave

**mannigfach, mahnn**-ik-fahk, *adj* manifold, varied

**mannigfaltig, mahnn**-ik-fahlt-ik, *adj* manifold, multifarious

**männlich, men**-lik, *adj* male, masculine

**Mansarde,** mahnn-**zard**-e, *f* attic, garret

**manschen, mahnn**-shen, *v* *fam* to mess around

**Manschette,** mahnn-**shet**-e, *f* cuff, wristband; **–nknopf,** *m* cuff-link

**Mantel, mahnn**-tel, *m* mantle, coat, cloak; casing

**Manufaktur,** mahnn-oo-fahck-**toor**, *f* factory; (textile) mill; **–waren,** *pl* manufactured goods (especially textiles)

**Manuskript,** mahnn-oo-**skript**, *nt* manuscript

**Mappe, mahpp**-e, *f* portfolio, album, satchel

**Marathon, mah**-rah-tohnn, *m* marathon

**Märchen, mair**-ken, *nt* fairy-tale, fable, romance; **–prinz,** *m* Prince Charming

**märchenhaft, mair**-ken-hahft, *adj* legendary, like a fairy-tale

**Margarine,** mahr-gah-**ree**-ne, *f* margarine

**Marienkäfer,** mah-**ree**-en-kayf-er, *m* lady-bird

**Marihuana,** mah-ree-**hwah**-nah, *nt* marijuana

**Marine,** mah-**reen**-e, *f* navy, fleet

**marinieren,** mah-ree-**neer**-en, *v* to pickle, to marinate

**Mark,** mark, *nt* marrow; pith; vigour; *f* (German) mark

**markant,** mark-**ahnt**, *adj*

clear-cut, striking, marked

**Marke, mark**-*e*, *f* token, sign; stamp; brand; **–nartikel**, *m* proprietary article

**markieren, mark**-eer-en, *v* to emphasize; to pretend

**Markstein, mark**-shtine, *m* milestone; boundary stone; epoch

**Markt, markt**, *m* market; fair; trade, business; **–bude**, *f* market-stall; **–flecken**, *m* market-town; **–forschung**, *f* market research; **–lücke**, *f* gap in the market; **–platz**, *m* market-place; **–wirtschaft**, *f* market economy

**Marmelade, mar**-me-**lahd**-*e*, *f* jam

**Marmor, mar**-mohr, *m* marble; **–bild**, *nt* marble statue

**Marokko, mah**-**rock**-oh, *nt* Morocco

**Marone, mah**-**rohn**-*e*, *f* sweet chestnut

**Marsch, marsh**, *m* march; *f* marshy land

**marschbereit, marsh**-be-rite, *adj* ready to march

**marschieren, marsh**-eer-en, *v* to march

**Marter, mar**-ter, *f* torture, torment, agony

**martern, mar**-tern, *v* to torture, to torment, to put on the rack

**Märtyrer, mairt**-EE-rer, *m*

martyr; **–tum**, *nt* martyrdom

**März, mairts**, *m* March

**Marzipan, mar**-tsee-pahn, *nt* marzipan

**Masche, mahsh**-*e*, *f* mesh, stitch

**Maschine, mahsh**-ee-ne, *f* machine, engine

**maschinell, mahsh**-ee-**nel**, *adj* machine-made, mechanical

**Maschinenbauer, mahsh**-ee-nen-**bow**-er, *m* mechanical engineer

**Maschinengewehr, mahsh**-ee-nen-gay-ver, *nt* machine gun

**Maschinenschaden, mahsh**-ee-nen-shah-den, *m* mechanical fault

**Masern, mah**-zern, *pl* measles

**Maß, mahss**, *nt* measure; rate, proportion; extent; size; *f* litre (of beer)

**Masse, mahss**-*e*, *f* bulk, mass, volume; quantity; **–nartikel**, *m* mass-produced article; **–medien**, *pl* mass media

**massenhaft, mahss**-en-hahft, *adj & adv* massed together, numerous; *fam* heaps of

**Massenkarambolage, mahss**-en-kah-rahmm-boh-lah-zhe, *f* multiple car accident

**maßgebend, mahss**-gayb-ent, *adj* decisive,

authoritative, leading

**massieren, mahss**-eer-en, *v* to massage

**massig, mahss**-ik, *adj* solid, massive, bulky

**mäßig, mace**-ik, *adj* moderate; temperate; frugal

**mäßigen, mace**-ig-en, *v* to moderate; to modify

**Maßkrug, mahss**-krook, *m* litre (beer) mug

**Maßnahme, mahss**-nahm-*e*, *f* step; measure

**Maßregel, mahss**-rayg-el, *f* measure

**Maßstab, mahss**-shtahp, *m* rule(r); scale

**Mast, mahst**, *m* mast, pole, pylon; *f* fattening, feed

**mästen, mest**-en, *v* to fatten; to batten

**Material, maht**-air-ee-**ahl**, *nt* material

**Materie, maht**-**air**-ee-*e*, *f* matter; subject

**Mathematik, mahtt**-e-mah-**tick**, *f* mathematics

**Matratze, maht**-**rahtt**-se, *f* mattress

**Matrose, maht**-**roh**-ze, *m* seaman, sailor, mariner

**Matsch, mahtsh**, *m* slush, slop, pulp, mash

**matschig, mahtsh**-ik, *adj* muddy, messy, sloppy

**matt, mahtt**, *adj* exhausted, jaded, lifeless; dull; faint; mat; (chess) mate

**Matte, mahtt**-*e*, *f* mat(ting);

mead, meadow

**Mauer,** mow-er, *f* wall; partition; **–blümchen,** *nt* wallflower

**mauern,** mow-*ern, v* to build walls

**Maul,** mowl, *nt* snout, muzzle; *fam* big mouth; **–beere,** *f* mulberry; **–esel,** *m* mule; **–korb,** *m* muzzle (of animal); **–sperre,** *f* lock-jaw; **–tier,** *nt* mule; **–wurf,** *m* mole

**Maurer,** mowr-*er, m* bricklayer, mason; builder

**Maus,** mows, *f* mouse

**mäuschenstill,** moys-ken-shtill, *adj* quiet as a mouse

**Mausefalle,** mow-ze-fahll-e, *f* mouse-trap

**mausen,** mowz-*en, v* to catch mice; to sneak

**mausern,** mow-*zern, v* to moult

**mausetot,** mow-ze-toht, *adj* stone-dead

**Maut,** mowt, *f* toll; **–gebühr,** *f* toll (charge); **–straße,** *f* toll road

**maximal,** mahks-ee-mahl, *adj & adv* maximal, maximum; maximally, at most

**Mayonnaise,** mah-yoh-neh-ze, *f* mayonnaise

**Mechanik,** mek-ahn-ik, *f* mechanics, mechanism; **–er,** *m* mechanic; fitter

**Mechanismus,** mek-ahn-is-mooss, *m* mechanism

**meckern,** meck-*ern, v* to

bleat

**Medaille,** may-**dahll**-ye, *f* medal

**Medien,** meh-dee-en, *pl* the media

**Medikament,** may-dee-kah-**ment,** *nt* medicine

**Medizin,** may-dee-**tseen,** *f* medicine, physic; medication; **–er,** *m* doctor

**Meer,** mair, *nt* sea, ocean; **–busen,** *m* gulf, bay; **–enge,** *f* straits, channel

**Meeresfrüchte,** mair-es-frEEk-te, *pl* seafood

**Meeresspiegel,** mair-es-shpeeg-el, *m* sea-level

**Meerrettich,** mair-ret-ik, *m* horse-radish

**Meerschweinchen,** mair-shvine-ken, *nt* guinea-pig

**Megaphon,** maig-ah-fohn, *nt* megaphone

**Mehl,** mail, *nt* flour, meal

**mehlig,** mail-ik, *adj* floury, mealy

**Mehlspeise,** mail-shpy-ze, *f* floury food; pudding

**mehr,** mair, *adv* more

**mehrdeutig,** mair-doyt-ik, *adj* ambiguous

**mehren,** mair-en, *v* to multiply, to increase

**mehrere,** mair-e-re, *adj* several, a few, different

**mehrfach,** mair-fahk, *adj* manifold; *adv* repeatedly, on several occasions

**Mehrheit,** mair-hite, *f* majority; plurality

**mehrmal(s),** mair-mahl(s),

*adv* several times

**Mehrwertsteuer,** mair-vairt-shtoy-er, *f* value added tax

**Mehrzahl,** mair-tsahl, *f* greater part, majority

**meiden,** my-den, *v* to avoid, to shun

**Meile,** my-le, *f* mile

**meilenweit,** my-len-vite, *adj* stretching for miles, miles away

**mein, meine(r/s),** mine, mine-e(r/s), *adj* my; *pron* mine

**Meineid,** mine-ite, *m* perjury, false oath

**meinen,** mine-en, *v* to mean, to signify; to think; to assert

**meinerseits,** mine-er-zites, *adv* for my part

**meinesgleichen,** my-nes-gly-ken, *pron* people like myself

**meinesteils,** my-nes-tiles, *adv* for my part

**meinethalben,** my-net-hahllb-en, *adv* on my account, for my sake

**meinetwegen,** my-net-vay-gen, *adv* on my account, for my sake

**meinetwillen,** my-net-vil-en, *adv* on my account, for my sake

**Meinung,** my-noong, *f* opinion; intention, wish

**Meißel,** my-sel, *m* chisel

**meißeln,** my-seln, *v* to carve, to chisel

**meist**, my'st, *adj* most, greatest

**meistbietend**, my'st-beet-ent, *adj* bidding most (at auctions)

**meistens**, my-stens, *adv* mostly, in most cases, generally

**Meister**, my-ster, *m* master; champion (sport)

**meisterhaft**, my-ster-hahft, *adj* masterly; *adv* to perfection

**meistern**, my-stern, *v* to master

**Meisterschaft**, my-ster-shahft, *f* championship, mastery

**Meisterwerk**, my-ster-vairk, *nt* masterpiece

**Meistgebot**, my'st-ge-boht, *nt* highest bid

**Melasse**, may-lahss-e, *f* molasses, treacle

**melden**, meld-en, *v* to announce, to inform, to report; **sich –**, to get in touch; to report

**Meldung**, meld-oong, *f* notification; report

**melken**, melk-en, *v* to milk

**Melone**, mel-oh-ne, *f* melon

**Memme**, mem-e, *f* coward

**Menge**, meng-e, *f* crowd, quantity, swarm

**mengen**, meng-en, *v* to mix; **sich –**, *v* to meddle

**Meningitis**, men-in-gee-tis, *f* meningitis

**Mensch**, mensh, *m* man, human being; *nt* hussy

**Menschenalter**, men-shen-ahlt-er, *nt* generation; lifetime

**Menschenfeind**, men-shen-fy'nt, *m* misanthrope

**Menschenfreund**, men-shen-froynt, *m* philanthropist

**Menschenkenner**, men-shen-ken-er, *m* judge of character

**menschenmöglich**, men-shen-merk-lik, *adj* feasible; humanly possible

**menschenscheu**, men-shen-shoy, *adj* unsociable, shy

**Menschenschlag**, men-shen-shlahk, *m* kind of people

**Menschenverstand**, men-shen-fair-shtahnt, *m* common-sense

**Menschheit**, mensh-hite, *f* mankind; humankind

**menschlich**, mensh-lik, *adj* human(e)

**Menschlichkeit**, mensh-lik-kite, *f* humaneness

**Menstruation**, mens-troo-ahts-yohn, *f* menstruation

**Mensur**, men-zoor, *f* fencing bout; duel

**Mentalität**, men-tahl-ee-tait, *f* mentality

**merken**, mairk-en, *v* to mark, to note, to observe

**merkenswert**, mairk-ens-vairt, *adj* noteworthy

**merklich**, mairk-lik, *adj* perceptible; visible

**Merkmal**, mairk-mahl, *nt* characteristic

**merkwürdig**, mairk-vEErd-ik, *adj* strange, curious

**merkwürdigerweise**, mairk-vEErd-ig-er-vy-ze, *adv* curiously (enough)

**meßbar**, mess-bahr, *adj* measurable

**Meßbecher**, mess-bek-er, *m* measuring cup

**Messe**, mess-e, *f* mass; fair; **–gelände**, *nt* exhibition centre; **–halle**, *f* exhibition hall

**messen**, mess-en, *v* to measure; to gauge

**Messer**, mess-er, *nt* knife

**Messing**, mess-ing, *nt* brass

**Metall**, met-ahll, *nt* metal

**metallisch**, met-ahll-ish, *adj* metallic

**Meter**, mayt-er, *m* metre; **–maß**, *nt* (metric) measuring tape; metre rule

**Methode**, met-oh-de, *f* method

**Metier**, met-ee-ay, *nt* calling, vocation

**Mettwurst**, met-voorst, *f* (soft) German sausage

**metzeln**, mets-eln, *v* to massacre

**Metzger**, mets-ger, *m* butcher

**Meuchelmord**, moyk-el-mort, *m* assassination

**Meuchelmörder**, moyk-el-merd-er, *m* assassin

**meuchlerisch**, moyk-ler-ish, *adj* treacherous, like an assassin

**Meute,** moyt-*e*, *f* pack (of hounds)

**Meuterei,** moyt-*e*-**ry,** *f* mutiny

**Meuterer,** moyt-*er*-*er*, *m* mutineer

**meutern,** moyt-*ern*, *v* to mutiny

**Mexiko,** mek-sik-oh, *nt* Mexico

**mich,** mik, *pron (accusative)* me

**Mieder,** meed-*er*, *nt* girdle, bodice

**Miene,** meen-*e*, *f* mien, air, look

**Miete,** meet-*e*, *f* hire; rent; tenancy

**mieten,** meet-*en*, *v* to hire, to rent; to charter

**Mieter,** meet-*er*, *m* tenant

**Mietskaserne,** meets-kah-zairn-*e*, *f* tenement-building

**Mietvertrag,** meet-fer-trahk, *m* lease

**Mietwagen,** meet-vah-gen, *m* hire car

**Migräne,** mee-**gray**-ne, *f* migraine

**Mikrofon,** meek-roh-**fohn**, *nt* microphone

**Mikrowelle,** meek-roh-**vel**-*e*, *f* microwave

**Milch,** milk, *f* milk; soft roe (of fish)

**milchig,** milk-ik, *adj* milky

**Milchspeise,** milk-shpy-ze, *f* milk diet; milk-pudding

**Milchstraße,** milk-shtrahs-*e*, *f* milky-way

**Milchwirtschaft,** milk-veert-shahft, *f* dairy-farm

**mild(e),** milt (**mild**-*e*), *adj* mild, gentle, soft; lenient

**Milde,** mild-*e*, *f* mildness, gentleness, softness; leniency

**mildern,** mild-*ern*, *v* to soothe; to mitigate

**mildherzig,** milt-hairt-sik, *adj* tender-hearted

**mildtätig,** milt-tait-ik, *adj* charitable

**Milieu,** mil-**yer**, *nt* sphere; atmosphere, tone

**militant,** mee-lee-**tahnt**, *adj* militant

**Milz,** milts, *f* spleen

**minder,** min-der, *adj & adv* less(er); smaller; minor

**Minderheit,** min-der-hite, *f* minority

**minderjährig,** min-der-yair-ik, *adj* under age

**mindern,** min-dern, *v* to lessen, to decrease

**minderwertig,** min-der-vairt-ik, *adj* inferior

**mindest,** min-dest, *adv* least, lowest, smallest

**Mindestalter,** min-dest-ahll-ter, *nt* minimum age

**mindestens,** min-dest-ens, *adv* at least, no less than

**Mindestmaß,** min-dest-mahs, *nt* minimum

**Mine,** meen-*e*, *f* mine

**Mineralwasser,** min-e-**rahl**-vahss-er, *nt* mineral water

**Minibus,** min-e-booss, *m* minibus

**Minimum,** min-im-oom, *nt* minimum

**Minirock,** min-e-rock, *m* mini-skirt

**Ministerium,** min-ist-**air**-ee-oomm, *nt* ministry

**Ministerpräsident,** minn-ist-er-pray-zee-**dent**, *m* prime minister

**Minorität,** meen-o-ree-**tayt**, *f* minority

**Minute,** meen-**oot**-*e*, *f* minute

**Minze,** min-tse, *f* mint

**mir,** meer, *pron (dative)* (to) me

**Mischbrot,** mish-broht, *nt* bread (made from a mixture of flours)

**mischen,** mish-*en*, *v* to mix; to alloy; to mingle; to shuffle (cards)

**Mischling,** mish-ling, *m* hybrid, cross-breed

**Mischmasch,** mish-mahsh, *m* jumble; mess

**mißachten,** miss-**ahkt**-*en*, *v* to disregard; to despise, to disdain

**Mißbehagen,** miss-be-hahg-en, *nt* uneasiness; discontent

**mißbilligen,** miss-bil-ig-en, *v* to disapprove (of)

**Mißbrauch,** miss-browk, *m* misuse, abuse

**mißbrauchen,** miss-**browk**-en, *v* to misuse

**missen,** miss-*en*, *v* to miss; to go without

**Mißerfolg,** miss-**air**-folk, *m*

failure, ill-success

**Missetat, miss-***e*-taht, *f* misdeed; crime

**Missetäter, miss-***e*-tayt-*er*, *m* evil-doer; criminal

**mißfallen, miss-fahll-***en*, *v* to displease

**Mißgeburt, miss-***ge*-boort, *f* deformed person

**Mißgeschick, miss-***ge*-shick, *nt* misfortune

**mißgestaltet, miss-***ge*-shtahlt-*et*, *adj* misshapen, deformed

**mißgestimmt, miss-***ge*-shtimt, *adj* depressed, low-spirited

**mißgönnen, miss-gern-***en*, *v* to begrudge

**Mißgunst, miss-***goonst, *f* jealousy, envy; grudge

**mißhandeln, miss-hahnn-**deln, *v* to ill-treat, to maltreat

**Missionar, miss-yohn-ahr**, *m*, missionary

**Mißkredit, miss-**kraid-it, *m* discredit

**mißlich, miss-**lik, *adj* awkward, delicate; doubtful

**mißliebig, miss-**leeb-ik, *adj* unpopular; obnoxious

**mißlingen, miss-ling-***en*, *v* to fail, to be abortive

**mißmutig, miss-**moot-ik, *adj* discontented, bad-tempered

**mißraten, miss-raht-***en*, *adj* badly brought up

**Mißstand, miss-**shtahnt, *m*

disgrace, outrage; bad state of affairs

**Mißtrauen, miss-**trow-*en*, *nt* mistrust, distrust

**mißtrauen, miss-**trow-*en*, *v* to distrust, to mistrust

**mißtrauisch, miss-**trow-ish, *adj* distrustful, suspicious

**Mißverständnis, miss-**fer-shtent-niss, *nt* misunderstanding

**mißverstehen, miss-**fer-shtay-*en*, *v* to misunderstand

**Mißwirtschaft, miss-**veert-shahfft, *f* mismanagement

**Mist, mist**, *m* manure, dung; rubbish

**mit, mit**, *prep* with; *adv* too; along (with)

**Mitarbeit, mit-**ahr-bite, *f* co-operation, assistance; **–er**, *m* co-worker, colleague

**mitbringen, mit-**bring-*en*, *v* to bring along

**Mitbringsel, mit-**bring-zel, *nt* gift, souvenir

**miteinander, mit-**ine-ahnn-der, *adv* with one another

**Mitesser, mit-**ess-*er*, *m* blackhead

**Mitgefühl, mit-***ge*-fEEl, *nt* sympathy

**Mitgift, mit-**gift, *f* dowry

**Mitglied, mit-**gleet, *nt* member

**Mithilfe, mit-**hilf-*e*, *f* aid, help, assistance

**mithin, mit-**hin, *adv* therefore consequently;

thus, so

**mitkommen, mit-**komm-*en*, *v* to come along

**Mitleid, mit-**lite, *nt* sympathy; compassion

**Mitleidenschaft, mit-**ly-den-shahft, *f* **jdn in – ziehen,** *v* to affect sb (detrimentally)

**mitmachen, mit-**mahk-*en*, *v* to join in, to participate

**Mitmensch, mit-**mensh, *m* fellow-man

**mitreden, mit-**rayd-*en*, *v* to join in (a conversation)

**Mitschuld, mit-**shoolt, *f* complicity

**Mittag, mit-**tahk, *m* midday, noon; lunch break; **–essen,** *nt* lunch; **–(s)schlaf,** *m* afternoon nap, siesta

**mittags, mit-**tahks, *adv* at noon/midday

**Mittäter, mit-**tayt-*er*, *m* accomplice

**Mitte, mit-***e*, *f* middle, centre; midst

**mitteilen, mit-**tile-*en*, *v* to inform, to advise

**Mitteilung, mit-**tile-oong, *f* communication, information

**mittel, mit-***el*, *adj* central, middle; medium

**Mittel, mit-***el*, *nt* means; remedy, medicine; medium

**Mittelalter, mit-***el*-ahlt-*er*, *nt* Middle Ages

**mittelbar, mit-***el*-bar, *adj*

intermediate; indirect

**Mitteleuropa**, mit-el-oy-roh-pah, *nt* Central Europe

**Mittelgebirge**, mit-el-ge-bir-ge, *nt* low mountain range

**mittellos**, mit-el-lohs, *adj* impoverished; powerless

**mittelmäßig**, mit-el-maiss-ik, *adj* mediocre, middling

**Mittelmeer**, mit-el-mair, *nt* Mediterranean

**Mittelpunkt**, mit-el-poonkt, *m* centre, focus

**mittels**, mit-els, *prep* by means of

**Mittelstand**, mit-el-shtahnt, *m* middle-classes

**Mittelstufe**, mit-el-shtoof-e, *f* intermediate classes/years (in school)

**Mittelweg**, mit-el-vaik, *m* middle course

**mitten**, mit-en, *adv* in the midst of; –durch, *adv* right through the centre

**Mitternacht**, mit-er-nahkt, *f* midnight

**mittlere(r/s)**, mit-ler-e(r/s), *adj* middle, central; intermediate

**mittlerweile**, mit-ler-vy-le, *adv* meanwhile

**mittun**, mit-toon, *v* to join/help in

**mitunter**, mit-oont-er, *adv* occasionally

**Mitwelt**, mit-velt, *f* contemporary world

**mitwirken**, mit-virk-en, *v* to co-operate in

**Mittwoch**, mit-vok, *m* Wednesday

**mitzählen**, mit-tsayl-en, *v* to take into account

**Möbel**, merb-el, *nt* (piece of) furniture

**Mobiliar**, moh-bil-ee-ahr, *nt* household effect(s), furniture

**Mobiltelefon**, moh-beel-tay-le-fohn, *nt* mobile phone

**möblieren**, merb-leer-en, *v* to furnish

**Mode**, mohd-e, *f* fashion; vogue, craze, fad

**Modell**, moh-dell, *nt* model, mould; pattern

**modellieren**, moh-del-eer-en, *v* to model, to mould

**Moder**, mohd-er, *m* mould(ering), mustiness

**moderig**, mohd-er-ik, *adj* musty, mouldy, decaying

**modern**, mohd-ern, *v* to rot; to go mouldy

**modern**, mohd-airn, *adj* modern

**Modeschöpfer**, mohd-e-sherpp-fer, *m* fashion designer

**Modewort**, mohd-e-vort, *nt* fashionable word, buzz word

**modisch**, mohd-ish, *adj* stylish, fashionable

**mogeln**, mohg-eln, *v* to cheat, to trick

**mögen**, merg-en, *v* to like (to); may

**möglich**, merk-lik, *adj* possible

**möglicherweise**, merk-lik-er-vy-ze, *adv* possibly

**Möglichkeit**, merk-lik-kite, *f* possibility

**Mohn**, mohn, *m* poppy

**Möhre**, mer-re, *f* carrot

**Mohrrübe**, mohr-rEEb-e, *f* carrot

**Mokka**, mock-ah , *m* Mocha coffee

**Molkerei**, molk-e-ry, *f* dairy-farm(ing)

**Moll**, moll, *nt mus* minor

**mollig**, mol-ik, *adj* comfortable, cosy, snug; plump

**Moment**, moh-ment, *m* moment; *nt* motive; momentum; –aufnahme, *f* snap-shot

**momentan**, moh-men-tahn, *adj* momentary; immediate

**Monat**, moh-naht, *m* month; –sheft, *nt* (monthly) magazine

**monatlich**, moh-naht-lik, *adj* monthly

**Monatskarte**, moh-nahts-kahr-te, *f* monthly ticket

**Mönch**, mernk, *m* monk; friar

**Mond**, mohnt, *m* moon; –finsternis, *f* eclipse of the moon; –schein, *m* moonshine, moonlight; –sichel, *f* crescent (moon)

**mondsüchtig**, mohnt-zEEkt-ik, *adj* moonstruck; somnambulistic

**Monopol**, mo-noh-pohl, *nt* monopoly

**Montag, mohn**-tahk, *m*
Monday

**Montage, mon**-**tah-she**, *f*
installation, erection,
assembly

**montieren, mont**-**eer-en**, *v*
to instal, to erect, to
assemble

**Moor, mohr**, *nt* swamp, bog,
fen, marsh

**Moos, mohs**, *nt* moss

**moosig, moh**-zik, *adj* mossy

**Moral, moh**-**rahl**, *f* morality

**Morast, moh**-**rahst**, *m* bog,
swampy soil, mud, morass

**Mord, mort**, *m* murder

**morden, mord**-en, *v* to
murder

**Mörder, merd**-er, *m*
murderer

**mörderisch, merd**-er-ish, *adj*
murderous; *fig* dreadful

**Mordgier, mort**-geer, *f*
bloodthirstiness

**Mordskerl, morts**-kairl, *m*
*fig* devil

**mordsmäßig, morts**-maiss-
ik, *adj* enormous, awful

**Mordsspaß, morts**-shpahs,
*m* great fun

**Mordsspektakel, morts**-
shpeck-**tahk**-el, *m* terrible
noise

**Morgen, morg**-en, *m*
morning

**morgen, morg**-en, *adv*
tomorrow; – **abend**, *adv*
tomorrow evening – **früh**,
*adv* tomorrow morning

**Morgenblatt, morg**-en-
blahtt, *nt* (morning)
newspaper

**morgendlich, morg**-ent-lik,
*adj* of/in the morning

**Morgengrauen, morg**-en-
grow-en, *nt* daybreak

**Morgenland, morg**-en-
lahnt, *nt* Orient, East

**Morgenrock, morg**-en-rock,
*m* housecoat, dressing-
gown

**Morgenrot, morg**-en-roht,
*nt* sunrise, dawn

**morgens, morg**-ens, *adv* in
the morning; every
morning

**morsch, morsh**, *adj* rotten,
decayed

**Mörser, merz**-er, *m* mortar

**Mörtel, mert**-el, *m* mortar;
plaster

**Moschee, mosh**-ay, *f*
mosque

**Moschus, mosh**-ooss, *m*
musk

**Moselwein, moh**-zel-vine, *m*
Moselle (wine)

**Moskau, moss**-kow, *nt*
Moscow

**Moskito, moss**-kee-toh, *m*
mosquito

**Moslem, moss**-laim, *m*
Muslim

**moslemisch, moss**-laim-ish,
*adj* muslim

**Most, mosst**, *m* new wine,
unfermented fruit juice

**motivieren, moh**-teev-eer-
en, *v* to motivate

**Motor, moh**-tohr, *m* engine,
motor; –**boot**, *nt* motor
boat; –**fahrzeug**, *nt* motor
vehicle; –**haube**, *f* bonnet;
–**schaden**, *m* engine
failure

**Motorrad, mo**-tohr-raht, *nt*
motor-cycle

**Motte, mot**-e, *f* moth

**moussieren, mooss**-eer-en, *v*
to froth, to fizz

**Möwe, merv**-e, *f* (sea-)gull,
mew

**Mücke, mEEck**-e, *f* gnat,
midge

**mucken, moock**-en, *v* to
growl, to mutter

**Mückenstich, mEEck**-en-
shtik, *m* gnat-bite

**müde, mEEd**-e, *adj* tired,
fatigued

**Müdigkeit, mEEd**-ik-kite, *f*
tiredness, fatigue

**muffig, mooff**-ik, *adj* sulky;
stuffy, fusty

**Mühe, mEE**-e, *f* trouble;
labour; effort; pains

**mühelos, mEE**-e-lohs, *adj*
without effort

**mühen (sich), mEE**-en (zik),
*v* to take pains, to make
an effort

**Mühle, mEEl**-e, *f* mill;
grinder

**Mühsal, mEE**-zahl, *f*
hardship, trouble; toil

**mühsam, mEE**-zahmm, *adj*
wearisome; troublesome;
painstaking

**mühselig, mEE**-zail-ik, *adj*
laborious; wretched

**Mulde, moold**-e, *f* hollow;
trough; skip (for rubbish)

**Müll, mEEll**, *m* rubbish,

refuse; **–eimer,** m dustbin

**Müller, m**EELL-er, m miller

**Mumie, m**oom-ee-e, f mummy

**München, m**EEn-ken, nt Munich

**Mund,** moont, m mouth

**Mundart,** moont-*art,* f dialect; idiom

**munden,** moon-den, v to taste good

**münden, m**EEn-den, v to run into (river)

**mundgerecht,** moont-ge-rekt, *adj* palatable; suitable

**mündig, m**EEn-dik, *adj* of age; mature, responsible

**mündlich, m**EEnt-lik, *adj* verbal; oral

**Mundstück,** moont-shtEEck, nt mouthpiece; tip (of cigarette)

**Mündung, m**EEn-doong, f mouth (of river); estuary; muzzle (of gun)

**munkeln,** moonk-eln, v to rumour; to whisper

**Münster, m**EEnst-er, nt cathedral, minster

**munter,** moont-er, *adj* vigorous; lively; merry

**Münze, m**EEnt-se, f coin(age); cash; mint

**Münztelefon, m**EEnts-tay-le-fohn, nt pay-phone

**mürb(e), m**EErb(-e), *adj* crumbly; rotten; soft, tender; ripe; well-done

**Mürbeteig, m**EEr-be-tike, m shortcrust pastry

**murmeln,** moorm-eln, v to

murmur

**murren,** moorr-en, v to grumble; to murmur

**mürrisch, m**EErr-ish, *adj* sulky, ill-tempered, sullen

**Mus,** moos, nt mush; puree; jam

**Muschel, m**oosh-el, f mussel; shell

**Muscheltier,** moosh-el-teer, nt shell-fish

**Museum,** moo-**zai**-oom, nt museum

**Musik,** moo-**zeek,** f music

**musikalisch,** moo-zee-**kahl**-ish, *adj* musical

**Musikant,** moo-zee-**kahnt,** m (amateur) musician

**Musikautomat,** moo-**zeek**-ow-toh-maht, m musical box

**Musiker,** moo-**zeek**-er, m (professional) musician

**musizieren,** moo-zee-**tseer**-en, v to play music

**Muskat(nuß),** moos-**kaht**(-nooss), m (f), nutmeg

**Muskel, m**ooss-kel, m muscle

**muskulös,** moos-koo-**lers,** *adj* muscular

**Muße, m**oos-e, f leisure; spare time

**Müsli, m**EEs-lee, nt muesli

**müssen, m**EEss-en, v to have to, to be obliged to, must

**müßig, m**EEss-ik, *adj* idle, lazy; useless

**Müßiggang, m**EEss-ik-gahng, m idleness, sloth

**Muster,** moost-er, nt sample; design; pattern; model; **–beispiel,** nt typical example

**mustergültig,** moost-er-gEEL-tik, *adj* exemplary, model

**musterhaft,** moost-er-hahft, *adj* exemplary, model

**mustern,** moost-ern, v to muster; to review; to figure

**Mut,** moot, m courage, bravery

**mutig,** moot-ik, *adj* courageous, brave

**mutlos,** moot-lohs, *adj* disheartened, despondent

**mutmaßen,** moot-mahs-en, v to presume

**mutmaßlich,** moot-mahs-lik, *adj* presumably

**Mutter,** moott-er, f mother; **–leib,** m womb

**mütterlich, m**EEtt-er-lik, *adj* motherly, maternal

**Muttermal,** moott-er-mahl, nt birthmark, mole

**Muttermilch,** moott-er-milk, f mother's milk

**mutterseelenallein,** moott-er-zail-en-ahll-ine, *adj* all alone

**Mutwille,** moot-vil-e, m wilfulness, malice

**mutwillig,** moot-vil-ik, *adj* mischievous; wilful

**Mütze, m**EEtt-se, f cap, bonnet

**MwSt,** *abbr*
  **Mehrwertsteuer,** VAT

**na!** nah, *interj* now! now then! well!

**na gut**, nah **goot**, *interj* okay then

**Nabel**, nahb-el, *m* navel

**nach**, nahk, *prep & adv* after; to(wards); according to; past

**nachäffen**, nahk-eff-en, *v* to ape, to copy

**nachahmen**, nahk-ahm-en, *v* to imitate, to copy

**Nachbar**, nahk-bar, *m* neighbour; **–schaft**, *f* neighbours; proximity; **–staat**, *m* neighbouring state

**nachdem**, nahk-daim, *adv & conj* after(wards)

**nachdenken**, nahk-dengken, *v* to reflect

**nachdenklich**, nahk-dengklik, *adj* meditative, pensive

**Nachdruck**, nahk-droock, *m* emphasis; (print) reproduction

**nachdrücklich**, nahkdrEEck-lik, *adj* emphatic

**nacheinander**, nahk-ineahnn-der, *adv* one after the other

**Nachfolger**, nahk-folg-er, *m* successor

**nachforschen**, nahk-forshen, *v* to investigate

**Nachfrage**, nahk-frahg-e, *f* demand; inquiry

**nachfüllen**, nahk-fEEll-en, *v* to refill

**nachgeben**, nahk-gayb-en, *v* to give in

**nachgehen**, nahk-gay-en, *v* to go after; to attend to; to investigate; (clock) to be slow

**Nachgeschmack**, nahk-geshmahck, *m* after-taste

**nachgiebig**, nahk-geeb-ik, *adj* indulgent; yielding, submissive

**nachgrübeln**, nahk-grEEb-eln, *v* to muse over

**nachhelfen**, nahk-helf-en, *v* to give help; to push forward

**nachher**, nahk-hair, *adv* afterwards; later on

**Nachhilfe**, nahk-hilf-e, *f* assistance, aid

**nachholen**, nahk-hohl-en, *v* to make up for; to recover

**Nachhut**, nahk-hoot, *f* rearguard

**Nachkomme**, nahk-kom-e, *m* descendant

**nachkommen**, nahk-komen, *v* to come after; to comply with

**Nachlaß**, nahk-lahss, *m* reduction; estate

**nachlassen**, nahk-lahss-en, *v* to bequeath; to abate; to deteriorate

**Nachlassenschaft**, nahk-lahss-en-shahft, *f* inheritance

**nachlässig**, nahk-less-ik, *adj* careless, negligent

**nachlösen**, nahk-lers-en, *v* to buy a ticket/supplement on the train

**nachmachen**, nahk-mahk-en, *v* to imitate; to counterfeit

**Nachmittag**, nahk-mit-ahg, *m* afternoon

**nachmittags**, nahk-mit-ahks, *adv* in/during the

afternoon

**Nachnahme, nahk**-nahm-*e*, *f* reimbursement; c.o.d.

**nachrechnen, nahk**-rek-nen, *v* to check, to verify

**Nachricht, nahk**-rikt, *f* information, report, news; **–en,** *pl* the news

**Nachruf, nahk**-roof, *m* obituary notice

**nachrufen, nahk**-roof-en, *v* to call after (sb)

**Nachsaison, nahk**-zay-zong, *f* off-season

**nachschicken, nahk**-shick-en, *v* to forward (mail)

**nachschlagen, nahk**-shlahg-en, *v* to look up (in a book)

**Nachschub, nahk**-shoop, *m* reinforcements; new batch

**nachsehen, nahk**-zay-en, *v* to look up a thing; to gaze after

**nachsenden, nahk**-zen-den, *v* to forward (mail)

**Nachsicht, nahk**-zikt, *f* indulgence, toleration

**nachsichtig, nahk**-zik-tik, *adj* indulgent, lenient

**nachsinnen, nahk**-zin-en, *v* to reflect, to ponder

**nachsitzen, nahk**-zits-en, *v* to be kept in school

**Nachspeise, nahk**-shpy-ze, *f* dessert, sweet, pudding

**nächst(e/r), naykst**-(*-e/er*), *adj* nearest; *adv* next, nearest

**nachstehen, nahk**-shtay-en, *v* to rank after

**nachstellen, nahk**-shtel-en, *v* to put back (clocks), to adjust; to pursue (sb)

**Nächstenliebe, nayk**-sten-leeb-*e*, *f* love of one's neighbour

**nächstens, nayk**-stens, *adv* shortly, very soon

**nachstöbern, nahk**-shterb-ern, *v* to rummage (after)

**nachsuchen, nahk**-zook-en, *v* to (have a) look

**Nacht, nahkt,** *f* night

**Nachteil, nahk**-tile, *m* drawback; injury, loss

**nachteilig, nahk**-ty-lik, *adj* detrimental, injurious

**Nachthemd, nahkt**-hemt, *nt* night-shirt

**Nachtigall, nahkt**-ee-gahll, *f* nightingale

**Nachtisch, nahk**-tish, *m* dessert, sweet, pudding

**Nachtleben, nahkt**-lay-ben, *nt* nightlife

**nächtlich, naykt**-lik, *adj* at night, nocturnal

**Nachtmahl, nahkt**-mahl, *nt* supper

**Nachtrag, nahk**-trahk, *m* postscript, supplement

**nachtragen, nahk**-trahg-en, *v* to bear a grudge, to append

**nachträglich, nahk**-traik-lik, *adj* supplementary; belated

**nachts, nahkts,** *adv* at/during the night

**nachtwandeln, nahkt**-vahnn-deln, *v* to walk in one's sleep

**Nachweis, nahk**-vice *m* information, particulars, proof

**nachweisbar, nahk**-vice-bar, *adj* manifest, demonstrable

**nachweisen, nahk**-vy-zen, *v* to indicate, to prove

**nachweislich, nahk**-vice-lik, *adj* evident, demonstrable

**Nachwelt, nahk**-velt, *f* posterity

**Nachwuchs, nahk**-vooks, *m* new generation(s); young shoot(s)

**nachzahlen, nahk**-tsahl-en, *v* to pay in addition

**nachzählen, nahk**-tsayl-en, *v* to count over

**nachziehen, nahk**-tsee-en, *v* to draw (drag) after; to follow

**Nachzügler, nahk**-tsEEg-ler, *m* straggler

**Nacken, nahck**-en, *m* nape/scruff of the neck

**nackt, nahckt,** *adj* naked, bare, nude

**Nadel, nahd**-el, *f* needle

**Nadelwald, nahd**-el-wahlt, *m* coniferous forest

**Nagel, nahg**-el, *m* nail

**nageln, nahg**-eln, *v* to nail

**nagelneu, nahg**-el-noy, *adj* brand-new

**nagen, nahg**-en, *v* to gnaw, to nibble

**nahe, nah**-e, *adj & adv* near(ly), close to

**Nähe, nay**-e, *f* proximity; neighbourhood

**nahebei, nah**-e-by, *adv* close

by, nearly

**nahelegen,** nah-*e*-lay-gen, *v* to urge sb to do sth

**naheliegen,** nah-*e*-lee-gen, *v* to be obvious, near at hand

**nahen,** nah-*en*, *v* to approach, to draw near

**nähen,** nay-*en*, *v* to sew; to do needlework

**näher,** nay-*er*, *adj* nearer, closer

**Nähere(s),** nay-*er*-es, *nt* particulars, details

**näherkommen,** nay-*er*-komm-*en*, *v* to approach; **sich –,** *v* to get closer

**nähern (sich),** nay-*ern* (zik), *v* to approach

**Nähgarn,** nay-garn, *nt* sewing cotton

**nähren,** nayr-*en*, *v* to nourish, to feed

**nahrhaft,** nahr-hahft, *adj* nourishing; rich, substantial

**Nahrung,** nahr-oong, *f* food, sustenance

**Nahrungsmittel,** nahr-oongs-mit-*el*, *nt* foodstuff

**Naht,** naht, *f* seam; joint

**Nahverkehr,** nah-fer-kair, *m* local traffic

**Name,** nahm-*e*, *m* name; reputation

**namens,** nahm-*ens*, *adv* by the name of, called, named; *prep* on behalf of

**Namensvetter,** nahm-*ens*-fet-*er*, *m* namesake

**namentlich,** nahm-*ent*-lik,

*adj & adv* by name; especially, particularly

**namhaft,** nahm-hahft, *adj* named, by name; renowned

**nämlich,** naim-lik, *adj & adv* the same; namely, that is to say

**Napf,** nahp'f, *m* basin, bowl, dish, mug

**Napfkuchen,** nahp'f-kook-*en*, *m* kind of madeira cake

**Narbe,** narb-*e*, *f* scar, mark

**Narr,** nahrr, *m* fool

**Narrenstreich,** nahrr-*en*-shtry'k, *m* foolish trick

**Narrheit,** nahrr-hite, *f* foolishness, folly

**närrisch,** nairr-ish, *adj* foolish, crazy; funny

**Narzisse,** nahrr-tsis-*e*, *f* narcissus, daffodil

**naschen,** nahsh-*en*, *v* to enjoy dainties on the sly, to nibble

**naschhaft,** nahsh-hahft, *adj* having a sweet tooth

**Naschkätzchen, –katze,** nahsh-kets-ke*n*, –kahts-*e*, *nt f* person with a sweet tooth

**Naschwerk,** nahsh-vairk, *nt* sweetmeats

**Nase,** nahz-*e*, *f* nose; snout, proboscis

**Nasenloch,** nahz-*en*-lok, *nt* nostril

**naseweis,** nahz-*e*-vice, *adj* forward, pert

**Nashorn,** nahs-horn, *nt*

rhinoceros

**naß,** nahss, *adj* wet; moist, damp, humid

**Nässe,** ness-*e*, *f* wet(ness); moisture

**nässen,** ness-*en*, *v* to wet, to moisten

**naßkalt,** nahss-kahlt, *adj* wet and cold

**Nation,** nahts-yohn, *f* nation

**Nationalfeiertag,** nahts-yohn-**ahl**-fy-er-tahk, *m* national holiday

**Nationalflagge,** nahts-yohn-**ahl**-flahgg-*e*, *f* national flag

**Nationalhymne,** nahts-yohn-**ahl**-hEEm-ne, *f* national anthem

**Nationalmannschaft,** nah-tse-ohn-**ahl**-mahnn-shahft, *f* national team

**Nationalpark,** nahts-yohn-**ahl**-park, *m* national park

**Natter,** nahtt-*er*, *f* viper, adder, asp

**Natur,** nah-toor, *f* nature

**Naturerscheinung,** nah-**toor**-air-shy-noong, *f* natural phenomenon

**Naturforscher,** nah-**toor**-forsh-er, *m* naturalist

**Naturgeschichte,** nah-**toor**-ge-shik-te, *f* natural history

**naturgetreu,** nah-**toor**-ge-troy, *adj* true to nature, life-like

**Naturkatastrophe,** nah-**toor**-kah-tah-stroh-fe, *f*

natural disaster

**natürlich,** nah-**tEEr**-lik, *adj & adv* natural(ly); of course

**Naturprodukt,** nah-**toor**-pro-dookt, *nt* natural product

**naturrein,** nah-**toor**-rine, *adj* pure

**Naturschutz,** nah-**toor**-shoots, *m* nature conservation; –**gebiet,** *nt* nature reserve

**Neapel,** nay-**ah**-pel, *nt* Naples

**Nebel,** nayb-el, *m* fog; mist; haze

**neb(e)lig,** nayb-(e-)lik, *adj* foggy; misty; hazy

**neben,** nayb-en, *prep* next to, beside(s); side by side

**nebenan,** nayb-en-**ahnn,** *adv* next door, adjoining

**nebenbei,** nayb-en-**by,** *adv* at the same; incidentally

**nebeneinander,** nayb-en-ine-**ahnn**-der, *adv* side by side

**Nebenfluß,** nayb-en-flooss, *m* tributary

**nebenher,** nayb-en-**hair,** *adv* in addition; at the same time; besides

**Nebensache,** nayb-en-sah*k*e, *f* minor matter, trifle

**nebensächlich,** nayb-en-sayk-lik, *adj* subordinate

**Nebensaison,** nayb-en-zay-zong, *f* low season

**Nebenstraße,** nayb-en-shtrahs-e, *f* side-street

**Nebenwirkung,** nai-ben-virk-oong, *f* side-effect

**nebst,** naip'st, *prep* (together) with

**necken,** neck-en, *v* to tease

**neckisch,** neck-ish, *adj* teasing, amusing

**Neffe,** nef-e, *m* nephew

**negativ,** neg-ah-teef, *adj* negative

**nehmen,** naym-en, *v* to take; to receive, to accept

**Neid,** nite, *m* envy, jealousy

**neidisch,** ny-dish, *adj* envious, jealous

**Neige,** ny-ge, *f* slope; depression; end; dregs

**neigen,** ny-gen, *v* to bend; to bow, to tilt; to incline

**Neigung,** ny-goong, *f* slope, incline, gradient; inclination, liking

**nein,** nine, *adv* no

**Nektarine,** neck-tah-**ree**-ne, *f* nectarine

**Nelke,** nelk-e, *f* carnation, pink; clove

**nennen,** nen-en, *v* to name, to call; to mention

**nennenswert,** nen-ens-vairt, *adj* worth mentioning

**Neon,** nay-on, *nt* neon; –**lampe,** *f* neon lamp; –**röhre,** *f* neon tube

**Nerv,** nairf, *m* nerve

**nervig,** nairv-ik, *adj* strong, terse; pithy

**nervös,** nairv-ers, *adj* excitable, irritable; nervy, having weak nerves

**Nerz,** nairts, *m* mink

**Nessel,** nes-el, *f* nettle

**Nest,** nest, *nt* nest; eyrie; small town/village

**Nesthäkchen,** nest-haik-ken, *nt* youngest child, baby of family

**nett,** net, *adj* nice; neat, tidy, pretty

**netto,** net-oh, *adv* net, clear

**Netz,** nets, *nt* net; network

**neu,** noy, *adj* new, novel; original; fresh

**Neubau,** noy-bow, *m* building under construction, new building

**neuerdings,** noy-er-dings, *adv* lately, latterly, of late; anew

**Neuerung,** noy-er-oong, *f* innovation, reform; novelty

**neu(e)stens** noy-(e-)stens, *adv* of late, recently

**Neugier(de)** noy-geer(-de), *f* curiosity

**neugierig,** noy-geer-ik, *adj* curious, inquisitive, nosy

**Neuheit,** noy-hite, *f* newness

**Neuigkeit,** noy-ik-kite, *f* (piece of) news; novelty

**Neujahr,** noy-yar, *nt* New Year('s Day)

**neulich,** noy-lik, *adj & adv* recent(ly); the other day

**Neuling,** noy-ling, *m* novice, beginner

**Neumond,** noy-mohnt, *m* new moon

**neun,** noyn, *num* nine

**neunzehn, noyn**-tsain, *num* nineteen

**neunzig, noyn**-tsik, *num* ninety

**neurotisch, noy-roht**-ish, *adj* neurotic

**Neuseeland, noy-zay**-lahnt, *nt* New Zealand

**Neuzeit, noy**-tsite, *f* modern times

**neuzeitlich, noy**-tsite-lik, *adj* modern, up-to-date

**nicht, nikt,** *adv* not

**Nichte, nik**-te, *f* niece

**nichtig, nik**-tik, *adj* void; vain, idle

**Nichtraucher, nikt**-rowk-er, *m* non-smoker

**nichts, nikts,** *pron* nothing, nought

**nichtsdestoweniger, nikts**-dest-oh-**vayn**-ig-er, *adv* nevertheless

**Nichtsnutz, nikts**-noots, *m* good-for-nothing

**nichtssagend, nikts**-zahg-ent, *adj* meaningless

**nichtswürdig, nikts**-vEErd-ik, *adj* worthless, vile

**nicken, nick**-en, *v* to nod

**nie, nee,** *adv* never

**nieder, need**-er, *adj & adv* common, low; down

**niederdrücken, need**-er-drEEck-en, *v* to press down; to oppress

**Niedergang, need**-er-gahng, *m* decline

**niedergeschlagen, need**-er-ge-shlahg-en, *adj* depressed, dejected

**Niederlage, need**-er-lahg-e, *f* defeat

**Niederlande, need**-er-lahn-de, *pl* Netherlands

**Niederländer, need**-er-len-der, *m* Dutchman; **–in**, *f* Dutchwoman

**niederländisch, need**-er-len-dish, *adj* Dutch

**niederlassen (sich), need**-er-lahss-en (zik), *v* to settle; to establish o.s.

**Niederlassung, need**-er-lahss-oong, *f* settlement; branch

**niedermetzeln, need**-er-met-seln, *v* to massacre

**Niederschlag, need**-er-shlahg, *m* precipitation; sediment

**niederschlagen, need**-er-shlah-gen, *v* to knock down; to cast down; to suppress

**niederste(r), need**-erst-e(r), *adj* lowest

**Niedertracht, need**-er-trahkt, *f* infamy, vileness

**niederträchtig, need**-er-trek-tik, *adj* vile, mean, base, infamous

**Niederung, need**-er-oong, *f* lowland, plain

**niedlich, need**-lik, *adj* dainty, neat; nice, pretty

**niedrig, need**-rik, *adj* low; base, vulgar

**niemals, nee**-mahls, *adv* never, at no time

**niemand, nee**-mahnt, *pron* nobody

**Niere, neer**-e, *f* kidney

**nieseln, neez**-eln, *v* to drizzle

**niesen, neez**-en, *v* to sneeze

**Niete, neet**-e, *f* blank (cartridge); dead loss; no-hoper

**nieten, neet**-en, *v* to rivet

**Nikotin, nee-ko-teen,** *nt* nicotine

**Nil, neel,** *m* Nile; **–pferd,** *nt* hippopotamus

**nimmer, nim**-er, *adv* never

**nimmersatt, nim**-er-saht, *adj* insatiable

**nippen, nip**-en, *v* to sip

**Nippes, nip**-es, *pl* knick-knacks, small ornaments

**nirgend(s), neerg**-ent(s), *adv* nowhere

**Nische, neesh**-e, *f* niche, recess

**nisten, nist**-en, *v* to (make a) nest

**Niveau, nee-voh,** *nt* level

**Nixe, nix**-e, *f* nymph, water-sprite

**nobel, nohb**-el, *adj* generous, liberal; noble

**noch, nok,** *adv* still, yet, besides; nor

**nochmals, nok**-mahls, *adv* once more, again

**Nonne, non**-e, *f* nun

**Nord-, nort,** *pref* North, northern

**Norden, nord**-en, *m* north

**Nordirland, nort-eer**-lahnt, *nt* Northern Ireland

**nordisch, nord**-ish, *adj* northern;

northerly; Norse

**nördlich, nert**-lik, *adj*
northerly; northern;
arctic; *adv* north (of)

**Nordlicht, nord**-likt, *nt*
aurora borealis, northern
lights

**Nordpol, nort**-pohl, *m*
North Pole

**Nordsee, nort**-zay, *f* North
Sea

**nörgeln, nerg**-eln, *v* to
grumble, to find fault
with, to nag

**Norm**, norm, *f* pattern,
model, standard

**Norwegen, nor**-vay-gen, *nt*
Norway

**Norweger, nor**-vay-ger, *m*
Norwegian (person)

**norwegisch, nor**-vay-gish,
Norwegian

**Not**, noht, *f* need, necessity;
distress, want; danger;
trouble

**Notar, noht**-ar, *m* notary,
solicitor

**notariell, noht**-ar-ee-**yel**, *adj*
notarial

**Notausgang, noht**-ows-
gahng, *m* emergency exit

**Notbehelf, noht**-be-help, *m*
stop-gap, makeshift,
expedient

**Notbremse, noht**-brem-se, *f*
emergency brake

**notdürftig, noht**-dEErft-ik,
*adj* meagre, poor;
makeshift

**Note, noht**-e, *f mus*
note; mark, certificate

(school); remark

**Noten, noht**-en, *pl* (sheet)
music

**Notfall, noht**-fahll, *m*
emergency

**notgedrungen, noht**-ge-
droong-en, *adj* from
necessity

**notieren, noht**-**eer**-en, *v* to
note, to jot down

**nötig, nert**-ik, *adj* necessary,
required

**nötigen, nert**-ig-en, *v* to
force, to oblige; to invite;
to urge

**Notiz, noht**-eets, *f* notice,
cognizance;
memorandum; **–block**,
**–buch**, *nt* notebook

**Notstand, noht**-shtahnt, *m*
(state of) emergency;
urgent need

**Notwehr, noht**-vair, *f* self-
defence

**notwendig, noht**-ven-dik,
*adj* necessary

**Novelle, noh**-**vel**-e, *f* short
story

**November, noh**-**vem**-ber, *m*
November

**Nu, noo**, *nt* moment,
instant

**Nuance, noo**-**ahng**-se, *f*
shade, tint

**nüchtern, nEEk**-tern, *adj*
sober; fasting; temperate,
frugal

**Nudel, nood**-el, *f* noodle,
vermicelli; **–n**, *pl* pasta

**Null, nooll**, *f* nought

**null, nooll**, *adj* void;

*num* zero

**Nullpunkt, nooll**-poonkt, *m*
zero; freezing-point

**numerieren, noomm**-er-**eer**-
en, *v* to number

**Nummer, noomm**-er, *f*
number; copy, issue; size

**nun, noon**, *adv* now, at
present; then; well now!

**nunmehr, noon**-mair, *adv &*
*conj* now, by (from) this
time

**nur, noor**, *adv* only, solely

**Nürnberg, nEErn**-bairg, *nt*
Nuremberg

**Nuß, nooss**, *f* nut;
**–knacker**, *m* nut-cracker

**Nüster, nEEst**-er, *f* nostril
(of animals)

**nutz(e), noots(-e)**, *adj*
profitable, useful

**Nutz(en), noots(-en)**, *m*
utility, use; gain,
advantage

**nutzen, noots**-en, *v* to be
useful

**nützen, nEEts**-en, *v* to use

**nützlich, nEEts**-lik, *adj*
useful

**nutzlos, noots**-lohs, *adj*
useless

**Nylon, ny**-lon, *nt* nylon;
**–hemd**, *nt* nylon shirt;
**–strümpfe**, *fpl* nylon
stockings

**ob,** op, *conj* whether, if

**Obacht,** oh-*bahkt*, *f* attention, heed

**Obdach,** op-*dahk*, *nt* shelter, lodging

**obdachlos,** op-*dahk*-lohs, *adj* homeless

**oben,** oh-ben, *adv* above, upstairs; overhead

**obenan,** oh-ben-*ahnn*, *adv* at the top/head of

**obendrein,** oh-ben-*drine*, *adv* into the bargain, over and above

**Ober,** oh-ber, *m* waiter

**ober(e/er/es),** oh-ber(-e/er/es), *adj* upper, higher, superior

**Oberbefehlshaber,** oh-ber-be-*fails*-hahb-er, *m* commander-in-chief

**Oberfläche,** oh-ber-flek-e, *f* surface

**oberflächlich,** oh-ber-flek-

lik, *adj* superficial, shallow

**oberhalb,** oh-ber-*hahlp*, *prep* above

**Oberhaupt,** oh-ber-*howpt*, *nt* chief, sovereign, head

**Oberhemd,** oh-ber-hemt, *nt* shirt

**Oberkellner,** oh-ber-kel-ner, *m* head-waiter

**Oberkiefer,** oh-ber-keef-er, *m* upper jaw

**Oberkörper,** oh-ber-kerp-er, *m* upper part of body, torso

**Oberleder,** oh-ber-layd-er, *nt* uppers (shoe)

**Oberlicht,** oh-ber-likt, *nt* sky-(top-)light

**Oberschenkel,** oh-ber-sheng-kel, *m* thigh

**Oberst,** oh-berst, *m* colonel

**obgleich,** op-*gly'k*, *conj* although, though

**Obhut,** op-hoot, *f*

protection, care, guardianship

**obig(e/er/es),** oh-bik (oh-big-e/er/es), *adj* foregoing, above(-mentioned)

**Oblate,** ob-laht-e, *f* wafer

**obligatorisch,** ob-lig-ah-tohr-ish, *adj* obligatory, compulsory

**Obmann,** op-mahnn, *m* chief, chairman, foreman

**Obrigkeit,** oh-brik-kite, *f* public authorities

**Obst,** ohp'st, *nt* fruit

**obwohl,** ob-vohl, *conj* although, though

**Ochs(e),** oks(-e), *m* ox, bullock

**öde,** erd-e, *adj* deserted, dreary

**Öde,** erd-e, *f* desert, wasteland

**oder,** oh-der, *conj* or

**Ofen,** oh-ffen, *m* stove, fire-place; oven; furnace

**offen,** off-en, *adj* open; candid, frank

**offenbar,** off-en-bahr, *adj* obvious, manifest, evident; **–en,** *v* to reveal, to manifest

**offenherzig,** off-en-hairt-sik, *adj* openhearted, frank

**offensichtlich,** off-en-zikt-lik, *adj* obvious

**offenstehen,** off-en-shtay-en; *v* to be open/permitted

**öffentlich,** erf-ent-lik, *adj* public

**Öffentlichkeit,** erf-ent-lik-kite, *f* public

**offerieren**, of-er-eer-en, *v* to offer

**Offerte**, of-*airt*-e, *f* offer

**öffnen**, erf-nen, *v* to open

**oft**, oft, *adv* often, frequently

**oh**, oh, *interj* oh

**ohne**, oh-ne, *prep* without

**ohnegleichen**, oh-*ne*-gly-ken, *adj* unparalleled

**Ohnmacht**, ohn-*mahkt*, *f* fainting fit, fainting

**ohnmächtig**, ohn-mekt-ik, *adj* unconscious; powerless

**Ohr**, ohr, *nt* ear

**Öhr**, er, *nt* eye (of needle); eyelet

**Ohrfeige**, ohr-fy-ge, *f* box on the ear

**Ohrring**, ohr-ring, *m* earring

**Ökoladen**, er-koh-lahd-en, *m* health-food shop

**Oktober**, ok-toh-ber, *m* October

**Öl**, erl, *nt* oil

**Ölbild**, erl-bilt, *nt* oil-painting

**Oldtimer**, old-time-er, *m* vintage car

**ölen**, erl-en, *v* to oil, to lubricate

**Ölfarbe**, erl-farb-e, *f* oil-paint

**ölig**, erl-ik, *adj* oily; unctuous

**Olympiade**, oh-lEEmp-ee-ahd-e, *f* Olympic Games

**Oma**, oh-mah, *f* granny

**Onkel**, ong-kel, *m* uncle

**Oper**, oh-per, *f* opera

**Operette**, oh-per-et-e, *f* light opera, musical comedy

**Opfer**, op-fer, *nt* victim; sacrifice; martyr

**Opferlamm**, op-fer-lahmm, *nt* sacrificial lamb; innocent victim

**opfern**, op-fern, *v* to sacrifice

**Orange**, oh-rahnge-zhe, *f* orange; –nsaft, *m* orange juice

**Orden**, ord-en, *m* order; distinction, decoration

**ordentlich**, ord-ent-lik, *adj* ordinary; orderly; regular

**ordinär**, ord-in-air, *adj* vulgar, common

**ordnen**, ord-nen, *v* to regulate; to put in order; to settle

**Ordnung**, ord-noong, *f* order, arrangement

**Orgel**, org-el, *f* organ

**orgeln**, org-eln, *v* to play/grind a (barrel-)organ

**orientieren (sich)**, or-ee-ent-eer-en (zik), *v* to find one's way; to collect information

**Orientierung**, or-ee-ent-eer-oong, *f* orientation; –ssinn, *m* sense of orientation

**Orkan**, or-kahn, *m* hurricane, gale

**Ort**, ort, *m* place, spot, locality; town

**örtlich**, ert-lik, *adj* local

**ortsansässig**, orts-ahnn-saiss-ik, *adj* local

**Ortschaft**, ort-shahft, *f* locality; township, place

**Ortssinn**, orts-sin, *m* sense of direction

**Öse**, erz-e, *f* loop, eye

**Ost-**, ost, *pref* East, eastern

**Osten**, ost-en, *m* east; East, Orient

**Osterei**, ohst-er-i, *nt* Easter-egg

**Osterglocke**, ohst-er-glock-e, *f* daffodil

**Ostermontag**, ohst-er-mohn-tahk, *m* Easter Monday

**Ostern**, ohst-ern, *pl* Easter

**Österreich**, erst-e-rike, *nt* Austria

**Österreicher**, erst-e-rike-er, *m* Austrian (person)

**österreichisch**, erst-e-rike-ish, *adj* Austrian

**östlich**, erst-lik, *adj* eastern, easterly

**Ostsee**, ost-zay, *f* Baltic (Sea)

**Otter**, ot-er, *m* otter; *f* adder

**Ozon**, oh-tsohn, *nt* ozone; –loch, *nt* ozone hole; –schicht, *f* ozone layer

**Paar,** pahr, *nt* pair; couple

**paar,** pahr, *adj* **ein –,** a few

**paaren,** pahr-en, *v* to pair, to couple; to match

**Pacht,** pahkt, *f* lease, tenancy; tenure

**pachten,** pahkt-en, *v* to lease, to rent; to farm

**Pächter,** pekt-er, *m* tenant (-farmer); leaseholder, lessee

**Pack,** pahck, *nt*; pack, packet, package; rabble, mob

**Päckchen,** peck-ken, *nt* small package/parcel

**packen,** pahck-en, *v* to pack; to seize

**Packesel,** pahck-ay-zel, *m* pack-mule; drudge

**paffen,** pahff-en, *v* to puff, to smoke

**Paket,** pah-kait, *nt* parcel, package; packet

**Palast,** pah-lahst, *m* palace

**panieren,** pah-neer-en, *v* to coat with breadcrumbs

**Paniermehl,** pah-neer-mail, *nt* breadcrumbs

**Panne,** pahnn-e, *f* breakdown (of car etc.)

**Pantoffel,** pahnn-toff-el, *m* slipper; **–held,** *m* henpecked husband

**Pantomime,** pahnn-toh-mee-me, *m* mime; *f* mime show

**Panzer,** pahnt-ser, *m* armour, (coat of) mail; tank

**panzern,** pahnt-sern, *v* to armour-plate

**Papa,** pahpp-ah, *m* dad

**Papagei,** pah-pah-guy, *m* parrot

**Papier,** pah-peer, *nt* paper

**Papierkorb,** pah-peer-korp, *m* waste-paper basket

**Papiertaschentuch,** pah-

**peer**-tah-shen-took, *nt* paper handkerchief

**Pappe,** pahpp-e, *f* cardboard; paste

**Pappel,** pahpp-el, *f* poplar

**Pappendeckel,** pahpp-en-deck-el, *m* cardboard, pasteboard

**Pappschachtel,** pahpp-shahk-tel, *f* cardboard box

**Paprika,** pahpp-ree-kah, *m* paprika; capsicum, pepper

**Papst,** pahpst, *m* Pope, Pontiff

**päpstlich,** paipst-lik, *adj* papal, pontifical; papist

**Parabolantenne,** pah-rah-bohl-ahnn-ten-e, *f* satellite dish

**Parfüm,** par-fEEm, *nt* perfume, scent

**parieren,** pah-reer-en, *v* to obey; to stop short; to wager; to parry

**Paris,** pah-rees, *nt* Paris

**Parkett,** par-kett, *nt* parquet (floor); stalls *theatre*

**Parkhaus,** park-hows, *nt* multi-storey car park

**Parkkralle,** park-krahll-e, *f* wheel clamp

**Parklücke,** park-lEEk-e, *f* parking space

**Parkplatz,** park-plahts, *m* car park, parking place

**Parkuhr,** park-oohr, *f* parking meter

**Parkverbot,** park-fair-boht, *nt* parking ban

**Partei,** par-ty, *f* party (political, contracting);

faction

**parteiisch**, par-**ty**-ish, *adj*
one-sided, biassed

**Parterre**, par-**tair**, *nt*
ground-floor; pit *theatre*

**Partie**, part-**ee**, *f* outing;
parcel; game

**Partitur**, part-ee-**toor**, *f mus*
score

**Partner**, part-ner, *m* partner;
–**stadt**, *f* twin town

**Party**, part-ee, *f* party

**Parzelle**, par-**tsel**-e, *f* plot
(of land), lot

**Paß**, pahss, *m* passport;
(mountain) pass; passage

**Passagier**, pahss-ah-**zheer**, *m*
passenger

**Passant**, pahss-**ahnnt**, *m*
passer-by

**passen**, pahss-en, *v* to fit; to
pass; to suit

**passieren**, pahss-**eer**-en, *v* to
pass, to cross; to happen,
to occur

**passiv**, pahss-eef, *adj* passive

**Passivrauchen**, pahss-eef-
rowk-en, *nt* passive
smoking

**Paste**, pahss-te, *f* paste; paté

**Pastete**, pahss-**tait**-e, *f* pie,
tart

**pasteurisiert**, pahss-ter-ree-
**zeert**, *adj* pasteurized

**Pastinake**, pahss-tee-**nahck**-
e, *f* parsnip

**Pastor**, pahss-tohr, *m*
(Protestant) clergyman

**Pate**, paht-e, *m* godfather;
–**nkind**, *nt* godchild

**Patient**, pahts-yent, *m*
patient

**Patrone**, pah-**trohn**-e, *f*
cartridge; model; pattern

**Patrouille**, pah-**trooll**-ye, *f*
patrol

**Patsche**, pahtt-she, *f* puddle;
mess; paw

**patzig**, pahtt-sik, *adj*
insolent, saucy

**Pauke**, powk-e, *f* drum,
tympanum

**pauken**, powk-en, *v* to beat
a drum, to thump; to fight
a duel; to cram

**Pauschalreise,
Pauschalurlaub**, pow-
shahl-ry-ze, pow-**shahl**-
oor-lowp, *f m* package
holiday

**Pause**, pow-ze, *f* interval;
pause, rest

**Pazifik**, pah-**tsee**-fick, *m*
Pacific Ocean

**PC**, peh-**tseh**, *m abbr*
**Personalcomputer**, PC

**Pech**, pek, *nt* pitch; hard
luck

**Pechvogel**, pek-fohg-el, *m*
unlucky person

**Pein**, pine, *f* pain, torment,
torture

**peinigen**, pine-ig-en, *v* to
torment

**peinlich**, pine-lik, *adj* very
careful; painful, awkward

**Peitsche**, pite-she, *f* whip,
lash

**Pelle**, pel-e, *f* skin, peel

**pellen**, pel-en, *v* to peel, to
skin

**Pellkartoffeln**, pel-kahrt-of-
eln, *pl* jacket potatoes

**Pelz**, pelts, *m* fur, pelt, skin

**Pendel**, pen-del, *nt*
pendulum; –**verkehr**, *m*
shuttle service; commuter
traffic

**Pendler**, pend-ler, *m*
commuter

**penibel**, pen-**eeb**-el, *adj*
fastidious; painful;
difficult to please

**Penicillin**, pen-ee-tsil-**een**,
*nt* penicillin

**Pension**, pahngs-**yohn**, *f*
pension; guest house; –**är**,
*m* pensioner; –**at**, *nt* girls'
boarding-school; –**ierung**,
*f* retirement

**Pergament**, pair-gah-**ment**,
*nt* parchment; grease-
proof paper

**Perle**, pairl-e, *f* pearl; bead

**perlen**, pairl-en, *v* to
sparkle; to fizz

**Perlmutt(er)**, pairl-**moott**(-
er), *nt (f)*, mother-of-pearl

**Personal**, pair-zohn-ahl, *nt*
personnel, staff; cast

**Personalcomputer**, pair-
zohn-ahl-kom-pyoo-ter, *m*
personal computer

**Personalien**, pair-zohn-**ahl**-
yen, *pl* (full) personal
particulars

**persönlich**, pair-**zern**-lik, *adj*
personal

**Perücke**, pair-**EEck**-e, *f* wig

**Pessimist**, pes-ee-**mist**, *m*
pessimist

**Pest**, pest, *f* plague,
pestilence; epidemic

**Petersilie**, pait-er-zeel-ye, *f*
  parsley

**petzen**, pet-sen, *v* to tell
  tales, to inform

**Pfad**, p'faht, *m* path

**Pfadfinder**, p'faht-fin-der, *m*
  path-finder; (Boy-)Scout

**Pfaffe**, p'fahff-e, *m fam*
  parson, priest

**Pfahl**, p'fahl, *m* post, pole,
  stake, prop

**Pfand**, p'fahnt, *nt* pledge,
  security; forfeit

**pfänden**, p'fend-en, *v* to
  seize as a pledge

**Pfänderspiel**, p'fen-der-
  shpeel, *nt* game of forfeits

**Pfandflasche**, p'fahnt-
  flahsh-e, *f* returnable
  bottle

**Pfandleiher**, p'fahnt-ly-er, *m*
  pawnbroker

**Pfanne**, p'fahnn-e, *f* (frying)
  pan

**Pfannkuchen**, p'fahnn-
  koohk-en, *m* pancake,
  fritter; doughnut

**Pfarrer**, p'fahrr-er, *m* vicar,
  minister

**Pfau**, p'fow, *m* peacock

**Pfeffer**, p'fef-er, *m* pepper;
  –**kuchen**, *m* gingerbread;
  –**minz**, *nt* peppermint

**pfeffern**, p'fef-ern, *v* to
  (season with) pepper; to
  chuck (out)

**Pfeife**, p'fy-fe, *f* (organ)
  pipe; whistle

**pfeifen**, p'fy-fen, *v* to
  whistle; to pipe; to squeak

**Pfeil**, p'file, *m* arrow; dart;

bolt

**Pfeiler**, p'fy-ler, *m* pillar,
  column, post

**Pfennig**, p'fenn-ik, *m*
  pfennig

**pferchen**, p'fairk-en, *v* to
  pen/cram together

**Pferd**, p'fairt, *nt* horse;
  –**estärke**, *f* horse-power

**Pfiff**, p'fif, *m* whistle; trick;
  ruse

**pfiffig**, p'fif-ik, *adj* cunning,
  sly

**Pfingsten**, p'fing-sten, *nt*
  Whitsun

**Pfirsich**, p'feer-zik, *m* peach

**Pflanze**, p'flahnt-se, *f* plant;
  *fam* person

**pflanzen**, p'flahnt-sen, *v* to
  plant

**Pflaster**, p'flahst-er, *nt*
  plaster; flagging,
  pavement

**pflastern**, p'flahst-ern, *v* to
  plaster; to pave

**Pflasterstein**, p'flahst-er-
  shtine, *m* paving-stone

**Pflaume**, p'flowm-e, *f* plum;
  –**nkucken**, *m* plum-tart;
  –**nmus**, *nt* (thick) plum-
  jam

**Pflege**, p'flaig-e, *f* care,
  nursing; maintenance;
  –**kind**, *nt* foster-child

**pflegen**, p'flaig-en, *v* to
  nurse; to tend; to care for;
  to apply oneself to

**Pflicht**, p'flikt, *f* duty;
  obligation; –**eifer**, *m* zeal;
  –**gefühl**, *nt* sense of duty

**Pflock**, p'flock, *m* peg,

wooden pin

**pflücken**, p'flEEck-en, *v* to
  pick; to pluck

**Pflug**, p'flook, *m* plough

**pflügen**, p'flEEg-en, *v* to
  plough

**Pforte**, p'fort-e, *f* gate,
  doorway, portal

**Pförtner**, p'fert-ner, *m*
  porter; doorkeeper; turn-
  key

**Pfote**, p'foht-e, *f* paw, foot;
  scrawl

**Pfrop(en)**, p'frop'f(-en), *m*
  bung; stopper; cork; clot;
  blockage

**Pfuhl**, p'fool, *m* pool,
  puddle, pit

**pfui**, p'foo-ee, *interj* ugh,
  yuk; tut tut

**Pfund**, p'foont, *nt* pound
  (money and weight)

**pfuschen**, p'foosh-en, *v* to
  botch, to bungle

**Pfütze**, p'fEEt-se, *f* puddle,
  mud-hole

**Phantasie**, fahnt-ah-zee, *f*
  imagination, fancy

**phantasieren**, fahnt-ah-
  zeer-en, to fantasize; to
  improvise

**Philister**, fi-list-er, *m*
  Philistine; uncultured
  person

**phlegmatisch**, fleg-mah-tish,
  *adj* lethargic, apathetic

**Phobie**, foh-bee, *f* phobia

**Photograph**, see **Fotograf**

**Photographie**, see
  **Fotografie**

**photographieren**, see

1 4 5

**fotografieren**

**Physik,** fEE-zick, *f* physics

**Pickel, pick**-el, *m* pimple; pickaxe

**Picknick, pick**-nick, *nt* picnic

**piep(s)en, peep**(s)-*en*, *v* to chirp, to squeak

**Piepmatz, peep**-mahts, *m* dicky-bird

**piesacken, pee**-sahck-en, *v* to torment, to torture

**Pik,** peek, *nt* (cards) spades

**pikfein, peek**-fine, *adj* very smart, elegant

**Pilger, pil**-ger, *m* pilgrim

**pilgern, pil**-gern, *v* to go on a pilgrimage

**Pille, pil**-e, *f* pill

**Pilz,** pilts, *m* mushroom, toadstool; fungus

**Pinsel, pin**-zel, *m* paintbrush

**pinseln, pin**-zeln, *v* to paint, to handle a brush

**Pionier,** pee-yohn-**eer**, *m* pioneer

**pirschen, peersh**-en, *v* to stalk (prey)

**Piste, pis**-te, *f* course; piste; runway

**Pizza, pits**-ah, *f* pizza

**Pkw,** peh-kah-weh, *m abbr* **Personenkraftwagen,** car, light goods vehicle

**plädieren,** play-**deer**-en, *v* to plead, to act as advocate

**Plage, plahg**-e, *f* worry, care; torment; nuisance

**plagen, plahg**-en, *v* to annoy, to torment; to

tease

**Plakat,** plah-**kaht**, *nt* placard, poster

**Plan,** plahn, *m* plan, scheme, project; plain, level country

**planen, plahn**-en, *v* to plan, to scheme, to plot

**Planke, plahng**-ke, *f* plank, thick board

**Plänkelei,** pleng-ke-ly, *f* squabble

**planmäßig, plahn**-mace-ik, *adj* according to plan, systematic

**planschen, plahn**-shen, *v* to splash, to paddle

**Plappermaul, plahpp**-er-mowl, *nt* chatterbox, prattler

**plappern, plahpp**-ern, *v* to chatter, to babble

**Plastik, plahss**-tick, *f* sculpture; *nt* plastic, polythene; **–beutel,** *m* plastic bag; **–folie,** *f* plastic film; **–tüte,** *f* plastic bag

**Platane,** plaht-**ahn**-e, *f* plane tree

**plätschern, plet**-shern, *v* to splash; to ripple

**platschnaß, plahtsh**-nahss, *adj* soaking wet

**platt,** plahtt, *adj* flat, even, level

**Plattdeutsch, plahtt**-doytsh, *nt* Low German

**Platte, plahtt**-e, *f* plate; dish; bare spot; board

**plätten, plet**-en, *v* to flatten; to iron; to press

**Plattenspieler, plahtt**-en-shpeel-er, *m* record player

**Platz,** plahts, *m* place, spot; square

**Plätzchen, plets**-ken, *nt* biscuit; small place

**platzen, plahts**-en, *v* to burst; to crack

**Platzkarte, plahts**-kart-e, *f* seat reservation

**Platzmangel, plahts**-mahng-el, *m* lack of space

**Plauderei,** plowd-e-**ry**, *f* chat, gossip(ing)

**plaudern, plowd**-ern, *v* to chat, to gossip

**Pleite, ply**-te, *f* bankruptcy, failure

**Plombe, plom**-be, *f* lead seal; filling (in tooth)

**plombieren,** plom-**beer**-en, *v* to seal; to fill (teeth)

**plötzlich, plerts**-lik, *adj* sudden, unexpected; *adv* suddenly

**plump,** ploomp, *adj* blunt, clumsy, coarse

**plumps,** ploomps, *interj* thump! thud! splash!

**Plunder, ploonn**-der, *m* rubbish, lumber, junk

**plündern, plEEnn**-dern, *v* to plunder, to loot

**Plüsch,** plEEsh, *m* plush

**PLZ,** *abbr* **Postleitzahl**

**Po,** poh, *m* bottom, bum

**Pöbel, perb**-el, *m* common people, rabble

**pochen, pok**-en, *v* to rap, to beat, to knock

**Pointe, pwang**-te, *f* point (of

a joke etc.)

**Pokal**, poh-**kahl**, *m* cup, goblet

**pökeln**, perk-eln, *v* to pickle, to salt

**Polen**, poh-len, *nt* Poland

**polieren**, poh-**leer**-en, *v* to polish

**Politur**, poh-lee-**toor**, *f* polish, gloss

**Polizei**, poh-lee-**tsy**, *f* police; **–beamte(r)**, *m* policeman; **–revier**, *nt* police-station; **–stunde**, *f* (pub) closing time; **–wache**, *f* police-station

**Polizist**, poh-lee-**tsist**, *m* policeman

**polnisch**, pol-nish, *adj* Polish

**Polster**, polst-er, *nt* cushion; upholstery; stuffing; **–möbel**, *pl* upholstered furniture

**polstern**, pol-stern, *v* to upholster, to stuff

**Polterabend**, polt-er-ahb-ent, *m* party on the eve of a wedding

**poltern**, polt-ern, *v* to crash (about)

**Polyester**, pohl-ee-**aist**-er, *m* polyester

**Pommes frites**, pom frit, *pl* chips, French fries

**Popcorn**, pop-korn, *nt* popcorn

**Popmusik**, pop-moo-zeek, *f* pop (music)

**Pornographie**, por-noh-grahff-**ee**, *f* pornography

**Porree**, por-ay, *m* leek

**Portemonnaie**, port-mon-ay, *nt* purse

**Portier**, port-yeh, *m* doorkeeper, porter

**Porto**, port-oh, *nt* postage

**Portugal**, port-oo-gahll, *nt* Portugal

**portugiesisch**, port-oo-geez-ish, *adj* Portuguese

**Porzellan**, por-tsel-**lahn**, *nt* porcelain, china

**Posaune**, poh-**zown**-e, *f* trombone, trumpet

**Positur**, poh-zee-**toor**, *f* posture, attitude

**possierlich**, pos-**eer**-lik, *adj* comical; funny

**Post**, post, *f* mail, post (-office); **–amt**, *nt* post-office (building); **–anweisung**, *f* money-order; **–bote**, *m* postman; **–fach**, *nt* post-office/P.O. box; **–karte**, *f* postcard

**Posten**, post-en, *m* item; lot; sentry; post

**postlagernd**, post-lahg-ernt, *adj* poste restante

**Postleitzahl**, post-lite-tsahl, *f* post code

**Poststempel**, post-shtem-pel, *m* postmark

**postwendend**, post-vendent, *adv* by return of post

**poussieren**, pooss-**eer**-en, *v* to flirt, to court

**Pracht**, prahkt, *f* splendour, pomp

**prächtig**, prek-tik, *adj* splendid, gorgeous, fine

**Prachtkerl**, prahkt-kairl, *m* splendid fellow; beauty

**Prachtstück**, prahkt-stEEck, *nt* showpiece

**prachtvoll**, prahkt-fol, *adj* (very) fine, magnificent

**prägen**, pray-gen, *v* to mint, to coin; to emboss, to stamp

**prahlen**, prahl-en, *v* to boast, to brag

**Prahlerei**, prahl-e-ry, *f* boasting

**prahlerisch**, prahl-er-ish, *adj* boastful

**Prahlhans**, prahl-hahns, *m* boaster

**praktisch**, prahck-tish, *adj* practical; useful

**praktizieren**, prahck-tee-tseer-en, *v* to practise (medicine etc.)

**Praline**, prahl-ee-ne, *f* truffle chocolate

**prall**, prahll, *adj* stretched tight; plump

**prallen**, prahll-en, *v* to crash into, to collide with

**Prämie**, praim-ye, *f* premium; bonus; prize

**präm(i)ieren**, praim-(ee-)eer-en, *v* to give an award/bonus

**prangen**, prahng-en, *v* to shine; to be resplendent

**Präparat**, pray-pah-**raht**, *nt* preparation; medicine

**präparieren**, pray-pah-reer-en, *v* to preserve; to dissect

**Prärie**, pray-ree, *f* prairie

**präsentieren,** pray-zent-**eer**-en, v to present

**Präservativ,** pray-zer-vah-teef, nt condom

**Präsidium,** pray-zeed-ee-oomm, nt presidency; headquarters

**prasseln,** prahss-eln, v to patter; to crackle

**prassen,** prahss-en, v to lead the high life

**prätentiös,** pray-ten-se-erss, adj pretentious

**Praxis,** prahck-siss, f practice; experience; connexion; (doctor's) surgery

**predigen,** pray-dee-gen, v to preach; to sermonize

**Prediger,** pray-dee-ger, m preacher, clergyman

**Predigt,** pray-dikt, f sermon

**Preis,** price, m price; prize

**Preiselbeere,** pry-sel-bair-e, f cranberry

**preisen,** pry-zen, v to praise; to extol

**preisgeben,** price-gay-ben, v to abandon; to expose; to betray

**preisgekrönt,** price-ge-krernt, adj prize-winning, award-winning

**preisgünstig,** price-gEEnst-ik, adj good value, inexpensive

**Preisliste,** price-list-e, f price-list

**Preisschild,** price-shilt, nt price tag

**preiswert,** price-vairt, adj good value

**prellen,** prel-en, v to overcharge; to dupe; to rebound

**Presse,** press-e, f press; journalism; **–agentur,** f press agency; **–bericht,** m news item, news story; **–fotograf,** m press photographer; **–freiheit,** f freedom of the press

**pressen,** press-en, v to press, to squeeze

**pressieren,** press-eer-en, v to be urgent

**prickeln,** prick-eln, v to prickle, to sting; to bubble

**Priester,** preest-er, m priest

**prima,** preem-ah, adj & interj excellent, great

**Primel,** preem-el, f cowslip, primrose

**Prinz,** prints, m prince

**Prinzessin,** prin-tsess-in, f princess

**Prinzip,** prin-tseep, nt principle

**prinzipiell,** prin-tseep-ee-ell, adj & adv on principle

**Prise,** preez-e, f pinch (of salt etc.)

**Pritsche,** prit-she, f flat-bed (of lorry); plank-bed

**Privatdozent,** pree-vaht-doh-tsent, m private lecturer

**Privatfernsehen,** pree-vaht-fairn-say-en, nt commercial television

**privatisieren,** pree-vaht-e-zeer-en, v to privatise

**Privatschule,** pree-vaht-shoo-le, f private school

**pro,** proh, prep for, per

**Probe,** proh-be, f trial, test; rehearsal; sample

**proben,** proh-ben, v to try; to rehearse

**probeweise,** proh-be-vy-ze, adv experimentally

**probieren,** proh-beer-en, v to try; to rehearse

**Produzent,** proh-doo-tsent, m producer, grower, maker

**produzieren,** proh-doo-tseer-en, v to produce, to make

**Profi,** proh-fee, m professional (sport etc.)

**profitieren,** proh-feet-eer-en, v to profit from

**Prokurist,** proh-koor-ist, m head-clerk (authorized to sign)

**Propaganda,** pro-pah-gahnn-dah, f propaganda

**prophezeien,** proh-fe-tsy-en, v to prophesy

**prosit,** proh-zit, interj cheers, to your health

**Prospekt,** proh-spekt, m brochure, leaflet; prospectus

**prost,** prohst, interj cheers, to your health

**protegieren,** proh-te-zheer-en, v to favour, to patronize

**protestieren,** proh-test-eer-en, v to protest

**Protokoll,** proh-toh-kol, nt minutes, record; protocol

**protzen, prot**-sen, v to boast, to show off

**protzig, prot**-sik, adj boastful

**Proviant,** proh-vee-**ahnt,** m provisions

**Provinz,** proh-**vints,** f province, county, country

**Provision,** proh-vee-zee-**ohn,** f commission

**provisorisch,** proh-ve-zohr-ish adj temporary, provisional

**Prozedur,** proh-tsay-**doohr,** f procedure, process

**Prozent,** proh-**tsent,** nt per cent

**Prozess,** proh-**tsess,** m lawsuit; process

**prozessieren,** proh-tsess-eer-en, v to litigate

**prüde, prEED**-e, adj prudish

**prüfen, prEEf**-en, v to test, to examine

**Prüfung, prEEf**-oong, f examination; affliction

**Prügel, prEEg**-el, m cudgel; pl thrashing; **–ei,** f fight, scuffle; **–knabe,** m scapegoat, whipping-boy

**prügeln, prEEg**-eln, v to thrash; **sich –,** to have a fight

**Prügelstrafe, prEEg**-el-shtrah-fe, f corporal punishment

**Prunk,** proonk, m pomp, splendour

**prunken,** proonk-en, v to be resplendent; to flaunt

**prusten,** proost-en, v to sneeze; to burst out

laughing

**PS,** abbr **Pferdestärke,** hp

**Psyche, psEE**-ke, f psyche

**Psychiater, psEEk**-yah-ter, m psychiatrist

**Psychoanalytiker, psEEk**-oh-ah-nah-lEEt-ee-ker, m psychoanalyst

**psychologisch, psEEk**-oh-loh-gish, adj psychological

**Psychopath, psEEk**-oh-**paht,** m psychopath

**Psychotherapeut, psEEk**-oh-tair-ah-**poyt,** m psychotherapist

**Publikum, poob**-lee-koomm, nt audience

**Pudel, pood**-el, m poodle

**Pudding, poodd**-ing, m blancmange

**Puder, pood**-er, m powder

**pudern, pood**-ern, v to powder

**Puderquaste, pood**-er-kvahst-e, f powder-puff

**Puff,** pooff, m bang; thump; pouffe; fam brothel

**Puffärmel, pooff**-airm-el, m puff(ed) sleeve

**Puffer, pooff**-er, m buffer; (potato) pancake

**Pulle, pooll**-e, f fam bottle

**Pullover, pooll**-oh-ver, m pullover

**Puls,** pools, m pulse

**Pulsader, pools**-ahd-er, f artery

**pulsieren,** pooll-zeer-en, v to pulsate; to throb

**Pulsschlag, pools**-shlahk, m pulsation, beating of pulse

**Pult,** poolt, nt (writing-) desk

**Pulver, pool**-ver, nt powder

**Pumpe, poomp**-e, f pump

**pumpen, poomp**-en, v to pump; fam to borrow/lend

**Pumpernickel, poomp**-er-nick-el, m black rye-bread

**Pumphose, poomp**-hoh-ze, f baggy trousers

**Punkt,** poonkt, m point; full-stop, period

**pünktlich, pEEnkt**-lik, adj punctual; exact

**Pünktlichkeit, pEEnkt**-lik-kite, f punctuality

**Pupille,** pooh-**pil**-e, f pupil (of eye)

**Puppe, poopp**-e, f doll, puppet; pupa, cocoon

**pur,** poor, adj pure, sheer

**Püree, pEEr**-ay, nt mash, puree

**pürieren, pEEr**-eer-en, v to liquidize

**purpurfarbig, poor**-poor-fahr-bik, adj crimson

**Purzelbaum, poort**-sel-bowm, m somersault

**purzeln, poort**-seln, v to tumble

**pusten, poost**-en, v to blow, to puff

**Pute, poot**-e, f turkey(-hen)

**Puter, poot**-er, m turkey (-cock)

**Putsch,** pootsh, m coup d'état, revolt, putsch

**Putz,** poots, m decoration; millinery; finery; plaster

**putzen, poots**-en, v to

polish; to clean(se); to
adorn

**putzig, poots**-ik, *adj* droll,
funny

**Putzfrau, poots**-frow, *f*
cleaning lady

**Putzkolonne, poots**-ko-lo-
ne, *f* cleaning staff

**Putzmittel, poots**-mit-el, *nt*
cleanser; polishing
material

**Putzzeug, poots**-tsoyk, *nt*
polishing material(s)

**Puzzle(spiel), poozz**-el
(-shpeel), *nt* jigsaw

**Pyrenäen,** pEE-ray-**nay**-en,
*pl* Pyrenees

**Quacksalber, kvahck**-zahlb-er, *m* quack (doctor); **–ei**, *f* quackery, quack medicine

**Quader, kvahd**-er, *m* cuboid

**Quadrat, kvah-draht**, *nt* square

**quaken, kvahk**-en, *v* to croak; to quack

**Qual, kvahl**, *f* torment, intense suffering

**quälen, kvay**-len, *v* to torture, to torment;

**Quälerei, kvay-le-ry**, *f* torture; worry

**quälerisch, kvay**-ler-ish, *adj* tormenting, annoying

**Quälgeist, kvail-gy'st**, *m* tormenter

**Qualität, kvahl-ee-tait**, *f* quality, kind, variety

**Qualifikation, kvahl-ee-fee-kahts-yohn**, *f* qualification

**qualifiziert, kvahl-ee-fee-tseert**, *adj* qualified

**Qualle, kvahll**-e, *f* jelly-fish

**Qualm, kvahlm**, *m* (thick) smoke; fumes

**qualmen, kvahll**-men, *v* to give off fumes/thick smoke; *fam* to smoke (cigarettes)

**qualmig, kvahll**-mik, *adj* smoky, full of fumes

**qualvoll, kvahl**-fol, *adj* agonizing

**Quantität, kvahnn-tee-tait**, *f* quantity

**Quantum, kvahnn**-toomm, *nt* quantity; quota; quantum

**Quappe, kvahpp**-e, *f* tadpole

**Quark, kvahrk**, *m* curds, cream-cheese; *fam* trash

**Quart, kvahrt**, *f mus* fourth

**Quartal, kvahrt-ahl**, *nt* quarter (of a year)

**Quarz, kvahrts**, *nt* quartz

**quasi, kvah**-zee, *adv* so to speak, as it were

**quasseln, kvahss**-eln, *v* to chatter

**Quasselstrippe, kvahss**-el-shtrip-e, *f* chatterbox

**Quaste, kvahst**-e, *f* tassel, pom-pom

**Quatsch, kvahtsh**, *m* nonsense, rubbish

**quatschen, kvahtt**-shen, *v* to talk rubbish; **kvaht**-shen, *v* to squash

**Quecksilber, kveck**-sil-ber, *nt* mercury, quick-silver

**Quelle, kvel**-e, *f* spring, source, fountain

**quellen, kvel**-en, *v* to pour, to stream, to well (up); to swell

**Quengelei, kveng**-e-ly, *f* bother, nagging, fault-finding

**quengelig, kveng**-el-ik, *adj* nagging, grumbling

**quengeln, kveng**-eln, *v* to nag, to grumble, to find fault

**quer, kvair**, *adj* slanting; *adv* across, diagonally; **– durch**, *adv* right across/through

**Quere, kvair**-e, *f* diagonal

**Querflöte, kvair**-flert-e, *f*
flute

**Querkopf, kvair**-kop'f, *m*
obstinate person

**Querschnitt, kvair**-shnitt,
*m* cross-section

**Querstraße, kvair**-shtrahs-
e, *f* side-street, turning

**quetschen, kvet**-shen, *v* to
crush, to pinch

**Quetschung, kvet**-shoong, *f*
bruise

**quieken, kveek**-en, *v* to
squeak, to squeal

**quietschen, kveet**-shen, *v* to
squeak, to creak

**Quirl, kvirl**, *m* whisk

**quirlen, kvirl**-en, *v* to
whisk; to twirl

**Quitte, kvit**-e, *f* quince

**quittieren, kvit-eer**-en, *v* to
give a receipt; to quit

**Quittung, kvit**-oong, *f*
receipt; penalty

**Quiz, kvis**, *nt* Quiz;
**–sendung,** *f* quiz show

**Quote, kvoht**-e, *f* share,
quota

**Rabatt,** rah-**bahtt**, m rebate, discount

**Rabbiner,** rah-**been**-er, m rabbi

**Rabe,** rah-be, m raven

**rabenschwarz,** rah-ben-shvahrts, adj jet-black

**rabiat,** rah-be-**aht**, adj rabid; rough; furious

**Rache,** rahk-e, f revenge, vengeance

**Rachen,** rahk-en, m throat, pharynx

**rächen,** rek-en, v to revenge, to avenge

**Rad,** raht, nt wheel; cycle, bike

**Radar,** rahd-ahr, m & nt radar; **–falle,** f speed trap; **–kontrolle,** f radar speed check

**Radau,** rah-dow, m loud noise, row

**Raddampfer,** raht-dahmp-fer, m paddle-steamer

**radebrechen,** rahd-e-brek-en, v to speak a language imperfectly

**radeln,** raht-eln, v to cycle

**rädern,** ray-dern, v to put on wheels

**radfahren,** raht-fahr-en, v to cycle

**Radfahrer,** raht-fahr-er, m cyclist

**radieren,** rah-deer-en, v to erase; to etch

**Radiergummi,** rah-deer-goomm-ee, m (india-) rubber

**Radiermesser,** rah-deer-mess-er, nt pen-knife

**Radierung,** rah-deer-oong, f etching; erasure

**Radieschen,** rah-dees-ken, nt radish

**radikal,** rah-dee-kahl, adj radical

**radioaktiv,** rah-dee-oh-ahck-**teef,** adj radioactive

**Radiosender,** rah-dee-oh-zen-der, m radio station

**Radler,** rahd-ler, m cyclist

**radschlagen,** raht-shlahg-en, v to turn a somersault

**Radweg,** raht-vaig, m cycleway, cycle path

**raffen,** rahff-en, v to amass; to gather; to take in (seams)

**Raffinerie,** rahff-een-er-ee, f refinery

**raffiniert,** rahff-een-eert, adj cunning; refined

**Rahm,** rahm, m cream

**rahmen,** rahm-en, v to frame; to form cream; to skim

**Rahmen,** rahm-en, m frame

**Rakete,** rah-kayt-e, f rocket

**rammen,** rahmm-en, v to ram; to stamp firm

**Rampe,** rahmp-e, f ramp, platform

**Ramsch,** rahmsh, m job-lot; junk; **–ware,** f cheap goods

**ran,** rahn, abbr heran

**Rand,** rahnt, m edge; rim; brink

**randalieren,** rahn-dah-lee-ren, v to (go on the) rampage

**Rang,** rahng, m rank, station; circle theatre

**rangieren,** rahng-zheer-en, v to shunt; to take rank

**Ranke,** rahng-ke, f tendril,

shoot

**ranken, rahng**-ken *v* to creep, to climb (of plants)

**Ranzen, rahnt**-sen, *m* satchel

**ranzig, rahnt**-sik, *adj* rancid, rank

**Rappe, rahpp**-e, *m* black horse

**rappeln, rahpp**-eln, *v* to rattle

**Raps,** rahpps, *m* rape (-seed), colza

**rar,** rahr, *adj* rare, scarce; exquisite

**Rarität,** rahr-ee-**tait**, *f* rarity; curio(sity)

**rasch,** rahsh, *adj* quick, brisk, speedy

**rascheln, rahsh**-eln, *v* to rustle; to crackle

**Rasen, rahz**-en, *m* lawn, turf; **–mäher,** *m* lawn-mower

**rasen, rahz**-en, *v* to rage; to rush; to be frenzied

**Raserei,** rahz-e-**ry,** *f* frenzy, madness

**Rasierapparat,** rahz-eer-ahpp-ah-raht, *m* (electric) shaver

**rasieren,** rahz-eer-en, *v* to shave

**Rasierklinge,** rahz-eer-kling-e, *f* razor-blade

**Rasierpinsel,** rahz-eer-pin-zel, *m* shaving-brush

**Raspel, rahsp**-el, *f* rasp

**raspeln, rahsp**-eln, *v* to rasp; to scrape

**Rasse, rahss**-e, *f* race, breed,

stock

**rasseln, rahss**-eln, *v* to rattle; to clank

**rassig, rahss**-ik, *adj* racy, sleek; spirited, lively

**Rassismus,** rahss-**is**-mooss, *m* racism

**Rassist,** rahss-**ist**, *m* racist

**Rast,** rahst, *f* rest; recreation; halt

**rasten, rahst**-en, *v* to rest; to halt

**Rat,** raht, *m* advice; council(lor)

**Rate, raht**-e, *f* instalment; rate

**raten, raht**-en, *v* to advise; to guess (see **erraten**)

**ratenweise, raht**-en-vy-ze, *adv* in instalments

**Ratgeber, raht**-gayb-er, *m* adviser, counsellor

**Rathaus, raht**-hows, *nt* town-hall

**rationalisieren,** rahts-yohn-ahl-ee-**zee**-ren, *v* to rationalise

**rationell,** rahts-yohn-**ell**, *adj* rational; efficient

**ratlos, raht**-lohs, *adj* helpless, at a loss

**ratsam, raht**-zahmm, *adj* advisable; commendable

**Ratschlag, raht**-shlahk, *m* advice, counsel

**Rätsel, rayt**-sel, *nt* riddle, puzzle; mystery

**rätselhaft, rayt**-sel-hahft, *adj* mysterious; puzzling

**Ratsherr, rahts**-hair, *m* councillor

**Ratskeller, rahts**-kel-er, *m* cellar under the town-hall

**Ratte, rahtt**-e, *f* rat; **–fänger,** *m* rat-catcher; Pied Piper

**rattern, rahtt**-ern, *v* to rattle

**Raub,** rowp, *m* robbery; abduction; prey

**rauben,** row-ben, *v* to rob, to steal

**Räuber,** roy-ber, *m* robber, thief

**Raubgier,** rowp-geer, *f* rapacity

**Raubtier,** rowp-teer, *nt* beast of prey

**Raubvogel,** rowp-fohg-el, *m* bird of prey

**Rauch,** rowk, *m* smoke

**rauchen,** rowk-en, *v* to smoke

**Raucher,** rowk-er, *m* smoker; **–abteil,** *nt* smoking compartment

**Rauchfang,** rowk-fahng, *m* chimney

**rauchig,** rowk-ik, *adj* smoky

**räuchern,** royk-ern, *v* to cure with smoke; to fumigate

**'rauf,** rowf, *abbr* **herauf**

**Raufbold,** rowf-bolt, *m* bully

**raufen,** rowf-en, *v* to pull up/out; to brawl

**rauh,** row, *adj* rough, rugged; severe, harsh

**Raum,** rowm, *m* room, space; locality

**räumen,** roym-en, *v* to clear; to remove

**Raumfahrt, rowm**-fart, *f* space travel

**räumlich, roym**-lik, *adj* in regard to space, spatial

**Räumlichkeit, roym**-lik-kite, *f* space; **–en**, *pl* rooms, premises

**raunen, rown**-en, *v* to whisper

**Raupe, rowp**-e, *f* caterpillar

**'aus, rowss,** *abbr* **heraus**

**Rausch, rowsh,** *m* ecstasy; intoxication

**rauschen, rowsh**-en, *v* to rush; to rustle; to roar

**Rauschgift, rowsh**-gift, *nt* drug; **–süchtige(r)**, *m & f*, drug addict

**räuspern (sich), roysp**-ern (zik), *v* to clear one's throat

**Razzia, rahtt**-see-ah, *f* raid

**Reagenzglas, ray**-ah-**gents**-glahs, *nt* test tube

**reagieren, ray**-ah-**geer**-en, *v* to react; to respond

**Realschule, ray**-ahl-**shool**-e, *f* type of secondary school

**Realität, ray**-ahl-ee-tait, *f* reality

**realitätsfern, realitätsfremd, ray**-ahl-ee-taits-fairn, -fremt, *adj* unrealistic

**Rebe, ray**-be, *f* vine; shoot

**Rebhuhn, rayp**-hoon, *nt* partridge

**Rechen, rek**-en, *m* rake; rack

**Rechenschaft, rek**-en-shahft, *f* account

**Recherche, ray**-**shair**-she, *f* investigation, inquiry

**rechnen, rek**-nen, *v* to reckon, to calculate

**Rechnung, rek**-noong, *f* bill, invoice; account

**Rechnungsauszug, rek**-noongs-ows-tsook, *m* statement of account

**recht, rekt,** *adj* right; right-hand; correct

**Recht, rekt,** *nt* right, privilege; justice; law

**rechtfertigen, rekt**-fairt-ig-en, *v* to justify; to defend

**rechthaberisch, rekt**-hahb-er-ish, *adj* dogmatic, pig-headed

**rechtlich, rekt**-lik, *adj* lawful, legal; fair

**rechtmäßig, rekt**-mace-ik, *adj* rightful, lawful

**rechts, rekts,** *adv* on the right; right

**Rechtsanwalt, rekts**-ahnn-vahlt, *m* solicitor; lawyer; barrister

**rechtschaffen, rekt**-shahff-en, *adj* upright, just

**Rechtschreibung, rekt**-shry-boong, *f* orthography

**Rechtsfall, rekts**-fahll, *m* case (court)

**rechtsgültig, rekts**-gEElt-ik, *adj* valid in law

**Rechtshänder, rekts**-hen-der, *m* right-handed person

**rechtskräftig, rekts**-kreft-ik, *adj* valid, legal

**rechtsum, rekts**-oomm, *adv* to the right; about (turn)

**Rechtsverkehr, rekts**-fair-kair, *m* right-hand traffic

**rechtswegen, rekts**-vaig-en, *adv* by rights

**rechtzeitig, rekt**-tsy-tik, *adv* in good time, punctually

**recken, reck**-en, *v* to stretch

**recyceln, ree**-**sike**-eln, *v* to recycle

**Recycling, ree**-**sike**-ling, *nt* recycling

**Redakteur, ray**-dahck-**ter**, *m* editor

**Redaktion, ray**-dahckts-yohn, *f* editor's office; editing

**Rede, ray**-de, *f* speech; talk; address

**Redefreiheit, ray**-de-fry-hite, *f* freedom of speech

**redegewandt, ray**-de-ge-vahnt, *adj* eloquent

**reden, ray**-den, *v* to talk, to speak

**Redensart, ray**-dens-art, *f* (hackneyed/empty) phrase; idiom

**redigieren, ray**-dee-geer-en, *v* to edit

**redlich, rayt**-lik, *adj* upright; open; straightforward

**Redner, rayd**-ner, *m* orator; speaker

**redselig, rayd**-zail-ik, *adj* talkative

**Reeder, rayd**-er, *m* ship-owner; shipper

**Reederei, rayd**-*e*-**ry**, *f* shipping(-business)

**reel, ray**-el, *adj* fair, honest;

respectable; real

**Referendar,** ref-*e*-ren-**dar,** *m* trainee; student (teacher); articled clerk

**Referent,** ref-*e*-rent, *m* speaker, reporter

**reflektieren,** ref-lek-**teer**-en, *v* to reflect; to think

**Refrain,** ray-**freng,** *m* chorus of a song

**Regal,** ray-**gahl,** *nt* shelves, shelving, pigeon-holes

**rege,** ray-ge, *adj* lively, brisk, active

**Regel,** ray-gel, *f* rule; regulation

**regelmäßig,** ray-gel-mace-ik, *adj* regular; orderly

**regeln,** ray-geln, *v* to regulate; to arrange

**regelrecht,** ray-gel-rekt, *adj* real, proper

**regen (sich),** ray-gen (zik), *v* to stir, to move

**Regen,** ray-gen, *m* rain;
   **–bogen,** *m* rainbow;
   **–mantel,** *m* raincoat;
   **–schirm,** *m* umbrella;
   **–wald,** *m* rain forest;
   **–wurm,** *m* earth-worm

**Regie,** ray-zhee, *f* production; direction (film)

**regieren,** ray-**gheer**-en, *v* to rule, to govern

**Regierung,** ray-**gheer**-oong, *f* government

**Regisseur,** ray-zhee-**ser,** *m* producer; (film) director

**regnen,** rayg-nen, *v* to rain

**regnerisch,** rayg-ner-ish, *adj*

rainy

**Reh,** ray, *nt* deer, roe(-buck)

**Rehbraten,** ray-braht-en, *m* roast venison

**reiben,** ry-ben, *v* to rub; to grate

**Reiberei,** ry-be-ry, *f* friction

**reich,** ry'k, *adj* rich

**Reich,** ry'k, *nt* empire, realm

**reichen,** ry'k-en, *v* to reach, to stretch; to pass

**reichhaltig,** ry'k-hahlt-ik, *adj* plentiful, abundant

**reichlich,** ry'k-lik, *adj* copious, plentiful

**Reichtum,** ry'k-toom, *m* riches, wealth

**reif,** rife, *adj* ripe, mature

**Reif,** rife, *m* ring; hoop; frost

**Reife,** ry-fe, *f* maturity, ripeness

**reifen,** ry-fen, *v* to ripen, to mature

**Reifen,** ry-fen, *m* hoop; tyre

**reiflich,** rife-lik, *adj* mature

**Reihe,** ry-e, *f* row; range; succession; turn

**reihen,** ry-en, *v* to string, to arrange in rows; to tack (sewing)

**Reihenfolge,** ry-en-folg-e, *f* succession, sequence

**Reiher,** ry-er, *m* heron

**Reim,** rime, *m* rhyme

**reimen,** ry-men, *v* to rhyme, to make up rhymes

**rein,** rine, *adj* pure; clean; chaste; net

**reinigen,** ry-nig-en, *v* to clean(se); to purify

**Reinigung,** ry-nee-goong, *f*

clean(s)ing; purification; dry cleaning

**reinlich,** rine-lik, *adj* clean; tidy

**Reis,** rice, *m* rice

**Reise,** ry-ze, *f* voyage, journey, trip; **–büro,** *nt* travel agency

**reisefertig,** ry-ze-fair-tik, *adj* ready for a journey

**Reiseführer,** *m* (tour) guide; guidebook

**reisen,** ry-zen, *v* to travel

**Reisekrankheit,** ry-ze-krahnk-hite, *f* travel sickness

**Reisende(r),** ry-zen-de(r), *m & f* traveller; passenger

**Reisepaß,** ry-ze-pahss, *m* passport

**Reisescheck,** ry-ze-sheck, *m* traveller's cheque

**Reisetasche,** ry-ze-tah-she, *f* travelling-bag, grip

**Reisig,** ry-zik, *nt* brushwood, faggots

**reißen,** ry-sen, *v* to tear; to pull; to break, to snap

**Reitbahn,** rite-bahn, *f* bridle path

**reiten,** ry-ten, *v* to ride (a horse)

**Reiter,** ry-ter, *m* rider

**Reithose,** rite-hoh-ze, *f* riding breeches; jodhpurs

**Reitweg,** rite-wayk, *m* bridle path

**Reiz,** rites, *m* irritation; charm

**reizbar,** rites-bahr, *adj* irritable, touchy

**reizen, rites**-en, *v* to irritate; to stimulate; to incite; to charm

**reizend, rites**-ent, *adj* charming, delightful

**reizvoll, rites**-fol, *adj* attractive; fascinating

**Reklamation,** ray-klah-mahts-**yohn**, *f* complaint; protest

**Reklame, ray-klah**-me, *f* advertising, advertisement; publicity

**reklamieren,** ray-klah-**meer**-en, *v* to complain; to claim

**rempeln, rem**-peln, *v* to jostle

**Rennbahn, ren**-bahn, *f* race-course

**rennen, ren**-en, *v* to run, to rush

**Rennpferd, ren**-pfairt, *nt* race-horse

**Renommee,** ray-nom-**ay**, *nt* renown; reputation

**renommiert,** ray-nom-**eert**, *adj* renowned

**renovieren,** ray-noh-**veer**-en, *v* to renovate, to redecorate; to refurbish

**rentabel,** ren-**tahb**-el, *adj* lucrative, profitable

**Rente, rent**-e, *f* pension; income; annuity

**rentieren (sich),** rent-**eer**-en (zik), *v* to be worthwhile/profitable, to pay

**Rentner, rent**-ner, *m* pensioner

**Reparatur,** ray-pah-raht-**oor**, *f* repair(ing); **–werkstatt,** *f* garage; repair shop

**reparieren,** ray-pah-**reer**-en, *v* to repair

**Reservierung,** ray-zer-**veer**-oong, *f* booking, reservation

**Residenz,** ray-zee-**dents**, *f* residence; seat (mansion)

**respektieren,** res-peck-**teer**-en, *v* to respect

**Rest,** rest, *m* rest, remainder; remnant

**restlos, rest-lohs**, *adj & adv* complete(ly), total(ly)

**Resultat,** ray-zooll-**taht**, *nt* result; outcome

**retour,** ray-**toor**, *adv* back

**retten, ret**-en, *v* to save, to rescue

**Rettich, ret**-ik, *m* radish

**Rettung, ret**-oong *f* rescue; salvation; escape

**Reue, roy**-e, *f* penitence, repentance

**revanchieren (sich),** ray-vahng-**sheer**-en (zik), *v* to return a compliment/service; to have one's revenge

**revidieren,** ray-vee-**deer**-en, *v* to examine

**Revision,** ray-veez-**yohn**, *f* auditing; examination; appeal

**Revisor,** ray-vee-**zohr**, *m* auditor

**Rezension,** ray-tsents-**yohn**, *f* review (of book etc.)

**Rezept,** ray-**tsept**, *nt* recipe; prescription

**Rezeption,** ray-tsepts-**yohn**, *f* reception (hotel etc.)

**Rhabarber,** rah-**barb**-er, *m* rhubarb

**Rhein,** rine, *m* Rhine

**Rheinwein,** rine-vine, *m* Rhine wine, hock

**richten, rik**-ten, *v* to set, to straighten; to direct; to judge

**Richter, rik**-ter, *m* judge

**Richtgeschwindigkeit, rikt**-ge-shvind-ik-kite, *f* recommended speed

**richtig, rik**-tik, *adj* right, correct; just, fair

**Richtigkeit, rik**-tik-kite, *f* correctness; fairness

**Richtlinie, rikt**-leen-ye, *f* guideline; directive

**Richtung, rikt**-oong, *f* direction, course

**riechen, reek**-en, *v* to smell

**Riege, reeg**-e, *f* team, squad

**Riegel, reeg**-el, *m* bolt

**Riemen, reem**-en, *m* strap, thong

**Riese, reez**-e, *m* giant; ogre

**rieseln, reez**-eln, *v* to trickle; to fall (snow)

**riesenartig, reez**-en-art-ik, *adj* like a giant

**Riesenerfolg, reez**-en-air-folk, *m* huge success

**riesengroß, reez**-en-grohs, *adj* gigantic

**riesig, reez**-ik, *adj* colossal, enormous

**Riff,** rif, *nt* reef; sandbank

**Rille,** ril-*e*, *f* groove; furrow

**Rind,** rint, *nt,* cow; beef

**Rinde,** rin-*de*, *f* bark, rind; crust

**Rindfleisch,** rint-fly'sh, *nt* beef

**Rindvieh,** rint-fee, *nt* cattle;*fam* blockhead

**Ring,** ring, *m* ring; circle; round

**Ringbahn,** ring-bahn, *f* circle line

**ringeln,** ring-eln, *v* to curl; to coil

**ringen,** ring-en, *v* to wrestle; to wring (hands)

**ringsherum, ringsumher,** rings-hair-oomm, -oomm-hair, *adv* round about

**Ringstraße,** ring-strahs-*e*, *f* ring road

**Rinne,** rin-*e*, *f* groove; gully; sewer

**rinnen,** rin-en, to trickle; to flow; to leak

**Rinnstein,** rin-shtine, *m* gutter

**Rippe,** rip-*e*, *f* rib; frame(work)

**Rippenspeer,** rip-en-shpair, *m* roast loin of pork

**Risiko,** ree-zee-koh, *nt* risk

**riskant,** risk-ahnt, *adj* risky

**riskieren,** risk-eer-en, *v* to risk

**Riß,** ris, *m* tear, fissure; gap, crack

**rissig,** ris-ik, *adj* cracked

**Ritt,** rit, *m* ride

**Ritter,** rit-er, *m* knight; cavalier

**Rittergut,** rit-er-goot, *nt* gentleman's estate

**ritterlich,** rit-er-lik, *adj* chivalrous; knightly

**rittlings,** rit-lings, *adj* astride

**Ritze,** rits-*e*, *f* slit; fissure; scratch

**ritzen,** rit-sen, *v* to slit; to scratch; to graze

**Rizinusöl,** rit-see-nooss-erl, *nt* castor-oil

**Robbe,** rob-*e*, *f* seal

**Roboter,** roh-boh-ter, *m* robot

**röcheln,** rerk-eln, *v* to groan; to give a death rattle

**Rock,** rock, *m* coat; skirt

**Rogen,** rohg-en, *m* hard roe

**Roggen,** rogg-en, *m* rye; **–brot,** *nt* rye-bread

**roh,** roh, *adj* raw; rough; brutal

**Roheit,** roh-hite, *f* rawness; roughness; brutality

**Rohr,** rohr, *nt* cane; tube; pipe; barrel (of gun)

**Röhre,** rer-*e*, *f* tube; channel; oven

**Rohrstock,** rohr-shtock, *m* cane, stick

**Rolle,** rol-*e*, *f* roller; reel; spool; roll; rôle

**rollen,** rol-en, *v* to roll; to rumble

**Rollmops,** rol-mops, *m* pickled herring, roll-mop

**Rollo,** rol-oh, *nt* roller-blind

**Rollschuh,** rol-shoo, *m* roller-skate

**Rollstuhl,** rol-shtool, *m* wheelchair; **–fahrer,** *m* wheelchair user

**Rolltreppe,** rol-trep-*e*, *f* escalator

**Rom,** rohm, *nt* Rome

**Roman,** roh-mahn, *m* novel

**Röntgenstrahlen,** rernt-gen-shtrahl-en, *pl* X-rays

**rosa,** roh-zah, *adj* pink

**Rose,** roh-ze, *f* rose

**Rosenkohl,** roh-zen-kohl, *m* brussels sprouts

**rosig,** roh-zik, *adj* rosy

**Rosine,** roh-zeen-*e*, *f* raisin; sultana

**Roß,** ross, *nt* horse, steed

**Rost,** rost, *m* rust; grate; gridiron

**Rostbraten,** rosst-braht-en, *m* roast joint (of beef)

**rosten,** rosst-en, *v* to rust

**rösten,** rerst-en, *v* to grill; to roast, to fry

**rostig,** rost-ik, *adj* rusty

**rot,** roht, *adj* red

**rotbäckig,** roht-beck-ik, *adj* rosy-cheeked

**Röte,** rert-*e*, *f* redness

**rothaarig,** roht-hahr-ik, *adj* red-haired

**Rotkehlchen,** roht-kayl-ken, *nt* robin (redbreast)

**Rotkraut,** roht-krowt, *nt* red cabbage

**Rotlichtbezirk,** roht-likt-be-tsirk, *m* red-light district

**Rotwein,** roht-vine, *m* red wine

**Rotte,** rot-*e*, *f* gang; band; swarm

**Rotwild,** roht-vilt, *nt* red

deer

**Roulade,** rool-**ahd**-*e*, *f* beef olive

**routiniert,** root-een-**eert**, *adj* experienced

**Rowdy,** row-dee, *m* vandal

**Rübe,** rEEb-*e*, *f* turnip

**rüber,** rEEb-*er*, *abbr* **herüber**

**Rubin,** roob-een, *m* ruby

**ruchlos,** rook-lohs, *adj* wicked, malicious

**Ruck,** roock, *m* jerk, push

**Rückblick,** rEEck-blick, *m* retrospect

**Rücken,** rEEck-en, *m* back; rear; ridge

**rücken,** rEEck-en, *v* to move, to shift

**Rückenmark,** rEEck-en-mark, *nt* spinal cord

**Rückfahrkarte,** rEEck-fahr-kart-*e*, *f* return ticket

**Rückfahrt,** rEEck-fahrt, *f* return journey

**Rückfall,** rEEck-fahll, *m* relapse

**Rückflug,** rEEck-flook, *m* return flight

**Rückgabe,** rEEck-gahb-*e*, *f* return, restitution

**Rückgang,** rEEck-gahng, *m* fall; decline

**Rückgrat,** rEEck-graht, *nt* backbone; spine

**Rückhalt,** rEEck-hahlt, *m* reserve; support

**Rückkehr,** rEEck, **Rückkunft,** rEEck-kair, -koonft, *f* return

**rücklings,** rEEck-lings, *adj* backwards

**Rückreise,** rEEck-ry-ze, *f* return journey

**Rucksack,** roock-zahck, *m* rucksack

**Rückseite,** rEEck-zy-te, *f* back, reverse

**Rücksicht,** rEEck-sikt, *f* consideration, regard

**Rücksichtnahme,** rEEck-sikt-nahm-*e*, *f* (taking into) consideration

**Rücksprache,** rEEck-shprahk-*e*, *f* consultation

**rückständig,** rEEck-shtend-ik, *adj* in arrears

**Rücktritt,** rEEck-trit, *m* retirement, resignation

**rückwärts,** rEEck-vairts, *adv* back(wards)

**Rückweg,** rEEck-vayk, *m* way back/home

**ruckweise,** roock-vy-ze, *adv* by jerks

**Rückzug,** rEEck-tsook, *m* retreat

**Rudel,** rood-*el*, *m* crowd; pack; herd

**Ruder,** rood-*er*, *nt* oar; rudder; helm

**rudern,** rood-*er*n, *v* to row

**Ruf,** roof, *m* call, shout, sound; reputation

**rufen,** roof-en, *v* to call, to shout

**Rufnummer,** roof-noomm-*er*, *f* telephone number

**Rüffel,** rEEff-*el*, *m* reprimand

**Rüge,** rEEg-*e*, *f* reproach, blame

**rügen,** rEEg-en, *v* to

reproach, to blame

**Ruhe,** rooh-*e*, *f* silence, quiet; recreation; rest

**ruhen,** rooh-en, *v* to rest

**Ruhestand,** rooh-*e*-shtahnt, *m* retirement

**Ruhetag,** rooh-*e*-tahg, *m* rest day, holiday

**ruhig,** rooh-ik, *adj* quiet; tranquil; calm; *interj* be quiet!

**Ruhm,** room, *m* glory; fame; praise

**rühmen,** rEEm-en, *v* to praise; to extol

**rühmlich,** rEEm-lik, *adj* praiseworthy; glorious

**Ruhr,** roor, *f* diarrhoea, dysentery

**Rührei,** rEEr-i, *nt* scrambled egg(s)

**rühren,** rEEr-en, *v* to stir; to move; to strike

**rührend,** rEEr-ent, *adj* touching, affecting

**rührig,** rEEr-ik, *adj* alert; active

**Rührung,** rEEr-oong, *f* emotion

**Rumänien,** roo-main-ee-en, *nt* Rumania

**Rummel,** roomm-*el*, *m* (loud) noise; trick(s); **–platz,** *m* fairground

**Rumpelkammer,** roomm-pel-kahmm-*er*, *f* lumber-room

**Rumpf,** roomp'f, *m* trunk; torso; hull

**rümpfen,** rEEmp-fen, *v* to wrinkle; to curl

**rund,** roont, *adj* round, circular; globular

**Runde, roonn**-de, *f* circle

**runden, roonn**-den, *v* to (make/become) round

**Rundfahrt, roonnt**-fahrt, *f* round trip; excursion

**Rundfunk, roont**-foonk, *m* broadcasting; **–sendung,** *f* (radio) broadcast/ programme

**rundherum, roont**-hair-oomm, *adv* round about

**Rundreise, roont**-ry-ze, *f* circular tour, round trip

**Rundschau, roont**-show, *f* review

**Rundschreiben, roont**-shry-ben, *nt* circular letter

**rundum, roont**-oomm, *adv* round about

**Rundwanderweg, roont**-vahnn-der-vaig, *m* circular path

**Runkelrübe, roonk**-el-rEEb-e, *f* swede

**Runzel, roonn**-tsel, *f* wrinkle; pucker

**runzelig, roonn**-tsel-ik, *adj* wrinkled, puckered

**runzeln, roonn**-tseln, *v* to wrinkle; to pucker

**Rüpel, rEEp**-el, *m* lout, yob(bo)

**rupfen, roopp**-fen, *v* to pluck; to pick

**ruppig, roopp**-ik, *adj* rough; gruff; wild

**Ruß, roos,** *m* soot

**Russe, roos**-e, *m* Russian (man)

**Rüssel, rEEss**-el, *m* trunk, snout

**rußig, roos**-ik, *adj* sooty; smutty

**Russin, roos**-in, *f* Russian (woman)

**russisch, roos**-ish, *adj* Russian

**Rußland, ross**-lahnt, *nt* Russia

**rüsten, rEEst**-en, *v* to arm; to equip

**rüstig, rEEst**-ik, *adj* active; nimble

**Rüstung, rEEst**-oong, *f* armour; preparation

**Rute, root**-e, *f* rod, birch, switch; brush

**Rutschbahn, rootsh**-bahn, *f* (children's) slide

**rutschen, roott**-shen, *v* to slide, to glide

**rütteln, rEEtt**-eln, *v* to shake (up); to jog

**Saal,** zahl, *m* hall, large room; ward

**Saat,** zaht, *f* seed(s); young crop(s); **–krähe,** *f* rook

**sabbern,** zahbb-ern, *v* to slobber, to slaver

**Säbel, zay**-bel, *m* sword

**sachdienlich, zahk**-deen-lik, *adj* suitable; serviceable; relevant

**Sache, zahk**-e, *f* thing; matter; affair

**Sachkenner, zahk**-ken-er, *m* expert; connoisseur

**sachkundig, zahk**-koonn-dik, *adj* expert

**Sachlage, zahk**-lahg-e, *f* circumstances

**sachlich, zahk**-lik, *adj* objective; matter-of-fact

**sächlich, zek**-lik, *adj* neuter

**sacht(e), zahkt**(-e), *adj* gentle, soft; gradual

**Sachverhalt, zahk**-fair-hahlt, *m* facts of the case

**Sachverständige(r), zahk**-fair-shten-dig-*e*(r), *m & f,* expert

**Sack,** zahck, *m* sack; bag; pocket; **–gasse,** *f* cul-de-sac

**säen, zay**-en, *v* to sow

**Safran, zahff**-rahn, *m* saffron

**Saft,** zahft, *m* sap, juice; fluid

**saftig, zahft**-ik, *adj* juicy; obscene

**Sage, zahg**-e, *f* saga, legend; rumour

**Säge, zayg**-e, *f* saw; **–mehl,** *nt* sawdust

**sagen, zahg**-en, *v* to say, to tell

**sägen, zayg**-en, *v* to saw

**sagenhaft, zahg**-en-hahft, *adj* legendary; mythical; fabulous

**Sägespäne, zayg-***e*-shpayn-*e*, *pl* wood-shavings; sawdust

**Sahne, zahn**-e, *f* cream

**Saison,** zay-**zong,** *f* season

**Saite, zy**-te, *f* string (of an instrument)

**Salami,** zahl-**ah**-mee, *f* salami

**Salat,** zahl-**aht,** *m* salad; lettuce; **–soße,** *f* salad dressing

**Salbe, zahlb**-e, *f* ointment; balm

**Salbei, zahlb**-i, *m & f* sage

**salben, zahlb**-en, *v* to anoint

**Salbung, zahlb**-oong, *f* anointment; unction

**Saldo, zahld**-oh, *m* balance, remainder

**Saline,** zahl-**een**-e, *f* salt-mine, salt works

**Salmonelle,** zahlm-ohn-**ell**-e, *f* salmonella

**Salon, zahl**-ong, *m* drawing-room; saloon; lounge

**salonfähig, zahl**-ong-fay-ik, *adj* presentable

**salopp, zahl**-op, *adj* casual

**Salz, zahlts, ** *nt* salt; seasoning

**salzarm, zahlts**-ahrm, *adj* low in salt

**salzen, zahlt**-sen, *v* to salt; to season

**salzig, zahlts**-ik, *adj* salt(y)

**Salzkartoffeln, zahlts**-kahr-tof-eln, *pl* boiled potatoes

**Salzstreuer, zahlts**-shtroy-er, *m* salt cellar

**Same(n), zahm**-*e*(n), *m* seed

**Sammelbecken, zahmm**-elbeck-en, nt reservoir

**sammeln, zahmm**-eln, v to collect, to gather

**Sammler, zahmm**-ler, m collector, gatherer

**Sammlung, zahmm**-loong, f collection

**Samstag, zahmms**-tahk, m Saturday

**Samt, zahmmt, m** velvet

**samt, zahmmt, adv together; – und sonders, adv** each and every

**sämtlich, zemt**-lik, adj all, complete

**Sand, zahnt, m** sand; grit

**sandig, zahnn**-dik, adj sandy; gritty

**Sandkuchen, zahnnt**-kook-en, m Madeira cake

**Sandstrand, zahnt**-shtrahnt, m sandy beach

**Sanduhr, zahnt**-oor, f hourglass

**sanft, zahnft, adj** gentle, sweet; soft; smooth

**Sänfte, zenf**-te, f sedan-chair

**Sanftmut, zahnft**-moot, f gentleness

**Sänger, zeng**-er, m singer

**Sanitäter, zahnn-ee-tayt**-er, m first-aider, stretcher-bearer

**Sanitätswagen, zahnn-ee-tayts**-vahg-en, m ambulance

**Sardelle, zard-el**-e, f anchovy

**Sarg, zark, m** coffin

**Satellit, zahtt-e-leet, m**

satellite; **–enfernsehen, nt** satellite TV

**satt, zahtt, adj** satisfied; sated

**Sattel, zahtt**-el, m saddle

**sattelfest, zahtt-el-fest, adj** firm in the saddle; well versed

**satteln, zahtt**-eln, v to saddle

**sättigen, zet-ig-en, v** to satisfy; to appease

**Satz, zahtts, m** sentence; set; leap; fixed sum; mus movement; **–ung, f** rule; statute; dogma

**Sau, zow, f** sow

**sauber, zow**-ber, adj clean; neat, tidy; fine

**säuberlich, zoy**-ber-lik, adj clean; decent

**säubern, zoyb**-ern, v to clean(se)

**Saubohne, zow-bohn**-e, f broad-bean

**Sauce, zoh**-se, f gravy, sauce

**sauer, zow**-er, adj sour, acid, tart; cross

**Sauerampfer, zow-er**-ahmpf-er, m sorrel

**Sauerbraten, zow-er-braht**-en, m joint soaked in vinegar

**Sauerei, zow-e**-ry, f mess, dirty business

**Sauerkraut, zow-er-krowt**, nt pickled shredded cabbage

**säuerlich, zoy-er-lik, adj** acidic

**säuern, zoy**-ern, v to make

sour; to leaven

**Sauerstoff, zow-er**-shtof, m oxygen

**Saufbold, zowf**-bolt, m drunkard

**saufen, zowf**-en, v to swill, to drink (animals); fam to booze

**Säufer, zoy**-fer, m drunkard

**Sauferei, zowf-e**-ry, f hard drinking

**saugen, zowg**-en, v to suck

**säugen, zoyg**-en, v to suckle, to nurse

**Säugetier, zoyg-e**-teer, nt mammal

**Säugling, zoyg**-ling, m baby

**Säule, zoyl**-e, f column, pillar

**Saum, zowm, m** seam, hem; edge

**saumäßig, zow**-mace-ik, adj lousy; tremendous

**säumen, zoym**-en, v to delay; to hem

**Sauna, zow**-nah, f sauna

**Säure, zoyr**-e, f acid; sourness

**saurer Regen, zow-rer ray**-gen, m acid rain

**säuseln, zoy**-zeln, v to murmur; to rustle; to purr

**sausen, zow**-zen, v to rush, to dash, to whiz

**SB, abbr Selbstbedienung**

**S-Bahn, ess**-bahn, f suburban railway

**Scampi, skahmm**-pee, pl scampi

**schaben, shahb**-en, v to scrape, to grate; to rasp

**schäbig,** shay-bik, *adj* shabby; mean

**Schablone,** shahb-lohn-e, *f* stencil; routine

**Schach,** shahk, *nt* chess

**schachern, shahk-**ern, *v* to barter; to haggle

**schachmatt, shahk-**mahtt, *adj* checkmate

**Schacht,** shahkt, *m* shaft, pit; hollow

**Schachtel, shahk-**tel, *f* (cardboard) box

**schade,** shahd-e, *adj* what a pity!

**Schädel, shay-**del, *m* skull

**schaden, shahd-**en, *v* to harm; to injure

**Schaden, shahd-**en, *m* damage; hurt; loss; **–ersatz,** *m* compensation; **–freude,** *f* malice, gloating

**schadenfroh, shahd-**en-froh, *adj* malicious, gloating

**schadhaft, shaht-**hahft, *adj* defective; damaged

**schädigen, shayd-**ig-en, *v* to harm; to wrong

**schädlich, shayt-**lik, *adj* harmful, hurtful

**schadlos, shaht-**lohs, *adj* unhurt; indemnified

**Schadstoff, shaht-**shtof, *m* pollutant, harmful substance

**Schaf,** shahf, *nt* sheep; *fam* stupid person

**Schäfer, shayf-**er, *m* shepherd

**Schäferhund, shayf-**er-

hoont, *m* sheepdog; German shepherd dog

**schaffen, shahff-**en, *v* to create; to be busy; to do, to manage

**Schaffner, shahff-**ner, *m* guard, conductor

**Schafott, shahff-**ot, *nt* scaffold

**Schaft,** shahft, *m* shaft, stock; leg (of boot); shank

**Schakal, shah-kahl,** *m* jackal

**schal,** shahl, *adj* stale, flat, insipid

**Schal,** shahl, *m* shawl, muffler

**Schale, shahl-**e, *f* shell; peel; bowl, basin

**schälen, shayl-**en, *v* to peel, to shell

**Schalk,** shahlk, *m* rogue, joker

**schalkhaft, shahlk-**hahft, *adj* roguish; arch

**Schall,** shahll, *m* sound, noise; peal

**schalldicht, shahll-**dikt, *adj* soundproof

**schallen, shahll-**en, *v* to sound; to ring

**Schaltbrett, shahlt-**bret, *nt* switchboard; dashboard

**schalten, shahlt-**en, *v* to command; to switch; to change gear

**Schalter, shahlt-**er, *m* booking-office, counter; switch; **–stunden,** *pl* hours of business

**Schaltjahr, shahlt-**yahr, *nt*

leap-year

**Scham,** shahm, *f* shame; modesty; bashfulness

**schämen (sich), shaym-**en (zik), *v* to be ashamed; to be shy

**Schamgefühl, shahm-**ge-fEEl, *nt* feeling of shame

**schamhaft, shahm-**hahft, *adj* shy; modest, coy

**schamrot, shahm-**roht, *adj* blushing

**schampunieren, shahm-**poo-**neer-**en, *v* to shampoo

**Schande, shahnd-**e, *f* shame, disgrace

**schänden, shend-**en, *v* to dishonour; to outrage; to violate

**schändlich, shent-**lik, *adj* shameful, disgraceful

**Schank,** shahnk, *m* sale of alcohol; bar; **–tisch,** *m* bar

**Schanze, shahnt-**se, *f* earthwork, trench

**Schar,** shahr, *f* troop; host; flock; plough-share

**scharen, shahr-**en, *v* to collect

**scharf,** shahrf, *adj* sharp; harsh; keen; smart

**Scharfblick, shahrf-**blick, *m* perspicacity; insight

**Schärfe, shairf-**e, *f* sharpness; keenness; severity

**schärfen, shairf-**en, *v* to sharpen; to strengthen

**Scharfrichter, shahrf-**rik-ter, *m* executioner

**Scharfsicht, shahrf**-zikt, f sharp sight

**Scharfsinn, shahrf**-zin, m acumen

**Scharlach, shahr**-lahk, m scarlet; scarlet fever

**Scharmützel, shahr-mEEtt**-sel, nt skirmish

**Scharnier, shahr-neer**, nt hinge

**Schärpe, shairp**-e, f sash; sling

**scharren, shahr**-en, v to scrape; to scratch

**Scharte, shahrt**-e, f notch; loophole; gap

**Schatten, shahtt**-en, m shadow; shade

**Schattierung, shahtt-eer**-oong, f shading; tint

**schattig, shahtt**-ik, adj shaded

**Schatz, shahts**, m treasure; riches; loved one

**Schatzamt, shahts**-ahmt, nt exchequer

**schätzen, shets**-en, v to estimate; to esteem

**Schätzung, shets**-oong, f estimate; estimation

**Schau, show**, f show, view; performance; **–bild**, nt diagram, graph

**Schauder, show**-der, m shudder(ing); horror

**schauderhaft, show**-der-hahft, adj dreadful

**schaudern, show**-dern, v to shudder

**schauen, show**-en, v to see; to gaze

**Schauer, show**-er, m shower; shudder

**schauerlich, show**-er-lik, adj gruesome

**Schaufel, show**-fel, f shovel; paddle(-boat)

**schaufeln, show**-feln, v to shovel

**Schaufenster, show**-fenst-er, nt shop-window; **–bummel**, m window shopping

**Schaukel, show**-kel, f swing, see-saw

**schaukeln, show**-keln, v to rock, to swing

**Schaum, show**m, m foam, froth, surf; lather

**schäumen, shoym**-en, v to foam, to froth

**Schauplatz, show**-plahts, m scene; theatre (of war)

**Schauspiel, show**-shpeel, nt scene; drama; **–er**, m actor, player; **–haus**, nt theatre

**Scheck, sheck**, m cheque

**scheckig, sheck**-ik, adj piebald; speckled

**Scheckkarte, sheck**-kahrt-e, f bank card, cheque card

**Scheibe, shy**-be, f disc; slice; pane; target; **–nwischer**, m windscreen wiper

**Scheide, shy**-de, f sheath; case; division; vagina

**scheiden, shy**-den, v to part, to separate; to divorce

**Scheideweg, shy**-de-vayk, m crossroads

**Scheidung, shy**-doong, f separation; divorce

**Schein, shine**, m shine; semblance; note, bill

**scheinbar, shine**-bar, adj apparent

**scheinen, shine**-en, v to shine; to seem

**scheinheilig, shine**-hile-ik, adj hypocritical

**Scheinwerfer, shine**-vair-fer, m searchlight; spotlight

**Scheit, shy't**, nt log; splinter

**Scheitel, shy**-tel, m crown of head; (hair) parting

**scheiteln, shy**-teln, v to part (hair)

**Scheiterhaufen, shy**-ter-howf-en, m stake, (funeral-)pyre

**scheitern, shy**-tern, v to fail; to be wrecked

**Schelle, shel**-e, f bell

**schellen, shel**-en, v to ring a bell

**Schellfisch, shel**-fish, m haddock

**Schelte, shelt**-e, f scolding

**schelten, shelt**-en, v to scold, to reprimand

**Schema, shaym**-ah, nt model; pattern

**Schemel, shaym**-el, m stool

**Schenke, sheng**-ke, f inn, tavern

**Schenkel, sheng**-kel, m thigh; shank; angle

**schenken, sheng**-ken, v to give (as a present); to pour out; to grant

**Schenkung, shenk**-oong, f donation

**Scherbe, shairb**-e, *f* fragment; shard

**Schere, shair**-e, *f* shears, scissors; shafts

**scheren, shair**-en, *v* to shear, to clip; **sich um etw –**, *v* to care about sth; **scher dich!** *interj* scram!

**Schererei, shair**-e-ry, *f* annoyance, trouble

**Scherz, shairts,** *m* joke

**scherzen, shairt**-sen, *v* to joke

**scherzhaft, shairts**-hahft, *adj* jovial

**Scheu, shoy,** *f* shyness; timidity; fear

**scheu, shoy,** *adj* shy; timid

**scheuchen, shoyk**-en, *v* to scare away

**Scheuer, shoy**-er, *f* barn; shelter

**scheuern, shoy**-ern, *v* to scrub, to scour

**Scheune, shoyn**-e, *f* barn

**Scheusal, shoy**-zahl, *nt* monster

**scheußlich, shoys**-lik, *adj* horrible, awful

**Schicht, shikt,** *f* layer, stratum; shift; class

**schichten, shikt**-en, *v* to layer, to stack

**Schick, shick,** *m* smartness, chic

**schick, shick,** *adj* smart, chic

**schicken, shick**-en, *v* to send, to dispatch

**schicklich, shick**-lik, *adj* seemly; decent

**Schicksal, shick**-zahl, *nt* fate, destiny

**Schiebedach, sheeb**-e-dahk, *nt* sun roof

**schieben, sheeb**-en, *v* to push, to slide; to wangle

**Schieber, sheeb**-er, *m* slider; pusher; wangler

**Schiebung, sheeb**-oong, *f* pushing; wangling

**Schiedsgericht, sheets**-ge-rikt, *nt* court of arbitration

**Schiedsrichter, sheets**-rik-ter, *m* arbitrator, referee, umpire

**schief, sheef,** *adj* crooked; slanting; sloping

**Schiefer, sheef**-er, *m* slate

**schielen, sheel**-en, *v* to squint, to be cross-eyed

**Schienbein, sheen**-bine, *nt* shin(-bone)

**Schiene, sheen**-e, *f* splint; rail; bar; hoop

**Schienennetz, sheen**-en-nets, *nt* railway-system

**schier, sheer,** *adj* pure; sheer; *adv* nearly

**schießen, shees**-en, *v* to shoot, to fire

**Schießscheibe, shees**-shy-be, *f* target

**Schiff, shif,** *nt* ship, vessel, craft; nave; shuttle

**Schiffahrt, shif**-fahrt, *f* shipping, navigation

**schiffbar, shif**-bahr, *adj* navigable

**Schiffbruch, shif**-brook, *m* shipwreck

**schiffen, shif**-en, *v* to ship;

to navigate

**Schild, shilt,** *nt* shield; signboard

**schildern, shild**-ern, *v* to describe

**Schilderung, shild**-er-oong, *f* description; sketch

**Schildkröte, shilt**-krert-e, *f* tortoise, turtle

**Schildpatt, shilt**-pahtt, *nt* tortoise-shell

**Schildwache, shilt**-vahk-e, *f* sentry

**Schilf(rohr), shilf**(-rohr), *nt* reed

**schillern, shil**-ern, *v* to shimmer

**Schimmel, shim**-el, *m* mildew, mould; white horse

**schimmelig, shim**-el-ik, *adj* mildewed, mouldy

**schimmeln, shim**-eln, *v* to go mouldy

**Schimmer, shim**-er, *m* glimmer; gleam; pomp

**schimmern, shim**-ern, *v* to gleam; to glitter

**Schimpf, shimp'f,** *m* insult; indignity; disgrace

**schimpfen, shimp'f**-en, *v* to scold; to grumble; to abuse

**schimpflich, shimp'f**-lik, *adj* disgraceful

**Schimpfwort, shimp'f**-vort, *nt* swear word

**schinden, shin**-den, *v* to maltreat, to overwork; to flay

**Schinder, shin**-der, *m* knacker; slave-driver; **–ei,**

*f* drudgery, grind

**Schinken, shing**-ken, *m* ham; **–speck,** *m* bacon

**Schippe, ship**-e, *f* spade; shovel; spades (cards)

**schippen, ship**-en, *v* to shovel

**Schirm,** sheerm, *m* umbrella; shelter; protection; peak (of cap); **–herrschaft,** *f* patronage

**schlabbern, shlahbb**-ern, *v* to slobber

**Schlacht,** shlahkt, *f* battle, action

**schlachten, shlahkt**-en, *v* to slaughter; to kill

**Schlachter, shlakt**-er, *m* butcher; **–ei,** *f* butcher's shop

**Schlächter, shlekt**-er, *m* butcher; **–ei,** *f* butcher's shop

**Schlachtfeld, shlahkt**-felt, *nt* battle-field

**Schlachthaus, shlahkt**-hows, *nt* slaughter-house, abattoir

**Schlachthof, shlahkt**-hohf, *m* slaughter-house, abattoir

**Schlacke, shlahck**-e, *f* slag

**Schlackwurst, shlahck**-voorst, *f* kind of sausage

**Schlaf,** shlahf, *m* sleep; **–abteil,** *m* sleeping compartment; **–anzug,** *m* pyjamas

**Schläfe, shlay**-fe, *f* temple (forehead)

**schlafen, shlahf**-en, *v*

to sleep

**Schläfer, shlayf**-er, *m* sleeper

**schläfrig, shlayf**-rik, *adj* sleepy, drowsy

**schlaff, shlahff,** *adj* slack, limp, flabby

**Schlaflosigkeit, shlahf**-lohz-ik-kite, *f* sleeplessness

**Schlafmittel, shlahf**-mit-el, *nt* sleeping-draught

**Schlafsack, shlahf**-zahck, *m* sleeping-bag

**Schlaftablette, shlahf**-tah-blet-e, *f* sleeping-pill

**schlaftrunken, shlahf**-troong-ken, *adj* heavy with sleep

**Schlafwagen, shlahf**-vahg-en, *m* sleeping-car

**schlafwandeln, shlahf**-vahnn-deln, *v* to sleep-walk

**Schlafzimmer, shlahf**-tsim-er, *nt* bedroom

**Schlag,** shlahk, *m* blow, stroke; slap; shock; beat; knock; kind; **–anfall,** *m* stroke; **–baum,** *m* barrier

**schlagen, shlahg**-en, *v* to beat; to strike, to hit, to knock

**Schlager, shlahg**-er, *m* hit (-song); bargain; draw (attraction)

**Schläger, shlayg**-er, *m* brawler; bat, racket, club; rapier

**Schlägerei,** shlayg-e-**ry,** *f* brawl

**schlagfertig, shlahk**-fairt-ik,

*adj* quick-witted

**Schlagloch, shlahk**-lok, *nt* pothole

**Schlagsahne, shlahk**-zahn-e, *f* whipped cream

**Schlagwort, shlahk**-vort, *nt* catchword, slogan

**Schlamm,** shlahmm, *m* mud, slime

**schlammig, shlahmm**-ik, *adj* muddy, slimy

**Schlange, shlahng**-e, *f* snake, serpent; queue

**schlank, shlahnk,** *adj* slim, slight, slender

**Schlankheitskur, shlahnk**-hites-koor, *f* (slimming) diet

**schlapp, shlahpp,** *adj* slack, limp; worn-out; run-down

**Schlappe, shlahpp**-e, *f* defeat; loss

**Schlapphut, shlahpp**-hoot, *m* floppy hat

**schlau, shlow,** *adj* sly, clever

**Schlauch, shlowk,** *m* tube, hose; **–boot,** *nt* rubber dinghy

**Schläue, shloy**-e, *f* cunning

**Schlauheit, shlow**-hite, *f* cleverness; cunning

**schlecht, shlekt,** *adj* bad, evil; wicked

**schlechterdings, shlekt**-er-dings, *adv* absolutely; virtually

**schlechthin, shlekt**-hin, *adv* plainly

**Schlechtigkeit, shlekt**-ik-kite, *f* wickedness; evil

**Schlegel, shlayg**-el, *m*

drumstick; mallet

**Schlehdorn, shlay**-dorn, *m* blackthorn, sloe

**Schlehe, shlay**-e, *f* sloe

**Schleie, shly**-e, *f* tench

**schleichen, shly**-ken, *v* to creep, to prowl

**Schleichhandel, shly'k**-hahnd-el, *m* illicit trade

**Schleier, shly**-er, *m* veil

**schleierhaft, shly**-er-hahft, *adj* hazy; veiled

**Schleife, shly**-fe, *f* loop; knot, bow

**schleifen, shly**-fen, *v* to grind, to sharpen, to polish; to drag; to demolish

**Schleifstein, shlife**-shtine, *m* grindstone

**Schleim, shlime,** *m* slime; phlegm, mucus

**schleimig, shly**-mik, *adj* slimy

**schlemmen, shlem**-en, *v* to feast, to live it up

**Schlemmer, shlem**-er, *m* glutton; gourmet

**schlendern, shlend**-ern, *v* to saunter

**schlenkern, shlenk**-ern, *v* to dangle; to jerk

**Schleppdampfer, shlep**-dahmp-fer, *m* tug(-boat)

**Schleppe, shlep**-e, *f* train (of dress)

**schleppen, shlep**-en, *v* to drag; to trail

**Schlepper, shlep**-er, *m* hauler; tug(-boat); smuggler

**Schleuder, shloy**-der, *f* sling; centrifuge

**schleudern, shloy**-dern, *v* to sling, to fling; to skid

**schleunig(st), shloy**-nig(st), *adj* prompt

**Schleuse, shloy**-ze, *f* lock, sluice

**Schlich(e), shlik**(-e), *m* (*pl*) trick, dodge

**schlicht, shlikt,** *adj* simple, homely, honest

**schlichten, shlikt**-en, *v* to arrange; to settle (a dispute)

**schließen, shlees**-en, *v* to lock; to close, to shut; to conclude

**Schließfach, shlees**-fak, *nt* locker

**schließlich, shlees**-lik, *adj* final; conclusive; *adv* finally, ultimately

**Schliff, shlif,** *m* cut; polish

**schlimm, shlim,** *adj* evil, bad; severe; serious; ill

**Schlinge, shling**-e, *f* sling; noose; snare

**Schlingel, shling**-el, *m* rascal

**schlingen, shling**-en, *v* to wind, to wrap; to gulp

**schlingern, shling**-ern, *v naut* to roll

**Schlingpflanze, shling**-pflahnt-se, *f* climbing plant, creeper

**Schlips, shlips,** *m* tie

**Schlitten, shlit**-en, *m* sledge, sleigh

**schlittern, shlit**-ern, *v*

to slide

**Schlittschuh, shlit**-shoo, *m* skate; – **laufen,** *v* to skate

**Schlittschuhbahn, shlit**-shoo-bahn, *f* ice-rink

**Schlitz, shlits,** *m* slit; slot; crack

**schlitzen, shlit**-sen, *v* to slit; to slash

**Schloß, shloss,** *nt* castle; palace; lock; clasp

**Schlosser, shloss**-er, *m* locksmith

**Schlot, shloht,** *m* chimney; funnel

**schlottern, shlot**-ern, *v* to shake; to hang loosely

**Schlucht, shlookt,** *f* gorge, gully, ravine

**schluchzen, shlook**-tsen, *v* to sob

**Schluck, shloock,** *m* mouthful, gulp; draught

**schlucken, shloock**-en, *v* to swallow; to gulp

**Schlummer, shloomm**-er, *m* slumber, light sleep

**schlummern, shloomm**-ern, *v* to slumber

**Schlund, shloont,** *m* gullet

**schlüpfen, shlEEpp**-fen, *v* to slip

**schlüpfrig, shlEEp'f**-rik, *adj* slippery; precarious

**Schlupfloch, shloopp'f**-lok, *nt* hiding-place; loop-hole

**Schlupfwinkel, shloopp'f**-vink-el, *m* hiding place, nook

**schlürfen, shlEErf**-en, *v* to drink (noisily); to slurp

**schlurfen, shloorf**-en, *v* to shuffle

**Schluß, shlooss,** *m* closing, end; conclusion

**Schlüssel, shlEEss**-el, *m* key; clef; **–bein,** *nt* collar-bone; **–blume,** *f* primrose; **–bund,** *nt* bunch of keys; **–loch,** *nt* keyhole

**schlüssig, shlEEss**-ik, *adj* logical, conclusive

**Schlußverkauf, shlooss**-fair-kowf, *m* clearance sale

**Schmach, shmah**k, *f* dishonour; disgrace; insult

**schmachten, shmahkt**-en, *v* to languish; to be parched

**schmächtig, shmekt**-ik, *adj* delicate; slight, slim

**schmackhaft, shmahck**-hahft, *adj* tasty, palatable

**schmähen, shmay**-en, *v* to vilify; to slander

**schmählich, shmay**-lik, *adj* abusive; disgraceful; *adv* badly, sadly

**schmal, shmahl,** *adj* narrow; slender; meagre

**schmälern, shmayl**-ern, *v* to narrow; to lessen

**Schmälerung, shmayl**-er-oong, *f* reduction, diminution

**Schmalz, shmahlts,** *nt* lard, dripping

**schmarotzen, shmah-rot**-sen, *v* to sponge

**Schmarotzer, shmah-rot**-ser, *m* sponger; cadger; parasite

**Schmarren, shmahrr**-en, *m* nonsense; dish made of pancakes

**schmatzen, shmahtt**-sen, *v* to smack one's lips; to eat noisily

**Schmaus, shmows,** *m* feast

**schmecken, shmeck**-en, *v* to taste

**Schmeichelei, shmy-***ke***-ly,** *f* flattery

**schmeicheln, shmy-**keln, *v* to coax; to flatter

**Schmeichler, shmy'***k***-ler,** *m* flatterer; wheedler

**schmeichlerisch, shmy'***k***-**ler-ish, *adj* wheedling; flattering

**schmeißen, shmy-**sen, *v* to throw, to chuck

**Schmelz, shmelts,** *m* glaze, enamel; melodiousness

**schmelzen, shmelt**-sen, *v* to melt; to smelt

**Schmerz, shmairts,** *m* pain, ache; grief; suffering

**schmerzen, shmairt**-sen, *v* to ache, to hurt

**Schmerzensgeld, shmairt**-sens-gelt, *nt* damages

**schmerzhaft, shmairts**-hahft, *adj* painful

**schmerzlich, shmairts**-lik, *adj* painful; grievous

**Schmerzmittel, shmairts**-mit-el, *nt* painkiller

**Schmetterling, shmet**-er-ling, *m* butterfly

**schmettern, shmet**-ern, *v* to shatter; to resound; to warble

**Schmied, shmeet,** *m* smith

**Schmiede, shmeed**-e, *f* smithy

**Schmiedeeisen, shmeed**-*e*-ize-en, *nt* wrought iron

**schmieden, shmeed**-en, *v* to forge; to devise

**schmiegen, shmeeg**-en, *v* to adhere, to nestle; to bend

**schmiegsam, shmeek**-zahm, *adj* flexible

**Schmiere, shmeer**-e, *f* grease, ointment; flea-pit; look-out

**schmieren, shmeer**-en, *v* to smear; to grease; to bribe

**Schmierfink, shmeer**-fink, *m fam* muck-raker

**schmierig, shmeer**-ik, *adj* smeary; greasy; dirty

**Schminke, shming**-*ke*, *f* make-up

**schminken, shming**-ken, *v* to make up, to put on make-up

**schmollen, shmol**-en, *v* to sulk; to pout

**Schmorbraten, shmohr**-braht-en, *m* pot roast

**schmoren, shmohr**-en, *v* to stew

**Schmuck, shmoock,** *m* finery; jewellery; decoration

**schmuck, shmoock,** *adj* trim; spruce; smart

**schmücken, shmEEck**-en, *v* to adorn; to decorate

**Schmucksachen, shmoock**-sak-en, *pl* jewels

**Schmuggel, shmoogg**-el, *m* smuggling

**schmuggeln, shmoogg-**eln, *v* to smuggle

**Schmuggler, shmoogg-**ler, *m* smuggler

**schmunzeln, shmoont-**seln, *v* to smile broadly; to smirk

**Schmutz,** shmoots, *m* dirt, filth

**schmutzen, shmoots-**en, *v* to soil (easily)

**schmutzig, shmoots-**ik, *adj* dirty, filthy; squalid

**Schnabel, shnahb-**el, *m* beak, bill

**schnäbeln, shnayb-**eln, *v* to bill and coo

**Schnalle, shnahll-**e, *f* buckle, clasp; *fam* silly woman

**schnallen, shnahll-**en, *v* to buckle, to fasten

**schnalzen, shnahlt-**sen, *v* to click; to snap

**schnappen, shnahpp-**en, *v* to snap; to catch; to tip

**Schnappschuß, shnahpp-**shooss, *m* snapshot

**Schnaps,** shnahps, *m* liquor; spirits

**schnarchen, shnark-**en, *v* to snore; to snort

**schnarren, shnahrr-**en, *v* to whiz; to rattle

**schnattern, shnahtt-**ern, *v* to rattle; to cackle

**schnauben, shnowb-**en, *v* to snort; to pant

**schnaufen, shnowf-**en, *v* to breathe hard; to snort

**Schnauzbart, shnowts-**bart, *m* moustache

**Schnauze, shnowt-**se, *f* snout, mouth (animals); jaw

**schnauzen, shnowt-**sen, *v* to scold roughly

**Schnecke, shneck-**e, *f* snail, slug

**Schnee,** shnay, *m* snow

**Schneeball, shnay-**bahll, *m* snowball

**schneebedeckt, shnay-**be-deckt, *adj* snow-covered

**Schneeflocke, shnay-**flock-e, *f* snowflake

**Schneegestöber, shnay-**ge-shter-ber, *nt* light snowstorm

**Schneeglöckchen, shnay-**glerck-ken, *nt* snowdrop

**Schneeketten, shnay-**ket-en, *pl* snow chains

**Schneeregen, shnay-**rayg-en, *m* sleet

**Schneeschuh, shnay-**shoo, *m* snow-shoe

**Schneesturm, shnay-**shtoorm, *m* snowstorm, blizzard

**Schneewehe, shnay-**vay-e, *f* snow-drift

**Schneewittchen, shnay-**vit-ken, *nt* Snow White

**Schneid,** shnite, *m* smartness

**Schneide, shny-**de, *f* cutter, cutting-edge

**schneiden, shny-**den, *v* to cut; to clip; to prune

**Schneider, shny-**der, *m* tailor; cutter

**Schneiderei, shny-**de-ry, *f* tailoring; dressmaking

**schneidern, shny-**dern, *v* to do tailoring/dress-making, to sew

**schneidig, shny-**dik, *adj* sharp, smart

**schneien, shny-**en, *v* to snow

**schnell, shnell,** *adj* quick; rapid; brisk

**schnellen, shnell-**en, *v* to toss; to jerk

**Schnelligkeit, shnell-**ik-kite, *f* rapidity; velocity

**Schnellimbiß, shnell-**im-bis, *m* snack; snack bar

**Schnellkochtopf, shnell-**kok-topf, *m* pressure cooker

**Schnellzug, shnell-**tsook, *m* express train

**Schnepfe, shnep-**fe, *f* snipe

**schneuzen (sich), shnoyt-**sen (zik), *v* to blow one's nose

**schniegeln (sich), shneeg-**eln (zik), *v* to smarten o.s. up

**schnippisch, shnip-**ish, *adj* snappish, uppish

**Schnitt,** shnit, *m* cut(ting); slash, wound; pattern

**Schnittbohnen, shnit-**bohn-en, *pl* French beans

**Schnitte, shnit-**e, *f* slice, cut; sandwich

**Schnittlauch, shnit-**lowk, *m* chive

**Schnittmuster, shnit-**moost-er, *nt* (dress)

pattern

**Schnitzel,** shnit-sel, *nt* chip, cut, scrap; cutlet

**schnitzen,** shnit-sen, *v* to carve

**Schnitzer,** shnit-ser, *m* (wood) carver; howler, blunder

**Schnitzerei,** shnit-se-ry, *f* carving

**schnöde,** shnerd-e, *adj* vile, base, despicable

**Schnorchel,** shnork-el, *m* snorkel

**schnorcheln,** shnork-eln, *v* to go snorkelling

**Schnörkel,** shnerk-el, *m* flourish; scroll; spiral

**schnorren,** shnorr-en, *v* to cadge; to beg; to scrounge

**Schnorrer,** shnorr-er, *m* cadger; beggar; scrounger

**schnüffeln,** shnEEff-eln, *v* to sniff; to spy out

**Schnupfen,** shnoopp-fen, *m* (head) cold

**schnupfen,** shnoopp-fen, *v* to take snuff

**Schnupftabak,** shnoopp'f-tah-bahck, *m* snuff

**schnuppe,** shnoopp-e, *adj* jdm – sein, to be all the same to sb

**schnuppern,** shnoopp-ern, *v* to sniff; to scent

**Schnur,** shnoor, *f* string, cord; braid

**schnüren,** shnEEr-en, *v* to cord; to tie; to lace

**schnurgerade,** shnoor-ge-rahd-e, *adj* straight as a die

**schnurlos,** shnoor-lohs, *adj* cordless

**Schnurrbart,** shnoorr-bart, *m* moustache

**schnurren,** shnoorr-en, *v* to purr; to buzz

**Schnürriemen,** shnEEr-reem-en, *m* (shoe-)lace

**Schnürschuhe,** shnEEr-shoo-e, *pl* lace-up shoes

**Schnürsenkel,** shnEEr-zen-kel, *m* shoe-lace

**schnurstracks,** shnoor-shtrahcks, *adv* straight away

**Schober,** shoh-ber, *m* shed; stack

**Schöffe,** sherff-e, *m* juror; –namt, *nt* jury service

**Schokolade,** shoh-koh-lah-de, *f* chocolate

**Scholle,** shol-e, *f* clod, lump; floe; plaice

**schon,** shohn, *adv* already; as yet, so far; indeed, sure enough; anyway

**schön,** shern, *adj* beautiful; fine; nice

**schonen,** shohn-en, *v* to spare; to take care; to preserve

**Schoner,** shohn-er, *m* schooner; antimacassar

**Schönheit,** shern-hite, *f* beauty; good looks; –soperation, *f* plastic surgery

**Schonkost,** shohn-kost, *f* (special) diet

**Schopf,** shop'f, *m* shock/tuft of hair

**schöpfen,** sherpp-fen, *v* to draw (water, breath etc.); to bale (water); to create

**Schöpfer,** sherpp-fer, *m* Creator; maker, producer

**schöpferisch,** sherpp-fer-ish, *adj* creative

**Schöpfung,** sherpp-foong, *f* creation; production

**Schorf,** shorf, *m* scab

**Schornstein,** shorn-shtine, *m* chimney; funnel; –feger, *m* chimney-sweep

**Schoß,** shohs, *m* shoot (plant); lap; womb

**Schoßhund,** shohs-hoont, *m* lap-dog

**Schote,** shoht-e, *f* pod, husk

**Schotte,** shot-e, *m* Scot, Scotsman

**Schottin,** shot-in, *f* Scot, Scotswoman

**schottisch,** shot-ish, *adj* Scottish

**Schottland,** shot-lahnt, *nt* Scotland

**schräg,** shrayk *adj* slanting, oblique; sloping; – gegenüber, *adv* diagonally across

**Schramme,** shrahmm-e, *f* scratch; scar

**Schrank,** shrahnk, *m* cupboard; cabinet; wardrobe

**Schranke,** shrahng-ke, *f* barrier; fencing

**Schraube,** shrowb-e, *f* screw

**schrauben,** shrowb-en, *v* to screw

**Schraubenschlüssel,**

**shrowb**-en-shlEEss-el, *m* spanner

**Schraubenzieher, shrowb**-en-tsee-er, *m* screwdriver

**Schreck(en), shreck**(-en), *m* shock; terror

**schrecken, shreck**-en, *v* to frighten, to scare

**schrecklich, shreck**-lik, *adj* terrible; fearful

**Schrei, shry, *m* cry, shout, shriek, scream

**schreiben, shry**-ben, *v* to write

**Schreibheft, shripe**-heft, *nt* exercise book

**Schreibkraft, shripe**-krahft, *f* typist

**Schreibmaschine, shripe**-mah-sheen-e, *f* typewriter

**Schreibtisch, shripe**-tish, *m* writing-desk

**Schreibwaren, shripe**-wahr-en, *pl* stationery

**schreien, shry**-en, *v* to cry, to scream, to yell

**Schrein, shrine, *m* shrine

**Schreiner, shrine**-er, *m* joiner, cabinet-maker

**schreiten, shry**-ten, *v* to step, to stride

**Schrift, shrift, *f* writing; character; manuscript

**Schriftführer, shrift**-fEEr-er, *m* secretary (of an organisation)

**Schriftleiter, shrift**-ly-ter, *m* editor

**Schriftleitung, shrift**-ly-toong, *f* editorial office

**schriftlich, shrift**-lik, *adj* in writing

**Schriftsteller, shrift**-shtel-er, *m* writer; author

**Schriftstück, shrift**-shtEEck, *nt* document

**Schriftverkehr, shrift**-fair-kair, *m* correspondence

**schrill, shrill, *adj* shrill, grating

**Schritt, shrit, *m* step; pace; footstep

**schrittweise, shrit**-vy-ze, *adv* step by step

**schroff, shrof, *adj* gruff, rough; rugged

**schröpfen, shrerpp**-fen, *v* to fleece; to bleed

**Schrot, shroht, *nt* shot; wholemeal

**Schrott, shrot, *m* srap metal; *fam* rubbish

**schrubben, shroobb**-en, *v* to scrub

**Schrubber, shroobb**-er, *m* scrubbing-brush

**schrumpfen, shroomp**-fen, *v* to shrink

**Schub, shoop, *m* batch; push, shove

**Schubkarre(n), shoop**-karr-e(n), *m & f,* wheelbarrow

**Schublade, shoob**-lahd-e, *f* drawer

**schüchtern, shEEk**-tern, *adj* shy, timid, bashful

**Schuft, shooft, *m* scoundrel, rogue

**schuften, shooft**-en, *v* to work very hard

**Schuh, shoo, *m* shoe; **–creme,** *f* shoe polish;

**–größe,** *f* shoe size; **–löffel,** *m* shoehorn; **–macher,** *m* cobbler; shoemaker; **–putzer,** *m* boot-black; **–riemen,** *m* shoelace; **–werk,** *nt* footwear

**Schularbeiten, shool**-ar-bite-en, *pl* homework

**Schuld, shoolt, *f* guilt; debt; fault

**schuldbewußt, shoold**-be-woost, *adj* feeling guilty

**schulden, shoold**-en, *v* to owe; to be indebted

**schuldig, shoold**-ik, *adj* guilty; indebted

**Schuldigkeit, shoold**-ik-kite, *f* obligation, duty; debt

**Schuldner, shoold**-ner, *m* debtor

**Schuldschein, shoolt**-shine, *m* I.O.U., promissory note

**Schule, shool**-e, *f* school; college

**schulen, shool**-en, *v* to train, to school

**Schüler, shEEl**-er, *m* scholar, pupil, student

**Schulferien, shool**-fair-ee-en, *pl* school holidays

**Schulklasse, shool**-klahss-e, *f* (school) class/form

**schulpflichtig, shool**-p'flikt-ik, *adj* of school age

**Schulunterricht, shool**-oon-ter-ikt, *m* (school) lessons

**Schulter, shoolt**-er, *f* shoulder; **–blatt,** *nt*

shoulder-blade

**schultern, shoolt**-ern, *v* to shoulder

**Schulzwang, shool**-tsvahng, *m* compulsory education

**Schund, shoont,** *m* trash; rubbish

**Schuppe, shoopp**-e, *f* scale; **–n,** *pl* dandruff

**Schuppen, shoopp**-en, *m* shed, shelter

**schuppen, shoopp**-en, *v* to scale, to remove scales

**schüren, shEEr**-en, *v* to rake/poke (a fire); *fig* to stir up, to fan flames

**Schurke, shoork**-e, *m* rascal; villain

**Schürze, shEErt**-se, *f* apron; pinafore

**Schuß, shooss,** *m* shot; shoot(ing)

**Schüssel, shEEss**-el, *f* dish, bowl; basin

**Schußwaffen, shooss**-vahff-en, *pl* firearms

**Schuster, shooss**-ter, *m* cobbler, shoemaker

**schustern, shooss**-tern, *v* to cobble; to botch

**Schutt, shoott,** *m* refuse; rubbish

**schütteln, shEEtt**-eln, *v* to shake

**schütten, shEEtt**-en, *v* to pour; to shoot; to throw

**Schutz, shoots,** *m* protection; screen; shelter

**Schütze, shEEts**-e, *m* marksman; hunter

**schützen, shEEts**-en, *v* to

protect, to guard

**Schutzengel, shoots**-eng-el, *m* guardian angel

**Schützengraben, shEEts**-en-grahb-en, *m* trench

**Schutzhütte, shoots**-hEEtt-e, *f* (mountain) shelter

**Schutzmarke, shoots**-mark-e, *f* trade-mark

**Schutztruppe, shoots**-troopp-e, *f* colonial troops

**schwach, shvahk,** *adj* weak, feeble; delicate

**Schwäche, shvek**-e, *f* weakness

**schwächen, shvek**-en, *v* to weaken; to lessen

**Schwachheit, shvahk**-hite, *f* weakness

**schwächlich, shvek**-lik, *adj* delicate, weakly

**Schwächling, shvek**-ling, *m* weakling

**schwachsichtig, shvahk**-zik-tik, *adj* weak-sighted

**schwachsinnig, shvahk**-zin-ik, *adj* feeble-minded

**Schwächung, shvek**-oong, *f* weakening

**Schwager, shvahg**-er, *m* brother-in-law

**Schwägerin, shvayg**-er-in, *f* sister-in-law

**Schwalbe, shvahlb**-e, *f* swallow; **–nschwanz,** *m* swallow-tail

**Schwall, shvahll,** *m* surge; heaving mass/crowd

**Schwamm, shvahmm,** *m* sponge; fungus

**schwammig, shvahmm**-ik,

*adj* spongy; fungoid

**Schwan, shvahn,** *m* swan

**schwanger, shvahng**-er, *adj* pregnant

**Schwangerschaft, shvahng**-er-shahft, *f* pregnancy

**Schwank, shvahnk,** *m* farce, burlesque; joke

**Schwankung, shvahnk**-oong, *f* fluctuation; uncertainty

**Schwanz, shvahnts,** *m* tail

**schwänzeln, shvent**-seln, *v* to wag (tail); *fig* to crawl

**schwänzen, shvent**-sen, *v* to saunter; to play truant

**Schwarm, shvahrm,** *m* swarm; flock; crowd

**schwärmen, shvairm**-en, *v* to swarm; to skirmish; to enthuse

**Schwarte, shvart**-e, *f* rind; skin

**schwarz, shvarts,** *adj* black; swarthy

**Schwarzbrot, shvarts**-broht, *nt* (dark) rye-bread

**Schwärze, shvairts**-e, *f* blackness; blacking

**schwärzen, shvairts**-en, *v* to blacken; to darken

**Schwarze Meer, shvarts**-e **mair,** *nt* Black Sea

**Schwarzmarkt, shvarts**-mahrkt, *m* black market

**Schwarzseher, shvarts**-zay-er, *m* pessimist

**Schwarzwald, shvarts**-vahlt, *m* Black Forest

**schwatzen, (schwätzen), shvahts**-en, **(shvets-en),** *v* to chatter

**Schwätzer,** shvets-*er,* *m* chatterbox

**schwatzhaft, shvahts-**hahft, *adj* talkative, chatty

**schweben, shvayb-**en, *v* to hover, to float; to be suspended

**Schweden, shvay-**den, *nt* Sweden

**schwedisch, shvay-**dish, *adj* Swedish

**Schwefel, shvay-**fel, *m* sulphur

**schwefelig, shvayf-**el-ik, *adj* sulphurous

**Schweif,** shvife, *m* tail

**schweifen, shvy-**fen, *v* to roam, to ramble; to curve

**schweigen, shvy-**gen, *v* to be silent

**schweigsam, shvike-**zahm, *adj* silent; taciturn

**Schwein,** shvine, *nt* pig, swine; good luck; **–ebraten,** *m* roast pork; **–efleisch,** *nt* pork; **–ehund,** *m pej* pig; **–erei,** *f* dirtiness; mess; **–eschmalz,** *nt* lard; **–skotelett,** *nt* pork-chop

**Schweiß,** shvice, *m* sweat

**schweißtriefend, shvice-**treef-ent, *adj* dripping with sweat

**Schweiz,** shvites, *f* Switzerland

**schweizerisch, shvy-**tser-ish, *adj* Swiss

**Schweizer Käse, shvy-**tser kay-ze, *m*

Emmental cheese

**schwelgen, shvelg-**en, *v* to indulge oneself

**Schwelle, shvel-**e, *f* threshold; beam; sleeper (train)

**schwellen, shvel-**en, *v* to swell; to swirl

**Schwemme, shvem-**e, *f* watering place; *fam* bar, pub

**Schwengel, shveng-**el, *m* clapper; handle; lout

**schwenken, shveng-**ken, *v* to brandish; to swing (round)

**schwer,** shvair, *adj* heavy; difficult, hard; serious; – **behindert,** *adj* severely handicapped

**Schwere, shvair-**e, *f* heaviness, weight; severity

**schwerfallen, shvair-**fahll-en, *v* to be(come) difficult

**schwerfällig, shvair-**fel-ik, *adj* ponderous; slow; clumsy

**schwerhörig, shvair-**her-ik, *adj* hard of hearing

**Schwerkraft, shvair-**krahft, *f* gravity

**schwerlich, shvair-**lik, *adv* scarcely; with difficulty

**Schwermut, shvair-**moot, *f* melancholy

**Schwerpunkt, shvair-**poonkt, *m* centre of gravity; *fig* emphasis, focal point

**Schwert,** shvairt, *nt* sword

**Schwester, shvest-**er, *f*

sister; nurse

**schwesterlich, shvest-**er-lik, *adj* sisterly

**Schwieger–, shveeg-**er, *pref* -in-law; **–eltern,** *pl* parents-in-law; **–mutter,** *f* mother-in-law; **–sohn,** *m* son-in-law; **–tochter,** *f* daughter-in-law; **–vater,** *m* father-in-law

**Schwiele, shveel-**e, *f* callus; welt

**schwierig, shveer-**ik, *adj* difficult; precarious; delicate

**Schwierigkeit, shveer-**ik-kite, *f* difficulty

**Schwimmbad, shvim-**baht, *nt* swimming pool

**schwimmen, shvim-**en, *v* to swim; to float

**Schwimmweste, shvim-**vest-e, *f* life jacket

**Schwindel, shvin-**del, *m* giddiness; swindle

**Schwindelei, shvin-**de-ly, *f* swindling

**schwind(e)lig, shvind(-e)-**lik, *adj* giddy, dizzy

**schwindeln, shvind-**eln, *v* to swindle, to cheat; to be dizzy

**schwinden, shvind-**en, *v* to dwindle, to grow less; to vanish

**Schwindler, shvind-**ler, *m* swindler, cheat

**Schwinge, shving-**e, *f* wing, pinion

**schwingen, shving-**en, *v* to swing, to wield

**Schwips,** shvips, *m* (slight) intoxication

**schwirren,** shvir-en, *v* to whir, to whiz, to hum

**Schwitzbad,** shvits-baht, *nt* Turkish bath

**schwitzen,** shvits-en, *v* to sweat, to perspire

**schwören,** shver-en, *v* to swear

**schwul,** shvool, *adj* gay (homosexual)

**schwül,** shvEEl, *adj* sultry, close

**Schwung,** shvoong, *m* swing(ing); rise; ardour

**schwunghaft,** shvoong-hahft, *adj* lively, brisk

**schwungvoll,** shvoong-fol, *adj* full of energy

**Schwur,** shvoor, *m* oath; **–gericht,** *nt* sessional court

**sechs,** zecks, *num* six

**Sechseck,** zecks-eck, *nt* hexagon

**sechste(r),** zecks-te(r), *adj* sixth

**Sechstel,** zecks-tel, *nt* sixth

**sechzehn,** zek-tsayn, *num* sixteen

**sechzig,** zek-tsik, *num* sixty

**See,** zay, *m* lake; *f* sea, ocean

**Seebad,** zay-baht, *nt* seaside resort

**seefest,** zay-fest, *adj* seaworthy; not subject to sea-sickness

**Seehund,** zay-hoont, *m* seal

**seekrank,** zay-krahnk, *adj* sea-sick

**Seele,** zayl-e, *f* soul

**Seelenheil,** zayl-en-hile, *nt* salvation

**Seelenruhe,** zayl-en-roo-e, *f* tranquillity of mind

**Seelöwe,** zay-lerv-e, *m* sea-lion

**Seelsorger,** zayl-zorg-er, *m* minister (of religion)

**Seemacht,** zay-mahkt, *f* naval power

**Seemöwe,** zay-merv-e, *f* sea-gull

**Seeräuber,** zay-royb-er, *m* pirate

**seetüchtig,** zay-tEEk-tik, *adj* seaworthy

**Seezunge,** zay-tsoong-e, *f* sole (fish)

**Segel,** zay-gel, *nt* sail; **–boot,** *nt* sailing boat, yacht; **–fliegen,** *nt* gliding

**segeln,** zay-geln, *v* to sail

**Segelschiff,** zay-gel-shif, *nt* sailing ship

**Segeltuch,** zay-gel-took, *nt* canvas, sail-cloth

**Segen,** zay-gen, *m* blessing

**Segler,** zayg-ler, *m* sailor, navigator; yachtsman

**segnen,** zayg-nen, *v* to bless

**sehen,** zay-en, *v* to see; to look

**Sehenswürdigkeit,** zay-ens-vEErd-ik-kite, *f* sight, place of interest

**Sehkraft,** zay-krahft, *f* (eye)sight

**Sehne,** zay-ne, *f* sinew, tendon; string (bow)

**sehnen (sich),** zayn-en

(zik), *v* to long (for)

**sehnig,** zayn-ik, *adj* sinewy; muscular

**sehnlich(st),** zayn-lik(st), *adj* ardent, eager

**Sehnsucht,** zayn-zookt, *f* longing, yearning

**sehnsüchtig,** zayn-zEEk-tik, *adj & adv* longing(ly); yearning

**sehr,** zair, *adv* very; greatly; highly; badly

**seicht,** zy'kt, *adj* shallow; superficial

**Seide,** zy-de, *f* silk

**Seidel,** zy-del, *nt* tankard, pot

**seiden,** zy-den, *adj* of silk, silken

**Seidenpapier,** zy-den-pah-peer, *nt* tissue-paper

**Seidenraupe,** zy-den-rowp-e, *f* silkworm

**Seife,** zy-fe, *f* soap; **–nschaum,** *m* lather

**Seil,** zile, *nt* rope, cable, line; **–bahn,** *f* cable railway

**sein,** zine, *v* to be; to exist

**sein, seine(r/s),** zine, zine-e(r/s), *adj & pron* his, its

**seiner,** zine-er, *pron* (genitive *m & nt*) of him/it

**seinerseits,** zine-er-zites, *adv* on his/its part

**seinesgleichen,** zine-es-gly-ken, *pron* people like him

**seinethalben, seinetwegen, seinetwillen,** zine-net-hahllb-en, -vaig-en, vil-en, *adv* for his sake

**seit**, zite, *prep* since; *conj* since, seeing that

**seitdem**, zite-daym, *adv* since (then)

**Seite**, zy-te, *f* side; page; party

**Seitengasse**, zy-ten-gahss-e, *f* side-street

**seitens**, zy-tens, *prep* on the part of

**seither**, zite-hair, *adv* since then

**seitlich**, zite-lik, *adj* beside, at the side

**seitwärts**, zite-vairts, *adv* sideways

**Sekretär**, zeck-re-tair, *m* writing-desk; secretary

**Sekt**, zeckt, *m* sparkling wine

**Sektion**, zeckts-yohn, *f* division; dissection; post-mortem

**sekundär**, zeck-oonn-dair, *adj* secondary, subordinate

**Sekunde**, zeck-oonn-de, *f* second

**selber**, zelb-er, *pron* my/your/him/her/it/oneself; our/your/themselves

**selbst**, zelp'st, *adv* even; *pron* my/your/him/her/it/oneself/our/your/themselves; in person

**selbständig**, zelp-shtend-ik, *adj* independent; self-employed

**Selbstbedienung**, zelpst-be-deen-oong, *f* self-service

**selbstbewußt**, zelpst-be-voost, *adj* self-confident

**Selbstgefühl**, zelpst-ge-fEEl, *nt* self-assurance, ego

**selbstgemacht**, zelpst-ge-makt, *adj* home-made

**Selbstgespräch**, zelpst-ge-shprayk, *nt* soliloquy

**selbstlos**, zelpst-lohs, *adj* unselfish

**Selbstmord**, zelpst-mort, *m* suicide

**Selbstmörder**, zelpst-merd-er, *m* (person committing) suicide

**selbstredend**, zelpst-rayd-ent, *adj* self-evident

**selbstsicher**, zelpst-zik-er, *adj* self-assured, self-confident

**selbstsüchtig**, zelpst-zEEkt-ik, *adj* selfish

**Selbstversorgung**, zelpst-fair-zohrg-oong, *f* self-catering

**Selbstvertrauen**, zelpst-fair-trow-en, *nt* self-confidence

**selbstverständlich**, zelpst-fair-shtent-lik, *adv* of course

**selig**, zayl-ik, *adj* relig blessed; happy

**Sellerie**, zel-er-ee, *m & f* celery

**selten**, zelt-en, *adj* rare, seldom, scarce

**seltsam**, zelt-zahm, *adj* curious, strange

**Semester**, zay-mest-er, *nt* term (university)

**senden**, zend-en, *v* to send; to broadcast

**Sendung**, zend-oong, *f*

consignment; dispatch; programme

**Senf**, zenf, *m* mustard

**sengen**, zeng-en, *v* to single, to scorch

**Senior**, zehn-yohr, *m* (old-age) pensioner; **–enheim**, *nt* old people's home; **–enpaß**, *m* senior citizen's pass/railcard

**senken**, zeng-ken, *v* to sink, to lower; to dip

**senkrecht**, zenk-rekt, *adj* vertical

**Sense**, zen-ze, *f* scythe

**sensibel**, zen-zee-bel, *adj* sensitive

**September**, zep-tem-ber, *m* September

**servieren**, zairv-eer-en, *v* to serve

**Serviette**, zairv-ee-ett-e, *f* napkin

**Sessel**, zess-el, *m* easy-chair; **–lift**, *m* chairlift

**setzen**, zets-en, *v* to set, to place; **sich –**, *v* to sit down

**Seuche**, zoyk-e, *f* epidemic; plague

**seufzen**, zoyf-tsen, *v* to sigh

**Sexismus**, seks-is-mooss, *m* sexism

**sexistisch**, seks-ist-ish, *adj* sexist

**sezieren**, zay-tseer-en, *v* to dissect

**Shampoo**, shahmm-poo, *nt* shampoo

**sich**, zik, *refl pron* oneself

**Sichel**, zik-el, *f* sickle

**sicher**, zik-er, *adj* certain,

sure; safe, secure

**Sicherheit, zik**-er-hite, *f*
security; safety; certainty;
**–sgurt,** *m* safety belt;
**–snadel,** *f* safety pin

**sicherlich, zik**-er-lik, *adv*
surely, certainly

**sichern, zik**-ern, *v* to secure;
to safeguard; to ensure

**sicherstellen, zik**-er-shtel-
en, *v* to secure; to make
sure

**Sicht, zikt,** *f* sight, vision;
view

**sichtbar, zikt**-bahr, *adj*
visible; perceptible

**sichten, zikt**-en, *v* to sight

**sichtlich, zikt**-lik, *adj*
visible; *adv* evidently

**sickern, zick**-ern, *v* to ooze;
to trickle

**Sie, zee,** *pron* (formal) you

**sie, zee,** *pron* she, her; it;
they, them

**Sieb, zeep,** *nt* sieve; strainer

**sieben, zee**-ben, *v* to sift, to
sieve; *num* seven

**sieb(en)te, zeeb**(-en)-te, *adj*
seventh

**siebzehn, zeep**-tsain, *num*
seventeen

**siebzig, zeep**-tsik, *num*
seventy

**siechen, zeek**-en, *v* to pine
away; to be in ill-health

**siedeln, zeed**-eln, *v* to settle

**sieden, zeed**-en, *v* to boil; to
seethe

**Siedler, zeed**-ler, *m* settler,
colonist

**Siedlung, zeed**-loong, *f*

housing estate

**Sieg, zeek,** *m* victory

**Siegel, zeeg**-el, *nt* seal;
signet

**siegen, zeeg**-en, *v* to be
victorious

**Sieger, zeeg**-er, *m* victor

**siegreich, zeek**-ry'k, *adj*
victorious

**Silbe, zilb**-e, *f* syllable

**Silber, zilb**-er, *nt* silver

**silbern, zilb**-ern, *adj* of silver

**Silvester(abend), zil-vest**-
er(-ahb-ent), *nt* (*m*), New
Year's Eve

**singen, zing**-en, *v* to sing

**sinken, zing**-ken, *v* to sink

**Sinn, zin,** *m* sense; mind;
nature; disposition

**sinnen, zin**-en, *v* to ponder;
to reflect, to meditate

**sinnlich, zin**-lik, *adj* sensual;
sensuous; sensory

**Sinnlichkeit, zin**-lik-kite, *f*
sensuality; sensuousness

**sinnlos, zin**-lohs, *adj*
pointless; meaningless

**sinnvoll, zin**-fol, *adj*
meaningful; wise; sensible

**Sintflut, zint**-floot, *f* deluge,
flood

**Sippe, zip**-e, *f* relations,
family, clan

**Sippschaft, zip**-shahft, *f*
relations, family, clan

**Sitte, zit**-e, *f* habit, custom,
usage; **–n,** *pl* morals

**sittlich, zit**-lik, *adj* moral;
respectable

**Sittlichkeit, zit**-lik-kite, *f*
morality; moral code

**sittsam, zit**-zahm, *adj*
modest; respectable;
decent

**Sitz, zits,** *m* seat; residence

**sitzen, zit**-sen, *v* to sit, to be
seated; to fit

**Sitzplatz, zits**-plahts, *m* seat

**Sitzung, zit**-soong, *f*
meeting; session

**Skala, skah**-lah, *f mus* scale

**Skandal, skahnn-dahl,** *m*
noise; scandal

**Skandinavien, skahnn-dee-
nah**-vee-en, *pl*
Scandinavia

**Skat, skaht,** *m* German card
game

**Skateboard, skayt**-bort, *nt*
skateboard

**Ski, shee,** *m* ski; **–lauf,** *m*
skiing; **–laufen,** *v* to ski;
**–läufer,** *m* skier; **–lift,** *m*
ski lift; **–piste,** *f* ski slope,
piste

**Skizze, skit**-se, *f* sketch;
draft

**skizzieren, skit-seer**-en, *v* to
sketch

**Sklave, sklahv**-e, *m* slave

**Sklaverei, sklahv**-e-*ry*, *f*
slavery

**Skonto, skont**-oh, *m*
discount, rebate

**Slovakei, slo-vah-ky,** *f*
Slovakia

**Slowenien, slo-vay-nee-en,**
*nt* Slovenia

**Smaragd, smah-rahkt,** *m*
emerald

**Smog, smog,** *m* smog

**Smoking, smoh**-king, *m*

dinner jacket

**sb.,** *abbr* for **siehe oben, zee-e oh-ben,** see above

**so,** zoh, *adv* so, like this; such; *conj* therefore

**sobald,** zoh-**bahlt,** *conj* as soon as

**Socke,** zohck-e, *f* sock

**Sockel,** zock-el, *m* base, foot

**sodann,** zoh-**dahnn,** *adv* after that; then

**soeben,** zoh-**ayb-**en, *adv* just now

**sofern,** zoh-**fairn,** *conj* in so far as; if

**sofort,** zoh-**fort,** *adv* at once, immediately

**Software,** soft-wair, *f* software

**sog.,** *abbr* **sogenannt,** zoh-ge-nahnt, *adj* so-called

**sogar,** zoh-**gar,** *adv* even

**sogleich,** zoh-**gly'k,** *adv* at once, immediately

**Sohle,** zohl-e, *f* (in)sole; bottom, floor

**Sohn,** zohn, *m* son

**Soja,** zoh-jah, *f* soya; **–bohne,** *f* soya bean; **–soße,** *f* soya sauce

**solange,** zoh-**lahng-**e, *conj* so long as

**solch,** zolk, *pron* such; – **ein(e),** such a

**solche(r/s),** zol-ke(r/s), *adj* such; **ein(e) –,** such a

**Soldat,** zol-**daht,** *m* soldier

**Söldner,** zerlt-ner, *m* hireling, mercenary

**solid(e),** zol-**eed**(-e), *adj* steady, respectable; solid

**sollen,** zol-en, *v* to be obliged to; to have to; ought to; shall

**Solo,** zoh-loh, *nt* solo

**somit,** zoh-mit, *adv* hence, therefore, thus

**Sommer,** zom-er, *m* summer; **–sprossen,** *pl* freckles

**Sonderangebot,** zon-der-ahn-ge-boht, *nt* special offer

**sonderbar,** zon-der-bar, *adj* strange; unusual

**sondergleichen,** zon-der-gly-ken, *adj* unequalled

**sonderlich,** zon-der-lik, *adj* notable; *adv* particularly

**Sonderling,** zon-der-ling, *m* eccentric (person)

**sondern,** zon-dern, *conj* but (after negation)

**Sonnabend,** zon-ah-bent, *m* Saturday

**Sonne,** zon-e, *f* sun

**sonnen (sich),** zon-en (zik), *v* to sun oneself; to bask

**Sonnenaufgang,** zon-en-owf-gahng, *m* sunrise

**Sonnenblume,** zon-en-bloom-e, *f* sunflower

**Sonnenbad,** zon-en-baht, *nt* sunbathing

**Sonnenbrand,** zon-en-brahnt, *m* sunburn

**Sonnenbräune,** zon-en-broy-ne, *f* sun tan

**Sonnenbrille,** zon-en-brill-e, *f* sun glasses

**Sonnencreme,** zon-en-kraim, *f* sun cream

**Sonnenenergie,** zon-en-en-air-gee, *f* solar power

**Sonnenklar,** zon-en-klahr, *adj* clear as day

**Sonnenkollektor,** zon-en-kol-ek-tohr, *m* solar panel

**Sonnenschein,** zon-en-shine, *m* sunshine

**Sonnenschirm,** zon-en-sheerm, *m* sunshade, parasol

**Sonnenschutz,** zon-en-shoots, *m* sun protection

**Sonnenstich,** zon-en-shtik, *m* sunstroke

**Sonnenstrahl,** zon-en-shtrahl, *m* sunbeam

**Sonnenuntergang,** zon-en-oont-er-gahng, *m* sunset

**sonnenverbrannt,** zon-en-fair-brahnnt, *adj* sunburnt

**sonnig,** zon-ik, *adj* sunny

**Sonntag,** zon-tahk, *m* Sunday

**sonst,** zonst, *adv* otherwise; besides

**sonstige(r/s),** zons-ti-ge(r/s), *adj* former; other

**sonstwie,** zonst-vee, *adv* in some other way

**sonstwo,** zonst-voh, *adv* elsewhere

**sonstwoher,** zonst-voh-hair, *adv* from elsewhere

**Sorge,** zorg-e, *f* sorrow; anxiety; worry

**sorgen,** zorg-en, *v* to attend to; to procure; **sich –,** to worry

**Sorgfalt,** zorg-fahlt, *f* attention; care

**sorgfältig,** zorg-felt-ik, *adj*

careful; attentive; exact

**sorgsam**, zorg-zahm, *adj* particular; careful

**Sorte**, zort-e, *f* kind; sort; variety

**sortieren**, zort-eer-en, *v* to (as)sort; to arrange

**Soße**, zoh-se, *f* sauce, gravy

**Souffleur**, zooff-ler, *m* prompter

**soviel**, zoh-feel, *conj* as far as

**soweit**, zoh-vite, *conj* in so far as

**sowie**, zoh-vee, *conj* as soon as; as well as

**sowieso**, zoh-vee-soh, *adv* in any case

**sowohl**, zoh-vohl, *conj* as well; – ... als auch ..., *conj* both ... and ...

**Sozialhilfe**, zo-tsee-ahl-hilf-e, *f* income support

**Sozialversicherung**, zo-tsee-ahl-fair-zik-er-oong, *f* social security

**spähen**, shpay-en, *v* to look out for; to spy

**Spalier**, shpah-leer, *nt* trellis; row, line (of people)

**Spalt**, shpahlt, *m* cleft; slit; crevasse

**Spalte**, shpahlt-e, *f* column; cleft; slit; crevasse

**spalten**, shpahlt-en, *v* to split; to crack

**Span**, shpahn, *m* chip, splinter

**Spanferkel**, shpahn-fairk-el, *nt* suckling pig

**Spange**, shpahng-e, *f*

buckle, clasp

**Spanien**, shpah-nee-en, *nt* Spain

**spanisch**, shpah-nish, *adj* Spanish

**Spann**, shpahnn, *m* instep

**Spanne**, shpahnn-e, *f* span; stretch

**spannen**, shpahnn-en, *v* to stretch; to tighten; to tie

**Spannung**, shpahnn-oong, *f* tension; tightness; strain; suspense; voltage

**Sparbüchse**, shpahr-bEEks-e, *f* money box

**sparen**, shpahr-en, *v* to save; to spare

**Spargel**, shpahrg-el, *m* asparagus

**Sparkasse**, shpahr-kahss-e, *f* savings bank

**spärlich**, shpair-lik, *adj* scanty, sparse; meagre

**sparsam**, shpahr-zahm, *adj* saving; thrifty; economical

**Sparschwein**, shpahr-shvine, *nt* piggy bank

**Spaß**, shpahs, *m* fun; joking; amusement

**spaßen**, shpahs-en, *v* to joke

**spaßhaft**, shpahs-hahft, *adj* funny; for fun

**spaßig**, shpahs-ik, *adj* amusing, funny

**spät**, shpayt, *adj* late, belated

**Spaten**, shpaht-en, *m* spade

**späterhin**, shpayt-er-hin, *adv* later on

**spätestens**, shpayt-est-ens, *adv* at the latest

**Spatz**, shpahts, *m* sparrow

**spazieren**, shpaht-seer-en, *v* to stroll; –fahren, *v* to go for a drive; –gehen, *v* to go for a walk

**Spazierfahrt**, shpaht-seer-fahrt, *f* drive, ride

**Spaziergang**, shpaht-seer-gahng, *m* walk, ramble; stroll

**Spazierstock**, shpaht-seer-shtock, *m* walking-stick

**Specht**, shphekt, *m* woodpecker

**Speck**, shpeck, *m* bacon

**Spediteur**, shpay-de-ter, *m* forwarding-agent; furniture remover

**Speer**, shpair, *m* spear; lance; javelin (sport)

**Speiche**, shpy-ke, *f* spoke (wheel)

**Speichel**, shpy-kel, *m* spittle, saliva

**Speicher**, shpy-ker, *m* granary; warehouse; attic

**speichern**, shpy-kern, *v* to store; to warehouse

**Speise**, shpy-ze, *f* food; nourishment; –kammer, *f* pantry; –karte, *f* menu; –lokal, *nt* restaurant

**speisen**, shpy-zen, *v* to eat, to dine

**Speisesaal**, shpy-ze-zahl, *m* dining-room

**Speisewagen**, shpy-ze-vahg-en, *m* restaurant-car

**Speisezimmer**, shpy-ze-tsim-er, *nt* dining-room

**Spektakel**, shpeck-tahk-el,

*m* noise, row

**Spelunke**, shpay-**loong**-ke, *f*
*fam* dive

**Spende**, shpend-e, *f*
donation, gift; distribution

**spenden**, shpend-en, *v* to
donate; to give

**spendieren**, shpend-**eer**-en,
*v* to buy (for), to stand
(drink etc.)

**Sperber**, shpairb-er, *m*
sparrow-hawk

**Sperling**, shpair-ling, *m*
sparrow

**Sperre**, shpairr-e, *f* closure;
blockade; stoppage

**sperren**, shpairr-en, *v* to
bar, to obstruct; to
interrupt

**Sperrsitz**, shpairr-zits, *m*
stall *theatre*

**Sperrstunde**, shpairr-
shtoond-e, *f* closing time

**Spesen**, shpay-zen, *pl*
expenses; charges

**spicken**, shpick-en, *v* to
lard; to bribe; *fam* to crib

**Spiegel**, shpeeg-el, *m* mirror

**Spiegelei**, shpeeg-el-i, *nt*
fried egg

**spiegelglatt**, shpeeg-el-
glahtt, *adj* smooth as glass

**spiegeln**, shpeeg-eln, *v* to
reflect; to shine

**Spiel**, shpeel, *nt* play; game;
pastime

**spielen**, shpeel-en, *v* to play;
to perform; to gamble

**Spieler**, shpeel-er, *m* player;
gambler

**Spielerei**, shpeel-e-ry, *f*

play(ing); pastime;
triviality

**Spielhölle**, shpeel-herll-e, *f*
gambling den

**Spielsachen**, shpeel-sahk-
en, *pl* toys

**Spielverderber**, shpeel-fair-
dairb-er, *m* spoil-sport

**Spielwaren**, shpeel-vahr-en,
*pl* toys

**Spielzeug**, shpeel-tsoyk, *nt*
plaything(s), toy(s)

**Spieß**, shpees, *m* spear; pike;
(roasting-)spit

**Spießbürger**, shpees-bEErg-
er, *m* bourgeois, Philistine

**Spießer**, shpees-er, *m*
bourgeois, Philistine

**Spinat**, shpeen-**aht**, *m*
spinach

**Spind**, shpint, *m* & *nt*
locker, cupboard

**Spindel**, shpin-del, *f* spindle

**Spinne**, shpinn-e, *f* spider

**spinnen**, shpinn-en, *v* to
spin; to purr; *fam* to
imagine things, to be mad

**Spinnwebe**, shpinn-vaib-e, *f*
spider's web

**Spion**, shpee-ohn, *m* spy;
scout

**Spionage**, shpee-ohn-**ahzh**-
e, *f* espionage, spying

**spionieren**, shpee-ohn-**eer**-
en, *v* to spy; to pry

**Spiritismus**, shpeer-ee-tis-
mooss, *m* spiritualism

**Spirituosen**, shpeer-it-oo-
**ohz**-en, *pl* spirits

**Spital**, shpee-**tahl**, *nt*
hospital

**spitz**, shpits, *adj* pointed;
sharp

**Spitz**, shpits, *m* Pomeranian
(dog)

**Spitzbube**, shpits-boob-e, *m*
rogue; rascal, scamp

**Spitze**, shpit-se, *f* point;
peak; tip; spire; lace

**Spitzel**, shpit-sel, *m*
detective; police spy

**spitzen**, shpit-sen, *v* to
point; to sharpen

**spitzfindig**, shpits-fin-dik,
*adj* nit-picking

**Spitzname**, shpits-nahm-e,
*m* nickname

**Splitter**, shplitt-er, *m*
splinter

**splittern**, shplitt-ern, *v* to
splinter; to shatter

**splitternackt**, shplitt-er-
nahckt, *adj* stark naked

**sponsern**, shpon-sern, *v* to
sponsor

**Sponsor**, shpon-sohr, *m*
sponsor

**Sporn**, shporn, *m* spur

**spornen**, shporn-en, *v* to
spur

**sportlich**, shport-lik, *adj*
relating to sport

**Spott**, shpott, *m* mockery;
derision

**spottbillig**, shpot-bil-ik, *adj*
dirt-cheap

**Spöttelei**, shpertt-e-ly, *f*
mocking (remark)

**spötteln**, shpertt-eln, *v* to
mock, to poke fun at

**spotten**, shpot-en, *v* to
mock; to jeer

**Spötter, shpertt**-er, *m* mocker; blasphemer

**spöttisch, shpertt**-ish, *adj* mocking, sneering, derisive

**Spottpreis, shpot**-price, *m* ridiculous(ly low) price

**Sprache, sphrahk**-e, *f* language; speech

**Sprachfehler, shprahk**-fail-er, *m* speech defect

**sprachkundig, shprahk**-koond-ik, *adj* good at (foreign) languages

**Sprachkurs, shprahk**-koors, *m* language course

**sprachlos, shprahk**-lohs, *adj* speechless

**Sprachrohr, shprahk**-rohr, *nt* megaphone; *fig* mouthpiece

**Spray, shpray, nt** spray; **–dose,** *f* aerosol, spray

**sprechen, shprek**-en, *v* to speak, to talk; to converse

**Sprecher, shprek**-er, *m* speaker; spokesman; news reader

**Sprechstunde, shprek**-shtoonn-de, *f* office-hour; surgery

**Sprechzimmer, shprek**-tsim-er, *nt* consulting-room

**spreizen, shpry**-tsen, *v* to spread out

**sprengen, shpreng**-en, *v* to force apart; to blow up; to sprinkle

**Sprengstoff, shpreng**-shtof, *m* explosive

**sprenkeln, shpreng**-keln, *v* to speckle, to spot

**Spreu, shproy,** *f* chaff

**Sprichwort, shprik**-vort, *nt* proverb

**sprichwörtlich, shprik**-vert-lik, *adj* proverbial

**sprießen, shprees**-en, *v* to sprout, to germinate

**Springbrunnen, shpring**-broonn-en, *m* fountain

**springen, shpring**-en, *v* to jump; to spring; to burst; to crack

**Springer, shpring**-er, *m* jumper; knight (chess)

**Spritze, shprit**-se, *f* syringe; hose; injection

**spritzen, shprit**-sen, *v* to squirt; to splash

**spröde, shprerd**-e, *adj* fragile; brittle; rough; coy, prudish

**Sproß, shpross,** *m* shoot, sprout; offspring

**Sprosse, shpross**-e, *f* rung, step

**sprossen, shpross**-en, *v* to sprout, to shoot

**Sprößling, shprerss**-ling, *m* shoot, sprout; offspring

**Spruch, shprook,** *m* sentence; verdict; maxim, saying

**Sprudel, shprood**-el, *m* bubbling spring; flow; sparkling water

**sprudeln, shprood**-eln, *v* to gush forth, to bubble

**Sprühdose, shprEE**-doh-ze, *f* aerosol

**sprühen, shprEE**-en, *v* to sparkle; to send out sparks

**Sprung, shproong,** *m* jump, leap; **–brett,** *nt* diving-board, springboard (also *fig*); **–feder,** *f* (spiral) spring

**sprungfertig, shproong**-fairt-ik, *adj* ready to jump

**Spucke, shpoock**-e, *f* spit(tle)

**spucken, shpoock**-en *v* to spit

**Spucknapf, shpoock**-nahp'f, *m* spittoon

**Spuk, shpook,** *m* spook, spectre, ghost

**spuken, shpook**-en, *v* to haunt, to walk (ghosts)

**Spule, shpool**-e, *f* bobbin, spool; coil

**spulen, shpool**-en, *v* to reel; to spin

**spülen, shpEEl**-en, *v* to rinse; to wash up

**Spülmaschine, shpEEl**-mah-shee-ne, *f* dishwasher

**Spülmittel, shpEEl**-mit-el, *nt* washing-up liquid

**Spur, shpoor,** *f* spoor; track; trail

**spüren, shpEEr**-en, *v* to perceive, to feel

**spurlos, shpoor**-lohs, *adj* without (leaving any) trace

**Spurweite, shpoor**-vite-e, *f* gauge (of railway); track (of car)

**sputen (sich), shpoot**-en (zik), *v* to make haste

**Staat, shtaht,** *m* state;

show, pomp

**staatlich, shtaht**-lik, *adj* (of the) state

**Staatsangehörige(r), shtahts**-ahnn-ge-her-rige(r), *m & f* subject (of a state), national

**Staatsanwalt, shtahts**-ahnn-vahlt, *m* public prosecutor

**Staatsbeamte(r), shtahts**-be-ahmt-e(r), *m* civil servant

**Staatsdienst, shtahts**-deenst, *m* civil service

**Staatswesen, shtahts**-vayz-en, *nt* state

**Stab, shtahp**, *m* staff, stick; bar

**Stachel, shtahk**-el, *m* spike; sting; thorn; prickle; barb; **–beere,** *f* gooseberry; **–draht,** *m* barbed wire

**stachelig, shtahk**-el-ik, *adj* thorny, prickly

**Stachelschwein, shtahk**-el-shvine, *nt* porcupine

**Stadion, shtahd**-yohn, *nt* stadium

**Stadt, shtahtt**, *f* town

**Städter, shtayt**-er, *m* town-/city-dweller

**städtisch, shtayt**-ish, *adj* municipal; urban

**Stadtmitte, shtahtt-mit**-e, *f* town/city centre

**Stadtplan, shtahtt**-plahn, *m* street plan

**Stadtrat, shtahtt**-raht, *m* town-council(lor)

**Stadtrundfahrt, shtahtt**-roont-fahrt, *f* city tour

**Stadtteil, shtahtt**-tile, *m* district, quarter

**Stadtverordnete(r), shtahtt**-fair-ord-net-e(r), *m & f* town councillor

**Staffel, shtahff**-el, *f* degree, step; bracket; (sport) relay

**Staffelei, shtahff-el-y**, *f* easel

**Stahl, shtahl**, *m* steel

**stählen, shtayl**-en, *v* to steel; to harden

**stählern, shtayl**-ern, *adj* (of/like) steel

**Stall, shtahll**, *m* stable, stall, sty; **–knecht,** *m* stable-boy, groom; **–ung,** *f* stabling; mews

**Stamm, shtahmm**, *m* stem, stalk; trunk; tribe; stock; **–baum,** *m* genealogical tree; pedigree

**stammeln, shtahmm**-eln, *v* to stammer

**stammen, shtahmm**-en, *v* to descend (from); to spring (from)

**Stammgast, shtahmm**-gahsst, *m* regular customer (in pub)

**stämmig, shtem**-ik, *adj* robust, stocky, sturdy

**Stammkneipe, Stammlokal, shtahmm**-knipe-e, **-loh**-kahl, *f nt* favourite pub, local

**Stammtisch, shtahmm**-tish, *m* table reserved for regular customers (in pub)

**stampfen, shtahmp**-fen, *v* to stamp; to trample; to paw

**Stand, shtahnt**, *m* stand;

position; state; **–bild,** *nt* statue

**Ständchen, shtent**-ken, *nt* serenade

**Ständer, shtend**-er, *m* stand; post; pedestal

**Standesamt, shtahnd**-es-ahmt, *nt* register office

**Standesbeamte(r), shtahnd**-es-be-ahmt-e(r), *m* registrar

**standesgemäß, shtahnd**-es-ge-mace, *adj* according to one's station

**standhaft, shtahnt**-hahft, *adj* firm, steadfast, resolute

**standhalten, shtahnt-hahl**-ten, *v* to stand firm

**ständig, shtend**-ik, *adj* constant; permanent

**Standort, shtahnt**-ort, *m* location, position; base

**Standpunkt, shtahnt**-poonkt, *m* point of view; position

**Standuhr, shtahnt**-oor, *f* clock

**Stange, shtahng**-e, *f* rod, perch, stake

**stänkern, shtenk**-ern, *v* to make mischief

**Stanniol, shtahnn**-yohl, *nt* tin foil, silver paper

**stanzen, shtahnt**-sen, *v* to stamp, to punch

**Stapel, shtahp**-el, *m* stack, pile; store, depot; stocks; **–lauf,** *m* launch(ing)

**stapeln, shtahp**-eln, *v* to heap up; to stack

**Star, shtar**, *m* starling;

cataract (eye); (pop/film etc.) star

**stark,** shtark, *adj* strong; sturdy; severe

**Stärke, shtairk**-e, *f* strength, power; starch

**stärken, shtairk**-en, *v* to strengthen; to starch

**Stärkung, shtairk**-oong, *f* strengthening; reinforcement

**starr,** shtarr, *adj* rigid, stiff; fixed, staring

**starren, shtarr**-en, *v* to stare; to be(come) numb

**Starrheit, shtarr**-hite, *f* rigidity; numbness

**starrköpfig, shtarr**-kerpp-fik, *adj* stubborn; headstrong

**Starrsinn, shtarr**-zin, *m* stubbornness

**Startbahn, shtart**-bahn, *f* runway

**Station,** shtahts-**yohn,** *f* station; bus stop; (hospital) ward; **–svorsteher,** *m* station-master

**Statist, shtaht**-ist, *m* supernumerary, *theatre* extra

**statt,** shtahtt, *prep* instead of

**Stätte, shtet**-e, *f* place; abode; site

**stattfinden, shtahtt**-fin-den, *v* to take place

**statthaft, shtahtt**-hahft, *adj* permitted; legal

**Statthalter, shtahtt**-hahlt-er, *m* governor; viceroy

**stattlich, shtahtt**-lik, *adj* splendid, stately; commanding

**Stau,** shtow, *m* traffic jam; blockage

**Staub,** shtowp, *m* dust; (fine) powder

**stauben, shtowb**-en, *v* to give off/create dust

**stäuben, shtoyb**-en, *v* to dust; to powder

**Staubgefäß, shtowp**-ge-face, *nt* stamen

**staubig, shtowb**-ik, *adj* dusty; powdery

**Staubsauger, shtowp**-sow-ger, *m* vacuum cleaner

**Staude, shtowd**-e, *f* bush, shrub

**stauen, shtow**-en, *v* to stow; to dam

**staunen, shtown**-en, *v* to be surprised/astonished

**Stausee, shtow**-zay, *m* reservoir

**Std.,** *abbr* **Stunde,** hour; o'clock

**stechen, shtek**-en, *v* to stab; to pierce; to prick

**Stechginster, shtek**-ginst-er, *m* gorse, furze

**Stechpalme, shtek**-pahlm-e, *f* holly

**Steckbrief, shteck**-breef, *m* warrant

**Steckdose, shteck**-doh-ze, *f* (electrical) socket

**Stecken, shteck**-en, *m* staff, stick

**stecken, shteck**-en, *v* to stick; to be stuck; to put, to set; **–bleiben,** *v* to be/get stuck

**Steckenpferd, shteck**-en-p'fairt, *nt* hobby-horse; fad

**Steckling, shteck**-ling, *m* shoot, cutting; slip

**Stecknadel, shteck**-nahd-el, *f* pin

**Steckrübe, shteck**-rEEb-e, *f* swede

**Steg,** shtayk, *m* path; footbridge; bridge (of violin)

**Stegreif, shtayk**-rife, *m* **aus dem – spielen,** to improvise

**stehen, shtay**-en, *v* to stand, to be standing (up); **–bleiben,** *v* to stop; to remain standing

**Stehkragen, shtay**-krahg-en, *m* stand-up collar

**stehlen, shtayl**-en, *v* to steal

**Stehplatz, shtay**-plahts, *m* standing-room

**steif,** shtife, *adj* stiff, rigid; thick

**steifen, shty**-fen, *v* to stiffen; to starch

**Steig,** shtike, *m* steep track; **–bügel,** *m* stirrup

**steigen, shty**-gen, *v* to climb, to mount; to rise

**steigern, shty**-gern, *v* to raise; to increase; to intensify

**Steigerung, shty**-ger-oong, *f* increase; raising; comparing

**Steigung, shty**-goong, *f* rise; gradient

**steil,** shtile, *adj* steep, sheer

**Stein,** shtine, *m* stone

**steinalt**, *shtine*-ahlt, *adj* very old

**Steinbock**, *shtine*-bock, *m* ibex; capricorn

**Steinbruch**, *shtine*-brook, *m* quarry

**Steinbutt**, *shtine*-boott, *m* turbot

**steinern**, *shtine*-ern, *adj* (of) stone; (of) earthenware

**Steingut**, *shtine*-goot, *nt* earthenware

**steinhart**, *shtine*-hart, *adj* as hard as stone

**steinig**, *shtine*-ik, *adj* stony; rocky

**steinigen**, *shtine*-ig-en, *v* to stone (to death)

**Steinkohle**, *shtine*-kohl-e, *f* hard coal

**Steinmetz**, *shtine*-mets, *m* stone-mason

**Steinpflaster**, *shtine*-p'flahst-er, *nt* stone paving

**steinreich**, *shtine*-ry'k, *adj* very rich

**Steiß**, *shtice*, *m* rump, buttock; posterior

**Stelldichein**, *shtel*-dik-ine, *nt* appointment; rendezvous

**Stelle**, *shtel*-e, *f* place, spot; job; situation; digit

**stellen**, *shtel*-en, *v* to place; to stand; to set

**stellenweise**, *shtel*-en-vy-ze, *adv* in places

**Stellung**, *shtel*-oong, *f* position; placement, employment

**Stellvertreter**, *shtel*-fair-

traiyt-er, *m* representative; substitute, deputy

**Stelze**, *shtelt*-se, *f* stilt

**Stemmeisen**, *shtem*-i-zen, *nt* crowbar

**stemmen**, *shtem*-en, *v* to support; to dam; to stem

**Stempel**, *shtemp*-el, *m* stamp; mark; pistil

**stempeln**, *shtemp*-eln, *v* to stamp; to mark

**Stengel**, *shteng*-el, *m* stem, stalk; handle

**Steppdecke**, *shtep*-deck-e, *f* quilt

**steppen**, *shtep*-en, *v* to quilt

**Sterbebett**, *shtairb*-e-bet, *nt* death-bed

**sterben**, *shtairb*-en, *v* to die

**sterbenskrank**, *shtairb*-ens-krahnk, *adj* fatally/terminally ill

**sterblich**, *shtairp*-lik, *adj* mortal

**Sterblichkeit**, *shtairp*-lik-kite, *f* mortality

**Stereoanlage**, *shtay*-ray-oh-ahnn-lah-ge, *f* stereo (system)

**Stern**, *shtairn*, *m* star; asterisk

**Sterndeuter**, *shtairn*-doyt-er, *m* astrologer

**sternhell**, *shtairn*-hel, *adj* starry

**Sternkunde**, *shtairn*-koonn-de, *f* astronomy

**Sternschnuppe**, *shtairn*-shnoopp-e, *f* shooting star

**Sternwarte**, *shtairn*-vart-e, *f* observatory

**Sternzeichen**, *shtairn*-tsyk-en, *nt* star sign

**stet**, *shtayt*, *adj* fixed, steady; constant

**stetig**, *shtayt*-ik, *adj* steady; continual; constant

**stets**, *shtayts*, *adv* always, ever

**Steuer**, *shtoy*-er, *nt* rudder, tiller; *f* tax, duty; **–berater**, *m* tax consultant; **–bord**, *nt* starboard; **–mann**, *m* helmsman; mate

**steuern**, *shtoy*-ern, *v* to steer, to navigate; to control

**Steuerung**, *shtoy*-er-oong, *f* steering(-wheel); control

**Stewardeß**, *st'yoo*-ahr-dess, *f* stewardess

**Stich**, *shtik*, *m* stitch; sting, bite; stab

**sticheln**, *shtik*-eln, *v* to sneer; to tease

**stichhaltig**, *shtik*-hahlt-ik, *adj* plausible, sound

**Stichwaffe**, *shtik*-vahff-e, *f* foil, sword, dagger

**Stichwort**, *shtik*-vort, *nt* cue; catch-word; headword

**sticken**, *shtick*-en, *v* to embroider

**Stickerei**, *shtick*-e-ry, *f* embroidery

**stickig**, *shtick*-ik, *adj* stuffy, choking

**Stickstoff**, *shtick*-shtof, *m* nitrogen

**Stief–**, *shteef*, *pref* step-; **–bruder**, *m* stepbrother;

**–mutter,** *f* stepmother;

**–schwester,** *f* stepsister;

**–sohn,** *m* stepson;

**–tochter,** *f* stepdaughter;

**–vater,** *m* stepfather

**Stiefel, shteef**-el, *m* boot

**stiefeln, shteef**-eln, *v fam* to hoof it

**Stiefmütterchen, shteef-**mEEtt-*er*-ken, *nt* pansy

**Stiege, shteeg**-e, *f* stair(s)

**Stieglitz, shteeg**-lits, *m* goldfinch

**Stiel, shteel,** *m* handle; stalk; stem

**stier, shteer,** *adj* staring; vacant

**Stier, shteer,** *m* bull; steer

**stieren, shteer**-en, *v* to stare; to look vacant

**Stierkampf, shteer**-kahmp'f, *m* bull-fight

**Stift, shtift,** *m* peg; tag; bolt; pencil; *nt* convent; charitable foundation

**stiften, shtift**-en, *v* to found; to create; to endow

**Stiftung, shtift**-oong, *f* foundation; endowment; **–sfest,** *nt* commemoration day

**Stigma, s(h)tig**-mah, *nt* stigma

**Stil, shteel,** *m* style

**still, shtil,** *adj* still, quiet; silent; peaceful

**Stille, shtil**-e, *f* quiet, stillness; calm

**Stilleben, shtil**-layb-en, *nt* still-life

**stillen, shtil**-en, *v* to still; to

stanch; to appease; to quench; to breast-feed

**Stille(r) Ozean, shtil**-e(r) oh-tsay-ahn, *m* Pacific Ocean

**stillschweigend, shtil**-shvy-gent, *adj* silent; tacit

**Stillstand, shtil**-shtahnt, *m* stoppage

**Stimmband, shtim**-bahnt, *nt* vocal chord

**Stimme, shtim**-e, *f* voice; vote

**stimmen, shtim**-en, *v* to tally; to tune; to harmonize

**Stimmgabel, shtim**-gahb-el, *f* tuning-fork

**Stimmung, shtim**-oong, *f* mood, humour; atmosphere

**Stimmwechsel, shtim-**vecks-el, *m* breaking of the voice

**stinken, shtink**-en, *v* to stink

**Stinktier, shtink**-teer, *nt* skunk

**Stirn, shteern,** *f* forehead; brow; **–runzeln,** *nt* frown(ing)

**stöbern, shterb**-ern, *v* to rummage

**stochern, shtok**-ern, *v* to poke, to stir up

**Stock, shtock,** *m* stick, cane; storey

**stocken, shtock**-en, *v* to stop (short); to slacken

**stockfinster, shtock**-finst-er, *adj* pitch-dark

**Stockfisch, shtock**-fish, *m* dried cod

**Stockung, shtock**-oong, *f* stoppage; block; congestion

**Stockwerk, shtock**-vairk, *nt* storey

**Stoff, shtof,** *m* stuff; substance; fabric, material; subject

**Stoffel, shtof**-el, *m* blockhead

**stöhnen, shtern**-en, *v* to groan, to moan

**Stollen, shtol**-en, *m* tunnel; gallery (in mine); fruit loaf

**stolpern, shtolp**-ern, *v* to stumble

**stolz, shtolts,** *adj* proud; haughty

**Stolz, shtolts,** *m* pride; vanity

**stolzieren, shtolts-eer**-en, *v* to stalk, to strut

**stopfen, shtop**-fen, *v* to stuff, to cram; to darn

**Stoppel, shtop**-el, *f* stubble

**Stöpsel, shterpp**-sel, *m* stopper

**stöpseln, shterpp**-seln, *v* to stop (up); to cork

**Stör, shter,** *m* sturgeon

**Storch, shtork,** *m* stork

**stören, shter**-en, *v* to disturb; to interrupt

**Störenfried, shter**-en-freet, *m* mischief-maker

**stornieren, shtorn-eer**-en, *v* to cancel

**störrisch, shter**-ish, *adj*

stubborn; wayward

**Störung, shter**-oong, f
disturbance; interruption

**Stoß**, shtohs, m thrust, push;
stroke; blow; blast; heap

**stoßen, shtohs**-en, v to
push, to thrust; to pound;
to knock

**Stoßzahn, shtohs**-tsahn, m
tusk

**stottern, shtot**-ern, v to
stutter, to stammer

**Str.,** abbr **Straße**

**stracks**, shtrahcks, adv
straight away; directly

**strafbar, shtrahf**-bar, adj
punishable; criminal

**Strafe, shtrahf**-e, f
punishment; penalty;
chastisement

**strafen, shtrahf**-en, v to
punish; to correct

**straff**, shtrahff, adj taut,
tight; stretched; severe

**straffen, shtrahff**-en, v to
tighten, to stretch

**Strafgesetz, shtrahf**-ge-zets,
nt criminal code

**sträflich, shtrayf**-lik, adj
criminal; punishable

**Sträfling, shtrayf**-ling, m
convict

**Strafrecht, shtrahf**-rekt, nt
criminal law

**Strafsache, shtrahf**-sahk-e, f
criminal case

**Strafzettel, shtrahf**-tset-el,
m (speeding, parking etc.)
ticket

**Strahl**, shtrahl, m beam, ray;
jet

**strahlen, shtrahl**-en, v to
beam; to radiate; to shine

**Strahlung, shtrahl**-oong, f
radiation

**Strähne, shtrayn**-e, f strand;
plait

**stramm**, shtrahmm, adj
sturdy; stiff

**strampeln, shtrahmp**-eln, v
to struggle; to fidget, to
kick

**Strand**, shtrahnt, m beach,
shore, strand

**stranden, shtrahnd**-en, v to
be stranded; to founder

**Strang**, shtrahng, m rope;
track; trace

**Strapaze, shtrah-paht**-se, f
hardship; toil; exertion

**Straße, shtrahs**-e, f street,
road; straits; **–bahn,** f
tramway; **–nfest,** nt street
fair; **–nkarte,** f road map;
**–nmusikant,** m busker;
**–nverkehr,** m traffic

**Strategie, shtrah-tay-gee,** f
strategy

**sträuben (sich), shtroyb**-en
(zik), v to stand on end; to
struggle against

**Strauch, shtrowk,** m bush,
shrub

**straucheln, shtrowk**-eln, v
to stumble

**Strauß, shtrows,** m ostrich;
bouquet

**streben, shtrayb**-en, v to
aspire; to strive

**Streber, shtrayb**-er, m
ambitious person

**strebsam, shtrayp**-zahm, adj

zealous; ambitious

**Strecke, shtreck**-e, f stretch;
tract; track

**strecken, shtreck**-en, v to
stretch, to extend

**Streich, shtry'k,** m stroke;
trick; action

**streicheln, shtry**-keln, v to
stroke, to pat

**streichen, shtry**-ken, v to
stroke; to delete; to
spread; to paint

**Streichholz, shtry'k**-holts,
nt match

**Streifband, shtrife**-bahnt, nt
wrapper

**Streifen, shtrife**-en, m strip,
stripe

**streifen, shtrife**-en, v to
brush against; to touch; to
roam

**Streifzug, shtrife**-tsook, m
expedition, incursion

**Streik, shtrike,** m strike

**streiken, shtrike**-en, v to
strike, to down tools

**Streit, shtrite,** m dispute,
quarrel; fight

**streiten, shtrite**-en, v to
quarrel, to dispute

**Streitfrage, shtrite**-frah-ge, f
dispute

**streitig, shtrite**-ik, adj
contested, in dispute

**Streitigkeit, shtrite**-ik-kite,
f dispute; quarrel

**Streitkräfte, shtrite**-kreft-e,
pl mil forces

**streitsüchtig, shtrite**-SEEkt-
ik, adj quarrelsome

**streng, shtreng,** adj strict;

severe; harsh

**Strenge, shtreng**-*e*, *f* severity; strictness

**Streß, shtres**, *m* stress

**streuen, shtroy**-en, *v* to strew, to scatter

**Streuselkuchen, shtroy**-sel-kook-en, *m* cake with crumble topping

**Strich, shtrik**, *m* stroke, line

**Strick, shtrick**, *m* cord, rope, line

**stricken, shtrick**-en, *v* to knit

**Strickwaren, shtrick**-vahr-en, *pl* knitwear

**striegeln, shtreeg**-eln, *v* to brush

**Striemen, shtreem**-en, *m* stripe; weal

**Strippe, shtrip**-e, *f* string; strap; *fam* phone

**Stroh, shtroh**, *nt* straw; –**dach**, *nt* thatched roof; –**feuer**, *nt* *fig* passing fancy; –**halm**, *m* (drinking) straw; –**mann**, *m* scarecrow; dummy; –**witwer**, *m* grass-widower

**Strolch, shtrolk**, *m* tramp; rascal

**Strom, shtrohm**, *m* stream; current; large river; –**ausfall**, *m* power cut; –**bett**, *nt* river-bed

**strömen, shtrerm**-en, *v* to stream; to flow, to run

**Stromschnelle, shtrohm**-shnel-e, *f* rapid(s)

**Strömung, shtrerm**-oong, *f* current; streaming,

flowing

**Strophe, shtrohf**-e, *f* verse; stanza

**strotzen, shtrot**-sen, *v* to be full (of); to be crammed (with)

**Strudel, shtrood**-el, *m* whirlpool, eddy; strudel

**strudeln, shtrood**-eln, *v* to swirl, to eddy

**Strumpf, shtroomp'f**, *m* stocking; sock; –**band**, *nt* garter; –**hose**, *f* (pair of) tights; –**waren**, *pl* hosiery

**Strunk, shtroonk**, *m* stump, stalk

**struppig, shtroopp**-ik, *adj* dishevelled; scrubby

**Stube, shtoob**-e, *f* room

**stubenrein, shtoob**-en-rine, *adj* house-trained

**Stück, shtEEck**, *nt* piece; portion; play; –**chen**, *nt* little piece

**stückeln, shtEEck**-eln, *v* to cut into (small) pieces

**stückig, shtEEck**-ik, *adj* in pieces

**stückweise, shtEEck**-vy-ze, *adv* piecemeal

**Stückwerk, shtEEck**-vairk, *nt* patchwork; piece-work

**Student, shtoo-dent**, *m* (university) student

**Studienplan, shtoo**-dee-en-plahn, *m* syllabus

**studieren, shtoo-deer**-en, *v* to study

**Studium, shtood**-ee-oomm, *nt* study, studies

**Stufe, shtoof**-e, *f* step;

grade; rung; standard

**stufenweise, shtoof**-en-vy-ze, *adv* by steps/degrees

**Stuhl, shtool**, *m* chair; –**gang**, *m* bowel movement

**Stulle, shtooll**-e, *f* piece of bread and butter; sandwich

**stülpen, shtEElp**-en, *v* to turn up/out/in

**stumm, shtoomm**, *adj* dumb, mute

**Stummel, shtoomm**-el, *m* stump; fag-end

**Stümper, shtEEmp**-er, *m* botcher, bungler, clumsy person

**stümpern, shtEEmp**-ern, *v* to botch, to bungle

**stumpf, shtoomp'f**, *adj* blunt

**Stumpf, shtoomp'f**, *m* stump; fag-end

**Stumpfsinn, shtoomp'f**-zin, *m* stupidity; dullness

**Stunde, shtoonn**-de, *f* hour; lesson

**stunden, shtoonn**-den, *v* to give time for payment

**Stundenkilometer, shtoonn**-den-kee-loh-may-ter, *m* kilometers per hour

**stundenlang, shtoonn**-den-lahng, *adv* for hours

**Stundenplan, shtoonn**-den-plahn, *m* timetable

**stündlich, shtEEnt**-lik, *adj* hourly

**stur, shtoor**, *adj* obstinate

**Sturm, shtoorm**, *m*

storm, gale

**stürmen,** shtEErm-en, v to storm; to charge; to dash

**Stürmer,** shtEErm-er, m forward (sport); *fam* go-getter

**stürmisch,** shtEErm-ish, *adj* stormy; impetuous

**Sturz,** shtoorts, m (down)fall; crash; collapse; **–bach,** m mountain stream

**stürzen,** shtEErt-sen, v to fall; to collapse; to crash; to dash

**Stute,** shtoot-e, f mare

**Stütze,** shtEEtt-se, f support; stay; help

**stutzen,** shtoott-sen, v to trim, to cut short; to hesitate

**stützen,** shtEEtt-sen, v to support; to rely

**stutzig,** shtoott-sik, *adj* startled; perplexed

**Styropor®,** shtEEr-oh-pohr, nt polystyrene

**s.u.,** *abbr* **siehe unten,** zee-e oont-en, see below

**subtrahieren,** zoopp-trah-heer-en, v to subtract

**Subvention,** zoopp-vents-yohn, f subsidy

**subventionieren,** zoopp-vents-yohn-eer-en, v to subsidize

**Suche,** zook-e, f search

**suchen,** zook-en, v to seek, to look for

**Sucht,** zookt, f mania, passion; addiction

**süchtig,** zEEk-tik, *adj* addicted

**Süd-,** zEEt, *pref* South, southern; **–früchte,** pl citrus/tropical fruits; **–see,** f South Pacific

**Sudelei,** zood-e-ly, f scrawl; graffiti

**sudeln,** zood-eln, v to scrawl; to daub

**Süden,** zEEd-en, m South

**südlich,** zEEt-lik, *adj* southern, southerly

**Suff,** zooff, m *fam* drunkenness, drink(ing)

**süffig,** zEEff-ik, *adj* light and sweet (beverage)

**Sühne,** zEEn-e, f atonement; reconciliation

**sühnen,** zEEn-en, v to expiate; to atone

**Summe,** zoomm-e, f sum, amount; total

**summen,** zoomm-en, v to buzz, to hum

**Summer,** zoomm-er, m buzzer

**Sumpf,** zoomp'f, m bog, swamp, marsh

**sumpfig,** zoomp-fik, *adj* boggy, marshy

**Sünde,** zEEnn-de, f sin, trespass; **–nbock,** m scapegoat; **–r,** m sinner

**sündhaft,** zEEnt-hahft, *adj* sinful

**sündigen,** zEEnn-dig-en, v to sin

**Supermarkt,** zoop-er-mahrkt, m supermarket

**Suppe,** zoopp-e, f soup, broth; **–nfleisch,** nt boiled beef; **–nlöffel,** m soup spoon

**Surfbrett,** serf-bret, nt surfboard

**surfen,** serf-en, v to surf

**surren,** zoorr-en, v to buzz, to whiz

**süß,** zEEs, *adj* sweet

**süßen,** zEEs-en, v to sweeten

**Süßholz,** zEEs-holts, nt liquorice; soft-soap

**Süßigkeit,** zEEs-ik-kite, f sweets, sweetness

**süßlich,** zEEs-lik, *adj* (slightly) sweet; sickly, sugary

**Süßstoff,** zEEs-shtoff, m artificial sweetener

**Süßwasser,** zEEs-vahss-er, nt fresh water

**Sweatshirt,** svet-shert, nt sweatshirt

**synthetisch,** zEEn-tayt-ish, *adj* synthetic

**Szene,** s'tsayn-e, f scene

**Tabak, tah**-bahck, *m* tobacco; **–sbeutel,** *m* tobacco-pouch

**Tabelle, tah-bel-***e,* *f* table, schedule, index

**Tablett, tah-blet,** *nt* tray

**Tablette, tah-blet-***e,* *f* tablet

**Tadel, tahd-**el, *m* blame; reproach

**tadellos, tahd-**el-lohs, *adj* faultless; splendid

**tadeln, tahd-**eln, *v* to blame

**Tafel, tahf-**el, *f* table; tablet; slate; board; (chococlate) bar

**täfeln, tay-**feln, *v* to panel

**Taft, tahft,** *m* taffeta

**Tag, tahk,** *m* day; **–ebuch,** *nt* diary, journal; **–edieb,** *m* idler

**tagelang, tahg-**e-lahng, *adj & adv* for days (on end)

**Tagelöhner, tahg-**e-lern-er, *m* (day-)labourer

**tagen, tahg-**en, *v* to dawn; to hold a meeting

**Tagesanbruch, tahg-**es-ahnn-brook, *m* daybreak

**tag(es)hell, tahg(**-es)-hel, *adj* as light as day

**Tageslicht, tahg-**es-likt, *nt* daylight

**Tagesordnung, tahg-**es-ord-noong, *f* agenda

**Tageszeitung, tahg-**es-tsite-oong, *f* daily paper

**Tagewerk, tahg-**e-vairk, *nt* day's work

**täglich, tayk-**lik, *adj* daily; *adv* per/every day

**tags, tahks,** *adv* on the day; by day

**tagsüber, tahks-**EEb-er, *adv* by/during the day

**tagtäglich, tahk-tayk-**lik, *adj* (happening) daily

**Tagung, tahg-**oong, *f* session, conference; **–sort,**

*m* venue

**Taille, tahll-**ye, *f* waist

**Takt, tahckt,** *m* rhythm, time; tact

**Tal, tahl,** *nt* valley, dale

**Talg, tahlk,** *m* tallow, suet

**Talk, tahlk,** *m* talc(um)

**Talkessel, tahl-**kess-el, *m* circular valley

**Talsperre, tahl-**shpairr-e, *f* dam across valley

**talwärts, tahl-**vairts, *adv* towards the valley

**Tampon, tahmm-**pong, *m* tampon

**Tändelei, tend-**e-ly, *f* dallying, trifling; dawdling

**tändeln, tend-**eln, *v* to dally, to trifle; to dawdle

**Tang, tahng,** *m* sea-weed

**Tank, tahnck,** *m* tank; **–stelle,** *f* petrol station

**Tanne, tahnn-***e,* *f* fir(-tree); **–nbaum,** *m* fir/Christmas tree; **–nnadel,** *f* pine needle; **–nwald,** *m* forest of fir-trees; **–nzapfen,** *m* fir-cone

**Tante, tahnt-***e,* *f* aunt

**Tanz, tahnts,** *m* dance

**tänzeln, tent-**seln, *v* to frisk; to amble; to prance

**tanzen, tahnt-**sen, *v* to dance

**Tänzer, tent-**ser, *m* dancer

**Tanzfläche, tahnts-**flaik-e, *f* dance-floor

**Tanzlokal, tahnts-**loh-kahl, *nt* dance-hall

**Tanzstunde, tahnts-**shtoonn-de, *f*

dancing-lesson

**Tapete,** tahpp-**ayt**-e, f wallpaper

**tapezieren,** tahpp-e-**tseer**-en, v to wallpaper

**Tapezierer,** tahpp-e-**tseer**-er, m (interior) decorator

**tapfer,** tahpp-fer, adj brave, valiant, plucky

**Tapferkeit,** tahpp-fer-kite, f valour, bravery

**tappen,** tahpp-en, v to grope; to walk clumsily

**Tarnung,** tarn-oong, f camouflage

**Tasche,** tahsh-e, f pocket; bag, pouch; **–nbuch,** nt paperback (book); **–ndieb,** m pickpocket; **–nkrebs,** m common crab; **–nlampe,** f torch; **–nmesser,** nt penknife; **–ntuch,** nt handkerchief

**Tasse,** tahss-e, f cup

**Taste,** tahst-e, f (piano etc.) key

**tasten,** tahst-en, v to grope, to feel one's way

**Tat,** taht, f deed, action; achievement; **–bestand,** m facts of the matter

**Täter,** tayt-er, m doer; culprit, perpetrator

**tätig,** tayt-ik, adj active, busy, engaged (in)

**Tätigkeit,** tayt-ik-kite, f activity, action; occupation

**Tatkraft,** taht-krahft, f energy

**tätlich,** tayt-lik, adj

violent; physical

**Tatsache,** taht-zahk-e, f fact

**tatsächlich,** taht-**zaik**-lik, adj & adv actual(ly)

**Tatze,** tahtt-se, f paw

**Tau,** tow, nt cable, rope; m dew

**taub,** towp, adj deaf, hard of hearing; hollow

**Taube,** towb-e, f pigeon, dove; **–nschlag,** m dovecote

**Taubheit,** towp-hite, f deafness

**taubstumm,** towp-shtoom, adj deaf and dumb

**tauchen,** towk-en, v to dip; to plunge; to dive

**Taucher,** towk-er, m diver; **–anzug,** m wetsuit

**tauen,** tow-en, v to thaw; to cover with dew

**Taufbecken,** towf-beck-en, nt (baptismal) font

**Taufe,** towf-e, f baptism, christening

**taufen,** towf-en, v to baptize, to christen

**Taufname,** towf-nahm-e, m Christian name

**Taufpate,** towf-paht-e, m godfather

**Taufschein,** towf-shine, m baptism certificate

**taugen,** towg-en, v to be of value; to serve a purpose

**Taugenichts,** towg-e-nikts, m good-for-nothing

**tauglich,** towk-lik, adj serviceable; fit; useful

**Taumel,** towm-el, m

giddiness; delirium; frenzy

**taumeln,** towm-eln, v to totter, to stagger; to tumble

**Tausch,** towsh, m exchange; barter

**tauschen,** towsh-en, v to exchange; to barter

**täuschen,** toysh-en, v to deceive, to trick, to delude

**Täuschung,** toysh-oong, f delusion; deception

**tausend,** towz-ent, num thousand

**Tauwetter,** tow-vet-er, nt thaw

**Taxe,** tahcks-e, f rate, charge; tax

**Taxi,** tahcks-ee, nt taxi

**taxieren,** tahcks-eer-en, v to estimate, to assess

**Technik,** tek-nick, f technology; technique, skill; **–er,** m engineer; technician

**Technologie,** tek-noh-loh-gee, f technology

**Tee,** tay, m tea; (herb) infusion; **–beutel,** m tea bag; **–gebäck,** nt cake, biscuits; **–kanne,** f teapot; **–löffel,** m teaspoon

**Teer,** tayr, m tar

**teeren,** tayr-en, v to tar

**Teich,** ty'k, m pond

**Teig,** tike, m dough, paste

**Teil,** tile, m part, share, division

**teilen,** tile-en, v to share; to divide; to distribute

**Teilhaber, tile**-hahb-er, *m* partner

**Teilnahme, tile**-nahm-e, *f* sympathy; participation

**teilnahmslos, tile**-nahms-lohs, *adj* apathetic

**teilnehmen, tile**-naym-en, *v* to take part; to join (in)

**teils,** tiles, *adv* partly, in part

**Teilung, tile**-oong, *f* division; partition

**teilweise, tile**-vy-ze, *adv* partially, partly

**Teilzahlung, tile**-tsahl-oong, *f* part-payment

**Teilzeitarbeit, tile**-tsite-ahr-bite, *f* part-time work

**Teint,** teng, *m* complexion

**Telefax, tay**-le-fahcks, *nt* fax

**Telefon, tay**-le-fohn, *nt* telephone; **–anruf,** *m* telephone call; **–nummer,** *f* telephone number; **–zelle,** *f* telephone box; **–zentrale,** *f* switchboard

**Teller, tel**-er, *m* plate

**Tempel, temp**-el, *m* temple

**Temperament, temp**-er-ah-ment, *nt* temperament, liveliness

**Tempo, temp**-oh, *nt* time, measure; rhythm; **–limit,** *nt* speed limit

**Tennis, ten**-is, *nt* tennis; **–platz,** *m* tennis court; **–schläger,** *m* tennis racket

**Teppich, tep**-ik, *m* carpet; **–boden,** *m* carpeting

**Termin, tairm**-een, *m* appointment; (due-)date; hearing (court); term

**Terpentin, tairp**-en-teen, *nt* turpentine

**Terrain, tair**-reng, *nt* country; ground, plot

**Terrasse, tair**-ahss-e, *f* terrace, patio

**Terrine, tair**-reen-e, *f* tureen

**Terrorist, tair**-ohr-ist, *m* terrorist

**Terzett, tairt**-set, *nt* trio

**Tesafilm®, tay**-sah-film, *m* Sellotape®

**teuer, toy**-er, *adj* dear; expensive

**Teu(e)rung, toy**(-e)-roong, *f* rise in prices, inflation

**Teufel, toyf**-el, *m* devil

**Teufelei, toyf**-e-ly, *f* devilry

**teuflisch, toyf**-lish, *adj* devilish

**Text,** text, *m* text; words; libretto; wording; **–verarbeitung,** *f* word processing

**Theater, tay**-aht-er, *nt* theatre; stage; **–kasse,** *f* box-office; **–stück,** *nt* play

**Thema, taym**-ah, *nt* theme, subject; topic

**Themse, tem**-ze, *f* Thames

**Therapie, tay**-rah-pee, *f* therapy

**Thermalbad, tair**-mahl-baht, *nt* (thermal) spa; thermal bath

**Thron,** trohn, *m* throne; **–besteigung,** *f* accession to the throne; **–folger,** *m* successor to the throne

**Thymian, tEEm**-ee-ahn, *m* thyme

**tief,** teef, *adj* deep; profound; low

**Tiefe, teef**-e, *f* depth; profundity

**Tiefebene, teef**-ay-be-ne, *f* plain

**Tiefgarage, teef**-gah-rah-zhe, *f* underground car park

**Tiefkühlkost, teef**-kEEl-kost, *f* frozen food

**Tiefsinn, teef**-zin, *m* thoughtfulness; melancholy

**Tiegel, teeg**-el, *m* crucible

**Tier,** teer, *nt* animal; beast; **–arzt,** *m* vet; **–bändiger,** *m* animal trainer; **–garten,** *m* zoo

**tierisch, teer**-ish, *adj* bestial; of animals

**Tierklinik, teer**-kleen-ick, *f* veterinary clinic

**Tierkunde, teer**-koonn-de, *f* zoology

**Tierpark, teer**-park, *m* zoo

**Tierquälerei, teer**-kvayl-e-ry, *f* cruelty to animals

**Tierreich, teer**-ry'k, *nt* animal kingdom

**Tierwelt, teer**-velt, *f* wildlife

**Tiger, teeg**-er, *m* tiger

**tilgen, tilg**-en, *v* to destroy; to wipe out; to pay off

**Tilgung, tilg**-oong, *f* destruction; discharge (of debts)

**Tinte, tin**-te, *f* ink; **–nfaß,** *nt* inkstand; **–nfisch,** *m* cuttlefish, octopus; **–nklecks,** *m* ink-stain

**tippen**, tip-en, v to touch lightly; to type; to bet

**Tisch**, tish, m table; **–decke**, f table-cloth; **–gebet**, nt grace before/after meal; **–ler**, m joiner; **–tennis**, nt table tennis; **–tuch**, nt table-cloth; **–zeit**, f dinner-time

**Titel**, teet-el, m title; **–bild**, nt frontispiece

**titulieren**, tit-oo-leer-en, v to title, to style

**toben**, toh-ben, v to rage, to rave

**Tobsucht**, tohp-zookt, f frenzy

**Tochter**, tohk-ter, f daughter

**töchterlich**, terk-ter-lik, adj like a daughter

**Tod**, toht, m death

**Todesstrafe**, tohd-es-shtrahf-e, f capital punishment

**Todfeind**, toht-fine't, m mortal enemy

**tödlich**, tert-lik, adj mortal, fatal, deadly

**todschick**, toht-shick, adj flash, classy

**Toilette**, toy-let-e, f toilet; **–npapier**, nt toilet paper; **–ntsch**, m dressing table

**toll**, tol, adj foolish, mad; terrific

**Tolle**, tol-e, f head-dress; crest, tuft

**tollen**, tol-en, v to frolic

**Tollheit**, tol-hite, f madness; folly

**tollkühn**, tol-kEEn, adj

rash, foolhardy

**Tollwut**, tol-vooht, f hydrophobia, rabies

**Tolpatsch**, tol-pahtsh, m clumsy person

**Tölpel**, terl-pel, m fool

**tölpelhaft**, terl-pel-hahft, adj clumsy, awkward

**Ton**, tohn, m clay; tone, sound, note

**tonangebend**, tohn-ahn-gayb-ent, adj leading

**Tonart**, tohn-art, f pitch; mus key

**Tonband**, tohn-bahnt, nt (magnetic) tape; **–gerät**, nt tape recorder

**tönen**, tern-en, v to sound, to ring

**tönern**, tern-ern, adj made of clay; clayey

**Tonfall**, tohn-fahll, m modulation

**Tonkunst**, tohn-koonst, f music

**Tonleiter**, tohn-ly-ter, f mus scale

**Tonne**, ton-e, f ton; tun, butt, barrel

**Topf**, top'f, m pot; vessel, saucepan; jug, jar

**Töpfer**, terpp-fer, m potter

**Töpferei**, terpp-fer-i, f pottery

**töpfern**, terpp-fern, v to make pottery

**Tor**, tohr, nt gate(way); m fool, simpleton

**Torf**, torf, m peat, turf

**Torheit**, tohr-hite, f folly, foolishness

**Torhüter**, tohr-hEEt-er, m gate-keeper; goalkeeper

**töricht**, terr-ikt, adj foolish; silly

**torkeln**, tork-eln, v to reel

**Tornister**, tor-nist-er, m satchel, knapsack, pack

**Torte**, tort-e, f tart, cake

**Torwart**, tohr-vart, m goalkeeper

**Torweg**, tohr-vayk, m gateway, archway

**tosen**, tohz-en, v to roar, to howl; to crash

**tot**, toht, adj dead, deceased

**Tote(r)**, toht-e(r), m & f, dead person, corpse

**töten**, tert-en, v to kill

**totenähnlich**, toht-en-ayn-lik, adj deathlike

**totenblaß**, toht-en-blahss, adj deathly pale

**Totenfeier**, toht-en-fy-er, f funeral (ceremony)

**Totengräber**, toht-en-grayb-er, m grave-digger, sexton

**Totengruft**, toht-en-grooft, f tomb

**Totenhemd**, toht-en-hemt, nt shroud

**Totenkopf**, toht-en-kop'f, m skull

**totenstill**, toht-en-shtil, adj deathly still/quiet

**totfahren**, toht-fahr-en, v to run over

**totlachen (sich)**, toht-lahk-en (zik), v to die laughing

**totschießen**, toht-shees-en, v to shoot dead

**Totschlag**, toht-shlahk, m

manslaughter

**totschlagen, toht**-shlahg-en, *v* to kill (also *fig*)

**totschweigen, toht**-shvy-gen, *v* to suppress (news, facts etc.)

**Tötung, tert**-oong, *f* manslaughter, killing

**Trab,** trahp, *m* trot

**traben, trahb**-en, *v* to trot

**Tracht,** trahkt, *f* dress, fashion; load

**trachten, trahkt**-en, *v* to strive (for)

**Tragbahre, trahk**-bahr-e, *f* litter, stretcher

**tragbar, trahk**-bar, *adj* portable; acceptable

**träge, trayg**-e, *adj* indolent, lazy; sleepy

**tragen, trahg**-en, *v* to carry, to bear, to support; to wear

**Träger, trayg**-er, *m* carrier; porter; girder; bearer

**Tragetasche, trahg**-e-tahsh-e, *f* carrier bag

**Trägheit, trayk**-hite, *f* laziness, indolence

**Tragödie, trah-gerd**-ye, *f* tragedy

**traktieren,** trahck-**teer**-en, *v* to maltreat

**Traktor, trahck**-tohr, *m* tractor

**trällern, trel**-ern, *v* to hum, to sing

**trampeln, trahmm**-peln, *v* to trample, to stamp

**Trampeltier, trahmm**-pel-teer, *nt* camel; *fam* clumsy

person

**trampen, tramp**-en, *v* to hitch-hike

**Tran,** trahn, *m* blubber, fish-oil

**tranchieren,** trahng-**sheer**-en, *v* to carve (meat)

**Träne, train**-e, *f* tear

**tränen, train**-en, *v* to run (with tears)

**tranig, trahn**-ik, *adj* like oil; sluggish

**Trank,** trahnk, *m* drink, beverage

**tränken, treng**-ken, *v* to give to drink; to soak, to drench

**Transpiration,** trahnn-spee-rahts-**yohn**, *f* perspiration

**transpirieren,** trahnn-spee-**reer**-en, *v* to perspire

**Traube, trowb**-e, *f* bunch of grapes

**trauen, trow**-en, *v* to trust; to rely; to marry

**Trauer, trow**-er, *f* mourning; sorrow, grief

**trauern, trow**-ern, *v* to mourn, to grieve

**Trauerspiel, trow**-er-shpeel, *nt* tragedy

**Trauerweide, trow**-er-vy-de, *f* weeping-willow

**Traufe, trowf**-e, *f* gutter

**träufeln, troyf**-eln, *v* to drip, to drop, to trickle

**Traum,** trowm, *m* dream

**Trauma, trowm**-ah, *nt* trauma

**träumen, troym**-en, *v* to dream

**traurig, trow**-rik, *adj* sad

**Trauring, trow**-ring, *m* wedding-ring

**Trauschein, trow**-shine, *m* marriage certificate

**traut,** trowt, *adj* beloved; intimate

**Trauung, trow**-oong, *f* wedding(-ceremony)

**Treff,** tref, *m* meeting-point

**treffen, tref**-en, *v* to hit (the mark), to strike; to meet

**Treffer, tref**-er, *m* good hit; goal

**trefflich, tref**-lik, *adj* excellent

**Treffpunkt, tref**-poonkt, *m* meeting place

**treiben, try**-ben, *v* to drive, to set in motion

**Treibhaus, tripe**-hows, *nt* conservatory, hot-house

**Treibholz, tripe**-holts, *nt* drift-wood

**Treibstoff, tripe**-shtof, *m* fuel

**trennbar, tren**-bar, *adj* separable

**trennen, tren**-en, *v* to separate, to detach

**treppab, trep**-ahpp, *adv* downstairs

**treppauf, trep**-owf, *adv* upstairs

**Treppe, trep**-e, *f* stairs, staircase; –**ngeländer,** *nt* banister(-rail)

**treten, trayt**-en, *v* to tread, to step; to kick

**treu,** troy, *adj* faithful, true; sincere

**Treue, troy**-e, *f* faithfulness; loyalty

**treuherzig, troy**-hairt-sik, *adj* frank; true-hearted

**Tribüne,** tree-**bEEn**-e, *f* platform; grandstand

**Trichter, trik**-ter, *m* funnel

**Trieb,** treep, *m* driving, momentum; force; impulse; shoot

**Triebfeder,** treep-**fayd**-er, *f* main spring; *fig* main motive

**triefen, treef**-en, *v* to drip; to be dripping

**triftig, trift**-ik, *adj* well-founded, cogent

**Trikot, trick**-oh, *nt* (cotton) jersey; (sports) shirt

**trillern, tril**-ern, *v* to trill, to warble

**Trimester,** tree-**mest**-er, *nt* (three month) term

**trinken, trink**-en, *v* to drink

**Trinkgeld, trink**-gelt, *nt* gratuity, tip

**Trinkhalle, trink**-hahll-e, *f* refreshment kiosk

**Trinkwasser, trink**-vahss-er, *nt* drinking water

**trippeln, trip**-eln, *v* to trip along

**Tritt,** trit, *m* tread; step; pace; kick; **–brett,** *nt* running-board; **–leiter,** *f* step-ladder

**trocken, trock**-en, *adj* dry; parched, arid

**trocknen, trock**-nen, *v* to dry

**Trödel, trerd**-el, *m*

lumber, rubbish

**trödeln, trerd**-eln, *v* to dawdle, to loiter

**Trog,** trohk, *m* trough

**Trommel, trom**-el, *f* drum; **–fell,** *nt* ear-drum; drum skin

**trommeln, trom**-eln, *v* to drum

**Trompete,** trom-**payt**-e, *f* trumpet

**trompeten,** trom-**payt**-en, *v* to (sound the) trumpet

**Tropf,** trop'f, *m* simpleton; wretch

**tröpfeln, trerp**-feln, *v* to fall in drops, to trickle

**Tropfen, trop**-fen, *m* drop

**tropfen, trop**-fen, *v* to drip, to trickle

**Trost,** trohst, *m* consolation, solace

**trösten, trerst**-en, *v* to console, to comfort

**trostlos, trohst**-lohs, *adj* bleak

**Trottel, trot**-el, *m fam* fool

**Trottoir,** trohtt-**wahr**, *nt* pavement

**Trotz,** trots, *m* stubbornness; defiance

**trotz,** trots, *prep* in spite of; **–dem,** *adv* nevertheless

**trotzen, trots**-en, *v* to defy; to sulk

**trotzig, trots**-ik, *adj* defiant, obstinate; haughty

**trüb(e),** trEEp (**trEEb**-e), *adj* gloomy, muddy, murky; sad

**trüben, trEEb**-en, *v* to dim;

to trouble; to make muddy

**Trübsal, trEEp**-zahl, *f* misery; affliction

**trübselig, trEEp**-zayl-ik, *adj* melancholy, sad

**Trübsinn, trEEp**-zin, *m* melancholy, sadness

**Trug,** troohk, *m* delusion; deception

**trügen, trEEg**-en, *v* to deceive, to delude

**trügerisch, trEEg**-er-ish, *adj* deceptive, deceitful

**Trugschluß, trook**-shlooss, *m* false conclusion

**Truhe, troo**-e, *f* chest, trunk

**Trümmer, trEEmm**-er, *pl* debris, rubbish

**Trumpf,** troomp'f, *m* trump(s)

**Trunk,** troonk, *m* drink; draught; drunkenness

**trunken, troonk**-en, *adj* drunk, intoxicated

**Trunkenbold, troonk**-en-bolt, *m* drunkard

**Trunkenheit, troonk**-en-hite, *f* drunkenness

**Trunksucht, troonk**-zookt, *f* dipsomania, alcoholism

**Truthahn, trooht**-hahn, *m* turkey-cock

**Tschechien, tshek**-ee-en, *nt* Czech Republic

**T-Shirt,** tee-shirt, *nt* T-shirt

**tschüs,** tshEEs, *interj* bye

**Tuch,** took, *nt* cloth, stuff, material; scarf; towel

**tüchtig, tEEk**-tik, *adj* (cap)able, efficient; thorough

**Tücke, tEEck**-*e*, *f* spite, malice; cunning

**tückisch, tEEck**-ish, *adj* spiteful; crafty

**Tugend, toog**-ent, *f* virtue

**tugendhaft, toog**-ent-hahft, *adj* virtuous

**Tulpe, toolp**-*e*, *f* tulip

**tummeln (sich), toomm**-eln (*zik*), *v* to stir, to exercise; to wheel

**Tümpel, tEEmp**-el, *m* pool, puddle

**tun, toon, v to do, to make, to perform, to act**

**tünchen, tEEn**-ken, *v* to whitewash

**Tunke, toong**-ke, *f* gravy

**tunken, toong**-ken, *v* to dip, to soak

**tunlich, toon**-lik, *adj* feasible; expedient; practical

**tunlichst, toon**-likst, *adv* if possible

**Tüpfelchen, tEEpp**-fel-ken, *nt* dot, point

**Tupfen, toopp**-fen, *m* dot, spot

**tupfen, toopp**-fen, *v* to touch lightly; to dab; to spot

**Türkei, tEEr**-ky, *f* Turkey

**Tür(e), tEEr**(-*e*), *f* door

**Türkis, tEEr**-kees, *m* turquoise

**türkisch, tEErk**-ish, *adj* Turkish

**Türklinke, tEEr**-kling-ke, *f* door-handle

**Turm, toorm, m tower;** castle

**türmen, tEErm**-en, *v* to tower; to pile up; to run away

**turnen, toorn**-en, *v* to do gymnastics

**Turner, toorn**-er, *m* gymnast

**Turnhalle, toorn**-hahll-*e*, *f* gym

**Turnier, toorn**-**eer**, *nt* tournament

**Turnschuhe, toorn**-shoo-*e*, *pl* trainers

**Turnverein, toorn**-fair-ine, *m* gymnastic club

**Türschwelle, tEEr**-shvel-*e*, *f* threshold

**Tusch, toosh, m flourish (of trumpets)**

**Tusche, toosh**-*e*, *f* Indian ink

**tuschen, toosh**-en, *v* to draw with Indian ink

**tuscheln, toosh**-eln, *v* to whisper

**Tuschkasten, toosh**-kahst-en, *m* paintbox

**Tüte, tEEt**-*e*, *f* paper-bag

**TÜV, tEEf, m abbr Technischer Überwachungsverein, MOT**

**U-Bahn,** oo-bahn, *f* tube, underground

**übel,** EEb-*el*, *adj* evil, bad; sick

**Übel,** EEb-*el*, *nt* evil, ill; malady; **–keit,** *f* nausea, (feeling of) sickness

**übelnehmen,** EEb-*el*-naym-en, *v* to take amiss

**üben,** EEb-en, *v* to practise; to exercise

**über,** EEb-er, *prep* over, above; about; via

**überall,** EEb-er-ahll, *adv* everywhere

**überarbeiten,** EEb-er-arb-ite-en, *v* to overwork; to revise

**überaus,** EEb-er-ows, *adv* extremely

**überbieten,** EEb-er-beet-en, *v* to outbid; to surpass

**Überbleibsel,** EEb-er-blipe-sel, *nt* remnant, remains

**Überblick,** EEb-er-blick, *m* survey; summary; overall view

**überblicken,** EEb-er-blick-en, *v* to survey; to overlook

**überbringen,** EEb-er-bring-en, *v* to convey, to deliver

**überdies,** EEb-er-dees, *adv* moreover

**Überdruß,** EEb-er-drooss *m* weariness; surfeit

**überdrüssig,** EEb-er-drEEss-ik, *adj* weary of

**überdurchschnittlich,** EEb-er-doork-shnit-lik, *adj* above average; *adv* exceptionally

**übereilen,** EEb-er-ile-en, *v* to precipitate; to hurry too much

**übereinander,** EEb-er-ine-ahnn-der, *adv* one above the other

**Übereinkommen, Übereinkunft,** EEb-er-ine-kom-en, *nt* –koonft, *f* agreement, understanding

**übereinstimmen,** EEb-er-ine-shtim-en, *v* to agree

**überfahren,** EEb-er-fahr-en, *v* to run over; to pass over

**Überfahrt,** EEb-er-fahrt, *f* crossing

**Überfall,** EEb-er-fahll, *m* (sudden) attack, raid

**überfallen,** EEb-er-fahll-en, *v* to attack suddenly

**überfällig,** EEb-er-fel-ik, *adj* overdue

**Überfluß,** EEb-er-flooss, *m* abundance, plenty

**überflüssig,** EEb-er-flEEss-ik, *adj* superfluous, unnecessary; redundant

**überfordern,** EEb-er-ford-ern, *v* to ask too much; to overstrain

**überführen,** EEb-er-fEEr-en, *v* to transfer; to convict

**überfüllen,** EEb-er-fEEll-en, *v* to overcrowd

**Übergabe,** EEb-er-gahb-e, *f* handing over; surrender

**Übergang,** EEb-er-gahng, *m* crossing; transition

**übergeben,** EEb-er-gayb-en, *v* to hand over; to surrender; **sich –,** *v* to vomit

**übergehen,** EEb-er-gay-en, *v* to pass over; to omit

**übergreifen,** EEb-er-gry-fen, *v* to overlap; to encroach on

**überhandnehmen,** EEb-er-**hahnnt**-naym-en, v to gain ground

**überhängen,** EEb-er-**heng**-en, v to overhang

**überhäufen,** EEb-er-**hoyf**-en, v to overburden; to overwhelm

**überhaupt,** EEb-er-**howpt,** adv generally; actually; – **nicht,** not at all

**überheblich,** EEb-er-**heb**-lik, adj arrogant

**überholen,** EEb-er-**hohl**-en, v to overtake; to overhaul

**überhören,** EEb-er-**her**-en, v not to hear; to ignore

**überkochen,** EEb-er-**kohk**-en, v to boil over

**überlassen,** EEb-er-**lahss**-en, v to leave over; to relinquish

**überlaufen,** EEb-er-**lowf**-en, v to run over; to desert

**überleben,** EEb-er-**layb**-en, v to survive; to outlive

**überlegen,** EEb-er-**layg**-en, v to think over; adj superior

**Überlegenheit,** EEb-er-**layg**-en-hite, f superiority

**Überlegung,** EEb-er-**layg**-oong, f consideration; deliberation

**überliefern,** EEb-er-**leef**-ern, v to deliver; to hand down

**Überlieferung,** EEb-er-**leef**-er-oong, f tradition

**überlisten,** EEb-er-**list**-en, v to outwit; to dupe

**überm,** EEb-erm, = **über dem,** over the

**Übermacht,** EEb-er-**mahkt,** f superior strength

**übermannen,** EEb-er-**mahnn**-en, v to overpower

**übermäßig,** EEb-er-**mace**-ik, adj immoderate; profuse

**Übermensch,** EEb-er-**mensh,** m superman

**übermitteln,** EEb-er-**mit**-eln, v to transmit

**übermorgen,** EEb-er-**morg**-en, adv the day after tomorrow

**Übermut,** EEb-er-**moot,** m high spirits; impertinence

**übermütig,** EEb-er-**mEEt**-ik, adj high spirited; impertinent

**übernachten,** EEb-er-**nahk**-ten, v to pass the night

**Übernachtung,** EEb-er-**nahkt**-oong, f overnight stay

**Übernahme,** EEb-er-**nahm**-e, f taking over

**übernehmen,** EEb-er-**naym**-en, v to take over; to take on; **sich –,** v to take on too much, to overdo it

**überqueren,** EEb-er-**kvayr**-en, v to cross

**überragen,** EEb-er-**rahg**-en, v to tower above; to project, to protrude

**überraschen,** EEb-er-**rahsh**-en, v to surprise

**überreden,** EEb-er-**rayd**-en, v to persuade

**überreichen,** EEb-er-**ry**-ken, v to hand over

**Überrest,** EEb-er-**rest,** m remnant, remains; ruin

**überrumpeln,** EEb-er-**roomp**-eln, v to take by surprise

**übers,** EEb-ers, = **über das,** over the

**überschätzen,** EEb-er-**shet**-sen, v to over-estimate

**überschreiten,** EEb-er-**shry**-ten, v to overstep; to step over

**Überschrift,** EEb-er-**shrift,** f heading, title

**Überschuß,** EEb-er-**shooss,** m surplus; balance

**überschüssig,** EEb-er-**shEEss**-ik, adj surplus; left over

**überschwemmen,** EEb-er-**shvem**-en, v to flood; to overflow

**Überschwemmung,** EEb-er-**shvem**-oong, f flood

**überschwenglich,** EEb-er-**shveng**-lik, adj gushing; excessive

**übersehen,** EEb-er-**say**-en, v to overlook; to look over

**übersenden,** EEb-er-**send**-en, v to send; to transmit

**übersetzen,** EEb-er-**set**-sen, v to translate; EEb-er-set-sen, v to cross over

**Übersicht,** EEb-er-**zikt,** f survey; summary, sketch

**übersichtlich,** EEb-er-**zikt**-lik, adj clear

**übersiedeln,** EEb-er-**zeed**-eln, v to emigrate

**überspringen,** EEb-er-**shpring**-en, v to jump over; fig to skip

**überstehen,** EEb-er-**shtay**-en,

*v* to overcome; to endure

**Überstunden,** EEb-er-shtoond-en, *pl* overtime

**überstürzen,** EEb-er-**shtEEr**tsen, *v* to precipitate

**übertragen,** EEb-er-**trahg**-en, *v* to carry forward; to transfer; to broadcast

**übertreffen,** EEb-er-tref-en, *v* to excel, to eclipse

**übertreiben,** EEb-er-**try**-ben, *v* to exaggerate

**übertreten,** EEb-er-**trayt**-en, *v* to transgress; EEb-er-trayt-en, *v* to overstep; to convert

**übertrieben,** EEb-er-treeb-en, *adj* exaggerated

**übervorteilen,** EEb-er-**fohr**-tile-en, *v* to take advantage

**überwachen,** EEb-er-vahk-en, *v* to watch over; to superintend

**überwältigen,** EEb-er-velt-ig-en, *v* to overwhelm

**überweisen,** EEb-er-**vy**-zen, *v* to transfer; to refer (a patient)

**überwiegen,** EEb-er-veeg-en, *v* to outweigh; to prevail

**überwinden,** EEb-er-vin-den, *v* to overcome; to conquer

**überwintern,** EEb-er-vint-ern, *v* to hibernate

**überwuchern,** EEb-er-**voohk**-ern, *v* to overgrow

**überzeugen,** EEb-er-**tsoyg**-en, *v* to convince

**Überzeugung,** EEb-er-**tsoyg**-oong, *f* conviction; persuasion

**überziehen,** EEb-er-tsee-en, *v* to cover; to pull over; EEb-er-**tsee**-en, *v* to overdraw (account)

**Überziehungskredit,** EEb-er-**tsee**-oongs-kray-dit, *m* overdraft provision

**Überzug,** EEb-er-tsook, *m* cover, case, pillow-case; coating

**üblich,** EEb-lik, *adj* usual, customary

**U-Boot,** oo-boht, *nt abbr* **Unterseeboot,** U-boat

**übrig,** EEb-rik, *adj* over, left over, remaining

**übrigens,** EEb-rig-ens, *adv* by the way; moreover

**Übung,** EEb-oong, *f* exercise, practice

**Ufer,** oof-er, *nt* bank, beach, shore

**Uhr,** oor, *f* clock; watch; o'clock; **–macher,** *m* watchmaker; **im –zeigersinn,** *adv* clockwise; **gegen den –zeigersinn,** *adv* anti-clockwise; **–zeit,** *f* time of day

**Ulk,** oolk, *m* lark, practical joke

**ulkig,** oolk-ik, *adj* funny

**Ulme,** oolm-e, *f* elm(-tree)

**Ultraschall,** ool-trah-shahll, *m* ultrasound

**um,** oom, *prep* (a)round; about; at; for; by; *conj* in order to

**umändern,** oomm-end-ern,

*v* to alter; to change

**umarmen,** oomm-**arm**-en, *v* to embrace

**Umbau,** oomm-bow, *m* reconstruction; rebuilding; conversion

**umbauen,** oomm-bow-en, *v* to rebuild

**umbinden,** oomm-bin-den, *v* to tie round; to put on

**umblicken (sich),** oomm-blick-en (zik), *v* to look round

**umbringen,** oomm-bring-en, *v* to kill

**umbuchen,** oomm-book-en, *v* to change one's booking

**umdrehen,** oomm-dray-en, *v* to turn round/over

**umfallen,** oomm-fahll-en, *v* to fall over

**Umfang,** oomm-fahng, *m* size, circumference; extent

**umfangreich,** oomm-fahng-rike, *adj* voluminous; extensive

**umfassen,** oomm-**fahss**-en, *v* to embrace, to clasp

**Umfrage,** oomm-frahg-e, *f* survey, poll

**Umgang,** oomm-gahng, *m* contact, dealings, relations, company

**umgänglich,** oomm-geng-lik, *adj* easy to get on with

**Umgangssprache,** oomm-gahngs-shprahk-e, *f* colloquial language

**umgeben,** oomm-gayb-en, *v* to surround

**Umgebung,** oomm-**gayb**-

oong, *f* neighbourhood, surroundings

**Umgegend,** oomm-gayg-ent, *f* environs, vicinity

**umgehen,** oomm-**gay**-en, *v* to evade; to circumvent; oomm-gay-en, *v* to haunt; to have dealings (with)

**Umgehungsstraße,** oomm-**gay**-oongs-shtrahs-*e*, *f* bypass

**umgekehrt,** oomm-ge-kairt, *adj* contrary, reverse; *adv* vice versa

**umgraben,** oomm-grahb-en, *v* to dig (up)

**umher,** oomm-hair, *adv* around; on every side

**umhüllen,** oomm-hEEll-en, *v* to wrap; to veil

**umkehren,** oomm-kair-en, *v* to turn back/round

**umkippen,** oomm-kip-en, *v* to tip over, to upset

**umklammern,** oomm-klahmm-ern, *v* to clasp

**Umkleide(raum),** oomm-kly-de(-rowm), *m & f,* changing room

**umkleiden (sich),** oomm-kly-den (zik), *v* to change (clothes)

**umkommen,** oomm-komm-en, *v* to perish; to die

**Umkreis,** oomm-krice, *m* circumference; vicinity

**Umlauf,** oomm-lowf, *m* circulation; rotation; –bahn, *f* orbit

**Umlaut,** oomm-lowt, *m* umlaut (¨)

**Umleitung,** oomm-lite-oong, *f* (traffic) diversion

**umrahmen,** oomm-**rahm**-en, *v* to frame

**Umrechnungskurs,** oomm-rek-noongs-koors, *m* exchange rate

**umringen,** oomm-**ring**-en, *v* to surround

**Umriß,** oomm-riss, *m* outline; sketch

**umrühren,** oomm-rEEr-en, *v* to stir

**ums,** ooms, = um das, round the; for the

**Umsatz,** oomm-zahts, *m* turnover

**Umschau,** oomm-show, *f* look(ing) out

**umschauen (sich),** oomm-show-en (zik), *v* to look round

**Umschlag,** oomm-shlahk, *m* envelope; wrapper; poultice; change; *comm* turnover

**umschließen,** oomm-**shlees**-en, *v* to enclose

**umschnallen,** oomm-shnahll-en, *v* to buckle on

**umschulen,** oomm-shool-en, *v* to re-train

**umschütten,** oomm-shEEtt-en, *v* to spill, to overturn; to pour out

**Umschwung,** oomm-shvoong, *m* about-turn, sudden change

**umsehen (sich),** oomm-zay-en (zik), *v* to look round/about

**umsetzen,** oomm-zet-sen, *v* to transplant; to transpose; to convert; **sich** –, *v* to change places

**umsichtig,** oomm-zik-tik, *adj* circumspect, prudent

**umsomehr,** oomm-zoh-**mair**, *adv* all the more

**umsonst,** oomm-**zonst**, *adv* in vain; free; gratis

**Umstand,** oomm-shtahnt, *m* circumstance

**umständlich,** oomm-shtentlik, *adj* fussy; complicated; troublesome

**umsteigen,** oomm-shty-gen, *v* to change (trains etc.)

**umstoßen,** oomm-shtohs-en, *v* to knock over; to overthrow; to cancel

**Umsturz,** oomm-shtoorts, *m* overthrow, crash

**umtauschen,** oomm-towsh-en, *v* to (ex)change

**umwälzen,** oomm-velt-sen, *v* to roll over; to overthrow; to revolutionize

**umwechseln,** oomm-veck-seln, *v* to (ex)change

**Umweg,** oomm-vayk, *m* roundabout way

**Umwelt,** oomm-velt, *f* environment

**umweltbewußt,** oomm-velt-be-voost, *adj* with concern for the environment

**umweltfreundlich,** oomm-velt-froynt-lik, *adj* environmentally friendly

**umweltschädlich,** oomm-velt-shait-lik, *adj* harmful to the environment

**Umweltschutz, oomm**-velt-shoots, *m* environmental protection

**Umweltschützer, oomm**-velt-shEEts-*er*, *m* environmentalist

**Umweltverschmutzung, oomm**-velt-fair-shmoots-oong, *f* (environmental) pollution

**umwenden, oomm**-vend-en, *v* to turn over/round

**umwerfen, oomm**-vairf-en, *v* to knock over, to overturn, to upset

**umzäunen, oomm**-tsoyn-en, *v* to fence round/in

**umziehen, oomm**-tsee-en, *v* to move (house); **sich –**, *v* to change (clothes)

**umzingeln, oomm**-tsing-eln, *v* to surround

**Umzug, oomm**-tsook, *m* removal; procession

**unabhängig, oonn**-ahpp-heng-ik, *adj* independent

**unangenehm, oonn**-ahnn-ge-naym, *adj* unpleasant

**Unannehmlichkeit, oonn**-ahnn-naym-lik-kite, *f* unpleasantness, inconvenience

**unanständig, oonn**-ahnn-shtend-ik, *adj* indecent

**unartig, oonn**-art-ik, *adj* naughty

**unausstehlich, oonn**-ows-shtay-lik, *adj* intolerable

**unbedingt, oonn**-be-dingt, *adj* unconditional; absolute; *adv* absolutely

**unbeholfen, oonn**-be-holfen, *adj* awkward, clumsy

**unbeliebt, oonn**-be-leept, *adj* unpopular

**unberufen, oonn**-be-roofen, *adj* unauthorized; *interj* touch wood

**unbesonnen, oonn**-be-zonen, *adj* careless; indiscreet

**unbeweglich, oonn**-be-vayk-lik, *adj* immobile; fixed

**unbewußt, oonn**-be-voost, *adj* unaware; unconscious

**unbrauchbar, oonn**-browk-bar, *adj* unusable

**und, oont** *conj* and

**Undank, oonn**-dahnk, *m* ingratitude

**undankbar, oonn**-dahnk-bar, *adj* ungrateful

**undenkbar, oonn**-denk-bar, *adj* unthinkable; inconceivable

**undeutlich, oonn**-doyt-lik, *adj* indistinct

**Unding, oonn**-ding, *nt* absurdity

**unduldsam, oonn**-doolt-zahm, *adj* intolerant

**undurchdringlich, oonn**-doork-dring-lik, *adj* impenetrable

**uneben, oonn**-ayb-en, *adj* uneven, rough (ground)

**unecht, oonn**-ekt, *adj* spurious, counterfeit; sham

**unehelich, oonn**-ay-e-lik, *adj* illegitimate

**unehrlich, oonn**-ayr-lik, *adj* dishonest

**unendlich, oonn**-ent-lik, *adj* infinite, endless

**unentbehrlich, oonn**-ent-bair-lik, *adj* indispensable

**unentgeltlich, oonn**-ent-gelt-lik, *adj* free (of charge)

**unerfahren, oonn**-air-fahr-en, *adj* inexperienced

**unerhört, oonn**-air-hert, *adj* unheard of

**unermeßlich, oonn**-air-mess-lik, *adj* immeasurable

**unermüdlich, oonn**-air-mEEt-lik, *adj* untiring

**unerreicht, oonn**-air-ry'kt, *adj* unequalled, unrivalled

**unerschrocken, oonn**-air-shrock-en, *adj* dauntless

**unerwünscht, oonn**-air-vEEnsht, *adj* undesired, unwelcome

**Unfall, oonn**-fahll, *m* accident, mishap

**unfaßbar, oonn**-fahss-bar, *adj* inconceivable

**unfehlbar, oonn**-fayl-bar, *adj* infallible

**unförmig, oonn**-ferm-ik, *adj* shapeless; monstrous

**unfrankiert, oonn**-frahng-keert, *adj* unstamped, not prepaid

**unfreundlich, oonn**-froynt-lik, *adj* unfriendly, unkind

**Unfrieden, oonn**-freed-en, *m* discord, strife

**Unfug, oonn**-fook, *m*

offence; mischief; wrong

**Ungar,** oong-gar, *m*
Hungarian (person)

**Ungarn,** oong-garn, *nt*
Hungary

**ungeachtet,** oonn-ge-ahk-tet, *prep* irrespective of

**ungebildet,** oonn-ge-bild-et, *adj* uneducated

**ungebührlich,** oonn-ge-bEEr-lik, *adj* improper; undue

**ungebunden,** oonn-ge-boond-en, *adj* unattached

**Ungeduld,** oonn-ge-doolt, *f* impatience

**ungeduldig,** oonn-ge-dool-dik, *adj* impatient

**ungeeignet,** oonn-ge-ike-net, *adj* unsuitable

**ungefähr,** oonn-ge-fair, *adj* approximate; *adv* about, approximately

**Ungeheuer,** oonn-ge-hoy-er, *nt* monster

**ungeheuer(lich),** oonn-ge-hoy-er(-lik), *adj* huge, immense; monstrous

**ungelegen,** oonn-ge-layg-en, *adj* inopportune, inconvenient

**ungemein,** oonn-ge-mine, *adj* uncommon; extraordinary

**ungemütlich,** oonn-ge-mEEt-lik, *adj* uncomfortable; unsociable

**ungeniert,** oonn-zhay-neert, *adj* unceremonious, unrestrained

**ungenießbar,** oonn-ge-nees-

bar, *adj* uneatable; undrinkable

**ungerade,** oonn-ge-rahd-e, *adj* uneven; odd (numbers); not straight

**ungeraten,** oonn-ge-raht-en, *adj* spoilt

**ungerecht,** oonn-ge-rekt, *adj* unjust, unfair

**ungern,** oonn-gairn, *adv* unwillingly, reluctantly

**ungeschickt,** oonn-ge-shickt, *adj* clumsy, awkward

**ungeschliffen,** oonn-ge-shlif-en, *adj* uncut; uncouth

**ungestüm,** oonn-ge-shtEEm, *adj* impetuous; hot-headed

**Ungetüm,** oonn-ge-tEEm, *nt* monster

**ungewohnt,** oonn-ge-vohnt, *adj* unaccustomed

**Ungeziefer,** oonn-ge-tseef-er, *nt* vermin

**ungezogen,** oonn-ge-tsohg-en, *adj* naughty; ill-mannered

**ungezwungen,** oonn-ge-tsvoong-en, *adj* unconstrained

**Unglaube,** oonn-glowb-e, *m* incredulity; lack of faith

**ungläubig,** oonn-gloyb-ik, *adj* disbelieving

**unglaublich,** oonn-glowp-lik, *adj* incredible, beyond belief

**ungleich,** oonn-gly'k, *adj* uneven, odd; varying, changeable; unequal

**Unglück,** oonn-glEEck, *nt* misfortune; bad luck; accident, disaster

**unglücklich,** oonn-glEEck-lik, *adj* unhappy; unfortunate; **–erweise,** *adv* unfortunately

**unglückselig,** oonn-glEEck-zayl-ik, *adj* disastrous

**Unglücksfall,** oonn-glEEcks-fahll, *m* misfortune, disaster, accident

**Ungnade,** oonn-g'nahd-e, *f* disfavour; disgrace

**ungnädig,** oonn-g'nayd-ik, *adj* ungracious; ill-humoured

**ungünstig,** oonn-gEEnst-ik, *adj* unfavourable

**Unheil,** oonn-hile, *nt* evil, trouble

**unheimlich,** oonn-hime-lik, *adj* uncanny, weird; sinister

**Universität,** oon-ee-vair-zee-tayt, *f* university

**unkenntlich,** oonn-kent-lik, *adj* unrecognizable

**Unkenntnis,** oonn-kent-niss, *f* ignorance

**unklug,** oonn-klook, *adj* unwise, imprudent

**Unkosten,** oonn-kost-en, *pl* expense(s)

**Unkraut,** oonn-krowt, *nt* weed(s)

**unlängst,** oonn-lengst, *adv* recently, not long since

**unlauter,** oonn-lowt-er, *adj* impure, unfair

**unleserlich,** oonn-lay-zer-lik, *adj* illegible

**Unmasse, oonn**-mahss-e, *f* immense number/quantity

**unmäßig, oonn**-mace-ik, *adj* excessive, immoderate

**Unmenge, oonn**-meng-e, *f* huge number

**Unmensch, oonn**-mensh, *m* inhuman creature

**unmenschlich, oonn**-mensh-lik, *adj* inhuman, barbarous

**unmittelbar, oonn**-mit-el-bar, *adj & adv* immediate(ly); direct(ly)

**unnötig, oonn**-nert-ik, *adj* unnecessary

**unnütz, oonn**-nEEts, *adj* useless; idle; pointless

**unordentlich, oonn**-ord-ent-lik, *adj* messy, untidy

**Unordnung, oonn**-ort-noong, *f* disorder

**unparteiisch, oonn**-part-i-ish, *adj* impartial, unbiassed

**unpassend, oonn**-pahss-ent, *adj* unsuitable; improper

**unpäßlich, oonn**-pess-lik, *adj* indisposed, unwell

**Unrat, oonn**-raht, *m* rubbish; refuse

**Unrecht, oonn**-rekt, *nt* wrong; injury

**unrecht, oonn**-rekt, *adj* wrong; incorrect; unfair; **–mäßig,** *adj* illegal; illegitimate

**unregelmäßig, oonn**-rayg-el-mace-ik, *adj* irregular

**unrein, oonn**-rine, *adj* impure; unclean

**unrichtig, oonn**-rik-tik, *adj* wrong, incorrect

**Unruhe, oonn**-roo-e, *f* unrest, anxiety; commotion

**unruhig, oonn**-roo-ik, *adj* uneasy; alarmed; restless

**uns, oons,** *pron (accusative & dative)* us, to us

**unsagbar, oonn**-zahk-bar, *adj* unspeakable; unutterable

**unsauber, oonn**-zowb-er, *adj* unclean, impure

**unschädlich, oonn**-shayt-lik, *adj* harmless

**unscheinbar, oonn**-shine-bar, *adj* insignificant; plain

**Unschuld, oonn**-shoolt, *f* innocence; purity (of heart)

**unschuldig, oonn**-shoold-ik, *adj* innocent, not guilty

**unser, unsere(r/s), oonn**-zer, **oonn**-ze-re(r/s), *adj* our; *pron* ours

**unsereiner, oonn**-zer-ine-er, *pron* one of our kind

**unsichtbar, oonn**-zikt-bar, *adj* invisible

**Unsinn, oonn**-zin, *m* nonsense

**unsinnig, oonn**-zin-ik, *adj* nonsensical, absurd

**unsozial, oonn**-zo-tsee-ahl, *adj* anti-social

**unsterblich, oonn**-shtairp-lik, *adj* immortal

**Unsterblichkeit, oonn**-stairp-lik-kite, *f* immortality

**unstet, oonn**-shtayt, *adj* unstable, inconstant

**Unsumme, oonn**-zoomm-e, *f* immense sum

**untauglich, oonn**-towk-lik, *adj* unfit; unsuitable

**unten, oonn**-ten, *adv* below; underneath; down(stairs)

**unter, oonn**-ter, *prep* under(neath); beneath, below; among

**Unterarm, oonn**-ter-arm, *m* forearm

**unterbleiben, oonn**-ter-bly-ben, *v* not to happen; to cease

**unterbrechen, oonn**-ter-brek-en, *v* to interrupt

**unterbringen, oonn**-ter-bring-en, *v* to give/find shelter for; to lodge

**unterdessen, oonn**-ter-dess-en, *adv* meanwhile

**unterdrücken, oonn**-ter-drEEck-en, *v* to suppress, to oppress; to repress

**untereinander, oonn**-ter-ine-ahnn-der, *adv* together; one underneath the other

**Unterernährung, oonn**-ter-er-nair-oong, *f* malnutrition

**unterfassen, oonn**-ter-fahss-en, *v* jdn –, *v* to take sb's arm

**Unterführung, oonn**-ter-fEEr-oong, *f* underpass, subway

**Untergang, oonn**-ter-gahng,

*m* sinking; going down, setting; decline

**Untergebene(r),** oonn-ter-**gayb**-en-e(r), *m & f*, subordinate

**untergehen,** oonn-ter-**gay**-en, *v* to sink; to go down

**untergeordnet,** oonn-ter-ge-**ord**-net, *adj* inferior, subordinate

**untergraben,** oonn-ter-**grahb**-en, *v* to undermine

**Untergrundbahn,** oonn-ter-**groont**-bahn, *f* underground railway

**unterhalb,** oonn-ter-**hahlp,** *adv* below

**Unterhalt,** oonn-ter-**hahlt,** *m* maintenance; sustenance

**unterhalten,** oonn-ter-**hahlt**-en, *v* to maintain; to entertain; to keep; **sich –,** *v* to converse, to enjoy o.s.

**Unterhaltung,** oonn-ter-**hahlt**-oong, *f* conversation; entertainment

**Unterhändler,** oonn-ter-**hend**-ler, *m* negotiator

**Unterhemd,** oonn-ter-**hemt,** *nt* vest, undershirt

**Unterhose(n),** oonn-ter-**hoh**-ze(n), *f (pl)* (under)pants, briefs

**unterirdisch,** oonn-ter-**eerd**-ish, *adj* underground, subterranean

**unterkommen,** oonn-ter-**kom**-en, *v* to find shelter

**Unterkühlung,** oonn-ter-**kEEl**-oong, *f* hypothermia

**Unterkunft,** oonn-ter-**koonft,** *f* accommodation

**Unterlage,** oonn-ter-**lahg**-e, *f* pad; layer; document

**unterlassen,** oonn-ter-**lahss**-en, *v* to refrain from

**unterlegen,** oonn-ter-**layg**-en, *v* to lay a thing under; oonn-ter-**layg**-en, *adj* inferior; defeated

**Unterleib,** oonn-ter-**lipe,** *m* abdomen

**unterliegen,** oonn-ter-**leeg**-en, *v* to succumb; to be subject to

**Unterlippe,** oonn-ter-**lip**-e, *f* lower lip

**unterm,** oonn-**term,** = **unter dem,** under the

**Unternehmen,** oonn-ter-**naym**-en, *nt* enterprise, undertaking

**unternehmen,** oonn-ter-**naym**-en, *v* to undertake

**Unternehmer,** oonn-ter-**naym**-er, *m* contractor, entrepreneur

**Unterredung,** oonn-ter-**rayd**-oong, *f* conversation, conference

**Unterricht,** oonn-ter-**rikt,** *m* teaching, lesson

**unterrichten,** oonn-ter-**rikt**-en, *v* to instruct; to inform

**Unterrock,** oonn-ter-**rock,** *m* petticoat

**unters,** oonn-**ters,** = **unter das,** under the

**untersagen,** oonn-ter-**zahg**-en, *v* to prohibit; to forbid

**Untersatz,** oonn-ter-**zahts,** *m* base, stand, pedestal

**unterscheiden,** oonn-ter-**shy**-den, *v* to discern, to distinguish; to differ

**Unterschied,** oonn-ter-**sheet,** *m* difference

**unterschlagen,** oonn-ter-**shlahg**-en, *v* to embezzle; oonn-ter-**shlahg**-en, *v* to cross (legs)

**Unterschlupf,** oonn-ter-**shloop´f,** *m* refuge, hiding place

**unterschreiben,** oonn-ter-**shry**-ben, *v* to sign

**Unterschrift,** oonn-ter-**shrift,** *f* signature

**Unterseeboot,** oonn-ter-**zay**-boht, *nt* submarine

**Untersetzer,** oonn-ter-**zets**-er, *m* tablemat, coaster

**untersetzt,** oonn-ter-**zetst,** *adj* thick-set, squat

**unterst(e/r),** oonn-**terst** (-e/er), *adj* lowest

**Unterstand,** oonn-ter-**shtahnt,** *m* shelter; dug-out

**unterstehen,** oonn-ter-**shtay**-en, *v* to be subordinate to; **sich –,** *v* to dare (to)

**unterstreichen,** oonn-ter-**shtry**-ken, *v* to underline (also *fig*)

**unterstützen,** oonn-ter-**shtEEt**-sen, *v* to support

**Unterstützung,** oonn-ter-**shtEEtt**-soong, *f* support; relief

**untersuchen,** oonn-ter-**zook**-en, *v* to examine; to investigate

**Untersuchung,** oonn-ter-**zook**-oong, *f* inquiry; investigation; examination

**Untertan,** oonn-ter-tahn, *m* subject (of state)

**untertänig,** oonn-ter-**tayn**-ik, *adj* humble; submissive

**Untertasse,** oonn-ter-**tahss**-e, *f* saucer

**untertauchen,** oonn-ter-**towk**-en, *v* to submerge, to dip; *fig* to disappear

**Untertitel,** oonn-ter-**tee**-tel, *m* subtitle

**Unterwäsche,** oonn-ter-**vaish**-e, *f* underwear

**unterwegs,** oonn-ter-**vayks**, *adv* on the road/way

**unterweisen,** oonn-ter-**vy**-zen, *v* to instruct

**unterwerfen,** oonn-ter-**vairf**-en, *v* to subject

**unterwürfig,** oonn-ter-**vEErf**-ik, *adj* obsequious, humble

**unterzeichnen,** oonn-ter-**tsy'k**-nen, *v* to sign; to ratify

**unterziehen,** oonn-ter-**tsee**-en, *v* to subject to

**Untier,** oonn-teer, *nt* monster

**untreu,** oonn-troy, *adj* unfaithful; disloyal

**untröstlich,** oonn-**trerst**-lik, *adj* inconsolable

**Untugend,** oonn-**toog**-ent, *f* vice, bad habit

**ununterbrochen,** oonn-oonn-ter-**brok**-en, *adj* continuous

**unverbesserlich,** oonn-fair-**bess**-er-lik, *adj* incorrigible

**unverbindlich,** oonn-fair-**bint**-lik, *adj* not binding

**unverblümt,** oonn-fair-**blEEmt**, *adj* blunt, direct

**unverdient,** oonn-fair-**deent**, *adj* unmerited, undeserved

**unverdorben,** oonn-fair-**dorb**-en, *adj* unspoilt

**unverdrossen,** oonn-fair-**dross**-en, *adj* indefatigable

**unvereinbar,** oonn-fair-**ine**-bar, *adj* incompatible

**unvergeßlich,** oonn-fair-**gess**-lik, *adj* unforgettable

**unvergleichlich,** oonn-fair-**gly'k**-lik, *adj* incomparable

**unverhofft,** oonn-fair-**hohft**, *adj* unexpected, unforeseen

**unverletzt,** oonn-fair-**letst**, *adj* unharmed, uninjured

**unvermeidlich,** oonn-fair-**mite**-lik, *adj* inevitable

**unvermutet,** oonn-fair-**moot**-et, *adj* unsuspected, unlooked for

**unvernünftig,** oonn-fair-**nEEnft**-ik, *adj* unreasonable, absurd

**unverschämt,** oonn-fair-**shaymt**, *adj* impudent, brazen

**Unverschämtheit,** oonn-fair-**shaymt**-hite, *f* impertinence, impudence

**unverschuldet,** oonn-fair-**shoold**-et, *adj* through no fault of one's own; not in debt

**unversehens,** oonn-fair-**zay**-ens, *adv* unexpectedly

**unversehrt,** oonn-fair-**zairt**, *adj* unhurt, undamaged

**Unverstand,** oonn-fair-**shtahnt**, *m* lack of judgement; folly, foolishness

**unverständlich,** oonn-fair-**shtent**-lik, *adj* incomprehensible

**unverträglich,** oonn-fair-**trayk**-lik, *adj* incompatible

**unverwundbar,** oonn-fair-**voont**-bar, *adj* invulnerable

**unverzagt,** oonn-fair-**tsahkt**, *adj* intrepid, fearless

**unverzeihlich,** oonn-fair-**tsy**-lik, *adj* unpardonable

**unverzüglich,** oonn-fair-**tsEEk**-lik, *adj* without delay

**Unwahrheit,** oonn-**vahr**-hite, *f* untruth, lie

**unwahrscheinlich,** oonn-**vahr**-shine-lik, *adj* improbable, unlikely

**unweit,** oonn-vite, *prep* not far from, close to

**Unwetter,** oonn-**vet**-er, *nt* stormy/foul weather

**unwiderruflich,** oonn-**veed**-er-**roof**-lik, *adj* irrevocable

**unwiderstehlich,** oonn-**veed**-er-**shtay**-lik, *adj* irresistible

**unwillig, oonn**-vil-*ik*, *adj*
reluctant, unwilling

**unwillkürlich, oonn**-vil-
kEER-*lik*, *adj* involuntary

**unwirsch, oonn**-veersh, *adj*
surly, gruff; uncouth

**unwissend, oonn**-viss-ent,
*adj* ignorant;
unsuspecting;
inexperienced

**Unwissenheit, oonn**-viss-
en-hite, *f* ignorance

**unwissentlich, oonn**-viss-
ent-*lik*, *adj* unwitting

**unwürdig, oonn**-vEErd-*ik*,
*adj* unworthy

**Unzahl, oonn**-tsahl, *f*
immense number

**unzählbar, oonn**-tsayl-*bar*,
*adj* innumerable, countless

**unzählig, oonn**-tsayl-*ik*, *adj*
innumerable, countless

**Unze, oont**-se, *f* ounce

**unzeitgemäß, oon**-tsite-ge-
mace, *adj* ill-timed;
premature

**unzertrennlich, oonn**-tsert-
trenn-*lik*, *adj* inseparable

**Unzucht, oonn**-tsookt, *f*
sexual offence;
prostitution

**unzufrieden, oonn**-tsoo-
free-den, *adj* dissatisfied

**unzugänglich, oonn**-tsoo-
geng-*lik*, *adj* inaccessible

**unzulänglich, oonn**-tsoo-
leng-*lik*, *adj* inadequate,
insufficient

**Unzulänglichkeit, oonn**-
tsoo-leng-*lik*-kite, *f*
inadequacy

**unzurechnungsfähig, oonn**-
tsoo-rek-noongs-fay-*ik*, *adj*
not responsible for one's
actions

**unzureichend, oonn**-tsoo-
ry-kent, *adj* insufficient

**unzuverlässig, oonn**-tsoo-
fair-less-*ik*, *adj* unreliable;
uncertain

**unzweckmäßig, oon**-tsveck-
mace-*ik*, *adj* inappropriate

**unzweideutig, oonn**-tsvy-
doyt-*ik*, *adj* simple;
unambiguous

**unzweifelhaft, oonn**-tsvy-
fel-hahft, *adj* undoubted

**üppig, EEpp**-*ik*, *adj*
luxuriant; rich; sensual,
voluptuous

**Üppigkeit, EEpp**-*ik*-kite, *f*
luxury; plenty;
voluptuousness

**Urahn, oor**-ahn, *m*
ancestor, great-
grandfather

**uralt, oor**-ahlt, *adj* ancient,
very old

**Uranfang, oor**-ahnn-fahng,
*m* very beginning

**urbar, oor**-bar, *adj* tilled;
arable

**Urbedeutung, oor**-be-doyt-
oong, *f* original meaning

**Urbestandteil, oor**-be-
shtahnt-tile, *m* original
component

**Urbewohner, oor**-be-vohn-
er, *m* native, original
inhabitant; Aborigine

**Urbild, oor**-bilt, *nt* original

**ureigen, oor**-eye-gen, *adj*
original, innate

**Ureltern, oor**-elt-ern, *pl*
ancestors

**Urenkel, oor**-eng-kel, *m*
great-grandchild

**Urform, oor**-form, *f* original
form

**urgemütlich, oor**-ge-mEEt-
lik, *adj* extremely
comfortable

**Urgeschichte, oor**-ge-shik-
te, *f* dawn of history

**Urgroß–, oor**-grohs, *pref*;
**–eltern,** *pl* great-
grandparents; **–mutter,** *f*
great-grandmother;
**–vater,** *m* great-
grandfather

**Urheber, oor**-hayb-er, *m*
originator, author; **–recht,**
*nt* copyright

**urinieren, oor**-ee-neer-en, *v*
to urinate

**urkomisch, oor**-kohm-ish,
*adj* very comical

**Urkunde, oor**-koonn-de, *f*
document, deed

**urkundlich, oor**-koont-lik,
*adj* documentary

**Urlaub, oor**-lowp, *m* leave
(of absence), holiday(s);
**im –,** on holiday

**Urne, oorn**-e, *f* urn

**urnenförmig, oorn**-en-ferm-
ik, *adj* urn-shaped

**urplötzlich, oor**-plerts-lik,
*adj & adv* very sudden(ly)

**Urquell, oor**-kvel, *m*
origin(al source)

**Ursache, oor**-zahk-e, *f*
cause, motive

**ursächlich,** oor-zek-lik, *adj*
causative

**Ursprung,** oor-shproong, *m*
origin; source

**ursprünglich,** oor-**shprEEng**-lik, *adj* original, primal

**Ursprungsland,** oor-shproongs-lahnt, *nt*
country of origin

**Urstoff,** oor-shtof, *m* raw material

**Urteil,** oor-tile, *nt*
judgement; verdict; opinion

**urteilen,** oor-tile-en, *v* to pass judgement; to judge

**Urteilskraft,** oor-tiles-krahft, *f* judgement; discernment

**Urteilsspruch,** oor-tiles-shprook, *m* sentence, judgement

**Urtext,** oor-text, *m* original text

**urtümlich,** oor-tEEm-lik, *adj* original

**Urvater,** oor-faht-er, *m* forefather

**urväterlich,** oor-fayt-er-lik, *adj* ancestral

**Urvolk,** oor-fohlk, *nt* primitive people

**Urwald,** oor-vahlt, *m* primeval forest; jungle

**urwüchsig,** oor-vEEks-ik, *adj* natural; original

**Urzeit,** oor-tsite, *f* primeval period; antiquity

**Urzustand,** oor-tsoo-shtahnt, *m* primitive condition

**Urzweck,** oor-tsveck, *m* original/chief purpose

**Usus,** ooz-ooss, *m* custom

**usw.,** *abbr* **und so weiter,** etc.

**Valentinstag,** vah-len-teens-tahk, *m* Valentine's Day

**Valuta,** vah-loot-ah, *f* foreign currency; monetary standard

**Vanille,** vahn-ill-(y)e, *f* vanilla

**Vater,** faht-er, *m* father; **–land,** *nt* fatherland, motherland

**väterlich,** fayt-er-lik, *adj* fatherly

**Vaterstadt,** faht-er-shtaht, *f* native town

**Vaterunser,** faht-er-oonn-zer, *nt* Lord's Prayer

**v. Chr.,** *abbr* **vor Christo/Christus,** B.C.

**Vegetarier,** vay-ge-tar-ee-er, *m* vegetarian

**vegetarisch,** vay-ge-tar-ish, *adj* vegetarian

**vegetieren,** vay-ge-teer-en, *v* to vegetate; to exist

**Veilchen,** file-ken, *nt* violet

**Vene,** vayn-e, *f* vein

**Venedig,** ven-ay-dik, *nt* Venice

**Ventil,** ven-teel, *nt* valve; stop; piston

**Ventilator,** ven-tee-laht-ohr, *m* (electric) fan

**verabreden,** fair-ahpp-rayd-en, *v* to agree; to appoint (a time)

**Verabredung,** fair-ahpp-rayd-oong, *f* appointment; arrangement

**verabreichen,** fair-ahpp-ry-ken, *v* to tender; to dispense

**verabscheuen,** fair-ahpp-shoy-en, *v* to loathe, to detest

**verabschieden,** fair-ahpp-sheed-en, *v* to dismiss; **sich –,** *v* to take leave

**verachten,** fair-ahkt-en, *v* to despise; to disdain

**verächtlich,** fair-ekt-lik, *adj* contemptuous; contemptible

**Verachtung,** fair-ahkt-oong, *f* contempt; scorn

**verallgemeinern,** fair-ahllge-mine-ern, *v* to generalize

**veralten,** fair-ahlt-en, *v* to grow obsolete

**veränderlich,** fair-end-er-lik, *adj* changeable

**verändern,** fair-end-ern, *v* to change; to vary

**Veränderung,** fair-end-er-oong, *f* change; alteration

**veranlagt,** fair-ahnn-lahkt, *adj* suited to, gifted for; disposed to

**Veranlagung,** fair-ahnn-lahg-oong, *f* talent; disposition

**veranlassen,** fair-ahnn-lahss-en, *v* to cause

**Veranlassung,** fair-ahnn-lahss-oong, *f* cause, occasion, impulse

**veranschaulichen,** fair-ahnn-show-lik-en, *v* to make clear; to demonstrate

**Veranschaulichung,** fair-ahnn-show-lik-oong, *f* demonstration; illustration

**veranstalten,** fair-ahnn-shtahl-ten, *v* to organize; to arrange

**verantworten,** fair-ahnt-vort-en, *v* to be

responsible; **sich –,** *v* to justify oneself

**Verantwortlichkeit,** fair-**ahnt**-vort-lik-kite, *f* responsibility

**Verantwortung,** fair-**ahnt**-vort-oong, *f* responsibility, risk

**verarbeiten,** fair-**ahr**-by-ten, *v* to consume; to manufacture; to process

**verärgert,** fair-**airg**-ert, *adj* vexed, annoyed

**verarmen,** fair-**arm**-en, *v* to (be) impoverish(ed)

**verausgaben,** fair-**ows**-gahb-en, *v* to spend; **sich –,** *v* to exhaust oneself

**veräußern,** fair-**oys**-ern, *v* to dispose of

**Verband,** fair-**bahnt,** *m* bandage, dressing; union, association

**verbannen,** fair-**bahnn**-en, *v* to banish, to exile

**Verbannung,** fair-**bahnn**-oong, *f* exile; expulsion

**verbergen,** fair-**bairg**-en, *v* to hide, to conceal

**verbessern,** fair-**bess**-ern, *v* to improve, to (a)mend

**verbeugen (sich),** fair-**boyg**-en (zik), *v* to bow

**Verbeugung,** fair-**boyg**-oong, *f* bow

**verbiegen,** fair-**beeg**-en, *v* to bend out of shape

**verbieten,** fair-**beet**-en, *v* to forbid, to prohibit

**verbilligen,** fair-**bil**-ig-en, *v* to cheapen

**verbilligt,** fair-**bil**-ikt, *adj* reduced

**verbinden,** fair-**bin**-den, *v* to unite, to connect; to bandage

**verbindlich,** fair-**bint**-lik, *adj* binding; courteous

**Verbindlichkeit,** fair-**bint**-lik-kite, *f* courtesy; liability

**Verbindung,** fair-**bin**-doong, *f* communication, connection; compound

**verbitten (sich),** fair-**bit**-en (zik), *v* to refuse to tolerate

**verbittern,** fair-**bit**-ern, *v* to embitter

**verblassen,** fair-**blahss**-en, *v* to fade

**Verbleib,** fair-**blipe,** *m* whereabouts

**verbleiben,** fair-**bly**-ben, *v* to remain; to continue

**verbleit,** fair-**blite,** *adj* leaded (petrol)

**verblenden,** fair-**blend**-en, *v* to dazzle; to blind

**Verblendung,** fair-**blend**-oong, *f* delusion

**verblüffen,** fair-**blEEff**-en, *v* to dumbfound

**verblühen,** fair-**blEE**-en, *v* to fade, to wither

**verbluten,** fair-**bloot**-en, *v* to bleed to death

**verbohrt,** fair-**bohrt,** *adj* stubborn, cranky

**verborgen,** fair-**borg**-en, *adj* hidden

**Verborgenheit,** fair-**borg**-en-

hite, *f* obscurity

**Verbot,** fair-**boht,** *nt* prohibition

**verboten,** fair-**boht**-en, *adj* prohibited, forbidden

**Verbrauch,** fair-**browk,** *m* consumption (of goods)

**verbrauchen,** fair-**browk**-en, *v* to use up, to consume

**Verbraucher,** fair-**browk**-er, *m* consumer

**verbrechen,** fair-**brek**-en, *v* to commit (a crime)

**Verbrechen,** fair-**brek**-en, *nt* crime

**Verbrecher,** fair-**brek**-er, *m* criminal

**verbrecherisch,** fair-**brek**-er-ish, *adj* criminal

**verbreiten,** fair-**bry**-ten, *v* to spread, to circulate, distribute

**Verbreitung,** fair-**bry**-toong, *f* spreading, circulation, distribution; radiation

**verbrennen,** fair-**bren**-en, *v* to burn up; to be consumed by fire

**Verbrennung,** fair-**bren**-oong, *f* burning (up); cremation

**verbringen,** fair-**bring**-en, *v* to spend time

**verbrüdern (sich),** fair-**brEEd**-ern (zik), *v* to fraternize

**verbrühen,** fair-**brEE**-en, *v* to scald

**verbummeln,** fair-**boomm**-eln, *v* to waste (time); to get lazy

**verbunden,** fair-**boonn**-den, *adj* obliged; bandaged

**verbünden (sich),** fair-**bEEnn**-den (zik), *v* to form an alliance

**Verbündete(r),** fair-**bEEnn**-de-te(r), *m & f*, ally

**verbürgen,** fair-**bEErg**-en, *v* to warrant, to guarantee

**Verdacht,** fair-**dakt**, *m* suspicion; distrust

**verdächtig,** fair-**dekt**-ik, *adj* suspected, suspicious

**verdächtigen,** fair-**dek**-tig-en, *v* to suspect

**verdammen,** fair-**dahmm**-en, *v* to condemn

**verdammt,** fair-**dahmmt**, *adj & interj* damned

**Verdammung,** fair-**dahmm**-oong, *f* damnation; condemnation

**verdampfen,** fair-**dahmp**-fen, *v* to evaporate, to vaporise

**verdanken,** fair-**dahng**-ken, *v* to be indebted to

**verdauen,** fair-**dow**-en, *v* to digest

**verdaulich,** fair-**dow**-lik, *adj* digestible

**Verdauung,** fair-**dow**-oong, *f* digestion

**Verdeck,** fair-**deck**, *nt* deck; roof, hood

**verdecken,** fair-**deck**-en, *v* to cover up; to veil

**Verderb(en),** fair-**dairp** (fair-**dairb**-en), *m* (*nt*), ruin; decay

**verderben,** fair-**dairb**-en, *v* to spoil; to ruin; to rot

**verderblich,** fair-**dairp**-lik, *adj* fatal, pernicious; corruptible

**Verderbnis,** fair-**dairp**-niss, *f* depravity

**verderbt,** fair-**dairp't**, *adj* demoralized; corrupt

**verdeutlichen,** fair-**doyt**-lik-en, *v* to make clear

**verdienen,** fair-**deen**-en, *v* to earn; to merit; to deserve

**Verdienst,** fair-**deenst**, *m* earnings; merit

**verdoppeln,** fair-**dop**-eln, *v* to double

**verdorben,** fair-**dorb**-en, *adj* spoilt, bad, polluted; corrupt

**verdorren,** fair-**dorr**-en, *v* to wither, to dry up

**verdrängen,** fair-**dreng**-en, *v* to displace; to push aside; to repress

**verdrehen,** fair-**dray**-en, *v* to distort

**verdreht,** fair-**drayt**, *adj* crazy, cranky

**verdrießen,** fair-**drees**-en, *v* to vex; to grieve

**verdrießlich,** fair-**drees**-lik, *adj* vexed, annoyed; grieved

**Verdrießlichkeit,** fair-**drees**-lik-kite, *f* moroseness

**verdrossen,** fair-**dross**-en, *adj* morose; unwilling; reluctant

**verdrucken,** fair-**droock**-en, *v* to misprint

**Verdruß,** fair-**drooss**, *m* annoyance; indignation

**verdunkeln,** fair-**doong**-keln, *v* to darken; to grow dim; *fig* to obscure

**verdünnen,** fair-**dEEnn**-en, *v* to dilute

**verdursten,** fair-**doorst**-en, *v* to die of thirst

**verdüstern,** fair-**dEEst**-ern, *v* to darken; to grow dim; *fig* to obscure

**verdutzt,** fair-**dootst**, *adj* taken aback

**veredeln,** fair-**ayd**-eln, *v* to ennoble; to graft

**verehelichen,** fair-ay-e-lik-en, *v* to marry

**verehren,** fair-**ayr**-en, *v* to venerate; to admire

**Verehrer,** fair-**ayr**-er, *m* admirer

**Verehrung,** fair-**ayr**-oong, *f* veneration; admiration

**vereidigen,** fair-**ide**-ig-en, *v* to swear in

**Verein,** fair-**ine**, *m* society, association, club, union

**vereinbaren,** fair-**ine**-bar-en, *v* to agree to

**vereinen,** fair-**ine**-en, *v* to unite, to combine

**vereinfachen,** fair-**ine**-fahk-en, *v* to simplify

**vereinigen,** fair-**ine**-ig-en, *v* to unite, to combine

**Vereinigte Staaten,** fair-**ine**-ick-te **shtaht**-en, *pl* United States

**Vereinte Nationen,** fair-**ine**-te nahts-**yohn**-en, *pl* United Nations

**vereiteln,** fair-**ite**-eln,

*v* to frustrate

**verenden,** fair-**end**-en, *v* to perish, to die (animals)

**verengen,** fair-**eng**-en, *v* to (become/make) narrow

**vererben,** fair-**airb**-en, *v* to bequeath

**verewigen,** fair-**ay**-vig-en, *v* to immortalize

**verfahren,** fair-**fahr**-en, *v* to proceed; **sich –,** *v* to get lost

**Verfahren,** fair-**fahr**-en, *nt* process, proceeding, procedure

**Verfall,** fair-**fahll**, *m* decay, ruin; lapse; expiry (of card etc.)

**verfallen,** fair-**fahll**-en, *v* to decay; to expire (card etc.)

**Verfallsdatum,** fair-**fahls**-dah-toom, *nt* expiry date, sell-by date

**verfälschen,** fair-**felsh**-en, *v* to adulterate

**verfärben,** fair-**fairb**-en, *v* to discolour

**verfassen,** fair-**fahss**-en, *v* to compose, to draw up

**Verfasser,** fair-**fahss**-er, *m* author

**Verfassung,** fair-**fahss**-oong, *f* constitution; disposition

**verfaulen,** fair-**fowl**-en, *v* to rot, to decay

**verfechten,** fair-**fek**-ten, *v* to defend, to advocate, to champion

**verfehlen,** fair-**fayl**-en, *v* to miss; to fall

**verfeinden,** fair-**fine**-den, *v* to make enemies

**verfeinern,** fair-**fine**-ern, *v* to refine; to improve

**verfertigen,** fair-**fairt**-ig-en, *v* to manufacture, to prepare

**verfinstern,** fair-**finst**-ern, *v* to darken

**verfliegen,** fair-**fleeg**-en, *v* to fly off; to evaporate

**verfließen,** fair-**flees**-en, *v* to elapse

**verfluchen,** fair-**flook**-en, *v* to curse, to damn

**verfolgen,** fair-**foll**-gen, *v* to pursue; to follow

**Verfolgung,** fair-**folg**-oong, *f* persecution; pursuit

**verfügbar,** fair-**fEEg**-bar, *adj* available

**verfügen,** fair-**fEEg**-en, *v* to dispose; to decree

**Verfügung,** fair-**fEEg**-oong, *f* decree; disposition

**verführen,** fair-**fEEr**-en, *v* to tempt; to seduce

**verführerisch,** fair-**fEEr**-er-ish, *adj* tempting; seductive

**Verführung,** fair-**fEEr**-oong, *f* seduction

**vergällen,** fair-**gel**-en, *v* to spoil (enjoyment etc.); to embitter

**vergangen,** fair-**gahng**-en, *adj* past; bygone

**Vergangenheit,** fair-**gahng**-en-hite, *f* past; history

**vergänglich,** fair-**geng**-lik, *adj* transient, fleeting;

perishable

**vergeben,** fair-**gayb**-en, *v* to forgive; to give away

**vergebens,** fair-**gayb**-ens, *adv* in vain; to no avail

**vergeblich,** fair-**gayp**-lik, *adj* futile, vain, fruitless

**Vergebung,** fair-**gayb**-oong, *f* forgiveness

**vergehen,** fair-**gay**-en, *v* to pass (of time), to elapse; **sich –,** *v* to commit an offence

**Vergehen,** fair-**gay**-en, *nt* trespass

**vergelten,** fair-**gelt**-en, *v* to repay, to requite

**vergessen,** fair-**gess**-en, *v* to forget

**Vergessenheit,** fair-**gess**-en-hite, *f* oblivion

**vergeßlich,** fair-**gess**-lik, *adj* forgetful

**vergeuden,** fair-**goyd**-en, *v* to squander; to lavish

**vergewaltigen,** fair-ge-**vahlt**-ig-en, *v* to assault; to rape

**vergewissern,** fair-ge-**viss**-ern, *v* to make sure

**vergießen,** fair-**gees**-en, *v* to shed (tears); to spill

**vergiften,** fair-**gift**-en, *v* to poison; to taint

**Vergiftung,** fair-**gift**-oong, *f* poisoning

**Vergißmeinnicht,** fair-**giss**-mine-nikt, *nt* forget-me-not

**vergittern,** fair-**git**-ern, *v* to fence in

**Vergleich,** fair-**gly'k**, *m*

comparison; agreement

**vergleichen**, fair-**gly**-ken, *v* to compare

**verglühen**, fair-**glEE**-en, *v* to fade/die away, to burn out

**Vergnügen**, fair-g'**nEEg**-en, *nt* amusement, pleasure

**vergnügen**, fair-g**nEEg**-en, *v* to amuse; **sich –**, *v* to enjoy o.s.

**vergnüglich**, fair-g'**nEEg**-lik, *adj* delightful; pleased

**vergnügt**, fair-g'**nEEgt**, *adj* delighted; cheerful

**Vergnügung**, fair-g'**nEEg**-oong, *f* amusement

**vergolden**, fair-**goll**-den, *v* to gild

**vergönnen**, fair-**gernn**-en, *v* to permit, to grant

**vergöttern**, fair-**gertt**-ern, *v* to idolize

**vergraben**, fair-**grahb**-en, *v* to bury; to burrow

**vergreifen**, fair-**gry**-fen, *v* to make a mistake; **sich an etw –**, to misappropriate; to lay hands on

**vergriffen**, fair-**grif**-en, *adj* out of print; out of stock

**vergrößern**, fair-**grers**-ern, *v* to enlarge; to increase

**Vergrößerung**, fair-**grers**-er-oong, *f* enlargement; **–sglas**, *nt* magnifying glass

**vergünstigen**, fair-**gEEnst**-ig-en, *v* to grant (privileges)

**Vergünstigung**, fair-**gEEnst**-ig-oong, *f* privilege; benefit

**vergüten**, fair-**gEEt**-en, *v* to

make good; to refund; to compensate

**verhaften**, fair-**hahft**-en, *v* to arrest

**Verhaftung**, fair-**hahft**-oong, *f* arrest

**verhallen**, fair-**hahll**-en, *v* to die away (sounds)

**verhalten**, fair-**hahlt**-en, *v* to suppress; to behave; to be (in a position); *adj* restrained

**Verhalten**, fair-**hahlt**-en, *nt* conduct, behaviour

**Verhältnis**, fair-**helt**-niss, *nt* relation; proportion; (love) affair; **–se**, *pl* conditions, state of affairs

**verhältnismäßig**, fair-**helt**-niss-mace-ik, *adj* proportionate, relative; *adv* comparatively

**verhandeln**, fair-**hahnn**-deln, *v* to negotiate

**Verhandlung**, fair-**hahnd**-loong, *f* negotiation; trial

**verhängen**, fair-**heng**-en, *v* to cover; to decree; to impose

**Verhängnis**, fair-**heng**-niss, *nt* fate; doom

**verhängnisvoll**, fair-**heng**-niss-fol, *adj* fateful

**verharmlosen**, fair-**harm**-loh-zen, *v* to play down

**verhaßt**, fair-**hahsst**, *adj* hated, odious

**verhätscheln**, fair-**hayt**-sheln, *v* to pamper

**verhauen**, fair-**how**-en, *v* to thrash; to fail (exams)

**verheben (sich)**, fair-**hayb**-en (zik), *v* to injure oneself by lifting

**verheerend**, fair-**hayr**-ent, *adj* disastrous

**verhehlen**, fair-**hayl**-en, *v* to dissemble, to conceal

**verheimlichen**, fair-**hime**-lik-en, *v* to conceal

**verheiraten**, fair-**hy**-raht-en, *v* to marry

**Verheiratung**, fair-**hy**-raht-oong, *f* marriage

**verheißen**, fair-**hy**-sen, *v* to hold out promise

**Verheißung**, fair-**hy**-soong, *f* promise

**verhelfen**, fair-**helf**-en, *v* to assist in obtaining

**verherrlichen**, fair-**hairr**-lik-en, *v* to glorify

**verhexen**, fair-**hecks**-en, *v* to bewitch

**verhindern**, fair-**hin**-dern, *v* to prevent

**verhöhnen**, fair-**hern**-en, *v* to mock; to jeer

**Verhöhnung**, fair-**hern**-oong, *f* derision; mockery

**Verhör**, fair-**her**, *nt* evidence, interrogation

**verhören**, fair-**her**-en, *v* to interrogate; to mishear

**verhüllen**, fair-**hEEll**-en, *v* to wrap up, to muffle

**verhungern**, fair-**hoong**-ern, *v* to starve (to death)

**verhüten**, fair-**hEEt**-en, *v* to prevent, to avert; to use contraceptives

**Verhütung**, fair-**hEEt**-oong, *f*

prevention; contraception; **–smittel**, *nt* contraceptive

**verirren (sich)**, fair-**eerr**-en (zik), *v* to get lost

**verjubeln**, fair-**yoob**-eln, *v* to lavish

**verjüngen**, fair-**yEEng**-en, *v* to rejuvenate; to taper, to narrow

**verkalken**, fair-**kahlk**-en, *v* to calcify; *fam* to become senile

**Verkauf**, fair-**kowf**, *m* selling, sale

**verkaufen**, fair-**kowf**-en, *v* to sell; **sich –**, *v* to market o.s.; to present o.s.

**Verkäufer**, fair-**koyf**-er, *m* salesman; seller; shop assistant

**verkäuflich**, fair-**koyf**-lik, *adj* saleable

**Verkehr**, fair-**kair**, *m* traffic; contact, communication; business

**verkehren**, fair-**kair**-en, *v* to do business; to frequent; to associate (with)

**Verkehrsamt**, fair-**kairs**-ahmt, *nt* tourist office

**Verkehrsberuhigung**, fair-**kairs**-be-roo-ee-goong, *f* traffic calming

**verkehrsgünstig**, fair-**kairs**-gEEnst-ik, *adj* convenient, easy to reach (by car etc.)

**Verkehrsmittel**, fair-**kairs**-mit-el, *nt* means of transport

**Verkehrsunfall**, fair-**kairs**-

oonn-fahll, *m* road accident

**Verkehrsverein**, fair-**kairs**-fair-ine, *m* tourist office

**verkehrt**, fair-**kairt**, *adj* wrong; inverted

**verkennen**, fair-**kenn**-en, *v* to mistake, to misjudge

**verklagen**, fair-**klahg**-en, *v* to sue

**Verklärung**, fair-**klair**-oong, *f* transfiguration; ecstasy

**verkleiden (sich)**, fair-**kly**-den (zik), *v* to disguise o.s.

**Verkleidung**, fair-**kly**-doong, *f* disguise

**verkleinern**, fair-**kly**-nern, *v* to make small(er), to reduce

**Verkleinerung**, fair-**kly**-ner-oong, *f* reduction

**verklingen**, fair-**kling**-en, *v* to die away (sounds)

**verknüpfen**, fair-**k'nEEpp**-fen, *v* to connect

**verkohlen**, fair-**kohl**-en, *v* to char; to pull someone's leg

**verkommen**, fair-**kom**-en, *v* to decay; to go downhill

**verkorken**, fair-**kork**-en, *v* to cork up

**verkörpern**, fair-**kerp**-ern, *v* to embody

**verkraften**, fair-**krahft**-en, *v* to bear; to cope

**verkriechen (sich)**, fair-**kreek**-en (zik), *v* to creep into hiding

**verkrüppeln**, fair-**krEEpp**-eln, *v* to cripple

**verkümmern**, fair-**kEEmm**-

ern, *v* to pine, to atrophy (also *fig*)

**verkünd(ig)en**, fair-**kEEnd**(-ig)-en, *v* to make known, to proclaim

**Verkünd(ig)ung**, fair-**kEEnd**(-ig)-oong, *f* publication, announcement

**verkupfern**, fair-**koopp**-fern, *v* to copper(-plate)

**verkuppeln**, fair-**koopp**-eln, *v* to couple together

**verkürzen**, fair-**kEErt**-sen, *v* to shorten

**Verkürzung**, fair-**kEErt**-soong, *f* shortening

**verladen**, fair-**lahd**-en, *v* to load; to ship

**Verlag**, fair-**lahk**, *m* publishing house

**verlangen**, fair-**lahng**-en, *v* to demand; to long for

**Verlangen**, fair-**lahng**-en, *nt* desire; longing

**verlängern**, fair-**leng**-ern, *v* to lengthen; to extend

**Verlängerung**, fair-**leng**-er-oong, *f* prolongation; lengthening; extra time *sport*

**verlangsamen**, fair-**lahng**-zahm-en, *v* to retard; to slow down

**Verlaß**, fair-**lahss**, *m* reliance

**verlassen**, fair-**lahss**-en, *v* to leave, to quit; **sich –**, *v* to rely, to trust

**verläßlich**, fair-**less**-lik, *adj* reliable

**Verlauf**, fair-**lowf**, m passage of time; progress; course

**verlaufen**, fair-**lowf**-en, v to pass (time); **sich –**, v to get lost

**verlegen**, fair-**layg**-en, v to publish; to transfer; to mislay; **sich – auf**, to specialize in; adj embarrassed

**Verlegenheit**, fair-**layg**-en-hite, f embarrassment

**Verleger**, fair-**layg**-er, m publisher

**verleiden**, fair-ly-den, v to disgust; to spoil

**Verleih**, fair-**ly**, m hire service

**verleihen**, fair-**ly**-en, v to loan, to lend

**verleiten**, fair-**ly**-ten, v to lead astray

**verlernen**, fair-**lairn**-en, v to forget (something learned)

**verlesen**, fair-**layz**-en, v to read out; to misread; to sort out

**verletzen**, fair-**lets**-en, v to injure, to hurt; to damage

**verletzlich**, fair-**lets**-lik, adj vulnerable, sensitive

**Verletzung**, fair-**lets**-oong, f injury; damage; infringement

**verleugnen**, fair-**loyg**-nen, v to deny

**Verleugnung**, fair-**loyg**-noong, f denial

**verleumden**, fair-**loym**-den, v to defame, to slander

**Verleumdung**, fair-**loym**-doong, f defamation, slander, libel

**verlieben (sich)**, fair-**leeb**-en (zik), v to fall in love

**verliebt**, fair-**leept**, adj in love, enamoured

**verlieren**, fair-**leer**-en, v to lose

**Verließ**, fair-**leess**, nt dungeon, keep

**verloben (sich)**, fair-**lohb**-en (zik), v to become engaged

**verlobt**, fair-**lohpt**, adj betrothed, engaged

**Verlobte(r)**, fair-**lohpt**-e(r), m & f, fiancé(e)

**Verlobung**, fair-**lohb**-oong, f betrothal, engagement

**verlocken**, fair-**lock**-en, v to allure, to entice

**verlogen**, fair-**lohg**-en, adj habitually untruthful

**verlöschen**, fair-**lersh**-en, v to extinguish

**verlosen**, fair-**lohz**-en, v to raffle

**verlöten**, fair-**lert**-en, v to solder

**verlottern**, fair-**lott**-ern, v to go to ruin

**Verlust**, fair-**loost**, m loss; bereavement

**vermachen**, fair-**mahk**-en, v to bequeath

**Vermächtnis**, fair-**mekt**-nis, nt legacy

**vermählen**, fair-**mayl**-en, v to marry; **sich –**, to get married

**Vermählung**, fair-**mayl**-oong, f marriage; wedding

**vermarkten**, fair-**markt**-en, v to market

**vermehren**, fair-**mayr**-en, v to increase

**vermeiden**, fair-**my**-den, v to avoid; to evade

**vermengen**, fair-**meng**-en, v to confuse; to mix up

**Vermerk**, fair-**mairk**, m remark, note; entry

**vermerken**, fair-**mairk**-en, v to note; to (re)mark

**vermessen**, fair-**mess**-en, v to survey; adj presumptuous

**Vermessung**, fair-**mess**-oong, f survey(ing)

**vermieten**, fair-**meet**-en, v to let

**vermindern**, fair-**min**-dern, v to lessen; to impair

**vermischen**, fair-**mish**-en, v to mix

**vermissen**, fair-**miss**-en, v to miss

**vermitteln**, fair-**mit**-eln, v to mediate; to intervene

**vermittels(t)**, fair-**mit**-els(t), prep by means of

**Vermittlung**, fair-**mit**-loong, f mediation; intercession; agency; **–sgebühr**, f commission

**Vermittler**, fair-**mit**-ler, m intermediary; agent

**vermodern**, fair-**mohd**-ern, v to fall to dust

**vermögen**, fair-**merg**-en, v to be able (to)

**Vermögen**, fair-**merg**-en, nt

capability; fortune

**vermögend**, fair-**merg**-ent, *adj* well-to-do

**vermuten**, fair-**moot**-en, *v* to conjecture; to presume; to suppose

**vermutlich**, fair-**moot**-lik, *adj* probable; supposed

**Vermutung**, fair-**moot**-oong, *f* conjecture; supposition

**vernachlässigen**, fair-**nahk**-less-ig-en, *v* to neglect

**vernageln**, fair-**nahg**-eln, *v* to nail up

**vernarben**, fair-**nahrb**-en, *v* to (leave a) scar

**vernarrt**, fair-**nahrt**, *adj* infatuated

**vernehmen**, fair-**naym**-en, *v* to perceive, to understand, to learn; *law* to examine (in court)

**Vernehmung**, fair-**naym**-oong, *f law* examination

**verneigen (sich)**, fair-**ny**-gen (*zik*), *v* to bow

**verneinen**, fair-**nine**-en, *v* to deny

**Verneinung**, fair-**nine**-oong, *f* denial; negation

**vernichten**, fair-**nik**-ten, *v* to destroy

**Vernichtung**, fair-**nik**-toong, *f* destruction

**vernieten**, fair-**neet**-en, *v* to rivet

**Vernunft**, fair-**noonft**, *f* reason, intellect; (common) sense

**vernünftig**, fair-**nEEnft**-ik, *adj* sensible; reasonable

**veröden**, fair-**erd**-en, *v* to lay waste; to become deserted

**veröffentlichen**, fair-**erff**-ent-lik-en, *v* to publish; to make known

**verordnen**, fair-**ord**-nen, *v* to prescribe; to order

**Verordnung**, fair-**ord**-noong, *f* order; edict

**verpachten**, fair-**pahk**-ten, *v* to lease

**verpacken**, fair-**pahck**-en, *v* to pack; to wrap

**Verpackung**, fair-**pahck**-oong, *f* packing

**verpassen**, fair-**pahss**-en, *v* to let slip; to miss up

**verpfänden**, fair-p'**fend**-en, *v* to pledge; to pawn

**verpflanzen**, fair-p'**flahnt**-sen, *v* to transplant

**verpflegen**, fair-p'**flayg**-en, *v* to look after, to nurse; to board

**Verpflegung**, fair-p'**flayg**-oong, *f* provisioning; board(ing); tending

**verpflichten**, fair-p'**flik**-ten, *v* to bind, to oblige

**verpfuschen**, fair-p'**foosh**-en, *v* to spoil; to botch

**verpönt**, fair-**pernt**, *adj* frowned (up)on

**verprügeln**, fair-**prEEg**-eln, *v* to thrash

**Verrat**, fair-**raht**, *m* treason; treachery

**verraten**, fair-**raht**-en, *v* to betray; to divulge

**Verräter**, fair-**rayt**-er, *m* traitor

**verräterisch**, fair-**rayt**-er-ish, *adj* treacherous; treasonable

**verrauchen**, fair-**rowk**-en, *v* to go up in smoke; to cool down

**verrechnen**, fair-**rek**-nen, *v* to adjust accounts; **sich –**, *v* to miscalculate

**Verrechnung**, fair-**rek**-noong, *f* miscalculation; adjustment; **–sscheck**, *m* crossed cheque

**verrecken**, fair-**reck**-en, *v fam* to perish, to die (like an animal)

**verregnen**, fair-**rayg**-nen, *v* to spoil by rain

**verreisen**, fair-**ry**-zen, *v* to go out of town, to travel

**verrenken**, fair-**reng**-ken, *v* to dislocate, to sprain

**verrichten**, fair-**rik**-ten, *v* to perform; to carry out

**verriegeln**, fair-**reeg**-eln, *v* to bolt (door)

**verringern**, fair-**ring**-ern, *v* to reduce, to diminish

**verrinnen**, fair-**rin**-en, *v* to elapse; to run off

**verrosten**, fair-**rost**-en, *v* to get rusty

**verrucht**, fair-**rookt**, *adj* villainous, infamous

**verrücken**, fair-**rEEck**-en, *v* to shift, to displace

**verrückt**, fair-**rEEckt**, *adj* mad, insane

**Verrücktheit**, fair-**rEEckt**-hite, *f* madness, insanity, lunacy

**Verruf**, fair-**roof**, m ill repute

**verrufen**, fair-**roof**-en, adj ill-reputed, notorious

**Vers**, fairs, m verse; poetry; stanza

**versagen**, fair-**zahg**-en, v to fail, to break down; to refuse

**versalzen**, fair-**zahlt**-sen, v to oversalt; fig to spoil

**versammeln**, fair-**zahmm**-eln, v to assemble

**Versammlung**, fair-**zahmm**-loong, f assembly, meeting

**Versand**, fair-**zahnt**, m export(ation), dispatch; **–haus**, nt mail-order business

**versaufen**, fair-**zowf**-en, v fam to spend on drink

**versäumen**, fair-**zoym**-en, v to neglect; to miss

**verschachern**, fair-**shahk**-ern, v to sell off

**verschaffen**, fair-**shahff**-en, v to provide, to supply; **sich –**, v to obtain, to acquire

**verschämt**, fair-**shaymt**, adj bashful; ashamed

**verschärfen**, fair-**shairf**-en, v to make more severe, to intensify

**verscheiden**, fair-**shy**-den, v to pass away

**verschenken**, fair-**sheng**-ken, v to give away

**verscherzen**, fair-**shairts**-en, v to forfeit

**verscheuchen**, fair-**shoyk**-en, v to scare away

**verschicken**, fair-**shick**-en, v to forward

**verschieben**, fair-**sheeb**-en, v to shift; to postpone

**verschieden**, fair-**sheed**-en, adj different; diverse; **–artig**, adj varied

**Verschiedenheit**, fair-**sheed**-en-hite, f difference; variety

**verschiedentlich**, fair-**sheed**-ent-lik, adj on several occasions

**verschiffen**, fair-**shif**-en v to ship, to dispatch

**verschimmeln**, fair-**shim**-eln, v to go mouldy

**verschlafen**, fair-**shlahf**-en, v to oversleep; fig to miss; adj drowsy, sleepy

**Verschlag**, fair-**shlahk**, m locker, shed; partition

**verschlagen**, fair-**shlahg**-en, v to board up; adj cunning, devious

**verschlechtern**, fair-**shlek**-tern, v to make worse; to worsen

**verschleiern**, fair-**shly**-ern, v to veil

**Verschleiß**, fair-**shlys**, m wear and tear

**verschleißen**, fair-**shly**-sen, v to wear out

**verschleudern**, fair-**shloy**-dern, v to squander; to sell off

**verschließen**, fair-**shlees**-en, v to lock; to shut

**verschlimmern**, fair-**shlim**-ern, v to aggravate; to demoralize

**verschlingen**, fair-**shling**-en, v to gulp; to gobble; to entangle

**verschlucken**, fair-**shloock**-en, v to swallow; **sich –**, v to swallow the wrong way

**Verschluß**, fair-**shlooss**, m lock; shutter; fastener

**verschmähen**, fair-**shmay**-en, v to scorn

**verschmerzen**, fair-**shmairt**-sen, v to forget/get over a loss

**verschmitzt**, fair-**shmitst**, adj mischievous

**verschmutzen**, fair-**shmoots**-en, v to soil; to pollute

**verschnupft**, fair-**shnoop**'ft, adj having a cold; fam to be miffed

**verschollen**, fair-**shol**-en, adj lost, forgotten

**verschonen**, fair-**shohn**-en, v to spare

**verschöne(r)n**, fair-**shern**-e(r)n, v to beautify, to improve

**verschreiben**, fair-**shry**-ben, v to prescribe; **sich –**, v to make a mistake in writing; to devote o.s. to

**verschrotten**, fair-**shrott**-en, v to scrap

**verschüchtern**, fair-**shEEk**-tern, v to intimidate

**verschulden**, fair-**shooll**-den, v to be guilty of

**verschuldet**, fair-**shooll**-det,

*adj* in debt

**verschwägert,** fair-shvay-gert, *adj* related by marriage

**verschwenden,** fair-shvend-en, *v* to waste, to squander

**Verschwender,** fair-shvend-er, *m* spendthrift

**verschwenderisch,** fair-shvend-er-ish, *adj* wasteful

**verschwiegen,** fair-shveeg-en, *adj* reserved, discreet

**Verschwiegenheit,** fair-shveeg-en-hite, *f* reticence; discretion

**verschwimmen,** fair-shvim-en, *v* to dissolve; to grow hazy

**verschwinden,** fair-shvin-den, *v* to disappear

**verschwommen,** fair-shvom-en, *adj* indistinct

**verschwören,** fair-shverr-en, *v* to conspire; to curse

**Verschwörer,** fair-shverr-er, *m* plotter

**Verschwörung,** fair-shverr-oong, *f* conspiracy

**versehen,** fair-zay-en, *v* to provide; to carry out; **sich –,** *v* to make a mistake

**Versehen,** fair-zay-en, *nt* oversight; mistake

**versenden,** fair-zend-en, *v* to send off; to export

**versengen,** fair-zeng-en, *v* to singe

**versenken,** fair-zeng-ken, *v* to sink; to lower

**versessen,** fair-zess-en, *adj*

keen (on), crazy (about)

**versetzen,** fair-zet-sen, *v* to misplace; to displace; to transfer; to pawn; to reply; to put

**Versetzung,** fair-zet-soong, *f* displacement; transfer

**verseuchen,** fair-zoyk-en, *v* to contaminate

**versichern,** fair-zik-ern, *v* to insure; to assure; to ensure; to ascertain

**Versicherung,** fair-zik-er-oong, *f* insurance; assurance

**versiegeln,** fair-zeeg-eln, *v* to seal up

**versilbern,** fair-zil-bern, *v* to silver

**versinken,** fair-zing-ken, *v* to sink

**versoffen,** fair-zof-en, *adj fam* drunk

**versöhnen,** fair-zern-en, *v* to reconcile

**Versöhnung,** fair-zern-oong, *f* reconciliation

**versorgen,** fair-zorg-en, *v* to provide (with)

**Versorgung,** fair-zorg-oong, *f* provision

**verspäten (sich),** fair-shpayt-en (zik), *v* to be late

**Verspätung,** fair-shpayt-oong, *f* delay; lateness

**verspeisen,** fair-shpy-zen, *v* to eat

**versperren,** fair-shpairr-en, *v* to obstruct

**verspielen,** fair-shpeel-en, *v*

to gamble away

**verspotten,** fair-shpot-en, *v* to mock; to tease

**versprechen,** fair-shprek-en, *v* to promise; **sich –,** *v* to make a slip of the tongue

**Versprechen,** fair-shprek-en, *nt* promise

**verspüren,** fair-shpEEr-en, *v* to feel; to perceive

**Verstand,** fair-shtahnt, *m* reason; understanding; mind; wit; intellect

**verständig,** fair-shten-dik, *adj* sensible, reasonable; prudent

**verständigen,** fair-shten-dig-en, *v* to advise; to inform; **sich –,** *v* to communicate; to agree on (sth)

**verständlich,** fair-shtent-lik, *adj* intelligible; understandable

**Verständnis,** fair-shtent-nis, *nt* comprehension; understanding

**verstärken,** fair-shtairk-en, *v* to strengthen

**Verstärker,** fair-shtairk-er, *m* amplifier

**Verstärkung,** fair-shtairk-oong, *f* strengthening; reinforcement; amplification

**verstauben,** fair-shtowb-en, *v* to get dusty

**verstauchen,** fair-shtowk-en, *v* to sprain

**Versteck,** fair-shteck, *nt* hiding-place; concealment

**verstecken,** fair-**shteck**-en, *v* to hide

**verstehen,** fair-**shtay**-en, *v* to understand

**versteigern,** fair-**shty**-gern, *v* to auction

**Versteigerung,** fair-**shty**-ger-oong, *f* auction

**verstellbar,** fair-**shtel**-bar, *adj* adjustable

**verstellen,** fair-**shtel**-en, *v* to shift; to block (way); **sich –,** *v* to dissemble, to disguise

**versteuern,** fair-**shtoy**-ern, *v* to tax

**verstimmen,** fair-**shtim**-en, *v* to put out of tune; *fam* to annoy

**verstohlen,** fair-**shtohl**-en, *adj* stealthy, furtive

**verstopfen,** fair-**shtop**-fen, *v* to stop up; to block

**Verstopfung,** fair-**shtop**-foong, *f* constipation; obstruction

**verstorben,** fair-**shtorb**-en, *adj* deceased; late

**Verstörtheit,** fair-**shtert**-hite, *f* bewilderment

**Verstoß,** fair-**shtohs**, *m* offence, breach

**verstoßen,** fair-**shtohs**-en, *v* to offend, to violate

**verstreichen,** fair-**shtry**-ken, *v* to elapse

**verstümmeln,** fair-**shtEEmm**-eln, *v* to mutilate

**verstummen,** fair-**shtoomm**-en, *v* to become

silent/dumb

**Versuch,** fair-**zook**, *m* attempt; try, trial; experiment

**versuchen,** fair-**zook**-en, *v* to try; to attempt; to tempt

**Versuchskaninchen,** fair-**zooks**-kahn-een-ken, *nt fig* guinea-pig

**Versuchung,** fair-**zook**-oong, *f* temptation

**versumpfen,** fair-**zoomp**-fen, *v* to become boggy; to go to pot

**versündigen (sich),** fair-**zEEnn**-dig-en (zik), *v* to sin; to trespass

**versüßen,** fair-**zEEs**-en, *v* to sweeten

**vertagen,** fair-**tahg**-en, *v* to postpone; to adjourn

**vertauschen,** fair-**towsh**-en, *v* to exchange; to mix up

**verteidigen,** fair-**ty**-dig-en, *v* to defend

**Verteidiger,** fair-**ty**-dig-er, *m* defender

**Verteidigung,** fair-**ty**-dig-oong, *f* defence

**verteilen,** fair-**ty**-len, *v* to distribute; to apportion

**verteuern,** fair-**toy**-ern, *v* to make dearer

**verteufelt,** fair-**toyf**-elt, *adj* devilish; damned, confounded

**vertiefen,** fair-**teef**-en, *v* to deepen; **sich –,** *v* to become engrossed

**vertilgen,** fair-**tilg**-en, *v* to eradicate; to destroy; to

eat up

**Vertilgung,** fair-**tilg**-oong, *f* extermination

**Vertrag,** fair-**trahk**, *m* agreement; contract; treaty

**vertragen,** fair-**trahg**-en, *v* to bear, to endure; **sich –,** *v* to get on (with sb); to go well together

**vertraglich,** fair-**trahk**-lik, *adj & adv* contractual(ly)

**verträglich,** fair-**traik**-lik, *adj* sociable; compatible; easily digestible

**vertrauen,** fair-**trow**-en, *v* to trust

**Vertrauen,** fair-**trow**-en, *nt* trust; confidence

**vertraulich,** fair-**trow**-lik, *adj* in confidence

**vertraut,** fair-**trowt**, *adj* familiar

**vertreiben,** fair-**try**-ben, *v* to dispel; to sell; to pass (time)

**Vertreibung,** fair-**try**-boong, *f* exile, expulsion

**vertreten,** fair-**trayt**-en, *v* to represent; to bar (way)

**Vertreter,** fair-**trayt**-er, *m* representative; salesman

**Vertretung,** fair-**trayt**-oong, *f* agency

**Vertrieb,** fair-**treep**, *m* sale; distribution department

**vertrocknen,** fair-**trock**-nen, *v* to dry up; to wither

**vertrösten,** fair-**trerst**-en, *v* to put off with promises

**vertun,** fair-**toon**, *v* to waste;

sich –, *v* to make a mistake

**vertuschen,** fair-**toosh**-en, *v* to hush up; to gloss over

**Vertuschung,** fair-**toosh**-oong, *f* cover-up

**verübeln,** fair-**EEb**-eln, *v* to take amiss; to blame for

**verüben,** fair-**EEb**-en, *v* to commit (crime)

**verunglücken,** fair-**oonn**-glEEck-en, *v* to come to grief; to have an accident

**verunreinigen,** fair-**oonn**-rine-ig-en, *v* to pollute; to soil

**verunstalten,** fair-**oonn**-shtahlt-en, *v* to deface

**verursachen,** fair-**oor**-zahk-en, *v* to cause

**verurteilen,** fair-**oor**-tile-en, *v* to condemn; to sentence

**Verurteilung,** fair-**oor**-tile-oong, *f* (passing of) sentence, verdict; condemnation

**vervielfachen,** fair-**feel**-fak-en, *v* to multiply

**vervielfältigen,** fair-**feel**-felt-ig-en, *v* to copy, to duplicate

**vervollkommnen,** fair-**fol**-kom-nen, *v* to perfect

**vervollständigen,** fair-**fol**-shten-dig-en, *v* to complete

**verwachsen,** fair-**vahcks**-en, *v* to heal up; to outgrow; to interlace; *adj* deformed

**verwahren,** fair-**vahr**-en, *v* to guard; to keep (safe)

**verwahrlosen,** fair-**vahr**-lohz-en, *v* to be uncared for

**Verwahrung,** fair-**vahr**-oong, *f* safe keeping

**verwaisen,** fair-**vy**-zen, *v* to become orphaned

**verwaist,** fer-**vy'st**, *adj* orphaned; abandoned, deserted

**verwalten,** fair-**vahlt**-en, *v* to administer, to manage; to govern

**Verwalter,** fair-**vahlt**-er, *m* administrator; trustee

**Verwaltung,** fair-**vahlt**-oong, *f* management; administration

**verwandeln,** fair-**vahnn**-deln, *v* to transform

**Verwandlung,** fair-**vahnd**-loong, *f* transformation

**verwandt,** fair-**vahnt**, *adj* related

**Verwandte(r),** fair-**vahnt**-e(r), *m & f,* relative, relation

**Verwandtschaft,** fair-**vahnt**-shahft, *f* relationship; relatives, relations

**verwarnen,** fair-**vahrn**-en, *v* to caution

**verwechseln,** fair-**vecks**-eln, *v* to mistake for

**Verwechslung,** fair-**vecks**-loong, *f* mistake; confusion

**verwegen,** fair-**vayg**-en, *adj* bold, rash; daring

**Verwegenheit,** fair-**vayg**-en-hite, *f* audacity

**verweigern,** fair-**vy**-gern, *v* to refuse

**Verweigerung,** fair-**vy**-ger-oong, *f* refusal, denial

**verweilen,** fair-**vy**-len, *v* to stay, to remain

**Verweis,** fair-**vice**, *m* reproof, reprimand; reference

**verweisen,** fair-**vy**-zen, *v* to reprimand; to refer

**verwelken,** fair-**velk**-en, *v* to wither, to fade

**verwenden,** fair-**vend**-en, *v* to use; to utilize

**Verwendung,** fair-**vend**-oong, *f* use

**verwerflich,** fair-**vairf**-lik, *adj* reprehensible

**verwerten,** fair-**vairt**-en, *v* to utilize

**verwesen,** fair-**vayz**-en, *v* to decay, to rot

**Verwesung,** fair-**vayz**-oong, *f* putrefaction

**verwickeln,** fair-**vick**-eln, *v* to entangle, to involve

**verwickelt,** fair-**vick**-elt, *adj* complicated, complex

**verwildern,** fair-**vil**-dern, *v* to grow wild; to run to seed

**verwirken,** fair-**veerk**-en, *v* to forfeit

**verwirklichen,** fair-**veerk**-lik-en, *v* to realize

**verwirren,** fair-**veerr**-en, *v* to confuse; to (en)tangle

**Verwirrung,** fair-**veerr**-oong, *f* confusion

**verwischen,** fair-**vish**-en, *v*

to become blurred, to
obscure

**verwittern,** fair-**vit**-ern, v to
weather

**verwöhnen,** fair-**vern**-en, v
to pamper; to spoil

**verworren,** fair-**vorr**-en, adj
confused

**verwundbar,** fair-**voont**-bar,
adj vulnerable

**verwunden,** fair-**voonn**-den,
v to wound, to injure

**verwundern,** fair-**voonn**-
dern, v to surprise

**Verwunderung,** fair-**voonn**-
der-oong, f amazement,
surprise, astonishment

**Verwundung,** fair-**voond**-
oong, f wound, injury

**verwünschen,** fair-**vEEnn**-
shen, v to curse; to
enchant

**verwüsten,** fair-**vEEst**-en, v
to devastate

**Verwüstung,** fair-**vEEst**-
oong, f devastation

**verzagen,** fair-**tsahg**-en, v to
despair; to lose courage

**verzaubern,** fair-**tsowb**-ern,
v to bewitch

**verzehren,** fair-**tsayr**-en, v to
devour; to absorb, to
consume

**verzeichnen,** fair-**tsy'k**-nen,
v to record

**Verzeichnis,** fair-**tsy'k**-nis,
nt schedule, list, record,
index

**verzeihen,** fair-**tsy**-en, v to
pardon

**verzeihlich,** fair-**tsy**-lik, adj

pardonable

**Verzeihung,** fair-**tsy**-oong, f
pardon, forgiveness; interj
I'm sorry

**verzerrt,** fair-**tsairt**, adj
distorted

**Verzicht,** fair-**tsikt**, m
resignation; renunciation

**verzichten,** fair-**tsikt**-en, v to
renounce

**verziehen,** fair-**tsee**-en, v to
distort; to spoil (children)

**verzieren,** fair-**tseer**-en, v to
decorate

**Verzierung,** fair-**tseer**-oong,
f decoration,
embellishment

**verzinken,** fair-**tsing**-ken, v
to galvanize

**verzinsen,** fair-**tsin**-zen, v to
pay interest on

**verzögern,** fair-**tserg**-ern, v
to retard; to delay

**verzollen,** fair-**tsol**-en, v to
pay duty on

**verzuckern,** fair-**tsoock**-ern,
v to coat with sugar; to
sweeten (also fig)

**Verzug,** fair-**tsook**, m delay

**verzweifeln,** fair-**tsvy**-feln, v
to despair

**Verzweiflung,** fair-**tsvy**-
floong, f despair

**Vetter,** fet-er, m (male)
cousin

**vgl.,** abbr vergleiche, cf.

**Video,** vee-day-oh, nt video;
**–gerät,** nt video recorder

**Vieh,** fee, nt cattle; live
stock; **–zucht,** f cattle-
breeding

**viel,** feel, adj much; **–e,** feel-
e, adj many

**vielerlei,** feel-er-ly, adj many
kinds of

**vielfach,** feel-fahk, adj
multiple; adv often

**Vielfalt,** feel-fahlt, f variety

**Vielfraß,** feel-frahs, m
glutton

**vielleicht,** feel-ly'kt, adv
perhaps, maybe

**vielmals,** feel-mahls, adv
often, frequently

**vielmehr,** feel-mair, adv
rather; on the contrary

**vielseitig,** feel-zy-tik, adj
many-sided; versatile

**vier,** feer, num four

**Viereck,** feer-eck, nt square,
quadrangle

**viereckig,** feer-eck-ik, adj
square, four-cornered

**Vierfüßler,** feer-fEES-ler, m
quadruped

**viermal,** feer-mahl, adv four
times

**vierte(r),** feert-e(r), adj
fourth

**Viertel,** feert-el, nt quarter;
fourth

**Vierteljahr,** feert-el-yahr, nt
quarter (of a year)

**vierteljährlich,** feert-el-yair-
lik, adj quarterly

**Viertelstunde,** feert-el-
shtoonn-de, f quarter of
an hour

**vierzehn,** feer-tsain, num
fourteen

**vierzig,** feer-tsik, num forty

**Villa,** vil-ah, f villa

**Violine,** vee-oh-**leen**-*e*, *f* violin

**Virus,** vee-rooss, *nt* virus

**Visitenkarte,** vee-zeet-en-kart-*e*, *f* visiting-card

**Visum,** vee-zoomm, *nt* visa

**Vitamin,** vee-tah-meen, *nt* vitamin

**Vogel,** fohg-*el*, *m* bird; fowl; **–käfig,** *m* bird-cage; **–scheuche,** *f* scarecrow

**Vokabel,** voh-**kahb**-*el*, *f* word (usually in a foreign language); **–n,** *pl* vocabulary

**Vokal,** voh-**kahl**, *m* vowel

**Volk,** folk, *nt* people; nation; race; **–sabstimmung,** *f* referendum; **–sfest,** *nt* fair; **–slied,** *nt* folk-song

**volkstümlich,** folks-tEEm-lik, *adj* popular

**Volksvertreter,** folks-fair-trayt-*er*, *m* member of parliament

**Volkswirtschaft,** folks-veert-shahft, *f* political economy, economics

**voll,** fol, *adj* full; filled; complete; **–auf,** *adv* abundantly, in plenty

**Vollbart,** foll-bart, *m* (full) beard, whiskers

**Vollblut,** foll-bloot, *nt* thoroughbred

**vollbringen,** foll-bring-*en*, *v* to achieve; to carry out

**vollenden,** foll-end-*en*, *v* to complete; to finish

**vollendet,** foll-end-*et*, *adj* complete; perfect

**vollends,** foll-ends, *adv* entirely, wholly

**Vollendung,** foll-end-oong, *f* completion; perfection

**Völlerei,** ferll-*e*-ry, *f* gluttony

**Vollgas,** foll-gahs, *nt* full throttle; **mit –,** at full tilt

**völlig,** ferll-ik, *adj* complete; *adv* wholly, entirely

**volljährig,** foll-yayr-ik, *adj* of age

**vollkommen,** foll-kom-*en*, *adj* perfect; thorough; absolute

**Vollkommenheit,** foll-kom-en-hite, *f* perfection

**Vollkorn,** foll-korn, *nt* wholemeal; **–brot,** *nt* wholemeal bread

**vollmachen,** foll-mahk-*en*, *v* to fill

**Vollmacht,** foll-mahkt, *f* power of attorney

**Vollmilch,** foll-milk, *f* full-cream milk

**Vollmond,** foll-mohnt, *m* full moon

**Vollpension,** foll-pengs-yohn, *f* full-board

**vollständig,** foll-shten-dik, *adj* complete; *adv* altogether

**vollstrecken,** foll-shtreck-*en*, *v* to execute

**Vollwertkost,** foll-vairt-kost, *f* wholefood

**vollzählig,** foll-tsayl-ik, *adj* complete (numerically)

**vollziehen,** foll-tsee-*en*, *v* to complete; to execute

**Volontär,** voll-on-tair, *m* volunteer; trainee

**vom,** fom, = **von dem,** of the, from the

**von,** fon, *prep* of; from; by

**vor,** for, *prep* before, in front of; previous; ago; because of

**Vorabend,** for-ahb-ent, *m* evening before

**vorahnen,** for-ahn-en, *v* to have a premonition

**voran,** for-ahnn, *adv* at the/in front; **–kommen,** *v* to make progress

**voraus,** for-ows, *adv* before, in advance

**vorausahnen,** for-ows-ahn-en, *v* to have a premonition

**vorausgehen,** for-ows-gay-en, *v* to lead the way; to precede

**voraussagen,** for-ows-zahg-en, *v* to predict

**voraussetzen,** for-ows-zet-sen, *v* to presume

**Voraussetzung,** for-ows-zet-soong, *f* assumption; prerequisite

**voraussichtlich,** for-ows-zikt-lik, *adj* prospective; *adv* probably

**Vorbedacht,** for-be-dahkt, *m* forethought

**Vorbedingung,** for-be-ding-oong, *f* precondition

**Vorbehalt,** for-be-hahlt, *m* reservation

**vorbei,** for-by, *adv* by, past;

over

**vorbereiten, for**-be-ry-ten, *v* to prepare

**vorbestellen, for**-be-shtel-en, *v* to book (in advance)

**vorbeugen, for**-boyg-en, *v* to bend forward; to take precaution

**Vorbild, for**-bilt, *nt* model, pattern; prototype

**vorbildlich, for**-bilt-lik, *adj* pattern, model; representative

**vordem,** for-**daym**, *adv* formerly

**vordere(r), for**-der-e(r), *adj* (in) front

**Vorderfuß, ford**-er-foos, *m* forefoot

**Vordergrund, ford**-er-groont, *m* foreground

**Vorderrad, ford**-er-raht, *nt* front wheel

**vordrängen, for**-dreng-en, *v* to press forward

**vordringen, for**-dring-en, *v* to push forward, to advance

**voreilig, for**-ile-ik, *adj* rash, overhasty

**voreingenommen, for**-ine-ge-nomm-en, *adj* prepossessed

**vorenthalten, for**-ent-hahlt-en, *v* to withhold

**vorerst, for**-airst, *adv* for the present; first of all

**Vorfahr(e), for**-fahr(-e), *m* ancestor

**Vorfahrt, for**-fart, *f* right of way

**Vorfall, for**-fahll, *m* incident, occurrence

**vorfallen, for**-fahll-en, *v* to happen, to occur

**vorfinden, for**-fin-den, *v* to find; to discover

**Vorfreude, for**-froy-de, *f* anticipation

**vorführen, for**-fEEr-en, *v* to demonstrate, to show

**Vorgang, for**-gahng, *m* process; proceedings; file

**Vorgänger, for**-geng-er, *m* predecessor

**vorgehen, for**-gay-en, *v* to be fast (clock); to proceed; to advance

**vorgestern, for**-gest-ern, *adv* the day before yesterday

**vorhaben, for**-hahb-en, *v* to intend; to have on

**vorhanden, for**-hahnn-den, *adj* at hand; present; existing

**Vorhang, for**-hahng, *m* curtain

**vorher, for**-hair, *adv* previously

**vorhersagen,** for-hair-zahg-en, *v* to predict

**vorhersehen, for**-hair-zay-en, *v* to foresee

**vorhin,** for-**hin**, *adv* just now; recently

**vorig(e/r), for**-ik (**for**-ig-e/er), *adj* last, previous; past

**Vorkehrung, for**-kair-oong, *f* provision; precautionary measure

**Vorkenntnis, for**-kent-niss, *f* previous knowledge

**vorkommen, for**-kom-en, *v* to occur, to happen

**vorläufig, for**-loyf-ik, *adj* provisional; preliminary

**vorlaut, for**-lowt, *adj* cheeky, impertinent

**vorlegen, for**-layg-en, *v* to lay before; to submit

**vorlesen, for**-layz-en, *v* to read aloud

**Vorlesung, for**-layz-oong, *f* lecture, reading

**vorletzt(e/r), for**-letst(-e/er), *adj* last but one

**Vorliebe, for**-leeb-e, *f* preference

**vormals, for**-mahls, *adv* formerly

**vormerken, for**-mairk-en, *v* to make a note; to mark

**Vormittag, for**-mit-ahg, *m* morning

**vormittags, for**-mit-ahgs, *adv* in the morning; a.m.

**Vormund, for**-moont, *m* guardian

**vorn(e), forn**(-e), *adv* in front

**Vorname, for**-nahm-e, *m* first/Christian name

**vornehm, for**-naym, *adj* elegant; aristocratic; distinguished

**vornehmen, for**-naym-en, *v* to do, to carry out; **sich –,** *v* to resolve/intend (to do sth)

**Vorort, for**-ort, *m* suburb(s)

**Vorposten, for**-post-en, *m* outpost

**Vorrat, for**-raht, *m* stock; store; **–skammer,** *f* larder, store cupboard

**Vorrichtung, for**-rik-toong, *f* device, arrangement

**vorrücken, for**-rEEck-en, *v* to advance

**Vorsaison, for**-zay-zong, *f* early season

**Vorsatz, for**-zahts, *m* resolution; design; purpose

**Vorschau, for**-show, *f* preview; trailer

**Vorschein, for**-shine, *m* appearance

**Vorschlag, for**-shlahk, *m* proposal

**vorschlagen, for**-shlahg-en, *v* to propose; to suggest

**vorschreiben, for**-shry-ben, *v* to prescribe; to stipulate

**Vorschrift, for**-shrift, *f* order; prescription

**Vorschule, for**-shool-*e,* *f* preparatory school

**Vorschuß, for**-shoos, *m* advance (of money)

**vorschützen, for**-shEEtt-sen, *v* to pretend

**vorsehen, for**-zay-en, *v* to provide for; **sich –,** *v* to be careful

**Vorsehung, for**-zay-oong, *f* (divine) providence

**vorsetzen, for**-zet-sen, *v* to place before; to move forward

**Vorsicht, for**-zikt, *f* foresight; care; caution

**vorsichtig, for**-zik-tik, *adj* careful, cautious

**Vorsichtsmaßregel, for**-zikts-mahs-rayg-*el,* *f* measure of precaution

**Vorsitzende(r), for**-zits-end-*e*(r), *m & f,* president, chair(person)

**Vorsorge, for**-zorg-*e,* *f* provision

**vorsorgen, for**-zorg-en, *v* to provide, to make provisions

**Vorspeise, for**-shpy-ze, *f* hors d'oeuvre, starter

**vorspiegeln, for**-shpeeg-eln, *v* to delude, to deceive

**Vorspiel, for**-shpeel, *nt* prelude; overture

**vorsprechen, for**-shprek-en, *v* to call on someone; to recite

**Vorsprung, for**-shproong, *m* projection; start, lead; advantage

**Vorstadt, for**-shtahtt, *f* suburb

**Vorstand, for**-shtahnt, *m* committee, board; director

**vorstehen, for**-shtay-en, *v* to superintend; to project

**Vorsteher, for**-shtay-er, *m* superintendent, chief

**vorstellen, for**-shtel-en, *v* to introduce; to represent; to personify; **sich –,** *v* to imagine, to visualize; to go for a (job) interview

**Vorstellung, for**-shtel-oong, *f* introduction; imagination; performance, show; **–sgespräch,** *nt* (job)

interview

**Vorstoß, for**-shtohs, *m* push forward; advance, attack

**vorstoßen, for**-shtohs-en, *v* to project; to push forward

**Vorstrafe, for**-shtrah-fe, *f* previous conviction

**vorstrecken, for**-shtreck-en, *v* to stretch forward; to advance (money)

**Vorteil, for**-tile, *m* advantage, gain

**vorteilhaft, for**-tile-hahft, *adj* advantageous

**Vortrag, for**-trahk, *m* lecture; performance; recital

**vortragen, for**-trahg-en, *v* to carry forward; to recite; to express

**vortrefflich, for**-tref-lik, *adj* excellent; superior

**vortreten, for**-trayt-en, *v* to step forward

**vorüber, for**-EEb-er, *adv* past, over, gone; **–gehen,** *v* to go past; to pass

**Vorurteil, for**-oohr-tile, *nt* prejudice

**Vorverkauf, for**-fair-kowf, *m* advance sale

**Vorwahl, for**-vahl, *f* area code

**Vorwand, for**-vahnt, *m* pretext, subterfuge

**vorwärts, for**-vairts, *adv* forward(s); onward(s)

**vorwerfen, for**-vairf-en, *v* to throw in front of; to reproach

**vorwiegend, for**-veeg-ent,

*adj* predominant

**Vorwort, for**-vort, *nt*
preface

**Vorwurf, for**-voorf, *m*
reproach

**vorzeigen, for**-tsy-gen, *v* to
produce, to show; to
present

**vorzeitig, for**-tsy-tik, *adj*
premature

**vorziehen, for**-tsee-en, *v* to
draw forth; to prefer

**Vorzimmer, for**-tsim-*er*, *nt*
anteroom; reception
(area)

**Vorzug, for**-tsook, *m*
preference; privilege;
precedence

**vorzüglich, for**-**tsEEk**-lik, *adj*
excellent; choice

**Waage,** vahg-*e*, *f* scales

**waagrecht,** vahk-rekt, *adj* horizontal

**Waagschale,** vahk-shahl-*e*, *f* scale (of balance)

**Wabe,** vahb-*e*, *f* honeycomb

**wach,** vah*k*, *adj* awake; alive; brisk

**Wache,** vahk-*e*, *f* guard (-house); watch; police-station

**wachen,** vahk-*en*, *v* to watch; to be awake

**Wachs,** vah*cks*, *nt* wax

**wachsam,** vahk-zahm, *adj* watchful, vigilant

**wachsen,** vah*cks*-*en*, *v* to grow; to wax

**Wachstuch,** vah*cks*-took, *nt* American (wax) cloth

**Wachstum,** vah*cks*-toom, *nt* growth

**Wachtel,** vahk-tel, *f* quail (bird)

**Wächter,** vek-ter, *m* watchman; guard(ian)

**Wachtmeister,** vahkt-my-ster, *m* sergeant-major; police sergeant

**wack(e)lig,** vahck(-*e*)-lik, *adj* rickety; shaky

**wackeln,** vahck-*eln*, *v* to shake; to rock; to stagger

**wacker,** vahck-er, *adj* good, decent, honest

**Wade,** vahd-*e*, *f* calf (of leg)

**Waffe,** vahff-*e*, *f* weapon, arm

**Waffel,** vahff-el, *f* wafer; waffle

**Waffenstillstand,** vahff-en-shtil-shtahnt, *m* armistice; cease-fire

**wagen,** vahg-*en*, *v* to dare, to venture; to stake

**Wagen,** vahg-*en*, *m* carriage; car; vehicle

**wägen,** vayg-*en*, *v* to weigh (up)

**Waggon,** vahgg-ong, *m* railway-truck; carriage

**Wagnis,** vahg-nis, *nt* risk, hazard; venture

**Wahl,** vahl, *f* choice, selection; election

**wählen,** vayl-*en*, *v* to choose, to select; to elect

**Wähler,** vayl-er, *m* elector

**wählerisch,** vayl-er-ish, *adj* fastidious

**Wahlkampf,** vahl-kahmp'f, *m* election campaign

**Wahlkreis,** vahl-krise, *m* constituency

**Wahlrecht,** vahl-rekt, *nt* franchise; suffrage

**Wahlstimme,** vahl-shtim-*e*, *f* vote

**Wahn,** vahn, *m* delusion, illusion; mania

**wähnen,** vayn-*en*, *v* to fancy; to think wrongly

**Wahnsinn,** vahn-zin, *m* madness; insanity; far out!

**wahnsinnig,** vahn-zin-ik, *adj* mad, insane; *adj fam* incredibly

**wahr,** vahr, *adj* true; genuine; proper

**wahren,** vahr-*en*, *v* to preserve (from)

**währen,** vayr-*en*, *v* to last; to hold out

**während,** vayr-ent, *prep* during; *conj* while

**wahrhaftig,** vahr-hahft-ik,

*adj* true; *interj* really, actually

**Wahrheit, vahr**-hite, *f* truth; reality

**wahrlich, vahr**-lik, *adv* really; indeed

**wahrnehmen, vahr**-naym-en, *v* to perceive

**wahrsagen, vahr**-zahg-en, *v* to predict; to tell fortunes

**Wahrsager, vahr**-zahg-er, *m* fortune-teller

**wahrscheinlich, vahr**-**shine**-lik, *adj* probable; *adv* probably

**Währung, vayr**-oong, *f* currency; sterling

**Waise, vy**-ze, *f* orphan

**Wal, vahll, *m* whale

**Wald, vahlt, *m* wood, forest; –**brand, *m* forest fire

**Walfisch, vahll**-fish, *m* whale

**Waliser, vah**-**lee**-zer, *m* Welshman; –**in, *f* Welshwoman

**walisisch, vah**-**lee**-zish, *adj* Welsh

**Wall, vahll, *m* rampart(s); dam

**Wallach, vahll**-ahk, *m* gelding

**wallen, vahll**-en, *v* to flow; to bubble up

**Wallfahrt, vahll**-fahrt, *f* pilgrimage

**Walnuß, vahll**-nooss, *f* walnut

**Walroß, vahll**-ross, *nt* walrus

**walten, vahlt**-en, *v* to rule;

to act

**Walze, vahlt**-se, *f* roller; cylinder; barrel

**walzen, vahlt**-sen, *v* to roll (flat)

**wälzen, velt**-sen, *v* to turn about; to roll over

**Walzer, vahlt**-ser, *m* waltz

**Wand, vahnt, *f* wall; partition; side; panel

**Wandel, vahnn**-del, *m* change

**wandeln, vahnn**-deln, *v* to wander, to walk; to change

**Wanderer, vahnn**-de-rer, *m* traveller (on foot)

**Wanderlust, vahnn**-der-loost, *f* desire to travel

**wandern, vahnn**-dern, *v* to wander; to go walking

**Wanderschaft, vahnn**-der-shahft, *f* journey, travelling

**Wandervogel, vahnn**-der-fohg-el, *m* bird of passage; *fig* hiker

**Wanderweg, vahnn**-der-vayg, *m* footpath, trail

**Wanduhr, vahnt**-oor, *f* wall clock

**Wange, vahng**-e, *f* cheek

**wanken, vahng**-ken, *v* to flinch; to budge

**wann, vahnn, *adv* when

**Wanne, vahnn**-e, *f* bath (-tub)

**Wanze, vahnt**-se, *f* bug

**Wappen, vahpp**-en, *nt* coat-of-arms, crest

**Ware, vahr**-e, *f* good(s),

ware, commodity; –**nhaus,** *nt* warehouse, department-store; –**nzeichen,** *nt* trademark

**warm, varm, *adj* warm

**Wärme, vairm**-e, *f* warmth; heat

**wärmen, vairm**-en, *v* to warm; to heat

**Wärmflasche, vairm**-flahsh-e, *f* hot water bottle

**warnen, varn**-en, *v* to warn; to caution

**Warnung, varn**-oong, *f* warning; caution

**Warschau, var**-show, *nt* Warsaw

**warten, vart**-en, *v* to wait; to stay

**Wärter, vairt**-er, *m* attendant

**Wartesaal, vart**-e-zahl, *m* waiting-room

**warum, vah**-**roomm**, *adv* why

**Warze, vart**-se, *f* wart; nipple

**was, vahss, *pron* what; (that) which, that

**Waschbecken, vahsh**-beck-en, *nt* wash-basin

**Wäsche, vesh**-e, *f* wash(ing); linen, clothes

**waschecht, vahsh**-ekt, *adj* (colour-)fast; *fig* genuine

**waschen, vahsh**-en, *v* to wash

**Wäscherei, vesh**-e-ry, *f* laundry

**Waschküche, vahsh**-kEEk-e, *f* laundry room

**Waschlappen, vahsh**-lahpp-en, *m* (face-) flannel

**Waschmaschine, vahsh**-mah-shee-ne, *f* washing machine

**Waschmittel, vahsh**-mit-el, *nt* detergent

**Waschpulver, vahsh**-poollfer, *nt* washing powder

**Waschsalon, vahsh**-sahlong, *m* launderette

**Wasser, vahss**-er, *nt* water

**wasserdicht, vahss**-er-dikt, *adj* water-tight, waterproof

**Wasserfall, vahss**-er-fahll, *m* waterfall

**Wasserhahn, vahss**-er-hahn, *m* water-tap

**wässerig, vess**-er-ik, *adj* watery

**Wasserkessel, vahss**-er-kessel, *m* kettle; boiler

**Wasserleitung, vahss**-er-lytoong, *f* water-supply

**wässern, vess**-ern, *v* to water

**wasserscheu, vahss**-er-shoy, *adj* afraid of water

**Wassersport, vahss**-ershport, *m* watersports

**Wasserstoff, vahss**-er-shtof, *m* hydrogen

**Wassersucht, vahss**-erzookt, *f* dropsy

**wäßrig, vess**-rik, *adj* watery

**waten, vaht**-en, *v* to wade

**watscheln, vaht**-sheln, *v* to waddle

**Watt, vahtt**, *nt* mud flats; watt

**Watte, vahtt**-e, *f* cottonwool

**weben, vayb**-en, *v* to weave

**Weber, vayb**-er, *m* weaver

**Weberei, vay**-be-ry, *f* weaving (mill); woven article

**Webstuhl, vayp**-shtool, *m* loom

**Wechsel, vecks**-el, *m* change; fluctuation; *fm* bill of exchange; **–geld**, (*nt*) (small) change; **–jahre**, *pl* menopause; **–kurs**, *m* exchange rate

**wechseln, vecks**-eln, *v* to change; to interchange

**wecken, veck**-en, *v* to awaken, to rouse

**Wecker, veck**-er, *m* alarm-clock

**wedeln, vayd**-eln, *v* to wag (tail); to fan

**weder, vayd**-er, *conj* neither; **– ... noch**, neither ... nor

**Weg, vayk**, *m* way, path, track, road, street

**weg, veck**, *adv* away; gone; (far) off

**wegbegeben (sich), veck**-be-gayb-en (zik), *v* to go away, to drift away

**wegbleiben, veck**-bly-ben, *v* to remain/stay away

**wegblicken, veck**-blick-en, *v* to look away

**wegbringen, veck**-bring-en, *v* to take away

**wegen, vayg**-en, *prep* on account of, because of

**wegfahren, veck**-fahr-en, *v* to drive away; to depart

**weggehen, veck**-gay-en, *v* to go away, to leave

**wegjagen, veck**-yahg-en, *v* to chase/drive away

**weglassen, veck**-lahss-en, *v* to leave out; to allow someone to go

**weglaufen, veck**-lowf-en, *v* to run away

**wegmüssen, veck**-mEEss-en, *v* to be obliged to leave

**wegnehmen, veck**-naym-en, *v* to take away

**wegräumen, veck**-roym-en, *v* to clear away

**wegreißen, veck**-ry-sen, *v* to tear away/off

**wegrennen, veck**-ren-en, *v* to run away

**wegschicken, veck**-shick-en, *v* to send away

**wegschleppen, veck**-shlep-en, *v* to drag away

**wegschließen, veck**-shlees-en, *v* to lock away

**wegsehen, veck**-zay-en, *v* to look away

**wegsenden, veck**-zend-en, *v* to send off/away

**wegsetzen, veck**-zet-sen, *v* to move/put aside/away

**wegstecken, veck**-shteck-en, *v* to hide away; *fig* to cope

**wegstellen, veck**-shtel-en, *v* to put away

**wegstürzen, veck**-shtEErt-sen, *v* to dash/rush away

**wegtragen, veck**-trahg-en, *v*

to carry off/away

**wegtreten,** veck-trayt-*en*, *v* to step aside; to break ranks

**wegtun,** veck-toon, *v* to put away; to hide

**Wegweiser,** vayg-vy-z*er*, *m* sign-post

**wegwerfen,** veck-vairf-*en*, *v* to throw away

**Wegwerfwindel,** veck-vairf-vin-del, *f* disposable nappy

**wegwollen,** veck-vol-*en*, *v* to want to get away

**wegziehen,** veck-tsee-*en*, *v* to drag away; to move away

**weh,** vay, *adj* painful, sore; **–tun,** *v* to hurt

**Weh,** vay, *nt* pain, woe, pang; **–en,** *pl* labour pains

**weh(e),** vay(-*e*), *interj* alas! don't you dare!

**wehen,** vay-*en*, *v* to waft; to blow; to flutter

**Wehgeschrei,** vay-*ge*-shry, *nt* lamentation

**wehklagen,** vay-klahg-*en*, *v* to wail, to lament

**Wehmut,** vay-moot, *f* melancholy; sadness

**wehmütig,** vay-mEEt-ik, *adj* doleful

**Wehr,** vayr, *f* resistance, defence; guard, troop(s); *nt* weir; **–dienst,** *m* military service

**wehren (sich),** vay-ren, (zik), *v* to resist, to defend o.s.

**wehrlos,** vayr-lohs, *adj*

defenceless

**Wehrpflicht,** vayr-p'flikt, *f* compulsory military service

**Weib,** vipe, *nt* woman, female; wife; **–chen,** *nt* female animal

**weiblich,** vipe-lik, *adj* feminine

**weich,** vy'k, *adj* soft; mild, delicate

**Weiche,** vy-ke, *f* shunt(ing); switch

**weichen,** vy-ken, *v* to soften; to yield; to withdraw

**weichherzig,** vy'k-hairt-sik, *adj* soft-hearted

**weichlich,** vy'k-lik, *adj* flabby; effeminate

**Weide,** vy-de, *f* pasture (-land); willow(-tree)

**weiden,** vy-den, *v* to pasture, to graze

**weigern(sich),** vy-gern (zik), *v* to refuse, to decline

**Weigerung,** vy-ge-roong, *f* refusal

**Weihe,** vy-*e*, *f* dedication, ordination; inauguration

**weihen,** vy-*en*, *v* to consecrate, to ordain

**Weiher,** vy-*er*, *m* fish-pond

**Weihnacht(en),** vy-nahkt (-en), *f* (nt), Christmas; **–sabend,** *m* Christmas Eve; **–sbaum,** *m* Christmas-tree; **–sfest,** *nt* Christmas celebration(s); **–skind,** *nt* child Jesus;

**–lied,** *nt* Christmas carol; **–smann,** *m* Santa Claus

**Weihrauch,** vy-rowk, *m* incense

**weil,** vile, *conj* because; since, as

**Weile,** vile-*e*, *f* while; short time

**weilen,** vile-*en*, *v* to abide; to stay; to linger

**Wein,** vine, *m* wine; vine; creeper; **–bau,** *m* cultivation of grapes; **–berg,** *m* vineyard

**weinen,** vine-*en*, *v* to weep, to cry

**weinerlich,** vine-*er*-lik, *adj* whining, whimpering

**Weinfaß,** vine-fahss, *nt* wine-cask

**Weinkarte,** vine-kart-*e*, *f* wine-list

**Weinkelter,** vine-kelt-*er*, *f* wine-press

**Weinkrampf,** vine-krahmpf, *m* fit of hysterical weeping

**Weinlese,** vine-lay-ze, *f* vintage

**Weinrebe,** vine-rayb-*e*, *f* (grape)vine

**Weintraube,** vine-trow-be, *f* (bunch of) grape(s)

**weise,** vy-ze, *adj* wise, prudent; shrewd

**Weise,** vy-ze, *f* manner, way; *mus* tune; *m* wise man, sage

**weisen,** vy-zen, *v* to point, to show

**Weisheit,** vice-hite, *f* wisdom, prudence

**weismachen**, vice-mahk-en, v jdm etw –, to make sb believe sth

**weiß**, vice, adj white

**weissagen**, vice-zahg-en, v to prophesy; to predict

**Weißbier**, vice-beer, nt pale ale

**Weißbrot**, vice-broht, nt white bread

**Weiße(r)**, vice-e(r), m & f, white (wo)man

**Weißkohl**, vice-kohl, m (white) cabbage

**Weisung**, vy-zoong, f instruction(s); direction

**weit**, vite, adj distant; wide; extensive; broad

**Weite**, vite-e, f width, breadth; spaciousness; distance

**weiten**, vite-en, v to widen; to stretch

**weiter**, vite-er, adj wider; more distant; adv farther, further; –gehen, v to walk/go on; –hin, adv further/farther on

**weitgreifend**, vite-gry-fent, adj far-reaching

**weither**, vite-hair, adv from afar

**weitläufig**, vite-loyf-ik, adj extensive; spacious, rambling; long drawn-out; adv at great length

**weitsichtig**, vite-zik-tik, adj far-sighted; far-seeing

**Weizen**, vite-sen, m wheat; –mehl, nt wheat flour

**welche(r/s)**, velk-e(r/s), pron who, which, what; some, any

**welk**, velk, adj faded, withered; wrinkled

**Wellblech**, vell-blek, nt corrugated iron

**Welle**, vell-e, f wave; billow; shaft; –nlänge, f wavelength

**wellig**, vell-ik, adj wavy

**Welt**, velt, f world; –all, nt universe

**weltberühmt**, velt-be-rEEmt, adj world-famous

**welterfahren**, velt-air-fahren, adj worldly wise

**Weltgeschichte**, velt-geshik-te, f world history

**weltlich**, velt-lik, adj worldly; temporal

**Weltmacht**, velt-mahkt, f world-power

**Weltstadt**, velt-shtahtt, f metropolis

**weltweit**, velt-vite, adj worldwide

**wem**, vaim, pron (dative m & nt) to whom, whom

**wen**, vain, pron (accusative m) whom

**Wendeltreppe**, ven-del-trep-e, f winding staircase

**wenden**, vend-en, v to turn; sich – an, to apply to, to turn to

**Wendepunkt**, vend-e-poonkt, m turning point

**Wendung**, vend-oong, f turn(ing); crisis; phrasing

**wenig**, vayn-ik, adj little; –e, few; –er, less; fewer

**wenigstens**, vayn-ig-stens, adv at least

**wenn**, ven, conj if, when

**wer**, vair, pron who

**Werbegeschenk**, vairb-e-geshenk, nt freebee

**werben**, vairb-en, v to woo; to recruit; to advertise

**Werbung**, vairb-oong, f advertising; promotion; publicity

**werden**, vaird-en, v to become; shall, will (future)

**werfen**, vairf-en, v to throw, to fling, to hurl

**Werft**, vairft, f shipyard; hangar

**Werk**, vairk, nt work; labour; enterprise; –statt, f workshop; –tag, m weekday; –zeug, nt tool, instrument

**wert**, vairt, adj worth

**Wert**, vairt, m value, worth; –sachen, pl valuables

**wertvoll**, vairt-fol, adj valuable; precious

**Wesen**, vayz-en, nt being; existence; condition; essence

**wesentlich**, vayz-ent-lik, adj essential

**weshalb**, ves-halp, adv why

**Wespe**, vesp-e, f wasp

**wessen**, ves-en, pron whose

**West-**, vest, pref West, western

**Weste**, vest-e, f waistcoat

**Westen**, vest-en, m West

**westlich**, vest-lik, adj

west(ern), westerly

**weswegen,** ves-vayg-en, *adv* why

**Wettbewerb,** vet-be-vairp, *m* competition

**Wette,** vet-e, *f* wager, bet

**Wetteifer,** vet-ife-er, *m* emulation

**wetten,** vet-en, *v* to bet, to wager

**Wetter,** vet-er, *nt* weather; **–bericht,** *m* weather report; **–karte,** *f* weather chart; **–leuchten,** *nt* sheet-lightning; **–vorhersage,** *f* weather forecast

**Wettfahrt,** vet-fahrt, *f* race (boat, cycle etc.)

**Wettkampf,** vet-kahmp'f, *m* contest

**Wettlauf,** vet-lowf, *m* (running) race

**Wettrennen,** vet-ren-en, *nt* (horse)race

**Wettstreit,** vet-shtrite, *m* competition; emulation; match

**wetzen,** vet-sen, *v* to whet, to sharpen

**Wicht,** vikt, *m* goblin; *fam* titch, little devil

**wichtig,** vik-tik, *adj* important, weighty

**Wichtigkeit,** vik-tik-kite, *f* importance

**wickeln,** vick-eln, *v* to wind; to coil; to reel

**Wickelraum,** vick-el-rowm, *m* (nappy) changing room

**wider,** veed-er, *prep* against, contrary to

**widerfahren** veed-er-fahr-en, *v* to occur, to happen

**Widerhall,** veed-er-hahll, *m* echo, reverberation

**widerlegen,** veed-er-layg-en, *v* to refute, to disprove

**widerlich,** veed-er-lich, *adj* repulsive; sickly

**Widerrede,** veed-er-rayd-e, *f* contradiction, objection

**widerrufen,** veed-er-roof-en, *v* to contradict; to retract

**Widerschein,** veed-er-shine, *m* reflexion

**widersetzen (sich),** veed-er-zets-en (zik), *v* to resist

**widersinnig,** veed-er-zin-ik, *adj* contradictory; paradoxical

**widerspenstig,** veed-er-shpenst-ik, *adj* obstinate

**widerspiegeln,** veed-er-shpeeg-eln, *v* to reflect

**widersprechen,** veed-er-shprek-en, *v* to contradict

**Widerspruch,** veed-er-shprook, *m* contradiction; opposition

**Widerstand,** veed-er-shtahnt, *m* resistance

**widerstehen,** veed-er-shtay-en, *v* to resist

**widerwärtig,** veed-er-vairt-ik, *adj* disgusting; adverse

**Widerwille(n),** veed-er-vil-e(n), *m* repugnance; aversion

**widmen,** vit-men, *v* to dedicate

**widrig,** veed-rik, *adj* contrary, adverse;

obnoxious

**wie,** vee, *adv* how; *conj* (such) as; like

**wieder,** veed-er, *adv* again, once more, afresh

**wiederaufbereiten,** veed-er-owf-be-rite-en, *v* to recycle

**wiederbekommen,** veed-er-be-kom-en, *v* to get back

**wiederbringen,** veed-er-bring-en, *v* to bring back

**wiedererkennen,** veed-er-air-ken-en, *v* to recognize

**wiederfinden,** veed-er-fin-den, *v* to find again; to recover

**wiedergeben,** veed-er-gayb-en, *v* to give back; to repeat

**wiederherstellen,** veed-er-hair-shtel-en, *v* to restore

**wiederholen,** veed-er-hohl-en, *v* to repeat

**Wiederkäuer,** veed-er-koy-er, *m* ruminant

**wiederkehren,** veed-er-kayr-en, *v* to return

**wiederkommen** veed-er-kom-en, *v* to come back/again

**wiedersehen,** veed-er-zay-en, *v* to see again

**wiederum,** veed-er-oomm, *adv* again; on the other hand

**Wiedervereinigung,** veed-er-fair-ine-ee-goong, *f* reunification

**wiederverwerten,** veed-er-fair-vairt-en, *v* to recycle

**Wiege**, veeg-e, f cradle

**wiegen**, veeg-en, v to weigh; to have a weight; to rock

**Wiegenlied**, veeg-en-leet, nt cradle song; lullaby

**wiehern**, vee-ern, v to neigh

**Wien**, veen, nt Vienna

**Wiese**, veez-e, f meadow

**Wiesel**, veez-el, nt weasel

**wieso**, vee-zoh, adv why, how

**wieviel**, vee-feel, adv how much

**wild**, vilt, adj wild; savage

**Wild**, vilt, nt game, venison;
  **–bret**, nt game; venison;
  **–erer**, m poacher

**wildern**, vild-ern, v to poach

**Wildleder**, vilt-layd-er, nt suede

**Wildnis**, vilt-niss, f wilderness

**Wildschwein**, vilt-shvine, nt (wild) boar

**Wille**, vil-e, m will, desire, willingness

**willig**, vil-ik, adj willing; ready; docile

**willkommen**, vil-kom-en, adj welcome

**Willkür**, vil-kEEr, f free will; arbitrary power

**willkürlich**, vil-kEEr-lik, adj despotic, arbitrary

**wimmeln**, vim-eln, v to swarm, to abound in

**wimmern**, vim-ern, v to whine, to whimper

**Wimper**, vimp-er, f eyelash

**Wind**, vint, m wind, breeze;
  **–beutel**, m cream bun

**Winde**, vin-de, f winch, windlass

**Windel**, vin-del, f nappy

**winden**, vin-den, v to twist, to wind

**Windenergie**, vint-en-air-gee, f wind power

**Windhund**, vint-hoont, m greyhound

**windig**, vin-dik, adj windy, breezy

**Windmühle**, vint-mEEl-e, f windmill

**Windschutzscheibe**, vint-shoots-shy-be, f windscreen

**windstill**, vint-shtil, adj calm, without breeze

**Windzug**, vint-tsook, m draught, current of air

**Wink**, vink, m hint, beckoning; suggestion

**Winkel**, ving-kel, m angle; nook, quiet corner

**winken**, ving-ken, v to beckon, to wave (hand)

**winseln**, vin-zeln, v to whimper, to wail

**Winter**, vin-ter, m winter;
  **–garten**, m conservatory;
  **–schlaf**, m hibernation;
  **–sport**, m winter sports

**Winzer**, vint-ser, m wine-grower

**winzig**, vint-sik, adj minute, diminutive; petty

**Wipfel**, vip-fel, m tree-top

**wippen**, vip-en, v to rock, to balance; to tip

**wir**, veer, pron we

**Wirbel**, veerb-el, m whirl;

vertebra; top of head; fuss

**wirbeln**, veerb-eln, v to whirl; to warble

**Wirbelsäule**, veerb-el-zoyl-e, f spine

**wirken**, veerk-en, v to work; to be effective

**wirklich**, veerk-lik, adj real, actual, substantial

**Wirklichkeit**, veerk-lik-kite, f reality

**wirksam**, veerk-zahm, adj efficacious, effective; powerful

**Wirksamkeit**, veerk-zahm-kite, f efficacy

**Wirkung**, veerk-oong, f effect; result

**wirr**, veerr, adj confused, tangled

**Wirre**, veerr-e, f disorder, chaos; muddle

**Wirrwarr**, veerr-vahrr, m confusion, chaos

**Wirsing(kohl)**, veer-zing (-kohl), m savoy cabbage

**Wirt**, veert, m landlord; host; master of house;
  **–schaft**, f inn; economy

**wirtschaften**, veert-shahft-en, v to manage

**wirtschaftlich**, veert-shahft-lik, adj economical; economic

**Wirtshaus**, veerts-hows, nt inn, pub(lic-house)

**wischen**, vish-en, v to wipe

**wißbegierig**, vis-be-geer-ik, adj thirsting for knowledge, inquisitive

**wissen**, vis-en, v to know, to

be aware

**Wissenschaft, vis**-en-shahft, *f* science

**wissenschaftlich, vis**-en-shahft-lik, *adj* scientific

**wissenswert, vis**-ens-vairt, *adj* worth knowing

**wissentlich, vis**-ent-lik, *adj* conscious; wilful

**wittern, vit**-ern, *v* to scent, to smell; to suspect

**Witterung, vit**-er-oong, *f* weather(-conditions); scent

**Witwe, vit**-ve, *f* widow; **–r,** *m* widower

**Witz, vits,** *m* joke, jest; wit; **–bold,** *m* joker, comedian

**witzig, vits**-ik, *adj* witty, funny

**wo, voh,** *adv* where

**woanders, voh**-ahnn-ders, *adv* elsewhere

**Woche, voh**-e, *f* week; **–nende,** *nt* weekend

**wochenlang, vok**-en-lahng, *adj* for weeks (on end)

**Wochentag, vok**-en-tahg, *m* week-day

**wöchentlich, verk**-ent-lik, *adj* weekly

**Wodka, vot**-kah, *m* vodka

**wodurch, voh**-doohrk, *adv* through what; whereby, through which

**Woge, vohg**-e, *f* wave

**wogen, vohg**-en, *v* to surge, to swell

**woher, voh**-hair, *adv* where from; whence, from where

**wohin, voh**-hin, *adv* where

to; to where

**wohingegen, voh**-hin-gayg-en, *conj* whereas

**wohl, vohl,** *adv* well, in good health; indeed

**Wohlbefinden, vohl**-be-fin-den, *nt* well-being

**Wohlbehagen, vohl**-be-hahg-en, *nt* comfort

**wohlbehalten, vohl**-be-hahlt-en, *adv* safely

**Wohlfahrt, vohl**-fahrt, *f* welfare

**Wohlgefallen, vohl**-ge-fahll-en, *nt* liking; pleasure

**Wohlgeruch, vohl**-ge-rook, *m* scent, perfume

**wohlhabend, vohl**-hahb-ent, *adj* well-to-do

**Wohlklang, vohl**-klahng, *m* harmony, melody

**Wohlstand, vohl**-shtahnt, *m* wealth

**Wohltäter, vohl**-tayt-er, *m* benefactor

**wohltätig, vohl**-tayt-ik, *adj* charitable

**Wohltätigkeit, vohl**-tayt-ik-kite, *f* charity

**wohlweislich, vohl**-vice-lik, *adv* prudently

**Wohlwollen, vohl**-vol-en, *nt* goodwill

**wohnen, voh**-nen, *v* to live, to dwell, to reside

**Wohngemeinschaft, vohn**-ge-mine-shahft, *f* people sharing a flat/house

**Wohnmobil, vohn**-moh-beel, *nt* campervan

**Wohnort, voh**-nort, *m*

dwelling-place

**Wohnsitz, vohn**-zits, *m* (place of) residence

**Wohnstube, vohn**-shtoob-e, *f* living-room

**Wohnung, voh**-noong, *f* dwelling; home; flat

**Wohnwagen, vohn**-vahg-en, *m* caravan

**Wohnzimmer, vohn**-tsim-er, *nt* living-room

**wölben, verlb**-en, *v* to vault, to arch

**Wolf, volf,** *m* wolf

**Wolke, volk**-e, *f* cloud; **–nbruch,** *m* cloud-burst, heavy shower; **–nkratzer,** *m* skyscraper

**wolkig, volk**-ik, *adj* cloudy, clouded

**Wolle, vol**-e, *f* wool

**wollen, vol**-en, *v* to want to; *adj* woollen

**wollig, vol**-ik, *adj* woolly

**Wollust, vol**-loost, *f* lust; sensuality

**womit, voh**-mit, *adv* what with; with/by which

**Wonne, von**-e, *f* bliss, joy, ecstasy

**woran, voh**-rahnn, *adv* at/by what; at/by which

**worauf, voh**-rowf, *adv* on what; on which

**woraus, voh**-rows, *adv* out of what; whence, out of which

**worin, voh**-rin, *adv* in what; wherein, in which

**Wort, vort,** *nt* word

**Wörterbuch, vert**-er-book,

nt dictionary

**wörtlich, vert**-lik, *adj* literal; verbal; verbatim

**Wortschatz, vort**-shahts, *m* vocabulary

**worüber,** voh-**rEEb**-er, *adv* about what; over/about which

**worunter,** voh-**roont**-er, *adv* under what; under/among which

**wovon,** voh-**fon**, *adv* what from; from which, whereof

**wovor,** voh-**for**, *adv* before what; before which

**wozu,** voh-**tsoo**, *adv* what for, why; for which

**Wrack,** vrahck, *nt* wreck(age); debris

**wringen, vring**-en, *v* to wring (out)

**Wucherer, vook**-e-rer, *m* usurer; profiteer

**wuchern, vook**-ern, *v* to grow rampant, to proliferate; to practise usury

**Wuchs,** voocks, *m* growth

**Wucht,** vookt, *f* impetus, force; weight

**wuchtig, vook**-tik, *adj* weighty, heavy

**wühlen, vEEl**-en, *v* to delve; to burrow; to agitate

**wund,** voont, *adj* sore, chafed

**Wunde, voonn**-de, *f* wound; hurt; injury

**Wunder, voonn**-der, *nt* miracle; marvel; wonder

**wunderbar, voonn**-der-bar, *adj* wonderful

**wunderhübsch, voonn**-der-hEEpsh, *adj* very pretty

**wunderlich, voonn**-der-lik, *adj* strange, curious, odd

**wundern, voonn**-dern, *v* to astonish; **sich –,** *v* to marvel, to be astonished

**wunderschön, voonn**-der-shern, *adj* very beautiful, exquisite

**wundervoll, voonn**-der-fol, *adj* wonderful

**Wunsch,** voonsh, *m* wish, desire; request

**wünschen, vEEnn**-shen, *v* to wish; to request; **–swert,** *adj* desirable

**Würde, vEErd**-e, *f* dignity; honour; office; virtue

**würdig, vEErd**-ik, *adj* worthy; estimable; **–en,** *v* to deem worthy; to deign; to value

**Wurf,** voorf, *m* throw; cast; litter

**Würfel, vEErf**-el, *m* dice; cube

**würfeln, vEErf**-eln, *v* to throw dice; to jumble together

**würgen, vEErg**-en, *v* to choke; to swallow with difficulty

**Wurm,** voorm, *m* worm; serpent

**wurmig, voorm**-ik, *adj* wormy, worm-eaten

**Wurst,** voorst, *f* sausage

**Würstchen, vEErst**-ken, *nt* saveloy; small sausage

**Würze, vEErt**-se, *f* seasoning, flavouring

**Wurzel, voort**-sel, *f* root

**wurzeln, voort**-seln, *v* to take root

**würzen, vEErt**-sen, *v* to season, to spice

**würzig, vEErt**-sik, *adj* aromatic; piquant, spicy

**Wust,** voost, *m* confused heap; chaos

**wüst,** vEEst, *adj* desolate, deserted; waste; repulsive

**Wüste, vEEst**-e, *f* desert; wilderness

**Wut,** voot, *f* rage, anger, wrath; mania

**wüten, vEEt**-en, *v* to rage

**wütend, vEEt**-ent, *adj* raging, wrathful; furious

**Wüterich, vEEt**-er-ik, *m* tyrant; frantic person

**Xanthippe,** xahnn-**tip**-*e*, *f*
shrew
**X-Beine, icks**-by-n*e*, *pl*
knock-knees
**x-beliebig, icks**-b*e*-lee-bi*k*,
*adj* any old
**x-mal, icks**-mahl, *adv*
umpteen times

**Yacht,** yah*k*t, *f* yacht
**Yoghurt, yoh**-goort, *m*
  yoghurt
**Yucca, yook**-ah, *f* yucca

**Zacke(n), tsahck**-*e*(*n*), *m & f*, tooth of comb; prong; peak

**zackig, tsahck**-ik, *adj* jagged; toothed

**zaghaft, tsahk**-hahft, *adj* timid; nervous

**zäh, tsay**, *adj* tough; gluey, glutinous; leathery

**Zahl, tsahl**, *f* number, figure

**zahlen, tsahl**-en, *v* to pay

**zählen, tsayl**-en, *v* to count; to reckon; to amount to

**Zähler, tsayl**-er, *m* meter (gas/electricity meter)

**zahlreich, tsahl**-ryk, *adj* numerous

**Zahlung, tsahl**-oong, *f* payment

**Zählung, tsayl**-oong, *f* counting; (e)numeration

**zahm, tsahm**, *adj* tame(d); domesticated

**zähmen, tsaym**-en, *v* to tame; to break in; to domesticate

**Zähmung, tsaym**-oong, *f* taming

**Zahn, tsahn**, *m* tooth; tusk; *mech* cog; **–arzt**, *m* dentist; **–bürste**, *f* tooth-brush; **–fleisch**, *nt* gums; **–pasta**, *f* tooth-paste; **–rad**, *nt* cog-wheel; **–schmerz**, *m* toothache; **–stocher**, *m* toothpick; **–weh**, *nt* toothache

**Zange, tsahng**-e, *f* tongs; pliers; tweezers

**Zank, tsahnk**, *m* quarrel, altercation, dispute

**zanken, tsahng**-ken, *v* to quarrel; to scold

**zänkisch, tseng**-kish, *adj* quarrelsome; nagging

**Zapfen, tsahpp**-fen, *m* tap; bung, spigot; plug

**zapfen, tsahpp**-fen, *v* to tap (barrel)

**Zapfenstreich, tsahpp**-fen-stry'k, *m* lights-out; tattoo

**Zapfsäule, tsahp'f**-zoy-le, *f* petrol pump

**zappelig, tsahpp**-el-ik, *adj* fidgety

**zappeln, tsahpp**-eln, *v* to fidget; to jerk; to kick about

**Zar, tsar**, *m* Tsar

**zart, tsart**, *adj* tender; delicate; frail, weak

**zartfühlend, tsart**-fEEl-ent, *adj* tender-hearted

**zärtlich, tsairt**-lik, *adj* affectionate; tender

**Zärtlichkeit, tsairt**-lik-kite, *f* affection, tenderness; **–en**, *pl* affectionate words, sweet nothings

**Zauber, tsowb**-er, *m* magic, charm, enchantment

**Zauberei, tsowb**-e-ry, *f* magic; witchcraft

**Zauberer, tsowb**-e-rer, *m* magician; sorcerer

**zauberhaft, tsowb**-er-hahft, *adj* magical, enchanting

**Zauberkünstler, tsowb**-er-kEEnst-ler, *m* conjurer

**zaubern, tsowb**-ern, *v* to practise magic

**zaudern, tsowd**-ern, *v* to hesitate; to waver; to hang back

**Zaum, tsowm**, *m* bridle, rein

**zäumen, tsoym**-en, *v* to bridle

**Zaumzeug, tsowm**-tsoyk, *nt* bridle

**Zaun,** tsown, *m* fence; rail(ing); **–könig,** *m* wren **z.B.,** *abbr* **zum Beispiel,** e.g.

**Zeche,** tsek-*e*, *f* bill, reckoning; score; mine

**zechen,** tsek-*en*, *v* to carouse, to booze

**Zechprellerei,** tsek-prel-*e*-ry, *f* not paying one's bill

**Zeder,** tsay-der, *f* cedar

**Zeh(e),** tsay-(-*e*), *m* (*f*), toe; **–enspitze,** *f* tip of toe

**zehn,** tsain, *num* ten; **–fach,** *adj* tenfold, ten times; **–te(r),** *adj* tenth

**Zehntel,** tsain-tel, *nt* tenth

**zehren,** tsayr-*en*, *v* to live off, to feed on; to weaken, to sap, to wear (sb) out

**Zeichen,** tsy-ken, *nt* sign, mark, brand; indication

**zeichnen,** tsy'k-nen, *v* to draw, to design; to sign

**Zeichner,** tsy'k-ner, *m* draughtsman

**Zeichnung,** tsy'k-noong, *f* drawing, sketch(ing)

**Zeigefinger,** tsy-ge-fing-er, *m* index finger, forefinger

**zeigen,** tsy-gen, *v* to show; to point; to manifest

**Zeiger,** tsy-ger, *m* hand (of clock/instrument); indicator

**Zeile,** tsy-le, *f* line (of print); row (of houses)

**Zeit,** tsite, *f* time; era, epoch; period; **–alter,** *nt* age; **–arbeit,** *f* temporary job; **–geist,** *m* spirit of the age; **–genosse,** *m* contemporary

**zeitig,** tsite-ik, *adj* timely; opportune; in good time

**zeitigen,** tsite-ig-en, *v* to mature; to come to a head

**Zeitlang,** tsite-lahng, *f* (for) some time

**zeitlebens,** tsite-layb-ens, *adv* for life

**zeitlich,** tsite-lik, *adj* temporal; earthly

**Zeitlupe,** tsite-loop-*e*, *f* slow motion

**Zeitpunkt,** tsite-poonkt, *m* moment; epoch

**Zeitraum,** tsite-rowm, *m* period (of time)

**Zeitschrift,** tsite-shrift, *f* periodical, journal

**Zeitung,** tsite-toong, *f* newspaper

**Zeitverschwendung,** tsite-fair-shvend-oong, *f* waste of time

**Zeitvertreib,** tsite-fair-tripe, *m* pastime

**zeitweilig,** tsite-vile-ik, *adj* temporary

**zeitweise,** tsite-vy-ze, *adv* for a time

**Zeitwort,** tsite-vort, *nt* verb

**Zelle,** tsel-*e*, *f* cell

**Zelt,** tselt, *nt* tent; awning; **–platz,** *m* campsite

**zensieren,** tsen-zee-ren, *v* to censure; to give marks (school)

**Zensur,** tsen-zoor, *f* censorship; (school) mark

**Zentimeter,** tsen-tee-mayt-er, *m* centimetre

**Zentrale,** tsent-rahl-*e*, *f* central office; (telephone) exchange

**Zepter,** tsep-ter, *nt* sceptre; mace

**zerbrechen,** tsair-brek-en, *v* to break to pieces

**zerbrechlich,** tsair-brek-lik, *adj* brittle; breakable; fragile

**zerdrücken,** tsair-drEEck-en, *v* to crush

**Zerfall,** tsair-fahll, *m* decay, ruin

**zerfallen,** tsair-fahll-en, *v* to fall to pieces

**zerfetzen,** tsair-fets-en, *v* to tear to shreds; to slit

**zerfleischen,** tsair-fly-shen, *v* to tear to pieces

**zergehen,** tsair-gay-en, *v* to dissolve

**zergliedern,** tsair-gleed-ern, *v* to dismember

**zerhacken,** tsair-hahck-en, *v* to hack to pieces

**zerhauen,** tsair-how-en, *v* to smash

**zerkauen,** tsair-kow-en, *v* to chew well

**zerkleinern,** tsair-klyn-ern, *v* to reduce to small pieces; to grind; to chop

**zerknirscht,** tsair-k'neersht, *adj* contrite, penitent

**zerknittern,** tsair-k'nitt-ern, *v* to crush

**zerkratzen,** tsair-krahtt-sen, *v* to spoil by scratching

**zerlegen,** tsair-layg-en, *v* to dissect

**zerlumpt**, tsair-**loompt**, *adj* in rags, ragged

**zermahlen**, tsair-**mahl**-en, *v* to grind up

**zermalmen**, tsair-**mahlm**-en, *v* to grind to powder; to smash up

**zerplatzen**, tsair-**plahtt**-sen, *v* to explode; to burst

**zerquetschen**, tsair-**kvet**-shen, *v* to crush, to squash

**zerreiben**, tsair-**ry**-ben, *v* to rub to powder

**zerreißen**, tsair-**ry**-sen, *v* to tear (to pieces)

**zerren**, **tsairr**-en, *v* to tug, to drag

**zerrinnen**, tsair-**rin**-en, *v* to dissolve; to melt (away)

**Zerrung**, tsair-oong, *f* pulled muscle

**zerrütten**, tsair-**rEEt**-en, *v* to ruin, to wreck

**zerschellen**, tsair-**shel**-en, *v* to dash to pieces

**zerschlagen**, tsair-**shlahg**-en, *v* to smash up; *fig* to shatter

**zerschmettern**, tsair-**shmet**-ern, *v* to shatter

**zerschneiden**, tsair-**shny**-den, *v* to cut up

**zersetzen**, tsair-**zet**-sen, *v* to disintegrate

**zersplittern**, tsair-**shplit**-ern, *v* to splinter

**zerspringen**, tsair-**shpring**-en, *v* to burst; to split

**zerstampfen**, tsair-**shtahmp**-fen, *v* to pound

**Zerstäuber**, tsair-**shtoyb**-er, *m* atomizer

**zerstören**, tsair-**shter**-en, *v* to destroy

**Zerstörung**, tsair-**shter**-oong, *f* destruction

**zerstreuen**, tsair-**shtroy**-en, *v* to scatter; to divert

**zerstreut**, tsair-**shtroyt**, *adj* scattered; absent-minded

**Zerstreuung**, tsair-**shtroy**-oong, *f* diversion; distraction

**zerstückeln**, tsair-**shtEEck**-eln, *v* to dismember; to chop up

**zerteilen**, tsair-**ty**-len, *v* to split up; to divide

**zertreten**, tsair-**trayt**-en, *v* to tread under foot

**zertrümmern**, tsair-**trEEmm**-ern, *v* to wreck; to demolish

**zerzausen**, tsair-**tsowz**-en, *v* to crumple; to crease; to tousle

**zetern**, **tsayt**-ern, *v* to cry out in protest; to nag

**Zettel**, **tset**-el, *m* label, slip of paper; note; form

**Zeug**, tsoyk, *nt* stuff, material; thing(s); utensils

**Zeuge**, **tsoyg**-e, *m* witness

**zeugen**, **tsoyg**-en, *v* to give evidence; to witness; to beget

**Zeugnis**, **tsoyk**-nis, *nt* testimony; certificate

**Zichorie**, tseek-**ohr**-ye, *f* chicory

**Zicke**, **tsick**-e, *f* goat; *fam* silly cow

**zickzack**, **tsick**-tsahck, *adv* (in) zigzag

**Ziege**, **tseeg**-e, *f* nanny-goat; **–nbock**, *m* billy-goat

**Ziegel**, **tseeg**-el, *m* tile; brick; **–stein**, *m* brick

**ziehen**, **tsee**-en, *v* to draw; to pull; to be draughty; to move; to rear; to train

**Ziehharmonika**, tsee-har-**mohn**-ick-ah, *f* accordion

**Ziel**, tseel, *nt* goal; aim; destination; target

**zielen**, **tseel**-en, *v* to (take) aim

**Zielscheibe**, **tseel**-shy-be, *f* target, butt

**zielstrebig**, tseel-**shtraib**-ik, *adj* purposeful, determined

**ziemen (sich)**, **tseem**-en (zik), *v* to be seemly

**ziemlich**, **tseem**-lik, *adj* fair; moderate; passable; *adv* fairly, rather

**Zierat**, **tseer**-aht, *m* decoration; ornament

**Zier(de)**, **tseer**(-de), *f* ornament

**zieren**, **tseer**-en, *v* to grace; to decorate

**zierlich**, **tseer**-lik, *adj* dainty; graceful; neat

**Ziffer**, **tsif**-er, *f* figure; number; cypher; **–blatt**, *nt* dial

**Zigarette**, tsee-gah-**ret**-e, *f* cigarette

**Zigarre**, tsee-**gahrr**-e, *f* cigar

**Zigeuner**, tsee-**goyn**-er, *m* gipsy

**Zimmer**, **tsim**-er, *nt* room,

chamber; **–mädchen**, *nt* chambermaid; **–mann**, *m* carpenter; **–service**, *m* room-service

**zimmern, tsim**-ern, *v* to do carpentry; to chop with an axe

**zimperlich, tsimp**-er-lik, *adj* squeamish; prudish

**Zimt, tsimt**, *m* cinnamon

**Zink, tsink**, *nt* zinc

**Zinke, tsing**-ke, *f* prong; (comb) tooth

**Zinn, tsin**, *nt* tin

**Zinne, tsin**-e, *f* battlement; pinnacle

**Zins(en), tsins**(-en), *m (pl)* interest; **–satz**, *m* rate of interest

**Zipfel, tsip**-fel, *m* tip, point; corner

**zirka, tseer**-kah, *(abbr* ca.*)* *adv* about, approximately

**Zirkel, tseer**-kel, *m* compasses; circle; society

**zirkulieren, tseer-koo-leer**-en, *v* to circulate

**zirpen, tseer**-pen, *v* to chirp; to squeak

**zischeln, tsish**-eln, *v* to whisper

**zischen, tsish**-en, *v* to hiss; to sizzle; to fizzle

**Zitat, tsee**-taht, *nt* quotation, quoted passage

**Zither, tsit**-er, *f* zither; lute

**zitieren, tsee-teer**-en, *v* to quote; to cite

**Zitrone, tsee-trohn**-e, *f* lemon

**zittern, tsit**-ern, *v* to tremble; to shiver; to quake

**Zitze, tsit**-se, *f* nipple, teat

**Zivil, tsee-veel**, *nt* plain clothes; **–courage**, *f* courage of one's convictions; **–dienst**, *m* community service (as alternative to military service)

**Zivilisation, tsee-vee-lee-zahts-yohn**, *f* civilisation; **–skrankheit**, *f* stress caused by modern-living

**zögern, tserg**-ern, *v* to hesitate; to linger; to draw back

**Zögling, tserk**-ling, *m* pupil; charge

**Zoll, tsol**, *m* toll; (import) duty; customs; inch; **–amt**, *nt* customs house; **–beamte(r)**, *m & f* customs officer

**zollen, tsol**-en, *v* to acknowledge, to respect, to admire

**zollfrei, tsol**-fry, *adj* duty-free

**Zoo, tsoh**, *m* zoo

**Zoom(objektiv), zoom**(-op-yeck-teef)*, nt* zoom lens

**Zopf, tsop'f**, *m* plait, pigtail

**Zorn, tsorn**, *m* wrath, anger, indignation

**zornig, tsorn**-ik, *adj* angry, indignant

**Zote, tsoht**-e, *f* obscenity, dirty joke

**zotig, tsoht**-ik, *adj* obscene, smutty

**zottig, tsot**-ik, *adj* shaggy; tousled

**z.T.**, *abbr* **zum Teil**, *adv* partly

**zu, tsoo**, *prep* to, at, by, for, in; *adv* too

**Zubehör, tsoo**-be-her, *nt* equipment, accessories

**zubereiten, tsoo**-be-ry-ten, *v* to prepare

**zubinden, tsoo**-bin-den, *v* to tie/bind up

**zubleiben, tsoo**-bly-ben, *v* to remain shut

**zubringen, tsoo**-bring-en, *v* to spend (time)

**Zubringer, tsoo**-bring-er, *m* approach road

**Zucchini, tsook**-ee-nee, *pl* courgettes

**Zucht, tsookt**, *f* breeding; training; cultivation; discipline; decency

**züchten, tsEEk**-ten, *v* to breed; to grow

**Züchter, tsEEk**-ter, *m* breeder; keeper; cultivator

**Zuchthaus, tsookt**-hows, *nt* prison

**züchtig, tsEEk**-tik, *adj* chaste; demure, modest

**züchtigen, tsEEk**-tig-en, *v* to chastise, to punish

**Züchtigung, tsEEk**-tig-oong, *f* chastisement

**Züchtung, tsEEk**-toong, *f* breeding; cultivation; variety

**zucken, tsoock**-en, *v* to twitch, to quiver; to jerk

**zücken, tsEEck**-en, *v* to

draw (sword, dagger)

**Zucker,** tsoock-er, m sugar; **–guß,** nt icing

**zuckerig,** tsoock-er-ik, adj sugary

**Zuckerkrankheit,** tsoock-er-krahnk-hite, f diabetes

**zuckern,** tsoock-ern, v to (sweeten with) sugar

**Zuckerrohr,** tsoock-er-rohr, nt sugar-cane

**Zuckerrübe,** tsoock-er-rEEb-e, f sugar-beet

**zudecken,** tsoo-deck-en, v to cover (up)

**zudem,** tsoo-**daym**, adv moreover, besides

**zudrehen,** tsoo-dray-en, v to turn off (tap)

**zudringlich,** tsoo-dring-lik, adj obtrusive; forward

**Zudringlichkeit,** tsoo-dring-lik-kite, f forwardness

**zudrücken,** tsoo-drEEck-en, v to press shut

**zueinander,** tsoo-ine-**ahnn**-der, adv to one another

**zuerst,** tsoo-airst, adv (in the) first (place)

**Zufahrt,** tsoo-fahrt, f approach; drive(way)

**Zufall,** tsoo-fahll, m chance, accident

**zufallen,** tsoo-fahll-en, v to fall shut, to swing to; to accrue to

**zufällig,** tsoo-fel-ik, adj by chance, casual

**zufassen,** tsoo-fahss-en, v to grasp hold of; to help

**zufliegen,** tsoo-fleeg-en, v to

fly towards; fig to come easily

**Zufluß,** tsoo-flooss, m influx; tributary

**Zuflucht,** tsoo-flookt, f shelter, refuge

**zufolge,** tsoo-**folg**-e, prep owing to, according to

**zufrieden,** tsoo-freed-en, adj satisfied, contented

**Zufriedenheit,** tsoo-freed-en-hite, f contentment

**zufriedenstellen,** tsoo-freed-en-shtel-en, v to satisfy

**zufrieren,** tsoo-freer-en, v to freeze up

**zufügen,** tsoo-fEEg-en, v to add (to); to inflict

**Zug,** tsook, m train; drawing; draught (air); march, procession; trait; move

**Zugabe,** tsoo-gahb-e, f supplement, make-weight; encore

**Zugang,** tsoo-gahng, m access, admittance

**zugänglich,** tsoo-geng-lik, adj accessible; approachable

**zugeben,** tsoo-gayb-en, v to add; to admit; to grant

**zugegen,** tsoo-**gayg**-en, adj in attendance

**zugehen,** tsoo-gay-en, v to close (up); to reach; to happen

**zugehörig,** tsoo-ge-her-ik, adj proper; requisite; belonging to

**Zügel,** tsEEg-el, m bridle

**zügellos,** tsEEg-el-lohs, adj unbridled; unrestrained

**zügeln,** tsEEg-eln, v to bridle

**Zugeständnis,** tsoo-ge-shtent-nis, nt concession

**zugetan,** tsoo-ge-tahn, adj devoted, fond of

**Zugführer,** tsook-fEEr-er, m guard (train)

**zugig,** tsoo-ik, adj draughty

**zügig,** tsEEg-ik, adj quick, swift

**zugleich,** tsoo-**gly'k**, adv at the same time

**Zugluft,** tsook-looft, f draught (air)

**zugraben,** tsoo-grahb-en, v to cover with earth

**zugreifen,** tsoo-gry-fen, v to seize; to help oneself; **greif zu!,** fam dig in!

**zugrunde,** tsoo-groonn-de, adv to destruction; to the bottom

**Zugtier,** tsook-teer, nt draught animal

**zugunsten,** tsoo-goonn-sten, prep in favour of

**zugute,** tsoo-goot-e, adv to the benefit of

**Zugvogel,** tsook-fohg-el, m bird of passage

**zuhaken,** tsoo-hahk-en, v to fasten with a hook

**zuhalten,** tsoo-hahlt-en, v to keep closed

**Zuhälter,** tsoo-helt-er, m pimp

**Zuhause,** tsoo-how-se, nt home

**zuheilen,** tsoo-hile-en, v to

heal up

**zuhorchen, tsoo**-hork-en, *v* to listen attentively

**zuhören, tsoo**-her-en, *v* to listen

**zukehren (sich), tsoo**-kayr-en (zik), *v* to turn to

**zuklappen, tsoo**-klahpp-en, *v* to close with a bang

**zuknöpfen, tsoo**-k'nerpp-fen, *v* to button up

**zukommen, tsoo**-kom-en, *v* to come up to; to be due to

**Zukunft, tsoo**-koonft, *f* future

**zukünftig, tsoo**-kEEnft-ik, *adj* future

**zulächeln, tsoo**-lek-eln, *v* to smile at

**Zulage, tsoo**-lahg-e, *f* bonus, raise

**zulangen, tsoo**-lahng-en, *v* to help o.s.

**zulänglich, tsoo**-leng-lik, *adj* adequate, sufficient

**zulassen, tsoo**-lahss-en, *v* to admit; to leave shut; to permit

**zulässig, tsoo**-less-ik, *adj* admissible

**Zulauf, tsoo**-lowf, *m* concourse, rush of people

**zulaufen, tsoo**-lowf-en, *v* to rush towards; to flock to

**zulegen, tsoo**-layg-en, *v* to add; **sich –,** *v* to provide o.s. with; to buy

**zuleiten, tsoo**-ly-ten, *v* to lead towards; to pass on

**zuletzt, tsoo**-letst, *adv* at

last; ultimately

**zuliebe, tsoo**-leeb-e, *adv* for love of; as a favour

**zum, tsoomm,** = **zu dem,** for/to the

**zumachen, tsoo**-mahk-en, *v* to shut, to close; to fasten

**zumal, tsoo**-mahl, *adv* especially; chiefly

**zumauern, tsoo**-mow-ern, *v* to brick up

**zumeist, tsoo**-my'st, *adv* for the most part

**zumute, tsoo**-moot-e, *adv* in a mood

**zumuten, tsoo**-moot-en, *v* **jdm etw –,** to ask/expect sb to do sth; **sich zu viel –,** to take on too much

**Zumutung, tsoo**-moot-oong, *f* unreasonable demand/expectation

**zunächst, tsoo**-naykst, *adv* first (of all)

**zunageln, tsoo**-nahg-eln, *v* to nail up

**Zunahme, tsoo**-nahm-e, *f* increase; growth

**Zuname, tsoo**-nahm-e, *m* family name, surname

**zünden, tsEEnn**-den, *v* to light, to ignite; to set fire to

**Zündholz, tsEEnt**-holts, *nt* match

**Zündkerze, tsEEnt**-kairt-se, *f* spark-plug

**zunehmen, tsoo**-naym-en, *v* to increase; to grow; to gain weight

**Zuneigung, tsoo**-ny-goong, *f*

inclination; sympathy

**Zunft, tsoonft,** *f* guild, corporation

**Zunge, tsoong**-e, *f* tongue

**züngeln, tsEEng**-eln, *v* to leap up (fire)

**zungenfertig, tsoong**-en-fairt-ik, *adj* fluent

**zunichte, tsoo**-nikt-e, *adv;* **–machen** *v* to ruin, to destroy

**zunicken, tsoo**-nick-en, *v* to nod towards someone

**zuoberst, tsoo**-oh-berst, *adv* right on top

**zupfen, tsoopp**-fen, *v* to pluck, to unravel; to pull

**zuraten, tsoo**-raht-en, *v* to advise to

**zurechnen, tsoo**-rek-nen, *v* to number among; to attribute to

**zurechnungsfähig, tsoo**-rek-noongs-fay-ik, *adj* accountable for one's actions; sane

**zurecht, tsoo**-rekt, *adv* in (good) order; right; **–kommen,** *v* to cope; **–legen, –machen,** *v* to prepare, to lay out; **–setzen,** *v* to set right; **–weisen,** *v* to reprimand

**zureden, tsoo**-rayd-en, *v* to advise; to urge; to comfort

**zureiten, tsoo**-ry-ten, *v* to break in (horses)

**zurichten, tsoo**-rik-ten, *v* to make ready; to dress; to injure badly

**zuriegeln, tsoo**-reeg-eln, *v*

to bolt (shut)

**zürnen,** tsEErn-en, v to be angry (with)

**zurück,** tsoo-rEEck, adv back, backward(s)

**zurückbekommen,** tsoo-rEEck-be-kom-en, v to get back; to recover

**zurückbleiben,** tsoo-rEEck-bly-ben, v to remain/lag behind

**zurückdrängen,** tsoo-rEEck-dreng-en, v to push back

**zurückeilen,** tsoo-rEEck-ile-en, v to hurry back

**zurückerhalten,** tsoo-rEEck-air-hahlt-en, v to receive back

**zurückerstatten,** tsoo-rEEck-air-shtaht-en, v to return; to refund

**zurückfahren,** tsoo-rEEck-fahr-en, v to drive back; to recoil

**zurückfinden,** tsoo-rEEck-fin-den, v to find one's way back

**zurückführen,** tsoo-rEEck-fEEr-en, v to lead/trace back; to attribute to

**zurückgezogen,** tsoo-rEEck-ge-tsohg-en, adj secluded

**zurückhalten,** tsoo-rEEck-hahlt-en, v to keep/hold back

**Zurückhaltung,** tsoo-rEEck-hahlt-oong, f reserve, retention

**zurückkehren,** tsoo-rEEck-kair-en, v to return

**zurückkommen,** tsoo-

rEEck-kom-en, v to come back

**zurücklassen,** tsoo-rEEck-lahss-en, v to leave behind

**zurücklegen,** tsoo-rEEck-layg-en, v to cover (distance); to put back/by

**zurücknehmen,** tsoo-rEEck-naym-en, v to take back; to retract

**zurückrufen,** tsoo-rEEck-roof-en, v to call back; to recall

**zurückschicken,** tsoo-rEEck-shick-en, v to send back

**zurückschlagen,** tsoo-rEEck-shlahg-en, v to hit/throw back

**zurückschrecken,** tsoo-rEEck-shreck-en, v to shrink back; to frighten off

**zurücksetzen,** tsoo-rEEck-set-sen, v to set back; to slight; to reduce

**zurückstehen,** tsoo-rEEck-shtay-en, v to stand back; to be inferior

**zurückstellen,** tsoo-rEEck-shtel-en, v to put back

**zurücktreten,** tsoo-rEEck-trayt-en, v to step back; to retire

**zurückweichen,** tsoo-rEEck-vy-ken, v to recede, to yield

**zurückweisen,** tsoo-rEEck-vy-zen, v to reject

**zurückzahlen,** tsoo-rEEck-tsahl-en, v to repay

**zurückziehen,** tsoo-rEEck-tsee-en, v to withdraw

**zurufen,** tsoo-roof-en, v to call to, to call after

**Zusage,** tsoo-zahg-e, f promise; assent

**zusagen,** tsoo-zahg-en, v to promise; to assent

**zusammen,** tsoo-zahmm-en, adv together

**zusammenarbeiten,** tsoo-zahmm-en-ahr-by-ten, v to work together/in a team; to liaise

**zusammenbrechen,** tsoo-zahmm-en-brek-en, v to collapse

**zusammenbringen,** tsoo-zahmm-en-bring-en, v to bring together; to amass

**zusammenfahren,** tsoo-zahmm-en-fahr-en, v to be startled

**zusammenfallen,** tsoo-zahmm-en-fahll-en, v to collapse; to wither (away)

**zusammenfassen,** tsoo-zahmm-en-fahss-en, v to summarize

**zusammenfinden (sich),** tsoo-zahmm-en-fin-den (zik), v to meet

**zusammenfügen,** tsoo-zahmm-en-fEEg-en, v to join, to unite

**zusammengesetzt,** tsoo-zahmm-en-ge-zetzt, adj composed (of); compound, composite

**Zusammenhalt,** tsoo-zahmm-en-hahlt, m

holding together; coherence; solidarity; unity

**zusammenhalten,** tsoo-**zahmm**-en-hahlt-en, *v* to cling/hold together

**Zusammenhang,** tsoo-**zahmm**-en-hahng, *m* context, cohesion, connection

**zusammenklappen,** tsoo-**zahmm**-en-klahpp-en, *v* to fold up/together

**Zusammenkunft,** tsoo-**zahmm**-en-koonft, *f* meeting; conference

**zusammenlegen,** tsoo-**zahmm**-en-layg-en, *v* to place together; to fold; to combine; to club together

**zusammennehmen,** tsoo-**zahmm**-en-naym-en, *v* to take together; **sich –,** *v* to pull oneself together

**zusammenschließen,** tsoo-**zahmm**-en-shlees-en, *v* to combine; to chain together; **sich –,** *v* to join up

**zusammenschrecken,** tsoo-**zahmm**-en-shreck-en, *v* to startle

**zusammenschrumpfen,** tsoo-**zahmm**-en-shroomp-fen, *v* to shrink

**zusammensetzen,** tsoo-**zahmm**-en-zet-sen, *v* to put together; to combine; to compose: **sich –,** *v* to come together

**zusammenstellen,** tsoo-**zahmm**-en-shtel-en, *v* to assemble, to put together; to compile

**Zusammenstoß,** tsoo-**zahmm**-en-shtohs, *m* collision

**Zusammensturz,** tsoo-**zahmm**-en-shtoorts, *m* collapse, crash

**zusammentreffen,** tsoo-**zahmm**-en-tref-en, *v* to coincide; to meet (up)

**zusammentun,** tsoo-**zahmm**-en-toon, *v* to put together; **sich –,** *v* to unite

**zusammenziehen,** tsoo-**zahmm**-en-tsee-en, *v* to contract; to draw together; to move together

**Zusatz,** tsoo-zahts, *m* addition; additive; postscript

**zuschauen,** tsoo-show-en, *v* to watch, to look on

**Zuschauer,** tsoo-show-er, *m* spectator; **–raum,** *m* auditorium

**zuschicken,** tsoo-shick-en, *v* to send (to)

**zuschieben,** tsoo-sheeb-en, *v* to push to; to push shut

**zuschießen,** tsoo-shees-en, *v* to contribute

**Zuschlag,** tsoo-shlahk, *m* addition; surcharge

**zuschlagen,** tsoo-shlahg-en, *v* to slam; to close; to knock down; to add

**zuschließen,** tsoo-shlees-en, *v* to lock up

**zuschneiden,** tsoo-shny-den, *v* to cut (out)

**zuschreiben,** tsoo-shry-ben, *v* to attribute; to ascribe

**Zuschrift,** tsoo-shrift, *f* letter

**Zuschuß,** tsoo-shooss, *m* bonus; allowance; subsidy

**zusehen,** tsoo-zay-en, *v* to look on; to see to

**zusehends,** tsoo-zay-ents, *adv* visibly; more and more

**zusetzen,** tsoo-zet-sen, *v* to add to; to alloy with; to pester

**zusichern,** tsoo-zik-ern, *v* to assure of, to promise

**zuspitzen,** tsoo-shpits-en, *v* to point; to taper; to become critical

**zusprechen,** tsoo-shprek-en, *v* to cheer up, to comfort; to award

**Zustand,** tsoo-shtahnt, *m* condition, state, lot

**zustandekommen,** tsoo-**shtahnn**-de-kom-en, *v* to come about

**zuständig,** tsoo-shten-dik, *adj* competent; responsible

**zustehen,** tsoo-shtay-en, *v* to be proper/right

**zustellen,** tsoo-shtel-en, *v* to deliver

**zustimmen,** tsoo-shtim-en, *v* to agree; to assent

**zustoßen,** tsoo-shtohs-en, *v* to slam shut; to befall

**zutage,** tsoo-tahg-e, *adv* to the light of day

**Zutat,** tsoo-taht, *f* ingredient; trimming

**zuteilen,** tsoo-tile-en, *v* to apportion; to allot, to allocate

**zuträglich,** tsoo-trayk-lik, *adj* wholesome; useful, beneficial

**zutrauen,** tsoo-trow-en, *v* to think capable of

**Zutrauen,** tsoo-trow-en, *nt* confidence

**zutraulich,** tsoo-trow-lik, *adj* trusting; friendly

**zutreffend,** tsoo-tref-ent, *adj* correct; apt

**Zutritt,** tsoo-trit, *m* admittance; admission

**Zutun,** tsoo-toon, *nt* assistance; action

**zuverlässig,** tsoo-fair-les-ik, *adj* reliable

**Zuversicht,** tsoo-fair-zikt, *f* confidence; faith, trust

**zuvorkommen,** tsoo-fohr-kom-en, *v* to forestall

**zuvorkommend,** tsoo-fohr-kom-ent, *adj* obliging, courteous

**Zuwachs,** tsoo-vahcks, *m* increase; growth

**zuwege,** tsoo-vayg-e, *adv*; **etw –bringen** to achieve sth

**zuweisen,** tsoo-vy-zen, *v* to allot; to assign

**zuwenden,** tsoo-vend-en, *v* to turn to; to bestow

**zuwerfen,** tsoo-vairf-en, *v* to throw to; to slam

**zuwider,** tsoo-veed-er, *adj* contrary; distasteful

**zuziehen,** tsoo-tsee-en, *v* to draw together; to incur; to consult; **sich –,** *v* to tighten; to cloud over

**zuzüglich,** tsoo-tsEEk-lik, *prep* plus

**Zwang,** tsvahng, *m* compulsion; coercion

**zwängen,** tsveng-en, *v* to force; to constrain; to squeeze

**zwanghaft,** tsvang-hahft, *adj* compulsive

**zwanglos,** tsvang-lohs, *adj* informal, unceremonious

**zwanzig,** tsvahnt-sik, *num* twenty

**zwar,** tsvahr, *adv* indeed, it's true; **und –,** in fact, actually

**Zweck,** tsveck, *m* purpose; object, aim

**zweckmäßig,** tsveck-mace-ik, *adj* suitable

**zwecks,** tsvecks, *prep* for the purpose of

**zwei,** tsvy, *num* two; **–deutig,** *adj* ambiguous; **–erlei,** *adj* of two kinds

**Zweifel,** tsvy-fel, *m* doubt, uncertainty

**zweifelhaft,** tsvy-fel-hahft, *adj* doubtful

**zweifeln,** tsvy-feln, *v* to doubt

**Zweig,** tsvike, *m* branch, twig, bough; **–stelle,** *f* branch (bank, shop)

**Zweikampf,** tsvy-kahmpʼf, *m* one-to-one combat

**zweimal,** tsvy-mahl, *adv* twice

**Zweirad,** tsvy-raht, *nt* bicycle

**zweisprachig,** tsvy-shprahk-ik, *adj* bilingual

**zweispurig,** tsvy-shpoor-ik, *adj* two-lane

**zweite(r),** tsvy-te(r), *adj* second

**zweitrangig,** tsvite-rahng-ik, *adj* of secondary importance

**Zwerg,** tsvairk, *m* dwarf

**Zwetsch(g)e, tsvetsh-(g)e,** *f* plum

**zwicken,** tsvick-en, *v* to pinch, to nip

**Zwieback,** tsvee-bahck, *m* rusk, biscuit

**Zwiebel,** tsveeb-el, *f* onion; (plant) bulb

**Zwiegespräch,** tsvee-ge-shprayk, *nt* dialogue

**Zwiespalt,** tsvee-shpahlt, *m* disagreement; inner conflict

**Zwietracht,** tsvee-trahkt, *f* discord

**Zwilling,** tsvil-ing, *m* twin

**Zwinge,** tsving-e, *f* ferrule; tip; clamp

**zwingen,** tsving-en, *v* to compel, to force

**Zwinger,** tsving-er, *m* kennel; cage (usually wild animals)

**zwinkern,** tsving-kern, *v* to wink; to twinkle

**Zwirn,** tsveern, *m* thread; twine, yarn

**zwischen, tsvish**-en, *prep*
 between; among(st)

**Zwischenbericht, tsvish**-en-
 be-rikt, *m* interim report

**Zwischendeck, tsvish**-en-
 deck, *nt* between decks

**Zwischending, tsvish**-en-
 ding, *nt* cross (between)

**zwischendurch, tsvish**-en-
 **doohrk**, *adv* in between
 times, in the meantime

**Zwischenfall, tsvish**-en-
 fahll, *m* incident

**Zwischenglied, tsvish**-en-
 gleet, *nt* connecting link

**Zwischenhändler, tsvish**-
 en-hend-ler, *m* middleman

**zwischenher, tsvish**-en-
 **hair**, *adv* in the meantime

**zwischenmenschlich,**
 **tsvish**-en-mensh-lik, *adj*
 interpersonal

**Zwischenraum, tsvish**-en-
 rowm, *m* gap, space

**Zwischenwand, tsvish**-en-
 vahnt, *f* partition

**Zwist(igkeit), tsvist**(-ik-
 kite), *m* (*f*), discord;
 quarrel

**zwitschern, tsvit**-shern, *v* to
 chirp, to twitter

**zwo, tsvoh,** = **zwei,** *num* two
 (used on telephone)

**zwölf, tsverlf,** *num* twelve;
 **–te(r)**, *adj* twelfth

**Zylinder, tsee-lin**-der, *m*
 cylinder; top hat

**Zypern, tsEEp**-ern, nt
 Cyprus

ENGLISH · GERMAN
ENGLISCH · DEUTSCH

**a,** eh/e, *indefinite art* ein(e)

**abandon,** e-**bänn**-d'n, *v* verlassen; (give up) aufgeben; **–ed,** *adj* verlassen; (morally) verworfen

**abate,** e-**beht,** *v* nachlassen

**abattoir,** **äbb**-be-tu'ahr, *n* Schlachthof *m*

**abbey,** **äbb**-i, *n* Abtei *f*

**abbreviate,** e-**brie**-wi-eht, *v* abkürzen

**abbreviation,** e-brie-wi-**eh**-sch'n, *n* Abkürzung *f*

**abdicate,** **äbb**-di-keht, *v* abdanken; entsagen

**abdomen,** **äbb**-de-men, *n* Bauch *m*, Unterleib *m*

**abduction,** äbb-**dack**-sch'n, *n* Entführung *f*

**abet,** e-**bett,** *v* mithelfen

**abhorrent,** eb-ho-**rent,** *adj* zuwider, verhaßt

**abide,** e-**beid,** *v* verweilen,

bleiben; **– by,** gehorchen, sich halten an

**ability,** e-**bill**-i-ti, *n* Fähigkeit *f*, Tüchtigkeit *f*

**abject,** **äbb**-dschekt, *adj* erbärmlich, elend; (poverty) bitter; (apology) demütig

**ablaze,** e-**blehs,** *adj & adv* brennend, lodernd

**able,** eh-b'l, *adj* fähig, tüchtig; **to be – to,** *v* können

**ably,** eh-bli, *adv* fähig, geschickt

**abnormal,** äbb-**nor**-mel, *adj* abnorm, regelwidrig; (misshapen) mißgestaltet

**aboard,** e-**bord,** *adv* an Bord

**abode,** e-**bohd,** *n* Wohnsitz *m*

**abolish,** e-**boll**-isch, *v* abschaffen

**abominable,** e-**bomm**-in-e-

b'l, *adj* abscheulich

**aborigine,** äbb-e-**ridsch**-i-ni, *n* Ureinwohner *m*

**abortion,** e-**bor**-sch'n, *n* Abtreibung *f*; (miscarriage) Fehlgeburt *f*

**abound,** e-**baund,** *v* reichlich vorhanden sein

**about,** e-**baut,** *adv* (approximately) etwa, ungefähr; (around) (rings) herum; *prep* (place) um; (subject) über; **to be – to,** *v* im Begriff sein

**above,** e-**baw,** *adv* oben; *prep* über

**abrasion,** e-**breh**-sch'n, *n* Hautabschürfung *f*

**abreast,** e-**brest,** *adv* nebeneinander

**abridge,** e-**bridsch,** *v* abkürzen, verkürzen

**abroad,** e-**bro'ad,** *adv* im Ausland, ins Ausland

**abrupt,** e-**brapt,** *adj* (manner) schroff; (step) jäh

**abscess,** **äbb**-ssess, *n* Abszeß *m*, Geschwür *nt*

**abscond,** eb-**skond,** *v* durchgehen, flüchten

**absence,** **äbb**-ssenss, *n* Abwesenheit *f*

**absent,** **äbb**-ssent, *adj* abwesend; **–ee,** *n* Abwesende(r) *m & f*; **– minded,** *adj* zerstreut

**absent,** **äbb**-ssent, *v* – **oneself,** fernbleiben

**absolute,** **äbb**-sse-luht, *adj* absolut; unbedingt

**absolve**, eb-**solw**, *v*
lossprechen; – **from**,
freisprechen, entheben

**absorb**, eb-**sorb**, *v*
aufsaugen; *fig* ganz in
Anspruch nehmen

**abstain**, eb-**stehn**, *v* (parl
etc.) sich der Stimme
enthalten; – **from**, sich
enthalten

**abstemious**, eb-**stie**-mi-ess,
*adj* enthaltsam

**abstention**, eb-**stenn**-sch'n,
*n* (parl etc.)
Stimmenthaltung *f*

**abstinence**, **äbb**-sti-nenss, *n*
Enthaltsamkeit *f*

**abstract**, **äbb**-sträckt, *adj*
abstrakt; *n*
Zusammenfassung *f*

**abstract**, **äbb**-sträckt, *v*
wegnehmen;
zusammenfassen

**absurd**, eb-**ssörd**, *adj* albern;
unvernünftig

**abundance**, e-**bann**-denss, *n*
Überfluß *m*

**abundant**, e-**bann**-d'nt, *adj*
reichlich, im Überfluß

**abuse**, e-**bjuhss**, *n*
Mißbrauch *m*; (affront)
Beschimpfung *f*

**abuse**, e-**bjuhs**, *v*
mißbrauchen;
beschimpfen

**abusive**, e-**bjuhss**-iw, *adj*
beleidigend, Schimpf-

**abyss**, e-**biss**, *n* Abgrund *m*

**academy**, e-**kädd**-e-mi, *n*
Akademie *f*; Hochschule *f*

**accede**, eck-**ssied**, *v*

einwilligen; – **to**, (throne)
besteigen

**accelerate**, eck-**ssell**-e-reht,
*v* beschleunigen

**accelerator**, eck-**ssell**-e-reh-
ter, *n* Gaspedal *nt*

**accent**, **äck**-ssent, *n* Akzent
*m*; Betonung *f*

**accept**, eck-**ssept**, *v*
annehmen; akzeptieren;
–**able**, *adj* akzeptabel,
annehmbar; –**ance**, *n*
Annahme *f*;
Zustimmung, *f*

**access**, **äck**-ssess, *n* Zutritt
*m*, Zugang *m*

**accessible**, eck-**ssess**-i-b'l,
*adj* zugänglich

**accessory**, eck-**ssess**-e-ri, *n*
Accessoire *nt*, Zubehör *nt*

**accident**, **äck**-ssi-dent, *n*
Unfall *m*; Zufall *m*

**accidental**, äck-ssi-**denn**-t'l,
*adj* versehentlich, zufällig

**acclaim**, e-**klehm**, *n* Beifall
*m*; *v* Beifall zurufen

**acclimatize**, e-**klei**-me-tais, *v*
akklimatisieren; – **to**, sich
gewöhnen an

**accommodate**, e-**komm**-e-
deht, *v* (lodge)
unterbringen; – (oneself)
**to**, sich anpassen

**accommodation**, e-**komm**-e-
**deh**-sch'n, *n* (lodging)
Unterkunft *f*; (agreement)
Übereinkommen *nt*

**accompany**, e-**kamm**-pe-ni,
*v* begleiten

**accomplice**, e-**kamm**-pliss, *n*
Komplize *m*,

Mitschuldige(r) *m & f*

**accomplish**, e-**kamm**-plisch,
*v* vollführen; (purpose)
erreichen; –**ed**, *adj*
erreicht; kompetent;
–**ment**, *n* Vollendung *f*;
(performance) Leistung *f*

**accord**, e-**kord**, *n*
Übereinstimmung *f*; of
one's own –, freiwillig

**accord**, e-**kord**, *v*
übereinstimmen; – **with**,
entsprechen; –**ing to**, *prep*
gemäß; nach; –**ingly**, *adv*
demgemäß

**accordance**, e-**kor**-denss, *n*
in –**ance with**, *prep*
gemäß, entsprechend

**accost**, e-**kosst**, *v*
ansprechen; belästigen

**account**, e-**kaunt**, *n* (bill)
Rechnung *f*; (bank)
Konto *nt*; – **for**, *v*
Rechenschaft ablegen für,
verantwortlich sein für;
**on –**, auf Rechnung; **on
no –**, auf keinen Fall;
–**able**, *adj* verantwortlich

**accountant**, e-**kaun**-tent, *n*
Wirtschaftsprüfer *m*

**accrue**, e-**kruh**, *v*
erwachsen; – **from**,
entstehen aus

**accumulate**, e-**kjuh**-mju-
leht, *v* (gather)
ansammeln, anhäufen;
(collect) sich ansammeln,
sich anhäufen

**accuracy**, **äck**-ju-re-ssi, *n*
Genauigkeit *f*

**accurate**, **äck**-ju-ret, *adj*

genau; richtig

**accuse**, e-**kjuhs**, v anklagen, beschuldigen

**accustom**, e-**kass**-tem, v gewöhnen

**ace**, ehss, n As nt; adj Star-

**ache**, ehk, n Schmerz m; v schmerzen

**achieve**, e-**tschiew**, v vollbringen; erringen; –**ment**, n (attainment) Errungenschaft f; (performance) Leistung f

**acid**, äss-idd, adj sauer; n Säure f; – **rain**, n saurer Regen m

**acidity**, e-**ssidd**-i-ti, n Säure f

**acknowledge**, ek-**noll**-idsch, v anerkennen; (receipt) bestätigen

**acknowledg(e)ment**, ek-**noll**-idsch-ment, n Anerkennung f; (receipt) Bestätigung f

**acne**, **äck**-ni, n Akne f

**acorn**, eh-korn, n Eichel f

**acoustics**, e-**kuh**-sticks, n Akustik f

**acquaint**, e-**ku'ehnt**, v bekannt machen; (familiarize) vertraut machen

**acquaintance**, e-**ku'ehn**-tenss, n Bekanntschaft f; (person) Bekannte(r) m & f

**acquiesce**, äck-ku'i-**ess**, v einwilligen

**acquire**, e-**ku'eir**, v erwerben, erlangen

**acquisition**, äck-ku'i-**sisch**-'n, n Erwerb m; Akquisition f

**acquit**, e-**ku'itt**, v freisprechen, entlasten

**acquittal**, e-**ku'itt**-'l, n Freispruch m

**acre**, eh-ker, n (measurement) Morgen m

**acrid**, **äck**-ridd, adj beißend, scharf

**acrobat**, **äck**-re-bätt, n Akrobat m

**across**, e-**kross**, adv hinüber; prep durch; (quer) über

**acrylic**, e-**krill**-ick, adj Acryl nt

**act**, äckt, n Tat f; (of a play) Akt m; law Gesetz nt; v handeln; (in theatre) spielen

**action**, **äck**-sch'n, n Handlung f; law Prozeß m; mil Gefecht nt

**activate**, **äck**-ti-weht, v aktivieren

**active**, **äck**-tiw, adj wirksam; belebt; tätig

**activity**, äck-**tiw**-i-ti, n Betätigung f, Tätigkeit f

**actor**, **äck**-ter, n Schauspieler m

**actress**, **äck**-triss, n Schauspielerin f

**actual**, äck-tschu-el, adj tatsächlich; wirklich; –**ly**, adv tatsächlich

**acute**, e-**kjuht**, adj spitz; (pain) scharf; (senses) scharfsinnig; med akut

**adamant**, **ädd**-e-ment, adj beharrlich

**adapt**, e-**däpt**, v anpassen, umarbeiten, umbauen; (plays etc.) bearbeiten; –**er**, n (elec etc.) Adapter m, Zwischenstecker m

**adaptation**, ädd-**äpp-teh**-sch'n, n Anpassung f; (plays etc.) Bearbeitung f

**add**, ädd, v addieren; hinzufügen; beitragen

**addict**, **ädd**-ikt, n Süchtige(r) m & f

**addicted**, e-**dick**-tidd, adj süchtig

**addiction**, e-**dick**-sch'n, Sucht f

**addition**, e-**disch**-'n, n Addition f; Zusatz m; –**al**, adj zusätzlich

**additive**, **ädd**-i-tiw, n Zusatz m

**address**, e-**dress**, n Anschrift f, Adresse f; (talk) Anrede f, Ansprache f; v adressieren; (orally) ansprechen

**adept**, **ädd**-ept, adj geschickt

**adequate**, **ädd**-i-ku'et, adj genügend; hinreichend

**adhere**, ed-**hier**, v anhaften; kleben; – **to**, festhalten an

**adherent**, ed-**hier**-ent, n Anhänger m

**adhesive**, ed-**hie**-ssiw, adj klebend; n Klebstoff m

**adjacent**, ed-**dscheh**-ss'nt, adj angrenzend

**adjective**, **ädd**-dscheck-tiw, n Adjektiv nt

**adjoin**, ed-**dscheun**, v angrenzen; –**ing**, adj

angrenzend

**adjourn**, ed-**dschörn**, v
vertagen, aufschieben;
**–ment**, n Vertagung f

**adjust**, ed-**dschast**, v mech
einstellen; **– (oneself) to**,
(sich) anpassen; **–able**, adj
verstellbar; **–ment**, n
Anpassung f; mech
Einstellung f

**administer**, ed-**minn**-iss-ter,
v verwalten; (medicine)
verabreichen

**administration**, ed-minn-iss-
**treh**-sch'n, n Verwaltung
f; Regierung f

**admirable**, **ädd**-mi-re-b'l, adj
bewundernswert

**admiration**, ädd-mi-**reh**-
sch'n, n Bewunderung f

**admire**, ed-**meir**, v
bewundern

**admission**, ed-**misch**-'n, n
(entry) Zutritt m, Einlaß
m; (confession)
Geständnis nt; **– fee**,
n Eintritt m,
Eintrittsgebühr f

**admit**, ed-**mitt**, v einlassen;
(concede) zugeben;
**–tance**, n Zulassung f;
(fee) Eintritt m,
Eintrittsgebühr f

**admonish**, ed-**monn**-isch, v
ermahnen; verweisen

**ado**, e-**duh**, n Tun nt;
Treiben nt

**adolescence**, ädd-e-**less**-'nss,
n Jugend f, Pubertät f

**adolescent**, ädd-e-**less**-'nt,
adj jugendlich; n

Jugendliche(r) m & f

**adopt**, e-**dopt**, v adoptieren,
annehmen; **–ion**, n
Adoption f, Annahme f

**adore**, e-**dor**, v schwärmen
(für), sehr lieben; (God)
anbeten

**adorn**, e-**dorn**, v schmücken;
verzieren

**adrift**, e-**drift**, adv (floating)
treibend; (lost) verloren

**adroit**, e-**dreut**, adj gewandt,
behende

**adult**, e-**dalt**/ädd-**alt**, adj
erwachsen; n
Erwachsene(r) m & f

**adulterate**, e-**dall**-te-reht, v
verfälschen, verpanschen

**adultery**, e-**dal**-te-ri, n
Ehebruch m

**advance**, ed-**wahnss**, n
(progress) Fortschritt m;
(money) Vorschuß m; v
(progress) vorrücken;
(lend) vorschießen; **in –**,
adv im voraus

**advantage**, ed-**wahn**-tidsch,
n Vorteil m

**advantageous**, ädd-wahn-
**teh**-dschess, adj vorteilhaft

**advent**, **ädd**-went, n
Ankunft f; Advent m

**adventure**, ed-**wenn**-tscher,
n Abenteuer nt

**adventurous**, ed-**wenn**-
tsche-ress, adj
abenteuerlich; (bold)
kühn

**adverb**, **ädd**-wörb, n
Adverb nt

**adversary**, **ädd**-wer-se-ri, n

Gegner m

**adverse**, **ädd**-wörss, adj
nachteilig; widrig

**advert**, **ädd**-wört, n
Annonce f, Anzeige f

**advertise**, **ädd**-wer-teis, v
werben, Reklame machen;
**–ising**, n Werbung f

**advertisement**, ed-**wör**-tiss-
ment, n Anzeige f

**advice**, ed-**weiss**, n Rat m;
(information)
Benachrichtigung f

**advisable**, ed-**weis**-e-b'l, adj
ratsam

**advise**, ed-**weis**, v raten;
(inform) benachrichtigen;
**ill –d**, adj unklug,
unüberlegt; **well –d**, adj
wohlüberlegt

**adviser**, ed-**wei**-ser, n
Ratgeber m

**advocate**, **ädd**-ve-ket, n
Befürworter m

**advocate**, **ädd**-ve-keht, v
befürworten

**aerial**, **ähr**-ri-el, adj Luft-; n
Antenne f

**aerobics**, **ähr**-**roh**-bicks, n
Aerobic nt

**aerodynamic**, ähr-roh-dei-
**nämm**-ick, adj
aerodynamisch

**aeroplane**, **ähr**-roh-plehn, n
Flugzeug nt

**aerosol**, **ähr**-roh-ssol, n
Aerosol nt, Sprühflasche f

**afar**, e-**fahr**, adv [von]
weither

**affable**, **äff**-e-b'l, adj
freundlich, umgänglich

**affair**, e-**fähr**, n (love)
Affäre f; (matter)
Angelegenheit f, Sache f

**affect**, e-**fekt**, v angehen,
betreffen; (move) rühren;
**–ed**, adj affektiert;
(moved) gerührt

**affection**, e-**feck**-sch'n, n
Zuneigung f, Liebe f; **–ate**,
adj liebevoll, zärtlich

**affidavit**, äff-i-**deh**-witt, n
eidliche Erklärung f

**affiliate**, e-**fill**-i-eht, v –
**to/with**, sich anschließen,
sich angliedern

**affinity**, e-**finn**-i-ti, n
(liking) Anziehung f;
(relationship)
Verwandtschaft f; chem
Affinität f

**affirm**, e-**förm**, v
bekräftigen, bestätigen

**affirmation**, äff-er-**meh**-
sch'n, n Bekräftigung f,
Bestätigung f

**affirmative**, e-**förm**-e-tiw,
adj bejahend, zustimmend;
n Bejahung f

**affix**, e-**ficks**, v anheften,
anbringen

**afflict**, e-**flikt**, v
heimsuchen; betrüben;
**–ion**, n Gebrechen nt,
Leiden nt

**affluence**, **äff**-luh-enss, n
(wealth) Reichtum m

**affluent**, **äff**-luh-ent, adj
(rich) wohlhabend

**afford**, e-**ford**, v
(time/money) sich leisten;
(opportunity) gewähren;

(pleasure) bereiten

**Africa**, **äff**-rick-e, n Afrika
nt; **–n**, adj afrikanisch; n
Afrikaner m

**affront**, e-**frant**, n
Beleidigung f; v beleidigen

**afloat**, e-**floht**, adj & adv
flott, schwimmend

**afraid**, e-**frehd**, adj
ängstlich, bange; **to be –
(of)**, v sich fürchten,
Angst haben (vor); **I'm –
(that)**, leider, ich fürchte
(daß)

**afresh**, e-**fresch**, adv von
neuem

**after**, **ahf**-ter, prep nach; adv
nachher, danach; conj
nachdem; **– sales service**,
n Kundendienst m

**aftermath**, **ahf**-ter-mahth, n
Auswirkungen pl Folgen pl

**afternoon**, **ahf**-ter-**nuhn**, n
Nachmittag m

**aftershave**, **ahf**-ter-schehw,
n Aftershave nt,
Rasierwasser nt

**afterthought**, **ahf**-ter-thort,
n nachträgliche Idee f

**afterwards**, **ahf**-ter-werds,
adv nachher, später,
danach

**again**, e-**gehn**, adv wieder,
nochmals; außerdem; **–
and –**, immer wieder

**against**, e-**genst**, prep gegen

**age**, ehdsch, n Alter nt;
(period) Zeitalter nt; **–
group**, n Altersgruppe f; **–
limit**, n Altersgrenze f; **to
be of –**, volljährig sein

**aged**, eh-dschidd, adj alt,
bejahrt

**agency**, eh-dschen-ssi, n
Agentur f, Vertretung f; fig
Vermittlung f

**agenda**, e-**dschenn**-de, n
Tagesordnung f

**agent**, eh-dschent, n
Vertreter m, Agent m

**aggravate**, **ägg**-re-weht, v
(person) ärgern;
(situation) verschlimmern

**aggregate**, **ägg**-ri-get, adj
gesamt; n Anhäufung f,
Summe f

**aggregate**, **ägg**-ri-geht, v
anhäufen, ansammeln

**aggression**, e-**gresch**-'n, n
Aggression f; (attack)
Angriff m, Überfall m

**aggressive**, e-**gress**-iw, adj
streitlustig; aggressiv

**aghast**, e-**gahst**, adj bestürzt,
entsetzt

**agile**, **ädd**-dscheil, adj
behende, flink

**agitate**, **ädd**-dschi-teht, v
(shake) schütteln; (upset)
erregen; (cause trouble)
agitieren

**agitation**, ädd-dschi-**teh**-
sch'n, n (mental)
Erregung f, Aufregung f;
(trouble) Agitation f

**ago**, e-**goh**, adv vor, her;
**long –**, adv lange her

**agonize**, **ägg**-e-neis, v sich
quälen, unentschlossen
sein

**agony**, **ägg**-e-ni, n Qual f,
Pein f

**agree**, *e-grie*, *v* einig sein, übereinstimmen; **– to**, einwilligen in; **–able**, *adj* angenehm; **–ment**, *n* Übereinstimmung *f*; (contract) Vertrag *m*

**agricultural**, *ägg-ri-kall-tsche-rel*, *adj* landwirtschaftlich

**agriculture**, *ägg-ri-kall-tscher*, *n* Landwirtschaft *f*

**aground**, *e-graund*, *adv* gestrandet

**ahead**, *e-hedd*, *adv* voran, voraus

**aid**, *ehd*, *n* Hilfe *f*; (money) Unterstützung *f*; *v* helfen

**AIDS**, *ehds*, *n* AIDS *nt*

**ailing**, *eh-ling*, *adj* kränklich

**ailment**, *ehl-ment*, *n* Leiden *nt*, Krankheit *f*

**aim**, *ehm*, *n* Ziel *nt*, Zweck *m*; *v* zielen; **–less**, *adj* ziellos

**air**, *ähr*, *n* Luft *f*; (manner) Miene *f*; *mus* Melodie *f*; *v* (clothes etc.) lüften; **– conditioning**, *n* Klimaanlage *f*; **– gun**, *n* Luftgewehr *nt*; **– mail**, *n* Luftpost *f*

**aircraft**, *ähr-krahft*, *n* Flugzeug *nt*

**airline**, *ähr-lein*, *n* Fluggesellschaft *f*

**airplane**, *ähr-plehn*, *n* Flugzeug *nt*

**airport**, *ähr-port*, *n* Flughafen *m*

**airtight**, *ähr-teit*, *adj* luftdicht

**aisle**, *eil*, *n* Gang *m*

**ajar**, *e-dschahr*, *adj* angelehnt, halboffen

**akin**, *e-kinn*, *adj* verwandt; gleicher Art

**alabaster**, *äll-e-bahss-ter*, *n* Alabaster *m*

**alarm**, *e-lahrm*, *n* Alarm *m*; *v* beunruhigen; **– call**, *n* Weckruf *m*; **– clock**, *n* Wecker *m*

**alarming**, *e-lahr-ming*, *adj* beunruhigend

**album**, *äll-bem*, *n* Album *nt*; (record) Langspielplatte *f*

**alcohol**, *äll-ke-holl*, *n* Alkohol *m*; **– free**, *adj* alkoholfrei

**alcoholic**, *äll-ke-holl-ick*, *adj* alkoholisch; *n* Alkoholiker *m*

**alcoholism**, *äll-ke-holl-ism*, *n* Alkoholismus *m*

**alert**, *e-lört*, *adj* wachsam; **on the – (for)**, auf der Hut (vor); **–ness**, *n* Wachsamkeit *f*; (nimbleness) Flinkheit *f*

**alias**, *eh-li-ess*, *adv* alias; *n* Deckname *m*

**alien**, *eh-li-en*, *adj* fremd, ausländisch; (sci-fi) außerirdisch; *n* Fremde(r) *m & f*; Ausländer *m*; (sci-fi) Außerirdische(r) *m & f*

**alienate**, *eh-li-en-eht*, *v* entfremden

**alight**, *e-leit*, *adj* brennend; erleuchtet; *v* absteigen, aussteigen

**align**, *e-lein*, *v* ausrichten; anpassen

**alike**, *e-leik*, *adj* gleich, ähnlich

**alimony**, *all-i-me-ni*, *n* Unterhalt *m*

**alive**, *e-leiw*, *adj* (living) lebendig; (lively) lebendig, rege, munter

**all**, *o'al*, *adj* alle, alles; ganz; *adv* gänzlich; **– along**, die ganze Zeit; **– right**, in Ordnung, schon gut; **– the more**, um so mehr; **above –**, vor allem; **not at –**, gar nicht; gern geschehen

**allay**, *e-leh*, *v* beruhigen; beschwichtigen

**allegation**, *äll-i-geh-sch'n*, *n* Behauptung, *f*

**allege**, *e-ledsch*, *v* aussagen; behaupten; **–d**, *adj* angeblich; **–dly**, *adv* angeblich

**allegiance**, *e-lie-dschenss*, *n* Treue *f*

**allergy**, *äll-er-dschi*, *n* Allergie *f*

**allergic**, *e-lör-dschick*, *adj* allergisch

**alleviate**, *e-lie-wi-eht*, *v* lindern

**alley**, *äll-i*, *n* Gasse *f*; **blind –**, Sackgasse *f*

**alliance**, *e-lei-enss*, *n* Bündnis *nt*, Allianz *f*

**allied**, *äll-eid*, *adj* verbündet, alliiert; **– to**, verwandt (mit)

**allocate**, *äll-e-keht*, *v* zuteilen

**allot**, *e-lott*, *v* zuteilen,

zuerkennen

**allotment**, e-**lott**-ment, n
Zuteilung f; (ground)
Schrebergarten m

**allow**, e-**lau**, v (permit)
erlauben; (concede)
zugeben; – **for**,
berücksichtigen

**allowance**, e-**lau**-enss, n
Unterstützung f,
Unterhaltsgeld nt; (pocket
money) Taschengeld nt;
(rebate) Nachlaß m; **to
make –ances**,
berücksichtigen,
Zugeständnisse machen

**alloy**, **äll**-eu, n Legierung f

**all-round**, o'al-**raund**, adj
Allround-

**all-time**, o'al-**teim**, adj aller
Zeiten

**allude (to)**, e-**luhd** (tu), v
anspielen (auf)

**alluring**, e-**luhr**-ring, adj
verlockend; verführerisch

**allusion**, e-**luh**-sch'n, n
Anspielung f

**ally**, **äll**-ei, n Verbündete(r)
m & f, Alliierte(r) m

**ally**, e-**lei**, v – o.s. with, sich
vereinigen mit

**almighty**, o'al-**mei**-ti, adj
allmächtig; **the Almighty**,
n der Allmächtige m

**almond**, **ah**-mend, n
Mandel f

**almost**, o'al-**mohst**, adv fast,
beinahe

**alms**, ahms, npl Almosen pl;
**–house**, n Armenhaus nt

**aloft**, e-**loft**, adv in

der/die Luft

**alone**, e-**lohn**, adv allein,
nur

**along**, e-**long**, adv vorwärts;
prep längs, entlang; –
**with**, prep zusammen mit

**alongside**, e-**long**-sseid, adv
nebenher, daneben; prep
neben

**aloof**, e-**luhf**, adj unnahbar;
adv fern; **stay –**, sich
abseits halten

**aloud**, e-**laud**, adv laut;
hörbar

**alphabet**, **äll**-fe-bett, n
Alphabet nt

**alphabetical(ly)**, äll-fe-**bett**-
i-k'l(-i), adj & adv
alphabetisch

**alpine**, **äll**-pein, adj Alpen-
**Alps**, älpss, npl Alpen pl

**already**, o'al-**redd**-i, adv
schon, bereits

**also**, **o'al**-ssoh, conj auch,
ebenfalls; außerdem

**altar**, **o'al**-ter, n Altar m

**alter**, **o'al**-ter, v ändern

**alteration**, o'al-te-**reh**-sch'n,
n Änderung f

**alternate**, o'al-**tör**-net, adj
abwechselnd; **on – days**,
jeden zweiten Tag

**alternate**, **o'al**-ter-neht, v
abwechseln

**alternative**, o'al-**tör**-ne-tiw,
adj Alternativ-, andere(r);
n Wahl f; Alternative f;
**–ly**, adv als Alternative,
oder

**although**, o'al-**dhoh**, conj
obwohl

**altitude**, **äll**-ti-tjuhd, n
Höhe, f

**altogether**, o'al-tu-**gedh**-er,
adv im ganzen;
vollkommen

**aluminium**, äll-juh-**minn**-
jem, n Aluminium nt

**always**, **o'al**-u'ehs, adv
immer, jederzeit

**a.m.** eh emm, adv (abbr **ante
meridiem**), vormittags

**amass**, e-**mäss**, v anhäufen,
ansammeln

**amateur**, **ämm**-e-tör, adj
Amateur-, Hobby-; n
Amateur m; pej Dilettant
m; **–ish**, adj dilettantisch

**amaze**, e-**mehs**, v in Staunen
(ver)setzen; **–d**, adj
erstaunt

**amazement**, e-**mehs**-ment, n
Erstaunen nt

**amazing**, e-**meh**-sing, adj
erstaunlich

**ambassador**, ämm-**bäss**-e-
der, n Botschafter m; fig
Vertreter m

**amber**, **ämm**-ber, n
Bernstein m; (traffic light)
Gelb nt

**ambiguity**, ämm-bi-**gjuh**-i-
ti, n Zweideutigkeit f

**ambiguous**, ämm-**bigg**-ju-
ess, adj zweideutig

**ambition**, ämm-**bisch**-'n, n
Ehrgeiz m

**ambitious**, ämm-**bisch**-ess,
adj ehrgeizig

**ambulance**, **ämm**-bju-lenss,
n Krankenwagen m

**ambush**, **ämm**-busch, n

Hinterhalt *m*, Überfall (aus dem Hinterhalt); *v* (aus dem Hinterhalt) überfallen

**amenable**, *e*-mie-ne-b'l, *adj* zugänglich; empfänglich

**amend**, *e*-mend, *v* (ab)ändern; **–ment**, *n* Änderung *f*

**amends**, *e*-mends, *npl* **make – (for)**, *v* wiedergutmachen

**America**, *e*-me-ri-ke, *n* Amerika; **–n**, *adj* amerikanisch; *n* Amerikaner *m*

**amethyst**, ämm-*i*-thist, *n* Amethyst *m*

**amiable**, eh-mi-*e*-b'l, *adj* liebenswürdig; freundlich

**amicable**, ämm-i-ke-b'l, *adj* freundschaftlich; (settlement) gütlich

**amid(st)**, *e*-mid(st), *prep* inmitten, mitten in

**amiss**, *adj*-miss, *adj & adv* **there's something –**, da stimmt irgend etwas nicht; **to take sth –**, etw übelnehmen

**ammonia**, *e*-moh-ni-*e*, *n* Ammoniak *nt*

**ammunition**, ämm-ju-nisch-'n, *n* Munition *f*

**amnesia**, ämm-nie-si-*e*, *n* Gedächtnisschwund *m*

**amnesty**, ämm-niss-ti, *n* Amnestie *f*

**amok**, *e*-mack, *adv* **run –**, *v* Amok laufen

**among(st)**, *e*-mang(st), *prep*

unter, zwischen

**amoral**, eh-mo-rel, *adj* amoralisch

**amorous**, ämm-*e*-ress, *adj* verliebt

**amount**, *e*-maunt, *n* Menge *f*; (money) Betrag *m*; **– to**, *v* betragen, sich belaufen auf; *fig* hinauslaufen auf

**amp(ere)**, ämp-(ähr), *n* Ampere *nt*

**ample**, ämp-'l, *adj* reichlich; (roomy) geräumig

**amplifier**, ämp-li-fei-er, *n* Verstärker *m*

**amplify**, ämp-li-fei, *v* verstärken

**amputate**, ämp-ju-teht, *v* amputieren

**amuse**, *e*-mjuhs, *v* amüsieren; (entertain) unterhalten

**amusement**, *e*-mjuhs-ment, *n* Belustigung *f*; (entertainment) Unterhaltung *f*; **–s**, *pl* Freizeitangebot *nt*; (slot machines) Spielhalle *f*

**an**, änn/*e*n, *art* ein, eine, ein

**anaemia**, *e*-nie-mi-*e*, *n* Anämie *f*, Blutarmut *f*

**anaemic**, *e*-nie-mick, *adj* blutarm

**anaesthetic**, änn-ess-thett-ick, *n* Betäubungsmittel *nt*; **general –**, Vollnarkose *f*

**analogue**, änn-*e*-logg, *adj* Analog-

**analogy**, *e*-näll-*e*-dschi, *n* Analogie *f*

**analysis**, *e*-näll-*i*-ssiss, *n* Analyse *f*

**analyse**, änn-*e*-leis, *v* analysieren

**anarchy**, änn-er-ki, *n* Anarchie *f*

**ancestor**, änn-ssess-ter, *n* Vorfahr *m*

**ancestry**, änn-ssess-tri, *n* Abstammung *f*, Herkunft *f*

**anchor**, äng-ker, *n* Anker *m*; *v* ankern; verankern

**anchovy**, änn-tsche-wi, *n* Sardelle *f*

**ancient**, ehn-sch'nt, *adj* alt; (clothes etc.) uralt; (monument) historisch

**and**, ännd, *conj* und; **– so on**, und so weiter; **bigger – bigger**, immer größer

**Andes**, änn-dies, *npl* Anden *pl*

**anew**, *e*-njuh, *adv* aufs neue, von neuem

**angel**, ehn-dsch'l, *n* Engel *m*

**anger**, äng-ger, *n* Zorn *m*, Ärger *m*; *v* ärgern

**angle**, äng-g'l, *n* Winkel *m*; *fig* Standpunkt *m*

**angler**, äng-gler, *n* Angler *m*, Fischer *m*

**Anglican**, äng-gli-k'n, *adj* anglikanisch; *n* Anglikaner *m*

**angling**, äng-gling, *n* Angeln *nt*, Fischen *nt*

**angry**, äng-gri, *adj* ärgerlich, böse; (enraged) zornig

**anguish**, äng-gu'isch, *n* Qual *f*

**animal**, änn-i-mel, *n* Tier *nt*;

*adj* tierisch

**animate,** *änn-*i-met, *adj*
lebendig

**animate,** *änn-*i-meht, *v*
beleben; animieren; **–d,**
*adj* lebhaft, belebt; **–d**
**film,** *n* Zeichentrickfilm *m*

**animosity,** *änn-*i-moss-i-ti, *n*
Feindseligkeit *f*

**aniseed,** *änn-*i-ssied, *n*
Anis *m*

**ankle,** *äng-*k'l, *n*
(Fuß)knöchel *m*

**annex,** *änn-*eks, *n* (to
document) Anhang *m*; (to
building) Anbau *m*

**annex,** *e-*neks, *v*
annektieren

**annihilate,** *e-*nei-i-leht, *v*
vernichten, zerstören

**anniversary,** *änn-*i-wör-se-
ri, *n* Jahrestag *m*;
(wedding) Hochzeitstag *m*

**annotate,** *änn-*e-teht, *v*
kommentieren

**announce,** *e-*naunss, *v*
ankündigen; **–ment,** *n*
Ankündigung *f*; (official)
Bekanntmachung *f*

**announcer,** *e-*naun-sser, *n*
Ansager *m*

**annoy,** *e-*neu, *v* ärgern;
**be/get –ed,** *v* sich ärgern;
**–ance,** *n* Verärgerung *f*;
**–ing,** *adj* ärgerlich

**annual,** *änn-*ju-el, *adj*
jährlich, Jahres-; *n* (plant)
einjährige Pflanze; (book)
Jahresalbum *nt*

**annul,** *e-*nall, *v* für ungültig
erklären, aufheben

**anomalous,** *e-*nomm-e-less,
*adj* anormal, abweichend

**anomaly,** *e-*nomm-e-li, *n*
Abweichung *f*

**anonymous,** *e-*nonn-i-mess,
*adj* anonym

**anonymity,** *änn-*e-ni-mi-ti,
*n* Anonymität *f*

**anorak,** *änn-*e-rack, *n*
Anorak *m*

**anorexia,** *änn-*e-reck-ssi-e, *n*
Magersucht *m*, Anorexie *f*

**another,** *e-*nadh-er, *adj &*
*pron* ein(e) andere(r/s),
noch ein(e); **one –,**
einander

**answer,** *ahn-*sser, *n* Antwort
*f*; *v* antworten; **– the door,**
aufmachen; **– the phone,**
das Telefon abnehmen

**answerable,** *ahn-*sse-re-b'l,
*adj* verantwortlich

**answering machine,** *ahn-*
sse-ring me-schien, *n*
Anrufbeantworter *m*

**ant,** *ännt,* *n* Ameise *f*

**antagonism,** *änn-*tägg-e-
nism, *n* Antagonismus *m*

**antagonize,** *änn-*tägg-e-neis,
*v* gegen sich aufbringen

**Antarctic,** *änn-*tark-tick,
*adj* antarktisch; **the –,**
**Antarctica,** *n* die
Antarktis *f*

**antelope,** *änn-*ti-lohp, *n*
Antilope *f*

**antenatal,** *änn-*ti-neh-t'l, *adj*
vor der Geburt,
Schwangerschafts-

**anthem,** *änn-*them, *n*
Hymne *f*

**anti-,** *änn-*ti, *pref* Anti-,
Gegen-

**anti-aircraft,** *änn-*ti-ähr-
krahft, *adj* Flugabwehr-

**antibiotic,** *änn-*ti-bei-ott-
ick, *adj* antibiotisch; *n*
Antibiotikum *nt*

**anticipate,** *änn-*tiss-i-peht, *v*
(expect) vorhersehen,
erwarten; (precede)
zuvorkommen

**anticipation,** *änn-*tiss-i-peh-
sch'n, *n* Erwartung *f*; **in –,**
im voraus

**anticlimax,** *änn-*ti-klei-
macks, *n* Enttäuschung *f*

**anticlockwise,** *änn-*ti-
klock-u'eis, *adj & adv*
gegen den Uhrzeigersinn

**antidote,** *änn-*ti-doht, *n*
Gegenmittel *nt*

**antifreeze,** *änn-*ti-fries, *n*
Frostschutzmittel *nt*

**antihistamine,** *änn-*ti-
hiss-te-mien, *n*
Antihistamin *nt*

**antiquated,** *änn-*ti-kueh-
tidd, *adj* antiquiert,
veraltet

**antique,** *änn-*tiek, *adj* antik;
*n* Antiquität *f*

**antiseptic,** *änn-*ti-ssepp-
tick, *adj* antiseptisch; *n*
Antiseptikum *nt*

**antisocial,** *änn-*ti-ssoh-sch'l,
*adj* unsozial

**antlers,** *änt-*lers, *npl*
Geweih *nt*

**anvil,** *änn-*will, *n* Amboß *m*

**anxiety,** *äng-*sei-i-ti, *n*
Besorgnis *f*, Sorge *f*; *med*

Angstneurose f

**anxious, äng-schess,** *adj*
besorgt, ängstlich; **be –
(about),** *v* sich Sorgen
machen (um)

**any, enn-i, adj & adv** (in
questions) etwas; welche
*pl*; (whichever) jede(r/s);
(any one) irgend eine(r/s);
**not –,** kein(e); **(not) –
more,** (nicht) mehr; **in –
case,** auf jeden Fall;
überhaupt

**anybody, enn-i-bodd-i,** *pron*
(irgend) jemand; **not –,**
niemand

**anyhow, enn-i-hau,** *conj* auf
jeden Fall, immerhin

**anyone, enn-i-u'an,** *pron*
(irgend) jemand; **not –,**
niemand

**anything, enn-i-thing,** *pron*
(irgend) etwas; alles; **not
–,** nichts

**anyway, enn-i-u'eh,** *adv* auf
jeden Fall, immerhin;
überhaupt

**anywhere, enn-i-u'ähr,** *adv*
irgendwo(hin); **not –,**
nirgendwo(hin)

**apart, e-part,** *adv* (aside)
abseits, beiseite;
(separated) auseinander; **–
from,** *prep* außer

**apartheid, e-part-eit,** *n*
Apartheid f

**apartment, e-part-ment,** *n*
Wohnung f

**apathetic, äpp-e-thett-ick,**
*adj* apathisch,
teilnahmslos

**apathy, äpp-e-thi,** *n* Apathie
f; Teilnahmslosigkeit f

**ape, ehp,** *n* Affe m; *v*
nachäffen

**aperitif, e-pe-ri-tief,** *n*
Aperitif m

**aperture, äpp-er-tscher,** *n*
Öffnung f; *photog*
Blende f

**apex, eh-pecks,** *n* Gipfel m;
Spitze f

**apiece, e-piess,** *adv* pro
Stück; pro Person

**apologetic, e-poll-e-dsche-**
tick, *adj* entschuldigend

**apologize, e-poll-e-dscheis,** *v*
sich entschuldigen

**apology, e-poll-e-dschi,** *n*
Entschuldigung f

**apostle, e-poss-'l,** *n* Apostel
m

**apostrophe, e-poss-tre-fi,** *n*
Apostroph m

**appal, e-po'al,** *v* entsetzen;
**–ling,** *adj* entsetzlich

**apparatus, äpp-e-reh-tess,** *n*
Apparat m, Geräte *pl*

**apparent, e-pä-rent,** *adj*
(obvious) offenbar, klar;
(seeming) scheinbar; **–ly,**
*adv* anscheinend

**apparition, äpp-e-risch-'n,** *n*
Erscheinung f

**appeal, e-piel,** *n* Aufruf m;
*law* Berufung f; *v*
(dringend) bitten; *law*
Berufung einlegen; **– to,**
(turn to) appellieren an;
(be attractive to) zusagen,
gefallen

**appear, e-pier,** *v* erscheinen;

(seem) scheinen; *theatre*
auftreten; **–ance,** *n*
Erscheinen nt; *theatre*
Auftritt m; (looks)
Aussehen nt

**appease, e-pies,** *v*
besänftigen,
beschwichtigen

**appendage, e-pend-idsch,** *n*
Anhang m, Zubehör m;
(limb) Gliedmaße f

**appendicitis, e-pend-i-ssai-**
tiss, *n*
Blinddarmentzündung f

**appendix, e-pend-icks,** *n* (to
book) Anhang m; *med*
Blinddarm m

**appetite, äpp-i-teit,** *n*
Appetit m; *fig* Lust f

**appetizer, äpp-i-tei-ser,** *n*
Appetitanreger m; (food)
Vorspeise f

**appetizing, äpp-i-tei-sing,**
*adj* appetitlich

**applaud, e-plo'ad,** *v*
applaudieren, Beifall
klatschen

**applause, e-plo'as,** *n*
Applaus m, Beifall m

**apple, äpp-'l,** *n* Apfel m; **–
tree,** Apfelbaum m

**applicable, e-plick-e-b'l,** *adj*
zutreffend

**appliance, e-plei-enss,** *n*
Gerät nt

**applicant, äpp-li-kent,** *n*
Bewerber m

**application, äpp-li-keh-**
sch'n, *n* (use) Anwendung
f, Gebrauch m;
(candidacy) Bewerbung f;

(effort) Fleiß m; – **form**, n Bewerbungsformular nt

**apply**, e-plei, v (be appropriate) zutreffen; (use) anwenden; (lay on) auflegen, auftragen; – **for**, sich bewerben um; – **to**, sich wenden an

**appoint**, e-peunt, v (to post) ernennen; (agree) festsetzen

**appointment**, e-peunt-ment, n (to post) Ernennung f; (meeting) Verabredung f; (post) Stelle f

**appraisal**, e-preh-s'l, n Abschätzung f, Beurteilung f

**appreciable**, e-prie-schi-e-b'l, adj merklich

**appreciate**, e-prie-schi-eht, v (recognize) anerkennen, einsehen; (value) schätzen, zu schätzen wissen; (be grateful) dankbar sein; (in value) im Wert steigen

**appreciation**, e-prie-schi-eh-sch'n, n Anerkennung f; Schätzung; Steigerung f

**apprehend**, äpp-ri-**hend**, v (arrest) festnehmen; (understand) verstehen; (perceive) wahrnehmen

**apprehension**, äpp-ri-**henn**-sch'n, n (fear) Angst f; (arrest) Verhaftung f

**apprehensive**, äpp-ri-**henn**-ssiw, adj besorgt, ängstlich

**apprentice**, e-prenn-tiss, n Lehrling m; –**ship**, Lehre

f, Lehrzeit f

**approach**, e-prohtsch, n Annäherung f; (access) Zugang m, Zufahrt f; (to problem) Ansatz m; v sich nähern; (person) herantreten an; (problem) angehen

**appropriate(ly)**, e-proh-pri-et(-li), adj & adv angemessen, passend

**appropriate**, e-proh-pri-eht, v sich aneignen

**approval**, e-pruh-wel, n Billigung f, Beifall m

**approve**, e-pruhw, v billigen

**approximate(ly)**, e-prock-ssi-met(-li), adj & adv ungefähr, annähernd

**approximate (to)**, e-prock-ssi-meht (tu), v nahekommen

**apricot**, eh-pri-kott, n Aprikose f

**April**, eh-prill, n April m

**apron**, eh-pren, n Schürze f

**apse**, äpps, n Apsis f

**apt**, äppt, adj (fit) passend; (inclined) geneigt; (capable) fähig

**aptitude**, äpp-ti-tjuhd, n Begabung f, Talent nt

**aquarium**, e-kwähr-ri-em, n Aquarium nt

**Aquarius**, e-kwähr-ri-ess, n Wassermann m

**aquatic**, e-kwätt-ick, adj Wasser-

**Arab**, ä-reb, adj arabisch; n Araber m

**Arabic**, ä-re-bick, adj

(language) arabisch; n Arabisch nt

**aqueduct**, äck-u'i-dackt, n Aquädukt m/nt

**arable**, ä-re-b'l, adj bebaubar, nutzbar

**arbitrary**, ahr-bi-tre-ri, adj willkürlich

**arbitrate**, ahr-bi-treht, v schlichten, vermitteln

**arbitration**, ar-bi-treh-sch'n, n Schlichtung f

**arbitrator**, ahr-bi-treh-ter, n Schlichter m, Vermittler m

**arc**, ark, n Bogen m; – **lamp**, Bogenlampe f

**arcade**, ark-ehd, n Arkade f; (shopping) Passage f

**arch**, artsch, n Bogen m; v sich wölben

**archaeologist**, ar-ki-oll-e-dschist, n Archäologe m

**archaeology**, ar-ki-oll-e-dschi, n Archäologie f

**archaic**, ar-keh-ick, adj veraltet

**archbishop**, artsch-**bisch**-ep, n Erzbischof m

**archer**, artsch-er, n Bogenschütze m; –**y**, n Bogenschießen n

**archetype**, ahr-ki-teip, n Urbild nt

**archipelago**, ar-ki-pell-e-goh, n Archipel m

**architect**, ahr-ki-tekt, n Architekt m, Baumeister m

**architecture**, ahr-ki-teck-tscher, n Architektur f

**archive(s), ahr**-keiw(s), n(pl) Archiv nt

**archway, artsch**-u'eh, n (Tor)bogen m

**Arctic, ark**-tick, adj arktisch, Polar-; **the –**, n die Arktis f

**ardent, ahr**-d'nt, adj feurig, glühend

**ardour, ahr**-der, n (passion) Leidenschaft f; (zest) Eifer m

**arduous, ahr**-djuh-ess, adj mühsam, schwierig

**area, ähr**-ri-e, n (expanse) Fläche f; (district) Gebiet nt, Gegend f

**arena, e**-rie-ne, n Arena f

**Argentina, ar**-djschen-tie-ne, n Argentinien nt

**Argentinian, ar**-djschen-tinn-jen, adj argentinisch; n Argentinier m

**argue, ahr**-gjuh, v (debate) diskutieren; (dispute) (sich) streiten

**argument, ahr**-gju-ment, n Diskussion f; Auseinandersetzung f; (reason) Begründung f

**arise, e**-reis, v (occur) entstehen, vorkommen; (of protest) sich erheben; (of question) sich stellen; **– from**, sich ergeben aus

**aristocracy, ä**-ri-stock-re-ssi, n Aristokratie f, Adel m

**aristocratic, ä**-ri-ste-krätt-ick, adj aristokratisch

**arithmetic, e**-rith-me-tick, n Rechnen nt

**Ark, ark**, n **– of the Covenant**, Bundeslade f; **Noah's –**, die Arche Noah f

**arm, arm**, n Arm m; (branch) Zweig m; v (sich) bewaffnen; (equip) ausrüsten; **–s**, npl (weapons) Waffen pl; **coat of –s**, Wappen nt

**armament, ahr**-me-m'nt, n Aufrüstung f; **–s**, npl Ausrüstung f

**armchair, ahr**-tschähr, n Sessel m

**armistice, ahr**-miss-tiss, n Waffenstillstand m

**armour, ahr**-mer, n Rüstung f

**armoured, ahr**-merd, adj Panzer-

**armoury, ahr**-me-ri, n Waffenlager nt

**armpit, arm**-pitt, n Achselhöhle f

**army, ahr**-mi, n Heer nt Armee f

**aromatic, ä**-re-mätt-ick, adj würzig, aromatisch

**aroma, e**-roh-me, n Duft m, Aroma nt

**around, e**-raund, adv (rings) herum; prep um… herum

**arouse, e**-raus, v (auf)wecken; (excite) erregen

**arrange, e**-rehndsch, v (objects) (an)ordnen; (meeting) ansetzen; (obtain) besorgen; (agree) vereinbaren

**array, e**-reh, n (line-up) Aufstellung f; (collection) Ansammlung f

**arrears, e**-riers, n Rückstand m; **fall into –**, in Rückstand geraten

**arrest, e**-rest, n Verhaftung f, Festnahme f; v verhaften, festnehmen; (stop) unterbinden

**arrival, e**-raiw-'l, n Ankunft f; (person) Ankömmling m; (goods) Lieferung f

**arrive, e**-raiw, v ankommen; **– at a decision**, zu einer Entscheidung kommen

**arrogance, ä**-re-genss, n Arroganz f

**arrogant, ä**-re-gent, adj arrogant

**arrow, ä**-roh, n Pfeil m

**arse, arss**, n vulg Arsch m

**arsenal, ahr**-ss'n-'l, n Arsenal nt, Waffenlager nt

**arsenic, ahr**-ss'n-ick, n Arsen nt

**arson, ahr**-ss'n, n Brandstiftung f

**art, art**, n Kunst f; (skill) Geschick nt; **–s**, Geisteswissenschaften pl

**arterial road, ar**-tier-ri-el rohd, n Verkehrsader f

**artery, ahr**-te-ri, n Schlagader f, Arterie f

**artful, art**-full, adj (sly) schlau

**artichoke, ahr**-ti-tschohk, n Artischocke f; **Jerusalem –**, Topinambur m

**article, ahr**-ti-k'l, n Artikel

m; – of clothing, Kleidungsstück nt

**articulate**, ar-tick-ju-let, adj (speech) deutlich; (speaker) gewandt; **to be –**, v sich gut ausdrücken

**articulate**, ar-tick-ju-leht, v artikulieren; (state) darlegen; **–d lorry**, Sattelschlepper m

**artificial**, ahr-ti-fisch-'l, adj künstlich

**artillery**, ar-till-e-ri, n Artillerie f

**artisan**, ahr-ti-sänn, n (Kunst)handwerker m

**artist**, ahr-tist, n Künstler m; **–ic**, adj künstlerisch

**as**, äs, conj (time) als; (manner) wie, so wie; (reason) da; so wie; **– for**, was… betrifft; **– if/though**, als ob; **– from/of**, ab; **– good –**, so gut wie; **– to**, in Bezug auf; **– well**, auch; **– well –**, sowohl… als auch; **– yet**, bis jetzt

**asbestos**, äs-bess-tess, n Asbest m

**ascend**, e-ssend, v besteigen; hinaufgehen

**ascent**, e-ssent, n Aufstieg m; Besteigung f

**ascertain**, äss-er-tehn, v feststellen

**ascribe to**, e-skreib tu, v zuschreiben

**ash**, äsch, n Asche f; (tree) Esche f; **–tray**, Aschenbecher m; **Ash**

**Wednesday**, Aschermittwoch m

**ashamed**, e-schehmd, adj beschämt; **be – (of)**, sich schämen (für)

**ashore**, e-schohr, adv an(s) Land

**Asia**, eh-sche, n Asien nt; **–n**, adj asiatisch; n Asiat m

**aside**, e-sseid, adv beiseite, abseits; n beiläufige Bemerkung f

**ask**, ahsk, v (enquire) fragen; (Frage) stellen; (permission, request) bitten; (invite) einladen; **– after**, fragen nach; **– for**, bitten um

**askew**, e-skjuh, adv schief

**asleep**, e-sliep, adj schlafend; **be –**, v schlafen; **fall –**, v einschlafen

**asparagus**, e-spä-re-gess, n Spargel m

**aspect**, äss-peckt, n Aspekt m, Seite f

**aspen**, äss-p'n, n Espe f

**aspersion**, äss-pör-sch'n, n **cast –s (on)**, v abfällige Bemerkungen machen (über)

**asphyxiation**, äss-fick-ssi-eh-sch'n, n Erstickung f

**asphyxiate**, äss-fick-ssi-eht, v ersticken; **be –d**, ersticken

**aspiration**, äss-pi-reh-sch'n, n Ziel nt; **have –s (towards)**, v streben (nach)

**aspire to**, e-speir tu, v streben nach

**aspirin**, äss-pi-rinn, n Aspirin nt

**ass**, äss, äss n Esel m

**assail**, e-ssehl, v angreifen; (of doubts) plagen

**assailant**, e-sseh-lent, n Angreifer m

**assassin**, e-ssäss-in, n Attentäter m

**assassinate**, e-ssäss-i-neht, v ermorden

**assassination**, e-ssäss-i-neh-sch'n, v (geglücktes) Attentat nt; **– attempt**, n Attentat nt

**assault**, e-ssolt, n Angriff m; v angreifen; (sexually) herfallen über

**assemble**, e-ssemm-b'l, v (people) versammeln; (parts) zusammensetzen; (of group) sich versammeln

**assembly**, e-ssemm-bli, n (meeting) Versammlung f; (construction) Zusammensetzen nt, Montage f

**assent**, e-ssent, n Zustimmung f; **– (to)**, v zustimmen

**assert**, e-ssört, v behaupten; **–ion**, n Behauptung f

**assess**, e-ssess, v (ein)schätzen; (tax) festsetzen; **–ment**, n Einschätzung f; (of tax) Festsetzung f; **–or**, n Schätzer m; Prüfer m

**asset, äss**-itt, n Vorteil m;
*fin* Vermögenswert m;
**–s,** *pl fin* Aktiva *pl*
Vermögen *nt*

**assiduous,** e-ssidd-*juh-ess*,
*adj* (hard-working) fleißig;
(attentive) aufmerksam

**assign,** e-ssein, v zuteilen;
übertragen; **–ment,**
Übertragung *f*; (task)
Aufgabe *f*

**assist,** e-ssist, v helfen;
**–ance,** n Hilfe *f*; (money)
Unterstützung *f*; **–ant,**
Mitarbeiter m; (shop) **–,**
Verkäufer m

**associate,** e-ssoh-ssi-et, n
Kollege m; (partner)
Teilhaber m; **– (member),**
n außerordentliches
Mitglied *nt*

**associate (with),** e-ssoh-ssi-
et (u'idh), v (ideas etc.)
assoziieren (mit); (of
people) verkehren (mit)

**association,** e-ssoh-ssi-eh-
sch'n, n (link) Assoziation
*f*, Zusammenhang m;
(group) Verein m

**assorted,** e-ssor-tidd, *adj*
gemischt

**assortment (of),** e-ssort-
ment (ew), n Auswahl *f*
(an), Sortiment *nt* (von)

**assume,** e-ssjuhm, v
(presume, take on)
annehmen;
(responsibility)
übernehmen; **–ing that,**
angenommen/
vorausgesetzt, daß

**assumption,** e-ssamp-sch'n,
n Annahme *f*

**assurance,** e-schor-renss, n
(insurance) Versicherung
*f*; (promise) Zusicherung *f*

**assure,** e-schor, v (promise,
insure) versichern; (make
certain) sichern

**asterisk, äss**-te-risk, n
Sternchen *nt*

**astern,** e-störn, *adv* (nach)
achtern, achteraus

**astonish,** e-stonn-isch, v
erstaunen, in Erstaunen
setzen; **–ment,** n
Erstaunen *nt*

**astound,** e-staund, v
verblüffen

**astray,** e-streh, *adj* verloren;
**go –,** v fehlgehen; **lead –,**
v irreführen

**astride,** e-streid, *prep*
rittlings auf

**astrologer,** e-stroll-e-dscher,
n Astrologe m

**astrology,** e-stroll-e-dschi, n
Astrologie *f*

**astronaut, äss**-tre-no'at, n
Astronaut m

**astronomer,** e-stronn-e-mer,
n Astronom m

**astronomy,** e-stronn-e-mi, n
Astronomie *f*

**astute,** e-stjuht, *adj* schlau

**asylum,** e-ssei-lem, n Asyl
*nt*; (mental) Anstalt *f*

**at, ätt**/ett, *prep* an, zu, bei,
in; (hour) um; (price) zu;
(speed) mit; **– home,** zu
Hause; **– once,** sofort; **–
times,** manchmal

**atheist,** eh-thie-ist, n
Atheist m

**Athens, äth**-ens, n Athen *nt*

**athlete, äth**-liet, n Athlet m,
Sportler m

**athletic,** äth-lett-ick, *adj*
athletisch; (person)
sportlich; **–s,** n
Leichtathletik *f*

**Atlantic, ätt**-länn-tick, *adj*
atlantisch; **the – (Ocean),**
n der Atlantik m

**atlas, ätt**-less, n Atlas m

**atmosphere, ätt**-mess-fier, n
Atmosphäre *f*

**atom, ätt**-em, n Atom *nt*;
**–ic,** *adj* atomar, Atom-;
**–(ic) bomb,** n
Atombombe *f*; **–ic energy,**
n Atomenergie *f*

**atone (for),** e-tohn (for), v
sühnen; **–ment,** n Sühne *f*

**atrocious,** e-troh-schess, *adj*
scheußlich, gräßlich

**atrocity,** e-tross-i-ti, n (act)
Greueltat *f*

**attach (to),** e-tätsch, v (to a
letter etc.) anheften;
(value etc.) legen (auf);
zuschreiben; **be –ed to,**
(fond of) hängen an;
**–ment,** n (accessory)
Zusatzteil m; (fondness)
Zuneigung *f*

**attack,** e-täck, n Angriff m;
(illness) Anfall m; v
angreifen; **–er,** n
Angreifer m

**attain,** e-tehn, v erreichen,
erlangen; **–ment,** n (act)

Erreichen nt, Erlangen nt;
**–ments,** pl (talents)
Kenntnisse pl
**attempt,** e-tempt, n Versuch
m; (attack) Attentat nt; v
versuchen
**attend,** e-tend, v (be at)
anwesend sein; (regularly)
besuchen; **– to,** (person)
sich kümmern um; (task)
erledigen; **–ance,** n
(presence) Anwesenheit f;
(number present)
Teilnehmerzahl f
**attendant,** e-tenn-dent, adj
damit verbunden; n
(keeper) Wärter m,
Wächter m; (companion)
Begleiter m
**attention,** e-tenn-sch'n, n
Aufmerksamkeit f; mil –!,
Achtung!; **for the – of,** zu
Händen von; **pay – (to),** v
beachten
**attentive,** e-tenn-tiw, adj
aufmerksam
**attest (to),** e-test (tu), v
(testify) bescheinigen;
(prove) bezeugen
**attic,** ätt-ick, n
Dachboden m; **– (room),**
Dachzimmer nt
**attitude,** ätt-i-tjuhd, n
(mental) Einstellung f;
(manner) Haltung f
**attorney,** e-tör-ni, n
Rechtsanwalt m; **power of
–,** Vollmacht f
**attract,** e-träkt, v anziehen;
(attention) erregen, auf
sich ziehen; **–ion,** n

(power) Anziehungskraft
f; (personal) Reiz m;
(thing) Attraktion f; **–ive,**
adj attraktiv, anziehend
**attribute,** ätt-ribb-juht, n
Attribut nt
**attribute (to),** e-tribb-juht
(tu), v zuschreiben,
beimessen
**aubergine,** oh-ber-dschien,
n Aubergine f
**auburn,** o'a-börn, adj
rotbraun
**auction,** o'ak-sch'n, n
Versteigerung f, Auktion
f; v versteigern; **–eer,** n
Auktionator m
**audacious,** o'a-deh-schess,
adj (bold) verwegen;
(impudent) dreist
**audacity,** o'a-däss-i-ti, n
Kühnheit f; Dreistigkeit f
**audible,** o'a-di-b'l, adj
hörbar
**audience,** o'a-di-enss, n
(public) Publikum nt;
(interview) Audienz f
**audio,** o'a-di-oh, adj Audio-;
**–visual,** audiovisuell
**audit,** o'a-ditt, n
Buchprüfung f; v prüfen;
**–or,** n Buchprüfer m
**audition,** o'a-disch-'n, n
theatre Vorsprechprobe f;
mus Probespiel nt,
Vorsingen nt
**auditor,** o'a-di-ter, n
Buchprüfer m
**augment,** o'ag-ment, v
vermehren, vergrössern
**augur,** o'a-ger, n – **well (ill),**

Gutes (nichts Gutes)
verheißen
**August,** o'a-gest, n
August m
**aunt,** ahnt, n Tante f
**au pair,** oh-pähr, n Au-pair-
(Mädchen) nt
**auspicious,** o'ass-pisch-ess,
adj günstig, glücklich
**austere,** oss-tier, adj
(person) streng; (room
etc.) karg, schmucklos
**austerity,** oss-te-ri-ti, n
(severity) Strenge f;
(simplicity)
Schmucklosigkeit f;
(hardship) Entbehrung f
**Australia,** oss-treh-li-e, n
Australien nt; **–n,** adj
australisch; n Australier m
**Austria,** oss-tri-e, n
Österreich nt; **–n,** adj
österreichisch; n
Österreicher m
**authentic,** o'a-thenn-tick,
adj authentisch; echt
**author,** o'a-ther, n Verfasser
m, Schriftsteller m
**authoritarian,** o'a-tho-ri-
tähr-ri-en, adj autoritär
**authoritative,** o'a-tho-ri-te-
tiw, adj (definitive)
maßgebend;
(commanding) bestimmt
**authority,** o'a-tho-ri-ti, n
Autorität f; **the –s,** pl die
Verwaltung f
**authorize,** o'a-the-reis, v
(empower) ermächtigen;
(permit) genehmigen
**autobiography,** o'a-te-bei-

**ogg**-re-fi, *n*
Autobiographie *f*

**autograph**, o'a-te-grahf, *n*
Autogramm *nt*

**automatic**, o'a-te-mätt-ick,
*adj* automatisch; *n*
(engine) Automatik *f*;
(weapon)
Schnellfeuerwaffe *f*

**automatically**, o'a-te-mätt-
ick-e-li, *adv* automatisch

**automobile**, o'a-te-me-biel,
*n* Auto(mobil) *nt*

**autumn**, o'a-tem, *n*
Herbst *m*

**auxiliary**, o'ag-sill-i-e-ri, *adj*
helfend, Hilfs-

**avail**, e-wehl, *n* to no –,
vergebens

**available**, e-weh-le-b'l, *adj*
(thing) verfügbar,
erhältlich; (person) frei,
erreichbar

**availability**, e-weh-le-bill-i-
ti, *n* (of thing)
Erhältlichkeit *f*

**avalanche**, äw-e-lahntsch, *n*
Lawine *f*

**avarice**, äw-e-riss, *adj*
Habsucht *f*, Geiz *m*

**avenge**, e-wendsch, *v*
rächen

**avenue**, äw-e-njuh, *n* Allee *f*

**average**, äw-e-ridsch, *adj*
durchschnittlich; *n*
Durchschnitt *m*; on –, *adv*
durchschnittlich

**averse (to)**, e-wörss (tu),
*adj* abgeneigt

**aversion (to)**, e-wör-sch'n
(tu), *n* (dislike)

Abneigung *f* (gegen);
(horror) Abscheu *f* (vor)

**avert**, e-wört, *v* (turn away)
abwehren, abwenden;
(prevent) abwenden,
verhüten

**aviary**, eh-wi-e-ri, *n*
Vogelhaus *nt*

**aviation**, eh-wi-eh-sch'n, *n*
Luftfahrt *f*

**avid (for)**, äw-idd (for), *adj*
gierig (nach), süchtig
(nach)

**avocado**, äw-e-kah-doh, *n*
Avocado *f*

**avoid**, e-weud, *v* vermeiden;
(obstacle) ausweichen

**avoidance**, e-weud-'nss, *n*
Vermeidung *f*

**await**, e-u'eht, *v* erwarten

**awake**, e-u'ehk, *adj* wach; *v*
(wake up) aufwachen;
(arouse) aufwecken;
–**ning**, *n* Erwachen *nt*

**award**, e-uord, *n* Preis *m*;
(mil etc.) Auszeichnung *f*;
*v* (prize) zuerkennen;
(damages) zusprechen

**aware (of)**, e-u'ähr (ew), *adj*
bewußt; **be – (of)**, sich
bewußt sein

**away**, e-u'eh, *adv* weg, fort;
**1 km –**, 1 km entfernt

**awe**, o'ah, *n* Ehrfurcht *f*

**awesome**, o'a-s'm, *adj*
ehrfurchtgebietend

**awful**, o'a-full, *adj* furchtbar,
entsetzlich; –**ly**, *adv*
furchtbar; *fam* sehr

**awhile**, e-u'eil, *adv* eine
Weile, eine Zeitlang

**awkward**, o'ak-u'ed, *adj*
(inconvenient) ungünstig;
(embarrassing) peinlich;
(clumsy) ungeschickt;
–**ness**, *n* (embarrassment)
Verlegenheit *f*

**awning**, o'a-ning, *n* (of
shop) Markise *f*; (of
caravan) Vordach *nt*

**awry**, e-**rei**, *adj* & *adv* schief,
krumm; **go –**, *v*
schiefgehen

**axe**, äcks, *n* Axt *f*

**axis**, äck-ssiss, *n* (*pl* axes),
Achse *f*

**axle**, äck-ss'l, *n mech*
Achse *f*

**azure**, äs-juhr, *adj*
himmelblau

**B & B,** bie end bie (*abbr* **bed and breakfast**), Übernachtung *f* mit Frühstück, Gästezimmer *pl*

**babble, bäbb-'l,** *v* plappern; (stream) plätschern

**baby, beh-**bi, *n* Baby *nt*

**baby-sit, beh-**bi-ssitt, *v* babysitten; **–er,** *n* Babysitter *m*

**bachelor, batsch-**e-ler, *n* Junggeselle *m*; **Bachelor of Arts/Science,** *n* Bakkalaureus der philosophischen Fakultät/der Naturwissenschaften *m*

**back, bäck,** *adv* (nach) hinten; zurück; *n* (of person/animal) Rücken *m*; (of cheque etc.) Rückseite *f*; *v* (support) unterstützen; (bet) wetten auf; (go backwards) rückwärts gehen/fahren; **– down,** nachgeben; **– out,** sich zurückziehen

**backbone, bäck-**bohn, *n* Rückgrat *nt*

**background, bäck-**graund, *n* Hintergrund *m*; (social) Verhältnisse *pl*

**backing, bäck-**ing, *n* (support) Unterstützung *f*

**backlash, bäck-**läsch, *n* Gegenreaktion *f*

**backpack, bäck-**päck, *n* Rucksack *m*

**back seat, bäck** ssieht, *n* Rücksitz *m*; **take a –,** *v fig* sich zurückhalten

**backside, bäck-**sseid, *n fam* Hinterteil *nt*

**backstage, bäck-stehdsch,** *adj & adv* hinter den Kulissen

**back-up, bäck-**app, *n* (support) Unterstützung *f*;

*comp* Sicherungskopie *f*

**backward, bäck-**u'ed, *adj* rückständig

**backwards, bäck-**u'eds, *adv* rückwärts

**backwater, bäck-**u'o'a-ter, *n* totes Wasser *nt*; *fig* hinterste Provinz *f*

**backyard, bäck** jahrd, *n* Hinterhof *m*

**bacon, beh-**k'n, *n* Speck *m*

**bacteria, bäck-tier-**ri-e, *npl* Bakterien *pl*

**bad, bäd,** *adj* schlecht; (grave) schlimm; (wicked) böse; (smell etc.) schlecht

**badge, bädsch,** *n* Abzeichen *nt*, Plakette *f*

**badger, bädsch-**er, *n* Dachs *m*; *v* (pester) belästigen

**badly, bäd-**li, *adv* schlecht, schlimm; **– injured,** schwerverletzt; **need –,** dringend brauchen

**badminton, bädd-**minn-t'n, *n* Badminton *nt*, Federball *nt*

**baffle, bäff-'l,** *v* verwirren, verblüffen

**bag, bäg,** *n* (sack) Beutel *m*; (handbag) Tasche *f*; (paper/plastic) Tüte *f*; **–s of,** *fam* eine Menge

**baggage, bägg-**idsch, *n* Gepäck *nt*

**baggy, bägg-**i, *adj* (zu) weit

**bagpipes, bägg-**peips, *npl* Dudelsack *m*

**Bahamas, be-hah-**mes, *npl* **the –,** die Bahamas *pl*

**bail, behl,** *n* Kaution *f*; *v*

gegen Kaution freilassen; **– out,** die Kaution stellen für; *fig* aus der Klemme helfen

**bailiff,** beh-liff, *n* Gerichtsvollzieher *m*

**bait,** beht, *n* Köder *m*; *v* (hook) ködern; (animal) hetzen

**bake,** behk, *v* backen; **–r,** *n* Bäcker *m*; **–ry,** *n* Bäckerei *f*

**balance,** bäll-'nss, *n* Gleichgewicht *nt*; (scales) Waage *f*; *fin* Kontostand *m*; **– of payments,** Zahlungsbilanz *f*; *v* balancieren; *n comm* ausgleichen; **– the books,** die Bilanz ziehen; **– sheet,** *n* Bilanz *f*

**balcony,** bäll-*ke*-ni, *n* Balkon *m*

**bald,** bo'ald, *adj* kahl; *fig* knapp; **be –,** *v* eine Glatze haben

**bale,** behl, *n* (of hay) Ballen *m*; **– out,** *v* (boat) ausschöpfen; (from plane) abspringen

**ball,** bo'al, *n* Ball *m*; (billiards, bullet) Kugel *f*; (wool) Knäuel *nt*

**ballet,** bäll-eh, *n* Ballett *nt*; **– dancer,** Balletttänzer *m*

**balloon,** be-*luhn*, *n* Ballon *m*

**ballot,** bäll-*et*, *n* Abstimmung *f*, Wahl *f*; *v* abstimmen

**ballpoint (pen),** bo'al-peunt

(penn), *n* Kugelschreiber *m*

**balm,** bahm, *n* Balsam *m*

**Baltic,** bo'al-tick, *adj* Ostsee-; *n* **the – (Sea),** die Ostsee *f*

**bamboo,** bämm-*buh*, *n* Bambus *m*

**ban,** bänn, *n* Verbot *nt*; *v* verbieten

**banana,** be-*nah*-ne, *n* Banane *f*

**band,** bänd, *n* (strip) Band *nt*; (group) Gruppe *f*; (gang) Bande *f*; *mus* Band *f*, Kapelle *f*; **– together,** *v* sich zusammenschließen

**bandage,** bänn-didsch, *n* Verband *m*; *v* verbinden; (limb) bandagieren

**bandy,** bänn-di, *adj* **– legged,** o-beinig; *v* **– about,** herumerzählen

**bang,** bäng, *n* Knall *m*; *v* knallen

**Bangladesh,** bäng-gle-*desch*, *n* Bangladesch *nt*

**bangle,** bäng-g'l, *n* Armreif(en) *m*

**banish,** bänn-isch, *v* verbannen, ausweisen

**banister(s),** bänn-iss-ter(s), *n(pl)* Treppengeländer *nt*

**bank,** bänk, *n* (fin etc.) Bank *f*; (of river) Ufer *nt*; (of earth) Damm *m*; (money) einzahlen; (of plane) in die Querlage gehen; **– on,** rechnen mit, sich verlassen auf; **– account,** *n* Bankkonto *nt*;

**–(er's) card,** *n* Scheckkarte *f*; **– holiday,** *n* öffentlicher Feiertag *m*; **–note,** *n* Banknote *f*, Geldschein *m*; **– statement,** *n* Kontoauszug *m*

**banker,** bäng-ker, *n* Bankier *m*

**bankrupt,** bänk-rapt, *adj* bankrott; **go –,** Bankrott machen; **–cy,** *n* Bankrott *m*

**banner,** bänn-er, *n* Banner *nt*

**banquet,** bäng-ku'itt, *n* Bankett *nt*, Festessen *nt*

**baptism,** bäpp-tism, *n* Taufe *f*

**baptize,** bäpp-teis, *v* taufen

**bar,** bar, *n* (for drinks) Bar *f*; (rod) Stange *f*; *mus* Takt *m*; (of chocolate) Tafel *f*; (fig obstacle) Hindernis *nt*; *law* **the Bar,** die Anwaltschaft *f*; *v* (route) versperren; (person) ausschließen; **– none,** ohne Ausnahme; **behind –s,** hinter Gittern

**barbaric,** bar-bä-rick, *adj* barbarisch; (cruel) grausam

**barbarity,** bar-bä-ri-ti, *n* Barbarei *f*; (cruelty) Grausamkeit *f*

**barbecue,** bar-bi-kjuh, *n* Grillparty *f*, Barbecue *nt*; *v* grillen

**barbed wire,** barbd u'eir, *n* Stacheldraht *m*

**barber, bar**-ber, n
Herrenfriseur m

**barcode, bar**-kohd, n
Strichcode m

**bare, bähr,** adj nackt, bloss;
(country) kahl; v
entblößen; **–faced,**
schamlos; **–foot,** barfuß;
**–headed,** ohne Hut

**barely, bähr-**li, adv kaum

**bargain, bar**-ginn, n
(agreement) Handel m;
(cheap item)
Schnäppchen nt; **– (for),**
v handeln (um); **get more
than one –ed for,** fig sein
blaues Wunder erleben

**barge, bardsch,** n (freight)
Lastkahn m; (houseboat)
Hausboot nt; **– in,** v
hereinplatzen; fig sich
einmischen; **– into,** v
(person) anrempeln

**bark, bark,** n (of dog) Bellen
nt; (of tree) Rinde f; v (of
dog) bellen

**barley, bar-**li, n Gerste f

**barmaid, bar-**mehd, n
Bardame f

**barman, bar-**männ, n
Barmann m, Barkellner m

**barn, barn,** n Scheune f

**barometer, be-romm-**i-ter, n
Barometer nt

**barracks, bä-reks,** npl
Kaserne f

**barrage, bä-rahdsch,** n (of
stones/words) Hagel m;
(dam) Talsperre f

**barrel, bä-rel,** n Faß nt,
Tonne f; (of gun) Lauf m

**barren, bä-ren,** adj
unfruchtbar; (land) öde

**barricade, bä-ri-kehd,** n
Barrikade f; v
verbarrikadieren

**barrier, bä-ri-er,** n Schranke
f; fig Hindernis nt

**barrister, bä-riss-ter,** n
Rechtsanwalt m

**barrow, bä-roh,** n
Schubkarren m

**bartender, bar-**tenn-der, n
Barkeeper m, Barkellner m

**barter, bar-**ter, v (exchange)
Tauschhandel treiben;
(bargain) handeln

**base, behss,** n Basis f;
(pedestal) Sockel m;
(centre) Stützpunkt m; **–
on,** v gründen/basieren
auf; **be –d on,** v
ruhen/basieren auf

**baseball, behss-**bo'al, n
Baseball m

**basement, behss-**ment, n
Untergeschoß nt,
Kellergeschoß nt

**bash, bätt-**er, v (fam)
(person) schlagen; (car
etc.) eindellen; **– down,**
einschlagen

**bashful, bäsch-**full, adj
schüchtern

**basic, bäh-**ssick, adj
(fundamental)
grundsätzlich, Grund-;
(minimal) elementar; **the
–s,** npl das Wesentliche nt;
**–ally,** adv im Grunde

**basil, bä-**sill, n Basilikum nt

**basin, beh-**ss'n, n (dish)

Schüssel f; **(wash)–,**
Waschbecken nt

**basis, beh-**ssiss, n Basis f,
Grundlage f

**bask, bahsk,** v sich sonnen,
sich wärmen

**basket, bahss-**kitt, n Korb m

**basketball, bahs-**kitt-bo'al,
n Basketball m

**bass, behss,** n mus Baß m

**bassoon, be-**ssuhn, n
Fagott nt

**bastard, bahss-**ted, n
Bastard m; (fig, fam)
Scheißkerl m

**bat, bätt,** n (animal)
Fledermaus f; sport
Schläger m; v sport
schlagen; **not – an eyelid,**
nicht (mal) mit der
Wimper zucken

**batch, bätsch,** n (of work,
letters) Stoß m; (of goods)
Sendung f

**bath, bahth,** n Bad nt;
**–(tub),** n Badewanne f;
**have a –,** v baden;
**(swimming) –s,** npl
Schwimmbad nt

**bathroom, bahth-**rum, n
Bad nt, Badezimmer nt

**bathe, behdh,** v baden; **–r,** n
Badende(r) m, & f

**batter, bätt-**er, n Teig m; v
(strike) verprügeln;
(damage) verbeulen; **–
down,** v einschlagen; **–ed,**
adj (object) verbeult;
(wife) mißhandelt

**battery, bätt-**e-ri, n
Batterie f

**battle, bätt-'l**, n Schlacht f; v kämpfen; **–field**, n Schlachtfeld nt; **–ship**, n Schlachtschiff nt

**Bavaria**, be-**vähr**-ri-e, n Bayern nt; **–n**, adj bay(e)risch; n Bayer m

**bawl**, bo'al, v laut schreien

**bay**, beh, n (of sea) Bucht f; (horse) braunes Pferd nt; v bellen; **–(leaf/tree)**, n Lorbeer(blatt/baum) nt/m

**be**, bie, v sein; (in passives) werden, sein; (imperative) sei!, seid!, seien Sie!; **how are you?**, wie geht es Ihnen?; **I'm hot/cold**, mir ist heiß/kalt; **isn't it?/aren't they?**, nicht wahr?; **there is/are**, es gibt

**beach**, bietsch, n Strand m; v auf Strand setzen

**beacon, bie-k'n**, n Leuchtturm nt

**bead**, bied, n (of glass) Perle f; (drop) Tropfen m

**beak**, biek, n Schnabel m

**beaker, bie-ker**, n Becher m

**beam**, biem, n (of wood) Balken m; (of light) Strahl m; v strahlen; **–ing**, adj strahlend

**bean**, bien, n Bohne f

**bear**, bähr, n Bär m; v (carry, produce) tragen; (endure) aushalten, leiden; (offspring) gebären; **– left/right**, sich links/rechts halten; **– out**, bestätigen

**bearable**, adj erträglich

**beard**, bierd, n Bart m; **–ed**,

adj bärtig

**bearing, hähr-ring**, n (behaviour) Verhalten nt; mech (Kugel)lager nt; (relevance) **– on**, Bezug m auf; **–s**, npl Orientierung f; mech (Kugel)lager nt

**beast**, biest, n Tier nt; (cattle) Vieh nt; fig Bestie f; **–ly**, adv & adj fig roh, gemein

**beat**, biet, n (stroke) Schlag m; mus Takt m; v (strike, defeat) schlagen; (thrash) (ver)prügeln; **– it**, fam abhauen; **– up**, zusammenschlagen

**beautiful, bjuh-ti-full**, adj schön; **–ly**, adv schön; (well) hervorragend

**beautify, bjuh-ti-fei**, v verschönern, schmücken

**beauty, bjuh-ti**, n Schönheit f; **– spot**, (mole) Schönheitsfleck m; (place) schöne Gegend f

**beaver, bie-wer**, n Biber m

**because, be-kos**, conj weil; **– of**, prep wegen

**beckon (to), beck-en** (tu), v winken

**become, bi-kamm**, v werden; **becoming**, adj (conduct) schicklich; (dress) kleidsam

**bed**, bedd, n Bett nt; (in garden) Beet nt; **– clothes**, npl Bettwäsche f; **–ding**, n Bettzeug nt; **–ridden**, adj bettlägerig; **–room**, n Schlafzimmer nt; **–sit(ter)**,

**–sitting room**, n möbliertes Zimmer nt, Wohnschlafzimmer nt

**bee**, bie, n Biene f

**beech**, bietsch, n Buche f

**beef**, bief, n Rindfleisch nt; **–burger**, Hamburger m

**beehive, bie-heiw**, n Bienenstock m

**beer**, bier, n Bier nt

**beet**, biet, n Rübe f

**beetle, bie-t'l**, n Käfer m

**beetroot, biet-ruht**, n rote Beete/Rübe f

**before, bi-for**, adv vorher, früher; (already) schon; conj bevor; prep vor

**beforehand, bi-for-händ**, adv im voraus

**beg (for)**, beg (for), v (request) dringend bitten (um); (for alms) betteln; **–gar**, n Bettler m

**begin, bi-ginn**, v beginnen, anfangen; **–ner**, n Anfänger m; **–ning**, n Anfang m

**begrudge, bi-gradsch**, v mißgönnen, beneiden

**behalf, bi-hahf**, n **on – of**, im Namen von, für

**behave, bi-hehw**, v sich benehmen, sich betragen

**behaviour, bi-hehw-jer**, n Benehmen nt, Verhalten nt

**behead, bi-hedd**, v enthaupten, köpfen

**behind, bi-heind**, adv hinten; n (inf) Hinterteil nt; prep hinter; **–(hand)**, *adv* im Rückstand

**behold,** bi-**hohld**, *v* erblicken; **–!,** siehe da!

**being,** bie-ing, *n* (existence) Dasein *nt*; (creature) Wesen *nt*

**belated,** bi-**leh**-tidd, *adj* verspätet

**belch,** beltsch, *v* rülpsen, aufstoßen; (smoke etc.) ausspeien

**belfry,** bell-fri, *n* Glockenturm *m*

**Belgian,** bell-dschen, *adj* belgisch; *n* Belgier *m*

**Belgium,** bell-dschem, *n* Belgien *nt*

**belie,** bi-lei, *v* Lügen strafen

**belief,** bi-lief, *n* (faith) Glaube *m*; (opinion) Meinung *f*

**believable,** bi-liew-e-b'l, *adj* glaubhaft, glaubwürdig

**believe (in),** bi-liew (inn), *v* glauben (an); **–r,** *n* Gläubige(r) *m & f*

**belittle,** bi-litt-'l, *v* schlechtmachen

**bell,** bell, *n* (church etc.) Glocke *f*; (door etc.) Klingel *f*

**belligerent,** bi-lidsch-e-rent, *adj* (nation) kriegslustig; (person) streitlustig

**bellow,** bell-oh, *v* brüllen

**bellows,** bell-ohs, *npl* Blasebalg *m*

**belly,** bell-i, *n* Bauch *m*

**belong (to),** bi-long (tu), *v* gehören; (club etc.) angehören, Mitglied sein

**belongings,** bi-long-ings, *npl* Sachen *pl* Besitz *m*

**beloved,** bi-lavd, *adj* geliebt, lieb; *n* Geliebte(r) *m & f*

**below,** bi-loh, *adv* unten; *prep* unter, unterhalb

**belt,** belt, *n* (clothing) Gürtel *m*; *mech* (Treib)riemen *m*; *v* den Gürtel zumachen; (fam hit) knallen; (fam run) rasen; **– up,** *fam* die Klappe halten

**bench,** bentsch, *n* Bank *f*; *law* the –, (judges) Richter *pl*; (in court) Richterbank *f*

**bend,** bend, *n* Biegung *f*; (in road) Kurve *f*; *v* biegen; (back, knee, rules) beugen

**beneath,** bi-nieth, *adv* unten; *prep* unter, unterhalb

**benefactor,** benn-i-**fäck**-ter, *n* Wohltäter *m*

**beneficial,** benn-i-**fisch**-'l, *adj* vorteilhaft; (healing) heilsam

**beneficiary,** be-ni-**fisch**-*e*-ri, *n* Nutznießer m

**benefit,** benn-i-fitt, *n* (advantage) Vorteil *m*, Nutzen *m*; (allowance) Beihilfe *f*; (social security) Sozialhilfe *f*; *v* nützen; **– (from),** Nutzen ziehen (aus)

**benevolence,** bi-**new**-*e*-lenss, *n* Wohlwollen *nt*

**benevolent,** bi-**new**-*e*-lent,

*adj* wohlwollend

**benign,** bi-**nein**, *adj* (person) gütig; (influence) günstig; (tumour) gutartig

**bent,** bent, *adj* gebogen; (fam dishonest) korrupt; (fam homosexual) schwul; *n* (inclination) Neigung *f*; **be – on (doing),** *v* entschlossen sein (zu tun)

**bequeath (to),** bi-**ku'iedh** (tu), *v* vermachen, hinterlassen

**bequest,** bi-**ku'est**, *n* Vermächtnis *nt*

**bereaved,** bi-**riewd**, *adj* vom Verlust betroffen; **the –,** *npl* die Hinterbliebenen

**bereavement,** bi-**riew**-ment, *n* Trauerfall *m*

**Bermuda,** ber-**mjuh**-de, *n*; **the –s,** *npl* die Bermudas *pl*

**berry,** be-ri, *n* Beere *f*

**berth,** börth, *n* (cabin) Koje *f*; (on train) Bett *nt*; (anchorage) Ankerplatz *m*; *v* anlegen

**beseech,** bi-**ssietsch**, *v* anflehen

**beset,** bi-**ssett**, *v* bedrängen; **– with,** *adj* geplagt mit

**beside,** bi-**sseid**, *prep* neben, dicht bei; **be – o.s. (with),** *v* außer sich sein (vor); **be – the point,** *v* nicht zur Sache gehören

**besides,** bi-**sseids**, *adv* außerdem; *prep* außer

**besiege,** bi-**ssiedsch**, *v* bedrängen; *mil* belagern

**best,** best, *adj* beste(r/s); *adv* am besten; **all the –!,** alles Gute!; **at –,** bestenfalls; **do one's –,** *v* sein Bestes tun; **– man,** *n* Trauzeuge *m*

**bet,** bett, *n* Wette *f*; *v* wetten

**betray,** bi-treh, *v* verraten

**better,** bett-er, *adj & adv* besser; (like, enjoy) mehr; (healthy) gesund; *v* verbessern; **get the – of,** *v* unterkriegen; **you had – (do),** *v* Sie (tun) lieber/besser

**betting,** bett-ing, *n* Wetten *nt*

**between,** bi-tu'ien, *adv* dazwischen; *prep* zwischen; **– ourselves,** unter uns gesagt

**beverage,** bew-e-ridsch, *n* Getränk *nt*

**bevy,** bew-i, *n* Schwarm *m*, Schar *f*

**bewail,** bi-u'ehl, *v* beklagen, beweinen

**beware (of),** bi-u'ähr (ew), *v* sich hüten (vor); **–!,** Vorsicht!

**bewildered,** bi-u'ill-derd, *adj* verwirrt

**bewitched,** bi-u'itscht, *v* bezaubert

**beyond,** bi-jond, *adv* jenseits, über… hinaus; **– belief,** nicht zu glauben

**bias,** bei-ess, *n* (prejudice) Vorurteil *nt*; (viewpoint) Ausrichtung *f*; **–(s)ed,** *adj* voreingenommen

**Bible,** bei-b'l, *n* Bibel *f*

**bicker,** bick-er, *v* zanken

**bicycle,** bei-ssick-'l, *n* Fahrrad *nt*

**bid,** bidd, *n* (at sale, cards) Gebot *nt*; (attempt) Versuch *m*; *v* (at sale, cards) bieten; **– farewell to,** *v* Abschied nehmen von

**bidder,** bidd-er, *n* Bietende(r) *m & f*; **the highest –,** *n* der/die Meistbietende *m & f*

**bide,** beid, *v* abwarten

**bifocal,** bei-foh-k'l, *adj* Bifokal-; **–s,** *npl* Bifokalbrille *f*

**big,** bigg, *adj* groß; (important) wichtig

**bigot,** bigg-et, *n* Frömmler *m*; **–ed,** *adj* bigott, borniert; **–ry,** *n* Bigotterie *f*, Borniertheit *f*

**bike,** beik, *n* (Fahr)rad *nt*

**bikini,** bi-kie-ni, *n* Bikini *m*

**bilberry,** bill-be-ri, *n* Heidelbeere *f*, Blaubeere *f*

**bile,** beil, *n* Galle *f*

**bilingual,** bei-ling-gu'el, *adj* zweisprachig

**bill,** bill, *n* (account) Rechnung *f*; *law* Gesetzentwurf *m*; (of bird) Schnabel *m*; *v* (charge) berechnen; **– of fare,** *n* Speisekarte *f*; **fill/fit the –,** der/die/das richtige sein

**billet,** bill-itt, *n* Quartier *nt*

**billiards,** bill-jerds, *npl* Billard *nt*

**billion,** bill-jen, *n* (in Britain: 10¹²) Billion *f*; (in USA: 10⁹) Milliarde *f*

**bin,** bin, *n* Kasten *m*; (refuse) Mülleimer *m*

**bind,** beind, *v* binden; (commit) verpflichten; (person) fesseln; **–ing,** *adj* verbindlich; *n* (of book) Einband *m*

**binge,** bindsch, *n* *fam* (drinking) Sauferei *f*; (eating) Fresserei *f*

**binoculars,** bi-nock-ju-lers, *npl* Fernglas *nt*

**biography,** bei-ogg-re-fi, *n* Biographie *f*

**biological,** bei-e-lodsch-i-k'l, *adj* biologisch

**biology,** bei-oll-e-dschi, *n* Biologie *f*

**birch,** börtsch, *n* Birke *f*

**bird,** börd, *n* Vogel *m*; **–'s eye view,** *n* (Blick aus der) Vogelschau *f*; **– watcher,** *n* Vogelbeobachter *m*

**birth,** börth, *n* Geburt *f*; **– control,** *n* Geburtenkontrolle *f*; **–day,** *n* Geburtstag *m*; **–place,** *n* Geburtsort *m*; **–rate,** *n* Geburtenziffer *f*

**biscuit,** biss-kitt, *n* Keks *m*

**bisect,** bei-ssekt, *v* halbieren

**bishop,** bisch-ep, *n* Bischof *m*; (chess) Läufer *m*

**bit,** bitt, *n* (part) Stück *nt*; (horse) Gebiß *nt*; *comp* Bit *nt*; **a –,** etwas, ein bißchen

**bitch,** bitsch, *n* Hündin *f*;

(*pej* woman) Schlampe *f*; *v*
*fam* meckern

**bite,** beit, *n* Biß *m*;
(mouthful) Bissen *m*; *v*
beißen

**biting,** beit-ing, *adj* beißend;
(wind) schneidend

**bitter,** bitt-er, *adj* bitter;
(struggle) erbittert;
(person) verbittert; *n*
(halb)dunkles Bier *nt*;
**–ness,** *n* Bitterkeit *f*

**black,** bläck, *adj* schwarz;
(dark, gloomy) finster, *v*
schwärzen; (shoes)
wichsen; (boycott)
boykottieren; **– eye,** *n*
blaues Auge *nt*; **– and
blue,** grün und blau; **– and
white,** (*photog* etc.)
Schwarzweiß-; **B– Forest,**
*n* Schwarzwald *f*; **–
market,** *n* Schwarzmarkt
*m*; **B– Sea,** *n* Schwarzes
Meer *nt*

**blackberry,** bläck-be-ri, *n*
Brombeere *f*

**blackbird,** bläck-börd, *n*
Amsel *f*

**blackcurrant,** bläck-*ka*-
rent, *n* schwarze
Johannisbeere *f*

**blacken,** bläck-'n, *v*
schwärzen; *fig* verleumden

**blackleg,** bläck-legg, *n*
Streikbrecher *m*

**blackmail,** bläck-mehl, *n*
Erpressung *f*; *v* erpressen;
**–er,** *n* Erpresser *m*

**blackout,** bläck-aut, *n med*
Ohnmachtsanfall *m*;

(wartime) Verdunkelung *f*

**blacksmith,** bläck-smith, *n*
Schmied *m*

**bladder,** bládd-er, *n* Blase *f*

**blade,** blehd, *n* (of weapon)
Klinge *f*; (of grass) Halm
*m*; (of oar) Blatt *nt*

**blame,** blehm, *n* (censure)
Tadel *m*; (fault) Schuld *f*,
Verantwortung *f*; *v* –
**(for),** die Schuld geben
(an); **to be to – (for),**
schuld sein (an)

**blameless,** blehm-liss, *adj*
schuldlos, tadellos

**bland,** bländ, *adj* freundlich,
mild; *pej* fade

**blank,** blänk, *n adj* (vacant)
leer; (page)
unbeschrieben; (look)
ausdruckslos; *n* (space)
Lücke *f*; (cartridge)
Platzpatrone *f*; **; – cheque,**
*n* Blankoscheck *m*; *fig*
Freibrief *m*; **– verse,** *n*
Blankvers *m*; **go –,** *v fam*
Mattscheibe haben

**blanket,** bläng-kitt, *n* Decke
*f*; *v* bedecken

**blare,** blähr, *v* schmettern

**blaspheme,** bläss-*fiem,* *v*
Gott lästern

**blasphemy,** bläss-fi-mi, *n*
Gotteslästerung *f*

**blast,** blahst, *n* (of wind)
Windstoß *m*; (explosion)
Explosion *f*; *v* (explode)
sprengen; **–!,** *fam*
verdammt!; **–ed,** *adj fam*
verdammt

**blatant,** bleh-t'nt, *adj*

offensichtlich,
unverhohlen

**blaze,** blehs, *n* Feuer *nt*,
Brand *m*; *v* lodern; **– a
trail,** *v fig* den Weg
bahnen; **– of light,** *n*
Lichtstrahl *m*

**bleach,** blietsch, *v* bleichen;
*n* Bleichmittel *nt*

**bleak,** bliek, *adj* (wind)
rauh; (country) kahl, öde

**bleary,** blier-ri, *adj* (sleepy)
verschlafen

**bleat,** bliet, *v* blöken; *fig*
meckern

**bleed,** blied, *v* bluten; (draw
blood) zur Ader lassen

**blemish,** blemm-isch, *n*
Makel *m*; *v* beschädigen;
*fig* beflecken

**blend,** blend, *v* (sich)
vermischen; *n* Mischung *f*

**bless,** bless, *v* segnen; **–
you!,** Gesundheit!; **–ed,**
*adj* gesegnet; **–ing,** *n*
Segen *m*; (good fortune)
Glück *nt*

**blight,** bleit, *n* (on plant)
Braunfäule *f*; (eyesore)
Schandfleck *m*; *v*
verderben

**blind,** bleind, *adj* blind;
(corner) unübersichtlich;
*n* (for window) Rouleau
*nt*; (venetian) Jalousie *f*; *v*
blenden; **– spot,** *n* toter
Winkel; *fig* schwacher
Punkt *m*; **the –,** *npl* die
Blinden *pl*

**blindfold,** bleind-fohld, *n*
Augenbinde *f*; *v* die

Augen verbinden
**blindly, bleind**-li, *adv*
Blindlings
**blindness, bleind**-niss, *n*
Blindheit *f*
**blink,** blink, *v* (of eyes)
blinzeln; (of light)
blinken
**blinkers, blink**-ers, *npl* (for
horse) Scheuklappen *pl*
**bliss,** bliss, *n* Seligkeit *f*;
**–ful,** *adj* (person) selig;
(experience) herrlich
**blister, bliss**-ter, n Blase *f*; *v*
(paint) Blasen werfen;
(skin) Blasen bekommen
**blitz,** blitz, *n* Luftkrieg *m*
**blizzard, blis**-erd, *n*
Schneesturm *m*
**bloated, bloht**-idd, *adj*
aufgedunsen; (*fig* full)
vollgestopft
**blob,** blob, *n fam* Klacks *m*,
Fleck *m*
**block,** block, *n* Block *m*; **–**
**of flats,** Wohnblock *m*;
**mental –,** geistige Sperre *f*
**blockade, block**-ehd, *n*
Blockade *f*
**blockage, block**-idsch, *n*
Verstopfung *f*
**blockbuster, block**-bass-ter,
*n* Knüller *m*
**bloke,** blohk, *n fam* Typ *m*
**blond(e),** blond, *adj* blond;
**blonde,** *n* Blondine *f*
**blood,** bladd, *n* Blut *nt*; **–**
**donor,** *n* Blutspender *m*; **–**
**group,** *n* Blutgruppe *f*; **–**
**pressure,** *n* Blutdruck *m*;
**–shed,** *n* Blutvergießen *nt*;

**–shot,** *adj* blutunterlaufen;
**–thirsty,** *adj* blutdürstig;
**–y,** *adj* blutig; *fam*
verdammt; **–minded,** *adj*
*fam* stur
**bloom,** bluhm, *n* Blüte *f*; *v*
blühen; **–ing,** *adj* blühend
**blossom, bloss**-em, *n* Blüte
*f*; *v* blühen
**blot,** blott, *n* Klecks *m*; *fig*
Fleck *m*; *v* beklecksen;
(dry) löschen; *fig*
verderben; **–ting paper,**
Löschpapier *nt*
**blotchy, blotsch**-i, *adj*
fleckig
**blouse,** blaus, *n* Bluse *f*
**blow,** bloh, *n* Schlag *m*; *v*
blasen; (of wind) wehen;
(nose) putzen; **– over,**
(storm, dispute) sich
legen; **– up,** (tyres etc.)
aufblasen; (explode)
sprengen
**blow-dry, bloh**-drei, *v*
fönen; **have a –,** *v* sich
föhnen lassen
**blue,** bluh, *adj* blau;
(obscene) Porno-; (*fam*
sad) melancholisch; **out**
**of the –,** aus heiterem
Himmel
**bluebell, bluh**-bell, *n*
Sternhyazinthe *f*;
(in Scotland)
Glockenblume *f*
**blueprint, bluh**-print, *n*
Blaupause *f*; *fig* Entwurf *m*
**blues,** bluhs, *npl* **the –,** *mus*
der Blues; **have the –,** *fam*
melancholisch sein

**bluff,** blaff, *n* Bluff *m*; *v*
bluffen; **call sb's –,** *v* es
darauf ankommen lassen
**blunder, blan**-der, *n* grober
Fehler *m*; *v* einen Bock
schießen
**blunt,** blant, *adj* (blade)
stumpf; (words)
unverblümt; *v* (blade)
stumpf machen; (senses)
abstumpfen; **–ness,** *n*
Stumpfheit *f*;
Unverblümtheit *f*
**blurred,** blörd, *adj* (image)
verschwommen; (writing)
verschmiert
**blurt out,** blört aut, *v*
herausplatzen mit
**blush,** blasch, *n* Erröten *nt*;
*v* erröten
**boar,** bor, *n* Eber *m*; **wild –,**
Wildschwein *nt*
**board,** bord, *n* (of wood)
Brett *nt*; (black-) Tafel *f*;
(of company) Aufsichtsrat
*m*; (of officials) Behörde *f*;
*v* (lodge) (in Pension)
wohnen; (floor) mit
Brettern auslegen; (train,
bus) einsteigen in; (plane,
ship) besteigen; **– and**
**lodging,** *n* Unterkunft *f*
und Verpflegung *f*; **–er,** *n*
(guest) Pensionsgast *m*;
(pupil) Internatsschüler
*m*; **–ing house,** *n* Pension
*f*; **–ing-school,** *n* Internat
*nt*; **across the –,** *adv*
generell; **on –,** *adv* an
Bord

**boast,** bohst, *n* Prahlerei *f*; *v*

prahlen, sich rühmen; **–er**, n Prahler m

**boat**, boht, n Boot nt; (rowing) Kahn m; **–-hook**, n Bootshaken m; **–ing**, adj Boots-; n Bootfahren nt

**boatswain**, boh-ss'n, n Bootsmann m

**bob**, bobb, v **– about**, **bob up and down**, (auf dem Wasser) schaukeln; **– up**, auftauchen

**bobbin**, bobb-in, n Spule f

**bobsleigh**, bobb-slei, n Bob m

**bode**, bohd, v **– well/ill**, ein gutes/schlechtes Zeichen sein

**bodily**, bodd-i-li, adj & adv körperlich; (in one piece) ganz

**body**, bodd-i, n Körper m; (corpse) Leiche f; **–guard**, Leibwächter m; (group) Leibwache f; **–work**, Karosserie f

**bog**, bogg, n Sumpf m; **get –ged down**, v steckenbleiben; **–gy**, adj sumpfig

**bogus**, boh-gess, adj falsch

**boil**, beul, n med Geschwür nt; v kochen; (of water) sieden; **– down to**, fig hinauslaufen auf

**boiled**, beuld, adj gekocht; **– potatoes**, npl Salzkartoffeln pl

**boiler**, beu-ler, n (domestic) Boiler m; (in engine) (Dampf)kessel m

**boisterous**, beuss-te-ress, adj ausgelassen, wild

**bold**, bohld, adj (brave) mutig; (impudent) dreist; (pattern etc.) kräftig

**bolster**, bohl-ster, n Nackenrolle f; **– up**, v stützen; fig Mut machen

**bolt**, bohlt, n Riegel m; (lightning) Blitzstrahl m; v verriegeln; (of horse) durchgehen; **– upright**, adv kerzengerade

**bomb**, bomm, n Bombe f; v bombardieren

**bombard**, bonm-**bahrd**, v bombardieren

**bond**, bond, n (obligation) Verpflichtung f; (fig link) Band nt; (fin stock) Bond m; in **–**, (customs) unter Zollverschluß

**bondage**, bonn-didsch, n Sklaverei f

**bone**, bohn, n Knochen m; (of fish) Gräte f; v (meat) die Knochen herauslösen, entbeinen; (fish) entgräten; **–d**, adj ohne Knochen; ohne Gräten

**bonfire**, bonn-feir, n (Freuden)feuer nt

**bonnet**, bonn-itt, n Haube f; Häubchen nt; (of car) Motorhaube f

**bonus**, boh-ness, n (annual) Prämie f; (supplement) Zuschlag m; (special) Bonus m

**bony**, boh-ni, adj knochig

**book**, buck, n Buch nt; v

(tickets) bestellen; **–case**, n Bücherregal nt; **–ed (up)**, adj ausverkauft, ausgebucht; **–ing office**, n rail Fahrkartenschalter m; theatre Vorverkaufsstelle f; **–keeper**, n Buchhalter m; **–keeping**, n Buchführung f; **–mark**, n Lesezeichen nt; **–seller**, n Buchhändler m; **–shop**, n Buchhandlung f; **–stall**, n Bücherstand m; **–worm**, n Bücherwurm m

**boom**, buhm, n comm Hochkonjunktur f; naut Baum m; (noise) Dröhnen nt; v (of business) einen Aufschwung nehmen; (of noise) dröhnen

**boon**, buhn, n Segen m

**boost**, buhst, n Auftrieb m; v (output etc.) ankurbeln; fig stärken; **give a – to**, v Auftrieb geben; **–er**, n (med injection) Wiederholungsimpfung f

**boot**, buht, n Stiefel m; (of car) Kofferraum m; v (kick) einen Fußtritt geben; comp laden; **– out**, v fam rausschmeißen; **to –**, adv noch dazu

**booth**, buhdh, n (voting etc.) Kabine f; (fair) Bude f; (telephone) Zelle f

**booty**, buh-ti, n Beute f

**booze**, buhs, fam n Alkohol m; v saufen

**border**, bor-der, adj Grenz-; n (frontier) Grenze f;

(edge) Rand m; (flowerbed) Rabatte f; v (country) grenzen an; (surround) umschließen; – **on,** v fig grenzen an; **–ing,** adj angrenzend

**borderline,** bor-der-lein, n Grenze f; **– case,** Grenzfall m

**bore,** bor, v (drill) bohren; (weary) langweilen; n (of gun) Kaliber nt; (person) Langweiler m; (thing) Plage f

**boring,** bor-ring, adj langweilig

**born,** born, adj geboren

**borough,** ba-re, adj Stadt-; n (Stadt)bezirk m

**borrow,** bo-roh, v borgen

**bosom,** bus-em, n Busen m

**boss,** boss, n Boß m, Chef m; **– about/around,** v herumkommandieren; **–y,** adj herrisch

**botanist,** bott-e-nist, n Botaniker m

**botany,** bott-e-ni, n Botanik f

**botch (up),** botsch (app), v verpfuschen

**both,** bohth, adj beide, beides; **– … and …,** sowohl… als auch…

**bother,** bodh-er, n (trouble) Mühe f; (nuisance) Plage f; v (pester) belästigen; (take trouble) sich Mühe geben

**bottle,** bott-'l, n Flasche f; v in Flaschen abfüllen; –

**bank,** n Altglascontainer m; **– opener,** n Flaschenöffner m

**bottom,** bott-em, adj untere(r/s), unterste(r/s); n Boden m, Grund m; (fam of person) Hinterteil m; **–less,** adj bodenlos

**bough,** bau, n Ast m, Zweig m

**bounce,** baunss, n Aufprall m; v (of ball) (auf)springen; (fam of cheque) platzen

**bound,** baund, adj (book, hands) gebunden; (obliged) verpflichtet; n (jump) Sprung m; (limit) Grenze f; v (jump) springen; (border) begrenzen; **be – for,** v auf dem Weg sein nach; **out of –s,** Betreten verboten

**boundary,** baun-de-ri, n Grenze f

**bounty,** baun-ti, n (reward) Kopfgeld nt

**bouquet,** bu-keh, n (of flowers) Strauß m; (of wine) Blume f

**bout,** baut, n (of illness) Anfall m; (fig sport) Kampf m

**bow,** boh, n (archery, violin) Bogen m; (tie, knot) Schleife f

**bow,** bau, n (of body) Verbeugung f, Verneigung f; naut Bug m; v sich verbeugen; **– to,** fig sich beugen (vor)

**bowel,** bau-el, n Darm m;

**–s,** pl fig das Innere nt

**bowl,** bohl, n Schale f, Schüssel f; (ball) Kugel f; v die Kugel rollen; (cricket) den Ball werfen

**bowling,** boh-ling, n Bowling nt; Kegeln nt; (cricket) Werfen nt; **–ing alley,** n Kegelbahn f; **–ing green,** n Rasenfläche f zum Bowling

**bowls,** bohls, npl Bowling nt

**bow tie,** boh tei, n Fliege f

**box,** bocks, n Schachtel f; (chest) Kiste f; theatre Loge f; (fam TV) Glotze f; v sport boxen; (pack) verpacken; **– sb's ears,** v jdm eine Ohrfeige geben

**boxing,** bock-ssing, n Boxen nt; **Boxing Day,** n zweiter Weihnachtstag m; **– match,** Boxkampf m

**box office,** bocks-off-iss, n (Theater/Kino)kasse f

**boxroom,** bocks-ruhm, n Abstellraum m

**boy,** beu, n Junge m

**boycott,** beu-kott, n Boykott m; v boykottieren

**boyfriend,** beu-frend, n Freund m

**bra,** brah (abbr brassière), n BH

**brace,** brehss, n mech Strebe f; med Klammer f; (two) Paar nt; v mech verstreben; (invigorate) stärken; **– oneself for,** v sich gefaßt machen auf; **–s,** npl Hosenträger pl

**bracelet, brehss**-let, *n*
 Armband *nt*

**bracing, breh**-ssing, *adj*
 stärkend, kräftigend

**bracken, bräck**-'n, *n*
 Farnkraut *nt*

**bracket, bräck**-itt, *n mech*
 (Regal)träger *m*;
 (parenthesis) Klammer *f*;
 (group) Gruppe *f*, Klasse *f*;
 *v* einklammern;
 **(together)**, *v fig* in
 Verbindung bringen

**brag, brägg**, *v* prahlen;
 **–gart**, *n* Prahler *m*

**braid, brehd**, *n* (of hair)
 Flechte *f*; (trimming)
 Borte *f*; *v* flechten

**brain(s), brehn**(s), *n(pl)*
 (physical) Gehirn *nt*;
 (mind) Verstand *m*;
 **–wave**, *n* Geistesblitz *m*;
 **–y**, *adj* gescheit; **have sth
 on the –**, *v* etw im Kopf
 haben

**braise, brehs**, *v* schmoren

**brake, brehk**, *n* Bremse *f*; *v*
 bremsen

**bramble, brämm**-b'l, *n*
 Brombeere *f*

**bran, bränn**, *n* Kleie *f*

**branch, brahntsch**, *n* Ast *m*,
 Zweig, *m*; *comm*
 Zweigstelle *f*; **– off**, *v*
 abzweigen

**brand, bränd**, *n comm*
 Marke *f*; (mark) Brandmal
 *m*; *v fig* brandmarken

**brandish, bränn**-dish, *v*
 schwingen

**brand-new, bränd-njuh**, *adj*

nagelneu

**brandy, bränn**-di, *n* Kognak
 *m*, Branntwein *m*

**brass, brahss**, *n* Messing *nt*;
 *mus* die Blechbläser *pl*; **–
 band**, *n* Blaskapelle *f*

**bravado, bre-vah**-doh, *n*
 Wagemut *m*

**brave, brehw**, *adj* tapfer,
 mutig; *v* (weather) trotzen

**bravery, breh**-we-ri, *n*
 Tapferkeit *f*

**brawl, bro'al**, *n* Schlägerei *f*;
 *v* sich schlagen

**brawn, bro'an**, *n* (cooking)
 Sülze *f*; (strength)
 Muskelkraft *f*; **–y**, *adj*
 muskulös, kräftig

**bray, breh**, *v* schreien

**brazen, breh-s'n**, *adj*
 unverschämt

**brazier, breh-si-er**, *n*
 Kohlenfeuer *nt*

**Brazil, bre-sill**, *n* Brasilien
 *nt*; **–ian**, *adj* brasilianisch;
 *n* Brasilianer *m*; **--nut**, *n*
 Paranuß *f*

**breach, brietsch**, *n* (gap)
 Lücke *f*; (of contract etc.)
 Bruch *m*; (of law)
 Übertretung *f*; (of
 discipline) Verstoß *m*; *v*
 durchbrechen

**bread, bredd**, *n* Brot *nt*; **–
 and butter**, *n* Butterbrot
 *nt*; *fig* tägliches Brot *nt*

**breadth, brédth**, *n* Breite *f*

**break, brehk**, *n* (fracture)
 Bruch *m*; (gap) Lücke *f*;
 (pause) Pause *f*; *v*
 (zer)brechen,

kaputtmachen; (promise)
 brechen; (habit) sich
 abgewöhnen; (horse)
 zureiten; (of glass etc.)
 zerbrechen, kaputtgehen;
 **– down**, *v* (of car) eine
 Panne haben; (of
 negotiatons) scheitern; **–
 even**, *v* die Kosten
 decken; **have a good/bad
 –**, *v* Glück/Pech haben

**breakage, breh**-kidsch, *n*
 Bruch *m*

**breakdown, brehk**-daun, *n*
 *mech* Panne *f*; (of person)
 Zusammenbruch *m*

**breakfast, breck**-fest, *n*
 Frühstück *nt*

**breakthrough, brehk**-thruh,
 *n* Durchbruch *m*

**breakwater, brehk-u'oa-ter**,
 *n* Wellenbrecher *m*

**bream, briem**, *n* Brassen *m*

**breast, brest**, *n* Brust *f*

**breath, breth**, *n* Atem(zug)
 *m*; *fig* Hauch *m*; **under
 one's –**, *adv* leise,
 flüsternd

**breathalyse, breth-e**-leis, *v*
 ins Röhrchen blasen
 lassen; **Breathalyser ®** *n*
 Alcotest *m*

**breathe, briedh**, *v* atmen

**breathless, breth**-less, *adj*
 atemlos, außer Atem

**breeches, brie**-tschis, *npl*
 Kniehosen *f*; (riding)
 Reithosen *f*

**breed, bried**, *n* Rasse *f*; *v*
 züchten; *fig* erzeugen; **–er**,
 *n* Züchter *m*; **–ing**, *n* (of

stock) Zucht f;
(education) Bildung f
**breeze,** bries, n Brise f
**breezy, brie**-si, adj (weather)
windig; (manner) flott,
lustig
**brevity, brew-i**-ti, n Kürze f
**brew,** bruh, v brauen; **–er,**
n Brauer m; **–ery,** n
Brauerei f
**bribe,** breib, n Bestechung f,
Bestechungsgeld nt; v
bestechen; **–ry,** n
Bestechung f
**brick,** brick, n Backstein m,
Ziegelstein m; **–layer,** n
Maurer m
**bridal, brei-**d'l, adj Braut-
**bride,** breid, n Braut f;
**–groom,** Bräutigam m;
**–smaid,** Brautjungfer f
**bridge,** bridsch, n Brücke f;
(cards) Bridge nt; v
überbrücken
**bridle, brei-**d'l, n Zaum m; v
aufzäumen
**brief,** brief, adj kurz; n
Auftrag m; v informieren,
unterweisen; **–s,** npl
Slip m
**briefcase, brief-**keiss, n
Aktentasche f
**brigadier, brigg-e-dier,** n
Brigadegeneral m
**bright,** breit, adj (light) hell;
(clever) intelligent;
(lively) aufgeweckt;
(cheerful) heiter; **–en**
(up), v aufheitern; (of
weather) sich aufklären
**brilliance, brill-**jenss, n

Glanz m
**brilliant, brill-**jent, adj
glänzend; (achievement)
hervorragend
**brim,** brimm, n Rand m; (of
hat) Krempe f; **–full,** adj
randvoll; **– over,** v
überlaufen
**brine,** brein, n Salzwasser nt,
(Salz)lake f
**bring,** bring, v bringen;
**– forward,** comm
übertragen; **– in,**
hereinbringen; **– off,**
(succeed with) schaffen;
**– up,** (educate) erziehen;
(topic) erwähnen
**brink,** brink, n Rand m
**brisk,** brisk, adj (lively)
lebhaft; (agile) flink
**brisket, briss-**kitt, n
Bruststück nt
**bristle, briss-**'l, n Borste f; v
sich sträuben
**British, britt-**isch, adj
britisch; **the –,** npl die
Briten pl; **the – Isles,** npl
die Britischen Inseln pl
**brittle, britt-**'l, adj spröde,
zerbrechlich
**broach,** brohtsch, v
anschneiden
**broad,** bro'ad, adj (wide)
breit; (vague) grob, weit;
(accent) breit; **–cast,** v
(Rundfunk)sendung f; v
senden; **–en,** v (sich)
verbreitern; **–ly,** adv
allgemein gesagt;
**–minded,** adj tolerant
**broccoli, brock-**e-li, n

Brokkoli m
**brochure, broh-**scher, n
Broschüre f
**broken, broh-**k'n, adj
(object) kaputt; (bone,
heart, promise) gebrochen
**broker, broh-**ker, n
Makler m
**bronchitis,** brong-**kei-**tiss, n
Bronchitis f
**bronze,** brons, n Bronze f
**brooch,** brohtsch, n
Brosche f
**brood,** bruhd, n Brut f; v
brüten
**brook,** bruck, n Bach m; v
erdulden
**broom,** bruhm, n Besen m;
(plant) Ginster m
**broth,** broth, n Brühe f
**brothel, broth-**'l, n Bordell
nt
**brother, bra-**dher, n Bruder
m; **–hood,** Bruderschaft f;
**– -in-law,** Schwager m
**brow,** brau, n (eyebrow)
(Augen)braue f;
(forehead) Stirn f; (of
hill) (Berg)kuppe f
**brown,** braun, adj braun;
bräunen; **– bread,** n
Mischbrot nt,
Vollkornbrot nt; **– paper,**
n Packpapier nt
**browse,** braus, v **– (around),**
sich umsehen; **– through,**
(book) schmöckern in
**bruise,** bruhs, n blauer Fleck
m; v (body) einen blauen
Fleck verpassen; (feelings)
verletzen; (of body) einen

blauen Fleck bekommen

**brunette**, bru-**nett**, n Brünette f

**brunt**, brant, n volle Wucht f

**brush**, brasch, n Bürste f; (paint) Pinsel m; (skirmish) Zusammenstoß m; v bürsten; (sweep) fegen; **– up**, v auffrischen; **–wood**, n Reisig nt

**brusque**, bruhsk, adj brüsk, schroff

**Brussels**, **brass**-'ls, n Brüssel nt; **– sprouts**, npl Rosenkohl m

**brutal**, **bruh**-t'l, adj brutal, roh

**brutality**, bru-**täll**-i-ti, n Brutalität f, Roheit f

**brute**, bruht, n Bestie f; fig Unmensch m

**bubble**, **babb**-'l, n Blase f; v perlen, sprudeln; **– bath**, n Schaumbad nt

**buck**, back, n Bock m; **– up!**, (hurry up) halt dich ran!; (cheer up) Kopf hoch!; **pass the – (to)**, v die Verantwortung abschieben (auf)

**bucket**, **back**-itt, n Eimer m

**buckle**, **back**-'l, n Schnalle f; v zuschnallen; (bend) verbiegen

**bud**, bad, n Knospe f; v knospen, ausschlagen

**budge**, badsch, v sich rühren; fig weichen

**budget**, **badsch**-itt, n Budget nt; parl Haushaltsplan m; **–**

**for**, v einplanen

**buff**, baff, adj braungelb; n (enthusiast) Fan m

**buffalo**, **baff**-e-loh, n Büffel m

**buffer**, **baff**-er, n (railway) Puffer m; comp Pufferspeicher m

**buffet**, bu-**feh**, n (food) Büfett nt; (bar) Imbißstube f; **– car**, Speisewagen m

**buffet**, **baff**-itt, v hin und her stoßen

**buffoon**, be-**fuhn**, n Hanswurst m

**bug**, bag, n (also fig) Wanze f

**buggy**, **bagg**-i, n Kinderwagen m

**bugle**, **bjuh**-g'l, n Bügelhorn nt

**build**, bild, n (Körper)bau m; v bauen; **–er**, Bauunternehmer m; **–ing**, Gebäude nt, Bau m

**built-in**, bilt-**inn**, adj eingebaut

**built-up**, bilt-**app**, adj bebaut

**bulb**, balb, n (of plant) Blumenzwiebel f; (lamp) (Glüh)birne f

**bulge**, baldsch, n Wölbung f; fig Anschwellen nt; v anschwellen

**bulk**, balk, n (size) Größe f; (major part) Großteil m; **in –**, comm en gros; **–y**, adj umfangreich

**bull**, bull, n Bulle m, Stier

m; **–dog**, Bulldogge f; **–dozer**, Planierraupe f

**bullet**, **bull**-itt, n Kugel f

**bulletin**, **bull**-e-tinn, n Bulletin nt, Bericht m

**bulletproof**, **bull**-itt-pruhf, adj kugelsicher

**bullion**, **bull**-jen, n Gold-/Silberbarren pl

**bull's eye**, **bulls**-ei, n (target) das Schwarze nt; (shot) Volltreffer m

**bully**, **bull**-i, n Tyrann m; v tyrannisieren

**bum**, bamm, n fam (backside) Hinterteil m; (good-for-nothing) Rumtreiber m; **– (off)**, v (fam scrounge) schnorren (bei)

**bumble-bee**, **bamm**-b'l-bie, n Hummel f

**bump**, bamp, n (blow) Stoß m; (swelling) Beule f; v stoßen; **– into**, stoßen gegen; fig treffen; **–y**, adj holprig

**bumper**, **bamm**-per, adj Rekord-, Sonder-; n (of car) Stoßstange f

**bunch**, bantsch, n (of flowers) Strauß m; (of keys) Bund m; **– of grapes**, Weintrauben pl

**bundle**, **bann**-d'l, n Bündel nt; v (zusammen)bündeln

**bung**, bang, n Zapfen m; (fam throw) schmeißen; **– (up)**, verstopfen

**bungalow**, **bang**-ge-loh, n Bungalow m

**bungle, bang**-g'l, n
Stümperei f; v
verpfuschen; **–r,** n
Stümper m

**bunion, banm**-jen, n
Entzündung f am
Fußballen

**bunker, bang**-ker, n
Bunker m

**bunting, banm**-ting, n
Wimpel pl

**buoy,** beu, n Boje f; **–ant,** adj
(floatable) schwimmfähig;
(cheerful) heiter

**burden, bör**-d'n, n Last f; fig
Bürde f; v belasten,
beladen; **–some,** adj
beschwerlich

**bureau, bjue**-roh, n (desk)
Sekretär m; (chest)
Kommode f; (office) Büro
nt; (official body) Amt nt

**bureaucracy, bjue-rock-re**-ssi, n Bürokratie f

**bureaucrat, bjue**-re-krätt, n
Bürokrat m

**burglar, bör**-gler, n
Einbrecher m; **–y,** n
Einbruch m

**burial, be**-ri-el, n
Beerdigung f

**burly, bör**-li, adj stämmig,
stark

**burn, börn,** n Brandwunde f;
(stream) Bach m; v (of fire
etc.) brennen; (oneself,
food etc.) verbrennen; **–
down,** abbrennen,
niederbrennen; **–er,** n
Brenner m

**burrow, ba**-roh, n Bau m; v
graben

**bursar, bör**-sser, n
Schatzmeister m

**burst, börst,** n (in pipe)
Bruch m; (of anger etc.)
Ausbruch m; v platzen;
(pipe etc.) sprengen; **–
into,** (room) platzen in;
(tears) ausbrechen in;
(flames) aufgehen in; **–
out laughing,** in
Gelächter ausbrechen

**bury, be**-ri, v begraben;
(conceal) vergraben

**bus,** bass, n (Omni)bus m

**bush,** busch, n Busch m,
Strauch m; **–y,** adj buschig,
dicht

**business, bis**-niss, n comm
Geschäft nt; (concern)
Sache f; Angelegenheit f;
**–like,** adj geschäftsmäßig;
**–man,** n Geschäftsmann
m; **–woman,** n
Geschäftsfrau f; **on –,** adv
geschäftlich; **that's none
of your –,** das geht dich
nichts an

**busker, bass**-ker, n
Straßenmusikant m

**bus stop, bass** stopp, n
Bushaltestelle f

**bust,** bast, adj (fam broken)
kaputt; (bankrupt) pleite;
n Büste f; **go –,** v pleite
machen

**bustle, bass**-'l, n Getriebe
nt; v geschäftig sein, hin
und her rennen

**bustling, bass**-ling, adj
(person) geschäftig;
(place) belebt

**busy, bi**-si, adj (person)
beschäftigt; (place)
belebt; (phone) besetzt; **–
oneself (with),** v sich
beschäftigen (mit)

**busybody, bi**-si-bodd-i, n
Wichtigtuer m

**but,** batt, conj aber; (on the
contrary) sondern; prep
außer; **all –,** so gut wie;
**nothing –,** nichts als, nur;
**the last – one,** der/die/das
vorletzte

**butcher, butsch**-er, n
Metzger m; v schlachten;
**–'s (shop),** n Metzgerei f

**butler, batt**-ler, n Butler m

**butt, batt,** n (for water)
Tonne f; (of gun) Kolben
m; (of cigarette) Stummel
m; v (mit dem Kopf)
stoßen; **– in (on),** sich
einmischen (in)

**butter, batt**-er, n Butter f; v
mit Butter bestreichen,
buttern; **–cup,** n
Butterblume f; **–dish,** n
Butterdose f; **–fingers,** n
Schussel m; **–fly,** n
Schmetterling m

**buttocks, batt**-ecks, npl
Gesäß nt

**button, batt**-'n, n Knopf m;
v zuknöpfen; **–hole,** n
Knopfloch nt

**buttress, batt**-riss, n
Strebepfeiler m; v stützen

**buxom, back**-ss'm, adj drall

**buy,** bei, v kaufen; **–er,** n
Käufer m

**buzz,** b*a*s, *n* Summen *nt*;
*v* summen; **–er,** *n*
Summer *m*

**buzzard,** b*a*s-ed, *n* Bussard *m*

**by,** bei, *prep* (agent) durch;
(means) mit, per; (via)
über, durch; (during) bei;
(near) neben, an; (before)
bis; **– oneself,** allein; **–
the way,** übrigens; **one –
one,** einer nach dem
anderen; *adv* **go/pass –,**
vorbeigehen

**by(e)-law,** bei-lo'a, *n*
Verordnung *f*

**by(e)-election,** bei-i-leck-
sch'n, *n* Nachwahl *f*

**bypass,** bei-pahss, *n*
Umgehungsstraße *f*; *v*
umgehen

**bystander,** bei-stänn-der, *n*
Umstehende(r) *m & f*,
Zuschauer *m*

**byte,** beit, *n comp* Byte *nt*

**cab,** käbb, n Taxi nt

**cabaret,** käbb-*e*-reh, n Kabarett nt

**cabbage,** käbb-idsch, n Kohl m; (head of cabbage) Kohlkopf m

**cabin,** käbb-in, n (on ship) Kabine f; (hut) Hütte f

**cabinet,** käbb-i-nitt, n Schränkchen nt; (display) Vitrine f; parl Kabinett nt; **--maker,** n Kunsttischler m

**cable,** keh-b'l, n Tau nt; elec Kabel nt; (telegram) Telegramm nt; v kabeln, telegraphieren; – television, n Kabelfernsehen nt

**cackle,** käck-'l, n Gackern nt; (chatter) Geschwätz nt; (laughter) Lachen nt; v gackern; (chatter) schwatzen;

(laugh) lachen

**cactus,** käck-*tess*, n Kaktus m

**caddie,** kädd-i, n Golfjunge m

**caddy,** kädd-i, n (Tee)büchse f

**cadet,** ke-dett, n Kadett m

**cadge,** kädsch, v schnorren; **–r,** n Schnorrer m

**café,** käff-eh, n Café nt

**cafeteria,** käff-i-tier-ri-e, n Cafeteria f, Selbstbedienungsrestaurant nt

**cage,** kehdsch, n Käfig m; **–y,** adj geheimnistuerisch, ausweichend

**cajole,** ke-dschohl, – sb into sth, v jdn zu etw überreden

**cake,** kehk, n Kuchen m; (of soap) Stück nt; v verkrusten

**calamity,** ka-lämm-i-ti, n

Kalastrophe f; Unglück nt

**calcium,** käll-ssi-em, n Kalzium nt

**calculate,** käll-kju-leht, v berechnen, kalkulieren

**calculation,** käll-kju-leh-sch'n, n Berechnung f

**calculator,** käll-kju-leh-ter, n Rechner m

**calendar,** käll-in-der, n Kalender m

**calf,** kahf, n (animal) Kalb nt; (leg) Wade f

**calibre,** käll-i-ber, n Kaliber nt

**call,** ko'al, n (shout) Ruf m; (phone) Anruf m; v rufen; (name) nennen; – for, (collect) abholen; (demand) erfordern; – off, (cancel) absagen; – on, (visit) besuchen; be –ed, heißen

**caller,** ko'a-ler, n (visitor) Besucher m; (phone) Anrufer m

**callous,** käll-ess, adj gefühllos, herzlos

**calm,** kahm, n Ruhe f, Stille f; naut Flaute f; adj ruhig; v beruhigen; – down, sich beruhigen

**calorie,** käll-e-ri, n Kalorie f

**camber,** kämm-ber, n Wölbung f

**camcorder,** kämm-kor-der, n Camcorder m

**camel,** kämm-'l, n Kamel nt

**cameo,** kämm-i-oh, n Kamee f

**camera,** kämm-e-re, n

(stills) Fotoapparat m; (cine, TV) Kamera f; **in –**, unter Ausschluß der Öffentlichkeit

**camouflage, kämm-**e-flahsch, n Tarnung f; v tarnen

**camp, kämp,** adj fam tuntenhaft; n Lager nt; v zelten, campen

**campaign, kämm-pehn,** n mil Feldzug m; fig Kampagne f; v (in election) den Wahlkampf führen; **– (for/against),** sich einsetzen (für/gegen)

**camper, kämm-**per, n (person) Camper m; (vehicle) Wohnmobil nt

**campsite, kämp-**sseit, n Campingplatz m

**campus, kämm-**pess, n Campus m, Universitätsgelände nt

**can, känn,** n Kanne f; (tin) Dose f; v (preserve) einmachen

**can, känn,** v (be able) können; (be permitted) können, dürfen

**Canada, känn-**e-de, n Kanada nt

**Canadian, ke-neh-**di-en, adj kanadisch; n Kanadier m

**canal, ke-näll,** n Kanal m

**canary, ke-nähr-**ri, n Kanarienvogel m

**cancel, känn-**ss'l, v (appointment) absagen; (train) streichen; (ticket) entwerten

**cancellation, känn-sse-leh-**sch'n, n (of appointment) Absage f; (of train) Streichung f; (of ticket) Entwertung f

**cancer, känn-**sser, n (med, star sign) Krebs m

**candid, känn-**didd, adj offen, ehrlich

**candidate, känn-**di-det, n Kandidat m, Bewerber m

**candle, känn-**d'l, n Kerze f; **–stick,** Kerzenhalter m

**candour, känn-**der, n Offenheit f

**candy, känn-**di, n Kandis(zucker) m; (sweets) Bonbons pl; v kandieren; **–floss,** n Zuckerwatte f

**cane, kehn,** n Rohr nt; (plant/walking stick) Stock m; v prügeln

**canine, keh-**nein, adj Hunde-; n (tooth) Eckzahn m

**canister, känn-**iss-ter, n Blechdose f

**cannabis, kän-**e-bis, n Cannabis m

**cannibal, kän-**i-b'l, n Kannibale m

**cannon, känn-**en, n Kanone f

**canny, känn-**i, adj schlau

**canoe, ke-nuh,** n Kanu nt; v Kanu fahren

**can-opener, känn-**oh-p'n-er, n Dosenöffner m

**canopy, känn-**e-pi, n Baldachin m

**cantankerous, känn-täng-**ke-ress, adj zänkerisch

**canteen, känn-tien,** n (restaurant) Kantine f; (cutlery) Besteckkasten m

**canter, känn-**ter, n Kanter m; v langsam galoppieren

**canvas, känn-**wess, n Segeltuch nt; (painting) Leinwand f; **under –,** im Zelt

**canvass, känn-**wess, v comm werben; (in election) um Stimmen werben

**canyon, känn-**jen, n Felsschlucht f

**cap, käpp,** n (hat) Mütze f; (of bottle) Deckel m; (of pen) Kappe f; (of radiator/tank) Verschluß m; v (close) verschließen; (exceed) übertreffen; (limit) einschränken

**capable, keh-**pe-b'l, adj fähig; **– of,** imstande zu

**capacity, ke-päss-**i-ti, n (size) Inhalt m; (ability) Fähigkeit f; (position) Eigenschaft f

**cape, kehp,** n geog Kap nt; (cloak) Umhang m

**caper, keh-**per, n (pickle) Kaper f; (prank) Eskapade f

**capital, käpp-**i-t'l, n fin Kapital nt; (city) Hauptstadt f; (letter) Großbuchstabe m; **–ism,** n Kapitalismus m; **–ist,** adj kapitalistisch; n Kapitalist m; **– punishment,**

**Todesstrafe** f

**capitulate,** ka-**pitt**-juh-leht, v kapitulieren

**capricious,** ke-**prisch**-ess, adj launisch, eigensinnig

**capsize,** käpp-**sseis,** v kentern

**capsule,** käpp-sjuhl, n Kapsel f

**captain,** käpp-tinn, n naut Kapitän m; mil Hauptmann m; v anführen; naut befehligen

**captive,** käpp-tiw, n Gefangene(r) m & f; adj gefangen

**captivity,** käpp-tiw-i-ti, n Gefangenschaft f

**capture,** käpp-tscher, n Eroberung f, Gefangennahme f; data –, Datenerfassung f; v (person) gefangennehmen; (town) einnehmen; (interest) erregen

**car,** kahr, n Wagen m, Auto nt; rail Wagen m

**carafe,** ke-**räff,** n Karaffe f

**caramel,** kä-re-mel, n Karamel m; (toffee) Karamelle f

**carat,** kä-ret, n Karat nt

**caravan,** kä-re-wän, n Wohnwagen m; – site, Campingplatz m für Wohnwagen

**carbon,** kahr-ben, n Kohlenstoff m; – copy, Durchschlag m; – paper, Kohlepapier nt

**carburettor,** kahr-be-**rett**-er, n Vergaser m

**carcass,** kahr-kess, n Kadaver m

**card,** kahrd, n Karte f; –board, Pappe f; –board box, Karton m

**cardiac,** kahr-di-ack, adj Herz-; – arrest, n Herzstillstand m

**cardigan,** kahr-di-gen, n Strickjacke f

**cardinal,** kahr-di-n'l, adj Haupt-; (number) Kardinal-; n Kardinal m

**care,** kehr, n (attention) Sorgfalt f; (caution) Vorsicht f; (anxiety) Sorge f; (tending) Pflege f; – (about), v sich kümmern (um); (like) mögen; I don't – das ist mir egal; take –, aufpassen; take –! Vorsicht!; take – of, sorgen für

**career,** ke-rier, n Karriere f, Laufbahn f

**carefree,** kehr-frie, adj sorglos

**careful,** kehr-full, adj vorsichtig, sorgfältig

**careless,** kehr-liss, adj nachlässig; –ness, n Nachlässigkeit f

**caress,** ke-ress, n Liebkosung f; v liebkosen

**caretaker,** kehr-teh-ker, n Hausmeister m

**car ferry,** kahr fe-ri, n Autofähre f

**cargo,** kahr-goh, n Ladung f

**car hire,** kahr heir, n Autovermietung f

**Caribbean,** kä-ri-bie-en, adj karibisch; n (Sea) Karibik f

**caricature,** kä-ri-ke-tjuhr, n Karikatur f

**caring,** kehr-ring, adj (person) warmherzig, liebevoll; (society) sozial

**carnage,** kahr-nidsch, n Blutbad nt

**carnal,** kahr-n'l, adj sinnlich, fleischlich

**carnation,** kar-neh-sch'n, n Nelke f

**carnival,** kahr-ni-w'l, n Karneval m, Fasching m

**carnivorous,** kar-ni-ve-ress, adj fleischfressend

**carol,** kä-rel, n (Weihnachts)lied nt

**carp,** kahrp, n (fish) Karpfen m; v nörgeln

**car park,** kahr pahrk, n Parkplatz m; (multi-storey) Parkhaus nt

**carpenter,** kahr-p'n-ter, n Zimmermann m

**carpet,** kahr-pitt, n Teppich m; (fitted) Teppichboden m; v (mit Teppichboden) auslegen

**car phone,** kahr fohn, n Autotelefon nt

**carriage,** kä-ridsch, n rail Wagen m; comm Beförderung(skosten) f(pl); (deportment) Haltung f

**carrier,** kä-ri-er, n comm

Spediteur m; (luggage rack) Gepäckhalter m; --bag, Tragetasche f; --pigeon, Brieftaube f

**carrot**, kä-ret, n Karotte f, Möhre f

**carry**, kä-ri, v tragen; – on, (continue) weitermachen; (fuss) Theater machen; (conduct) führen; – out, (order) ausführen; (plan) durchführen

**cart**, kahrt, n Wagen m; v schleppen

**carton**, kahr-ten, n Karton m; (of milk) Tüte f

**cartoon**, kahr-tuhn, n Karikatur f; (film) Zeichentrickfilm m; (strip) Comic m

**cartridge**, kahr-tridsch, n Patrone f

**carve**, kahrw, v (wood) schnitzen; (meat) tranchieren

**carving**, kahr-wing, n Schnitzerei f

**car wash**, kahr u'osch, n Autowäsche f

**cascade**, käss-**kehd**, n Wasserfall m, Kaskade f

**case**, kehss, n (matter) Fall m; (suitcase) Koffer m; (box) Kiste f; (spectacle etc.) Etui nt; **in any –**, auf jeden Fall; **in –**, im Falle, falls

**cash**, käsch, n Bargeld nt; v einlösen; – **book**, n Kassenbuch nt; – **card**, n Geldautomatenkarte f; –

**dispenser**, n Geldautomat nt; **in –**, bar

**cashier**, käsch-**ier**, n Kassierer m

**cashmere**, käsch-mier, n Kaschmir m

**casino**, ke-ssie-noh, n Kasino nt

**cask**, kahsk, n Faß nt

**casket**, kahss-kitt, n Kästchen nt

**casserole**, käss-e-rohl, n Kasserolle f; (stew) Eintopf m

**cassette**, ke-ssett, n Kassette f; – **player**, n Kassettenspieler m; – **recorder**, n Kassettenrekorder m

**cast**, kahst, n (throw) Wurf m; theatre Besetzung f; (metal) Guß m; v (throw) werfen; (metal etc.) gießen; theatre besetzen

**castanet**, käss-te-**nett**, n Kastagnette f

**caste**, kahst, n Kaste f

**cast iron**, kahst ei-en, n Gußeisen nt

**castle**, kah-ss'l, n Schloß nt, Burg f; (chess) Turm m; v (chess) rochieren

**castor**, kahss-ter, n (wheel) Laufrolle

**castor oil**, kahss-ter eul, n Rizinusöl nt

**casual**, käsch-ju-el, adj (clothes) leger, Freizeit-; (attitude) ungezwungen; (meeting) zufällig; (work) Gelegenheits-

**casualty**, käsch-ju-el-ti, n Opfer nt; – (**department**), Unfallstation f

**cat**, kät, n Katze f; **tom–**, Kater m

**catalogue**, kätt-e-log, n Katalog m; v katalogisieren

**catalytic converter**, kätt-e-litt-ick ken-wör-ter, n Katalysator m

**cataract**, kätt-e-räkt, n (med) grauer Star; (rapids) Katarakt m

**catarrh**, ke-tahr, n Katarrh m

**catastrophe**, ke-täss-tre-fi, n Katastrophe f

**catch**, kätsch, n (of fish) Fang m; (snag) Haken m; (on door) Schnapper m; v fangen; (seize) fassen; (an illness) sich holen; – **fire**, Feuer fangen; – **up**, einholen

**catching**, kätt-sching, adj ansteckend

**catch phrase**, kätsch frehs, n Schlagwort nt

**catchy**, kätt-schi, adj eingängig

**category**, kätt-i-ge-ri, n Kategorie f, Klasse f

**cater**, keh-ter, v mit Speisen und Getränken versorgen; – **for**, (function) ausrichten; (needs) eingestellt sein auf; –**ing**, n Bewirtung f; (trade) Gastronomie f

**caterer**, keh-ter-er, n

Speiselieferant *m*

**caterpillar, kätt**-er-pill-er, *n*
Raupe *f*

**cathedral,** ke-**thie**-drel, *n*
Kathedrale *f*, Dom *m*

**catholic, käth**-e-lick, *adj*
*relig* katholisch; (broad)
vielseitig; *n* Katholik *m*

**cattle, kätt**-'l, *n* Vieh *nt*

**cauliflower, koll**-i-flau-er, *n*
Blumenkohl *m*

**cause,** ko-as, *n* Grund *m*,
Ursache *f*; (ideal) Sache *f*;
*v* verursachen

**causeway, ko'as**-u'eh, *n*
Damm *m*

**caustic, ko'ass**-tick, *adj*
ätzend, kaustisch; *fig* bissig

**caution, ko'a**-sch'n, *n* (care)
Vorsicht *f*; (warning)
Verwarnung *f*; *v*
verwarnen

**cautious, ko'a**-schess, *adj*
vorsichtig

**cavalier,** käw-*e*-**lier**, *n*
*adj* unbekümmert; *n*
Kavalier *m*

**cavalry, käw**-el-ri, *n*
Kavallerie *f*

**cave,** kehw, *n* Höhle *f*; – **in,**
*v* einstürzen; (give in)
nachgeben

**cavern, käw**-ern, *n* Höhle *f*;
–**ous,** *adj* (hollow) hohl;
(gaping) gähnend

**caviar(e), käw**-i-ahr, *n*
Kaviar *m*

**cavity, käw**-i-ti, *n* Höhlung
*f*; (in tooth) Loch *nt*

**CD,** ssie-**die** (*abbr* compact
disc), CD *f*; – **player,** *n*

CD-Spieler *m*; –-**ROM,** *n*
CD-ROM *f*

**cease,** ssiess, *v* aufhören;
–-**fire,** *n* Waffenruhe *f*;
–**less,** *adj* unaufhörlich

**cedar, ssie**-der, *n* Zeder *f*

**cede,** ssied, *v* abtreten,
überlassen

**ceiling, ssie**-ling, *n* Decke *f*;
*fig* Höchstgrenze *f*

**celebrate, ssell**-i-breht, *v*
feiern; –**d,** *adj* berühmt

**celebration, ssell**-i-**breh**-
sch'n, *n* Feier *f*

**celebrity, ssi-lebb**-ri-ti, *n*
(person) berühmte
Persönlichkeit *f*; (fame)
Berühmtheit *f*

**celery, ssell**-e-ri, *n* Sellerie
*m & f*

**celestial, ssi-less**-ti-el, *adj*
himmlisch

**celibacy, ssell**-i-be-ssi, *n*
Zölibat *m/nt*

**cell,** ssell, *n* Zelle *f*

**cellar, ssell**-er, *n* Keller *m*

**cello, tschell**-oh, *n*
(Violon)cello *nt*

**cellphone, ssell**-fohn, *n*
Funktelefon *nt*

**cellular, ssell**-ju-ler, *adj*
zellular, Zell-

**celluloid, ssell**-ju-leud, *n*
Zelluloid *nt*

**Celt,** kelt/sselt, *n* Kelte *m*,
Keltin *f*; –**ic,** *adj* keltisch

**cement,** ssi-**ment**, *n* Zement
*m*; (glue) Klebstoff *m*; *v*
zementieren; leimen; –
**mixer,** *n*
Betonmischmaschine *f*

**cemetery, ssemm**-i-tri, *n*
Friedhof *m*

**censor, ssenn**-sser, *n* Zensor
*m*; *v* zensieren; –**ship,** *n*
Zensur *f*

**census, ssenn**-ssess, *n*
Volkszählung *f*

**centenary, ssenn-tie**-ne-ri, *n*
Jahrhundertfeier *f*

**centigrade, ssenn**-ti-grehd,
*adj* Celsius-

**centimetre, ssenn**-ti-mie-
ter, *n* Zentimeter *m*

**central, ssenn**-trel,
*adj* zentral; (main)
Haupt-; – **heating,** *n*
Zentralheizung *f*

**centralize, ssenn**-tre-leis, *v*
zentralisieren

**centre, ssenn**-ter, *n*
Mittelpunkt *m*, Zentrum
*nt*; *v* zentrieren

**century, ssenn**-tsche-ri, *n*
Jahrhundert *nt*

**ceramic, ssi-rämm**-ick,
*adj* keramisch; –**s,**
*npl* Keramik *f*;
Keramikwaren *pl*

**cereal, ssier**-ri-el, *n* (crop)
Getreide *nt*; (food)
Getreideflocken *pl*

**ceremony, sse**-ri-me-ni, *n*
Zeremonie *f*; (formality)
Förmlichkeit *f*

**certain(ly), ssör**-t'n(-li), *adj*
& *adv* gewiß, sicher,
bestimmt

**certainty, ssör**-t'n-ti, *n*
Gewißheit *f*

**certificate, sser**-tidd-i-ket, *n*
Bescheinigung *f*; (of

health, qualifications)
Zeugnis nt

**certify**, ssör-ti-fei, v
bescheinigen

**cervical**, ssör-wi-k'l, adj
Gebärmutterhals-

**cervix**, ssör-wicks, n
Gebärmutterhals m

**cessation**, sse-sseh-sch'n, n
Aufhören nt; (of
hostilities) Einstellung f

**cf.** (abbr = compare), vgl.

**CFC** ssie eff ssie (abbr
chlorofluorocarbon), n
FCKW

**chafe**, tschef, v (rub)
scheuern; (fret) aufgeregt
werden

**chaffinch**, tschäff-intsch, n
Buchfink m

**chain**, tschehn, n Kette f; –
up, v anketten

**chair**, tschehr, n Stuhl m;
(armchair) Sessel m; (of
committee) Vorsitz m; v
den Vorsitz führen

**chairman**, tschehr-men, n
Vorsitzende(r) m & f

**chalet**, schall-eh, n
Chalet nt

**chalice**, tschäll-iss, n
Kelch m

**chalk**, tscho'ak, n Kreide f

**challenge**, tschäll-indsch, n
Herausforderung f; (to
authority) Infragestellung
f; v herausfordern;
(authority) in Frage
stellen; fig fordern;
**challenging**, adj
(provocative)

herausfordernd;
(demanding)
anspruchsvoll

**chamber**, tschehm-ber, n
Kammer f; –maid, n
Zimmermädchen nt; –
**music**, n Kammermusik f;
–s, npl (of barrister)
Kanzlei f

**chamois**, schämm-u'a, adj, n
Gemse f, Waschleder nt

**champagne**, schämm-pehn,
n Champagner m;
(sparkling wine) Sekt m

**champion**, tschämm-pi-en,
n sport Meister m; (of
cause) Verfechter m;
–ship, n Meisterschaft f

**chance**, tschahnss, n (luck)
Zufall m; (opportunity)
Gelegenheit f;
(possibility) Möglichkeit
f; adj zufällig; v riskieren;
**by –**, adv zufällig

**chancel**, tschahn-ss'l, n
Chor m

**chancellor**, tschahn-ss'l-er,
n Kanzler m; – of the
**Exchequer**, n
Finanzminister m

**chandelier**, schänn-di-lier, n
Kronleuchter m

**change**, tschehndsch, n
(alteration) Veränderung
f; (small money)
Kleingeld nt; (money
returned) Wechselgeld nt;
v (alter) ändern;
(transform) verwandeln;
(money, gear, etc.)
wechseln; (swap)

tauschen; (trains etc.)
umsteigen; (clothes) sich
umziehen; – one's mind,
es sich anders überlegen;
–able, adj wechselhaft

**changing room**, tschehn-
dsching ruhm, n
Umkleideraum m

**channel**, tschänn-'l, n Kanal
m; v (water) leiten; fig
lenken; (English)
**Channel**, n Ärmelkanal
m; **Channel Islands**, npl
Kanalinseln pl; **Channel
Tunnel**, n Kanaltunnel m

**chant**, tschahnt, n Gesang
m; v singen

**chaos**, keh-oss, n Chaos nt

**chaotic**, keh-ott-ick, adj
chaotisch

**chap**, tschäpp, n Kerl m

**chapel**, tschäpp-'l, n Kapelle
f

**chaperon(e)**, schäpp-e-
rohn, n Anstandsdame f; v
begleiten

**chaplain**, tschäpp-linn, n
Kaplan m

**chapped**, tschäpt, adj
aufgesprungen, rauh

**chapter**, tschäpp-ter, n
Kapitel m

**char**, tschar, n (charlady)
Putzfrau f; v (scorch)
verkohlen; (clean) putzen

**character**, kä-rick-ter, n
(nature) Charakter m;
(figure) Gestalt f; (letter)
Buchstabe m; –istic, adj
charakteristisch, typisch;
n Merkmal nt

**charade**, sche-*rahd*, n
Scharade f

**charcoal**, *tschar*-kohl, n
Holzkohle f

**charge**, tschardsch, n (price)
Preis m; (fee) Gebühr f;
(explosive) Ladung f; *law*
Anklage f; v (bill)
berechnen; *law* anklagen;
*mil* angreifen; – **card**, n
Kundenkarte f; **free of –**,
kostenlos; **in – (of)**,
verantwortlich (für)

**charitable**, tschä-ri-te-b'l,
*adj* wohltätig

**charity**, tschä-ri-ti, n (good
causes) Wohlfahrt f;
(organization)
Wohltätigkeitsverein nt;
(virtue) Nächstenliebe f

**charlady**, tschar-*leh*-di, n
Putzfrau f

**charm**, tscharm, n Charme
m, Reiz m; (spell) Bann m;
(amulet) Talisman m; v
bezaubern; –**ing**, *adj*
reizend, bezaubernd

**chart**, tschart, n (naut,
weather) Karte f;
(diagram) Schaubild nt; v
erfassen

**charter**, tschar-ter, n
Freibrief m; v chartern;
–**ed accountant**, n
Wirtschaftsprüfer m

**charwoman**, tschar-u'umm-
en, n Putzfrau f

**chase**, tschehss, n Jagd f; v
jagen; (pursue) verfolgen

**chasm**, käs-'m, n Abgrund m

**chassis**, schä-ssi, n

Fahrgestell nt

**chaste**, tschehst, *adj* keusch

**chastity**, tschäss-ti-ti, n
Keuschheit f

**chat**, tschätt, n Plauderei f; v
plaudern; – **show**, n
Talkshow f; –**ter**, n
Geschwätz nt; v
schwatzen; (of teeth)
klappern; –**terbox**, n
Quasselstrippe f; –**ty**, *adj*
geschwätzig

**chauffeur**, schoh-fer, n
Chauffeur m

**chauvinist**, schoh-wi-nist,
n Chauvinist m; *fam*
Chauvi m

**cheap(ly)**, tschiep(-li), *adj*
& *adv* billig

**cheat**, tschiht, n Betrüger m;
v betrügen; –**ing**,
n Betrügen nt;
Falschspielen nt

**check**, tscheck, n (restraint)
Hemmung f; (chess)
Schach nt; (verification)
Kontrolle f; (pattern)
Karo nt; v hemmen; (stop)
einhalten; (verify)
kontrollieren; (examine)
prüfen; – **in**, v
einchecken, sich
anmelden; (luggage)
abfertigen lassen; –**in**, n
Abfertigung f; –**mate**, n
Schachmatt nt; v matt
setzen; – **out**, v sich
abmelden, abreisen; –-
**out**, n Kasse f; – **up**, v
überprüfen; –-**up**, n (med)
Untersuchung f

**cheek**, tschiek, n Backe f;
(impudence)
Unverschämtheit f; –**y**,
*adj* frech

**cheer**, tschier, n
Fröhlichkeit f; (applause)
Beifallsruf m; v (applaud)
zujubeln; (comfort)
aufmuntern; –**ful**, *adj*
fröhlich; –**less**, freudlos,
traurig; –**s!**, Prost!; – **up!**
Kopf hoch!

**cheerio**, tschier-ri-oh, *interj*
tschüs

**cheese**, tschies, n Käse m;
–**board**, n Käseplatte f

**chef**, scheff, n
Küchenchef m

**chemical**, kemm-i-k'l, *adj*
chemisch; n Chemikalie f

**chemist**, kemm-ist, n
(expert) Chemiker m; (in
shop) Apotheker m,
Drogist m; –**ry**, n Chemie
f; –**'s**, n Apotheke f,
Drogerie f

**cheque**, tscheck, n Scheck
m; –**book**, n Scheckbuch nt;
– **card**, n Scheckkarte f

**chequered**, tscheck-erd, *adj*
(pattern) kariert; (career,
history) bewegt

**cherish**, tsche-risch, v
(person) lieben; (illusion)
sich hingeben

**cherry**, tsche-ri, n Kirsche f

**chess**, tschess, n
Schach(spiel) nt

**chest**, tschest, n Brust f;
(trunk) Truhe f; (box)
Kiste f; – **of drawers**,

Kommode f

**chestnut, tschess**-natt, n
Kastanie f

**chew,** tschuh, v kauen; **–ing
gum,** n Kaugummi m

**chic,** schiek, adj schick,
elegant

**chick,** tschick, n Küken n

**chicken, tschick**-inn, n
(bird) Huhn nt; (food)
Hähnchen nt; **– out,** v fam
kneifen; **–pox,** n
Windpocken pl

**chief,** tschief, n adj Haupt-;
(boss) Chef m; (of tribe)
Häuptling m; **– executive,**
n Geschäftsführer m; **–ly,**
adv hauptsächlich

**chilblain, tschill**-blehn, n
Frostbeule f

**child,** tscheild, n (pl
**children**), Kind nt; **–birth,**
n Geburt f; **–ish,** adj
kindisch; **–like,** adj
kindlich; **–minder,** n
Tagesmutter f

**Chile, tschill**-i, n Chile nt;
**–an,** adj chilenisch; n
Chilene m, Chilenin f

**chill,** tschill, n Frische f;
(med) Erkältung f; fig
Abkühlung f; v kühlen

**chilli, tschill**-i, adj Chili m

**chilly, tschill**-i, adj kühl; fig
frostig

**chime,** tscheim, n
Glockenspiel nt; v läuten;
**– in,** sich einmischen

**chimney, tschimm**-ni, n
Schornstein m; **– sweep,**
Schornsteinfeger m

**chimpanzee, tschimm**-pänn-
**sie,** n Schimpanse m

**chin,** tschinn, n Kinn nt

**china, tschei**-ne, n
Porzellan nt

**China, tschei**-ne, n
China nt

**Chinese, tschei**-nies, adj
chinesisch; n Chinese m,
Chinesin f; (language)
Chinesisch nt

**chink,** tschink, n (gap)
Spalt m, Ritze f; (clink)
Klimpern m; v klimpern

**chip,** tschipp, n (of wood
etc.) Splitter m; v (cup
etc.) anschlagen; (wood
etc.) abstoßen; **– in,** v sich
einmischen; **–s,** npl
Pommes frites pl

**chiropodist,** ki-**ropp**-e-dist,
n Fußpfleger m

**chirp,** tschörp, n Zwitschern
nt; v zwitschern

**chisel, tschis**-'l, n Meißel m;
v meißeln

**chit,** tschitt, n Zettel m

**chitchat, tschitt**-tschätt, n
Geschwätz nt

**chivalrous, schi**-wel-ress, adj
ritterlich

**chives,** tscheiws, npl
Schnittlauch m

**chlorine, klor**-rien, n
Chlor nt

**chock,** tschock, n
Bremsklotz m; **– full,** adj
knüppelvoll

**chocolate, tschock**-e-let, n
Schokolade f

**choice,** tscheuss, n

(decision) Wahl f;
(variety) Auswahl f; adj
Qualitäts-, auserlesen

**choir,** ku'eir, n Chor m

**choke,** tschohk, v
(suffocate) ersticken;
(strangle) erwürgen

**cholera, koll**-e-re, n
Cholera f

**cholesterol,** ko-**less**-te-rel, n
Cholesterin m

**choose,** tschuhs, v wählen,
auswählen

**chop,** tschopp, n Kotelett nt;
v (wood) spalten; (food)
(zer)hacken; **get the –,** v
fam rausgeschmissen
werden

**chopper, tschopp**-er, n
(axe) Hackbeil nt;
(fam helicopter)
Hubschrauber m

**choppy, tschopp**-i, adj
bewegt

**chopstick, tschopp**-stick, n
Stäbchen nt

**choral, kor**-rel, adj Chor-

**chord,** kord, n (string) Saite
f; mus Akkord m

**chore,** tschor, n Pflicht f;
(domestic) **–s,** npl
Hausarbeit f

**chorister,** ko-**riss**-ter, n
Chorsänger m

**chorus, kor**-ress, n (singers)
Chor m; (in song) Refrain
m

**Christ,** kreist, n Christus m

**christen, kriss**-'n, v taufen;
**–ing,** n Taufe f

**Christian, kriss**-ti-en, adj

christlich; n Christ m; –
**name,** n Vorname m
**Christianity, kriss-ti-änn-i-**
ti, n Christentum nt
**Christmas, kriss-mess,** n
Weihnachten pl; **– card,** n
Weihnachtskarte f; **– Day,**
n erster Weihnachtstag m;
**– Eve,** n Heiligabend m;
**Merry –!** Frohe
Weihnachten!
**chrome, krohm,** n Chrom nt
**chronic, kronn-ick,** adj
chronisch
**chronicle, kronn-i-k'l,** n
Chronik f
**chronological, kronn-e-**
lodsch-ick-'l, adj
chronologisch
**chubby, tschabb-i,** adj
rundlich; (cheeks)
pausbäckig
**chuck, tschakk,** v fam
schmeißen; **– out,**
(person) rausschmeißen;
(object) wegschmeißen
**chuckle, tschakk-'l,** n
Kichern nt; v vor sich hin
lachen
**chug, tschagg,** v tuckern
**chum, tschamm,** n fam
Kumpel m
**chunk, tschank,** n (großes)
Stück nt
**church, tschörtsch,** n Kirche
f; **–yard,** Kirchhof m
**churlish, tschör-lisch,** adj
mürrisch, grob
**churn, tschörn,** n (butter)
Butterfaß nt; (milk)
Milchkanne f; v buttern; –

**out,** v massenweise
produzieren
**chute, schuht,** n Rutsche
f; (rubbish)
Müllschlucker m
**cider, ssei-der,** n
Apfelwein m
**cigar, ssi-gahr,** n Zigarre f
**cigarette, ssi-ge-rett,** n
Zigarette f
**cinders, ssinn-ders,** npl
Asche f
**cine-camera, ssinn-i-kämm-**
e-re, n (Schmal)
filmkamera f
**cine-film, ssinn-i-film,** n
Schmalfilm m
**cinema, ssinn-i-me,** n
Kino nt
**cinnamon, ssinn-e-men,** n
Zimt m
**cipher, ssei-fer,** n Chiffre f,
Code m
**circle, ssör-k'l,** n Kreis m;
theatre Rang m; v kreisen
(um) (surround)
umgeben
**circuit, ssör-kitt,** n (course)
Rennbahn f; (lap) Runde
f; elec Stromkreis m
**circuitous, ssör-kjuh-itt-ess,**
adj umständlich
**circular, ssör-kju-ler,** n
(letter) Rundschreiben nt;
(leaflet) Wurfsendung f;
adj kreisförmig; rund
**circulate, ssör-kju-leht,** v
(of blood, traffic) fließen;
(of news, rumour) sich
verbreiten; (memo)
zirkulieren lassen;

(rumour) in Umlauf
bringen
**circulation, ssör-kju-leh-**
sch'n, n Umlauf m; (of
blood) Kreislauf m; (of
newspaper) Auflage f
**circumcise, ssör-kem-sseis,**
v beschneiden
**circumference, sser-kamm-**
fe-renss, n Umfang m
**circumspect, ssör-kem-**
speckt, adj umsichtig
**circumstances, ssör-kem-**
sten-ssis, npl Umstände pl
Verhältnisse pl
**circumstantial, ssör-kem-**
stänn-sch'l, adj
umständlich; **– evidence,**
n Indizienbeweis m
**circumvent, ssör-kem-went,**
v umgehen
**circus, ssör-kess,** n Zirkus m
**cistern, ssiss-tern,** n (tank)
Zisterne f; (of WC)
Spülkasten m
**cite, sseit,** v zitieren
**citizen, ssitt-i-s'n,** n Bürger
m; **–ship,** n
Staatsbürgerschaft f
**citrus, ssitt-ress,** adj Zitrus-
**city, ssitt-i,** n Stadt f,
Großstadt f; **– centre,** n
Stadtmitte f; **City (of
London),** n das Londoner
Bankenviertel nt
**civic, ssiw-ick,** adj Stadt-,
Bürger-
**civil, ssiw-il,** adj (of society)
bürgerlich; (polite)
höflich; **– servant,** n
Staatsbeamte(r) m & f; –

**war,** n Bürgerkrieg m

**civilian,** ssi-**will**-jen, adj zivil; n Zivilist m

**civilization,** ssi-wi-lei-**seh**-sch'n, n Kultur f, Zivilisation f

**civilized,** ssiw-i-leisd, adj zivilisiert, zivil

**claim,** klehm, n (demand) Anspruch m; comm Forderung f; (assertion) Behauptung f; v (apply for) beantragen; (assert) behaupten; **–ant,** n Antragsteller m

**clairvoyant,** klähr-**weu**-ent, n adj hellseherisch; n Hellseher m

**clamber,** klämm-ber, v klettern

**clammy,** klämm-i, adj klamm, feucht

**clamour,** klämm-er, n Geschrei nt, Lärm m; – **for,** v schreien nach, fordern

**clamp,** klämp, n Schraubzwinge f; v einspannen; – **down (on),** v durchgreifen (gegen)

**clan,** klänn, n Clan m

**clandestine,** klänn-**dess**-tinn, adj geheim

**clang,** kläng, n Klappern nt; v klappern

**clank,** klänk, n Klirren nt; v klirren

**clap,** kläpp, n (of hands) Klatschen nt; (of thunder) Schlag m; v (Beifall) klatschen; **–ping,**

(Beifall)klatschen nt; – **trap,** n Blödsinn m

**claret,** klä-ritt, n Bordeauxwein m

**clarify,** klä-ri-fei, v klären

**clarinet,** klä-ri-**nett,** n Klarinette f

**clash,** kläsch, n Zusammenstoß m; fig Konflikt m; v zusammenstoßen; (of colours) sich beißen; fig in Konflikt kommen

**clasp,** klahsp, n (catch) Spange f; (grasp) Griff m; v (grasp) ergreifen; (embrace) umarmen

**class,** klahss, n Klasse f; v klassifizieren

**classic,** kläss-ick, adj klassisch; n Klassiker m; **–al,** adj klassisch; (ancient) antik

**classified,** kläss-i-feid, adj klassifiziert; (secret) Geheim-; – **ad(vertisement),** n Kleinanzeige f

**classify,** kläss-i-fei, v klassifizieren

**classroom,** klahss-ruhm, n Klassenzimmer nt

**clatter,** klätt-er, n Geklapper nt; v klappern

**clause,** klo'as, n law Klausel f; gram Satz m

**claustrophobia,** kloss-tre-**foh**-bi-e, n Klaustrophobie f

**claw,** klo'a, n Klaue f; (sharp) Kralle f; (of crab

etc.) Schere f; v kratzen; – **at,** sich krallen an

**clay,** kleh, n Lehm m; (potter's) Ton m; **–ey,** adj lehmig

**clean,** klien, adj sauber; v putzen; (clothes etc.) reinigen; **–er,** n (domestic) Putzfrau f; (office) Reiniger m; **–ing,** n Putzen nt; (clothes etc.) Reinigung f; – **out,** v (gründlich) saubermachen; – **up,** v saubermachen; (tidy) aufräumen

**cleanliness, klenn**-li-niss, n Reinlichkeit f

**cleanse,** klenns, v reinigen

**clean-shaven,** klien-**scheh**-wen, adj glattrasiert

**clear,** klier, adj klar; (unobstructed) frei; v (of weather) aufklaren; (of fog etc.) sich auflösen; (remove) beseitigen; (jump over) überspringen; (approve) abfertigen; (road) freimachen; (table) abräumen; (suspect) freisprechen; **–ance,** n Beseitigung f; (space) Spielraum m; (customs) Abfertigung f; (sale) Räumungsverkauf m; – **cut,** adj eindeutig; **–ing,** n Lichtung f; **–ly,** adv klar; fig selbstverständlich; – **off,** v fam abhauen; – **out,** v ausräumen; – **up,** v (tidy) aufräumen;

(mystery) aufklären

**cleaver, klie**-wer, n
Hackbeil nt

**clef, kleff,** n mus
(Noten)schlüssel m

**cleft, kleft,** n Spalte f

**clematis, klemm**-e-tiss, n
Klematis f

**clemency, klemm**-en-ssi, n
Milde f

**clench, klentsch,** v (teeth)
zusammenbeißen; (fist)
ballen

**clergy, klör**-dschi, n die
Geistlichen pl; **–man,** n
Geistlicher m

**clerical, kle**-ri-k'l, adj
(office) Schreib-, Büro-;
relig geistlich; **– error,** n
Schreibfehler m

**clerk, klark,** n
(Büro)angestellte(r) m & f

**clever, klew**-er, adj klug,
schlau; (dextrous)
geschickt; **–ness,** n
Klugheit f, Geschicktheit f

**cliché, klie**-scheh, n
Klischee nt

**click, klick,** n (of switch,
fingers) Knipsen nt; (of
joint) Knacken nt; v
knipsen; knacken; (of
heels) klappern; (fam
become clear) funken

**client, klei**-ent, n Kunde m,
Kundin f; Klient m; **–ele,**
n Kundschaft f

**cliff, kliff,** n Klippe f,
Felsen m

**climate, klei**-mitt, n
Klima nt

**climax, klei**-mäcks, n
Höhepunkt m

**climb, kleim,** n Aufstieg m;
v klettern; (mountain)
besteigen; **– down,** v
absteigen; (give in)
nachgeben; **–er,** n (rock)
Kletterer m; (mountain)
Bergsteiger m

**clinch, klintsch,** n Clinch
m; v (settle) abmachen

**cling (to), kling** (tu), v sich
festklammern (an); fig
sich festhalten (an)

**clinic, klinn**-ick, n Klinik f

**clink, klink,** n Klirren nt; v
klirren

**clip, klipp,** n Klammer f;
(clasp) Spange f; v
scheren; **–ping,** n (article)
Ausschnitt m

**cloak, klohk,** n Umhang m;
v bedecken, hüllen;
**–room,** n Garderobe f;
(WC) Toilette f

**clock, klock,** n Uhr f; **alarm
–,** Wecker m; **– in/on,** v
(den Arbeitsbeginn)
stempeln; **– off/out,** v (das
Arbeitsende) stempeln

**clockwise, klock**-u'eis, adv
im Uhrzeigersinn

**clockwork, klock**-u'örk, adj
(toy) zum Aufziehen; n
Uhrwerk nt;
Aufziehmechanismus m;
**like –,** adv wie am
Schnürchen

**clog, klogg,** n Holzschuh m;
v **– (up),** verstopfen

**cloister, kleuss**-ter, n

Kreuzgang m

**clone, klohn,** n Klon m; v
klonen

**close, klohss,** adj nahe, in
der Nähe; (relative) nahe;
(friend, connection) eng;
(weather) schwül; (result)
knapp; (study) genau; adv
nahe; **– behind,** prep dicht
hinter; **– by,** adv in der
Nähe; **– to,** prep nahe bei,
dicht an, in der Nähe von

**close, klohs,** n Schluß m; v
schließen; adj
geschlossen, zu; **– down,** v
schließen, stillegen

**closet, klos-itt,** n (cupboard)
Wandschrank m; (room)
Kabinett nt

**closure, kloh**-scher, n
Schließung f; (of road)
Sperrung f

**clot, klott,** n Klumpen nt;
(of blood) Blutgerinnsel
nt; (fool) Trottel m; v (of
blood) gerinnen

**cloth, kloth,** n Tuch nt, Stoff
m; (cleaning) Lappen m;
(table) Tischdecke f

**clothe, klohdh,** v kleiden

**clothes, klohdhs,** n Kleider
pl; **bed–,** n Bettwäsche f;
**–brush,** n Kleiderbürste f;
**–line,** n Wäscheleine f

**clothing, kloh**-dhing, n
Kleidung f

**cloud, klaud,** n Wolke f; v fig
trüben; **–burst,** n
Wolkenbruch m; **–less,** adj
wolkenlos; **–y,** adj (sky)
bewölkt; (liquid) trüb

**clout,** klaut, n (fam blow)
Schlag m; (strength)
Schlagkraft f; v schlagen;
fam hauen

**clove,** klohw, n
Gewürznelke f; (of garlic)
(Knoblauch)zehe f

**clover,** kloh-wer, n Klee m;
v **to be in –,** üppig leben

**clown,** klaun, n Clown m;
(fool) Hanswurst m; v –
**(about/around),**
herumkaspern

**club,** klabb, n Klub m, Club
m; (weapon) Keule f;
(golf) Schläger m; **–house,**
n Klubhaus nt; **–s,** npl
(cards) Kreuz nt

**cluck,** klack, n Glucken nt;
v glucken

**clue,** kluh, n Anhaltspunkt
m; (crossword) Frage f; **I
haven't (got) a –,** ich
habe keine Ahnung

**clump,** klamp, n (of trees
etc.) Gruppe f

**clumsy, klamm**-si, adj
(person) ungeschickt;
(unwieldy) plump

**cluster, klass**-ter, n (of
trees, islands) Gruppe f;
(of fruit) Büschel nt; v –
**(round),** sich drängen
(um)

**clutch,** klatsch, n Griff m;
(motor) Kupplung f; v
(grasp) umklammern;
(grab) packen

**clutter, klatt**-er, n
Durcheinander nt; v
(mind, room) vollstopfen;

(desk) übersäen

**c/o** (abbr care of), c/o, z. Hd.

**coach,** kohtsch, n (bus)
(Reise)bus m; (horse-
drawn) Kutsche f; sport
Trainer m; (school)
Nachhilfelehrer m; v sport
trainieren; (school)
Nachhilfeunterricht
geben

**coagulate,** koh-**ägg**-ju-leht,
v gerinnen

**coal,** kohl, n Kohle f; **–
cellar,** n Kohlenkeller m

**coalition,** koh-e-**lisch**-'n, n
Koalition f

**coalmine, kohl**-mein, n
Kohlenbergwerk nt

**coarse,** korss, a, grob; (joke,
laugh) derb

**coast,** kohst, n Küste f; v im
Leerlauf fahren; **–guard,** n
Küstenwache f; **–line,** n
Küste(nlinie) f

**coat,** koht, n Mantel m; (of
animal) Fell nt; (of paint)
Schicht f; v (paint)
überstreichen; **–hanger,** n
Kleiderbügel m; **–ing,** n
Überzug m; (of paint)
Schicht f; **– of arms,** n
Wappen nt

**coax,** kohkss, v überreden

**cob,** kobb, n (horse) kleines
Pferd nt; (corn)
(Mais)kolben m

**cobble, kobb**-'l, n Kopfstein
m; **–s,** npl
Kopfsteinpflaster nt

**cobbler, kobb**-ler, n
(Flick)schuster m

**cobblestone, kobb**-'l-stohn,
n Kopfstein m

**cobweb, kobb**-u'ebb, n
(threads) Spinnenweben
pl; (net) Spinnennetz nt

**cocaine,** koh-**kehn,** n
Kokain m

**cock,** kock, n (bird, tap,
valve) Hahn m; (vulg
penis) Schwanz m; v (gun)
spannen; (ears) spitzen;
**–erel,** junger Hahn m; **–-
eyed,** adj (crooked) schief;
(absurd) widersinnig

**cockle, kock**-'l, n
Herzmuschel f

**Cockney, kock**-ni, n
eingeborener Londoner m

**cockpit, kock**-pitt, n
Cockpit m

**cockroach, kock**-rohtsch, n
Küchenschabe f

**cocktail, kock**-tehl, n
Cocktail m

**cocoa,** koh-koh, n Kakao m

**coconut,** koh-ke-natt, n
Kokosnuß f

**cocoon,** ke-**kuhn,** n Kokon
m; v einhüllen

**cod,** kodd, n Kabeljau m

**coddle, kodd**-'l, v
verhätscheln

**code,** kohd, n law
Gesetzbuch nt; (cipher)
Kode m; comp Code m; v
verschlüsseln; comp
kodieren

**cod-liver oil, kodd**-li-wer
eul, n Lebertran m

**coerce,** koh-**örss,** v zwingen

**coffee, koff**-i, n Kaffee m; **–**

289

**pot**, n Kaffeekanne f; –
**table**, n Couchtisch m

**coffin**, koff-in, n Sarg m

**cog**, kogg, n Zahn m; –-
**wheel**, Zahnrad nt

**cogent**, koh-dschent, adj
zwingend

**cogitate**, kodsch-i-teht, v
nachdenken

**cognac**, konn-jäk, n
Kognak m

**coherent**, koh-hier-rent, adj
zusammenhängend

**cohesion**, koh-hie-sch'n, n
Kohäsion f

**coil**, keul, n Rolle f;
(contraceptive) Spirale f;
elec Spule f; v aufrollen

**coin**, keun, n Münze f; v
prägen; –-box, n (phone)
Münzfernsprecher m; –-
**operated**, adj Münz-

**coincide**, koh-inn-sseid, v
zusammenfallen,
übereinstimmen

**coke**, kohk, n Koks m;
(carbonated drink) Cola f;
(drug) Kokain nt; – (up),
v verkoken

**colander**, koll-en-der, n
Sieb nt

**cold**, kohld, n Kälte f; (med)
Erkältung f; adj kalt; **catch**
–, v sich erkälten; **I'm** –,
mir ist kalt

**coleslaw**, kohl-slo'a, n
Krautsalat m

**collaborate**, ke-läbb-e-reht,
v zusammenarbeiten

**collaboration**, ke-läbb-e-
reh-sch'n, n

Zusammenarbeit f; (with
enemy) Kollaboration f

**collapse**, ke-läps, n (of
person) Zusammenbruch
m; (of building) Einsturz
m; v (of person)
zusammenbrechen; (of
building) einstürzen

**collar**, koll-er, n Kragen m;
(for dog) Halsband nt;
–bone, n Schlüsselbein nt

**collate**, ke-leht, v
kollationieren

**collateral**, ke-lätt-e-rel, adj
nebensächlich; fin
zusätzlich; n fin
(zusätzliche) Sicherheit f

**colleague**, koll-ieg, n
Kollege m

**collect**, ke-lekt, v sammeln;
(fetch) abholen;–ion,
Sammlung f; (money)
Kollekte f; (post) Leerung
f; –ive, adj gemeinsam;
–or, n Sammler m; (tax)
(Steuer)einnehmer m

**college**, koll-idsch, n
Hochschule f,
Berufsschule f;
(university) College nt

**collide**, ke-leid, v
zusammenstoßen

**colliery**, kol-je-ri, n Zeche f

**collision**, ke-lisch-'n, n
Zusammenstoß m

**colloquial**, ke-loh-ku'i-el, adj
umgangssprachlich

**collusion**, ke-luh-sch'n, n
(geheime) Absprache f

**colon**, koh-lonn, n (writing)
Doppelpunkt m; (med)

Dickdarm m

**colonel**, köh-n'l, n Oberst m

**colonial**, ke-loh-ni-el, adj
Kolonial-; n Bewohner m
der Kolonien

**colonnade**, koll-e-nehd, n
Säulengang m

**colonize**, koll-e-neis, v
kolonisieren

**colony**, koll-e-ni, n
Kolonie f

**colossal**, ke-loss-'l, adj
kolossal, riesig

**colour**, kall-er, n Farbe f; v
färben; – bar, n
Rassenschranke f; –blind,
adj farbenblind; –fast, adj
farbecht; –ful, adj bunt;
–ing, n (complexion)
Gesichtsfarbe f

**colt**, kohlt, n Fohlen nt

**column**, koll-em, n Säule f;
(print) Spalte f; mil
Kolonne f

**coma**, koh-me, n (med)
Koma nt

**comb**, kohm, n Kamm m;
(honey) (Honig)wabe f; v
kämmen; fig
durchkämmen

**combat**, komm-bätt, n
Kampf m; v bekämpfen

**combination**, komm-bi-neh-
sch'n, n Kombination f; in
–, adv gemeinsam

**combine**, komm-bein, n
comm Konzern m;
– (harvester), n
Mähdrescher m

**combine**, kem-bein, v
verbinden

**combustion,** kem-**bass**-tsch'n, n Verbrennung f

**come,** kamm, v kommen; – **across,** (find) stoßen auf; – **down,** (of price) fallen; – **from,** herkommen, kommen aus; – **in,** hereinkommen; – **off,** (detach) abgehen; (succeed) gelingen; – **out,** herauskommen; – **round/to,** (med) wieder zu sich kommen; – **to,** (sum) sich belaufen auf; – **up,** hochkommen; (of sun) aufgehen; (of problem) auftauchen; – **up against,** stoßen auf

**comedian,** ke-**mie**-di-en, n Komiker m

**comedy,** komm-**e**-di, n Komödie f

**comet,** komm-itt, n Komet m

**comfort,** kamm-fet, n Komfort m; (consolation) Trost m; v trösten; **–able,** adj bequem; (income) ausreichend; (life) angenehm

**comic,** komm-ick, adj komisch; n (book) Comic m, Comic-Heft nt; (comedian) Komiker m

**coming,** kamm-ing, adj künftig; n Kommen nt

**comma,** komm-e, n Komma nt

**command,** ke-mahnd, n Befehl m; mil Kommando nt; (mastery)

Beherrschung f; v befehlen; beherrschen; mil kommandieren

**commandeer,** komm-en-dier, v requirieren

**commander,** ke-mahn-der, n Kommandant m

**commanding,** ke-mahn-ding, adj mil befehlshabend; (tone) gebieterisch; (location) beherrschend

**commandment(s),** ke-mahnd-ment(s), n(pl) Gebot(e) nt(pl)

**commemorate,** ke-memm-e-reht, v gedenken

**commence,** ke-menss, v beginnen

**commencement,** ke-menss-ment, n Anfang m

**commend,** ke-mend, v (recommend) empfehlen; (praise) loben

**commensurate (with),** ke-menn-sju-ret (u'idh), adj entsprechend

**comment,** komm-ent, n Bemerkung f; v bemerken; **–ary,** n Kommentar m; **–ator,** n Kommentator m; (sports etc.) Reporter m; – **on,** v sich äußern über/zu

**commerce,** komm-örss, n Handel m

**commercial,** ke-mör-sch'l, adj kommerziell; Geschäfts-, Handels-; (TV) Werbespot m; – **break,** (TV) Werbung f

**commiserate (with),** ke-

mis-e-reht u'idh, v mitfühlen (mit)

**commission,** ke-misch-'n, n (fee) Provision f; (order) Auftrag m; mil Patent nt; (committee) Kommission f; v (person) beauftragen; (work) in Auftrag geben; (officer) ernennen; **–aire,** Portier m

**commit,** ke-mitt, v (resources) einsetzen; (crime) begehen; (to prison etc.) einweisen; **–ment,** n Verpflichtung f; – **oneself (to),** v sich festlegen (auf), sich verpflichten (zu)

**committee,** ke-mitt-i, n Ausschuß m

**commodity,** ke-modd-i-ti, n Ware f

**common,** komm-en, adj (usual; vulgar) gewöhnlich; (universal) allgemein; (communal) gemeinsam; n (public ground) Gemeindeland nt; **–er,** Bürgerliche(r) m & f; **–place,** adj alltäglich; – **room,** n Aufenthaltsraum m; **Commons,** npl parl Unterhaus nt; – **sense,** n gesunder Menschenverstand m; **Commonwealth,** n Commonwealth nt

**commotion,** ke-moh-sch'n, n Aufsehen nt

**commune,** komm-juhn, n Kommune f

**communicate,** ke-**mjuh**-ni-keht, v in Verbindung stehen; (be understood) sich verständigen; (news) mitteilen

**communication,** ke-mjuh-ni-**keh**-sch'n, n (act) Kommunikation f; (message) Mitteilung f

**Communion,** ke-**mjuh**-ni-en, n relig Abendmahl nt

**communism, komm**-ju-nism, n Kommunismus m

**communist, komm**-mju-nist, adj kommunistisch; n Kommunist m

**community,** ke-**mjuh**-ni-ti, n (group) Gemeinde f; (ideal) Gemeinschaft f; – **centre,** n Gemeindezentrum nt

**commute,** ke-**mjuht,** v pendeln; –**r,** n Pendler m

**compact,** kem-**päckt,** adj kompakt; (soil) fest; – **disc,** n Compact Disc f, CD f

**compact, komm**-päckt, n (agreement) Vereinbarung f; (for powder) Puderdose f

**companion,** kem-**pänn**-jen, n Begleiter m; (spouse) Gefährte m; –**ship,** Gesellschaft f

**company, kamm**-pe-ni, n (people) Gesellschaft f; (firm) Firma f, Gesellschaft f, Unternehmen nt; mil Kompanie f; **keep sb –,** jdm Gesellschaft leisten

**comparative,** kem-**pä**-re-tiw, adj relativ; n gram Komparativ m; –**ly,** adv verhältnismäßig

**compare,** kem-**pähr,** v vergleichen

**comparison,** kem-**pä**-ri-ss'n, n Vergleich m; **in – (with),** im Vergleich (zu)

**compartment,** kem-**pahrt**-ment, n rail Abteil nt; (in fridge etc.) Fach nt

**compass, kamm**-pess, n (magnetic) Kompaß m; (range) Umkreis m; (a pair of) –**es,** npl Zirkel m

**compassion,** kem-**päsch**-'n, n Mitleid nt; –**ate,** adj mitfühlend

**compatible,** kem-**pätt**-i-b'l, adj passend, entsprechend; comp kompatibel

**compel,** kem-**pell,** v zwingen

**compensate, komp**-penn-sseht, v entschädigen; – **for,** ausgleichen

**compensation, komm**-penn-**sseh**-sch'n, n Entschädigung f

**compete,** kem-**piet,** v (take part) teilnehmen; (vie) konkurrieren; – **for,** kämpfen um

**competent, komm**-pi-tent, adj fähig, kompetent

**competition, komm**-pi-**tisch**-'n, n (comm etc.) Konkurrenz f; sport Wettbewerb m

**competitive,** kem-**pett**-i-tiw, adj Konkurrenz-; (price

etc.) konkurrenzfähig

**competitor,** kem-**pett**-i-ter, n (participant) Teilnehmer m; comm Konkurrent m

**compile,** kem-**peil,** v zusammenstellen; (publication) verfassen

**complacent,** kem-**pleh**-ss'nt, adj selbstgefällig

**complain,** kem-**plehn,** v beklagen, sich beschweren

**complaint,** kem-**plehnt,** n Klage f; (formal) Beschwerde f; (med) Krankheit f

**complement, komm**-pli-ment, n Ergänzung f; v ergänzen

**complete,** kem-**pliet,** adj ganz, vollständig; (finished) fertig; v vervollständigen; (finish) abschließen; –**ly,** adv ganz

**completion,** kem-**plie**-sch'n, n Beendigung f; Abschluß m

**complex, komm**-plecks, adj verwickelt, kompliziert; n Komplex m

**complexion,** kem-**pleck**-sch'n, n Gesichtsfarbe f; fig **put a new – on,** v in einem neuen Licht erscheinen lassen

**compliance,** kem-**plei**-enss, n Einwilligung f; (with rules) Einhalten nt; – **with,** gemäß

**complicate, komm**-pli-keht, v komplizieren

**compliment, komm**-pli-

ment, n Kompliment nt;
–s, npl Grüße pl; –s slip, n
Empfehlungszettel m

compliment, komm-pli-
ment, v Komplimente
machen

comply (with), kem-plei
(u'idh), v entsprechen,
erfüllen

component, kem-poh-nent,
n Bestandteil m

compose, kem-pohs, v
(constitute) bilden;
(music) komponieren;
(poetry) verfassen; –d, adj
gefaßt; –r, n Komponist m

composite, komm-pe-sitt,
adj zusammengesetzt

composition, komm-pe-
sisch-'n, n (make-up)
Zusammensetzung f;
(essay) Aufsatz m; (mus,
art) Komposition f

compost, komm-post, n
Kompost m

composure, kem-poh-scher,
n Fassung f

compound, komm-paund, n
chem Verbindung f;
(enclosure) Lager nt; adj
zusammengesetzt; –
fracture, n komplizierter
Bruch m; – interest, n
Zinseszins m

compound, kem-paund, v
chem mischen; (worsen)
verschlimmern

comprehend, komm-pri-
hend, v begreifen

comprehension, komm-
pri-henn-sch'n, n

Verständnis nt

comprehensive, komm-pri-
henn-siw, adj umfassend; –
(school), n Gesamtschule
f

compress, komm-press, n
Kompresse f

compress, kem-press, v
komprimieren

comprise, kem-preis, v
umfassen

compromise, komp-re-meis,
n Kompromiß m; v
kompromittieren; einen
Kompromiß schließen

compulsion, kem-pall-sch'n,
n Zwang m

compulsive, kem-pall-ssiw,
adj zwanghaft

compulsory, kem-pall-sse-ri,
adj obligatorisch

compute, kem-pjuht, v
berechnen

computer, kem-pjuh-ter, n
Computer m; – game, n
Computerspiel nt; –ize, v
(data) computerisieren;
(method, system) auf
Computer umstellen; –
programmer, n
Programmierer m

comrade, komm-ridd, n
Kamerad m; Genosse m

con, konn, n Schwindel;
v hereinlegen

concave, konn-kehw/konn-
kehw, adj konkav

conceal, ken-ssiel, v (object,
feelings) verbergen; (fact)
verheimlichen

concede, ken-ssied, v

(admit) zugeben; (give
up) gewähren

conceit, ken-ssiet, n
Einbildung f; –ed, adj
eingebildet

conceive, ken-ssiew, v
(comprehend) sich
vorstellen; (med)
empfangen

concentrate, konn-ssen-
treht, v konzentrieren; –
(on), sich konzentrieren
(auf)

concentration, konn-ssen-
treh-sch'n, n
Konzentration f; – camp,
n Konzentrationslager nt,
KZ nt

concept, konn-ssept, n
Begriff m

conception, ken-ssepp-
sch'n, n Vorstellung f;
(med) Empfängnis f

concern, ken-ssörn, n
(affair) Sache f; (firm)
Unternehmen nt;
(disquiet) Sorge f; v
betreffen; be –ed (about),
sich Sorgen machen (um);
–ing, prep bezüglich

concert, konn-ssert, n
Konzert m

concerted, ken-ssör-tidd, adj
gemeinsam

concerto, ken-tschähr-toh,
n Konzert nt, Concerto nt

concession, ken-ssesch-'n, n
Konzession f

conciliation, ken-ssill-i-eh-
sch'n, n Versöhnung f;
(procedure) Schlichtung f

**conciliatory,** ken-**ssill**-i-e-tri, *adj* besänftigend

**concise,** ken-**sseiss,** *adj* kurz, bündig

**conclude,** ken-**kluhd,** *v* (finish) beenden; (agree) abschließen; – **(from),** (infer, decide) schließen (aus)

**conclusion,** ken-**kluh**-sch'n, *n* Abschluß *m*; (inference, decision) Schluß *m*

**conclusive,** ken-**kluh**-ssiw, *adj* entscheidend

**concoct,** ken-**kokt,** *v* (cooking etc.) zusammenstellen; (scheme) aushecken; –**ion,** *n* (food) Kreation *f*; (drink) Gebräu *nt*

**concourse,** kong-korss, *n* Vorplatz *m*; **(station)** –, Bahnhofshalle *f*

**concrete,** kong-kriet, *adj* konkret; *n* Beton *m*

**concur,** ken-**kör,** *v* übereinstimmen

**concurrent(ly),** ken-**ka**-rent(-li), *adj & adv* gleichzeitig

**concussion,** ken-**kasch**-'n, *n* (med) Gehirnerschütterung *f*

**condemn,** ken-**demm,** *v* verurteilen; (building/food) abbruchreif/für den Verzehr ungeeignet erklären

**condensation,** konn-denn-sseh-sch'n, *n*

(vaporization) Kondensation *f*

**condense,** ken-**denss,** *v chem* kondensieren; (book) abkürzen; –**d milk,** *n* Kondensmilch *f*

**condescend,** konn-di-**ssend,** *v* sich herablassen; –**ing,** *adj* herablassend

**condition,** ken-**disch**-'n, *n* Bedingung *f*; (state) Zustand *m*; –**al,** *adj* bedingt; –**er,** *n* (for hair) Spülung *f*; –**s,** *npl* Verhältnisse *pl*

**condolences,** ken-**doh**-len-ssis, *npl* Beileid *nt*

**condom,** konn-domm, *n* Kondom *m/nt*

**condone,** ken-**dohn,** *v* dulden

**conducive (to),** ken-**djuh**-ssiw (tu), *adj* förderlich, dienlich

**conduct,** konn-dackt, *n* Benehmen *nt*; (management) Führung *f*

**conduct,** ken-**dackt,** *v* (manage) leiten, führen; *mus* dirigieren; –**ed tour,** *n* Führung *f*; –**or,** *n elec* Leiter *m*; (bus) Schaffner *m*; *mus* Dirigent *m*

**cone,** kohn, *n* Kegel *m*; (for ice-cream) Tüte *f*; (fir-cone) Zapfen *m*

**confectioner,** ken-**feck**-sch'n-er, *n* Konditor *m*; –**'s,** *n* Konditorei *f*; –**y,** *n* Süßigkeiten *pl*

**confederate,** ken-**fedd**-e-ret,

*n* Verbündete(r) *m*

**confederation,** ken-fedd-erreh-sch'n, *n* Bund *m*

**confer,** ken-**för,** *v* konferieren; – **(on),** (bestow) verleihen

**conference,** konn-fe-renss, *n* Konferenz *f*

**confess,** ken-**fess,** *v* gestehen; *relig* beichten

**confession,** ken-**fesch**-'n, *n* Geständnis *nt*; *relig* Beichte *f*

**confide,** ken-**feid,** *v* anvertrauen; – **in sb,** sich jdm anvertrauen

**confidence,** konn-fi-denss, *n* (faith) Vertrauen *nt*; (self-) Selbstvertrauen *nt*; – **trick,** *n* Schwindel *m*

**confident,** konn-fi-dent, *adj* überzeugt; (self-) selbstsicher

**confidential,** konn-fi-**denn**-sch'l, *adj* vertraulich

**confine (to),** ken-**fein** (tu), *v* (limit) beschränken (auf); (lock up) einsperren (in); –**d,** *adj* beschränkt; –**ment,** *n* (childbirth) Wochenbett *nt*; (prison) Haft *f*

**confines,** konn-feins, *npl* Grenzen *pl*

**confirm,** ken-**förm,** *v* bestätigen; *relig* konfirmieren

**confirmation,** konn-fer-meh-sch'n, *n* Bestätigung *f*; *relig* Konfirmation *f*

**confiscate,** konn-fiss-keht, *v*

beschlagnahmen

**conflagration,** konn-fle-greh-sch'n, n Brand m

**conflict, konn**-flikt, n Konflikt m; (combat) Kampf m

**conflict,** ken-**flikt,** v im Widerspruch stehen; –ing, adj widersprechend

**conform,** ken-**form,** v sich anpassen; – **to,** sich richten nach, entsprechen

**confound,** ken-**faund,** v verwirren

**confront,** ken-**frant,** v (face) entgegentreten; – **with,** gegenüberstellen, konfrontieren mit

**confrontation,** konn-fren-**teh**-sch'n, n Konfrontation f

**confuse,** ken-**fjuhs,** v (bewilder) verwirren; (mix up) verwechseln

**confusing,** ken-**fjuh**-sing, adj verwirrend

**confusion,** ken-**fjuh**-sch'n, n (bewilderment) Verwirrung f; (disorder) Durcheinander nt

**congeal,** ken-**dschiel,** v (of blood) gerinnen; (of fat) fest werden

**congenial,** ken-**dschie**-ni-el, adj angenehm

**congenital,** ken-**dschenn**-i-tel, adj angeboren

**congested,** ken-**dschess**-tidd, adj überfüllt

**congestion,** ken-**dschess**-tsch'n, n Stau m,

Verstopfung f

**conglomerate,** ken-**glomm**-e-ret, n Konglomerat nt

**congratulate,** ken-**grätt**-ju-leht, v gratulieren; (on birthday etc.) beglückwünschen

**congratulations,** ken-**grätt**-ju-**leh**-sch'ns, npl Glückwünsche pl

**congregate,** kong-gri-geht, v sich versammeln

**congregation,** kong-gri-**geh**-sch'n, n Gemeinde f

**congress,** kong-gress, n Kongreß m

**conical,** kon-i-k'l, adj kegelförmig

**conifer,** kon-i-fer, n Nadelbaum m

**conjecture,** ken-**dscheck**-tscher, n Vermutung f; v vermuten

**conjugal, konn**-dschu-gel, adj ehelich

**conjunction,** ken-**dschank**-sch'n, n Verbindung f; gram Bindewort nt

**conjunctivitis,** ken-dschank-ti-**wei**-tiss, n Bindehautentzündung f

**conjure, kann**-dscher v zaubern; – **up,** beschwören; fig heraufbeschwören; –**r,** n Zauberkünstler m

**con man, konn** männ, n Schwindler m

**connect,** ke-**neckt,** v verbinden; elec anschließen; –**ion,** n

Verbindung f; elec, rail Anschluß m

**connive,** ke-**neiw,** v (conspire) gemeinsame Sache machen; – **at,** (overlook) stillschweigend dulden

**connoisseur,** konn-e-**ssör,** n Kenner m

**conquer,** kong-ker, v (territory) erobern; (enemy, feelings) besiegen; –**or,** n Eroberer m

**conquest,** kong-ku'est, n Eroberung f; Sieg m

**conscience, konn**-sch'nss, n Gewissen nt

**conscientious,** konn-schi-**enn**-schess, adj gewissenhaft

**conscious, konn**-schess, adj bewußt; (med) bei Bewußtsein; –**ness,** n Bewußtsein nt

**conscript, konn**-skript, n Wehrpflichtige(r) m

**consecrate, konn**-ssi-kreht, v weihen

**consecutive,** ken-**sseck**-juh-tiw, adj aufeinanderfolgend

**consensus,** ken-**ssen**-ssess, n allgemeine Meinung f; (agreement) Übereinstimmung f

**consent,** ken-**ssent,** n Einwilligung f; v – **(to),** einwilligen (in)

**consequence, konn**-ssi-ku'enss, n (result) Folge f;

(importance) Wichtigkeit f

**consequently, konn-**ssi-ku'ent-li, adv folglich

**conservation, konn-**sser-**weh-**sch'n, n Schutz m

**conservative, ken-**ssör-we-tiw, adj konservativ

**conservatory, ken-**ssör-we-tri, n Wintergarten m; mus Konservatorium nt

**conserve, ken-**ssörw, n Eingemachtes nt; v (maintain) erhalten; (fruit etc.) einmachen

**consider, ken-**ssidd-er, v (reflect) überlegen; (view) betrachten als; (take account of) berücksichtigen; **–able,** adj beträchtlich; **–ate,** rücksichtsvoll; **–ation,** n (reflection) Überlegung f; (thoughtfulness) Rücksicht f; **–ing,** conj eigentlich; prep in Anbetracht

**consign, ken-**ssein, v anvertrauen; **–ment,** n Sendung f

**consist (of), ken-**ssist (ew), v bestehen (aus)

**consistency, ken-**ssiss-ten-ssi, n (of substance) Konsistenz f; (logic) Konsequenz f

**consistent, ken-**ssiss-tent, adj konsequent

**consolation, konn-**sse-**leh-**sch'n, n Trost m

**console, konn-**ssohl, n

comp, mech Kontrollpult nt

**console, ken-**ssohl, v trösten

**consolidate, ken-**ssoll-i-deht, v konsolidieren

**consonant, konn-**sse-nent, n Konsonant m

**consortium, ken-**ssor-ti-em, n Konsortium nt

**conspicuous, ken-**spick-ju-ess, adj (striking) auffallend; (distinguished) hervorragend

**conspiracy, ken-**spi-re-ssi, n Verschwörung f

**conspire, ken-**speir, v sich verschwören

**constable, konn-**ste-b'l, n Polizist m

**constabulary, ken-**stäbb-ju-ler-ri, n Polizei f

**constant, konn-**stent, adj (continuous) ständig; (unchanging) konstant; (faithful) treu

**constellation, konn-**ste-**leh-**sch'n, n Sternbild nt

**consternation, konn-**ster-**neh-**sch'n, n Bestürzung f

**constipation, konn-**sti-**peh-**sch'n, n Verstopfung f

**constituency, ken-**stitt-ju-en-ssi, n Wahlkreis m

**constituent, ken-**stitt-ju-ent, n (part) Bestandteil m; (voter) Wähler m

**constitute, konn-**sti-tjuht, v ausmachen, bilden; (equate to) darstellen

**constitution, konn-**sti-**tjuh-**sch'n, n (administration)

Verfassung f; (health) Konstitution f; **–al,** adj Verfassungs-

**constraint, ken-**strehnt, n (force) Zwang m; (limit) Einschränkung f

**constrict, ken-**strikt, v einschränken

**construct, ken-**strakt, v bauen; (sentence) bilden; **–ion,** n Bau m; (interpretation) Auslegung f; **–ive,** adj konstruktiv

**consul, konn-**ss'l, n Konsul m; **–ate,** n Konsulat nt

**consult, ken-**ssalt, v konsultieren; **–ant,** n Berater m; (med) Facharzt m; **–ation,** n Beratung f

**consume, ken-**ssjuhm, v (food etc.) konsumieren; (fuel, money) verbrauchen; **–r,** n Verbraucher m; **–r goods,** npl Verbrauchsgüter pl; **–r society,** n Konsumgesellschaft f

**consummate, konn-**sse-met, adj vollkommen

**consummate, konn-**sse-meht, v vollziehen

**consumption, ken-**ssamp-sch'n, n Verbrauch m; (of food etc.) Konsum m; (med) Schwindsucht f

**contact, konn-**täckt, n Kontakt m, Verbindung; (physical) Berührung f; v sich in Verbindung setzen mit; **– lenses,** npl

Kontaktlinsen *pl*
**contagious**, ken-**teh**-dschess, *adj* ansteckend
**contain**, ken-**tehn**, *v* enthalten; **–er**, *n* Behälter; *comm* Container *m*
**contaminate**, ken-**tämm**-i-neht, *v* verunreinigen
**contemplate**, **konn**-tem-pleht, *v* nachdenken über
**contemporary**, ken-**temm**-pe-re-ri, *adj* zeitgenössisch; *n* Zeitgenosse *m*
**contempt**, ken-**tempt**, *n* Verachtung *f*; **–ible**, *adj* verachtenswert, verächtlich; **–uous**, *adj* verächtlich
**contend**, ken-**tend**, *v* (maintain) behaupten; **– (with sb for)**, kämpfen/konkurrieren (mit jdn um); **–er**, *n* Kandidat *m*; *sport* Wettkämpfer *m*
**content(ed)**, ken-**tent**(-idd), *adj* zufrieden; *v* befriedigen
**content(s)**, **konn**-tent(s), *n(pl)* Inhalt *m*, Gehalt *m*
**contention**, ken-**tenn**-sch'n, *n* Behauptung *f*
**contentious**, ken-**tenn**-schess, *adj* (person) streitsüchtig; (issue) umstritten
**contentment**, ken-**tent**-ment, *n* Zufriedenheit *f*
**contest**, **konn**-test, *n* Kampf *m*; *sport* Wettkampf *m*
**contest**, ken-**test**, *v* bestreiten; *law* anfechten

**contestant**, ken-**test**-'nt, *n* (quiz, *parl*) Kandidat *m*; (sport, quiz) Teilnehmer *m*
**context**, **konn**-tekst, *n* Zusammenhang *m*
**continent**, **konn**-ti-nent, *n* Festland *nt*, Kontinent *m*
**continental**, konn-ti-**nenn**-t'l, *adj* kontinental; (European) europäisch
**contingency**, ken-**tinn**-dschen-ssi, *n* Eventualität *f*
**contingent**, ken-**tinn**-dschent, *adj* abhängig; *n* Kontingent *m*
**continual**, ken-**tinn**-ju-el, *adj* fortwährend; **–ly**, *adv* immer wieder
**continuation**, ken-tinn-ju-**eh**-sch'n, *n* Fortsetzung *f*
**continue**, ken-**tinn**-juh, *v* (of person) weitermachen; (of event) weitergehen; (activity) fortsetzen
**continuity**, ken-tinn-**juh**-i-ti, *n* Kontinuität *f*
**continuous**, ken-**tinn**-ju-ess, *adj* ununterbrochen; **– stationery**, *n* Endlospapier *nt*
**contortion**, ken-**tor**-sch'n, *n* Verrenkung *f*
**contraband**, **konn**-tre-bänd, *n* Schmuggelware *f*
**contraception**, konn-tre-**ssepp**-sch'n, *n* Empfängnisverhütung *f*
**contraceptive**, konn-tre-**ssepp**-tiw, *adj*

empfängnisverhütend; empfängnisverhütendes Mittel *nt*
**contract**, **konn**-träckt, *n* Vertrag *m*
**contract**, ken-**träckt**, *v* (shrink) (sich) zusammenziehen; (illness) erkranken an; **–ion**, *n* Zusammenziehung *f*; (med) Wehe *f*; **–or**, *n* Auftragnehmer *m*; (builder) Unternehmer *m*; **–ual**, *adj* vertraglich
**contradict**, konn-tre-**dikt**, *v* widersprechen; **–ion**, *n* Widerspruch *m*; **–ory**, *adj* widersprüchlich
**contraption**, ken-**träpp**-sch'n, *n* Apparat *m*
**contrary**, ken-**trähr**-ri, *adj* widerspenstig
**contrary**, **konn**-tre-ri, *adj* entgegengesetzt; *n* Gegenteil *nt*; **on the –**, im Gegenteil
**contrast**, **konn**-trahst, *n* Gegensatz *m*; (visual, TV) Kontrast *m*
**contrast**, ken-**trahst**, *v* gegenüberstellen; **– with**, in Kontrast stehen zu
**contravene**, konn-tre-**wien**, *v* verstoßen gegen
**contribute (to)**, ken-**tribb**-juht (tu), *v* beitragen
**contribution**, kon-tri-**bjuh**-sch'n, *n* Beitrag *m*
**contrivance**, ken-**treiw**-'nss, *n* Vorrichtung *f*
**contrive**, ken-**treiw**, *v*

(scheme) ersinnen; (arrange) arrangieren

**control,** ken-**trohl,** v (manage) kontrollieren, leiten; (master) beherrschen; n Kontrolle f; (of feelings etc.) Beherrschung f; **–s,** npl Kontrollpult nt; (of car) Steuerung f; **out of –,** außer Kontrolle; **under –,** unter Kontrolle

**controversial,** kon-tre-**wör**-sch'l, adj umstritten

**controversy, konn**-tre-wör-ssi, n Kontroverse f

**conurbation,** konn-ör-**beh**-sch'n, n Ballungsgebiet nt

**convalescence,** konn-we-**less**-enss, n Genesung f

**convalescent,** konn-we-**less**-n't, adj genesend; n Genesende(r) m & f

**convector (heater),** ken-**weck**-ter (hie-ter), n Heizlüfter m

**convene,** ken-**wien,** v (meeting) zusammenrufen; (gather) sich versammeln

**convenience,** ken-**wie**-ni-enss, n Annehmlichkeit f; (WC) Toilette f; **with all modern –s,** mit allem Konfort

**convenient,** ken-**wie**-ni-ent, adj praktisch, günstig

**convent,** konn-went, n (Frauen)kloster nt

**convention,** ken-**wenn**-sch'n, n (gathering)

Versammlung f; (custom) Konvention f, Brauch m; **–al,** adj konventionell

**converge,** ken-**wördsch,** v zusammenlaufen

**conversant (with),** ken-**wör**-ss'nt (u'idh), adj vertraut (mit)

**conversation,** konn-wer-**sseh**-sch'n, n Gespräch nt, Unterhaltung f

**converse,** ken-**wörss,** v sich unterhalten

**conversion,** ken-**wör**-sch'n, n Umwandlung f; (of building etc.) Umbau m; relig Bekehrung f

**convert, konn**-wört, n Bekehrte(r) m & f

**convert,** ken-**wört,** v umwandeln; umbauen; bekehren; **–ible,** adj umwandelbar; fin konvertierbar; n Kabriolett nt

**convex, konn**-weks, adj konvex

**convey,** ken-**weh,** v (goods) befördern; (message) vermitteln; **–or (belt),** n Fließband nt

**convict, konn**-wikt, n Sträfling m

**convict,** ken-**wikt,** v verurteilen; **–ion,** n Verurteilung f; (belief) Überzeugung f

**convince,** ken-**winss,** v überzeugen

**convoluted, konn**-we-luh-tidd, adj verwickelt

**convoy, konn**-weu, n Konvoi m

**convulse,** ken-**walss,** v (muscles) zusammenziehen; fig erschüttern; **–d with laughter,** gekrümmt vor Lachen

**convulsion,** ken-**wall**-sch'n, n Krampf m; fig Erschütterung f

**coo,** kuh, v gurren; **–ing,** n Gurren nt

**cook,** kuck, n Koch m, Köchin f; v (do cooking) kochen; (prepare) zubereiten; **– book,** Kochbuch nt

**cooker, kuck**-er, n Herd m; **–y,** n Kochen nt

**cool,** kuhl, adj kühl; v abkühlen; **– down,** (sich) abkühlen; **–ness,** n Kühle f; (nerve) Kaltblütigkeit f

**coop,** kuhp, n Hühnerkorb m; **– up,** v einsperren

**co-operate,** koh-**opp**-e-reht, v zusammenarbeiten

**co-operation,** koh-opp-e-**reh**-sch'n, n Zusammenarbeit f

**co-operative,** koh-**opp**-e-re-tiw, adj hilfsbereit; comm Genossenschafts-; n Kooperative f, Genossenschaft f

**co-ordinate,** koh-**or**-di-neht, v koordinieren

**co-ordination,** koh-or-di-**neh**-sch'n, n Koordination f

**cop,** kopp, n (*fam* policeman) Bulle m

**cope,** kohp, v; es schaffen; – **with,** fertig werden mit

**copious,** koh-pi-ess, *adj* reichlich; zahlreich

**copper,** kopp-er, n Kupfer nt; (*fam* policeman) Bulle m; –**s,** *npl* Kleingeld nt

**coppice,** kopp-iss, n Wäldchen nt

**copse,** kopps, n Wäldchen nt

**copy,** kopp-i, n Kopie f; (of book) Exemplar nt; v kopieren; (write out) abschreiben; –**right,** Copyright nt, Urheberrecht nt

**coral,** ko-rel, n Koralle f; – **reef,** n Korallenriff nt

**cord,** kord, n Schnur f; (belt) Kordel f

**cordial,** kor-di-el, *adj* herzlich; n (alcoholic) Likör m; (fruit) Fruchtsaft m

**cordon,** kor-den, n Kordon m; – **off,** v absperren

**corduroy,** kor-dju-reu, n Kord(samt) m

**core,** kor, n Kern m; v entkernen

**cork,** kork, n (material) Kork m; (stopper) Korken m; v zukorken; –**screw,** n Korkenzieher m

**cormorant,** kor-me-rent, n Kormoran m

**corn,** korn, n (wheat) Korn nt; (on foot) Hühnerauge

nt; –**d beef,** n Corned beef nt; – **on the cob,** n Maiskolben m; (**sweet**)–, n (maize) Mais m

**corner,** kor-ner, n Ecke f; (bend) Kurve f; v comm monopolisieren; (trap) in die Enge treiben

**cornet,** kor-nitt, n mus Kornett nt; (for ice-cream) Tüte f

**cornflour,** korn-flau-er, n Stärkemehl nt

**corny,** kor-ni, *adj* (joke) blöd; (sentimental) kitschig

**coronary,** ko-re-ne-ri, n Herzinfarkt m

**coronation,** ko-re-neh-sch'n, n Krönung f

**coroner,** ko-re-ner, n amtlicher Leichenschauer m

**corporal,** kor-pe-rel, n Obergefreite(r) m; *adj* körperlich; – **punishment,** n Prügelstrafe f

**corporate,** kor-pe-ret, *adj* gemeinsam; comm Firmen-

**corporation,** kor-pe-reh-sch'n, n comm Aktiengesellschaft f, Körperschaft f; (town) Gemeinde f

**corps,** kor, n Korps nt

**corpse,** korps, n Leiche f

**corpuscle,** kor-pass-'l, n Blutkörperchen nt

**correct,** ke-rekt, *adj* (right) richtig; (proper) korrekt; v berichtigen, korrigieren;

–**ion,** n Verbesserung f

**correspond,** ko-riss-**pond,** v – (**to**), (equate) entsprechen; – (**with**), (write) korrespondieren (mit); –**ence,** n Korrespondenz f; –**ence course,** n Fernkurs m; –**ent,** n Korrespondent m

**corridor,** ko-ri-dor, n Korridor m, Gang m

**corroborate,** ke-**robb**-e-reht, v bestätigen

**corroboration,** ke-robb-e-reh-sch'n, n Bestätigung f

**corrode,** ke-rohd, v korrodieren, zerfressen

**corrosion,** ke-roh-sch'n, n Korrosion f

**corrugated,** ko-re-geh-tidd, *adj* gewellt; – **iron,** n Wellblech nt; – **paper,** Wellpappe f

**corrupt,** ke-rapt, *adj* (bribable) korrupt, bestechlich; (text) verdorben; v korrumpieren; (bribe) bestechen; –**ion,** n (moral) Verdorbenheit f; (bribery) Bestechung f

**corset,** kor-ssitt, n Korsett nt

**Corsica,** kor-ssi-ke, n Korsika f

**cortege,** kor-tesch, n (funeral) Leichenzug m

**cosh,** kosch, n Totschläger m

**cosmetic,** kos-**mett**-ick, *adj* kosmetisch; –**s,** *npl*

Kosmetika *pl*

**cosmic, kos**-mick, *adj* kosmisch

**cosmopolitan,** kos-me-**poll**-i-t'n, *adj* kosmopolitisch, international

**cosmos, kos**-moss, *n* Kosmos *m*

**cost,** kost, *n* Preis *m*; (expense) Kosten *pl*; *v* kosten; **--effective,** *adj* rentabel; **--ly,** *adj* teuer; **– of living,** *n* Lebensunterhaltungskos-ten *pl*; **–s,** *npl law* Kosten *pl*; **at all –s,** um jeden Preis

**costume, koss**-tjuhm, *n* Kostüm *nt*

**cosy, koh**-si, *adj* gemütlich

**cot,** kott, *n* (child's) Kinderbett *nt*

**cottage, kott**-idsch, *n* kleines Haus *nt*, Häuschen *nt*; **– cheese,** *n* Hüttenkäse *m*; **– industry,** *n* Heimindustrie *f*

**cotton, kott**-'n, *n* Baumwolle *f*; (thread) Garn *nt*; **– wool,** Watte *f*

**couch,** kautsch, *n* Sofa *nt*, Couch *f*

**couchette,** ku-**schett**, *n* Liegewagen *m*

**cough,** koff, *n* Husten *m*; *v* husten; **--drop/pastille,** *n* Hustenbonbon *nt*

**could,** kudd, *v* (*past & conditional of* can)

**council, kaun**-ssil, *n* Rat *m*; **– housing,** *n* Sozialwohnung *f*; **--lor,** *n*

Stadtrat *m*, Stadträtin *f*

**counsel, kaun**-ss'l, *v* beraten; *n law* Anwalt; **--lor,** *n* Berater *m*

**count,** kaunt, *v* zählen; *n* (numbering) Zählung *f*; (aristocrat) Graf *m*; **– on,** *v* (assume) rechnen mit; (rely on) zählen auf

**countdown, kaunt**-daun, *n* Countdown *m*

**countenance, kaun**-te-nenss, *n* face; *v* gutheißen

**counter, kaun**-ter, *n* (shop) Ladentisch *m*; (café) Theke *f*; (post office) Schalter *m*; (games) Spielmarke *f*; *v* kontern; **–act,** *v* entgegenwirken; **--feit,** *adj* gefälscht; *n* Fälschung *f*; *v* fälschen; **--foil,** *n* (Kontroll) abschnitt *m*; **--mand,** *v* widerrufen; **--part,** (person) *n* Gegenüber *nt*; (object) Gegenstück *nt*; **--sign,** *v* gegenzeichnen; **--to,** *prep* gegen

**countess, kaun**-tiss, *n* Gräfin *f*

**countless, kaunt**-liss, *adj* zahllos

**country, kant**-ri, *n* Land *nt*; **– dancing,** *n* Volkstanz *m*; **--man,** Landmann *m*; (compatriot) Landsmann *m*; **--side,** *n* Landschaft *f*

**county, kaun**-ti, *n* Grafschaft *f*

**coup,** kuh, *n* Coup *m*; **–**

**(d'état),** *n* Putsch *m*

**coupé, kuh**-peh, *n* Coupé *nt*

**couple, kapp**-'l, *n* Paar *nt*; *v* (mate) (sich) paaren; (link) koppeln

**coupon, kuh**-ponn, *n* Gutschein *m*

**courage, ka**-ridsch, *n* Mut *m*

**courageous,** ke-**reh**-dschess, *adj* mutig

**courgette,** kur-**schett**, *n* Zucchini *f*

**courier,** ku-ri-er, *n* (messenger) Kurier *m*; (delivery) Zusteller *m*; (guide) Reiseleiter *m*

**course,** korss, *n* (river, direction) Lauf *m*; (tuition, *naut*) Kurs *m*; (of race) Bahn *f*; (golf) Platz *m*; (of meal) Gang *m*; **of –,** *adv* natürlich

**court,** kort, *n* (royal) Hof *m*; *law* Gericht *nt*; *v* (danger) herausfordern; (woman) den Hof machen

**courteous, kör**-ti-ess, *adj* höflich

**courtesy, kör**-ti-si, *n* Höflichkeit *f*

**courtier, kor**-ti-er, *n* Höfling *m*

**court-martial,** kort-**mahr**-sch'l, *n* Kriegsgericht *nt*; *v* vor ein Kriegsgericht stellen

**courtroom, kort**-ruhm, *n* Gerichtssaal *m*

**courtship, kort**-schip, *n* (wooing) Werben *nt*

**courtyard, kort**-jahrd, n
Hof m

**cousin, kas**-inn, n Cousin
m, Kusine f

**cove,** kohw, n geog Bucht f

**covenant, ka**-we-nent, n
Abkommen nt; relig
Bund m

**cover, ka**-wer, n (cloth)
Decke f; (lid) Deckel m;
(of book, magazine)
Umschlag m; (insurance)
Versicherung f; mil
Deckung f; v bedecken;
(insure) versichern; (fin,
mi) decken; (distance)
zurücklegen; (report on)
berichten über; –**age,** n
Berichterstattung f; –
**charge,** n Bedienungsgeld
nt; –**ing,** n Decke f; –
**note,** n vorläufiger
Versicherungsschein m

**covert, koh**-wört, adj
geheim

**cover up, ka**-wer app, v
zudecken; (conceal)
verschleiern; **cover-up,** n
Verschleierung f

**covet, ka**-witt, v begehren

**cow,** kau, n Kuh f; v
einschüchtern

**coward, kau**-ed, n Feigling
m; –**ice,** Feigheit f; –**ly,** adj
feige

**cowboy, kau**-beu, n Cowboy
m

**cower, kau**-er, v kauern

**coxswain, kock**-ss'n, n
Steuermann m

**coy,** keu, adj (shy)

schüchtern; (coquettish)
neckisch

**crab,** kräb, n (food, large)
Krabbe f; (small) Krebs m;
––**apple,** n Holzapfel m

**crack,** kräck, n Riß m,
Sprung m; (noise) Knall
m; (drug) Crack nt; v (of
whip) knallen; (of china
etc.) springen; (nut, safe)
knacken; –**er,** n (firework)
Kracher m; (Christmas)
Knallbonbon m; (biscuit)
Keks m; –**le,** v knistern; –
**up,** v fig
zusammenbrechen

**cradle, kreh**-d'l, n Wiege f; v
wiegen

**craft,** krahft, n (trade)
Gewerbe nt, Handwerk nt;
naut Schiff nt; (skill)
Handfertigkeit f; –**sman,**
Handwerker m

**crafty,** krahf-ti, adj schlau

**crag,** krägg, n Felsspitze f

**cram,** krämm, v vollstopfen;
(coach) einpauken; –
**into,** hineinstopfen in

**cramp,** krämp, n Krampf m;
v einengen; –**ed,** adj eng

**cranberry, känn**-be-ri, n
Preiselbeere f

**crane,** krehn, n (hoist)
Krahn m; (bird) Kranich

**crank,** kränk, n mech Kurbel
f; (eccentric) Spinner m; v
kurbeln

**crash,** kräsch, n (collision)
Zusammenstoß m; (plane)
Absturz m; (noise) Krach
m; fin Zusammenbruch m;

v (collide)
zusammenstoßen;
(of plane) abstürzen;
(of stock market)
zusammenbrechen; –
**course,** n Intensivkurs m;
– **helmet,** n Sturzhelm m;
– **landing,** n
Bruchlandung f

**crate,** kreht, n Kiste f

**crater, kreh**-ter, n Krater m

**crave,** krehw, v sich sehnen
nach

**craving, kreh**-wing, n
Begierde f

**crawl, kro**'al, n Kriechen nt;
(swimming) Kraul nt; v
kriechen

**crayfish, kreh**-fisch, n
(freshwater) Krebs m;
(saltwater) Languste f

**crayon, kreh**-onn, n
Buntstift m

**craze,** krehs, n Fimmel m,
große Mode f

**crazy, kreh**-si, adj verrückt;
– **paving,** n Mosaikpflaster
nt

**creak,** kriek, v knarren

**cream,** kriem, n (dairy)
Rahm m, Sahne f;
(artificial, lotion) Creme
f; – **cheese,** n Frischkäse
m; –**y,** adj sahnig, cremig

**crease,** kriess, v zerknittern;
(deliberately) eine Falte
machen in; n Falte f

**create,** kri-eht, v erschaffen;
(cause) verursachen

**creation,** kri-eh-sch'n, n
Schöpfung f

**creative**, kri-**eh**-tiw, *adj*
(power) schöpferisch;
(attitude) kreativ

**creator**, kri-**eh**-ter, *n*
Schöpfer *m*

**creature**, **krie**-tscher, *n*
Geschöpf *nt*, Wesen *nt*

**crèche**, kresch, *n*
Kinderkrippe *f*

**credentials**, kri-**denn**-sch'ls, *npl*
Beglaubigungsschreiben *nt*, Zeugnis *nt*

**credible**, **kredd**-i-b'l, *adj*
glaubwürdig, glaubhaft

**credit**, **kredd**-itt, *n* Kredit *m*; *v* glauben; *fin* gutschreiben; **–able**, *adj* lobenswert; **– card**, *n* Kreditkarte *f*; **–or**, *n* Gläubiger *m*

**creed**, kried, *n* Glaubensbekenntnis *nt*

**creek**, kriek, *n* kleine Bucht *f*

**creep**, kriep, *v* kriechen; (glide) schleichen; **–er**, *n* (plant) Kletterpflanze *f*; **–y**, *adj* unheimlich

**cremate**, kri-**meht**, *v* einäschern

**cremation**, kri-**meh**-sch'n, *n* Einäscherung *f*

**crematorium**, kremm-*e*-**tor**-ri-em, *n* Krematorium *nt*

**crescent**, kres-'nt, *n* Halbmond *m*

**cress**, kress, *n* Kresse *f*

**crest**, krest, *n* (of hill, bird) Kamm *m*; (heraldry) Wappen *nt*; **–fallen**, *adj* niedergeschlagen

**Crete**, kriet, *n* Kreta *nt*

**crevice**, **krew**-iss, *n* Spalte *f*

**crew**, kruh, *n* Besatzung *f*

**crib**, kribb, *n* Krippe *f*; *v* (*fam* copy) abschreiben

**crick**, krick, *n* **– in one's neck**, steifes Genick *nt*

**cricket**, **krick**-itt, *n* (insect) Grille *f*; *sport* Kricket *nt*

**crime**, kreim, *n* Verbrechen *nt*

**criminal**, **krimm**-i-n'l, *n* Verbrecher *m*; *adj* verbrecherisch, strafbar, Straf-

**crimson**, **krimm**-s'n, *adj* blutrot; (blushing) knallrot

**cringe**, krindsch, *v* schaudern; **– before sb**, kriechen vor, kuschen

**crinkle**, **kring**-k'l, *n* Falte *f*; *v* knittern

**cripple**, **kripp**-'l, *n* Krüppel *m*; *v* verkrüppeln; *fig* lahmlegen

**crisis**, **krei**-ssiss, *n* (*pl* **crises**), Krise *f*

**crisp**, krisp, *adj* knusprig; *n* Chip *m*

**criterion**, krei-**tier**-ri-en, *n* (*pl* **criteria**), Kriterium *nt*

**critic**, **kritt**-ick, *n* Kritiker *m*; **–al**, *adj* kritisch

**criticism**, **kritt**-i-ssism, *n* Kritik *f*

**criticize**, **kritt**-i-sseis, *v* kritisieren

**croak**, krohk, *v* (frog) quaken; (crow, person) krächzen

**crochet**, **kroh**-scheh, *v* häkeln; *n* Häkelei *f*

**crockery**, **krock**-*e*-ri, *n* Geschirr *nt*

**crocodile**, **krock**-*e*-deil, *n* Krokodil *nt*

**crocus**, **kroh**-kes, *n* Krokus *m*

**crook**, kruck, *n* (staff) Stab *m*; (criminal) Gauner *m*

**crooked**, **kruck**-idd, *adj* krumm; *fig* unehrlich

**crop**, kropp, *n* Ernte *f*; *v* stutzen; **– up**, *v* aufkommen

**croquet**, **kroh**-keh, *n* Krocket *nt*

**croquette**, kre-**kett**, *n* Krokette *f*

**cross**, kross, *adj* böse; *n* Kreuz *nt*; *v* (road etc.) überqueren; (legs) übereinanderschlagen; (arms) verschränken; **–– examine**, *v* ins Kreuzverhör nehmen; **–ing**, *n* (junction) Kreuzung *f*; (sea) Überfahrt *f*; **– out**, *v* ausstreichen; **be at – purposes**, aneinander vorbeireden; **–road(s)**, *n* Kreuzung *f*; **–word (puzzle)**, *n* Kreuzworträtsel *nt*

**crotch**, krotsch, *n* (body, trousers) Schritt *m*

**crotchet**, **krott**-schitt, *n* *mus* Viertelnote *f*; **–y**, *adj* nörgelig

**crouch**, krautsch, v kauern

**crow**, kroh, n Krähe f; v krähen; (*fam* boast) sich brüsten

**crowbar**, **kroh**-bahr, n Brecheisen nt

**crowd**, kraud, n Menge f; v drängen; (room etc.) überfüllen

**crown**, kraun, n Krone f; (of head) Scheitel m; v krönen

**crucial**, **kruh**-sch'l, *adj* entscheidend

**crucifix**, **kruh**-ssi-ficks, n Kruzifix nt; **–ion**, n Kreuzigung f

**crucify**, **kruh**-ssi-fei, v kreuzigen; *fig* verreißen

**crude**, kruhd, *adj* (oil etc.) roh; (manners) grob; (implement etc.) primitiv

**cruel**, **kru**-el, *adj* grausam; **–ty**, n Grausamkeit f

**cruet**, **kru**-itt, n Gewürzständer m

**cruise**, kruhs, n Kreuzfahrt f; v eine Kreuzfahrt machen; **–r**, n *mil* Kreuzer m; (pleasure boat) Vergnügungsjacht f

**crumb**, kramm, n Krümel nt, Krume f

**crumble**, **kramm**-b'l, v zerbröckeln; (of resistance) sich auflösen

**crumple**, **kramm**-p'l, v zusammenknüllen, zerknittern

**crunch**, krantsch, n Knirschen nt; (*fig* crisis point) Knackpunkt m; v knirschen; **–y**, *adj* (apple) knackig; (biscuit) knusprig

**crush**, krasch, n Gedränge nt; v zerdrücken; (spices) zerstoßen; (opposition) unterdrücken

**crust**, krast, n Kruste f; **–y**, *adj* knusprig; *fig* barsch

**crutch**, kratsch, n Krücke f

**cry**, krei, n Schrei m; (call) Ruf m; v schreien; (call) rufen; (weep) weinen; **– off**, v absagen

**crypt**, kript, n Krypta f; **–ic**, *adj* rätselhaft; (clue) verschlüsselt

**crystal**, **kriss**-t'l, n Kristall m; (glass) Kristall nt; **–lize**, v *chem* kristallisieren; (fruit) kandieren; *fig* sich herauskristallisieren

**cub**, kab, n Junges nt

**Cuba**, **kjuh**-be, n Kuba nt

**cube**, kjuhb, n Würfel m; (maths) dritte Potenz f; v (maths) hoch drei nehmen

**cubic capacity**, **kjuh**-bick ke-**päss**-i-ti, n Fassungsvermögen nt

**cubicle**, **kjuh**-bi-k'l, n Kabine f

**cuckoo**, **kuck**-uh, n Kuckuck m; **– clock**, n Kuckucksuhr f

**cucumber**, **kjuh**-kamm-ber, n Gurke f

**cuddle**, **kadd**-'l, v liebkosen, schmusen

**cue**, kjuh, n *theatre* Stichwort nt; (billiards) Queue m/nt

**cuff**, kaff, n (of sleeve) Manschette f; (blow) Klaps m; v einen Klaps geben; **–link**, n Manschettenknopf m

**culinary**, **kall**-i-ne-ri, *adj* Koch-

**cull**, kall, v (flowers) pflücken; (seals, deer, etc.) abtöten

**culminate**, **kall**-mi-neht, v gipfeln

**culpable**, **kall**-pe-b'l, *adj* schuldig

**culprit**, **kalp**-ritt, n Schuldige(r) m & f, Täter m

**cult**, kalt, n Kult m

**cultivate**, **kall**-ti-weht, v kultivieren

**cultural**, **kall**-tsche-r'l, *adj* kulturell, Kultur-

**culture**, **kall**-tscher, n Kultur f

**cumbersome**, **kamm**-ber-ssem, *adj* (clothing) behinderlich; (parcel etc.) unhandlich; (procedure) beschwerlich

**cumulative**, **kjuh**-mju-le-tiw, *adj* kumulativ

**cunning**, **kann**-ing, *adj* listig, schlau; n Gerissenheit f, Schläue f

**cup**, kapp, n Tasse f; (mug) Becher m; (trophy) Pokal m

**cupboard**, **kabb**-erd, n

Schrank *m*

**curate, kjuhr-ritt,** *n* Vikar *m*

**curator, kjuhr-reh-ter,** *n* Kustos *m*

**curb, körb,** *n* Beschränkung *f*; *v* einschränken

**curdle, kör-d'l,** *v* gerinnen

**cure, kjuhr,** *n* (remedy) Heilmittel *nt*; (treatment) Heilverfahren *nt*; *v* (med) heilen; (smoke) räuchern; (salt) pökeln; (dry) trocknen

**curfew, kör-fjuh,** *n* Ausgangssperre *f*

**curiosity, kjuhr-ri-oss-i-ti,** *n* (inquisitiveness) Neugier *f*; (object) Kuriosität *f*

**curious, kjuhr-i-ess,** *adj* (inquisitive) neugierig; (peculiar) seltsam

**curl, körl,** *n* Locke *f*; *v* (sich) locken; **–er,** *n* Lockenwickler *m*; **–y,** *adj* lockig

**currant, ka-rent,** *n* (dried) Korinthe *f*

**currency, ka-ren-ssi,** *n* Währung *f*

**current, ka-rent,** *adj* (present) aktuell; (widespread) gebräuchlich; *n* Strom *m*; **– account,** *n* Girokonto *nt*

**curriculum, ke-rick-ju-lem,** *n* Lehrplan *m*; **– vitae,** *n* Lebenslauf *m*

**curry, ka-ri,** *n* Curry *m/nt*; *v* mit Currygewürzen zubereiten; **– favour (with),** sich

einschmeicheln (bei)

**curse, körss,** *n* Fluch *m*; *v* fluchen; verwünschen

**cursor, kör-sser,** *n comp* Cursor *m*

**cursory, kör-sser-ri,** *adj* flüchtig

**curt, kört,** *adj* kurz, knapp, barsch

**curtail, ker-tehl,** *v* (ab)kürzen

**curtain, kör-ten,** *n* Vorhang *m*, Gardine *f*

**curts(e)y, kört-ssi,** *n* Knicks *m*; *v* knicksen

**curve, körw,** *n* Kurve *f*; *v* sich biegen; (of road etc.) einen Bogen machen

**cushion, kusch-'n,** *n* Kissen *nt*; *v* dämpfen

**custard, kass-terd,** *n* (runny) Vanillesoße *f*; (set) Pudding *m*

**custody, kass-te-di,** *n* (detention) Haft *f*; (care) Aufsicht *f*

**custom, kass-tem,** *n* Brauch *m*; (trade) Kundschaft *f*; **–ary,** *adj* gebräuchlich, üblich; **–er,** *n* Kunde *m*, Kundin *f*; **–ize,** *v* speziell ausrüsten; **––made,** *adj* (clothes etc.) nach Maß; (car) speziell angefertigt

**customs, kass-tems,** *n* Zoll *m*; **–s duty,** *n* Zoll *m*, Zollabgabe *f*

**cut, kart,** *n* Schnitt *m*; (share) Anteil *m*; (in price) Herabsetzung *f*; (in salary, hours, text)

Kürzung; *v* schneiden; (grass) mähen; (price) herabsetzen; (expenses, wages, text) kürzen; (production) einschränken; (cards) abheben; **– back (on),** einschränken; **– down,** (tree) fällen; (expenses) einschränken; **– off,** abschneiden

**cute, kjuht,** *adj* niedlich

**cuticle, kjuh-ti-k'l,** *n* Nagelhaut *f*

**cutlery, katt-le-ri,** *n* Besteck *nt*

**cutlet, katt-litt,** *n* Kotelett *nt*

**cut-price, katt preiss,** *adj* herabgesetzt, ermäßigt

**cut-throat, katt-throht,** *adj* mörderisch, gnadenlos

**cutting, katt-ing,** *adj* schneidend; *n* (article) Ausschnitt *m*; (plant) Ableger *m*

**CV,** ssie wie (*abbr* **curriculum vitae**), Lebenslauf *m*

**cycle, sei-k'l,** *n* (bicycle) Fahrrad *nt*; (sequence) Zyklus *m*; *elec* Periode *f*

**cycling, sei-kling,** *n* Radfahren *nt*

**cyclist, sei-klist,** *n* Radfahrer *m*

**cylinder, si-linn-der,** *n* Zylinder *m*

**cymbals, simm-b'ls,** *npl* Becken *nt*

**cynic, sinn-ick,** *n* Zyniker

*m*; **–al,** *adj* zynisch
**cypress, sei**-press, *n*
Zypresse *f*
**Cyprus, sei**-press, Zypern *nt*
**cyst,** ssisst, *n* Zyste *f*; **–itis,** *n*
Blasenentzündung *f*
**czar,** zahr, *n* Zar *m*
**Czech,** tscheck, *adj*
tschechisch; *n* Tscheche
*m*, Tschechin *f*; **–**
**Republic,** *n* Tschechische
Republik *f*, Tschechien *nt*

**dab,** däbb, n Tupfer m; v (be)tupfen

**dabble,** däbb-'l, v – **in,** sich in etw versuchen; –**r,** n Amateur m

**dad(dy),** dädd(-i), n Vati m

**daffodil,** däff-e-dill, n Osterglocke f, Narzisse f

**daft,** däft, adj doof

**dagger,** dägg-er, n Dolch m

**dahlia,** deh-li-e, n Dahlie f

**daily,** deh-li, adj & adv täglich, Tages-

**dainty,** dehn-ti, adj zierlich

**dairy,** dähr-ri, adj Milch-; n (works) Molkerei f; (shop) Milchgeschäft nt; – **produce,** n Molkereiprodukte pl

**dais,** deh-iss, n Podium nt

**daisy,** deh-si, n Gänseblümchen nt

**dale,** dehl, n Tal nt

**dam,** dämm, n Damm m; v stauen

**damage,** dämm-idsch, n Schaden m; v beschädigen; –**s,** npl Schadenersatz m

**damn,** dämm, fam n **I don't give a –,** das ist mir piepegal; v verdammen; – **(it)!** verdammt!

**damning,** dämm-ing, adj vernichtend

**damp,** dämp, adj feucht; n Feuchtigkeit f; v anfeuchten

**dance,** dahnss, n Tanz m; v tanzen; –**r,** n Tänzer m

**dandelion,** dänn-di-lei-en, n Löwenzahn m

**dandruff,** dänn-dreff, n Schuppen pl

**Dane,** dehn, n Däne m, Dänin f

**danger,** dehn-dscher, n Gefahr f; –**ous,** adj gefährlich

**dangle,** däng-g'l, v baumeln (lassen)

**Danish,** deh-nish, adj dänisch; n (language) Dänisch nt

**Danube,** dänn-juhb, n Donau f

**dapper,** däpp-er, adj fein, elegant

**dare,** dähr, v (have courage) es wagen; (challenge) herausfordern; **I – say,** es kann gut sein

**daring,** dähr-ring, adj (brave) waghalsig; (audacious) verwegen

**dark,** dahrk, adj dunkel; fig düster; –**ness,** n Dunkelheit f; –**room,** n Dunkelkammer f; **be in the – (about),** im Dunkeln sein (über)

**darling,** dahr-ling, adj sehr lieb; n Liebling m

**darn,** dahrn, v stopfen

**dart,** dahrt, n (weapon) Pfeil m; (in clothes) Abnäher m; v – **(about),** (herum)sausen; –**s,** n Darts m

**dash,** däsch, n (punctuation) Gedankenstrich m; (small amount) bißchen; v (rush) stürzen; (destroy) zunichte machen; **make a – for,** stürzen auf

**dashboard,** däsch-bord, n Armaturenbrett nt

**dashing,** däsch-ing, adj

schneidig

**data,** deh-te, n(pl) Angaben pl; (comp etc.) Daten pl; **–base,** n Datenbank f; – **processing,** n Datenverarbeitung f

**date,** deht, n Datum nt; (appointment) Verabredung f; (fruit) Dattel f; v (letter) datieren; (go out with) gehen mit; **–d,** adj altmodisch; **– of birth,** n Geburtsdatum nt; **out of –,** überholt; **up to date,** (clothes etc.) modisch; (news etc.) aktuell

**daughter,** do'a-ter, n Tochter f; **–-in-law,** n Schwiegertochter f

**daunting,** do'an-ting, adj entmutigend

**dawdle,** do'a-d'l, v bummeln, trödeln

**dawn,** do'an, n (Morgen)dämmerung f; v dämmern

**day,** deh, n Tag m; **the –after tomorrow,** übermorgen; **the – before yesterday,** vorgestern; **–break,** n Tagesanbruch m; **–dream,** n Tagtraum m; **–light,** n Tageslicht nt; **–time,** n in/during the tagsüber; **–-to-day,** adj alltäglich

**daze,** deis, n in a –, benommen; **–d,** adj benommen

**dazzle,** däs-'l, v blenden

**D-day, die-**deh, n der Tag X m

**deacon,** die-k'n, n Diakon m

**dead,** dedd, adj tot; (limb, finger) abgestorben; adv (exactly) genau; ( fam very) total; npl die Toten pl; **–en,** v (pain) abtöten; (sound) dämpfen; (blow) auffangen; **–end,** n Sackgasse f; **– heat,** n totes Rennen nt; **–line,** n Termin m; **–lock,** n Stillstand m; **–ly,** adj tödlich

**deaf,** deff, adj taub; **–en,** v taub machen; **–ness,** n Taubheit f

**deal,** diel, n comm Geschäft nt; v (cards) geben, austeilen; **–er,** n Händler m; (cards) Geber m; **– in,** v handeln mit; **– with,** v comm verhandeln mit; (attend to) sich befassen mit; (sort out) fertig werden mit; (of book etc.) handeln von; **a great – (of),** eine Menge f

**dean,** dien, n Dekan m

**dear,** dier, adj lieb; (costly) teuer; n Liebling m; **Dear Mr X/Sir,** Sehr geehrter Herr X/Herr; **Dear James,** Lieber James

**death,** deth, n Tod m; (fatality) Todesfall m; **– penalty,** n Todesstrafe f

**debar (from),** di-bahr (frem), v ausschließen (von)

**debase,** di-behss, v (person) entwürdigen; (currency) entwerten

**debate,** di-beht, n Debatte f; v debattieren

**debauchery,** di-bo'a-tsche-ri, n Ausschweifung f

**debilitating,** di-bill-i-teh-ting, adj schwächend

**debit,** debb-itt, n fin Soll nt; v (account) belasten

**debris,** debb-rie, n Trümmer pl

**debt,** dett, n Schuld f; **–or,** n Schuldner m; **in –,** verschuldet

**début,** deh-bjuh, n Debüt nt

**decade,** deck-ehd, n Jahrzehnt nt

**decadence,** deck-e-denss, n Dekadenz f

**decaffeinated,** die-käff-ie-neh-tidd, adj koffeinfrei

**decanter,** di-känn-ter, n Karaffe f

**decapitate,** di-käpp-i-teht, v köpfen, enthaupten

**decay,** di-keh, n (decline) Verfall m; (rot) Fäule f; v verfallen; (of food) verderben

**deceased,** di-ssiesst, adj verstorben

**deceit,** di-ssiet, n Betrug m, Täuschung f; **–ful,** adj falsch, hinterlistig

**deceive,** di-ssiew, v täuschen

**December,** di-ssemm-ber, n Dezember m

**decency,** die-ssen-ssi, n

Anstand *m*

**decent, die**-ssent, *adj*
anständig

**deception**, di-**ssepp**-sch'n, *n*
Betrug *m*, Täuschung *f*

**deceptive**, di-**ssepp**-tiw, *adj*
trügerisch

**decide**, di-**sseid**, *v* (sich)
entscheiden; **-d(ly)**, *adj* &
*adv* (without question)
entschieden; (very)
ausgesprochen

**deciduous**, di-**sidd**-ju-ess,
*adj* Laub-

**decimal**, **dess**-i-m'l, *adj*
Dezimal-; **- point**, *n*
Komma *nt*

**decipher**, di-**ssei**-fer, *v*
entziffern

**decision**, di-**ssisch**-'n, *n*
Entscheidung *f*,
Beschluß *m*

**decisive**, di-**ssei**-ssiw, *adj*
entscheidend

**deck**, deck, *n* Deck *nt*; **-
chair**, *n* Liegestuhl *m*; **-
out**, *v* schmücken

**declaration**, deck-le-**reh**-
sch'n, *n* Erklärung *f*

**declare**, di-**klähr**, *v* erklären;
(at customs) verzollen

**declension**, di-**klen**-sch'n, *n*
*gram* Deklination *f*

**decline**, di-**klein**, *n*
(reduction) Rückgang *m*;
(deterioration) Verfall *m*;
*v* (deteriorate) verfallen;
(reject) ablehnen; (be
reduced) zurückgehen;
*gram* deklinieren

**declutch**, die-**klatsch**, *v*

auskuppeln

**decode**, die-**kohd**, *v*
entschlüsseln; **-r**, *n* (TV
etc.) Decoder *m*

**decompose**, die-kom-**pohs**, *v*
(sich) zersetzen

**décor**, **deh**-kor, *n* (room)
Ausstattung *f*; *theatre*
Dekor *m/nt*

**decorate**, **deck**-*e*-reht, *v*
(make festive)
schmücken; (paint)
(an)streichen; (paper)
tapezieren; (cake)
verzieren; (honour)
auszeichnen

**decoration**, deck-*e*-**reh**-
sch'n, *n mil* Auszeichnung
*f*; (ornament) Verzierung
*f*; **-s**, *npl* Schmuck *m*

**decoy**, die-**keu**, *n*
Lockvogel *m*

**decrease**, **die**-kriess, *n*
Abnahme *f*,
Verminderung *f*

**decrease**, di-**kriess**, *v*
abnehmen

**decree**, di-**krie**, *n* Erlaß *m; v*
verordnen

**decrepit**, di-**krepp**-itt, *adj*
altersschwach,
heruntergekommen

**dedicate**, **dedd**-i-keht, *v*
widmen; *relig* weihen; **-d**,
*adj* ergeben

**deduce (from)**, di-**djuhs**
(frem), *v* ableiten (aus)

**deduct**, di-**dakt**, *v*
abziehen; **-ion**, *n* (of
money) Abzug *m*;
(conclusion) Folgerung *f*

**deed**, died, *n* (action) Tat *f*;
(document) Urkunde *f*

**deem**, diem, *v* halten für

**deep**, diep, *adj* tief; **-en**, *v*
vertiefen; **--frozen**, *adj*
tiefgefroren; (food)
Tiefkühl-; **--sea**, *adj*
(diving) Tiefsee-; (fishing)
Hochsee-; **--seated**, *adj*
tiefsitzend

**deer**, dier, *n* Hirsch *m*; (roe)
Reh *nt*

**deface**, di-**fehss**, *v*
verunstalten, entstellen

**defamation**, deff-*e*-**meh**-
sch'n, *n* Verleumdung *f*

**default**, di-**fo'alt**, *n* (non-
payment) Nichtzahlung *f*;
(non-performance)
Versäumnis *f*; *v* säumig
sein; *law* nicht erscheinen;
**-er**, *n* Säumige(r) *m & f*

**defeat**, di-**fiet**, *n* Niederlage
*f*; *v* schlagen, **-ist**, *adj*
defätistisch; *n* Defätist *m*

**defect**, **die**-fekt, *n* Fehler *m*;
*mech* Defekt *m*

**defective**, di-**feck**-tiw, *adj*
mangelhaft; *mech* defekt

**defence**, di-**fenss**, *n*
Verteidigung *f*; **-less**, *adj*
schutzlos, wehrlos

**defend**, di-**fend**, *v*
verteidigen; **-ant**, di-**fen**-
dent, *n* Angeklagte(r) *m*
& *f*; **-er**, *n* Verteidiger *m*

**defensive**, di-**fen**-ssiw, *adj*
defensiv

**defer**, di-**för**, *v* (delay)
verschieben; **- (to)**,
(submit) sich fügen

**deference, deff**-e-renss, *n*
Achtung *f;* **in – to,** aus
Achtung vor

**defiance,** di-**fei**-enss, *n* Trotz
*m;* **in – of sb/sth,** jdm/etw
zum Trotz

**defiant,** di-**fei**-ent, *adj*
trotzig

**deficiency,** di-**fisch**-en-ssi, *n*
(shortage) Mangel *m;*
(defect) Schwäche *f*

**deficient,** di-**fisch**-ent, *adj*
mangelhaft, unzulänglich

**deficit, deff**-i-ssitt, *n*
Defizit *nt*

**defile,** di-**feil,** *v*
verschmutzen

**define,** di-**fein,** *v* (word etc.)
definieren; (powers etc.)
bestimmen

**definite, deff**-i-nitt, *adj*
(agreed) fest; (positive)
bestimmt; (distinct)
eindeutig; **–ly,** *adv* fest,
eindeutig

**definition, deff**-i-**ni**-sch'n, *n*
(of word etc.) Definition
*f;* (of powers etc.)
Bestimmung *f*

**deflect,** di-**fleckt,** *v*
ablenken

**deform,** di-**form,** *v*
verunstalten, deformieren

**defraud,** di-**fro'ad,** *v*
betrügen

**defray,** di-**freh,** *v*
übernehmen

**defrost,** die-**frost,** *v* (fridge,
windscreen) abtauen;
(food) auftauen

**deft,** deft, *adj* flink

**defunct,** di-**fankt,** *adj*
(person) verstorben;
(machine etc.) überholt,
stillgelegt

**defuse,** die-**fjuhs,** *v*
entschärfen

**defy,** di-**fei,** *v* trotzen;
(challenge) herausfordern

**degenerate,** di-**dschenn**-e-
ret, *adj* entartet,
degeneriert

**degenerate,** di-**dschenn**-e-
reht, *v* entarten,
degenerieren

**degradation,** degg-re-**deh**-
sch'n, *n* Erniedrigung *f*

**degrade,** di-**grehd,** *v*
erniedrigen

**degree,** di-**grie,** *n* Grad *m;* –
**course,** *n* Universitätskurs
*m*

**dehydrated,** die-hei-**dreh**-
tidd, *adj* ausgetrocknet;
(food) Trocken-

**de-ice,** die-**eiss,** *v* enteisen;
**–r,** *n* Enteiser *m*

**deity,** die-i-ti, *n* Gottheit *f*

**deject,** di-**dscheckt,** *v*
niederschlagen; **–ion,** *n*
Niedergeschlagenheit *f*

**delay,** di-**leh,** *n*
(postponement) Aufschub
*m;* (lateness) Verspätung *f;*
*v* (postpone) verschieben;
(detain) aufhalten;
**without –,** unverzüglich

**delectable,** di-**leck**-te-b'l, *adj*
(delicious) köstlich;
(delightful) reizend

**delegate, dell**-i-get, *n*
Delegierte(r) *m & f*

**delegate, dell**-i-geht, *v*
delegieren

**delete,** di-**liet,** *v* streichen

**deliberate(ly),** di-**libb**-e-
ret(-li), *adj & adv*
(intentional) absichtlich;
(slow) bedächtig

**deliberate,** di-**libb**-e-reht, *v*
nachdenken

**delicacy,** di-**li-ke**-ssi, *n*
(food) Delikatesse *f;*
(sensitivity) Feingefühl *nt;*
(daintiness) Zartheit *f*

**delicate, dell**-i-ket, *adj*
(sensitive) feinfühlig;
(dainty, weak) zart

**delicatessen,** dell-i-ke-**tess**-
'n, *n* (food) Feinkost *f;*
(shop) Feinkostgeschäft *nt*

**delicious,** di-**lisch**-ess, *adj*
lecker

**delight,** di-**leit,** *n* Wonne *f;* –
entzücken; **–ed,** *adj*
entzückt; **–ful,** *adj*
entzückend, reizend

**delinquency,** di-**ling**-ku'en-
ssi, *n* Kriminalität *f*

**delinquent,** di-**ling**-ku'ent, *n*
Straffällige(r) *m & f*

**delirious,** di-**li**-ri-ess, *adj*
(med) im Delirium; *fig* im
Freudentaumel

**deliver,** di-**liw**-er, *v* (goods)
liefern; (letter) zustellen;
(speech) halten; (baby)
zur Welt bringen; **–y,** *n* (of
goods) Lieferung *f;* (of
letters) Zustellung *f;* (of
baby) Entbindung *f*

**delude,** di-**luhd,** *v* täuschen

**deluge, dell**-juhdsch, *n*

Überschwemmung *f; fig*
Flut *f*

**delusion,** di-**luh**-sch'n, *n*
Täuschung *f*

**delve into,** delw **inn**-tu, *v*
tief greifen in; *fig* sich
vertiefen in

**demand,** di-**mahnd,** *n*
Forderung *f; comm*
Nachfrage *f; v* verlangen,
fordern; **–ing,** *adj*
anspruchsvoll

**demean (oneself),** di-**mien**
(u'ann-sself), *v* (sich)
erniedrigen

**demeanour,** di-**mie**-ner, *n*
Benehmen *nt*

**demented,** di-**menn**-tidd, *adj*
verrückt

**demise,** di-**meis,** *n* Ableben
*nt*

**demo, demm**-oh, *n (abbr*
**demonstration),** Demo *f*

**democracy,** di-**mock**-re-ssi,
*n* Demokratie *f*

**democrat,** demn-*e*-krätt, *n*
Demokrat *m*

**democratic,** demn-*e*-krätt-
ick, *adj* demokratisch

**demolish,** di-**moll**-isch, *v*
(building) abreißen;
(theory) vernichten

**demon, die**-men, *n*
Dämon *m*

**demonstrate, demm**-en-
streht, *v* demonstrieren

**demonstration,** demm-en-
**streh**-sch'n, *n*
Demonstration *f*

**demonstrator, demm**-
en-streh-ter, *n*

**Demonstrant** *m*

**demoralize,** die-**mo**-*re*-leis, *v*
demoralisieren

**demote,** di-**moht,** *v*
degradieren

**demure,** di-**mjuhr,** *adj*
spröde, sittsam

**den,** denn, *n* (of animal)
Höhle *f;* (private room)
Bude *f*

**denial,** di-**nei**-el, *n*
Leugnung *f;* (official)
Dementi *nt;* (refusal)
Ablehnung *f*

**denim, denn**-imm, *n*
Denim-, Jeans-; **–s,** *npl*
(Blue) Jeans *pl*

**Denmark, denn**-mark, *n*
Dänemark *nt*

**denomination,** di-nomm-i-
**neh**-sch'n, *n relig*
Bekenntnis *nt; fin* Wert *m*

**denominator,** di-**nomm**-i-
neh-ter, *n* Nenner *m*

**denote,** di-**noht,** *v*
bezeichnen

**denounce,** de-**naunss,** *v*
(accuse) brandmarken;
(inform against)
denunzieren

**dense,** denss, *adj* dicht; (*fam*
stupid) dumm

**density, denn**-ssi-ti, *n*
Dichte *f*

**dent,** dent, *n* Delle *f; v*
(metal) einbeulen;
(wood) eine Delle
machen in

**dental,** dent-'l, *adj* Zahn-

**dentist, denn**-tist, *n*
Zahnarzt *m;* **–ry,** *n*

Zahnheilkunde *f*

**dentures, denn**-tschers, *npl*
Gebiß *nt*

**denude,** di-**njuhd,** *v*
entblößen

**deny,** di-**nei,** *v* (accusation)
ableugnen; (officially)
dementieren; (request)
abschlagen

**deodorant,** die-**oh**-*de*-rent, *n*
Deodorant *nt*

**depart,** di-**pahrt,** *v* abfahren;
*fig* abweichen

**department,** di-**pahrt**-ment,
*n* Abteilung *f;* **– store,**
Warenhaus *nt*

**departure,** di-**pahr**-tscher, *n*
(of train, bus) Abfahrt *f;*
(of plane) Abflug *m;* (of
person) Abreise *f; fig* neue
Richtung *f;* **– lounge,** *n*
Abflughalle *f*

**depend (on),** di-pend (onn),
*v* (be conditional on)
abhängen von; (rely on)
sich verlassen auf; **–ant,** *n*
Angehörige(r) *m & f;*
**–ent,** *adj* abhängig; **that
–s,** es kommt darauf an

**depict,** di-**pikt,** *v* darstellen

**depleted,** di-**plie**-tidd, *adj*
erschöpft

**deplorable,** di-**plor**-*re*-b'l, *adj*
bedauerlich

**deplore,** di-**plor,** *v* bedauern,
mißbilligen

**deploy,** di-**pleu,** *v* einsetzen

**deport,** di-**port,** *v*
abschieben

**deportation,** die-port-**eh**-
sch'n, *n* Abschiebung *f*

**depose,** di-pohs, *v* absetzen

**deposit,** di-pos-itt, *n* (payment) Anzahlung *f*; (security) Kaution *f*; (in bank) Guthaben *nt*; (sediment) Ablagerung *f*; *v* (money) einzahlen; (load) ablegen; **– account,** *n* Sparkonto *nt*

**depot,** depp-oh, *n* Depot *nt*, Lagerhaus *nt*

**depraved,** di-prehwd, *adj* verdorben

**depreciate,** di-prie-schi-eht, *v* an Wert verlieren

**depreciation,** di-prie-schi-eh-sch'n, *n* Wertminderung *f*

**depress,** di-press, *v* (press down) niederdrücken; *fig* deprimieren

**depression,** di-presch-'n, *n* (low mood) Depression *f*; (economic) Wirtschaftskrise *f*; (in ground) Vertiefung *f*; (atmospheric) Tief *nt*

**deprivation,** depp-ri-weh-sch'n, *n* (taking) Beraubung *f*; (lack) Entbehrung *f*

**deprive (of),** di-preiw (ew), *v* berauben; **–d,** *adj* benachteiligt

**depth,** depth, *n* Tiefe *f*

**deputize (for),** depp-ju-teis (vor), *v* vertreten

**deputy,** depp-ju-ti, *n* Stellvertreter *m*

**derailed,** di-rehld, **be –,** *v* entgleisen

**derailment,** di-rehl-ment, *n* Entgleisung *f*

**deranged,** di-rehndschd, *adj* geistesgestört

**derelict,** de-ri-lickt, *adj* verlassen

**deride,** di-reid, *v* auslachen

**derisory,** di-rei-sse-ri, *adj* (sum) lächerlich; (laughter) spöttisch

**derive (from),** di-reiw (frem), *v* (deduce) ableiten (von); (obtain) gewinnen (aus)

**derogatory,** di-rogg-e-tri, *adj* abfällig

**descend,** di-ssend, *v* (person) hinuntergehen; (vehicle) hinunterfahren; (lower o.s.) sich erniedrigen; **–ant,** *n* Nachkomme *m*; **be –ed from,** *v* abstammen von

**descent,** di-ssent, *n* Abstieg *m*; (ancestry) Abstammung *f*

**describe,** di-skreib, *v* beschreiben

**description,** di-skripp-sch'n, *n* Beschreibung *f*

**descriptive,** di-skripp-tiw, *adj* anschaulich

**desecrate,** dess-i-kreht, *v* entweihen

**desert,** des-ert, *n* Wüste *f*

**desert,** di-sört, *v* verlassen; *mil* desertieren; **–er,** *n* *mil* Deserteur *m*; **–ion,** *n* Verlassen *nt*; *mil* Desertion *f*

**deserve,** di-sörw, *v* verdienen

**deserving,** di-sör-wing, *adj* verdienstvoll

**design,** di-sein, *n* (intention) Absicht *f*; (sketch) Entwurf *m*; (of machine) Konstruktion *f*; (pattern) Muster *nt*; *v* (sketch) entwerfen; (machine) konstruieren

**designate,** des-igg-net, *adj* designiert

**designate,** des-igg-neht, *v* ernennen

**designer,** di-sei-ner, *n* Designer *m*

**desirable,** di-seir-re-b'l, *adj* wünschenswert

**desire,** di-seir, *n* (wish) Wunsch *m*; (craving) Verlangen *nt*; *v* (sich) wünschen; (sexually) begehren

**desist (from),** di-sist (frem), *v* absehen von

**desk,** desk, *n* Schreibtisch *m*; (school) Pult *nt*; (reception) Empfang *m*

**desolate,** dess-e-let, *adj* trostlos

**despair,** diss-pähr, *n* Verzweiflung *f*; **– (of),** *v* verzweifeln (an)

**despatch,** diss-pätsch, *n* (sending) Absendung *f*; (message) Meldung *f*; *v* abschicken

**desperate,** dess-pe-ret, *adj* verzweifelt; (urgent) dringend

**desperation,** dess-pe-reh-sch'n, n Verzweiflung f

**despicable,** diss-**pick**-*e*-b'l, *adj* verächtlich

**despise,** diss-**peis,** *v* verachten

**despite,** diss-**peit,** *prep* trotz

**despondent,** diss-**ponn**-dent, *adj* niedergeschlagen

**despot,** dess-pet, *n* Despot *m*

**dessert,** di-**sört,** *n* Nachtisch *m*, Dessert *nt*

**destination,** dess-ti-**neh**-sch'n, *n* (of goods) Bestimmungsort *m*; (of person) Reiseziel *nt*

**destiny,** dess-ti-ni, *n* Schicksal *nt*

**destitute,** dess-ti-tjuht, *adj* mittellos

**destroy,** diss-**treu,** *v* zerstören, vernichten

**destruction,** diss-**track**-sch'n, *n* Zerstörung f

**destructive,** diss-**track**-tiw, *adj* zerstörend

**detach,** di-**tätsch,** *v* (loosen) loslösen; (take off) abnehmen; **–ed,** (house) Einzel-; (attitude) distanziert; **–ment,** *n mil* Sonderkommando *nt*; (attitude) Abstand *m*

**detail,** die-tehl, *n* Einzelheit f; *v* (relate) erzählen; (list) aufführen; **–ed,** *adj* detailliert

**detain,** di-**tehn,** *v* (delay) aufhalten; (imprison) in Haft halten

**detect,** di-tekt, *v* entdecken; **–ion,** *n* Entdeckung f;

**–ive,** *n* Detektiv *m*; **–ive story,** *n* Kriminalgeschichte f, Krimi *m*

**détente,** deh-tahnt, *n* Entspannung f

**detention,** di-**tenn**-sch'n, *n* (captivity) Haft f; (school) Nachsitzen *nt*

**deter,** di-tör, *v* abschrecken

**detergent,** di-**tör**-dschent, *n* Waschmittel *nt*

**deteriorate,** di-**tier**-ri-e-reht, *v* sich verschlechtern

**determination,** di-tör-mi-**neh**-sch'n, *n* Entschlossenheit f

**determine,** di-tör-minn, *v* bestimmen; **–d,** *adj* entschlossen

**deterrent,** di-te-rent, *n* Abschreckungsmittel *nt*

**detest,** di-test, *v* verabscheuen

**detonate,** dett-*e*-neht, *v* explodieren lassen

**detour,** die-tuhr, *n* Umweg *m*

**detract (from),** di-**träckt** (frem), *v* beeinträchtigen, schmälern

**detrimental,** dett-ri-**menn**-t'l, *adj* schädlich

**devaluation,** dee-**wäll**-juh-**eh**-sch'n, *n* Abwertung f

**devalue,** di-**wäll**-juh, *v* abwerten

**devastate,** dew-ass-teht, *v* verwüsten; *fig* umhauen

**develop,** di-**well**-ep, *v* entwickeln; **–ing country,**

*n* Entwicklungsland *nt*; **–ment,** *n* Entwicklung f

**deviate (from),** die-wi-eht (frem), *v* abweichen (von)

**device,** di-**weiss,** *n* Gerät *nt*

**devil,** dew-'l, *n* Teufel *m*; **–ish,** *adj* teuflisch

**devious,** die-wi-ess, *adj* (method, act) fragwürdig; (person, mind) verschlagen

**devise,** di-**weis,** *v* sich ausdenken

**devoid of,** di-**weud** ew, *prep* ohne, frei von

**devote (to),** di-**woht** (tu), *v* (self, time) widmen; (resources) bestimmen (für); **–d,** *adj* ergeben

**devotion,** di-**woh**-sch'n, *n* (loyalty) Ergebenheit f; (duty) Hingabe f; **–s,** *npl relig* Andacht f

**devour,** di-**wau**-er, *v* verschlingen

**devout,** di-**waut,** *adj* fromm

**dew,** djuh, *n* Tau *m*

**dexterity,** decks-te-ri-ti, *n* Geschicklichkeit f

**diabetes,** dei-*e*-**bie**-ties, *n* Zuckerkrankheit f

**diabetic,** dei-*e*-bett-ick, *adj* (person) zuckerkrank; (food) Diabetiker-; *n* Diabetiker *m*

**diabolical,** dei-e-boll-i-k'l, *adj* teuflisch

**diagnose,** dei-*e*-gnohs, *v* diagnostizieren

**diagnosis,** dei-*e*-gnoh-ssiss, *n* Diagnose f

**diagonal,** dei-**ägg**-e-n'l, *adj*
diagonal; n Diagonale f

**diagram,** dei-e-**grämm,** n
Diagramm nt

**dial,** dei-el, n (clock)
Zifferblatt nt; (telephone)
Wählscheibe f; *v* wählen

**dialect,** dei-e-lekt, n
Mundart f, Dialekt m

**dialogue,** dei-e-logg, n
Dialog m

**diameter,** dei-**ämm**-i-ter, n
Durchmesser m

**diamond,** dei-e-mend, n
Diamant m; **–s,** *npl* (cards)
Karo nt

**diaphragm,** dei-e-främm, n
(anatomy) Zwerchfell nt;
(contraceptive) Pessar nt

**diarrhoea,** dei-e-**rie**-e, n
Durchfall m

**diary,** dei-e-ri, n (for
appointments)
Terminkalender m;
(journal) Tagebuch nt

**dice,** deiss, *npl* Würfel *pl*

**dictate,** dick-**teht,** *v*
diktieren

**dictation,** dick-**teh**-sch'n, n
Diktat nt

**dictator,** dick-**teh**-ter, n
Diktator m; **–ship,** n
Diktatur f

**dictionary,** dick-schen-e-ri,
n Wörterbuch nt

**die,** dei, n Würfel m; *v*
sterben; **– away,** (of
sound) leiser werden; (of
wind, anger) sich legen; **–
out,** aussterben

**diesel,** die-s'l, n Diesel m

**diet,** dei-et, n (food)
Nahrung f; (slimming)
Abmagerungskur f;
(special) Diät f; *v* eine
Abmagerungskur machen

**differ,** diff-er, *v* (be
dissimilar) sich
unterscheiden; (disagree)
nicht übereinstimmen;
**–ence,** n Unterschied m;
(between amounts)
Differenz f; **–ent,** *adj*
verschieden

**difficult,** diff-i-k'lt, *adj*
schwer, schwierig; **–y,** n
Schwierigkeit f

**diffident,** diff-i-dent, *adj*
zaghaft, schüchtern

**diffuse,** diff-**juhss,** *adj*
weitschweifig

**diffuse,** diff-**juhs,** *v*
verbreiten

**dig,** dig, *v* graben; **– in,** *mil*
sich eingraben; (*fam* eat)
reinhauen; **– up,**
ausgraben

**digest,** di-**dschest,** *v*
verdauen; **–ion,** n
Verdauung f

**digit,** didsch-itt, n Ziffer f;
**–al,** *adj* Digital-

**dignified,** digg-ni-feid, *adj*
würdevoll

**dignitary,** digg-ni-te-ri, n
Würdenträger m

**dignity,** digg-ni-ti, n
Würde f

**digress,** dei-**gress,** *v*
abschweifen

**dilapidated,** di-**läpp**-i-deh-
tidd, *adj* verfallen

**dilate,** dei-**leht,** *v* (sich)
weiten

**dilemma,** dei-**lemm**-e, n
Dilemma nt

**diligent,** dill-i-dschent, *adj*
fleißig

**dilute,** dei-**luht,** *v*
verdünnen

**dim,** dimm, *adj* trüb,
schwach; (*fam* stupid)
dumm; *v* verdunkeln

**dimension,** dei-**menn**-sch'n,
n Dimension f

**diminish,** di-**minn**-isch, *v*
(sich) verringern

**diminutive,** di-**minn**-ju-tiw,
*adj* winzig

**dimple,** dimm-p'l, n
Grübchen nt

**din,** dinn, n Getöse nt

**dine,** dein, *v* speisen

**dingy,** dinn-dschi, *adj* düster

**dinghy,** ding-gi, n (sailing)
Dinghy nt; (inflatable)
Schlauchboot nt

**dining car,** dei-ning kahr, n
Speisewagen m

**dining room,** dei-ning
ruhm, n Eßzimmer nt,
Speisezimmer nt

**dinner,** dinn-er, n (evening)
Abendessen nt; (midday)
Mittagessen nt; (formal)
Essen nt; **– jacket,** n
Smoking m

**dip,** dipp, n (slope) Abfall
m; (swim) kurzes Bad nt; *v*
(of ground) sich senken;
(into liquid) eintauchen;
(headlights) abblenden

**diploma,** di-**ploh**-me, n

Diplom *nt*

**diplomacy,** di-**ploh**-me-ssi, *n* Diplomatie *f*

**diplomat, dipp**-le-mätt, *n* Diplomat *m*; **–ic,** *adj* diplomatisch

**dire,** deir, *adj* entsetzlich

**direct,** dei-**reckt,** *adj* direkt; *v* (manage) leiten; (order) anweisen; (film) Regie führen; **– sb (to),** jdm den Weg sagen (zu); **–ion,** *n* (way) Richtung *f*; (management) Leitung *f*; (of film) Regie *f*; **–ions,** *npl* (to place) Wegbeschreibung *f*; (for use) Bedienungsanleitung *f*

**directly,** di-**rekt**-li, *adv* direkt; (immediately) sofort

**director,** di-**reck**-ter, *n* (manager) Direktor *m*, Leiter *m*; (of film) Regisseur *m*; **–y,** *n* (telephone) Telefonbuch *nt*; (trade) Verzeichnis *nt*

**dirt,** dört, *n* Schmutz *m*; **– cheap,** *adj* spottbillig; **–y,** *adj* schmutzig

**disability,** diss-e-**bill**-i-ti, *n* Behinderung *f*

**disabled,** diss-**eh**-b'ld, *adj* behindert

**disadvantage,** diss-ed-**wahn**-tidsch, *n* Nachteil *m*

**disagree,** diss-e-**grie,** *v* nicht übereinstimmen; **–able,** *adj* unangenehm; **–ment,** *n* (between opinions)

Uneinigkeit *f*; (between figures etc.) Diskrepanz *f*

**disallow,** diss-e-**lau,** *v* nicht zulassen

**disappear,** diss-e-**pier,** *v* verschwinden; **–ance,** *n* Verschwinden *nt*

**disappoint,** diss-e-**peunt,** *v* enttäuschen; **–ment,** *n* Enttäuschung *f*

**disapproval,** diss-e-**pruh**-w'l, *n* Mißbilligung *f*

**disapprove (of),** diss-e-**pruhw** (ew), *v* mißbilligen

**disarm,** diss-**ahrm,** *v* (person) entwaffnen; *mil* abrüsten; **–ament,** *n* Abrüstung *f*

**disaster,** di-**sahss**-ter, *n* Katastrophe *f*

**disastrous,** di-**sahss**-tress *adj* verheerend

**disc, disk,** *n* Scheibe *f*; (record) Platte *f*; (CD) Compact Disc *f*

**discard,** diss-**kahrd,** *v* (throw away) ausrangieren; (reject) verwerfen; (cards) abwerfen

**discern,** di-**ssörn,** *v* (distinguish) unterscheiden; (perceive) wahrnehmen; **–ing,** *adj* kritisch

**discharge,** diss-**tschardsch,** *n* (dismissal) Entlassung *f*; (of gun) Abfeuern *nt*; *med* Ausfluß *m*; *elec* Entladung *f*; *v* (fulfil) nachkommen; (release) freisprechen;

(dismiss) entlassen; (cargo) ausladen; (gun) abfeuern

**disciple,** di-**ssei**-p'l, *n* Jünger *m*

**discipline,** di-**ssi**-plinn, *n* Disziplin *f*

**disc jockey, disk** dscho-ki, *n* Diskjockey *m*

**disclaim,** diss-**klehm,** *v* abstreiten

**disclose,** diss-**klohs,** *v* bekanntmachen; enthüllen

**disclosure,** diss-**kloh**-scher, *n* Enthüllung *f*

**disco,** diss-koh, *n* (*abbr* **discotheque**), Disko *f*

**discolour,** diss-**kall**-er, *v* verfärben

**discomfort,** diss-**kamm**-fert, *n* Unbehagen *nt*

**disconcerted,** diss-ken-**ssör**-tidd, *adj* beunruhigt

**disconnect,** diss-ke-**nekt,** *v* (objects) trennen; (power etc.) abstellen

**discontent,** diss-ken-**tent,** *n* Unzufriedenheit *f*; **–ed,** *adj* unzufrieden

**discontinue,** diss-ken-**tinn**-juh, *v* (production) einstellen; (conversation, project) abbrechen

**discord,** diss-kord, *n* Zwietracht *f*; *mus* Dissonanz *f*

**discordant,** diss-**kor**-d'nt, *adj* unharmonisch; *mus* dissonant

**discount,** diss-kaunt, *n*

Skonto m/nt; (trade) Rabatt m; **at a –**, mit Rabatt

**discount,** diss-**kaunt**, v (reduce) diskontieren; (ignore) nicht berücksichtigen

**discotheque,** diss-ke-**teck**, n Diskothek f

**discourage,** diss-**ka**-ridsch, v (dishearten) entmutigen; (dissuade) abraten

**discourteous,** diss-**kör**-ti-ess, adj unhöflich

**discover,** diss-**ka**-wer, v entdecken; **–y,** n Entdeckung f

**discredit,** diss-**kredd**-itt, v unglaubwürdig machen

**discreet,** diss-**kriet**, adj diskret

**discrepancy,** diss-**krepp**-en-ssi, n Diskrepanz f

**discriminate,** diss-**krimm**-i-neht, v – **(between),** unterscheiden (zwischen); – **(against),** diskriminieren

**discriminating,** diss-**krimm**-i-neh-ting, adj kritisch

**discrimination,** diss-**krimm**-i-**neh**-sch'n, n (judgement) Urteilsvermögen nt; (unfair) Diskriminierung f

**discuss,** diss-**kass**, v diskutieren, besprechen; **–ion,** n Diskussion f, Besprechung f

**disdain,** diss-**dehn**, n Verachtung f; v verachten;

**–ful,** adj verächtlich

**disease,** di-**sies**, n Krankheit f; **–d,** adj krank

**disembark,** diss-imm-**bark**, v von Bord gehen

**disenchanted,** diss-inn-**tschahn**-tidd, adj desillusioniert

**disengage,** diss-inn-**gehdsch**, v (detach) losmachen; (clutch) auskuppeln

**disentangle,** diss-inn-**täng**-g'l, v entwirren

**disfigure,** diss-**figg**-er, v entstellen

**disgrace,** diss-**grehss**, n Schande f; v Schande bringen über; **–ful,** adj skandalös

**disgruntled,** diss-**grann**-t'ld, adj verstimmt

**disguise,** diss-**geis**, n Verkleidung f; v verkleiden; fig verschleiern

**disgust,** diss-**gast**, n Ekel m; v anekeln

**dish,** disch, n (bowl) Schüssel f; (food) Gericht nt; **–cloth,** Spüllappen m; – **up,** v auftischen

**dishearten,** diss-**hahr**-t'n, v entmutigen

**dishevelled,** di-**schew**-'ld, adj (hair) zerzaust; (clothes) unordentlich

**dishonest,** diss-**onn**-ist, adj unehrlich

**dishonour,** diss-**onn**-er, n Unehre f; v entehren

**dishwasher,** disch-u'osch-er,

n Geschirrspülmaschine f

**disillusion,** di-ssi-**luh**-sch'n, v ernüchtern, desillusionieren

**disincentive,** diss-inn-**senn**-tiw, n Entmutigung f

**disinfect,** diss-inn-**fekt**, v desinfizieren

**disintegrate,** diss-inn-ti-greht, v zerfallen

**disjointed,** diss-**dscheun**-tidd, adj zusammenhanglos

**disk,** disk, n comp (hard) Festplatte f; (floppy) Diskette f; – **drive,** n Diskettenlaufwerk nt

**dislike,** diss-**leik**, n Abneigung f; v nicht mögen

**dislocate,** diss-le-keht, v med verrenken; fig in Verwirrung bringen

**dislodge,** diss-**lodsch**, v entfernen, lösen

**disloyal,** diss-**leu**-el, adj treulos

**dismal,** dis-mel, adj (place) düster; (failure) kläglich

**dismantle,** diss-**männ**-t'l, v demontieren

**dismay,** diss-**meh**, n Bestürzung f; v bestürzen

**dismiss,** diss-**miss**, v (person) entlassen; (idea) abtun

**dismount,** diss-**maunt**, v absteigen

**disobedient,** diss-e-bie-di-ent, adj ungehorsam

**disobey,** diss-e-beh, v nicht gehorchen

**disorder,** di-ssor-der, *n* (untidiness) Unordnung *f*; (disturbance) Unruhen *pl*; *med* Beschwerden *pl*; **–ly,** *adj* (untidy) unordentlich; (unruly) undiszipliniert

**disorganized,** di-ssor-ge-neisd, *adj* chaotisch

**disorientated,** di-ssor-ri-en-teh-tidd, *adj* verwirrt

**disown,** di-ssohn, *v* nicht anerkennen; (person) verstoßen

**disparaging,** diss-pä-ri-dsching, *adj* geringschätzig

**disparity,** diss-pä-ri-ti, *n* Ungleichheit *f*

**dispatch,** *see* despatch

**dispel,** diss-pell, *v* vertreiben

**dispensary,** diss-penn-se-ri, *n* Apotheke *f*

**dispense,** diss-penss, *v* verteilen; *med* abgeben; **– with,** verzichten auf

**dispensing chemist,** diss-penn-ssing kemm-ist, *n* Apotheker *m*

**disperse,** diss-pörss, *v* (sich) zerstreuen

**displaced person,** diss-plehst pör-ss'n, *adj* Verschleppte(r) *m & f*

**display,** diss-pleh, *n* (of goods) Auslage *f*; (show) Schau *f*; *v* (goods) ausstellen; (interest etc.) zeigen; (show off) vorführen

**displease,** diss-plies, *v* mißfallen; **–d,** *adj* verstimmt

**displeasure,** diss-plesch-er, *n* Mißfallen *nt*

**disposable,** diss-poh-se-b'l, *adj* Wegwerf-; (bottle) Einweg-; **– nappy,** *n* Wegwerfwindel *f*

**disposal,** diss-poh-sel, *n* (throwing away) Beseitigung *f*, Entsorgung *f*; **be at sb's –,** *v* (be available) jdm zur Verfügung stehen

**dispose of,** diss-pohs ew, *v* (throw away) beseitigen, entsorgen; (have available) verfügen über

**disposed,** diss-pohsd, *adj* geneigt

**disposition,** diss-pe-sisch-'n, *n* Natur *f*

**disproportionate,** diss-pre-por-sche-net, *adj* unverhältnismäßig

**disprove,** diss-pruhw, *v* widerlegen

**dispute,** diss-pjuht, *n* Streit *m*; *v* bestreiten

**disqualify,** diss-ku'o-li-fai, *v* disqualifizieren

**disquiet,** diss-ku'ai-et, *n* Unruhe *f*; *v* beunruhigen

**disregard,** diss-ri-gahrd, *n* Nichtbeachtung *f*; *v* nicht beachten

**disreputable,** diss-repp-ju-te-b'l, *adj* verrufen; (appearance) unansehnlich

**disrepute,** diss-ri-pjuht, *n* Verruf *m*

**disrespect,** diss-ri-spekt, *n* Respeklosigkeit *f*; **–ful,** *adj* respektlos

**disrupt,** diss-rapt, *v* stören; **–ion,** *n* Störung *f*

**dissatisfied,** di-ssätt-iss-sfeid, *adj* unzufrieden

**dissect,** di-ssekt, *v* sezieren

**disseminate,** di-ssemm-in-eht, *v* verbreiten

**dissent,** di-ssent, *n* Meinungsverschiedenheit *f*; *v* anderer Meinung sein

**dissident,** diss-i-dent, *adj* dissident; *n* Dissident *m*

**dissimilar,** diss-ssimm-i-ler, *adj* unähnlich

**dissipate,** diss-i-peht, *v* (use up) verschwenden; (disappear) (sich) auflösen

**dissociate,** di-ssoh-ssi-eht, *v* trennen; **– o.s. from,** *v* distanzieren von

**dissolute,** diss-e-luht, *adj* zügellos

**dissolve,** di-solw, *v* (sich) auflösen

**dissuade (from),** di-ssu'ehd (frem), *v* ausreden

**distance,** diss-tenss, *n* Entfernung *f*; (gap) Abstand *m*; *v* **– o.s. from,** sich distanzieren von; **in the –,** in der Ferne

**distant,** diss-tent, *adj* (in space) entfernt, fern; (in time) fern; (in attitude) distanziert

**distaste,** diss-tehst, *n* Widerwille *m*; **–ful,** *adj* zuwider

**distended,** diss-**tenn**-didd, *adj* aufgebläht

**distil,** diss-**till,** *v* destillieren; **–lery,** *n* Brennerei *f*

**distinct,** diss-**tinkt,** *adj* (clear) deutlich; (different) verschieden; **–ion,** *n* (difference) Unterschied *m*; (eminence) Auszeichnung *f*; **–ive,** *adj* unverwechselbar

**distinguish,** diss-**ting**-gu'isch, *v* unterscheiden; **–ed,** *adj* berühmt; **–ing,** *adj* kennzeichnend; **– o.s.,** *v* sich auszeichnen

**distort,** diss-**tort,** *v* verdrehen, verrenken

**distract,** diss-**träckt,** *v* ablenken; **–ion,** *n* (interruption) Ablenkung *f*; (distress) Verstörung *f*

**distress,** diss-**tress,** *n* (danger) Not *f*; (worry) Sorge *f*; (pain) Leiden *nt*; *v* **– sb/o.s.,** jdm/sich Sorgen machen; **–ing,** *adj* bedrückend, bestürzend

**distribute,** diss-**tribb**-juht, *v* verteilen

**distribution,** diss-tribb-**juh**-sch'n, *n* Verteilung *f*

**distributor,** diss-**tribb**-juh-ter, *n* (car) Verteiler *m*; (wholesaler) Großhändler *m*

**district,** diss-**trikt,** *n* Bezirk *m*

**distrust,** diss-**trast,** *n* Mißtrauen *nt; v* mißtrauen

**disturb,** diss-**törb,** *v* (disrupt) stören; (worry) beunruhigen; **–ance,** *n* Störung *f*; (trouble) Unruhe *f*; **–ing,** *adj* störend; beunruhigend

**disuse,** diss-**juhss,** *n* **fall into –,** *v* außer Gebrauch kommen

**disused,** diss-**juhsd,** *v* außer Gebrauch; (building) leerstehend; (factory etc.) stillgelegt

**ditch,** ditsch, *n* Graben *m; v fam* fallenlassen

**dither,** didh-er, *v fam* zaudern

**ditto,** ditt-oh, *adv* gleichfalls, dito

**dive,** deiw, *n* (by swimmer) Kopfsprung *m*; (by plane) Sturzflug *m; v* (jump) springen; (under water) tauchen; **–r,** *n* (under water) Taucher *m*

**diverge,** dei-**wördsch,** *v* (voneinander) abweichen

**diverse,** dei-**wörss,** *adj* verschieden

**diversion,** dei-**wör**-sch'n, *n* (distraction) Ablenkung *f*; (from route) Umleitung *f*; (amusement) Zerstreuung *f*

**diversity,** dei-**wör**-ssi-ti, *n* Vielfalt *f*

**divert,** dei-**wört,** *v* (distract) ablenken; (re-route) umleiten; (amuse) zerstreuen

**divide,** di-**weid,** *v* (separate) trennen; (split up) (sich) teilen

**diving,** dei-**wing,** *n* (into water) Springen *nt*; (under water) Tauchen *nt*; **– board,** *n* Sprungbrett *nt*

**divine,** di-**wein,** *v* göttlich

**division,** di-**wisch**-'n, *n* (separation) Teilung *f*; (part) Teil *m*; (maths, mil) Division *f*; (disagreement) Uneinigkeit *f*

**divorce,** di-**worss,** *n* Scheidung *f; v* sich scheiden lassen (von); **–d,** *adj* geschieden

**divulge,** dei-**waldsch,** *v* preisgeben

**DIY,** die ei u'ei, *abbr* do-it-yourself

**dizzy,** dis-i, *adj* schwindlig

**DJ,** die djschei, *abbr* disc jockey

**do,** duh, *v* tun, machen; (clean) putzen; (be suitable) passen; (be adequate) reichen; **– up,** (fasten) zumachen; (renovate) renovieren; **– without,** ohne auskommen; **can/could – with;** brauchen können; **he's –ing well/badly;** es geht ihm gut/schlecht; **how do you – ?** Guten Tag; **make – (with);** auskommen (mit)

**docile,** doh-sseil, *adj* lenksam

**dock,** dock, *n* Dock *nt; law* Anklagebank *f; v* (of ship) anlegen; (of spaceship) docken; **–er**, n Hafenarbeiter m; **–s**, npl Hafen m; **–yard**, n Werft f

**doctor, dock**-ter, n (medical) Arzt m, Ärztin f; (title) Doktor m; v (evidence) verfälschen; (food, drink) etw beimischen

**document, dock**-ju-ment, n Urkunde f, Dokument nt; **–ary**, n (film) Dokumentarfilm m; adj urkundlich

**dodge, dodsch,** n Kniff m; v ausweichen

**dog, dogg,** n Hund m; **– collar**, n Hundehalsband nt; (vicar's) Kragen m

**dogged, dogg-idd,** adj hartnäckig

**dogmatic, dogg-mätt-ick,** adj dogmatisch

**do-it-yourself, duh itt yor-self,** n Do-it-yourself nt

**dole, dohl,** n fam Stempelgeld nt; **be on the –**, v fam stempeln gehen; **– out**, v austeilen

**doleful, dohl-full,** adj traurig

**doll, doll,** n Puppe f

**dollar, doll-er,** n Dollar m

**dolphin, doll-finn,** n Delphin m

**dome, dohm,** n Kuppel f

**domestic, de-mess-tick,** n Hausangestellte(r) m & f; adj Haus-; (not international) Innen-, Binnen-; **–ated**, adj

häuslich

**dominant, domm-i-nent,** adj dominierend

**dominate, domm-i-neht,** v beherrschen

**domineering, domm-i-nier-ring,** adj tyrannisch

**dominion, de-minn-jen,** n (territory) Staatsgebiet nt

**donate, doh-neht,** v spenden

**donation, doh-neh-sch'n,** n Spende f

**donkey, dong-ki,** n Esel m

**donor, doh-ner,** n Spender m

**doodle, duh-d'l,** v kritzeln

**doom, duhm,** n Verhängnis nt; **be –ed**, v verdammt sein; **Doomsday,** n jüngster Tag m

**door, dor,** n Tür f; **–bell,** n Türklingel f; **on the –step,** fig direkt vor der Tür; **–way,** n Eingang m

**dope, dohp,** n fam Rauschgift nt; sport Aufputschmittel nt; v dopen; **–y,** adj (stupid) bekloppt; (sleepy) benebelt

**dormant, dor-ment,** adj ruhend

**dormitory, dor-mi-tri,** n Schlafsaal m; **– town,** n Schlafstadt f

**dosage, doh-ssidsch,** n Dosierung f

**dose, dohss,** n Dosis f

**dot, dott,** n Punkt m; **–ted,** adj (line) punktiert;

(scattered) verstreut; (patterned) übersät; **on the –,** pünktlich

**double, dabb-'l,** adj & adv doppelt; n Doppelte nt; (likeness) Doppelgänger m; v (sich) verdoppeln; **–bass,** n Kontrabaß m; **–bed,** n Doppelbett nt; **–cross,** v hintergehen; **–room,** n Doppelzimmer nt; **–s,** npl (tennis) Doppel nt

**doubt, daut,** n Zweifel m; v bezweifeln; **–ful,** adj zweifelhaft; **–less,** adv ohne Zweifel

**dough, doh,** n Teig m; **–nut,** n Berliner m

**dove, daw,** n Taube f; **- -cot,** Taubenschlag m

**dowdy, dau-di,** adj altmodisch

**down, daun,** adv & prep herunter, hinunter; n (feathers) Flaum m; **–and-out,** n Tramp m; **–cast,** adj niedergeschlagen; **–fall,** n Sturz m; **–hill,** adv bergab; **–pour,** n Platzregen m; **Downs,** npl (hills) Hügelland nt; **–stairs,** adv (nach) unten; **–-to-earth,** adj praktisch; **–wards,** adv abwärts, nach unten

**doze, dohs,** n Nickerchen nt; v dösen; **– off,** einnicken

**dozen, das-en,** n Dutzend nt

**drab, dräbb,** adj langweilig

**draft, drahft,** n (rough) Entwurf m; fin Wechsel m;

*v* entwerfen

**drag**, drägg, *v* (object) schleppen; (behind) hinterherhinken; *n fam* Plage *f*; **in –**, in Frauenkleidung

**dragon**, drägg-en, *n* Drache *m*; **–fly**, Libelle *f*

**drain**, drehn, *n* Abfluß *m*; *fig* Belastung *f*; *v* (land) entwässern; (vegetables) abtropfen lassen; (resources) auslaugen; **–age**, *n* Kanalisation *f*; **– away**, *v* (of liquid) ablaufen

**drama**, drah-me, *n* Drama *nt*

**dramatic**, dre-**mätt**-ick, *adj* dramatisch

**drastic**, **dräss**-tick, *adj* drastisch

**draught**, drahft, *adj* (beer) vom Faß *n*; (air) Zug *m*; (drink) Schluck *m*; (sketch) Entwurf *m*; *naut* Tiefgang *m*; **–board**, Damebrett *nt*; **–s,** *pl* Damespiel *nt*

**draughtsman**, drahfts-men, *n* Zeichner *m*

**draw**, dro'a, *n* (lottery) Ziehung *f*; (tie) unentschiedenes Spiel *nt*; *v* (pull) ziehen; (sketch) zeichnen; (crowd) anlocken; (money) abheben; (cheque) ausstellen; **–back**, *n* Nachteil *m*

**drawer**, dro'a, *n* (furniture) Schublade *f*; (bill)

Aussteller *m*; **–s**, *npl* Unterhosen *pl*

**drawing**, dro'a-ing, *n* (picture) Zeichnung *f*; (act) Zeichnen *nt*; **– room**, Salon *m*

**drawl**, dro'al, *v* schleppend sprechen

**dread**, dredd, *n* Furcht *f*; *v* fürchten; **–ful**, *adj* furchtbar

**dream**, driem, *n* Traum *m*; *v* träumen; **–y**, *adj* verträumt

**dreary**, drier-ri, *adj* (dull) trüb; (boring) langweilig

**dredge**, dredsch, *v* ausbaggern; **–r**, *n* Bagger *m*

**dregs**, dreggs, *npl* (Boden)satz *m*; *fig* Abschaum *m*

**drench**, drentsch, *v* durchnässen

**dress**, dress, *n* (garment) Kleid *nt*; (clothing) Kleidung *f*; *v* (sich) anziehen; (wound) verbinden; **get –ed**, *v* sich anziehen; **–ing**, *n med* Verband *m*; (cooking) (Salat)soße *f*, Dressing *nt*; **–ing gown**, *n* Bademantel *m*; **–ing room,** *n* (in house) Ankleidezimmer *nt*; *sport* Umkleideraum *m*; *theatre* Garderobe *f*; **– table**, *n* Toilettentisch *m*; **–maker**, *n* (Damen)schneider *m*; **– up**, *v* (smart) sich feinmachen; (disguise) sich verkleiden

**dribble**, dribb-'l, *v* (saliva) sabbern; *sport* dribbeln (mit)

**drift**, drift, *n* (current) Strömung *f*; (snow etc.) Wehe *f*; (tendency) Richtung *f*; *v* treiben; *fig* sich treiben lassen

**drill**, drill, *n mil* Drill *m*; (tool) Bohrer *m*; *v mil* exerzieren; (bore) bohren

**drink**, drink, *n* Getränk, *nt*; *v* trinken; **–ing water**, *n* Trinkwasser *nt*

**drip**, dripp, *n* Tropfen *nt*; *v* tropfen; **–ping,** *n* Bratenfett *nt*

**drive**, dreiw, *n* (journey) Fahrt *f*; (approach) Einfahrt *f*; (energy) Schwung *m*; *v* (set in motion) treiben; (vehicle) fahren; (machine) antreiben; *v* –**r**, *n* Fahrer *m*; **disk/CD-ROM –**, *n* Disketten-/CD-ROM-Laufwerk *nt*

**drivel**, driw-'l, *n fam* Blödsinn *m*

**driving licence**, drei-wing lei-ssenss, *n* Führerschein *m*

**drizzle**, dris-'l, *n* Nieselregen *m*; *v* nieseln

**droll**, drohl, *adj* drollig

**drone**, drohn, *n* (of bee) Summen *nt*; (of engine) Brummen *nt*; *v* summen; brummen

**droop**, druhp, *v* (of eyelids) herunterhängen; (of head) hängen lassen; (of plant) verwelken

**drop,** dropp, n (fall) Fall m; (of liquid) Tropfen m; v (fall) fallen; (let fall) fallen lassen; – **off,** v einschlafen; –**out,** n Aussteiger m

**drought,** draut, n Dürre f

**drown,** draun, v (be drowned) ertrinken; (cause to drown) ertränken

**drowsy,** drau-si, adj schläfrig

**drudgery,** dradsch-e-ri, n Schufterei f

**drug,** dragg, n med Medikament nt; (addictive) Droge f; v betäuben; – **addict,** n Rauschgiftsüchtige(r) m & f

**drum,** dramm, n Trommel f; v trommeln; –**s,** npl Schlagzeug nt; –**mer,** n Trommler m; – **up,** v auftreiben

**drunk,** drank, adj betrunken; n Säufer m; –**ard,** n Trinker m; –**enness,** Betrunkenheit f

**dry,** drei, adj trocken; v trocknen; – **cleaning,** n chemische Reinigung f; – **up,** v (of well etc.) austrocknen; (dishes) abtrocknen

**dual,** djuh-el, adj doppelt; – **carriageway,** n zweispurige Fahrbahn f

**dubious,** djuh-bi-ess, adj

zweifelhaft

**duchess,** datsch-ess, n Herzogin f

**duck,** dack, n Ente f; v sich ducken

**dud,** dadd, adj fam (cheque) ungedeckt; (bad) mies; n (blank, person) Niete f

**due,** djuh, n (share) Anteil m; (rights) Recht nt; adj (owing) fällig; (fitting) gebührend; – **east,** adv nach Osten, östlich; – **to,** prep wegen

**duel,** djuh-el, n Duell nt; v sich duellieren

**dues,** djuhs, npl Gebühren fpl

**duet,** dju-ett, n Duett nt

**duke,** djuhk, n Herzog m

**dull,** dall, adj (weather, colour) trüb; (boring) langweilig; (metal) matt; (sound, pain) dumpf

**duly,** djuh-li, adv (properly) gebührend; (officially) ordnungsgemäß

**dumb,** damm, adj stumm; (fam stupid) doof; –**founded,** adj verblüfft

**dummy,** damm-i, n (mannequin) Schaufensterpuppe f; (fake) Attrappe f; (cards) Strohmann m; (baby's) Schnuller m; – **run,** n Probe f

**dump,** damp, n Müllplatz m; (pej place) Kaff nt; –**ing,** n Schuttabladen nt; (comm of exports) Dumping nt

**dumpling,** damp-ling, n Kloß m, Knödel m

**dune,** djuhn, n Düne f

**dung,** dang, n Dung m, Dünger m

**dungarees,** dang-ge-ries, npl Latzhose f

**dungeon,** dann-dschen, n Verließ nt

**dupe,** djuhp, n Angeführte(r) m & f; v anführen

**duplicate,** djuh-pli-ket, adj doppelt; n Duplikat nt

**duplicate,** djuh-pli-keht, v (repeat) wiederholen; (make copies) kopieren, vervielfältigen

**durable,** djur-re-b'l, adj (lasting) dauerhaft; (hardwearing) strapazierfähig

**duration,** djur-reh-sch'n, n Dauer f

**duress,** djur-ress, n under –, unter Zwang

**during,** djur-ring, prep während

**dusk,** dask, n Dämmerung f

**dust,** dast, n Staub m; v abstauben; (cooking) bestäuben; –**bin,** n Mülleimer m; –**er,** n Staubtuch nt; –**man,** n Müllmann m; –**y,** adj staubig

**Dutch,** datsch, adj holländisch, niederländisch; n (language) Niederländisch nt; npl (people) Holländer pl, Niederländer pl; –**man,**

n Holländer *m*,
Niederländer *m*
**dutiful, djuh**-ti-full, *adj*
pflichtbewußt
**duty, djuh**-ti, *n* Pflicht *f*;
(tax) Zoll *m*; **on –**, im
Dienst
**duvet, duh**-weh/**djuh**-weh,
*n* Federbett *nt*
**dwarf,** du'orf, *n* Zwerg *m*; *v*
überragen
**dwell,** duell, *v* wohnen; **–er**,
*n* Bewohner *m*; **–ing**,
Wohnung *f*; **– on**, grübeln
über
**dwindle, du'inn**-d'l, *v*
schwinden, abnehmen
**dye,** dei, *n* Farbstoff *m*; *v*
färben
**dying, dei**-ing, *adj* (person)
sterbend; (species)
aussterbend
**dynamic,** dei-**nämm**-ick, *adj*
dynamisch
**dynamite, dei**-ne-meit, *n*
Dynamit *nt*
**dynamo, dei**-ne-moh, *n*
Dynamo *m*
**dyslexia,** diss-**leck**-ssi-*e*, *n*
Legasthenie *f*
**dyslexic,** diss-**leck**-ssick, *adj*
legasthenisch; *n*
Legastheniker *m*

**each,** ietsch, *adj & pron*
jede(r/s); **– other,** uns/sich
(gegenseitig), einander;
**two –,** je zwei

**eager(ly),** ie-ger, *adj & adv*
eifrig; **–ness,** n Eifer m

**eagle,** ie-g'l, n Adler m

**ear,** ier, n Ohr nt; (of wheat)
Ähre f

**earl,** örl, n Graf m

**early,** ör-li, *adj & adv* früh

**earmark,** ier-mark, v
bestimmen

**earn,** örn, v verdienen

**earnest,** ör-nist, *adj*
ernsthaft; n Ernst m; **in –,**
im Ernst

**earnings,** ör-nings, *npl*
Verdienst m

**earphones,** ier-fohns, *npl*
Kopfhörer m

**earring,** ier-ring, n
Ohrring m

**earshot,** ier-schott, n

**(with)in –** in Hörweite f

**earth,** örth, n Erde f; v
(electricity) erden;
**–enware,** n Steingut nt;
**–ly,** *adj* irdisch; **no –
reason,** *fam* nicht der
geringste Grund

**earthquake,** örth-ku'ehk, n
Erdbeben nt

**earwig,** ier-u'igg, n
Ohrwurm m

**ease,** ies, n (comfort)
Behagen nt; (simplicity)
Leichtigkeit f; v (pain)
lindern; (mind, task)
erleichtern; **at (one's) –,**
ungezwungen

**easel,** ie-s'l, n Staffelei f

**easily,** ie-si-li, *adv* leicht

**east,** iest, *adj* östlich, Ost-;
*adv* östlich, nach Osten; n
Osten m

**Easter,** iess-ter, *adj* Oster-; n
Ostern nt

**easterly,** iess-ter-li, *adj*
östlich

**eastern,** iess-tern, *adj*
östlich, Ost-; orientalisch

**easy,** ie-si, *adj & adv*
(simple) leicht; (relaxed)
ungezwungen; **– chair,** n
Sessel m; **––going,** *adj*
gelassen

**eat,** iet, v essen; (of animals)
fressen; **– away,** (corrode)
zerfressen; **– into,**
(corrode) zerfressen; (use
up) angreifen

**eavesdrop,** iews-dropp, v
lauschen; **–er,** n Horcher
m; **– on,** v belauschen

**ebb,** ebb, n Ebbe f; **–
(away),** v abebben

**ebony,** ebb-e-ni, n
Ebenholz nt

**ebullient,** i-ball-jent, *adj*
übersprudelnd

**eccentric,** ek-ssent-rick,
*adj* exzentrisch; n
Exzentriker m

**ecclesiastical,** eck-lie-si-äss-
tick-'l, *adj* kirchlich

**echo,** eck-oh, n Echo nt; v
widerhallen

**eclipse,** i-klipss, n Finsternis
f; v verfinstern

**ecology,** i-koll-e-dschi, n
Ökologie f

**economic,** ie-ke-nomm-ick,
*adj* wirtschaftlich,
Wirtschafts-; **–al,** *adj*
wirtschaftlich; (thrifty)
sparsam; **–s,** n
Volkswirtschaft f

**economize,** i-konn-e-meis, v

sparen

**economy**, i-**konn**-*e*-mi, *n* Wirtschaft *f*; (saving) Sparmaßnahme *f*; (thrift) Sparsamkeit *f*

**ecstasy**, **eck**-ste-ssi, *n* Ekstase *f*, Verzückung *f*; (drug) Ecstasy *f*

**eczema**, **eck**-si-me, *n* Ekzem *nt*

**eddy**, **edd**-i, *n* Wirbel *m*; *v* wirbeln

**edge**, edsch, *n* (of knife) Schneide *f*; (brink) Rand *m*; *v* (border) einfassen; (move carefully) sich vorsichtig bewegen; – **away**, sich davonstehlen

**edgy**, **edsch**-i, *adj* nervös

**edible**, **edd**-i-b'l, *adj* eßbar, genießbar

**edifice**, **edd**-i-fiss, *n* Gebäude *nt*

**edit**, **edd**-itt, *v* (text) redigieren; (film, tape) schneiden; (publish) herausgeben; –**ion**, *n* Ausgabe *f*; (of book) Auflage *f*; –**or**, *n* Redakteur *m*; –**orial**, *adj* Redaktions-; *n* Leitartikel *m*

**educate**, **edd**-ju-keht, *v* (aus)bilden; (child) erziehen

**education**, ed-ju-**keh**-sch'n, *n* Erziehung *f*; (Aus)bildung *f*; –**al**, *adj* pädagogisch, Erziehungs-

**eel**, iel, *n* Aal *m*

**eerie**, **ier**-ri, *adj* unheimlich

**efface**, eff-**ehss**, *v* auswischen; *fig* tilgen

**effect**, eff-**ekt**, *n* Wirkung *f*; *v* bewirken; –**ive**, *adj* wirksam; **in** –, eigentlich; **take** –, *v* in Kraft treten

**effeminate**, eff-**emm**-i-net, *adj* unmännlich

**effervescent**, eff-er-**wess**-'nt, *adj* sprudelnd

**efficacious**, eff-i-**keh**-schess, *adj* wirksam

**efficiency**, eff-**isch**-en-ssi, *n* Leistungsfähigkeit *f*

**efficient**, eff-**isch**-n't, *adj* (person) tüchtig; (machine) leistungsfähig

**effort**, **eff**-ert, *n* Anstrengung *f*; –**less(ly)**, *adj & adv* mühelos; **make an** –, *v* sich anstrengen

**effrontery**, eff-**rann**-te-ri, *n* Unverschämtheit *f*

**effusive**, eff-**juh**-ssiw, *adj* überschwenglich

**e.g.**, ie dschie, *abbr*, z.B.

**egalitarian**, egg-äll-i-**tähr**-ri-en, *adj* egalitär, Gleichheits-

**egg**, egg, *n* Ei *nt*; –-**cup**, Eierbecher *m*; – **on**, *v fam* anstacheln

**ego**, ie-goh, *n* Ich *nt*; (self-confidence) Selbstbewußtsein *nt*

**egotism**, **egg**-*e*-tism, *n* Ichbezogenheit *f*

**egotist**, **egg**-*e*-tist, *n* Egozentriker *m*

**Egypt**, ie-dschipt, *n* Ägypten *n*

**eiderdown**, ei-der-daun, *n* Federbett *nt*

**eight**, eht, *num* acht; –**een**, *num* achtzehn; –**h**, *adj* achte(r/s); *n* Achtel *nt*; –**y**, *num* achtzig

**Eire**, **ähr**-re, *n* Irland *nt*

**either**, ei-dher, *adj & pron* eine(r/s) von beiden; *adv* (in negatives) auch nicht; *conj* – ... **or** ..., entweder ... oder ...

**eject**, i-**dscheckt**, *v* ausstoßen, hinauswerfen

**elaborate**, i-**läbb**-*e*-ret, *adj* kompliziert; (detailed) sorgfältig ausgearbeitet

**elaborate**, i-**läbb**-*e*-reht, *v* (work out) ausarbeiten; (describe) ausführen

**elapse**, i-**läpps**, *v* vergehen

**elastic**, i-**läss**-tick, *n* Gummiband *nt*; *adj* elastisch; – **band**, *n* Gummiband *nt*

**elated**, i-**leh**-tidd, *adj* freudig erregt

**elbow**, **ell**-boh, *n* Ellbogen *m*; – **one's way through**, *v* sich durchdrängen

**elder**, **ell**-der, *adj* ältere(r/s); *n* Ältere(r) *m & f*; (tree) Holunder *m*; –**ly**, *adj* ältlich, ältere(r/s); *npl* Älteren *pl*

**eldest**, **ell**-dist, *adj* älteste(r/s); *n* Älteste(r) *m & f*

**elect**, i-**lekt**, *adj* designiert; *v* wählen; –**ion**, *n* Wahl *f*; –**or**, *n* Wähler *m*; –**orate**, *n* Wählerschaft *f*

**electric(al),** i-leck-trick(-'l), *adj* elektrisch, Elektro-; – **blanket,** *n* Heizdecke *f*

**electrician,** i-leck-trisch-'n, *n* Elektriker *m*

**electricity,** i-leck-**triss**-i-ti, *n* Elektrizität *f*

**electrify,** i-leck-tri-fei, *v* elektrifizieren; *fig* elektrisieren

**electrocute,** i-leck-tre-kjuht, *v* durch Stromschlag töten

**electronic,** i-leck-**tronn**-ick, *adj* elektronisch; – **mail,** *n* E-Mail *f*; –**s,** *n* Elektronik *f*

**elegance,** ell-i-genss, *n* Eleganz *f*

**elegant,** ell-i-gent, *adj* elegant

**element,** ell-i-ment, *n* Element *nt*; –**ary,** *adj* elementar; (simple) einfach; (basic) Grund-

**elephant,** ell-i-fent, *n* Elefant *m*

**elevate,** ell-i-weht, *v* erhöhen; *fig* erheben

**eleven,** i-lew-en, *num* elf; –**th,** *adj* elfte(r/s)

**elf,** elf, *n* (*pl* **elves**), Elfe *f*, Kobold *m*

**elicit,** i-liss-itt, *v* entlocken

**eligible,** ell-i-dschi-b'l, *adj* (electable) wählbar; (entitled) berechtigt

**eliminate,** i-limm-i-neht, *v* ausscheiden

**elite,** i-liet, *n* Elite *f*

**elm,** elm, *n* Ulme *f*

**elongated,** ie-long-geh-tidd, *adj* langgestreckt

**elope,** i-lohp, *v* durchbrennen; –**ment,** *n* Durchbrennen *nt*

**eloquence,** ell-*e*-ku'enss, *n* Beredtheit *f*

**eloquent,** ell-*e*-ku'ent, *adj* beredt

**else,** elss, *adv* andere(r/s), sonst; **or –,** *conj* sonst, oder

**elsewhere,** elss-u'ähr, *adv* woanders(hin), sonstwo(hin)

**elucidate,** i-luh-ssi-deht, *v* erläutern; (mystery) aufklären

**elude,** i-luhd, *v* entkommen

**elusive,** i-luhss-iw, *adj* schwer faßbar; (vague) ausweichend

**emaciated,** i-meh-ssi-eh-tidd, *adj* abgezehrt

**e-mail,** ie-mehl, *n* (*abbr* **electronic mail**), E-Mail *f*

**emanate (from),** emm-*e*-neht (frem), *v* (flow out) ausströmen (von); (originate) stammen aus

**emancipate,** i-männ-ssi-peht, *v* emanzipieren; (slave) freilassen

**embalm,** im-bahm, *v* einbalsamieren

**embankment,** im-bänk-ment, *n* (river) Uferböschung *f*; (road) Straßendamm *m*; (railway) Bahndamm *m*

**embargo,** im-bar-goh, *n* Embargo *nt*

**embark,** im-bark, *v* (sich) einschiffen; – **on,** *fig* anfangen

**embarrass,** im-bä-ress, *v* in Verlegenheit bringen; –**ed,** *adj* verlegen; –**ing,** *adj* peinlich; –**ment,** *n* Verlegenheit *f*

**embassy,** emm-be-ssi, *n* Botschaft *f*

**embedded,** imm-**bedd**-idd, *adj* verankert

**embellish,** emm-bell-isch, *v* verschönern

**embers,** emm-bers, *npl* Glut *f*

**embezzle,** imm-bes-'l, *v* unterschlagen, veruntreuen; –**ment,** *n* Unterschlagung *f*

**embitter,** imm-bitt-er, *v* verbittern

**embody,** imm-bodd-i, *v* (personify) verkörpern; (include) aufnehmen

**embrace,** imm-brehss, *v* (hug) umarmen; (contain) umfassen

**embroider,** imm-breu-der, *v* (be)sticken; *fig* ausschmücken; –**y,** *n* Stickerei *f*

**embroiled (in),** imm-breuld (inn) *adj* verwickelt (in)

**emerald,** emm-*e*-reld, *n* Smaragd *m*

**emerge,** i-mördsch, *v* auftauchen; (truth) sich herausstellen

**emergency,** i-mör-dschen-ssi, n Notfall m; **– exit,** n Notausgang m; **– landing,** n Notlandung f

**emetic,** i-mett-ick, n Brechmittel nt

**emigrant,** emm-i-grent, n Auswanderer m

**emigrate,** emm-i-greht, v auswandern

**eminence,** emm-i-nenss, n (distinction) hoher Rang m; (title) Eminenz f

**eminent,** emm-i-nent, adj (hoch)angesehen

**emission,** i-misch-'n, n (of rays) Ausstrahlung f; (of heat, smoke) Abgabe f; (of gas) Ausströmen nt; **–s,** npl Emissionen pl

**emit,** i-mitt, v ausstrahlen; abgeben; ausströmen

**emotion,** i-moh-sch'n, n Gefühl nt; **–al,** adj emotional; (moving) gefühlsgeladen; (person) leicht erregbar

**emperor,** emm-pe-rer, n Kaiser m

**emphasis,** emm-fe-ssiss, n Betonung f, Nachdruck m

**emphasize,** emm-fe-sseis, v betonen

**emphatic(ally),** emm-fätt-ick-(e-li), adj & adv nachdrücklich

**empire,** emm-peir, n Reich nt

**employ,** imm-pleu, v (person) beschäftigen; (use) anwenden; **–ee,** n

Angestellte(r) m & f; **–er,** n Arbeitgeber m; **–ment,** n Beschäftigung f; (post) Arbeitsstelle f

**empower,** imm-pau-er, v ermächtigen

**empress,** emm-priss, n Kaiserin f

**emptiness,** emp-ti-niss, n Leere f

**empty,** emp-ti, adj leer; v leeren; (drain away) abfließen; (become empty) sich leeren

**emulate,** emm-ju-leht, v nachstreben

**emulation,** emm-ju-leh-sch'n, n Nacheiferung f

**enable,** i-neh-b'l, v – sb to do sth, es jdm ermöglichen, etw zu tun

**enact,** i-näckt, v (play) aufführen; (role) spielen; law erlassen

**enamel,** i-nämm-'l, n Email nt; (tooth) Zahnschmelz m; v emaillieren

**encased (in),** inn-kehst (inn), adj eingeschlossen (in)

**enchant,** inn-tschahnt, v bezaubern, entzücken; **–ing,** adj bezaubernd, entzückend

**enchantment,** inn-tschahnt-ment, n Entzücken nt

**encircle,** inn-ssör-k'l, v umgeben, umfassen

**enclose,** inn-klohs, v einschließen; (with letter)

beilegen; **–d,** adj & adv (with letter) beiliegend

**enclosure,** inn-kloh-scher, n (with letter) Anlage f; (fence) Umzäunung f; (for animals) Gehege nt

**encompass,** inn-kamm-pess, v umfassen

**encore,** ong-kohr, n Zugabe f

**encounter,** inn-kaun-ter, n Begegnung f; mil Zusammenstoß m; v treffen; (enemy, difficulties) stoßen auf

**encourage,** inn-ka-ridsch, v ermutigen; **–ment,** n Ermutigung f

**encouraging,** inn-ka-ridsching, adj ermutigend

**encroach on,** inn-krohtsch on, v (rights) eingreifen in; (time) in Anspruch nehmen

**encrusted (with),** inn-krass-tidd (u'idh), adj besetzt (mit)

**encumbered,** inn-kamm-berd, adj – by, (clothes etc.) behindert durch; – with, (load) beladen mit; (debts etc.) belastet mit

**encumbrance,** inn-kamm-brenss, n (load) Last f; (responsibility) Belastung f

**encyclop(a)edia,** inn-sseik-le-pie-di-e, n (Konversations)lexikon nt

**end,** endd, n Ende nt; (conclusion) Schluß m; v

(be)enden; **–less**, *adj*
endlos; **– up**, *v* landen,
enden; **in the –**, zum
Schluß; **on –**, (upright)
hochkant; **for days on –**,
tagelang

**endanger**, inn-**dehn**-dscher,
*v* gefährden

**endear**, inn-**dier**, **– o.s. to
sb**, *v* sich bei jdm beliebt
machen; **–ing**, *adj* reizend

**endeavour**, inn-**dew**-er, *n*
Bemühung *f*; *v* sich
bemühen

**ending**, **enn**-ding, *n* Ende *nt*;
(of story) Ausgang *m*

**endive**, **enn**-diw, *n*
Endiviensalat *m*

**endorse**, inn-**dorss**, *v* (sign)
unterzeichnen; (approve)
billigen; **–ment**, *n*
(approval) Billigung *f*; (on
driving licence)
Strafvermerk *m*

**endow**, inn-**dau**, *v* (pay for)
stiften; **– sb with**,
(money) jdm etw stiften;
(gift) jdm etw schenken

**endurance**, inn-**djuhr**-renss,
*n* Ausdauer *f*

**endure**, inn-**djuhr**, *v*
aushalten, ertragen

**enema**, **enn**-i-me, *n*
Einlauf *m*

**enemy**, **enn**-i-mi, *adj*
feindlich; *n* Feind *m*

**energetic**, enn-er-**dschett**-
ick, *adj* aktiv, tatkräftig

**energy**, **enn**-er-dschi, *n*
Energie *f*

**enforce**, inn-**forss**, *v*

(obedience) erzwingen;
(the law) durchsetzen

**engage**, inn-**gehdsch**, *v*
(employ) anstellen; *mil*
angreifen; *mech*
einschalten; **– sb in
conversation**, jdn in ein
Gespräch verwickeln; **– in**,
(take part) sich beteiligen
an

**engaged**, inn-**gehdschd**, *adj*
(to marry) verlobt; (busy)
beschäftigt; (toilet,
telephone) besetzt; ; **get –**,
*v* sich verloben

**engagement**, inn-**gehdsch**-
ment, *n* (appointment)
Verabredung *f*; (to
marry) Verlobung *f*; *mil*
Gefecht *nt*

**engaging**, inn-**geh**-dsching,
*adj* gewinnend

**engender**, inn-**dschen**-der, *v*
erzeugen

**engine**, **enn**-dschinn, *n*
Maschine *f*; (car) Motor
*m*; *rail* Lokomotive *f*

**engineer**, enn-dschi-**nier**, *n*
Ingenieur *m*; *v* (contrive)
arrangieren; **–ing**, *n*
Technik *f*; (trade)
Ingenieurswesen *nt*

**England**, **ing**-glend, *n*
England *nt*

**English**, **ing**-glisch, *adj*
englisch; *n* (language)
Englisch *nt*; **the –**, *npl* die
Engländer *pl*; **the –
Channel**, *n* der
Armelkanal *m*; **–man**, *n*
Engländer *m*; **–woman**, *n*

Engländerin *f*

**engraving**, inn-**greh**-wing, *n*
Stich *m*

**engrossed**, inn-**grohst**, *adj*
vertieft

**engulf**, inn-**galf**, *v*
verschlingen

**enhance**, inn-**hahnss**, *v*
steigern

**enigma**, i-**nigg**-me, *n* Rätsel
*nt*

**enjoy**, inn-**dscheu**, *v*
genießen; **– o.s.**, sich
amüsieren; *n*
Vergnügen *nt*; (of rights
etc.) Genuß *m*

**enlarge**, inn-**lahrdsch**, *v*
vergrößern; **–ment**, *n*
Vergrößerung *f*

**enlighten**, inn-**lei-t'n**, *v*
aufklären; **–ment**, *n*
Aufklärung *f*

**enlist**, inn-**list**, *v mil* sich
melden; (support,
sympathy) gewinnen

**enliven**, inn-**lei**-wen, *v*
beleben

**enmity**, **enn**-mi-ti, *n*
Feindschaft *f*

**enormity**, i-**nor**-mi-ti, *n*
Ungeheuerlichkeit *f*

**enormous(ly)**, i-**nor**-mess(-
li), *adj & adv* enorm,
ungeheuer

**enough**, i-**naff**, *adj*
genügend, genug; *adv*
genug; **be –**, *v* reichen

**enquire**, inn-**ku'eir**, *see*
**inquire**

**enrage**, inn-**rehdsch**, *v*
wütend machen

**enrol,** inn-**rohl,** v (sich)
einschreiben; (for course)
sich anmelden **–ment,** n
Einschreibung f;
Anmeldung f

**ensign,** inn-ssein, n (naval
flag) Flagge f; (rank)
Fähnrich m

**enslave,** inn-**sslehw,** v zum
Sklaven machen

**ensue,** inn-**sjuh,** v (darauf)
folgen

**entail,** inn-**tehl,** v mit sich
bringen

**entangle,** inn-**täng-g'l,** v
verfangen; fig verstricken;
**become –d (in),** sich
verwickeln; sich
verfangen in; fig sich
verstricken in

**enter,** enn-ter, v (walk into,
join) eintreten (in);
(competition) sich
melden (zu); (in book)
eintragen; **– into,**
(discussions) eingehen;
(calculations) eine Rolle
spielen bei

**enterprise,** enn-ter-preis, n
(firm, project)
Unternehmen nt;
(initiative) Initiative f

**enterprising,** enn-ter-prei-
sing, adj (person)
unternehmungslustig;
(idea) kühn

**entertain,** enn-ter-**tehn,** v
(amuse) unterhalten;
(guest) bewirten;
(consider) erwägen; **–er,** n
Entertainer m; **–ing,** adj

unterhaltsam; **–ment,** n
Unterhaltung f

**enthrall,** inn-**thro'al,** v
fesseln

**enthusiasm,** inn-**thjuh**-si-
äs-em, n Begeisterung f

**enthusiast,** inn-**thjuh**-si-äst,
n Enthusiast m; **–ic,** adj
begeistert

**entice,** inn-**teiss,** v
verführen

**entire,** inn-**teir,** adj ganz;
**–ly,** adv völlig; **–ty,** n
Gesamtheit f

**entitled,** inn-**tei**-t'ld, adj
(book) mit dem Titel;
(person) berechtigt; **be –
(to),** v das Recht haben
(auf); (have a claim)
Anspruch haben auf

**entitlement (to),** inn-**tei**-t'l-
ment (tu), n Berechtigung
f (zu); Anspruch m (auf)

**entrance,** enn-trenss, n
Eingang m; (for vehicles)
Einfahrt f; (action)
Eintritt m; **– fee,** n
Eintrittsgeld nt

**entrance,** enn-**trahnss,** v
entzücken

**entrant,** enn-trent, n sport
Teilnehmer m; (for exam)
Kandidat m

**entreat,** inn-**triet,** v
anflehen

**entrenched,** inn-**trentscht,**
adj verwurzelt

**entrepreneur,** onn-tre-pre-
**nör,** n Unternehmer m

**entrust,** inn-**trast,** v **– to sb,**
jdm anvertrauen; **– sb**

**with,** jdn betrauen mit

**entry,** enn-tri, n (way in)
Eingang m, Einfahrt f;
(entering) Eintritt m,
Einfahrt f; (in book)
Eintrag m; (in account)
Eintragung f; **– form,** n
Anmeldeformular nt; **–
visa,** n Einreisevisum nt;
**no –,** Eintritt/Einfahrt
verboten

**enumerate,** i-**njuh**-me-reht,
v aufzählen

**envelop,** inn-**well**-ep, v
einhüllen

**envelope,** enn-we-lohp, n
Umschlag m

**enviable,** enn-wi-e-b'l, adj
beneidenswert

**envious,** enn-wi-ess, adj
neidisch

**environment,** inn-**weir**-ren-
ment, n (general) Umwelt
f; (local) Umgebung f; **–al,**
adj Umwelt-; **–ally
friendly,** adj
umweltfreundlich

**environs,** enn-**weir**-rens, npl
Umgebung f

**envisage,** inn-**wi**-sidsch, v
sich vorstellen

**envoy,** enn-weu, n
Gesandte(r) m & f

**envy,** enn-wi, n Neid m; v
beneiden

**ephemeral,** i-**femm**-e-rel, adj
flüchtig

**epic,** epp-ick, adj episch;
(achievement) gewaltig; n
Epos nt

**epidemic,** epp-i-**demm**-ick,

*n adj* epidemisch;
Epidemie *f*

**epilepsy, epp-i-lepp-ssi,** *n*
Epilepsie *f*

**epileptic, epp-i-lepp-tick,**
*adj* epileptisch; *n*
Epileptiker *m*

**episode, epp-i-ssohd,** *n* (of
story) Episode *f*;
(incident) Begebenheit *f*

**epoch, ie-pock,** *n* Zeitalter
*nt*

**equal, ie-ku'el,** *n adj* gleich;
Gleichgestellte(r) *m & f*; *v*
gleichkommen; (maths)
gleichen

**equality, i-ku'oll-i-ti,**
*n* Gleichheit *f*;
(equal rights)
Gleichberechtigung *f*

**equalize, ie-ku'e-leis,** *v*
gleich machen; *sport*
ausgleichen

**equally, ie-ku'e-li,** *adv* gleich

**equate (with), i-ku'eht**
(u'idh), *v* gleichsetzen

**equation, i-ku'eh-sch'n,** *n*
Gleichung *f*

**equator, i-kueh-ter,** *n*
Äquator *m*

**equilibrium, ie-ku'i-libb-ri-**
em, *n* Gleichgewicht *nt*

**equinox, ie-ku'i-nocks,** *n*
Tagundnachtgleiche *f*

**equip, i-ku'ipp,** *v* ausrüsten;
**–ment,** *n* Ausrüstung *f*,
Ausstattung *f*;
(implements) Geräte *pl*

**equitable, eck-u'i-te-b'l,** *adj*
(just) gerecht; (fair) billig

**equity, eck-u'i-ti,** *n*

Gerechtigkeit *f*;
Billigkeit *f*

**equivalent, i-ku'iw-e-lent,**
*adj* (equal) gleichwertig;
(similar) entsprechend;
*n* (counterpart)
Gegenstück *nt*; (in
value) Gegenwert *m*

**equivocal, i-ku'iw-e-k'l,** *adj*
zweideutig

**era, ier-re,** *n* Epoche *f*

**eradicate, i-rädd-i-keht,** *v*
ausrotten

**erase, i-rehs,** *v* ausradieren;
(from tape, *comp*) löschen;
**–r,** *n* Radiergummi *m/nt*

**erect, i-rekt,** *adj* aufrecht; *v*
(building) errichten;
(sign, furniture, system)
aufstellen

**erection, i-reck-sch'n,** *n*
Errichten *nt*; Aufstellen
*nt*; (of penis) Erektion *f*

**ergonomics, ör-ge-nomm-**
icks, *n* Ergonomie *f*

**erode, i-rohd,** *v* (land)
auswaschen; (rock)
verwittern; (confidence)
untergraben

**erotic, i-rott-ick,** *adj*
erotisch

**err, örr,** *v* sich irren

**errand, e-rend,** *n*
Besorgung *f*

**erratic, i-rätt-ick,** *adj*
(unreliable)
unberechenbar; (irregular)
unregelmäßig

**erroneous, i-roh-ni-ess,** *adj*
irrig

**error, e-rer,** *n* Fehler *m*

**erupt, i-rapt,** *v* ausbrechen;
**–ion,** *n* Ausbruch *m*

**escalate, ess-ke-leht,** *v mil*
(sich) ausweiten; (costs)
(sich) schnell erhöhen

**escalator, ess-ke-leh-ter,** *n*
Rolltreppe *f*

**escape, iss-kehp,** *n* Flucht *f*;
(of gas) Ausströmen *nt*; *v*
entkommen, fliehen

**escort, ess-kort,** *n* (guard)
Eskorte *f*; (companion)
Begleiter *m*

**escort, ess-kort,** *v* begleiten;
*mil* eskortieren

**especially, iss-pesch-e-li,** *adv*
besonders

**espionage, ess-pi-e-nahsch,**
*n* Spionage *f*

**essay, ess-eh,** *n* Aufsatz *m*

**essence, ess-enss,** *n* (nature)
Wesen *nt*; (core)
Wesentliche(s) *nt*;
(extract) Essenz *f*

**essential, i-ssenn-sch'l,** *adj*
(fundamental) wesentlich;
(necessary) unbedingt
nötig; **–ly,** *adv* im
wesentlichen

**establish, iss-täbb-lisch,** *v*
(set up) gründen;
(determine) feststellen;
**–ed,** *adj* (belief,
government) herrschend;
(truth, method)
anerkannt; **–ment,** *n*
(institution) Anstalt *f*;
(setting up) Einrichtung *f*;
**the Establishment,**
Establishment *nt*

**estate, iss-teht,** *n* (land) Gut

nt; (of deceased) Nachlaß m; (housing) Siedlung f; – **agent,** n Grundstücksmakler m; – **car,** n Kombiwagen m

**esteem,** iss-**tiem,** n (opinion) Achtung f; (good opinion) Wertschätzung f; v schätzen

**estimate,** ess-ti-met, n Schätzung f; comm (of costs) (Kosten)-voranschlag m

**estimate,** ess-ti-meht, v schätzen

**estranged,** iss-**trehndschd,** adj entfremdet

**estuary,** ess-tju-e-ri, n Mündung f

**etc.,** abbr et cetera, usw.

**etching,** ett-tsching, n Kupferstich m

**eternal,** i-tör-n'l, adj ewig

**eternity,** i-tör-ni-ti, n Ewigkeit f

**ether,** ie-ther, n Äther m

**ethical,** i-ss-ick-'l, adj ethisch

**ethics,** eth-icks, n (study) Ethik f; npl (morality) Moral f

**ethnic,** eth-nick, adj ethnisch, Volks-; – **minority,** n ethnische Minderheit f

**etiquette,** ett-i-kett, n Etikette f

**EU,** ie juh, n (abbr **European Union**), EU f

**euphemism,** juh-fe-mism, n

**Euphemismus** m

**Euro,** juhr-ro, n Euro m

**Europe,** juhr-rep, n Europa nt; –**an,** adj europäisch; n Europäer m

**evacuate,** i-**wäck-**ju-eht, v (people) evakuieren; (place) räumen

**evade,** i-**wehd,** v (blow, question) ausweichen; (pursuer, justice) sich entziehen

**evaluate,** i-**wäll-**ju-eht, v bewerten

**evaporate,** i-wäpp-e-reht, v verdunsten; fig schwinden; –**d milk,** Kondensmilch f

**evasive,** i-weh-ssiw, adj ausweichend

**eve,** iew, n Vorabend m; **Christmas Eve,** n Heiligabend m

**even,** ie-wen, adj (surface) eben; (layer) gleichmäßig; (score) unentschieden; (number) gerade; adv sogar; – **if,** selbst wenn; **get – (with),** heimzahlen; – **though,** obwohl; – **out,** v (sich) ausgleichen

**evening,** iew-ning, n Abend m; – **class(es),** n(pl); Abendkurs m; – **dress,** n (man's) Gesellschaftsanzug m; (woman's) Abendkleid nt

**event,** i-went, n (incident) Ereignis nt; (function) Veranstaltung f; –**ful,** adj ereignisreich; **in the –,** im Endeffekt; **in the – of,** im

Falle

**eventual(ly),** i-went-ju-el(-i), adj & adv schließlich, zum Schluß

**ever,** ew-er, adv (always) immer; (at any time) je(mals); –**green,** adj immergrün; –**lasting,** adj ewig; – **since,** adv & conj seitdem; prep seit; **for – (and ever),** für immer; **not –,** nie(mals)

**every,** ew-ri, adj & pron jede(r/s); alle; –**body/one,** adj jeder(mann); –**day,** adj alltäglich, Alltags-; – **other,** jeder(r/s) zweite; –**thing,** alles; –**where,** adv überall

**evict,** i-wikt, v ausweisen

**eviction,** i-wick-sch'n, n Räumung f

**evidence,** ew-i-denss, n (proof) Beweis(e) m(pl.); (testimony) Aussage f

**evident,** ew-i-dent, adj offensichtlich

**evil,** ie-wil, n Böse nt; adj schlecht

**evoke,** i-wohk, v hervorrufen

**evolution,** ie-we-luh-sch'n, n (of life) Evolution f; (development) Entwicklung f

**evolve,** i-wolw, v (sich) entwickeln

**ewe,** juh, n Mutterschaf nt

**exacerbate,** ick-**säss-er-beht,** v verschlimmern

**exact,** igg-**säckt,** adj genau; v

fordern; **–ing**, *adj*;
anspruchsvoll; **–ly**, *adv*
genau

**exaggerate**, igg-**sädd**-dsche-
reht, *v* übertreiben

**exaggeration**, igg-**sädd**-
dsche-**reh**-sch'n, *n*
Übertreibung *f*

**exalted**, igg-**soll**-tidd, *adj*
(rank) hoch; (mood)
exaltiert

**exam**, igg-**sämm**, *n* (*abbr*
**examination**), (test)
Prüfung *f*

**examination**, igg-sämm-i-
**neh**-sch'n, *n* (test)
Prüfung *f*; (study, *med*)
Untersuchung *f*;
(inspection) Kontrolle *f*;
*law* Verhör *nt*

**examine**, igg-**sämm**-in, *v*
(test) prüfen; (study, *med*)
untersuchen; (inspect)
kontrollieren; *law*
verhören

**example**, igg-**sahm**-p'l, *n*
Beispiel, *nt*; **for –**, zum
Beispiel

**exasperate**, igg-**sahss**-pe-
reht, *v* zur Verzweiflung
bringen

**excavate**, **eks**-ke-veht, *v*
ausgraben

**exceed**, ick-**ssied**, *v*
überschreiten

**exceedingly**, ick-**ssie**-ding-li,
*adv* äußerst

**excel**, ick-**ssell**, *v* sich
auszeichnen

**excellence**, **eck**-sse-lenss, *n*
(quality/achievement)

hervorragende
Qualität/Leistung *f*;
Vortrefflichkeit *f*

**excellent**, **eck**-sse-lent, *adj*
ausgezeichnet, vortrefflich

**except**, ick-**ssept**, *prep*
außer; *v* ausnehmen; **–ion**,
*n* Ausnahme *f*; **take –ion
to**, *v* Anstoß nehmen an;
**–ional**, *adj*
außergewöhnlich

**excerpt**, **eck**-ssörpt, *n*
Auszug *m*

**excess**, ick-**ssess**, *n*
Übermaß *nt*; (charge)
Zuschlag *m*; **– baggage**, *n*
Mehrgepäck *nt*; **–ive**, *adj*
übermäßig, übertrieben

**exchange**, iks-**tschehndsch**,
*n* (of objects) Tausch *m*;
(of views, prisoners)
Austausch *m*; (telephone)
Zentrale *f*; *v* tauschen;
(money, letters) wechseln;
(views) austauschen; **–
rate**, Wechselkurs *m*

**Exchequer**, iks-**tscheck**-er, *n*
Schatzamt *nt*

**excise**, **eck**-sseis, *n*
Verbrauchssteuer *f*

**excise**, ick-**sseis**, *v*
herausschneiden

**excitable**, ick-**sseit**-e-b'l, *adj*
leicht erregbar

**excite**, ick-**sseit**, *v* erregen;
**–d**, aufgeregt; **–ment**, *n*
Aufregung *f*; **get –d
(about)**, *v* (annoyed) sich
aufregen (über);
(enthusiastic) sich (für
etw) begeistern

**exciting**, ick-**ssei**-ting, *adj*
aufregend; (story)
spannend

**exclaim**, iks-**klehm**, *v*
ausrufen

**exclamation**, eks-kle-**meh**-
sch'n, *n* Ausruf *m*; **–
mark**, *n* Ausrufezeichen *nt*

**exclude**, iks-**kluhd**, *v*
ausschließen

**exclusion**, iks-**kluh**-sch'n, *n*
Ausschluß *m*

**exclusive**, iks-**kluh**-ssiw, *adj*
(sole) ausschließlich;
(select) exklusiv; **–ly**, *adv*
ausschließlich

**excrement**, **eks**-kri-ment, *n*
Kot *m*

**excruciating**, iks-**kruh**-schi-
eh-ting, *adj* fürchterlich

**excursion**, iks-**kör**-sch'n, *n*
Ausflug *m*

**excuse**, iks-**kjuhss**,
*n* Ausrede *f*,
Entschuldigung *f*

**excuse**, iks-**kjuhs**, *v*
entschuldigen; **– me!**
Entschuldigung!

**execute**, **eck**-ssi-kjuht, *v*
(carry out) ausführen;
(put to death) hinrichten

**execution**, eck-ssi-**kjuh**-
sch'n, *n* Ausführung *f*;
Hinrichtung *f*; **–er**, *n*
Scharfrichter *m*

**executive**, igg-**seck**-ju-tiw,
*adj* Exekutiv-; *comm*
geschäftsführend; *n*
(government) Exekutive *f*;
*comm* Manager *m*

**executor**, igg-**seck**-ju-ter, *n*

Testamentsvollstrecker *m*
**exemplary,** igg-**semm**-ple-ri, *adj* musterhaft
**exemplify,** igg-**semm**-pli-fei, *v* erläutern
**exempt,** igg-**semmt,** *v* befreien; **–ion,** *n* Befreiung *f*
**exercise, eck**-sser-sseis, *n* Ubung *f*; (physical) Bewegung *f*; *v* üben; *mil* exerzieren; (power) ausüben; (take exercise) sich Bewegung verschaffen; **– book,** *n* Heft *nt*
**exert,** igg-**sört,** *v* ausüben; **- o.s.,** sich anstrengen; **–ion,** *n* Anstrengung *f*
**exhale, eks-hehl,** *v* ausatmen
**exhaust,** igg-**so'ast,** *v* erschöpfen; **–ed,** *adj* erschöpft; *n mech* Auspuff *m*; (gases) Abgase *pl*; **–ion,** *n* Erschöpfung *f*; **–ive,** *adj* umfassend
**exhibit,** igg-**sibb**-itt, *n* Ausstellungsstück *nt*; *v* ausstellen
**exhibition, eck**-ssi-**bisch**-'n, *n* Ausstellung *f*; (shop) Auslage *f*; **–ist,** *n* Exhibitionist *m*
**exhilarating,** igg-**sil**;-e-reh-ting, *adj* belebend, fröhlich stimmend
**exhort,** igg-**sort,** *v* ermahnen
**exile, eck**-sseil, *n* Exil *nt*, Verbannung *f*; (person)

Verbannte(r) *m & f*; *v* verbannen
**exist,** igg-**sist,** *v* existieren; **–ence,** *n* Existenz *f*; **–ing,** *adj* gegenwärtig
**exit, eck-**ssitt, *n* (way out) Ausgang *m*, Ausfahrt *f*; (departure) Abgang *m*; *v* hinausgehen
**exodus, eck**-sse-dess, *n* Auszug *m*
**exonerate,** igg-**sonn**-e-reht, *v* entlasten
**exorbitant,** igg-**sor**-bi-tent, *adj* übermäßig
**exotic,** igg-**sott**-ick, *adj* exotisch
**expand,** iks-**pänd,** *v* (sich) ausdehnen
**expanse,** iks-**pänss,** *n* Fläche *f*
**expansion,** iks-**pänn**-sch'n, *n* (physics) Ausdehnung *f*; (comm etc.) Erweiterung *f*
**expect,** iks-**pekt,** *v* (suppose) annehmen; (await, demand) erwarten; **–ant,** *adj* erwartungsvoll; **- mother,** *n* werdende Mutter *f*
**expectation,** eks-peck-**teh**-sch'n, *n* Erwartung *f*
**expedience, expediency,** iks-**pie**-di-enss, iks-**pie**-di-en-ssi, *n* Zweckdienlichkeit *f*
**expedient,** iks-**pie**-di-ent, *n* Hilfsmittel *nt*; *adj* zweckdienlich
**expedition,** eks-pi-**disch**-'n, *n* Expedition *f*
**expel,** iks-**pell,** *v* ausstoßen,

ausweisen
**expend,** iks-**pend,** *v* verwenden; **–iture,** *n* (spending) Ausgabe *f*; (money spent) Ausgaben *pl*
**expense,** iks-**penss,** *n* Kosten *pl*; **–s,** *npl* Unkosten *pl*; (account) Spesen *pl*
**expensive,** iks-**penn**-ssiw, *adj* teuer, kostspielig
**experience,** iks-**pier**-ri-enss, *n* (knowledge) Erfahrung *f*; (event) Erlebnis *nt*; *v* erleben; **–d,** *adj* erfahren
**experiment,** iks-pe-ri-ment, *n* Versuch *m*; *v* experimentieren
**expert, eks**-pört, *n* Fachmann *m*, Experte *m*, Expertin *f*; *adj* erfahren
**expertise,** eks-per-**ties,** *n* Sachverstand *m*
**expire,** iks-**peir,** *v* (run out) ablaufen; (die) versterben
**expiry,** iks-**peir**-ri, *n* Ablauf *m*
**explain,** iks-**plehn,** *v* erklären
**explanation,** eks-ple-**neh**-sch'n, *n* Erklärung *f*
**explanatory,** iks-**plänn**-e-te-ri, *n* erklärend
**explicit,** iks-**pli**-ssitt, *adj* deutlich
**explode,** iks-**plohd,** *v* explodieren; (cause to explode) sprengen
**exploit, eks**-pleut, *n* Heldentat *f*

**exploit**, iks-**pleut**, v (use) ausnutzen; (treat unfairly) ausbeuten

**exploratory**, iks-**plo**-re-te-ri, adj Probe-

**explore**, iks-**plor**, v erforschen

**explosion**, iks-**ploh**-sch'n, n Explosion f

**explosive**, iks-**ploh**-ssiw, adj explosiv; n Sprengstoff m

**export**, eks-**port**, adj Export-; n Export m

**export**, eks-**port**, v ausführen, exportieren; **–er**, n Exporteur m

**expose**, iks-**pohs**, v (to danger) aussetzen; (fraud etc.) aufdecken; (person) entlarven; photog belichten

**exposure**, iks-**poh**-scher, n (unmasking) Bloßstellung f, Entlarvung f; photog Belichtung f; med Unterkühlung f

**expound**, iks-**paund**, v auslegen, erläutern

**express**, iks-**press**, adj (fast) Eil-; (explicit) ausdrücklich; n rail Schnellzug m; v ausdrücken; **–ion**, n Ausdruck m; **–ive**, adj ausdrucksvoll; **–ly**, adv ausdrücklich; (by) –, per Expreß

**expulsion**, iks-**pall**-sch'n, n Ausweisung f

**exquisite**, iks-**ku'is**-itt, adj erlesen, köstlich

**extend**, iks-**tend**, v (enlarge) erweitern; (house) anbauen, ausbauen; (hand, arm) ausstrecken; (prolong) verlängern; (cover) sich ausdehnen

**extension**, iks-**tenn**-sch'n, n (enlargement) Erweiterung f; (building) Anbau m; (in time) Verlängerung; (telephone) Apparat m

**extensive**, iks-**tenn**-ssiw, adj (area) weit; (research etc.) umfangreich; (use) weitgehend

**extent**, iks-**tent**, n (scope) Umfang m; (degree) Maß m; (area) Ausdehnung f

**extenuating**, eks-tenn-ju-eh-ting, adj mildernd

**exterior**, iks-**tier**-ri-er, adj äußere(r/s), Außen-; n Äußere nt

**exterminate**, eks-**tör**-mi-neht, v ausrotten

**external**, eks-**tör**-n'l, adj äußere(r/s)

**extinct**, iks-**tinkt**, adj (volcano) erloschen; (species) ausgestorben

**extinguish**, iks-**ting**-gu'isch, v auslöschen

**extort**, iks-**tort**, v erpressen; **–ion**, n Erpressung f

**extra**, eks-**tre**, adj zusätzlich, Zusatz-; adv besonders; n (for car) Extra nt; **–s**, npl comm zusätzliche Kosten pl

**extract**, eks-**träct**, n (cooking) Extrakt m; (from text) Auszug m

**extract**, iks-**träckt**, v (her)ausziehen

**extradite**, eks-tre-deit, v ausliefern

**extramarital**, eks-tre-mä-ri-t'l, adj außerehelich

**extraordinary**, iks-**tror**-di-ne-ri, adj (unusual) außerordentlich; (special) Sonder-; (strange) seltsam

**extravagance**, iks-**träw**-e-genss, n Verschwendung f

**extravagant**, iks-**träw**-e-gent, adj verschwenderisch; (exaggerated) extravagant

**extreme**, iks-**triem**, adj äußerste(r/s); (politics) extrem; **–ly**, adv äußerst

**extremity**, iks-**tremm**-i-ti, n (end) äußerstes Ende nt; (need) Not f; (action) äußerstes Mittel nt

**extricate**, eks-tri-keht, v befreien

**extrovert**, eks-tre-vört, n extravertierter Mensch m

**exuberant**, igg-**sjuh**-be-rent, adj überschwenglich

**eye**, ei, n Auge nt; **–ball**, n Augapfel m; **–brow**, n Augenbraue f; **–drops**, npl Augentropfen pl; **–lash**, n Augenwimper f; **–let**, n Schnürloch nt; **–lid**, n Augenlid nt; **–shadow**, n Lidschatten m; **–sight**, n Sehkraft f; **–witness**, n Augenzeuge m

**fable, feh**-b'l, *n* Fabel *f*,
Märchen *nt*; **-d,** *adj*
(famous) berühmt

**fabric, fább**-rick, *n* Gewebe
*nt*; (building) Struktur *f*

**fabrication, fább**-ri-**keh**-
sch'n, *n* Herstellung *f*;
(lie) Lüge *f*

**fabulous, fább**-ju-less, *adj* (
*fam* marvellous) fabelhaft

**façade, fe**-**ssahd,** *n* Fassade *f*

**face, fehss,** *n* Gesicht *nt*;
(clock) Zifferblatt *nt*; *v*
(opposite) gegenüber sein;
(deal with)
gegenübertreten; **-cream,**
*n* Gesichtscreme *f*; **-lift,** *n*
Facelifting *nt*; *fig*
Verschönerung *f*

**facetious, fe-ssie**-schess, *adj*
witzig, frech

**facial, feh**-schel, *adj*
Gesichts-

**facile, fáss**-eil, *adj* leicht;

(superficial) oberflächlich

**facilitate, fe-ssill**-i-teht, *v*
erleichtern

**facilities, fe-ssill**-i-tis, *npl*
(equipment)
Einrichtungen *pl*;
(opportunities)
Möglichkeiten *pl*

**facsimile, fáck-ssimm**-i-li, *n*
Faksimile *nt*; (message)
Telefax *nt*

**fact, fáckt,** *n* Tatsache *f*;
Wirklichkeit *f*

**faction, fáck-**sch'n, *n*
Splittergruppe *f*

**factor, fáck**-ter, *n* Faktor *m*

**factory, fáck-**te-ri, *n* Fabrik
*f*, Werk *nt*

**faculty, fáck-**'l-ti, *n*
Fähigkeit *f*; (university)
Fakultät *f*

**fad, fád,** *n* *fam* Masche *f*

**fade, fehd,** *v* verwelken,
verblassen; (colour)

verschießen

**fag, fágg,** *n* *fam* Kippe *f*

**fail, fehl,** *v* fehlschlagen;
(voice, light etc.)
versagen; (neglect)
unterlassen; (go/get
wrong) mißlingen; (exam)
durchfallen; (bankrupt)
Konkurs machen; **– to do
sth,** *v* etw nicht tun, etw
unterlassen; **–ing,** *n*
Schwäche *f*; **–ure,** *n*
Mißerfolg *m*; (insolvency)
Konkurs *m*; **without –,** auf
jeden Fall

**faint, fehnt,** *adj* schwach; *n*
Ohnmacht *f*; *v*
ohnmächtig werden

**fair, fáhr,** *adj* (just) fair;
(hair) blond; (weather)
heiter; *n* (trade) Messe *f*;
(funfair) Jahrmarkt *m*;
**–ness,** *n* Gerechtigkeit *f*

**fairy, fáhr**-ri, *n* Fee *f*; **– tale,**
*n* Märchen *nt*

**faith, fehth,** *n* Glaube *m*;
(confidence) Vertrauen
*nt*; **–ful,** *adj* treu;
**–less,**
treulos; **Yours –fully,** Mit
freundlichen Grüßen

**fake, fehk,** *n* Fälschung *f*; *v*
fälschen

**falcon, foll**-k'n, *n* Falke *m*

**fall, fo'al,** *n* Fall *m*, Sturz *m*;
*v* fallen, stürzen; **– for,**
(love) sich in jdn
verlieben; (be taken in)
auf etw hereinfallen; **–
through,** ins Wasser fallen

**fallacy, fáll**-e-ssi, *n* Irrtum *m*;
(false conclusion)

Trugschluß *m*

**fallible, fäll**-i-b'l, *adj* fehlbar

**fallout, fo'al**-aut, *n*
radioaktiver Niederschlag
*m*; (consequences)
Konsequenzen *pl*

**false,** folss, *adj* falsch; –
**teeth,** *npl* Gebiß *nt*

**falsify, foll**-ssi-fei, *v*
(ver)fälschen

**falter, foll**-ter, *v* stocken;
(speech) stammeln

**fame,** fehm, *n* Ruhm *m*; **–d,**
*adj* berühmt

**familiar,** fe-**mill**-yer, *adj*
vertraut; (intimate) intim

**family, fämm**-i-li, *n* Familie
*f*; – **doctor,** *n* Hausarzt *m*,
Hausärztin *f*

**famine, fämm**-inn, *n*
Hungersnot *f*

**famished, fämm**-ischt, *adj*
ausgehungert

**famous, feh**-mess, *adj*
berühmt

**fan,** fänn, *n* Fächer *m*;
Ventilator *m*; (admirer)
Fan *m*; *v* fächeln

**fanatic,** fe-**nätt**-ick, *adj*
fanatisch; *n* Fanatiker *m*

**fancy, fänn**-ssi, *adj*
ausgefallen; *n* Idee *f*;
(desire) Neigung *f*, Lust *f*;
*v* (imagine) sich
einbilden; (like) Lust
haben zu/auf; – **dress,** *n*
Maskenkostüm *nt*

**fang,** fäng, *n* Fang *m*;
(snake) Giftzahn *m*

**fantastic, fänn-täss**-tick, *adj*
phantastisch

**fantasy, fänn**-te-si, *n*
Phantasie *f*

**far,** fahr, *adj & adv* weit; –
**away,** weit entfernt

**farce,** fahrss, *n* Farce *f*

**farcical, fahr-**ssi-k'l, *adj*
lächerlich

**fare,** fähr, *n* Fahrpreis *m*;
(food) Kost *f*

**farewell, fähr-w**'ell, *n*
Abschied *m*; *interj* lebe
wohl!

**Far East,** fahr iest, *n* Ferner
Osten *m*

**farm,** fahrm, *n* Bauernhof *m*;
*v* bewirtschaften; **–er,** *n*
Landwirt *m*; **–house,** *n*
Bauernhaus *nt*; **–ing,** *n*
Landwirtschaft *f*; **–yard,** *n*
Bauernhof *m*

**far-reaching,** fahr-**riet-**
tsching, *adj* weitreichend

**fascinate, fäss**-i-neht, *v*
faszinieren; bezaubern

**fascism, fäsch**-ism, *n*
Faschismus *m*

**fashion, fäsch**-'n, *n* Mode *f*;
*v* bilden; **–able,** *adj*
modisch; **in –,** modern

**fast,** fahst, *adj* schnell; (firm,
fixed, tight) fest; (colour)
farbecht; *n* Fasten *nt*; *v*
fasten; **be –,** *v* (of clock)
vorgehen; – **food,** *n* Fast
food *nt*

**fasten, fah-**ss'n, *v*
befestigen; fest zumachen;
**–er,** *n* Verschluß *m*

**fastidious, fäss-tidd**-i-ess, *adj*
pingelig

**fat,** fätt, *adj* fett, dick;

*n* Fett *nt*

**fatal, feh-**t'l, *adj* tödlich

**fatality, fe-täll**-i-ti, *n*
tödliches Unglück *nt*

**fate,** feht, *n* Schicksal *nt*; **–d,**
*adj* vorbestimmt; **–ful,** *adj*
verhängnisvoll

**father, fah-**dher, *n* Vater *m*;
**–in-law,** Schwiegervater
*m*; **–ly,** *adj* väterlich

**fathom, fädh-**em, *n* Klafter
*f*; *naut* Faden *m*; *v*
ergründen; (to sound)
sondieren

**fatigue,** fe-**tieg,** *n* Ermüdung
*f*; *mil* Arbeitsdienst *m*; *v*
ermüden

**fatten (up), fätt-**'n (app), *v*
mästen

**fault, fo'alt,** *n* (blame,
cause) Schuld *f*; (defect,
mistake) Fehler *m*; **–less,**
*adj* fehlerlos, tadellos; **–y,**
*adj* fehlerhaft, mangelhaft

**favour, feh**-wer, *n* Gunst *f*;
(kindness) Gefallen *m*; *v*
begünstigen; **–able,** *adj*
günstig

**favourite, feh-**we-ritt, *adj*
Lieblings…; *n* Liebling *m*;
*sport* Favorit *m*

**fawn,** fo'an, *adj* rehbraun; *n*
Rehkalb *nt*; *v* kriechen

**fax,** fäcks, *n* (*abbr*
**facsimile**) Fax *nt*; *v* faxen

**fear,** fier, *n* Furcht *f*; *v*
fürchten; befürchten;
**–ful,** *adj* schrecklich;
(timid) furchtsam; **–less,**
furchtlos

**feasible, fie-**si-b'l, *adj*

möglich, ausführbar

**feast, fiest,** n Fest nt; v
schmausen

**feat, fiet,** n Tat f;
(achievement) Leistung f

**feather, fe**-dher, n Feder f;
**–s,** pl Gefieder nt

**feature, fiet**-tscher, n
Merkmal nt; (face)
Gesichtszug m

**February, febb**-ru-e-ri, n
Februar m

**federal, fedd**-e-rel, adj
Bundes-

**federation, fedd**-e-**reh**-sch'n,
n Bund m, Verband m

**fed up, fedd app,** adj be **–,** v
die Nase voll haben

**fee, fie,** n Gebühr f; (for
person) Honorar nt

**feeble, fie**-b'l, adj schwach

**feed, fied,** v füttern, nähren.
n Futter nt; **–back,** n
Feedback m

**feel, fiel,** v (sich) fühlen;
(touch) befühlen; n
Fühlen nt, Gefühl nt;
**–er,** n Fühler m; **–ing,** n
Gefühl nt

**feet, fiet,** pl of **foot**

**feign, fehn,** v heucheln, sich
verstellen

**feline, fie**-lein, adj
katzenartig

**fell, fell,** v fällen; (person)
niederschlagen

**fellow, fell**-oh, adj Mit-; n
Kerl m; (member)
Mitglied nt; **–ship,**
Verbundenheit f

**felony, fell**-e-ni, n schweres

Verbrechen nt

**felt, felt,** n Filz m; **--tip pen,**
n Filzstift m

**female, fie**-mehl, adj
weiblich; n Weibchen nt

**feminine, femm**-i-ninn, adj
weiblich

**feminist, femm**-i-nist, adj
feministisch, Feministen-;
n Feministin f, Feminist m

**fen, fenn,** n Marschland nt

**fence, fenss,** n Zaun m; v
einzäunen; (combat)
fechten

**fencing, fenn**-ssing, n sport
Fechten nt; (fence) Zaun
m

**fender, fenn**-der, n (hearth)
Kaminschutz m; (ship)
Fender m

**ferment, fer**-ment, v gären,
gären lassen

**fern, förn,** n Farn m

**ferocious, fe-roh**-schess, adj
wild; (strong) heftig

**ferret, fe**-ritt, n Frettchen
nt; **– about,** v
herumstöbern

**ferry, fe**-ri, n Fähre f; v
übersetzen

**fertile, för**-teil, adj fruchtbar

**fertilize, för**-ti-leis, v
befruchten; (feed)
düngen; **–r,** n Dünger m

**fervent, fer**-went, adj
leidenschaftlich

**fester, fess**-ter, v eitern

**festival, fess**-ti-w'l, n Fest
nt, Festtag m

**festive, fess**-tiw, adj festlich

**festoon, fess-tuhn,** n

Girlande f; v bekränzen

**fetch, fetsch,** v holen; (call
for) abholen

**fête, feht,** n Fest nt

**feud, fjuhd,** n Fehde f; **–al,**
adj feudal

**fever, fie**-wer, n Fieber nt;
**–ish,** adj fiebrig; (excited)
erregt

**few, fjuh,** adj wenige; **a –,**
einige, ein paar

**fiancé, fi-onn**-sseh, n
Verlobter m; **–e,** n
Verlobte f

**fib, fibb,** fam n Flunkerei f; v
flunkern, schwindeln

**fibre, fei**-ber, n Faser f

**fickle, fick**-'l, adj
unbeständig

**fiction, fick**-sch'n, n
erzählende Literatur f;
(book) Roman m; **–al,** adj
erdichtet

**fictitious, fick-ti**-schess, adj
erfunden; (false) unecht

**fiddle, fidd**-'l, n mus Geige f;
fam Gaunerei f; v mus
geigen; fig krumme Dinger
drehen; **– with,** v
herumspielen mit

**fidelity, fi-dell**-i-ti, n Treue f

**fidget, fid**-dschitt, n
Zappelphilipp m; v
zappelig sein

**field, field,** n Feld nt; v
aufstellen; (deal with)
fertig werden mit

**fiend, fiend,** n Teufel m;
**–ish,** adj teuflisch

**fierce, fierss,** adj wild;
(strong) heftig

**fiery, feir**-ri, adj feurig; (temper) hitzig

**fifteen**, fiff-tien, num fünfzehn; **–th**, adj fünfzehnte(r/s)

**fifth**, fifth, adj fünfte(r/s); n Fünftel m

**fifty**, fiff-ti, num fünfzig

**fig**, figg, n Feige f; **- -tree**, Feigenbaum m

**fight**, feit, n Kampf m; Schlägerei f; v kämpfen; **–er**, n Kämpfer m; (plane) Kampfflugzeug nt

**figment**, figg-ment, n **a – of the imagination,** Hirngespinst nt

**figure**, figg-er, n Figur f, Gestalt f; (number) Ziffer f; v (sich) vorstellen; **–head**, n Galionsfigur f; **– out**, v verstehen, herausfinden

**filch**, filtsch, v mausen, stibitzen

**file**, feil, n (tool) Feile f; mil Reihe f; (office) Ordner m; v feilen; (letters etc.) ablegen

**filing**, fei-ling, n Ablage f; **– cabinet,** n Aktenschrank m

**fill**, fill, v füllen; (teeth) plombieren; **– in,** v (form) ausfüllen; (details) erläutern

**filling**, fill-ing, n Füllung f; (teeth) Plombe f; **– station,** n Tankstelle f

**film**, film, n photog Film m; (cinema) Film m; (layer) Belag m; v filmen, verfilmen

**filter**, fill-ter, n Filter m; v filtern

**filth**, filth, n Dreck m; **–y,** adj schmutzig

**fin**, finn, n Flosse f

**final**, fei-nel, adj definitiv; (last) letzte(r/s); **–ist,** n Finalist m; **–ize,** v abschließen(d besprechen); **–ly,** adv (lastly) schließlich; (in the end) endlich

**finance**, fei-nänss, n Finanzierung f; (department) Rechnungsabteilung f; v finanzieren; **–s,** npl Finanzlage f

**financial**, fei-nän-schel, adj finanziell m

**finch**, fintsch, n Fink m

**find**, feind, n Fund; v finden; law erklären; **– out,** v herausfinden; (person) erwischen

**fine**, fein, adj fein; (weather) schön; n Geldstrafe f; v zu einer Geldstrafe verurteilen; **– art(s),** n(pl.), schöne Künste pl

**finery**, fei-ne-ri, n Glanz m, Pracht f

**finger**, fing-ger, n Finger m; v befühlen, betasten; **–nail,** n Fingernagel m; **–print,** n Fingerabdruck m

**finish**, finn-isch, v beenden; (cease) aufhören; n Ende nt, Schluß m; (goods)

Ausführung f; sport Finish nt; **–ing line,** n Ziellinie f

**finite**, fei-neit, adj begrenzt

**Finland**, finn-lend, n Finnland nt

**Finn**, finn, n Finne m, Finnin f; **–ish,** adj finnisch; n Finnisch nt

**fir**, för, n Tanne f; **– cone,** Tannenzapfen m

**fire**, feir, n Feuer nt; (conflagration) Brand m; v anzünden; (inspire) begeistern; (fam sack) feuern; **– alarm,** n Feuermelder nt; **–arm,** n Schußwaffe f **– brigade,** n Feuerwehr f; **– engine,** n Feuerwehrauto nt; **– escape,** n Feuertreppe f; **– exit,** n Notausgang m; **– extinguisher,** n Feuerlöscher m; **–man,** n Feuerwehrmann m; (stoker) Heizer m; **–place,** n offener Kamin m; **–proof,** adj feuerfest; **–works,** npl Feuerwerk nt

**firing squad**, feir-ring sku'odd, n Exekutionskommando nt

**firm**, förm, adj fest; (resolute) standhaft; n Firma f

**first**, först, adj & n erste(r/s); adv zuerst; **– aid,** n Erste Hilfe f; **–-aid kit,** n Erste-Hilfe-Kasten m; **– class,** adj (travel) erster Klasse; (excellent) erstklassig; **– name,** n Vorname m

**fish,** fisch, *n* Fisch *m*; *v* fischen, angeln; **–bone,** *n* Gräte *f*; **–erman,** Fischer *m*; **– hook,** Angelhaken *m*; **–ing,** *n* Angeln *nt*; **– rod,** Angelrute *f*; **–monger,** Fischhändler *m*

**fissure,** fisch-er, *n* Spalte *f*

**fist,** fist, *n* Faust *f*

**fit,** fitt, *adj* passend, geeignet; *n* (paroxysm) Anfall *m*; *v* passen; (erect, set up, mount etc.) montieren; **–ness,** *n* Eignung *f*; *sport* Fitneß *f*; **–ted carpet,** *n* Teppichboden *m*; **–ting,** *adj* angemessen, geeignet; **–ting room,** *n* Anproberaum *f*; **–tings,** *npl* Ausstattung *f*

**five,** feiw, *num* fünf

**fix,** ficks, *n fig* Klemme *f*; *v* befestigen, reparieren; **–ture,** *n sport* Spieldatum *nt*; **–tures,** *npl*, unbewegliches Inventar *nt*;

**fizzle out,** fis-'l aut, *v* im Sand verlaufen

**fizzy,** fis-i, *adj* sprudelnd, Sprudel-

**flabby,** fläbb-i, *adj* schlaff, schwammig

**flag,** flägg, *n* Fahne *f*, Flagge *f*; *v* (languish) erschlaffen; **– down,** *v* anhalten; **– up,** *v* hervorheben

**flagrant,** fleh-grent, *adj* flagrant, schamlos

**flair,** flähr, *n* Gespür *nt*, Talent *nt*

**flake,** flehk, *n* (of snow etc.) Flocke *f*; (of rust, paint) Schuppe *f*; **– (off),** *v* abbröckeln, abblättern

**flamboyant,** flämm-**beu**-ent, *adj* extravagant

**flame,** flehm, *n* Flamme *f*; *v* lodern

**flammable,** flämm-e-b'l, *adj* brennbar

**flan,** flänn, *n* Torte *f*

**flank,** flänk, *n* Flanke *f*; *v* flankieren

**flannel,** flänn-'l, *n* Flanell *m*; (facecloth) Waschlappen *m*

**flap,** fläpp, *n* (table etc.) Klappe *f*; *v* (wings) flattern

**flare,** flähr, *n* flackerndes Licht *nt*; (signal) Leuchtsignal *nt*; **– up,** *v* aufflackern; (break out) (wieder) ausbrechen

**flash,** fläsch, *n* Aufleuchten *nt*; *photog* Blitz *m*; *v* blitzen; **–back,** *n* Rückblende *f*; **–y,** *adj* auffallend

**flask,** flahsk, *n* Flachmann *m*; (Thermos ®) Thermosflasche *f*

**flat,** flätt, *adj* flach, platt; (business) flau; *n*; (dwelling) Wohnung *f*; *mus* b *nt*; **–ly,** *adv* rundweg, glatt; **–ten,** *v* flach machen, eben machen

**flatter,** flätt-er, *v* schmeicheln; **–ing,** *adj*

**flavour,** fleh-wer, *n* Geschmack *m*; (wine) Blume *f*; *v* würzen; **–ing,** Würze *f*

**flaw,** flo'a, *n* Fehler *m*; (crack) Riß *m*; **–less,** makellos

**flax,** fläcks, *n* Flachs *m*

**flea,** flie, *n* Floh *m*

**fleck,** fleck, *n* Tupfen *m*

**flee,** flie, *v* fliehen

**fleece,** fliess, *n* Flies *nt*; *v fam* ausnehmen

**fleet,** fliet, *n* Flotte *f*; **–ing,** *adj* flüchtig

**flesh,** flesch, *n* Fleisch *nt*

**Flemish,** flemm-isch, *adj* flämisch

**flex,** flecks, *n* Kabel *nt*; *v* beugen; **–ible,** *adj* biegsam, flexibel

**flicker,** flick-er, *n* Flackern *nt*; *v* flackern

**flight,** fleit, *n* Flug *m*

**flimsy,** flimm-si, *adj* (material, paper) dünn; (structure) schwach

**flinch,** flintsch, *v* (zusammen)zucken

**fling,** fling, *v* werfen, schleudern

**flint,** flint, *n* Feuerstein *m*

**flip,** flipp, *v* drehen; (go crazy) durchdrehen

**flippant,** flipp-'nt, *adj* leichtfertig

**flipper,** flipp-er, *n* Flosse *f*

**flirt,** flört, *n* Flirt *m*; *v* flirten

**float,** floht, *n* (raft) Floß *nt*;

(angler's) Schwimmer m; v treiben; (ship) flott machen; (stock exchange) an die Börse gehen

**flock,** flock, n (cattle) Herde f; (birds) Schwarm m; v zusammenströmen

**flog,** flogg, v (whip) peitschen; (fam sell) verhökern, verscheuern

**flood,** fladd, n Flut f; (inundation) Überschwemmung f; v überschwemmen; **–light,** n Flutlicht nt

**floor,** flohr, n Boden m, Fußboden m; (storey) Stock m; v überfordern

**flop,** flopp, n (failure) Reinfall m; v (fail) durchfallen; (fall) plumpsen; **–py,** adj schlaff; **– disk,** n comp Diskette f

**floral,** flor-rel, adj Blumen-

**florid,** flo-ridd, adj blühend

**florist,** flo-rist, n Blumenhändler m

**flounder,** flaun-der, n Flunder f; v (stumble) stolpern; (struggle) sich quälen

**flour,** flau-er, n Mehl nt

**flourish,** fla-risch, n mus Fanfare f; (writing) Schnörkel m; v (brandish) schwenken; (go well) gutgehen, florieren

**flout,** flaut, v mißachten

**flow,** floh, n Strom m; v fließen, strömen

**flower,** flau-er, n Blume f; v

blühen; **–bed,** n Blumenbeet nt; **–pot,** n Blumentopf m

**flu,** fluh, n (abbr influenza), Grippe f

**fluctuate,** flack-tju-eht, v schwanken

**flue,** fluh, n Rauchfang m

**fluency,** fluh-en-ssi, n (Rede)gewandtheit f

**fluent,** fluh-ent, adj gewandt; (language) fließend

**fluff,** flaff, n Fussel f; **–y,** adj flockig, flaumig

**fluid,** fluh-idd, adj flüssig; n Flüssigkeit f

**fluke,** fluhk, n Glücksfall m

**flurry,** fla-ri, n Aufregung f; v durcheinander bringen

**flush,** flasch, adj (level) bündig; n Erröten nt; v (redden) erröten; (rinse) ausspülen; **–ed,** adj rot

**flustered,** flass-terd, adj nervös

**flute,** fluht, n mus Flöte f; **–d,** adj (grooved) gerillt

**flutter,** flatt-er, n Geflatter nt; v flattern

**fly,** flei, n Fliege f; v fliegen; (flag) wehen; **–ing,** n Fliegen nt; **– saucer,** n fliegende Untertasse f

**foal,** fohl, n Fohlen nt

**foam,** fohm, n Schaum m; v schäumen

**fob off,** fobb off, v jdn mit etw abspeisen

**focal,** foh-k'l, adj Brenn-; **– point,** n Brennpunkt m

**focus,** foh-kess, n Brennpunkt m; **– (on),** v (camera etc.) einstellen (auf); (efforts etc.) konzentrieren (auf); **in –,** scharf; **out of –,** unscharf

**fodder,** fodd-er, n Futter nt

**foe,** foh, n Feind m

**fog,** fogg, n Nebel m; **–gy,** adj neb(e)lig; **–lamp,** n (car) Nebelscheinwerfer m

**foil,** feul, n (metal) Folie f; (fencing) Florett nt; v vereiteln

**foist on,** feust on, v aufhalsen

**fold,** fohld, n (clothes etc.) Falte f; v falten; (arms) kreuzen; **–er,** Mappe f; **–ing,** adj Klapp-

**foliage,** foh-li-idsch, n Laub nt

**folk,** fohk, adj Volks-; Folklore-; n Leute pl Volk nt

**follow,** foll-oh, v folgen; fig befolgen; **–er,** n Anhänger m; (disciple) Jünger m; **–ing,** adj folgend; n Anhängerschaft f

**folly,** foll-i, n Torheit f

**fond,** fond, adj be – of, v gern haben

**fondle,** fonn-d'l, v liebkosen, hätscheln

**font,** font, n Taufbecken nt

**food,** fuhd, n Speise f; Nahrung f (for animals) Futter nt; **– poisoning,** n Lebensmittelvergiftung f;

**– processor,** n Küchenmaschine f

**fool,** fuhl, n Narr m; v täuschen, hereinlegen; **–hardy,** adj tollkühn; **–ish,** adj töricht, närrisch; **–proof,** adj narrensicher

**foot,** futt, n Fuß m; **– the bill,** v die Rechnung bezahlen; **–ball,** n Fußball m; **–baller,** n Fußballspieler m; **–bridge,** n Fußgängerbrücke f; **–hill,** n (Gebirgs)ausläufer m; **–hold,** n Halt m, Stützpunkt m; **–man,** n Diener m; **–path,** n Fußweg m; **–print,** n Fußabdruck m; **–step,** n Schritt m

**for,** for, prep (purpose, future time) für; (distance) auf, weit; (purpose) zu; (reason) aus; (past time) seit; conj denn

**forage,** fo-ridsch, n (Vieh)Futter nt; v nach Nahrung suchen; (rummage) stöbern

**forbear,** for-behr, v unterlassen; (be patient) sich gedulden; **–ance,** n Nachsicht f

**forbid,** fe-bidd, v verbieten; **–den,** adj verboten; **–ding,** adj furchteinflößend; (grim) unwirtlich

**force,** forss, n Gewalt f; (power) Kraft f; v (compel) zwingen; (break open) aufbrechen; **–ful,**

adj stark; (person) energisch; **–s,** npl Streitkräfte pl

**forceps,** for-ssepss, npl (Geburts)zange f

**forcibly,** for-ssi-bli, adj gewaltsam

**ford,** ford, n Furt f; v durchwaten

**fore,** for, n Vordergrund m; **to the –,** im/in den Vordergrund

**forearm,** for-ahrm, n Unterarm m

**foreboding,** for-boh-ding, n Vorahnung f

**forecast,** for-kahst, n Prognose f, Voraussage f; (weather etc.) Wetterbericht m; v vorhersagen

**forecourt,** for-kort, n Vorplatz m

**forefathers,** for-fah-dhers, npl Vorfahren pl

**forefinger,** for-fing-ger, n Zeigefinger m

**forefront,** for-frant, n **to be in the –,** in vorderster Linie stehen

**forego,** for-goh, v verzichten auf

**foregone,** for-gonn, **it is a – conclusion,** n es steht von vornherein fest

**foreground,** for-graund, n Vordergrund m

**forehead,** for-hedd, n Stirn f

**foreign,** fo-rinn, adj ausländisch, fremd; **–er,** n Ausländer m

**foreman,** for-men, n Vorarbeiter m; Werkmeister m; (law of jury) Sprecher m

**foremost,** for-mohst, adj vorderste(r/s); erste(r/s)

**forensic,** fe-renn-sick, s., gerichtsmedizinisch

**forerunner,** for-rann-er, n Vorläufer m

**foresee,** for-ssie, v vorhersehen; **–able,** adj vorhersehbar

**foreshadow,** for-schädd-oh, v vorausdeuten auf

**foresight,** for-sseit, n Weitblick m, Voraussicht f

**forest,** fo-rist, n Wald m

**forestall,** for-sto'al, v zuvorkommen

**forestry,** fo-riss-tri, n Forstwirtschaft f

**foretaste,** for-tehst, n Vorgeschmack m

**foretell,** for-tell, v vorhersagen, prophezeien

**forever,** for-ew-er, adv immer

**foreword,** for-u'örd, n Vorwort nt

**forfeit,** for-fitt, v (life, goods etc.) verlieren, verwirken; n (games) Pfand nt; (fine) Strafe f

**forge,** fohrdsch, n Schmiede f; v schmieden; (falsify) fälschen; **– ahead,** v vorankommen

**forger,** for-dscher, n Fälscher m; Falschmünzer m; **–y,** n Fälschung f

**forget,** fe-gett, v vergessen;
–**ful,** adj vergeßlich;
–**fulness,** n Vergeßlichkeit
f; –**me-not,**
Vergißmeinnicht nt

**forgive,** fe-giw, v vergeben;
–**ness,** n Verzeihung f,
Vergebung f

**fork,** fork, n Gabel f; (road)
Gabelung f; – **out,** v fam
blechen

**forlorn,** fe-lorn, adj
verlassen, einsam

**form,** form, n (shape) Form
f; (class) Klasse f; (seat)
Bank f; (to fill in)
Formular nt; v bilden; (a
plan) entwerfen; mil sich
formieren

**formal,** for-mel, adj
förmlich, formell; (stiff)
steif

**formality,** fe-mäll-i-ti,
n Förmlichkeit f,
Formalität f

**format,** for-mätt, n Format
nt; v comp formatieren

**formation,** for-meh-sch'n, n
Gestaltung f; (mil &
geological) Bildung f

**former,** for-mer, adj früher;
–**ly,** adv vormals

**formidable,** for-mi-deb-'l,
adj gewaltig,
beeindruckend

**formula,** for-mju-le, n
Formel f

**formulate,** for-muj-leht, v
formulieren

**forsake,** fe-ssehk, v
verzichten auf; (desert)

verlassen

**fort,** fort, n Fort nt

**forth,** forth, adv fort, weiter;
(out) hervor; (ahead)
vorwärts; **and so** –, und so
weiter; –**coming,** adj
bevorstehend; –**right,** adj
direkt; –**with,** adv
unverzüglich

**fortification,** for-ti-fi-keh-
sch'n, n Befestigung f

**fortify,** for-ti-fei, v
(military) befestigen;
(strengthen) stärken

**fortitude,** for-ti-tjuhd, n
innere Stärke f

**fortnight,** fort-neit, n
vierzehn Tage mpl.

**fortress,** fort-riss, n
Festung f

**fortuitous,** for-tjuh-i-tess,
adj zufällig

**fortunate,** for-tju-net, adj
glücklich

**fortune,** for-tjuhn, n
Vermögen nt; (luck)
Glück nt; – **teller,** n
Wahrsager m

**forty,** for-ti, num vierzig

**forward,** for-u'erd, adj
(advance) Voraus-;
(advanced) frühreif;
(cheeky) direkt; adv
vorwärts; v (send)
nachschicken; (further)
vorantreiben

**fossil,** foss-'l, n Fossil nt

**foster,** foss-ter, v pflegen,
fördern; – **parents,** npl
Pflegeeltern pl

**foul,** faul, adj widerlich,

schmutzig; n sport Foul nt;
v beschmutzen

**found,** faund, v gründen;
–**ation,** n Gründung f;
–**ations,** npl Fundament
nt; –**er,** n Gründer m; –**ry,**
n Gießerei f

**fountain,** faun-tin, n
Springbrunnen m; – **pen,**
Füller m

**four,** for, num vier; –**teen,**
num vierzehn; –**th,** adj
vierte(r/s); n Viertel nt

**fowl,** faul, n Huhn nt;
(poultry) Geflügel nt

**fox,** focks, n Fuchs m; v
täuschen; –**glove,** n
Fingerhut m; –**terrier,**
Foxterrier m

**foyer,** feu-ei, n Foyer nt

**fraction,** fräck-sch'n, n
Bruchstück nt;
(mathematical) Bruch m

**fracture,** fräck-tscher, n
Bruch m; v brechen

**fragile,** frädd-dscheil, adj
zerbrechlich

**fragment,** frägg-ment, n
Bruchstück nt

**fragrance,** freh-grenss, n
Duft m

**fragrant,** freh-grent, adj
duftend

**frail,** frehl, adj zart; (health)
gebrechlich

**frame,** frehm, n Rahmen m;
v einrahmen; –**work,** n
Gerüst nt; (panelling)
Fachwerk nt

**France,** frahnss, n
Frankreich nt

**franchise, fränn-**tscheis, *n* Wahlrecht *nt*; *comm* Lizenz *f*

**frank, fränk,** *adj* aufrichtig; **–ly,** *adv* offen gesagt; **–ness,** *n* Offenheit *f*

**frantic, fränn-**tick, *adj* hektisch, stürmisch; **be –,** *v* außer sich sein

**fraternal, fre-tör-**n'l, *adj* brüderlich

**fraternity, fre-tör-**ni-ti, *n* Brüderlichkeit *f*; (club) Vereinigung *f*

**fraught (with), fro'at** (u'idh), *adj* -geladen

**fraud, fro'ad,** *n* Betrug *m*, Schwindel *m*; **–ulent,** *adj* betrügerisch

**fray, freh,** *n* (scuffle) Tumult *m*; *v* abnützen; **–ed,** (cuff etc.) abgescheuert; *fig* angespannt

**freak, friek,** *n* Freak *m*; (abnormal) Mißgeburt *f*; **–ish,** *adj* launisch, verrückt

**freckle, freck-**'l, *n* Sommersprosse *f*

**free, frie,** *adj* frei; *v* befreien; **–dom,** *n* Freiheit *f*; **–lance,** *adj* freischaffend; **–mason,** Freimaurer *m*; **––range,** *adj* (egg) Land-; **– trade,** Freihandel *m*; **of one's own – will,** aus freien Stücken

**freeze, fries,** *v* frieren, gefrieren; **–r,** *n* Tiefkühltruhe *f*

**freezing, frie-**sing, *adj* eisig;

**– point,** *n* Gefrierpunkt *m*

**freight, freht,** *n* Ladung *f*; (cost) Fracht *f*; *v* befrachten

**French, frentsch,** *adj* französisch; *n*; (language) Französisch *nt*; *npl* (people) Franzosen *pl*; **– bean,** *n* grüne Bohne *f*; **– fries,** *npl* Pommes frites *pl*; **–man,** *n* Franzose *m*; **–woman,** *n* Französin *f*; **– window,** Verandatür *f*

**frenzied, frenn-**sidd, *adj* rasend

**frenzy, frenn-**si, *n* Raserei *f*, Wahnsinn *m*

**frequency, frie-ku'en-**ssi, *n* Häufigkeit *f*; (physics) Frequenz *f*

**frequent, frie-**ku'ent, *adj* häufig

**frequent, fri-ku'ent,** *v* besuchen

**fresh, fresch,** *adj* frisch; (cheeky) frech, keck; **–en up,** *v* (sich) frischmachen; **–ness,** *n* Frische *f*; **–water,** *adj* Süßwasser-

**fret, frett,** *v* beunruhigt sein; **–ful,** *adj* unruhig; (child) quengelig; **–saw,** *f* Laubsäge *f*

**friar, frei-**er, *n* Mönch *m*, Frater *m*

**friction, frick-**sch'n, *n* Reibung *f*, Friktion *f*

**Friday, frei-**deh, *n* Freitag *m*

**fridge, fridsch,** *n* Kühlschrank *m*

**friend, frend,** *n* Freund *m*,

**Freundin** *f*; **–ly,** *adj* freundschaftlich, befreundet; **–ship,** *n* Freundschaft *f*

**frieze, fries,** *n* Fries *m*

**fright, freit,** *n* Schreck *m*, Furcht *f*; **–en,** *v* (people) erschrecken; (animals) verscheuchen; **–ening,** *adj* schrecklich; **–ful,** *adj* schrecklich, furchtbar; **be –ened,** *v* Angst haben

**frigid, fridd-**dschidd, *adj* eisig; *fig* frostig

**frill, frill,** *n* Krause *f*; *v* kräuseln

**fringe, frindsch,** *n* Franse *f*; (edge) Rand *m*; *v* säumen

**frisk, frisk,** *v* durchsuchen

**frisky, friss-**ki, *adj* ausgelassen; (horse) tänzelnd

**fritter, fritt-**er, *n* (sweet) Ausgebackenes *nt*; **– away,** *v* vergeuden

**frivolous, friw-e-**less, *adj* frivol, leichtfertig

**frizzy, fris-**i, *adj* kraus

**fro, froh,** *adv* **to and –,** hin und her, auf und ab

**frock, frock,** *n* Kleid *nt*

**frog, frogg,** *n* Frosch *m*

**frolic, froll-**ick, *n* Spaß *m*; *v* (herum)springen

**from, fromm,** *prep* (distance) von; (origin) aus; (cause) vor; (past time) seit; **– ... to ...,** von ... bis ...; **where –?** woher?

**front, frant,** *adj* Vorder-; *n*

Vorderteil nt, Vorderseite f; *mil* Front f; **– door**, Haustür f; **in –**, *adv* vorne; **in – of**, *prep* vor; **front page**, n Titelseite f

**frontier**, **frann**-tier, n Grenze f

**frost**, frost, n Frost m; v mit Reif überziehen **–bitten**, *adj* erfroren; **–erer**, n Milchglas nt; **–y**, *adj* frostig, eisig

**froth**, froth, n Schaum m; v schäumen

**frown**, fraun, n Stirnrunzeln nt; v die Stirne runzeln

**frugal**, fruh-g'l, *adj* (meal) spärlich; (person) sparsam

**fruit**, fruht, n (singly) Frucht f; (collectively) Obst nt; **–erer**, n Obsthändler m; **–ful**, *adj* fruchtbar

**fruition**, fru-**isch**-'n, n Reife f; *fig* Genuß m

**fruitless**, **fruht**-liss, *adj* unfruchtbar, fruchtlos

**fruit machine**, fruht me-**schien**, n Spielautomat m

**frustrate**, **frass**-treht, v vereiteln; **–d**, *adj* frustriert

**fry**, frei, v braten; **–ing pan**, n Bratpfanne f

**fudge**, fudsch, n Fondant m; v ausweichen

**fuel**, fju-el, n Brennstoff m; v treiben

**fugitive**, **fjuh**-dschi-tiw, n Flüchtling m

**fulfil**, full-**fill**, v erfüllen; **–ment**, n Erfüllung f

**full**, full, *adj* voll; **– moon**, n Vollmond m; **--scale**, *adj* (drawing) in Originalgröße; (complete) total; **– stop**, n Punkt m; **--time**, *adj* Ganztags-; **-y**, *adv* völlig, gänzlich; **in –**, vollständig

**fulsome**, **full**-sem, *adj* übertrieben

**fume**, fjuhm, v dampfen; (be angry) wütend sein; **–s**, *npl* Abgase pl

**fun**, fann, n Scherz m, Spaß m; **make – of**, v sich lustig machen über

**function**, **fank**-sch'n, n Veranstaltung f; Funktion f; v funktionieren; **–al**, *adj* zweckmäßig

**fund**, fand, n Fonds m; v finanzieren; **–s**, *npl* Mittel pl

**fundamental**, fan-de-**menn**-t'l, *adj* grundlegend, wesentlich

**funeral**, **fjuh**-ne-rel, n Beerdigung f; **– service**, n Trauergottesdienst m

**funfair**, **fann**-fähr, n Jahrmarkt m

**fungus**, **fang**-gess, n Pilz m

**funnel**, **fann**-'l, n Trichter m; (of engine, steamer) Schlot m; v schleusen

**funny**, **fann**-i, *adj* komisch, witzig

**fur**, för, n Pelz m, Fell nt

**furbish**, **för**-bisch, v ausstatten

**furious**, **fjuhr**-ri-ess, *adj*

wütend, rasend

**furlong**, **för**-long, n Achtelmeile f

**furlough**, **för**-loh, n Urlaub m

**furnace**, **för**-niss, n Ofen m

**furnish**, **för**-nisch, v möblieren

**furniture**, **för**-nit-tscher, n Möbel npl

**furrow**, **fa**-roh, n Furche f

**further**, **för**-dher, *adj* weiter; *adv* übrdies, ferner; v fördern; **– education**, n Weiterbildung f; (for adults) Erwachsenenbildung f; **–more**, *adv* ferner

**furtive**, **för**-tiw, *adj* verstohlen

**fury**, **fjuhr**-ri, n Wut f

**fuse**, fjuhs, n Zünder m; (electric) Sicherung f; v verschmelzen; durchbrennen; **– box**, n Sicherungskasten m

**fuselage**, **fjuh**-se-lahsch, n (Flugzeug) Rumpf m

**fusion**, **fjuh**-sch'n, n Verschmelzung f

**fuss**, fass, n Theater nt, Rummel m; v viel Aufhebens machen; **–y**, *adj* wählerisch

**futile**, **fjuh**-teil, *adj* vergeblich, nutzlos

**futility**, fju-**till**-i-ti, n Sinnlosigkeit f

**future**, **fjuh**-tscher, *adj* zukünftig; n Zukunft f

**gabble, gäbb-'l,** v brabbeln

**gable, geh-b'l,** n Giebel m

**gadget, gädd-**dschitt, n Gerät nt

**Gaelic, geh-**lick, adj gälisch; n (language) Gälisch nt

**gaffe, gäff,** n Fauxpas m, Fehler m

**gag, gägg,** n Knebel m; (joke) Gag m; v knebeln; (silence) zum Schweigen bringen; (choke) würgen

**gaiety, geh-**i-ti, n Fröhlichkeit f

**gaily, geh-**li, adv lustig

**gain, gehn,** n Gewinn m; v (win) gewinnen; (obtain) erhalten; (watch) vorgehen

**gait, geht,** n Gang m

**gala, gah-**le, adj Gala-; n Gala f, Fest nt

**galaxy, gäll-**äck-si, n Milchstraße f, Galaxis f

**gale, gehl,** n Sturm m

**gall, go'al,** n (cheek) Frechheit f

**gallant, gäll-**ant, adj tapfer; ritterlich; **-ry,** n (courage) Tapferkeit f; (manners) Aufmerksamkeit f

**gallery, gäll-**e-ri, n Galerie f

**galling, go'a-**ling, adj ärgerlich

**gallon, gäll-**en, n Gallone f

**gallop, gäll-**epp, n Galopp m; v galoppieren

**gallows, gäll-**ohs, npl Galgen m

**galore, ga-**lor, adv in Menge, in Fülle

**galvanize, gäll-**ve-neis, v (fig rouse) wachrütteln, galvanisieren

**gamble, gämm-**b'l, n Glücksspiel nt; (risk) Wagnis; v spielen; (risk) riskieren, aufs Spiel setzen; **-r,** n Spieler m

**gambol, gämm-**b'l, n Luftsprung m; v hüpfen

**game, gehm,** n Spiel nt; Partie f; (animals) Wild nt; (fam prostitution) Prostitution f; **-keeper,** Wildhüter m

**gammon, gämm-**en, n geräucherter Schinken m

**gamut, gämm-**et, n Tonleiter f; Umfang m

**gang, gäng,** n Trupp m; (of robbers etc.) Bande f

**gangster, gäng-**ster, n Gangster m

**gangway, gäng-**u'eh, n (passage) Gang m; (ship's) Gangway f

**gaol, dschehl,** n Gefängnis nt

**gap, gäpp,** n Lücke f

**gape, gehp,** v gaffen, glotzen

**gaping, geh-**ping, adj gähnend

**garage, gä-**rahsh, n Garage f

**garb, gahrb,** n Tracht f

**garbage, gahr-**bidsch, n Abfall m

**garble, gahr-**b'l, v durcheinanderbringen

**garden, gahr-**d'n, n Garten m; v im Garten arbeiten; **-er,** n Gärtner m; **-ing,** n Gartenarbeit f

**gargle, gahr-**g'l, n Gurgelwasser nt; v gurgeln

**garish, gähr-**risch, adj auffallend, grell

**garlic, gahr-**lick, n Knoblauch m

**garment, gahr**-ment, *n*
Kleidungsstück *nt*

**garnish, gahr**-nisch, *n*
Garnierung *f*; *v* garnieren

**garret**, gä-ritt, *n* Dachstube *f*

**garrison**, gä-ri-ss'n, *n*
Garnison *f*

**garrulous**, gä-rju-less, *adj*
schwatzhaft

**garter, gahr**-ter, *n*
Strumpfband *nt*

**gas**, gäss, *n* Gas *nt*; (petrol)
Benzin *nt*

**gaseous**, gä-ssi-ess, *adj*
gasig, gasartig

**gash**, gäsch, *n* klaffende
Wunde *f*; *v* tief ins Fleisch
schneiden

**gasket**, gäss-kitt, *n*
Dichtung *f*

**gasp**, gahsp, *n* Keuchen *nt*; *v*
nach Luft schnappen

**gastric**, gäss-trick, *adj*
gastrisch, Magen-

**gate**, geht, *n* (small) Pforte *f*;
(large) Tor *nt*; (airport)
Flugsteig *m*

**gather**, gädh-er, *v*
(ver)sammeln; (infer)
schließen, erfahren; **–ing**,
*n* Versammlung *f*

**gauche**, gohsch, *adj* linkisch;
(tactless) plump

**gaudy**, go'a-di, *adj* (colour)
grell; (appearance)
prunkhaft

**gauge**, gehdsch, *n* (size)
Normalmaß *nt*; (tool)
Maßstab *m*; (rails)
Spurweite *f*; (petrol)
Benzinuhr *f*; *v* ausmessen;

*fig* abschätzen

**gaunt**, go'ant, *adj* hager, dürr

**gauntlet**, go'ant-litt, *n*
Fehdehandschuh *m*

**gauze**, go'as, *n* Gaze *f*; (wire)
Drahtgeflecht *nt*

**gawky**, go'a-ki, *adj* linkisch;
(tall and thin) schlaksig

**gay**, geh, *adj* (happy)
fröhlich; (colour) lebhaft;
(homosexual) schwul

**gaze**, gehs, *n* Blick *m*; *v*
starren; **– at**, anstarren

**GB**, *abbr* Great Britain

**gear**, gier, *n mech* Getriebe
*nt*; (*fam* equipment)
Ausrüstung *f*; **–box**, *n*
Getriebekasten *m*; **be –ed
to**, *v* ausgerichtet sein auf:
**bottom –**, niedrigster
Gang *m*; **reverse –**,
Rückwärtsgang *m*; **top –**,
höchster Gang *m*

**gelatine**, dschell-**e**-tien, *n*
Gelatine *f*

**gem**, dschemm, *n*
Edelstein *m*

**Gemini**, dschemm-i-ni, *n*
Zwillinge *pl*

**gender**, dschenn-der, *n*
Geschlecht *nt*

**general**, dschenn-e-rel, *adj*
allgemein; *n* General *m*;
**–ize**, *v* verallgemeinern;
**–ly**, *adv* im allgemeinen; **–
practitioner**, *n* praktischer
Arzt *m*

**generate**, dschenn-e-reht, *v*
erzeugen

**generation**, dschenn-*e*-reh-
sch'n, *n* Generation *f*;

(production) Erzeugung *f*

**generator**, dschenn-*e*-reh-
ter, *n* Stromerzeuger *m*;
Generator *m*

**generosity**, dschenn-*e*-ross-
i-ti, *n* Großzügigkeit *f*;
(magnanimity) Großmut *f*

**generous**, dschenn-*e*-ress,
*adj* großzügig

**genetic**, dschenn-**nett**-ick, *adj*
genetisch; **–s**, *n* Genetik *f*

**Geneva**, dschi-**nie**-we, *n*
Genf *m*

**genial**, dschie-**ni**-el, *adj*
angenehm; (person)
liebenswürdig

**genitals**, dschenn-i-t'ls, *npl*
Genitalien *pl*

**genius**, dschie-**ni**-ess, *n*
Genie *nt*

**genocide**, dschenn-*e*-sseid, *n*
Völkermord *m*

**genteel**, dschenn-**tiel**, *adj*
fein, vornehm

**gentle**, dschenn-t'l, *adj*
sanft, mild; **–man**, *n*
Gentleman *m*, Herr *m*;
**–ness**, *n* Sanftheit *f*;
Milde *f*

**gently**, dschent-li, *adv* sanft

**gents**, dschents, *n* (toilet)
Herren *pl*

**genuine**, dschenn-ju-inn,
*adj* echt; **–ness**, *n*
Echtheit *f*

**geographic(al)**, dschi-*e*-
**gräff**-ick(-'l), *adj*
geographisch

**geography**, dschi-**ogg**-re-fi, *n*
Geographie *f*

**geological**, dschi-*e*-lodsch-ik'l, *adj* geologisch

**geology,** dschi-**oll**-*e*-dschi, *n* Geologie *f*

**geometric(al),** dschi-*e*-**mett**-rick(-'l), *adj* geometrisch

**geometry,** dschi-**omm**-i-tri, *n* Geometrie *f*

**geranium,** dschi-**reh**-ni-em, *n* Gerane *f*

**geriatric,** dsche-ri-**ätt**-rick, *adj* Alten-; *n* alter Mensch *m*

**germ,** dschörm, *n* Keim *m*; *med* Bazillus *m*

**German,** dschör-men, *adj* deutsch; *n* (language) Deutsch *nt*; (person) Deutsche(r) *m & f*

**Germany,** dschör-me-ni, *n* Deutschland *nt*

**germinate,** dschör-mi-neht, *v* keimen, sprossen

**gesticulate,** dschess-**tick**-ju-leht, *v* gestikulieren

**gesture,** dschess-tscher, *n* Geste *f*

**get,** gett, *v* (obtain, catch) bekommen; (earn) verdienen; (fetch) bringen, holen; (become) werden; – **back,** (return) zurückkommen; – **by,** (manage) durchkommen; – **down,** (descend) (dismount) absteigen; – **down to,** in Angriff nehmen; – **in(to),** einsteigen (in); – **off,** (alight) aussteigen; (escape) loskommen; – **on,** (progress)

weiterkommen; – **out,** herauskommen; – **over,** (illness, shock) sich erholen von; – **round,** (circumvent) herumkommen um; – **round to (it),** dazu kommen; –**get sth done,** etw machen lassen; – **(to),** (arrive) ankommen (in); – **through (to),** durchkommen (zu); – **up,** aufstehen

**ghastly,** gahst-li, *adj* gräßlich

**gherkin,** gör-kinn, *n* Gewürzgurke *f*

**ghetto,** gett-oh, *n* G(h)etto *nt*; – **blaster,** *n fam* (lauter) Radiorekorder

**ghost,** gohst, *n* Gepenst *nt*; –**ly,** *adj* geisterhaft

**giant,** dschei-ent, *adj* riesig; *n* Riese *m*

**gibberish,** dschibb-*e*-risch, *n* Kauderwelsch *nt*

**gibe,** dscheib, *n* Spott *m*; *v* verspotten

**giblets,** dschibb-lits, *npl* (Geflügel)innereien *pl*

**giddiness,** gidd-i-niss, *n* Schwindelanfall *m*

**giddy,** gidd-i, *adj* schwindlig

**gift,** gift, *n* (present) Gabe *f*, Geschenk *nt*; (talent) Begabung *f*; –**ted,** *adj* begabt

**gigantic,** dschai-**gänn**-tick, *adj* riesenhaft; riesig

**giggle,** gigg-'l, *n* Gekicher *nt*; *v* kichern

**gild,** gild, *v* vergolden; –**ing,**

*n* Vergoldung *f*

**gills,** gills, *npl* Kiemen *pl*

**gilt,** gilt, *adj* vergoldet; *n* Vergoldung *f*

**gimmick,** gimm-ick, *n* Gag *m*

**gin,** dschinn, *n* (drink) Gin *m*, (Wacholder)schnaps *m*; (trap) Schlinge *f*

**ginger,** dschinn-dscher, *n* Ingwer *m*; – **beer,** *n* Ingwerbier *nt*; –**bread,** *n* Pfefferkuchen *m*; –**haired,** rothaarig; –**ly,** *adv* behutsam

**gipsy,** dschipp-ssi, *n* Zigeuner *m*

**giraffe,** dschi-**rahf,** *n* Giraffe *f*

**girder,** gör-der, *n* Träger *m*

**girdle,** gör-d'l, *n* Hüftgürtel *m*

**girl,** görl, *n* Mädchen *nt*; –**friend,** *n* Freundin *f*

**giro,** dschai-roh, *n* (bank) Giro *nt*; (post office) Postscheck *m*

**girth,** görth, *n* (strap) Sattelgurt *m*; (circumference) Umfang *m*

**gist,** dschist, *n* Wesentliches *nt*, Kern *m*

**give,** giw, *v* geben; (present) schenken; (confer) erteilen; – **away,** verschenken; – **in,** nachgeben; – **up,** aufgeben; – **way,** (to traffic) Vorfahrt gewähren; (collapse, yield) nachgeben, einstürzen

**glacier, gláss**-i-er, *n* Gletscher *m*

**glad,** gládd, *adj* froh; (news) erfreulich; **–ly,** *adv* gern(e)

**glamorous, glámm**-*e*-ress, *adj* glamourös

**glamour, glámm**-er, *n* Glanz *m*

**glance,** glahnss, *n* Blick *m*; *v* blicken; **– off,** *v* abprallen (von)

**gland,** gländ, *n* Drüse *f*

**glare,** glähr, *n* (brightness) grelles Licht *nt*; (stare) wilder Blick *m*; *v* blenden; (stare) anstarren

**glaring, glähr**-ring, *adj* blendend; (striking) auffallend; (obvious) kraß

**glass,** glahss, *adj* Glas-; *n* Glas *nt*; **–es,** *npl* (spectacles) Brille *f*; **– house,** *n* Gewächshaus *nt*; **– ware,** *n* Glas *nt*; **–works,** *n* Glashütte *f*; **–y,** *adj* (stare) glasig; (smooth) spiegelglatt

**glaze,** glehs, *n* Glasur *f*; *v* (door etc.) verglasen; (pottery etc.) glasieren; **– over,** glasig werden

**glazier, glehs**-jer, *n* Glaser *m*

**gleam,** gliem, *n* Schimmer *m*; (ray) Strahl *m*; *v* schimmern, strahlen

**glean,** glien, *v* herausfinden

**glee,** glie, *n* Freude *f*

**glib,** glibb, *adj pej* aalglatt

**glide,** gleid, *v* gleiten; **–r,** *n*

(aircraft) Segelflugzeug *nt*

**glimmer, glimm**-er, *n* Schimmer *m*; *v* schimmern

**glimpse,** glimps, *n* flüchtiger Blick *m*; *v* flüchtig sehen

**glint,** glint, *n* Lichtschein *m*; *v* scheinen

**glisten, gliss**-'n, *v* glitzern, glänzen

**glitter, glitt**-er, *n* Glitzern *nt*; *v* glitzern

**gloat (over),** gloht (oh-wer), *v* sich an etw weiden; (sadistic pleasure) schadenfroh sein

**global, gloh**-b'l, *adj* global, Welt-; **– warming,** *n* globale Erwärmung *f*

**globe,** glohb, *n* (sphere) Kugel *f*; (earth) Erdball *m*; (map) Globus *m*

**globular, globb**-ju-ler, *adj* kugelförmig

**gloom,** gluhm, *n* Düsterheit *f*

**gloomy, gluh**-mi, *adj* düster; (person) schwermütig

**glorify, glo'a**-ri-fei, *v* verherrlichen

**glorious, glo'a**-ri-ess, *adj* glorreich; (excellent) herrlich

**glory, glo'a**-ri, *n* Ruhm *m*; (honour) Ehre *f*; **– in,** *v* sich an etw rühmen; (take pleasure) sich an etw erfreuen

**gloss,** gloss, *n* Glanz *m*; (paint) Lackfarbe *f*; **– over,** *v* beschönigen; **–y,**

*adj* glänzend

**glove,** glaw, *n* Handschuh *m*

**glow,** gloh, *n* Glut *f*, Glühen *nt*; (of sky) Röte *f*; *v* glühen

**glue,** gluh, *n* Klebstoff *m*; *v* kleben

**glum,** glamm, *adj* mißgelaunt

**glut,** glatt, *n* Überfülle *f*; *v* überschwemmen

**glutton, glatt**-'n, *n* Vielfraß *m*; **–y,** *n* Völlerei *f*

**gnarled,** nahrld, *adj* knorrig

**gnash,** näsch, *v* knirschen

**gnat,** nätt, *n* Mücke *f*

**gnaw,** no'a, *v* nagen (an), zernagen

**go,** goh, *n* Schwung *m*; *v* gehen; (drive) fahren; (travel) reisen; (depart) abfahren; (function) funktionieren; (become) werden; **– away,** weggehen; (on journey) verreisen; **– back,** zurückgehen; **– down,** hinuntergehen; (sink) untergehen; **– for,** holen; (attack) angreifen; (like) mögen; **– off,** (depart) abgehen; (of light) ausgehen; (explode) losgehen; (go bad) schlecht werden; (cease to like) nicht mehr mögen; **– on,** (continue) weitergehen; *pej* reden und reden; (of light) angehen; (happen) passieren; **– out,**

346

ausgehen; – **up**,
hinaufsteigen; – **with**,
passen zu; – **without**,
verzichten auf; **be –ing to**,
werden; **have a – (at)**,
versuchen

**goad**, gohd, *n* anstacheln

**go-ahead**, goh-*e*-hedd, *adj*
unternehmungslustig; *n*
(*fig* permission) grünes
Licht *nt*

**goal**, gohl, *n* (aim) Ziel *nt*;
*sport* Tor *nt*; **–keeper**, *n*
Torwart *m*

**goat**, goht, *n* Ziege *f*

**gobble**, gobb-'l, *v*
hinunterschlingen

**goblet**, gobb-litt, *n* Pokal *m*

**goblin**, gobb-linn, *n*
Kobold *m*

**god**, godd, *n* Gott *m*; **–child**,
*n* Patenkind *nt*; **–dess**, *n*
Göttin *f*; **–father**, *n* Pate
*m*; **– fearing**, *adj*
gottesfürchtig; **–forsaken**,
*adj* gottverlassen; **–liness**,
*n* Frömmigkeit *f*; **–ly**, *adj*
fromm; **–mother**, *n* Patin
*f*; **–send**, *n* Gottesgabe *f*

**goggle-eyed**, gogg-'l-eid, *adj*
glotzäugig

**goggles**, gogg-'ls, *npl*
Schutzbrille *f*

**going**, goh-ing, *adj* (current)
gängig; (viable)
gutgehend; *n* (progress)
Vorankommen *nt*

**gold**, gohld, *adj* golden,
Gold-; *n* Gold *nt*; **–en**, *adj*
golden; **–finch**, *n* Stieglitz
*m*; **–fish**, Goldfisch *m*;

**–mine**, Goldgrube *f*;
**–smith**, Goldschmied *m*

**golf**, golf, *n* Golf *nt*; **– club**,
*n* (organization) Golfklub
*m*; (stick) Golfschläger *m*;
**– course**, *n* Golfplatz *m*;
**–er**, *n* Golfspieler *m*

**gondola**, gonn-de-le, *n*
Gondel *f*

**gong**, gong, *n* Gong *m*

**good**, gudd, *adj* gut; *n*
(goodness) Güte *nt*; (use)
Nutzen *m*; (benefit) Wohl
*nt*; **– afternoon!** guten
Tag!; **–bye!** auf
Wiedersehen!; (on
telephone) auf
Wiederhören; **– morning!**
guten Morgen!; **– night!**
gute Nacht!; **G– Friday**, *n*
Karfreitag *m*; **–looking**,
*adj* gutaussehend; **–-
natured**, *adj* gutmütig

**goodness**, gudd-niss, *n* Güte
*f*; (virtue) Tugend *f*

**goods**, gudds, *npl* Waren *pl*
Güter *pl*; **– train**, *n*
Güterzug *m*

**goodwill**, gudd-u'ill, *n*
Wohlwollen *nt*; *comm*
Goodwill *m*

**goose**, guhss, *n* Gans *f*

**gooseberry**, gus-be-ri, *n*
Stachelbeere *f*

**gooseflesh**, guhss-flesch, *n*
Gänsehaut *f*

**goose pimples**, guhss pimm-
p'ls, *npl* Gänsehaut *f*

**gore**, gor, *n* Blut *nt*; *v*
durchbohren

**gorge**, gordsch, *n*

Bergschlucht *f*; *v* **– (o.s.)**,
sich vollstopfen

**gorgeous**, gor-dschess, *adj*
prächtig; (person)
hinreißend

**gorilla**, ge-rill-*e*, *n* Gorilla *m*

**gorse**, gorss, *n* Stechginster
*m*

**gory**, go'a-ri, *adj* blutig

**gosling**, goss-ling, *n* junge
Gans *f*, Gänschen *nt*

**gospel**, goss-p'l, *n*
Evangelium *nt*

**gossip**, goss-ipp, *n* (talk)
Klatsch *m*; (person)
Klatschbase *f*; *v* klatschen

**gouge (out)**, gaudsch (aut),
*v* (aus)bohren

**gout**, gaut, *n* Gicht *f*; **–y**, *adj*
gichtkrank

**govern**, gaw-ern, *v* regieren;
**–ess**, *n* Gouvernante *f*;
**–ment**, Regierung *f*; **–or**,
Prinzipal *m*; (of province)
Statthalter *m*; *mech*
Regulator *m*

**gown**, gaun, *n* Kleid *nt*;
(official) Talar *m*;
(academic) Robe *f*

**GP**, dschie pie, *abbr* **general
practitioner**

**grab**, gräbb, *v* packen

**grace**, grehss, *n* (blessing)
Gnade *f*; (prayer)
Tischgebet *nt*; (charm)
Anmut *f*; *v* zieren; **–ful**,
*adj* graziös, anmutig;
**–fulness**, *n* Grazie *f*;
Anmut *f*; **–less**, *adj*
taktlos, schroff

**gracious**, greh-schess, *adj*

liebenswürdig; (merciful) gnädig

**gradation,** gre-**deh**-sch'n, n Abstufung f

**grade,** grehd, n Grad m, Rang m; (class) Klasse f; v einstufen

**gradient,** greh-di-ent, n Neigung f

**gradual(ly),** grädd-ju-el(-li), adj & adv allmählich

**graduate,** grädd-ju-et, n Akademiker m

**graduate,** grädd-ju-eht, v (from university) absolvieren

**graft,** grahft, n (botany) Edelreis nt; med Transplantat nt; (fam corruption) Schiebung f; (fam hard work) Schufterei f; v (tree) pfropfen; med transplantieren; (fam work hard) schuften

**grain,** grehn, n (of corn, salt, photog etc.) Korn nt; (cereal) Getreide nt; (of wood) Maserung f

**gram,** grämm, n Gramm nt

**grammar,** grämm-er, n Grammatik f; – **school,** n Gymnasium nt

**gramme,** grämm, n Gramm nt

**granary,** gränn-e-ri, n Kornspeicher m; – **bread,** n Vollkornbrot m

**grand,** gränd, adj grandios, großartig; –**child,** n Enkelkind nt; –**daughter,**

Enkelin f; –**father,** Großvater m; –**iose,** adj grandios; –**mother,** Großmutter f; –**parents,** npl Großeltern pl; – **piano,** n Flügel m; –**son,** n Enkel m

**grant,** grahnt, n Zuschuß m; (scholarship) Stipendium nt; v bewilligen, gewähren; zugeben

**granted,** grahn-tidd, **take for –,** v als selbstverständlich hinnehmen

**grape,** grehp, n Traube f

**grapefruit,** grehp-fruht, n Pampelmuse f, Grapefruit f

**graph,** grahf, n Schaubild nt

**graphic,** gräff-ick, adj (vivid) anschaulich; (drawn) graphisch; –**s,** n Grafik f

**grapple with,** gräpp-'l u'idh, fig. ernstlich anpacken

**grasp,** grahsp, n Griff m; v greifen; (mentally) begreifen; –**ing,** adj habgierig

**grass,** grahss, n Gras nt; (lawn) Rasen m; –**hopper,** n Heuschrecke f; –**roots,** adj Basis-, von der Basis ausgehend; –**y,** adj grasig; v (fam tell) singen

**grate,** greht, n Kamin m; v (cheese etc.) reiben; (scrape) knirschen; (annoy) auf die Nerven gehen

**grateful,** greht-full, adj

dankbar

**gratification,** grätt-i-fi-keh-sch'n, n Genugtuung f; (satisfaction) Befriedigung f

**gratify,** grätt-i-fei, v freuen; (satisfy) befriedigen; –**ing,** adj erfreulich

**grating,** greh-ting, adj (rasping) knirschend; (shrill) schrill; n Gitter nt

**gratis,** greh-tiss, adv gratis, umsonst

**gratitude,** grätt-i-tjuhd, n Dankbarkeit f

**gratuitous,** gre-tjuh-i-tess, adj grundlos

**gratuity,** gre-tjuh-i-ti, n Geschenk nt; (tip) Trinkgeld nt

**grave,** grehw, adj ernst; n Grab nt

**gravel,** gräw-'l, n Kies m

**gravestone,** grehw-stohn, n Grabstein m

**graveyard,** grehw-jahrd, n Friedhof m

**gravitate (towards),** gräw-i-teht (tu-u'ords), v angezogen werden (von)

**gravity,** gräw-i-ti, n (physics) Schwere f; (seriousness) Ernsthaftigkeit f

**gravy,** greh-wi, n Soße f

**graze,** grehs, n Abschürfung f; v (touch) streifen; (scrape skin) aufschürfen; (feed) grasen

**grease,** griess, n Fett nt; (lubricant) Schmierfett;

*v* einfetten; (lubricate) schmieren

**greasy**, grie-ssi, *adj* (oily) fettig; (road) schlüpfrig

**great**, greht, *adj* groß; (renowned) berühmt; (*fam* good) toll

**Great Britain**, greht britt-'n, *n* Großbritannien *nt*

**great-grandfather**, greht gränd-fah-dher, *n* Urgroßvater *m*

**great-grandmother**, greht gränd-madh-er, *n* Urgroßmutter *f*

**greatly**, greht-li, *adv* sehr

**greatness**, greht-niss, *n* Größe *f*

**Greece**, griess, *n* Griechenland *nt*

**greed**, gried, *n* Gier *f*; (gluttony) Gefräßigkeit *f*; **–ily**, *adv* gierig, gefräßig; **–iness**, *n* Gier *f*; **–y**, *adj* gierig, gefräßig

**Greek**, griek, *adj* griechisch; *n* (language) Griechisch *nt*; (person) Grieche *m*, Griechin *f*

**green**, grien, *adj* grün; (environmentally friendly) umweltfreundlich; *n* Grün *nt*; (open ground) Wiese *f*; *v* grünen; **–gage**, *n* Reineclaude *f*; **–grocer**, Gemüsehändler *m*; **–house**, Gewächshaus *nt*; **–house gas**, Treibhausgas *nt*; **–ish**, *adj* grünlich; **–s**, *npl* Grüngemüse *nt*

**greet**, griet, *v* begrüßen; **–ing**, *n* Gruß *m*

**gregarious**, gri-gähr-ri-ess, *adj* gesellig

**grenade**, gre-nehd, *n* Granate *f*

**grey**, greh, *adj* grau; **–hound**, *n* Windhund *m*

**grief**, grief, *n* Kummer *m*, Trauer *f*

**grievance**, grie-wenss, *n* Beschwerde *f*

**grieve**, griew, *v* trauern; (vex) betrüben

**grievous**, griew-ess *adj* (serious) schwer; (distressing) schmerzlich

**grill**, grill, *n* Rost *m*, Grill *m*; *v* auf dem Rost braten, grillen

**grim**, grimm, *adj* (dismal) finster; (fierce) grimmig

**grimace**, gri-mehss, *n* Grimasse *f*; *v* das Gesicht verziehen

**grime**, greim, *n* Schmutz *m*

**grin**, grinn, *n* Grinsen *nt*; *v* grinsen

**grind**, greind, *v* (coffee etc.) mahlen; (knife) schleifen; (teeth) knirschen mit; **–er**, *n* Mühle *f*

**grip**, gripp, *n* Griff *m*; *v* greifen, packen; **–ping**, *adj* spannend

**grisly**, gris-li, *adj* gräßlich, grausig

**gristle**, griss-'l, *n* Knorpel *m*

**grit**, gritt, *n* (gravel) Splitt *m*; (*fam* courage) Schneid *m*; *v* (teeth)

zusammenbeißen; (road) streuen; **–ty**, *adj* sandig

**groan**, grohn, *n* Stöhnen *nt*, Ächzen *nt*; *v* stöhnen

**grocer**, grohss-er, *n* Lebensmittelhändler *m*; **–ies**, *npl* Lebensmittel *pl*; **–'s**, **–y**, *n* Lebensmittelgeschäft *nt*

**groin**, greun, *n* Leisten *fpl*.

**groom**, gruhm, *n* Pferdeknecht *m*; (bridegroom) Bräutigam *m*; *v* sich zurechtmachen; (horse) striegeln; **well–ed**, *adj* gepflegt

**groove**, gruhw, *n* Rinne *f*, Furche *f*

**grope**, grohp, *v* tasten, tappen

**gross**, grohss, *adj* (thick) dick; (coarse) grob; *comm* brutto; *n* (12 dozen) Gros *nt*; **– weight**, Bruttogewicht *nt*; **–ly**, *adv* ungeheuer

**ground**, graund, *v* gründen auf; *naut* stranden; *n* Grund *m*, Boden *m*; *sport* Platz *m*; **–floor**, *n* Erdgeschoß *nt*; **–ing**, *n* Grundlagen *pl*; **–less**, *adj* grundlos; **–s**, *npl* (park) Anlagen *fpl*.; (coffee etc.) Satz *m*; **–sheet**, *n* Zeltboden *m*; **–work**, *n* Grundlage *f* (preparation) Vorarbeit *f*

**group**, gruhp, *n* Gruppe *f*; *v* gruppieren

**grouse**, grauss, *n* Waldhuhn

nt; v fam murren

**grove**, grohw, n Hain m

**grovel**, grow-'l, v kriechen

**grow**, groh, v wachsen; (become) werden; (cultivate) anbauen; **–er**, n Produzent m; **–n up**, adj erwachsen; **–th**, n Wachstum nt; med Geschwür nt; (increase) Zunahme f; (of beard) Wuchs m

**growl**, graul, n Brummen nt; v brummen

**grub**, grabb, n Larve f; (fam food) Futter nt; **–by**, adj schmutzig

**grudge**, gradsch, n Groll m; v mißgönnen; **bear a –**, v einen Groll hegen

**gruelling**, gruh-e-ling, adj zermürbend

**gruesome**, gruh-sem, adj grausig, grauenhaft

**gruff**, graff, adj mürrisch; (voice) rauh

**grumble**, gramm-b'l, v murren

**grumpy**, gramm-pi, adj schlechtgelaunt

**grunt**, grant, n Grunzen nt; v grunzen

**guarantee**, gä-ren-tie, n Garantie f; v garantieren

**guard**, gahrd, n Wache f; (railway) Schaffner m; (machine) Schutzvorrichtung f; (corps) Garde f; v bewachen; **–ed**, adj zurückhaltend; (cautious)

vorsichtig; **–ian**, n Hüter m; (trustee) Vormund m

**guerrilla**, ge-rill-e, n Guerilla m; **– war(fare)**, n Guerillakrieg m

**guess**, gess, n Vermutung f; v raten; **–work**, n Raten nt

**guest**, gest, n Gast m; **–house**, Pension f; **–room**, n Gästezimmer nt

**guidance**, gei-denss, n Leitung f, Führung f; (advice) Rat m

**guide**, geid, n Führer m; (book) Reiseführer m; v führen; **–book**, n Reiseführer m; **– dog**, n Blindenhund m; **–lines**, npl Richtlinien pl

**guild**, gild, n Gilde f

**guile**, geil, n Arglist f; **–less**, adj arglos

**guilt**, gilt, n Schuld f; **–y**, adj schuldig

**guinea**, ginn-i, n Guinee f; **– pig**, Meerschweinchen nt; fig Versuchskaninchen nt

**guise**, geis, n **in the – of sth**, in Gestalt eines/des

**guitar**, gi-tahr, n Gitarre f

**gulf**, galf, n (sea) Golf m; (abyss) Abgrund m

**gull**, gall, n Möwe f

**gullet**, gall-itt, n Kehle f

**gullible**, gall-i-b'l, adj leichtgläubig

**gulp**, galp, n Schluck m; v schlucken

**gum**, gamm, n (glue) Klebstoff m; (in mouth) Zahnfleisch nt; v

gummieren

**gun**, gann, n Gewehr nt; (cannon) Geschütz nt; **– down**, v erschießen; **–fire**, n Geschützfeuer nt; **–man**, n einer Schutzwaffe bewaffneter Mann m; **–powder**, n Schießpulver nt

**gurgle**, gör-gl, v glucksen

**gush**, gasch, n Erguß m; v hervorströmen; (fig enthuse) schwärmen

**gust**, gast, n Windstoß m; **–y**, adj böig, stürmisch

**gut**, gatt, n Darm m; **–s**, npl (fam courage) Schneid m

**gutter**, gatt-er, n (in street) Gosse f; (on roof) Dachrinne f

**guy**, gei, n (fam man) Typ m; (effigy) Strohpuppe f; **–rope**, n Zeltschnur f

**gym**, dschimm, n (abbr **gymnasium/gymnastics**)

**gymnasium**, dschimm-neh-si-em, n Turnhalle f, Fitneßstudio nt

**gymnast**, dschimm-näst, n Turner m

**gymnastics**, dschimm-näss-tiks, n Turnen nt, Gymnastik f

**gym shoes**, dschimm schuhs, npl Turnschuhe pl

**gynaecologist**, gai-ni-koll-e-dschist, n Gynäkologe m, Frauenarzt m

**gynaecology**, gai-ni-koll-e-dschi, n Gynäkologie f, Frauenheilkunde f

**haberdashery**, häbb-er-däsch-*e*-ri, *n* Kurzwaren *pl*

**habit**, häbb-itt, *n* Gewohnheit *f*; (addiction) Sucht *f*

**habitable**, häbb-i-te-b'l, *adj* (be)wohnbar

**habitat**, häbb-i-tätt, *n* Lebensraum *m*

**habitual**, he-bitt-ju-el, *adj* gewohnt, gewohnheitsmäßig; **-ly**, *adv* gewöhnlich

**hack**, häck, *n* (pej writer) Schreiberling *m*; (pej horse) Gaul *m*; *v comp* hacken

**hacker**, häck-er, *n comp* Hacker *m*

**hackneyed**, häck-nidd, *adj* abgedroschen

**haddock**, hädd-ek, *n* Schellfisch *m*

**haemorrhage**, hemm-e-

ridsch, *n* Blutung *f*

**hag**, hägg, *n* Hexe *f*; **-gard**, *adj* (worn) ausgezehrt; (worry) abgehärmt

**haggle**, hägg-'l, *v* handeln, feilschen

**Hague**, hehg, *n* **The –**, Den Haag *nt*

**hail**, hehl, *n* Hagel *m*; *v* hageln; (call) rufen; (welcome) zujubeln

**hair**, hähr, *n* Haar *nt*; **-brush**, *n* Haarbürste *f*; **-cut**, *n* Haarschnitt *m*; **-do**, *n* Frisur *f*; **-dresser**, *n* Friseur *m*; **-drier**, *n* Fön *m*; **-pin**, *n* Haarnadel *f*; **-pin bend**, *n* Haarnadelkurve *f*; **--raising**, *adj* haarsträubend; **-style**, *n* Frisur *f*; **-y**, *adj* haarig

**hake**, hehk, *n* Seehecht *m*

**hale**, hehl, *adj* gesund; (robust) kräftig

**half**, hahf, *adj & adv* halb; *n* Hälfte *f*; (beer) kleines Bier *nt*; (child's ticket) halbe Fahrkarte *f*; **– an hour**, eine halbe Stunde *f*; **– board**, *n* Halbpension *f*; **--hearted**, *adj* halbherzig; **--price**, *adj* zum halben Preis; **– term**, *n* Ferien *pl* in der Mitte des Trimesters; **– time**, *n sport* Halbzeit *f*; (work) Kurzarbeit *f*; **-way**, *adj* halb; *adv* zur Hälfte; **one and a –**, anderthalb; **two and a –**, zweieinhalb

**halibut**, häll-i-bet, *n* Heilbutt *m*

**hall**, ho'al, *n* (building) Halle *f*; (room) Saal *m*; (hallway) Flur *m*; **-mark**, *n* (Feingehalts)stempel *m*

**hallo = hello**

**hallowed**, häll-ohd, *adj* geheiligt, heilig

**Hallowe'en**, häll-oh-ien, *n* Halloween *nt*

**hallucinate**, he-lu-ssi-neht, *v* halluzinieren

**hallucination**, he-lu-ssi-neh-sch'n, *n* Halluzination *f*

**hallway**, ho'al-u'eh, *n* Flur *m*

**halo**, heh-loh, *n* Heiligenschein *m*; (moon's) Hof *m*

**halt**, hollt, *n* Halt *m*; *v* anhalten; (stop) stoppen

**halve**, hahw, *v* halbieren

**ham**, hämm, *n* Schinken *m*

**hamburger**, hämm-bör-ger,

*n* Hamburger *m*

**hamlet, hämm**-litt, *n* Dörfchen *nt*

**hammer, hämm**-er, *n* Hammer *m*; *v* hämmern

**hammock, hämm**-ek, *n* Hängematte *f*

**hamper, hämm**-per, *n* Picknickkorb *m*; *v* hindern

**hand,** händ, *n* Hand *f*; (of clock) Zeiger *m*; (worker) Arbeiter *m*; *v* reichen; – **in,** (s abgeben; **–bag,** *n* Handtasche *f*; **–bill,** *n* Flugblatt *nt*; **–book,** *n* Handbuch *nt*; **–cuffs,** *npl* Handschellen *pl*; **–ful,** *n* Handvoll *f*; (*fam* nuisance) Plage *f*; **–icap,** *n* (sport etc.) Handikap (physical/mental) Behinderung; *v* benachteiligen; **–icapped,** *adj* behindert; **–icraft,** *n* (Kunst)handwerk *nt*; **–kerchief,** *n* Taschentuch *nt*; **–le,** (n Griff *m*; (knob) Türknopf *m*; *v* handhaben, anfassen; – **luggage,** *n* Handgepäck *nt*; **–made,** *adj* handgemacht; **–out,** *n* (charity) Gabe *f*; (leaflet) Flugblatt *nt*; **–rail,** *n* Geländer *nt*; **at –,** nahe, **in –,** (cash) auf die Hand; (underway) in Arbeit; **give/lend a –,** helfen; **on (the) one –/on the other hand,** einerseits/andererseits; **out**

of –, außer Kontrolle

**handsome, hänn**-ss'm, *adj* gutaussehend; ansehnlich

**handy, hänn**-di, *adj* (convenient) praktisch; (skilled) geschickt; **–man,** *n* Bastler *m*

**hang,** häng, *v* aufhängen; hängen; – **about/around,** herumhängen, lungern; – **on,** *fam* warten; – **up,** (phone) auflegen; **get the – of,** etw in Griff bekommen, mit etw klarkommen

**hangar, häng**-er, *n* Hangar *m*

**hanger, häng**-er, *n* Kleiderbügel *m*

**hang-gliding, häng**-glei-ding, *n* Drachenfliegen *nt*

**hangover, häng**-oh-wer, *n* Kater *m*

**hanker (after), häng**-ker (ahf-ter), *v* sich sehnen (nach)

**hanky,** *abbr* **handkerchief**

**haphazard, häpp**-häs-erd, *adj* willkürlich

**happen, häpp**-en, *v* geschehen, passieren

**happily, häpp**-i-li, *adv* (joyfully) glücklich; (fortunately) glücklicherweise

**happiness, häpp**-i-niss, *n* Glück *nt*

**happy, häpp**-i, *adj* glücklich; – **birthday!** Herzlichen Glückwunsch zum Geburtstag!; – **New Year!** Frohes Neues Jahr!

**harangue,** he-räng, *n* Tirade *f*; *v fam* predigen

**harass,** hä-ress, *v* plagen; **–ment,** *n* Belästigung *f*

**harbour, hahr**-ber, *n* Hafen *m*; *v* (criminal etc.) beherbergen; (suspicion etc.) hegen

**hard,** hahrd, *adj* hart; (difficult) schwer; (character) unbeugsam; *adv* (work) hart; (push) fest; **–back,** *n* gebundene Ausgabe *f*, Hard-cover-Ausgabe *f*; – **disk,** *n comp* Festplatte *f*; **–en,** *v* härten; hart werden; **–en o.s.,** sich hartmachen; **–ly,** *adv* kaum; **–ness,** *n* Härte *f*; **–ship,** *n* Not *f*; – **shoulder,** *n* Seitenstreifen *m*; – **up,** *adj* knapp bei Kasse; **–ware,** *n* Eisenwaren *pl*; *comp* Hardware *f*; – **working,** *adj* fleißig; **–y,** *adj* (person) abgehärtet; (plant) winterhart

**hare,** hähr, *n* Hase *m*; **--lip,** *n* Hasenscharte *f*

**harm,** hahrm, *n* Schaden *m*; *v* schädigen; **–ful,** *adj* schädlich; **–less,** harmlos

**harmonious,** har-**moh**-ni-ess, *adj* harmonisch

**harmonize, hahr**-me-neis, *v* harmonieren; *mus* harmonisieren; – **(with),** harmonieren (mit)

**harness, hahr**-niss, *n* Geschirr *nt*; *v* anschirren; (forces) ausnützen

**harp,** hahrp, n Harfe f; **– on (about),** fam (immer wieder) über etw reden

**harpoon,** har-puhn, n Harpune f; v harpunieren

**harrowing,** hä-roh-ing, adj entsetzlich

**harsh,** hahrsch, adj (sound) barsch; (severe) streng; (colour) grell

**harvest,** hahr-wist, n Ernte f; v ernten

**hash,** häsch, n (meat) Haschee nt; (chaos) Wirrwarr m

**hashish,** häsch-isch, n Haschisch nt

**hassle,** häss-'l, n Ärger m

**haste,** hehst, n Eile f

**hasten,** heh-ss'n, v beschleunigen; eilen, sich beeilen

**hastily,** hehss-ti-li, adv rasch

**hasty,** hehss-ti, adj rasch; pej voreilig

**hat,** hätt, n Hut m

**hatch,** hätsch, n (in wall) Durchreiche f; n (naut) Luke f; v ausbrüten; (plot) aushecken; **–back,** n Schräghecklimousine f

**hatchet,** hätt-schitt, n Beil nt

**hate,** heht, n Haß m; v hassen; **–ful,** adj verhaßt; gehässig

**hatred,** heht-ridd, n Haß m

**haughty,** ho'a-ti, adj stolz, hochmütig

**haul,** ho'al, v ziehen; (tow) schleppen; n (catch) Fang m; **–age,** n Spedition f; **a long –,** ein weiter Weg m

**haunch,** ho'antsch, n Schenkel m; (meat) Keule f

**haunt,** ho'ant, n Treffpunkt m; v (of ghost) spuken in; (of memory etc.) plagen; (frequent) verkehren in

**have,** häw, v (possess) haben; (baby) bekommen; **– breakfast,** frühstücken; **– lunch/dinner,** zu Mittag/Abend essen; **– sth done,** etw machen lassen

**haven,** heh-wen, n Zufluchtsort m

**havoc,** häw-ek, n Verheerung f

**hawk,** ho'ak, n Habicht m; v hausieren; **–er,** n Hausierer m

**hawthorn,** ho'a-thorn, n Hagedorn m

**hay,** heh, n Heu nt; **– fever,** n Heuschnupfen m; **–stack,** n Heuschober m

**hazard,** häs-erd, n (danger) Gefahr f; (chance) Schicksal nt; (risk) Risiko nt; v riskieren; **–ous,** adj gefährlich

**haze,** hehs, n Dunst m

**hazel,** heh-s'l, adj (colour) hellbraun; n Haselnußstrauch m; **–nut,** n Hazelnuß f

**hazy,** heh-si, adj dunstig; (unclear) verschwommen

**he,** hie, pron er

**head,** hedd, adj Ober-; n Kopf m; (boss) Chef m; (forefront) Spitze f; v (lead) leiten; (ball) köpfen; **–ache,** n Kopfschmerzen pl; **– first,** adv mit dem Kopf zuerst/voran; kopfüber; **(for),** v fahren in Richtung; **–,** n Überschrift f; **–lamp,** n Scheinwerfer m; **–land,** n Vorgebirge nt; **–light,** n Scheinwerfer m; **–line,** n Schlagzeile f; **–long,** adj ungestüm; kopfüber; **–master,** n Schuldirektor m; **–mistress,** n Schuldirektorin f; **– office,** n Zentrale f; **–phones,** npl Kopfhörer pl; **–quarters,** npl Zentrale f; mil Hauptquartier nt; **–s or tails,** Kopf oder Zahl; **–strong,** adj eigensinnig; **–waiter,** n Oberkellner m; **–way,** n Fortschritte pl; **–y,** adj berauschend

**heal,** hiel, v heilen; verheilen; **–ing,** adj heilsam

**health,** helth, n Gesundheit f; **– food,** n Reformkost f; **–y,** adj gesund

**heap,** hiep, n Haufen m; v häufen

**hear,** hier, v hören; **–ing,** Gehör nt; law Verhandlung f; **–ing aid,** n Hörgerät nt; **–say,** n Hörensagen nt

**hearse,** hörss, n
  Leichenwagen m
**heart,** hahrt, n Herz nt;
  (core) Kern m; (cards)
  Herz nt; **– attack,** n
  Herzanfall m; **–breaking,**
  adj herzzerreißend;
  **–broken,** adj untröstlich;
  **–burn,** n Sodbrennen nt;
  **–felt,** adj aufrichtig
**hearth,** hahrth, n Herd m
**heartily,** hahr-ti-li, adv
  herzlich
**heartless,** hahrt-liss, adj
  herzlos
**hearty,** hahr-ti, adj (meal,
  appetite) herzhaft;
  (cheerful) herzlich
**heat,** hiet, n Hitze f; sport
  Ausscheidungsrunde f; v
  heizen, erhitzen; **–er,** n
  (Heiz)ofen m
**heath,** hieth, n Heide f
**heathen,** hie-dhen, adj
  heidnisch; n Heide m,
  Heidin f
**heather,** hedh-er, n
  Heidekraut nt
**heating,** hie-ting, n Heizung
  f
**heatstroke,** hiet-strohk, n
  Hitzschlag m
**heatwave,** hiet-u'eiw, n
  Hitzewelle f
**heave,** hiew, n (throw)
  Schwung m; (effort)
  Anstrengung f; v (throw)
  werfen; (lift) heben;
  (drag) schleppen; (sigh)
  ausstoßen
**heaven,** hew-en, n Himmel

m; **–ly,** adj himmlisch
**heavy,** hew-i, adj schwer
**Hebrew,** hie-bruh, adj
  hebräisch; n (language)
  Hebräisch nt
**Hebrides,** hebb-ri-dies, npl
  Hebriden pl
**heckle,** heck-'l, v
  dazwischenrufen
**hectic,** heck-tick, adj
  hektisch
**hedge,** hedsch, n Hecke f; v
  (be evasive) ausweichen;
  **– one's bets,** sich
  absichern
**hedgehog,** hedsch-hogg, Igel
  m
**heed,** hied, v beachten; n
  Acht f; **–ful,** adj achtsam;
  **–less,** achtlos
**heel,** hiel, n (of foot) Ferse f;
  (of shoe) Absatz m
**hefty,** heff-ti, adj kräftig,
  groß
**heifer,** heff-er, n Färse f
**height,** heit, n (of object)
  Höhe f; (of person) Größe
  f; **–en,** v erhöhen;
  (intensify) verstärken
**heinous,** heh-ness, adj
  abscheulich
**heir,** ähr, n Erbe m; **–ess,**
  Erbin f; **–loom,** n Erbstück
  nt
**helicopter,** hell-i-kop-ter, n
  Hubschrauber m
**hell,** hell, n Hölle f;–!
  verdammt!; **–ish,** adj
  höllisch
**hello,** he-loh, interj hallo,
  guten Tag

**helm,** helm, n Steuer nt;
  **–sman,** n Steuermann m
**helmet,** hell-mitt, n Helm m
**help,** help, n Hilfe f; v
  helfen; **–er,** n Helfer m;
  **–ful,** adj hilfreich; **–ing,** n
  Portion f; **–less,** adj hilflos;
  **– oneself,** v sich
  bedienen; **I can't – it,** ich
  kann nichts dafür
**hem,** hemm, n Saum m; v
  säumen; **– in,**
  einschließen
**hemisphere,** hemm-iss-fier,
  n Halbkugel f
**hemp,** hemp, n Hanf m
**hen,** hen, n (chicken)
  Henne f; (female bird)
  Weibchen nt
**hence,** henss, adv (thus)
  daher; **five years –,** in
  fünf Jahren
**henceforth,** henss-forth, adv
  von nun an
**her,** hör, adj ihr; pron
  (accusative) sie; (dative)
  ihr
**herald,** he-reld, n Vorbote
  m; v ankündigen
**heraldry,** he-reld-ri, n
  Wappenkunde f
**herb,** hörb, n Kraut nt;
  (cookery) Gewürzkraut nt
**herd,** hörd, n Herde f; v
  zusammenpferchen;
  **–sman,** n Hirte m
**here,** hier, adv hier(her);
  **–abouts,** adv hier ungefähr
  hier; **–after,** adv künftig; n
  Jenseits nt; **–by,** adv
  hiermit

**hereditary,** hi-redd-i-te-ri, *adj* erblich; (property) ererbt

**herewith,** hier-u'idh, *adv* hiermit; (enclosed) anbei

**heresy,** he-ri-si, *n* Ketzerei *f*

**heretic,** he-ri-tick, *n* Ketzer *m*

**heritage,** he-ri-tidsch, *n* Erbschaft *f*, Erbe *nt*

**hermetic(al),** hörrmett-ick(-'l), *adj* hermetisch

**hermit,** hör-mitt, *n* Einsiedler *m*; **–age,** *n* Einsiedelei *f*

**hernia,** hör-ni-e, *n* Bruch *m*

**hero,** hier-roh, *n* Held *m*; **–ic,** *adj* heldenhaft

**heroin,** he-roh-in, *n* Heroin *nt*

**heroine,** he-roh-in, *n* Heldin *f*

**heroism,** he-roh-ism, *n* Heldentum *nt*

**heron,** he-ren, *n* Reiher *m*

**herring,** he-ring, *n* Hering *m*

**hers,** hörs, *pron* ihre(r/s)

**herself,** hör-sself, *pron* (*refl*) sich (selbst); (*emphatic*) selbst; **by –,** *adv* alleine

**hesitant,** he-si-tent, *adj* zögernd

**hesitate,** he-si-teht, *v* zögern

**hesitation,** he-si-teh-sch'n, *n* Zögern *nt*

**heterosexual,** he-te-roh-seck-ssju-el, *adj* heterosexuell; *n* Heterosexuelle(r) *m & f*

**hew,** hjuh, *v* hauen, hacken

**hexagon,** heck-sse-gen, *n* Sechseck *nt*

**heyday,** heh-deh, *n* Blüte *f*

**hi,** *interj* hallo

**hiatus,** hei-eh-tess, *n* Unterbrechung *f*

**hibernate,** hei-ber-neht, *v* Winterschlaf *m* halten

**hiccough, hiccup,** hick-app, *n* Schluckauf *m*

**hidden,** hidd-'n, *adj* verborgen

**hide,** heid, *n* Haut *f*, Fell *nt*; *v* (sich) verstecken, (sich) verbergen; (keep secret) verheimlichen

**hideous,** hidd-i-ess, *adj* scheußlich, gräßlich

**hiding,** hei-ding, *n* (beating) Tracht *f* Prügel.; **–place,** *n* Versteck *nt*; **in –,** versteckt

**hi-fi,** hei-fei, *n* Hi-Fi *nt*

**high,** hei, *adj* hoch; (wind) stark; **–brow,** *adj* intellektuell; **–er,** *adj* höher; **–er education,** *n* Hochschulbildung *f*; **–est,** *adj* höchste(r/s); **–heeled,** *adj* hochhackig; **H–lands,** *npl* schottisches Hochland *nt*; **–light,** *n* (in hair) Strähne *f*; *fig* Höhepunkt *m*; **–ness,** *n* Höhe *f*; **H–ness,** *n* (title) Hohheit *f*; **–rise building,** *n* Hochhaus *nt*; **– street,** *n* Hauptstraße *f*; **–way,** *n* öffentliche Straße *f*

**hijack,** hei-dschäck, *v* entführen; **–ing,** *n* Entführung *f*

**hike,** heik, *n* Wanderung *f*; *v* wandern; **–r,** *n* Wanderer *m*

**hilarious,** hi-lähr-ri-ess, *adj* sehr lustig

**hill,** hill, *n* Berg *m*; (small) Hügel *m*; (incline) Steigung *f*; **–side,** *n* Berghang *m*; **–y,** *adj* hügelig

**hilt,** hilt, *n* Heft *nt*, Griff *m*; **up to the –,** voll und ganz

**him,** himm, *pron* (accusative) ihn; (dative) ihm; **–self,** *pron* (refl) sich (selbst); (emphatic) selbst; **by –,** *adv* alleine

**hind,** heind, *adj* hinter, Hinter-; *n* (deer) Hirschkuh *f*

**hinder,** hinn-der, *v* behindern

**hindmost,** heind-mohst, *adj* hinterste(r/s)

**hindrance,** hinn-drenss, *n* Hindernis *nt*

**hindsight,** heind-sseit, *n* **with (the benefit of) –,** im nachhinein

**hinge,** hindsch, *n* Scharnier *nt*; (on door) Angel *f*; **– on,** *v* abhängen von

**hint,** hint, *n* (indication) Hinweis *m*; (trace) Spur *f*; *v* andeuten

**hip,** hipp, *adj fam* in; *n* Hüfte *f*

**hire,** hei-er, *n* Miete *f*; (car) Verleih *m*; *v* (car etc.) mieten; (staff) anstellen; **–car,** *n* Leihwagen *m*; **–**

**purchase,** n Ratenkauf m

**his,** his, adj sein; *pron* seine(r/s)

**hiss,** hiss, n Zischen nt; v zischen

**historian,** hiss-**tor**-ri-en, n Historiker m

**historic,** hiss-to-rick, adj historisch

**historical,** hiss-to-rick-'l, adj geschichtlich, historisch

**history,** hiss-te-ri, n Geschichte f

**hit,** hitt, n (blow) Schlag m; (score) Treffer m; (success) Erfolg m; v (strike) schlagen; (wound, damage, score) treffen; **--and-run accident,** n Unfall m mit Fahrerflucht

**hitch,** hitsch, n Haken m; v (pull up) hochziehen; (hook on) anhängen; (make fast) festmachen; – **off,** v ausgliedern **a lift,** v trampen

**hitch-hike, hitsch-heik,** v trampen; **–r,** n Tramper m

**hi-tech, hei-teck,** adj Hi-tech-

**hitman,** hitt-**männ,** n Killer m

**hither,** hidh-er, adv hierher; **–to,** adv bisher

**hive,** heiw, n Bienenstock m; **–off,** v ausgliedern

**hoard,** hord, n Hort m; v hamstern

**hoarding, hor**-ding, n Bauzaun m

**hoarse,** horss, adj heiser

**hoax,** hohks, n Streich m; v

anführen

**hob,** hobb, n Kochplatte f, Kochstelle f

**hobble, hobb-**'l, v humpeln

**hobby, hobb-**i, n Hobby nt; **--horse,** n Steckenpferd nt

**hock,** hock, n (wine) weißer Rheinwein m; (leg) Hachse f

**hoe,** hoh, n Hacke f; v hacken

**hog,** hogg, n Schwein nt; v für sich beanspruchen; **go the whole –,** v fam etw konsequent durchziehen, Nägel mit Köpfen machen

**hoist,** heust, v Winde f; (flag) hissen hochheben;

**hold,** hohld, n (grasp) Halt m; (power) Macht f; *naut* Laderaum m; v halten; (contain) enthalten; (possess) besitzen, haben; (conversation) führen; (on telephone) am Apparat bleiben; **– back,** zurückhalten; **– down,** v festhalten; (job) behalten; (prices) niedrig halten; **–er,** n (receptacle) Behälter m; (owner) Inhaber m; **–ing,** n Pachtgut nt; (share) Anteil m; **– on,** v sich festhalten; (wait) warten; **– one's own,** v sich behaupten; **– out,** v (resist) aushalten; **– up,** v (delay) aufhalten; (attack) überfallen; **--up,** n (delay)

Verzögerung f; (attack) Überfall m

**hole,** hohl, n Loch nt

**holiday, holl**-i-deh, n (day) Feiertag m; (vacation) Urlaub m; **– resort,** n Ferienort m; **–s,** npl Ferien pl

**holiness, hoh-**li-niss, n Heiligkeit f

**Holland, holl-**end, n Holland nt

**hollow, holl**-oh, adj hohl; (sound) dumpf; (fig empty) leer; n Vertiefung f; **– out,** v aushöhlen

**holly, holl-**i, n Stechpalme f

**holocaust, holl-**e-korst, n Holocuast m

**hologram, holl-**e-grämm, n Hologramm nt

**holy, hoh-**li, adj heilig; **H-Week,** Karwoche f

**homage, homm-**idsch, n Huldigung f; **pay – to,** v huldigen

**home,** hohm, adv nach Hause; (at home) zu Hause n Zuhause nt; Heim nt; **at –,** adv zu Hause; **--coming,** n Heimkehr f; **–land,** n Heimat f; **–less,** adj obdachlos; **–ly,** adj häuslich; **–made,** adj selbstgemacht, Hausmacher-; **–ward,** adj Heim-, Rück-; adv nach Hause, heimwärts; **be –sick,** v Heimweh haben

**homoeopathic,** hoh-mi-o-

**päth**-ick, *adj* homöopathisch

**homosexual**, hoh-moh-**seck**-ssju-el, *adj* homosexuell; *n* Homosexuelle(r) *m & f*

**honest**, **onn**-ist, *adj* ehrlich; **–y**, *n* Ehrlichkeit *f*

**honey**, **hann**-i, *n* Honig *m*; **–moon**, *n* Hochzeitsreise *f*, Flitterwochen *pl*; **–suckle**, *n* Geißblatt *nt*

**honk**, hongk, *v* hupen

**honorary**, **onn**-e-re-ri, *adj* Ehren-

**honour**, **onn**-er, *n* Ehre *f*; *v* ehren; **–able**, *adj* ehrenhaft

**hood**, hudd, *n* Kapuze *f*; (of car) Verdeck *nt*

**hoodwink**, **hudd**-u'ink, *v* täuschen

**hoof**, huhf, *n* Huf *m*

**hook**, huck, *n* Haken *m*; *v* festhaken; (catch) fangen; **– and eye**, *n* Haken und Öse *pl*

**hooligan**, **huh**-li-gen, *n* Rowdy *m*

**hoop**, huhp, *n* (toy) Reifen *m*; (band) Band *nt*

**hooray**, huh-**rei**, *interj* hurra; *n* Hurra *nt*

**hoot**, huht, *v* (of owl) heulen; (of horn) hupen; **–er**, *n* (car's) Hupe *f*; (*fam* nose) Zinken *m*

**hoover** ®, **huh**-wer, *n* Staubsauger *m*; *v* Staub saugen

**hop**, hopp, *n* Hüpfer *m*;

(plant) Hopfen *m*; *v* hüpfen

**hope**, hohp, *n* Hoffnung *f*; *v* hoffen; **–ful**, *adj* (person) hoffnungsvoll; (situation) vielversprechend; **–fully**, *adv* (with hope) hoffnungsvoll; (it is hoped) hoffentlich; **–less**, *adj* hoffnungslos

**horizon**, he-**rei**-sen, *n* Horizont *m*

**horizontal**, ho-ri-**son**-t'l, *adj* wagrecht, horizontal

**hormone**, **hor**-mohn, *n* Hormon *nt*

**horn**, horn, *n* Horn *nt*; (car's) Hupe *f*

**hornet**, **hor**-nitt, *n* Hornisse *f*

**horny**, **hor**-ni, *adj fam* geil

**horrible**, **ho**-ri-b'l, *adj* schrecklich

**horrid**, **ho**-ridd, *adj* entsetzlich; (person) gemein

**horrify**, **ho**-ri-fei, *v* entsetzen

**horror**, **ho**-rer, *n* Entsetzen *nt*; Greuel *m*; **– film**, *n* Horrorfilm *m*

**hors d'oeuvre**, or **dörw(r)**, *n* Vorspeise *f*

**horse**, horss, *n* Pferd *nt*; **– chestnut**, *n* Roßkastanie *f*; **–man**, *n* Reiter *m*; **–power**, *n* Pferdestärke *f*; **–racing**, *n* Pferderennen *nt*; **–radish**, *n* Meerrettich *m*; **–riding**, *n* Reiten *nt*; **–shoe**, *n* Hufeisen *nt*;

**–woman**, *n* Reiterin *f*; **on –back**, *adv* zu Pferde

**horticulture**, **hor**-ti-kall-tscher, *n* Gartenbau *m*

**hose**, hohs, *n* (rubber tube) Schlauch *m*; (stockings) Strümpfe *pl*

**hosiery**, **hohs**-je-ri, *n* Strumpfwaren *pl*

**hospitable**, hoss-**pitt**-e-b'l, *adj* gastfreundlich, gastlich

**hospital**, **hoss**-pit-'l, *n* Krankenhaus *nt*

**hospitality**, hoss-pi-**täll**-i-ti, *n* Gastfreundschaft *f*

**host**, hohst, *n* Gastgeber *m*; (innkeeper) Wirt *m*; (army) Heer *nt*; *relig* Hostie *f*

**hostage**, **hoss**-tidsch, *n* Geisel *f*

**hostel**, **hoss**-t'l, *n* Herberge *f*; (youth) Jugendherberge *f*; **–ry**, *n* Gasthof *m*

**hostess**, **hohss**-tess, *n* Gastgeberin *f*

**hostile**, **hoss**-teil, *adj* feindlich; (unfriendly) feindselig

**hot**, hott, *adj* heiß; (food, drink) warm; (spicy) scharf

**hotel**, hoh-**tell**, *n* Hotel *nt*

**hothouse**, **hott**-hauss, *n* Treibhaus *nt*

**hotline**, **hott**-lein, *n* heißer Draht *m*, Hotline *f*

**hotly**, **hott**-li, *adv* hitzig

**hound**, haund, *n* Jagdhund *m*; *v* hetzen

**hour**, au-er, *n* Stunde *f*; **–ly**,

*adj* stündlich

**house,** hauss, n Haus nt;
**–boat,** n Hausboot nt;
**–hold,** n Haushalt m;
**–keeper,** n Haushälterin f;
**–keeping,** n
Hauswirtschaft f; **H– (of Commons),** n Unterhaus nt; **––warming (party),** n
Einweihungsparty f;
**–wife,** n Hausfrau f;
**–work,** n Hausarbeit f

**house,** haus, v unterbringen

**housing,** hau-sing, n
Wohnungen pl; (cover)
Gehäuse nt; **– estate,** n
Wohnsiedlung f

**hovel,** how-'l, n elende
Hütte f

**hover,** how-er, v schweben;–
**about,** v fig herumhängen;
**–craft,** n
Luftkissenfahrzeug nt

**how,** hau, adv wie; **–ever,**
adv wie auch; conj jedoch;
**– far?** wie weit? **– much?**
wieviel? **– many?** wie
viele?

**howl,** haul, n Geheul nt; v
heulen

**HQ,** abbr headquarters

**hub,** habb, n Nabe f; fig
Mittelpunkt m

**huddle (together),** hadd-'l
(tu-gedh-er), v sich
(zusammen)drängen

**hue,** hjuh, n Farbton m; **–
and cry,** n Gezeter nt

**hug,** hagg, n Umarmung f; v
umarmen

**huge,** hjuhdsch, adj riesig

**hulk,** halk, n naut Hulk
m/nt; (fam person)
Klotz m

**hull,** hall, n naut
Schiffsrumpf m

**hum,** hamm, n (of insect)
Summen nt; (of engine)
Brummen nt; v summen;
brummen

**human,** hjuh-men, adj
menschlich; **– (being),** n
Mensch m

**humane,** hju-mehn, adj
human

**humanitarian,** hju-männ-i-
**tähr**-ri-en, adj humanitär

**humanity,** hju-**männ**-i-ti, n
Menschheit f; (kindness)
Humanität f

**humble,** hamm-b'l, adj
demütig; v demütigen

**humbug,** hamm-bagg, n
(nonsense) Humbug
m; (sweet)
Pfefferminzbonbon nt

**humdrum,** hamm-dramm,
adj Alltags-

**humid,** hjuh-midd, adj
feucht

**humidity,** hju-**midd**-i-ti, n
Feuchtigkeit f

**humiliate,** hju-**mill**-i-eht, v
erniedrigen

**humiliation,** hju-mill-i-eh-
sch'n, n Erniedrigung f

**humorous,** hjuh-me-ress, adj
lustig, komisch

**humour,** hjuh-mer, n (wit)
Humor m; (mood) Laune
f; **– sb** v jdm seinen
Willen lassen

**hunch,** hantsch, n
Buckel m; (suspicion)
Ahnung f; **–back,** n
Bucklige(r) m & f;
**–ed,** adj gekrümmt

**hundred,** **hann**-dred, num
hundert; **–th,** adj
hundertste(r/s), n
Hundertstel nt;
**–weight,** Zentner m

**Hungarian,** hang-**gähr**-ri-
en, adj ungarisch; n
(language) Ungarisch nt;
(person) Ungar m

**Hungary,** hang-ge-ri, n
Ungarn nt

**hunger,** hang-ger, n Hunger
m; **– after/for,** v hungern
nach

**hungry,** hang-gri, adj
hungrig; **be –,** v Hunger
haben

**hunt,** hant, n Jagd f; v jagen;
**–er,** n Jäger m; **– for,** v
suchen

**hurdle,** hör-d'l, n Hürde f

**hurl,** hörl, v schleudern

**hurrah,** he-**rah,** interj hurra

**hurray = hurrah**

**hurricane,** **ha**-ri-ken, n
Orkan m

**hurried,** **ha**-ridd, adj eilig;
**–ly,** adv hastig

**hurry,** **ha**-ri, n Eile f; v
eilen, sich beeilen; (rush)
übereilen; **be in a –,** v es
eilig haben

**hurt,** hört, adj verletzt; v
(pain) weh tun; (injure)
verletzen; **–ful,** adj
verletzend

**hurtle, hör**-t'l, *v* sausen
**husband, has**-bend, *n*
(Ehe)mann *m*
**hush,** hasch, *interj* Ruhe!;
Stille *f*; **– up,** *v* (quieten)
zum Schweigen bringen;
(conceal) vertuschen
**husk,** hask, *n* Hülse *f*,
Schale *f*
**husky, hass**-ki, *adj* heiser; *n*
(dog) Husky *m*
**hustle, hass**-'l, *v* (jostle)
stoßen; (hurry) drängen
**hut,** hatt, *n* Hütte *f*
**hutch,** hatsch, *n* (rabbit)
Stall *m*; (hamster) Käfig *m*
**hyacinth, hei**-*e*-ssinth, *n*
Hyazinthe *f*
**hybrid, hei**-bridd, *adj*
Misch-; *n* Kreuzung *f*
**hydrant, hei**-drent, *n*
Hydrant *m*
**hydraulic, hei**-**dro**-lick, *adj*
hydraulisch
**hydro-electric, hei**-droh-i-
**leck**-trick, *adj* (power)
Wasserkraft-, durch
Wasserkraft erzeugt
**hydrofoil, hei**-dre-feul, *n*
Tragflügelboot *nt*
**hydrogen, hei**-dri-dschen, *n*
Wasserstoff *m*
**hygiene, hei**-dschien, *n*
Hygiene *f*
**hygienic, hei**-**dschien**-ick,
*adj* hygienisch
**hymn,** himm, *n* Hymne *f*
**hype,** heip, *n* Rummel *m*
**hypermarket, heip**-er-mahr-
kitt, *n* Hypermarket *m*
**hyphen, hei**-fen, *n*

Bindestrich *m*
**hypnotic,** hipp-**nott**-ick, *adj*
hypnotisch
**hypnotize, hipp**-ne-teis, *v*
hypnotisieren
**hypocrisy,** hi-**pock**-ri-ssi, *n*
Heuchelei *f*
**hypocrite, hipp**-*e*-kritt, *n*
Heuchler *m*
**hypothermia,** heip-oh-**thör**-
mje, *n* Unterkühlung *f*
**hypothesis,** hei-**poth**-i-ssiss,
*n* Hypothese *f*
**hypothetic(al),** heip-*e*-
**thett**-ick-'l, *adj*
hypothetisch
**hysterical,** hiss-**te**-rick-'l, *adj*
hysterisch

**I,** ei, *pers. pron* ich

**ice,** eiss, *n* Eis *nt*; **–berg,** *n* Eisberg *m*; **– cream,** *n* Eis *nt*; **– cube,** *n* Eiswürfel *m*; **– rink,** *n* Schlittschuhbahn *f*; **– skating,** *n* Schlittschuhlaufen *nt*

**icicle,** eiss-i-k'l, *n* Eiszapfen *m*

**icing,** eiss-ing, *n* Zuckerguß *m*; **– sugar,** *n* Puderzucker *m*

**icon,** ei-kon, *n* Ikone *f*

**icy,** eiss-i, *adj* eisig

**idea,** ei-di-e, *n* Idee *f*, Einfall *m*

**ideal,** ei-di-el, *adj* ideal; *n* Ideal *nt*; **–ist,** *n* Idealist *m*

**identical,** ei-denn-ti-k'l, *adj* gleichartig, identisch

**identification,** ei-denn-ti-fi-keh-sch'n, *n* Identifizierung *f*; **(means of) –,** Ausweispapiere *pl*

**identify,** ei-denn-ti-fai, *v* identifizieren

**identity,** ei-denn-ti-ti, *n* Identität *f*; **– card,** *n* Personalausweis *m*

**idiom,** idd-i-em, *n* (phrase) Redewendung *f*; (dialect) Idiom *nt*

**idiomatic,** idd-i-e-mätt-ick, *adj* idiomatisch

**idiosyncratic,** idd-i-oh-ssing-krätt-ick, *adj* eigenwillig

**idiot,** idd-i-et, *n* Idiot *m*

**idiotic,** idd-i-ott-ick, *adj* idiotisch

**idle,** ei-d'l, *adj* (lazy) faul; (inactive) tatenlos; (empty) leer; *v* faulenzen; **–ness,** *n* Untätigkeit *f*; **–r,** *n* Faulenzer *m*

**idol,** ei-d'l, *n* Idol *nt*; **–ize,** *v* vergöttern

**idyllic,** i-dill-ick, *adj* idyllisch

**if,** iff, *conj* wenn; (whether) ob; **– not,** wenn nicht; **– only,** wenn… nur; **– so,** wenn ja; **even –,** selbst wenn

**ignite,** igg-nait, *v* (set fire to) anzünden; (catch fire) sich entzünden

**ignition,** igg-ni-sch'n, *n* Zündung *f*; **– key,** *n* Zündschlüssel *m*

**ignorance,** igg-ne-renss, *n* Unwissenheit *f*

**ignorant,** igg-ne-rent, *adj* unwissend

**ignore,** igg-nor, *v* ignorieren; unbeachtet lassen

**ill,** ill, *adj* (unwell) krank; (nauseous) übel; *n* Übel *nt*

**illegal,** i-lie-gel, *adj* illegal

**illegible,** i-ledsch-i-b'l, *adj* unleserlich

**illegitimate,** i-li-dschitt-i-met, *adj* (child) unehelich; (action, conclusion) unzulässig

**ill feeling,** ill fie-ling, *n* Verstimmung *f*

**illiterate,** i-litt-e-ret, *adj* analphabetisch; (uneducated) ungebildet

**illness,** ill-niss, *n* Krankheit *f*

**illogical,** i-lodsch-i-k'l, *adj* unlogisch

**illuminate,** i-luh-mi-neht, *v* beleuchten

**illumination,** i-lu-mi-**neh-**

**sch'n,** n Beleuchtung f

**illusion,** i-**luh**-sch'n, n
Täuschung f, Illusion f

**illusory,** i-**luh**-se-ri, adj
illusorisch

**illustrate, ill-**e-streht, v
(text) illustrieren;
(explain)
veranschaulichen

**illustration,** ill-e-**streh**-
sch'n, n (picture)
Illustration f; (example)
Beispiel nt

**illustrious,** i-**lass**-tri-ess, adj
berühmt

**image, imm-**idsch, n
(picture) Bild nt;
(reputation) Image nt

**imaginary,** i-**mädsch**-i-ne-ri,
adj Phantasie-; (not real)
eingebildet

**imagination,** i-mädsch-i-
**neh**-sch'n, n Phantasie f,
Einbildung(skraft) f

**imagine,** i-**mädsch**-inn, v
(picture to o.s.) sich
vorstellen; (delude o.s.)
sich einbilden

**imbecile, imm-**bi-ssiel, n
Schwachsinnige(r) m & f

**imbibe, imm-baibb,** v
trinken

**imbue, imm-bjuh,** v
durchdringen; fig erfüllen

**imitate, imm-**i-teht, v
nachahmen, imitieren

**immaculate,** i-**mäck**-ju-litt,
adj makellos; relig
unbefleckt

**immaterial,** i-me-**tier**-ri-el,
adj unwichtig

**immature,** i-me-**tjuhr,** adj
unreif

**immediate,** i-**mie**-di-et, adj
unmittelbar; sofortig; **–ly,**
adv (time) sofort; (place)
direkt

**immense,** i-**menss,** adj
ungeheuer

**immensity,** i-**menss**-i-ti, n
Ungeheuerlichkeit f

**immerse (in),** i-**mörss**
(inn), v (ein)tauchen (in)

**immigrant, imm**-i-grent, n
Einwanderer m,
Immigrant m

**immigrate, imm-**i-greht, v
einwandern, immigrieren

**immigration,** i-mi-**greh**-
sch'n, n Einwanderung f,
Immigration f

**imminent, imm-**i-nent, adj
unmittelbar bevorstehend

**immobile,** i-**moh**-beil, adj
unbeweglich

**immobilize,** i-**moh**-bi-lais, v
unbeweglich machen; fig
lähmen

**immodest,** i-**modd**-ist, adj
unbescheiden; (improper)
unanständig

**immoral,** i-**mo**-rel, adj
unmoralisch

**immorality,** i-me-**räll**-i-ti, n
Unsittlichkeit f

**immortal,** i-**mor**-t'l, adj
unsterblich; **–ize,** v
verewigen

**immovable,** i-**muh**-we-b'l,
adj unbeweglich, fest

**immune,** i-**mjuhn,** adj med
immun; (safe) geschützt

**immunity,** i-**mjuh**-ni-ti, n
(med, law) Immunität f

**imp,** imp, n Kobold m;
(rascal) Schelm m

**impact, imm-**päckt, n
(Zusammen)Stoß m; fig
Wirkung f

**impair,** imm-**pähr,** v
beeinträchtigen

**impale,** imm-**pehl,** v
aufspießen

**impart,** imm-**pahrt,** v
mitteilen

**impartial,** imm-**pahr**-schel,
adj unparteiisch

**impassable,** imm-**pah**-sse-b'l,
adj unpassierbar

**impasse, äm-**päss, v
Sackgasse f

**impassive,** imm-**päss**-iw, adj
ausdruckslos

**impatience,** imm-**peh**-
schenss, n Ungeduld f

**impatient,** imm-**peh**-schent,
adj ungeduldig

**impeach,** imm-**pietsch,** v
beschuldigen; **–ment,** n
Beschuldigung f

**impeccable,** imm-**peck**-e-b'l,
adj tadellos

**impede,** imm-**piedd,** v
behindern

**impediment,** imm-**pedd**-i-
ment, n Hindernis nt; (in
speech) Sprachfehler m

**impending,** imm-**penn**-ding,
adj bevorstehend;
(threatening) drohend

**imperative,** imm-**pe**-re-tiw,
adj gebieterisch;
(necessary) erforderlich; n

*gram* Imperativ *m*

**imperfect,** imm-**pör**-fikt, *adj*
mangelhaft; *n gram*
Imperfekt *nt*

**imperfection,** imm-per-**feck**-sch'n, *n*
Unvollkommenheit *f*;
Defekt *m*

**imperial,** imm-**pier**-ri-el, *adj*
kaiserlich, Reichs-; **–ism,**
*n* Imperialismus *m*

**impersonal,** imm-**pör**-sse-n'l,
*adj* unpersönlich

**impersonate,** imm-**pör**-se-neht, *v* (pretend to be)
sich ausgeben als; (mimic)
imitieren

**impertinence,** imm-**pör**-ti-nenss, *n* Frechheit *f*

**impertinent,** imm-**pör**-ti-nent, *adj* unverschämt

**impervious (to),** imm-**pör**-vi-ess (to), *adj*
unempfänglich (für)

**impetuous,** imm-**pett**-ju-ess, *adj* ungestüm, hitzig

**impetus,** imm-pi-tess, *adj*
Antrieb *m*, Anstoß *m*

**impinge (on),** imm-**pindsch** (onn), *v* beeinträchtigen

**implement,** imm-pli-ment, *n*
Gerät *nt*; *v* durchführen,
umsetzen

**implicate,** imm-pli-keht, *v*
belasten, verwickeln

**implication,** imm-pli-**keh**-sch'n, *n* (suggestion)
Implikation *f*

**implicit,** imm-**pliss**-itt, *adj*
(implied) implizit,
unausgesprochen;

(unquestioning)
unbedingt

**implore,** imm-**plor**, *v*
anflehen

**imply,** imm-**plai**, *v*
bedeuten; (suggest)
andeuten

**impolite,** imm-pe-**lait**, *adj*
unhöflich

**import,** imm-**port**, *n* (goods)
Import *m*, Einfuhr *f*;
(meaning) Bedeutung *f*; **–duty,** *n* Einfuhrzoll *m*

**import,** imm-**port**, *v*
einführen

**importance,** imm-**port**-enss, *n* Wichtigkeit *f*

**important,** imm-**por**-tent, *adj* wichtig

**importer,** imm-**por**-ter, *n*
Importeur *m*

**impose (on),** imm-**pohs** (onn), *v* auferlegen

**imposing,** imm-**poh**-sing, *adj* imposant

**imposition,** imm-pe-**si**-sch'n, *n* Auferlegung *f*,
Erhebung *f*; (taking
advantage) Ausnützung *f*

**impossibility,** imm-poss-i-**bill**-i-ti, *n*
Unmöglichkeit *f*

**impossible,** imm-**poss**-i-b'l, *adj* unmöglich

**impostor,** imm-**poss**-ter, *n*
Betrüger *m*

**impotent,** imm-pe-tent, *adj*
(powerless) unfähig;
(sexually) impotent

**impound,** imm-**paund**, *v* in
Beschlag nehmen

**impoverished,** imm-**pow**-e-rischt, *adj* verarmt

**impracticable,** imm-**präck**-ti-ke-b'l, *adj* unpraktisch

**imprecation,** imm-pri-**keh**-sch'n, *n* Fluch *m*

**impregnable,** imm-**pregg**-ne-b'l, *adj* uneinnehmbar

**impregnate,** imm-**pregg**-neht, *v* imprägnieren

**impress,** imm-**press**,
*v*(influence) Eindruck
machen (auf); (mark)
(ein)prägen; **–ion,** *n*
Eindruck *m*; (mark)
Abdruck *m*; **–ive,** *adj*
eindrucksvoll

**imprint,** imm-**print**, *n*
Abdruck *m*

**imprison,** imm-**pris**-'n, *v*
einsperren; **–ment,** *n* Haft
*f*

**improbable,** imm-**probb**-e-b'l, *adj* unwahrscheinlich

**impromptu,** imm-**promp**-tjuh, *adj & adv*
improvisiert

**improper,** imm-**propp**-er, *adj*
unschicklich

**improve,** imm-**pruhw**, *v*
verbessern; **–ment,** *n*
Verbesserung *f*

**improvize,** imm-**pre**-weis, *v*
improvisieren

**imprudent,** imm-**pruh**-dent, *adj* unklug

**impudence,** imm-pju-denss, *n* Unverschämtheit *f*

**impudent,** imm-pju-dent, *adj* unverschämt, frech

**impulse,** imm-palss, *n*

Impuls *m*; (An)stoß *m*

**impure,** imm-**pjuhr,** *adj*
(dirty) unrein; (morally)
unkeusch

**impurity,** imm-**pjuhr**-ri-ti, *n*
Unreinheit *f*

**in,** inn, *adv* **be –,** (at
home/work) da sein; (in
fashion) in sein; **sb is –
for sth,** jdm steht etw
bevor; **be – on,** Bescheid
wissen über; **come –,**
(person) hereinkommen;
(train etc.) ankommen

**in,** inn, *prep in*; **– 1960,**
1960, im Jahre 1960; **– the
morning/afternoon,** am
Morgen/Nachmittag; **–
German/English,** auf
deutsch/englisch; **1 – 3,**
jede(r/s) dritte

**inability,** inn-e-**bill**-i-ti, *n*
Unfähigkeit *f*

**inaccessible,** inn-äck-**ssess**-
i-b'l, *adj* unzugänglich

**inaccuracy,** i-**näck**-ju-re-ssi,
*n* Ungenauigkeit *f*

**inaccurate,** i-**näck**-ju-ret, *adj*
(wrong) unrichtig;
(imprecise) ungenau

**inadequate,** i-**nädd**-i-kuet,
*adj* unzulänglich

**inadvertent(ly),** inn-ed-**vört**-
tent(-li), *adj & adv*
versehentlich

**inane,** i-**nehn,** *adj* albern

**inanimate,** i-**nänn**-i-met, *adj*
leblos

**inappropriate,** inn-e-**prohp**-
pri-et, *adj* unpassend,
unangemessen

**inasmuch as,** inn-es-**matsch**
äs, *conj* insofern als

**inaudible,** i-**no'a**-di-b'l, *adj*
unhörbar

**inaugurate,** i-**no'a**-gju-reht,
*v* (building) einweihen;
(person, policy) einführen

**inborn,** inn-**born,** *adj*
angeboren

**inbred,** inn-**bred,** *adj*
angeboren

**incalculable,** inn-**käll**-kju-
le-b'l, *adj* unermeßlich;
(unpredictable)
unberechenbar

**incapable,** inn-**keh**-pe-b'l,
*adj* unfähig

**incapacitate,** inn-ke-**päss**-i-
teht, *v* unfähig machen

**incapacity,** inn-ke-**päss**-i-ti,
*n* Unfähigkeit *f*

**incarnation,** inn-kar-**neh**-
sch'n, *n* Verkörperung *f*;
*relig* Fleischwerdung *f*

**incendiary,** inn-**ssenn**-di-e-
ri, *adj* Brand-; *n*
Brandstifter *m*

**incense,** inn-ssenss, *n*
Weihrauch *m*

**incense,** inn-**ssenss,** *v*
erzürnen

**incentive,** inn-**ssenn**-tiw, *n*
Ansporn *m*;
(performance)
Leistungsanreiz *m*

**incessant(ly),** inn-**ssess**-
ent(-li), *adj & adv*
unaufhörlich

**inch,** intsch, *n* Zoll *m*; *v* sich
ganz langsam
voranbewegen

**incident,** inn-**ssi-dent,** *n*
Vorfall *m*

**incidental,** inn-ssi-**denn**-t'l,
*adj* beiläufig; (music)
Begleit-; **-ly,** *adv* übrigens

**incinerator,** inn-**ssinn**-e-
reh-ter, *n*
Verbrennungsofen *m*

**incision,** inn-**ssisch**-'n, *n*
Einschnitt *m*

**incite,** inn-**sseit,** *v*
aufstacheln

**inclination,** inn-kli-**neh**-
sch'n, *n* Neigung *f*

**incline,** inn-**klein,** *n*
Neigung *f*, Abhang *m*

**incline,** inn-**klein,** *v* sich
neigen; **be –ed (to),**
geneigt sein (zu)

**include,** inn-**kluhd,** *v*
einschließen

**including,** inn-**kluh**-ding,
*prep* einschließlich,
inbegriffen

**inclusive (of),** inn-**kluh**-
ssiw (ew), *adv*
einschließlich

**incoherent,** inn-ke-**hier**-
rent, *adj*
unzusammenhängend;
(rambling) unverständlich

**income,** inn-**kamm,** *n*
Einkommen *nt*; **– tax,** *n*
Einkommensteuer *f*

**incoming,** inn-**kamm**-ing,
*adj* (train etc.)
ankommend; (president
etc.) nachfolgend

**incomparable,** inn-**komm**-
pe-re-b'l, *adj*
unvergleichlich

**incompatible,** inn-kemm-**pätt**-i-b'l, *adj* unvereinbar

**incompetence,** inn-**komm**-pi-tenss, *n* Unfähigkeit *f*

**incompetent,** inn-**komm**-pi-tent, *adj* unfähig

**incomplete,** inn-kemm-**plieht,** *adj* unvollständig

**incomprehensible,** inn-komm-pri-**henn**-ssi-b'l, *adj* unbegreiflich, unverständlich

**inconceivable,** inn-kenn-**ssie**-we-b'l, *adj* unvorstellbar

**inconclusive,** inn-kenn-**kluh**-ssiw, *adj* ergebnislos, unschlüssig

**incongruous,** inn-**kong**-gru-ess, *adj* absurd; (inappropriate) unpassend

**inconsiderate,** inn-konn-**ssidd**-e-ret, *adj* rücksichtslos

**inconsistent,** inn-konn-**ssiss**-tent, *adj* (contradictory) widersprüchlich; (irregular) unbeständig; (self-contradictory) inkonsequent

**inconsolable,** inn-konn-**ssoh**-le-b'l, *adj* untröstlich

**inconspicuous,** inn-konn-**spick**-ju-ess, *adj* unauffällig

**incontinent,** inn-**konn**-ti-nent, *adj med* inkontinent

**inconvenience,** inn-konn-**wie**-ni-enss, *n* Unbequemlichkeit *f*; *v*

Unannehmlichkeiten bereiten

**inconvenient,** inn-konn-**wie**-ni-ent, *adj* unbequem, ungünstig

**incorporate (into),** inn-**kor**-pe-reht (**inn**-tu), *v* aufnehmen (in), einbringen (in)

**incorrect,** inn-ke-**rekt,** *adj* unrichtig

**incorrigible,** inn-ko-ri-dschi-b'l, *adj* unverbesserlich

**increase, inn**-kriess, *n* (in pay) Erhöhung *f*; (in size) Vergrößerung *f*; (in number) Zunahme *f*

**increase,** inn-**kriess,** *v* (raise) erhöhen; (in size) vergrößern; (in number) (sich) vermehren, zunehmen

**incredible,** inn-**kredd**-i-b'l, *adj* unglaublich

**incredulous,** inn-**kredd**-ju-less, *adj* skeptisch

**incriminate,** inn-**krimm**-i-neht, *v* beschuldigen

**incubator, inn**-kju-beh-ter, *n* Brutkasten *m*

**incumbent,** inn-**kamm**-bent, *adj* – **on,** obliegend; *n* Amtsinhaber *m*

**incur,** inn-**kör,** *v* sich zuziehen, erleiden

**incurable,** inn-**kjuhr**-re-b'l, *adj* unheilbar; *fig* unverbesserlich

**indebted (to),** inn-**dett**-id (tu), *adj* (owing money)

verschuldet; (obliged) verpflichtet

**indecent,** inn-**die**-ssent, *adj* unanständig

**indecision,** inn-di-**ssi**-sch'n, *n* Unentschlossenheit *f*

**indecisive,** inn-di-**ssei**-ssiw, *adj* ergebnislos, unschlüssig

**indecorous,** inn-di-ko-ress, *adj* unziemlich

**indeed,** inn-**died,** *adv* tatsächlich, in der Tat

**indefensible,** inn-di-**fenn**-ssi-b'l, *adj* unhaltbar; (inexcusable) nicht zu entschuldigen

**indefinitely,** inn-**deff**-i-nitt-li, *adv* auf unbestimmte Zeit

**indelible,** inn-**dell**-i-b'l, *adj* unauslöschlich; (stain) nicht zu entfernen

**indemnify,** inn-**demm**-ni-fai, *v* entschädigen

**indemnity,** inn-**demm**-ni-ti, *n* Entschädigung *f*

**independence,** inn-di-**penn**-dens, *n* Unabhängigkeit *f*

**independent,** inn-di-**penn**-dent, *adj* unabhängig

**indescribable,** inn-diss-**krei**-be-b'l, *adj* unbeschreiblich

**indestructible,** inn-diss-**track**-ti-b'l, *adj* unzerstörbar

**indeterminate,** inn-di-**tör**-mi-nitt, unbestimmt

**index, inn**-dex, *n* Index *m*; (in book) Register *nt*; **index finger,** *n*

Zeigefinger *m*

**India, inn**-di-e, *n* Indien *nt*; **–n,** *adj* indisch; *n* (language) Indisch *nt*; Inder *m*; **(American) –,** *n* Indianer *m*

**indicate, inn**-di-keht, *v* andeuten

**indication, inn**-di-keh-sch'n, *n* (An)zeichen *nt*

**indicative, inn-dick**-*e*-tiw, *adj* **be – of,** *v* auf etw schließen lassen; *n gram* Indikativ *m*

**indicator, inn**-di-keh-ter, *n* (sign) (An)zeichen *nt*; (car's) Blinker *m*

**indict, inn-dait,** *v* anklagen; **–ment,** *n* Anklage *f*

**indifference, inn-diff**-*e*-renss, *n* Gleichgültigkeit *f*

**indifferent, inn-diff**-*e*-rent, *adj* (uncaring) gleichgültig; (mediocre) mittelmäßig

**indigestible, inn**-di-dschess-ti-b'l, *adj* unverdaulich

**indigestion, inn**-di-**dschess**-tschen, *n* Verdauungsstörung *f*

**indignant, inn-digg**-nent, *adj* entrüstet

**indignation, inn-digg-neh**-sch'n, *n* Entrüstung *f*

**indignity, inn-digg**-ni-ti, *n* Demütigung *f*

**indirect(ly), inn**-di-**reckt**(-li), *adj & adv* indirekt

**indiscreet, inn**-diss-**kriet,** *adj* indiskret

**indiscriminate, inn**-diss-

**krimm**-i-net, *adj* unkritisch; (random) willkürlich

**indispensable, inn**-diss-**penn**-sse-b'l, *adj* unentbehrlich

**indisposed, inn**-diss-**pohsd,** *adj* (disinclined) abgeneigt; (unwell) unwohl

**indisputable, inn**-diss-**pjuh**-te-b'l, *adj* unbestreitbar

**indistinct, inn**-diss-**tinkt,** *adj* undeutlich

**indistinguishable, inn**-diss-**ting**-gu'isch-*e*-b'l, *adj* ununterscheidbar

**individual, inn**-di-**widd**-ju-*e*l, *adj* individuell, Einzel-; *adv* einzeln; *n* Individuum *nt*

**indolent, inn**-de-lent, *adj* träge

**indoor, inn**-dor, *adj* (plant, game, etc.) Zimmer-; (clothes) Haus-; *sport* Hallen-

**indoors, inn**-dors, *adv* (in) drinnen, im Hause; (into) ins Haus

**induce, inn-djuhss,** *v* (persuade) veranlassen; (cause) herbeiführen; **–ment,** *n* Anreiz *m*

**induction, inn-dack**-sch'n, *n* Einführung *f*

**indulge, inn-daldsch,** *v* sich hingeben; **– in,** sich etw gönnen; **–nce,** *n* (pleasure) Genuß *m*; **–nt,** inn-**dall**-dschent, *adj*

genüßlich; (forgiving) nachsichtig

**industrial, inn-dass**-tri-*e*l, *adj* industriell, Industrie-; **– estate,** *n* Industriegebiet *nt*

**industrialization, inn-dass**-tri-*e*-lai-**seh**-sch'n, *n* Industrialisierung *f*

**industrious, inn-dass**-tri-ess, *adj* fleißig

**industry, inn**-dess-tri, *n* Industrie *f*; (hard work) Fleiß *m*

**inebriated, i-nie**-bri-eh-tidd, *adj* betrunken

**inedible, i-nedd**-i-b'l, *adj* ungenießbar

**ineffective, i-ni-feck**-tiw, *adj* wirkungslos

**ineffectual, i-ni-feck**-tju-*e*l, *adj* untauglich

**inefficiency, i-ni-fisch**-en-ssi, *n* Unfähigkeit *f*

**inefficient, i-ni-fisch**-ent, *adj* unwirksam; unfähig

**inept, i-nept** *adj* (inappropriate) ungeeignet; (clumsy) ungeschickt

**inequality, i-ni-ku'oll**-i-ti, *n* Ungleichheit *f*

**inert, i-nört,** *adj* träge; (chemical) inaktiv

**inertia, i-nör**-sche, *n* Trägheit *f*

**inescapable, i-niss-keh**-pe-b'l, *adj* unvermeidlich

**inevitable, i-new**-i-te-b'l, *adj* unvermeidlich

**inevitably, i-new**-i-teb-li,

*adv* zwangsläufig

**inexact**, i-nigg-**säckt**, *adj* (inaccurate) ungenau; (incorrect) unrichtig

**inexcusable**, i-nicks-**kjuh**-se-b'l, *adj* unverzeihlich

**inexhaustible**, i-nigg-**so'ass**-ti-b'l, *adj* unerschöpflich

**inexorable**, i-**neckss**-*e-re*-b'l, *adj* unerbittlich

**inexpensive**, i-nickss-**penn**-ssiw, *adj* preiswert

**inexperience**, i-nickss-**pier**-ri-enss, n Unerfahrenheit *f*; **–d**, *adj* unerfahren

**inexplicable**, i-nickss-**plick**-*e*-b'l, *adj* unerklärlich

**inextricable**, i-nickss-**trick**-*e*-b'l, *adj* unentwirrbar

**infallible**, inn-**fäll**-i-b'l, *adj* unfehlbar

**infamous**, **inn**-fe-mess, *adj* berüchtigt

**infamy**, **inn**-fe-mi, n Unehre *f*; Schande *f*

**infancy**, **inn**-fen-ssi, n Kindheit *f*; **in its –**, *fig* noch in den Kinderschuhen

**infant**, **inn**-fent, n kleines Kind *nt*; *law* Unmündige(r) *m & f*; **–ile**, *adj* kindisch; **– school**, n Vorschule *f*

**infantry**, **inn**-fen-tri, n Infanterie *f*

**infatuated (with)**, inn-**fätt**-ju-eh-tid (u'idh), *adj* vernarrt (in)

**infect**, inn-**feckt**, *v* anstecken; **–ed**, *adj*

(person) infiziert; (wound) entzündet; **–ion**, n Ansteckung *f*, Infektion *f*; **–ious**, *adj* ansteckend

**infer**, inn-**för**, *v* ableiten, schließen (aus)

**inference**, **inn**-fe-renss, n Folgerung *f*, Schluß *m*

**inferior**, inn-**fier**-ri-er, *adj* minderwertig

**inferiority**, inn-fier-ri-o-ri-ti, n Minderwertigkeit *f*; **– complex**, n Minderwertigkeits-kom-plex *m*

**infernal**, inn-**för**-nel, *adj* teuflisch, höllisch

**infertile**, inn-**för**-teil, *adj* unfruchtbar

**infertility**, inn-fer-**till**-i-ti, n Unfruchtbarkeit *f*

**infested**, inn-**fess**-tidd, *adj* **be – with**, wimmeln von

**infidelity**, inn-fi-**dell**-i-ti, n, Untreue *f*

**infinite(ly)**, **inn**-fi-nit(-li), *adj & adv* unendlich

**infinity**, inn-**finn**-i-ti, n Unendlichkeit *f*

**infirm**, inn-**förm**, *adj* gebrechlich; **–ary**, n Krankenhaus *nt*; (sick-quarters) Krankenstation *f*

**inflame**, inn-**flehm**, *v* (enrage) aufbringen; *med* entzünden

**inflammable**, inn-**flamm**-*e*-b'l, *adj* feuergefährlich, leicht entzündlich

**inflammation**, inn-fle-**meh**-sch'n, n Entzündung *f*

**inflate**, inn-**fleht**, *v* aufblasen; (tyre) aufpumpen; (price) steigern

**inflation**, inn-**fleh**-sch'n, n Inflation *f*

**inflexible**, inn-**fleck**-ssi-b'l, *adj* unbiegsam; *fig* unbeugsam

**inflict (on)**, inn-**flickt** (onn), *v* zufügen; aufbürden

**influence**, **inn**-fluh-enss, n Einfluß *m*; *v* beeinflussen

**influential**, inn-fluh-**enn**-schel, *adj* einflußreich

**influenza**, inn-fluh-**enn**-*se*, n Grippe *f*

**influx**, **inn**-flacks, n Zufluß *m*

**inform**, inn-**form**, *v* benachrichtigen, informieren; **–al**, *adj* zwanglos; **–ant**, n Informant *m*

**information**, inn-fer-**meh**-sch'n, n Auskünfte *pl*, Information *f*; **a piece of –**, eine Auskunft *f*

**informer**, inn-**for**-mer, n *pej* Denunziant *m*

**infrequent(ly)**, inn-**frie**-ku'ent(-li), *adj & adv* selten

**infringe**, inn-**frindsch**, *v* verstoßen gegen; *law* verletzen; **–ment**, n Verstoß *m*; Verletzung *f*

**infuriate**, inn-**fjuhr**-ri-eht, *v* wütend machen

**infusion**, inn-**fjuh**-sch'n, n

Aufguß *m*

**ingenious,** inn-**dschie**-ni-ess, *adj* geschickt; (cleverly designed) genial

**ingenuity,** inn-dschinn-**juh**-i-ti, *n* Einfallsreichtum *m*

**ingenuous,** inn-**dschenn**-juh-ess, *adj* naiv

**ingot,** ing-gett, *n* Barren *m*

**ingrained,** inn-**grehnd**, *adj* eingewurzelt; (person) eingefleischt

**ingratiate oneself (with),** inn-**greh**-schi-eht u'an-**sself** (u'idh), *v* sich einschmeicheln (bei)

**ingratitude,** inn-**grätt**-i-tjuhd, *n* Undankbarkeit *f*

**ingredient,** inn-**grie**-di-ent, *n* Zutat *f*, Bestandteil *m*

**ingrowing,** inn-**groh**-ing, *adj* nach innen wachsend

**inhabit,** inn-**häbb**-itt, *v* bewohnen; **–able,** *adj* bewohnbar; **–ant,** *n* Einwohner *m*

**inhale,** inn-**hehl**, *v* einatmen, inhalieren

**inherent (in),** inn-**hier**-rent (inn), *adj* innewohnend; (natural) natürlich

**inherit,** inn-**he**-ritt, *v* erben; **–ance,** *n* Erbe *nt*

**inhibited,** inn-**hibb**-i-tidd, *adj* gehemmt

**inhibition,** inn-hi-**bi**-sch'n, *n* Hemmung *f*

**inhospitable,** inn-hoss-**pitt**-e-b'l, *adj* (climate etc.) unwirtlich; (person) ungastlich

**inhuman,** inn-**hju**-men, *adj* unmenschlich

**inimitable,** i-**nimm**-i-te-b'l, *adj* unnachahmlich

**iniquitous,** i-**nick**-u'i-tess, *adj* ungerecht

**initial,** i-**nisch**-el, *adj* Anfangs-, anfänglich; *n* Initiale *f*; **–ly,** *adv* anfangs, zu Anfang

**initiate,** i-**nisch**-i-eht, *v* (person) einweihen; (proceedings) einleiten

**initiative,** i-**nisch**-e-tiw, *n* Initiative *f*

**inject,** inn-**dscheckt**, *v* (ein)spritzen; **–ion,** *n* Spritze *f*

**injunction,** inn-**dschank**-sch'n, *n law* Verfügung *f*

**injure,** inn-**dscher**, *v* verletzen, schädigen

**injury,** inn-**dsche**-ri, *n* Verletzung *f*; *fig* Unrecht *nt*; **– time,** *n sport* Nachspielzeit *f*

**injustice,** inn-**dschass**-tiss, *n* Ungerechtigkeit *f*

**ink,** ink, *n* Tinte *f*

**inkling,** ink-ling, *n* Ahnung *f*

**inlaid,** inn-**lehd**, *adj* eingelegt

**inland,** inn-**länd**, *adj* inländisch, Binnen-; *adv* landeinwärts; *n* **I–Revenue,** *n* Finanzamt *nt*

**in-laws,** inn-**lo'as**, *npl* (parents-in-law) Schwiegereltern *pl*; (family) angeheiratete

Verwandte *pl*

**inlet,** inn-lett, *n mech* Zuleitung *f*; *geog* Bucht *f*

**inmate,** inn-meht, *n* Insasse *m*

**inn,** inn, *n* Gasthaus *m*

**innate,** i-**neht**, *adj* angeboren

**inner,** inn-er, *adj* inner, Innen-; **– city,** *n* Innenstadt *f*

**innkeeper,** inn-kie-per, *n* Gastwirt *m*

**innocent,** inn-*e*-ssent, *adj* unschuldig

**innocuous,** i-**nock**-ju-ess, *adj* harmlos

**innovation,** i-ne-**weh**-sch'n, *n* Neuerung *f*

**innuendo,** inn-ju-**enn**-doh, *n* Anspielung *f*

**innumerable,** i-**njuh**-me-re-b'l, *adj* unzählig

**inoculate,** i-**nock**-ju-leht, *v* (ein)impfen

**inoffensive,** i-ne-**fenn**-ssiw, *adj* harmlos

**inopportune,** inn-opp-er-tjuhn, *adj* ungelegen

**inordinately,** i-**nor**-di-net-li, *adj* unmäßig

**input,** inn-putt, *n* (contribution) Beitrag *m*; *comp* Input *m*

**inquest,** inn-ku'est, *n* gerichtliche Untersuchung *f*; *fig* nachträgliche Analyse *f*

**inquire (about),** inn-**ku'air** (e-baut), *v* sich erkundigen (nach); **–**

**into,** untersuchen

**inquiry,** inn-**ku'air**-ri, *n* Erkundigung *f*; (investigation) Untersuchung *f*; **– office,** *n* Auskunftsbüro *nt*

**inquisition,** inn-ku'i-**sisch**-'n, *n* Inquisition *f*

**inquisitive,** inn-**ku'i**-si-tiw, *adj* neugierig

**inroad,** inn-rohd, *n* Eingriff *m*

**insane,** inn-**ssehn,** *adj* wahnsinnig; *med* geisteskrank

**insanity,** inn-**ssänn**-i-ti, *n* Wahnsinn *m*

**insatiable,** inn-**sseh**-schi-e-b'l, *adj* unersättlich

**inscribe,** inn-**skraib,** *v* einschreiben

**inscription,** inn-**skrip**-sch'n, *n* Inschrift *f*

**insect,** inn-ssekt, *n* Insekt *nt*

**insecure,** inn-ssi-**kjuhr,** *adj* unsicher

**insemination,** inn-semm-i-**neh**-sch'n, *n* (artificial) Befruchtung *f*

**insensible,** inn-ssenn-ssi-b'l, *adj* unempfindlich; (unconscious) bewußtlos

**inseparable,** inn-**ssepp**-e-re-b'l, *adj* unzertrennlich; *gram* untrennbar

**insert,** inn-**ssört,** *v* einsetzen; (words) einfügen; (advertisement) setzen; **–ion,** *n* Einlegen *nt*; (words) Einfügung *f*; (advertisement) Anzeige

**inside,** inn-**ssaid,** *adj* inner, Innen-; *adv* drinnen; nach innen; *n* Innenseite *f*, Innere(s) *nt*; **inside out,** *adv* (reversed) falsch herum; (thoroughly) in- und auswendig

**insidious,** inn-**ssidd**-i-ess, *adj* hinterlistig

**insight,** inn-**sseit,** *n* Einsicht *f*, Verständnis *nt*

**insignificant,** inn-ssigg-**niff**-i-kent, *adj* unbedeutend

**insincere,** inn-ssinn-**ssier,** *adj* unaufrichtig

**insinuate,** inn-**ssinn**-ju-eht, *v* andeuten

**insipid,** inn-**ssipp**-idd, *adj* fade, geschmacklos

**insist** (on), inn-**ssist** (onn), *v* bestehen (auf); **–ent,** *adj* beharrlich

**insolence,** inn-**sse**-lenss, *n* Unverschämtheit *f*

**insolent,** inn-**sse**-lent, *adj* unverschämt, frech

**insolvent,** inn-**ssoll**-went, *adj* zahlungsunfähig

**inspect,** inn-**spekt,** *v* inspizieren; **–ion,** *n* Inspektion *f*; **–or,** *n* Inspektor *m*; (bus, factory) Kontrolleur *m*

**inspiration,** inn-spi-**reh**-sch'n, *n* Inspiration *f*

**inspire,** inn-**speir,** *v* einflößen; inspirieren

**instal(l),** inn-**sto'al,** *v* einsetzen; installieren; **–ation,** *n* Installation *f*;

**instalment,** inn-**sto'al**-ment, *n* (payment) Rate *f*; (episode) Fortsetzung *f*; **to pay by – s,** *v* auf Rate zahlen

**instance,** inn-stenss, *n* Beispiel *nt*; Fall *m*; **for –,** zum Beispiel

**instant,** inn-stent, *adj* sofortig; *n* Augenblick *m*; **–aneous,** *adj* augenblicklich; **–ly,** *adv* sofort

**instead,** inn-**stedd,** *adv* statt dessen; **– of,** *prep* anstatt

**instep,** inn-stepp, *n* Spann *m*

**instigate,** inn-sti-geht, *v* anstiften

**instil,** inn-still, *v* einflößen

**instinct,** inn-stinkt, *n* Instinkt *m*

**institute,** inn-sti-tjuht, *n* Institut *nt*; *v* einleiten, einführen

**instruct,** inn-**strakt,** *v* (teach) unterrichten; (direct) anweisen; **–ion,** *n* (teaching) Unterricht *m*; (direction) Anweisung; **–or,** *n* Lehrer *m*

**instrument,** inn-stru-ment, *n* Instrument *nt*

**insubordination,** inn-sse-bor-di-**neh**-sch'n, *n* Widersetzlichkeit *f*

**insufferable,** inn-**ssaff**-e-re-b'l, *adj* unerträglich

**insufficient,** inn-sse-**fisch**-ent, *adj* ungenügend

**insular,** inn-ssju-ler, *adj*
Insel-; *fig* engstirnig

**insulation,** inn-ssju-leh-
sch'n, *n* Isolierung *f*

**insulin,** inn-ssju-linn, *n*
Insulin *nt*

**insult,** inn-ssalt, *n*
Beleidigung *f*

**insult,** inn-ssalt, *v*
beleidigen

**insurance,** inn-schor-renss,
*n* Versicherung *f*

**insure,** inn-schor, *v*
versichern

**insurrection,** inn-sse-reck-
sch'n, *n* Aufstand *m*

**intact,** inn-takt, *adj* intakt

**intangible,** inn-tänn-schi-
b'l, nicht greifbar

**integral,** inn-tegg-rel, *adj*
wesentlich

**integrate (into),** inn-tigg-
reht **(inn-**tu), *v*
eingliedern (in)

**integrity,** inn-tegg-ri-ti, *n*
Seriosität *f*

**intellect,** inn-ti-lekt, *n*
Verstand *m*

**intelligence,** inn-tell-i-
dschenss, *n* Intelligenz *f*

**intelligent,** inn-tell-i-
dschent, *adj* intelligent

**intend,** inn-tend, *v*
beabsichtigen

**intense,** inn-tenss, *adj* stark,
intensiv; (person)
ernsthaft; –ly, *adv*
intensiv; (very) äußerst

**intensify,** inn-tenn-ssi-fei, *v*
verstärken

**intensive,** inn-tenn-ssiw, *adj*

intensiv; **– care (unit),** *n*
Intensivstation *f*

**intensity,** inn-tenn-si-ti, *n*
Intensität *f*

**intent (on),** inn-tent (onn),
*adj* (determined)
entschlossen;
(concentrating)
konzentriert (auf);**–ion,** *n*
Absicht *f*; **–ional,** *adj*
absichtlich; **–ly,** *adv*
konzentriert

**interact,** inn-te-räkt, *v*
gemeinsam handeln; *n*
Wechselwirkung *f*

**intercept,** inn-ter-ssept, *v*
auffangen

**interchange,** inn-ter-
tschehndsch, *n*
(exchange) Austausch
*m*; (junction)
Verkehrskreuz *m*

**interchange,** inn-ter-
tschehndsch, *v*
austauschen

**intercom,** inn-ter-komm, *n*
(Gegen)sprechanlage *f*

**intercourse,** inn-ter-korss, *n*
(sexual, social) Verkehr
*m*; *comm* Beziehungen *pl*

**interest,** inn-te-rest, *n*
Interesse *nt*; *fin* Zinsen *pl*;
*comm* Anteil *m*; *v*
interessieren; **–ed,**
interessiert; (involved)
beteiligt; **–ing,** *adj*
interessant; **be –ed in,** *v*
sich interessieren für

**interface,** inn-ter-feiss, *n*
Schnittstelle *f*; *comp*
Interface *nt*

**interfere,** inn-ter-fier, *v* –
**(in),** (meddle) sich
einmischen; **– with,**
(radio etc.) stören;
(property etc.) sich an etw
zu schaffen machen

**interference,** inn-ter-fier-
renss, *n* (meddling)
Einmischung *f*; (radio
etc.) Störung *f*

**interior,** inn-tier-ri-er, *adj*
inner, Innen-; *n* Inneres
*nt*; **– designer,** *n*
Innenarchitekt *m*

**intermediary,** inn-ter-mie-
di-e-ri, *n* Vermittler *m*

**intermediate,** inn-ter-mie-
di-et, *adj* dazwischen
liegend; Mittel-,
Zwischen-

**intermittent(ly),** inn-ter-
mitt-ent(-li), *adj & adv*
periodisch

**intern,** inn-törn, *v*
internieren

**internal,** inn-tör-nel, *adj*
inner, Innen-; (inland)
Inlands-; **–ly,** *adv*
innerlich, inner

**international,** *adj*
international; *n sport*
(player) Nationalspieler
*m*; (match) Länderspiel *nt*

**interpret,** inn-tör-pritt, *v*
(translate) dolmetschen;
(explain) deuten; *theatre,*
*mus* interpretieren;
**–ation,** *n* Interpretation *f*;
**–er,** *n* (translator)
Dolmetscher *m*; *theatre,*
*mus* Interpret *m*

**interrogate,** inn-**te**-*re*-geht, *v* verhören

**interrogation,** inn-te-re-**geh**-sch'n, *n* Verhör *nt*

**interrupt,** inn-*te*-**rapt,** *v* unterbrechen; **–ion,** *n* Unterbrechung *f*

**intersect,** inn-ter-**ssekt,** *v* (sich) schneiden; **–ion,** *n* (of roads) Kreuzung *f*

**interspersed (with),** inn-ter-**spörst** (u'idh), *adj* durchsetzt (mit)

**interval,** inn-**ter**-vel, *n* (distance) Abstand *m*; *theatre* etc. Pause *f*

**intervene,** inn-ter-**wien,** *v* (person) eingreifen; (space, time) dazwischenliegen

**intervention,** *n* Eingreifen *nt*

**interview,** Interview *nt*; **(job) –,** *n* Vorstellungsgespräch *nt*; *v* interviewen; **–er,** *n* Interviewer *m*

**intestine,** inn-**tess**-tin, *n* Darm *m*

**intimacy,** inn-ti-*me*-ssi, *n* Intimität *f*

**intimate,** inn-ti-met, *adj* (familiar, close) vertraut; (sexually) intim; (private) persönlich

**intimate,** inn-ti-meht, *v* andeuten

**intimidate,** inn-ti-mi-deht, *v* einschüchtern

**intimidation,** inn-ti-mi-**deh**-sch'n, *n* Einschüchterung *f*

**into,** inn-tu, *prep* in, in… hinein

**intolerable,** inn-**toll**-*e*-*re*-b'l, *adj* unerträglich

**intolerance,** inn-**toll**-*e*-renss, *n* Intoleranz *f*

**intoxicate,** inn-**tock**-ssi-keht, *v* berauschen; **–d,** *adj* betrunken

**intractable,** inn-**träck**-te-b'l, *adj* hartnäckig

**intransigent,** inn-**tränn**-si-dschent, *adj* unnachgiebig

**in-tray,** inn-treh, *n* Ablage *f* für Eingänge

**intrepid,** inn-**trepp**-idd, *adj* unerschrocken

**intricate,** inn-tri-ket, *adj* verwickelt

**intrigue,** inn-trieg, *n* Intrige *f*

**intrigue,** inn-trieg, *v* faszinieren

**intriguing,** inn-**trie**-ging, *adj* faszinierend

**intrinsic,** inn-**trinn**-sick, *adj* (inherent) innewohnend; (essential) wesentlich

**introduce,** inn-tre-**djuhss,** *v* (bring in) einführen; (person) vorstellen

**introduction,** inn-tre-**dak**-sch'n, *n* Einführung *f*; (to book etc.) Einleitung *f*; (to person) Vorstellung *f*

**introductory,** inn-tre-**dak**-te-ri, *adj* Einführungs-; einleitend

**intrude (on),** inn-**truhd** (onn), *v* stören; **–r,** *n* Eindringling *m*

**intrusive,** inn-**truh**-ssiw, *adj* aufdringlich, störend

**intuition,** inn-tju-**isch**-'n, *n* Intuition *f*

**inundate,** inn-an-deht, *adj* überschwemmen

**invade,** inn-**wehd,** *v* einfallen (in); **–r,** *n* Angreifer *m*

**invalid,** inn-**wäll**-idd, *adj* ungültig

**invalid,** inn-*we*-lidd, *adj* (disabled) invalide; (ill) krank; *n* (disabled) Invalide *m*; (ill) Kranke(r) *m* & *f*; **– chair,** *n* Rollstuhl *m*

**invaluable,** inn-**wäll**-ju-*e*-b'l, *adj* unschätzbar

**invariable,** inn-**wehr**-ri-*e*-b'l, *adj* unveränderlich

**invariably,** inn-**wehr**-ri-eb-li, *adv* ausnahmslos

**invasion,** inn-**weh**-sch'n, *n* Einfall *m*

**invent,** inn-**went,** *v* erfinden; **–ion,** *n* Erfindung *f*; **–ive,** *adj* erfinderisch; **–or,** *n* Erfinder *m*

**inventory,** inn-went-ri, *n* Inventar *m*

**invert,** inn-**wört,** *v* umkehren, umdrehen; **–ed commas,** *pl* Anführungszeichen *pl*

**invest,** inn-**west,** *v* investieren

**investigate,** inn-wess-ti-geht, *v* untersuchen

**investigation,** inn-wess-ti-

**geh**-sch'n, *n*
Untersuchung *f*

**investment,** inn-**west**-ment, *n* Investition *f*, Kapitalanlage *f*

**investor,** inn-**wess**-ter, *n* Investor *m*, Kapitalanleger *m*

**inveterate,** inn-**wett**-e-ret, *adj* eingefleischt

**invigorating,** inn-**wigg**-e-reh-ting, *adj* belebend

**invincible,** inn-**winn**-ssi-b'l, *adj* unüberwindlich

**invisible,** inn-**wis**-i-b'l, *adj* unsichtbar

**invitation,** inn-wi-**teh**-sch'n, *n* Einladung *f*

**invite,** inn-**weit,** *v* einladen

**invoice,** inn-**weuss,** *n* Rechnung *f*; *v* – **sb for sth,** jdm für etw eine Rechnung ausstellen

**invoke,** inn-**wohk,** *v* anrufen

**involuntary,** inn-**woll**-en-te-ri, *adj* unwillkürlich

**involve,** inn-**wolw,** *v* (entail) mit sich bringen; **– in,** verwickeln in; **–ed,** *adj* (complicated) verwickelt; **get –ed (in),** mitmachen (bei); sich verwickeln (in)

**inward,** inn-u'ed, *adj* inner, Innen-; *adv* nach innen; **–ly,** innerlich; **–s,** nach innen, einwärts

**iodine,** ei-*o*-dien, *n* Jod *nt*

**IOU,** ei oh juh, *n abbr* **I owe you**), Schuldschein *m*

**IRA,** ei ahr eh, *n* (*abbr* **Irish Republican Army**), IRA *f*

**irate,** ei-**reht,** *adj* wütend

**Ireland,** eir-lend, *n* Irland *nt*

**iris,** ei-riss, *n* (plant) Schwertlilie *f*; (eye) Regenbogenhaut *f*

**Irish,** ei-rish, *adj* irisch; **the –,** *npl* Iren *pl* Irländer *pl*; **–man,** Ire *m*, Irländer *m*; **–woman,** Irin *f*, Irländerin *f*

**irksome,** örk-sem, *adj* lästig

**iron,** ei-en, *adj* eisern, Eisen-; *n* (metal) Eisen *nt*; (appliance) Bügeleisen *nt*; *v* bügeln; **I– Curtain,** eiserner Vorhang *m*

**ironic(al),** ei-**ronn**-ick(-'l), *adj* ironisch

**ironing,** ei-e-ning, *n* (action) Bügeln *nt*; (clothes) Bügelwäsche *f*; **– board,** *n* Bügelbrett *nt*

**ironmonger,** ei-en-mang-ger, *n* Eisenwarenhandlung *f*

**irony,** ei-*ro*-ni, *n* Ironie *f*

**irrational,** i-**räsch**-e-nel, *adj* irrational

**irreconcilable,** i-reck-*on*-sseil-e-b'l, *adj* unvereinbar

**irrefutable,** i-ri-**fjuh**-te-b'l, *adj* unwiderlegbar

**irregular,** i-**regg**-ju-ler, *adj* (uneven, *gram*) unregelmäßig; (shape) ungleichmäßig; (extraordinary) unüblich

**irrelevant,** i-**rell**-e-went, *adj* nebensächlich

**irreparable,** i-**repp**-e-re-b'l,

*adj* nicht wiedergutzumachend

**irreplaceable,** i-ri-**pleh**-sse-b'l, *adj* unersetzlich

**irreproachable,** i-ri-**proh**-tsche-b'l, *adj* tadellos

**irresistible,** i-ri-**siss**-ti-b'l, *adj* unwiderstehlich

**irrespective (of),** i-riss-**peck**-tiw (ev), *adj* ungeachtet

**irresponsible,** i-riss-**ponn**-ssi-b'l, *adj* unverantwortlich; verantwortungslos

**irretrievable,** i-ri-**trie**-we-b'l, *adj* unwiederbringlich

**irreverent,** i-**rew**-e-rent, *adj* respektlos

**irrigate,** i-ri-geht, *v* bewässern

**irritable,** i-ri-*te*-b'l, *adj* reizbar

**irritate,** i-ri-teht, *v* irritieren; *med* reizen

**Islam,** is-lahm, Islam *m*; **–ic,** *adj* islamisch

**island,** ei-lend, *n* Insel *f*; **–er,** *n* Inselbewohner *m*

**isle,** eil, *n* Eiland *nt*, Insel *f*

**isolate,** ei-sse-leht, *v* isolieren; **–d,** *adj* isoliert; (unique) einzeln, Einzel-

**isolation,** ei-sse-**leh**-sch'n, *n* Isolierung *f*

**Israel,** is-reh-el, *n* Israel *nt*; **–i,** *adj* israelisch; *n* Israeli *m & f*

**issue,** iss-juh, *n* (subject) Frage *f*, Thema *nt*; (of newspaper) Ausgabe *f*; (of

shares) Emission *f*; *v*
(publish) herausgeben;
(shares) emittieren;
(order) erteilen; (passport,
certificate) ausstellen

**isthmus, iss**-mes, *n*
Landenge *f*, Isthmus *m*

**it,** itt, *pron* er/sie/es;
ihn/sie/es; ihm/ihr/ihm

**Italian,** i-**täll**-jen, *adj*
italienisch; *n* (person)
Italiener *m*; (language)
Italienisch *nt*

**italic,** i-**täll**-ick, *adj* kursiv;
**–s,** *npl* Kursivschrift *f*

**Italy, itt**-*e*-li, *n* Italien *nt*

**itch,** itsch, *n* Krätze *f*; *fig*
Drang *m*; *v* jucken; **–y,** *adj*
juckend

**item, ei**-tem, *n* (thing)
Gegenstand *m*; (in list)
Posten *m*; (of news)
Artikel *m*; **–ize,** *v* einzeln
aufführen

**itinerant,** i-**tinn**-*e*-rent, *adj*
wandernd

**itinerary,** ei-**tinn**-*e*-re-ri, *n*
Reiseroute *f*

**its,** its, *adj* sein *m/nt* ihr *f*;
dessen

**itself,** itt-**sself,** *pron* (*refl*)
sich (selbst); (*emphatic*)
selbst

**ivory, ei**-we-ri, *n*
Elfenbein *nt*

**ivy, ei**-wi, *n* Efeu *m*

**jab,** dschäbb, n (blow)
Schlag m; (with needle)
Stich m; (fam injection)
Spritze f; v stechen

**jabber,** dschäbb-er, v
plappern

**jack,** dschäck, n mech
Wagenheber m; (cards)
Bube m; – **up,** v (car)
aufbocken

**jackal,** dschäck-'l, n
Schakal m

**jacket,** dschäck-itt, n Jacke
f; (of book)
Schutzumschlag m

**jackknife,** dschäck-neif, v
querstellen

**jackpot,** dschäck-pott, n
Hauptgewinn m

**jade,** dschehd, n Jade f

**jaded,** dscheh-didd, adj
(tired) abgespannt;
(worn) abgestumpft

**jagged,** dschägg-idd, adj
zackig

**jail,** dschehl, n Gefängnis nt;
–**er,** n Gefängniswärter m

**jam,** dschäm, n (conserve)
Marmelade f; (traffic)
Stau m; v (sich)
verklemmen; (broadcast)
stören; – **in(to),**
hineinzwängen (in)

**jangle,** dschäng-g'l, v klirren

**January,** dschänn-ju-e-ri, n
Januar m

**Japan,** dsche-pänn, n Japan
nt; –**ese,** adj japanisch; n
(person) Japaner m;
(language) Japanisch nt

**jar,** dschahr, n (container)
Glas nt; (jolt) Ruck m; v
(of sound) kreischen; (of
colours, opinions) nicht
harmonieren; (jolt)
erschüttern

**jargon,** dschahr-gen, n
Fachsprache f; pej Jargon
m

**jaundice,** dscho'an-diss, n
Gelbsucht f; –**d,** adj
zynisch

**jaunt,** dscho'ant, n Ausflug
m; –**y,** adj unbeschwert

**javelin,** dschäw-lin, n
Speer m

**jaw,** dscho'ah, n Kiefer m; v
fam schwatzen

**jay,** dscheh, n
Eichelhäher m

**jazz,** dschäs, n Jazz m; –**y,**
adj poppig

**jealous,** dschell-ess, adj
eifersüchtig; –**y,** n
Eifersucht f

**jeans,** dschiens, npl Jeans pl

**jeer (at),** dschier (et), v
höhnen, verhöhnen

**jelly,** dschell-i, n Gelee nt;
(sweet) Grütze f; –**fish,** n
Qualle f

**jeopardize,** dschepp-er-dais,
v gefährden

**jeopardy,** dschepp-er-di, n
Gefahr f

**jerk,** dschörk, n Ruck m; v
rucken; (fam idiot) Trottel
m

**jersey,** dschör-si, n Pullover
m; sport Trikot nt

**jest,** dschest, n Scherz m; v

scherzen

**jet,** dschett, n (of liquid)
Strahl m; (nozzle)
Mundstück m; (plane)
Düsenflugzeug nt;
(mineral) Jett nt; –
**engine,** n Düsentriebwerk
nt; **–lag,** n Jet-lag m

**jettison,** dschett-i-ss'n, v
über Bord werfen

**jetty,** dschett-i, n Mole f

**jewel,** dschuh-el, n Juwel nt;
**–ler,** n Juwelier m; **–lery,** n
Schmuck m

**Jewish,** dschuh-isch, adj
jüdisch

**jibe,** dscheib, n Stichelei f

**jig,** dschigg, n Jig f; **– about,**
v herumhüpfen

**jigsaw,** dschigg-so'a, n
Puzzle nt

**jingle,** dsching-g'l, n
(advertising)
Werbespruch m; v
klimpern

**job,** dschobb, n (position)
Stellung f; (task) Arbeit f;
**–less,** adj arbeitslos

**jockey,** dschock-i, n
Jockei m

**jocular,** dschock-ju-ler, adj
scherzhaft

**jog,** dschogg, v (run) joggen;
(nudge) anstoßen; **–ging,**
n Jogging nt

**join,** dscheun, n Naht f; v
verbinden; (club etc.)
beitreten; **–er,** n Schreiner
m; **– in,** v mitmachen
(bei)

**joint,** dscheunt, adj

gemeinsam; n (of meat)
Braten m; (carpentry)
Verbindung nt; (anatomy)
Gelenk nt; (fam bar etc.)
Spelunke f; **–ly,** adv
gemeinschaftlich

**joke,** dschohk, n Spaß m,
Witz m; v scherzen; **–r,**
n Witzbold m; (cards) Joker
m

**jolly,** dscholl-i, adj lustig,
munter; **– good!** fam
prima!

**jolt,** dscholt, n Stoß m; fig
Schock m; v stoßen; fig
aufrütteln

**jostle,** dschoss-'l, v
anrempeln, anstoßen

**journal,** dschör-nel, n
(periodical) Zeitschrift f;
(diary) Tagebuch nt; **–ism,**
n Journalismus m; **–ist,** n
Journalist m

**journey,** dschör-ni, n Reise
f, Fahrt f

**jovial,** dschoh-wi-el, adj
heiter, jovial

**joy,** dscheu, n Freude f; **–ful,**
adj freudig; **––ride,** n
Spritztour f in einem
gestohlenen Auto

**jubilant,** dschuh-bi-lent, adj
jubelnd, freudestrahlend

**jubilee,** dschuh-bi-lie, n
Jubiläum nt

**judge,** dschadsch, n law
Richter m; (critic) Kenner
m; v (assess) beurteilen;
(law case) verhandeln;
**–ment,** n law Urteil nt;
relig Gericht nt; (opinion)

Meinung f

**judicial,** dschuh-disch-'l, adj
gerichtlich

**judicious,** dschuh-disch-ess,
adj verständig, weise

**judo,** dschuh-doh, n Judo nt

**jug,** dschagg, n Krug m

**juggle,** dschagg-'l, v
jonglieren; **–r,** n Jongleur
m

**juice,** dschuhss, n Saft m

**juicy,** dschuh-ssi, adj saftig

**jukebox,** dschuhk-bocks, n
Jukebox f

**July,** dschu-lei, n Juli m

**jumble,** dschamm-b'l, n
Wirrwarr m; v
durcheinanderwerfen; **–d,**
adj verwirrt; **– sale,** n
Basar m

**jumbo,** dschamm-boh, n
Jumbo m; **– (jet),** n
Jumbo(-Jet) m

**jump,** dschamp, n Sprung m;
v springen; (start)
zusammenfahren; **–er,** n
sport Springer m;
(pullover) Pullover m

**junction,** dschank-sch'n, n
(of roads) Kreuzung f; (of
motorways)
(Autobahn)kreuz nt;
(railway) Knotenpunkt m

**June,** dschuhn, n Juni m

**jungle,** dschang-g'l, n
Dschungel m

**junior,** dschuh-ni-er, adj
(younger) jünger,
Junioren-; (subordinate)
untergeordnet; n
Jüngere(r) m & f; –

**school,** n Grundschule f
**junk,** dschank, n Trödel m;
  **– food,** n Junk-food nt; **–
  mail,** n Wurfsendung f
**jurisdiction,** dschuhr-riss-
  **dick**-sch'n, n
  Gerichtsbarkeit f
**juror, dschuhr**-rer, n law
  Geschworene(r) m & f
**jury, dschuhr**-ri, n law
  Geschworene pl;
  (competition) Jury f
**just,** dschast, adj gerecht;
  adv (now) soeben, gerade;
  (only) nur; (exactly)
  genau; (simply) mal; **– as
  good,** genauso gut; **–ice,** n
  Gerechtigkeit f;
  **–ification,** Rechtfertigung
  f; **–ify,** v rechtfertigen; **–ly,**
  adv mit Recht
**jut (out),** dschott (aut), v
  hervorragen
**juvenile, dschuh**-we-neil,
  adj jugendlich, Jugend-;
  pej kindisch; n
  Jugendliche(r) m & f

**kangaroo,** käng-ge-**ruh,** n Känguruh nt

**karate,** ke-**rah**-ti, n Karate nt

**kebab,** ki-**bäbb,** n Kebab m

**keel,** kiel, n Kiel m

**keen,** kien, adj begeistert; (blade, intellect) scharf

**keep,** kiep, n Unterhalt f; v (retain) behalten; (preserve) erhalten; (animal, promise) halten; (remain) bleiben; (of food) sich halten; – **back,** zurückhalten; **–er,** n Wärter m; **--fit,** n Fitneßübungen pl; – **left/right,** v sich links/rechts halten; – **(on) doing,** v (continue) weitermachen; (repeat) immer wieder machen; – **out!** Eintritt verboten!; **–sake,** n Andenken nt; –

**to,** v daranhalten; – **up,** v (continue) fortsetzen; – **up (with),** v Schritt halten (mit)

**keg,** kegg, n Fäßchen nt

**kennel, kenn-**'l, n Hundehütte f

**kerb,** körb, n Bordstein m

**kernel, körn-**'l, n Kern m

**kettle, kett-**'l, n Kessel m; **–drum,** n Pauke f

**key,** kie, n Schlüssel m; (of typewriter etc.) Taste f; mus Tonart f; **–board,** n Tastatur f; **–hole,** n Schlüsselloch nt; **–ring,** n Schlüsselring m; v – **(in),** eingeben

**khaki,** kah-ki, adj k(h)aki; n K(h)aki nt

**kick,** kick, n Tritt m; (thrill) Kitzel m; v treten; (of horse) ausschlagen

**kid,** kidd, n (young goat)

Zicklein nt; (fam child) Kind nt; (leather) Glacéleder nt; v anführen, Spaß machen

**kidnap, kidd-**näpp, v entführen; **–er,** n Enführer m

**kidney, kidd-**ni, n Niere f

**kill,** kill, n (hunt) Erlegen nt; (prey) Beute f; v töten; (person) umbringen; **–er,** n Mörder m; **–ing,** n Mord m; (fam gain) Coup m

**kiln,** kiln, n Brennofen m

**kilo,** kie-loh, n (abbr kilogram(me)) Kilo nt

**kilobyte, kill-**e-beit, n comp Kilobyte nt

**kilogram(me),** kill-e-grämm, n Kilogramm nt

**kilometre,** ki-lomm-i-ter, n Kilometer m

**kind,** keind, adj liebenswürdig, freundlich; n Art f; **what – of,** was für (ein)

**kindergarten, kinn-**der-gahr-ten, n Kindergarten m

**kindle, kinn-**d'l, v anzünden; fig erwecken

**kindly, keind-**li, adj freundlich; adv freundlicherweise; **would you –ly …?** würden Sie bitte …?

**kindness, keind-**niss, n (goodness) Liebenswürdigkeit f; (favour) Gefallen m, Gefälligkeit f

**king,** king, n König m;
–**dom,** n Königreich nt

**kinky, king**-ki, adj (hair)
wellig; (bizarre) spleenig

**kiosk, kie**-osk, n Kiosk m;
(telephone) Telefonzelle f

**kipper, kipp**-er, n
Bückling m

**kiss,** kiss, n Kuß m; v (sich)
küssen

**kit,** kitt, n (equipment)
Ausrüstung f; (set) Satz m

**kitchen, kitt**-schinn, n
Küche f; – **sink,** n
Spülbecken nt

**kite,** keit, n (toy) Drachen
m; (bird) Milan m

**kitten, kitt**-'n, n
Kätzchen nt

**kitty, kitt**-i, n Kasse f; (fam
kitten) Mieze f

**knack,** näck, n Kniff m

**knapsack, näpp**-ssäck, n
Rucksack m; mil
Tornister m

**knead,** nied, v kneten

**knee,** nie, n Knie nt; –**cap,** n
Kniescheibe f

**kneel,** niel, v knien

**knell,** nell, n Grabgeläute nt

**knickers, nick**-ers, n
Schlüpfer m

**knife,** neif, n Messer nt; v
erstechen

**knight,** neit, n Ritter m;
(chess) Springer m;
–**hood,** n Ritterwürde f

**knit,** nitt, v stricken; –**ting,**
n Strickzeug nt; –**wear,** n
Strickwaren pl

**knob,** nobb, n Knopf m; (on

door) Griff m; – **of butter,**
n kleines Stück nt Butter

**knock,** nock, v (on door)
klopfen (an); (strike)
schlagen; (fam criticize)
kritisieren; – **against,** v
stoßen gegen; – **down,** v
niederschlagen; (with car)
anfahren; –**er,** n (door)
Türklopfer m; – **off,** v (do
quickly) schnell erledigen;
(fam steal) klauen; (stop
work) Feierabend
machen; – **out,** v k.o.-
schlagen

**knock-out, nock**-aut, adj
(fam great) toll; n (blow)
K.o.-Schlag m; fam
Wucht f

**knot,** nott, n Knoten m; v
(ver)knüpfen

**knotty, nott**-i, adj (problem)
verwickelt; (wood)
knorrig

**know,** noh, v (fact) wissen;
(be acquainted with)
kennen; (experience)
erleben; (language)
können; – **about,** v
Bescheid wissen über; –
**how to do sth,** etw tun
können

**know-how, noh**-hau, n
Know-how nt

**knowledge, noll**-idsch, n
Wissen nt; Kenntnis f

**knuckle, nack**-'l, n
Knöchel m

**lab**, läbb, n (*abbr* **laboratory**), Labor nt

**label**, leh-b'l, n Etikett nt; v etikettieren

**laboratory**, le-bo-re-te-ri, n Labor nt

**laborious**, le-bo-ri-ess, adj mühsam, anstrengend

**labour**, leh-ber, n Arbeit f; med Wehen pl; v (work hard) sich abmühen; (work with difficulty) sich quälen; **–ed**, adj schwer, mühsam, **–er**, n Arbeiter m; **go into –**, v med Wehen bekommen

**laburnum**, le-bör-nem, n Goldregen m

**lace**, lehss, n Spitze f; (shoe) Schnürsenkel m; v **– (up)**, (zu)schnüren

**lack**, lack, n **– of**, Mangel m an; v **– sth**, kein(e, en)... haben; **be –ing**, fehlen

**lacquer**, läck-er, n Lack m; v lackieren

**lad**, lädd, n Junge m

**ladder**, lädd-er, n (steps) Leiter f; (in fabric) Laufmasche f

**laden**, leh-den, adj beladen

**ladies**, leh-dis, n (toilet) Damen pl

**lady**, leh-di, n Dame f; **–bird**, n Marienkäfer m; **–like**, adj damenhaft

**lag**, lägg, v isolieren; **– behind**, zurückbleiben

**lair**, lähr, n Unterschlupf nt

**lake**, lehk, n See m

**lamb**, lämm, n (animal) Lamm nt; (meat) Lamm(fleisch) nt; v lammen; **– chop**, n Lammkotelett nt

**lame**, lehmm, adj lahm; v lähmen; **–ness**, n Lahmheit f

**lament**, le-ment, n Klage f; v beklagen

**lamp**, lämp, n Lampe f; (in street) Laterne f; **–post**, n Laternenpfahl m; **–shade**, n Lampenschirm m

**land**, länd, n Land nt; (property) Grundstück nt; v landen; naut an Land gehen; (fam obtain) kriegen; **–fill**, n Müllgrube f; **–ing**, n Landung f; (on stairs) Treppenabsatz m; **–lady**, (lodgings) n Hauswirtin f; (pub) Wirtin f; **–lord**, (lodgings) n Hauswirt m; (pub) Wirt m; **–mark**, n Wahrzeichen nt; fig Markstein m; **–scape**, n Landschaft f; **–scape gardener,** n Gartengestalter m; **–slide**, n Erdrutsch m; (fig victory) Erdrutschsieg m

**lane**, lehn, n (narrow road) Weg m; (of carriageway) (Fahr)spur f; sport Bahn f

**language**, läng-gu'idsch, n Sprache f; **bad/strong –**, derbe Ausdrücke pl

**languid**, läng-gu'idd, adj schlaff

**languish**, läng-gu'isch, v schmachten

**lank**, länk, adj (tall) hager; (limp) glatt herabhängend; **–y**, lang und dünn

**lantern**, länn-tern, n Laterne f

**lap**, läpp, n Schoß m; sport

Runde f; v (of water) plätschern; *sport* überrunden; **– up,** (drink) auflecken

**lapel,** le-**pell**, n Revers nt

**lapse,** läpss, n (of time) Zeitraum m; (error) Fehler m; v verfallen

**larceny,** lahr-sse-ni, n Diebstahl m

**lard,** lahrd, n Schweineschmalz nt

**large,** lahrdsch, adj groß; **–ly,** adv größtenteils; **–-scale,** adj (change, event) in großem Rahmen; (map) in großem Maßstab

**lark,** lahrk, n Lerche f; (fam fun) Scherz m; **– about,** v herumalbern

**laryngitis,** lä-rin-**dschei**-tiss, n Kehlkopfentzündung f

**laser,** leh-ser, n Laser m

**lash,** läsch, n (stroke) Hieb m; (eyelash) Augenwimper f; v (whip) peitschen; (tie) festbinden; **– out,** (fight) um sich schlagen; (spend heavily) sich etw leisten/gönnen

**last,** lahst, adj letzte(r/s); adv zuletzt; v (object) halten; (situation) dauern; (resources) ausreichen; **–ing,** adj dauerhaft; **at –,** adv endlich; **– but one,** adj vorletzte(r/s);

**latch,** lätsch, n Klinke f; **–key,** n Hausschlüssel m

**late,** leht, adj spät; (belated)

verspätet; (former) ehemalig; (deceased) verstorben; adv spät; (belatedly) zu spät

**latecomer,** leht-kamm-er, n Spätankömmling m

**lately,** leht-li, adv in letzter Zeit

**lateral,** lätt-e-rel, adj seitlich, Seiten-

**latest,** leh-tist, adj neueste(r/s)

**lathe,** lehdh, n Drehbank f

**lather,** lah-dher, n Seifenschaum m; v (ein)schäumen

**Latin,** lätt-in, adj lateinisch; n Latein nt; **– America,** Lateinamerika nt

**latitude,** lätt-i-tjuhd, n geog Breite f; fig Spielraum m

**latter,** lätt-er, adj letztere(r/s)

**lattice,** lätt-iss, n Gitterwerk nt

**laugh,** lahf, n Lachen nt; **– (at),** v lachen (über); **–able,** adj lächerlich; **–ing stock,** n Gespött nt; **–ter,** Gelächter nt

**launch,** lo'antsch, n (of ship) Stapellauf m; (of rocket) Start m; (of product, venture) Vorstellung f, Einführung f; v (ship) vom Stapel lassen; (product, venture) einführen

**launderette,** lo'an-de-rett, n Waschsalon m

**laundry,** lo'an-dri, n

Wäsche f; **do the –,** v (Wäsche) waschen

**lavatory,** läw-e-te-ri, n Toilette f

**lavender,** läw-in-der, n Lavendel m

**lavish,** läw-isch, adj freigebig; v **– (money) on sth,** (Geld) für etw verschwenden; **– (gifts) on sb,** jdn mit (Geschenken) überhäufen

**law,** lo'ah, n (act) Gesetz nt; (study) Jura; **––abiding,** adj gesetzestreu; **– court,** n Gerichtshof m; **–ful,** adj rechtmäßig; **–less,** adj gesetzlos; (person) zügellos

**lawn,** lo'ahn, n Rasen m; **–mower,** n Rasenmäher m

**lawsuit,** lo'a-suht, n Prozeß m

**lawyer,** lo'a-jer, n Rechtsanwalt m, Rechtsanwältin f

**lax,** läcks, adj lose, locker

**laxative,** läx-e-tiw, n Abführmittel nt

**lay,** leh, adj Laien-; v (egg) legen; (table) decken; **– down,** v (arms) niederlegen; (rule, condition) festlegen; **– on,** (food etc.) bieten; (power, water) anschließen

**layabout,** leh-e-baut, n Faulenzer m

**layby,** leh-bei, n Haltebucht f

**layer,** leh-er, n Schicht f

**layman,** leh-men, n Laie m

**layout, leh**-aut, n
(arrangement) Anlage f;
(design) Layout nt

**laze (about), lehs** (e-**baut**),
v faulenzen

**laziness, leh**-si-niss, n
Faulheit f

**lazy, leh**-si, adj faul, träge

**lb., abbr pound** (weight)

**lead, ledd,** adj Blei-; n Blei
nt; (for pencil) Mine f

**lead, lied,** n (distance
ahead) Vorsprung m; (first
position) Führung f;
(example) Beispiel nt;
(clue) Spur f; (theatre, mus
role) Hauptrolle f; (dog's)
Leine f; v führen, leiten;
**–er,** n Leiter m, Führer m;
(of party) Vorsitzende(r)
m & f; (article) Leitartikel
m; **–ership,** n Leitung f,
Führung f

**lead-free, ledd**-frie, adj
bleifrei

**leading,** adj führend;
(principal) Haupt-; **–
article,** n Leitartikel m

**leaf, lief,** n Blatt nt; **–
through,** v durchblättern;
**turn over a new –,** v
einen neuen Anfang
machen

**leaflet, lief**-litt, n (handout)
Flugblatt nt; (instructions)
Merkblatt nt

**leafy, lief**-i, adj belaubt

**league, lieg,** n Bund m; sport
Liga f; naut Seemeile f

**leak, liek,** n Leck nt;
(information) undichte

Stelle f; v (liquid) lecken;
**– out,** (of liquid)
auslaufen; (of
information) durchsickern

**lean, lien,** adj mager; v **–
against,** sich lehnen
gegen; **– forward,** sich
vorbeugen; **– on,** sich
lehnen an; **– out,**
hinauslehnen; **– towards,**
fig tendieren zu

**leaning, lie**-ning, adj schräg;
n Neigung f

**leap, liep,** n Sprung m; v
springen; **– year,** n
Schaltjahr nt

**learn, lörnn,** v lernen;
(news, experience)
erfahren; **–ed,** adj gelehrt;
**–er,** n Lernende(r) m & f;
(pupil) Schüler m;
(beginner) Anfänger m;
**–ing,** n Lernen nt;
(knowledge) Wissen nt

**lease, liess,** n
(accommodation)
Mietvertrag m; (land etc)
Pachtvertrag m; v mieten,
pachten; **– (out),**
vermieten, verpachten

**leash, liesch,** n Leine f

**least, liest,** adj geringste(r/s);
adv am wenigsten; **at –,**
mindestens, wenigstens;
**not in the –,** gar nicht

**leather, ledh**-er, n Leder nt

**leave, liew,** n (permission)
Erlaubnis f; (of absence)
Urlaub m; v lassen;
(depart) abreisen; (desert)
verlassen; (bequeath)

hinterlassen; **– behind,**
zurücklassen; (forget)
liegenlassen; **– off,**
aufhören; **– out,** auslassen;
**– to,** (hand over)
überlassen

**lecherous, letsch**-e-ress, adj
lüstern

**lecture, lek**-tscher, n
Vortrag m; (at university)
Vorlesung f; (telling-off)
Strafpredigt f; v einen
Vortrag halten; (tell off)
jdm eine Strafpredigt
halten; **–r,** n (at
university) Dozent m

**ledge, ledsch,** n (of window)
Sims m; (of rock)
Vorsprung m

**ledger, ledsch**-er, n
Hauptbuch nt

**leech, lietsch,** n Blutegel m

**leek, liek,** n Lauch m

**leer, lier,** v fam angaffen

**left, left,** adj (side)
linke(r/s); (remaining)
übrig; adv links; n linke
Seite f; (politics) Linke f; **–
handed,** adj linkshändig;
**–hand side,** n linke Seite
f; **– luggage (office),** n
Gepäckaufbewahrung f;
**–overs,** npl Reste pl; **be –
(over),** v übrigbleiben; **on
the –,** links; **to the –,**
nach links

**leg, legg,** n Bein nt; (of
meat) Keule f; (stage)
Etappe f

**legacy, legg**-e-ssi, n
Vermächtnis nt

**legal, lie**-g'l, *adj* (lawful)
legal; (imposed by law)
gesetzlich; (advice,
matter) juristisch; **–ize,** *v*
legalisieren; **– tender,** *n*
gesetzliches
Zahlungsmittel *nt*

**legend, ledsch**-end, *n* Sage *f*,
Legende *f*; **–ary,** *adj*
legendär; (famous)
berühmt

**leggings, legg**-ings, *npl*
Leggings *pl*

**legible, ledsch**-i-b'l, *adj*
leserlich

**legion, lie**-dschen, *n*
Legion *f*

**legislate, ledsch**-iss-leht, *v*
Gesetze erlassen

**legislation, ledsch**-iss-leh-
sch'n, *n* Gesetzgebung *f*

**legitimate, le-dschitt**-i-met,
*adj* legitim; (child)
ehelich

**leisure, lesch**-er, *n* Muße *f*,
Freizeit *f*; **– centre,** *n*
Freizeitzentrum *nt*; **–ly,**
*adv* gemächlich

**lemon, lemm**-en, *adj*
Zitronen-; *n* (fruit)
Zitrone *f*; (colour)
Zitronengelb *nt*; **–ade,**
Limonade *f*

**lend, lend,** *v* leihen

**length, length,** *n* Länge *f*;
(of time) Dauer *f*; (of
cloth etc.) Stück *nt*; **–en,**
*v* verlängern; **–ways,** *adj*
Längs-; *adv* der Länge
nach; **–y,** *adj* lang,
weitschweifig; **at –,** (fully)

ausführlich; (finally)
schließlich; **for the – of
…, … entlang**

**lenient, lie**-ni-ent, *adj* mild,
gelind

**lens, lens,** *n* Linse *f*; *photog*
Objektiv *nt*

**Lent, lent,** *n* Fastenzeit *f*

**lentil, lenn**-till, *n* Linse *f*

**Leo, lie**-oh, *n* Löwe *m*

**leopard, lepp**-erd, *n* Leopard
*m*

**leotard, lie**-*e*-tahrd, *n*
Turnanzug *m*

**leper, lepp**-er, *n*
Leprakranke(r) *m & f*

**leprosy, lepp**-re-ssi, *n* Lepra *f*

**lesbian, les**-bi-en, *adj*
lesbisch; *n fam* Lesbe *f*;
Lesbierin *f*

**less, less,** *adj adv pron*
weniger; **– and less,**
immer weniger; **– than,**
weniger als

**lessen, less**-en, *v*
vermindern, abnehmen

**lesser, less**-er, *adj* geringer

**lesson, less**-en, *n* (school)
Stunde *f*; (in book etc.)
Lektion *f*; *fig* Lehre *f*

**let, lett,** *v* (allow) lassen;
(house etc.) vermieten;
(land) verpachten; **–
down,** (clothes) länger
machen; (disappoint)
enttäuschen; **– off,** (gun
etc.) abfeuern; (not
punish) laufenlassen; **–
out,** (clothes) weiter
machen; (prisoner)
entlassen; **– on,** (*fam* tell)

etw verraten; (*fam*
pretend) so tun, als ob; **–
up,** nachlassen

**lethal, lie**-thel, *adj* tödlich

**lethargic, le-thahr**-dschick,
*adj* träge

**letter, lett**-er, *n* (message)
Brief *m*; (of alphabet)
Buchstabe *m*; **–box,** *n*
Briefkasten *m*; **–ing,** *n*
Beschriftung *f*; **– of credit,**
*n* Kreditbrief *m*

**lettuce, lett**-iss, *n* Kopfsalat
*m*

**leukaemia, lu-kie-mi-***e*,
Leukämie *f*

**level, lew**-el, *adj* (flat) eben;
(at same height) auf
gleicher Höhe; (head)
kühl; *adv* gleich, auf
gleicher Höhe; *n* (height)
Höhe *f*; (position) Niveau
*nt*; (instrument)
Wasserwaage *f*; *v* **–
(off/out),** (of ground)
eben werden; (of
inequalities) sich
ausgleichen; **– (out/up),**
(ground) einebnen;
(differences) ausgleichen;
**– crossing,** *n*
Bahnübergang *m*; **be –
with,** *v fam* ehrlich sein
mit; **on the –,** *adj fam*
ehrlich

**lever, lie**-wer, *n* Hebel *m*; *fig*
Druckmittel *nt*; **– open,** *v*
aufstemmen

**levity, lew**-i-ti, *n*
Leichtfertigkeit *f*

**levy, lew**-i, *n* (raising)

Erhebung f; (tax) Steuer f; v (tax) erheben; (fine) auferlegen

**lewd,** ljuhd, *adj* anzüglich; **–ness,** n Anzüglichkeit f

**liability,** lei-*e*-bill-i-ti, n (duty) Pflicht f; (responsibility) Haftung f; (burden) Belastung f; *fin* Verbindlichkeit f

**liable,** lei-*e*-b'l, *adj* **– for,** (responsible) haftbar; **– to,** (prone) anfällig; (subject) -pflichtig

**liar,** lei-*er*, n Lügner m

**liaise (with),** lie-**ehs** (u'idh), v zusammenarbeiten (mit), sich mit jdm absprechen

**liaison,** lie-**eh**-sonn, n Verbindung f; (sexual) Liaison f

**libel,** lei-b'l, n Verleumdung f; v verleumden; **–lous,** *adj* verleumderisch

**liberal,** libb-*e*-rel, *adj* (tolerant) liberal; (generous) freigebig; (tolerant person) liberal denkender Mensch m; (politics) Liberale(r) m & f

**liberate,** libb-*e*-reht, v befreien

**liberty,** libb-*er*-ti, n (freedom) Freiheit f; (cheek) Frechheit f; **take liberties (with),** v sich etwas herausnehmen

**Libra,** lie-bre, n Waage f

**librarian,** lei-**breht**-ri-en, n

Bibliothekar m

**library,** lei-bre-ri, n Bücherei f, Bibliothek f

**licence,** lei-ssenss, n Genehmigung f, Schein m; (driving) Führerschein m

**license,** lei-ssenss, v genehmigen; konzessionieren; **–d,** *adj* genehmigt; (to sell alcohol) mit Schankerlaubnis

**licentious,** lei-**ssenn**-shess, *adj* zügellos

**lichen,** lei-ken, n Flechte f

**lick,** lick, n Lecken nt; v lecken; **at a good –,** (*fam* fast) mit einem Affenzahn

**lid,** lidd, n Deckel m; (eye)**–,** (Augen)lid nt

**lie,** lei, n (untruth) Lüge f; v (rest) liegen; (tell lies) lügen; **– low,** untertauchen; **– down,** sich hinlegen

**lieu,** ljuh, n **in – of,** *prep* anstatt

**lieutenant,** lef-**tenn**-ent, n Leutnant m

**life,** leif, n Leben nt; **–belt,** n Rettungsring m; **–boat,** n Rettungsboot nt; **– cycle,** Lebenszyklus m; **– insurance,** n Lebensversicherung f; **– jacket,** n Schwimmweste f; **–less,** *adj* leblos; **–like,** *adj* lebensecht; **–long,** *adj* lebenslang; **– sentence,** n lebenslängliche

Freiheitsstrafe f; **–-size(d),** *adj* lebensgroß

**lifetime,** leif-teim, n Lebensdauer f; **in one's –,** während seines Lebens; **once in a –,** einmal im Leben, einmalig

**lift,** lift, n (elevator) Fahrstuhl m, Aufzug m, Lift m; v (object) hochheben; (restriction) aufheben; **give sb a –,** (in car) jdn mitnehmen; *fig* jdn aufmuntern; **--off,** n Abheben nt

**light,** leit, n Licht nt; (for cigarette) Feuer nt; *adj* (bright, pale) hell; (in weight) leicht; v (fire) anzünden; (illuminate) beleuchten; **– bulb,** n Glühbirne f; **–en,** (brighten) erhellen; (in weight) erleichtern; **–er,** n Feuerzeug nt; **--headed,** *adj* schwindlig; **--hearted,** *adj* leichtherzig; **–house,** n Leuchtturm m; **–ing,** n Beleuchtung f; **–ly,** *adv* (gently) leicht; (casually) leichthin; (unpunished) glimpflich; **–ness,** n (in colour) Helligkeit f; (in weight) Leichtheit f

**lightning,** leit-ning, n Blitz m; **– conductor,** n Blitzableiter m

**lights,** leits, *npl* (traffic lights) (Verkehrs)ampel f; (on car) Scheinwerfer pl

**like,** leik, *adj* (the same)

gleich; (similar) ähnlich; *prep* (in comparisons) wie; (similar to) ähnlich; *v* gern haben, mögen; **–lihood,** *n* Wahrscheinlichkeit *f*; **–ly,** *adj* wahrscheinlich; **–ness,** *n* Ähnlichkeit *f*; (portrait) Porträt *nt*; **– this,** *adv* so; **–wise,** *adv* gleichfalls; **what (is it) like?** wie (ist es)?; **would –: I would –** **…,** ich möchte …, ich hätte gern …; **would you** **– …?** möchten Sie …?, hätten Sie gern …?

**liking, lei-**king, *n* Vorliebe *f*

**lilac, lei-**lek, *adj* (colour) lila; *n* Flieder *m*

**lilt, lilt,** *n* singender Tonfall *m*

**lily, lill-**i, *n* Lilie *f*; **– of the** **valley,** Maiglöckchen *nt*

**limb, limm,** *n* Glied *nt*

**limber up, limm-**ber app, *v* warm machen; (prepare) sich vorbereiten

**limbo, limm-**bo, *n* **in –,** in der Schwebe

**lime, leim,** *n* (substance) Kalk *m*; (fruit) Limone *f*; (tree) Linde *f*; **–light,** *n* Rampenlicht *m*

**limit, limm-**itt, *n* Grenze *f*; *v* begrenzen, beschränken; **–ation,** *n* Einschränkung *f*; **–ed,** *adj* beschränkt; **–ed** **company,** *n* Gesellschaft *f* mit beschränkter Haftung

**limp, limp,** schlaff; *n* Hinken *nt*; *v* hinken

**limpet, limm-**pitt, *n* Napfschnecke *f*; *fig* Klette *f*

**line, lein,** *n* Linie *f*; (of writing) Zeile *f*; (row) Reihe *f*; (rope, fishing etc.) Leine *f*; (railway) Strecke *f*; (telephone) Leitung *f*, Verbindung *f*; (business) Branche *f*; *v* (clothes) füttern; (street etc.) säumen;

**linear, linn-**i-er, linear, Längen-

**lined, leind,** *adj* (paper) liniert; (face) faltig

**line manager,** lein männ-i-dscher, *n* unmittelbarer Vorgesetzter *m*

**linen, linn-**in, *n* (cloth) Leinen *nt*; (laundry) Wäsche *f*

**liner, lei-**ner, *n* Linienschiff *nt*

**line up, lein** app, *v* (get in line) sich aufstellen; (put in line) aufstellen; (prepare) planen, arrangieren

**linger, ling-**ger, *v* (remain) bleiben; (hesitate) zaudern

**lingerie, länn-**dsche-rie, *n* Damenunterwäsche *f*

**lingering, lingg-**er, *adj* (illness) langwierig; (doubt) anhaltend

**linguist, ling-**gu'ist, *n* Sprachkundige(r) *m & f*; **–ic,** *adj* sprachlich; **–s,** *n* Sprachwissenschaft *f*

**lining, lei-**ning, *n* Futter *nt*

**link, link,** *n* (in chain) Glied *nt*; (connection) Verbindung *f*; *v* verbinden; **–s,** *npl* Golfplatz *m*; **– up,** *v* (bring together) in Verbindung bringen; (come together) sich zusammenschließen

**lino, lei-**noh, *abbr* **linoleum**

**linoleum, linn-oh-**li-em, *n* Linoleum *nt*

**linseed oil, linn-**ssied eul, *n* Leinöl *nt*

**lint, lint,** *n* (dressing) Mull *m*; (fluff) Fussel *m*

**lion, lei-**en, *n* Löwe *m*; **–ess,** *n* Löwin *f*

**lip, lipp,** *n* Lippe *f*; (of cup etc.) Rand *m*; **–read,** *v* von den Lippen ablesen; **give – service,** ein Lippenbekenntnis ablegen; **–stick,** *n* Lippenstift *m*

**liqueur, li-kör,** *n* Likör *m*

**liquid, lick-**u'idd, *adj* flüssig; *n* Flüssigkeit *f*; **–ate,** *v* liquidieren; (debts) bezahlen; **–ation,** *n* Liquidation *f*; **–ize,** *v* pürieren; **–izer,** *n* Mixer *m*

**liquor, lick-**er, *n* Alkohol *m*; **–ice,** *n* Lakritze *f*

**lisp, lisp,** *n* Lispeln *nt*; *v* lispeln

**list, list,** *n* Liste *f*; *naut* Schlagseite *f*; *v* (in writing) aufschreiben; (orally) aufzählen; *naut* Schlagseite haben

383

**listen, liss-**'n, *v* horchen; – **to**, zuhören; (radio) hören; **–er,** *n* Zuhörer *m*; (radio) Hörer *m*

**literacy, litt-**e-*re*-ssi, *n* Lese- und Schreibfertigkeit *f*

**literal(ly), litt-**e-rel(-i), *adj & adv* wörtlich

**literary, litt-**e-re-ri, *adj* literarisch

**literate, litt-**e-*ret, adj* lese- und schreibkundig; (educated) gebildet

**literature, lit-**re-tscher, *n* Literatur *f*

**litigation, litt-**i-*geh-*sch'n, *n* Rechtsstreit *m*

**litre, lie-**ter, *n* Liter *m*

**litter, litt-**er, *n* (rubbish) Abfall *m*; (stretcher) Trage *f*; (animals) Wurf *m*; *v* verstreuen; **– bin,** *n* Abfalleimer *m*; **–ed with,** übersät mit

**little, litt-**'l, *adj* (small) klein; (not much) wenig; *adv & n* wenig; **a –**, ein wenig, ein bißchen

**live, liw,** *v* leben; (reside) wohnen; **– down,** Gras wachsen lassen über; **– up to,** (expectation) gerecht werden; (standard) erreichen

**live, leiw,** *adj* (living) lebend; (ammunition) scharf; (electrically) geladen; (broadcast) live; *adv* live, direkt

**livelihood, leiw-**li-hud, *n* Lebensunterhalt *m*

**lively, leiw-**li, *adj* lebhaft, lebendig

**liven up, leiw-**en app, *v* beleben

**liver, liw-**er, *n* Leber *f*

**livid, liw-**idd, *adj* (colour) blau; (furious) wütend

**living, liw-**ing, *adj* lebend(ig); *n* Leben(sunterhalt *m*) *nt*; **– room,** *n* Wohnzimmer *nt*; **– standards,** *npl* Lebensstandard *m*

**lizard, lis-**erd, *n* Eidechse *f*

**load, lohd,** *n* (cargo) Ladung *f*; (burden) Last *f*; *v* beladen; (*comp*, gun) laden; **–s of,** *fam* massenhaft; **–ed,** *adj* beladen; (question) suggestiv; (*fam* rich) steinreich

**loaf, lohf,** *n* Laib *m*; *v* **– (about/around),** herumlungern

**loam, lohm,** *n* Lehm *m*; **–y,** *adj* lehmig

**loan, lohn,** *n* Leihgabe *f*; (public) Anleihe *f*; *fin* Darlehen *nt*; *v* leihen; **on –,** *adj* geliehen; *adv* leihweise

**loath (to), lohth** (tu), *adj* ungern

**loathe, lohdh,** *v* verabscheuen

**loathing, loh-**dhing, *n* Abscheu *m*, Ekel *m*

**lobby, lobb-**i, *n* (in house) Vorhalle *f*; (in hotel, theatre) Foyer *nt*; (pressure group) Lobby *f*; *v* **– (for),** sich für etw einsetzen

**lobe, lohb,** *n* (of ear) Ohrläppchen *nt*

**lobster, lobb-**ster, *n* Hummer *m*

**local, loh-**k'l, *adj* Orts-, hiesig; *n* (pub) Stammkneipe *f*; (person) Einheimische(r) *m & f*; **– anaesthetic,** *n* örtliche Betäubung *f*; **– call,** *n* (telephone) Ortsgespräch *nt*; **– government,** *n* Kommunalverwaltung *f*; **–ly, loh-**ke-li, *adv* am Ort

**locality, loh-**käll-i-ti, *n* Ort *m*

**locate, loh-**keht, *v* auffinden

**location, loh-**keh-sch'n, *n* Lage *f*; Stelle *f*; **on –,** vor Ort

**lock, lock,** *n* Schloß *nt*; *naut* Schleuse *f*; (of hair) Locke *f*; *v* verschließen; **–er,** *n* Schließfach *nt*; **–et,** *n* Medaillon *nt*; *v* **– out,** aussperren; **–smith,** *n* Schlosser *m*; **– up,** *v* einschließen

**locomotive, loh-**ke-moh-tiw, *n* Lokomotive *f*

**locust, loh-**kest, *n* Heuschrecke *f*

**lodge, lodsch,** *n* (gatehouse) Pförtnerhaus *nt*; (masonic) Loge *f*; *v* (stick) stecken; **– (with),** wohnen (bei); **–r,** *n* Untermieter *m*

**lodging, lodsch-ing, board and –,** n Kost und Logis; **–s,** npl Unterkunft f; (flat) Wohnung f

**loft,** loft, n Dachboden m; **–y,** adj hoch m

**log,** logg, n (wood) Klotz m; **–(book),** Logbuch nt

**logic, lodsch-ick,** n Logik f; **–al,** adj logisch

**loin,** leun, n Lende f

**loiter, leu-**ter, v (go slowly) bummeln; (stand about) herumlungern; **–er,** n Herumlungerer m

**London, lann-**den, n London nt

**lone,** lohn, adj einzeln; **–liness,** n Einsamkeit f; **–ly,** adj einsam; **–r,** n Einzelgänger m

**long,** long, adj (time, size) lang; (journey) weit; adv lange; v **– (for),** sich sehnen (nach); **– distance,** adj Fern-; **–ing,** n Sehnsucht f, Sehnen nt; **–itude,** n Länge f; (degree of) Längengrad m; **– jump,** n Langsprung m; **– range,** adj (plane) Langstrecken-; (forecast) langfristig; **–suffering,** adj schwer geprüft; **–term,** adj langfristig; **–winded,** adj langatmig; **a – way (away),** weit (entfernt); **as – as,** solange; **before –,** bald; **no –er,** nicht mehr

**loo,** luh, n fam Klo nt

**look,** luck, n Blick m; v schauen; (appear) aussehen; **– after,** v sorgen für; **– at,** v ansehen; **– down on,** v herabsehen auf; **– for,** v suchen; **– forward to,** v sich freuen auf; **–ing-glass,** n Spiegel m; **– into,** (investigate) untersuchen; **– out,** v hinaussehen; (take care) aufpassen; interj Achtung!; **–out,** n (watch) Ausschau f; (person) Wachposten m; **– up,** aufblicken; (word) nachschlagen; **–s,** npl Aussehen nt

**loom,** luhm, n Webstuhl m; v bedrohlich werden

**loony,** luh-ni, adj verrückt

**loop,** luhp, n Schleife f; (rope) Schlaufe f; **–hole,** n fig Lücke f

**loose,** luhss, adj (fit, connection, conduct) lose; (knot, weave, morals) locker; (translation) frei; **– change,** n Kleingeld nt; **–n,** v lockern; **be at a – end,** nichts zu tun haben

**loot,** luht, n Beute f; v plündern

**lop,** lopp, v zustutzen; **– off,** v abhauen; **–sided,** adj schief

**lord,** lord, n Herr m; (title) Lord m; **the L–,** relig der Herr; **the L–s,** npl parl das Oberhaus nt

**lorry,** lo-ri, n Lastwagen m

**lose,** luhs, v verlieren; (of watch) nachgehen; **–r,** n Verlierer m

**loss,** loss, n Verlust m; **be at a –,** v nicht weiter wissen

**lost,** lost, adj verloren; **– property,** n Fundsachen pl; **– property office,** n Fundbüro nt

**lot,** lott, n (item, fate) Los nt; (quantity) Menge f; **a –,** adv viel; **a – of, –s of,** eine Menge, viel(e); **the –,** alles; pl alle

**lotion,** loh-sch'n, n Lotion f

**lottery, lott-**e-ri, n Lotterie f; fig Glücksspiel nt

**loud,** laud, adj (noise) laut; (colour, style) grell; **–speaker,** n Lautsprecher m

**lounge,** laundsch, n (in house) Wohnzimmer nt; (in hotel etc.) Gesellschaftszimmer nt; v **– (about),** herumsitzen; **– suit,** n Straßenanzug m

**louse,** lauss, n Laus f; pej Ratte f

**lout,** laut, n Lümmel m

**love,** law, adj Liebes-; n Liebe f; (person) Liebling m; (zero) null; v (person) lieben; (thing/activity) sehr gern haben/mögen; **– affair,** n Verhältnis nt; **–ly,** adj schön, reizend; **–r,** n Liebhaber m; (of animals etc.) Freund m; **in – (with),** adj verliebt (in); **make –,** v (sex) mit jdm schlafen

**low,** loh, *adj* niedrig; (note, level) tief; (voice) leise; (light) schwach; (morale) schlecht; (spirits) gedrückt; (density, quality) gering; *adv* (fly, sink, aim) tief; (quietly) leise; *n* (pressure) Tief *m*; (point) Tiefpunkt *m*; *v* (of cattle) muhen

**lower,** loh-er, *v* (price) herabsetzen; (load etc.) herunterlassen; (flag) einholen; (eyes, gun) senken; **– o.s.,** sich erniedrigen

**low-cut,** loh-**katt,** *adj* tiefausgeschnitten

**low-fat,** loh-**fatt,** *adj* fettarm

**lowland(s),** loh-lend(s), *n(pl.),* Tiefland *nt*

**low tide,** *n* Ebbe *f*

**loyal,** leu-el, *adj* treu; **–ty,** *n* Treue *f*

**lozenge,** los-indsch, *n* Pastille *f*

**Ltd,** limm-i-tidd, *n* (*abbr* **limited company**), GmbH

**lubricant,** luh-bri-kent, *n* Schmiermittel *nt*

**lubricate,** luh-bri-keht, *v* schmieren

**lucid,** luh-ssidd, *adj* klar

**luck,** lack, *n* Glück *nt*; **bad –,** Pech *nt*; **good –!** viel Glück!; **–ily,** *adv* glücklicherweise; **–y,** *adj* Glücks-; (chance) glücklich; **be –y,** Glück haben

**lucrative,** luh-kre-tiw, *adj* einträglich

**ludicrous,** luh-di-kress, *adj* lächerlich

**lug,** lagg, *v fam* schleppen

**luggage,** lagg-idsch, *n* Gepäck *nt*; **– office,** *n* Gepäckabgabe *f*; **– rack,** *n* Gepäckablage *f*

**lukewarm,** luhk-u'oarm, *adj* lau, lauwarm

**lull,** lall, *n* Pause *f*; *v* einlullen; beruhigen

**lullaby,** lall-e-bei, *n* Wiegenlied *nt*

**lumbago,** lamm-**beh**-goh, *n* Hexenschuß *m*

**lumber,** lamm-ber, *n* Gerümpel *nt*; (timber) Holz *nt*; **–jack,** *n* Holzfäller *m*; **– room,** *n* Abstellkammer *f*; *v* **– sb with sth,** jdm etw aufhalsen

**luminous,** luh-mi-ness, *adj* leuchtend

**lump,** lamp, *n* Klumpen *m*; (sugar) Stück *nt*; *med* Knoten *m*; **– it,** *v fam* sich mit etw abfinden; **– together,** *v* zusammenwerfen; **–y,** *adj* klumpig

**lunacy,** luh-ne-ssi, *n* Wahnsinn *m*

**lunar,** luh-ner, *adj* Mond-

**lunatic,** luh-ne-tick, *adj* wahnsinnig; *n* Wahnsinnige(r) *m & f*; **– asylum,** *n pej* Irrenanstalt *f*

**lunch(eon),** lantsch(-en), *n* Mittagessen *nt*

**lunch hour,** lantsch **au**-er, *n* Mittagspause *f*

**lunchtime,** lantsch-teim, *n* Mittag *m*; **at –,** mittags

**lung,** lang, *n* Lunge *f*

**lurch,** lörtsch, *n* Ruck *m*; *naut* Schlingern *nt*; *v* (of person) taumeln; (of vehicle) rucken; *naut* schlingern; **leave in the –,** *v* im Stich lassen

**lure,** ljuhr, *v* (an)locken

**lurid,** ljuhr-ridd, *adj* (colour) grell; (tale etc.) grausig

**lurk,** lörk, *v* lauern

**luscious,** lasch-ess, *adj* üppig; saftig

**lust,** last, *n* (desire) Wollust *f*; (greed) Gier *f*; **– (after/for),** *v* gelüsten (nach); **–ful,** *adj* lüstern

**lusty,** lass-ti, *adj* kräftig

**lute,** luht, *n* Laute *f*

**luxuriant,** lack-**schuhr**-ri-ent, *adj* üppig

**luxurious,** lack-**schuhr**-ri-ess, *adj* luxuriös

**luxury,** lack-sche-ri, *adj* Luxus-; *n* Luxus *m*

**lying,** lei-ing, *n* Lügen *nt*

**lymph,** limff, *n* Lymphe *f*

**lynch,** lintsch, *v* lynchen

**lyric(al),** li-rick(-'l), *adj* lyrisch

**lyrics,** li-ricks, *npl* Text *m*

**mac**, mäck, *abbr*
  **mackintosh**
**macaroni**, mäck-e-**roh**-ni, *n*
  Makkaroni *pl*
**machine**, me-**schien**, *n*
  Maschine *f*; **– gun**, *n*
  Maschinengewehr *nt*; **–ry**,
  *n* Maschinerie *f*
**mackerel**, **mäck**-e-rel, *n*
  Makrele *f*
**mackintosh**, **mäck**-inn-
  tosch, *n* Regenmantel *m*
**mad**, mädd, *adj* (crazy)
  verrückt; (angry) wütend;
  **– about**, vernarrt in
**madam**, **mädd**-em, *n* gnädige
  Frau *f*
**madden**, **mädd**-'n, *v* (make
  angry) wütend machen;
  (make crazy) verrückt
  machen
**madly**, **mädd**-li, *adv*
  wahnsinnig
**madman**, **mädd**-men, *n*
  Verrückter *m*
**madwoman**, **mädd**-u'u-men,
  *n* Verrückte *f*
**magazine**, mäg-e-**sien**, *n*
  (periodical) Zeitschrift *f*;
  *mil* Magazin *nt*
**madness**, **mädd**-niss, *n*
  Wahnsinn *m*
**maggot**, **mägg**-et, *n* Made *f*
**magic**, **mädsch**-ick, *adj*
  magisch, Zauber-; *n*
  Zauberei *f*
**magician**, me-**dschisch**-'n, *n*
  Zauberer *m*
**magistrate**, **mädsch**-iss-
  treht, *n* Friedensrichter *m*
**magnanimous**, mägg-**nänn**-
  i-mess, *adj* großmütig
**magnesium**, mägg-**nie**-si-em,
  *n* Magnesium *nt*
**magnet**, **mägg**-nitt, *n*
  Magnet *m*; **–ic**, *adj*
  magnetisch; **–ism**, *n*
  Magnetismus *m*; *fig*

unwiderstehlich; **–ize**, *v*
  magnetisieren
**magnificent**, mägg-ni-fi-
  ssent, *adj* prächtig
**magnify**, **mägg**-ni-fei, *v*
  vergrößern; **–ing glass,**
  *n* Lupe *f*,
  Vergrößerungsglas *nt*
**magnitude**, **mägg**-ni-**tjuhd**,
  *n* (size) Größe *f*;
  (importance) Bedeutung *f*
**magpie**, **mägg**-pei, *n* Elster *f*
**mahogany**, me-**hogg**-e-ni, *n*
  Mahagoni *nt*
**maid**, mehd, *n*
  Dienstmädchen *nt*; **old –,**
  *n pej* alte Jungfer *f*
**maiden**, **meh**-d'n, *adj*
  Jungfern-; *n* Maid *f*
**mail**, mehl, *n* Post *f*; *v*
  aufgeben; **– bag,** *n*
  Postsack *m*; **–box,** *n*
  Briefkasten *m*; **– order,** *adj*
  auf Bestellung, Katalog-;
  Versand-; *n*
  Versandhandel *m*
**maim**, mehm, *v*
  verstümmeln
**main**, mehn, *adj*
  hauptsächlich, Haupt-; *n*
  (water, gas) Hauptleitung
  *f*; **–land**, *n* Festland *nt*; **–ly**,
  *adv* hauptsächlich; **–s**, *npl*
  (water, gas)
  Versorgungsnetz *nt*;
  **–stream**, *n* (art, *mus*)
  Mainstream *m*; (trend)
  Trend *m*
**maintain**, mehn-**tehn**, *v*
  (claim) behaupten;
  (support) unterhalten;

(keep in repair) instand halten

**maintenance, mehn-**te-nenss, n (support) Unterhalt m; (repair) Instandhaltung f

**maize,** mehs, n Mais m

**majestic,** me-**dschess-**tick, adj majestätisch

**majesty, mädsch-**iss-ti, n Majestät f

**major, meh-**dscher, adj (important) Haupt-; (size) größer; (mus key) Dur nt; n mil Major m

**Majorca,** me-**jor-**ke, n Mallorca nt

**majority,** me-**dscho-**ri-ti, n Mehrheit f; (age) Volljährigkeit f

**make,** mehk, n Marke f; v machen; (manufacture) herstellen; (decision) treffen; (cause) dazu bringen; **–believe,** n Phantasie f; **– do (with),** v auskommen (mit); **– it,** v es schaffen; **–r,** n Fabrikant m; **–shift,** adj Behelfs-; **–up,** n Schminke f; v (face) schminken; (story) erfinden; (be reconciled) sich versöhnen

**making, meh-**king, n **in the –,** angehend

**malaise,** me-**lehs,** n Unbehagen nt

**malaria,** me-**lähr-**ri-e, n Malaria f

**male,** mehl, adj männlich; n

(animal) Männchen nt; (human) Mann m

**malevolent,** me-**lew-**e-lent, adj böswillig

**malfunction, mäll-**fank-sch'n, n Störung f; (machine) Funktionsstörung f; v nicht richtig funktionieren

**malice, mäll-**iss, n Groll m; Haß m

**malicious,** me-**lisch-**ess, adj boshaft; böswillig

**malign,** me-**lein,** adj böse; v verleumden

**malignant,** me-**ligg-**nent, adj bösartig

**malinger,** me-**ling-**ger, v sich krank stellen

**mallet, mäll-**itt, n Holzhammer m

**malnutrition, mäll-**njuh-**trisch-**'n, n Unterernährung f

**malpractice, mäll-präck-**tiss, n (law, med) Kunstfehler m

**malt,** mo'alt, n Malz nt

**maltreat, mäll-triet,** v mißhandeln

**mammal, mämm-**'l, n Säugetier nt

**man,** männ, n Mann m; (human race) Menschheit f; v bemannen

**manage, männ-**idsch, v (control) leiten, führen; (accomplish) fertigbringen; **–able,** adj machbar; **–ment,** n

Management nt, Leitung f, Führung f; (managers) Vorstand m; **–r,** n Manager m, Leiter m, Geschäftsführer m; **–ress,** n Managerin f, Leiterin f, Geschäftsführerin f

**managerial, männ-**idsch-**ier-**ri-el, adj leitend

**mandate, männ-**deht, n Verfügung f; law Mandat nt

**mandatory, männ-**de-te-ri, adj obligatorisch

**mane,** mehn, n Mähne f

**manger, mehn-**dscher, n Krippe f

**mangle, mäng-**g'l, n Rolle f; v mangeln

**mango, mäng-**goh, n Mango f

**manhandle, männ-hänn-**d'l, v (roughly) grob behandeln

**manhole, männ-**hohl, n Einstiegsluke f

**manhood,** n (quality) Männlichkeit f; (age) Mannesalter nt

**mania, meh-**ni-e, n Manie f, Sucht f; **–c,** n Verrückte(r) m & f

**manic, männ-**ick, adj manisch

**manicure, männ-**i-kjuhr, n Maniküre f

**manifest, männ-**i-fest, adj offenbar; v offenbaren; **–ation,** n Ausdruck m, Anzeichen nt

**manifesto, männ-**i-**fess-**toh,

*n* Manifest *nt*

**manipulate,** me-**nipp**-ju-leht, *v* handhaben

**mankind, männ-keind,** *n* Menschheit *f*

**manly, männ**-li, *adj* männlich

**manner, männ**-er, *n* Weise *f*; (kind) Art *f*; **–ism,** *n* Eigenart *f*; **–s,** *npl* Manieren *fpl*.

**man-made, männ**-mehd, *adj* künstlich, Kunst-

**manoeuvre,** me-**nuh**-wer, *n* Manöver *nt*; *mil* Feldzug *m*; *v* manövrieren

**manor, männ**-er, *n* Landgut *nt*; **– house,** *n* Herrenhaus *nt*

**manpower, männ**-pau-er, *n* Arbeitskräfte *pl*

**mansion, männ**-sch'n, *n* Herrensitz *m*

**manslaughter, männ**-slo'a-ter, *n* Totschlag *m*

**mantelpiece, männ**-t'l-piess, *n* Kaminsims *m*

**manual, männ**-ju-el, *adj* manuell, Hand-; *n* Handbuch *nt*; **– labour,** *n* manuelle Tätigkeit *f*

**manufacture, männ**-juh-**fäck**-tscher, *n* Herstellung *f*; *v* herstellen; **–r,** *n* Hersteller *m*

**manure,** me-**njuhr,** *n* Dung *m*; (fertilizer) Dünger *m*; *v* düngen

**manuscript, männ**-juh-skript, *n* Manuskript *nt*

**many, menn**-i, *adj & pron*

viele; **– a,** manch ein

**map, mäpp,** *n* Karte *f*; (of town) Plan *m*; *v* aufzeichnen; **– out,** planen

**maple, meh**-p'l, *n* Ahorn *m*

**mar, mahr,** *v* verderben; stören

**marathon, mä**-re-thonn, *n* *sport* Marathonlauf *m*; *fig* Marathon *m*

**marble, mahr**-b'l, *n* Marmor *m*; (toy) Murmel *f*

**march, mahrtsch,** *n* Marsch *m*; *v* marschieren

**March, mahrtsch,** *n* März *m*

**mare, mähr,** *n* Stute *f*

**margarine, mahr**-dsche-**rien,** *n* Margarine *f*

**margin, mahr**-dschin, *n* Rand *m*; (in margin) Rand-; (slight) unbedeutend; **–al seat,** *n* mit knapper Mehrheit gewonnener Sitz *m*; **–alize,** *v* an den Rand drängen

**marigold, mä**-ri-gohld, *n* Ringelblume *f*

**marijuana, mä**-ri-u'ah-ne, *n* Marihuana *nt*

**marina,** me-**rie**-ne, *n* Yachthafen *m*

**marinate, mä**-ri-neht, *v* marinieren

**marine,** me-**rien,** *adj* See-; *n* Seesoldat *m*

**marital, mä**-ri-tel, *adj* Ehe-; **– status,** *n* Familienstand *m*

**maritime, mä**-ri-teim, *adj*

See-, Marine-

**mark, mahrk,** *n* (sign) Zeichen *nt*; (stain) Fleck *m*; (currency) Mark *f*; (in exam) Note *f*; *v* (identify) markieren; (characterize) kennzeichnen; (stain) Flecken machen; (exam) korrigieren; **–ed,** *adj* deutlich; **make one's –,** *v* sich einen Namen machen

**market, mahr**-kitt, *n* Markt *m*; *fin* Börse *f*; *v* vermarkten; **– gardening,** *n* Gemüseanbau *m*; **–ing,** *n* Marketing *nt*- **research,** *n* Marktforschung *f*

**marksman, mahrks**-men, *n* Scharfschütze *m*

**marmalade, mahr**-me-lehd, *n* Orangenmarmelade *f*

**maroon,** me-**ruhn,** *adj* kastanienbraun; *v* aussetzen

**marriage, mä**-ridsch, *adj* Heirats-; *n* (ceremony) Hochzeit *f*; (state) Ehe *f*

**married, mä**-ridd, *adj* verheiratet, **– couple,** *n* Ehepaar *nt*

**marrow, mä**-roh, *n* (bone) Mark *nt*; (vegetable) Kürbis *m*

**marry, mär**-i, *v* (get married to) heiraten; (perform ceremony) trauen

**marsh, mahrsch,** *n* Sumpf *m*

**marshy, mahr**-schi, *adj* sumpfig

**martial, mahr**-schel, *adj*

kriegerisch, Kriegs-; – **law**, *n* Kriegsrecht *nt*

**martyr, mahr**-ter, *n* Märtyrer *m*; *v* peinigen; **–dom**, *n* Märtyrertum *nt*

**marvel, mahr**-wel, *n* Wunder *nt*; *v* – **(at)**, sich wundern (über); **–lous**, *adj* wunderbar

**Marxism, marck**-ssism, *n* Marxismus *m*

**marzipan, mahr**-si-pänn, *n* Marzipan *m*

**mascara, mäss-kah-re**, *n* Wimperntusche *f*

**masculine, mäss**-kjuh-linn, *adj* männlich

**mash, mäsch**, *v* zerdrücken; **–ed potato(es)**, *n*(*pl.*), Kartoffelpüree *nt*

**mask, mahsk**, *n* Maske *f*; *v* maskieren

**mason, meh**-ssen, *n* Maurer *m*, Steinhauer *m*; (freemason) Freimaurer *m*

**masonic, me-ssonn**-ick, *adj* freimaurerisch

**masonry, meh**-ssen-ri, *n* Mauerwerk *nt*

**masquerade, mäss-ke-rehd**, *n* Maskerade *f*; *v* – **(as)**, sich als etw/jd ausgeben

**mass, mäss**, *adj* Massen-; *n* Masse *f*, Menge *f*; *relig* Messe *f*; *v* sich sammeln; **–es of**, eine Menge; **the –es**, *npl* die Massen *pl*

**massacre, mäss-e-ker**, *n* Gemetzel *nt*; *v* massakrieren

**massage, mäss**-ahsch, *n*

Massage *f*; *v* massieren

**massive, mäss-iw**, *adj* massiv

**mast, mahst**, *n* Mast *m*

**master, mahss**-ter, *n* Herr *m*; (artist) Meister *m*; (teacher) Lehrer *m*; **M–**, (graduate) Magister *m*; *v* beherrschen; **–ful**, *adj* herrisch; **–ly**, *adv* meisterhaft; **–mind**, *n* (An)führer *m*; *v* (an)führen; **–piece**, *n* Meisterwerk *nt*; **–y**, *n* Können *nt*

**masticate, mäss**-ti-keht, *v* kauen, zerkauen

**masturbate, mäss**-ter-beht, *v* masturbieren

**mat, mätt**, *n* Matte *f*

**match, mätsch**, *n* Streichholz *nt*; *sport* Spiel *nt*, Match *nt*; (equal) Ebenbürtige(r) *m & f*; *v* (go well) passen zu; (go together) zusammenpassen; (equal) gleichkommen; **–ing**, *adj* passend

**mate, meht**, *n* (friend) Kumpel; (of animal) Männchen *nt*, Weibchen *nt*; *naut* Maat *m*; *v* (sich) paaren

**material, me-tier**-ri-el, *adj* (physical) materiell; (significant) wesentlich; *n* Material *nt*; (cloth) Stoff *m*; **–istic**, *adj* materialistisch; **–ize**, *v* (plan etc.) sich verwirklichen; (ghost

etc.) erscheinen; **–s**, *npl* Materialien *pl*

**maternal, me-tör**-nel, *adj* mütterlich, Mutter-

**mathematics, mäth-i-mätt**-icks, *n* Mathematik *f*

**maths, mäths**, *n* (*abbr* **mathematics**), Mathe *f*

**matinée, mätt**-i-neh, *n* Frühvorstellung *f*

**matrimonial, mätt-ri-moh**-ni-el, *n* ehelich, Ehe-

**matrimony, mätt**-ri-me-ni, *n* Ehestand *m*

**matrix, meh**-tricks, *n* Matrize *f*

**matron, meh**-tren, *n* (hospital) Oberschwester *f*; (school) Hausmutter *f*

**matter, mätt**-er, *n* (substance) Materie *f*; (substance) Stoff *m*; (affair) Angelegenheit *f*; *v* etwas ausmachen; **–-of-fact**, *adj* sachlich, nüchtern; **it doesn't –**, es macht nichts

**matting, mätt**-ing, *n* Geflecht *nt*; (mats) Matten *pl*

**mattress, mätt**-ress, *n* Matratze *f*

**mature, me-tjuhr**, *adj* reif; *v* reifen

**maturity, me-tjuhr**-ri-ti, *n* Reife *f*

**maul, mo'al**, *v* verletzen

**mauve, mohw**, *adj* hell lila

**maxim, mäck**-ssimm, *n* Grundsatz *m*

**maximize, mäck**-ssi-meis, *v*

maximieren

**maximum, mäck**-ssi-mem, *adj* maximal, Maximal-; *n* Maximum *nt*

**may, meh, *v*** (be permitted) dürfen; (be possible) können; (be probable) mögen

**May, meh, *n*** Mai *m*

**maybe, meh**-bie, *adj* vielleicht

**May Day, meh** deh, *n* der erste Mai *m*; (Labour Day) Tag *m* der Arbeit

**mayhem, meh**-hemm, *n* Chaos *nt*

**mayonnaise, meh**-e-nehs, *n* Mayonnaise *f*

**mayor, meh**-er, *n* Bürgermeister *m*

**maze, mehs, *n*** Irrgarten *m*

**me, mie, *pron*** (accusative) mich; (dative) mir; (emphatic) ich

**meadow, medd**-oh, *n* Wiese *f*

**meagre, mie**-ger, *adj* mager; (scanty) karg

**meal, miel, *n*** (food) Essen *nt*, Mahlzeit *f*; (flour) Mehl *nt*; **–time,** *n* Essenszeit *f*

**mean, mien, *adj*** (miserly) geizig; (nasty) gemein; *n* Durchschnitt *m*; *v* (signify) bedeuten; (have in mind) meinen; (intend) wollen; **be –t to,** sollen

**meander, mie**-änn-der, *v* sich schlängeln; *fig* abschweifen

**meaning, mie**-ning, *n* Bedeutung *f*; (purpose) Sinn *m*; **–ful,** *adj* bedeutungsvoll, sinnvoll; **–less,** *adj* bedeutungslos, sinnlos

**means, miens, *npl*** Mittel *pl*; **by – of,** durch, mit Hilfe von; **by all –,** selbstverständlich; **by no –,** keineswegs

**meantime, mien**-teim, *adv* **(in the) –,** inzwischen

**meanwhile, mien**-u'eil, *adv* inzwischen

**measles, mie**-sels, *npl* Masern *pl*

**measure, mesch**-er, *n* (tool, unit) Maß *nt*; (step) Maßnahme *f*; *v* messen; **–d,** *adj* gemessen; **–ment,** Maß *nt*

**meat, miet, *adj*** Fleisch-; *n* Fleisch *nt*; **–y,** *adj* fleischig; *fig* gehaltvoll

**mechanic, mi**-känn-ick, *n* Mechaniker *m*; **–al,** *adj* mechanisch; **–s,** *n* Mechanik *f*

**mechanism, meck**-e-nism, *n* Mechanismus *m*

**mechanize, meck**-e-neis, *v* mechanisieren

**medal, medd**-'l, *n* Medaille *f*

**meddle (in), medd**-'l (inn), *v* sich einmischen (in)

**media, mie**-di-e, *adj* Medien-; *npl* Medien *pl*

**mediaeval = medieval**

**mediate, mie**-di-eht, *v* vermitteln

**mediator, mie**-di-eh-ter, *n* Vermittler *m*

**medical, medd**-i-k'l, *adj* ärztlich, medizinisch; *n* (examination), (ärztliche) Untersuchung *f*

**medication, medd**-i-keh-sch'n, *n* Medikamente *pl*

**medicinal, me**-diss-i-n'l, *adj* medizinisch

**medicine, medd**-ssinn, *n* Medizin *f*, Arznei *f*

**medieval, medd**-i-ie-vel, *adj* mittelalterlich

**mediocre, mie**-di-oh-ker, *adj* mittelmäßig

**meditate, medd**-i-teht, *v* meditieren; (think) nachdenken

**Mediterranean, medd**-i-te-reh-ni-en, *adj* Mittelmeer-; (person) südländisch; *n* (person) Südländer *m*; **the – (Sea),** das Mittelmeer *nt*

**medium, mie**-di-em, *adj* mittlere(r/s), Mittel-; **– (-sized),** mittelgroß; *n* (midpoint) Mittel *nt*; (person, channel) Medium *nt*

**meek, miek, *adj*** sanftmütig

**meet, miet, *v*** (by arrangement) sich treffen mit; (by chance) begegnen; (get to know) kennenlernen; (difficulty) begegnen; (obligation) nachkommen; **–ing,** *n* (chance) (Zusammen)treffen;

(formal) Besprechung f;
**pleased to – you!** es freut
mich!

**mega-, megg-**e, *pref*
Mega-; **–byte,** n *comp*
Megabyte nt; **–phone,** n
Megaphon nt

**melancholy, mell-**en-koll-i,
*adj* melancholisch; n
Melancholie f

**mellow, mell-**oh, *adj* mild;
(tone) weich; (mood)
heiter gestimmt; v reifen;
*fig* weicher werden

**melodious,** mi-**loh**-di-ess, *adj*
melodisch

**melody, mell-**e-di, n
Melodie f

**melon, mell-**en, n Melone f

**melt,** melt, v schmelzen; **–
away,** (person) sich
auflösen; (anger)
abklingen; **–down,** n
Kernschmelze f; **–ing
point,** n Schmelzpunkt m

**member, memm-**ber, n (of
club) Mitglied nt; **M– of
Parliament,**
Abgeordnete(r) m & f;
**–ship,** n Mitgliedschaft f;
**–ship card,** n
Mitgliedskarte f

**membrane, memm-**brehn, n
Membran f

**memento,** mi-**menn-**toh, n
Andenken nt

**memo, memm-**oh, n (*abbr*
**memorandum**), Memo nt,
Mitteilung f; (on file)
Aktennotiz f

**memoirs, memm-**u'ahrs, *npl*

Memoiren *pl*

**memorable, memm-**e-re-b'l,
*adj* unvergeßlich

**memorandum, memm-**e-
**ränn-**dem, n
Memorandum nt,
Mitteilung f; (on file)
Aktennotiz f

**memorial,** mi-**mohr**-ri-el, *adj*
Gedenk-; n Denkmal nt

**memorize, memm-**e-reis, v
sich merken; (by heart)
auswendig lernen

**memory, memm-**e-ri, n
(faculty) Gedächtnis nt;
(thing recalled)
Erinnerung f; *comp*
Speicher m

**menace, menn-**iss, n
Drohung f; v bedrohen

**menagerie,** mi-**nädsch-**e-ri,
n Menagerie f

**mend,** mend, n reparierte
Stelle; v reparieren; (sew)
flicken; (of injury,
patient) kurieren

**menial, mie-**ni-el, *adj*
niedrig

**meningitis, menn-**in-
**dschei-**tiss, n
Hirnhautentzündung f

**menopause, menn-**e-po'as, n
Wechseljahre *pl*

**menstruation, menn-**stru-
eh-sch'n, n Menstruation f

**mental, menn-**t'l, *adj* geistig,
Geistes-; (*fam* mad)
verrückt; **– arithmetic,** n
Kopfrechnen nt; **–
breakdown,** n
Nervenzusammenbruch

m; **– cruelty,** n seelische
Grausamkeit; **– hospital,** n
Nervenklinik f

**mentality, menn-täll-**i-ti, n
Mentalität f

**mention, menn-**sch'n, n
Erwähnung f; v erwähnen;
**don't – it!** bitte (sehr)!

**menu, menn-**juh, n
Speisekarte f; *comp* Menü
nt

**mercenary, mör-**ssi-sne-ri,
*adj* geldgierig; n Söldner m

**merchandise, mör-**tschen-
deis, n Ware f

**merchant, mör-**tschent, n
Kaufmann m; **– navy,**
Handelsmarine f

**merciful, mör-**ssi-full, *adj*
gnädig; **–ly,** (kindly)
gnädig; (fortunately)
glücklicherweise

**merciless, mör-**ssi-liss, *adj*
erbarmungslos

**mercury, mör-**kju-ri, n
Quecksilber nt

**mercy, mör-**ssi, n (action)
Gnade f; (feeling)
Erbarmen nt

**mere,** mier, *adj* bloß; **–ly,** *adv*
bloß

**merge, mördsch,** v
verschmelzen; *comm* sich
zusammenschließen,
fusionieren; **–r,** n
Zusammenschluß m,
Fusion f

**meridian,** me-**ridd-**i-enn, n
Längengrad m

**meringue,** me-**räng,** n
Baiser nt

**merit, me**-ritt, *n*
(achievement) Verdienst
*nt*; (advantage) Vorzug *m*;
(distinction)
Auszeichnung *f*; *v*
verdienen

**mermaid, mör**-mehd, *n*
Meerjungfrau *f*

**merry, me**-ri, *adj* fröhlich,
heiter; **– Christmas!**
fröhliche Weihnachten!

**mesh,** mesch, *n* Masche *f*;
(netting) Geflecht *nt*

**mesmerize, mes**-me-reis, *v*
faszinieren

**mess,** mess, *n* (disorder)
Unordnung *f*; (dirt)
Schmutz *m*; (bungle)
Durcheinander *f*; *mil*
Kasino *nt*; **–
about/around,** *v*
herumalbern; **–
about/around with,** *v* an
etw herumbasteln;
(interfere) sich
einmischen; **– up,** *v*
(make untidy)
Unordnung machen;
(make dirty) schmutzig
machen; (bungle)
durcheinanderbringen

**message, mess**-idsch, *n*
Mitteilung *f*

**messenger, mess**-inn-
dscher, *n* Bote *m*

**messy,** *adj* (untidy)
unordentlich; (dirty)
schmutzig

**metal, mett**-'l, *n* Metall *nt*;
**–ic,** *adj* metallisch

**metaphor, mett**-e-for, *n*

Metapher *f*

**meteor, mie**-ti-er, *n* Meteor
*m*

**meteorology, mie**-ti-e-roll-e-
dschi, *n* Meteorologie *f*

**meter, mie**-ter, *n* (electricity
etc.) Zähler *m*

**method, meth**-edd, *n*
Methode *f*

**methodical,** mi-**thodd**-i-k'l,
*adj* methodisch

**Methodist, meth**-e-dist, *n*
Methodist *m*

**meths, meths,** *abbr*
**methylated spirit(s)**

**methylated spirit(s), me**-
thi-leh-tidd **spi**-ritt(s), *n*
Brennspiritus *m*

**meticulous, mi-tick**-ju-less,
*n* sorgfältig

**metre, mie**-ter, *n* Meter *m/nt*

**metric, mett**-rick, *adj*
metrisch

**metropolis, mi-tro**-pe-liss,
*n* Metropole *f*, Weltstadt *f*

**metropolitan, mett-re-poll**-
i-ten, *adj* Groß-;
großstädtisch

**mew,** mjuh, *v* miauen

**mews,** mjuhs, *n* Gasse *f*

**Mexico, meck**-ssi-koh, *n*
Mexiko *nt*

**micro-, mei**-kroh, *pref*
Mikro-; **–chip,** *n*
Mikrochip *m*; **–computer,**
*n* Mikrocomputer *m*;
**–phone,** *n* Mikrophon *nt*;
**–scope,** *n* Mikroskop *nt*;
**–wave,** *n* Mikrowelle *f*; *v*
in der Mikrowelle
zubereiten; **–wave oven,** *n*

Mikrowellenherd *nt*

**mid,** midd, *adj* Mittel-; **in –
March,** Mitte März; **in –
air,** in der Luft

**middle, midd**-'l, *adj*
mittlere(r/s), Mittel-; **in –**
Mitte *f*; **––aged,** *adj*
mittleren Alters; **M–
Ages,** *npl* Mittelalter *nt*;
**M– East,** *n* Naher Osten
*m*; **––class,** *adj*
Mittelstands-; *pej* spießig;
**–man,** Zwischenhändler
*m*; **– name,** *n* zweiter
Vorname *m*; **in the – of,**
*prep* mitten in, inmitten
von

**middling, midd**-ling, *adj*
mittelmäßig

**midge, midsch,** *n* Mücke *f*

**midget, midsch**-itt, *n*
Liliputaner *m*, Zwerg *m*

**midnight, midd**-neit, *n*
Mitternacht *f*

**midst, mids**'t, *prep* **in the –
of,** mitten in

**midsummer, midd-samm**-er,
*n* Hochsommer *m*

**midweek, midd-wiek,** *adj* &
*adv* in der Wochenmitte

**midwife, midd**-u'eif, *n*
Hebamme *f*

**midwinter, midd-u'inn**-ter,
*n* (Mitt)winter *m*

**might,** meit, *n* Macht *f*,
Gewalt *f*; *v* (*past* &
*conditional of* **may**); **–y,** *adj*
& *adv* mächtig

**migraine, mie**-grehn, *n*
Migräne *f*

**migrate, mei**-greht, *v*

(people) wandern; (birds) ziehen

**migration,** mei-greh-sch'n, n Wanderung f

**Milan,** mi-länn, n Mailand nt

**mild,** meild, adj (weather, flavour) mild; (medicine, beer) leicht; (person, criticism) sanft; (slight) leicht

**mildew,** mill-djuh, n Schimmel m

**mile,** meil, n Meile f; **–age,** (Anzahl f der) Meilen pl; **–stone,** n Meilenstein m

**militant,** mill-i-tent, adj militant; n Militante f

**military,** mill-i-te-ri, adj militärisch, Militär-; n Militär nt

**militate (against),** mill-i-teht (e-genst), v sich gegen etw aussprechen

**militia,** mi-lisch-e, n Miliz f

**milk,** milk, n Milch f; v melken; **– shake,** n Milkshake m; **–y,** adj milchig; **–y way,** n Milchstraße f

**mill,** mill, n Mühle f; (factory) Fabrik f; v mahlen; **– around/about,** durcheinanderlaufen

**millennium,** mi-lenn-i-em, n Jahrtausend nt

**miller,** mill-er, n Müller m

**milli-,** mill-i, pref Milli-; **–gram(e),** n Milligramm nt; **–metre,** n Millimeter m

**million,** mill-jen, n Million

f; **–aire,** n Millionär m

**mime,** meim, n (act) Pantomime f; (actor) Pantomime m; v pantomimisch darstellen

**mimic,** mimm-ick, v nachahmen; **–ry,** n Nachahmung f

**mince,** minss, n Hackfleisch nt; v zerhacken; **–meat,** n Hackfleisch nt; (sweet) süße Pastetenfüllung f; **– pie,** n Pastete f mit süßer Füllung

**mind,** meind, n Sinn m, Gemüt nt, Geist m; v aufpassen (auf); **–ful (of sth),** adj mit etw im Sinn; **–less,** adj sinnlos; **change one's –,** v es sich anders überlegen; **I don't mind,** es macht mir nichts aus; **make up one's –,** v sich entschließen; **never –!** macht nichts!, nicht schlimm!

**mine,** mein, n (pit) Grube f; (explosive) Mine f; v Bergbau betreiben

**mine,** mein, pron meine(r/s)

**miner,** mei-ner, n Bergmann m

**mineral,** minn-e-rel, adj mineralisch, Mineral-; n Mineral nt; **– water,** n Mineralwasser nt

**mingle (with),** ming-g'l (u'idh), v sich mischen (unter)

**miniature,** minn-i-tscher, adj Miniatur-; n Miniatur f

**minibus,** minn-i-bass, n Kleinbus m

**minim,** minn-imm, n halbe Note f

**minimal,** minn-i-mel, adj minimal, Mindest-

**minimize,** minn-i-meis, v verringern

**minimum,** minn-i-mem, adj minimal, Mindest-; n Minimum nt; **– temperature,** n Tiefsttemperatur f

**mini-skirt,** minn-i-skört, n Minirock m

**minister,** minn-iss-ter, n (government) Minister m; relig Pfarrer m; **– to,** v sich kümmern um

**ministry,** minn-iss-tri, n (government) Ministerium nt; relig geistliches Amt nt

**mink,** mink, n Nerz m

**minor,** mei-ner, adj (unimportant) unbedeutend; (small) kleiner; (mus key) Moll nt; n Minderjährige(r) m & f

**minority,** mei-no-ri-ti, n Minderheit f

**mint,** mint, n (herb) Minze f; (sweet) Pfefferminzbonbon nt; (for coinage) Münze f; v (coins) prägen; **make a –,** v fam abstauben

**minus,** mei-ness, adv weniger, minus, Minus-

**minute,** mei-njuht, adj

(tiny) winzig; (precise)
genau

**minute, minn**-itt, n (60
seconds) Minute f;
(moment) Augenblick m;
**–s, pl** Protokoll nt

**miracle, mi**-re-k'l, n
Wunder nt

**miraculous,** mi-**räck**-ju-less,
adj wunderbar

**mirage,** mi-**rahsch**, n Fata
Morgana f

**mire,** meir, n Morast m

**mirror,** mi-rer, n Spiegel m;
v widerspiegeln

**mirth,** mörth, n Frohsinn m;
Heiterkeit f

**misadventure,** miss-ed-
**wenn**-tscher, n
Mißgeschick m

**misanthropist,** mi-**sänn**-
thre-pist, n
Menschenfeind m

**misapprehension,** miss-äpp-
ri-henn-sch'n, n
Mißverständnis nt

**misappropriate,** miss-e-
**proh**-pri-eht, v
unterschlagen

**misbehave,** miss-bi-**hehw**, v
sich schlecht benehmen

**miscalculate,** miss-**käll**-klu-
leht, v falsch berechnen;
(misjudge) falsch
einschätzen

**miscarriage,** miss-kä-ridsch,
n med Fehlgeburt f; **– of
justice,** n Justizirrtum m

**miscellaneous,** miss-e-leh-
ni-ess, adj
verschieden(erlei)

**mischief, miss**-tschiff, n
(playfulness) Unfug m;
(harm) Unheil nt

**mischievous, miss**-tschi-
wess, adj (playful)
spitzbübisch; (harmful)
bösartig

**misconduct,** miss-**konn**-
dakt, n schlechtes
Betragen nt; (professional)
unkorrektes Verhalten nt

**misconstrue,** miss-ken-
**struh**, v mißdeuten,
mißverstehen

**miscount,** miss-**kaunt**, v
falsch rechnen

**misdeed,** miss-**died**, n
Missetat f

**misdemeanour,** miss-di-mie-
ner, n Vergehen nt

**miser, mei**-ser, n Geizhals m

**miserable,** mis-e-re-b'l, adj
(poor) elend; (unhappy)
unglücklich; (dreadful)
elend

**miserly,** mei-ser-li, adj geizig

**misery,** mis-e-ri, n Elend nt

**misfire,** miss-**feir**, v
(engine) fehlzünden;
(gun) nicht losgehen;
(plan) fehlschlagen

**misfit,** miss-**fitt**, n
Außenseiter m

**misfortune,** miss-**fohr**-
tjuhn, n Unglück nt

**misgiving,** miss-**giw**-ing, n
Bedenken pl

**misguided,** miss-**gei**-didd,
adj unangebracht

**mishap, miss**-häpp, n
Mißgeschick nt

**misinform,** miss-in-**form**, v
falsch informieren

**misinterpret,** miss-in-**tör**-
pritt, v falsch auslegen

**misjudge,** miss-**dschadsch**, v
falsch beurteilen

**mislay,** miss-**leh**, v verlegen

**mislead,** miss-**lied**, v
irreleiten, irreführen

**mismanage,** miss-**männ**-
idsch, v schlecht leiten

**misnomer,** miss-**noh**-mer, n
falsche Bezeichnung f

**misogynist,** miss-**ssodsch**-i-
nist, n Frauenfeind m

**misplace,** miss-**plehss**, v
verlegen

**misprint, miss**-print, n
Druckfehler m

**misrepresent,** miss-repp-ri-
**sent**, v falsch darstellen

**miss,** miss, n Fehlschuß m; v
(train, appointment etc.)
versäumen; (person)
vermissen; (not hit/catch)
verfehlen; **– out,** auslassen

**Miss,** miss, n Fräulein nt

**missile,** miss-eil, n
Geschoß nt

**missing,** adj (object)
fehlend; (person)
verloren; mil vermißt; **be
–,** fehlen

**mission, misch**-en, n
(delegation) Mission f;
relig Mission f; (embassy)
Gesandtschaft f; **–ary,**
Missionar m

**misspent,** miss-**spent**, adj
vergeudet

**mist,** mist, n Nebel m

**mistake, miss-tehk,** n Fehler m; **– for,** v verwechseln mit; **make a –,** v sich irren, einen Fehler machen

**mistaken, miss-teh-k'n,** adj (idea) falsch; **– identity,** n Verwechslung f; **be –,** v sich irren

**mistletoe, miss-'l-toh,** n Mistel f

**mistress, miss-triss,** n (house) Herrin f; (teacher) Lehrerin f; (lover) Geliebte f; (Mrs) Frau f

**mistrust, miss-trast,** n Mißtrauen nt; v mißtrauen

**misty, miss-ti,** adj neblig

**misunderstand, miss-an-der-ständ,** v mißverstehen; **–ing,** n Mißverständnis nt

**misuse, miss-juhs,** v mißbrauchen

**mitigate, mitt-i-geht,** v lindern, abschwächen

**mitten, mitt-'n,** n Fäustling m

**mix, micks,** v mischen, vermischen; **–ed,** adj gemischt; **–ed up,** adj (things) ducheinander; (person) verwirrt; **–er,** n Mixer m; **–ture,** n Mischung f; **– up,** v verwechseln; **– with,** v (associate with) mit jdm verkehren

**moan, mohn,** n (groan) Stöhnen nt; (complaint) Beschwerde f; v (groan)

stöhnen; (complain) jammern, sich beschweren

**moat, moht,** n Burggraben m

**mob, mobb,** n Pöbel m; v belagern

**mobile, moh-beil,** adj beweglich, mobil; **– phone,** n Funktelefon nt

**mobility, moh-bill-i-ti,** n Beweglichkeit f

**mobilize, moh-bi-leis,** v mobilisieren

**mock, mock,** adj falsch, Schein-; v verspotten; **–ery,** n Spott m; **–ing(ly),** adj & adv spöttisch; **–-up,** n (graphics) Layout nt; (three-dimensional) Modell nt

**mode, mohd,** n Weise f

**model, modd-'l,** adj (ideal) beispielhaft, Muster-; (toy etc.) Modell-; n (toy etc.) Modell nt; (ideal) Vorbild nt; (fashion) Model nt; v (make models) modellieren; (work as a model) als Model arbeiten; (clothes) vorführen, modeln

**modem, moh-demm,** n Modem nt

**moderate, modd-e-ret,** adj mäßig; n Gemäßigte(r) m & f

**moderate, modd-e-reht,** v (sich) mäßigen

**moderation, modd-e-reh-sch'n,** n Mäßigkeit f; **in –,** in/mit Maßen

**modern, modd-ern,** adj

modern, neu; **–ize,** v modernisieren

**modest, modd-ist,** adj bescheiden; **–y,** n Bescheidenheit f

**modification, modd-i-fi-keh-sch'n,** n Änderung f

**modify, modd-i-fei,** v ändern, modifizieren

**moist, meust,** adj feucht; **–en,** v anfeuchten; **–ure,** n Feuchtigkeit f

**molar, moh-ler,** n Backenzahn m

**mole, mohl,** n (animal) Maulwurf m; (mark) Muttermal nt; (jetty) Mole f

**molecule, moll-i-kjuhl,** n Molekül nt

**molest, me-lest,** v belästigen

**molten, mohl-t'n,** adj geschmolzen

**moment, moh-ment,** n Moment m, Augenblick m; **–ary,** adj kurz, vorübergehend

**momentous, me-menn-tess,** adj bedeutsam

**momentum, me-menn-tem,** n Schwung m

**monarch, monn-erk,** n Monarch m; **–y,** n Monarchie f

**monastery, monn-ess-tri,** n (Mönchs)kloster nt

**Monday, mann-deh,** n Montag m

**monetary, mann-i-te-ri,** adj Geld-

**money, mann-i,** n Geld nt;

**–lender,** n Geldverleiher m; **– order,** n Postanweisung f

**mongrel, mang**-grel, n (dog) Promenadenmischung f

**monitor, monn**-i-ter, n (observer) Beobachter m; (school) Aufsichtsschüler m; comp Monitor m; v überwachen

**monk,** mank, n Mönch m

**monkey, mang**-ki, n Affe m; **– nut,** n Erdnuß f

**monochrome, monn**-e-krohm, adj einfarbig

**monopolize,** me-**nopp**-e-leis, v monopolisieren

**monopoly,** mo-**nopp**-e-li, n Monopol nt

**monotonous,** me-**nott**-e-ness, adj eintönig

**monster, monn**-ster, n Ungeheuer nt

**monstrosity,** monn-**stross**-i-ti, n Monstrosität f

**monstrous, monn**-stress, adj (large) kolossal; (dreadful) schrecklich

**month,** manth, n Monat m; **–ly,** adj monatlich, Monats-; adv monatlich, einmal im Monat

**monument, monn**-ju-ment, n Denkmal nt

**monumental,** monn-ju-**menn**-t'l, adj gewaltig

**mood,** muhd, n Stimmung f; (temper) Laune f; gram Modus m; **–y,** adj launisch

**moon,** muhn, n Mond m; **–light,** n Mondlicht nt; v

schwarz arbeiten; **–lighting,** n Schwarzarbeit f

**moor,** mohr, n Heideland nt, Ödland nt; v (ship) festlegen; **–ing,** n Anlegeplatz m

**mop,** mopp, n Mop m; v wischen; **– up,** v aufwischen

**mope,** mohp, v fam Trübsal blasen

**moral,** mo-rel, adj moralisch; sittlich; n Moral f; **–s,** npl Moral f

**morale,** mo-**rahl,** n Moral f

**morality,** mo-**räll**-i-ti, n Sittlichkeit f

**morass,** me-**räss,** n Morast m

**morbid, mohr**-bidd, adj krankhaft; (macabre) makaber

**more,** mohr, adj & pron (in number, size) mehr; (additional) noch (mehr); adv mehr; **– ... than,** ...er als; **– and –,** immer mehr, immer ...er; **no –,** adj kein... mehr; pron nichts mehr; **not any –,** (no longer) nicht mehr; **once –,** noch einmal

**moreover,** mohr-**roh**-wer, adv überdies, ferner

**morning, mohr**-ning n Morgen m; **in the –,** am Morgen, morgens

**Morocco,** me-**rock**-oh, n Marokko nt

**moron, mohr**-ronn, n pej Schwachkopf m

**morose,** me-**rohss,** adj vergrämt

**morphine, mohr**-fien, n Morphium nt

**morsel, mohr**-s'l, n Stückchen nt

**mortal, mohr**-t'l, adj sterblich; (fatal) tödlich; Sterbliche(r) m & f

**mortality,** mohr-**täll**-i-ti, n Sterblichkeit f

**mortar, mohr**-ter, n (cement) Mörtel m; (gun) Mörser m

**mortgage, mohr**-gidsch, n Hypothek f; v, mit einer Hypothek belasten; **–e,** Hypothekar m

**mortified, mohr**-ti-feid, adj beschämt

**mortuary, mohr**-tju-e-ri, n Leichenhaus nt

**mosaic,** me-**seh**-ick, n Mosaik nt

**Moscow, moss**-koh, n Moskau nt

**Moslem, mas**-lem, adj moslemisch; n Moslem m

**mosque,** mosk, n Moschee f

**mosquito,** moss-**kie**-toh, n Mücke f

**moss,** moss, n Moos nt

**most,** mohst, adj meiste(r/s); (superlative) -ste(r/s); adv am meisten; (extremely) höchst, sehr; pron das meiste, die meisten; **–ly,** adv meistens, größtenteils

**moth,** moth, n Nachtfalter m; (in clothes) Motte f; **–ball,** n Mottenkugel f

**mother, madh**-er, n Mutter f; v bemuttern; **–hood,** n Mutterschaft f; **–in-law,** n Schwiegermutter f; **–ly,** adj mütterlich; **– of pearl,** n Perlmutt m; **– tongue,** n Muttersprache f

**motif,** moh-**tief**, n Motiv nt

**motion,** moh-**sch'n,** n Bewegung f; (proposal) Antrag m; **–less,** adj bewegungslos; **put/set in –,** v in Gang bringen

**motivation,** moh-tiw-eh-sch'n, n Motivierung f

**motive,** moh-tiw, n Motiv nt, Beweggrund m

**motor,** moh-ter, adj Motor-; n Motor m; (car) Auto nt; **–bike,** n Motorrad nt; **–car,** Auto nt; **–cycle,** n Motorrad nt; **–ing,** n Autofahren nt; **–ist,** n Autofahrer m; **–way,** n Autobahn f

**mottled, mott**-l'd, adj gesprenkelt

**motto, mott**-oh, n Motto nt, Wahlspruch m

**mould,** mohld, n (pattern) Form f; (mildew) Schimmel m; v formen; **–er,** v verschimmeln; **–y,** adj schimmlig

**moult,** mohlt, v (sich) mausern

**mound,** maund, n Erdhügel m

**mount,** maunt, n (horse) Pferd nt; (for picture) Montierung f; (for jewel) Fassung f; v (horse) besteigen; (jewel) fassen; (organize) organisieren; **– (up),** (increase) sich häufen

**mountain, maun**-tinn, n Berg m; **– bike,** n Mountainbike nt; **–eer,** n Bergsteiger m; **–ous,** adj bergig; **– range,** n Bergkette f; **–side,** n Berghang m

**mourn,** mohrn, v (be)trauern; **–er,** n Trauernde(r) m & f; **–ful,** adj traurig; **–ing,** n Trauer f; (clothes) Trauerkleidung f

**mouse,** mauss, n (animal, comp) Maus f; **–trap,** n Mausefalle f

**mousse,** muhss, n (food) Mousse f; (for hair) Haarschaum m, Schaumfestiger m

**moustache,** mess-**tahsch**, n Schnurrbart m

**mousy, mau**-ssi, adj (colour) mattbraun; (shy) scheu

**mouth,** mauth, n Mund m; (of animal) Maul nt; (of river) Mündung f; **–ful,** n Mundvoll m; **–piece,** n Mundstück nt; fig Sprachrohr nt; **-- watering,** adj lecker

**movable,** muh-we-b'l, adj beweglich

**move,** muhw, n (step) Schritt m; (in game) Zug m; (of house) Umzug m; v (sich) bewegen; (house) umziehen; (object) bewegen, verstellen; (affect) rühren; **– in,** v (to house) einziehen; **–ment,** n Bewegung f; (in clock) Uhrwerk nt; **– on,** v weitergehen; **– out,** v (of house) ausziehen; **get a – on,** v sich beeilen

**movie, muh**-wie, n fam Film m; **go to the –s,** v ins Kino gehen

**moving, muh**-wing, adj (in motion) beweglich; (affecting) rührend

**mow,** moh, v mähen; **– down,** v niedermähen; **(lawn) –er,** n Rasenmäher m

**Mr,** miss-ter, n Herr m

**Mrs,** miss-is, n Frau f

**Ms,** mes, n Frau f

**much,** matsch, adj & pron viel; adv viel, sehr; **as – (as),** soviel; **how –?** wieviel?; **too –,** zuviel

**muck,** mack, n Schmutz m; **– about,** v fam herumalbern; **–y,** adj dreckig

**mud,** madd, n Schlamm m

**muddle, madd**-'l, n Wirrwarr m; **– (up),** v verwirren; **– through,** v fam sich durchwursteln

**muddy, madd**-i, adj schlammig, schmutzig

**muffle, maff**-'l, v (wrap) einhüllen; (sound) dämpfen

**mug,** magg, n (beaker)
Becher m; (fam face)
Fratze f; (fam idiot) Depp
m; v überfallen; **–ging,** n
Überfall m; **–gy,** adj
schwül

**mule,** mjuhl, n Maulesel m

**mull over,** mall oh-wer, v
nachdenken über

**multi-,** mall-ti, pref, Multi-;
**–coloured,** adj bunt,
mehrfarbig

**multiple, mall-**ti-p'l,
adj mehrfach; **– sclerosis,** n
multiple Sklerose f

**multiplication,** mall-ti-pli-**keh-**sch'n, n
Multiplikation f

**multiply, mall-**ti-plei, v
(increase) sich
vermehren; **– (by),**
(arithmetic)
multiplizieren (mit)

**multi-purpose, mall-**ti-pör-pess, adj Mehrzweck-

**multi-storey,** mall-ti-**stohr-**ri, adj mehrstöckig; **– car park,** n Parkhaus nt

**multitude, mall-**ti-tjuhd, n
Menge f

**mum,** mamm, n Mutti f;
**keep – (about),** v den
Mund halten (über)

**mumble, mamm-**b'l, v
murmeln

**mummy, mamm-**i, n
(mother) Mutti f; (corpse)
Mumie f

**mumps,** mamps, n Mumps m

**munch,** mantsch, v kauen

**mundane, mann-**dehn, adj

banal

**municipal,** mju-**niss-**i-p'l,
adj städtisch, Gemeinde-

**mural, muhr-**rel, n
Wandgemälde nt

**murder, mör-**der, n Mord m;
v ermorden; **–er,** n Mörder
m; **–ess,** n Mörderin f;
**–ous,** adj mörderisch

**murky, mör-**ki, adj finster,
trüb

**murmur, mör-**mer, n
Gemurmel nt; v murmeln

**muscle, mass-**'l, n Muskel m

**muscular, mass-**kju-ler, adj
(of the muscle) Muskel-;
(strong) muskulös

**muse,** mjuhs, n Muse f; v
sinnen

**museum,** mjuh-**sie-**em, n
Museum nt

**mushroom, mash-**ruhm, n
Pilz m, Champignon m; v
wie Pilze aus dem Boden
schießen

**music, mjuh-**sick, n Musik f;
(score) Noten pl; **–al,** adj
musikalisch; **–al
instrument,** n
Musikinstrument nt

**musician,** mjuh-**sisch-**en, n
Musiker m

**musk,** mask, n Moschus m

**Muslim, mas-**limm, adj
moslemisch; n Moslem m

**muslin, mas-**linn, n
Musselin m

**mussel, mass-**'l, n Muschel f

**must,** mast, v müssen; **– not,**
nicht dürfen

**mustard, mass-**terd, n

Senf m

**muster, mass-**ter, v (sich)
zusammenrufen; fig
aufbringen

**musty, mass-**ti, adj muffig,
schimmelig

**mute,** mjuht, adj stumm; n
Stumme(r) m & f

**mutilate, mjuh-**ti-leht, v
verstümmeln

**mutiny, mjuh-**ti-ni, n
Meuterei f

**mutter, matt-**er, v murmeln,
murren

**mutton, matt-**'n, n
Hammelfleisch nt

**mutual(ly), mjuh-**tju-el(-i),
adj & adv gegenseitig

**muzzle, mas-**'l, n (for
animal) Maulkorb m;
(nose) Schnauze f; (of
gun) Mündung f; v
(animal) einen Maulkorb
anlegen; (silence) knebeln

**my,** mei, adj mein

**myriad,** mi-ri-ädd, n
Unzahl f

**myself,** mei-**sself,** pron (refl)
mich (selbst), mir (selbst);
(emphatic) selbst

**mysterious,** miss-**tier-**ri-ess,
adj geheimnisvoll

**mystery, miss-**te-ri, n
(secret) Geheimnis f;
(puzzle) Rätsel nt

**mystify, miss-**ti-fei, v
verwirren

**myth,** mith, n Mythos m; fig
Legende f; **–ical,** adj
mythisch; fig erfunden;
**–ology,** n Mythologie f

**n/a,** *abbr* **not applicable,** nicht zutreffend

**nab,** näbb, *v* (sich) schnappen

**nag,** nägg, *n* (horse) Gaul *m*; (person) Nörgler *m*; *v* nörgeln

**nail,** nehl, *n* Nagel *m*; *v* nageln; **–brush,** *n* Nagelbürste *f*; **– down,** *v* festnageln; **–file,** *n* Nagelfeile *f*; **– polish, – varnish,** *n* Nagellack *m*

**naïve,** nei-iew, *adj* naiv

**naked,** neh-kidd, *adj* nackt

**name,** nehm, *n* Name *nt*; (reputation) Ruf *m*; *v* nennen; (appoint) ernennen; **–less,** *adj* namenlos; **–ly,** *adv* nämlich; **–sake,** *n* Namensvetter *m*

**nanny,** nänn-i, *n* Kindermädchen *nt*; (grandmother) Oma *f*

**nap,** näpp, *n* Schläfchen *nt*; (on cloth) Noppe *f*

**nape,** nehp, *n* Nacken *m*, Genick *nt*

**napkin,** näpp-kinn, *n* Serviette *f*

**Naples,** neh-p'ls, *n* Neapel *nt*

**nappy,** näpp-i, *n* Windel *f*; **– rash,** *n* Windelausschlag *m*

**narcissus,** nar-ssiss-ess, *n* Narzisse *f*

**narcotic,** nar-kott-ick, *n* Betäubungsmittel *nt*

**narrate,** ne-reht, *v* erzählen

**narrative,** nä-re-tiw, *n* Erzählung *f*

**narrator,** ne-reh-ter, *n* Erzähler *m*

**narrow,** nä-roh, *adj* schmal, eng; *v* sich verengen; **– down (to),** *v* einengen

(auf); **–ly,** *adv* knapp; **-- minded,** *adj* engstirnig; **have a – escape,** *v* mit knapper Not entkommen

**nasal,** neh-sel, *adj* nasal, Nasen-

**nasty,** nahss-ti, *adj* eklig

**nation,** neh-sch'n, *n* Nation *f*

**national,** näsch-en-el, *adj* national, National-; *n* Staatsangehörige(r) *m & f*; **–ism,** *n* Nationalismus *m*; **–ist(ic),** *adj* nationalistisch; **–ize,** *n* verstaatlichen

**nationality,** näsch-en-äll-i-ti, *n* Staatsangehörigkeit *f*

**native,** neh-tiw, *adj* (country etc.) Heimat-; (plant etc.) einheimisch; (person) gebürtig; (inborn) angeboren; *n* Einheimische(r) *m & f*; **– language, – tongue,** *n* Muttersprache *f*

**natural,** nätt-sche-rel, *adj* natürlich, Natur-; (inborn) angeboren; **–ist,** *n* Naturforscher *m*; **–ized,** *adj* eingebürgert; **–ly,** *adv* natürlich

**nature,** neh-tscher, *n* Natur *f*

**naught,** no'at, *n* Null *f*; **come to –,** *v* zunichte werden

**naughty,** no'a-ti, *adj* unartig, ungehörig

**nausea,** no'a-si-e, *n* (sickness) Übelkeit *f*;

(disgust) Ekel f; **–ting,** adj
widerlich

**nautical, no'a-ti-k'l,** adj
nautisch, See-

**naval, neh-wel,** Marine-; **–
officer,** n Marineoffizier m

**nave, nehw,** n
Kirchenschiff nt

**navel, neh-wel,** n Nabel m

**navigate, näw-i-geht,** v (in
ship) befahren,
navigieren; (in car) lotsen

**navigation, näw-i-geh-sch'n,**
n Navigation f

**navigator, näw-i-geh-ter,** n
(in ship) Seefahrer m; (in
car) Lotse m

**navvy, näw-i,** n Bau-
/Straßenarbeiter m

**navy, näw-i,** n Marine f; **–
(blue),** adj marineblau

**Nazi, nah-zi,** n Nazi m

**near, nier,** adj nahe; adv &
prep in der Nähe; v sich
nähern; **–by,** adj nahe; adv
in der Nähe; **–ly,** adv
beinahe, fast; **–side,** n
Beifahrerseite f; **–sighted,**
adj kurzsichtig

**neat, niet,** adj (tidy)
ordentlich; (skilful)
elegant; (undiluted) pur

**necessarily, ness-e-sse-ri-li,**
adv notwendigerweise

**necessary, ness-e-sse-ri,** adj
nötig, notwendig

**necessitate, ni-ssess-i-teht,**
v erfordern

**necessity, ni-ssess-i-ti,** n
Notwendigkeit f; (need)
Not f

**neck, neck,** n Hals m; v
fam knutschen; **– and –,**
Kopf an Kopf; **–lace,** n
Halskette f; **–tie,**
Krawatte f

**née, neh,** adj geborene

**need, nied,** v brauchen; n
(requirement) Bedürfnis
nt; (necessity)
Notwendigkeit f;
(poverty) Not f; v
brauchen; **– to,** müssen,
brauchen zu; **be in – of,** v
brauchen

**needle, nie-d'l,** n Nadel f; v
fam ärgern

**needless, nied-liss,** adj
unnötig; **– to say,**
selbstverständlich

**needy, nie-di,** adj dürftig,
arm

**negation, ni-geh-sch'n,** n
Verneinung f

**negative, negg-e-tiw,** adj
verneinend; n Negativ nt

**neglect, ni-gleckt,** n
Vernachlässigung f; v
vernachlässigen; **–ful,** adj
nachlässig

**negligence, negg-li-
dschenss,** n Nachlässigkeit
f

**negligible, negg-li-dschib-'l,**
adj unerheblich

**negotiate, ni-goh-schi-eht,** v
(discuss) verhandeln; (get
past) bewältigen; (corner)
nehmen; comm einlösen

**negotiation, ni-goh-schi-eh-
sch'n,** n (discussion)
Verhandlung f; (getting

past) Bewältigung f

**negotiator,** n ni-goh-schi-
eh-ter, n Unterhändler m

**negro, nie-groh,** n Neger m

**neigh, neh,** v wiehern

**neighbour, neh-ber,** n
Nachbar m; **–hood,** n
Nachbarschaft f; **–ing,** adj
benachbart; **–ly,** adj
nachbarlich

**neither, nei-dher,** adj & pron
keine(r/s) (von beiden);
adv & conj auch nicht; **–
… nor,** weder… noch

**neon, nie-onn,** n Neon nt

**nephew, neff-yuh,** n Neffe
m

**nerve, nörw,** n Nerv m;
(courage) Mut m; (cheek)
Frechheit f; **––racking,** adj
nervenaufreibend

**nervous, nör-wess,** adj (of
the nerves) Nerven-;
(timid) nervös, befangen;
**– breakdown,** n
Nervenzusammenbruch m

**nest, nest,** n Nest nt; v nisten

**nestle (up to), ness-'l** (app
tu), v sich anschmiegen

**net, nett,** adj netto, Netto-;
n Netz nt; v fangen; **–ball,**
n Netzball m; **– curtain,** n
Store m, Tüllgardine f

**Netherlands, nedh-er-lends,**
npl Niederlande pl

**nett, nett,** adj netto, Netto-

**nettle, nett-'l,** n Nessel f

**network, nett-u'erk,** n
Netz(werk) m

**neuralgia, njuhr-räll-dschi-
e,** n Nervenschmerz m

**neurotic,** njuhr-**rott**-ick, *adj* neurotisch; *n* Neurotiker *m*

**neuter, njuh**-ter, *adj gram* sächlich; *v* kastrieren

**neutral, njuh**-trel, *adj* neutral; *n* (person) Neutrale(r) *m & f*; (gear) Leerlauf *m*; **–ize,** *v* ausgleichen

**never, new-**er, *adv* nie(mals); **––ending,** *adj* endlos; **–theless,** *adv* trotzdem

**new,** njuh, *adj* neu; **––born,** *adj* neugeboren; **––fangled,** *adj pej* neumodisch; **–ly,** *adv* frisch; **–lyweds,** *npl* Frischvermählte *pl*

**news,** njuhs, *n* Nachrichten *pl*; (piece of) Neuigkeit *f*; **–agent,** *n* Zeitungshändler *m*; **– flash,** *n* Kurzmeldung *f*; **–letter,** *n* Rundschreiben *nt*; **–paper,** *n* Zeitung *f*; **–reader,** *n* Nachrichtensprecher *m*

**new year, njuh jier,** *n* neues Jahr *nt*; **N– Y–'s Day,** *n* Neujahr *nt*, Neujahrstag *m*; **N– Y–'s Eve,** *n* Silvester *m*

**New Zealand, njuh sie**-lend, *n* Neuseeland *nt*; **–er,** *n* Neuseeländer *m*

**next,** next, *adj* nächste(r/s); (following) folgend; *adv* dann; **–door,** *adj* von nebenan; *adv* nebenan; **– of kin,** *n* nächste(r) Verwandte(r) *m & f*; **–**

time, das nächste Mal; **– to,** *prep* neben

**nib,** nibb, *n* Feder *f*

**nibble, nibb**-'l, *v* nagen, annagen

**nice,** neiss, *adj* (pleasant) nett, sympathisch; (attractive) hübsch; (thing, idea) schön

**nick,** nick, *n* Kerbe *f*, Einschnitt *m*; *v fam* klauen; **in the – of time,** gerade rechtzeitig

**nickel, nick**-'l, *n* (metal) Nickel *m*; (5 cents) Nickel *m*

**nickname, nick**-nehm, *n* Spitzname *m*

**nicotine, nick**-*e*-tien, *n* Nikotin *nt*

**niece,** niess, *n* Nichte *f*

**niggle, nigg**-'l, *v* sich mit Einzelheiten aufhalten; (grumble about) herumnörgeln

**night,** neit, *n* Nacht *f*; **–cap,** *n* Schlummertrunk *m*; **–club,** *n* Nachtklub *m*; **–dress,** *n* Nachthemd *nt*; **–fall,** *n* Einbruch *m* der Nacht; **–ingale,** *n* Nachtigall *f*; **–life,** *n* Nachtleben *nt*; **–ly,** *adv* jede Nacht, jeden Abend; **–mare,** *n* Alptraum *m*; **–time,** *n* Nacht *f*; **at –,** *adv* nachts, abends

**nil,** nill, *n* Null *f*

**Nile,** neil, *n* Nil *m*

**nimble, nimm**-b'l, *adj* flink, gewandt

**nine,** nein, *num* neun; **–teen,** *num* neunzehn; **–ty,** *num* neunzig

**ninth,** neinth, *adj* neunte(r/s); *n* Neuntel *nt*

**nip,** nipp, *n* Biß *m*; *v* zwicken; **– out,** *v fam* kurz weggehen

**nipple, nipp**-'l, *n* Zitze *f*; Brustwarze *f*

**nippy, nipp**-i, *adj* (*fam* fast) flink; (cold) frisch

**nitrogen, nei**-tre-dschen, *n* Stickstoff *m*

**no,** noh, *adj* kein; *adv* nein; *n* Nein *nt*; **– parking,** Parken verboten

**nobility,** ne-**bill**-i-ti, *n* Adel *m*

**noble, noh**-b'l, *adj* (character etc.) edel; (rank) adlig

**nobody, noh**-be-di, *pron* niemand, keiner; *n* Null *f*

**nocturnal,** nock-**tör**-nel, *adj* Nacht-

**nod,** nodd, *n* Nicken *nt*; *v* nicken

**noise,** neus, *n* (loud) Lärm *m*; (sound) Geräusch *nt*; **–less(ly),** *adj & adv* geräuschlos

**noisy, neu**-si, *adj* laut

**nominal, nomm**-i-nel, *adj* nominell

**nominate, nomm**-i-neht, *v* (propose) nominieren; (appoint) ernennen

**nominee, nomm**-i-**nie,** *n* Kandidat *m*

**none (of),** nann (ev), *pron*

keine(r/s) (von)

**nonentity,** nonn-**enn**-ti-ti, n
Null f

**non-fiction,** nonn-**fick**-sch'n, n Sachbuch nt,
Sachbücher pl

**nonetheless,** nann-dhe-**less**,
adv trotzdem

**nonplussed,** nonn-**plasst**,
adj verwirrt

**nonsense,** nonn-ssenss, n
Unsinn m

**non-smoker,** nonn-**ssmoh**-ker, n Nichtraucher m

**non-stop, nonn**-stopp, adj
nonstop, Nonstop-;
(train) durchgehend

**non-stick, nonn**-stick, adj
mit Antihaftbeschichtung

**noodles, nuh**-d'ls, npl
Nudeln pl

**nook,** nuck, n Winkel m

**noon,** nuhn, n Mittag m

**no one,** noh u'an, pron
niemand, keiner

**noose,** nuhss, n Schlinge f

**nor,** nohr, adv & conj auch
nicht; **neither... –,**
weder... noch

**norm,** norm, n Norm f

**normal, nohr**-mel, adj
normal

**north,** north, adj nördlich,
Nord-; adv nördlich, nach
Norden; n Norden m; **–-east,** n Nordosten m;
**–erly,** adj nördlich; **–ern,**
adj nördlich, Nord-;
**N–ern Ireland,** n
Nordirland nt; **N– Pole,** n
Nordpol m; **N– Sea,** n

Nordsee f; **–-west,** n
Nordwesten m

**Norway, nohr**-u'ei, n
Norwegen nt

**Norwegian,** nor-**u'ie**-dschen, adj norwegisch; n
(person) Norweger m;
(language) Norwegisch nt

**nose,** nohs, n Nase f; **–
(about/around),** v
herumschnüffeln; **–bleed,**
n Nasenbluten nt

**nostril, noss**-trill, n
Nasenloch nt

**nosy, noh**-si, adj neugierig

**not,** nott, adv nicht; **– any,**
kein; **– only,** nicht nur; **–
yet,** noch nicht

**notable, noh**-te-b'l, adj
bemerkenswert

**notch,** notsch, n Kerbe f; v
kerben, einschneiden

**note,** noht, n mus Note f;
(letter) Briefchen nt;
(comment) Anmerkung f;
v (notice) bemerken; (in
writing) notieren; **–book,**
n Notizbuch nt; **–d,** adj
berühmt, bekannt; **–pad,** n
Notizblock m; **–paper,** n
Briefpapier nt; **take – of,** v
achten auf; **take –s,** v
Notizen machen

**nothing, nath**-ing, adv &
pron nichts; **for –,**
umsonst

**notice, noh**-tiss, n (to quit)
Kündigung f; (public)
Bekanntmachung; v
bemerken; **at short
notice,** adv kurzfristig; be

**given –,** gekündigt
werden; **give (one's) –,** v
kündigen; **take – of,** v
beachten; **–able, noh**-tiss-e-b'l, adj merklich; **–
board,** n Anschlagtafel f,
Schwarzes Brett nt

**notify, noh**-ti-fei, v
anzeigen, benachrichtigen

**notion, noh**-sch'n, n Idee f;
Begriff m

**notorious,** noh-**tohr**-ri-ess,
adj berüchtigt

**notwithstanding,** not-uidh-s'tänn-ding, adv trotzdem;
prep ungeachtet, trotz

**nought,** no'at, n Null f

**noun,** naun, n gram
Hauptwort nt

**nourish, na**-risch, v nähren,
ernähren; **–ing,** adj
nahrhaft; **–ment,** n
Nahrung f

**novel, now**-el, adj neuartig;
n Roman m; **–ist,** n
Romanautor m; **–ty,** n
Neuheit f

**November,** noh-**wemm**-ber,
n November m

**novice, now**-iss, n Neuling
m; relig Novize m & f

**now,** nau, adv nun, jetzt;
**– and again, – and then,** ab
und zu; **by –,** inzwischen;
**just –,** gerade; **right –,**
sofort, jetzt

**nowadays,** nau-e-dehs, adv
heutzutage

**nowhere,** noh-u'ähr, adv
nirgends, nirgendwo

**noxious,** nok-schess, adj

schädlich, giftig

**nozzle, nos-'l,** *n*
Mundstück *nt*

**nuclear, njuh-klier,** *adj*
Atom-, Kern-

**nucleus, njuh-kli-ess,** *n*
Kern *m*

**nude, njuhd,** *adj* nackt; **in the –,** nackt

**nudge, nadsch,** *n* Stoß *m*; *v*
anstoßen

**nudist, njuh-dist,** *n* Nudist *m*

**nuisance, njuh-ssenss,** *n*
Lästigkeit *f*; Unfug *m*

**null, nall,** *adj* null, nichtig; **– and void,** null und nichtig; **–ify,** *v* für null und nichtig erklären; (proof) entkräften

**numb, namm,** *adj* starr; (sensation) gefühllos

**number, namm-ber,** *n*
Nummer *f*; (figure) Zahl *f*; (quantity) Anzahl *f*; *v* numerieren; (count) zählen; **–less,** *adj* zahllos, unzählig; **– plate,** *n* Nummernschild *nt*; **a – of,** mehrere

**numerate, njuh-me-ret,** *adj*
rechenkundig

**numerical, njuh-me-ri-k'l,** *adj* numerisch

**numerous, njuh-me-ress,** *adj* zahlreich

**nun, nann,** *n* Nonne *f*; **–nery,** Nonnenkloster *nt*

**nurse, nörss,** *n*
Krankenpfleger *m*; (children's)

Kindermädchen *nt*; *v*
pflegen; (suckle) säugen; *fig* hegen

**nursery, nör-sse-ri,** *n*
(children's) Kinderstube *f*; (for plants) Gärtnerei *f*; **– rhyme,** Kinderlied *nt*; **– school,** *n* Kindergarten *m*; **– slope,** *n fam* Idiotenhügel *m*

**nursing, nör-ssing,** *n*
Krankenpflege *f*; **– home,** *n* Pflegeheim *nt*

**nut, natt,** *n* Nuß *f*; (for screw) Mutter *f*; **–(case),** *n fam* Verrückte(r) *m & f*

**nutcrackers, natt-kräck-ers,** *npl* Nußknacker *m*

**nutmeg, natt-megg,** *n*
Muskatnuß *f*

**nutrient, njuh-tri-ent,** *n*
Nährstoff *m*

**nutrition, njuh-trisch-en,** *n*
Nahrung *f*

**nutritious, njuh-trisch-ess,** *adj* nahrhaft

**nutshell, natt-schell,** *n*
Nußschale *f*; **in a –,** kurz gesagt

**nylon, nei-lonn,** *adj* Nylon-; *n* Nylon *nt*

**oak,** ohk, *a* Eichen-; *n* Eiche *f*

**oar,** or, *n* Ruder *nt*; **–sman,** *n* Ruderer *m*

**oasis,** oh-**eh**-ssiss, *n* Oase *f*

**oath,** ohth, *n* (declaration) Eid *m*; (curse) Fluch *m*

**oatmeal,** **oht**-miel, *n* Hafermehl *nt*

**oats,** ohts, *npl* Hafer *m*

**obedience,** *e*-**bie**-di-enss, *n* Gehorsam *m*

**obedient,** *e*-**bie**-di-ent, *adj* gehorsam

**obese,** oh-**biess,** *adj* fett(leibig)

**obesity,** oh-**biess**-i-ti, *n* Fettheit *f*, Fettleibigkeit *f*

**obey,** *e*-**beh,** *v* gehorchen, folgen

**obituary,** *e*-**bitt**-ju-*e*-ri, *n* Nachruf *m*; **– notice,** *n* Todesanzeige *f*

**object,** **obb**-dschikt, *n* (thing) Gegenstand *m*; (purpose) Ziel *nt*; *gram* Objekt *nt*; **money is no –,** Geld spielt keine Rolle

**object,** eb-**dschekt,** *v* (be opposed) dagegen sein; **– (to),** (protest) protestieren, Einspruch erheben (gegen); **–ion,** *n* Einwand *m*; **–ionable,** *adj* unangenehm; (speech, behaviour) anstößig; **–ive,** *adj* objektiv; *n* Ziel *nt*

**obligation,** obb-li-**geh**-sch'n, *n* Verpflichtung *f*; **without –,** unverbindlich

**obligatory,** eb-**ligg**-*e*-te-ri, *adj* verbindlich

**oblige,** eb-**leidsch,** *v* (please) einen Gefallen tun; (compel) zwingen; **–d,** *adj* verbunden, dankbar

**obliging,** eb-**leidsch**-ing, *adj* gefällig

**oblique,** eb-**liek,** *adj* (angle, look) schief; (hint) indirekt

**obliterate,** eb-**litt**-*e*-reht, *v* auslöschen

**oblivion,** eb-**liw**-i-en, *n* Vergessenheit *f*

**oblivious (of/to),** eb-**liw**-i-ess (ew/tu), *adj* nicht bewußt

**oblong,** **obb**-long, *adj* länglich; *n* Rechteck *nt*

**obnoxious,** eb-**nock**-schess, *adj* widerlich

**obscene,** eb-**ssien,** *adj* obszön, widerlich

**obscure,** eb-**skjuhr,** *adj* (unclear, indistinct) unklar; (unknown) unbekannt; *v* (hide) verdecken; (confuse) unverständlich machen

**observance,** eb-**sör**-wenss, *n* Beachtung *f*; *relig* Einhalten *nt*

**observant,** eb-**sör**-went, *adj* aufmerksam

**observation,** obb-ser-**weh**-sch'n, *n* Beobachtung *f*; (remark) Bemerkung *f*

**observatory,** eb-**sör**-we-te-ri, *n* Observatorium *f*, Sternwarte *f*

**observe,** eb-**sörw,** *v* (watch) beobachten; (notice, remark) bemerken; (obey) einhalten

**obsess,** eb-**ssess,** **–ed (by/with),** *adj* besessen (von); **be –ed (by/with),** *v* besessen sein von; **–ion,** *n*

Besessenheit f; –ive, adj
zwanghaft

**obsolete**, obb-**sse**-liet, adj
veraltet

**obstacle**, obb-**ste**-k'l, n
Hindernis nt

**obstinate**, obb-**sti**-net, adj
stur

**obstruct**, eb-**strakt**, v
(hinder) hindern; (block)
sperren; (tube) verstopfen;
–**ion**, n Hindernis nt,
Sperre f; med Verstopfung
f, Obstruktion f

**obtain**, eb-**tehn**, v erhalten

**obtrusive**, eb-**truh**-ssiw, adj
aufdringlich

**obtuse**, eb-**tjuss**, adj stumpf,
dumm

**obviate**, obb-wi-eht, – **the
need of sth**, v etw unnötig
machen

**obvious**, obb-wi-ess, adj klar,
offenbar; –**ly**, adv
offensichtlich

**occasion**, e-**keh**-sch'n, n
Gelegenheit f; (event,
cause) Anlaß m; v
veranlassen; –**al(ly)**, adj &
adv gelegentlich

**occult**, e-**kalt**, adj
verborgen, geheim; n das
Okkulte nt

**occupation**, ock-ju-**peh**-
sch'n, n Beschäftigung f;
(job) Beruf m; mil
Besetzung f

**occupied**, ock-ju-peid, adj
(person) beschäftigt;
(seat, room) belegt

**occupier**, ock-ju-pei-er, n
(of post) Inhaber m; (of
property) Bewohner m

**occupy**, ock-ju-pei, v
(property) bewohnen;
(space, location)
einnehmen; (post)
innehaben; mil besetzen; –
**oneself**, v sich
beschäftigen

**occur**, e-**kör**, v vorkommen;
– **to sb**, jdm einfallen

**occurrence**, e-**ka**-renss, n
Vorfall m

**ocean**, oh-sch'n, n Ozean m,
Meer nt, See f

**o'clock**, e-**klock**, adv **it is
six** –, es ist sechs Uhr

**octagonal**, ock-**tägg**-e-n'l, adj
achtseitig, achteckig

**octave**, ock-tiw, n Oktave f

**October**, ock-**toh**-ber, n
Oktober m

**octopus**, ock-te-puss, n
Tintenfisch m

**odd**, odd, adj (number)
ungerade; (single) einzeln;
(strange) seltsam; –**ity**, n
(object) Kuriosität f;
(person) Sonderling m; –
**job**, n Gelegenheitsarbeit
f; –**ly**, adv
seltsam(erweise); **be the** –
**one out**, (person)
überzählig sein; (thing)
nicht passen

**odds**, odds, npl (betting)
Odds pl; (chances)
Aussichten npl; – **and
ends**, pl allerlei Sachen

**odious**, oh-di-ess, adj

gehässig, abscheulich

**odour**, oh-der, n Geruch m;
(fragrant) Wohlgeruch m

**of**, ow, prep (belonging to)
von; (made of) aus; **a cup
– coffee**, eine Tasse
Kaffee; **a litre – milk**, ein
Liter Milch

**off**, off, adj (light etc.) aus;
(food) schlecht;
(cancelled) abgesagt; adv
(clothes) aus; (distant)
entfernt; prep ab, von; –
**and on**, ab und zu; **go** –,
(dislike) nicht mehr
mögen; (leave)
(weg)gehen; **day** –, freier
Tag m; **well** –, gut gestellt

**offal**, off-'l, n Innereien pl

**offbeat**, off-biet, adj
unkonventionell

**offchance**, off-tschahnss, n
**on the** –, in der vagen
Hoffnung

**offence**, e-**fenss**, n (insult)
Beleidigung f; (crime)
Verstoß m; **take** –, v
beleidigt sein

**offend**, e-fend, v (insult)
beleidigen; (commit
crime) ein Verbrechen
begehen; –**er**, n Täter m

**offensive**, e-**fenn**-ssiw, adj
(insulting) beleidigend;
(unpleasant) widerlich;
(weapon) Angriffs-; n
Angriff m

**offer**, off-er, v anbieten; n
Angebot nt; –**ing**, Gabe f;
(sacrifice) Opfer nt

**offhand**, off-händ, adj & adv

spontan

**office**, off-iss, n (place) Büro nt; (post) Amt nt; **– hours**, npl Dienstzeit f; **–r**, n Beamte(r) m, Beamtin f; mil Offizier m

**official**, e-fisch-'l, adj amtlich, offiziell; n Beamte(r) m, Beamtin f;

**officious**, e-fisch-ess, adj übereifrig

**off-licence**, off-lei-ssenss, n Wein- und Spirituosenhandlung f

**off-peak**, off-piek, adj außerhalb der Stoßzeiten

**off-putting**, off-putt-ing, adj abstoßend

**off-season**, off-ssie-sen, adj außerhalb der Hauptsaison

**offside**, off-sseid, adj im Abseits; adv abseits

**offside**, off-sseid, n (of car) Fahrerseite f

**offspring**, off-spring, n Nachwuchs m

**off-stage**, off-stehdsch, adv hinter den Kulissen

**off-the-cuff**, off-dhe-kaff, adj aus dem Stegreif

**often**, off-'n, adv oft, öfters

**ogle**, oh-g'l, v beäugeln

**oh**, oh, interj ach, oh

**oil**, eul, n Öl nt; v ölen, mech schmieren; **–fired**, adj Öl-; **–y**, adj ölig, ölhaltig

**ointment**, eunt-ment, n Salbe f

**OK**, oh keh, adj in Ordnung, OK; n

Zustimmung f; v genehmigen

**old**, ohld, adj alt; **– age**, n Alter nt; **–age pensioner**, n Rentner m; **–fashioned**, adj altmodisch

**olive**, oll-iw, adj Oliven-; (colour) olivgrün; n Olive f

**Olympic**, e-limm-pick, adj olympisch; **the – Games**, npl die olympischen Spiele pl

**omelet(te)**, omm-let, n Omelett f

**omen**, oh-men, n Omen nt, Vorbedeutung f

**ominous**, omm-i-ness, adj unheilvoll

**omission**, e-misch-'n, n (thing left out) Auslassung f; (neglect) Unterlassung f

**omit**, e-mitt, v (leave out) auslassen; (neglect) versäumen, unterlassen

**omnibus**, omm-ni-bess, n (bus) Autobus m; (compendium) Sammelausgabe f

**on**, onn, adj (light etc.) an; adv (clothes) an; (onward) weiter; prep (on top of) auf; (date, day, TV) an; (foot, horseback) zu; (train, bus) mit; **– holiday**, im Urlaub; **– Monday**, am Montag; **– Mondays**, montags; **– the left/right**, links/rechts; **– to**, prep (movement) auf;

**be –**, v (of event) stattfinden; (fam be acceptable) in Ordnung sein

**once**, u'anss, adv einmal; **all at –**, plötzlich; **at –**, sofort, sogleich; **– more**, noch einmal; **– upon a time**, es war einmal

**oncoming**, onn-kamm-ing, adj entgegenkommend; **– traffic**, n Gegenverkehr m

**one**, u'ann, num eins; (with noun) ein(e); (only) einzig; pron eine(r/s); (impersonal) man; **– day**, eines Tages; **– another**, einander, sich; **a good –**, ein(e) gute(r/s); **this –**, diese(r/s); **that –**, der/die/das

**onerous**, oh-ne-ress, adj lästig, beschwerlich

**oneself**, u'ann-sself, pron (refl) sich (selbst); (emphatic) selbst; **by –**, adv alleine

**one-sided**, u'ann-ssei-didd, adj einseitig

**one-way**, u'ann-u'ei, adj (street) Einbahn-; (ticket) einfach

**ongoing**, onn-goh-ing, adj andauernd; (current) aktuell

**onion**, ann-jen, n Zwiebel f

**online**, onn-lein, adj comp Online-

**only**, ohn-li, adj einzig; (child) Einzel-; adv & conj nur, bloß; **not – … but**

**also ...**, nicht nur ..., sondern auch ...

**onset**, onn-ssett, n Beginn m; med Ausbruch m

**onslaught**, onn-slo'at, n (heftige) Attacke f

**onto**, onn-tu, (= on to) prep auf

**onus**, oh-ness, n Last f

**onward(s)**, onn-u'erd(s), adv vorwärts, weiter; **from ... –**, von ... an

**ooze**, uhs, n Schlamm m; v (liquid) sickern; quellen

**opaque**, oh-pehk, adj undurchsichtig

**open**, oh-p'n, adj offen, auf; (to public) öffentlich; v öffnen, aufmachen; **–er**, n Öffner m; **–ing**, n Öffnung f; (hole) Loch nt; **– learning**, n Selbststudium nt mit Tutorenunterstützung; **--minded**, adj aufgeschlossen; ; **--plan**, adj offen ausgelegt; **--plan office**, n Großraumbüro nt

**opera**, opp-e-re, n Oper f; **-- glass**, Opernglas nt; **-- house**, Opernhaus nt

**operate**, opp-e-reht, v (of machine) funktionieren, laufen; ; (of business) aktiv sein; (activate) betätigen; **– (on)**, (affect) hinwirken (auf); med operieren

**operation**, opp-e-reh-sch'n, n med Operation f; (business) Betrieb m; mil

Einsatz m

**operator**, opp-e-reh-ter, n (of machine) (Maschinen)bediener m; (telephone) Telefonist m; Operator m

**opinion**, e-pinn-jen, n Meinung f; **– poll**, n Meinungsumfrage f

**opponent**, e-poh-nent, n Gegner m, Opponent m

**opportunity**, opp-er-tjuh-ni-ti, n Gelegenheit f

**oppose**, e-pohs, v gegenüberstellen; (object) sich wenden gegen; sich aussprechen gegen; **as –d to**, im Gegensatz zu

**opposing**, e-poh-sing, adj entgegengesetzt; (team) gegnerisch

**opposite**, opp-e-sitt, adj entgegengesetzt; adv gegenüber; prep gegenüber; n Gegenteil nt

**opposition**, opp-e-sisch-'n, n (competition) Gegner m; (objection) Einrede f; (contrast) Gegensatz m; parl Opposition(spartei) f

**oppress**, e-press, v unterdrücken; **–ion**, n Unterdrückung f; **–ive**, (climate) drückend; (regime) repressiv

**opt**, opt, v **– for**, sich entscheiden für; **– out**, austreten aus

**optical**, opp-ti-k'l, adj optisch

**optician**, opp-tisch-'n, n

Optiker m

**optimist**, opp-ti-mist, n Optimist m; **–ic**, adj optimistisch

**option**, opp-sch'n, n Wahl f; (subject) Wahlfach nt; **–al**, adj (subject) wahlfrei; (feature) auf Wunsch

**opulent**, op-juh-lent, adj reich

**or**, or, conj oder; (in negative) noch; **– else**, sonst

**oral**, or-rel, adj mündlich

**orange**, o-rindsch, adj (colour) orange; n Apfelsine f, Orange f

**orator**, o-re-ter, n Redner m

**orbit**, or-bit, n Umlaufbahn f; v umkreisen

**orchard**, or-tscherd, n Obstgarten m

**orchestra**, or-kiss-tre, n Orchester nt

**orchestral**, or-kess-trel, adj orchestral, Orchester-

**orchid**, or-kidd, n Orchidee f

**ordain**, or-dehn, v bestimmen; relig ordinieren

**ordeal**, or-diel, n Qual f

**order**, or-der, n comm Bestellung f, Auftrag m; (command) Befehl m; (sequence) Reihenfolge f; (tidiness, civil) Ordnung f; (relig, decoration) Orden m; v (arrange) ordnen; comm bestellen; (command) befehlen; **–ly**,

*adj* ordentlich; *n med*
Krankenpfleger *m*; **in – to,**
um zu

**ordinary,** or-di-ne-ri, *adj*
gewöhnlich

**ore,** or, *n* Erz *nt*

**organ,** or-gen, *n mus* Orgel *f*;
(*med, fig*) Organ *nt*

**organic,** or-gänn-ick, *adj* aus
biologischem Anbau,
organisch

**organization,** or-ge-nei-seh-
sch'n, *n* Organisation *f*

**organize,** or-ge-neis, *v*
organisieren; **–r,** *n*
Organisator *m*,
Veranstalter *m*

**orgasm,** or-gäsm, *n*
Orgasmus *m*

**orgy,** or-dschi, *n* Orgie *f*

**Orient,** or-ri-ent, *n*
Orient *m*

**oriental,** or-ri-enn-t'l, *adj*
orientalisch

**origin,** o-ridsch-inn, *n*
Ursprung *m*

**original,** *e*-**ri**-dschinn-'l, *adj*
(*earliest*) ursprünglich;
(*idea, person*) originell; *n*
Original *nt*

**originate,** *e*-**ridsch**-i-neht, *v*
(*arise*) entstehen; (*create*)
schaffen; (*invent*)
erfinden

**ornament,** or-ne-ment, *n*
(*decoration*) Schmuck *m*;
(*object*) Ziergegenstand *m*

**ornamental,** or-ne-menn-t'l,
*adj* verzierend, Zier-

**orphan,** or-fen, *n* Waise *f*;
**–age,** Waisenhaus *nt*

**orthodox,** or-*the*-docks, *adj*
orthodox; **–y,** *n*
Orthodoxie *f*; *fig*
Konvention *f*

**orthopaedic,** or-*the*-pie-
dick, *adj* orthopädisch; **–s,**
*n* Orthopädie *f*

**oscillate,** oss-i-leht, *v*
schwanken

**ostensible,** oss-tenn-ssib-'l,
*adj* Schein-

**ostentatious,** oss-ten-teh-
schess, *adj* prahlerisch

**ostrich,** oss-tritsch, *n*
Strauß *m*

**other,** *adh*-er, *adj & pron*
andere(r/s); **–s,** *pl* andere;
**– than,** außer; **somehow
or –,** irgendwie

**otherwise,** *adh*-er-u'eis, *adv*
(*or else*) sonst;
(*differently*) anders

**ought (to),** o'at (tu), *v*
sollte(st, n); **– to have ...,**
hätte ... sollen

**ounce,** aunss, *n* Unze *f*

**our,** au-er, *adj* unser; **–s,**
*pron* unsere(r/s)

**ourselves,** aur-sselws, *pron*
(*refl*) uns (selbst);
(*emphatic*) selbst; **by –,** *adv*
alleine

**out,** aut, *adv* (*absent*) nicht
da, nicht zu Hause;
(*outside*) draußen;
(*motion*) hinaus, heraus;
(*not lit*) aus; **– of,** hinaus,
aus, außerhalb; **– of order,**
außer Betrieb; **be – of
(money),** *v* kein (Geld)
mehr haben

**outback,** aut-bäck, *n*
Hinterland *nt*

**outboard,** aut-bord, *adj*
Außenbord-

**outbreak,** aut-brehk, *n*
Ausbruch *m*

**outburst,** aut-börst, *n*
Ausbruch *m*

**outcast,** aut-kahst, *n*
Verstoßene(r) *m & f*

**outcome,** aut-kamm, *n*
Ergebnis *nt*

**outcry,** aut-krei, *n*
Aufschrei *m*

**outdated,** aut-deh-tidd, *adj*
überholt, altmodisch

**outdo,** aut-duh, *v*
übertreffen

**outdoor,** aut-dor, *adj*
Außen-; (pool) Frei-;
(sport, activity) im Freien;
**–s,** *adv* im Freien

**outer,** au-ter, *adj* äußere(r/s);
**– space,** *n* Weltraum *m*

**outfit,** aut-fitt, *n* (clothes)
Kleidung *f*; (*fam* business)
Laden *m*; **–ter,** *n*
Herrenausstatter *m*

**outgoing,** aut-goh-ing, *adj*
(departing) (aus dem
Amt) scheidend;
(extrovert)
kontaktfreudig; **–s,** *npl*
Ausgaben *pl*

**outgrow,** aut-groh, *v*
entwachsen; (overcome)
überwinden

**outing,** au-ting, *n* Ausflug *m*

**outlast,** aut-lahst, *v*
überdauern

**outlaw,** aut-lor, *n*

Geächtete(r) m & f; v
ächten; (prohibit)
verbieten

**outlay, aut-**leh, n
Ausgaben npl

**outlet, aut-**lett, n Ablauf m;
(market) (Absatz)markt
m; fig Ventil nt

**outline, aut-**lein, n Umriß m

**outlive, aut-**liw, v überleben

**outlook, aut-**luck, n
Aussicht f

**outlying, aut-**lei-ing, adj
entfernt liegend

**outnumber, aut-numm-**ber,
v zahlenmäßig überlegen
sein

**out-of-date, aut-**ew-**deht,** adj
(outmoded) veraltet;
(expired) verfallen

**outpatient, aut-**peh-schent,
n ambulanter Patient m

**outpost, aut-**pohst, n
Vorposten m

**output, aut-**putt, n
Produktion f; comp
Ausgabe f

**outrage, aut-**rehdsch, n
(crime) Verbrechen);
(violation) Verstoß m

**outrage, aut-rehdsch,** v
empören; **–ous,** adj
(immoral) unverschämt;
(cruel) grausam

**outright, aut-**reit, adj
(complete) total;
(unashamed)
gereadeheraus; adv
(completely) ganz; (kill)
gleich; (deny) glatt

**outset, aut-**ssett, n

Anfang m

**outside, aut-**sseid, adj
Außen-; adv (nach)
draußen; prep außerhalb; n
Außenseite f; **at the –,**
höchstens

**outsize, aut-**sseis, adj
überdimensional;
(clothes) in Übergröße

**outskirts, aut-**skörts, npl
Randgebiete pl

**outspoken, aut-spoh-**k'n, adj
freimütig

**outstanding, aut-stänn-**
ding, adj (excellent)
hervorragend; (debts)
ausstehend; (work)
unerledigt

**outstrip, aut-stripp,** v
übertreffen

**outward, aut-**wed, adj
äußere(r/s); adv nach
außen; **–bound,** adj
(shipping) auslaufend;
(course) Abenteuer-; **–ly,**
adv äußerlich

**outwit, aut-u'itt,** v
überlisten

**oval, oh-**wel, adj oval; n
Oval nt

**ovation, e-weh-**sch'n, n
Ovation f, begeisterter
Beifall m

**oven, a**w-en, n (Back)ofen
m

**over, oh-**wer, adv (there)
drüben; (motion) hinüber,
herüber; (finished) vorbei;
(remaining) übrig; prep
über; **(all) – again,** wieder,
noch einmal; **all –,**

(everywhere) überall;
(finished) vorbei

**overall, oh-we-ro'al,** adj
(general) allgemein;
(total) gesamt, Gesamt-;
(majority) absolut

**overall, oh-we-ro'al,** adv
(generally) im großen und
ganzen; (in total)
insgesamt

**overalls, oh-**we-ro'als, npl
Overall m

**overawed, oh-we-ro'ad,** adj
eingeschüchtert

**overbalance, oh-wer-bäll-**
enss, v aus dem
Gleichgewicht kommen

**overbearing, oh-wer-behr-**
ring, adj arrogant

**overboard, oh-**wer-bord, adv
über Bord; **go –,** v es
übertreiben

**overcast, oh-wer-kahst,** adj
bewölkt

**overcharge, oh-wer-**
**tschardsch,** v zuviel
berechnen

**overcoat, oh-wer-koht,** n
Mantel m

**overcome, oh-wer-kamm,** v
überwinden

**overcrowded, oh-wer-krau-**
didd, adj überfüllt

**overdo, oh-wer-duh,** v
(exaggerate) übertreiben;
(overcook) verkochen

**overdose, oh-wer-dohss,** n
Überdosis f; v eine
Überdosis nehmen

**overdraft, oh-wer-drahft,** n
(Konto)überziehung f

**overdrawn**, oh-wer-**dro'an**, *adj* überzogen

**overdue**, oh-wer-**djuh**, *adj* (train) verspätet; (debt) überfällig

**overflow**, oh-wer-**floh**, *n* Überlaufrohr *nt*

**overflow**, oh-wer-**floh**, *v* überlaufen

**overgrown**, oh-wer-**grohn**, *adj* überwuchert

**overhaul**, oh-wer-**ho'al**, *v* überholen

**overhear**, oh-wer-**hier**, *v* (zufällig) hören

**overjoyed**, oh-wer-**dscheud**, *adj* überglücklich

**overland**, oh-wer-**länd**, *adj* Überland-

**overlap**, oh-wer-**läpp**, *v* (sich) überschneiden

**overleaf**, oh-wer-**lief**, *adv* umseitig

**overload**, oh-wer-**lohd**, *v* überladen

**overlook**, oh-wer-**luck**, *v* (miss) übersehen; (have view of) überblicken

**overnight**, oh-wer-**neit**, *adj* Nacht-; – **stay/stop**, *n* Übernachtung *f*

**overnight**, oh-wer-**neit**, *adv* über Nacht; **stay** –, *v* übernachten

**overpower**, oh-wer-**pau**-er, *v* überwältigen

**overrated**, oh-we-**reh**-tidd, *adj* überschätzt

**overriding**, oh-we-**rei**-ding, *adj* wichtigste(r/s)

**overrule**, oh-we-**ruhl**, *v* verwerfen

**overrun**, oh-we-**rann**, *v* länger dauern als vorgesehen; – **(with)**, *adj* überlaufen von

**overseas**, oh-wer-**ssies**, *adj* Übersee-; *adv* nach/in Übersee

**overshadow**, oh-wer-**schädd**-oh, *v* überschatten

**oversight**, oh-wer-**sseit**, *n* Versehen *nt*

**oversleep**, oh-wer-**ssliep**, *v* verschlafen

**overstatement**, oh-wer-**steht**-ment, *n* Übertreibung *f*

**overstep**, oh-wer-**stepp**, *v* überschreiten

**overt**, oh-**wört**, *adj* unverhohlen

**overtake**, oh-wer-**tehk**, *n* (catch up) einholen; (pass) überholen

**overthrow**, oh-wer-**throh**, *v* stürzen; (defeat) besiegen

**overtime**, oh-wer-**teim**, *n* Überstunden *pl*

**overture**, oh-wer-**tjuhr**, *n* *mus* Ouvertüre *f*; (approach) Annäherungsversuch *m*

**overturn**, oh-wer-**törn**, *v* stürzen; (decision) aufheben

**overweight**, oh-wer-**u'eit**, *adj* übergewichtig

**overwhelm**, oh-wer-**u'elm**, *v* überwältigen

**overwork**, oh-wer-**u'örk**, *n* Überlastung *f*; *v*

(somebody) mit Arbeit überlasten; (oneself) sich überarbeiten

**overwrought**, oh-we-**ro'at**, *adj* überreizt

**owe**, oh, *v* schulden

**owing**, oh-ing, *adj* schuldig; – **to**, *prep* wegen

**owl**, aul, *n* Eule *f*

**own**, ohn, *adj* eigen; *v* besitzen; (admit) gestehen; **–er**, *n* Besitzer *m*, Eigentümer *m*; – **up (to)**, *v* zugeben; **get one's – back**, *v* sich revanchieren; **on one's –**, allein

**ox**, ocks, *n* Ochse *m*; **–tail soup**, *n* Ochsenschwanzsuppe *f*

**oxygen**, ock-ssi-dschen, *n* Sauerstoff *m*

**oyster**, euss-ter, *n* Auster *f*

**ozone**, oh-sohn, *n* Ozon *nt*; **–friendly**, *adj* ozonsicher; (without CFCs) FCKW-frei; – **layer**, *n* Ozonschicht *f*

**pace,** pehss, n (step) Schritt m; (speed) Tempo nt; v schreiten; (sport) Schritt machen; **–maker,** n Schrittmacher m

**pacific,** pe-**ssi**-fick, adj friedlich; **the P– (Ocean),** der Pazifik m

**pacifist,** **päss**-i-fisst, n Pazifist m

**pacify,** **päss**-i-fei, v besänftigen

**pack,** päck, n (bundle) Pack m; (of cards) Spiel nt; (gang) Bande f; (of hounds) Meute f; v packen; **–age,** n Paket nt; **–age holiday,** n Pauschalreise f; **–ed lunch,** n Lunchpaket nt; **–et,** n Päckchen nt; **–ing,** n Verpackung f

**pact,** päkt, n Pakt m, Vertrag m

**pad,** pädd, n (wad) Polster nt; (of paper) Block m; v polstern; **–ding,** n Wattierung f

**paddle,** **pädd**-'l, n Paddel nt; v (boat) paddeln; (in water) planschen; **– steamer,** n Raddampfer m

**paddock,** **pädd**-eck, n (meadow) Wiese f; (at races) Sattelplatz m

**padlock,** **pädd**-lock, n Vorhängeschloß nt; v verschliessen

**paediatrician,** pie-di-e-**trisch**-'n, n Kinderarzt m

**pagan,** **peh**-gen, adj heidnisch; n Heide m, Heidin f

**page,** pehdsch, n Seite f; **–(boy),** n Page m; (haircut) Pagenkopf m; v ausrufen lassen

**pageant,** **pädsch**-ent, n Prunkaufzug m

**pager,** **peh**-dscher, n Pager m, Piepser m

**pail,** pehl, n Eimer m

**pain,** pehn, n Schmerz m; **–ful,** adj (physically) schmerzhaft; (distressing) schmerzlich; **–killer,** n Schmerzmittel nt; **–less,** adj schmerzlos; **take –s,** v sich Mühe geben

**paint,** pehnt, n Farbe f; v anstreichen; (art) malen; **–brush,** n Pinsel m; **–er,** n Maler m; **–ing,** n Gemälde nt

**pair,** pähr, n Paar nt; **– of glasses,** n Brille f; **– of trousers,** n Hose f

**pal,** päll, n fam Kumpel m

**palace,** **päll**-iss, n Palast m

**palatable,** **päll**-e-te-b'l, adj genießbar; (acceptable) akzeptabel

**palate,** **päll**-itt, n Gaumen m

**pale,** pehl, adj blaß; v erbleichen; **–ness,** n Blässe f

**Palestine,** **päll**-iss-tein, n Palästina nt

**palette,** **päll**-itt, n Palette f

**pall,** po'al, n Wolke f; v langweilig werden

**pallid,** **päll**-idd, adj bleich, blaß

**palm,** pahm, n (tree) Palme f; (of hand) Handfläche f; **– sth off on sb,** v etw auf jdn abschieben; **P– Sunday,** n Palmsonntag m

**palpitation,** **päll**-pi-**teh**-

sch'n, n Herzklopfen nt

**paltry, po'al-tri,** adj armselig, lumpig

**pamper, pämm-per,** v verhätscheln

**pamphlet, pämm-flitt,** n Broschüre f

**pan, pänn,** n Topf m; **frying –, n** Bratpfanne f

**panache, pe-näsch,** n Schwung m

**pancake, pänn-kehk,** n Pfannkuchen m

**panda, pänn-de,** n Panda m

**pandemonium, pänn-di-moh-ni-em,** n Chaos nt

**pander (to), pänn-der (tu),** v allzu sehr engegenkommen, schmeicheln

**pane, pehn,** n Scheibe f

**panel, pänn-'l,** n (of wood etc.) Tafel f; (of people) Podium nt; **–ling, n** Täfelung f

**pang, päng,** n (of hunger) Stich; (of remorse) Reue

**panic, pänn-ick,** n Panik f; v in Panik versetzen

**pansy, pänn-si,** n (flower) Stiefmütterchen nt; (fam homosexual man) Schwuler m, (lesbian) Lesbe f

**pant, pänt,** v keuchen; (of dog) hecheln

**panther, pänn-ther,** n Panther m

**panties, pänn-tis,** npl (Damen)slip m

**pantomime, pänn-te-meim,** n Pantomime f; (entertainment) Kinderstück nt; (fuss) Aufhebens nt

**pantry, pänn-tri,** n Speisekammer f

**pants, pänts,** npl (underwear) Unterhose f; (trousers) Hose f

**papal, peh-pel,** adj päpstlich

**paper, peh-per,** adj aus Papier; n Papier nt; (newspaper) Zeitung f; v tapezieren; **–back, n** Taschenbuch nt; **– bag, n** Tüte f; **–clip, n** Büroklammer f; **– handkerchief, n** Papiertaschentuch nt; **–s, npl** Ausweis m, Papiere pl

**par, pahr,** n (golf) Par nt; **below –,** nicht auf der Höhe; **on a – with,** gleichgestellt mit

**parable, pä-re-b'l,** n Gleichnis nt

**parachute, pä-re-schuht,** n Fallschirm m

**parade, pe-rehd,** n Parade f; v paradieren; fig zur Schau stellen

**paradise, pä-re-deiss,** n Paradies nt

**paradox, pä-re-docks,** n Paradox nt; **–ical,** adj paradox

**paraffin, pä-re-finn,** n Paraffin m

**paragraph, pä-re-grahf,** n Absatz m

**parallel, pä-re-lell,** adj parallel

**paralyse, pä-re-leis,** v lähmen

**paralysis, pe-räll-i-ssiss,** n Lähmung f

**parameter, pe-rämm-i-ter,** n Parameter m

**paramount, pä-re-maunt,** adj höchter(r/s); von höchster Bedeutung

**paranoid, pä-re-neud,** adj paranoid

**parapet, pä-re-pett,** n Brüstung f

**paraphrase, pä-re-frehs,** v umschreiben

**paraplegic, pä-re-plie-dschick,** n Querschnittsgelähmte(r) m & f

**parasite, pä-re-sseit,** n Schmarotzer m, Parasit m

**parasol, pä-re-ssoll,** n Sonnenschirm m

**paratrooper, pä-re-truh-per,** n Fallschirmjäger m

**parcel, pahr-s'l,** n Paket nt

**parched, pahrtsch,** adj ausgetrocknet; (person) sehr durstig

**parchment, pahrtsch-ment,** n Pergament nt

**pardon, pahr-d'n,** n Verzeihung f; law Begnadigung f; v verzeihen; law begnadigen; **(I beg your) –?** wie bitte?; **I beg your –!** Verzeihung!

**parent, pähr-rent,** n, Elternteil m; **–s, npl**

Eltern *pl*

**parental**, pe-**renn**-t'l, *adj*
elterlich, Eltern-

**parentheses**, pe-**renn**-the-
ssies, *npl* Klammern *pl*

**parish**, pä-risch, *n*
Gemeinde *f*

**park**, pahrk, *n* Park *m*,
Anlagen *pl*; *v* parken;
**–ing**, *n* Parken *m*; **–ing
meter**, *n* Parkuhr *f*; **–ing
place**, *n* Parkplatz *m*; **–
ticket**, *n* Strafzettel *m*

**parliament**, pahr-le-ment, *n*
Parlament *nt*; **–ary**, *adj*
parlamentarisch,
Parlaments-

**parlour**, pahr-ler, *n* Salon *m*

**parole**, pe-**rohl**, *n*
Bewährung *f*

**paroxysm**, pä-**reck**-ssism, *n*
Anfall *m*

**parrot**, pä-ret, *n* Papagei *m*

**parry**, pä-ri, *v* parieren,
abwehren

**parsimonious**, pahr-ssi-
**moh**-ni-ess, *adj* geizig

**parsley**, pahrss-li, *n*
Petersilie *f*

**parsnip**, pahrss-nipp, *n*
Pastinake *f*

**parson**, pahr-ss'n, *n* Pfarrer
*m*; **–age**, *n* Pfarrhaus *nt*

**part**, pahrt, *n* (piece) Teil *m*;
*mech* Teil *nt*; *theatre* Rolle
*f*; *v* (divide) teilen;
(separate) sich trennen;
(the hair) scheiteln

**partial**, pahr-sch'l, *adj*
teilweise; **be – to**, *v* eine
Vorliebe haben für

**participant**, pahr-**tiss**-i-pent,
*n* Teilnehmer *m*

**participate (in)**, pahr-**tiss**-i-
peht (inn), *v* teilnehmen
(an)

**participle**, pahr-tiss-i-p'l, *n*
Partizip *nt*

**particle**, pahr-**tick**-'l, *n*
Teilchen *nt*

**particular**, pe-**tick**-kju-ler,
*adj* besondere(r/s); (fussy)
wählerisch; (exact) genau;
**–s**, *npl* (details)
Einzelheiten *pl*; (personal)
Daten *pl*

**parting**, pahr-ting, *n*
(leaving) Abschied *m*; (of
hair) Scheitel *m*

**partition**, par-**tisch**-'n, *n*
(wall) Scheidewand *f*; (of
country) Teilung *f*

**partly**, pahrt-li, *adv*
teilweise, zum Teil

**partner**, pahrt-ner, *n*
Partner *m*; *comm*
Teilhaber *m*; **–ship**, *n*
Partnerschaft *f*; *comm*
Teilhaberschaft *f*

**partridge**, pahrt-ridsch, *n*
Rebhuhn *nt*

**part-time**, pahrt-**teim**, *adj*
Teilzeit-; **work –**, *v*
Teilzeit arbeiten

**party**, pahr-ti, *n* (event)
Party *f*; (political) Partei *f*;
(person involved) Partei *f*

**pass**, pahss, *n* Paß *m*; *v*
vorbeigehen (an),
vorbeifahren (an); (not
speak) passen;
(examination) bestehen;

(time) verbringen; (hand
to) reichen; (of time)
verstreichen; **– away**, *v*
(die) versterben; **– up**, *v*
(renounce) ausschlagen

**passage**, päss-idsch, *n*
(corridor) Durchgang *m*;
(journey) Überfahrt *f*;
(text) Passage *f*

**passbook**, pahss-buck, *n*
Sparbuch *nt*

**passenger**, päss-in-dscher, *n*
Passagier *m*

**passer-by**, pahss-er-**bei**, *n*
Passant *m*

**passing**, pah-ssing,
*adj* (traffic) vorbei-
fahrend; (fleeting)
vorübergehend; **– place**, *n*
Ausweichstelle *f*

**passion**, päsch-'n, *n*
Leidenschaft *f*; (anger)
Zorn *m*; **–ate**, *adj*
leidenschaftlich

**passive**, päss-iw, *adj* passiv;
*n gram* Passiv *nt*

**Passover**, pahss-oh-wer, *n*
Passah *nt*

**passport**, pahss-port, *n*
(Reise)paß *m*

**password**, pahss-u'örd, *n*
Paßwort *nt*

**past**, pahst, *adj* vergangen;
*adv* vorbei, vorüber; *n*
Vergangenheit *f*; *prep* an
... vorbei; (telling time)
nach

**pasta**, päss-ter, *n* Pasta *f*,
Teigwaren *pl*

**paste**, pehst, *n* (glue)
Kleister *m*; Teig *m*; (gem)

Paste f; v kleben

**pasteurized, pahss**-tsche-reisd, adj pasteurisiert

**pastime, pahss**-teim, n Zeitvertreib m, Hobby nt

**pastry, pehss**-tri, n (dough) Teig m; (cakes) Gebäck nt

**pasture, pahss**-tscher, n Weide f

**pat,** pätt, n Klaps m; v streicheln

**patch,** pätsch, n (mend) Flicken m; (period) Phase f; v flicken; – **up,** v fig beilegen; –**y,** adj vereinzelt

**pâté, pätt**-eh, n Pastete f

**patent, peht**-'nt, n Patent nt; v patentieren lassen; – **leather,** n Lackleder nt

**paternal,** pe-tör-n'l, adj väterlich

**path,** pahth, n Pfad m, Weg m; (course) Bahn f

**pathetic,** pe-thett-ick, adj herzergreifend; (contemptible) armselig

**patience, peh**-schenss, n Geduld f

**patient, peh**-schent, n Patient m; adj geduldig

**patio, pätt**-i-oh, n Terrasse f

**patriot, peh**-tri-et, n Patriot m

**patriotic,** peh-tri-ott-ick, adj patriotisch

**patrol,** pe-**trohl,** n Patrouille f; v die Runde machen; mil patrouillieren

**patron, peh**-tren, n (customer) Kunde m, Kundin f; (supporter)

Gönner m

**patronize, pätt**-re-neis, v (support) fördern; (condescend to) herablassend behandeln; (frequent) besuchen

**patter, pätt**-er, n (of feet) Trappeln nt; (talk) Gerede nt

**pattern, pätt**-ern, n Muster m

**paunch,** po'ansch, n Bauch m

**pauper, po'a**-per, n Arme(r) m & f

**pause,** po'as, n Pause f; v pausieren

**pave,** pehw, v pflastern; –**ment,** n Pflaster nt; – **the way (for),** v den Weg bahnen (für)

**paving, peh**-wing, n Pflaster nt; – **stone,** n Pflasterstein m

**paw,** po'a, n Pfote f, Tatze f; v scharren; (fam touch) befummeln

**pawn,** po'an, n (pledge) Pfand nt; (chess) Bauer m; v versetzen; –**shop,** n Leihaus nt

**pay,** peh, n Lohn m; v (be)zahlen; (be profitable) sich lohnen; – **a visit to,** v besuchen; –**able,** adj zahlbar; – **attention (to),** v beachten, Aufmerksamkeit schenken; – **for,** v bezahlen; –**ment,** n Bezahlung f; –**phone,** n

(coins) Münzfernsprecher m; (public telephone) öffentliches Telefon nt

**PC,** pie ssie, abbr **personal computer**

**pea,** pie, n Erbse f

**peace,** piess, n Friede m; –**ful,** adj friedlich; –– **keeping,** adj Friedens-

**peach,** pietsch, n Pfirsich m

**peacock, pie**-kock, n Pfau m

**peak,** piek, n Gipfel m

**peal,** piel, n (of bells) Geläute nt; (of thunder) Schlag m; – **of laughter,** n schallendes Gelächter nt

**peanut, pie**-natt, n Erdnuß f

**pear,** pähr, n Birne f

**pearl,** pörl, n Perle f

**peasant, pes**-'nt, n Bauer m; –**ry,** n Landvolk nt

**peat,** piet, n Torf m

**pebble, pebb**-'l, n Kieselstein m

**peck,** peck, n (kiss) Küßchen nt; v picken; (kiss) flüchtig küssen; –**ish,** n hungrig

**peculiar,** pi-kjuh-li-er, adj sonderbar; –**ity,** n Eigenheit f

**pedal, pedd**-'l, n Pedal nt; v radfahren

**pedantic,** pi-**dänn**-tick, adj pedantisch, kleinlich

**peddler, pedd**-ler, n Hausierer m

**pedestal, pedd**-iss-t'l, n Sockel m

**pedestrian,** pi-**dess**-tri-en, adj Fußgänger-; fig

trocken, langweilig; n
Fußgänger m

**pedigree, pedd**-i-grie, n
Stammbaum m

**pedlar, pedd**-ler, n
Hausierer m

**peel**, piel, n Schale f, Rinde
f; v (fruit) schälen; (of
paint etc.) abblättern

**peep**, piep, n (look) Blick m;
(sound) Piepsen nt; v
(look) gucken; (make
sound) piepsen

**peer**, pier, n (noble) Peer m;
(equal) Gleichgestellte(r)
m & f; v gucken; **–age**, n
Adelsstand m; **–less**, adj
unvergleichlich

**peeved**, piewd, adj verärgert

**peevish**, pie-wisch, adj
verdrießlich

**peg**, pegg, n (for tent etc.)
Pflock m; (of violin)
Wirbel m; (for washing)
Klammer f; (for clothes)
Kleiderhaken m; v mit
Klammern aufhängen; fig
stabil halten

**pellet, pell**-itt, n Kügelchen
nt; (shot) Schrot m

**pelt**, pelt, n Fell nt; Pelz m; v
bewerfen; (of rain)
prasseln

**pelvis, pell**-wiss, n Becken
nt

**pen**, penn, n Feder f; (for
sheep) Pferch m

**penal**, pie-n'l, adj Straf-;
**–ize**, v bestrafen

**penalty, penn**-'l-ti, n Strafe
f; (football) Elfmeter m

**penance, penn**-enss, n
Buße f

**pence**, penss, npl Pence pl

**pencil, penn**-ssill, n Bleistift
m; **– sharpener**, n
Bleistiftspitzer m

**pendant, penn**-dent, n
Anhänger m

**pending, penn**-ding, adj
unerledigt; prep bis

**pendulum, penn**-dju-lem, n
Pendel nt

**penetrate, penn**-i-treht, v
durchdringen

**penfriend, penn**-frend, n
Brieffreund m

**penguin, peng**-gu'in, n
Pinguin m

**penicillin, penn**-i-ssill-in, n
Penizillin nt

**peninsula, pi-ninn**-ssju-le, n
Halbinsel f

**penis, pie**-niss, n Glied nt,
Penis m

**penitent, penn**-i-tent, adj
reuig

**penknife, penn**-neif, n
Taschenmesser nt

**penniless, penn**-i-liss, adj
mittellos

**penny, penn**-i, n Penny m

**pension, penn**-sch'n, n
Rente f; **–r**, n Rentner m

**pensive, penn**-ssiw, adj
nachdenklich

**penthouse, pent**-hauss, n
Penthouse nt

**penultimate, pi-nall**-ti-met,
adj vorletzte(r/s)

**people, pie**-p'l, n (nation)
Volk nt; npl Leute pl; v

bevölkern

**pepper, pepp**-er, n (spice)
Pfeffer m; (vegetable)
Paprika f; **–mint**, n
(sweet) Pfefferminz nt;
(plant) Pfefferminze f

**per**, pör, prep pro, durch

**perceive**, per-ssiew, v
wahrnehmen

**per cent**, per ssent, n
Prozent nt

**percentage**, per-ssenn-
tidsch, n Prozentsatz m

**perception**, per-ssepp-sch'n,
n Wahrnehmung f

**perceptive**, per-ssepp-tiw,
adj aufmerksam

**perch**, pörtsch, n (of bird)
Stange f; (fish) Barsch m;
v hocken

**percolate**, pör-ke-leht, v
filtern

**percussion**, per-kasch-'n, n
Schlagzeug nt

**peremptory**, pe-remp-te-ri,
adj kategorisch

**perennial**, pe-renn-i-el, adj
(plant) mehrjährig;
(lasting) immerwährend;
n mehrjährige Pflanze f

**perfect, pör**-fikt, adj
vollkommen; n gram
Perfekt nt

**perfect**, per-fekt, v
vervollkommnen; **–ion**, n
Vollkommenheit f

**perforate**, pör-fe-reht, v
perforieren, durchlöchern

**perform**, per-form, v (task)
leisten; theatre etc.
aufführen; (operation)

**ausführen, –ance,** n theatre etc. Vorstellung f; (carrying out) Ausführung f; (productivity) Leistung f

**perfume, pör-**fjuhm, n Parfüm nt

**perfunctory,** per-**fank**-te-ri, adj oberflächlich

**perhaps,** per-**häpss,** adv vielleicht

**peril, pe-**rill, n Gefahr f; **–ous,** adj gefährlich

**period, pier-**ri-ed, n (time, menstruation) Periode f; **–ic(al),** adj periodisch; **–ical,** n Zeitschrift f

**peripheral,** pe-**riff**-e-rel, adj peripher

**periscope, pe-**ri-skohp, n Periskop nt

**perish, pe-**risch, v (spoil) verderben; (die) umkommen; **–able,** adj leicht verderblich

**perjury, pör-**dsche-ri, n Meineid m

**perk,** pörk, n Vergünstigung f; **– up,** v (person) aufleben; fig in Gang kommen

**perm,** pörm, n Dauerwelle f

**permanent, pör-**me-nent, adj beständig, fest

**permeate, pör-**mi-eht, v durchdringen

**permissible,** per-**miss**-i-b'l, adj zulässig

**permission,** per-**misch**-'n, n Erlaubnis f

**permissive,** per-**miss**-iw, adj tolerant, großzügig

**permit, pör-**mitt, n Genehmigung f

**permit,** per-**mitt,** v erlauben

**pernicious,** pe-**nisch**-ess, adj übel

**perpendicular,** per-pen-**dick**-ju-ler, adj senkrecht

**perpetrate, pör-**pi-treht, v begehen

**perpetual,** per-**pett**-ju-el, adj immerwährend

**perplex,** per-**plecks,** v verwirren

**persecute, pör-**ssi-kjuht, v verfolgen

**persecution,** pör-ssi-**kjuh**-sch'n, n Verfolgung f

**perseverance,** pör-ssi-**wier**-renss, n Ausdauer f

**persevere,** pör-ssi-**wier,** v beharren

**persist,** per-**ssist,** v (insist) beharren; (remain) anhalten; **–ence,** n Beharrlichkeit f

**person, pör-**ss'n, n Person f; **–al(ly),** adj & adv persönlich; **–al computer,** n Computer m, Rechner m; **–ality,** n Persönlichkeit f; **–al stereo,** n Walkman ® m

**personify,** per-**ssonn**-i-fei, v verkörpern

**personnel,** per-se-**nell,** n Personal nt

**perspective,** per-**speck**-tiw, n Perspektive f

**perspiration,** per-spi-**reh**-sch'n, n Schweiß m

**perspire,** per-**speir,** v schwitzen

**persuade,** per-**ssu'ehd,** v überreden

**persuasion,** per-**ssu'eh**-sch'n, n Überzeugung(skraft) f

**pert,** pört, adj frech; (pretty) hübsch

**pertain (to),** per-**tehn** (tu), v gehören (zu), betreffen

**pertinent, pör-**ti-nent, adj relevant

**perturb,** per-**törb,** v beunruhigen

**pervade,** per-**wehd,** v durchdringen

**perverse,** per-**wörss,** adj (perverted) pervers; (awkward) verstockt

**pervert, pör-**wört, n perverser Mensch m

**pervert,** per-**wört,** v verdrehen, entstellen

**pessimist, pess-**i-mist, n Pessimist m

**pest,** pest, n Pest f; **–er,** v plagen

**pet,** pett, n (animal) Haustier nt; (person) Liebling m; v liebkosen

**petal, pett-'**l, n Blumenblatt nt

**petition,** pi-**tisch**-'n, n Unterschriftensammlung f

**petrify, pett-**ri-fei, v versteinern; (terrify) erschrecken

**petrol, pett-**rel, n Benzin nt; Treibstoff m

**petroleum,** pi-**troh**-li-em, n Erdöl nt

**petrol pump**, pett-rel pamp, n Zapfsäule f

**petrol station**, pett-rel steh-sch'n, n Tankstelle f

**petticoat**, pett-i-koht, n Unterrock m

**petty**, pett-i, adj kleinlich; – **cash**, n Portokasse f

**pew**, pjuh, n Kirchenbank f; fam Platz m

**pewter**, pjuh-ter, n Zinn m

**pharmacy**, fahr-me-ssi, n Apotheke f

**phase**, fehs, n Phase f; – **in/out**, v allmählich einführen/auslaufen lassen

**pheasant**, fes-'nt, n Fasan m

**phenomenon**, fi-nomm-i-nen, n Phänomen nt

**philanthropist**, fi-länn-thre-pist, n Menschenfreund m

**philosopher**, fi-loss-e-fer, n Philosoph m

**philiosophy**, fi-loss-e-fi, n Philosophie f

**phlegm**, flemm, n Phlegma nt; med Schleim m

**phobia**, foh-bi-e, n Phobie f

**phone**, fohn, n abbr **telephone**; --**in**, n Phone-in nt

**photo**, foh-toh, n Foto nt

**photocopier**, foh-te-kopp-i-er, n Kopiergerät nt

**photocopy**, foh-te-kopp-i, n Fotokopie f

**photograph**, foh-te-grahf, n Foto(grafie) f, Aufnahme f; v fotografieren

**photographer**, fe-togg-re-fer, n Fotograf m

**phrase**, frehs, n gram Phrase f; (expression) Ausdruck m; v formulieren; –**book**, n Sprachführer m

**physical**, fis-ick-'l, adj körperlich; – **education**, n Sportunterricht m

**physician**, fi-sisch-'n, n Arzt m, Ärztin f

**physicist**, fi-si-ssist, n Physiker m

**physics**, fi-sicks, n Physik f

**physiotherapie**, fi-si-oh-the-re-pi, n Physiotherapie f

**pianist**, pi-e-nist, n Pianist m

**piano**, pi-änn-oh, n Klavier nt; (grand) Flügel m

**pick**, pick, n (choice) Auswahl f; (tool) Pickel m; v (choose) wählen; (gather) pflücken; (teeth) stochern; – **out**, v aussuchen; – **up**, v aufheben; (collect) abholen; (fam learn) aufschnappen

**pickle**, pick-'l, v pökeln; –**s**, npl Pickles pl

**pickpocket**, pick-pock-itt, n Taschendieb m

**picnic**, pick-nick, n Picknick nt

**picture**, pick-tscher, n Bild nt; (painting) Gemälde nt; v sich vorstellen; –**s**, npl Kino nt; –**sque**, adj malerisch

**pie**, pei, n (savoury) Pastete f; (sweet) Torte f

**piece**, piess, n Stück nt;

–**meal**, adv stückweise; – **together**, v zusammenfügen; –**work**, n Akkordarbeit f

**pier**, pier, n Pier m

**pierce**, pierss, v durchstechen

**piercing**, pier-ssing, adj durchdringend

**piety**, pei-i-ti, n Frömmigkeit f

**pig**, pigg, n Schwein nt

**pigeon**, pidsch-inn, n Taube f; –**hole**, n Fach nt; v einordnen

**pigheaded**, pigg-hedd-idd, adj stur

**piglet**, pigg-litt, n Ferkel nt

**pigsty**, pigg-stei, n Schweinestall m

**pike**, peik, n (fish) Hecht m

**pilchard**, pill-tscherd, n Sardine f

**pile**, peil, n (heap) Haufen m, Stapel m; (stake) Pfahl m; (of carpet) Flor m; – (up), v (sich) anhäufen

**piles**, peils, n Hämorrhoiden pl

**pile-up**, peil-app, n Massenzusammenstoß m

**pilfer**, pill-fer, v stehlen

**pilgrim**, pill-grimm, n Pilger m; –**age**, n Wallfahrt f

**pill**, pill, n Pille f

**pillage**, pill-idsch, v plündern

**pillar**, pill-er, n Pfeiler m, Säule f

**pillory**, pill-e-ri, v an den Pranger stellen

**pillow, pill**-oh, n Kopfkissen nt; **–case,** n Kissenbezug m

**pilot, pi**-let, adj Versuchs-; n Pilot m; naut Lotse m; v führen; naut lotsen; **– light,** n Zündflamme f

**pimp,** pimp, n Zuhälter m

**pimple, pimm**-p'l, n Pickel m, Bläschen f

**pin,** pinn, n (sewing) Nadel f; (of brooch) Nadel f; (of bolt) Bolzen m; v stecken, heften; **–s and needles,** npl Kribbeln nt

**pinafore, pin**-e-for, n Schürze f

**pincers, pinn**-ssers, npl Kneifzange f

**pinch,** pintsch, n Kniff m; (of salt etc.) Prise f; v kneifen; (of shoe) drücken; (fam steal) klauen

**pine,** pein, n Kiefer f; v sich grämen; **–apple,** n Ananas f; **– for,** v sich sehnen nach

**ping,** ping, n (bell) Klingeln nt; **–pong,** n Tischtennis nt

**pink,** pink, adj rosa; n (colour) Rosa nt; (flower) Nelke f

**pinnacle, pinn**-e-k'l, n Gipfel m

**pinpoint, pinn**-peunt, v genau bestimmen

**pint,** peint, n Schoppen m; (of beer) großes Bier nt

**pioneer, pei-**e-nier, n Pionier m; fig

Bahnbrecher m

**pious, pei**-ess, adj fromm

**pip,** pipp, n Kern m; **– sb at the post,** v jdn knapp schlagen

**pipe,** peip, n (tube) Rohr nt; (smoking) Pfeife f; v pfeifen, schrillen; **– down,** v fam ruhig sein; **–dream,** n Luftschloß nt; **–line,** n Pipeline f; **–r,** n mus Dudelsackbläser m

**pirate, peir**-ret, n Seeräuber m; **– radio,** n Piratensender m

**Pisces, pei**-ssies, n Fische pl

**piss,** piss, v fam pissen; **–ed,** adj fam besoffen

**pistol, piss**-t'l, n Pistole f

**piston, piss**-t'n, n Kolben m

**pit,** pitt, n Grube f; theatre Parkett nt; **– o.s. against,** v sich an etw messen

**pitch,** pitsch, n (tar) Pech nt; mus Tonhöhe f; (sport) Feld nt; v (throw) werfen; naut stampfen; (tent) aufschlagen; **–ed battle,** n offene Schlacht f

**pitcher, pitsch**-er, n Krug m

**piteous, pitt**-i-ess, adj kläglich

**pitfall, pitt**-fo'al, n Falle f

**pith,** pith, n Mark nt; **–y,** adj fig prägnant

**pitiable, pitt**-i-e-b'l, adj kläglich, elend

**pitiful, pitt**-i-full, adj elend

**pitiless, pitt**-i-liss, adj erbarmungslos

**pittance, pitt**-'nss, n

Hungerlohn m

**pitted, pitt**-idd, adj voller Vertiefungen

**pity, piw**-i, n Mitleid nt; v bemitleiden; pej bedauern; **what a –!** wie schade!

**pivot, piw**-et, n Drehpunkt m; v sich drehen

**pizza, pie**-tse, n Pizza f

**placard, plä**-kahrd, n Plakat nt

**placate, ple**-keht, v besänftigen

**place, plehss,** n Platz m; (locality) Ort m; (home) Wohnung f; v (put) stellen; (lay) legen; **take –,** v stattfinden

**placid, pläss**-idd, adj gelassen, friedlich

**plagiarism, pleh**-dschje-rism, n Plagiat nt

**plague, plehg,** n Seuche f; fig Plage f; v plagen

**plaice, plehss,** n Scholle f

**plain, plehn,** adj (simple) einfach; (looks) unansehnlich; (clear) klar; n Ebene f; **–clothes,** adj in Zivil

**plaintiff, plehn**-tiff, n Kläger m

**plaintive, plehn**-tiw, adj klagend

**plait, plätt,** n Zopf m; v flechten

**plan, plänn,** n Plan m; (draft) Entwurf m; v planen; (intend) vorhaben

**plane, plehn,** n (aeroplane)

Flugzeug nt; (tool) Hobel m; v hobeln; **– tree,** n Platane f

**planet, plänn-**itt, n Planet m

**plank, plänk,** n Planke f, Brett nt

**plant,** plahnt, n Pflanze f; (factory) Fabrik f; mech Anlage f; v pflanzen; **–ation,** n Plantage f

**plaque, plahk** n (board) Gedenktafel f; (on teeth) Belag m

**plaster, plahss-**ter, n Gips m; (building) Verputz m; med Gipsverband m; (sticking) Pflaster nt; v (wall) verputzen; (fig cover) beschmieren

**plastic, pläss-tick,** adj (of plastic) Plastik-; (arts) plastisch; n Kunststoff m; **– bag,** n Plastiktüte f; **– surgery,** n plastische Chirurgie f

**plate, pleht,** n (dish) Teller m; (sheet) Platte f; (silver) Silber nt; v (gold) vergolden; (silver) versilbern

**plateau, plätt-oh,** n Hochebene f

**plate glass, pleht** glahss, n Flachglas nt

**platform, plätt-**form, n (in hall) Plattform f; Tribüne f; (railway) Bahnsteig m

**platinum, plätt-**i-nem, n Platin nt

**plausible, plo'a-**si-b'l, adj plausibel

**play,** pleh, n Spiel nt; theatre Stück nt; v spielen; **–er,** n Spieler m; **–ful,** adj verspielt; (fun) scherzhaft; **–ground,** n Spielplatz; **–group,** n Krabbelgruppe f; **–ing field,** n Spielfeld nt; **–mate,** n Spielkamerad m

**plea,** plie, n (request) Bitte f; law Verteidigungsrede f

**plead,** plied, v (give as excuse) sich entschuldigen; law plädieren; **– for sth,** um etw bitten; **– with sb,** v an jdn appellieren

**pleasant, ples-**'nt, adj angenehm

**please,** plies, v gefallen; **–!** bitte!; **–d,** adj angenehm; **–d to meet you,** angenehm; **– yourself!** ganz wie du willst!

**pleasing, plie-**sing, adj angenehm

**pleasure, plesch-**er, n Vergnügen nt; **with –,** gern (geschehen)

**pledge, pledsch** n (object) Pfand nt; (oath) Gelübde nt; v (pawn) verpfänden; (promise) versprechen

**plenty, plenn-**ti, n Fülle f; **– of,** viel, genügend

**pleurisy, pluhr-**ri-ssi, n Rippenfellentzündung f

**pliable, plei-**e-b'l, adj geschmeidig

**pliers, plei-**ers, npl Drahtzange f

**plight,** pleit, n Notlage f

**plimsoll, plimm-**ss'l, n Turnschuh m

**plod,** plodd, v (walk slowly) trotten; (work) sich abmühen; **– along,** v dahintrotten; **–der,** n Arbeitstier nt

**plot,** plott, n (conspiracy) Komplott nt; (land) Grundstück nt; (story) Handlung f; v (heimlich) planen

**plotter, plott-**er, n (conspirator) Verschwörer m; (machine) Plotter m

**plough,** plau, n Pflug m; v pflügen; **– through,** v (sich) durchkämpfen

**ploy,** pleu, n Trick m, Taktik f

**pluck,** plack, n Mut m; v (fruit) pflücken; (poultry) rupfen; (string) zupfen; **– up the courage to do sth,** v den Mut zu etw finden

**plug,** plagg, n Pflock m; elec Stecker m; (car) Zündkerze f; v zustopfen; (fam advertise) für etw werben; **– in,** anschließen

**plum,** plamm, n Pflaume f

**plumage, pluh-**midsch, n Gefieder nt

**plumb,** plamm, adj senkrecht; n Senkblei nt; v sondieren

**plumber, plamm-**er, n Klempner m

**plumbing, plamm-**ing, n (fittings) Rohre pl; (work)

Installationsarbeiten *pl*

**plump,** plamp, *adj* mollig; (animal) fett; **– for,** *v fam* sich entscheiden für

**plunder, plann-**der, *n* Beute *f*; *v* plündern

**plunge,** plandsch, *n* Sturz *m*; *v* tauchen; (dagger) stoßen

**plural,** pluhr-rel, *n* Mehrzahl *f*, Plural *m*

**plus,** plass, *prep* plus; 100 **-,** mehr als hundert

**plush(y),** plasch(-i), *adj* feudal

**ply,** plei, *n* (wood) Sperrholz *nt*; *v* (travel) verkehren; (trade) betreiben; **–wood,** *n* Sperrholz *nt*; **3–,** *adj* (wool) dreifädig

**PM,** *abbr* Prime Minister

**p.m.,** pie emm, *adv* (*abbr* **post meridiem**) nachmittags

**pneumatic,** nju-mätt-ick, *adj* pneumatisch, Luft-

**pneumonia,** nju-moh-ni-*e*, *n* Lungenentzündung *f*

**poach,** pohtsch, *v* (cook) pochieren; (for game) wildern; **–ed egg,** *n* verlorenes Ei *nt*; **–er,** *n* Wilddieb *m*

**pocket, pock-**itt, *n* Tasche *f*; *v* einstecken; **–money,** *n* Taschengeld *nt*

**pod,** podd, *n* Hülse *f*; (of peas) Schote *f*

**poem,** poh-imm, *n* Gedicht *nt*

**poet,** poh-itt, *n* Dichter *m*;

**–ic,** *adj* poetisch; **–ry,** *n* Lyrik *f*, Poesie *f*

**poignant, peun-**jent, *adj* ergreifend

**point,** peunt, *n* (tip) Spitze *f*; (score, position, *gram*) Punkt *m*; (purpose) Zweck *m*; (aspect) Seite *f*; *v* zeigen; **–ed,** *adj* spitz; **–er,** Zeiger *m*; **–less,** *adj* zwecklos; **– out,** *v* hinweisen auf; **– to,** zeigen auf; **– of view,** *n* Standpunkt *m*; (opinion) Meinung *f*; **be on the – of,** *v* drauf und dran sein, etw zu tun; **come/get to the –,** *v* zur Sache kommen

**poise,** peus, *n* Haltung *f*

**poison, peu-s'**n, *n* Gift *nt*; *v* vergiften; **–ous,** *adj* giftig

**poke,** pohk, *n* Stoß *m*; *v* stoßen; (fire) schüren; **–r,** *n* Schüreisen *nt*; (cards) Poker *m*

**poky, poh-**ki, *adj* winzig, eng

**Poland, poh-**lend, *n* Polen *m*

**polar, poh-**ler, *adj* polar, Polar-; **– bear,** *n* Eisbär *m*; **–ize,** *v* polarisieren

**pole,** pohl, *n* Stange *f*; (geog, *elec*) Pol *m*; **– vault,** *n* Stabhochsprung *m*

**police, pe-liess,** *n* Polizei *f*; **–man,** *n* Polizist *m*; **– station,** *n* Polizeiwache *f*; **–woman,** *n* Polizistin *f*

**policy, poll-**i-ssi, *n* Politik *f*; (insurance) Police *f*

**polish, poll-**isch, *n* (for

furniture) Politur *f*; (for floor) Wachs *nt*; (for shoes) Schuhcreme *f*; *fig* Glanz *m*; *v* polieren; wichsen; *fig* ausfeilen; **– off,** *v fam* verdrücken

**polite,** pe-leit, *adj* höflich; **–ness,** *n* Höflichkeit *f*

**political, pe-litt-**i-k'l, *adj* politisch

**politician, poll-i-tisch-**en, *n* Politiker *m*

**politics, poll-**i-ticks, *n* Politik *f*

**poll,** pohl, *n* (election) Wahl *f*; (of opinion) Umfrage *f*; (in votes) erhalten; **go to the –s,** *v* zur Wahl gehen

**pollen, poll-**en, *n* Pollen *m*

**polling, poh-**ling, *adj* Wahl-

**pollute,** pe-luht, *v* verunreinigen, verschmutzen

**pollution, pe-luh-**sch'n, *n* Verschmutzung *f*

**polo, poh-**loh, *n* Polo *nt*; **– neck,** *n* Rollkragenpullover *m*; **– shirt,** *n* Polohemd *nt*

**polyester, poll-i-ess-**ter, *n* Polyester *m*

**polystyrene, poll-i-stei-**rien, *n* Styropor ® *nt*

**polythene, poll-**i-thien, *n* Plastik *nt*; **– bag,** *n* Plastiktüte *f*

**pomegranate, pomm-i-**gränn-itt, *n* Granatapfel *m*

**pomp,** pomp, *n* Prunk *m*; **–ous,** *adj* großspurig

**pond,** pond, *n* Teich *m*

**ponder,** ponn-der, *v* nachdenken (über); **–ous,** *adj* schwerfällig

**pony,** poh-ni, *n* Pony *nt*; **–tail,** *n* Pferdeschwanz *m*

**poodle,** puh-d'l, *n* Pudel *m*

**pool,** puhl, *n* (swimming) Bad *nt*; (of blood etc.) Lache *f*; (kitty) (gemeinsame) Kasse *f*; (billiards) Poolspiel *nt*; *v* zusammenlegen; **(football) –s,** *npl* Toto *nt*

**poor,** por, *adj* (not rich, unfortunate) arm; (not good) schlecht, schwach; **–ly,** *adj & adv* schlecht; **the –,** *npl* die Armen *pl*

**pop,** popp, *n* (sound) Knall *m*; *mus* Popmusik *f*; (drink) Sprudel *m*, Brause *f*; *v* (sound) knallen; (burst) platzen; (*fam* put) stecken; **–corn,** *n* Popcorn *nt*; **– in/out,** *v* kurz vorbeikommen/weggehen

**Pope,** pohp, *n* Papst *m*

**poplar,** popp-ler, *n* Pappel *f*

**popper,** popp-er, *n* Druckknopf *m*

**poppy,** popp-i, *n* Mohn *m*

**populace,** popp-ju-liss, *n* Volk *nt*

**popular,** popp-ju-ler, *adj* (liked) beliebt; (of the people) Volks-, verbreitet

**popularity,** popp-ju-lä-ri-ti, *n* Beliebtheit *f*, Popularität *f*

**populate,** popp-ju-leht, *v* bevölkern

**population,** popp-juh-leh-sch'n, *n* Bevölkerung *f*

**populous,** popp-ju-less, *adj* stark bevölkert

**porcelain,** por-ssi-linn, *n* Porzellan *nt*

**porch,** portsch, *n* Vorhalle *f*; Portal *nt*

**porcupine,** por-kju-pein, *n* Stachelschwein *nt*

**pore,** por, *n* Pore *f*; **– over,** *v* über etw (gründlich) nachdenken

**pork,** pork, *n* Schweinefleisch *nt*

**pornography,** por-nogg-re-fi, *n* Pornographie *f*

**porous,** por-ress, *adj* porös

**porpoise,** por-pess, *n* Schweinswal *m*

**porridge,** po-ridsch, *n* Haferbrei *m*

**port,** port, *n* (wine) Portwein *m*; (harbour) Hafen *m*; (*naut* left) Backbord *nt*; **–hole,** *n* Bullauge *nt*

**portable,** port-e-b'l, *adj* tragbar

**portent,** por-tent, *n* Vorzeichen *nt*

**porter,** por-ter, *n* (doorman) Portier *m*; (of luggage) Träger *m*; **–age,** *n* Trägerlohn *m*

**portfolio,** port-foh-li-oh, *n* (case) Mappe *f*; (ministerial, artist's) Portefeuille *nt*

**portion,** por-sch'n, *n* (of food) Portion *f*; (share) (An)teil *m*

**portly,** port-li, *adj* beleibt, korpulent

**portrait,** port-reht, *n* Porträt *nt*

**portray,** por-treh, *v* darstellen

**Portugal,** port-ju-gel, *n* Portugal *nt*

**Portuguese,** port-ju-gies, *adj* portugiesisch; *n* (person) Portugiese *m*, Portugiesin *f*; (language) Portugiesisch *nt*

**pose,** pohs, *n* Stellung *f*; *v* posieren; **– as,** *v* sich ausgeben für

**position,** pe-sisch-'n, *n* Lage *f*; (job) Stellung *f*; (opinion) Standpunkt *m*; *v* plazieren

**positive,** pos-i-tiw, *adj* positiv; (certain) sicher

**possess,** pe-sess, *v* besitzen; **–ion,** *n* Besitz *m*; **–ive,** *adj* besitzergreifend

**possibility,** poss-i-bill-i-ti, *n* Möglichkeit *f*

**possible,** poss-i-b'l, *adj* möglich

**possibly,** poss-i-bli, *adv* möglicherweise, vielleicht; **not –,** unmöglich

**post,** pohst, *n* (mail) Post *f*; (pole) Pfosten *m*, Stange *f*; (job) Stelle *f*; (place) Posten *m*; *v* (letter) aufgeben; (notice) aushängen; **–age,** *n* Porto

nt; **–al order,** n
Postanweisung f; **–box,** n
Briefkasten m; **–card,** n
Postkarte f; **–code,** n
Postleitzahl f; **–date,** v
nachdatieren

**poster, poh-**ster, n Plakat nt,
Poster nt

**posterior, poss-tier-**ri-er, n
Hinterteil nt

**posterity, poss-te-**ri-ti, n
Nachwelt f

**postgraduate, pohst-
grädd-**ju-et, n
Graduierte(r) m & f

**posthumous, post-**ju-mess,
adj postum

**postman, pohst-**men, n
Briefträger m

**post-mortem, pohst-mor-**
tem, n Obduktion f

**post office, pohst off-**iss, n
(organization) Post f;
(office) Postamt nt

**postpone, pohss-pohn,** v
aufschieben

**postscript, pohst-**skript, n
Nachschrift f

**posture, poss-**tscher, n
Stellung f, Positur f

**pot,** pott, n (plant, cooking)
Topf m; (coffee, tee)
Kanne f; (fam cannabis)
Hasch m; v (plant)
eintopfen

**potato,** pe-**teh-**toh, n
Kartoffel f

**potent, poh-**tent, adj kräftig,
stark

**potential,** pe-**tenn-**sch'l, adj
potentiell; n Potential nt

**pothole, pott-**hohl, n (cave)
Höhle f; (in road)
Schlagloch nt

**potion,** poh-**sch'n,** n
Trank m

**potted, pott-**idd, adj (plant)
Topf– f; (food) eingemacht;
(condensed)
zusammengefaßt

**potter, pott-**er, n Töpfer m; **–y,**
n Steingut nt

**potty, pott-**i, adj verrückt; n
fam Töpfchen nt

**pouch,** pautsch, n Beutel m

**poultry, pohl-**tri, n
Geflügel nt

**pounce (on),** paunss (onn),
v sich stürzen (auf)

**pound,** paund, n (weight,
currency) Pfund nt;
(enclosure) Abstellplatz
m; (for dogs) Zwinger; v
zerstampfen

**pour,** por, v (rain, liquid)
gießen; (crowd) strömen;
**–ing,** adj strömend; **– out,**
(drink) einschenken

**pout,** paut, n Schmollmund
m; v schmollen

**poverty, pow-**er-ti, n Armut
f; **–-stricken,** adj
notleidend

**powder, pau-**der, n Pulver
nt; (face) Puder m; v
pudern; **– room,** n
Damentoilette f

**power, pau-**er, n Macht f,
Gewalt f; (faculty)
Fähigkeit f; mech Kraft f;
elec Strom m; v betreiben;
**– cut,** n Stromausfall m;

**–driven,** adj Motor-,
Elektro-; **–ed,** adj
betrieben; **–ful,** adj
mächtig, stark; **–less,** adj
machtlos; **– point,** n
(elektrischer) Anschluß
m; **– station,** n
Kraftwerk nt

**practicable, präck-**ti-ke-b'l,
adj praktikabel

**practical, präck-**ti-k'l, adj
praktisch

**practice, präck-**tiss, n Praxis
f; (custom) Gebrauch m;
(exercise) Übung f;
(doctor's) Praxis f; **in –,** in
der Praxis; **out of –,** außer
Übung

**practise, präck-**tiss, v
(exercise) üben; med
praktizieren; (profession)
ausüben

**practitioner, präck-tisch-e-**
ner, n med praktischer
Arzt m, praktische
Ärztin f

**pragmatic, prägg-mätt-**ick,
adj pragmatisch

**prairie, prehr-**ri, n Prärie f

**praise,** prehs, n Lob nt; v
loben; **–worthy,** adj
lobenswert

**pram,** präm, n
Kinderwagen m

**prance, prahnss,** v
stolzieren; **– about,** v
herumhüpfen

**prank,** pränk, n Streich m

**prattle, prätt-**'l, n
Geschwätz nt; v schwatzen

**prawn, pro'an,** n Garnele f

**pray**, preh, v beten; *fig* bitten

**prayer**, prähr, n Gebet nt; **–book**, n Gebetbuch nt; **the Lord's P–**, Vaterunser nt

**pre-**, prie, *pref* Vor-, Voraus-

**preach**, prietsch, v predigen; **–er**, n Prediger m

**precarious**, pri-**kehr**-ri-ess, *adj* prekär, riskant

**precaution**, pri-**ko'a**-sch'n, n Vorsichtsmaßnahme f

**precede**, pri-**ssied**, v vorangehen

**precedence**, press-i-denss, n Priorität f, Vortritt m

**precedent**, press-i-dent, n Präzedenzfall m

**precept**, prie-ssept, n Lehre f, Regel f; *law* Befehl m

**precinct**, prie-ssinkt, n (district) Bezirk m; (surroundings) Gelände nt; **pedestrian –**, n Fußgängerzone f; **shopping –**, n Einkaufsviertel nt

**precious**, presch-ess, *adj* kostbar, Edel-

**precipice**, press-i-piss, n Abgrund m

**precipitate**, pri-**ssipp**-i-tet, *adj* übereilt

**precipitate**, pri-**ssipp**-i-teht, v schleudern; *fig* stürzen

**precise**, pri-**sseiss**, *adj* genau

**precision**, pri-**ssisch**-'n, n Präzision f

**preclude**, pri-**kluhd**, v ausschließen

**precocious**, pri-**koh**-schess, *adj* altklug, frühreif

**preconceived**, prie-ken-**ssiewd**, *adj* vorgefaßt

**precursor**, pri-**kör**-sser, n Vorgänger m

**predator**, predd-e-ter, n Raubtier nt

**predecessor**, prie-di-**ssess**-er, n Vorgänger m

**predicament**, pri-**dick**-e-ment, n Zwangslage f

**predict**, pri-**dikt**, v prophezeien, vorhersagen; **–able**, *adj* vorhersagbar; **–ion**, n Vorhersage f

**predominant**, pri-**domm**-i-nent, *adj* vorherrschend; **–ly**, *adv* überwiegend

**pre-eminent**, prie-**emm**-i-nent, *adj* hervorragend

**pre-empt**, prie-**empt**, v vorwegnehmen

**preface**, preff-iss, n Vorwort nt

**prefect**, prie-fekt, n Präfekt m; (in school) Aufseher m

**prefer**, pri-**för**, v vorziehen; bevorzugen; lieber tun/haben

**preferably**, preff-e-reb-li, *adv* lieber

**preference**, pref-e-renss, n Vorzug m

**prefix**, prie-ficks, n Vorsilbe f; v voransetzen

**pregnancy**, pregg-nen-ssi, n Schwangerschaft f

**pregnant**, pregg-nent, *adj* schwanger; (animal) trächtig

**prejudice**, predsch-ju-diss, n Vorurteil nt; v beeinträchtigen; **–d**, *adj* voreingenommen; **without –**, *comm* unter Vorbehalt

**prejudicial**, predsch-ju-**disch**-'l, *adj* nachteilig

**preliminary**, pri-**limm**-i-ne-ri, *adj* einleitend; n Vorbereitung f

**prelude**, prell-juhd, n Vorspiel nt; *fig* Auftakt m

**premature**, premm-e-tschuhr, *adj* vorzeitig

**premeditated**, prie-medd-i-teh-tidd, *adj* vorbedacht

**premier**, premm-i-er, *adj* erste(r/s); n Premierminister m

**premise**, premm-iss, n Voraussetzung f, **–s**, *npl* (building) Gebäude nt; (buildings and land) Gelände nt

**premium**, prie-mi-em, *adj* erstklassig; n Prämie f; **be at a –**, hoch im Kurs stehen

**preparation**, prepp-e-**reh**-sch'n, n Vorbereitung f

**prepare**, pri-**pähr**, v (sich) vorbereiten; **– for**, sich vorbereiten auf

**preponderance**, pri-**ponn**-de-renss, n Übergewicht nt

**preposition**, pre-pe-**sisch**-'n, n Präposition f

**preposterous**, pri-**poss**-te-ress, *adj* absurd

**prerogative**, pri-**rogg**-e-tiv, n

Vorrecht *nt*

**prescribe,** pri-**skreib,** *v* vorschreiben; *med* verschreiben

**prescription,** priss-**kripp**-sch'n, *n med* Rezept *nt*

**presence,** pres-*enss,* *n* Gegenwart *f;* **– of mind,** Geistesgegenwart *f*

**present,** pres-*ent, adj* gegenwärtig; anwesend; *n* Gegenwart *f;* (gift) Geschenk *nt;* **–ation,** *n* Vorstellung *f;* (of gift) Überreichung *f;* **–ly,** *adv* sofort

**present,** pri-**sent,** *v* präsentieren, vorstellen; **– sb with sth,** jdm etw schenken

**preservation,** pres-er-**weh**-sch'n, *n* Erhaltung *f*

**preservative,** pri-**sör**-we-tiw, *n* Konservierungsmittel *nt*

**preserve,** pri-**sörw,** *n* Eingemachtes *nt; v* (maintain) erhalten; (fruit etc.) einmachen

**preside (over),** pri-**seid** (oh-wer), *v* vorsitzen

**president,** pres-i-**dent,** *n* Präsident *m;* (chairman) Vorsitzende(r) *m & f*

**press,** press, *n* Presse *f; v* drücken; (clothes) bügeln; (encourage) drängen; **– conference,** *n* Pressekonferenz *f;* **–ing,** *adj* dringend

**pressure,** presh-**er,** *n* Druck *m;* **– group,** *n* Pressure-group *f,* Interessenverband *m*

**prestige,** press-**tiesch,** *n* Prestige *nt*

**prestigious,** press-**tidsch**-ess, *adj* renommiert

**presumably,** pri-**sjuh**-meb-li, *adv* vermutlich

**presume,** pri-**sjuhm,** *v* vermuten

**presumption,** pri-**samp**-sch'n, *n* (assumption) Annahme *f;* (arrogance) Anmaßung *f*

**pretence,** pri-**tenss,** *n* Vorwand *m*

**pretend,** pri-**tend,** *v* vorgeben

**pretentious,** pri-**tenn**-schess, *adj* großspurig

**pretext,** prie-**tekst,** *n* Vorwand *m*

**pretty,** pritt-i, *adj* hübsch; *adv fam* ziemlich

**prevail,** pri-**wehl,** *v* vorherrschen; **– upon sb,** auf jdn einwirken

**prevalent,** prew-*e*-lent, *adj* vorherrschend

**prevent,** pri-**went,** *v* verhindern; **–ion,** *n* Verhinderung *f;* **–ive,** *adj* vorbeugend

**preview,** prie-**wjuh,** *n* Vorschau *f*

**previous(ly),** prie-wi-ess(-li), *adj & adv* früher

**prey,** preh, *n* Beute *f,* Raub *m;* **– on,** *v* rauben; *fig* sehr zusetzen

**price,** preiss, *n* Preis *m;*

**–less,** *adj* unschätzbar

**prick,** prick, *n* Stich *m; v* stechen

**prickle,** prick-'l, *n* Stachel *m*

**prickly,** prick-li, *adj* stachelig

**pride,** preid, *n* Stolz *m;* **– o.s. (on),** *v* sich brüsten (mit)

**priest,** priest, *n* Priester *m*

**prig,** prigg, *n* Besserwisser *m*

**prim,** primm, *adj* steif

**primary,** prei-me-ri, *adj* (original) ursprünglich; (main) Haupt-; **– school,** *n* Grundschule *f*

**primate,** prei-mitt, *n* (ape) Primat *m*

**prime,** preim, *adj* (main) Haupt-; (quality) erstklassig; (number) Prim-; *n* Blüte *f; v* (prepare) vorbereiten; (gun) laden; **P– Minister,** *n* Premierminister *m*

**primitive,** primm-i-tiw, *adj* primitiv

**primrose,** primm-rohs, *n* Primel *f*

**prince,** prinss, *n* Prinz *m,* Fürst *m*

**princely,** prinss-li, *adj* fürstlich

**princess,** prinn-ssess, *n* Prinzessin *f,* Fürstin *f*

**principal,** prinn-ssi-p'l, *adj* hauptsächlich, Haupt-; (school) Direktor *m;* (chief) Chef *m*

**principle,** prinn-ssi-p'l, *n*

Prinzip nt, Grundsatz m; **in –**, im Prinzip; **on –**, aus Prinzip

**print**, print, n Druck m; *photog* Abzug m; v drucken; (in capitals) in Druckbuchstaben schreiben; **–er**, n Drucker m; **–ing**, n Druck m; *photog* Abziehen nt; **–ing works**, n Druckerei f; **out of –**, adj vergriffen

**prior**, **prei**-er, adj früher; n Prior m; **– to**, conj bevor; *prep* vor

**priority**, prei-o-ri-ti, n (precedence) Vorrang m; (urgent thing) Priorität f

**prise open**, preis oh-pen, v aufstemmen

**prison**, **pris**-'n, n Gefängnis nt; **–er**, Gefangene(r) m & f

**pristine**, **priss**-tien, adj unberührt

**privacy**, **priw**-e-ssi, n Zurückgezogenheit f, Privatsphäre f

**private**, **prei**-witt, adj privat, Privat-; n einfacher Soldat m; **– eye**, n Privatdetektiv m; **in –**, privat

**privatize**, **prei**-we-teis, v privatisieren

**privilege**, **priw**-i-lidsch, n Vorrecht nt, Privileg nt; **–d**, adj privilegiert

**prize**, preis, n Preis m; v schätzen; **– idiot**, n fam Vollidiot m; **–winner**, n Preisträger m

**pro**, proh, n Profi m; *prep* für; **the –s and cons**, das Für und Wider

**probability**, probb-e-bill-i-ti, n Wahrscheinlichkeit f

**probable**, probb-e-b'l, adj wahrscheinlich

**probably**, probb-e-bli, adv wahrscheinlich

**probation**, pre-beh-sch'n, n Probezeit f; *law* Bewährung f

**probe**, prohb, v sondieren, prüfen

**problem**, probb-lem, n Problem nt, Aufgabe f

**procedure**, pre-ssie-dscher, n Verfahren nt

**proceed**, pre-ssied, v (act) vorgehen; (continue) fortfahren; (go forward) weiterfahren, weitergehen; **–ings**, npl (events) Vorgänge pl; *law* Verfahren nt

**proceeds**, proh-ssieds, npl Ertrag m

**process**, proh-ssess, v Verfahren nt; *chem* Prozeß m

**procession**, pre-ssesch-'n, n Prozession f

**proclaim**, pre-klehm, v bekanntmachen

**proclamation**, prock-le-meh-sch'n, n Proklamation f

**procrastination**, pre-krässti-neh-sch'n, n Aufschub m, Verzögerung f

**procure**, pre-kjuhr, v

verschaffen; (sex) kuppeln

**prod**, prodd, n Stich m; v stoßen, stechen

**prodigal**, prodd-i-g'l, adj verschwenderisch; n Verschwender m

**prodigious**, pre-didsch-ess, adj ungeheuer

**prodigy**, prodd-i-dschi, n Wunder nt; **child –**, n Wunderkind nt

**produce**, prodd-juss, n Erzeugnis nt

**produce**, pre-djuss, v (crop) erzeugen; (goods) herstellen; (effect) hervorrufen; (play) produzieren, inszenieren

**producer**, pre-djuh-sser, n Produzent m; (theatre, film) Produzent m

**product**, prodd-akt, n Produkt nt, Erzeugnis nt

**production**, pre-dack-sch'n, n Produktion f, Herstellung f; *theatre* Inszenierung f; **– line**, n Fließband nt

**profane**, pre-fehn, adj (secular) profan; (language) profan

**profess**, pre-fess, v vorgeben

**profession**, pre-fesch-'n, n Beruf m; **–al**, adj Berufs-; n Profi m

**professor**, pre-fess-er, n Professor m

**proficiency**, pre-fisch-en-ssi, n Tüchtigkeit f

**proficient**, pre-fisch-ent, adj bewandt

**profile,** proh-feil, n Profil nt; fig Umriß m

**profit,** proff-itt, n Gewinn m; v gewinnen; **–able,** adj einträglich; **–eer,** n Schieber m

**profound,** pre-faund, adj tief; (thorough) gründlich

**profuse,** pre-fjuss, adj reichlich; **–ly,** adv (thanks) überschwenglich; (sweat) stark

**profusion (of),** pre-fjuh-sch'n (ew), n Überfluß m (an)

**program,** proh-grämm, n comp Programm nt; v programmieren

**programme,** proh-grämm, n Programm nt; (broadcast) Sendung f

**programmer,** proh-grämm-er, n comp Programmierer m

**progress,** proh-gress, n Fortschritt m; **in –,** im Gang

**progress,** pre-gress, v vorwärts kommen

**progression,** pre-gresch-'n, n (succession) Folge f; (development) Fortschritt m

**prohibit,** pre-hibb-itt, v verbieten; **–ed,** adj verboten

**prohibition,** proh-i-bisch-'n, n Verbot nt

**prohibitive,** pro-hibb-i-tiw, adj untragbar

**project,** prodsch-ekt, n Projekt nt

**project,** pre-dschekt, v (predict) prognostizieren; (stick out) herausragen; **–ile,** n Geschoß nt; **–ion,** n (prediction) Prognose f; (protrusion) Vorsprung m

**proletariat,** proh-li-tähr-ri-et, n Proletariat nt

**prolific,** pre-liff-ick, adj fruchtbar; fig produktiv

**prologue,** proh-logg, n Prolog m

**prolong,** pre-long, v verlängern

**prom,** promm, abbr **promenade concert**

**promenade,** prom-i-nahd, n (walk) Spaziergang m; (avenue) Promenade f; **– concert,** n Promenadenkonzert nt

**prominent,** promm-i-nent, adj (important) hervorragend; (striking) auffallend

**promiscuous,** pre-miss-kju-ess, adj häufig den Partner wechselnd

**promise,** promm-iss, n Versprechen nt; v versprechen

**promising,** promm-iss-ing, adj vielversprechend

**promote,** pre-moht, v fördern

**promoter,** pre-moh-ter, n Förderer m; (organiser) Veranstalter m

**promotion,** pre-moh-sch'n,

n (of person) Beförderung f; (of product) Werbung f

**prompt,** prompt, adj prompt; v theatre souffliieren; (induce) anregen; **–er,** n Souffleur m; **–ly,** adv schnell; sofort

**prone,** prohn, adj langgestreckt, liegend; **– to,** geneigt zu

**prong,** prong, n Zinke f

**pronoun,** proh-naun, n Pronomen nt, Fürwort nt

**pronounce,** pre-naunss, v aussprechen; (judgement) verkünden; **–d,** adj ausgesprochen; **–ment,** n Erklärung f

**pronunciation,** pre-nann-ssi-eh-sch'n, n Aussprache f

**proof,** pruhf, adj standhaft; n Beweis m; (printer's) Abzug m; (alcoholic strength) Alkoholgehalt m

**prop,** propp, n Stütze f; theatre Requisite f; **– up,** v stützen

**propaganda,** propp-e-gänn-de, n Propaganda f

**propagate,** propp-e-geht, v fortpflanzen; fig verbreiten

**propel,** pre-pell, v treiben; **–lant,** n Treibmittel nt; **–ler,** n Propeller m

**proper,** propp-er, adj passend; (decent) anständig; **–ly,** adv richtig

**property,** propp-er-ti, n (possession) Eigentum nt;

(land) Immobilien pl;
(quality) Eigenschaft f

**prophecy, proff**-i-ssi, n
Prophezeiung f

**prophesy, proff**-i-ssei, v
prophezeien

**prophet, proff**-itt, n
Prophet m

**proportion, pre-por-**sch'n, n
Verhältnis nt; (share)
Anteil m; **–al,** adj
proportional; **–s,** npl
Proportionen pl

**proposal, pre-poh-**s'l, n
Vorschlag m; (of marriage)
Heiratsantrag m

**propose, pre-pohs**, v
vorschlagen; (marriage)
einen Heiratsantrag
machen

**proprietor, pre-prei**-e-ter, n
Besitzer m, Eigentümer m

**proprietress, pro-prei**-e-triss,
n Besitzerin f

**propriety, pre-prei**-e-ti, n
Schicklichkeit f

**pro rata,** proh rah-te, adv
anteilmäßig

**prose,** prohs, n Prosa f

**prosecute, pross**-i-kjuht, v
law anklagen

**prosecution, pross-i-kjuh-**
sch'n, n Anklage f

**prospect, pross**-pekt, n
Aussicht f

**prospective, pre-speck**-tiw,
adj zukünftig

**prospectus, pre-speck**-tess, n
Prospekt m; (university)
Studienführer m

**prosper, pross**-per, v

gedeihen

**prosperity, pross-pe**-ri-ti, n
Wohlstand m

**prosperous, pross-pe**-ress,
adj wohlhabend

**prostitute, pross**-ti-tjuht, n
Prostituierte f; v
prostituieren

**prostrate, pross**-treht, adj
(lying) ausgestreckt; fig
niedergeschlagen

**protect, pre-tekt**, v
beschützen; **–ion,** n
Schutz m; **–ive,** adj
schützend, Schutz-

**protein, proh**-tien, n
Protein n

**protest, proh**-test, n
Einspruch m, Protest m

**protest, pre-test**, v (declare)
beteuern; **– (against),**
protestieren (gegen); **–er,**
n Demonstrant m

**protracted, pre-träck**-tidd,
adj langwierig

**protrude, pre-truhd**, v
herausragen

**proud (of),** praud (ew), adj
stolz (auf)

**prove,** pruhw, v
(demonstrate) beweisen;
(turn out) sich erweisen

**proverb, prow**-örb, n
Sprichwort nt; **–ial,** adj
stichwörtlich

**provide, pre-weid**, v
versorgen; **– for,**
vorsorgen für

**provided (that), pre-wei-**
didd (dhet), conj
vorausgesetzt (, daß)

**providence, prow**-i-denss, n
Vorsehung f

**providing (that), pre-wei-**
ding (dhet), conj
vorausgesetzt (, daß)

**province, prow**-inss, n
Provinz f; fig Bereich m

**provincial, pre-winn**-sch'l,
adj Provinz-; pej
provinzlerisch

**provision, pre-wisch-**'n, n
Vorkehrung f; **–al,** adj
provisorisch; **–s,** npl
Lebensmittel pl

**proviso, pre-wei**-soh, n
Bedingung f

**provocation, prow-e-keh-**
sch'n, n Provokation f,
Herausforderung f

**provocative, pre-wock**-e-
tiw, adj provozierend;
(sexually) aufreizend

**provoke, pre-wohk**, v
(irritate) herausfordern,
reizen; (cause)
hervorrufen

**prow,** prau, n Bug m

**prowess, prau**-ess, n
(valour) Tapferkeit f;
(skill) Können nt

**prowl,** praul, v
herumstreifen; **–er,** n
jemand, der herumstreift

**proximity, prock**-ssi-mi-ti, n
Nähe f

**proxy, prock**-ssi, n
Stellvertreter m; **by –,** in
Vertretung; durch einen
Bevollmächtigten

**prudence, pruh**-denss, n
Überlegtheit f

**prudent, pruh**-dent, *adj* vorsichtig, überlegt

**prudish, pruh**-disch, *adj* prüde

**prune, pruhn, n** Backpflaume *f; v* (be)schneiden

**pry (into),** prei (**inn**-tu), *v* herumschnüffeln

**PS,** pie ess, *abbr* **postscript**

**psalm,** ssahm, n Psalm *m*

**pseudonym, sjuh**-de-nimm, n Pseudonym *nt*

**psychiatric,** sei-ki-**ätt**-rick, *adj* psychiatrisch

**psychiatrist,** sei-**kei**-e-trist, n Psychiater *m*

**psychic, sei**-kick, *adj* (phenomenon, person) übersinnlich; *n* Hellseher *m*

**psychoanalyst,** sei-koh-** änn**-e-list, n Psychoanalytiker *m*

**psychological,** sei-ke-**lodsch**-ick-'l, *adj* psychologisch

**psychology,** sei-**koll**-e-dschi, n Psychologie *f*

**psychopath,** sei-koh-päth, n Psychopath *m*

**PTO,** pie tie oh, *abbr* **please turn over,** bitte wenden

**pub,** pabb, n Kneipe *f*

**public, pabb**-lick, *adj* öffentlich; n Öffentlichkeit *f*

**publican, pabb**-li-ken, n (Gast)wirt *m*

**publication,** pabb-li-**keh**-sch'n, n Veröffentlichung *f*

**public house, pabb**-lick hauss, n Wirtshaus *nt*

**publicity,** pabb-**liss**-i-ti, n Werbung *f*

**publish, pabb**-lisch, *v* veröffentlichen; **–er,** n Verleger *m;* **–ing,** n Verlagswesen *nt*

**pucker, pack**-er, *v* runzeln

**pudding, pudd**-ing, n Pudding *m;* **black –,** n Blutwurst *f*

**puddle, padd**-'l, n Pfütze *f,* Lache *f*

**puerile, pjuhr**-reil, *adj* kindisch

**puff,** paff, n (breath) Hauch m; (of wind) Stoß m; (of cigarette) Zug m; *v* schnaufen; **–ed,** *adj fam* außer Puste; **– pastry,** n Blätterteig m; **– up,** sich aufblasen; **–y,** *adj* geschwollen; **powder–,** n Puderquaste *f*

**pull,** pull, n Zug m; (attraction) Anziehungskraft *f; v* ziehen; reißen; **– down,** (demolish) abreißen; **– one's weight,** sich voll einsetzen; **– o.s. together,** sich zusammenreißen; **– sb's leg,** jdn anführen

**pulley, pull**-i, n Rolle *f,* Flaschenzug *m*

**pullover, pull**-oh-wer, n Pullover *m*

**pulp,** palp, n Brei m; (fruit) Fruchtfleisch nt; *v* zu Brei machen; **wood–,** n

Holzschliff *m*

**pulpit, pull**-pitt, n Kanzel *f*

**pulse,** palss, n Puls *m*

**pulverize, pall**-we-reis, *v* pulverisieren

**pumice-stone, pamm**-iss-stohn, n Bimsstein *m*

**pump,** pamp, n Pumpe *f; v* pumpen; **– up,** aufpumpen

**pun,** pann, n Wortspiel *nt*

**punch,** pantsch, n (blow) Schlag m; (tool) Locheisen nt; (drink) Punsch m; *v* schlagen, boxen; **–line,** n Pointe *f*

**punctual, pank**-tju-el, *adj* pünktlich

**punctuate, pank**-tju-eht, *v* (text) mit Satzzeichen versehen; (interrupt) unterbrechen

**punctuation,** pank-tju-**eh**-sch'n, n Zeichensetzung *f*

**puncture, pank**-tscher, n Stich m; (in tyre) Reifenpanne *f; v* durchstechen; (tyre) platt werden

**pungent, pann**-dschent, *adj* scharf, beißend

**punish, pann**-isch, *v* bestrafen, strafen; **–able,** *adj* strafbar; **–ment,** n Strafe *f*

**punitive, pjuh**-ni-tiw, *adj* rigoros

**punt,** pant, n Stechkahn m; *v* staken; **–er,** n *fam* Zocker m

**puny, pjuh**-ni, *adj* schwächlich

**pupil, pjuh**-pill, *n* (at school) Schüler *m*; (of eye) Pupille *f*

**puppet, papp**-itt, *n* Marionette *f*

**puppy, papp**-i, *n* Hündchen *nt*

**purchase, pör**-tschiss, *n* (buy) Einkauf *m*; (grasp) Halt *m*; *v* einkaufen; **–r**, *n* Käufer *m*

**pure(ly), pjuhr** (-li), *adj & adv* rein

**puree, pjuhr**-reh, *n* Püree *nt*; *v* pürieren

**purgatory, pör**-ge-te-ri, *n* Fegefeuer *nt*

**purge, pördsch**, *v* reinigen; *med* abführen

**purify, pjuhr**-ri-fei, *v* reinigen

**purity, pjuhr**-ri-ti, *n* Reinheit *f*

**purple, pör**-p'l, *adj* lila, violett; *n* Lila *nt*, Violett *nt*

**purport, per**-port, *v* besagen

**purpose, pör**-pess, *n* (intention) Absicht *f*; (goal) Zweck *m*; **–ful**, *adj* zielstrebig; **–ly**, *adv* absichtlich; **on –**, *adv* absichtlich

**purr, pörr**, *v* schnurren

**purse, pörss**, *n* Geldbeutel *m*; Portemonnaie *nt*; *v* kräuseln

**purser, pör**-sser, *n* Zahlmeister *m*

**pursue, per**-ssjuh, *v* (prey) verfolgen; (aim)

nachstreben

**pursuit, per**-ssjuht, *n* (chase) Verfolgung *f*; (occupation) Beschäftigung *f*

**purveyor, per**-weh-er, *n* Lieferant *m*

**pus, pass**, *n* Eiter *m*

**push, pusch**, *n* Stoß *m*, Schub *m*; *v* stoßen, schieben; (press) drücken; (put forward) fördern; **–y**, *adj* (allzu) ehrgeizig

**puss(y), puss** (-i), *n* Miezekatze *f*

**put, putt**, *v* (lay) legen; (stand) stellen; (set) setzen; **– across**, erklären; **– away**, wegräumen; **– down**, (animal) einschläfern; (rebellion) unterdrücken; **– off**, (delay) aufschieben; **– sb off sth**, (discourage) jdn von etw abbringen; **– on**, (clothes) anziehen; (event) veranstalten; (light etc.) anschalten; **– out**, (light etc.) ausschalten; (circulate) verbreiten; **– up**, (lodge) unterbringen; **– up with**, sich gefallen lassen

**putrefy, pjuh**-tri-fei, *v* verfaulen

**putrid, pjuh**-tridd, *adj* faul

**putt, patt**, *n* Putt *m*; *v* putten; **–ing**, *n* Putten *nt*

**putty, patt**-i, *n* Kitt *m*

**puzzle, pas**-'l, *n* Rätsel *nt*; Puzzle(spiel) *nt*; *v*

verwirren; **– over**, *v* herumrätseln an; **crossword –**, *n* Kreuzworträtsel *nt*

**pyjamas, pi**-dschah-mes, *npl* Schlafanzug *m*, Pyjama *m*

**pylon, pei**-len, *n* Pylon *m*, Mast *m*

**pyramid, pi**-re-midd, *n* Pyramide *f*

**Pyrenees, pi**-re-nies, *npl* Pyrenäen *pl*

**python, pei**-then, *n* Python *m*, Riesenschlange *f*

**quack,** ku'äck, *n* (sound) Quaken *nt*; (*pej* doctor) Quacksalber *m*; *v* quaken

**quadrangle, ku'odd**-räng-g'l, *n* (courtyard) Hof *m*; (shape) Viereck *nt*

**quadruple, ku'odd**-ru-p'l, *adj* vierfach

**quadruplets, ku'odd**-**ruh**-plet, *npl*, Vierlinge *pl*

**quagmire, ku'ägg**-meir, *n* Sumpf *m*

**quail,** ku'ehl, *n* Wachtel *f*; *v* verzagen

**quaint,** ku'ehnt, *adj* drollig, kurios

**quake, ku'ehk,** *v* beben; (earth)–, *n* Erdbeben *nt*

**qualification,** ku'oll-i-fi-**keh**-sch'n, *n*

(achievement) Qualifikation *f*; (limitation) Einschränkung *f*

**qualified, k'uoll**-i-feid, *adj* qualifiziert; (limited) eingeschränkt

**qualify, ku'oll**-i-fei, *v* sich qualifizieren; (entitle) berechtigen; (limit) einschränken

**quality, ku'oll**-i-ti, *n* Qualität *f*; (characteristic) Eigenschaft *f*

**qualms,** ku'ahms, *npl* Bedenken *pl*

**quandary, ku'onn**-de-ri, *n* Dilemma *nt*

**quantity, ku'onn**-ti-ti, *n* Menge *f*

**quarantine, ku'o**-ren-tien, *n* Quarantäne *f*

**quarrel, ku'o**-rel, *n* Streit *m*; *v* sich streiten; **–some,** *adj* streitsüchtig

**quarry, ku'o**-ri, *n* (pit) Steinbruch *m*; (prey) Beute *f*

**quart,** ku'ort, *n* Quart *nt*

**quarter, ku'or**-ter, *n* Viertel *nt*; (period) Vierteljahr *nt*; *v* vierteln; (*mil* lodge) einquartieren; **–ly,** *adj & adv* vierteljährlich; **–final,** *n* Viertelfinale *nt*; **–master,** *n* Quartiermeister *m*; **–s,** *npl* Quartier *nt*

**quartet, ku'or**-tett, *n* Quartett *nt*

**quartz,** ku'orts, *n* Quarz *m*

**quash,** ku'osch, *v law* aufheben

**quaver, ku'eh**-wer, *n mus* Achtelnote *f*; *v* zittern

**quay,** kie, *n* Kai *m*, Ufermauer *f*

**queasy, ku'ie**-si, *adj* übel

**queen,** ku'ien, *n* Königin *f*

**queer,** ku'ier, *adj* sonderbar; (homosexual) schwul; *n* (homosexual man) Schwuler *m*; (lesbian) Lesbe *f*

**quell,** ku'ell, *v* (rebellion) unterdrücken; (fears) stillen

**quench,** ku'entsch, *v* löschen

**querulous, ku'e**-ru-less, *adj* gereizt

**query,** ku'ier-ri, n Frage f; v in Frage stellen

**quest,** ku'est, n Suche f

**question,** ku'ess-tschen, n Frage f; v (doubt) bezweifeln; (enquire) fragen; (interrogate) verhören; –**able,** adj fraglich; – **mark,** n Fragezeichen nt; –**naire,** n Fragebogen m; **out of the –,** ausgeschlossen

**queue,** kjuh, n Schlange f; v anstehen, Schlange stehen

**quibble,** ku'ibb-'l, v streiten

**quick,** ku'ick, adj schnell; (wit) lebhaft; **cut to the –,** v tief treffen; –**en,** v beschleunigen; –**ly,** adv schnell; –**sand,** n Treibsand m; –**silver,** n Quecksilber nt; –-**witted,** adj schlagfertig

**quiet,** ku'ei-et, adj (peaceful) ruhig, still; (not loud) leise; n Ruhe f, Stille f; –**en,** v beruhigen; –**ly,** adj leise, ruhig

**quilt,** ku'ilt, n Steppdecke f; –**ing,** n Steppen nt; (material) gesteppter Stoff m

**quince,** ku'inss, n Quitte f

**quinine,** ku'i-nien, n Chinin nt

**quintuplets,** ku'inn-**tjuh**-plet, npl Fünflinge pl

**quit,** ku'itt, v (leave) verlassen; (resign) kündigen; (give up) aufgeben; (stop) aufhören

**quite,** ku'eit, adv (totally) ganz, völlig; (fairly) ziemlich; –! genau!

**quits,** ku'itts, adj quitt

**quiver,** ku'iw-er, n (sheath) Köcher m; v beben, zittern

**quiz,** ku'is, n Quiz nt; v befragen; –**zical,** adj fragend; (mocking) spöttisch

**quota,** ku'oh-te, n Quote f

**quotation,** ku'oh-**teh**-sch'n, n (text) Zitat nt; (price) Kostenvoranschlag m; – **marks,** npl Anführungszeichen pl

**quote,** ku'oht, n Kostenvoranschlag m; v (give price) (den Preis) angeben; (cite) zitieren

**rabbi, räbb**-ei, *n* Rabbiner *m*

**rabbit, räbb**-it, *n* Kaninchen *nt*

**rabble, räbb**-'l, *n* Gesindel *nt*, Pöbel *m*

**rabid, reh**-bidd, *adj* tollwütig; *fig* rasend, wütend

**rabies, reh**-bies, *n* Tollwut *f*

**race, rehss,** *n* (breed) Rasse *f*; (contest) Wettrennen *nt*; (motor) Rennen *nt*; *v* rennen; **–course,** *n* Rennstrecke *f*; **–horse,** *n* Rennpferd *nt*; **–s,** *npl* Pferderennen *nt*; **–track,** *n* Rennstrecke *f*

**racial, reh**-sch'l, *adj* rassisch

**racism, reh**-ssism, *n* Rassismus *m*

**racist, reh**-ssist, *adj* rassistisch; *n* Rassist *m*

**rack, räck,** *n* Gestell *nt*; (for luggage) Ablage *f*; (on vehicle) Gepäckträger *m*; *v* **– one's brains,** sich den Kopf zerbrechen

**racket, räck**-itt, *n* (noise) Lärm *m*; (swindle) Schwindel *m*; (tennis) (Tennis)schläger *m*

**racquet, räck**-itt, *n* (Tennis)schläger *m*

**radar, reh**-dar, *n* Radar *m/nt*

**radial, reh**-di-el, *adj* radial

**radiant, reh**-di-ent, *adj* strahlend

**radiate, reh**-di-eht, *v* ausstrahlen; **– from,** (of roads) strahlenförmig ausgehen von

**radiation, reh**-di-eh-sch'n, *n* Strahlung *f*

**radiator, reh**-di-eh-ter, *n* Heizkörper *m*; (in car) Kühler *m*

**radical, rädd**-i-k'l, *adj* radikal; *n* Radikale(r)

*m & f*

**radio, reh**-di-oh, *n* Radio *nt*; **–active,** *adj* radioaktiv; **– station,** *n* Rundfunkstation *f*

**radiotherapy, reh**-di-oh-**the**-re-pi, *n* Strahlentherapie *f*

**radish, rädd**-isch, *n* Radieschen *nt*; (mooli) Rettich *m*

**radius, reh**-di-ess, *n* Radius *m*; (area around) Umkreis *m*

**raffle, räff**-'l, *n* Verlosung *f*; *v* verlosen

**raft, rahft,** *n* Floß *nt*

**rafter, rahf**-ter, *n* Sparren *m*

**rag, rägg,** *n* Lumpen *m*; (fam newspaper) Käseblatt *nt*

**rage, rehdsch,** *n* Wut *f*; *v* wüten, rasen; **all the –,** der letzte Schrei

**ragged, rägg**-idd, *adj* ausgefranst, zerlumpt

**raid, rehd,** *n* Überfall *m*; *mil* Angriff *m*; (police) Razzia *f*; *v* überfallen

**rail, rehl,** *n* Eisenbahn-; *n* (railway) Schiene *f*; (stairs) Geländer *nt*; **–way,** *n* Eisenbahn *f*; **–way station,** *n* Bahnhof *m*; **by –,** mit dem Zug

**rain, rehn,** *n* Regen *m*; *v* regnen, **–bow,** *n* Regenbogen *m*; **–coat,** *n* Regenmantel *m*; **–fall,** *n* Niederschlag *m*; **– forest,** *n* Regenwald *m*; **–y,** *adj* regnerisch

**raise, rehs,** *v* (hoch)heben;

(increase) erhöhen;
(family) großziehen;
(money) aufbringen;
(voice) erheben

**raisin, reh**-sinn, n Rosine f

**rake, rehk**, n Rechen m;
(person) Draufgänger m; v
rechen; (fire) schüren;
(with gunfire) bestreichen

**rally, räll**-i, n (political)
Versammlung f; (car)
Rallye f; v (collect)
sammeln; – **round**, sich
zusammentun

**ram, rämm**, n (animal)
Widder m; (weapon)
Rammklotz m; v rammen

**ramble, rämm**-b'l, n
Wanderung f; v wandern;
(of mind) irre sein; (talk)
zusammenhanglos
quasseln

**ramp, rämp**, n Rampe f

**rampage, rämm**-pedsch, n
**go on the – the –**, v randalieren

**rampant, rämm**-pent, adj
zügellos

**rampart, rämm**-pahrt, n
(Festungs)wall m

**rancid, ränn**-ssidd, adj
ranzig

**random, ränn**-dem, adj
willkürlich; **at –**, adv
willkürlich, aufs
Geratewohl

**randy, ränn**-di, adj fam geil

**range, rehndsch**, n (choice)
Auswahl f, Sortiment nt;
(of mountains) Kette f;
(extent) Umfang m; (of
weapon) Schußweite f;

(cooker) Herd m; v
(roam) umherziehen;
(extend) reichen; (line
up) ordnen; **rifle –**, n
Schießplatz m

**ranger, rehndsch**-er, n
Aufseher m; (forest)
Förster m

**rank, ränk**, adj (offensive)
stark, stinkend; (utter)
total; n (grade) Rang m;
(row) Reihe f; v
klassifizieren; **– among**, v
gehören zu; **– and file**, n
Basis f; **taxi –**, n
n Taxistand m

**rankle, räng**-k'l, v fam
wurmen

**ransack, ränn**-ssäck, v
durchstöbern,
durchwühlen

**ransom, ränn**-ssem, n
Lösegeld nt; v auslösen

**rant, ränt**, v wettern

**rap, räpp**, n (blow) Schlag
m; mus Rap m; v (hit)
schlagen; (knock) klopfen

**rape, rehp**, n
Vergewaltigung f; (plant)
Raps m; v vergewaltigen

**rapid, räpp**-idd, adj rasch,
schnell; **–ity**, n
Schnelligkeit f; **–s**, npl
Stromschnelle f

**rapist, reh**-pist, n
Vergewaltiger m

**rapture, räpp**-tscher, n
Entzücken nt

**rare, rähr**, adj rar, selten;
(lightly cooked) englisch
(gebraten); **–ly**, adv selten

**rarity, rähr**-ri-ti, n
Seltenheit f

**rascal, rahss**-k'l, n Schelm
m, Spitzbube m

**rash, räsch**, adj unbesonnen;
n Hautausschlag m

**rasher, räsch**-er, n
Speckscheibe f

**rasp, rahsp**, n Raspel f; v
raspeln; (voice) rasseln

**raspberry, rahs**-be-ri, n
Himbeere f

**rat, rätt**, n Ratte f; (pej
person) Ratte f

**rate, reht**, n (speed) Tempo
nt; fin Kurs m; (charge)
Preis m; (proportion)
Verhältnis nt; (tax)
Grundsteuer f; v schätzen

**rather, rah**-dher, adv (fairly)
ziemlich; (preferably)
lieber

**ratify, rätt**-i-fei, v
bestätigen, ratifizieren

**ratio, reh**-schi-oh, n
Verhältnis nt

**ration, räsch**-en, n Ration f;
v rationieren

**rational, räsch**-en-'l, adj
vernünftig, rational; **–ize**,
v rationalisieren

**rattle, rätt**-'l, n (noise)
Gerassel nt; (toy) Rassel f;
v rasseln, klappern;
**–snake**, n
Klapperschlange f

**raucous, ro'a**-kess, adj wild

**ravage, räw**-idsch, v
verwüsten

**rave, rehw**, v (rage) rasen; **–
about**, (enthuse)

schwärmen über

**raven,** reh-wen, *n* Rabe *m*

**ravenous,** räw-en-ess, *adj* heißhungrig

**ravine,** re-wien, *n* Schlucht *f*

**raving,** reh-wing, *adj* (furious) rasend; (mad) wahnsinnig

**ravishing,** räw-isch-ing, *adj* entzückend, hinreißend

**raw,** ro'a, *adj* roh; (wound) wund; **a – deal,** *n* (*fam* unfair treatment) ungerechte Behandlung *f*; (bad luck) Pech *nt*

**ray,** reh, *n* Strahl *m*

**raze,** rehs, *v* vernichten

**razor,** reh-ser, *n* Rasierapparat *m*; **– blade,** *n* Rasierklinge *f*

**reach,** rietsch, *n* (stretch) Reichweite *f*; (length) Strecke *f*; *v* langen nach; (arrive at) erreichen; (pass) reichen; **(with)in –,** erreichbar

**react,** ri-äkt, *v* reagieren; **–ion,** *n* Reaktion *f*; **(nuclear) –or,** *n* (Kern)reaktor *m*

**read,** ried, *v* lesen; **–er,** *n* (person) Leser *m*; (book) Schmöker *m*

**readily,** redd-i-li, *adv* (willingly) bereitwillig; (easily) leicht

**reading,** rie-ding, *n* Lesen *nt*

**read out,** ried aut, *v* vorlesen

**ready,** redd-i, *adj* bereit,

fertig; **–made,** *adj* Fertig-; (clothes) Konfektions-; **– meal,** *n* Fertigmahlzeit *f*

**real,** ri-el, *adj* (actual) wirklich; (genuine) echt; **– estate,** *n* Immobilien *pl*; **–istic,** *adj* realistisch

**reality,** ri-äll-i-ti, *n* Wirklichkeit *f*

**realize,** ri-e-leis, *v* (understand) begreifen; (plan) verwirklichen; (income) (er)bringen

**really,** ri-e-li, *adv* wirklich, tatsächlich

**realm,** relm, *n* Reich *nt*

**reap,** riep, *v* ernten; **the grim –er,** *n* der Schnitter (Tod) *m*

**rear,** rier, *adj* hintere(r & s), Hinter-; *n* (back) Rückseite *f*; *mil* Nachhut *f*; *v* (child) großziehen; (prance) sich bäumen; **bring up the –,** *v* die Nachhut bilden; **in the –,** *adv* hinten

**rearmament,** rie-ahr-me-ment, *n* Wiederaufrüstung *f*

**reason,** rie-sen, *n* (cause, motive) Grund *m*; (intellect) Verstand *m*; (sense) Vernunft *f*; *v* diskutieren; **–able,** *adj* vernünftig; (price) mäßig; **–ably,** *adj* (sensibly) vernünftig; (fairly) ziemlich; **–ing,** *n* Argumentation *f*

**reassurance,** rie-e-schor-

renss, *n* Beruhigung *f*

**reassure,** rie-e-schor, *v* beruhigen

**rebate,** rie-beht, *n* Rabatt *m*, Nachlaß *m*

**rebel,** rebb-'l, *n* Rebell *m*

**rebel,** ri-bell, *v* rebellieren, sich auflehnen; **–lion,** *n* Aufstand *m*; **–lious,** *adj* rebellisch

**rebirth,** rie-börth, *n* Wiedergeburt *f*

**rebound,** rie-baund, *n* Rückprall *m*

**rebound,** ri-baund, *v* zurückprallen

**rebuff,** ri-baff, *n* Abweisung *f*; *v* abweisen

**rebuke,** ri-bjuhk, *n* Rüge *f*, Tadel *m*; *v* rügen, tadeln

**recalcitrant,** ri-käll-ssi-trent, *adj* aufsässig

**recall,** rie-ko'al, *n* (summons) Rückruf *m*; (memory) Erinnerungsvermögen *nt*

**recall,** ri-ko'al, *v* (call back) zurückrufen; (remember) sich erinnern an

**recap,** rie-käpp, = recapitulate

**recapitulate,** rie-ke-pitt-ju-leht, *v* rekapitulieren, (kurz) zusammenfassen

**recede,** ri-ssied, *v* zurückweichen

**receipt,** ri-ssiet, *n comm* Quittung *f*; (receiving) Empfang *m*; **–s,** *npl comm* Einnahmen *pl*

**receive,** ri-ssiew, *v* erhalten;

(visitor) empfangen; **–r**, *n* (telephone) Hörer *m*; (official) Konkursverwalter *m*; (of stolen goods) Hehler *m*

**recent**, rie-ssent, *adj* (period) letzte(r/s); (event) neueste(r/s); (invention etc.) neu; *adv* kürzlich, neulich

**receptacle**, ri-ssepp-te-k'l, *n* Behälter *m*

**reception**, ri-ssepp-sch'n, *n* Empfang *m*; (hotel) Rezeption *f*; **–ist**, *n* Empfangschef *m*, Empfangsdame *f*; (doctor's) Sprechstundenhilfe *f*

**receptive**, ri-ssepp-tiw, *adj* empfänglich

**recess**, ri-ssess, *n* (niche) Nische *f*; *parl* Ferien *pl*

**recharge**, rie-tschahrdsch, *v* (wieder)aufladen

**recipe**, ress-i-pi, *n* Rezept *nt*

**reciprocal**, ri-ssipp-re-kel, *adj* gegenseitig

**recital**, ri-ssei-t'l, *n mus* Konzert *nt*

**recite**, ri-sseit, *v* rezitieren; (list) aufzählen

**reckless**, reck-liss, *adj* (careless) leichtsinnig; (driving) fahrlässig

**reckon**, reck-'n, *v* (calculate) rechnen; (think) meinen

**reclaim**, ri-klehm, *v* (expenses) zurückfordern; (land) urbar machen

**recline**, ri-klein, *v* sich lehnen, zurücklehnen

**recluse**, ri-kluhss, *n* Einsiedler *m*

**recognition**, reck-eg-nisch-'n, *n* Wiedererkennen *nt*; (appreciation) Anerkennung *f*

**recognize**, reck-eg-neis, *v* erkennen; (appreciate) anerkennen

**recoil**, ri-keul, *v* zurückprallen; *fig* zurückschrecken

**recollect**, reck-e-lekt, *v* sich erinnern (an); **–ion**, *n* Erinnerung *f*

**recommend**, reck-e-mend, *v* empfehlen; **–ation**, *n* Empfehlung *f*

**recompense**, reck-emm-penss, *n* Entschädigung *f*; (reward) Belohnung *f*; *v* entschädigen; (reward) belohnen

**reconcile**, reck-en-sseil, *v* (people) versöhnen; (facts) in Einklang bringen; (dispute) beilegen

**reconditioned**, rie-ken-disch-'nd, *adj* überholt

**reconnoitre**, reck-e-neu-ter, *v* auskundschaften

**reconsider**, rie-ken-ssidd-er, *v* (noch einmal) überdenken

**reconstruct**, rie-ken-strakt, *v* wiederaufbauen; **–ion**, *n* Wiederaufbau *m*

**record**, reck-ord, *n* (sport)

Rekord *m*; *mus* Schallplatte *f*; (account) Protokoll *nt*, Aufzeichnung *f*; (achievement) Leistung *f*

**record**, ri-kord, *v mus* aufnehmen; (document) festhalten

**recording**, ri-kor-ding, *n* Aufnahme *f*

**record player**, reck-ord pleh-er, *n* Plattenspieler *m*

**recoup**, ri-kuhp, *v* zurückgewinnen

**recourse**, ri-korss, *n* Zuflucht *f*

**recover**, ri-kaw-er, *v* (retrieve) zurückgewinnen; (health) sich erholen

**re-cover**, ri-kaw-er, *v neu* überziehen

**recovery**, ri-kaw-e-ri, *n* (of health) Erholung *f*; (of belongings) Wiederfinden *nt*

**recreate**, rie-krie-eht, *v neu* bilden

**recreation**, reck-ri-eh-sch'n, *n* Erholung *f*; **–al**, *adj* Erholungs-; **– ground**, *n* Freizeitgelände *nt*; (playground) Spielplatz *m*

**recrimination**, ri-krimm-i-neh-sch'n, *n* Beschuldigung *f*

**recruit**, ri-kruht, *n* Rekrut *m*; *v* werben

**rectangle**, reck-täng-g'l, *n* Rechteck *nt*

**rectangular**, reck-täng-gju-ler, *adj* rechteckig

**rectify**, reck-ti-fei, *v* berichtigen

**rector**, reck-ter, *n* Pfarrer *m*; **–y**, Pfarrhaus *nt*

**recuperate**, ri-kuh-pe-reht, *v* sich erholen

**recur**, ri-kör, *v* wiedervorkommen; **–rence**, *n* Wiederholung *f*; **–rent**, *adj* wiederkehrend

**recycle**, rie-ssei-k'l, *v* recyceln, wiederverwerten; **–d**, *adj* recycelt; (paper) Alt-

**recycling**, rie-**sseik**-ling, *n* Recycling *nt*, Wiederverwertung *f*

**red**, redd, *adj* rot; *n* Rot *nt*; (communist) Rote(r) *m* & *f*; **R– Cross**, *n* Rotes Kreuz *nt*; **–den**, *v* rot werden; (blush) erröten; **–dish**, *adj* rötlich

**redeem**, ri-diem, *v* (pledge) einlösen; (soul) erlösen; **–ing**, *adj* ausgleichend

**red-handed**, redd **hänn**-didd, *adv* auf frischer Tat

**red herring**, redd **he**-ring, *n* falsche Spur *f*

**red-hot**, redd hott, *adj* rotglühend

**red-light district**, *n* Amüsierviertel *nt*

**redo**, rie-duh, *v* neu machen

**redouble**, rie-**dabb**-'l, *v* verdoppeln

**redress**, ri-dress, *n* Abhilfe *f*; *v* abhelfen

**red tape**, red tehp, *n*

(unnötige) Bürokratie *f*

**reduce**, ri-djuhss, *v* vermindern; (price) herabsetzen; (size) verkleinern

**reduction**, ri-**dack**-sch'n, *n* Verminderung *f*; (of price) Ermäßigung *f*

**redundant**, ri-**dann**-dent, *adj* überflüssig; (worker) arbeitslos

**reed**, ried, *n* (Schilf)rohr *nt*

**reef**, rief, *n* Riff *nt*; *naut* Reff *nt*; **–**, *v* reffen

**reek**, riek, *n* Gestank *m*; **(of)**, *v* stinken (nach)

**reel**, riel, *n* Rolle *f*, Haspel *m*; *v* (wind) aufspulen; (stagger) taumeln

**refer to**, ri-**för** tu, *v* (mention) sich beziehen auf; (send to) verweisen an; (consult) nachschlagen

**referee**, reff-e-**rie**, *n* (sport) Schiedsrichter *m*; (guarantor) Referenz *f*; *v* (sport) schiedsrichtern; (mediate) schlichten

**reference**, reff-e-renss, *n* (mention) Erwähnung *f*; (allusion) Anspielung *f*; (testimonial) Zeugnis *nt*, Referenz *f*; (identification) Zeichen *nt*; **– book**, *n* Nachschlagewerk *nt*; **terms of –**, Aufgabenbereich *m*; **with – to**, mit Bezug auf

**referendum**, reff-e-**renn**-

dem, *n* Volksabstimmung *f*

**refill**, rie-fill, *n* Nachfüll-; (for pencil, ballpoint) Ersatzmine *f*

**refill**, rie-fill, *v* nachfüllen

**refine**, ri-fein, *v* raffinieren; *fig* verfeinern; **–d**, *adj* fein, gebildet; **–ment**, *n* (person) Kultiviertheit *f*; (improvement) Verbesserung *f*

**refit**, ri-fitt, *v* überholen

**reflect**, ri-flekt, *v* (light) zurückstrahlen; *fig* widerspiegeln; **– (on)**, nachdenken (über); **–ion**, *n* (image) Spiegelbild *nt*; (thought) Überlegung *f*; (criticism) Kritik *f*; **–ive**, *adj* reflektierend; (thoughtful) nachdenklich

**reflex**, rie-flecks, *adj* Reflex-; *n* Reflex *m*; **–ive**, *adj* *gram* reflexiv

**reform**, ri-form, *n* Reform *f*; *v* (system etc.) reformieren; (person) (sich) bessern; **R–ation**, *relig* Reformation *f*

**refrain**, ri-frehn, *n* Refrain *m*; **– (from)**, *v* unterlassen

**refresh**, ri-fresch, *v* erfrischen; **–er course**, *n* Auffrischungskurs *m*; **–ing**, *adj* erfrischend; **–ment**, *n* Erfrischung *f*

**refrigerator**, ri-fridsch-e-reh-ter, *n* Kühlschrank *m*

**refuel**, rie-fju-el, *v* tanken

**refuge**, reff-juhdsch, *n*

Zufluchtsort m; **take –
(in),** v sich flüchten (in)

**refugee,** reff-juh-**dschie,** n
Flüchtling m

**refund, rie-**fand, n
Rückzahlung f

**refund,** ri-**fandd,** v
zurückzahlen

**refusal,** ri-**fjuh-**sel, n
Verweigerung f

**refuse,** ri-**fjuhs,** v
verweigern

**refuse, reff-**juhss, n Abfall
m, Müll m; **– disposal,** n
Müllbeseitigung f; **–
dump,** n Mülldeponie f

**regain,** ri-**gehn,** v
zurückgewinnen;
zurückbekommen; **–
consciousness,** v wieder
zu sich kommen

**regal, rie-**gel, adj königlich

**regale,** ri-**gehl,** v festlich
bewirten; (entertain)
unterhalten

**regard,** ri-**gahrd,** n (esteem)
Achtung f; (look) Blick
m; v betrachten; **–ing,** prep
in bezug auf; **–less,** adv
trotzdem; **–less of,** prep
ungeachtet, ohne
Rücksicht auf; **kind –s,**
herzliche Grüße

**regenerate,** ri-**dschen-e-**
reht, v neu beleben

**regent, rie-**dschent, n
Regent m

**régime, reh-**dschiem, n
Regime nt

**regiment, redsch-**i-ment, n
Regiment nt

**regiment, redsch-**i-ment, v
reglementieren

**region, rie-**dschen, n
Gegend f, Region f; **–al,**
adj regional; **in the – of,**
(so) ungefähr

**register, redsch-**iss-ter, n
Verzeichnis nt; Register nt;
v (course) einschreiben;
(record) eintragen; (sign
up) sich melden; (show)
zeigen; **–ed,** adj (letter)
eingeschrieben;
(trademark) eingetragen

**registrar, redsch-**iss-trar, n
Standesbeamter m;
Standesbeamtin f

**registration, redsch-**iss-**treh-**
sch'n, n Eintragung f;
Anmeldung f; **– number,**
n (on car)
amtliches/polizeiliches
Kennzeichen nt

**registry office, redsch-**iss-tri
**off-**iss, n Standesamt m

**regret,** ri-**grett,** n Bedauern
nt; v bedauern; **–table,** adj
bedauerlich

**regular, regg-**ju-ler, adj
regelmäßig; n
Stammkunde m

**regulate, regg-**ju-leht, v
regulieren

**regulation, regg-**ju-**leh-**
sch'n, n (rule) Vorschrift f;
(control) Regelung f

**rehabilitation, rie-**he-bill-i-
**teh-**sch'n, n
Rehabilitierung f

**rehearsal,** ri-**hör-**ss'l, n
Probe f

**rehearse,** ri-**hörss,** v proben

**reign, rehn,** n Herrschaft f; v
regieren

**reimburse,** rie-im-**börss,** v
(money) zurückzahlen;
(person) entschädigen

**rein, rehn,** n Zügel m; v
zügeln

**reincarnation, rie-inn-kahr-**
**neh-**sch'n, n Wiedergeburt
f

**reindeer, rehn-**dier, n
Ren(tier) nt

**reinforce, rie-inn-forss,** v
verstärken; **–ment,** n
Verstärkung f; **–ments,** npl
(mil etc.) Verstärkung f

**reinstate, rie-inn-steht,** v
wieder einsetzen

**reiterate, rie-itt-e-**reht, v
betonen

**reject, rie-**dschekt, n
Ausschuß m

**reject,** ri-**dschekt,** v
verwerfen; **–ion,** n
Ablehnung f

**rejoice,** ri-**dscheuss,** v sich
freuen

**rejuvenate,** ri-**dschu-**wen-
eht, v verjüngen

**relapse,** ri-**läpss,** n Rückfall
m; v (illness) einen
Rückfall bekommen;
(crime) rückfällig werden

**relate,** ri-**leht,** v (tell)
erzählen; (make
connection) einen
Zusammenhang
herstellen; **–d,** adj
verwandt

**relation,** ri-**leh-**sch'n, n

(connection) Beziehung f;
(relative) Verwandte(r) m
& f; **–ship,** n (connection)
Zusammenhang f; (family)
Verwandtschaft f;
(couple) Beziehung f

**relative, rell-***e*-tiw, *adj*
relativ; n Verwandte(r) m
& f; **–ly,** *adv*
verhältnismäßig

**relax,** ri-**läcks,** v (sich)
entspannen; **–ation,** n
Erholung f; **–ing,** *adj*
erholsam

**relay, rie-**leh, n (sport)
Staffel f; v (signal)
übertragen; (message)
ausrichten

**release,** ri-**liess,** n
Entlassung f; v (prisoner)
entlassen; (news)
bekanntgeben

**relent,** ri-**lent,** v nachgeben;
**–less(ly),** *adj & adv*
unbarmherzig

**relevant, rel-**i-went, *adj*
relevant

**reliable,** ri-**lei**-e-b'l, *adj*
zuverlässig

**reliance,** ri-**lei-**enss, n Verlaß
m, Vertrauen nt

**relic, rell-**ick, n
Überbleibsel nt; *relig*
Reliquie f

**relief,** ri-**lief,** n
Erleichterung f; (of
pain) Linderung f; *mil*
Ablösung f

**relieve,** ri-**liew,** v
erleichtern; (pain)
lindern; *mil* ablösen; **– sb**

**of sth,** jdm etw
abnehmen

**religion,** ri-**lidsch-**en, n
Religion f

**religious,** ri-**lidsch-**ess, *adj*
fromm, religiös

**relinquish,** ri-**link-**u'isch, v
aufgeben

**relish, rell-**isch, n (spice)
Relish nt; (enjoyment)
Geschmack; v genießen

**relocate,** rie-loh-**keht,** v
umziehen; (business)
verlegen

**reluctance,** ri-**lack-**tenss, n
Widerwillen m

**reluctant,** ri-**lack-**tent, *adj*
unwillig, widerwillig

**rely on,** ri-**lei** on, v sich
verlassen auf

**remain,** ri-**mehn,** v (stay)
bleiben; (be left over)
übrigbleiben; **–der,** n Rest
m; **–s,** *npl* (human)
Überreste *pl*

**remand,** ri-**mahnd,** n
Untersuchungshaft; v – **in
custody,** in
Untersuchungshaft
behalten

**remark,** ri-**mahrk,** n
Bemerkung f; v bemerken;
**–able,** *adj* bemerkenswert

**remedial,** ri-**mie-**di-el, *adj*
med Heil-; (measure)
Hilfs-; (teaching)
Nachhilfe-

**remedy, rem-**i-di, n Mittel
nt; v (ver)bessern,
abhelfen

**remember,** ri-**memm-**ber, v

sich erinnern (an)

**remembrance,** ri-**memm-**
brenss, n Erinnerung f

**remind (of),** ri-**meind,** v
erinnern (an)

**reminiscence,** remm-i-**niss-**
enss, n Erinnerung f

**reminiscent,** remm-i-**niss-**
ent, *adj* be – **of,** v erinnern
an

**remiss,** ri-**miss,** *adj*
nachlässig; **–ion,** n med
Remission f

**remit,** ri-**mitt,** v (money)
überweisen; (fine, etc.)
erlassen; **–tance,** n (of
money) Überweisung f

**remnant, remm-**nent, n
Rest m

**remorse,** ri-**morss,** n Reue f;
**–less(ly),** *adj & adv*
unerbittlich

**remote,** ri-**moht,** *adj*
(distant) entfernt;
(isolated) abgelegen; **–
control,** n Fernsteuerung f;
**–controlled,** *adj*
ferngesteuert

**removal,** ri-**muh**-wel, n
(taking away) Beseitigung
f; (house move) Umzug m;
**– van,** n Möbelwagen m

**remove,** ri-**muhw,** v (take
away) beseitigen;
(dismiss) entlassen

**remuneration,** ri-mjuh-ne-
**reh**-sch'n, n Entlohnung f

**rend,** rend, v (zer)reißen

**render, renn-**der, v (make)
machen; (assistance)
leisten; (interpret)

wiedergeben; **–ing,** n (*mus* etc.) Wiedergabe f, Interpretation f

**rendezvous,** ronn-deh-vuh, n Rendezvous nt; v sich treffen

**renew,** ri-njuh, v erneuern; **–al,** n Erneuerung f

**renounce,** ri-naunss, v (abandon) verzichten auf; (give up) aufgeben

**renovate,** renn-e-veht, v renovieren, restaurieren

**renown,** ri-naun, n Ruhm m; **–ed,** adj berühmt

**rent,** rent, n Miete f; v mieten; (let out) vermieten; **–al,** n Miete f

**renunciation,** ri-nun-ssi-eh-sch'n, n Verzicht m

**reorganize,** rie-or-ge-neis, v umorganisieren

**rep,** repp, n abbr comm **representative**

**repair,** ri-pähr, n (mend) Reparatur f; (state) Zustand m; v reparieren

**repartee,** repp-ahr-tie, n (witty remark) schlagfertige Antwort; (quality) Schlagfertigkeit f

**repay,** ri-pei, v zurückzahlen; **–ment,** n Zurückzahlung f

**repeal,** ri-piel, n Aufhebung f; v aufheben

**repeat,** ri-piet, n Wiederholung f; v wiederholen

**repel,** ri-pell, v zurückschlagen; fig abstoßen; **–lent,** adj

abstoßend; **insect –ent,** n Insektenschutzmittel nt

**repent (of),** ri-pent (ew), v bereuen

**repercussions,** rie-per-kasch-'ns, npl Nachwirkungen pl, Konsequenzen pl

**repetition,** repp-i-tisch-'n, n Wiederholung f

**repetitive,** ri-pett-i-tiw, adj eintönig

**replace,** ri-plehss, v ersetzen; **–ment,** n Ersatz m

**replenish,** ri-plenn-isch, v (wieder) auffüllen

**replica,** repp-lick-e, n Nachbildung f

**reply,** ri-plei, n Antwort f; v antworten

**report,** ri-port, n (account) Bericht m; (school) Zeugnis nt; v (give account) berichten; (notify police) anzeigen; (present o.s.) sich melden; **–er,** n Reporter m

**repose,** ri-pohs, n Ruhe f

**represent,** repp-ri-sent, v darstellen; (act for) vertreten; **–ation,** n Darstellung f; (agency) Vertretung f; **–ative,** adj repräsentativ; n Vertreter m

**repress,** ri-press, n unterdrücken; **–ion,** n Unterdrückung f

**reprieve,** ri-priew, n Begnadigung f; v

begnadigen

**reprimand,** repp-ri-mahnd, n Verweis m; v tadeln

**reprint,** rie-print, n Nachdruck m

**reprint,** rie-print, v nachdrucken

**reprisal,** ri-prei-s'l, n Vergeltungsakt m, Repressalie f

**reproach,** ri-prohtsch, n Vorwurf m; v **– sb with sth,** jdm etw vorwerfen

**reproduce,** rie-pre-djuhss, v reproduzieren

**reproduction,** rie-pre-dack-sch'n, n Reproduktion f

**reptile,** repp-teil, n Reptil nt

**republic,** ri-pabb-lick, n Republik f

**repudiate,** ri-pjuh-di-eht, v zurückweisen

**repugnant,** ri-pagg-nent, adj widerlich

**repulse,** ri-palss, v (enemy) zurückschlagen; (approach) abweisen

**repulsive,** ri-pall-ssiw, adj widerwärtig

**reputable,** repp-juh-te-b'l, adj angesehen

**reputation,** repp-juh-teh-sch'n, n Ruf m

**repute,** ri-pjuht, n Ansehen nt; **–ed(ly),** adj & adv angeblich

**request,** ri-ku'est, n Bitte f; v bitten um

**require,** ri-ku'eir, v (need) benötigen; (demand) verlangen; **–ment,** n

(need) Bedarf *m*;
(demand) Anforderung *f*

**requisite**, reck-u'i-sitt,
*adj* erforderlich; *n*
Erfordernis *nt*

**requisition**, reck-u'i-sisch-
'n, *v* beschlagnahmen

**rescue**, ress-kjuh, *n* Rettung
*f*; *v* retten; **–r**, *n* Retter *m*

**research**, ri-ssörtsch, *n*
Forschung *f*; *v* forschen,
erforschen; **–er**, *n*
Forscher *m*

**resemblance**, ri-semm-
blenss, *n* Ähnlichkeit *f*

**resemble**, ri-semm-b'l, *v*
gleichen, ähnlich sein

**resent**, ri-sent *v*
übelnehmen; **–ful**, *adj*
nachtragend; **–ment**, *n*
Groll *m*

**reservation**, res-*e*-weh-
sch'n, *n* (booking)
Reservierung *f*;
(qualification)
Vorbehalt *m*

**reserve**, ri-sörw, *n* (stock)
Reserve *f*; (reticence)
Zurückhaltung *f*;
(nature/game) Reservat
*nt*; *v* (book) reservieren;
(right) sich vorbehalten;
**–d**, *adj* reserviert

**reservoir**, res-er-wu'ahr, *n*
Reservoir *nt*

**reside**, ri-seid, *v* wohnen

**residence**, res-i-denss, *n*
(home) Wohnung *f*; (stay)
Aufenthalt *m*

**resident**, res-i-dent, *adj*
wohnhaft; *n* (of house)

Bewohner *m*; (in area)
Einwohner *m*

**residential**, res-i-denn-sch'l,
*adj* Wohn-

**resign**, ri-sein, *v*
zurücktreten, kündigen;
**–o.s. (to)**, sich mit etw
abfinden

**resignation**, res-igg-neh-
sch'n, *n* Rücktritt *m*,
Kündigung *f*

**resilient**, ri-sill-jent, *adj*
unverwüstlich

**resin**, ress-inn, *n* Harz *nt*

**resist**, ri-sist, *v* sich wehren
gegen; **–ance**, *n*
Widerstand *m*

**resolute**, res-*e*-luht, *adj*
entschlossen

**resolution**, res-*e*-luh-sch'n,
*n* (decision) Beschluß *m*;
(intention) Vorsatz *m*;
(determination)
Entschlossenheit *f*

**resolve**, ri-solw, *v* (decide)
beschließen; (solve) lösen

**resort**, ri-sort, *n* (place)
Urlaubsort *m*; **– to**, *v*
Zuflucht nehmen zu; **last
–**, *n* letzter Ausweg *m*

**resounding**, ri-saun-ding,
*adj* überwältigend

**resource**, ri-sorss, *n*
Hilfsmittel *nt*; **–s**, *npl*
(natural) Ressourcen *pl*;
(money) Geldmittel *pl*;
**–ful**, *adj* findig

**respect**, ri-spekt, *n* (aspect)
Hinsicht *f*; (esteem)
Respekt *m*; *v* achten;
**–able**, *adj* angesehen; **–ful**,

*adj* respektvoll; **–ing**, *prep*
bezüglich; **–ive**, *adj*
jeweils; **–ively**, *adv*
beziehungsweise; **with –
to**, hinsichtlich

**respite**, ress-peit, *n*
Aufschub *m*; (break)
(Ruhe)pause *f*

**respond (to)**, ri-spond (tu),
*v* (answer) antworten
(auf); (react) reagieren

**response**, riss-ponss, *n*
(answer) Antwort *f*;
(reaction) Reaktion *f*

**responsibility**, riss-ponn-ssi-
bill-i-ti, *n*
Verantwortlichkeit *f*,
Verantwortung *f*

**responsible**, riss-ponn-ssib-
'l, *adj* (answerable)
verantwortlich; (reliable)
verantwortungsvoll

**rest**, rest, *n* (repose) Ruhe *f*;
(remainder) Rest *m*;
(break) Pause *f*; (sleep)
Schlaf *m*; *v* (repose) sich
ausruhen; (take break)
Pause machen; **– on**, *v*
beruhen auf

**restaurant**, ress-te-rong, *n*
Restaurant *nt*; **– car**, *n*
Speisewagen *m*

**restful**, rest-full, *adj* ruhig

**restive**, ress-tiw, *adj* unruhig

**restless**, rest-liss, *adj* ruhelos

**restore**, riss-tor, *v* (give
back) zurückgeben;
(renovate) restaurieren;
(health, order)
wiederherstellen

**restrain**, riss-trehn, *v*

zurückhalten, **–ed**, *adj*
zurückhaltend; **–t**, *n*
(control) Zurückhaltung *f*;
(arrest) Haft *f*

**restrict**, riss-**trikt**, *v*
einschränken; **–ion**, *n*
Einschränkung *f*

**result**, ri-**salt**, *n* Resultat *nt*;
Folge *f*; *v* – **from sth**, aus
etw folgern; – **in**, zur Folge
haben

**resume**, ri-**sjuhm**, *v*
wiederaufnehmen

**resumption**, ri-**samp**-sch'n,
*n* Wiederaufnahme *f*

**resurgence**, re-**ssör**-
dschenss, *n*
Wiederaufleben *nt*

**resurrection**, res-e-**reck**-
sch'n, *n* Auferstehung *f*

**retail**, **rie**-tehl, *adj*
Einzelhandels-; *n*
Einzelhandel *m*; *v* im
Einzelhandel verkaufen;
**–er**, *n* Einzelhändler *m*

**retain**, ri-**tehn**, *v* behalten;
**–er**, *n* (fee) Kaution *f*

**retaliate**, ri-**täll**-i-eht, *v*
vergelten

**retarded**, ri-**tahr**-didd, *adj*
zurückgeblieben

**retch**, retsch, *v* würgen

**reticent**, **rett**-i-ssent, *adj*
zurückhaltend

**retinue**, **rett**-i-njuh, *n*
Gefolge *nt*

**retire**, ri-**teir**, *v* (from work)
in Rente/Pension gehen;
(withdraw) sich
zurückziehen; **–d**, *adj* in
Rente/Pension; **–ment**, *n*

(from work) Ruhestand *m*;
(from world)
Zurückgezogenheit *f*

**retort**, ri-**tort**, *n* Erwiderung
*f*; *v* erwidern

**retract**, ri-**träkt**, *v* (take
back) zurücknehmen;
(pull back) zurückziehen

**retreat**, ri-**triet**, *v*
(withdrawal) Rückzug *m*;
(place) Zufluchtsort *m*; *v*
sich zurückziehen

**retribution**, rett-ribb-**juh**-
sch'n, *n* Vergeltung *f*

**retrieve**, ri-**triew**, *v* (get
back) zurückgewinnen;
(rescue) retten; (of dog)
zurückholen

**return**, ri-**törn**, *adj* Rück-;
(of person) Rückkehr *f*;
(of object) Rückgabe *f*;
(profit) Ertrag *m*; *v* (come
back) zurückkommen; (go
back) zurückgehen; (give
back) zurückgeben; **–s**, *npl
comm* Umsatz *m*; –
**(ticket)**, *n* Rückfahrkarte
*f*; (plane) Rückflugkarte *f*

**reunion**, rie-**juh**-ni-en, *n*
(school) Treffen *nt*;
(politics)
Wiedervereinigung *f*

**reunite**, rie-ju-**neit**, *v*
wiedervereinigen

**rev**, rew, *n* Umdrehungen *pl*;
*v* (den Motor) auf Touren
bringen

**reveal**, ri-**wiel**, *v* offenbaren,
enthüllen; **–ing**, *adj*
aufschlußreich

**revel (in)**, rew-'l (inn), *v*

schwelgen in

**revelation**, rew-e-**leh**-sch'n,
*n* Offenbarung *f*

**revenge**, ri-**wendsch**, *n*
Rache *f*; *v* – **o.s. (on)**,
sich rächen (an)

**revenue**, **rew**-e-njuh, *n*
Einkünfte *pl* ; Umsatz *m*

**reverence**, **rew**-e-renss, *n*
Ehrfurcht *f*

**Reverend**, **rew**-e-rend, *adj*
ehrwürdig; *n* Pfarrer *m*

**reverse**, ri-**wörss**, *adj*
umgekehrt; *n* (back)
Rückseite *f*; (contrary)
Gegenteil *nt*; (gear)
Rückwärtsgang *m*; *v* (turn
over) umdrehen; (go
backwards) rückwärts
fahren

**revert to**, ri-**wört** (tu), *v*
zurückkommen auf

**review**, ri-**wjuh**, *n*
(checking) Überprüfung *f*;
(events) Rückschau *f*;
(critique) Rezension *f*;
*theatre* Revue *f*; *v* (check)
überprüfen; (critique)
rezensieren; *mil* mustern;
(reconsider) revidieren;
**–er**, *n* Rezensent *m*

**revile**, ri-**weil**, *v* schmähen,
lästern

**revise**, ri-**weis**, *v* revidieren

**revision**, ri-**wisch**-'n, *n*
(reconsideration)
Revision *f*; (for exam)
Wiederholung *f*, Lernen *nt*

**revitalize**, ri-**wei**-te-leis, *v*
neu beleben

**revival**, ri-**wei**-wel, *n*

Wiederbelebung f

**revive**, ri-**weiw**, v (play, custom) wiederaufnehmen; (recover) wieder aufleben

**revoke**, ri-**wohk**, v widerrufen

**revolt**, ri-**wohlt**, n Aufstand m; v (rebel) rebellieren; (disgust) anekeln; –**ing**, adj ekelhaft

**revolution**, rew-e-**luh**-sch'n, n (uprising) Revolution f; (turn) Umdrehung f

**revolve**, ri-**wolw**, v sich drehen; –**r**, n Revolver m

**reward**, ri-**u'ord**, n Belohnung f; v belohnen; –**ing**, adj lohnend

**rheumatism**, **ruh**-me-tism, n Rheuma m

**Rhine**, rein, n Rhein m

**rhinoceros**, rei-**noss**-e-ress, n Nashorn m

**rhubarb**, **ruh**-barb, n Rhabarber m

**rhyme**, reim, n Reim m; v reimen

**rhythm**, **ridh**-'m, n Rhythmus m

**rib**, ribb, n Rippe f

**ribbon**, **ribb**-en, n Band nt

**rice**, reiss, n Reis m

**rich**, ritsch, adj reich; (food) schwer; –**es**, npl Reichtum m

**rickety**, **rick**-itt-i, adj wackelig

**rid**, ridd, v befreien; **to get – of**, loswerden

**riddle**, **ridd**-'l, n Rätsel nt;

–**d with**, durchlöchert von

**ride**, reid, n (in vehicle) Fahrt f; (on horse) Ritt m; v (horse) reiten; (bicycle) radfahren; (in vehicle) fahren; –**r**, n (on horse) Reiter m; (vehicle) Fahrer m

**ridge**, ridsch, n (mountain) Kamm m; (roof) First m

**ridicule**, **ridd**-i-kjuhl, n Spott m; v lächerlich machen

**ridiculous**, ri-**dick**-juh-less, adj lächerlich

**riding**, n Reiten nt; – **school**, n Reitschule f

**rife**, adj weit verbreitet

**rifle**, **reif**-'l, n Gewehr nt; – **through**, v durchstöbern

**rift**, rift, n Spalte f; fig Unstimmigkeit f

**rig**, rigg n naut Takelung f; v naut auftakeln; (election) manipulieren; **oil –**, n Ölbohrinsel f

**right**, reit, adj (correct) recht, richtig; (side) rechte(r/s); adv (to the right) rechts; (correctly) richtig; (directly) genau; n rechte Seite; (justice) Recht nt; (politics) Rechte f; **(put) –**, v wiedergutmachen; **– away**, adv sofort; **––handed**, adj rechtshändig; **––hand side**, n rechte Seite f; **– now**, adv sofort; **– of way**, n Vorfahrt f; **(all) –**, gut; **be –**, (of person) recht

haben; (of fact) stimmen; **on/to the –**, nach rechts

**rigid**, **ridsch**-idd, adj starr, steif, fest

**rigorous**, **rigg**-e-ress, adj streng

**rigour**, **rigg**-er, n Strenge f

**rile**, reil, v reizen

**rim**, rimm, n Rand m; (of hat) Krempe f; (of wheel) (Rad)felge f

**rind**, reindd, n Rinde f

**ring**, ring, n (object) Ring m; (of bell, telephone) Klingeln nt; (circle) Kreis m; v (bell) klingeln; – **(up)**, (on telephone) anrufen; –**leader**, n Rädelsführer m; – **road**, n Ringstraße f

**rink**, rink, n (ice) Eisbahn f; (roller-skating) Rollschuhbahn f

**rinse**, rinss, v spülen, ausspülen

**riot**, **rei**-ett, n Aufruhr m; fig Explosion f; v randalieren; –**er**, n Aufrührer m

**rip**, ripp, n Riß m; v reißen

**ripe**, reip, adj reif; –**n**, v reifen

**rip-off**, **ripp**-off, n fam Nepp m

**ripple**, **ripp**-'l, n kleine Welle f; v (sich) kräuseln

**rise**, reis, n (slope) Steigung f; (in salary) Erhöhung f; (in price) Steigerung f; v (in price) steigen; (stand up) aufstehen; (revolt) sich erheben; (of sun)

aufgehen; **give – to,** v
führen zu

**risk,** risk, n Risiko nt,
Gefahr f; v riskieren; **take
a –,** v ein Risiko eingehen;
**–y,** adj riskant; **at –,**
gefährdet, in Gefahr

**rite,** reit, n Ritus m

**rival,** rei-w'l, adj
rivalisierend; n Rivale m;
(competitor) Konkurrent
m; v rivalisieren mit; **–ry,**
n Rivalität f;
(competition) Konkurrenz
f

**river,** riw-er, adj Fluß-; n
Fluß m; (large) Strom m

**rivet,** riw-itt, n Niete f; v
nieten

**road,** rohd, adj Straßen-; n
Straße f; **– map,** n
Straßenkarte f; **– sign,** n
Straßenschild m; **–works,**
npl Straßenbauarbeiten pl,
Baustelle f

**roam,** rohm, v
umherwandern

**roar,** ror, n Gebrüll nt; v
brüllen; (of storm)
brausen; **do a –ing trade,** v
ein Bombengeschäft
machen

**roast,** rohst, n Braten m; v
braten

**rob,** robb, v berauben; **–ber,**
n Räuber m; **–bery,** n
Raubüberfall m

**robe,** rohb, n (dress) Kleid
nt; (of office) Talar m;
(dressing gown)
Bademantel m

**robin,** robb-in, n
Rotkehlchen nt

**robot,** roh-bott, n Roboter
m

**robust,** re-bast, adj (health,
appetite) robust; (build)
kräftig; (flavour, manner)
ausgeprägt

**rock,** rock, n Felsen m; mus
Rock m; (sweet)
Zuckerstange f; v
schaukeln; (cradle)
wiegen; **– and roll,** n Rock
and Roll m; **–ery,**
Steingarten m; **on the –s,**
(marriage, business)
wackelig; (drink) mit Eis

**rocket,** rock-it, n Rakete f; v
(of prices) in die Höhe
schießen

**rocking,** rock-ing, adj
Schaukel-

**rocky,** rock-i, adj (stony)
felsig; (wobbly) wackelig

**rod,** rodd, n Stange m;
(cane) Rute f

**roe,** roh, n (deer) Reh nt; (of
fish) Rogen m

**rogue,** rohg, n Gauner m;
(in fun) Schelm m; **–ry,** n
Gaunerei f

**roll,** rohl, n Rolle f; (bread)
Brötchen nt; v rollen; **–
call,** n Aufrufen nt; **–er,** n
Walze f; **–er skate,** n
Rollschuh m; **–ing,** adj
wellig; **–ing pin,** n
Wellholz nt; **–over,** v
(sich) umdrehen; **– up,** v
(fam arrive)
kommen

**Roman,** roh-men, adj
römisch; n Römer m; **–
Catholic,** adj (römisch-)
katholisch; n Katholik m

**romance,** roh-mänss, n
(affair) Romanze f; (story)
Liebesroman m

**romantic,** roh-männ-tick,
adj romantisch

**romanticism,** roh-männ-ti-
ssism, n Romantik f

**Rome,** rohm, n Rom nt

**romp,** romp, v
(herum)tollen

**roof,** ruhf, n Dach nt; (of
mouth) Gaumen m; **–
rack,** n Dachständer m

**rook,** ruk, n Saatkrähe f;
(chess) Turm m

**room,** ruhm, n Zimmer nt;
(space) Platz m; **– service,**
n Zimmerservice m; **–y,** adj
geräumig

**roost,** ruhst, n
Hühnerstange f; v
schlafen; **–er,** n Hahn m

**root,** ruht, n Wurzel f; v **–
(about),** (herum)wühlen

**rope,** rohp, n Seil nt; **– in,** v
einspannen; **get –ed in,** v
eingespannt werden

**rosary,** roh-se-ri, n
Rosenkranz m

**rose,** rohs, adj rosa; n Rose f

**rosé,** roh-seh, adj rosé

**rosemary,** rohs-me-ri, n
Rosmarin m

**rostrum,** rost-rem, n
Tribüne f; mus
Dirigentenpult nt

**rosy,** rohs-i, adj rosig

**rot**, rott, n Fäulnis f; v
verfaulen

**rota**, roh-te, n
Arbeitsplan m

**rotate**, roh-**teht**, v (sich)
drehen; (take turns) sich
abwechseln

**rotten**, rott-'n, adj verfault,
faul; (person, act) gemein

**rough**, raff, adj (not smooth)
rauh; (treatment, finish)
grob; (approximate)
ungefähr; (sea) stürmisch;
(bumpy) holperig; **–age**, n
Ballaststoffe pl; **– copy**, n
Entwurf m; **–ly**, adj
(treatment) grob;
(approximately) ungefähr;
**–ness**, n Rauheit f,
Grobheit f

**round**, raund, adj rund; adv
ringsherum; prep (corner)
um; (area) um … herum;
n Runde f; (shot) Schuß
m; v abrunden; **– about**,
adv rundherum; **–about**,
adj umständlich; n
(traffic) Kreisverkehr m;
(child's) Karussell nt; **–ly**,
adv entschieden; **–ness**, n
Rundheit f; (figure)
Rundlichkeit f; **– up**, v
(criminals) hochnehmen;
(figure, price) aufrunden;
go **–**, v herumgehen um;
(visit sb) besuchen; (be
enough) ausreichen

**rouse**, raus, v aufwecken

**route**, ruht, n Route f, Weg
m; (bus) Linie f

**routine**, ruh-**tien**, adj

Routine-, routinemäßig; n
Routine f

**rove**, rohw, v herumstreifen

**row**, roh, n Reihe f; v rudern

**row**, rau, n (dispute) Streit
m; (noise) Lärm m; v sich
streiten

**rowdy**, rau-di, adj rowdyhaft

**royal**, reu-el, adj königlich,
Königs-; **–ty**, n Königshaus
nt; (fee) Tantieme f

**rub**, rabb, v reiben; **– off**, v
abreiben; fig abfärben; **–
out**, v ausradieren; **– sb
(up) the wrong way**, v
jdn reizen

**rubber**, rabb-er, n Gummi
m/nt; (eraser)
Radiergummi m; **– band**, n
Gummiband nt

**rubbish**, rabb-isch, n
(refuse) Abfall m;
(nonsense) Quatsch m; **–
bin**, n Mülleimer m; **–
dump/tip**, n Mülldeponie f

**rubble**, rabb-'l, n Schutt m

**ruby**, ruh-bi, adj rubinfarbig;
n Rubin m; **– wedding**, n
vierzigster Hochzeitstag m

**rucksack**, rack-ssäck, n
Rucksack m

**rudder**, radd-er, n
(Steuer)ruder nt

**ruddy**, radd-i, adj rötlich;
fam verdammt

**rude**, ruhd, adj (impolite)
unhöflich; (rough) grob;
(awakening, reminder)
unsanft

**rudimentary**, ruh-di-**menn**-
te-ri, adj (knowledge)

elementar; (tool etc.)
primitiv

**rue**, ruh, v bereuen; **–ful**, adj
(person) reuevoll;
(situation) kläglich

**ruffian**, raff-jen, n
Rohling m

**ruffle**, raff-'l, n Kräuseln; v
kräuseln; (upset) aus der
Fassung bringen

**rug**, ragg, n (blanket) Decke
f; (carpet) Teppich m,
Läufer m

**rugby**, ragg-bi, n Rugby nt

**rugged**, ragg-idd, adj
(landscape) zerklüftet;
(features) zerfurcht

**ruin**, ruh-in, n (building)
Ruine f; (downfall) Ruin
m; v ruinieren; **in –s**,
zerstört

**rule**, ruhl, n (regulation)
Regel nt; (reign)
Herrschaft f;
(government) Amtszeit f;
(ruler) Lineal nt; v (king)
herrschen (über);
(government) amtieren;
(decide) enscheiden;
(draw lines on) linieren;
**–r**, n Lineal nt; (royal)
Herrscher m

**rumble**, ramm-b'l, n
(thunder etc.) Rollen nt;
(stomach) Knurren nt; v
rollen; knurren

**rummage**, ramm-idsch, v
herumstöbern

**rumour**, ruh-mer, n
Gerücht nt

**rump**, ramp, n fam

Hinterteil nt; – **steak,** n Rumpsteak nt

**run,** rann, n Lauf m; (race) Rennen nt; v rennen, laufen; (flow) fließen; (of train etc.) fahren; – **away,** v weglaufen; –**away,** n (person, horse) Ausreißer m; – **down,** v (of battery) leer werden; (with car) überfahren; (reduce) abbauen; – **into,** v (meet) begegnen; (trouble, debt) geraten in; (collide with) fahren gegen; –**ning,** adj fließend; n (management) Leitung f; (sport) Rennen nt, Jogging nt; –**ny,** adj (liquid) flüssig; (nose) laufend; – **out,** v (expire) ablaufen; (be exhausted) ausgehen; – **out of sth,** v kein … mehr haben; – **over,** v überfahren; – **through,** v (read/explain quickly) durchgehen; –**way,** n (take-off) Startbahn f; (landing) Landebahn f

**rupture, rap-**tscher, n Bruch m

**rural, ruhr-**rel, adj ländlich

**rush, rasch,** n (panic) Gedränge nt; (surge) Andrang m; (reed) Binse f; v (hurry) stürzen; (move quickly) schnell transportieren; – **hour,** n Stoßzeit f; (traffic) Hauptverkehrszeit f

**Russia, rasch-**e, n Rußland nt; –**n,** adj russisch; n (person) Russe m, Russin f; (language) Russisch nt

**rust, rast,** n Rost m; v (ver)rosten

**rustic, rass-**tick, adj ländlich

**rustle, rass-**'l, v rauschen, rascheln; (steal cattle) stehlen

**rusty, rass-**ti, adj rostig; fig eingerostet

**rut, rat,** n Furche f, Spur f; fig Trott m

**ruthless, ruhth-**less, adj rücksichtslos

**rye, rei,** n Roggen m

**sabbath,** ssäbb-eth, n
Sabbat m

**sabotage,** ssäbb-e-tahdsch, n
Sabotage f; v sabotieren

**sachet,** ssäsch-eh, n
Beutel m

**sack,** ssäck, n Sack m; v
(dismiss) entlassen; mil
plündern; **–ing,** n
(dismissal) Entlassung f;
(cloth) Sackleinen nt; **get
the –,** v entlassen werden

**sacrament,** ssack-re-ment, n
Sakrament nt

**sacred,** sseh-kridd, adj heilig

**sacrifice,** ssäck-ri-feiss, n
Opfer nt; v opfern

**sacrilege,** ssäck-ri-lidsch, n
Sakrileg nt

**sad,** ssäd, adj traurig; **–den,**
traurig machen

**saddle,** ssädd-'l, n Sattel m;
v (horse) satteln; **– sb
with sth,** v jdm etw

aufbürden; **–bag,** n
Satteltasche f

**sadistic,** sse-diss-tick, adj
sadistisch

**sadly,** ssädd-li, adv
(unfortunately) leider;
(with sadness) traurig

**sadness,** ssädd-niss, n
Traurigkeit f

**safe,** ssehf, adj sicher; n
Geldschrank m; **––deposit
box,** n Banksafe m;
**–guard,** n Schutz m; v
beschützen; **––keeping,** n
sichere Verwahrung f; **–
sex,** n Safer Sex m

**safety,** ssehf-ti, n Sicherheit
f; **– belt,** n Sicherheitsgurt
m; **– pin,** n
Sicherheitsnadel f

**sag,** ssägg, v durchhängen

**sage,** ssehdsch, n (herb)
Salbei m; (wise person)
Weise(r) m & f

**Saggitarius,** ssädsch-i-*tähr*-
ri-*ess*, n Schütze m

**sail,** ssehl, n Segel nt; v
segeln; (leave) abfahren;
**– through,** v fam etw
spielend schaffen; **–ing,** n
Segeln nt; **–or,** n Matrose
m, Seemann m

**saint,** ssehnt, n Heilige(r) m
& f; **–ly,** adj heilig

**sake,** ssehk, **for … sake,** um
… willen

**salad,** ssäll-ed, n Salat m;
**– dressing,** n Salatsoße f

**salami,** sse-*lah*-mi, n
Salami f

**salary,** ssäll-e-ri, n Gehalt nt

**sale,** ssehl, n Verkauf m;
(bargain) Ausverkauf m;
**–able,** adj verkäuflich; **–s
assistant,** n Verkäufer m;
**–sman,** n Verkäufer m;
**–woman,** n Verkäuferin f;
**for –,** zu verkaufen

**salient,** sseh-li-ent, adj
auffallend

**saliva,** sse-*lei*-we, n
Speichel m

**sallow,** ssäll-oh, adj bleich

**salmon,** ssämm-en, n
Lachs m

**saloon,** sse-*luhn*, n (car)
Limousine f; (lounge)
Salon m

**salt,** ssolt, adj salzig, Salz-; n
Salz nt; v salzen; (cure)
pökeln; **– away,** v auf die
hohe Kante legen; **–
cellar,** n Salzstreuer m; **–
water,** n Salzwasser nt; **–y,**
adj salzig

**salute**, sse-**luht**, n mil Salut m; v – **sb**, mil jdn salutieren; (admire) sich vor jdm verneigen

**salvage**, ssäll-widsch, n Bergung f; v bergen

**salvation**, ssäll-**weh**-sch'n, n Rettung f; relig Seligkeit f; **S– Army**, n Heilsarmee f

**same**, ssehm, adj (identical) (der/die/das)selbe; (equivalent) (der/die/das) gleiche; **all the –**, trotzdem; **at the – time**, (simultaneously) gleichzeitig; (however) andererseits

**sample**, ssahm-p'l, n Muster nt; v probieren

**sanctify**, ssänk-ti-fei, v heiligen, weihen

**sanction**, ssänk-sch'n, n Genehmigung f; law Sanktion f; v sanktionieren

**sanctity**, ssänk-ti-ti, n Heiligkeit f

**sanctuary**, ssänk-tju-e-ri, n (refuge) Zufluchtsort m; (in church) Altarraum m

**sand**, ssänd, n Sand m

**sandal**, ssänn-d'l, n Sandale f

**sandcastle**, ssänd-kah-ss'l, n Sandburg f

**sand dune**, ssänd djuhn, n Sanddüne f

**sandpaper**, ssänd-peh-per, n Sandpapier nt

**sandwich**, ssänd-u'itsch, n Sandwich m/nt, belegtes Brot nt; v – **(between)**, einklemmen (zwischen); – **course**, n Ausbildung f mit theoretischen und praktischen Bestandteilen

**sandy**, ssänn-di, adj sandig; (hair) rötlich

**sane**, ssehn, adj geistig gesund; vernünftig

**sanitary**, ssänn-i-te-ri, adj Gesundheits-; – **towel**, n Damenbinde f

**sanity**, ssänn-i-ti, n geistige Gesundheit f

**sap**, ssäpp, n Saft m; v unterhöhlen

**sapphire**, ssäff-eir, n Saphir m

**sarcasm**, ssahr-käsm, n Sarkasmus m

**sarcastic**, ssar-käss-tick, adj sarkastisch

**sardine**, ssar-dien, n Sardine f

**sash**, ssäsch, n Schärpe f

**satchel**, ssätsch-'l, n Schultasche f

**satellite**, ssätt-i-leit, n Satellit m; – **dish**, n Satellitenschüssel f; – **television**, n Satellitenfernsehen nt

**satin**, ssätt-inn, n Satin m

**satire**, ssätt-eir, n Satire f

**satisfaction**, ssätt-iss-**fäck**-sch'n, n Befriedigung f

**satisfactory**, ssätt-iss-**fäck**-te-ri, adj befriedigend

**satisfy**, ssätt-iss-fei, v (content) befriedigen; (fulfil) erfüllen

**satsuma**, ssätt-**suh**-me, n Mandarine f

**saturate**, ssätse-e-reht, v durchtränken

**Saturday**, ssätt-er-deh, n Samstag m, Sonnabend m

**sauce**, sso'ass, n Soße f, Sauce f; –**pan**, n (Koch)topf m

**saucer**, sso'a-sser, n Untertasse f

**saucy**, sso'a-ssi, adj frech

**sauna**, sso'a-ne, n Sauna f

**saunter**, sso'an-ter, v schlendern

**sausage**, ssoss-idsch, n Wurst f

**sauté**, ssoh-teh, adj anbraten

**savage**, ssäw-idsch, adj wild; n Barbar m

**savagery**, ssäw-idsch-e-ri, n Grausamkeit f

**save**, ssehw, n sport Abwehr f; v (rescue) retten; (economize) sparen; (keep) aufbewahren; comp speichern; – **up**, sparen

**saving**, sseh-wing, n Ersparnis f; –**s**, npl Ersparnisse pl; –**s account**, n Sparkonto nt

**Saviour**, ssehw-jer, n relig Erlöser m

**savour**, sseh-wer, v genießen; –**y**, adj pikant; n Pikantes nt

**saw**, sso'a, n Säge f; v sägen

**say**, sseh, v sagen; –**ing**, n Spruch m; **have a – in**, Mitspracherecht haben bei; **that is to –**, das heißt

**scab, skább**, n Schorf m

**scaffold, skäff-ohld**, n
Schaffot nt; **–ing**, n
Baugerüst nt

**scald**, sko'ald, n Verbrühung
f; v verbrühen

**scale**, skehl, adj (drawing,
model) maßstabgetreu;
n(pl), (of fish) Schuppe f;
(measure) Skala f; (ratio)
Maßstab m; mus Tonleiter
f; v (fish) abschuppen;
(mountain) besteigen; **–s**,
npl Waage f

**scallop, skäll**-ep, n
Jakobsmuschel f

**scalp**, skälp, n Kopfhaut f

**scamp, skämp**, n
Schlingel m

**scamper, skämm**-per, v –
**away/off**, davoneilen,
ausreißen

**scampi, skämm**-pi, npl
Scampi pl

**scan**, skänn, n med Scan m;
v (examine, med)
untersuchen; (skim)
überfliegen; (of verse)
skandieren; comp scannen

**scandal, skänn**-d'l, n
Skandal m; **–ous**, adj
skandalös

**Scandinavia**, skänn-di-**neh**-
wi-e, n Skandinavien nt;
**–n**, adj skandinavisch; n
Skandinavier m

**scanty, skänn**-ti, adj knapp,
dürftig

**scapegoat, skehp**-goht, n
Sündenbock m

**scar**, skahr, n Narbe f; v
vernarben

**scarce**, skährss, adj rar,
selten; **–ly**, adv kaum

**scarcity, skähr**-ssi-ti, n
Knappheit f

**scare**, skähr, n Schreck m; v
erschrecken; **– away**, v
verscheuchen; **–crow**, n
Vogelscheuche f; **bomb –**,
n Bombendrohung f

**scarf**, skarf, n Schal m;
(headscarf) Kopftuch nt

**scarlet, skahr**-let, adj
scharlachrot; 
Scharlachrot nt; **– fever**, n
Scharlach m

**scary, skähr**-ri, adj fam
furchterregend

**scathing, skeh**-dhing, adj
scharf, verletzend

**scatter, skätt**-er, v (sich)
zerstreuen, ausstreuen;
**–brain**, n Schussel m

**scavenger, skäw**-in-dscher,
n fam Aasgeier m

**scene**, ssien, n (place,
theatre) Szene f; (view)
Anblick m; **–ry**, n theatre
Bühnenbild nt; (view)
Landschaft f

**scent**, ssent, n Parfüm nt; (of
flowers) Duft m; (trail)
Spur f; v parfümieren

**sceptical, skepp**-ti-k'l, adj
skeptisch

**schedule, schedd**-juhl, n
(list) Liste f, Verzeichnis
nt; (timetable) Zeitplan m;
v ansetzen; **on –**, adv
planmäßig; **–ed flight**, n

Linienflug m

**scheme**, skiem, n Plan m; pej
Intrige f; v planen; pej
aushecken

**scholar, skoll**-er, n
Gelehrte(r) m & f; (pupil)
Schüler m; **–ship**, n (prize)
Stipendium nt; (learning)
Gelehrsamkeit f

**school**, skuhl, n Schule f;
**–child**, n Schulkind nt; **–
days**, npl Schulzeit f;
**–master**, n Lehrer m;
**–mistress**, n Lehrerin f; **–
teacher**, n Lehrer(in f) m

**sciatica, ssei-ätt**-i-ke, n
Ischias m/nt

**science, ssei**-enss, n
Wissenschaft f

**scientific**, ssei-en-**tiff**-ick,
adj wissenschaftlich

**scientist, ssei**-en-tist, n
Wissenschaftler m

**scissors, ssis**-ers, npl
Schere f

**scoff**, skoff, v spotten; (fam
eat) fressen; **– at**,
verspotten

**scold**, skohld, v
(aus)schimpfen

**scoop**, skuhp, n Schippe f,
Schaufel f; v **– out**,
(hollow) aushöhlen;
(liquid) ausschöpfen

**scooter, skuh**-ter, n (motor)
Motorroller m

**scope**, skohp, n
(opportunity) Spielraum
m; (extent) Rahmen m

**scorch**, skortsch, v sengen,
anbrennen

**score,** skor, n (result)
Ergebnis nt; (points)
Punktzahl f; mus Partitur
f; (twenty) zwanzig; v
(goal) (ein Tor) schießen;
(points) bekommen;
(scratch) kerben; (keep
count) zählen

**scorn,** skorn, n Verachtung
f; v verachten; **–ful,** adj
verächtlich

**Scorpio, skor-**pi-oh, n
Skorpion m

**Scot,** skott, n Schotte m,
Schottin f

**scotch,** skotsch, n (whisky)
Scotch m

**Scotland, skott-**lend, n
Schottland nt

**Scots,** skots, adj schottisch;
**–man,** n Schotte m;
**–woman,** n Schottin f

**Scottish, skott-**isch, adj
schottisch

**scoundrel, skaun-**drel, n
Schurke m

**scour, skau-**er, v (scrub)
scheuern; (search)
durchkämmen

**scourge, skördsch,** n (whip)
Geißel f; fig Plage f

**scout,** skaut, n mil Späher m;
v – (for), Ausschau
halten nach; **boy –,** n
Pfadfinder m

**scowl,** skaul, n finsterer
Blick m; v finster blicken

**scrabble, skräbb-**'l, v
kratzen; **– around,** wühlen
nach

**scraggy, skrägg-**i, adj dürr,
hager

**scramble, skrämm-**b'l, n
(struggle) Getümmel nt;
(climb) klettern; v – **up,**
hochklettern; **– for,** sich
reißen um

**scrap,** skräpp, n (food)
Bissen m; (paper etc)
Fetzen m; (metal) Schrott
m; (fam fight) Rauferei f; v
(throw out) aufgeben;
(fam fight) raufen

**scrape,** skrehp, n (scratch)
Kratzen m; (fam trouble)
Klemme f; v kratzen;
(vegetables) schaben; **–r,**
n (boots) Abstreifer m;
(ice) Schaber m; **–
through,** v gerade noch
durchkommen

**scrap heap,** skräp heep, n
Schutthaufen m; fig altes
Eisen nt

**scrap merchant,** skräpp
**mör-**tschent, n
Schrotthändler m

**scraps,** skräps, npl Reste pl

**scratch, skrätsch,** adj (team)
zusammengeworfen;
(without handicap) ohne
Vorgabe f; n Schramme f;
v kratzen; sport streichen;
**start from –,** v von vorne
anfangen; **up to –,** adj auf
Vordermann

**scrawl,** skro'al, n Gekritzel
nt; v kritzeln

**scream,** skriem, n Schrei m;
v schreien

**screen,** skrien, n Schirm m;
(TV) Bildschirm m; comp

Monitor m; (cinema)
Leinwand f; v
(be)schirmen; (film etc.)
zeigen; (check)
überprüfen; **–ing,** n
(check) Überprüfung f;
(of film etc.) Vorführung
f; **– off,** v abtrennen

**screw,** skruh, n Schraube f; v
schrauben; vulg bumsen;
**–driver,** n
Schraubenzieher m; **– up,**
v (crumple) zerknüllen;
(fam ruin) vermasseln

**scribble, skribb-**'l, n
Gekritzel nt; v kritzeln

**script,** skript, n (writing)
Handschrift f; theatre
Regiebuch nt; (film)
Drehbuch nt

**Scripture, skripp-**tscher, n
Heilige Schrift f

**scroll,** skrohl, n Rolle f;
(sculptural) Schnörkel m

**scrounge, skr**aundcsh, v
schnorren; **–r,** n Schnorrer
m

**scrub,** skrabb, n Gestrüpp
nt; v scheuern

**scruff,** skraff, n **– of the
neck,** Genick nt; **–y,** adj
schäbig

**scrum,** skramm, n Gedränge
nt

**scruple, skruh-**p'l, n
Skrupel m

**scrupulous, skruh-**pju-less,
adj peinlich, gewissenhaft

**scrutinize, skruh-**ti-neis, v
prüfen, untersuchen

**scrutiny, skruh-**ti-ni, n

Prüfung f

**scuff,** skaff, v abstoßen

**scuffle, skaff**-'l, n
Handgemenge nt

**scullery, skall**-e-ri, n
Spülküche f

**sculptor, skalp**-ter, n
Bildhauer m

**sculpture, skalp**-tscher, n
(art) Bildhauerei f;
(statue) Skulptur f

**scum,** skammm, n
Abschaum m

**scupper, skapp**-er, v naut
versenken; fig zunichte
machen

**scurry, ska**-ri, v hasten

**scuttle, skatt**-'l, n
(Kohlen)eimer m; v naut
versenken; (scamper)
trippeln

**scythe,** seidh, n Sense f

**sea,** ssie, n See f, Meer nt;
**–food,** n Meeresfrüchte pl;
**–gull,** n Möwe f

**seal,** ssiel, n (stamp) Siegel
nt; (animal) Seehund m; v
versiegeln

**sea level,** ssie lew-'l,
Meeresspiegel m

**sea lion,** ssie lei-en, n
Seelöwe m

**seam,** ssiem, n (sewing)
Naht f; (in mine) Lager nt

**seamy, ssie**-mi, adj
zwielichtig

**search,** sörtsch, n Suche f;
(examination)
Durchsuchung f; v suchen;
durchsuchen; **– for,** v
suchen nach; **–ing,** adj

forschend; **–light,** n
Scheinwerfer m; **– party,** n
Suchtrupp m

**seasick, ssie**-ssick, adj
seekrank; **–ness,** n
Seekrankheit f

**seaside, ssie**-sseid, n Küste f;
**at the –,** am Meer

**season, ssie**-s'n, n Jahreszeit
f; (fashionable) Saison f; v
(food) würzen; (timber)
austrocknen; **–al,** adj
Saison-; **–ed,** adj erfahren;
**–ing,** n Würze f; **– ticket,**
n theatre Abonnement nt;
(public transport)
Dauerkarte f

**seat,** ssiet, n Sitz m,
(Sitz)platz m; (bench)
Bank f; (of trousers)
Hosenboden m; (estate)
Landsitz m; v (guests,
public) Sitzplätze bieten
für; **– belt,** n
Sicherheitsgurt m

**seaweed, ssie**-u'ied, n
Seetang m

**seaworthy, ssie**-u'ör-dhi, adj
seefest

**secluded, ssi**-kluh-didd, adj
einsam, abgeschlossen

**seclusion, ssi**-kluh-sch'n, n
Abgeschiedenheit f

**second, sseck**-end, adj
zweite(r/s); n (time, mus)
Sekunde f; comm zweite
Wahl f; (supporter)
Sekundant m; v
unterstützen; **–ary,** adj
untergeordnet; **–hand,** adj
aus zweiter Hand,

gebraucht; **– hand,** n
Sekundenzeiger m; **–ly,**
adv zweitens; **––rate,** adj
zweitklassig; **have –
thoughts,** v es sich anders
überlegen

**secrecy, ssie**-kriss-i, n
Heimlichkeit f

**secret, ssie**-kritt, adj
geheim, Geheim-; n
Geheimnis nt

**secretarial, sseck**-re-tähr-ri-
el, adj Sekretariats-

**secretary, sseck**-re-te-ri, n
Sekretär m

**secretion, ssi**-krie-sch'n, n
Ausscheidung f

**secretive, ssie**-kritt-iw, adj
geheimnisvoll

**sect,** ssekt, n Sekte f; **–arian,**
adj Konfessions-

**section, sseck**-sch'n, n
Abschnitt m; v
unterteilen

**sector, sseck**-ter, n Sektor m

**secular, sseck**-ju-ler, adj
Säkular-; weltlich

**secure, ssi**-kjuhr, adj (safe)
sicher; (fixed) fest; v
(make safe, obtain)
sichern; (fix) befestigen

**security, ssi**-kjuhr-ri-ti, n
(safety) Sicherheit f;
(pledge) Pfand nt

**sedate, ssi**-deht, adj gesetzt,
ruhig; v med ruhigstellen,
sedieren

**sedative, ssedd**-e-tiw, n
Beruhigungsmittel nt

**sedentary, ssedd**-'n-te-ri, adj
sitzend

**sediment, ssedd**-i-ment, n
Ablagerung f; (in liquid)
Satz m

**sedition,** ssi-**disch**-'n, n
Aufruhr m

**seduce,** ssi-**djuhss,** v
verführen

**seduction,** ssi-**dack**-sch'n, n
Verführung f

**see,** ssie, v sehen;
(understand) verstehen;
(visit) besuchen; – **that,**
dafür sorgen, daß; –
**through,** durchschauen; –
**to,** erledigen

**seed,** ssied, n Samen m; sport
gesetzter Spieler m; –**y,** adj
zwielichtig; **go/run to** –, v
fig herunterkommen

**seek,** ssiek, v suchen; (strive
for) streben nach

**seem,** ssiem, v scheinen;
–**ingly,** adv anscheinend;
–**ly,** adj anständig

**seep,** ssiep, v sickern

**seethe,** ssiedh, v (crowds)
wimmeln; (with anger)
kochen

**seize,** ssies, v ergreifen,
packen; (power) ergreifen;
(confiscate)
beschlagnahmen

**seizure,** ssie-scher, n
(confiscation)
Beschlagnahme f; med
Anfall m

**seldom, ssell**-dem, adv
selten

**select,** ssi-**lekt,** adj exklusiv;
v auswählen; –**ion,** n
Auswahl f

**self,** sself, adj Selbst-; (one
etc.)–, pron (refl) sich;
(emphatic) selber, selbst; –
**catering,** adj für
Selbstversorger; –
**centred,** adj egozentrisch;
–**confidence,** n
Selbstvertrauen nt; –
**conscious,** adj unsicher; –
**contained,** adj
abgeschlossen; – **defence,**
n Selbstverteidigung f; –
**employed,** adj selbständig;
–**ish,** adj selbstsüchtig;
–**ishness,** n Selbstsucht f;
–**less,** adj selbstlos; –**pity,**
n Selbstmitleid nt; –
**portrait,** n Selbstbildnis
nt; –**righteous,** adj
selbstgerecht; –**sacrifice,**
n Selbstaufopferung f; –
**service,** n
Selbstbedienung f; –
**sufficient,** adj unabhängig

**sell,** ssell, v verkaufen; –**by
date,** n Verfallsdatum; –
**out (of),** v ausverkaufen

**Sellotape ®, sell**-oh-tehp, n
Tesafilm ® m

**semblance, ssemm**-blenss, n
Anschein m

**semi, ssemm**-i, pref Halb-;
–**circle,** n Halbkreis m;
–**colon,** n Semikolon nt; –
**detached house,** n
Doppelhaushälfte f;
–**final,** n Halbfinale n

**semolina, ssemm**-e-lie-ne, n
Grieß m

**senate, ssenn**-itt, n Senat m

**send,** ssend, v senden,

schicken; –**er,** n Absender
m; – **for,** v holen lassen; –
**off,** v abschicken; sport
vom Platz stellen; – **up,** v
(satirize) parodieren

**senile, ssie**-neil, adj
altersschwach

**senior, ssie**-ni-er, adj (older)
älter; (higher)
höhergestellt; n (in age)
Ältere(r) m & f; (in rank)
Höhergestellte(r) m & f; –
**citizen,** n Rentner m

**seniority,** ssie-ni-o-ri-ti, n
(in age) höheres Alter nt;
(in rank) höherer Rang m

**sensation, ssenn-sseh**-sch'n,
n Gefühl f; (stir)
Aufsehen nt, Sensation f

**sense,** ssenss, n (faculty,
meaning) Sinn m;
(reason) Verstand m;
(feeling) Gefühl nt; v
spüren; –**less,** adj sinnlos;
(unconscious) bewußtlos;
**make** –, v Sinn ergeben

**sensible, ssenn**-ssi-b'l, adj
vernünftig

**sensitive, ssenn**-ssi-tiw, adj
empfindlich

**sensual, ssenn**-ssju-el, adj
sinnlich

**sentence, ssenn**-tenss, n
gram Satz m; law Urteil nt;
v verurteilen

**sentiment, ssenn**-ti-ment, n
Gefühl nt, Empfindung f;
(conviction) Gesinnung f;
–**al,** adj sentimental

**sentry, ssenn**-tri, n Posten
m; – **box,** Wachhaus nt

**separate**, ssepp-*e*-ret, *adj*
einzeln

**separate**, ssepp-*e*-reht, *v*
(sich) trennen; **–ly**, *adv*
getrennt

**separation**, ssepp-*e*-**reh**-sch'n, n Trennung *f*

**September**, ssepp-**temm**-ber,
n September *m*

**septic**, ssepp-tick, *adj*
septisch

**sequel**, ssie-ku'el, n Folge *f*

**sequence**, ssie-ku'enss, n
Reihenfolge *f*

**serenade**, sse-re-nehd, *v*
Ständchen *nt*

**serene**, ssi-**rien**, *adj* heiter;
(still) ungetrübt

**sergeant**, ssahr-dschent, n
*mil* Feldwebel *m*; (police)
Wachtmeister *m*

**serial**, ssier-ri-el, *adj* Serien-
; n (TV, radio) Serie *f*;
**–ize**, *v* in Fortsetzungen
bringen

**series**, ssier-ris, n Serie *f*,
Reihe *f*

**serious(ly)**, ssier-ri-ess(-li),
*adj & adv* ernst(haft);
(injury) schwer

**sermon**, ssör-men, n
Predigt *f*

**serpent**, ssör-pent, n
Schlange *f*

**servant**, ssör-went, n
Diener *m*

**serve**, ssörw, *v* (be)dienen;
(food) servieren; (tennis)
aufschlagen; (sentence)
verbüßen; **it –s you right!**
das geschieht dir recht!

**service**, ssör-wiss, n Service
*m*, Dienst *m*; (hotel etc.)
Bedienung *f*; (trains etc.)
Verbindung *f*; *relig*
Gottesdienst *m*; *mech*
Wartung *f*; *v mech* warten;
**– area**, n Raststätte *f*; **–
charge**, n Bedienung *f*;
**S–s**, *npl mil* Streitkräfte *pl*;
**– station**, n Tankstelle *f*

**serviette**, ssör-wi-ett, n
Serviette *f*

**servile**, ssör-weil, *adj*
unterwürfig

**session**, sse-sch'n, n Sitzung
*f*; **be in –**, *v* tagen

**set**, ssett, *adj* (fixed)
festgesetzt; (ready) bereit;
n (collection, tennis) Satz
*m*; (radio, TV) Apparat *m*;
(of china) Service *nt*;
*theatre* Bühnenbild *nt*; *v*
(type, to music etc.)
setzen; (trap, clock, task)
stellen; (example) geben;
(table) decken; (hair)
legen; (bone) einrenken;
(solidify) fest werden;
(jewel) fassen; (of sun)
untergehen; **–back**, n
Rückschlag *m*; **–
meal/menu**, n Tagesmenü
*nt*; **– off**, *v* (depart)
losfahren; (alarm, bomb)
losgehen lassen; **– on fire**,
*v* anzünden; **– out**, *v*
(arrange) arrangieren;
(explain) erklären;
(depart) losfahren; **– up**, *v*
(organization) einrichten;
(statue) aufstellen

**settee**, ssett-**ie**, n Sofa *nt*

**setting**, ssett-ing, n
Umgebung *f*; (of jewel)
Fassung *f*

**settle**, ssett-'l, *v* (calm)
beruhigen; (pay)
bezahlen; (decide)
entscheiden; (make one's
home) sich niederlassen;
(of dust, sediment) sich
setzen; **– down**, *v* (calm
down) sich beruhigen;
(get used to) sich
eingewöhnen; **– for**, *v* sich
zufriedengeben mit;
**–ment**, n (payment)
Begleichung *f*; (colony)
Siedlung *f*; (of
foundations) Senken *nt*;
(agreement) Vereinbarung
*f*; (bequest) Vermächtnis
*nt*; **– on**, *v* sich
entscheiden für; **–r**, n
Siedler *m*

**seven**, ssew-en, *num* sieben;
**–teen**, *num* siebzehn; **–th**,
*adj* siebte; n Siebtel *nt*;
**–ty**, *num* siebzig

**sever**, ssew-er, *v* trennen;
(break off) abbrechen

**several**, ssew-'rel, *adj & pron*
mehrere

**severe**, ssi-**wier**, *adj* (person)
streng; (injury) schwer;
(weather) rauh

**severity**, ssi-we-ri-ti, *n*
Strenge *f*; Schwere *f*

**sew**, ssoh, *v* nähen

**sewage**, ssjuh-idsch, n
Abwasser *nt*

**sewer**, ssjuh-er, n

Abwasserkanal m

**sex,** sseks, n Sex m;
Geschlecht nt; **–ist,** adj
sexistisch; n Sexist m,
Sexistin f; **–ual,** adj
geschlechtlich,
Geschlechts-; **–y,** adj sexy;
**have – (with),** v
Geschlechtsverkehr
haben (mit)

**shabby, schäbb**-i, adj
schäbig; (action) gemein

**shack,** schäck, n Hütte f

**shackle, schäck-**'l, n Fessel
f; v fesseln

**shade,** schehd, n Schatten
m; (colour) Farbton m;
(for lamp, eyes etc.)
Schirm m; v beschatten

**shadow, schädd**-oh, n
Schatten m; v nachspüren;
**–y,** adj schattenhaft

**shady, scheh**-di, adj
schattig; fig verdächtig

**shaft,** schahft, n (of spear)
Schaft m; mech Welle f;
(in mine) Schacht m; (of
light) Strahl m

**shaggy, schägg**-i, adj zottig

**shake,** schehk, v schütteln;
(tremble) zittern; (shock)
erschüttern; **–n,** adj
erschüttert

**shaky, scheh**-ki, adj
wackelig; (unreliable)
unzuverlässig

**shall,** schäll, v (future)
werden; (obligation)
sollen

**shallow, schäll**-oh, adj
seicht; fig oberflächlich

**sham,** schämm, adj falsch; n
Heuchelei f

**shame,** schehm, n (disgrace)
Schande f; (sense of)
Scham f; v beschämen;
**–ful,** adj schändlich; **–less,**
adj schamlos; **it's a –,** es ist
schade; **what a –!** schade!

**shampoo,** schämm-**puh,** n
Shampoo nt; v Haare
waschen

**shamrock, schämm**-rock, n
Klee m; (leaf) Kleeblatt nt

**shandy, schänn**-di, n
Radlermaß f

**shape,** schehp, n Form f; v
formen, bilden; **–ed,**
suffix -förmig; **–less,** adj
formlos; **–ly,** adj
wohlgeformt; **take –,** v
Form annehmen

**share,** schähr, n Teil m,
Anteil m; fin Aktie f; v
teilen; **–holder,** n
Aktionär m

**shark,** schark, n Haifisch m;
fig Geschäftemacher m

**sharp,** scharp, adj scharf;
spitz; (mind) scharfsinnig;
mus erhöht; n mus Kreuz
nt; **–en,** v schärfen;
(point) spitzen; **–ener,** n
Schleifgerät nt; (pencil)
Anspitzer m; **–ly,** adj
(clearly) deutlich;
(suddenly) plötzlich;
(harshly) scharf; **–ness,** n
Schärfe f

**shatter, schätt**-er, v
zerschmettern; (nerves)
erschüttern; **–ed,** adj

(exhausted) erledigt

**shave,** schehw, n Rasur f; v
(sich) rasieren; **–r,** n
Rasierapparat m

**shaving, scheh**-wing, n
Rasieren nt; **– brush,** n
Rasierpinsel m; **– cream,** n
Rasierseife f; **– foam,** n
Rasierschaum m

**shavings, scheh**-wings, npl
Hobelspäne mpl

**shawl,** scho'al, n Stola f

**she,** schie, adj weiblich, -
weibchen; pron sie

**sheaf,** schief, n (of corn)
Garbe f; (of papers)
Bündel nt

**shear,** schier, v scheren; **–s,**
npl (große) Schere f;
(garden) Gartenschere f

**sheath,** schieth, n
(scabbard) Scheide f;
(condom) Kondom m/nt

**shed,** schedd, n Schuppen
m; v (tears, blood)
vergießen; (hair, leaves
etc.) verlieren

**sheen,** schien, n Glanz m

**sheep,** schiep, n Schaf nt

**sheer,** schier, adj (pure)
lauter, rein; (steep) steil;
(fine) fein; adv steil

**sheet,** schiet, n (for bed)
Bettuch nt, Laken nt; (of
paper) Bogen m; (of metal
etc.) Platte f; (of water,
ice) Fläche f; **– lightning,**
Wetterleuchten nt

**shelf,** schelf, n Brett nt; (set
of shelves) Regal nt

**shell,** schell, n (of nut)

Schale f; (of pea) Hülse f; (seashell) Muschel f; mil Geschoß nt, Granate f; v schälen; pulen; mil bombardieren; **–fish,** n Schalentier nt; pl Meeresfrüchte pl

**shelter,** schell-ter, n Schutz m; (mountain) Hütte f; (air raid etc.) Bunker m; v (take shelter) sich unterstellen; (give shelter) schützen; **night –,** n Obdachlosenheim nt

**shelve,** schelw, v aufschieben; **–s,** npl see **shelf**

**shepherd, schepp-**erd, n Schäfer m

**sherry, sche-**ri, n Sherry m

**Shetland, schett-**lend, n **the Shetlands,** npl die Shetlandinseln pl

**shield,** schield, n Schild nt; fig Schirm m; v schützen

**shift,** schift, n (work) Schicht f; (change) Wandel m; v (move) (sich) bewegen; (change) wechseln; **– work,** n Schichtarbeit f; **–y,** adj (untrustworthy) verschlagen; (evasive) ausweichend

**shin,** schinn, n Schienbein nt

**shine,** schein, n Schein m; Glanz m; v scheinen, leuchten, glänzen

**shingle, sching-**g'l, n (pebbles) Kiesel m; (on roof) Schindel f; **–s,** n med Gürtelrose f

**shiny, schei-**ni, adj glänzend

**ship,** schipp, n Schiff nt; v versenden; **–ment,** n Sendung f; **–per,** n Spediteur m; **–ping,** n (traffic) Schiffahrt f; (sending) Versand m; **–wreck,** n Schiffbruch m; **–yard,** n Werft f

**shire,** scheir, n Grafschaft f

**shirk,** schörk, v ausweichen; **–er,** n Drückeberger m

**shirt,** schört, n Hemd nt; **–y,** adj sauer

**shit,** schitt, vulg n Scheiße f; v scheißen

**shiver, schiw-**er, n Schauer m; v zittern

**shoal, scho-**al, n (of fish) Schwarm m; (shallows) Sandbank f

**shock,** schock, n Stoß m; (fright) Schreck m; elec Schlag m; v (frighten) erschüttern; (offend) schockieren; **– absorber,** n Stoßdämpfer m; **–ing,** adj schrecklich, schockierend

**shoddy, schodd-**i, adj (work) schludrig; (goods) minderwertig

**shoe,** schuh, n Schuh m; (horse's) Hufeisen nt; v (horse) beschlagen; **–horn,** n Schuhanzieher m; **–lace,** n Schnürsenkel m; **– polish,** n Schuhcreme f

**shoot,** schuht, n (growth) Sprößling m; (hunt) Jagd f; v schießen; (kill) erschießen; (film) drehen; **– up,** v aufschießen; **–ing,** n Schießen nt; **–ing star,** n Sternschnuppe f

**shop,** schopp, n Laden m, Geschäft nt; v einkaufen gehen; **–assistant,** n Verkäufer m; **–keeper,** n Ladeninhaber m; **–lifting,** n Ladendiebstahl m; **–per,** n Käufer m; **–ping,** n (act) Einkaufen nt; (goods) Einkäufe pl; **– ping centre,** n Einkaufszentrum nt

**shore,** schor, n Ufer nt, Strand m; v **– up,** v abstützen

**shorn,** schorn, adj geschoren

**short,** schort, adj kurz; (person) klein; (supply) knapp; n (film) Kurzfilm m; elec Kurzschluß m; **–age,** n Mangel m; **– circuit,** n Kurzschluß m; **–coming,** n Fehler m; **– cut,** n Abkürzung f; **–en,** v (ab)kürzen; **–fall,** n Defizit nt; **–hand,** n Kurzschrift f; **–list,** n engere Wahl f; **–ly,** adv bald; **–sighted,** adj kurzsichtig; **–tempered,** adj aufbrausend; **–term,** adj kurzfristig; **be – for sth,** v die Kurzform von etw sein; **be – of ...,** v nicht genug ... haben

**shot,** schott, n Schuß m; (person) Schütze m; (pellet) Schrot m; photog

Aufnahme f; (fam attempt) Versuch m; like a –, wie der Blitz; –gun, n Schrotflinte f

**should,** schudd, v (past & conditional of **shall**)

**shoulder, schohl**-der, n Schulter f, v schultern; fig auf sich nehmen; – **blade,** n Schulterblatt nt; **hard –,** n Seitenstreifen m

**shout,** schaut, n Schrei m; Ruf m; v schreien; rufen

**shove,** schaw, n Schub m; v schieben

**shovel, scha**-w'l, n Schaufel f; v schaufeln

**show,** schoh, n (display) Schau f; theatre Vorstellung f; (exhibition) Ausstellung f; v zeigen; ausstellen; (pity etc.) erweisen; (be visible) sichtbar sein; – **off,** v angeben; **—off,** n Angeber m; – **up,** v (be visible) zu sehen sein; (arrive) erscheinen; (expose) bloßstellen

**shower, schau**-er, n (of rain) Schauer m; (wash) Dusche f; v duschen; – **with,** überschütten mit; **–proof,** adj regendicht; **–y,** adj regnerisch

**show jumping,** schoh dschamm-ping, n Turnierreiten nt

**showroom, schoh**-ruhm, n Ausstellungsraum m

**showy, schoh**-i, adj

auffallend; (ostentatious) protzig

**shred,** schredd, n Fetzen m; v zerfetzen; (cooking) raspeln

**shrewd,** schruhd, adj scharfsinnig

**shriek,** schriek, n Kreischen nt; v kreischen

**shrill,** schrill, adj schrill, gellend

**shrimp,** schrimp, n Garnele f

**shrine,** schrein, n Schrein m

**shrink,** schrink, v schrumpfen; – **from,** zurückschrecken vor

**shrivel, schri**-w'l, v – (up), (zusammen)schrumpfen

**shroud,** schraud, n Leichentuch nt; v einhüllen

**Shrove Tuesday,** schrohw tjuhs-deh, n Faschingsdienstag m

**shrub,** schrabb, n Strauch m; **–bery,** n Gebüsch nt

**shrug,** schragg, n Achselzucken nt; v die Achseln zucken; – **off,** v fig als unwichtig abtun

**shudder, schadd**-er, n Schauder m; v schaudern

**shuffle, schaff**-'l, v (feet) schlurfen; (cards) mischen

**shun,** schann, v meiden

**shunt,** schant, v rangieren

**shut,** schatt, v zumachen, schließen; – **up,** v fam den Mund halten; **–ter,** n Fensterladen m; photog

Verschluß m

**shuttle, schatt**-'l, n (train) Pendelzug m; (bus) Pendelbus m; (spaceship) Shuttle f; **–cock,** n Federball m; – **service,** n Pendelverkehr m

**shy,** schei, adj schüchtern; v (of horse) scheuen; – **away from,** fig zurückweichen vor; **–ness,** n Schüchternheit f

**sick,** ssick, adj (unwell) krank; (nauseous) übel; (in bad taste) makaber; **be –,** v (unwell) krank sein; (vomit) brechen, sich übergeben; **be – of sth,** v fam etw satt haben; **feel –,** v sich übel fühlen; **–en,** v (fall ill) krank werden; (disgust) anekeln; **–ening,** adj ekelhaft

**sickle, ssick**-'l, n Sichel f

**sickly, ssick**-li, adj (unwell) kränklich; (too sweet) zu süß

**sickness,** n Krankheit f

**sick pay,** ssick peh, n Krankengeld nt

**side,** sseid, adj Seiten-; n Seite f; (team) Mannschaft f; v – **with sb,** jds Partei ergreifen; **–board,** n Büffet nt; **–boards,** npl Koteletten pl; – **by –,** nebeneinander; **–car,** n Beiwagen m; – **effect,** n Nebenwirkung f; **–light,** adj Standlicht nt;

–**step**, v ausweichen; –
**street**, n Nebenstraße f;
**get –tracked**, v abgelenkt
werden; **–ways**, adv
seitwärts

**siding**, **sseid**-ing, n
Nebengleis nt

**siege**, ssiedsch, n Belagerung
f

**sieve**, ssiw, n Sieb nt; v
sieben; fig durchsieben

**sift**, ssift, v sieben; fig prüfen

**sigh**, ssei, n Seufzer m; v
seufzen

**sight**, sseit, n (faculty)
Sehkraft f; (view,
spectacle) Anblick m; (of
gun) Visier nt; v erblicken;
**at –**, vom Blatt; **by –**, vom
Sehen; **in/out of –**,
in/außer Sicht

**sights**, sseitss, npl
Sehenswürdigkeiten pl

**sightseeing**, sseit-ssie-ing, n
Sightseeing nt

**sign**, ssein, n (symbol)
Zeichen nt; (notice)
Schild nt; v
unterschreiben

**signal**, ssigg-nel, n Signal nt;
v signalisieren

**signature**, ssigg-ne-tscher, n
Unterschrift f

**significance**, ssigg-niff-i-
kenss, n Bedeutung f

**significant**, ssigg-niff-i-kent,
adj bedeutend

**signify**, ssigg-ni-fei, v
bedeuten

**sign language**, ssein läng-
gu'idsch, n

Zeichensprache f

**signpost**, ssein-pohst, n
Wegweiser m

**silence**, ssei-lenss, n (quiet)
Stille f; (not speaking)
Schweigen nt; v zum
Schweigen bringen; **–!**
Ruhe!; **–r**, ssei-len-sser, n
Schalldämpfer m

**silent**, ssei-lent, adj (quiet)
still; (not speaking)
schweigsam; **be/keep –**,
schweigen

**silhouette**, sill-uh-ett, n
Schattenbild nt

**silicon**, ssill-i-ken, n
Silicium nt; **– chip**, n
Siliciumchip m

**silk**, ssilk, adj seiden,
Seiden-; n Seide f; **–y**, adj
seidig

**silly**, ssill-i, adj albern

**silver**, ssill-wer, adj silbern,
Silber-, aus Silber; n Silber
nt; v versilbern; **–-plated**,
adj versilbert; **–smith**, n
Silberschmied m; **–y**, adj
silbern

**similar**, ssimm-i-ler, adj
ähnlich

**similarity**, ssimm-i-lä-ri-ti, n
Ähnlichkeit f

**similarly**, ssimm-i-ler-li, adv
ebensogut

**simile**, ssimm-i-li, n
Gleichnis nt

**simmer**, ssimm-er, v sieden
(lassen)

**simper**, ssimm-per, v
gekünstelt lächeln

**simple**, ssimm-p'l, adj

einfach; **–-minded**, adj
einfältig

**simplicity**, ssimm-pliss-i-ti,
n Einfachheit f

**simplify**, ssimp-li-fei, v
vereinfachen

**simply**, ssimp-li, adv einfach

**simultaneous(ly)**, ssimm-el-
teh-ni-ess(-li), adj & adv
gleichzeitig

**sin**, ssinn, n Sünde f; v
sündigen

**since**, ssinss, adv seitdem;
conj (time) seit(dem);
(because) da, weil; prep
seit

**sincere**, ssinn-ssier, adj
aufrichtig; **Yours –ly**, Mit
freundlichen Grüßen

**sincerity**, ssin-sse-ri-ti, n
Aufrichtigkeit f

**sinew**, ssinn-juh, n Sehne f

**sinful**, ssinn-full, adj
sündhaft

**sing**, ssing, v singen

**singe**, ssindsch, v versengen

**singer**, ssing-er, n Sänger m

**single**, ssing-g'l, adj (only)
einzig; (unmarried) ledig;
(ticket) einfach; n (ticket)
einfache Fahrkarte f;
(unmarried person) Single
m; **– bed**, n Einzelbett nt;
**– file**, n Gänsemarsch m;
**–-handed**, adj & adv
allein; **–-minded**, adj
zielstrebig; **– out**, v
aussondern; **– room**, n
Einzelzimmer nt; **–s**, n
(tennis) Einzel nt

**singly**, ssing-gli, adv einzeln;

(piece by piece)
stückweise

**singular, ssing**-gju-ler, *adj*
einmalig; *n* Einzahl *f*,
Singular *m*

**sinister, ssinn**-iss-ter, *adj*
unheilvoll

**sink, ssink**, *n* Waschbecken
*nt*; *v* sinken; (ship)
versenken; (shaft) senken;
– **in**, einsinken;
(comprehend) verstehen

**sinner, ssinn**-er, *n* Sünder *m*

**sinus, ssei**-ness, *n* Sinus *m*

**sip, ssipp**, *n* Schlückchen *nt*;
*v* schlückchenweise
trinken

**siphon, ssei**-fen, *n* Siphon
*m*; *v* – **off**, ablassen; *fig*
abzweigen

**sir**, ssör, *n* (address) mein
Herr *m*; (title) Sir *m*

**siren, sseir**-ren, *n* Sirene *f*

**sirloin, ssör**-leun, *n*
Lendenstück *nt*

**sister, ssiss**-ter, *n* Schwester
*f*; –**in-law**, *n* Schwägerin *f*

**sit, ssitt**, *v* sitzen; (of
committee etc.) tagen; –
**down**, *v* sich (hin)setzen; –
**up**, *v* (straight) sich
gerade setzen

**sitcom, ssitt**-komm, *n* (*abbr*
**situation comedy**),
Situationskomödie *f*

**site, sseit**, *n* (land)
Grundstück *nt*; (location)
Lage *f*, Standort *m*; *v*
legen; **building –**, *n*
Baustelle *f*

**sitting, ssitt**-ing, *n* Sitzung *f*;

**– room**, *n* Wohnzimmer *nt*

**situated, ssitt**-juh-eh-
tidd, *adj* gelegen; **be –**, *v*
liegen

**situation, ssitt**-juh-ee-sch'n,
*n* Lage *f*; (post) Stelle *f*

**six, ssiks**, *num* sechs; –**teen**,
*num* sechzehn; –**th**, *adj*
sechste(r/s); *n* Sechstel *nt*;
–**ty**, *num* sechzig

**size, sseis**, *n* Größe *f*;
(measure) Maß *nt*; –**able**,
*adj* beträchtlich; – **up**, *v*
einschätzen

**skate, skeht**, *n* Schlittschuh
*m*; (fish) Rochen *m*; *v*
Schlittschuh laufen;
–**board**, *n* Skateboard *nt*;
–**r**, *n* Schlittschuhläufer *m*

**skating, skeh**-ting, *n* (ice)
Schlittschuhlaufen *nt*;
(roller skates)
Rollschuhlaufen *nt*; –
**rink**, *n* (ice) Eisbahn *f*;
(roller skates)
Rollschuhbahn *f*

**skeleton, skell**-i-ten, *n*
Skelett *nt*; *fig* Gerippe *nt*

**sketch, sketsch**, *n* Skizze *f*;
*theatre* Sketch *m*; *v*
skizzieren

**skewer, skjuh**-er, *n* Spieß *m*;
*v* (auf)spießen

**ski, skie**, *n* Ski *m*; *v* Ski
laufen; – **boot**, *n* Skistiefel
*m*

**skid, skidd**, *v* ausrutschen;
(of car) schleudern

**skier, skie**-er, *n* Skiläufer *m*

**skilful, skill**-full, *adj*
geschickt, gewandt

**skiing, skie**-ing, *n*
Skilaufen *nt*

**ski lift, skie** lift, *n* Skilift *m*

**skill, skill**, *n*
Geschicklichkeit *f*; –**ed**, *n*
(worker) gelernt; (expert)
geschickt

**skim, skimm**, *v*
abschäumen; –**med milk**,
*n* Magermilch *f*

**skimp, skimp**, *v* knausern,
sparen; –**py**, *adj* knapp

**skin, skinn**, *n* Haut *f*; (peel)
Schale *f*; *v* abhäuten;
(peel) schälen; –**ny**, *adj*
dünn

**skip, skipp**, *n* (jump) Sprung
*m*; (container) Container
*m*; *v* (jump) hüpfen; (with
rope) seilspringen; (omit)
auslassen; –**per**, *n* Kapitän
*m*

**skirmish, skör**-misch, *n*
Rangelei *f*; (fight)
Gefecht *nt*; *v* streiten;
(fight) sich Gefechte
liefern

**skirt, skört**, *n* Rock *m*; *v*
umgehen

**ski slope, skie** slohp, *n*
Skipiste *f*

**skittle, skitt**-'l, *n* Kegel *m*;
–**s**, *n* Kegeln *pl*

**skive, skeiw**, *v fam*
schwänzen

**skull, skall**, *n* Schädel *m*

**skunk, skank**, *n* Skunk *m*,
Stinktier *nt*

**sky, skei**, *n* Himmel *m*;
–**light**, *n* Oberlicht *nt*;
–**scraper**, *n*

Wolkenkratzer m

**slab,** släbb, n Platte f

**slack,** släck, adj (loose) lose, schlaff; (careless) nachlässig; (business) flau; v (not work) bummeln; **–en,** v (work loose) locker werden; (loosen) lockern; (slow down) verlangsamen; **–er,** n Faulenzer m

**slam,** slamm, n (cards) Schlemm m; v zuschlagen

**slander,** slahn-der, n Verleumdung f; v verleumden; **–er,** n Verleumder m

**slang,** släng, n Slang m

**slant,** slahnt, n Schräge f; fig Neigung f; v schräg laufen; **–ing,** adj schief, schräg

**slap,** släpp, n Klaps m; v schlagen, klopfen

**slash,** släsch, n (cut) Schnitt m; (wound) Schnittwunde f; v aufschlitzen; (fig price) drastisch reduzieren; (spending) drastisch kürzen

**slate,** sleht, n (material) Schiefer m; (on roof) Dachziegel m; (list of candidates) Kandidatenliste f; v in der Luft zerreißen

**slaughter,** slo'a-ter, n (of animals) Schlachten nt; (massacre) Metzelei f; v schlachten; (massacre) niedermetzeln; **–house,** n Schlachthof m

**slave,** slehw, n Sklave m, Sklavin f; v sich schinden; **–ry,** n Sklaverei f; (hard work) Schinderei f

**slay,** sleh, v erschlagen, umbringen

**sledge,** sledsch, n Schlitten m; **–hammer,** n Schmiedehammer m

**sleek,** sliek, adj (smooth) glatt; (well fed) wohlgenährt

**sleep,** sliep, n Schlaf m; v schlafen; **–ing bag,** n Schlafsack m; **–ing car,** n Schlafwagen m; **–ing pill,** n Schlaftablette f; **–less,** adj schlaflos; **–lessness,** n Schlaflosigkeit f; **–walker,** n Schlafwandler m; **–y,** adj schläfrig

**sleet,** sliet, n Schneeregen m

**sleeve,** sliew, n Ärmel m; **–less,** adj ärmellos

**sleigh,** sleh, n Schlitten m

**sleight,** sleit, n **– of hand,** Taschenspielerei f

**slender,** slenn-der, adj schlank; fig karg

**slice,** sleiss, n Schnitte f, Scheibe f; v in Scheiben schneiden

**slick,** slick, adj glatt; (polished) professionell; n (oil) – Ölteppich m

**slide,** sleid, n (children's) Rutschbahn f; photog Dia nt; v rutschen, gleiten; **hair –,** n Haarspange f

**slight,** sleit, adj (small) gering; (figure) zierlich; n

Beleidigung f; v beleidigen

**slim,** slimm, adj (thin) schlank; (small) gering; v (diet) eine Schlankheitskur machen; (reduce) reduzieren

**slime,** sleim, n Schlamm m

**slimming, slimm**-ing, adj Schlankheits-; n (diet) Abnehmen nt; (reduction) Kürzen nt

**slimy,** slei-mi, adj schlammig, fig schmierig

**sling,** sling, n Schlinge f; v schleudern

**slink,** slink, v schleichen

**slip,** slipp, n (error) Fehler m; (petticoat) Unterrock m; v (glide) gleiten; (fall) ausrutschen; **– away,** v sich davonstehlen; **– off,** v sich davonstehlen; (clothes) abstreifen; **– on,** v (clothes) überstreifen; **– one's mind,** v vergessen; **give sb the –,** v jdm entkommen

**slipped disc,** slipt disk, n Bandscheibenvorfall m

**slipper, slipp**-er, n Pantoffel m, Hausschuh m

**slippery, slipp**-e-ri, adj schlüpfrig

**slip-road, slipp**-rohd, n (on) Auffahrt f; (off) Ausfahrt f

**slit,** slitt, n Schlitz m; v aufschlitzen

**sliver, sliw**-er, n Streifen m; (food) dünne Scheibe f

**slob,** slobb, n (fam lazy) fauler Sack m; (fam fat)

Fettsack m

**slog**, slogg, v fam schuften

**slogan**, sloh-gen, n Slogan m, Schlagwort nt

**slope**, slohp, n Abhang m; v schräg laufen

**slot**, slott, n Schlitz m; (for coins) Einwurf m; – **in**, v (insert) einfügen; (fit in) passen; – **machine**, n Automat m

**sloth**, slohth, n Faulheit f; (animal) Faultier nt

**slouch**, slautsch, v lümmeln

**slovenly**, slaw-en-li, adj schlampig

**slow**, sloh, adj langsam; (stupid) dicht; (business) flau; – **down**, v nachlassen, (sich) verlangsamen; **–ly**, adv langsam; **be –**, v (of watch) nachgehen

**slug**, slagg, n Nacktschnecke f; (fam sip) Schlückchen nt; (fam bullet) Kugel f; **–ish**, adj träge

**sluice**, sluhss, n Schleuse f; **–gate**, n Schleusentor nt

**slum**, slamm, n Armenviertel nt

**slumber**, slamm-ber, n Schlummer m; v schlummern

**slump**, slamp, n Rückgang m, Sturz m; v fallen; comm stark zurückgehen

**slur**, slör, n Verleumdung f; **–red**, adj undeutlich; v undeutlich sprechen

**slush**, slasch, n

Schneematsch m; **–y**, adj matschig; (sentimental) sentimental

**slut**, slatt, n Schlampe f

**sly**, slei, adj schlau, listig

**smack**, smäck, n Schlag m; v schlagen; – **one's lips**, schmatzen

**small**, smo'al, adj klein; – **ad**, n Kleinanzeige f; – **change**, n Kleingeld nt; – **hours**, npl früher Morgen m; **–pox**, n Pocken pl; **–print**, n das Kleingedruckte nt

**smart**, smart, adj (clever) clever; (elegant) schick; (quick) flink; v schmerzen; – **card**, n Chipkarte f; **–en up**, v (make elegant) sich herrichten; (fam get clever) sich am Riemen reißen; **–ly**, adv (quickly) schnell; (elegantly) schick

**smash**, smäsch, n (collision) Zusammenstoß m; fin Einbruch m; v zerschlagen, zerschmettern; **–ing**, adj fam toll

**smattering**, smätt-e-ring, n oberflächliche Kenntnis f

**smear**, smier, n Fleck m; (defame) Beschmutzung f; v (be)schmieren; (defamation) in den Schmutz ziehen

**smell**, smell, n Geruch m; v riechen; (good) duften

**smile**, smeil, n Lächeln nt; v lächeln

**smirk**, smörk, n Grinsen nt; v grinsen

**smith**, smith, n Schmied m

**smithy**, ssmidh-i, n Schmiede f

**smog**, smogg, n Smog m

**smoke**, smohk, n Rauch m; v rauchen; (cure) räuchern; **–d glass**, n Rauchglas nt; **–less**, adj rauchlos; **–r**, n Raucher m; **–screen**, n fig Vernebelung f

**smoking**, smoh-king, n Rauchen nt

**smoky**, smoh-ki, adj (flavour) rauchig; (room) verraucht

**smooth**, smuhdh, adj glatt; v glätten

**smother**, smadh-er, v ersticken

**smoulder**, smohl-der, v glimmen; **–ing**, adj glühend

**smudge**, smadsch, n (Schmutz)fleck m; v beschmutzen, beschmieren

**smug**, smagg, adj selbstzufrieden

**smuggle**, smagg-'l, v schmuggeln; **–r**, n Schmuggler m

**smuggling**, smagg-ling, n Schmuggeln nt

**smut**, smatt, n Rußfleck m; (lewd) Schund m; **–ty**, adj schmutzig

**snack**, snäck, n Snack m, Imbiß m

**snail,** snehl, n Schnecke f
**snake,** snehk, n Schlange f
**snap,** snapp, n (sound)
Schnappen nt; (breaking)
Knack m; photog
Schnappschuß m; v
(break) brechen; (of
person, animal)
schnappen; photog
knipsen; **–shot,** n
Schnappschuß m
**snare,** snähr, n Schlinge f; v
fangen; (ensnare) in eine
Falle locken
**snarl,** snarl, v knurren; **– up,**
durcheinanderbringen;
(traffic) stocken
**snatch,** snätsch, n (grab)
Griff m; (snippet)
Stückchen nt; v (grab)
wegnehmen; (steal)
klauen; (sleep, meal) sich
(schnell) genehmigen
**sneak,** sniek, n (fam telltale)
Petze f; v schleichen; **–er,**
n Turnschuh m
**sneer,** snier, v spöttisch
lächeln
**sneeze,** snies, n Niesen nt; v
niesen
**sniff,** sniff, n Schnüffeln nt;
v schnüffeln; (smell)
schnuppern
**snip,** snipp, n Schnitt m;
(fam bargain)
Schnäppchen nt; v
schnippeln; **– off,** v
abschnippeln
**sniper,** snei-per, n
Heckenschütze m
**snippet,** snipp-itt, n

Schnipsel m
**snivel,** sniw-'l, v schnüffeln
**snob,** snobb, n Snob m;
**–bish,** adj snobistisch
**snooker,** snuh-ker, n
Snooker nt
**snooze,** snuhs, n
Nickerchen nt; v dösen
**snore,** snor, v schnarchen
**snorkel,** snor-k'l, n
Schnorchel m; v
schnorcheln
**snort,** snort, n Schnauben
nt; v schnauben
**snout,** snaut, n Schnauze f
**snow,** snoh, n Schnee m; v
schneien; **–ball,** n
Schneeball; v fig schnell
zunehmen; **–bound,** adj
eingeschneit; **–drop,** n
Schneeglöckchen nt;
**–flake,** n Schneeflocke f;
**–plough,** n Schneepflug
m; **–storm,** n
Schneesturm m
**snub,** snabb, n Abfuhr f; v
vor den Kopf stoßen; **–-
nosed,** adj stupsnasig
**snuff,** snaff, n
Schnupftabak m
**snug,** snagg, adj mollig,
behaglich
**so,** ssoh, adv so; conj
(therefore) also; (so that)
so daß; **– as to ...,** conj
damit; (in order to) um ...
zu; **– do I** (etc.), ich auch;
**– far,** adv bis jetzt; **– that,**
conj (purpose) damit;
(result) so daß; **– what?**
na und; **... or –,** etwa ...

**soak,** ssohk, v einweichen;
(drench) durchnässen
**soap,** ssohp, n Seife f; **–
opera,** n (TV) Seifenoper
f; **– powder,** n
Waschpulver nt; **–y,** adj
seifig
**soar,** ssor, v auffliegen; (of
prices) steil ansteigen
**sob,** ssobb, n Schluchzen nt;
v schluchzen
**sober,** ssoh-ber, adj
nüchtern; v **– up,**
nüchtern werden
**so-called,** ssoh-ko'ald, adj
sogenannte(r/s)
**sociable,** ssoh-sche-b'l, adj
gesellig
**social,** ssoh-schel, adj sozial;
**– club,** n Klub m für
geselliges Zusammensein;
**– evening,** n gesellige
Abendveranstaltung f;
**–ism,** n Sozialismus m;
**–ize with sb,** v mit jdm
Umgang
pflegen/verkehren; **–
security,** n
Sozialversicherung f; **–
worker,** n Sozialarbeiter m
**society,** sse-ssei-i-ti, n
Gesellschaft f; (club)
Verein m
**sock,** ssock, n Socke f; (fam
blow) Schlag m
**socket,** ssock-itt, n elec
Steckdose f; (for eye,
tooth) Höhle f
**sod,** ssodd, n (grass)
Rasensode f; vulg Sau f
**soda,** ssoh-de, n Soda nt; **–**

**water**, n Sodawasser nt
**sofa**, ssoh-fe, n Sofa nt
**soft**, ssoft, adj weich; (quiet)
leise; (lenient)
nachsichtig; – **drink**, n
alkoholfreies Getränk nt;
**–en**, v (make soft)
aufweichen; (get soft)
weich werden; (blow)
lindern; **–ness**, n
Weichheit f; **–ware**, n
comp Software f
**soil**, sseul, n Erde f, Boden
m; v beschmutzen
**solace**, ssoll-iss, n Trost m; v
trösten
**solar**, ssoh-ler, adj Sonnen-;
– **panel**, n
Sonnenkollektor m; –
**power**, n Sonnenenergie f
**solder**, ssoll-der, n
Lötmetall nt; v löten
**soldier**, ssohl-dscher, n
Soldat m; v – **on**, sich
durchkämpfen
**sole**, ssohl, adj einzig; n (of
foot etc.) Sohle f; (fish)
Seezunge f; **–ly**, adv allein
**solemn**, ssoll-em, adj
(occasion) feierlich;
(person) ernst
**solicit**, sse-liss-itt, v bitten
um; (of prostitute) sich
anbieten; **–or**, n
Rechtsanwalt m,
Rechtsanwältin f
**solid**, ssoll-idd, adj (hard)
fest; (not hollow) massiv
**solidarity**, ssoll-i-dä-ri-ti, n
Solidarität f
**solidify**, sse-lidd-i-fei, v fest

werden
**solitary**, ssoll-i-te-ri, adj
einsam; (single) einzeln; –
**confinement**, n
Einzelhaft f
**solitude**, ssoll-i-tjuhd, n
Einsamkeit f
**solo**, ssoh-loh, adj Solo-; n
Solo nt; **–ist**, n Solist m
**soluble**, ssoll-ju-b'l, adj
löslich; (problem) lösbar
**solution**, sse-luh-sch'n, n
Lösung f
**solve**, ssolw, v lösen;
(puzzle) erraten
**solvency**, ssoll-wen-ssi, n
Zahlungsfähigkeit f
**solvent**, ssoll-went, adj fin
zahlungsfähig; n chem
Lösungsmittel nt
**sombre**, ssomm-ber, adj
düster
**some**, ssamm, adj & pron
etwas, pl einige, manche,
ein paar; (a little) ein
wenig; (some or other)
(irgend)ein; adv etwa
**somebody**, ssamm-be-di,
pron jemand
**somehow**, ssamm-hau, adv
irgendwie
**someone**, ssamm-u'ann,
pron jemand
**somersault**, ssamm-er-ssolt,
n Purzelbaum m
**something**, ssamm-thing,
pron etwas
**sometime**, ssamm-teim, adj
(former) ehemalig(e, r);
adv irgendwann
**sometimes**, ssamm-teims,

adv manchmal
**somewhat**, ssamm-u'ott, adv
etwas
**somewhere**, ssamm-u'ähr,
adv irgendwo
**son**, ssann, n Sohn m
**sonar**, ssoh-nahr, n Sonar nt
**sonata**, sse-nah-te, n Sonate
f
**song**, ssong, n Lied nt
**son-in-law**, sann-inn-lor, n
Schwiegersohn m
**soon**, ssuhn, adv bald; –
**after(wards)**, n, kurz
danach; **as – as**, sobald;
**–er**, adv (earlier) früher;
(rather) lieber
**soot**, ssutt, n Ruß m
**soothe**, ssuhdh, v (person)
beruhigen; (pain) lindern
**sophisticated**, sse-fiss-ti-
keh-tidd, adj (person)
kultiviert; (elaborate)
ausgeklügelt
**sopping wet**, ssopp-ing
u'ett, adj patschnaß
**soppy**, ssopp-i, adj schmalzig
**sorcerer**, ssor-sse-rer, n
Zauberer m
**sorcery**, ssor-sse-ri, n
Zauberei f, Hexerei f
**sordid**, ssor-didd, adj
(squalid) schmutzig;
(base) dreckig
**sore**, ssor, adj schmerzhaft; n
wunde Stelle f
**sorrow**, sso-roh, n Kummer
m; **–ful**, adj kummervoll
**sorry**, sso-ri, adj elend; **–?**
wie bitte?; **(I am) –**, es tut
mir leid; **I am/I feel – for**

**sb**, *v* jd tut mir leid
**sort**, ssort, *n* Sorte *f*; *v* –
 **(out)**, (arrange) sortieren;
 (solve) lösen; **a – of …**,
 eine Art …, so ein(e) …
**soul**, ssohl, *n* Seele *f*; *mus*
 Soul *m*; **--destroying**, *adj*
 nervtötend
**sound**, ssaund, *adj* (healthy)
 gesund; (thorough)
 gründlich; (sensible)
 vernünftig; (sleep) fest; *n*
 Laut *m*; (musical) Klang
 *m*; (of voice) Ton *m*; *v*
 ertönen; (seem) klingen; –
 **barrier**, *n* Schallmauer *f*;
 **–bite**, *n*
 (Nachrichten)happen *m*;
 **– effects**, *npl* Toneffekte
 *pl*–**ing**, *n naut* Lotung *f*;
 (investigation)
 Sondierung *f*; **–track**, *n*
 Soundtrack *m*; **– like**, *v*
 sich anhören wie
**soup**, ssuhp, *n* Suppe *f*;
 **–spoon**, *n* Suppenlöffel *m*
**sour**, ssau-er, *adj* sauer
**source**, ssorss, *n* Quelle *f*;
 (origin) Ursprung *m*
**south**, ssauth, *adj* südlich,
 Süd-; *adv* südlich, nach
 Süden; *n* Süden *m*; **S–
 Africa**, *n* Südafrika *nt*; **S–
 America**, *n* Südamerika
 *nt*; **--east**, *n* Südosten *m*;
 **–erly**, *adj* südlich; **–ern**,
 *adj* südlich, Süd-; **S– Pole**,
 *n* Südpol *m*; **--west**, *n*
 Südwesten *m*
**souvenir**, ssuh-we-**nier**, *n*
 Andenken *nt*, Souvenir *nt*

**sovereign**, ssow-**rin**, *adj*
 souverän; *n* Herrscher *m*;
 **–ty**, *n* Souveränität *f*
**soviet**, ssoh-wi-et, *adj*
 sowjetisch; **the – Union**,
 Sowjetunion *f*
**sow**, ssau, *n* Sau *f*
**sow**, ssoh, *v* (be)säen; **–er**, *n*
 Sämann *m*
**soya**, sseu-e-, **– bean**, *n*
 Sojabohne *f*
**space**, spehss, *n* Raum *m*;
 (universe) All *nt*,
 Weltraum *m*; (time
 interval) Zeitraum *m*;
 (gap) Zwischenraum *m*;
 (distance) Abstand *m*;
 **–craft**, **–ship**, *n*
 Raumschiff *nt*
**spacious**, speh-schess, *adj*
 geräumig, umfangreich
**spade**, spehd, *n* Spaten *m*;
 (cards) Pik *nt*
**Spain**, spehn, *n* Spanien *nt*
**span**, spänn, *n* Spanne *f*; (of
 arch) Spannweite *f*; *v*
 überspannen
**Spaniard**, spänn-jerd, *n*
 Spanier *m*
**spaniel**, spänn-jel, *n* Spaniel
 *m*
**Spanish**, spänn-isch, *adj*
 spanisch; *n* (language)
 Spanisch *nt*; *npl* (people)
 Spanier *pl*
**spank**, spänk, *v* hauen
**spanner**, spänn-er, *n*
 Schraubenschlüssel *m*
**spar**, spahr, *n naut* Spiere *f*; *v*
 boxen; (fight) kämpfen
**spare**, spähr, *adj*

(replacement) Ersatz-;
 (thin) dürr; (left over)
 übrig; *n* Ersatzteil *nt*; *v*
 (time, money) übrig
 haben; (person, feelings)
 (ver)schonen; **– part**, *n*
 Ersatzteil *nt*; **– time**, *n*
 Freizeit *f*
**sparing(ly)**, spähr-ring(-li),
 *adj & adv* sparsam
**spark**, spark, *n* Funken *m*; *v*
 Funken sprühen; **–(ing)
 plug**, *n* Zündkerze *f*
**sparkle**, spark-'l, *v* funkeln,
 glänzen
**sparkling**, spark-ling, *adj*
 funkelnd, glänzend;
 (wine) Schaum-; (water)
 mit Kohlensäure
**sparrow**, spä-roh, *n* Spatz *m*,
 Sperling *m*
**sparse**, sparss, *adj* spärlich
**spasm**, späsm, *n* Krampf *m*
**spasmodic**, späs-modd-ick,
 *adj* sporadisch
**spate**, speht, *n* (*fig* series)
 Serie *f*
**spatter**, spätt-er, *v*
 (be)spritzen
**spawn**, spo'an, *n* Laich *m*; *v*
 hervorbringen; (frog)
 laichen
**speak**, spiek, *v* sprechen;
 (talk) reden; **–er**, *n*
 (person) Redner *m*;
 (loudspeaker)
 Lautsprecher *m*; **– to**, *v*
 sprechen mit
**spear**, spier, *n* Speer *m*; *v*
 aufspießen
**special**, spesch-'l, *adj*

besondere(r/s); –**ist**, n
Experte m, Expertin f; med
Facharzt m, Fachärztin f;
–**ity**, n Spezialität f;
(subject) Fachgebiet nt; –
**ize (in)**, v sich
spezialisieren (auf);
–**ly**, adv (particularly)
besonders; (purposely)
speziell; –**ty**, n
Fachgebiet nt

**species**, spie-schies, n Art f
**specific(ally)**, spe-ssi-fick(-
e-li), adj & adv spezifisch
**specification**, spe-si-fi-keh-
sch'n, n Angabe f; comm
Spezifikation f
**specify**, spess-i-fei, v (list)
spezifizieren; (stipulate)
vorschreiben
**specimen**, spess-i-minn, adj
Probe-; n Exemplar nt;
med Probe f
**speck**, speck, n Fleck m;
–**led**, adj gesprenkelt
**spectacle**, speck-te-k'l, n
Anblick m; (pair of) –**s**,
npl Brille f
**spectacular**, speck-**täck**-ju-
ler, adj sensationell
**spectator**, speck-**teh**-ter, n
Zuschauer m
**spectre**, speck-ter, n
Gespenst nt
**speculate**, speck-juh-leht, v
spekulieren
**speech**, spietsch, n Sprache
f; (discourse) Rede f;
–**less**, adj sprachlos
**speed**, spied, n
Geschwindigkeit f; v

eilen; (in car) zu schnell
fahren; –**ing**, n
Geschwindigkeitsüber-
schreitung f; – **limit**, n
Geschwindigkeits-
beschränkung f; –**ometer**,
n Tacho m; – **up**, v (make
faster) beschleunigen; (get
faster) schneller werden;
–**y**, adj schnell
**spell**, spell, n (magic)
Zauber m; (period)
Zeitlang f; v
buchstabieren; –**ing**, n
Schreibweise f
**spend**, spend, v ausgeben;
–**thrift**, n Verschwender m
**sphere**, sfier, n (shape,
globe) Kugel f; (area)
Gebiet nt
**spherical**, sfe-rick-'l, adj
kugelförmig
**spice**, speiss, n Gewürz nt; v
würzen
**spicy**, speiss-i, adj pikant
**spider**, spei-der, n Spinne f
**spike**, speik, n Stachel m;
(shoe) Spike m; v (fam
add to drink) etw in den
Drink tun
**spill**, spill, n Auslaufen nt; v
verschütten; (run over)
überlaufen
**spin**, spinn, n (outing)
Spazierfahrt f; v (turn)
sich drehen; (thread)
spinnen; – **out**, v in die
Länge ziehen
**spinach**, spinn-itsch, n
Spinat m
**spinal**, spei-n'l, adj

Wirbelsäulen-
**spindly**, spind-li, adj
spindeldürr
**spin doctor**, spinn-dock-ter,
n Wortkünstler m (in der
Politik)
**spin-drier**, spinn-drei-er, n
Wäscheschleuder f
**spine**, speinn, n Wirbelsäule
f; fig Rückgrat nt
**spinning**, spinn-ing, adj
Spinn-; n Spinnen nt
**spin-off**, spinn-off, n
Konsequenz f
**spinster**, spin-ster, n
unverheiratete Frau f; pej
alte Jungfer f
**spiral**, spei-rel, adj
spiralförmig; n Spirale
f; – **staircase**, n
Wendeltreppe f
**spire**, speir, n Turmspitze f
**spirit**, spi-ritt, n Geist m;
(alcohol) Spirituosen pl;
(vitality) Lebhaftigkeit f;
–**ed**, adj (lively) lebhaft;
(bold) mutig; –**s**, npl
Spirituosen pl; –**ual**, adj
geistig; –**ualist**, n Spiritist
m; **in good –s**, guten
Mutes
**spit**, spitt, n (saliva) Spucke
f; (cooking) Spieß m; v
spucken; (rain) sprühen
**spite**, speit, n Groll m; v
ärgern; –**ful**, adj boshaft;
**in – of**, conj trotz
**spittle**, spitt-'l, n Speichel m
**splash**, spläsch, n Spritzer m;
v (be)spritzen
**splendid**, splenn-didd, adj

prächtig, glänzend

**splendour, splenn**-der, n Pracht f, Glanz m

**splint,** splint, n Schiene f

**splinter, splinn**-ter, n Splitter m; v zersplittern

**split,** splitt, n Spalte f; fig Trennung f; v spalten; fig trennen; – **up,** sich trennen

**spoil,** speul, v verderben; (indulge) verwöhnen; **–s,** npl Beute f

**spoke,** spohk, n Speiche f

**spokesman, spohkss**-men, n Sprecher m

**spokeswoman, spohkss-wu**-men, n Sprecherin f

**sponge,** spandsch, n Schwamm m; v schnorren; – **bag,** n Kulturbeutel m; – **on sb,** v von jdm schnorren

**sponsor, sponn**-ser, n Sponsor m; v sponsern; **–ship,** n Sponsoring nt, Sponsorschaft f

**spontaneous(ly),** sponn-**teh**-ni-ess(-li), adj & adv spontan

**spooky, spuh**-ki, adj gespentisch

**spool,** spuhl, n Spule f; v spulen

**spoon,** spuhn, n Löffel m; **–ful,** n Löffel(voll) m

**sport,** sport, n Sport m; **–ing,** adj fair; **–s car,** n Sportwagen m; **–sman,** n Sportler m; **–swoman,** n Sportlerin f; **–y,** adj

sportlich

**spot,** spott, n (mark) Fleck m; (dot) Punkt m; (place) Ort m, Stelle f; v (mark) beflecken; (notice) bemerken; – **check,** n Stichprobe f; **–less,** adj fleckenlos; **–light,** n Scheinwerfer(licht nt) m; (limelight) Rampenlicht nt; **–ted,** adj gefleckt; getüpfelt; **–ty,** adj (skin) pickelig

**spout,** spaut, n (of gutter) Ausguß m; (of jug) Schnabel m; (of water) Ausfluß m; v spritzen

**sprain,** sprehn, n Verrenkung f; v verrenken

**sprawl,** spro'al, v sich spreizen, sich rekeln

**spray,** spreh, n (sea) Gischt m; (on road) Spritzen nt; (for hair etc.) Spray m/nt; (of flowers) Strauß m; v (be)sprühen; (hair) sprayen

**spread,** spredd, n (for bread) Aufstrich m; (expanse) Verbreitung f; v (expand) (sich) ausbreiten; (butter etc.) (ver)streichen; (news) verbreiten

**spree,** sprie, n (shopping) Einkaufsorgie f

**sprig,** sprigg, n Reis nt, Sproß m

**sprightly, spreit**-li, adj munter, lebhaft

**spring,** spring, n (season) Frühling m; (leap) Sprung

m; (source) Quelle f; mech Feder f; v springen; **–cleaning,** n Frühjahrsputz m; **–y,** adj elastisch

**sprinkle, spring**-k'l, v (water) sprengen; (sugar etc.) streuen; **–r,** n Sprinkler m; (garden) Sprenger m; – **with,** v (liquid) besprengen mit; (sugar etc.) bestreuen mit

**sprint,** sprint, n Sprint m; v sprinten, rennen

**sprout,** spraut, n Sprößling m; (vegetable) Rosenkohl m; v sprossen

**spruce,** spruhss, adj gepflegt; n Fichte f

**spur,** spör, n Sporn m; fig Ansporn m; v – **(on),** anspornen

**spurious, spjuhr**-ri-ess, adj unecht, falsch

**spurn,** spörn, v verschmähen

**spurt,** spört, n (jet) Spurt m; (speed) Endspurt m; v spritzen

**spy,** spei, n Spion m; v spionieren; **–ing,** n Spionage f

**squabble, sku'obb**-'l, n Zank m; v (sich) zanken

**squad,** sku'odd, n mil Trupp m; sport Mannschaft f; **–ron,** n (air) Staffel f; (naval) Geschwader nt

**squalid, sku'oll**-idd, adj schäbig; (dirty) schmutzig

**squall,** sku'o'al, n Bö f

**squalor, sku'oll**-er, n Elend

nt; (dirtiness) Schmutz m

**squander**, sku'onn-der, v
verschwenden

**square**, skwähr, adj
viereckig; (meal)
anständig; (fam old-
fashioned) spießig;
(maths) Quadrat-; n
(maths) Quadrat nt; (open space)
Platz m; v (maths)
quadrieren; –ed, adj
(paper) kariert; (maths)
(im) Quadrat; – metre, n
Quadratmeter m; – with,
v (agree) übereinstimmen
mit; (make agree)
abstimmen; all –, quitt

**squash**, sku'osch, n sport
Squash m; (drink)
Fruchtsaftgetränk nt; v
(zer)quetschen; fig
erdrücken

**squat**, sku'ott, adj untersetzt;
v hocken; –ter, n
Hausbesetzer m

**squeak**, sku'iek, v (of
animal) quieken; (of
door) quietschen

**squeeze**, sku'ies, n Druck m;
v drücken; (fruit)
auspressen

**squiggle**, sku'igg-'l, n
Schnörkel m

**squint**, sku'int, n Schielen
nt; v schielen

**squirrel**, sku'i-rel, n
Eichhörnchen nt

**squirt**, sku'ört, n Spritze f; v
spritzen

**St**, abbr Street or Saint

**stab**, stäbb, n Stich m; (fam

attempt) Versuch m; v
stechen; (fatally)
erstechen

**stability**, ste-**bill**-i-ti, n
Stabilität f

**stabilize**, steh-**bill**-eis, v
(sich) stabilisieren

**stable**, steh-b'l, adj fest,
stabil; n Stall m

**stack**, stäck, n (of paper)
Stapel m; (of hay)
Schober m; (chimney)
Schornstein m; v
aufstapeln

**stadium**, steh-di-em, n
Stadion nt

**staff**, stahf, n (employees)
Personal nt; (teachers)
Lehrerschaft f; (stick, mil)
Stab m; v besetzen

**stag**, stägg, n Hirsch m

**stage**, stehdsch, n theatre
Bühne f; (point)
(Zeit)punkt m; (of
journey) Etappe f; v
veranstalten; theatre
aufführen; – manager, n
Inspizient m

**stagger**, stägg-er, v taumeln;
(astonish) verblüffen;
(offset) staffeln

**stagnate**, stägg-neht, v
stocken, stillstehen

**stag party**, stägg pahr-ti, n
Männerabend m (vor der
Hochzeit)

**staid**, stehd, adj gesetzt

**stain**, stehn, n (colour)
Beize f; (mark) Fleck m; v
(colour) beizen; (mark)
beflecken; –ed glass, n

Farbglas nt; –ed glass
window, n Fenster nt mit
Glasmalereien; –less, adj
(steel) rostfrei; –
remover,
n Fleckenentferner m

**stair**, stähr, n (Treppen)stufe
f; –s, npl Treppe f; –case, n
Treppenhaus nt

**stake**, stehk, n (post) Pfahl
m; (wager) Einsatz m;
(interest) Anteil m; v
(wager) setzen; at –, auf
dem Spiel

**stale**, stehl, adj alt; (bread)
altbacken; (beer) schal;
–mate, n Patt nt

**stalk**, sto'ak, n Stengel m; v
(game) pirschen; (person)
jdm hinterherschleichen;
–er, n jd, der einer Person
hinterherschleicht

**stall**, sto'al, n Stand m; v (of
car) abwürgen; (stop)
stehenbleiben; (be
evasive) ausweichen; –s,
npl theatre Parkett nt

**stalwart**, sto'al-u'ert, adj
wacker, standhaft; n treuer
Anhänger m

**stamina**, stämm-i-ne, n
Ausdauer f

**stammer**, stämm-er, v
Stottern m; v stottern;
–er, n Stotterer m

**stamp**, stämp, n (rubber
etc.) Stempel m; (postage)
Briefmarke f; v stempeln;
(post) frankieren; (foot)
stampfen; (memory)
einprägen; – collecting, n
Briefmarkensammeln nt

**stampede,** stämm-**pied,** n wilde Flucht f

**stance,** stänss, n Haltung f

**stand,** ständ, n (platform) Tribüne f; (support) Ständer m; (resistance) Widerstand m; v stehen; (put) stellen; (endure) aushalten; (for election) kandidieren; – **down,** v (resign) zurücktreten; – **for,** v (mean) bedeuten; (tolerate) dulden; – **up,** v aufstehen

**standard,** stann-derd, adj Normal-; n (norm) Norm f; (level) Niveau nt; (flag) Fahne f, **–ize,** v normen; – **of living,** s, npl (moral) Maßstäbe pl; (of achievement) Maß nt

**standing,** adj (permanent) ständig; (upright) stehend; n Ansehen nt; – **order,** n fin Dauerauftrag m; – **room,** n Stehplatz m

**standpoint,** ständ-peunt, n Standpunkt m

**standstill,** ständ-still, n Stillstand m

**staple,** steh-p'l, adj Haupt-; n (clip) Heftklamme f; (food) Hauptnahrungsmittel nt; v (clip) klammern; **–r,** n Hefter m

**star,** stahr, n Stern m; (person) Star m; v auftreten

**starboard,** stahr-berd, n

**Steuerbord** nt

**starch,** startsch, n Stärke f; v stärken

**stare,** stähr, n Starren nt; v – **(at),** (an)starren

**stark,** stark, adj (reality etc.) kraß; (landscape) kahl; – **naked,** adj splitternackt

**starling,** stahr-ling, n Star m

**starry,** adj sternenübersät

**start,** start, n (beginning) Anfang m; sport Start m; (shock) Schreck m; v (begin) anfangen; sport starten; (car) anspringen; (journey) antreten; (jump) sich erschrecken; **–er,** n (dish) Vorspeise f; mech Anlasser m

**startle,** start-'l, v erschrecken

**starvation,** stahr-weh-sch'n, n Verhungern nt

**starve,** stahrw, v (ver)hungern

**state,** steht, n (country) Staat m; (condition) Zustand m; v angeben, erklären; **–ly,** adj stattlich; **–ment,** n Erklärung f; (account) Aufstellung f; **–sman,** n Staatsmann m

**static,** adj stillstehend; elec statisch

**station,** steh-sch'n, n rail Bahnhof m; (police) Wache f; (position) Rang m; v stationieren; (place) stellen; **–ary,** adj stillstehend

**stationer,** steh-sch'n-er, n

Schreibwarenhändler m; **–y,** n Schreibwaren fpl

**statistics,** ste-tiss-ticks, n Statistik f; npl Statistiken pl

**statue,** stätt-juh, n Standbild m, Statue f

**status,** steh-tess, n Status m, Ansehen nt

**statute,** stätt-juht, n Statut nt, Gesetz nt

**staunch,** stoansch, adj treu, fest; v stillen

**stave,** stehw, n (stick) Stab m; mus Notenlinien pl; – **in,** v einschlagen; – **off,** v abwehren

**stay,** steh, n Aufenthalt m; (remain) bleiben; (lodge) wohnen; – **the night,** v übernachten

**stead,** stedd, n Stelle f; **in good –,** zustatten

**steadfast,** stedd-fahst, adj standhaft, fest

**steadily,** stedd-i-li, adv (rain) ununterbrochen; (balance, gaze) fest

**steady,** stedd-i, adj (stable) stabil, fest; (reliable) solide; (unshaking) ruhig; (gradual) stetig; (rain) ununterbrochen

**steak,** stehk, n Steak nt

**steal,** stiel, v stehlen; (creep) sich stehlen

**stealth,** stelth, n Heimlichkeit f; **–y,** adj verstohlen

**steam,** stiem, n Dampf m; v dampfen; (cooking)

dämpfen; **–er,** Dampfer *m*

**steel,** stiel, *n* Stahl *m*; *v* – **o.s.,** sich wappnen

**steep,** stiep, *adj* steil; *v* einweichen

**steeple,** stie-p'l, *n* Kirchturm *m*

**steer,** stier, *v* steuern; **– clear of,** *v fam* aus dem Weg gehen, vermeiden; **–ing wheel,** *n* Steuerrad *nt*, Lenkrad *nt*

**stem,** stemm, *n* Stiel *m*; *v* (stop) stemmen; **– from,** *v* stammen von

**stench,** stentsch, *n* Gestank *m*

**step,** step, *n* (pace, measure) Schritt *m*; (stair) Stufe *f*; *v* schreiten; **– down,** *v* (resign) abtreten; **–brother/daughter/father,** *n* Stiefbruder *m*/-tochter *f*/-vater *m*; **–ladder,** *n* Trittleiter *f*; **–mother/sister/son,** Stiefmutter *f*/-schwester *f*/-sohn *m*

**stereo,** ste-ri-oh, *adj* Stereo-; *n* Stereoanlage *f*

**stereotype,** ste-ri-oh-teip, *n* Stereotyp *nt*; *fig* Klischee *nt*; *v fig* in ein Klischee zwängen

**sterile,** ste-reil, *adj* unfruchtbar; *med* steril

**sterilize,** ste-ri-leis, *v* sterilisieren

**sterling,** stör-ling, *adj* (silver) Sterling-; (pound) Sterling; *fig* gediegen; *n*

Pfund Sterling *nt*

**stern,** störn, *adj* ernst, streng; *n naut* Heck *nt*

**stew,** stjuh, *n* Ragout *nt*, Eintopf *m*; *v* schmoren

**steward,** stjuh-erd, *n* Steward *m*; **–ess,** *n* Stewardeß *f*

**stick,** stick, *n* Stock *m*; *v* stecken; (paste) ankleben; (*fam* bear) dabeibleiben; **– out,** *v* hervorstehen; **– up for sb/sth,** *v* sich für jdn/etw einsetzen; **–er,** *n* Ankleber *m*; **–ing plaster,** *n* Heftpflaster *nt*; **–y,** *adj* klebrig

**stiff,** stiff, *adj* steif; (thick) dick; (strong) stark; **–en,** *v* (sich) versteifen

**stifle,** steif-'l, *v* ersticken; *fig* unterdrücken

**stigma,** stigg-me, *n* Stigma *nt*

**stigmatize,** stigg-me-teis, *v* brandmarken

**stile,** steil, *n* Zauntritt *m*

**still,** still, *adj* still; *adv* (immer) noch; (anyway) trotzdem; *conj* trotzdem; *n* Destillierapparat *m*; *v* beruhigen; **birth,** *n* Totgeburt *f*; **–born,** *adj* totgeboren

**stilted,** still-tidd, gestelzt

**stilts,** stilts, *npl* Stelzen *pl*

**stimulate,** stimm-juh-leht, *v* anregen

**stimulus,** stimm-juh-less, *n* Anreiz *m*

**sting,** sting, *n* Stich *m*;

(barb) Stachel *m*; *v* stechen; (be sore) brennen

**stingy,** stinn-dschi, *adj* geizig, filzig

**stink,** stink, *n* Gestank *m*; *v* stinken

**stint,** stint, *n* Pensum *nt*; *v* sparen

**stipulate,** stipp-ju-leht, *v* fordern

**stir,** stör, *n* (excitement) Aufsehen *nt*; *v* (sich) rühren; **– up,** *v fig* wecken

**stirrup,** sti-rep, *n* Steigbügel *m*

**stitch,** stitsch, *n* Stich *m*; (knitting) Masche *f*; *med* Faden *m*; (pain) Seitenstiche *pl*; *v* nähen

**stock,** stock, *adj* Standard-; *n* (store) Vorrat *m*; *comm* Warenbestand *m*; (of gun) Kolben *m*; (broth) Brühe *f*; (animals) Vieh *nt*; (flower) Levkoje *f*; *v* (goods) führen; **in –,** vorrätig; **out of –,** nicht vorrätig; **take –,** *v* Inventur machen; *fig* Bilanz ziehen

**stockbroker,** stock-broh-ker, *n* Börsenmakler *m*

**stock cube,** stock kjuhb, *n* Brühwürfel *m*

**stock exchange,** stock iks-tschehndsch, *n* Börse *f*

**stocking,** stock-ing, *n* Strumpf *m*

**stock market,** stock mahr-kitt, *n* Börse *f*

**stockpile, stock**-peil, *n* Vorrat *m*; *v* horten, anhäufen

**stocks,** stocks, *npl* Aktien *pl*; **– and shares,** Effekten *pl*

**stocktaking, stock**-teh-king, *n* Inventur *f*

**stoke,** stohk, *v* heizen; **–r,** *n* Heizer *m*

**stolid,** stoll-idd, *adj* stur

**stomach, stamm-**ek, *n* Magen *m*; **– ache,** *n* Magenschmerzen *pl*

**stone,** stohn, *n* Stein *m*; (pebble) Kieselstein *m*; (of fruit) Kern *m*; (weight) 6,35 kg; *v* (fruit) entkernen; (throw stones at) steinigen; **--deaf,** *adj* stocktaub

**stool,** stuhl, *n* Hocker *m*; *med* Stuhlgang *m*

**stoop,** stuhp, *v* sich bücken, sich beugen

**stop,** stopp, *n* Halt *m*, Haltestelle *f*; (punctuation) Punkt *m*; *v* anhalten; (payment) einstellen; (hole) verschließen; (cease) aufhören; (doing sth) aufhören mit; **–gap,** *n* Notbehelf *m*; **–page,** *n* Unterbrechung; (traffic, blockage) Stau *m*; (strike) Streik *m*; **–per,** *n* Stöpsel *m*; **– press,** *n* letzte Meldung *f*

**storage, stor-**ridsch, *n* Lagerung *f*

**store,** stor, *n* (supply) Vorrat *m*; (warehouse) Lager *nt*; (shop) Kaufhaus *nt*, Laden *m*; *v* lagern

**storey, stor-**ri, *n* Stock *m*, Etage *f*

**stork,** stork, *n* Storch *m*

**storm,** storm, *n* Sturm *m*; *v* stürmen; **–y,** *adj* stürmisch

**story, stor-**ri, *n* Geschichte *f*; (untruth) Lüge *f*; **–book,** *n* Kinderbuch *nt*; (fairy tales) Märchenbuch *nt*

**stout,** staut, *adj* (fat) dick; (brave) tapfer; *n* Malzbier *nt*

**stove,** stohw, *n* Ofen *m*; (cooker) Herd *m*

**stow,** stoh, *v* verstauen; **–away,** *n* blinder Passagier *m*

**straddle, strädd-'**l, *v* rittlings sitzen; *fig* überspannen

**straggle, strägg-'**l, *v* nachhinken; **–r,** *n* Nachzügler *m*; **–y,** *adj* zottig

**straight,** streht, *adj* gerade; (honest) ehrlich; (undiluted) pur; *adv* direkt; **– away,** *adv* sofort; **–en,** *v* gerade machen; **–forward,** *adj* einfach; (honest) redlich; **– on,** *adv* geradeaus

**strain,** strehn, *n* (tension) Spannung *f*; (effort) Anstrengung *f*; (type) Art *f*; *mus* Klang *m*; *v* sich anstrengen; (make tense) spannen; (ankle) verrenken; (liquid)

durchseihen; (water) abgießen; **– ed,** *adj* (tense) gespannt; (forced) gezwungen; **–er,** *n* Sieb *nt*

**strait,** streht, *n* Meerenge *f*; **–jacket,** *n* Zwangsjacke *f*

**strand,** stränd, *n* Faden *m*; (of hair) Strähne *f*; **–ed,** *adj* (*naut, fig*) gestrandet

**strange,** strehndsch, *adj* fremd; (peculiar) seltsam; **–r,** *n* Fremde(r) *m & f*

**strangle, sträng-**g'l, *v* erwürgen

**strap,** sträpp, *n* Riemen *m*; *v* festschnallen; **–ping,** *adj* stramm

**strategic,** stre-tie-dschick, a, strategisch

**strategy, strätt-**e-dschi, *n* Strategie *f*

**straw,** stro'a, *n* Stroh *nt*; (drinking) Strohhalm *m*; **–berry,** *n* Erdbeere *f*; **be the last –,** *v* das Faß zum Überlaufen bringen

**stray,** streh, *adj* (animal) verirrt; (rare) vereinzelt; *v* vom Weg abgehen

**streak,** striek, *n* Streifen *m*; (in hair) Strähne *f*; (characteristic) Eigenschaft *f*; *v* (go quickly) flitzen; (run naked) blitzen; **–er,** *n* Blitzer *m*; **–y,** *adj* gestreift; (bacon) durchwachsen

**stream,** striem, *n* (small river) Bach *m*; (current, *fig*) Strom *m*; *v* strömen; **–line,** *v* rationalisieren;

–**lined,** *adj*
stromlinienförmig;
(simplified) rationalisiert

**street,** striet, *adj* Straßen-; n
Straße *f*; – **map,** n
Stadtplan *m*; **be –wise,** v
wissen, wo's langgeht

**strength,** strength, n Stärke
*f*, Kraft *f*; –**en,** v
verstärken

**strenuous, strenn-juh-ess,**
*adj* (task) anstrengend;
(denial, effort) heftig

**stress,** stress, n *med* Streß *m*;
*mech* Belastung *f*;
(emphasis) Gewicht *nt*; v
betonen; belasten

**stretch,** stretsch, n Strecke *f*;
v (sich) strecken; –**er,** n
Tragbahre *f*; – **out,** v
(sich) ausstrecken

**strew,** struh, v übersäen

**strict(ly),** strikt(-li), *adj & adv* (severe) streng;
(precise) genau

**stride,** streid, n Schritt *m*; v
schreiten

**strident, strei-dent,** *adj*
schrill

**strife,** streif, n Streit *m*

**strike,** streik, n Streik *m*; v
(hit) schlagen; (stop
work) streiken; (occur to)
einfallen; (chime)
schlagen; (match)
anstreichen; – **out,**
v (delete) ausstreichen; (set
off) aufbrechen; –**r,** n
Streiker *m*

**string,** string, n Schnur *f*;
*mus* Saite *f*; (series) Reihe

*f*; – **out,** v (delay) in die
Länge ziehen; –**s,** *npl*
Streichinstrumente pl; –
**(together),** v
aneinanderreihen

**stringent, strinn-**dschent,
*adj* streng

**strip,** stripp, n Streifen *m*; v
(undress) (sich)
ausziehen; – **cartoon,** n
Comic(strip) *m*

**stripe,** streip, n Streifen *m*;
–**d,** *adj* gestreift

**strive (for),** streiw (for), v
streben (nach)

**stroke,** strohk, n Schlag *m*;
*sport* Stoß *m*; (of pen) Zug
*m*; *mech* Hub *m*; *med*
Schlaganfall *m*; v
streicheln

**stroll,** strohl, n Spaziergang
*m*; v spazierengehen,
schlendern

**strong,** strong, *adj* stark;
(firm) fest; (bright) grell;
–**hold,** n Hochburg *f*;
–**room,** n Tresor *m*

**stroppy,** *adj fam* pampig

**structure, strack**-tscher, n
(construction) Struktur *f*;
(building) Bau *m*

**struggle, stragg-**'l, n Kampf
*m*; v – **(for),** kämpfen
(um)

**strut,** stratt, n Strebe *f*; v
stolzieren

**stub,** stabb, n (of pencil
etc.) Stummel *m*; (of
cigarette) Kippe *f*; (of
cheque, ticket) Abschnitt
*m*; v – **one's toe (on),** sich

den Zeh stoßen (an); –
**out,** ausdrücken

**stubble, stabb**-'l, n
Stoppeln *pl*

**stubborn, stabb-**ern, *adj*
hartnäckig

**stud,** stadd, n (earring)
Ohrstecker *m*; (on boot)
Stollen *m*; (stallion)
Deckhengst *m*; (for
horses) Gestüt *nt*; v
übersäen

**student, stjuh-**dent, *adj*
Studenten-; n (university)
Student *m*; (school)
Schüler *m*

**studio, stjuh-**di-oh, n
Studio *nt*; – **apartment,**
– **flat,** n
Einzimmerwohnung *f*

**studious, stjuh-**di-ess, *adj*
lernbegierig

**study, stadd-**i, n (work)
Studium *nt*; (room)
Arbeitszimmer *nt*;
(investigation)
Untersuchung *f*; v
studieren; (investigate)
untersuchen

**stuff,** staff, n Stoff *m*; *fam*
Zeug *nt*; v stopfen;
(animal) ausstopfen, –**ing,**
n Füllung *f*; –**y,** *adj* schwül

**stumble, stamm-**b'l, v
stolpern; – **across/on,**
stoßen auf

**stump,** stamp, n Stumpf *m*;
(cricket) Torstab *m*; v *fam*
verwirren; – **up,** v *fam*
blechen

**stun,** stann, v betäuben;

**–ning,** adj (looks) toll; (shocking) bestürzend

**stunt,** stant, n Stunt m; **–ed,** adj verkümmert

**stupefied, stjuh**-pi-feid, adj verblüfft

**stupendous, stjuh**-penn-dess, adj kolossal

**stupid, stjuh**-pidd, adj dumm; **–ity,** n Dummheit f

**stupor, stjuh**-per, n Betäubung f

**sturdy, stör**-di, adj kräftig

**stutter, statt**-er, n Stottern nt; v stottern

**sty,** stei, n Schweinestall m

**style,** steil, n Stil m, Art f; (fashion) Mode f

**stylish, stei**-lisch, adj modisch, elegant

**subdue, sseb**-djuh, v (quell) unterwerfen; (soften) dämpfen; **–d,** adj gedämpft

**subject, sseb**-dschikt, n (topic) Thema nt; (school) Fach nt; gram Subjekt nt; (person) Untertan m; **– to,** adj (exposed to) ausgesetzt; (subordinate to) unterworfen; (depending on) abhängig von

**subject (to), ssabb**-dschekt (tu), v (rule) unterwerfen; (suffering, criticism) aussetzen

**subjective,** adj subjektiv

**subjunctive, sseb**-dschank-tiw, n Konjunktiv m

**sublime, sseb**-leim, adj

erhaben

**submarine, ssabb**-me-rien, adj unterseeisch; n Unterseeboot nt

**submerge, sseb**-mördsch, v untertauchen

**submission, sseb**-misch-'n, n (proposal) Vorschlag m; (yielding) Unterwerfung f

**submit, sseb**-mitt, v (yield) nachgeben; (proposal) vorlegen

**subordinate, sse**-bor-di-net, adj untergeordnet; n Untergebene(r) m & f

**subscribe (to), sseb**-skreib (tu), v (support) sich etw anschließen; (donate) beitragen; (to journal) abonnieren; **–r,** n Abonnent m

**subscription, sseb**-skripp-sch'n, n (donation) Beitrag m; (to journal) Abonnement nt

**subsequent, ssabb**-ssi-ku'ent, adj folgend; **–ly,** adv später

**subside, sseb**-sseid, v sich senken; (abate) abnehmen; **–nce,** n Senkung f; (liquid) Senken nt

**subsidiarity, ssabb**-ssidd-i-ä-ri-ti, n Subsidiarität f

**subsidiary, sseb**-ssidd-i-e-ri, adj Neben-; n comm Tochtergesellschaft f

**subsidize, ssabb**-ssi-deis, v subventionieren

**subsidy, ssabb**-ssi-di, n

Subvention f, Hilfsgeld nt

**subsistence, sseb**-ssiss-tenss, n Unterhalt m

**substance, ssabb**-stenss, n Substanz f

**substantial, sseb**-stänn-sch'l, adj beträchtlich; (solid) kräftig

**substantiate, sseb**-stänn-schi-eht, v erhärten

**substitute, ssabb**-sti-tjuht, n (thing) Ersatz m; sport Ersatzspieler m; v **– for** sb/sth, für jdn/etw einspringen; **– X for Y,** Y durch X ersetzen

**subterfuge, ssabb**-ter-fjuhdsch, n List f

**subterranean, ssabb**-te-reh-ni-en, adj unterirdisch

**subtle, ssatt**-'l, adj subtil, fein

**subtitle, ssabb**-tei-t'l, n Untertitel m

**subtotal, ssabb**-toh-t'l, n Zwischensumme f

**subtract (from), sseb**-träkt (frem), v abziehen (von)

**suburb, ssabb**-örb, n Vorort m

**suburban, sseb**-ör-ben, adj Vororts-; **–ia,** n Stadtrand m

**subway, ssabb**-u'eh, n Unterführung f; (underground train) U-Bahn f

**succeed, ssek**-ssied, v (person) Erfolg haben; (plan) gelingen; (heir) nachfolgen; **–ing,** adj nachfolgend

**success**, ssek-**ssess**, n Erfolg m; **–ful**, adj erfolgreich; **be – (in)**, v Erfolg haben (bei)

**succession**, ssek-**sesch**-'n, n (sequence) Folge f; (inheritance) Nachfolge f; **–or**, n Nachfolger m

**successive**, ssek-**sess**-iw, adj aufeinanderfolgende (r/s)

**succinct**, ssek-**ssinkt**, adj knapp; (clear) prägnant

**succumb (to)**, sse-**kamm** (tu), v erliegen

**such**, ssatsch, adj solche(r/s); **– a**, solch ein(e), ein solche(r/s; (so great) so ein(e); adv so; **– a lot**, so viel(e); **– as**, wie (etwa)

**suck**, ssack, v saugen; **–le**, v säugen

**suction**, ssack-sch'n, n Saugkraft f

**sudden(ly)**, ssadd-'n(-li), adj & adv plötzlich

**sue**, ssuh, v verklagen

**suede**, ssu'ehd, n Wildleder nt

**suet**, ssuh-itt, n Talg m

**suffer**, ssaff-er, v (er)leiden; **–er**, n Betroffene(r) m & f; (illness) Leidende(r) m & f; **–ing**, adj leidend; n Leiden nt

**suffice**, sse-**feiss**, v genügen

**sufficient(ly)**, sse-**fisch**-ent(-li), adj & adv genügend, genug

**suffocate**, ssaff-e-keht, v

ersticken

**suffrage**, ssaff-ridsch, n Wahlrecht nt

**sugar**, schugg-er, n Zucker m; v zuckern; **–y**, adj süßlich

**suggest**, sse-**dschest**, v (imply) andeuten; (propose) vorschlagen; **–ion**, n (hint) Andeutung f; (proposal) Vorschlag m; **–ive**, adj andeutend; (indecent) zweideutig

**suicide**, ssuh-i-sseid, n (act) Selbstmord m; (person) Selbstmörder m; **commit –**, v Selbstmord begehen

**suit**, ssuht, n (man's) Anzug m; (woman's) Kostüm nt; law Prozeß m; (cards) Farbe f; v passen; **–able**, adj passend; **–case**, n Koffer m

**suite**, ssu'iet, n (rooms) Suite f; (furniture) Garnitur f; (followers) Gefolge nt; mus Suite f

**sulk**, ssalk, v schmollen; **–y**, adj mürrisch

**sullen**, ssall-en, adj mürrisch

**sulphur**, ssall-fer, n Schwefel m

**sultry**, ssalt-ri, adj schwül; (sensual) sinnlich

**sum**, ssamm, n Summe f; (arithmetic) Ergebnis nt; **– up**, v (kurz) zusammenfassen

**summarize**, ssamm-e-reis, v zusammenfassen

**summary**, ssamm-e-ri, adj

summarisch; n Zusammenfassung f

**summer**, ssamm-er, adj Sommer-; n Sommer m

**summit**, ssamm-itt, n Gipfel m

**summon**, ssamm-en, v law vorladen; (people)einberufen; (strength etc.) aufbringen; **–s**, n law Vorladung f

**sumptuous**, ssamp-tju-ess, adj prächtig, kostbar

**sun**, ssann, n Sonne f; **–bathe**, v sich sonnen; **–beam**, n Sonnenstrahl m; **–burn**, n Sonnenbrand m; **– cream**, n Sonnencreme f

**Sunday**, ssann-deh, n Sonntag m

**sundial**, ssann-deil, n Sonnenuhr f

**sundries**, ssann-dris, npl Verschiedenes nt

**sunglasses**, ssann-glah-ssis, npl Sonnenbrille f

**sunlight**, ssann-leit, n Sonnenlicht nt

**sunny**, ssann-i, adj sonnig

**sunrise**, ssann-reis, n Sonnenaufgang m

**sunroof**, ssann-ruhf, n (elec elektrisches) Schiebedach nt, Sonnendach nt

**sunscreen**, ssann-skrien, n Sonnenschutz m

**sunset**, ssann-ssett, n Sonnenuntergang m

**sunshine**, ssann-schein, n Sonnenschein m

**sunstroke, ssann**-strohk, n
Sonnenstich m

**suntan, ssann**-tänn, n
(Sonnen)bräune f; –
**lotion,** n Sonnenmilch f

**super, ssuh**-per, adj fam
prima

**superb, ssuh**-pörb, adj
herrlich, ausgezeichnet

**supercilious, ssuh**-per-**ssill**-
i-ess, adj hochnäsig

**superficial, ssuh**-per-**fisch**-'l,
oberflächlich

**superfluous, ssuh**-**pör**-flu-
ess, adj überflüssig

**superintend, ssuh**-pe-rinn-
tend, v überwachen; **–ent,**
n (police) Kommissar m;
(hostel etc.) Leiter m

**superior, ssuh**-**pier**-ri-er, adj
(tool, goods) besser; (skill,
intellect) überlegen;
(authority) höher; n
Vorgesetzte(r) m & f

**supermarket, ssuh**-
per-mahr-kitt, n
Supermarkt m

**superlative, ssuh**-**pör**-le-tiw,
adj überragend; n gram
Superlativ m

**supernatural, ssuh**-per-
**nätsch**-e-rel, adj
übernatürlich

**superpower, ssuh**-per-pau-
er, n Weltmacht f

**supersede, ssuh**-per-**ssied,** v
ersetzen

**supersonic, ssuh**-per-**ssonn**-
ick, adj Überschall

**superstition, ssuh**-per-
**stisch**-'n, n Aberglaube f

**superstitious, ssuh**-per-
**stisch**-ess, adj
abergläubisch

**supervise, ssuh**-per-weis, v
beaufsichtigen

**supervision, ssuh**-per-
**wisch**-'n, n Aufsicht f

**supervisor, ssuh**-per-weis-er,
n Aufseher m; (manual
work) Vorarbeiter m;
(clerical work) Büroleiter
m

**supper, ssapp**-er, n
Abendessen nt

**supplant, sse**-**plahnt,** v
verdrängen

**supple, ssapp**-'l, adj
geschmeidig, biegsam

**supplement, ssapp**-li-ment,
n (to book) Nachtrag m;
(to newspaper) Beilage f;
(food) Zusatz m

**supplement, ssapp**-li-ment,
v ergänzen

**supplier, sse**-**plei**-er, n
Lieferant m

**supplies, sse**-**pleis,** npl
Vorräte pl

**supply, sse**-**plei,** n Vorrat m;
**(with),** v versehen,
versorgen (mit); (deliver)
liefern

**support, sse**-**port,** n (prop)
Stütze f; (aid)
Unterstützung f; v stützen,
unterstützen; **–er,** n
Anhänger m

**suppose, sse**-**pohs,** v
vermuten, annehmen;
**–edly,** adv angeblich; **be
–d to,** v sollen

**supposing, sse**-**poh**-sing, conj
angenommen

**supposition, ssapp**-e-**sisch**-
'n, n Annahme f

**suppress, sse**-**press,** v
unterdrücken; **–ion,** n
Unterdrückung f

**supremacy, ssuh**-**premm**-e-
ssi, n Souveränität f (over
others) Vorherrschaft f

**supreme, ssuh**-**priem,** adj
höchste(r/s), oberste(r/s)

**surcharge, ssör**-tschardsch,
n Zuschlag m; (postage)
Strafporto nt

**sure, schor,** adj sicher,
gewiß; adv fam klar; **make
– (of),** v sich
vergewissern; (check)
nachprüfen

**surf, ssörf,** n Brandung f; v
surfen; **–er,** n Surfer m

**surface, ssör**-fiss, adj
Oberflächen-; (mail) auf
dem Landweg; n
Oberfläche f; v auftauchen

**surfboard, ssörf**-bord, n
Surfboard nt

**surfing, ssör**-fing, Surfen nt

**surge, ssördsch,** n Woge f; v
(auf)schwellen, wogen

**surgeon, ssör**-dschen, n
Chirurg m

**surgery, ssör**-dsche-ri, n
(specialty) Chirurgie f;
(operation) Operation f;
(place) Praxis f; **–
hours/times,** npl
Sprechstunden pl

**surgical, ssör**-dschick-'l, adj
chirurgisch; **– spirit,** n

Wundalkohol nt

**surly, ssör**-li, adj mürrisch, schroff, grob

**surmount**, sser-**maunt**, v überwinden

**surname**, ssör-nehm, n Familienname m

**surpass**, sser-**pahss**, v übertreffen

**surplus**, ssör-pless, n Überschuß m

**surprise**, sser-**preis**, n Überraschung f; v überraschen

**surrender**, sse-**renn**-der, n Kapitulation f; (of weapon) Übergabe f; v sich ergeben; (weapon) aufgeben

**surround**, sse-**raund**, v umgeben

**surrounding**, sse-**raun**-ding, adj umliegende(r/s); **–s**, npl Umgebung f

**survey**, ssör-weh, n (report) Bericht m; (opinion poll) (Meinungs)umfrage f; (measurement) Vermessung f

**survey**, sser-**weh**, v (measure) vermessen; (question) befragen; (look over) überblicken; **–or**, n Landvermesser m

**survival**, sser-**wei**-wel, n Überleben nt

**survive**, sser-**weiw**, v überleben

**survivor**, sser-**wei**-wer, n Überlebende(r) m & f

**susceptible (to)**, sse-**ssepp**-ti-b'l (tu), adj (receptive) empfänglich (für); (sensitive) empfindlich (gegen)

**suspect**, ssass-pekt, adj verdächtig; n Verdächtige(r) m & f

**suspect**, ssass-**pekt**, v verdächtigen

**suspend**, ssess-**pend**, v (halt) einstellen; (defer) verschieben; (worker) suspendieren; (hang up) hängen; **–er belt**, n Strumpfhaltergürtel m; **–ers**, npl (Brit) Strumpfbänder pl; (US) Hosenträger m

**suspense**, ssess-penss, n Spannung f

**suspension**, ssess-penn-sch'n, n (of worker) Suspendierung f; (on car) Federung f; **– bridge**, Hängebrücke f

**suspicion**, ssess-pisch-'n, n Verdacht m

**suspicious**, ssess-**pisch**-ess, adj (person) mißtrauisch; (thing) verdächtig

**sustain**, ssess-**tehn**, v (suffer) erleiden; (nourish) ernähren; (maintain) (aufrecht)erhalten; **–able**, adj nachhaltig

**sustenance**, ssass-ti-nenss, n Nahrung f

**swagger**, ssu'agg-er, n Großtuerei f; v (walk) stolzieren; (boast) großtun

**swallow**, ssu'oll-oh, n

Schluck m; (bird) Schwalbe f; v (ver)schlucken

**swamp**, ssu'omp, n Sumpf m; v überschwemmen

**swan**, ssu'onn, n Schwan m

**swap**, ssu'opp, n Tausch m; v **– (for)**, tauschen (gegen)

**swarm**, ssu'orm, n Schwarm m; v schwärmen; (with people) wimmeln

**swastika**, ssu'oss-tick-e, n Hakenkreuz nt

**swat**, ssu'ott, v schlagen

**sway**, ssu'eh, n (power) Herrschaft f; (influence) Einfluß m; v (swing) schaukeln; (influence) beeinflussen; (rock) schwanken

**swear**, ssu'ähr, v (affirm) schwören; (curse) fluchen; **–word**, n Schimpfwort nt, Fluch m

**sweat**, ssu'ett, n Schweiß m; v schwitzen; **–er**, n Pullover m; **–shirt**, n Sweatshirt nt; **–y**, adj verschwitzt

**swede**, su'ied, n Steckrübe f

**Swede**, su'ied, n Schwede m, Schwedin f

**Sweden**, **ssu'ie**-den, n Schweden nt

**Swedish**, ssu'ie-disch, adj schwedisch; n Schwedisch nt

**sweep**, ssu'iep, n Schornsteinfeger m; v (clean) kehren; (go fast) rauschen; **–ing**, adj

(statement) umfassend;
(movement) ausholend

**sweet,** ssu'iet, *adj* süß; *n*
(confectionery) Bonbon
*nt;* (dessert) Nachtisch *m;*
**–corn,** *n* Zuckermais *m;*
**–en,** *v* (ver)süßen; **–ener,**
*n* (artificial) Süßstoff *m;*
(bribe) (kleine)
Bestechung *f;* **–heart,** *n*
Geliebte(r) *m & f;* **–ness,**
*n* Süße *f;* **– pea,**
Gartenwicke *f*

**swell,** ssu'ell, *n* Dünung *f; v*
aufschwellen; **–ing,** *n*
Geschwulst *f*

**swerve,** ssu'örw, *v* ausbiegen,
abweichen

**swift,** ssu'ift, *adj* schnell,
geschwind, rasch; *n* (bird)
Mauersegler *m*

**swim,** ssu'imm, *v*
schwimmen; **–mer,** *n*
Schwimmer *m;* **–ming,** *n*
Schwimmen *nt;* **–ming
baths,** *npl* Schwimmbad
*nt;* **–ming costume,** *n*
Badeanzug *m;* **–ming pool,**
*n* Schwimmbad *nt;* **–ming
trunks,** *n* Badehose *f;*
**–suit,** *n* Badeanzug *m*

**swindle,** ssu'ind-'l, *n*
Schwindel *m; v*
beschwindeln; **–r,** *n*
Schwindler *m*

**swine,** ssu'ein, *n* Schwein *nt*

**swing,** ssu'ing, *n* Schwung *m;*
(child's) Schaukel *f;*
*mus* Swing *m; v*
schwingen, schaukeln

**Swiss,** ssu'iss, *adj*

schweizerisch; *n*
Schweizer *m*

**switch,** ssu'itsch, *n elec*
Schalter *m;* (change)
Wechsel *m; v* (change)
wechseln; (swap)
tauschen; **–board,** *n*
Zentrale *f;* **– off,** *v*
ausschalten; **– on,** *v*
einschalten

**Switzerland,** ssu'itt-zer-
lend, *n* Schweiz *f*

**swivel,** ssu'iw-'l, *n*
Drehgelenk *nt; v* (sich)
drehen

**swoon,** ssu'uhn, *v* in
Ohnmacht fallen

**swoop,** ssu'uhp, *n* Sturz *m;*
(raid) Razzia *f; v –*
**(down),** *v* (herab)stürzen

**swot,** ssu'ott, *fam n* Streber
*m; v* büffeln

**sword,** ssord, *n* Schwert *nt*

**sworn,** ssu'orn, *adj*
eingeschworen

**syllable,** ssill-e-b'l, *n* Silbe *f*

**syllabus,** ssill-e-bess, *n*
Lehrplan *m*

**symbol,** ssimm-b'l, *n*
Symbol *nt*

**symbolic(ally)** ssimm-**boll**-
ick(-e-li), *adj & adv*
symbolisch

**symmetry,** ssimm-itt-ri, *n*
Symmetrie *f*

**sympathetic,** ssimm-pe-
**thett**-ick, *adj* mitfühlend

**sympathize (with),** ssimm-
pe-**theis** (u'idh), *v*
mitfühlen mit, Mitleid
haben mit

**sympathy,** ssimm-pe-thi, *n*
Mitleid *nt,* Mitgefühl
*nt;* (on bereavement)
Beileid *nt*

**symphony,** ssimm-fe-ni, *n*
Symphonie *f*

**symptom,** ssimp-tem, *n*
Symptom *nt*

**synagogue,** ssinn-e-gogg, *n*
Synagoge *f*

**synchronize,** ssing-kre-neis,
*v* synchronisieren

**syncopated,** ssing-ke-peh-
tidd, *adj* synkopiert

**syndicate,** ssinn-di-ket, *n*
Konsortium *nt*

**synonym,** ssinn-e-nimm, *n*
Synonym *nt*

**synonymous,** ssi-**nonn**-i-
mess, *adj* gleichbedeutend,
synonym

**synopsis,** ssi-**nopp**-ssiss, *n*
Zusammenfassung *f*

**synthetic,** ssinn-**thett**-ick,
*adj* synthetisch; (fibre)
Kunst-

**syphon,** ssei-fen, *n* Siphon
*m; v* **– off,** ablassen; *fig*
abzweigen

**syringe,** ssi-rindsch, *n*
Spritze *f; v* (aus)spritzen

**syrup,** ssi-rep, *n* Sirup *m;* **–y,**
*adj pej* zuckersüß

**system,** ssiss-tem, *n* System
*nt;* **–atic(ally),** *adj & adv*
systematisch; **–s analyst,**
*comp* Systemanalytiker *m*

**ta,** tah, *interj fam* danke

**table, teh**-b'l, *n* Tisch *m*; (list) Tabelle *f*; **–cloth,** *n* Tischtuch *nt*; **–spoon,** *n* Eßlöffel *m*

**tablet, täbb**-let, *n* Tafel *f*; (pill) Tablette *f*

**table tennis, teh**-b'l tenn-iss, *n* Tischtennis *nt*

**tabloid, täbb**-leud, *adj* – **(newspaper),** *n* Boulevardzeitung *f*

**tacit, täss**-itt, *adj* stillschweigend

**tack, täck,** *n* (nail) Stift *m*; (stitch) Heftstich *m*; (direction) Kurs *m*; *v* (nail) anschlagen; (sew) anheften; *naut* lavieren

**tackle, täck**-'l, *n* Ausrüstung *f*; *sport* Angriff *m*; *v* (task) anpacken; (person) in Angriff nehmen; *sport* angreifen

**tacky, täck**-i, *adj* (sticky) klebrig; (*fam* shoddy) geschmacklos

**tact,** täkt, *n* Takt *m*; **–ful,** *adj* taktvoll

**tactic, täck**-tick, *n* Taktik *f*; **–al,** *adj* taktisch; **–s,** *n* Taktik *f*; *npl* Taktiken *pl*; **–less,** *adj* taktlos

**tadpole, tädd**-pohl, *n* Kaulquappe *f*

**tag, tägg,** *n* Aufhänger *m*; *v* (goods) anhängen; (criminal) überwachen

**tail,** tehl, *n* Schwanz *m*; *v* beschatten; **– off,** *v* abfallen; **–or,** *n* Schneider *m*; **–coat,** *n* Frack *m*; **–gate,** *n* Heckklappe *f*; **–s,** (of coin) Zahl(seite) *f*; (tailcoat) Frack *m*

**taint,** tehnt, *v* verderben; *fig* beschmutzen

**take,** tehk, *v* nehmen; (*med,*

*comm,* fortress) einnehmen; (accept) annehmen; (along) mitnehmen; (accommodate) Platz haben für; *gram* dazugehören; **– away,** *v* wegnehmen; **–away,** *adj* zum Mitnehmen; *n* Imbißstube *f*; **-home pay,** *n* Nettolohn *m*; **– in,** *v* (understand) begreifen; (fool) einwickeln; (dress) enger machen; **– it (that),** davon ausgehen (, daß); **– off,** *v* (of plane) starten; (of project) in Schwung kommen; (clothes) ausziehen; (mimic) parodieren; **– on,** *v* (worker) einstellen; (task) übernehmen; **– over,** *v* übernehmen; **–over,** *n* Übernahme *f*; **– up,** *v* (dress) kürzer machen; (hobby) anfangen

**takings, teh**-kings, *npl* Einnahmen *pl*

**talc,** tälk, *abbr* talcum powder

**talcum powder, täll**-kem pau-der, *n* Talkumpuder *m*

**tale,** tehl, *n* Erzählung *f*; (fairy) Märchen *nt*; **tell –s,** *v* (betray confidence) petzen; (lie) schwindeln

**talent, täll**-ent, *n* Talent *nt*, Begabung *f*; **–ed,** *adj* begabt

**talk,** to'ak, *n* Gespräch *nt*; (speech) Vortrag *m*; *v* –

**(about),** sprechen (über), reden (über); **–ative,** *adj* gesprächig

**tall,** to'al, *adj* (high) hoch; (big) groß

**tally, täll-**i, *v* übereinstimmen; **keep a –,** *v* mitschreiben, Buch führen

**talon, täll-**en, *n* Kralle *f*

**tame,** tehm, *adj* (animal) zahm; (dull) lahm; *v* zähmen

**tamper (with), tämm-**per (u'idh), *v* herumpfuschen (an)

**tampon, tämm-**ponn, *n* Tampon *m*

**tan,** tänn, *adj* (hell)braun; *n* Bräune *f*; *v* (hides) gerben; (make brown) bräunen; (go brown) braun werden

**tangerine, tänn-**dsche-rien, *n* Mandarine *f*

**tangible, tänn-**dschi-b'l, *adj* greifbar; (real) wirklich

**tangle, täng-**g'l, *n* Verwicklung *f*

**tank,** tänk, *n* Tank *m*; *mil* Panzer *m*

**tankard, täng-**kerd, *n* Krug *m*

**tanker, täng-**ker, *n* (ship) Tanker *m*; (lorry) Tankwagen *m*

**tantalize, tänn-**te-leis, *v* quälen

**tantamount to, tänn-**te-maunt tu, *adj* gleichbedeutend mit

**tap,** täpp, *n* (cock) Hahn *m*;

**(knock)** Klopfen *nt*; *v* (knock) klopfen; (barrel, tree) anzapfen; (wire) abhören

**tape,** tehp, *n* Band *nt*; (adhesive) Klebeband *nt*; (recording) Tonband *nt*; *v* (record) auf Band aufnehmen; **– measure,** *n* Bandmaß *m*; **red –,** *n* (unnötige) Bürokratie *f*

**taper, teh-**per, *n* Wachsstock *m*; *v* spitz zulaufen

**tape recorder,** tehp ri-**kor-**der, *n* Tonbandgerät *nt*

**tapestry, täpp-**iss-tri, *n* Wandteppich *m*, Gobelin *m*

**tar,** tahr, *n* Teer *m*; *v* teeren

**tardy, tahr-**di, *adj* (slow) langsam; (late) spät

**target, tahr-**gitt, *n* Scheibe *f*; *fig* Ziel *nt*

**tariff, tä-**riff, *n* Tarif *m*; (tax) Zolltarif *m*

**tarnish, tahr-**nisch, *v* matt machen, matt werden; *fig* beflecken

**tarpaulin, tar-po'a-**linn, *n* Persenning *f*

**tart,** tart, *adj* herb; *n* Torte *f*; (fam prostitute) Nutte *f*

**tartan, tahr-**ten, *adj* Schotten-; *n* Schottenstoff *m*

**task,** tahsk, *n* Aufgabe *f*; **–force,** *n* Sondertruppe *f*; **take to –,** *v* zur Rechenschaft nehmen

**tassel, täss-**'l, *n* Quaste *f*, Troddel *f*

**taste,** tehst, *n* Geschmack *m*; *v* schmecken, kosten; **–ful,** *adj* geschmackvoll; **–less,** *adj* geschmacklos

**tasty, tehss-**ti, *adj* schmackhaft

**tattered, tätt-**erd, *adj* zerfetzt

**tatters, tätt-**ers, *n* Fetzen *pl*

**tattoo,** te-**tuh,** *n* (on skin) Tätowierung *f*; *mil* Zapfenstreich *m*; *v* (skin) tätowieren

**tatty, tätt-**i, *adj* schäbig

**taunt,** to'ant, *n* Hohn *m*; *v* verhöhnen

**Taurus, to'a-**ress, *n* Stier *m*

**taut,** to'at, *adj* gespannt

**tavern, täh-**vern, *n* Schenke *f*, Wirtshaus *nt*

**tawdry, to'a-**dri, *adj* geschmacklos

**tax,** täcks, *n* Steuer *f*; *v* besteuern; (strain) belasten; **– with,** *v* beschuldigen

**taxation, täcks-eh-**sch'n, *n* Besteuerung *f*

**tax-free, täcks-**frie, *adj* steuerfrei

**taxi, täck-**ssi, *n* Taxi *nt*; **–rank, – stand,** *n* Taxistand *m*

**tea,** tie, *n* (drink) Tee *m*; (meal) Nachmittagstee *m*; **–bag,** *n* Teebeutel *m*

**teach,** tietsch, *v* lehren; (subject) unterrichten; **–er,** *n* Lehrer *m*; **–ing,** *n* Lehren *nt*, Unterricht *m*; (relig etc.) Lehre *f*

**team,** tiem, *n* sport

Mannschaft *f*; (animals) Gespann *nt*; (workers) Team *nt*; **–work,** *n* Teamarbeit *f*

**teapot,** *n* Teekanne *f*

**tear,** tähr, *n* Riß *m*; *v* (zer)reißen; (muscle) zerren; (go fast) rasen

**tear,** tier, *n* Träne *f*; **–ful,** *adj* tränenüberströmt; **– gas,** *n* Tränengas *nt*

**tease,** ties, *n* Quälgeist *m*; *v* necken

**teaspoon,** tie-spuhn, *n* Teelöffel *m*

**teat,** tiet, *n* Zitze *f*; (for baby) Sauger *m*

**tea towel,** tie tau-el, *n* Geschirrtuch *nt*

**technical,** teck-nick-'l, *adj* technisch

**technician,** teck-nisch-'n, *n* Techniker *m*

**technique,** teck-niek, *n* Technik *f*

**technology,** teck-noll-e-dschi, *n* Technologie *f*

**teddy (bear),** tedd-i bähr, *n* Teddy(bär) *m*

**tedious,** tie-di-ess, *adj* langweilig; (tiring) ermüdend

**tedium,** tie-di-em, *n* Langeweile *f*

**teem (with),** tiem (u'idh), *v* wimmeln (von); (rain) gießen

**teenage,** tien-ehdsch, *adj* jugendlich, Teenie-; **–r,** *n* Teenie *m*, Teenager *m*, Jugendliche(r) *m* & *f*

**teens, tiens,** *npl* Teenageralter *nt*

**teeter,** tie-ter, *v* wanken

**teeth,** tjeth, *pl of* tooth

**teething,** tie-dhing, *n* Zahnen *nt*; **– troubles,** *npl fig* Anlaufprobleme *pl*

**teetotal,** tie-toh-t'l, *adj* abstinent; **–ler,** *n* Abstinenzler *m*

**telecommunications,** tell-i-ke-mjuh-ni-keh-sch'ns, *npl* Fernmeldewesen *nt*

**telegram(me),** tell-i-grämm, *n* Telegramm *nt*

**telegraph,** tell-i-grahf, *n* Telegraf *m*; *v* telegrafieren

**telephone,** tell-i-fohn, *n* Telefon *nt*; *v* anrufen; **– booth, – box,** *n* Telefonzelle *f*; **– call,** *n* Anruf *m*; **– conversation,** *n* Telefongespräch *nt*; **– directory,** *n* Telefonbuch *nt*; **– number,** *n* Telefonnummer *f*

**telephonist,** ti-leff-e-nist, *n* Telefonist *m*

**telephoto (lens),** tell-i-foh-toh (lens), *n* Teleobjektiv *nt*

**telescope,** tell-i-skohp, *n* Fernrohr *nt*

**televise,** tell-i-weis, *v* (im Fernsehen) übertragen

**television,** tell-i-wisch-'n, *n* Fernsehen *nt*; **– (set),** *n* Fernseher *m*; Fernsehapparat *nt*

**telex,** tell-ecks, *n* Telex *nt*

**tell,** tell, *v* (fact) sagen,

mitteilen; (story) erzählen; (secret) verraten; **– (by),** (recognize) erkennen (an); **–ing,** *adj* (effective) schlagend; (revealing) vielsagend; **– off,** *v* ausschimpfen; **–tale,** *adj* vielsagend; *n* Petzer *m*

**temper, temm**-per, *n* (character) Naturell *nt*; (mood) Laune *f*; (angry mood) Wutanfall *m*; *v* (steel) härten; (reduce) mäßigen; **be in a (bad) –,** wütend sein; **lose one's –,** die Geduld verlieren

**temperament, temm**-pe-re-ment, *n* Temperament *nt*

**temperamental, temm**-pe-re-**menn**-t'l, *adj* launisch

**temperance, temm**-pe-renss, *n* Mäßigkeit *f*; (abstinence) Abstinenz *f*

**temperate, temm**-pe-ret, *adj* gemäßigt

**temperature, temm**-pritt-tscher, *n* Temperatur *f*; *med* Fieber *nt*

**tempest, temm**-pist, *n* Sturm *m*, Ungewitter *nt*

**template, temm**-plet, *n* Schablone *f*

**temple, temp**-p'l, *n* Tempel *m*; (forehead) Schläfe *f*

**temporarily, temm**-pe-re-ri-li, *adv* vorübergehend

**temporary, temm**-pe-re-ri, *adj* vorübergehend

**tempt,** tempt, *v* (attract) verlocken; (urge)

verleiten; **–ation,** n Versuchung f; **–ing,** adj verlockend

**ten, tenn,** num zehn

**tenable, tenn-e-b'l,** adj haltbar

**tenacious, ti-neh-schess,** adj zäh, beharrlich

**tenacity, ti-näss-i-ti,** n Zähigkeit f

**tenancy, tenn-en-ssi,** n (rent) Mietverhältnis nt

**tenant, tenn-ent,** n Mieter m; (of land) Pächter m

**tend, tend,** v (nurse) pflegen; **– to do sth,** (be inclined) dazu neigen, etw zu tun; (have a habit) etw gewöhnlich tun, etw oft tun

**tendency, tenn-den-ssi,** n (inclination) Neigung f; (habit) Angewohnheit f

**tender, tenn-der,** adj zart; (painful) empfindlich; (loving) zärtlich; n comm Angebot nt; (public) Ausschreibung f; rail Tender m; **–-hearted,** adj weichherzig; **–ness,** n Zartheit f; (soreness) Empfindlichkeit f; (affection) Zärtlichkeit f

**tenement, tenn-i-ment,** n Mietshaus nt

**tennis, tenn-iss,** n Tennis nt; **– court,** n Tennisplatz m; **– racket/racquet,** n Tennisschläger m; **– shoe,** n Tennisschuh m

**tenor, tenn-er,** n Tenor m

**tense, tenss,** adj (tight) gespannt; fig angespannt; n gram Zeitform f

**tension, tenn-sch'n,** n Spannung f, Anspannung f

**tent, tent,** n Zelt nt

**tentative, tenn-te-tiw,** adj (hesitant) unsicher; (provisional) unverbindlich

**tenth, tenth,** adj zehnte(r/s); n Zehntel nt

**tenure, tenn-jer,** n (of property) Besitz m; (of office) Amtszeit f

**tepid, tepp-idd,** adj lauwarm

**term, term,** n (expression) Ausdruck m; (period) Zeitraum m; (school, university) Trimester nt; (expiry) Laufzeit f; **–s,** npl comm Bedingungen f; **be on good –s with,** v gut auskommen mit; **come to –s with,** v sich abfinden mit; **in the long/short –,** auf lange/kurze Sicht

**terminal, tör-mi-n'l,** adj Schluß-, End-; med unheilbar; n (bus station) Endstation f; (airport) Terminal m; comp Terminal m/nt

**terminate, tör-mi-neht,** v beenden

**terminus, tör-mi-ness,** n Endstation f

**terrace, te-ress,** n Terrasse f; (of houses) (Häuser)reihe f; **–d,** adj terrassenförmig

angelegt; **–d house,** n Reihenhaus nt

**terrain, te-rehn,** n Gelände nt

**terrible, te-ri-b'l,** adj schrecklich

**terrific, te-riff-ick,** adj irrsinnig; fam toll

**terrify, te-ri-fei,** v (er)schrecken

**territory, te-ri-te-ri,** n Gebiet nt

**terror, te-rer,** n Schrecken m; (terrorism) Terror m; **–ism,** n Terrorismus m; **–ist,** n Terrorist m; **–ize,** v terrorisieren

**terse, törss,** adj kurz und bündig

**test, test,** n Versuch m, Probe f; (examination) Prüfung f; v probieren, prüfen

**testicle, tess-ti-k'l,** n Hoden m

**testify, tess-ti-fei,** v aussagen; **– that/to,** bezeugen

**testimonial, tess-ti-moh-ni-el,** n (recommendation) Referenz f; (presentation) Geschenk nt

**testimony, tess-ti-me-ni,** n Zeugnis nt; law Aussage f

**test tube, test tjuhb,** Reagenzglas nt; **test-tube baby,** n Retortenbaby nt

**text, tekst,** n Text m; **–book,** n Lehrbuch nt

**textile, tecks-teil,** adj Textil-; n Stoff m; **–s,** npl

Textilien *pl*

**texture, tecks**-tscher, *n* Struktur *f*

**Thames,** tems, *n* Themse *f*

**than,** dhänn/dhen, *conj* als

**thank,** thänk, *v* danken; **– sb for sth,** jdm für etw danken; **–ful,** *adj* dankbar; **–less,** *adj* undankbar; **–s,** *interj* danke; *npl* Dank *m*; **–s to,** *prep* dank; **T–sgiving,** *n* (festival) Erntedankfest *nt*; **– you (very much)!** *interj* danke (schön)!

**that,** thätt, *adj* der/die/das, jene(r/s); *pron* (demonstrative) das; (relative) der/die/das, welche(r/s), was; *conj* daß; **– good/much,** so gut/soviel; **– one,** jene(r/s); **after/before –,** danach/davor; **who is –?** wer ist da?

**thatch,** thätsch, *n* Strohdach *nt*; *v* mit Stroh decken

**thaw,** tho'a, *n* Tauwetter *nt*; *v* tauen; (frozen food) auftauen lassen

**the,** dhie/dhe, *definite art* der/die/das; **– more ...,** **– more ...,** je mehr ..., desto mehr ...; **so much –** **...,** umso ...

**theatre, thie**-ter, *n* Theater *nt*; *med* Operationssaal *m*

**theatrical, thie-ätt-rick-'l,** *adj* Theater-; *fig* theatralisch

**theft,** theft, *n* Diebstahl *m*

**their,** dhähr, *adj* ihr; **–s,** *pron* ihre(r/s)

**them,** dhem, *pron* (accusative) sie; (dative) ihnen

**theme,** thiem, *n* Thema *nt*; *mus* Motiv *nt*; **– park,** *n* Themenpark *m*

**themselves,** dhem-**sselws,** *pron* (refl) sich (selbst); (emphatic) selbst

**then,** dhenn, *adj* damalig; *adv* (next) dann, darauf; (at that time) damals; *conj* also; **by –,** bis dahin

**theology,** thi-**oll**-*e*-dschi, *n* Theologie *f*

**theoretical(ly),** thi-*e*-**rett**-ick-'l(-i), *adj & adv* theoretisch

**theory,** thi-*e*-ri, *n* Theorie *f*; **in –,** *adv* theoretisch

**therapist,** the-*re*-pist, *n* Therapeut *m*

**therapy,** the-*re*-pi, *n* Therapie *f*

**there,** dhähr, *adv* da, dort; (movement) dahin, dorthin; **– is/are,** es ist/sind; (in existence) es gibt

**thereabouts,** dhähr-*re*-**bauts,** *adv* (place) dort irgendwo; **... or –,** (quantity) ungefähr ...

**thereafter,** dhähr-**ahf**-ter, *adv* danach

**thereby,** dhähr-**bei,** *adv* dadurch, damit

**therefore, dhähr**-for, *adv*

deshalb, daher

**thermal, thör**-m'l, *adj* thermal

**thermometer,** ther-**momm**-i-ter, *n* Thermometer *nt*

**thermostat, thör**-moh-stätt, *n* Thermostat *nt*

**these,** dhies, *adj & pron,* pl of **this**

**thesis, thie**-ssiss, *n* These *f*; (university) Doktorarbeit *f*

**they,** dheh, *pron* sie; (impersonal) man

**thick,** thick, *adj* dick; (liquid) dickflüssig; (hair, smoke, forest) dicht; (fam stupid) dumm; **–en,** *v* (of liquid) eindicken; (of smoke etc.) dichter werden; (of plot) kompliziert werden; **–et,** *n* Dickicht *nt*; **–ness,** *n* Dicke *f*; (density) Dichte *f*

**thief,** thief, *n* Dieb *m*

**thieve,** thiew, *v* stehlen

**thieving, thie**-wing, *adj* diebisch; *n* Stehlen *nt*

**thigh,** thei, *n* Schenkel *m*

**thimble,** thimm-b'l, *n* Fingerhut *m*

**thin,** thinn, *adj* dünn; (person) mager; (sparse) spärlich; *v* **– (down),** verdünnen

**thing,** thing, *n* (object) Ding *nt*; (matter) Sache *f*; **–s,** *npl* (belongings) Sachen *pl*; **first – (in the morning),** früh am Morgen; **the – is,** das

Problem ist

**think,** think, v denken;
(believe) glauben; –
**about,** (consider)
überlegen; (ponder)
nachdenken über; – **of,**
denken an; (opinion)
halten von; (intend)
vorhaben; – **over,**
überlegen; – **up,** sich
ausdenken

**third,** thörd, adj dritte(r/s); n
Drittel nt; **–ly,** adv
drittens; **the T– World,** n
die Dritte Welt f

**thirst,** thörrst, n Durst m; v
– **for,** dürsten nach; **–y,**
adj durstig

**thirteen,** thör-tien, num
dreizehn; **–th,** adj
dreizehnte(r/s)

**thirty,** thör-ti, num dreißig

**this,** dhiss, adj diese(r/s);
pron (demonstrative) dies,
das; – **big/high,** so
groß/hoch; –
**morning/evening,** heute
morgen/abend; – **one,**
diese(r/s)

**thistle,** thiss-'l, n Distel f

**thorn,** thorn, n Dorn m; **–y,**
adj dornig; (problem)
schwierig

**thorough,** tha-re, adj
gründlich; (real) wirklich;
**–bred,** adj reinrassig; n
Vollblut nt; **–fare,** n
Hauptstraße f; **no –fare,**
gesperrt

**those,** dhohs, pl adj die,
jene; pl pron die (da), jene

**though,** dhoh, adv aber,
doch; conj obwohl

**thought,** tho'at, n (idea)
Gedanke m; (thinking)
Denken nt; **–ful,** adj
nachdenklich;
(considerate)
rücksichtsvoll; (attentive)
aufmerksam; **–less,** adj
(inconsiderate)
rücksichtslos, achtlos

**thousand,** thau-send, num
tausend; **–s (of),** Tausende
(von); **–th,** adj
tausendste(r/s); n
Tausendstel nt

**thrash,** thräsch, v
verdreschen; (fam sport
etc.) vernichtend
schlagen; – **about,** sich
hin- und herwerfen; **–ing,**
n Tracht Prügel f

**thread,** thredd, n Faden m;
(of screw) Gewinde nt; v
einfädeln; **–bare,** adj
fadenscheinig

**threat,** thrett, n Drohung f;
(danger) Gefahr f; **–en,** v
(be)drohen

**three,** thrie, num drei

**thresh,** thresch, v dreschen

**threshold,** thresch-hohld, n
Schwelle f

**thrift,** thrift, n Sparsamkeit
f; **–less,** adj
verschwenderisch; **–y,** adj
sparsam

**thrill,** thrill, n Aufregung f;
v aufregen; **–ed,** adj
entzückt; **–ing,** adj
aufregend

**thrive (on),** threiw (onn), v
gedeihen; comm
erfolgreich sein

**throat,** throht, n Kehle f,
Hals m

**throb,** throbb, v pochen,
klopfen; **–bing,** n Pochen
nt, Klopfen nt

**throes,** throhs, npl in the –
**of,** mitten in etw

**throne,** throhn, n Thron m

**throng,** throng, n Gedränge
nt; v sich drängen (in)

**throttle,** thrott-'l, n mech
Gas(pedal) nt; v
erdrosseln

**through,** thruh, adj (train)
durchgehend; (finished)
fertig; adv durch; prep
(place, means) durch;
(time) während; – **and –,**
durch und durch; **–out,**
adv (place) überall; (time)
die ganze Zeit; prep (time)
überall in; (place)
der/die/das ganze …
hindurch; **–put,** n
Durchsatz m; **no – road,**
keine Durchfahrt

**throw,** throh, n Wurf m; v
werfen; – **a party,** eine
Party geben; – **up,** v
brechen

**thrush,** thrasch, n Drossel f

**thrust,** thrast, n Stoß m;
mech Schubkraft f; v
stoßen

**thud,** thadd, n dumpfer
Schlag m

**thumb,** thamm, n Daumen
m; v durchblättern; – **a**

**lift,** per Anhalter fahren

**thump,** thamp, n (noise) Pochen nt; (blow) Schlag m; v schlagen

**thunder, thann**-der, n Donner m; v donnern; **–bolt,** n Donnern nt; **–storm,** n Gewitter nt; **–y,** adj gewittrig

**Thursday, thörs**-dei, n Donnerstag m

**thus,** dhass, adv (in this way) so; (therefore) also, daher

**thwart,** thu'ort, v (plan) vereiteln; (person) jdm in die Quere kommen

**thyme,** teim, n Thymian m

**tick,** tick, n (sound) Ticken nt; (mark) Häkchen nt; v (of clock) ticken; (mark) anhaken; **– off,** v fam rüffeln; **– over,** v (of engine) im Leerlauf laufen; fig weiterlaufen

**ticket, tick**-itt, n (transport) Fahrkarte f; (admission) Eintrittskarte f; (price) Schild nt; (luggage) Schein m; (lottery) Schein m; **– office,** n (transport) Fahrkartenschalter m; theatre Kasse f; parking **–,** (for car park) Parkschein m; (fine) Strafzettel m; **season –,** n Dauerkarte f

**tickle, tick**-'l, n Kitzeln nt; v kitzeln

**ticklish, tick**-lisch, adj kitzlig

**tidal, tei**-d'l, adj Flut-

**tide,** teid, n fig Trend m; **high–,** Flut f; **low–,** Ebbe f

**tidy, tei**-di, adj ordentlich; v **– (up),** aufräumen

**tie,** tei, n (for neck) Krawatte f; (band) Band nt; sport Unentschieden nt; v (fasten) binden; (draw) unentschieden spielen; **– a knot in,** einen Knoten machen; **– up,** v (person) beschäftigen; (animal, boat) anbinden; **–d up,** adj beschäftigt

**tier,** tier, n Rang m

**tiff,** tiff, n Streit m

**tiger, tei**-ger, n Tiger m

**tight,** teit, adj (close) dicht, fest; (clothes) eng; (control) streng; (fam drunk) blau; **–en,** v anziehen; (controls) verschärfen; **–rope,** n Drahtseil nt; fig Balanceakt m; **–s,** npl Strumpfhose f

**tile,** teil, n (on roof) Ziegel m; (glazed) Kachel f; (on floor) Fliese f; v mit Ziegeln decken; mit Fliesen belegen

**till,** till, conj = until; n Kasse f; v (earth) bestellen; prep = until

**tiller, till**-er, n naut Ruderpinne f

**tilt,** tilt, n Neigung f; v kippen

**timber, timm**-ber, n Bauholz nt

**time,** teim, n Zeit f; (period) Zeitdauer f; (occasion) Mal nt; (hour) Uhr f; mus Takt m; v zeitlich abstimmen; sport stoppen; **– bomb,** n Zeitbombe f; **–less,** adj zeitlos; **– limit,** n Frist f; **–ly,** adj rechtzeitig; **–r,** n (period) Schaltuhr f; **–scale,** n Frist f; **–table,** n (transport) Fahrplan m; (school) Stundenplan m; **– zone,** n Zeitzone f; **have a good –,** sich amüsieren; **in –,** rechtzeitig; **on –,** pünktlich; **what – is it?/what is the –?** wieviel Uhr ist es?

**timid, timm**-idd, adj zaghaft, furchtsam

**timing, tei**-ming, n Timing nt

**tin,** tin, n (metal) Zinn nt; (can) Dose f, Büchse f; v einmachen; **–foil,** n Alufolie f

**tinge,** tindsch, n Färbung f; fig Anflug m; v leicht färben; **–d with,** fig angehaucht mit

**tingle, ting**-g'l, n Prickeln nt; v prickeln

**tinkle, tink**-'l, n Geklingel nt; v klingeln

**tinned,** tind, adj Dosen-

**tin opener, tinn**-oh-p'n-er, n Dosenöffner m

**tinsel, tinn**-ss'l, n Lametta nt

**tint,** tint, n Farbton m; v

**tönen,** –ed glass, n getöntes Glas nt

**tiny,** tei-ni, adj winzig

**tip,** tipp, n Spitze f; (hint) Wink m; (money) Trinkgeld nt; v kippen; (give money) ein Trinkgeld geben; **––off,** n Tip m; **– over,** umkippen

**tipsy,** tipp-si, adj beschwipst

**tiptoe,** tipp-toh, n **on –,** auf Zehenspitzen

**tire,** teir, v ermüden; **–d,** adj müde; **be –d of,** v satt haben; **–less(ly),** adj & adv unermüdlich; **–some,** adj lästig

**tiring,** teir-ring, adj ermüdend

**tissue,** tisch-uh, n Gewebe nt; (handkerchief) Papiertaschentuch nt; **– paper,** n Seidenpapier nt

**tit,** titt, n (bird) Meise f; (vulg'r breast) Titte f; **– for tat,** wie du mir, so ich dir

**titillate,** titt-i-leht, v erregen

**title,** tei-t'l, n Titel m; (right) Rechtstitel m; **– deed,** Eigentumsurkunde f; **– page,** Titelblatt f

**titter,** titt-er, n Gekicher f; v kichern

**to,** tuh, adv (shut) zu; prep (a place) zu; (town, country, direction) nach; (person) an; (per) pro; (as far as) bis; (attached) an; (before verb) zu; (purpose) um … zu; **– and fro,** hin und her;

**try – do sth,** versuchen, etw zu tun; **want –,** wollen

**toad,** tohd, n Kröte f; **–stool,** n (nicht eßbarer) Pilz m

**toast,** tohst, n Toast m; v (bread) toasten; (drink to) trinken auf; **–er,** n Toaster m

**tobacco,** te-bäck-oh, n Tabak m; **–nist,** n Tabakhändler m

**toboggan,** te-bogg-en, n Rodelschlitten m; v rodeln

**today,** tu-deh, adv heute; (nowadays) heutzutage; **–'s,** adj der/die/das heutige

**toddler,** todd-ler, n Kleinkind nt

**toe,** toh, n Zeh m, Zehe f; (of sock, shoe) Spitze f; **–nail,** n Zehennagel m

**toffee,** toff-ie, n Karamelbonbon nt

**together,** tu-gedh-er, adv zusammen

**toil,** teul, n Plackerei f; v schwer arbeiten

**toilet,** teu-litt, n Toilette f; **– bag,** n Kulturbeutel m; **– paper,** n Toilettenpapier nt; **–ries,** npl Toilettenartikel pl

**token,** toh-k'n, n Zeichen nt; (gift token) Gutschein m

**tolerable,** toll-e-re-b'l, adj (bearable) erträglich; (good enough) annehmbar

**tolerance,** toll-e-renns, n

Toleranz f, Duldsamkeit f

**tolerant,** toll-e-rent, adj duldsam

**tolerate,** toll-e-reht, v dulden

**toll,** tohl, n Gebühr f; (road) Maut f; v läuten

**tomato,** te-mah-toh, n Tomate f

**tomb,** tuhm, n Grab nt

**tomboy,** tomm-beu, n Wildfang m

**tombstone,** tuhm-stohn, n Grabstein m

**tomcat,** tomm-kätt, n Kater m

**tomfoolery,** tom-fuh-le-ri, n Blödsinn m

**tomorrow,** tu-mo-roh, adv morgen; **– morning,** morgen früh; **the day after –,** übermorgen

**ton,** tann, n Tonne f; **–s of,** fam eine Unmenge (von)

**tone,** tohn, n Ton m; v (muscles) Fitneß f; **– down,** mäßigen; **– up,** (ver)stärken; **– with,** in Einklang sein mit

**tongs,** tongs, npl Zange f

**tongue,** tang, n Zunge f; **––in-cheek,** scherzhaft; **––tied,** adj stumm; **––twister,** n Zungenbrecher m

**tonic,** tonn-ick, n Stärkungsmittel nt; **– (water),** Tonic nt

**tonight,** tu-neit, adv heute abend, heute nacht

**tonsil,** tonn-ssill, n Mandel f; **–litis,** n

Mandelentzündung f

**too**, tuh, *adv* (excessively) zu; (also) auch; **– much**, zuviel

**tool**, tuhl, *n* Werkzeug *nt*

**toot**, tuht, *n* Hupen *nt*; *v* hupen

**tooth**, tuhth, *n* Zahn *m*; **–ache**, *n* Zahnschmerzen *pl*; **–brush**, *n* Zahnbürste *f*; **–paste**, *n* Zahnpasta *nt*; **–pick**, *n* Zahnstocher *m*

**top**, topp, *adj* oberste(r/s); *n* Spitze *f*; (of mountain) Gipfel *m*; (of tree) Wipfel *m*; (toy) Kreisel *m*; *v* übertreffen; **– hat**, *n* Zylinderhut *m*; **–heavy**, *adj* kopflastig; **– up**, *v* auffüllen; **on top**, *adv* oben; **on – of**, *prep* darüber hinaus

**topic**, topp-ick, *n* Gesprächsstoff *m*, Thema *nt*; **–al**, *adj* aktuell

**topless**, topp-liss, *adj* oben ohne

**topple**, topp-'l, *v* stürzen; **– over**, umstürzen

**topsy-turvy**, topp-ssi-tör-wi, *adv* durcheinander

**torch**, tortsch, *n* (electric) Taschenlampe *f*; (burning) Fackel *f*

**torment**, tor-ment, *n* Qual *f*

**torment**, tor-ment, *v* quälen

**tornado**, tor-neh-doh, *n* Wirbelsturm *m*

**torpedo**, tor-pie-doh, *n* Torpedo *m*

**torrent**, to-rent, *n* reißender Strom *m*

**torrential**, te-renn-tsch'l, *adj* strömend

**torrid**, to-ridd, *adj* heiß

**tortoise**, tor-tess, *n* Schildkröte *f*; **–shell**, *n* Schildpatt *nt*

**tortuous**, tort-ju-ess, *adj* gequält

**torture**, tor-tscher, *n* Folter *f*; *v* foltern

**toss**, toss, *n* Wurf *m*; *v* werfen; (coin) losen; **– and turn**, **– about**, sich wälzen; **– up**, eine Münze werfen

**tot**, tott, *n* (child) kleines Kind *nt*; (small drink) Gläschen *nt*

**total**, toh-t'l, *adj* Gesamt-, total; *n* Gesamtheit *f*; (sum) Endsumme *f*; *v* (add up) zusammenrechnen; (come to) auf … kommen

**totalitarian**, toh-tall-i-tähr-ri-en, *adj* totalitär

**totally**, toh-te-li, *adv* total

**totter**, tott-er, *v* wanken, wackeln

**touch**, tatsch, *n* (touching) Berührung *f*; (faculty) (Tast)gefühl *nt*; *v* berühren; (emotionally) rühren; **–ing**, *adj* (emotional) rührend; **– on**, *v* erwähnen; **–y**, *fig* empfindlich; **get in – with sb**, mit jdm Kontakt aufnehmen; **keep in – with sb**, mit jdm in Kontakt bleiben

**tough**, taff, *adj* zäh; (fam difficult) schwierig; (fam unfair) hart; **–!** Pech!

**tour**, tuhr, *n* Reise *f*, Tour *f*; *v* bereisen; **–ism**, *n* Tourismus *m*, Fremdenverkehr *m*; **–ist**, *n* Tourist *m*; **–ist office**, *n* Verkehrsamt *nt*, Verkehrsbüro *nt*

**tournament**, tor-ne-ment, *n* Turnier *nt*

**tout**, taut, *n* Anlocker *m*; *v* **– for**, Kunden schleppen

**tow**, toh, *v* schleppen; (car) abschleppen

**toward(s)**, tu-u'ord(s), *prep* (time) gegen; (direction) nach; (a place) auf … zu

**towel**, tau-el, *n* Handtuch *nt*

**tower**, tau-er, *n* Turm *m*; **–block**, *n* Hochhaus *nt*; **–ing**, *adj* hoch aufragend

**town**, taun, *n* Stadt *f*; **–centre**, *n* Stadtzentrum *nt*, Stadtmitte *f*; **– hall**, *n* Rathaus *nt*

**towrope**, toh-rohp, *n* Abschleppseil *nt*

**toy**, teu, *n* Spielzeug *nt*; *v* **–with**, spielen mit; **–shop**, *n* Spielwarengeschäft *nt*

**trace**, trehss, *n* (track) Spur *f*; *v* (follow track of) nachspüren; (copy) durchpausen; (find) aufspüren

**tracing paper**, treh-ssing peh-per, *n* Pauspapier *nt*

**track**, träck, *n* (path) Weg *m*; (trace) Spur *f*; (for

race) Bahn *f*; *rail* Gleis *nt*;
*v* verfolgen; **–suit**, *n*
Trainingsanzug *m*

**tract**, träkt, *n* (area) Gebiet
*nt*; *relig* Traktat *m*

**traction**, träck-sch'n, *n*
*mech* Zugkraft *f*; *med*
Streckverband *m*; **–
engine**, *n* Zugmaschine *f*

**tractor**, träck-ter, *n*
Traktor *m*

**trade**, trehd, *n* (commerce)
Handel *m*; (occupation)
Gewerbe *nt*; (skilled
work) Handwerk *nt*; *v* **–
(in)**, handeln (mit); **– in**,
*v* in Zahlung geben; **–
mark**, *n* Warenzeichen
*nt*; **–r**, *n* Händler *m*;
**–sman**, *n* (shopkeeper)
Händler *m*; (worker)
Handwerker *m*; **– union**, *n*
Gewerkschaft *f*

**tradition**, tre-disch-'n, *n*
Tradition *f*; **–al**, *adj*
traditionell

**traffic**, träff-ick, *n* Verkehr
*m*; **– jam**, *n* (Verkehrs)stau
*m*; **– light(s)**, *n*(*pl*),
(Verkehrs)ampel *f*

**tragedy**, trädsch-i-di, *n*
Tragödie *f*

**tragic**, trädsch-ick, *adj*
tragisch

**trail**, trehl, *n* (path) Weg *f*;
(trace) Spur *f*; (of smoke)
Wolke *f*; *v* (follow)
verfolgen; (drag)
schleppen; (hang)
hängenbleiben; (be left
behind) zurückbleiben;

**–er**, *n* (vehicle) Anhänger
*m*; (TV, film) Vorschau *f*

**train**, trehn, *n* *rail* Zug *m*; (of
dress) Schleppe *f*; *v*
(teach) ausbilden; *sport*
trainieren; (animal)
dressieren; (study) eine
Ausbildung machen; *mil*
einexerzieren; **–ed**, *adj*
ausgebildet; **–ee**, *n*
Lehrling *m*; (person) Trainer *m*; (shoe)
Sportschuh *m*; **–ing**, *n*
Ausbildung *f*; (further
education) Weiterbildung
*f*; *sport* Training *nt*

**trait**, treht, *n* Zug *m*

**traitor**, treh-ter *n* Verräter *m*

**tram**, trämm, *n*
Straßenbahn *f*

**tramp**, trämp, *n* (beggar)
Landstreicher *m*; *v*
marschieren

**trample**, trämp-'l, *v*
niedertreten

**trance**, trahnss, *n* Trance *f*

**tranquil**, träng-ku-ill,
*adj* ruhig; (mind)
gelassen; **–lizer**, *n*
Beruhigunsmittel *nt*

**transact**, tränn-säkt, *v*
verrichten; (business) ausführen;
**–ion**, *n* Verrichtung *f*;
(business) Geschäft *nt*

**transcend**, trann-ssend, *v*
übersteigen

**transcribe**, träns-kreib, *v*
abschreiben

**transcript**, tränn-skript, *v*
Abschrift *f*; *law*
Protokoll *nt*

**transfer**, tränss-fer, *n*
(drawing) Abziehbild *nt*;
(of money) Überweisung
*f*; (of premises) Verlegung
*f*; (of person) Versetzung *f*

**transfer**, tränss-för, *v*
(money) überweisen;
(premises) verlegen;
(person) versetzen

**transform**, tränss-form, *v*
umgestalten

**transfusion**, tränss-fjuh-
sch'n, *n* Blutübertragung *f*

**transient**, tränn-si-ent, *adj*
vergänglich

**transistor**, tränn-siss-ter, *n*
Transistor *m*; **– (radio)**, *n*
Transistorradio *nt*

**transit**, tränn-sitt, *n* Transit
*m*; **in –**, unterwegs

**transition**, tränn-sisch-'n, *n*
Übergang *m*

**transitory**, tränn-sitt-*e*-ri,
*adj* flüchtig

**translate**, träns-leht, *v*
übersetzen

**translation**, träns-leh-sch'n,
*n* Übersetzung *f*

**translator**, träns-leh-ter, *n*
Übersetzer *m*

**transmission**, träns-misch-
'n, Übersendung *f*; (*elec*,
TV) Übertragung *f*,
Sendung *f*

**transmit**, träns-mitt, *v*
übersenden; (*elec*, TV)
übertragen, senden; **–ter**,
*n* Sender *m*

**transparent**, tränss-pä-rent,
*adj* durchsichtig; *fig*
offenkundig

**transpire**, tränss-**peir**, v sich herausstellen

**transplant**, **tränss**-plahnt, n med Transplantation f

**transplant**, tränss-**plahnt**, v (plant) umpflanzen; (med, fig) verpflanzen

**transport**, **tränss**-port, n Transport m

**transport**, tränss-**port**, v transportieren

**transportation**, tränss-por-**teh**-sch'n, n Transport m, Beförderung f

**transverse**, tränss-**wörss**, adj querlaufend

**trap**, träpp, n Falle f; (pej mouth) Klappe f; v (catch) fangen; (trick) überlisten; **–door**, n Falltür f

**trappings**, **träpp**-ings, npl äußere Zeichen pl

**trash**, träsch, n (rubbish) Plunder m; (nonsense) Unsinn m; **–y**, adj wertlos

**trauma**, tro'a-me, n Trauma nt

**traumatic**, tro'a-**mätt**-ick, adj traumatisch

**travel**, **träw**-el, v reisen; **– agent**, n (office) Reisebüro nt; (person) Reisebürokaufmann m/-kauffrau f; **–ler**, n Reisende(r) m & f; **–ler's cheque**, n Reisescheck m; **– sickness**, n Reisekrankheit f

**trawler**, tro'a-ler, n Trawler m

**tray**, treh, n Tablett nt; **ash–**, Aschenbecher m

**treacherous**, tretsch-e-ress, adj (untrustworthy) verräterisch; (dangerous) gefährlich

**treachery**, tretsch-e-ri, n Verrat m

**treacle**, trie-k'l, n Sirup m

**tread**, tredd, n (of feet) Tritt m; (on tyre) Profil nt; (of stair) Stufe f; v **– (on)**, treten (auf)

**treason**, trie-sen, n Verrat m

**treasure**, tresch-er, n Schatz m; v schätzen; **–r**, n Schatzmeister m

**treasury**, tresch-e-ri, n Schatzamt nt

**treat**, triet, n (reward) Belohnung f; (enjoyment) Genuß m; v behandeln; **– sb to sth**, jdm etw gönnen

**treatise**, trie-tiss, n Abhandlung f

**treatment**, triet-ment, n Behandlung f

**treaty**, trie-ti, n Vertrag m

**treble**, trebb-'l, adj dreifach; (mus clef) Violin–; n mus Diskant m; v verdreifachen

**tree**, trie, n Baum m; **family –**, n Stammbaum m

**trek**, treck, n Treck m; v trecken

**trellis**, trell-iss, n Spalier nt

**tremble**, tremm-b'l, v zittern

**tremendous**, tri-menn-dess, adj ungeheuer; fam großartig

**tremor**, tremm-er, n Zittern nt; (earthquake) Beben nt

**trench**, trentsch, n Graben m; mil Schützengraben m

**trend**, trend, n Tendenz f, Trend m; **–y**, adj modisch

**trespass (on)**, tress-pess (onn), v unbefugt betreten; **–er**, n Unbefugte(r) m & f

**trestle**, tress-'l, n Gestell nt, Bock m

**trial**, trei-el, n (test) Probe f; (hardship) Kraftprobe f; law Prozeß m; **– and error**, Ausprobieren

**triangle**, trei-äng-g'l, n Dreieck nt; mus Triangel f

**triangular**, trei-äng-gju-ler, adj dreieckig

**tribal**, trei-b'l, adj Stammes-

**tribe**, treib, n Stamm m

**tribunal**, trei-bjuh-n'l, n Tribunal nt

**tributary**, tribb-ju-te-ri, n Nebenfluß m

**tribute**, tribb-juht, n (praise) Lob nt; (gift) Abgabe f

**trick**, trick, n (trap) Falle f; (joke) Streich m; (ruse) Trick m; (cards) Stich m; v überlisten; **–ery**, n Gaunerei f; **–ster**, Gauner m

**trickle**, trick-'l, n Tröpfeln nt; v tröpfeln

**tricky**, trick-i, adj (difficult) schwierig; (sensitive) delikat

**trifle, trei**-f'l, n Kleinigkeit f; (dessert) Trifle nt

**trifling, treif**-ling, adj geringfügig

**trigger, trigg**-er, n Drücker m; v – (off), auslösen

**trill, trill,** n Triller m; v trillern

**trim, trimm,** adj proper; n (on car) Verzierung f; v (decorate) besetzen; (clip) stutzen; –ming, n (for clothes) Besatz m; –s, npl (extras) Zubehör nt

**Trinity, trinn**-i-ti, n Dreieinigkeit f

**trinket, tring**-kitt, n Schmuckstück nt

**trio, trie**-oh, n Trio nt, Terzett nt

**trip, tripp,** n (journey) Reise f; (stumble) Stolpern nt; v (stumble) stolpern

**tripe, treip,** n Kaldaunen pl; Gedärme pl; (rubbish) Quatsch m

**triple, tripp**-'l, adj dreifach; v verdreifachen

**triplets, tripp**-litts, n Drillinge pl

**tripod, trei**-podd, n photog Stativ nt

**trite, treit,** adj banal

**triumph, trei**-emf, n Triumph m; v – (over), triumphieren (über)

**trivial, tri**-wi-el, adj belanglos

**trolley, troll**-i, n Karren m; (shopping) Einkaufswagen m

**trombone, tromm**-bohn, n Posaune f

**troop, truhp,** n mil Trupp m; v sich scharen; –s, npl Truppen pl

**trophy, troh**-fi, n Trophäe f

**tropical, tropp**-ick-'l, adj tropisch

**tropics, tropp**-icks, npl Tropen pl

**trot, trott,** n Trab m; v traben

**trouble, trabb**-'l, n (worry) Sorge f; (inconvenience) Mühe f; (disturbance) Unruhen pl; (difficulty) Schwierigkeit f; med Beschwerde f; v (bother) sich bemühen; (disturb) stören; –maker, n Unruhestifter m; –some, adj lästig; (difficult) beschwerlich; be in –, v Probleme haben; make –, v Unruhe stiften

**trough, troff,** n Trog m; (low pressure) Tief m

**trounce, traunss,** v verprügeln

**trousers, trau**-sers, npl Hose f

**trout, traut,** n Forelle f

**trowel, trau**-el, n Kelle f

**truant, truh**-ent, n (Schul)schwänzer m; play –, v die Schule schwänzen

**truce, truhss,** n Waffenstillstand m

**truck, track,** n (lorry) Lastwagen m; rail Güterwagen m

**truculent, track**-ju-lent, adj aufsässig

**trudge, tradsch,** v sich schleppen

**true, truh,** adj (correct) wahr; (faithful) treu; (genuine) echt

**truffle, traff**-'l, n Trüffel f

**truly, truh**-li, adj wirklich; Yours –, Mit freundlichen Grüßen

**trump, tramp,** n Trumpf m; v trumpfen; –ed-up, adj übertrieben

**trumpet, tramm**-pitt, n Trompete f

**truncheon, trann**-tsch'n, n Knüttel m

**trunk, trank,** n (of tree) Stamm m; (elephant's) Rüssel m; (of body) Rumpf m; (box) Truhe f; –call, n Fernruf m; –s, npl Badehose f

**truss, trass,** n Bündel nt; med Bruchband nt; v fesseln; (poultry) dressieren

**trust, trast,** n Vertrauen nt; (law, fin) Trust m; v trauen; –ee, n (law, fin) Treuhänder m; –ing, adj vertrauensvoll; – to, v sich verlassen auf; –worthy, adj zuverlässig

**truth, truhth,** n Wahrheit f; –ful, adj ehrlich

**try, trei,** v (attempt) versuchen, probieren; (taste) kosten; law (einen Fall) verhandeln; –ing, adj schwierig; – on, v (clothes) anprobieren

**tub,** tabb, n Kübel m; (bath) Wanne f

**tube,** tjuhb, n (pipe) Rohr nt, Röhre f; (paint etc.) Tube f; (London underground) U-Bahn f; **inner –,** n Schlauch m

**tuck,** tack, n Falte f; v (gather) falten; (put) stecken; **– in,** (sheet etc.) einwickeln; (fam eat) es sich schmecken lassen

**Tuesday,** tjuhs-dei, n Dienstag m

**tuft,** taft, n Büschel nt

**tug,** tagg, n Ruck m; v (drag) schleppen; (pull) zerren; **–(boat),** n Schlepper m; **– of-war,** n Seilziehen nt

**tuition,** tjuh-isch-'n, n Unterricht m

**tulip,** tjuh-lipp, n Tulpe f

**tumble,** tamm-b'l, n Sturz m; v stürzen; **–down,** adj baufällig; **– drier,** n Trockner m; **–r,** n Wasserglas nt

**tummy,** tamm-i, n fam Bauch m, Magen m

**tumour,** tjuh-mer, n Tumor m

**tumultuous,** tjuh-malt-ju-ess, adj stürmisch

**tuna,** tjuh-ne, n Thunfisch m

**tune,** tjuhn, n Melodie f; v stimmen; **–ful,** adj melodisch; **– in (to),** v einschalten; **–r,** n (for radio) Tuner m; **be in**

**tune/out of tune with,** v fig in Einklang/nicht in Einklang stehen mit

**tunic,** tjuh-nick, n Kittel m; mil Waffenrock m

**tuning fork,** tjuh-ning fork, n Stimmgabel f

**tunnel,** tann-'l, n Tunnel m; v einen Tunnel graben

**turbulent,** tör-bju-lent, adj stürmisch

**tureen,** tu-rien, n Terrine f, (Suppen)schüssel f

**turf,** törf, n Rasen m; (piece of) Sode f; v mit Fertigrasen auslegen; **– out,** fam rausschmeißen

**turkey,** tör-ki, n Truthahn m, Puter m

**Turkey,** tör-ki, n Türkei f

**turmoil,** tör-meul, n Aufruhr m

**turn,** törn, n Drehung f; (of century, tide) Wende f; (shock) Schrecken m; v (rotate) (sich) drehen; (turn round) wenden; (become) werden; (page) umblättern; **– back,** v zurückkehren; (clock) zurückstellen; **– into,** v (sich) verwandeln in; **– off,** v (light) ausschalten; (tap) zudrehen; (in car) abbiegen; **– on,** (light) einschalten; (tap) aufdrehen; **– out,** v (develop) sich herausstellen als; (produce) produzieren; (expel) hinauswerfen; (light)

ausschalten; **– up,** v (appear) auftauchen; (volume) lauter stellen; **– to,** v sich wenden an; **do (sb) a good –,** (jdm) etw Gutes tun; **in –,** abwechselnd; **it's my –,** ich bin an der Reihe f; **take –s,** v abwechseln

**turning,** tör-ning, n Abzweigung f; **– point,** n Wendepunkt m

**turnip,** tör-nipp, n weiße Rübe f

**turnout,** tör-naut, n theatre etc. Publikum nt; (election) Wahlbeteiligung f

**turnover,** tör-noh-ver, n (income) Umsatz m; (of stock) Umschlag m; (of staff) Personalwechsel m

**turnstile,** törn-steil, n Drehkreuz nt

**turntable,** törn-teh-b'l, n Plattenteller m

**turnup,** tör-napp, n Aufschlag m

**turpentine,** tör-pen-tein, n Terpentin nt

**turquoise,** tör-ku'eus, n adj türkisfarben; n (gem) Türkis m

**turret,** ta-ret, n Türmchen nt; mil Panzerturm m

**turtle,** tör-t'l, n Schildkröte f; **– dove,** n Turteltaube f; **– neck,** n Pullover m mit Stehbundkragen

**tusk,** task, n Stoßzahn m

**tussle,** tass-'l, n Kampf m,

Rauferei f; v kämpfen

**tutor, tjuh**-ter, n Lehrer m;
(private) Hauslehrer m; v
schulen

**TV,** tie wie, n abbr
**television,** TV nt

**twang,** tu'äng, n (voice)
näselnde Sprache f;
(sound) heller Ton m

**tweezers, tu'ie**-sers, npl
Pinzette f

**twelfth,** tu'elfth, adj
zwölfte(r/s), n Zwölftel nt

**twelve,** tu'elw, num zwölf

**twenty, tu'enn**-ti, num
zwanzig

**twice,** tu'eiss, adv zweimal; –
**as much/good,** doppelt
soviel/so gut

**twig,** tu'igg, n Zweig m; v
fam kapieren

**twilight, tu'ei**-leit, n
Zwielicht nt

**twin, tu'inn,** adj Zwillings-;
fig Doppel-; n Zwilling m;
n (towns) Partnerstadt f; –
**beds,** npl zwei
Einzelbetten pl

**twine,** tu'ein, n Bindfaden
m; v sich winden

**twinge,** tu'indsch, n Stechen
nt, Stich m; v stechen

**twinkle, tu'ing**-k'l, n
Funkeln nt; v flimmern;
(of eyes) funkeln

**twin town,** tu'inn taun, n
Partnerstadt f

**twirl,** tu'örl, v
(herum)wirbeln

**twist,** tu'ist, n Drehung f;
(in road) Biegung f, Kurve

f; v (sich) drehen;
(contort) verdrehen; **–ing,
–y,** adj kurvenreich

**twit,** tu'itt, n fam Idiot m

**twitch,** tu'itsch, n Zucken
nt; v zucken

**twitter, tu'it**-ter, n
Gezwitscher nt; v
zwitschern

**two,** tuh, num zwei; **–-faced,**
adj falsch; **–fold,** adj
zweifach; **–-seater,** n
Zweisitzer m; **–some,** n
Paar nt; **–-way,** adj
(traffic) Gegen-;
(communication) in beide
Richtungen; **–-wheeler,** n
Zweirad nt

**tycoon, tei-kuhn,** n
Magnat m

**type,** teip, n (sort) Art f;
(printing) Schrift f; v mit
der Maschine schreiben,
tippen; **–writer,** n
Schreibmaschine f;
**–written,** adj
maschinegeschrieben

**typhoid, tei**-feud, n Typhus
m

**typical (of), tipp**-ick-'l (ew),
adj typisch (für)

**typing, tei**-ping, n Tippen
nt, Maschineschreiben nt

**typist, tei**-pist, n
Schreibkraft f

**tyrannical, ti-ränn**-ick-'l,
adj tyrannisch

**tyrant, teir**-rent, n Tyrann m

**tyre,** teir, n Reifen m; –
**pressure,** n Reifendruck m

**U-bend,** juh-bend, n (pipe) U-Rohr nt

**ubiquitous,** ju-bick-u'i-tess, adj allgegenwärtig

**udder,** add-er, n Euter nt

**UFO,** juh-foh, n (abbr **unidentified flying object**), UFO nt

**ugliness,** agg-li-niss, n Häßlichkeit f

**ugly,** agg-li, adj häßlich; (situation) unangenehm

**UK,** juh kei, abbr **United Kingdom**

**ulcer,** all-sser, n Geschwür nt

**ulterior,** all-tier-ri-er, adj – **motive,** n Hintergedanke m

**ultimate,** all-ti-met, adj allerletzte(r/s); –**ly,** adv letztendlich

**ultimatum,** all-ti-meh-tem, n Ultimatum nt

**ultrasound,** all-tre-ssaund, n Ultraschall m

**umbrella,** amm-brell-e, n Regenschirm m

**umpire,** amm-peir, n Schiedsrichter m

**umpteen,** amp-tien, num x; –**th,** adj x-te(r/s)

**UN,** juh enn, abbr **United Nations**

**unabashed,** ann-e-bäscht, adj ungeniert

**unable,** ann-eh-b'l, adj unfähig, unvermögend; **be – to,** v nicht können

**unacceptable,** ann-ek-ssept-te-b'l, adj unannehmbar, nicht akzeptabel

**unaccountable,** ann-ä-kaun-te-b'l, adj unerklärlich

**unaided,** ann-eh-didd, adj ohne fremde Hilfe

**unanimity,** juh-ne-nim-i-ti, n Einmütigkeit f

**unanimous(ly),** juh-nänn-i-mess(-li), adj & adv einstimmig

**unanswerable,** ann-ahn-sse-re-b'l, adj nicht beantwortbar; (argument) unwiderlegbar

**unapproachable,** ann-e-prohtsch-e-b'l, adj unnahbar

**unarmed,** ann-ahrmd, adj unbewaffnet

**unashamed,** ann-e-schehmd, adj schamlos

**unassuming,** ann-e-sjuh-ming, adj bescheiden

**unattached,** ann-e-tätscht, adj ungebunden

**unattainable,** ann-e-teh-ne-b'l, adj unerreichbar

**unattended,** ann-e-tenn-didd, adj unbewacht

**unauthorized,** ann-o'a-the-reisd, adj unbefugt

**unavoidable,** ann-e-weu-de-b'l, adj unvermeidlich

**unaware,** ann-e-u'ähr, adj nicht bewußt; –**s,** adv unerwartet

**unbearable,** ann-bähr-re-b'l, adj unerträglich

**unbeatable,** ann-bie-te-b'l, adj unschlagbar

**unbeknown(st),** ann-bi-nohn(st), adj – **to sb,** ohne jds Wissen

**unbelievable,** ann-bi-lie-we-b'l, adj unglaublich

**unbend,** ann-bend, v (make

straight) geradebiegen; (fig open up) aus sich herausgehen; **-ing**, adj unnachgiebig, unbeugsam

**unbiased**, ann-**bai**-est, adj unvoreingenommen

**unbleached**, ann-**blietscht**, adj ungebleicht

**unbreakable**, ann-**brehk**-e-b'l, adj unzerbrechlich

**unbridled**, ann-**brei**-d'ld, adj zügellos

**unburden**, ann-**börr**-d'n, v – **o.s. (of)**, sich von etw befreien

**unbutton**, ann-**batt**-'n, v aufknöpfen

**uncalled-for**, ann-**ko'ald**-for, adj unangebracht

**uncanny**, ann-**känn**-i, adj unheimlich

**uncared-for**, ann-**kährd**-for, adj (unloved) ungeliebt; (unheeded) vernachlässigt

**unceasing**, ann-**ssie**-ssing, adj unaufhörlich

**unceremonious**, ann-sse-ri-**moh**-ni-ess, adj formlos; (rude) brüsk

**uncertain**, ann-**ssörr**-t'n, adj unsicher; **-ty**, n Unsicherheit f

**unchanging**, ann-**tschehn**-dsching, adj unveränderlich

**uncivilized**, ann-**ssiw**-i-leisd, adj unzivilisiert

**uncle**, ang-k'l, n Onkel m

**uncomfortable**, ann-**kammf**-er-te-b'l, adj unbequem

**uncommon**, ann-**komm**-en,

adj ungewöhnlich

**uncompromising**, ann-**komm**-pre-mei-sing, adj kompromißlos

**unconcerned**, ann-ken-**ssörnd**, adj gleichgültig

**unconditional**, ann-ken-**disch**-e-n'l, adj bedingungslos

**uncongenial**, ann-ken-**dschie**-ni-el, adj unsympathisch

**unconscious**, ann-**konn**-schess, adj med bewußtlos; (unintended) unbewußt; **-ly**, adv unbewußt

**uncontrollable**, ann-ken-**trohl**-e-b'l, adj unkontrollierbar

**unconventional**, ann-ken-**wenn**-schen-'l, adj zwanglos

**uncork**, ann-**kork**, v entkorken

**uncouth**, ann-**kuhth**, adj grob

**uncover**, ann-**kaw**-er, v aufdecken; (reveal) entblößen

**uncultivated**, ann-**kall**-ti-weh-tidd, adj unkultiviert

**undecided**, ann-di-**ssai**-didd, adj unentschieden

**undeniable**, ann-di-**nai**-e-b'l, adj unleugbar

**under**, ann-der, adv unten, darunter; (movement) nach unten; prep unter; **-age**, adj nicht volljährig

**undercarriage**, ann-der-**kä**-ridsch, n Untergestell nt

**underclothing**, ann-der-kloh-dhing, n Unterwäsche f

**undercover**, ann-der-**kaw**-er, adj Geheim-

**undercurrent**, ann-der-**ka**-rent, n Unterströmung f; fig Unterton m

**undercut**, ann-der-**katt**, v unterbieten

**underdeveloped**, ann-der-di-**well**-ept, adj unterentwickelt; **– country**, n Entwicklungsland nt

**underdog**, ann-der-dogg, n Benachteiligte(r) m & f

**underdone**, ann-der-**dann**, adj halbgar, blutig

**underestimate**, ann-de-**ress**-ti-met, n Unterschätzung f

**underestimate**, ann-de-**ress**-ti-meit, v unterschätzen

**underexposed**, ann-de-rick-spohsd, adj photog unterbelichtet

**underfed**, ann-der-**fedd**, adj unterernährt

**undergo**, ann-der-**goh**, v durchmachen; med sich unterziehen

**undergraduate**, ann-der-**grädd**-ju-et, n Student m

**underground**, ann-der-graund, adj unterirdisch; n rail U-Bahn f

**undergrowth**, ann-der-grohth, n Unterholz nt, Gestrüpp nt

**underhand**, ann-der-händ, adj hinterlistig

**underline,** ann-der-**lein**, *v* unterstreichen

**underlying,** ann-der-**lei**-ing, *adj* zugrundeliegend

**undermine,** ann-der-**mein**, *v* untergraben; (health) angreifen

**underneath,** ann-der-**nieth**, *adv* unten; (movement) nach unten; *prep* unter

**underpaid,** ann-der-**pehd**, *adj* unterbezahlt

**underpants,** ann-der-**pänts**, *npl* Unterhose *f*

**underpass,** ann-der-**pahss**, *n* Unterführung *f*

**underprivileged,** ann-der-**priw**-i-lidschd, *adj* benachteiligt

**underrated,** ann-de-**reh**-tidd, *adj* unterschätzt

**underside, ann**-der-sseid, *n* Unterseite *f*

**understand,** ann-der-**ständ**, *v* verstehen, begreifen; (believe) glauben; **–ing,** *n* Verständnis nt; (accord) Einverständnis *nt*; (supposition) Annahme *f*

**understatement, ann**-der-steht-ment, *n* Untertreibung *f*

**understudy, ann**-der-staddi, *n* theatre zweite Besetzung *f*; fig Stellvertreter *m*

**undertake,** ann-der-**tehk**, *v* unternehmen

**undertaker, ann**-der-tehker, *n* Leichenbestatter *m*

**undertaking, ann**-der-teh-king, *n* Unternehmen nt; (task) Aufgabe *f*

**undertone, ann**-der-tohn, *n* Flüsterton *m*

**underwater, ann**-der-u'o'ater, *adj* Unterwasser-; *adv* unter Wasser

**underwear, ann**-der-u'ähr, *n* Unterwäsche *f*

**underworld, ann**-der-u'örld, *n* Unterwelt *f*

**underwriter,** ann-de-rei-ter, *n* Versicherer *m*

**undeserved,** ann-di-**sörwd**, *adj* unverdient

**undesirable,** ann-di-**sair**-reb'l, *adj* unerwünscht

**undies,** ann-dis, *npl* fam Unterwäsche *f*

**undignified,** ann-**digg**-nifeid, *adj* würdelos

**undisclosed,** ann-diss-**klohsd**, *adj* geheim(gehalten)

**undisputed,** ann-diss-**pjuh**-tidd, *adj* unbestritten

**undisturbed,** ann-diss-**törbd**, *adj* ungestört

**undo,** ann-**duh**, *v* (unfasten) aufmachen; (negate) zunichte machen; **–ing,** *n* Verderben *nt*

**undoubted,** ann-**dau**-tidd, *adj* unzweifelhaft; **–ly,** *adv* zweifellos

**undress,** ann-**dress**, *v* (sich) ausziehen

**undue,** ann-**djuh**, *adj* übermäßig

**undulating, ann**-dju-lehting, *adj* (countryside)

sanft hügelig

**unduly,** ann-**djuh**-li, *adv* übermäßig

**unearned,** ann-**örnd**, *adj* unverdient

**unearth,** ann-**örth**, *v* ausgraben; fig aufstöbern; **–ly,** *adj* unheimlich

**uneasy,** ann-**ie**-si, *adj* unruhig

**uneconomic(al),** ann-ie-ke-**nomm**-ick(-'l), *adj* unwirtschaftlich

**uneducated,** ann-**edd**-ju-keh-tidd, *adj* ungebildet

**unemployed,** ann-imm-**pleud**, *adj* arbeitslos

**unemployment,** ann-imm-**pleu**-ment, *n* Arbeitslosigkeit *f*

**unending,** ann-**enn**-ding, *adj* endlos

**unequal,** ann-**iek**-u'el, *adj* ungleich; **–led,** *adj* unvergleichlich

**unerring,** ann-**ör**-ring, *adj* unfehlbar

**uneven,** ann-**ie**-wen, *adj* (not level) uneben; (irregular) unregelmäßig

**unexpected,** ann-ick-**speck**-tidd, *adj* unerwartet

**unfailing,** ann-**feh**-ling, *adj* unerschöpflich; **–ly,** *adv* stets

**unfair,** ann-**fähr**, *adj* unfair

**unfaithful,** ann-**fehth**-full, *adj* untreu

**unfamiliar,** ann-fe-**mill**-je, *adj* (strange) ungewohnt; (unknown) unbekannt; **be**

– **with,** v nicht kennen

**unfashionable,** ann-**fäsch**-e-ne-b'l, adj unmodern

**unfasten,** ann-**fah**-ss'n, v aufmachen

**unfavourable,** ann-**feh**-we-re-b'l, adj ungünstig

**unfeeling,** ann-**fie**-ling, adj gefühllos

**unfinished,** ann-**finn**-ischt, adj unvollendet

**unfit,** ann-**fitt,** adj (unsuitable) ungeeignet; (not well) nicht fit

**unfold,** ann-**fohld,** v (sich) entfalten

**unforeseen,** ann-for-**ssien,** adj unvorhergesehen

**unforgettable,** ann-fer-**gett**-e-b'l, adj unvergeßlich

**unforgivable,** ann-fer-**giw**-e-b'l, adj unverzeihlich

**unfortunate,** ann-**for**-tju-net, adj unglücklich; **–ly,** adv unglücklicherweise, leider

**unfounded,** ann-**faun**-didd, adj unbegründet

**unfriendly,** ann-**frend**-li, adj unfreundlich

**unfurnished,** ann-**för**-nischt, adj unmöbliert

**ungainly,** ann-**gehn**-li, adj unbeholfen

**ungrateful,** ann-**greht**-full, adj undankbar

**unguarded,** ann-**gahr**-didd, adj unbewacht; fig unvorsichtig

**unhappiness,** ann-**häpp**-i-niss, n Bekümmertheit f

**unhappy,** ann-**häpp**-i, adj (sad) unglücklich; (dissatisfied) unzufrieden

**unharmed,** ann-**harmd,** adj unverletzt

**unhealthy,** ann-**hell**-thi, adj ungesund

**unheard-of,** ann-**hör**-dow, adj unbekannt; (outrageous) unerhört

**unhurt,** ann-**hört,** adj unverletzt

**unidentified,** ann-ei-**denn**-ti-feid, adj unbekannt; (body) nicht identifiziert

**unification,** juh-ni-fi-**keh**-sch'n, n Vereinigung f

**uniform,** juh-ni-**form,** n Uniform f; adj gleichförmig; **–ity,** n Gleichförmigkeit f

**unify,** **juh**-ni-fei, v vereinigen

**unilateral,** juh-ni-**lätt**-e-rel, adj einseitig

**unimaginative,** ann-i-**madsch**-i-ni-tiw, adj phantasielos

**uninhabited,** ann-inn-**habb**-i-tidd, adj unbewohnt

**unintentional,** ann-inn-**tenn**-sche-n'l, adj unabsichtlich

**union,** **juh**-ni-en, n (joining) Vereinigung f; (association) Union f; **(trade) –,** n Gewerkschaft f

**unique,** juh-**niek,** adj (only) einzig; (unequalled) einzigartig

**unison,** **juh**-ni-ss'n, n Einklang m; **in –,** einstimmig

**unit,** **juh**-nitt, n Einheit f

**unite,** juh-**nait,** v (sich) vereinigen; **–d,** adj geschlossen; **U–d Kingdom,** n Vereinigtes Königreich nt; **U–d Nations (Organization),** n Vereinte Nationen pl; **U–d States (of America),** n Vereinigte Staaten pl

**unity,** **juh**-ni-ti, n Einigkeit f

**universal,** juh-ni-**wör**-ss'l, adj universal, Universal-

**universe,** **juh**-ni-wörss, n (Welt)all nt

**university,** juh-ni-**wör**-ssi-ti, n Universität f

**unjust,** ann-**dschast,** adj ungerecht

**unkind,** ann-**kaind,** adj unfreundlich

**unknown,** ann-**nohn,** adj unbekannt

**unlawful,** ann-**lo'a**-full, adj gesetzwidrig

**unleaded,** ann-**ledd**-idd, adj bleifrei, unverbleit

**unless,** ann-**less,** conj wenn nicht, es sei denn

**unlike,** ann-**laik,** adj unähnlich; prep im Gegensatz zu; **–ly,** adv unwahrscheinlich

**unlimited,** ann-**limm**-i-tidd, adj unbegrenzt

**unload,** ann-**lohd,** v abladen

**unlock,** ann-**lock,** v

aufschließen

**unlucky,** ann-**lack**-i, *adj*
unglücklich

**unmarried,** ann-**mä**-ridd, *adj*
ledig

**unmistakable,** ann-miss-**teh**-ke-b'l, *adj*
unverkennbar

**unmitigated,** ann-**mitt**-i-geh-tidd, *adj* (severity)
ungemildert; (disaster)
vollkommen

**unnatural,** ann-**nätt**-tsche-rel, *adj* unnatürlich

**unnecessary,** ann-**ness**-e-sse-ri, *adj* unnötig

**unnoticed,** ann-**noh**-tist, *adj*
unbemerkt

**unobtainable,** ann-eb-**teh**-ne-b'l, *adj* nicht erhältlich

**unobtrusive,** ann-eb-**truh**-ssiw, *adj* unauffällig

**unofficial,** ann-e-**fisch**-'l, *adj*
inoffiziell

**unopposed,** ann-e-**pohsd**, *adj* (progress)
ungehindert; (proposal)
unbestritten

**unorthodox,** ann-**or**-the-docks, *adj*
unkonventionell

**unpack,** ann-**päck**, *v*
auspacken

**unpleasant,** ann-**ples**-'nt, *adj* unangenehm

**unpopular,** ann-**popp**-ju-ler, *adj* unpopulär; (person)
unbeliebt

**unprecedented,** ann-**press**-i-den-tidd, *adj* beispiellos

**unpredictable,** ann-pri-

**dick**-e-b'l, *adj*
unvorhersehbar;
(unreliable)
unberechenbar

**unprofessional,** ann-pre-**fesch**-en-'l, *adj*
unprofessionell

**unqualified,** ann-**kwoll**-i-feid, *adj* (person)
unqualifiziert; (complete)
uneingeschränkt

**unquestionably,** ann-**ku'ess**-tsche-neb-li, *adv*
fraglos

**unravel,** ann-**räw**-'l, *v*
entwirren; *fig* lösen

**unreal,** ann-**riel**, *adj*
unwirklich; **–istic,** *adj*
unrealistisch

**unreasonable,** ann-**rie**-se-ne-b'l, *adj* unvernünftig

**unrelated,** ann-ri-**leh**-tidd, *adj* (people) nicht
verwandt; (events)
unzusammenhängend

**unrelenting,** ann-ri-**lenn**-ting, *adj* unerbittlich

**unreliable,** ann-ri-**lei**-e-b'l, *adj* unzuverlässig

**unremitting,** ann-ri-**mitt**-ing, *adj* unablässig

**unreserved,** ann-ri-**sörwd**, *adj* nicht reserviert; **–ly,**
*adv* uneinschränkt

**unrest,** ann-**rest**, *n*
Unruhen *pl*

**unroll,** ann-**rohl**, *v* (sich)
aufrollen

**unruly,** ann-**ruh**-li, *adj*
ungehorsam

**unsafe,** ann-**ssehf**, *adj* nicht

sicher; (dangerous)
gefährlich

**unsatisfactory,** ann-ssätt-iss-**fäck**-te-ri, *adj*
unbefriedigend

**unsavoury,** ann-**sseh**-we-ri, *adj* abstoßend

**unscrew,** ann-**skruh**, *v*
aufschrauben

**unscrupulous,** ann-**skruh**-pju-less, *adj* skrupellos

**unselfish,** ann-**ssell**-fisch, *adj* selbstlos

**unsettled,** ann-**ssett**-l'd, *adj*
wechselhaft, unsicher

**unshaven,** ann-**scheh**-ven, *adj* unrasiert

**unshrinking,** ann-**schring**-king, *adj* unverzagt

**unsightly,** ann-**ssait**-li, *adj*
häßlich

**unskilled,** ann-**skiid**, *adj*
ungelernt

**unsolved,** ann-**ssolwd**, *adj*
ungelöst

**unstable,** ann-**steh**-b'l, *adj*
(structure, economy)
unsicher; (mentally) labil

**unstuck,** ann-**stack**, *adj*
**come –,** *v* sich lösen; *fig* in
die Binsen gehen

**unsuccessful,** ann-ssek-**ssess**-full, *adj* erfolglos

**unsuitable,** ann-**ssuh**-te-b'l, *adj* unpassend

**unsuited (to),** ann-**ssuh**-tidd (tu), *adj* ungeeignet

**unsuspecting,** ann-ssess-**peck**-ting, *adj*
nichtsahnend

**unsympathetic,** ann-simm-

pe-**thett**-ick, *adj* wenig
  mitfühlend
**unthinkable,** ann-**think**-e-
  b'l, *adj* unvorstellbar
**unthinking,** ann-**thing**-king,
  *adj* gedankenlos
**untidy,** ann-**tai**-di, *adj*
  unordentlich
**untie,** ann-**tai**, *v* (knot)
  lösen; (lace etc.)
  aufbinden
**until,** en-**till**, *conj prep* bis
**untimely,** ann-**taim**-li, *adv*
  (inopportune) ungelegen;
  (death) vorzeitig
**untold,** ann-**tohld** *adj*
  (wealth) unermeßlich;
  (countless) unzählig
**untouched,** ann-**tatscht** *adj*
  unberührt
**untoward,** ann-te-**u'ord**, *adj*
  ungünstig
**unusual,** ann-**juh**-schu-el,
  *adj* ungewöhnlich
**unveil,** ann-**wehl**, *v*
  enthüllen
**unwarranted,** ann-**u'o**-ren-
  tidd, *adj* ungerechtfertigt
**unwavering,** ann-**u'eh**-we-
  ring, *adj* standhaft
**unwelcome,** ann-**u'ell**-kem,
  *adj* (visitor)
  unwillkommen; (news
  etc.) unangenehm
**unwell,** ann-**u'ell**, *adj* be −,
  *v* sich nicht wohl fühlen
**unwieldy,** ann-**u'iel**-di, *adj*
  unhandlich
**unwilling,** ann-**u'ill**-ing, *adj*
  widerwillig; **be − to do
  sth,** nicht bereit sein, etw

zu tun
**unwind,** ann-u'**aind**, *v*
  abwickeln, abwinden; *fig*
  sich entspannen
**unwise,** ann-**u'ais**, *adj*
  unklug
**unwittingly,** ann-u'**itt**-ing-
  li, *adv* unwissentlich
**unworthy (of),** ann-**u'ör**-
  dhi (ew), *adj* unwürdig
**unwrap,** ann-**räpp**, *v*
  auswickeln, auspacken
**unwritten,** ann-**ritt**-'n, *adj*
  ungeschrieben
**unyielding,** ann-**jiel**-ding,
  *adj* unbeugsam
**up,** app, *adv* (position)
  oben; (movement) nach
  oben; *prep* hinauf; −**and-
  coming,** *adj* aufstrebend; −
  **and down,** *adv* auf und
  nieder; −**s and downs,** *npl*
  Höhen und Tiefen *pl*; −
  **here,** *adv* (position) hier
  oben; (movement) herauf;
  − **there,** *adv* (position)
  dort oben; (movement)
  hinauf; − **to,** *prep* bis; **be −
  to,** *v* (capable of) zu etw
  in der Lage sein; **be − to
  sth,** *fam* etw aushecken;
  **it's − to you,** das ist
  deine/Ihre Sache
**upbringing,** **app**-bring-ing, *n*
  Erziehung *f*
**update,** app-**deht**, *v* auf den
  neuesten Stand bringen
**upgrade,** app-**grehd**, *v*
  (product) verbessern;
  (person) befördern
**upheaval,** app-**hie**-w'l, *n*

Aufruhr *m*
**uphill,** app-**hill**, *adj* (path)
  bergauf führend; (task)
  mühsam; *adv* bergauf
**uphold,** app-**hohld**, *v*
  aufrechterhalten;
  (support) stützen
**upholster,** app-**hohl**-ster, *v*
  polstern; −**y,** *n*
  Polsterung *f*
**upkeep,** **app**-kiep, *n*
  Instandhaltung *f*
**uplifting,** app-**lift**-ting, *adj*
  erhebend
**upon,** e-**ponn**, *prep* auf
**upper,** **app**-er, *adj* obere(r/s),
  höhere(r/s), Ober-; −-
  **class,** *adj* Oberschicht-; −
  **hand,** *n* Oberhand *f*; −
  −**most,** *adj* oberste(r/s),
  höchste(r/s)
**upright,** **app**-rait, *adj*
  aufrecht; (honest)
  rechtschaffen; *adv*
  aufrecht; *n* − **(piano),**
  Klavier *nt*
**uprising,** **app**-rei-sing, *n*
  Aufstand *m*
**uproar,** **app**-ror, *n*
  Aufruhr *m*
**uproot,** app-**ruht**, *v*
  entwurzeln
**upset,** app-**ssett**, *adj*
  (person) bestürzt,
  aufgeregt; (stomach)
  verdorben; *v* (knock over)
  umwerfen; (worry)
  aufregen
**upshot,** **app**-schott, *n*
  Ergebnis *nt*
**upside-down,** app-sseid-

**daun**, *adv* verkehrt herum; (untidy) drunter und drüber

**upstairs**, app-**stährs**, *adj* obere(r/s); *adv* oben; *n* Obergeschoß *nt*; **go –**, *v* nach oben gehen, hinaufgehen

**upstart**, **a**pp-start, *n* Emporkömmling *m*

**upstream**, app-**striem**, *adv* stromaufwärts

**uptake**, **a**pp-tehk, *n* be **quick/low on the –**, *v* schnell verstehen/schwer von Begriff sein

**uptight**, app-**teit**, *adj* nervös

**up-to-date**, app-tu-**deht**, *adj & adv* auf dem neuesten Stand, aktuell

**upward**, **a**pp-u'erd, *adj* steigend; **–s**, *adv* aufwärts

**uranium**, juhr-**reh**-ni-em, *n* Uran *nt*

**urban**, ör-ben, *adj* städtisch, Stadt-

**urchin**, ör-tschinn, *n* Strolch *m*

**urge**, ördsch, *n* Drang *m*; *v* drängen

**urgency**, ör-dschen-ssi, *n* Dringlichkeit *f*

**urgent**, ör-dschent, *adj* dringend

**urinate**, juhr-ri-neht, *v* urinieren

**urine**, juhr-rinn, *n* Urin *m*, Harn *m*

**urn**, örn, *n* Urne *f*

**us**, ass, *pron* uns; *(emphatic)* wir

**US**, *abbr* United States

**USA**, *abbr* United States of America

**usage**, juhss-idsch, *n* Gebrauch *m*

**use**, juhss, *n* Gebrauch *m*; (utility) Nutzen *m*; **–ful**, *adj* nützlich; **–less**, *adj* nutzlos; **it's no –**, (pointless) es hat keinen Zweck; (useless) es ist nutzlos

**use**, juhs, *v* gebrauchen; (apply) anwenden; **–d**, *adj* gebraucht; **I –d to ...**, früher habe ich ...; **– up**, *v* verbrauchen; **be –d to sth**, *v* etw gewohnt sein

**usher**, asch-er, *n* (court) Gerichtsdiener *m*; (cinema etc.) Platzanweiser *m*; **– in**, *v* einführen

**usual**, juh-schu-el, *adj* gewöhnlich, gebräuchlich; **–ly**, *adv* gewöhnlich

**usurp**, juh-**sörp**, *v* sich widerrechtlich aneignen; **–er**, *n* Usurpator *m*

**utensil**, juh-**tenn**-ssill, *n* Gerät *nt*

**utility**, juh-**till**-i-ti, *n* (usefulness) Nützlichkeit *f*; (service provider) öffentlicher Versorgungsbetrieb *m*; **– room**, *n* Hausarbeitsraum *m*

**utilize**, juh-ti-lais, *v* benutzen, verwerten

**utmost**, att-mohst, *adj*

äußerste(r/s); **to the –**, (exertion) bis zum äußersten; (enjoy) völlig

**utter**, att-er, *adj* höchster(r/s), völlig; *v* äußern; ausstoßen; **–ance**, *n* Äußerung *f*; **–ly**, *adv* äußerst, völlig

**U-turn**, juh-törn, *n* (in car, fig) Wende *f* (um 180 Grad)

**vacancy,** weh-ken-ssi, n (job) freie Stelle; (room) (freies) Zimmer nt; (emptiness) Leere f

**vacant,** weh-kent, adj leer; (available) frei; (house) unbewohnt

**vacate,** we-keht, v räumen

**vacation,** we-keh-sch'n, n Ferien pl

**vaccinate,** wäck-ssi-neht, v impfen

**vaccination,** wäck-ssi-neh-sch'n, n Impfung f

**vacuum,** wäck-ju-em, n Vakuum nt; v Staub saugen; **– cleaner,** n Staubsauger m; **– flask,** n Thermosflasche ® f

**vagina,** we-dschei-ne, n Scheide f

**vagrant,** weh-grent, n (homeless person) Obdachlose(r) m & f

**vague,** wehg, adj (shape, question) vage; (person) zerstreut

**vain,** wehn, adj eitel; (attempt) vergeblich; **in –,** umsonst

**valentine,** wäll-en-tein, n – **(card),** n Valentinskarte f

**valet,** wäll-eh, n Diener m

**valiant,** wäll-jent, adj tapfer

**valid,** wäll-idd, adj (ticket etc.) gültig; (excuse) triftig; (argument) stichhaltig; (objection) berechtigt

**valley,** wäll-i, n Tal nt

**valour,** wäll-er, n Tapferkeit f

**valuable,** wäll-ju-e-b'l, adj wertvoll; **–s,** npl Wertsachen pl

**valuation,** wäll-ju-eh-sch'n, n Schätzung f

**value,** wäll-juh, n Wert m; v schätzen; **– added tax,** n Mehrwertsteuer f; **–d,** adj geschätzt; **–r,** n Schätzer m

**valve,** wälw, n Ventil m; (of heart) Klappe f; (radio) Röhre f

**vampire,** wämm-peir, n Vampir m

**van,** wänn, n Lieferwagen m; mil Vorhut f

**vandal,** wänn-d'l, n Vandale m; fig Rowdy m; **–ism,** n (mutwillige) Zerstörung f; **–ize,** n (mutwillig) beschädigen

**vanguard,** wänn-gard, n mil Vorhut f; fig Spitze f

**vanilla,** we-nill-e, n Vanille f

**vanish,** wänn-isch, v verschwinden

**vanity,** wänn-i-ti, n Eitelkeit f; **– bag,** n Kosmetiktäschchen nt

**vantage point,** wahn-tidsch peunt, n Aussichtspunkt m

**vapour,** weh-per, n Dunst m

**variable,** wehr-ri-e-b'l, adj veränderlich; (adjustable) regulierbar

**variance,** wehr-ri-ens, n Unterschied m; **be at – (with),** v uneinig sein (mit); (opinions) nicht übereinstimmen

**variation,** wehr-ri-eh-sch'n, n Veränderung f, Variation f; (fluctuation) Schwankung f

**varicose veins,** wä-ri-kohss wehns, npl Krampfadern pl

**varied, wehr**-ridd, *adj*
(mixed) gemischt;
(eventful) bewegt

**variegated, wehr**-ri-geh-
tidd, *adj* buntfarbig; (leaf)
geflammt

**variety, we-rei**-i-ti, *n*
(mixture) Vielfalt *f*;
(change) Abwechslung *f*;
(type) Art *f*; *theatre*
Varieté *nt*

**various, wehr**-ri-ess, *adj*
(different) verschieden;
(several) mehrere

**varnish, wahr**-nisch, *n* Lack
*m*; *v* lackieren

**vary, wehr**-ri, *v* (make
different) ändern;
(become different) sich
verändern; (be different)
sich unterscheiden;
(fluctuate) schwanken

**vase, wahs**, *n* Vase *f*

**vast, wahst**, *adj*
unermeßlich, riesig

**vat, watt**, *n* großes Faß *nt*

**vault, wo**'alt, *n* Gewölbe *nt*;
(burial) Gruft *f*;
(strongroom) Tresorraum
*m*; (jump) Sprung *m*; *v* –
**(over),** überspringen

**veal, wiel**, *n* Kalbfleisch *nt*

**veer, wier**, *v* (of wind) sich
drehen; (of car)
ausscheren

**vegetable, wedsch**-i-te-b'l, *n*
Gemüse *nt*; –**s,** *npl*
Gemüse *nt*

**vegetarian, wedsch**-i-**tähr**-
ri-en, *n* Vegetarier *m*

**vegetation, wedsch-i-teh**-

sch'n, *n* Vegetation *f*

**vehement, wie**-i-ment, *adj*
heftig, gewaltig

**vehicle, wie**-i-k'l, *n*
Fahrzeug *nt*

**veil, wehl**, *n* Schleier *m*; *v*
verschleiern

**vein, wehn**, *n* Ader *f*;
(mood) Stimmung *f*

**velocity, wi-loss**-i-ti, *n*
Geschwindigkeit *f*

**velvet, well**-witt, *adj* Samt-;
*n* Samt *m*

**vending machine, wenn**-
ding me-**schien**, *n*
(Verkaufs)automat *m*

**vendor, wenn**-der, *n*
Verkäufer *m*

**veneer, we-nier**, *n* Furnier
*nt*; *fig* Fassade *f*; *v*
furnieren

**venereal, wi** nier-ri-el,
**–disease,** *n*
Geschlechtskrankheit *f*

**vengeance, wenn**-dschenss,
*n* Rache *f*; **with a –,**
gewaltig

**Venice, wenn**-iss, *n*
Venedig *nt*

**venison, wenn**-i-s'n, *n*
Reh(fleisch) *nt*

**venom, wenn**-em, *n* Gift *nt*;
*fig* Groll *m*; –**ous,** *adj* giftig

**vent, went**, *n* Öffnung *f*; (in
cask) Spundloch *nt*; (in
coat) Schlitz *m*; *v*
abreagieren; **give – to,** *v*
etw freien Lauf lassen

**ventilate, wenn**-ti-leht, *v*
lüften; (discuss) erörtern

**ventilator, wenn**-ti-leh-ter,

*n* Ventilator *m*; *med*
Beatmungsgerät *nt*

**ventriloquist, wenn-trill**-e-
ku'ist, *n* Bauchredner *m*

**venture, wenn**-tscher, *n*
Unternehmung *f*; *v* (sich)
wagen

**venue, wenn**-juh, *n*
(Austragungs)ort *m*

**verb, wörb**, *n* Zeitwort *nt*,
Verb *nt*; –**al(ly),** *adj & adv*
mündlich

**verbatim, wer-beh**-timm, *adj*
& *adv* wortwörtlich

**verbose, wer-bohss**, *adj*
wortreich, schwülstig

**verdict, wör**-dikt, *n* Urteil
*nt*

**verge, wördsch**, *n* Rand *m*; *v*
**– on,** grenzen an

**verify, wer-ri**-fei, *v* (confirm)
bestätigen; (check)
überprüfen

**veritable, we-ritt**-e-b'l, *adj*
wahrhaftig

**vermin, wör**-minn, *n*
Ungeziefer *nt*; *fig*
Abschaum *m*

**vernacular, wer-näck**-ju-ler,
*n* Landessprache *f*

**versatile, wör**-sse-teil, *adj*
vielseitig

**verse, wörss**, *adj* Vers-; *n*
(stanza) Strophe *f*;
(poetry) Dichtung *f*,
Poesie *f*; *relig* Vers *m*

**versed (in), wörst** (inn), *adj*
bewandert in

**version, wör**-sch'n, *n*
Version *f*

**versus, wör**-ssess, *prep* gegen

**vertebrate**, wör-ti-bret, *adj* Wirbel-; *n* Wirbeltier *nt*

**vertical**, wör-tick-'l, *adj* senkrecht

**vertigo**, wör-ti-goh, *n* Schwindel(anfall) *m*

**very**, wei-e, *adj* (exact) genau; *adv* (extremely) sehr; (absolutely) aller-; – **much**, sehr; **thank you – much**, vielen Dank

**vessel**, wess-'l, *n* Gefäß *nt*; *naut* Schiff *nt*

**vest**, west, *n* Unterhemd *nt*

**vested**, wess-tidd, *adj* **have a – interest in**, *v* (financial) finanziell beteiligt sein an; (personal) ein persönliches Interesse haben an

**vestige**, wess-tidsch, *n* Spur *f*, Zeichen *nt*

**vestry**, wess-tri, *n* Sakristei *f*

**vet**, wett, *n* (*abbr* **veterinary surgeon**) Tierarzt *m*, Tierärztin *f*; *v* überprüfen

**veteran**, wett-e-ren, *n* Veteran *m*

**veterinary**, wett-ri-ne-ri, *adj* tierärztlich, Veterinär-; – **surgeon**, *n* Tierarzt *m*, Tierärztin *f*

**veto**, wie-toh, *n* Veto *nt*; *v* sein Veto einlegen

**vex**, wecks, *v* ärgern; **–ation**, *n* Ärger *m*; **–ed**, *adj* (person) verärgert; (question) umstritten

**via**, wei-e, *prep* über

**viable**, wei-e-b'l, *adj* (plan) durchführbar; (business) rentabel; (foetus, economy) lebensfähig

**viaduct**, wei-e-dakt, *n* Viadukt *m*

**vibrate**, wei-breht, *v* vibrieren; (shake) beben

**vibration**, wei-breh-sch'n, *n* Schwingung *f*, Vibrieren *nt*

**vicar**, wick-er, *n* Pfarrer *m*; **–age**, *n* Pfarrhaus *nt*

**vice**, weiss, *adj* stellvertretend; *n* Laster *m*; *mech* Schraubstock *m*; **–president**, *n* Vizepräsident *m*

**vice versa**, wei-ssi wör-sse, *adv* umgekehrt

**vicinity**, wi-ssinn-i-ti, *n* Nähe *f*, Nachbarschaft *f*

**vicious**, wisch-ess, *adj* (nasty) gemein; (wicked) übel; (dog etc.) bösartig; – **circle**, *n* Teufelskreis *m*

**victim**, wick-timm, *n* Opfer *nt*; **–ize**, *v* schikanieren

**victor**, wick-ter, *n* Sieger *m*

**victorious**, wick-tor-ri-ess, *adj* siegreich

**victory**, wick-te-ri, *n* Sieg *m*

**video**, widd-i-oh, *adj* Video-; *n* (film) Video *nt*; (recorder) Videorekorder *m*; *v* (auf Video) aufnehmen; **– cassette**, *n* Videokassette *f*; **– tape**, *n* Videoband *nt*

**vie (for)**, wei (for), *v* wetteifern (um)

**Vienna**, wi-enn-e, *n* Wien *nt*

**view**, wjuh, *n* (sight) Aussicht *f*; (opinion) Ansicht *f*; (intention) Absicht *f*; *v* betrachten; **–er**, *n* (TV) Zuschauer *m*; (for film) Filmbetrachter *m*; (for slides) Diabetrachter *m*; **–finder**, *n* *photog* Sucher *m*; **–point**, *n* Standpunkt *m*; **in – of**, angesichts

**vigil**, widsch-ill, *n* Nachtwache *f*; **–ance**, *n* Wachsamkeit *f*; **–ant**, *adj* wachsam

**vigorous**, wigg-e-ress, *adj* energisch

**vigour**, wigg-er, *n* Kraft *f*, Energie *f*

**vile**, weil, *adj* (thought, remark) gemein; (food, weather) scheußlich

**vilify**, will-i-fei, *v* verunglimpfen

**villa**, will-e, *n* Villa *f*

**village**, will-idsch, *n* Dorf *nt*; **–r**, *n* Dorfbewohner *m*

**villain**, will-en, *n* Schurke *m*, Schuft *m*; **–ous**, *adj* gemein, abscheulich

**vindicate**, winn-di-keht, *v* rechtfertigen

**vindictive**, winn-dick-tiw, *adj* rachsüchtig, rachgierig

**vine**, wein, *n* Rebstock *m*

**vinegar**, winn-i-ger, *n* Essig *m*

**vineyard**, winn-jahrd, *n* Weinberg *m*

**vintage**, winn-tidsch, *adj* (car) Oldtimer-; (wine)

edel; n Jahrgang m

**vinyl,** wei-nill, n Vinyl nt

**viola,** wi-oh-le, n Bratsche f

**violate,** wei-e-leht, v
(disturb) schänden; (rape)
vergewaltigen; (law,
rights) verletzen; (treaty)
brechen

**violence,** wei-e-lenss, n
(brutality) Gewalt f;
(force) Heftigkeit f

**violent,** wei-e-lent, adj
(strong) heftig; (brutal)
gewaltsam

**violet,** wei-e-let, adj violett;
n Veilchen nt

**violin,** wei-e-linn, n Violine
f, Geige f; **–ist,** Geiger m

**VIP,** wie ei pie, n (abbr very
**important person),** VIP m

**virgin,** wör-dschinn, adj fig
unberührt; n Jungfrau f

**Virgo,** wör-goh, n Jungfrau f

**virile,** wi-reil, adj männlich,
maskulin

**virtual,** wör-tju-el, adj
(near) praktisch; (math,
comp) virtuell; **–lly,** adv
praktisch; so gut wie

**virtue,** wör-tjuh, n
(goodness) Tugend f;
(advantage) Vorteil m; **by
– of,** aufgrund

**virtuous,** wör-tju-ess, adj
tugendhaft

**virulent,** wi-rju-lent, adj
med bösartig; fig heftig

**virus,** wei-ress, n (med,
comp) Virus m

**visa,** wi-se, n Visum nt

**visibility,** wis-i-bill-i-ti, n

Sicht(weite) f

**visible,** wis-i-b'l, adj
sichtbar

**visibly,** wis-ibb-li, adv
sichtlich

**vision,** wisch-'n, n (faculty)
Sehvermögen nt; (image)
Vision f; (foresight)
Weitblick m

**visit,** wis-itt, n Besuch m;
v besuchen; **–or,** n
Besucher m

**visor,** wei-ser, n (on helmet)
Visier nt; (in car) Blende f

**vista,** wiss-te, n Ausblick m

**visual,** wisch-ju-el, adj Seh-,
visuell; **–ize,** v sich
vorstellen

**vital,** wei-t'l, adj (of life)
Lebens-; (essential)
unerläßlich; (lively) vital;
**–ity,** n Vitalität f; **–ly,** adv
äußerst

**vitamin,** witt-e-minn, n
Vitamin nt

**vivacious,** wi-weh-schess,
adj lebhaft

**vivacity,** wi-wäss-i-ti, n
Lebhaftigkeit f

**vivid,** wi-widd, adj lebhaft;
(bright) leuchtend

**V-neck,** wie-neck, n V-
Ausschnitt m

**vocabulary,** we-käbb-ju-le-
ri, n Wortschatz f

**vocal,** woh-k'l, adj mus
Vokal-; (vociferous)
lautstark; **– cords,** npl
Stimmbänder pl

**vocation,** we-keh-sch'n, n

(profession) Beruf m;
(calling) Berufung f; **–al,**
adj Berufs-

**vociferous,** we-ssiff-e-ress,
adj lautstark

**vodka,** wodd-ke, n Wodka m

**vogue,** wohg, n Mode f; **in
–,** modisch

**voice,** weuss, n Stimme f; v
äußern

**void,** weud, adj (empty) leer;
(invalid) ungültig; n Leere
f

**volatile,** woll-e-teil, adj
(substance) flüchtig;
(person) impulsiv;
(situation) brisant

**volcano,** woll-keh-noh, n
Vulkan m

**volley,** woll-i, n mil Salve f;
(tennis) Volley m; (of
stones, insults) Hagel m; v
(tennis) einen Volley
schlagen; **–ball,** n
Volleyball m

**volt,** wohlt, n Volt nt; **–age,**
n Spannung f

**voluble,** woll-ju-b'l, adj
beredt; (chatty) redselig

**volume,** woll-juhm, n
(loudness) Lautstärke f;
(book) Band m; (bulk)
Volumen nt

**voluminous,** we-luh-mi-
ness, adj groß,
umfangreich

**voluntary,** woll-en-te-ri, adj
freiwillig

**volunteer,** woll-en-tier, n
Freiwillige(r) m & f; v sich
(freiwillig) melden

**voluptuous,** we-**lapp**-tju-ess,
  *adj* üppig
**vomit, womm**-itt, *n*
  Erbrochenes *nt*; *v* (sich)
  erbrechen
**vote,** woht, *n* (voice)
  Stimme *f*; (election) Wahl
  *f*; (franchise) Wahlrecht
  *nt*; *v* wählen; –
  **for/against,** stimmen
  für/gegen
**voter, woh**-ter, *n* Wähler *m*
**voucher, wautsch**-er, *n*
  Gutschein *m*
**vouch for,** wautsch for, *v*
  einstehen für
**vow,** wau, *n* Versprechen *nt*;
  *relig* Gelübde *nt*; *v* geloben
**vowel, wau**-el, *n* Vokal *m*
**voyage, weu**-idsch, *n* Reise
  *f*; *v* reisen
**vulgar, wall**-ger, *adj* vulgär
**vulnerable, wall**-ne-re-b'l,
  *adj* (helpless) wehrlos;
  (unprotected)
  ungeschützt; – **to,** anfällig
  für
**vulture, wall**-tscher, *n*
  Geier *m*

**wacky,** u'äck-i, *adj fam*
verrückt

**wad,** u'odd, n (paper)
Bündel nt; (cotton wool)
Bausch m; **–ding,** n
Füllmaterial nt

**waddle,** u'odd-'l, v
watscheln

**wade,** u'ehd, v waten

**wafer,** u'eh-fer, n Waffel f;
*relig* Hostie f

**wag,** u'ägg, n Spaßvogel m; v
wedeln (mit)

**wage,** u'ehdsch, n Lohn m; v
**– war (on),** Krieg führen
(gegen)

**wager,** u'eh-dscher, n Wette
f; v wetten

**wages,** u'ehdsch-is, npl
Lohn m, Gehalt nt

**waggle,** u'ägg-'l, v wackeln;
(tail) wedeln mit

**wag(g)on,** u'ägg-en, n rail
Wagen m; (horse-drawn)
Fuhrwerk nt

**wail,** u'ehl, n klagender
Schrei m; v jammern

**waist,** u'ehst, n Taille f;
**–coat,** n Weste f, **–line,** n
Taille f

**wait,** u'eht, n Wartezeit f; v
warten; **– at table,** v
servieren; **–er,** n Kellner
m, Bedienung f; **– for,** v
warten auf; **–ing,** n
Warten nt; (service) n
Bedienung f; **–ing room,**
*rail* Wartesaal m;
(doctor's) Wartezimmer
nt; **–ress,** n Bedienung f;
**on,** v bedienen; **lie in –
for,** v auflauern

**waive,** u'ehw, v verzichten
auf, aufgeben

**wake,** u'ehk, n naut
Kielwasser; v (self)
aufwachen; (sb else)
aufwecken; **– up to sth,**

*fig* sich etw bewußt
werden

**Wales,** u'ehls, n Wales nt

**walk,** u'o'ak, n Spaziergang
m; v gehen; (stroll)
spazierengehen; (hike)
wandern; **–er,** n Wanderer
m, Spaziergänger m; **–ing,**
*adj* Wander-; n Gehen nt;
Wandern nt; **ing stick,** n
Spazierstock m; **–over,** n
*fam* Spaziergang m

**wall,** u'o'al, n (exterior)
Mauer f; (interior) Wand
f; **–ed,** adj mit Mauern
umgeben

**wallet,** u'oll-itt, n
Brieftasche f

**wallflower,** u'o'al-flau-er, n
Goldlack m; *fig*
Mauerblümchen nt

**wallop,** u'oll-ep, fam n
Schlag m; v hauen

**wallow,** u'oll-oh, v sich
wälzen

**wallpaper,** u'o'al-peh-per, n
Tapete f

**wally,** u'oll-i, n fam Depp m

**walnut,** u'o'al-natt, n
Walnuß f

**walrus,** u'o'al-ress, n Walroß
nt

**waltz,** u'olts, n Walzer m; v
Walzer tanzen

**wander,** u'onn-der, v
wandern; (from subject)
abschweifen

**wane,** u'ehn, v abnehmen

**want,** u'ont, n (lack)
Mangel m; (distress) Not
f; v (need) brauchen; –

**(to),** wollen; **–ed,** *adj* gesucht; **–ing,** *adj* unzulänglich

**wanton,** u'onn-ten, *adj* zügellos; (lustful) liederlich

**war,** u'or, n Krieg m; **–like,** *adj* kriegerisch; **make –,** v Krieg führen

**ward,** u'ord, n (minor) Mündel nt; (in hospital) Krankensaal m; **–en,** n (guard) Aufseher m; (of college) Rektor m; **–er,** n Wärter m; **– off,** v abwehren; **–ress,** n Wärterin f

**wardrobe, u'ord**-rohb, n (cupboard) Kleiderschrank m; (clothes) Garderobe f

**warehouse, u'ähr**-hauss, n Lagerhaus nt

**wares,** u'ährs, *npl* Waren *pl*

**warhead, w'or**-hedd, n Sprengkopf m

**warily, u'ähr**-ri-li, *adv* vorsichtig, behutsam

**warm,** u'orm, *adj* warm; v wärmen; **– up,** v (get warm) warm werden; (make warm) aufwärmen **–th,** n Wärme f

**warn (against),** u'orn (*e*-genst), v warnen (vor); **–ing,** *adj* Warn-; n Warnung f

**warp,** u'orp, v sich werfen; **–ed,** *adj* verzogen; *fig* pervers

**warrant, u'o**-rent, n (for search) Durchsuchungsbefehl m; (for arrest) Haftbefehl m; *comm* Garantie f; **–y,** n Garantie f

**warren, u'o**-ren, n (rabbit's) Kaninchenbau m; *fig* Labyrinth nt

**warrior, u'o**-ri-er, n Krieger m

**Warsaw, u'or**-so'a, n Warschau nt

**warship, u'or**-schipp, n Kriegsschiff nt

**wart,** u'ort, n Warze f

**wartime, u'or**-teim, *adj* Kriegs-; n Krieg m; **in –,** in Kriegszeiten

**wary, u'ähr**-ri, *adj* bedachtsam

**wash,** u'osch, v (sich) waschen; (crockery) abwaschen; **–able,** *adj* waschbar; **– basin,** n Waschbecken m; **–er,** n *mech* Dichtungsring m; (machine) Waschmaschine f; **–ing,** n (laundry) Wäsche f; **–ing machine,** n Waschmaschine f; **–ing powder,** n Waschpulver nt; **–ing-up,** n Abwasch m; **–ing-up liquid,** n Spülmittel nt; **–out,** n *fam* Reinfall m; **– up,** v spülen

**wasp,** u'osp, n Wespe f

**waste,** u'ehst, *adj* Abfall-; n Verschwendung f; (rubbish) Abfall m; v verschwenden; (time)

vergeuden; **– away,** v dahinschwinden; **– disposal unit,** n Müllschlucker m; **–ful,** *adj* (person) verschwenderisch; (process) unwirtschaftlich; **–land,** n Einöde f; **––paper basket,** n Papierkorb m

**watch,** u'otsch, n (timekeeper) Uhr f, Armbanduhr f; (lookout) Wache f; v (TV) fernsehen; (guard) (be)wachen; (observe) beobachten; (look) zusehen; **–dog,** n Wachthund m; *fig* Aufsicht(sbehörde) f; **–ful,** *adj* wachsam; **–maker,** n Uhrmacher m; **–man,** n Wächter m; **– out,** v (be careful) aufpassen; **– television,** v fernsehen

**water, u'o'a**-ter, n Wasser nt; v (plant) gießen; (animal) tränken; (of eye) tränen; **(hot) – bottle,** n Wärmflasche f; **– closet,** n Toilette f; **–colour,** n Aquarell nt; **–cress,** n Brunnenkresse f; **–fall,** n Wasserfall m; **–ing can,** n Gießkanne f; **– level,** n Wasserstand m; **–lily,** n Seerose f; **–line,** n Wasserlinie f; **–logged,** *adj* vollgesogen; **–mark,** n (in paper) Wasserzeichen nt;

**–proof,** *adj* wasserdicht; *n* Regenhaut *f*; **–shed,** *n fig* Wendepunkt *m*; **–skiing,** *n* Wasserskilaufen *nt*; **– tank,** *n* Wasserbehälter *m*; **–tight,** *adj* wasserdicht; **–y,** *adj* wässerig

**wave,** u'ehw, *n* (sea, *elec*) Welle *f*; (hand) Winken *nt*; *v* (of flag) wehen; (with hand) winken; (hair) wellen; **–length,** *n* Wellenlänge *f*

**waver,** u'eh-wer, *v* zaudern; **–ing,** *adj* unschlüssig

**wavy,** u'eh-wi, *adj* wellig

**wax,** u'äks, *n* Wachs *nt*; *v* wachsen, wichsen; (of moon) zunehmen; (become) werden; **–works,** *npl* Wachsfigurenkabinett *nt*

**way,** u'eh, *adv fam* weit; *n* (route, path) Weg *m*; (direction) Richtung *f*; (manner) (Art *f* und) Weise *f*, **; – in,** *n* Eingang *m*, Einfahrt *f*; **–lay,** *v* auflauern; **– out,** *n* Ausgang *m*, Ausfahrt *f*; **–ward,** *adj* ungezügelt; **a long –,** weit; **by the –,** übrigens; **on the –,** unterwegs, auf dem Weg; **lose one's –,** sich verirren

**we,** u'ie, *pron* wir

**weak,** u'iek, *adj* schwach; **–en,** *v* (make weak) schwächen; (grow weak) schwach werden; **–ling,** *n* Schwächling *m*; **–ness,** *n* Schwäche *f*

**wealth,** u'elth, *n* (richness) Reichtum *m*; (abundance) Fülle *f*; **–y,** *adj* reich

**wean,** u'ien, *v* entwöhnen; *fig* abgewöhnen

**weapon,** u'epp-'n, *n* Waffe *f*

**wear,** u'ähr, *n* (wear and tear) Abnützung *f*; (clothes) Kleidung *f*; *v* tragen; (last) sich tragen; **– off,** *v* (layer) abgehen; *fig* nachlassen; **– out,** *v* verbrauchen; (clothes) abnützen; (person) erschöpfen

**weary,** u'ier-ri, *adj* müde; *v* (tire) ermüden; (bore) langweilen

**weasel,** u'ie-s'l, *n* Wiesel *nt*

**weather,** u'edh-er, *n* Wetter *nt*; *v* (survive) überstehen; (become worn) verwittern; **–beaten,** *adj* wettergegärbt; **– forecast,** *n* Wettervorhersage *f*; **– report,** *n* Wetterbericht *m*; **under the –,** *fam* nicht ganz auf dem Posten

**weave,** u'iew, *v* (cloth) weben; (zigzag) sich schlängeln; **–r,** *n* Weber *m*

**web,** u'ebb, *n* Gewebe *nt*; **–bing,** *n* Gurtband *nt*; **–bed,** *adj* Schwimm-

**wed,** u'edd, *v* heiraten

**wedding,** u'edd-ing, *n* Hochzeit *f*; **– ring,** *n* Ehering *m*

**wedge,** u'edsch, *n* Keil *m*; *v* einkeilen; **– in,**

einzwängen

**wedlock,** u'edd-lock, *n* Ehestand *m*

**Wednesday,** u'ens-dei, *n* Mittwoch *m*

**weed,** u'ied, *n* Unkraut *nt*; *v* jäten; **–killer,** *n* Unkrautvertilgungsmittel *nt*; **–s,** *npl* Unkraut *nt*; **–y,** *adj* (fam feeble) schmächtig

**week,** u'iek, *n* Woche *f*; **–day,** *n* Wochentag *m*; (on timetable) Werktag *m*; **–end,** *n* Wochenende *nt*; **–ly,** *adj* wöchentlich, Wochen-; *adv* wöchentlich; *n* (magazine) Wochenzeitschrift *f*

**weep,** u'iep, *v* weinen; **–ing willow,** *n* Trauerweide *f*

**weigh,** u'eh, *v* wiegen; **– down,** niederdrücken; **– up,** erwägen

**weighing-machine,** u'eh-ing me-schien, *n* Waage *f*

**weight,** u'eht, *n* Gewicht *nt*; **–y,** *adj* gewichtig; **lose –,** abnehmen; **put on –,** *v* zunehmen

**weir,** u'ier, *n* Wehr *nt*

**weird,** u'ierd, *adj* unheimlich; (fam odd) sonderbar

**welcome,** u'ell-kem, *adj* willkommen; *n* Willkommen *nt*; *v* willkommen heißen; **you're –,** nichts zu danken

**weld,** u'eld, n Schweißnaht f; v schweißen; **–er,** n Schweißer m; **–ing,** n Schweißen nt

**welfare, u'ell-fähr,** n (wellbeing) Wohl nt; (support) Fürsorge f; **– state,** n Wohlfahrtsstaat m

**well,** u'ell, adj gesund; adv gut; n (water) Brunnen m; (oil) Quelle f; **–being,** n Wohl nt; **–bred,** adj wohlerzogen; **––built,** adj kräftig gebaut; **– done,** (food) durchgebraten; **––known,** adj bekannt; **––meaning,** adj wohlmeinend; **––off,** adj wohlhabend; **–wisher,** n Gönner m; **as –,** auch; **… as – as …,** sowohl … als auch …; **I'm well,** es geht mir gut

**Welsh,** u'elsch, adj walisisch; n (language) Walisisch nt; pl (people) Waliser pl; **–man,** n Waliser m; **–woman,** n Waliserin f

**west,** u'est, adj westlich, West-; adv westlich, nach Westen; n Westen m; **–erly,** adj westlich; **–ern,** adj westlich, West-; n Western m; **the W–Indies,** npl die Westindischen Inseln pl

**wet,** u'ett, adj naß; (fam weak) weichlich; n Nässe f; v naß machen; **–suit,** n Taucheranzug m

**whack,** u'äck, n Schlag m; v schlagen

**whale,** u'ehl, n Wal m; **–r,** n Walfänger m

**wharf,** u'orf, n Kai m

**what,** u'ott, adj (which) welche(r/s); (what sort) was für ein(e); pron was; **– a …!** was für ein(e) …!; **– is your name/are you called?** wie heißen Sie?; **–ever,** adj welche auch immer; pron was auch (immer); **– kind/sort of,** was für ein(e)

**wheat,** u'iet, n Weizen m

**wheedle, u'ie-d'l,** v beschwatzen

**wheel,** u'iel, n Rad nt; v schieben; (wheelchair) fahren; **–barrow,** n Schubkarren m; **–chair,** n Rollstuhl m; **– clamp,** n Parkkralle f

**wheeze,** u'ies, v keuchen

**when,** u'enn, adv wann; conj (question) wann; (future, whenever) wenn; (past) als; **–ever,** adv (any time) wann auch immer; (every time) jedesmal; conj (any time) wenn (auch immer); (every time) jedesmal wenn

**where,** u'ähr, adv wo; (movement) wohin; **–about(s),** adv wo; n Verbleib m; **–as,** conj während, wo hingegen; **–by,** adv woran, wodurch, womit; **– from,** adv woher;

**– to,** adv wohin; **–upon,** conj worauf

**wherever,** u'ähr-ew-er, adv wo auch immer; (movement) wohin auch immer

**wherewithal, u'ähr-u'idh-o'al,** n (Geld)mittel pl

**whet,** u'ett, v (blade) wetzen; (appetite) anregen

**whether, u'edh-er,** conj ob

**which,** u'itsch, pron (interrogative) welche(r/s); (relative) der/die/das; was; **–ever,** pron welche(r/s) auch immer

**while,** u'eil, n Weile f, Zeitlang f; conj während; **– away,** v (sich) die Zeit vertreiben

**whim,** u'imm, n Grille f

**whimper, u'imm-per,** n Gewinsel nt; v winseln

**whine,** u'ein, n Heulen nt; v wimmern

**whip,** u'ipp, n Peitsche f; v peitschen; (cream, egg) schlagen; **–ed cream,** Schlagsahne f

**whirl,** u'orl, n Wirbel m; v wirbeln; **–pool,** n Strudel m; **–wind,** n Wirbelwind m

**whirr,** u'ör, v surren

**whisk,** u'isk, n Schneebesen m; v (cream, egg) schlagen; **– away,** schnell wegziehen

**whiskers, u'iss-kers,** npl (cat etc) Schnurrhaare pl;

(man's) Backenbart *m*

**whisky, u'iss**-ki, *n* Whisky *m*

**whisper, u'iss**-per, *n* Geflüster *nt*; *v* flüstern

**whistle, u'iss**-'l, *n* (instrument) Pfeife *f*; (sound) Pfiff *m*; *v* pfeifen

**white, u'eit**, *adj* weiß; (drink) mit Milch; *n* Weiß *nt*; (of egg) Eiweiß *nt*; – **elephant**, *n* nutzloser Besitz *m*; – **lie**, *n* Notlüge *f*; –**ness**, *n* Weiße *f*; –**wash**, *n* Tünche *f*; *fig* Schönfärberei *f*; *v* tünchen; *fig* übertünchen

**whiting, u'ei**-ting, *n* Weißfisch *m*

**Whitsun, u'itt**-ssen, *n* Pfingsten *nt*

**whiz, u'is**, *v* zischen, sausen

**who, huh**, *pron* (interrogative) wer, wen, wem; (relative) der/die/das; –**ever**, *pron* wer/wen/wem auch immer

**whole, hohl**, *adj* ganze(r/s); *n* Ganze(s) *nt*; –**heartedly**, *adv* mit ganzem Herzen; –**meal**, *adj* Vollkorn-; –**sale**, *adj* Großhandels-; *fig* Massen-; *adv* ohne weiteres; *n* Großhandel *m*; –**some**, *adj* gesund; **on the –**, im großen und ganzen; **the – of the ...**, der/die/das ganze ...

**wholly, hoh**-li, *adv* gänzlich, völlig

**whom, huhm**, *pron* (accusative, dative) (interrogative) wen, wem; (relative) den/die/das, dem/der/dem

**whooping cough, huh**-ping-koff, *n* Keuchhusten *m*

**whore, hor**, *n* Hure *f*

**whose, huhs**, *adj* wessen; *pron* (possessive) (interrogative) wessen; (relative) dessen/deren/dessen; – **is that?** wem gehört das?

**why, u'ei**, *adv* warum, weshalb; *conj* **that is –**, deshalb, deswegen

**wick, u'ick**, *n* Docht *m*

**wicked, u'ick**-idd, *adj* böse; –**ness**, *n* Bosheit *f*

**wicker, u'ick**-er, *n* Korbgeflecht *nt*; – **basket**, *n* Weidenkorb *m*

**wicket, u'ick**-itt, *n* Wicket *nt*

**wide, u'eid**, *adj* breit; (clothes, world) weit; (interests) vielfältig; *adv* (open, spread) weit; (throw) daneben; –**angle lens**, *n* Weitwinkelobjektiv *nt*; – **awake**, *adj* hellwach; –**ly**, *adv* weit; (known) überall; –**n**, *v* (sich) erweitern; –**spread**, *adj* weitverbreitet

**widow, u'idd**-oh, *n* Witwe *f*; –**ed**, *adj* verwitwet; –**er**, *n* Witwer *m*

**width, u'idth**, *n* Breite *f*, Weite *f*

**wield, u'ield**, *v* schwingen; (power) ausüben

**wife, u'eif**, *n* Frau *f*, (formal) Gattin *f*

**wig, u'igg**, *n* Perücke *f*

**wild, u'eild**, *adj* wild; (angry) wütend; (mad) verrückt

**wilderness, u'ill**-der-niss, *n* Wildnis *f*, Wüste *f*

**wildlife, u'eild**-leif, *n* Tierwelt *f*

**wildly, u'eild**-li, *adv* wild; **not –**, *fam* nicht so sehr

**wilful, u'ill**-full, *adj* (person) eigenwillig; (act) vorsätzlich

**will, u'ill**, *n* Wille *m*; *law* Testament *nt v* (in future) werden; (be willing) wollen

**willing, u'ill**-ing, *adj* bereit; –**ly**, *adv* bereitwillig; –**ness**, *n* Bereitwilligkeit *f*

**willow, u'ill**-oh, *n* Weide *f*

**willpower, u'ill**-pau-er, *n* Willenskraft *f*

**wily, u'ei**-li, *adj* schlau, listig

**win, u'inn**, *n* Sieg *m*; *v* gewinnen

**wince, u'inss**, *v* zucken, zusammenfahren

**winch, u'intsch**, *n* Winde *f*

**wind, u'ind**, *adj mus* Blas-; *n* Wind *m*; *med* Blähung *f*; *mus* Blasinstrumente *pl*

**wind, u'eind**, *v* winden; (meander) sich winden; (clock) aufziehen; – **up**, *v* (clock) aufziehen; (business) liquidieren

**windfall, u'ind**-fo'al, *n*

(luck) unverhoffte(r)
Glücksfall m; (fruit)
Fallobst nt

**winding, u'ein**-ding, adj
gewunden

**windmill, u'ind**-mill, n
Windmühle f

**window, u'inn**-doh, n
Fenster nt – **box,** n
Blumenkasten m; **--
dressing,** n
Schaufensterdekoration f;
fig Schönfärberei f; –
**ledge,** n Fensterbank f; –
**pane,** n Fensterscheibe f; –
**sill,** n Fensterbank f

**windpipe, u'ind**-peip, n
Luftröhre f

**wind power, u'ind pau**-er, n
Windenergie f

**windscreen, u'ind**-skrien, n
Windschutzscheibe f; –
**washer,** n
Scheibenwaschanlage f; –
**iper,** n Scheibenwischer
m

**windswept, u'ind**-ssu'ept,
adj (person) zerzaust;
(landscape)
windgepeitscht

**windy, u'inn**-di, adj windig

**wine, u'ein,** n Wein m; –
**glass,** Weinglas nt; –
**list,** n Weinkarte f; –
**merchant,** n Weinhändler
m; – **tasting,** n
Weinprobe f

**wing, u'ing,** n Flügel m; (of
car) Kotflügel m; **–s,** npl
Seitenkulisse f

**wink, u'ink,** n Zwinkern nt;

v zwinkern, blinzeln

**winner, u'inn**-er, n
Gewinner m; sport Sieger
m

**winning, u'inn**-ing, adj
(team) siegreich; (shot)
entscheidend; (smile)
einnehmend; – **post,** n
Ziel nt; **-s,** npl Gewinn m

**winter, u'inn**-ter, adj
Winter-; n Winter m; v
überwintern; – **sport(s),**
n(pl), Wintersport m

**wintry, u'int**-ri, adj
winterlich, rauh

**wipe, u'eip,** v (ab)wischen; –
**out,** v (erase) löschen;
(destroy) vernichten

**wire, u'eir,** n Draht m;
(telegram) Telegramm nt;
v telegrafieren

**wireless, u'eir**-liss, n Funk
m; (set) Radio nt

**wiring, u'eir**-ring, n
(elektrische) Leitungen pl

**wisdom, u'is**-dem, n
Weisheit f, Verstand m; –
**tooth,** n Weisheitszahn m

**wise, u'eis,** adj weise, klug

**wish, u'isch,** n Wunsch m; v
wünschen; best **-es,** (in
letter) herzliche Grüße;
(on birthday etc.)
herzliche Glückwünsche;
**–ful thinking,** n
Wunschdenken nt

**wisp, u'isp,** n Wölkchen nt;
(of hair) Strähne f

**wistful, u'iss**-full, adj
sehnsüchtig

**wit, u'itt,** n (intelligence)

Verstand; (humour) Witz
m; (funny person)
Spaßvogel m

**witch, u'itsch,** n Hexe f;
**–craft,** n Hexerei f

**with, u'idh,** prep mit; (in the
company of) bei; (as a
result of) vor

**withdraw, u'idh-dro'a,** v
zurückziehen; (money)
abheben; **–n,** adj
verschlossen

**wither, u'idh**-er, v
verwelken; **–ing,** adj
(look) vernichtend

**withhold (from), u'idh-
hohld** (frem), v
vorenthalten

**within, u'idh-inn,** adv
innen; prep innerhalb

**with it, u'idh itt,** adj auf
dem Laufenden

**without, u'idh-aut,** adv
draußen; prep ohne; –
**...ing,** ohne zu ...en

**withstand, u'idh-ständ,** v
widerstehen

**witness, u'itt-niss,** n Zeuge
m, Zeugin f; v (see) sehen;
(signature) bestätigen; –
**to,** bezeugen

**wits, u'itts,** npl Verstand m

**witticism, u'itt**-i-ssism, n
Witzelei f

**witty, u'itt-i,** adj witzig

**wizard, u'is-erd,** n Zauberer
m

**wobble, u'obb-'l,** v wackeln

**woe, u'oh,** n Jammer m;
**–ful,** adj jammervoll,
elend

**wolf,** u'ulf, n Wolf m
**woman, u'umm**-en, n Frau f;
 **–ly,** adj weiblich, feminin
**womb, u'uhm,** n
 Gebärmutter f
**women's lib, wimm**-ins libb,
 n Frauenbewegung f
**wonder, u'ann**-der, n
 (astonishment)
 Verwunderung f; (marvel)
 Wunder nt; v (ask oneself)
 sich fragen; **– at,** sich
 wundern über; **–ful(ly),**
 adj & adv wunderbar; **no
 –!** kein Wunder!
**woo,** u'uh, v umwerben
**wood,** u'udd, n Holz nt;
 (forest) Wald m; **–ed,** adj
 bewaldet; **–en,** adj hölzern,
 Holz-; **–pecker,** n Specht
 m; **–wind,** n adj Holzblas-;
 n Holzblasinstrumente pl;
 **–work,** n Arbeiten pl mit
 Holz
**wool,** u'ull, adj Woll-; n
 Wolle f; **–len,** adj Woll-;
 **–lens,** npl Wollsachen pl;
 **–ly,** adj wollig; (vague)
 undeutlich
**word,** u'örd, n Wort nt;
 (news) Bescheid m; v
 verfassen; **–ing,** n
 Wortlaut m; **– processing,**
 n Textverarbeitung f; **–
 processor,** n Text-
 verarbeitungsprogramm
 nt; **give one's –,** v sein
 Wort geben; **in other –s,**
 anders gesagt
**work,** u'örk, n Arbeit f; (of
 art) Werk nt; v (labour)

arbeiten; (function)
 funktionieren; (succeed)
 klappen; **– loose,** v sich
 lockern; **– out,** v (solve)
 lösen; (devise)
 ausarbeiten; (succeed)
 klappen; sport sich fit
 halten; **get –ed up,** sich
 aufregen
**workable, u'ör**-ke-b'l, adj
 durchführbar, machbar
**worker, u'ör**-ker, n
 Arbeiter m
**workforce, u'örk**-forss, n
 Personal n
**working, u'ör**-king, adj
 (functioning)
 betriebsfähig; (in work)
 berufstätig; n (effect)
 Wirken nt; **– class,** n
 Arbeiterklasse f
**workman, u'örk**-men, n
 Arbeiter m; **–ship,** n
 Ausführung f
**workplace, u'örk**-pleiss, n
 Arbeitsplatz m
**works, u'örks,** n Fabrik f; pl
 mech Werk nt
**workshop, u'örk**-schopp, n
 Werkstatt f
**work station, u'örk**-steh-
 sch'n, n Arbeitsplatz m
**world, u'örld,** adj Welt-; n
 Welt f; **–ly,** adj weltlich;
 **–wide,** adj & adv weltweit
**worm,** u'örm, n Wurm m;
 (screw) Gewinde nt
**worry, u'a**-ri, n Sorge f; v
 (be worried) sich sorgen;
 (make worried)
 beunruhigen

**worse, u'örss,** adj & adv
 schlechter, schlimmer; n
 Schlimmeres nt,
 Schlechtere nt; **–n,** v
 (sich) verschlimmern
**worship, u'ör**-schipp, n
 Verehrung f; v anbeten
**worst, u'örst,** adj
 schlechteste(r/s);
 schlimmste(r/s); adv am
 schlechtesten, am
 schlimmsten; n
 Schlimmste(s),
 Schlechteste(s) nt
**worsted, u'uss**-tidd, n
 Kammgarn nt
**worth, u'örth,** adj wert; n
 Wert m; **–less,** adj wertlos;
 (person) nichtswürdig;
 **–while,** adv der Mühe
 wert
**worthy, u'ör**-dhi, adj würdig
**would, u'udd,** v (past &
 conditional of **will**); **–be,**
 adj Möchtegern-
**wound, u'uhnd,** n Wunde f;
 v verletzen
**wrangle, räng**-g'l, n Streit
 m; v streiten
**wrap, räpp,** n (shawl)
 Umhang m; (cover)
 Verhüllung f; v
 einwickeln; **– up,** (sich)
 einwickeln
**wrapper, räpp**-er, n (of
 book) Umschlag m
**wrapping paper, räpp**-ing
 **peh**-per, Packpapier nt;
 (gifts) Geschenkpapier nt
**wrath,** roth, n Zorn m; **–ful,**
 adj zornig

**wreak,** riek, *v* (havoc)
anrichten; (vengeance)
üben

**wreath,** rieth, *n* Kranz *m*

**wreck,** reck, *n* Wrack *nt*; *v*
zerstören; **–age,** *n*
Trümmer *pl*

**vren,** renn, *n* Zaunkönig *m*

**wrench,** rentsch, *n* (jar)
Ruck *m*; (sprain)
Verrenkung *f*; (tool)
Schraubenschlüssel *m*; *v*
(sprain) verrenken; (pull)
reißen

**wrestle, ress-**'l, *v* ringen;
**–r,** *n* Ringer *m*,
Ringkämpfer *m*

**wretch,** retsch, *n* Elende(r)
*m & f*; **–ed,** *adj* elend; *fam*
elend

**wriggle, rigg-**'l, *n* Windung
*f*; *v* sich winden, sich
schlängeln

**wring,** ring, *v* (clothes)
(aus)wringen; (neck)
umdrehen; (hands) ringen

**wrinkle, ring-**k'l, *n* Falte *f*; *v*
(crumple) verknittern;
(get wrinkled) Falten
bekommen

**wrist,** rist, *n* Handgelenk *nt*;
**–watch,** *n* Armbanduhr *f*

**writ,** ritt, *n* Verfügung *f*

**write,** reit, *v* schreiben;
(cheque) ausstellen; **– off,**
(debt, car) abschreiben;
**–r,** *n* Schreiber *m*;
(author) Schriftsteller *m*

**writhe,** reidh, *v* sich
krümmen

**writing, rei-**ting, *n*
Schreiben *nt*; **(hand)–,**
(Hand)schrift *f*; **in –,** *adv*
schriftlich; **– paper,** *n*
Schreibpapier *nt*

**written, ritt-**en, *adj*
schriftlich

**wrong,** rong, *adj* falsch;
(morally) unrecht; *n*
Unrecht *nt*; *v* Unrecht
zufügen; **be –,** unrecht
haben, sich irren; **be in
the –,** im Unrecht sein;
**what's – (with …)?** was
ist (mit …) los?

**wrought iron,** ro'at **ei-**en, *n*
Schmiedeeisen *nt*

**wry,** rei, *adj* (joke, humour)
fein; (grin) ironisch

**xenophobic,** zenn-*e*-**foh**-bick, *adj* fremdenfeindlich
**Xmas,** *abbr* **Christmas**
**X-ray, ecks**-reh, *adj* Röntgen-; *n* (image) Röntgenaufnahme *f*; *v* röntgen; **–s,** *npl* Röntgenstrahlen *pl*
**xylophone, sai**-*le*-fohn, *n* Xylophon *nt*

**joghourt, yog(h)urt, jogg-ert,** n Joghurt m/nt

**yoke,** johk, n Joch nt; v ins Joch spannen

**yolk,** johk, n Eidotter m, Eigelb nt

**you,** juh, pron (fam) du/dich/dir; pl ihr/euch; (formal) Sie/Ihnen; (impersonal) man/einen/einem

**young,** jang, adj jung; **–ster,** n (child) Kleine m & f & nt; (young person) Jugendliche(r) m & f; **the –,** npl die Jungen pl

**your,** jor, adj (fam) s dein; pl euer, eure; (formal) Ihr; **–s,** pron (fam) s deine(r/s); pl eure(r/s); (formal) Ihre(r/s), **–self,** pron (refl) (fam) dich (selbst), dir (selbst); (formal) sich (selbst); (emphatic) selbst; **–selves,** pron pl (refl) (fam) euch (selbst); (formal) sich (selbst); (emphatic) selbst

**youth,** juhth, n Jugend f; (young man) junger Mann m; (young people) Jugendliche pl; **– club,** n Jugendzentrum nt; **–ful,** adj jugendlich; **– hostel,** n Jugendherberge f; **–s,** npl Jugendliche pl

**YWCA,** wei dabb-'l-juh ssie eh, n (abbr Young Women's Christian Association), CVJF m

---

**acht,** jott, n Jacht f, Yacht f; **–ing,** nt, Segeln nt

**yard,** jahrd, n Hof m; (measure) Yard nt; **–stick,** m fig Maßstab m

**yarn,** jahrn, n Garn nt; (story) Geschichte f

**yawn,** jo'an, n Gähnen nt; v gähnen; **–ing,** adj gähnend; n Gähnen nt

**year,** jier, n Jahr nt; **–ly,** adj jährlich; **X—old,** adj Xjährig

**yearn (for),** jörn (for), v sich sehnen (nach); **–ing,** adj sehnsuchtsvoll; n Sehnsucht f

**yeast,** jiest, n Hefe f

**yell,** jell, n (gellender) Schrei m; v (gellend) schreien

**yellow,** jell-oh, adj gelb; n Gelb nt

**yelp,** jelp, n Gekläff nt; v

kläffen

**yes,** jess, adv ja; (in contradiction) doch; n Ja nt

**yesterday,** jess-ter-deh, adv gestern; **– morning,** gestern früh; **the day before –,** vorgestern

**yet,** jett, adv (in question) schon; (still) noch; (so far) bisher; conj dennoch, doch; **not –,** noch nicht

**yew,** juh, n Eibe f

**yield,** jield, n Ertrag m v (give way) nachgeben; (give away) abgeben; (bring in) einbringen; (produce) hervorbringen

**YMCA,** wei emm ssie eh, n (abbr Young Men's Christian Association), CVJM m

**yoga,** joh-ge, n Yoga m/nt, Joga m/nt

---

zany, seh-ni, *adj* verrückt

zap, säpp, *v fam* erledigen

zeal, siel, *n* Eifer *m*

zealous, sell-ess, *adj* eifrig

zebra, sieb-re/sebb-re, *n*
Zebra *nt*; – crossing, *n*
Zebrastreifen *m*

zero, sier-roh, *n* (figure)
Null *f*; (on scale)
Nullpunkt *m*

zest, sest, *n* (of
lemon/orange)
Zitronen/Orangenschale
*f*; (enthusiasm)
Begeisterung *f*

zigzag, sigg-sägg, *n*
Zickzackmuster *nt*; *v* im
Zickzack laufen/fahren

zinc, sink, *n* Zink *nt*

zip, sipp, *n* Reißverschluß *m*;
*v* – (up), den
Reißverschluß zumachen

zodiac, soh-di-äck, *n*
Tierkreis *m*; –al sign, *n*
Tierkreiszeichen *nt*

zone, sohn, *n* Zone *f*

zoo, suh, *n* Zoo *m*,
Tiergarten *m*

zoology, suh-oll-e-dschi, *n*
Zoologie *f*

zoom, suhm, *n photog*
Zoom(objektiv) *nt*; *v*
(rush) sausen; – in on, *v*
*photog* zoomen; – lens, *n*
Zoomobjektiv *nt*